The Fielding Bible

Volume III

What others are saying about defensive analytics:

"All over baseball, teams are being remade along these lines. The plodding power hitters who dominated the Age of Steroids are being replaced with wispy infielders who can't hit home runs but make tough plays look easy, skinny outfielders who swing light bats but cover ground like gazelles, and catchers who got their jobs because they're actually rather good at catching."

— Matthew Futterman, *Wall Street Journal*

"Measuring defense is a less-exact science than assessing hitting and pitching, but it's rapidly gaining importance in front offices. The possible reasons are plentiful and probably a perfect storm of factors in a changing game."

— Paul White, *USA Today*

" Comparing players' defensive skills is no longer as scientific as sizing up Best Supporting Actress performances before the Oscars. In his first *Bill James Abstract*, in 1977, the oracle of statistical analysis lamented the inability to quantify defensive success with anything other than such antiquated statistics as errors and fielding percentage. It has taken three decades, but the mystery of defensive analysis, perhaps the last frontier in the statistical ether, has been cracked by sabermetricians who have devoted 15, 20 years to the cause."

— Albert Chen, *Sports Illustrated*

" Front offices have access to much more advanced metrics than the public, some specifically charting where each batted ball is hit, how hard, and how high. As that wealth of data expands and reaches the public, it will be possible to better evaluate individual defensive performances. "

— James Click, Director,
Baseball Research and Development,
Tampa Bay Rays

The Fielding Bible

Volume III

John Dewan & Ben Jedlovec

Baseball Info Solutions

www.baseballinfosolutions.com

Published by ACTA Sports

A Division of ACTA Publications

www.actasports.com

Cover by Tom A. Wright

Cover Photo by Jeff Griffith-US PRESSWIRE

First Edition: March 2012

Published by:
ACTA Sports, a division of ACTA Publications
4848 North Clark Street
Chicago, IL 60640
(800) 397-2282
www.actasports.com www.actapublications.com

ISBN: 978-0-87946-476-9
ISSN: 1946-7524

Printed in the United States of America

Table of Contents

To the wives and girlfriends, friends and family
who tolerate our negligence during ridiculous hours, nights, and weekends
spent satisfying our baseball obsessions.

Foreword:
Reflections on the Deepest Nature of "Defense"

Bill James

Let us begin with the observation that defense is much more difficult to measure than offense, and that this seems to be true in every sport. In baseball, a generation ago, we had excellent measures of batting skill, but very primitive measures of fielding. In football, we had measures of yards carried, receptions, yards gained passing, receiving yards, passing attempts, completions, field goals, field goal attempts, punts, punt yards, etc., long before we had measures of sacks or deflections. Even now, the measures we have of defensive play in football are crude and not terribly useful. When I was a kid all we had for defense were tackles and interceptions. Now we have sacks, half-sacks, assists on tackles, etc., but still...it is hard to say reliably what the specific accomplishments of a defensive star have been.

In basketball we have always had points and rebounds, and I think we have had blocked shots for a long time, but even "steals" are a fairly recent invention. It is quite easy to identify the best offensive player on any college team by looking at their stats. It is speculative and unreliable to attempt the same thing based on the sketchy defensive statistics that we have (basically blocks and steals). Defense is simply more difficult to measure, in every sport, than is offense. Why is this true?

Let me deal first with a distraction. You often hear it said about baseball that baseball is the only sport in which the defense has the ball. This is true, but at least for our present purposes, it is more a distraction than an insight. It is true that the defense has the ball at the start of the play, but it is also true that the pitcher has very limited options as to what he can do with the ball. There are 360 degrees surrounding the pitcher, and 359 and a half of them are "places that the pitcher can't throw the ball." Setting aside base runners—a distraction within a distraction—the only thing he can do with the ball is throw it to the offense. The action starts when the offense does something with it.

Baseball is profoundly different from other sports in that the hitter also has very limited control of the action. In football the coach calls a running play or a pass, a play going to the left or the right. In baseball, anyone's ability to anticipate or "plan" the play is very limited. You don't "call" a line drive to right field. But this is all a distraction; none of it is really relevant to the issue we are examining here, which is "why is defense so much more difficult to measure, in all sports, than offense?"

There are two theories that suggest themselves. One is that offense is the act of making something happen. Defense is the act of preventing something from happening. It is inherently more difficult to measure points NOT scored than it is to measure points that are scored. If points are scored, you can, at a minimum, record who scored them. When points are not scored, it is not universally apparent who prevented them from being scored.

A second theory is that offense can be planned, whereas defense is generally a matter of reacting. Since offense is planned, responsibility is *assigned* to a particular player by the offensive team before the play begins, whereas defensive responsibilities are reactive, and occur within the framework of the action, therefore cannot as easily be assessed on the basis of opportunities assigned.

Yes, the extent to which offense can be "planned" in baseball is limited in a certain sense, but the offense sets the lineup. The hitters take turns hitting, which means that the offense chooses the sequence. The fielders don't take turns. The offense can steal a base, start a runner. The defense reacts; their "planning" is planning to react.

The greatest use of spectator sports is that they are a playground of the mind, in which our ideas about complex issues can be worked out in a greatly simplified universe. Let us ask, then, whether these two truisms about "defense" would apply in the world at large, as they do in sports?

Taking first the idea of national defense, or military defense. It seems fairly obvious that both truisms would apply in the world as they do in sports. A military on *offense* would be a military that was attempting to invade or conquer another country. A military on *defense* would be a military that was assigned to prevent the invasion or conquest of the homeland or of another country.

It would obviously be much easier to measure progress or success in an offensive military campaign than it would in a defensive one. If you are planning to invade another country, you can establish a list of targets that you wish to conquer, assign values to them, and measure very accurately what percentage of your objectives you have achieved.

Measuring how successfully you have *defended* yourself from invasion, however, would be difficult. You could, of course, measure and value the targets attacked by the enemy, figuring thus that your losses must be equal to the enemy's gains, but this measurement lacks perspective. The aggressive military can say "We can conquer Atlantasandria if we can overrun and gain control of these 22 targets and destroy these 41 defensive assets. So far we have gained control of 5 targets and destroyed 11 defensive assets, so we are a little more than 25% successful in our objectives." The defending military may know that they have lost 5 targets, but they have no way of knowing whether this is 5 out of 7 that will be attacked or 5 out of 200, thus, no way of knowing where they are relative to the goals of the opposition; further, even if you *did* know what the enemy's objectives were, this would still be granting to the military which is on offense the power to define the battle.

But maybe I misstated that; maybe what I should have said is simply that the military which is on offense **has** the power to define the battle, and there is nothing that anybody can do about that. That is just the way it is. Because the military which is on offense has the power to define the objectives of the war, it is always going to be more expensive to "play" defense than to be on offense.

On offense, you can pick your target, therefore you can focus your resources on that target. On defense, you have no way of knowing what target will be drawn into the battle next, therefore you have to allocate resources to every target. The consequence of this is that it is much, much more expensive to be on defense than it is to be on offense; more expensive, and also more difficult.

Thinking about this in the simplest military universe, where neither country has anything except "troops." Let us say that one country has 100,000 troops and the other has 40,000. But if the country that has 100,000 troops has 400 targets that it must defend, that works out to 250 troops defending each target. It is relatively easy for the smaller country, on offense to allocate 800 troops toward one target, and overrun it. Thus, it is virtually impossible to prevent a weaker military from successfully attacking a stronger military in the short run.

This describes 9-11, I think; the United States is vastly stronger than Al-Qaeda, but the United States has millions of targets that it must defend; therefore, it is virtually impossible to prevent a weaker opponent from making a successful attack on some target—for the same reason that defense in all sports is more difficult to measure than offense.

This also describes, I think, both the genius and the failure of Donald Rumsfeld. I'm not trying to probe sensitive issues here; I am trying to generalize from what I have learned from studying sports to the world at large, so that we might understand the world around us just a little bit better. You may remember that just after 9-11 there was a huge push to harden targets. For a while there, you couldn't find a public trash can because people were afraid Al-Qaeda would put a bomb in a public trash can. Rumsfeld said—correctly, in my view—that that's crazy; you can't defend every trash can; it would bankrupt you, and Al-Qaeda would find a place to put a bomb just as easily anyway. You have to go on offense, and take these people out. You have to make *them* play defense.

This we did brilliantly; the United States military, both in Iraq and Afghanistan, handled the *offensive* portion of the campaign masterfully. The problem was that in both places, we made a too-quick, too-sudden transition from offense to defense—and failed to anticipate what this would mean. Rumsfeld insisted on having a small, lightweight military in Iraq—a smaller "footprint"—which worked great as long as we were on offense, and could choose the targets; we could easily focus our resources and overwhelm any Iraqi target. The problem was that, once the "Mission Accomplished" banner went up, we went on defense. From that time on, the "small footprint" plan was a disaster. You can't play defense with a small footprint; it simply can't be done. In baseball you've got one batter against nine fielders—and the batter very often wins. If it was one against three the batter would hit .700.

A corollary that we can draw from this analysis, I think, is that *defense is inherently wasteful.* Ninety percent of the resources that you put into defense are going to be wasted, because you simply never know what target will be attacked, so you inevitably wind up defending targets that will never be attacked. You *can*, if you choose, declare victory by saying that the fact that you were never attacked is a victory, so every dollar spent on defense was well-spent, but...it's kind of a BS argument. It defines as "victory" what is actually waste.

A well-known corollary of this analysis, in basketball and football, is that it takes much, much more energy to play defense than it does to play offense. The offense *knows* where the ball is supposed to go. The defense doesn't know, so they have to defend every inch of the floor or every inch of the field, which is like defending every trash can: it requires a lot of energy. In every football broadcast we hear about "wearing down the defense." I always think "If the offense has been on the field all that time, why isn't the offense worn down just as much?" I always think that, but in fact there is a logical reason for it: It requires much more energy to play defense than it does to play offense. Defense wastes energy, because you don't know what is going to happen.

I'm moving on here, so let me ask a wrap-up question. What do we learn from this, really? *Be aware when you are transitioning to defense.* Defense is inherently different. It is difficult to measure, it is expensive, it is wasteful, it burns energy, it cannot be done with a small footprint. It's different. Be aware. That's really all.

I note a suspect corollary here, in baseball. In baseball, the place where we waste the most money is pitching, which is, of course, defense. We tend, in baseball, to collect pitchers who are actually useless because they get hurt. Pretty much every successful baseball team is spending some serious money on injured pitchers. I am unsure whether this is a legitimate corollary or not; it could be an unrelated condition that has the similar effect of making defense expensive. I don't know.

But a more useful insight, perhaps, is that this may explain the over-valuing of speed in baseball. Speed is really of very limited value on offense in baseball; most

of the value of speed in baseball is on defense. But this value tends, in practice, to be a wasted resource, since the average defensive player doesn't have one play a game on which his speed is a meaningful asset.

Moving on...in generalizing "offense" and "defense" to military and military defense, I very much limited the discussion. In fact, almost every activity in life has an offensive and a defensive component. As is suggested by the adage "all's fair in love and war"; there is an offensive and defensive component to love. If you are a single person and you are trying to find your soul mate or trying to find somebody to spend a weekend in Aruba with, you are on offense. You can select targets; you can focus your resources, you can set objectives and measure yourself against them.

If, on the other hand, you are in a relationship and it is not going so well and you are trying to figure out how to prevent the relationship from falling apart, then you are playing defense. Playing defense is inherently more difficult. It is difficult to set objectives for it. What, get through the week without a major argument? It is difficult to set *positive* objectives while playing defense.

There is a parallel between love and marriage and the Iraq war. In Iraq, we went in on offense and did great, and then settled into defense and took a long time to figure out what the hell we were doing. Relationships, like wars, tend to transition without proper warning from offense to defense, from targets and objectives to survival and reaction. When you are working toward marriage, it is relatively easy to know where you are, witness the phrase "take the relationship to another level." After you have become a couple, it is difficult to *measure* where you are, thus very easy to get lost. You lose track of the objectives; you don't know what target to defend. It is almost impossible to focus your resources, which tend to be divided among a thousand responsibilities—house payments, car payments, insurance for this, insurance for that, phone bills, gas for the car, etc. That's "defense."

Your job, as well, has an offensive and a defensive component. If you are trying to get promoted, trying to move ahead in your profession, you are on offense. If you are spending a lot of time worrying about getting fired, you're on defense. Playing defense is hard.

In baseball, when you are in the field—when you are on defense—your objective is to get back on offense. When you are on offense, your objective is to stay on offense as long as you can. The same is partially true in basketball; if the other team has the ball, your objective is to get the ball back. But this is only partially true in basketball, because basketball has a different structure, in which success ends the possession. In baseball, *failure* ends the possession (except for walk-off wins); in basketball, possessions may end in failure or success.

This is a profound difference between the sports, but there is also a profound parallel to real life. Many times, when we are struggling, what we need is to get back on offense. Playing offense is rewarding. Playing defense is expensive, frustrating, and unsatisfying. What you need, when you are on defense, is to get back on offense. If you're thinking about avoiding getting fired, it is time to go look for another job—a better job. Get back on offense. If you've put on weight, you need to get back on offense with your weight. You can *measure* how much weight you've lost. If you're just trying to avoid slipping backward any further, how do you measure that?

With money, paying the bills is defense. *Investing* is offense. What the government offers to poor people, very often, is help playing defense. What poor people *need*, very often, is to learn how to get on offense.

In religion, avoiding sins is playing defense. If your religion consists of a series of "don't do this" commands, that's *defensive* religion. It wears you out, it requires a lot of energy, and sometimes it is not very satisfying. If your religion consists of reaching out to people and helping them, if it consists of defending those who are attacked and helping those who are in need of help, that's religion on offense.

In criminal trials, the prosecutor is on offense, the defendant is (redundantly) on defense. I suspect that what good criminal defense attorneys do is, they go on offense; they figure out how to put the offense on the defense. That has to be true, because otherwise you're stuck playing defense, and defense is, by its nature, wasteful, expensive and unsatisfying, precisely because *it is difficult to measure your successes, thus difficult to see that you are having success*.

In World War II, the Battle of the Bulge was the Nazis going back on offense. Early in the war the Nazis were on offense, attacking other countries, and they were really good at playing offense. But when the Allies went on offense and attacked Normandy, that put the Nazis on defense. By December, 1944, the huge cost and drain of playing defense was wearing the Nazis down. The Battle of the Bulge was the Nazis realizing that, in order to survive, they had to get back on offense. The "surge" was the same thing; it was General David Petraeus realizing that the US had to get back on offense.

Well. . .this is deteriorating into a lecture. We're all poor, or fat, or divorced, or something; we are all on defense a good deal of the time. Let me return to my general point, because I don't know how else to get out of this thing. Defense is inherently different than offense on a very profound level. We cannot resist the temptation to measure defense as if it was merely the complement of offense, but it isn't; it is something entirely different, and one of the ways in which it is inherently different is that it is just very hard to measure. That's what this book is about: addressing the riddle of how we measure defense.

Introduction

Welcome back, my friends
to the show that never ends.
"Karn Evil 9"
by Emerson, Lake & Palmer

Yes, welcome back, our friends. To the third volume of *The Fielding Bible*. If you missed the first two, don't worry. We'll catch you up. Everything you need is in this volume, and it is 100 percent new material.

Analyzing defense in baseball turns out to be an exciting show that never ends. Over the last nine years we've come a long way. We think we now have a good understanding of how to measure defense, how to tell if a player performed well defensively or not. Part of the ongoing show is this triennial book, in which we share what we've learned with you. Of course, we will continue to analyze defense and find better and better ways to measure it, just as the sabermetrics revolution has done in the past several decades measuring offense and pitching, but the analysis will never end and we still have a long way to go.

Let's put it this way. For hitters, we might be at the 85-90 percent mark of being able to measure offense. We have a lot of good tools like OPS (on-base plus slugging), Runs Created, Wins Above Replacement. For pitchers,

we are not quite as far along. Maybe we're at the 75 percent level of understanding pitcher effectiveness with our numerical tools like ERA, Batting Average on Balls in Play, and Opponent OPS. For defense, ten years ago we were probably around the 10th percentile. Now with three volumes of *The Fielding Bible* under our belts, plus the work of many other excellent sabermetricians, we are probably in the 60-70 percent range.

Go ahead and flip through the book. No need to go start to finish. One of the cool sections is our projections of how players will do on defense in 2012. We now have enough confidence in our methods that we think we can predict the future (page 83). Or maybe you might be interested in whether or not the crazy Ted Williams Shift makes any sense (page 43). Or maybe you'd like to know 101 things you didn't know about defense (page 95).

In any case, as Emerson, Lake & Palmer sang,

Come inside, the show's about to start
Guaranteed to blow your head apart
Rest assured you'll get your money's worth

John Dewan and Ben Jedlovec
Baseball Info Solutions
March 2012

Defensive Runs Saved

Since *The Fielding Bible—Volume II* came out three years ago we've been busy. We have literally spent several thousand man-hours of research working to improve our methods to evaluate defense in baseball. During those three years the Major League team clients of Baseball Info Solutions have benefitted from the results of that research. In this book we share those results with you.

We're at the point where we are starting to get a good handle on measuring defense. We know a lot more than we knew three years ago, or than we knew six years ago when the first *Fielding Bible* came out. Everything that we know summarizes into what we call Defensive Runs Saved. Some folks have started calling it DRS for short. That's OK. It comes in handy at times to have a short name for something. DRS or DRS System. Or just Runs Saved. All OK. Sometimes people have called it The Fielding Bible system. That's OK too. Or sometimes it's called the Plus/Minus System. That's OK too, but it's a bit of a misnomer. The Plus/Minus System was the focus of the first volume of *The Fielding Bible* and remains the cornerstone of the Defensive Runs Saved System. The Plus/Minus System is the most important methodology that we use to measure defense. But it is only one of eight major methodologies that summarize into Defensive Runs Saved.

Call it anything you want. We use Defensive Runs Saved internally.

DRS is a straightforward concept. If a player has positive Defensive Runs Saved, he has helped his team defensively. When we say Austin Jackson had 29 Defensive Runs Saved in 2011 for the Tigers, it means he has helped his team prevent 29 runs from scoring, compared to an average center fielder, because of his

excellent defense. That was the best performance by any defender at any position in baseball last year. Logan Morrison had -26 runs saved for the Marlins playing left field in 2011. A negative runs saved number is below average. Morrison cost his team 26 runs because of his poor defense, the worst defensive performance in baseball in 2011. A player with a runs saved total around zero is average. Kevin Youkilis was exactly average playing third base for Boston in 2011 with exactly 0 runs saved.

That's generally the range. The best players can save about 30 runs defensively in a single season, and the worst players get close to -30. Using the rule of thumb that 10 runs is about equal to a win, Austin Jackson's defense all by itself accounted for three Detroit Tiger wins in 2011.

New in Volume III

There are six major things that we have done in the last three years to improve Defensive Runs Saved.

1) Timer Plus/Minus—This is the most important new addition to the DRS System. In 2009, Baseball Info Solutions started timing every batted ball from the moment it was hit to the moment of the resolution of the play (hit or out). By using the timer, we have taken some key subjective elements of the system and made them objective. For example, we used to measure the velocity of a batted ball with an estimate, calling it softly hit, hard hit, or medium. Now, we know the exact velocity of every batted ball. We have added this into our cornerstone methodology, the Plus/Minus System. For

more on this, see "Timing Batted Balls" on page 33.

2) Good Plays and Misplays—This is a brand new methodology. When a player makes a play that is better than the norm, we want to give him more credit. Or if it's worse, we want to take credit away. We have 28 categories of Good Plays and 54 categories of Misplays. We have converted the ones that don't overlap with our other methodologies to Runs Saved estimates. With this system we especially made great strides in measuring catcher defense. See "Good Plays and Misplays" on page 61.

3) Outfielder Arms—Here we use the new batted ball timer to upgrade our system to measure the impact that outfielders make defensively with their throwing arms. We also now use a more precise location of batted balls to enhance this methodology. See "Evaluating Outfielder Throwing Arms" on page 285.

4) Double Plays—We've upgraded our system to measure how good infielders are at starting and turning the double play by doing something similar to what we do with our Outfield Arms technique: measuring the location and the velocity of the batted ball in a double play situation to determine how difficult the play is to turn into a double play. See "Groundball Double Plays and Pivots" on page 293.

5) Bunts—Same thing here. We now include the location of bunts, among other criteria, to better evaluate how fielders make plays on bunts. See "Fielding Bunts" on page 299.

6) Centering—No, this has nothing to do with hockey and centering a puck. It's still baseball. The intention of Defensive Runs Saved is that zero is average. If a player has a positive number of runs saved, it's an above-average performance. If he has a negative number of runs saved, it's below average. As we've added on to the system over the years, we veered away from zero a bit. To get back on track, we took every methodology and "centered" it at zero. See "Centering" on page 461.

Eight Methodologies in Defensive Runs Saved

We have eight methodologies that comprise Defensive Runs Saved:

1) Plus/Minus System – measures range

2) OF Arm Runs Saved – measure outfielder arms

3) GDP Runs Saved – measures double play ability

4) Bunt Runs Saved – measures ability to field bunts

5) Good Plays and Misplays Runs Saved – measures contributions on miscellaneous plays which prevented or allowed a batter or baserunner advancement

6) Catcher Stolen Base Runs Saved – measures the catcher's ability to control the running game

7) Pitcher Stolen Base Runs Saved – measures the pitcher's ability to control the running game

8) Adjusted Earned Runs Saved – measures the catcher's handling of pitchers

Here's a grid by position showing which methodologies are used for which positions:

Methodology	Position								
	P	C	1B	2B	3B	SS	LF	CF	RF
Plus/Minus	x		x	x	x	x	x	x	x
OF Arms							x	x	x
GDP			x	x	x	x			
Bunts	x	x	x		x				
GFP/DME	x	x	x	x	x	x	x	x	x
Catcher SB		x							
Pitcher SB	x								
Adj. ER		x							

Year-by-Year Summary of Enhancements

Before you peruse the charts on the next several pages, here's a year-by-year summary of enhancements we've made over the years. Sometimes it's all new methodologies and sometimes it's a tweak to improve an existing one. During upcoming seasons, you'll find all the updated numbers on BillJamesOnline.com and FanGraphs.com.

2004

- Baseball Info Solutions (BIS) team clients get the first "Specialized Fielding Report" based on the in-depth coding of batted ball locations by BIS
- The Plus/Minus System debuts in this report

2005

- Distinction made between liners and flyballs in the Plus/Minus System, instead of just a velocity coding of soft, medium and hard. Data changed back to 2003
- Team clients get the second "Specialized Fielding Report" through the 2004 season. It is renamed to the *Team Fielding Bible*, exclusive to BIS customers

2006

- New defensive analysis goes public with the publication of the first volume, *The Fielding Bible*
- Plus/Minus System introduced to the public
- Outfielder Arm, GDPs and Bunts – methodologies for each introduced
- Revised Zone Rating – an upgrade to the old Zone Rating system
- After the release of the book, "fliners" added as new category to outfield plus/minus
- After the book, vector system changed to polar coordinates allowing for use of the standard 360 circle for measurement
- After the book, we modified the Plus/Minus System to consider all outfielder balls in the air that are caught or land within five feet to be the same, and all infield balls in the air within three feet to be the same
- BIS team clients receive updated information based on new techniques added after the book

2007

- Manny Adjustment added – removing balls hit high off the wall from consideration as a fieldable ball in the Plus/Minus System

- BIS team clients get the Manny Adjustment included with their new information

2008

- Catcher Adjusted Earned Runs Saved introduced
- Catcher SB Runs Saved, Pitcher SB Runs Saved introduced
- All methodologies converted to Runs Saved
- BIS team clients continue to receive updated information and techniques

2009

- *The Fielding Bible—Volume II* comes out providing updates to the public
- Defensive Runs Saved introduced to public
- Home Run Saving Catches become the first Good Play or Misplay to be converted to Runs Saved
- Batted Ball Timer started by BIS
- After the book, outfield plus/minus revised to include batted ball timer
- After the book, GDP Runs Saved revised to include timer and hit location
- BIS team clients receive all adjustments

2010

- Infield plus/minus revised to include batted ball timer
- Outfield arm runs saved revised to include timer and hit location
- Outfield Plus/Minus modified to consider all outfielder balls in the air that are caught or land within about ten feet to be the same, and all infield flyballs and line drives within about eight feet to be the same.
- BIS team clients now receive all updated techniques and adjustments as part of the new system for them to access information on a daily basis

2011

- Good Plays/Misplays Runs Saved developed and added back to 2004
- BIS team clients receive this new technique as well

2012

- Centering of all runs saved methodologies takes place
- Bunts runs saved recalculated for all players back to 2003
- Pitcher SB Runs Saved recalculated and centered for all players back to 2003
- *The Fielding Bible—Volume III* is published

First Basemen - 3-Year Runs Saved

Player	Plus/Minus	Bunts	GDP	GFP/DME	Total
Albert Pujols	20	0	2	13	35
Daric Barton	22	1	0	2	25
Adrian Gonzalez	13	5	0	6	24
James Loney	9	0	3	8	20
Kevin Youkilis	18	-1	0	2	19
Daniel Murphy	16	2	1	0	19
Todd Helton	5	2	2	6	15
Ike Davis	12	1	1	-1	13
Casey Kotchman	11	-1	-1	4	13
Mark Teixeira	9	0	-2	4	11
Mark Trumbo	8	0	2	0	10
Lyle Overbay	9	-2	1	1	9
Adam LaRoche	5	1	1	2	9
Justin Morneau	5	1	0	1	7
Joey Votto	7	-1	-1	0	5
Aubrey Huff	-2	1	0	5	4
Russell Branyan	6	0	0	-3	3
Derrek Lee	3	-2	-1	2	2
Lance Berkman	-1	3	-1	0	1
Freddie Freeman	-3	0	0	1	-2
Chris Davis	-5	1	0	1	-3
Justin Smoak	-3	-2	0	1	-4
Carlos Pena	-5	0	0	1	-4
Gaby Sanchez	-3	0	0	-2	-5
Michael Cuddyer	-4	0	0	-3	-7
Jorge Cantu	-7	1	0	-1	-7
Ty Wigginton	-8	-1	0	0	-9
Miguel Cabrera	-8	-3	1	1	-9
Matt LaPorta	-5	-3	0	-5	-13
Billy Butler	-9	0	0	-5	-14
Garrett Jones	-3	-3	-1	-8	-15
Paul Konerko	-20	1	1	2	-16
Prince Fielder	-23	-1	0	-2	-26
Ryan Howard	-24	-1	0	-5	-30
Adam Dunn	-29	-1	-1	-7	-38

First Basemen - 2010 Runs Saved

Player	Team	Plus/Minus	Bunts	GDP	GFP/DME	Total
Daric Barton	Oak	16	1	0	1	18
Ike Davis	NYM	10	1	1	0	12
Justin Morneau	Min	5	0	1	2	8
Albert Pujols	StL	3	-1	1	5	8
Lyle Overbay	Tor	7	-1	1	0	7
Kevin Youkilis	Bos	7	-1	0	1	7
Aubrey Huff	SF	3	1	0	3	7
Mark Teixeira	NYY	5	0	0	1	6
Adam LaRoche	Ari	4	0	1	1	6
Todd Helton	Col	1	2	1	2	6
James Loney	LAD	-1	1	1	3	4
Xavier Nady	ChC	4	-1	0	0	3
Casey Kotchman	Sea	3	1	-1	0	3
Brett Wallace	Hou	2	0	0	1	3
Kendrys Morales	LAA	1	0	0	2	3
Joey Votto	Cin	-1	0	1	3	3
Derrek Lee	2 tms	3	-1	0	0	2
Russell Branyan	2 tms	4	0	0	-3	1
Mike Napoli	LAA	1	0	0	0	1
Lance Berkman	2 tms	1	2	-1	-1	1
Carlos Pena	TB	0	0	0	0	0
Ty Wigginton	Bal	-1	-1	0	1	-1
Matt LaPorta	Cle	1	0	0	-3	-2
Justin Smoak	2 tms	-2	-1	0	0	-3
Adrian Gonzalez	SD	-3	0	0	0	-3
Billy Butler	KC	-2	0	0	-2	-4
Miguel Cabrera	Det	-4	-1	0	0	-5
Michael Cuddyer	Min	-5	0	0	-3	-8
Troy Glaus	Atl	-6	-1	0	-1	-8
Gaby Sanchez	Fla	-8	0	0	-2	-10
Adam Dunn	Was	-9	1	-1	-2	-11
Garrett Jones	Pit	-4	-2	-1	-5	-12
Ryan Howard	Phi	-11	-1	0	-1	-13
Paul Konerko	CWS	-17	1	1	2	-13
Prince Fielder	Mil	-15	0	0	-2	-17

First Basemen - 2011 Runs Saved

Player	Team	Plus/Minus	Bunts	GDP	GFP/DME	Total
Adrian Gonzalez	Bos	7	3	0	2	12
James Loney	LAD	7	0	1	3	11
Albert Pujols	StL	7	0	1	2	10
Mark Trumbo	LAA	7	0	2	0	9
Daniel Murphy	NYM	6	1	0	1	8
Todd Helton	Col	5	-1	1	2	7
Carlos Lee	Hou	5	1	1	0	7
Gaby Sanchez	Fla	5	0	0	0	5
Brett Wallace	Hou	4	0	-1	2	5
Joey Votto	Cin	8	-1	-1	-2	4
Daric Barton	Oak	4	0	0	0	4
Mark Teixeira	NYY	4	0	-1	0	3
Casey Kotchman	TB	1	-1	0	3	3
Aubrey Huff	SF	2	-1	0	1	2
Jesus Guzman	SD	1	0	0	-1	0
Xavier Nady	Ari	-3	1	0	2	0
Brandon Allen	2 tms	0	0	0	-1	-1
Carlos Pena	ChC	-1	0	0	0	-1
Justin Smoak	Sea	-1	-1	0	1	-1
Carlos Santana	Cle	-2	1	0	-1	-2
Mitch Moreland	Tex	-3	1	0	0	-2
Freddie Freeman	Atl	-3	0	0	1	-2
Justin Morneau	Min	-2	0	0	-1	-3
Derrek Lee	2 tms	-3	1	0	-1	-3
Miguel Cabrera	Det	-5	-1	1	2	-3
Juan Miranda	Ari	-1	-2	0	-1	-4
Adam Lind	Tor	-2	0	-1	-1	-4
Paul Konerko	CWS	-4	-1	1	0	-4
Lyle Overbay	2 tms	-5	1	0	0	-4
Conor Jackson	2 tms	-5	0	0	0	-5
Michael Morse	Was	-7	-1	0	1	-7
Eric Hosmer	KC	-7	-1	-1	0	-9
Prince Fielder	Mil	-7	0	0	-2	-9
Matt LaPorta	Cle	-7	-3	0	-1	-11
Ryan Howard	Phi	-12	1	0	-2	-13

First Basemen - 2009 Runs Saved

Player	Team	Plus/Minus	Bunts	GDP	GFP/DME	Total
Albert Pujols	StL	10	1	0	6	17
Adrian Gonzalez	SD	9	2	0	4	15
Daniel Murphy	NYM	10	1	1	-1	11
Kevin Youkilis	Bos	10	0	0	1	11
Travis Ishikawa	SF	9	0	1	0	10
Kendrys Morales	LAA	7	0	1	0	8
Casey Kotchman	2 tms	7	-1	0	1	7
Lyle Overbay	Tor	7	-2	0	1	6
James Loney	LAD	3	-1	1	2	5
Derrek Lee	ChC	3	-2	-1	3	3
Daric Barton	Oak	2	0	0	1	3
Ryan Garko	2 tms	4	0	0	-2	2
Justin Morneau	Min	2	1	-1	0	2
Mark Teixeira	NYY	0	0	-1	3	2
Todd Helton	Col	-1	1	0	2	2
Paul Konerko	CWS	1	1	-1	0	1
Lance Berkman	Hou	-1	1	0	1	1
Russell Branyan	Sea	0	0	0	0	0
Hank Blalock	Tex	0	-1	0	1	0
Prince Fielder	Mil	-1	-1	0	2	0
Miguel Cabrera	Det	1	-1	0	-1	-1
Joey Votto	Cin	0	0	-1	-1	-2
Andy Marte	Cle	-1	-1	0	0	-2
Chad Tracy	Ari	-1	0	0	-1	-2
Victor Martinez	2 tms	-3	1	0	0	-2
Adam LaRoche	3 tms	-4	1	0	1	-2
Chris Davis	Tex	-4	0	0	1	-3
Carlos Pena	TB	-4	0	0	1	-3
Ryan Howard	Phi	-1	-1	0	-2	-4
Aubrey Huff	Bal	-7	1	0	1	-5
Jason Giambi	2 tms	-7	1	0	-1	-7
Jorge Cantu	Fla	-7	1	0	-1	-7
Billy Butler	KC	-5	0	0	-3	-8
Nick Johnson	2 tms	-9	1	0	-5	-13
Adam Dunn	Was	-18	-1	0	-4	-23

Second Basemen - 3-Year Runs Saved

Player	Plus/Minus	GDP	GFP/DME	Total
Ian Kinsler	40	5	2	47
Ben Zobrist	46	0	-1	45
Dustin Pedroia	29	2	6	37
Chase Utley	30	3	3	36
Mark Ellis	18	2	7	27
Brandon Phillips	12	-2	8	18
Robinson Cano	21	1	-5	17
Clint Barmes	9	2	4	15
Aaron Hill	18	-4	-1	13
Howie Kendrick	10	-1	1	10
Danny Espinosa	8	1	1	10
Placido Polanco	6	1	2	9
Luis Valbuena	5	1	1	7
Ryan Theriot	4	0	-1	3
Orlando Hudson	7	-5	0	2
Omar Infante	4	1	-3	2
Felipe Lopez	4	0	-3	1
Martin Prado	-1	0	0	-1
Jamey Carroll	-6	1	3	-2
Kelly Johnson	-8	3	2	-3
Jose Lopez	0	1	-4	-3
Gordon Beckham	-5	1	0	-4
Freddy Sanchez	-6	2	-2	-6
Blake DeWitt	-3	-3	0	-6
Brian Roberts	-10	1	1	-8
Chone Figgins	-12	1	1	-10
Neil Walker	-15	1	3	-11
Alexi Casilla	-11	-1	1	-11
Rickie Weeks	-7	1	-8	-14
Chris Getz	-12	-1	-2	-15
Adam Kennedy	-9	-2	-4	-15
Alberto Callaspo	-15	-2	0	-17
Jeff Keppinger	-19	-1	-3	-23
Skip Schumaker	-29	-2	1	-30
Dan Uggla	-28	-4	-2	-34

Second Basemen - 2010 Runs Saved

Player	Team	Plus/Minus	GDP	GFP/DME	Total
Sean Rodriguez	TB	15	1	2	18
Chase Utley	Phi	11	3	3	17
Robinson Cano	NYY	15	2	-1	16
Brandon Phillips	Cin	6	-1	5	10
Mark Ellis	Oak	6	1	1	8
Luis Valbuena	Cle	6	1	1	8
Ian Kinsler	Tex	8	-1	0	7
Jonathan Herrera	Col	5	0	1	6
Dustin Pedroia	Bos	3	1	1	5
Orlando Hudson	Min	6	-1	-1	4
David Eckstein	SD	2	0	2	4
Omar Infante	Atl	4	1	-2	3
Martin Prado	Atl	2	0	0	2
Clint Barmes	Col	1	0	1	2
Ryan Theriot	2 tms	2	-1	0	1
Luis Castillo	NYM	2	-1	0	1
Kelly Johnson	Ari	-3	1	2	0
Brian Roberts	Bal	-2	1	0	-1
Aaron Hill	Tor	0	-2	0	-2
Adam Kennedy	Was	1	-2	-1	-2
Chris Getz	KC	-3	0	1	-2
Will Rhymes	Det	3	-1	-4	-2
Julio Lugo	Bal	-1	0	-1	-2
Freddy Sanchez	SF	-2	-1	0	-3
Howie Kendrick	LAA	-4	-2	1	-5
Blake DeWitt	2 tms	-3	-2	0	-5
Gordon Beckham	CWS	-9	1	1	-7
Neil Walker	Pit	-10	2	0	-8
Mike Aviles	KC	-3	-3	-2	-8
Dan Uggla	Fla	-8	-1	0	-9
Chone Figgins	Sea	-12	1	1	-10
Jeff Keppinger	Hou	-10	1	-1	-10
Cristian Guzman	2 tms	-5	-2	-3	-10
Rickie Weeks	Mil	-12	1	-5	-16
Skip Schumaker	StL	-16	-1	0	-17

Second Basemen - 2011 Runs Saved

Player	Team	Plus/Minus	GDP	GFP/DME	Total
Ben Zobrist	TB	22	1	0	23
Dustin Pedroia	Bos	15	-1	4	18
Ian Kinsler	Tex	15	3	0	18
Mark Ellis	2 tms	12	1	4	17
Howie Kendrick	LAA	10	0	0	10
Dustin Ackley	Sea	9	1	0	10
Chase Utley	Phi	8	-1	0	7
Brandon Phillips	Cin	7	-1	0	6
Danny Espinosa	Was	5	0	0	5
Robert Andino	Bal	4	1	0	5
Omar Infante	Fla	4	0	0	4
Ramon Santiago	Det	4	0	0	4
Gordon Beckham	CWS	4	0	-1	3
Jose Altuve	Hou	1	1	1	3
Aaron Hill	2 tms	3	0	-1	2
Robinson Cano	NYY	0	2	-1	1
Kelly Johnson	2 tms	-3	2	2	1
Darwin Barney	ChC	3	-2	0	1
Alexi Casilla	Min	-1	0	2	1
Ruben Tejada	NYM	-1	0	2	1
Jonathan Herrera	Col	0	0	0	0
Chris Getz	KC	-1	0	-1	-2
Aaron Miles	LAD	-2	0	0	-2
Neil Walker	Pit	-5	-1	3	-3
Skip Schumaker	StL	-2	-1	0	-3
Orlando Cabrera	2 tms	-2	0	-2	-4
Rickie Weeks	Mil	-3	1	-3	-5
Maicer Izturis	LAA	-8	1	2	-5
Jemile Weeks	Oak	-6	0	0	-6
Freddy Sanchez	SF	-7	1	0	-6
Orlando Hudson	SD	-5	-3	0	-8
Jamey Carroll	LAD	-12	1	1	-10
Jeff Keppinger	2 tms	-7	-2	-2	-11
Dan Uggla	Atl	-10	-1	-2	-13
Justin Turner	NYM	-8	-3	-2	-13

Second Basemen - 2009 Runs Saved

Player	Team	Plus/Minus	GDP	GFP/DME	Total
Ian Kinsler	Tex	17	3	2	22
Ben Zobrist	TB	17	0	-1	16
Dustin Pedroia	Bos	11	2	1	14
Aaron Hill	Tor	15	-2	0	13
Clint Barmes	Col	8	2	3	13
Chase Utley	Phi	11	1	0	12
Maicer Izturis	LAA	3	2	2	7
Orlando Hudson	LAD	6	-1	1	6
Jamey Carroll	Cle	5	0	1	6
Placido Polanco	Det	2	1	2	5
Howie Kendrick	LAA	4	1	0	5
Freddy Sanchez	2 tms	3	2	-2	3
Brandon Phillips	Cin	-1	0	3	2
Mark Ellis	Oak	0	0	2	2
Mike Fontenot	ChC	1	0	1	2
Nick Punto	Min	-1	0	3	2
Anderson Hernandez	2 tms	3	0	-2	1
Robinson Cano	NYY	6	-3	-3	0
Kaz Matsui	Hou	-5	2	3	0
Luis Valbuena	Cle	-1	0	0	-1
Akinori Iwamura	TB	2	-1	-2	-1
Felipe Lopez	2 tms	0	0	-3	-3
Martin Prado	Atl	-3	0	0	-3
Jose Lopez	Sea	-1	1	-4	-4
David Eckstein	SD	-5	0	1	-4
Kelly Johnson	Atl	-2	0	-2	-4
Delwyn Young	Pit	-5	-1	1	-5
Manny Burriss	SF	-4	-2	0	-6
Brian Roberts	Bal	-8	0	0	-8
Skip Schumaker	StL	-11	0	1	-10
Chris Getz	CWS	-8	-1	-2	-11
Dan Uggla	Fla	-10	-2	0	-12
Luis Castillo	NYM	-8	-4	0	-12
Alexi Casilla	Min	-12	0	-1	-13
Alberto Callaspo	KC	-14	-2	0	-16

Third Basemen - 3-Year Runs Saved

Player	Plus/Minus	Bunts	GDP	GFP/DME	Total
Evan Longoria	43	7	5	6	61
Adrian Beltre	49	3	1	-1	52
Scott Rolen	31	0	0	6	37
Chone Figgins	29	1	0	-2	28
Ryan Zimmerman	25	0	-1	4	28
Brandon Inge	19	-4	2	3	20
Casey Blake	18	1	-1	2	20
Jack Hannahan	21	-2	-1	0	18
Placido Polanco	14	0	1	1	16
Chase Headley	14	0	-1	2	15
Alex Rodriguez	8	0	0	3	11
Jose Lopez	11	-1	-1	0	9
Ian Stewart	7	1	-1	1	8
Alberto Callaspo	7	3	1	-3	8
Kevin Kouzmanoff	11	-2	0	-3	6
Pablo Sandoval	2	2	0	1	5
Brent Morel	0	0	-1	2	1
Kevin Youkilis	1	0	-1	0	0
Miguel Tejada	-3	1	0	0	-2
Andy LaRoche	-3	1	-2	1	-3
Jhonny Peralta	-4	1	-1	-1	-5
David Freese	-9	1	2	-1	-7
Melvin Mora	-1	-2	-2	-3	-8
Chipper Jones	-9	-2	1	1	-9
Danny Valencia	-8	-1	0	-1	-10
Edwin Encarnacion	-13	0	0	-1	-14
Mark Teahen	-16	-1	-1	-2	-20
Pedro Alvarez	-18	-1	-1	-1	-21
Casey McGehee	-22	0	1	0	-21
Wilson Betemit	-18	-1	-1	-2	-22
Michael Young	-33	-1	1	4	-29
Chris Johnson	-31	1	0	0	-30
Mark Reynolds	-27	-3	0	-3	-33
David Wright	-27	-2	-3	-2	-34
Aramis Ramirez	-34	1	-2	-3	-38

Third Basemen - 2010 Runs Saved

Player	Team	Plus/Minus	Bunts	GDP	GFP/DME	Total
Evan Longoria	TB	13	3	2	2	20
Adrian Beltre	Bos	15	2	1	1	19
Chase Headley	SD	14	1	-1	0	14
Kevin Kouzmanoff	Oak	13	-1	1	-2	11
Ryan Zimmerman	Was	12	-1	-1	1	11
Jose Lopez	Sea	11	-1	0	0	10
Brandon Inge	Det	8	0	1	1	10
Scott Rolen	Cin	7	1	0	2	10
Casey Blake	LAD	9	0	-1	-1	7
Placido Polanco	Phi	4	0	2	1	7
Ian Stewart	Col	2	1	0	2	5
Alex Rodriguez	NYY	3	-1	1	0	3
Danny Valencia	Min	3	0	0	0	3
Jhonny Peralta	2 tms	2	0	0	0	2
Alberto Callaspo	2 tms	1	3	0	-2	2
Pablo Sandoval	SF	-3	0	1	3	1
Chipper Jones	Atl	2	-2	0	0	0
Felipe Lopez	2 tms	-1	0	0	0	-1
Edwin Encarnacion	Tor	-1	-1	0	-1	-3
Melvin Mora	Col	-2	-1	-1	-1	-5
Wes Helms	Fla	-4	0	0	-1	-5
David Freese	StL	-6	1	1	-1	-5
Mark Reynolds	Ari	-4	0	-1	-1	-6
Pedro Feliz	2 tms	-7	0	1	0	-6
Omar Vizquel	CWS	-6	0	0	-1	-7
Andy LaRoche	Pit	-5	0	-2	-1	-8
Miguel Tejada	2 tms	-8	0	0	-1	-9
Pedro Alvarez	Pit	-10	0	0	0	-10
Michael Young	Tex	-12	-1	0	2	-11
Wilson Betemit	KC	-10	0	-1	-1	-12
David Wright	NYM	-13	0	-1	0	-14
Jorge Cantu	2 tms	-13	0	-1	0	-14
Casey McGehee	Mil	-14	1	0	-1	-14
Aramis Ramirez	ChC	-10	-2	-1	-2	-15
Chris Johnson	Hou	-15	0	0	-1	-16

Third Basemen - 2011 Runs Saved

Player	Team	Plus/Minus	Bunts	GDP	GFP/DME	Total
Evan Longoria	TB	14	4	1	3	22
Pablo Sandoval	SF	15	1	0	-1	15
Adrian Beltre	Tex	14	0	0	-1	13
Alex Rodriguez	NYY	11	1	0	1	13
Scott Rolen	Cin	7	0	1	2	10
Placido Polanco	Phi	10	0	-1	0	9
Jack Hannahan	Cle	7	0	-1	0	6
Juan Uribe	LAD	5	1	0	-1	5
Alberto Callaspo	LAA	4	0	1	-1	4
Miguel Cairo	Cin	3	0	0	0	3
Lonnie Chisenhall	Cle	2	1	0	0	3
Casey McGehee	Mil	0	0	1	2	3
Mike Moustakas	KC	4	-2	0	0	2
Brent Morel	CWS	1	0	-1	2	2
Chase Headley	SD	0	-1	0	2	1
Kevin Youkilis	Bos	2	0	-1	-1	0
Chone Figgins	Sea	-1	1	0	-1	-1
Ty Wigginton	Col	-2	0	0	1	-1
David Freese	StL	-2	0	1	0	-1
Brandon Inge	Det	1	-2	0	-1	-2
Chipper Jones	Atl	-3	0	0	0	-3
Aaron Miles	LAD	-5	1	0	-1	-5
Ryan Zimmerman	Was	-8	1	0	2	-5
David Wright	NYM	-3	-1	-1	-1	-6
Daniel Descalso	StL	-5	-1	0	0	-6
Wilson Betemit	2 tms	-6	0	0	-1	-7
Ryan Roberts	Ari	-6	-1	0	0	-7
Kevin Kouzmanoff	2 tms	-7	0	0	0	-7
Greg Dobbs	Fla	-7	-2	0	0	-9
Pedro Alvarez	Pit	-8	-1	-1	-1	-11
Scott Sizemore	Oak	-9	-1	0	-1	-11
Chris Johnson	Hou	-14	1	0	1	-12
Danny Valencia	Min	-11	-1	0	-1	-13
Aramis Ramirez	ChC	-18	2	-1	-1	-18
Mark Reynolds	Bal	-18	-3	1	-2	-22

Third Basemen - 2009 Runs Saved

Player	Team	Plus/Minus	Bunts	GDP	GFP/DME	Total
Chone Figgins	LAA	30	0	0	-1	29
Ryan Zimmerman	Was	21	0	0	1	22
Adrian Beltre	Sea	20	1	0	-1	20
Evan Longoria	TB	16	0	2	1	19
Scott Rolen	2 tms	17	-1	-1	2	17
Joe Crede	Min	13	0	0	1	14
Jack Hannahan	2 tms	14	-2	0	0	12
Brandon Inge	Det	10	-2	1	3	12
Casey Blake	LAD	6	1	0	2	9
Pedro Feliz	Phi	4	1	1	3	9
Andy LaRoche	Pit	5	0	0	2	7
Kevin Kouzmanoff	SD	5	-1	-1	-1	2
Bill Hall	2 tms	2	0	0	-1	1
Kevin Youkilis	Bos	0	0	0	1	1
Ian Stewart	Col	4	-1	-1	-2	0
Melvin Mora	Bal	2	-1	0	-1	0
Emilio Bonifacio	Fla	1	1	-1	-1	0
Gordon Beckham	CWS	-2	1	1	-1	-1
Garrett Atkins	Col	-2	0	0	0	-2
Geoff Blum	Hou	-4	0	0	1	-3
Mark Reynolds	Ari	-5	0	0	0	-5
Aramis Ramirez	ChC	-6	1	0	0	-5
Alex Rodriguez	NYY	-6	0	-1	2	-5
Mark DeRosa	2 tms	-9	2	0	2	-5
Adam Kennedy	Oak	-5	0	-1	0	-6
Jeff Keppinger	Hou	-8	1	1	0	-6
Chipper Jones	Atl	-8	0	1	1	-6
Jhonny Peralta	Cle	-6	1	-1	-1	-7
Edwin Encarnacion	2 tms	-8	1	0	0	-7
Casey McGehee	Mil	-8	-1	0	-1	-10
Pablo Sandoval	SF	-10	1	-1	-1	-11
Mark Teahen	KC	-9	-1	-1	-1	-12
David Wright	NYM	-11	-1	-1	-1	-14
Mike Lowell	Bos	-17	0	1	1	-15
Michael Young	Tex	-17	0	1	1	-15

Shortstops - 3-Year Runs Saved

Player	Plus/Minus	GDP	GFP/DME	Total
Brendan Ryan	54	6	2	62
Troy Tulowitzki	27	8	8	43
Jack Wilson	31	2	2	35
Alex Gonzalez	22	1	8	31
Alexei Ramirez	24	4	1	29
Clint Barmes	29	-1	1	29
Cesar Izturis	20	1	3	24
Yunel Escobar	28	2	-7	23
Paul Janish	19	-2	3	20
Elvis Andrus	12	5	-2	15
Alcides Escobar	16	-3	1	14
Marco Scutaro	17	-2	-2	13
Stephen Drew	5	3	4	12
Ramon Santiago	9	-1	-1	7
Rafael Furcal	7	0	-1	6
J.J. Hardy	8	-3	0	5
Jhonny Peralta	8	1	-4	5
Erick Aybar	0	2	2	4
Josh Wilson	5	0	-2	3
Asdrubal Cabrera	-5	2	5	2
Jason Bartlett	2	-7	0	-5
Cliff Pennington	-14	4	5	-5
Jimmy Rollins	-11	4	1	-6
Ronny Cedeno	-6	0	-2	-8
Everth Cabrera	-9	0	0	-9
Ryan Theriot	-6	-2	-3	-11
Edgar Renteria	-6	-3	-2	-11
Ian Desmond	-7	-2	-4	-13
Starlin Castro	-3	-2	-9	-14
Jose Reyes	-18	1	-1	-18
Derek Jeter	-16	-4	-1	-21
Miguel Tejada	-20	-1	-1	-22
Orlando Cabrera	-27	-1	2	-26
Hanley Ramirez	-24	-4	-2	-30
Yuniesky Betancourt	-49	-1	-2	-52

Shortstops - 2010 Runs Saved

Player	Team	Plus/Minus	GDP	GFP/DME	Total
Alex Gonzalez	2 tms	19	2	6	27
Brendan Ryan	StL	19	3	0	22
Alexei Ramirez	CWS	18	1	1	20
Troy Tulowitzki	Col	13	4	2	19
Cliff Pennington	Oak	7	2	4	13
Yunel Escobar	2 tms	7	3	-1	9
Jack Wilson	Sea	6	0	2	8
Cesar Izturis	Bal	5	1	1	7
Josh Wilson	Sea	8	0	-1	7
Ramon Santiago	Det	8	0	-1	7
Alcides Escobar	Mil	5	1	0	6
Erick Aybar	LAA	7	-2	-1	4
Rafael Furcal	LAD	5	-1	0	4
Jimmy Rollins	Phi	0	2	1	3
Marco Scutaro	Bos	3	-1	-1	1
Jerry Hairston	SD	3	-1	-1	1
Stephen Drew	Ari	-3	2	1	0
Orlando Cabrera	Cin	1	0	-1	0
Jason Bartlett	TB	2	-3	0	-1
Asdrubal Cabrera	Cle	-5	1	3	-1
Jamey Carroll	LAD	1	-2	0	-1
Edgar Renteria	SF	-1	0	-1	-2
Miguel Tejada	SD	0	-1	-1	-2
Jose Reyes	NYM	-4	2	-2	-4
Starlin Castro	ChC	3	0	-7	-4
Tommy Manzella	Hou	-3	0	-1	-4
Juan Uribe	SF	-6	0	1	-5
J.J. Hardy	Min	-3	-1	-1	-5
Elvis Andrus	Tex	-4	0	-3	-7
Ian Desmond	Was	-3	-1	-3	-7
Derek Jeter	NYY	-8	0	-1	-9
Ronny Cedeno	Pit	-11	1	1	-9
Angel Sanchez	2 tms	-12	-1	0	-13
Hanley Ramirez	Fla	-16	-1	-2	-19
Yuniesky Betancourt	KC	-20	-4	-3	-27

Shortstops - 2011 Runs Saved

Player	Team	Plus/Minus	GDP	GFP/DME	Total
Brendan Ryan	Sea	16	1	1	18
Clint Barmes	Hou	14	-1	1	14
Troy Tulowitzki	Col	6	2	3	11
Alcides Escobar	KC	11	-3	2	10
Alex Gonzalez	Atl	9	-1	1	9
J.J. Hardy	Bal	8	-1	1	8
Alexei Ramirez	CWS	4	3	0	7
Elvis Andrus	Tex	5	3	-1	7
Yunel Escobar	Tor	8	0	-1	7
Reid Brignac	TB	7	0	0	7
Paul Janish	Cin	8	-2	0	6
Ronny Cedeno	Pit	9	-2	-2	5
Asdrubal Cabrera	Cle	2	-1	2	3
Stephen Drew	Ari	0	1	2	3
Brandon Crawford	SF	3	0	0	3
Jhonny Peralta	Det	4	0	-2	2
Marco Scutaro	Bos	2	0	-1	1
Edgar Renteria	Cin	3	-1	-1	1
Willie Bloomquist	Ari	0	0	1	1
Erick Aybar	LAA	-4	2	1	-1
Ian Desmond	Was	-2	-1	0	-3
Dee Gordon	LAD	-2	-1	0	-3
Rafael Furcal	2 tms	-4	0	-1	-5
Emilio Bonifacio	Fla	-5	0	0	-5
Jamey Carroll	LAD	-5	0	0	-5
Yuniesky Betancourt	Mil	-9	2	0	-7
Jimmy Rollins	Phi	-9	2	0	-7
Ryan Theriot	StL	-8	0	0	-8
Cliff Pennington	Oak	-10	1	0	-9
Jason Bartlett	SD	-8	0	-1	-9
Starlin Castro	ChC	-6	-2	-2	-10
Tsuyoshi Nishioka	Min	-7	-2	-3	-12
Jose Reyes	NYM	-14	0	1	-13
Hanley Ramirez	Fla	-12	-1	0	-13
Derek Jeter	NYY	-13	-1	-1	-15

Shortstops - 2009 Runs Saved

Player	Team	Plus/Minus	GDP	GFP/DME	Total
Jack Wilson	2 tms	25	2	1	28
Brendan Ryan	StL	19	2	1	22
Elvis Andrus	Tex	11	2	2	15
Cesar Izturis	Bal	11	0	3	14
Troy Tulowitzki	Col	8	2	3	13
Marco Scutaro	Tor	12	-1	0	11
Paul Janish	Cin	10	0	1	11
Stephen Drew	Ari	8	0	1	9
Adam Everett	Det	7	0	2	9
Rafael Furcal	LAD	6	1	0	7
Yunel Escobar	Atl	13	-1	-5	7
Jason Bartlett	TB	8	-4	1	5
Derek Jeter	NYY	5	-3	1	3
Robert Andino	Bal	2	1	0	3
Alexei Ramirez	CWS	2	0	0	2
Hanley Ramirez	Fla	4	-2	0	2
J.J. Hardy	Mil	3	-1	0	2
Alex Cora	NYM	1	1	0	2
Erick Aybar	LAA	-3	2	2	1
Ryan Theriot	ChC	5	-1	-4	0
Asdrubal Cabrera	Cle	-2	2	0	0
Nick Green	Bos	0	1	-1	0
Jimmy Rollins	Phi	-2	0	0	-2
Cristian Guzman	Was	-1	0	-1	-2
Ramon Santiago	Det	-2	-1	0	-3
Ronny Cedeno	2 tms	-4	1	-1	-4
Alex Gonzalez	2 tms	-6	0	1	-5
Nick Punto	Min	-7	1	1	-5
Brendan Harris	Min	-6	-1	0	-7
Everth Cabrera	SD	-8	0	0	-8
Cliff Pennington	Oak	-11	1	1	-9
Edgar Renteria	SF	-8	-2	0	-10
Miguel Tejada	Hou	-16	0	1	-15
Yuniesky Betancourt	2 tms	-20	1	1	-18
Orlando Cabrera	2 tms	-30	-1	2	-29

Left Fielders - 3-Year Runs Saved

Player	Plus/Minus	OF Arm	GFP/DME	Total
Brett Gardner	35	10	4	49
Gerardo Parra	20	2	1	23
Alex Gordon	8	15	0	23
Carl Crawford	14	4	0	18
Laynce Nix	11	8	-2	17
Ryan Raburn	6	6	2	14
Josh Hamilton	11	0	0	11
Travis Snider	7	4	-1	10
Matt Holliday	14	-4	-1	9
Scott Hairston	11	-3	1	9
Ryan Braun	14	-12	6	8
Jose Tabata	14	-6	0	8
Juan Rivera	-2	6	3	7
Lastings Milledge	3	1	3	7
Fred Lewis	10	-3	-2	5
Carlos Gonzalez	-1	3	3	5
Nolan Reimold	-1	2	3	4
David DeJesus	-3	5	2	4
Michael Saunders	3	0	1	4
David Murphy	10	-7	0	3
Jason Bay	-6	1	7	2
Seth Smith	8	-4	-3	1
Johnny Damon	-1	1	0	0
Josh Willingham	-6	1	2	-3
Ryan Ludwick	-2	-3	1	-4
Felix Pie	-16	4	0	-12
Carlos Lee	-13	-2	-2	-17
Chris Coghlan	-19	2	0	-17
Juan Pierre	-10	-10	1	-19
Manny Ramirez	-12	-7	-2	-21
Jonny Gomes	-18	0	-4	-22
Delmon Young	-19	-5	0	-24
Logan Morrison	-30	4	-5	-31
Raul Ibanez	-35	-2	1	-36
Alfonso Soriano	-22	-2	-13	-37

Left Fielders - 2010 Runs Saved

Player	Team	Plus/Minus	OF Arm	GFP/DME	Total
Brett Gardner	NYY	15	7	4	26
Gerardo Parra	Ari	10	1	0	11
Ryan Braun	Mil	11	-4	2	9
Carl Crawford	TB	7	0	1	8
Matt Holliday	StL	10	-1	-2	7
Josh Hamilton	Tex	7	0	0	7
Jose Tabata	Pit	7	-3	1	5
David Murphy	Tex	4	-1	2	5
Lastings Milledge	Pit	3	1	1	5
Travis Snider	Tor	6	-1	0	5
Jason Bay	NYM	2	0	1	3
Michael Saunders	Sea	0	2	1	3
Alex Gordon	KC	3	2	-2	3
Carlos Gonzalez	Col	1	0	2	3
Chris Coghlan	Fla	-4	3	3	2
Ryan Raburn	Det	1	1	0	2
Corey Patterson	Bal	2	0	0	2
Josh Willingham	Was	-2	2	1	1
Scott Hairston	SD	7	-5	-1	1
Pat Burrell	SF	-4	3	1	0
Felix Pie	Bal	-5	5	0	0
Seth Smith	Col	2	0	-2	0
Matt Diaz	Atl	3	-2	-1	0
Melky Cabrera	Atl	-5	2	0	-3
Austin Kearns	2 tms	-3	0	-1	-4
Fred Lewis	Tor	-2	-1	-2	-5
Logan Morrison	Fla	-7	3	-1	-5
Juan Pierre	CWS	-7	-4	2	-9
Raul Ibanez	Phi	-8	-3	0	-11
Juan Rivera	LAA	-10	0	-2	-12
Delmon Young	Min	-16	2	1	-13
Alfonso Soriano	ChC	-8	-4	-2	-14
Scott Podsednik	2 tms	-3	-7	-5	-15
Carlos Lee	Hou	-9	-6	-3	-18
Jonny Gomes	Cin	-17	-2	-2	-21

Left Fielders - 2011 Runs Saved

Player	Team	Plus/Minus	OF Arm	GFP/DME	Total
Brett Gardner	NYY	20	3	0	23
Alex Gordon	KC	5	13	2	20
Tony Gwynn	LAD	10	0	2	12
Gerardo Parra	Ari	9	2	0	11
Sam Fuld	TB	2	4	3	9
Michael Brantley	Cle	6	2	0	8
Martin Prado	Atl	4	2	1	7
Carlos Lee	Hou	2	3	2	7
Laynce Nix	Was	2	4	0	6
Brennan Boesch	Det	1	2	2	5
Josh Hamilton	Tex	4	0	0	4
Ryan Braun	Mil	8	-6	1	3
Jose Tabata	Pit	7	-3	-1	3
Desmond Jennings	TB	4	0	-1	3
Juan Rivera	2 tms	0	3	0	3
Carlos Gonzalez	Col	-1	2	1	2
J.D. Martinez	Hou	-2	2	2	2
Alex Presley	Pit	3	0	-1	2
David Murphy	Tex	6	-4	-1	1
Josh Willingham	Oak	-3	0	3	0
Jonny Gomes	2 tms	1	1	-2	0
Michael Morse	Was	-3	1	2	0
Matt Holliday	StL	0	-2	1	-1
Carl Crawford	Bos	-2	0	0	-2
Nolan Reimold	Bal	-3	-1	2	-2
Jason Bay	NYM	-5	0	2	-3
Delmon Young	2 tms	1	-3	-1	-3
Ryan Ludwick	2 tms	-3	-3	1	-5
Cody Ross	SF	-7	2	0	-5
Vernon Wells	LAA	-3	-2	-3	-8
Alfonso Soriano	ChC	-6	1	-4	-9
Eric Thames	Tor	-5	-2	-2	-9
Juan Pierre	CWS	-6	-4	-1	-11
Raul Ibanez	Phi	-18	-3	-2	-23
Logan Morrison	Fla	-23	1	-4	-26

Left Fielders - 2009 Runs Saved

Player	Team	Plus/Minus	OF Arm	GFP/DME	Total
Juan Rivera	LAA	8	3	5	16
Carl Crawford	TB	9	4	-1	12
Scott Hairston	2 tms	5	2	2	9
Wladimir Balentien	2 tms	1	5	2	8
Ryan Raburn	Det	2	5	1	8
Denard Span	Min	4	1	2	7
Scott Podsednik	CWS	5	0	1	6
Nyjer Morgan	Pit	6	0	0	6
Nolan Reimold	Bal	1	2	2	5
Laynce Nix	Cin	6	1	-2	5
David DeJesus	KC	-3	5	2	4
Lastings Milledge	Pit	1	1	2	4
Matt Holliday	2 tms	4	-1	0	3
Seth Smith	Col	7	-3	-1	3
Fred Lewis	SF	4	0	-1	3
Jason Bay	Bos	-3	1	4	2
Johnny Damon	NYY	1	0	0	1
Juan Pierre	LAD	3	-2	0	1
Gerardo Parra	Ari	1	-1	1	1
Ben Francisco	2 tms	-1	1	0	0
Raul Ibanez	Phi	-9	4	3	-2
David Murphy	Tex	0	-2	-1	-3
Ryan Braun	Mil	-5	-2	3	-4
Josh Willingham	Was	-1	-1	-2	-4
Chris Duncan	StL	-1	-2	-1	-4
Carlos Lee	Hou	-6	1	-1	-6
Adam Lind	Tor	-4	-2	0	-6
Delmon Young	Min	-4	-4	0	-8
Garret Anderson	Atl	-6	-4	-1	-11
Chase Headley	SD	-3	-7	-2	-12
Manny Ramirez	LAD	-5	-5	-2	-12
Carlos Quentin	CWS	-10	0	-2	-12
Adam Dunn	Was	-6	-3	-3	-12
Alfonso Soriano	ChC	-8	1	-7	-14
Chris Coghlan	Fla	-15	-1	-3	-19

Center Fielders - 3-Year Runs Saved

Player	Plus/Minus	OF Arm	GFP/DME	Total
Franklin Gutierrez	30	0	12	42
Austin Jackson	40	1	1	42
Michael Bourn	36	2	0	38
Chris Young	41	-5	-4	32
Tony Gwynn	33	-2	1	32
Carlos Gomez	20	1	4	25
Peter Bourjos	11	6	8	25
Curtis Granderson	7	5	5	17
Angel Pagan	12	6	-3	15
Cameron Maybin	23	-6	-2	15
Coco Crisp	14	-6	5	13
Rick Ankiel	-1	9	-1	7
Jacoby Ellsbury	13	-7	-2	4
Andres Torres	9	-2	-3	4
Aaron Rowand	4	-2	1	3
Shane Victorino	-8	7	3	2
Torii Hunter	5	-3	0	2
Drew Stubbs	-6	6	-1	-1
Denard Span	10	-12	1	-1
Nyjer Morgan	7	-2	-6	-1
Colby Rasmus	-1	1	-2	-2
Mike Cameron	6	-5	-5	-4
Cody Ross	1	-3	-2	-4
Marlon Byrd	-13	4	3	-6
Alex Rios	0	-7	-1	-8
Rajai Davis	-3	-4	-1	-8
Adam Jones	-38	23	5	-10
Dexter Fowler	-1	-8	-3	-12
Andrew McCutchen	-13	-1	1	-13
Melky Cabrera	-14	-1	2	-13
Grady Sizemore	-4	-8	-2	-14
Vernon Wells	-14	-2	-1	-17
Nate McLouth	-17	-4	-2	-23
B.J. Upton	-20	1	-7	-26
Matt Kemp	-53	7	0	-46

Center Fielders - 2010 Runs Saved

Player	Team	Plus/Minus	OF Arm	GFP/DME	Total
Michael Bourn	Hou	27	2	1	30
Chris Young	Ari	16	3	-1	18
Tony Gwynn	SD	16	0	2	18
Austin Jackson	Det	17	-1	-3	13
Angel Pagan	NYM	11	4	-2	13
Curtis Granderson	NYY	10	2	0	12
Julio Borbon	Tex	14	-3	0	11
Coco Crisp	Oak	5	-1	3	7
Cameron Maybin	Fla	7	-1	0	6
Carlos Gomez	Mil	5	1	-1	5
Marlon Byrd	ChC	-2	5	1	4
Andres Torres	SF	8	-2	-2	4
Aaron Rowand	SF	2	0	1	3
Dexter Fowler	Col	2	-4	4	2
Shane Victorino	Phi	-5	3	3	1
Franklin Gutierrez	Sea	-1	-3	4	0
Alex Rios	CWS	1	-3	1	-1
Drew Stubbs	Cin	-2	0	1	-1
Rick Ankiel	2 tms	-1	1	-1	-1
Mitch Maier	KC	-3	1	0	-2
Cody Ross	2 tms	-1	-2	-1	-4
Trevor Crowe	Cle	-3	0	-1	-4
Denard Span	Min	-3	-3	1	-5
Vernon Wells	Tor	-1	-3	-1	-5
Rajai Davis	Oak	0	-3	-2	-5
Carlos Beltran	NYM	-7	2	0	-5
Colby Rasmus	StL	-6	-1	1	-6
Adam Jones	Bal	-12	5	-1	-8
Andrew McCutchen	Pit	-10	1	1	-8
Nyjer Morgan	Was	1	-6	-3	-8
Torii Hunter	LAA	-7	-2	-1	-10
Michael Brantley	Cle	-12	-3	1	-14
B.J. Upton	TB	-12	-1	-6	-19
Nate McLouth	Atl	-17	-2	-2	-21
Matt Kemp	LAD	-30	-4	-3	-37

Center Fielders - 2011 Runs Saved

Player	Team	Plus/Minus	OF Arm	GFP/DME	Total
Austin Jackson	Det	23	2	4	29
Chris Young	Ari	22	-3	1	20
Cameron Maybin	SD	18	-2	-1	15
Carlos Gomez	Mil	9	3	3	15
Peter Bourjos	LAA	6	3	3	12
Franklin Gutierrez	Sea	5	1	4	10
Denard Span	Min	13	-3	-1	9
Rick Ankiel	Was	-1	8	1	8
Jacoby Ellsbury	Bos	9	-2	0	7
Andrew McCutchen	Pit	8	-3	0	5
Jon Jay	StL	4	0	0	4
Nyjer Morgan	Mil	7	-2	-2	3
Shane Victorino	Phi	3	-1	0	2
Coco Crisp	Oak	2	-3	2	1
Ezequiel Carrera	Cle	3	0	-2	1
Marlon Byrd	ChC	-4	2	2	0
Endy Chavez	Tex	1	-1	0	0
Ben Revere	Min	4	-3	-2	-1
Michael Bourn	2 tms	2	-3	-2	-3
Dexter Fowler	Col	3	-2	-4	-3
Andres Torres	SF	-2	0	-1	-3
Drew Stubbs	Cin	-8	5	-1	-4
Adam Jones	Bal	-12	8	0	-4
Colby Rasmus	2 tms	-1	-2	-1	-4
Matt Kemp	LAD	-11	4	2	-5
Curtis Granderson	NYY	-11	2	3	-6
Melky Cabrera	KC	-7	-1	2	-6
Grady Sizemore	Cle	-5	-1	0	-6
B.J. Upton	TB	-7	1	-1	-7
Jordan Schafer	2 tms	-4	-1	-2	-7
Nate McLouth	Atl	-3	-2	-2	-7
Angel Pagan	NYM	-5	-1	-2	-8
Alex Rios	CWS	-6	-1	-2	-9
Rajai Davis	Tor	-6	-4	1	-9
Chris Coghlan	Fla	-12	-1	0	-13

Center Fielders - 2009 Runs Saved

Player	Team	Plus/Minus	OF Arm	GFP/DME	Total
Franklin Gutierrez	Sea	26	2	4	32
Torii Hunter	LAA	12	-1	1	12
Curtis Granderson	Det	8	1	2	11
Michael Bourn	Hou	7	3	1	11
Tony Gwynn	SD	15	-3	-1	11
Angel Pagan	NYM	6	3	1	10
Colby Rasmus	StL	6	4	-2	8
Willy Taveras	Cin	4	3	0	7
Brett Gardner	NYY	4	2	1	7
Rajai Davis	Oak	3	3	0	6
Nate McLouth	2 tms	3	0	2	5
Carlos Gomez	Min	6	-3	2	5
Nyjer Morgan	2 tms	-1	6	-1	4
Adam Jones	Bal	-14	10	6	2
Cody Ross	Fla	4	-1	-1	2
Carlos Beltran	NYM	4	-1	-1	2
Mike Cameron	Mil	10	-5	-4	1
B.J. Upton	TB	-1	1	0	0
Josh Hamilton	Tex	-1	1	0	0
Rick Ankiel	StL	1	0	-1	0
Shane Victorino	Phi	-6	5	0	-1
Mitch Maier	KC	-4	3	0	-1
Aaron Rowand	SF	1	-2	-1	-2
Matt Kemp	LAD	-12	7	1	-4
Jacoby Ellsbury	Bos	1	-4	-2	-5
Grady Sizemore	Cle	1	-5	-1	-5
Denard Span	Min	0	-6	1	-5
Chris Young	Ari	3	-5	-4	-6
Kosuke Fukudome	ChC	-9	2	0	-7
Melky Cabrera	NYY	-5	-1	-1	-7
Vernon Wells	Tor	-11	1	0	-10
Andrew McCutchen	Pit	-11	1	0	-10
Marlon Byrd	Tex	-7	-3	0	-10
Dexter Fowler	Col	-6	-2	-3	-11
Willie Harris	Was	-5	-4	-3	-12

Right Fielders - 3-Year Runs Saved

Player	Plus/Minus	OF Arm	GFP/DME	Total
Jason Heyward	38	-7	-1	30
Jeff Francoeur	4	17	8	29
Ben Zobrist	11	8	4	23
Hunter Pence	9	10	1	20
Jay Bruce	16	1	3	20
Mike Stanton	15	4	-3	16
Will Venable	17	0	-2	15
Justin Upton	36	-11	-11	14
J.D. Drew	26	-11	-2	13
Shin-Soo Choo	-5	12	5	12
Torii Hunter	-2	5	5	8
Garrett Jones	5	2	0	7
Cody Ross	6	-1	0	5
David DeJesus	6	-5	3	4
Ryan Sweeney	0	2	2	4
Nate Schierholtz	-4	7	0	3
Matt Joyce	-4	2	5	3
Kosuke Fukudome	2	2	-2	2
Ryan Ludwick	2	-2	1	1
Corey Hart	11	-7	-4	0
Ichiro Suzuki	5	-13	7	-1
Jayson Werth	-10	11	-3	-2
Nelson Cruz	0	-3	0	-3
Carlos Beltran	-2	0	-1	-3
Jose Bautista	-25	13	7	-5
Seth Smith	3	-7	-5	-9
Jason Kubel	-16	4	1	-11
Nick Markakis	-24	4	8	-12
Nick Swisher	-13	3	-2	-12
Bobby Abreu	-17	7	-5	-15
Andre Ethier	-6	-12	0	-18
Brad Hawpe	-13	-7	-3	-23
Carlos Quentin	-8	-13	-3	-24
Michael Cuddyer	-34	2	4	-28
Magglio Ordonez	-28	-1	0	-29

Right Fielders - 2010 Runs Saved

Player	Team	Plus/Minus	OF Arm	GFP/DME	Total
Jay Bruce	Cin	18	-2	1	17
Jeff Francoeur	2 tms	8	8	1	17
Jason Heyward	Atl	19	-5	1	15
Mike Stanton	Fla	10	2	1	13
J.D. Drew	Bos	12	-2	-2	8
Ben Zobrist	TB	4	3	1	8
Ryan Ludwick	2 tms	10	-3	0	7
Will Venable	SD	7	0	0	7
Cody Ross	2 tms	6	0	0	6
Shin-Soo Choo	Cle	-10	10	5	5
Nate Schierholtz	SF	1	4	0	5
Corey Hart	Mil	5	-1	-1	3
Nelson Cruz	Tex	3	-1	1	3
Roger Bernadina	Was	3	1	-1	3
Hunter Pence	Hou	4	-1	-1	2
Justin Upton	Ari	9	-5	-2	2
Ryan Sweeney	Oak	0	-1	1	0
Ichiro Suzuki	Sea	2	-5	2	-1
Nick Swisher	NYY	-3	2	0	-1
Kosuke Fukudome	ChC	1	-1	-1	-1
Torii Hunter	LAA	-3	0	2	-1
Jayson Werth	Phi	-9	5	2	-2
David DeJesus	KC	-2	-2	2	-2
Jose Bautista	Tor	-13	6	4	-3
Michael Morse	Was	-4	1	-1	-4
Brad Hawpe	2 tms	-4	-2	-1	-7
Jose Guillen	2 tms	-2	-2	-3	-7
Jason Kubel	Min	-8	-1	0	-9
Brennan Boesch	Det	-9	2	-2	-9
Magglio Ordonez	Det	-8	-1	-1	-10
Michael Cuddyer	Min	-14	2	2	-10
Nick Markakis	Bal	-11	0	0	-11
Bobby Abreu	LAA	-7	0	-4	-11
Andre Ethier	LAD	-9	-5	0	-14
Carlos Quentin	CWS	-15	-7	-2	-24

Right Fielders - 2011 Runs Saved

Player	Team	Plus/Minus	OF Arm	GFP/DME	Total
Jason Heyward	Atl	19	-2	-2	15
Torii Hunter	LAA	1	5	3	9
Justin Upton	Ari	17	-5	-4	8
Josh Reddick	Bos	9	-1	-1	7
David DeJesus	Oak	7	-3	1	5
Will Venable	SD	6	0	-1	5
Andre Ethier	LAD	5	-2	1	4
Mike Stanton	Fla	5	2	-4	3
Shin-Soo Choo	Cle	2	2	-1	3
Chris Denorfia	SD	2	0	1	3
Nick Markakis	Bal	-6	2	6	2
Jeff Francoeur	KC	-7	5	3	1
Hunter Pence	2 tms	-4	5	0	1
Carlos Quentin	CWS	7	-6	-1	0
Corey Hart	Mil	5	-4	-2	-1
Brennan Boesch	Det	0	-1	0	-1
Jay Bruce	Cin	0	-2	0	-2
Kosuke Fukudome	2 tms	-3	3	-2	-2
Matt Joyce	TB	-5	0	3	-2
J.D. Drew	Bos	2	-4	0	-2
Ichiro Suzuki	Sea	-2	-3	2	-3
Carlos Beltran	2 tms	-2	0	-1	-3
Jason Kubel	Min	-9	5	1	-3
Nick Swisher	NYY	-8	3	1	-4
Jayson Werth	Was	-6	3	-1	-4
Garrett Jones	Pit	-3	-1	0	-4
Seth Smith	Col	2	-5	-3	-6
Nelson Cruz	Tex	-3	-3	0	-6
Jose Bautista	Tor	-13	3	3	-7
Ben Francisco	Phi	-6	1	-2	-7
Nate Schierholtz	SF	-9	1	0	-8
Magglio Ordonez	Det	-10	1	0	-9
Domonic Brown	Phi	-5	-2	-2	-9
Michael Cuddyer	Min	-11	0	1	-10
Lance Berkman	StL	-14	-2	-2	-18

Right Fielders - 2009 Runs Saved

Player	Team	Plus/Minus	OF Arm	GFP/DME	Total
Hunter Pence	Hou	9	6	2	17
Jeff Francoeur	2 tms	3	4	4	11
Ryan Church	2 tms	6	4	1	11
Ryan Sweeney	Oak	6	2	0	8
J.D. Drew	Bos	12	-5	0	7
Gabe Gross	TB	2	2	3	7
Randy Winn	SF	4	2	0	6
Nate Schierholtz	SF	4	2	0	6
Jay Bruce	Cin	-2	5	2	5
Brandon Moss	Pit	1	2	2	5
Jayson Werth	Phi	5	3	-4	4
Justin Upton	Ari	10	-1	-5	4
Shin-Soo Choo	Cle	3	0	1	4
Alex Rios	2 tms	1	4	-1	4
Ichiro Suzuki	Sea	5	-5	3	3
Jeremy Hermida	Fla	4	0	-1	3
Will Venable	SD	4	0	-1	3
Cody Ross	Fla	3	0	0	3
Nelson Cruz	Tex	0	1	-1	0
Clete Thomas	Det	-2	2	0	0
Bobby Abreu	LAA	-8	7	-1	-2
Corey Hart	Mil	1	-2	-1	-2
Elijah Dukes	Was	-1	1	-2	-2
Nick Markakis	Bal	-7	2	2	-3
Ryan Ludwick	StL	-6	2	1	-3
Milton Bradley	ChC	-1	-2	-2	-5
Matt Diaz	Atl	-4	-1	-1	-6
Nick Swisher	NYY	-2	-2	-3	-7
Andre Ethier	LAD	-2	-5	-1	-8
Michael Cuddyer	Min	-9	0	1	-8
Brian Giles	SD	-1	-6	-1	-8
Magglio Ordonez	Det	-10	-1	1	-10
Jermaine Dye	CWS	-12	-4	5	-11
Brad Hawpe	Col	-9	-5	-2	-16
Jose Guillen	KC	-12	-5	-2	-19

Catchers - 3-Year Runs Saved

Player	Adj ER	Stolen Bases	Bunts	GFP/DME	Total
Matt Wieters	10	8	3	5	26
Yadier Molina	0	10	0	15	25
Jeff Mathis	9	0	-1	14	22
Russell Martin	4	7	-1	9	19
Carlos Ruiz	5	0	1	11	17
Humberto Quintero	3	7	2	5	17
Kurt Suzuki	3	-3	1	12	13
Jason Varitek	11	-13	1	10	9
Miguel Montero	11	3	0	-6	8
Chris Iannetta	4	2	3	-1	8
Rod Barajas	2	-3	-2	8	5
Joe Mauer	9	-2	2	-4	5
Ryan Hanigan	9	1	0	-5	5
Rob Johnson	3	4	4	-7	4
Ivan Rodriguez	-9	9	1	2	3
Dioner Navarro	4	0	-1	-1	2
Gerald Laird	0	4	-2	-1	1
Lou Marson	-1	6	0	-4	1
Jonathan Lucroy	-1	-2	0	2	-1
Ronny Paulino	1	0	3	-6	-2
Jarrod Saltalamacchia	3	3	-1	-7	-2
Miguel Olivo	4	7	-1	-14	-4
Nick Hundley	-1	-2	-1	0	-4
Ryan Doumit	0	-9	0	5	-4
Geovany Soto	-2	-2	1	-2	-5
Yorvit Torrealba	1	-3	-5	1	-6
Kelly Shoppach	-5	1	-2	-1	-7
Chris Snyder	0	-5	2	-5	-8
Brian McCann	-12	1	4	-3	-10
Alex Avila	0	-4	-3	-4	-11
Mike Napoli	-8	-3	-2	2	-11
A.J. Pierzynski	3	0	-1	-16	-14
Ramon Hernandez	-14	-2	3	-4	-17
John Buck	-5	-10	-1	-3	-19
Victor Martinez	-14	-7	-2	1	-22

Catchers - 2010 Runs Saved

Player	Team	Adj ER	Stolen Bases	Bunts	GFP/DME	Total
Yadier Molina	StL	6	6	1	7	20
Miguel Olivo	Col	3	11	-1	-2	11
Kurt Suzuki	Oak	6	-2	1	3	8
Yorvit Torrealba	SD	6	1	-1	2	8
Buster Posey	SF	1	4	1	2	8
Matt Wieters	Bal	0	5	2	0	7
Carlos Ruiz	Phi	5	2	-1	1	7
Humberto Quintero	Hou	1	4	2	0	7
Russell Martin	LAD	0	4	-2	3	5
Jonathan Lucroy	Mil	-1	2	0	3	4
Jeff Mathis	LAA	2	-1	0	3	4
Joe Mauer	Min	4	-1	1	-1	3
Ronny Paulino	Fla	0	1	1	1	3
Ivan Rodriguez	Was	-4	2	0	4	2
Jason Kendall	KC	-3	-1	1	4	1
Miguel Montero	Ari	1	1	1	-2	1
A.J. Pierzynski	CWS	4	2	0	-6	0
Koyie Hill	ChC	0	-3	1	2	0
Brian McCann	Atl	-6	4	1	0	-1
Lou Marson	Cle	-1	1	-1	-1	-2
Bengie Molina	2 tms	-1	-1	0	-1	-3
Geovany Soto	ChC	1	-4	0	0	-3
Chris Snyder	2 tms	0	-3	2	-2	-3
Rod Barajas	2 tms	2	-4	-1	0	-3
Francisco Cervelli	NYY	3	-4	1	-3	-3
John Jaso	TB	-1	-2	0	0	-3
Gerald Laird	Det	2	-2	-1	-2	-3
Matt Treanor	Tex	1	-1	-1	-2	-3
Ryan Doumit	Pit	1	-8	0	3	-4
Alex Avila	Det	-2	-2	-2	-1	-7
Ramon Hernandez	Cin	-10	0	2	1	-7
Victor Martinez	Bos	-5	-2	-2	1	-8
Nick Hundley	SD	-5	-1	0	-2	-8
John Buck	Tor	-5	-3	-1	-2	-11
Jorge Posada	NYY	-2	-6	-1	-5	-14

Catchers - 2011 Runs Saved

Player	Team	Adj ER	Stolen Bases	Bunts	GFP/DME	Total
Matt Wieters	Bal	9	5	1	2	17
Chris Iannetta	Col	4	3	1	0	8
Jeff Mathis	LAA	3	1	-1	5	8
Russell Martin	NYY	0	2	-1	6	7
Humberto Quintero	Hou	1	1	0	4	6
Miguel Montero	Ari	3	3	0	-1	5
Nick Hundley	SD	-1	2	0	4	5
Kelly Shoppach	TB	-2	5	-1	1	3
Brayan Pena	KC	-1	2	-1	3	3
Rod Barajas	LAD	-1	-1	-1	5	2
Lou Marson	Cle	0	3	1	-2	2
Carlos Ruiz	Phi	-4	-2	1	5	0
Ryan Hanigan	Cin	4	-1	0	-3	0
Kurt Suzuki	Oak	-4	1	0	2	-1
Geovany Soto	ChC	-2	1	1	-1	-1
Drew Butera	Min	-6	3	2	0	-1
Jason Varitek	Bos	2	-5	0	2	-1
Alex Avila	Det	3	-2	0	-3	-2
Eli Whiteside	SF	-2	-1	1	0	-2
Matt Treanor	2 tms	2	0	-2	-2	-2
John Jaso	TB	2	-3	-1	-1	-3
Yadier Molina	StL	-6	0	-1	3	-4
Brian McCann	Atl	-2	-3	2	-1	-4
Jarrod Saltalamacchia	Bos	-2	4	-1	-5	-4
Josh Thole	NYM	-1	-4	0	1	-4
Carlos Santana	Cle	0	-1	0	-3	-4
Ramon Hernandez	Cin	-3	0	2	-3	-4
John Buck	Fla	0	-3	0	-2	-5
J.P. Arencibia	Tor	1	-5	1	-2	-5
Jonathan Lucroy	Mil	0	-4	0	-1	-5
Wilson Ramos	Was	-2	1	-1	-3	-5
Ronny Paulino	NYM	-1	-3	2	-4	-6
Miguel Olivo	Sea	0	-3	0	-6	-9
A.J. Pierzynski	CWS	-2	-3	-1	-3	-9
Yorvit Torrealba	Tex	-5	-1	-4	-2	-12

Catchers - 2009 Runs Saved

Player	Team	Adj ER	Stolen Bases	Bunts	GFP/DME	Total
Carlos Ruiz	Phi	4	0	1	5	10
Jeff Mathis	LAA	4	0	0	6	10
Yadier Molina	StL	0	4	0	5	9
Russell Martin	LAD	4	1	2	0	7
Jason Varitek	Bos	8	-8	1	6	7
Koyie Hill	ChC	2	5	0	0	7
Kurt Suzuki	Oak	1	-2	0	7	6
Gerald Laird	Det	-2	7	0	1	6
Rod Barajas	Tor	1	2	0	3	6
Ryan Doumit	Pit	2	0	1	3	6
Rob Johnson	Sea	4	4	1	-5	4
Chris Iannetta	Col	1	1	1	0	3
Jarrod Saltalamacchia	Tex	5	-1	0	-1	3
Joe Mauer	Min	4	-1	0	-1	2
Miguel Montero	Ari	7	-1	-1	-3	2
Matt Wieters	Bal	1	-2	0	3	2
Ryan Hanigan	Cin	0	2	0	-1	1
Ronny Paulino	Fla	2	2	0	-3	1
Ivan Rodriguez	2 tms	-6	4	2	-1	-1
Geovany Soto	ChC	-1	1	0	-1	-1
Nick Hundley	SD	5	-3	-1	-2	-1
Dioner Navarro	TB	0	0	-1	-1	-2
Gregg Zaun	2 tms	-4	-3	0	4	-3
Omir Santos	NYM	-1	-2	0	-1	-4
A.J. Pierzynski	CWS	1	1	0	-7	-5
Brian McCann	Atl	-4	0	1	-2	-5
Mike Napoli	LAA	-3	-4	-1	3	-5
Kelly Shoppach	Cle	0	-2	0	-3	-5
Miguel Olivo	KC	1	-1	0	-6	-6
Jason Kendall	Mil	-6	-2	-1	2	-7
Josh Bard	Was	0	-1	-1	-7	-9
Bengie Molina	SF	-7	-2	-1	0	-10
John Baker	Fla	-3	-5	-1	-2	-11
Victor Martinez	2 tms	-8	-4	0	0	-12
Jorge Posada	NYY	-10	-1	0	-3	-14

Pitchers - 3-Year Runs Saved

Player	Plus/Minus	SB	Bunts	GFP/DME	Total
Mark Buehrle	17	12	0	0	29
Zack Greinke	7	6	6	2	21
Jake Westbrook	17	1	1	1	20
Ricky Romero	8	5	4	0	17
Jon Garland	12	2	2	1	17
R.A. Dickey	11	2	2	2	17
Bronson Arroyo	10	0	4	2	16
Joe Saunders	4	6	2	0	12
Trevor Cahill	12	-1	-1	2	12
Brad Bergesen	10	2	0	0	12
Jeremy Guthrie	6	3	2	0	11
Javier Vazquez	8	1	2	0	11
Aaron Cook	5	5	0	1	11
Tim Stauffer	4	4	2	1	11
Justin Verlander	5	4	0	1	10
Bruce Chen	4	5	1	0	10
Randy Wolf	8	-1	2	0	9
Clayton Kershaw	-1	9	2	-1	9
John Danks	3	5	3	-2	9
Livan Hernandez	2	5	2	0	9
Jhoulys Chacin	7	2	0	0	9
Paul Maholm	4	3	0	1	8
Doug Fister	4	3	0	1	8
Wade LeBlanc	3	4	1	0	8
John Lannan	1	1	3	2	7
Johnny Cueto	2	6	0	-1	7
Jair Jurrjens	4	0	2	1	7
Carlos Zambrano	1	4	2	0	7
Ubaldo Jimenez	5	0	1	0	6
Wandy Rodriguez	5	0	1	0	6
Roy Oswalt	4	-1	3	0	6
Joel Pineiro	4	2	0	0	6
Barry Zito	3	3	0	0	6
Chris Narveson	5	3	-2	0	6
Brian Duensing	3	3	-1	1	6
Mike Leake	2	2	1	1	6
Jordan Zimmermann	3	4	0	-1	6
Jason Vargas	4	1	0	0	5
Ian Kennedy	3	0	2	0	5
Bud Norris	2	1	1	1	5
Jonathon Niese	3	3	0	-1	5
Jeff Francis	5	-1	1	0	5
Dan Haren	4	-2	2	0	4
Nick Blackburn	0	3	1	0	4
Tim Hudson	0	2	1	1	4
Zach Duke	1	3	0	0	4
Kyle Lohse	1	2	1	0	4
Shaun Marcum	2	2	0	0	4
Brett Cecil	3	2	0	-1	4
Kyle Kendrick	4	2	-2	0	4
James Shields	-5	8	0	0	3
Matt Cain	3	0	2	-2	3
Jon Lester	4	2	-3	0	3
Fausto Carmona	10	-5	0	-2	3
J.A. Happ	-1	3	1	0	3
Scott Feldman	4	-1	0	0	3
Dallas Braden	-2	7	-2	0	3
Scott Kazmir	0	2	1	0	3
Vicente Padilla	0	4	-1	0	3
Edward Mujica	1	1	1	0	3
Josh Tomlin	2	2	-1	0	3
D.J. Carrasco	3	1	0	-1	3
Matt Guerrier	2	0	1	0	3
Cole Hamels	4	0	-1	-1	2
Gavin Floyd	3	-2	0	1	2
David Price	-2	1	2	1	2
Hiroki Kuroda	2	0	1	-1	2
Scott Baker	-1	3	-1	1	2
Jorge de la Rosa	3	-2	0	1	2
Chris Capuano	1	1	0	0	2
Bartolo Colon	0	2	0	0	2
Chad Gaudin	-1	2	1	0	2
Jake Arrieta	4	-1	-1	0	2
Shawn Camp	1	0	1	0	2
Miguel Batista	2	0	0	0	2
Erik Bedard	1	2	-1	0	2
Jered Weaver	0	1	0	0	1
Chris Carpenter	-6	5	1	1	1
Ryan Dempster	4	-1	-1	-1	1
Yovani Gallardo	2	-2	1	0	1
Kevin Correia	2	2	-3	0	1
Clayton Richard	-3	8	-3	-1	1
Kevin Millwood	0	2	-1	0	1
Jeff Karstens	1	0	0	0	1
Wade Davis	-3	2	2	0	1
Brett Anderson	-3	3	1	0	1
Jaime Garcia	1	1	-1	0	1

Player	Plus/Minus	SB	Bunts	GFP/DME	Total
David Huff	1	0	0	0	1
Tyler Clippard	-1	1	1	0	1
Sean Marshall	1	0	1	-1	1
Mitch Talbot	-1	3	-1	0	1
Micah Owings	1	1	-2	1	1
Chad Billingsley	0	2	-2	0	0
Anibal Sanchez	-2	-1	2	1	0
Josh Johnson	0	-1	0	1	0
Clay Buchholz	0	1	0	-1	0
Armando Galarraga	-2	1	1	0	0
Tommy Hunter	-3	1	0	2	0
Craig Stammen	2	-2	0	0	0
Jeremy Hellickson	0	0	0	0	0
Gio Gonzalez	0	0	0	-1	-1
Daniel Hudson	0	1	-2	0	-1
Matt Harrison	-1	2	-1	-1	-1
Madison Bumgarner	-2	2	0	-1	-1
Jake Peavy	-2	-1	1	1	-1
Kevin Slowey	-1	0	0	0	-1
Doug Davis	-2	3	-2	0	-1
Kyle McClellan	-2	1	0	0	-1
Carlos Villanueva	3	-3	-1	0	-1
Phil Coke	-1	1	0	-1	-1
Aaron Laffey	-3	1	0	1	-1
Cliff Lee	-6	2	1	1	-2
Francisco Liriano	-2	2	-1	-1	-2
Jonathan Sanchez	0	-1	-1	0	-2
Aaron Harang	-1	0	-1	0	-2
Mat Latos	0	-2	1	-1	-2
Charlie Morton	-2	-1	1	0	-2
Phil Hughes	-2	-1	1	0	-2
Rodrigo Lopez	-1	0	0	-1	-2
Tom Gorzelanny	0	-1	-1	0	-2
Brandon McCarthy	-1	0	-1	0	-2
Brian Tallet	0	1	-2	-1	-2
Jason Berken	-2	0	0	0	-2
Edinson Volquez	1	-2	-1	0	-2
Alexi Ogando	-2	0	0	0	-2
Felix Hernandez	1	-3	-1	0	-3
Justin Masterson	-5	2	0	0	-3
Brett Myers	-3	2	-2	0	-3
Tim Wakefield	1	-4	-1	1	-3
Jason Marquis	0	-2	-1	1	-3
Homer Bailey	-3	0	-1	1	-3
Dave Bush	-1	-4	2	0	-3
Ross Ohlendorf	-3	1	-1	0	-3
James McDonald	-4	1	1	-1	-3
Brian Matusz	0	-2	-1	0	-3
Joba Chamberlain	-1	-3	1	0	-3
David Hernandez	-1	0	-2	0	-3
Carlos Marmol	0	-3	0	0	-3
Nick Masset	-2	0	0	-1	-3
Andy Sonnanstine	-1	0	-1	-1	-3
Luke Hochevar	-1	-5	2	0	-4
Brandon Morrow	-6	0	2	0	-4
Derek Holland	-9	5	-1	1	-4
Felipe Paulino	-6	2	1	-1	-4
Vin Mazzaro	-2	0	-2	0	-4
Carl Pavano	3	-8	0	0	-5
Matt Garza	-6	2	0	-1	-5
Max Scherzer	-8	3	0	0	-5
Jason Hammel	-1	-3	-1	0	-5
C.J. Wilson	1	-3	-2	-1	-5
Chris Volstad	-1	-4	0	0	-5
Joe Blanton	-3	-1	0	-1	-5
Colby Lewis	-4	0	-1	0	-5
Rich Harden	-4	2	-2	-1	-5
Roy Halladay	-4	-2	0	0	-6
Kyle Davies	-2	-3	-1	0	-6
Daisuke Matsuzaka	-1	-5	0	0	-6
Derek Lowe	-5	-1	-1	0	-7
Ted Lilly	6	-7	-5	-1	-7
Ricky Nolasco	-2	-1	-4	0	-7
CC Sabathia	-6	1	0	-3	-8
Josh Beckett	1	-8	-1	0	-8
Rick Porcello	-7	-1	1	-1	-8
Brandon League	-6	0	-2	0	-8
Edwin Jackson	-3	-5	-2	1	-9
A.J. Burnett	-4	-3	-1	-1	-9
Mike Pelfrey	-4	-3	-3	1	-9
Randy Wells	-5	-1	-2	-1	-9
Jeff Niemann	-5	-5	1	0	-9
Freddy Garcia	-3	-5	-1	0	-9
John Lackey	-2	-8	0	0	-10
Tommy Hanson	-1	-9	0	0	-10
Tim Lincecum	-7	-5	1	0	-11
Brad Penny	-7	-4	1	-1	-11
Ervin Santana	-7	-8	-1	1	-15

Pitchers - 2011 Runs Saved

Player	Team	Plus/Minus	SB	Bunts	GFP/DME	Total
R.A. Dickey	NYM	6	2	1	1	10
Jake Westbrook	StL	6	1	1	0	8
James Shields	TB	0	6	1	0	7
Joe Saunders	Ari	3	3	1	0	7
Mark Buehrle	CWS	4	4	-1	0	7
Hiroki Kuroda	LAD	5	1	1	0	7
Jhoulys Chacin	Col	6	2	-1	0	7
Tim Stauffer	SD	3	2	1	1	7
Jeremy Guthrie	Bal	3	2	1	0	6
Aaron Cook	Col	4	2	0	0	6
Justin Verlander	Det	4	1	-1	1	5
Clayton Kershaw	LAD	1	3	1	0	5
Ricky Romero	Tor	3	1	1	0	5
John Lannan	Was	2	1	1	1	5
Doug Fister	2 tms	4	1	-1	0	4
Bronson Arroyo	Cin	2	0	2	0	4
Jeff Francis	KC	4	-1	1	0	4
Zack Greinke	Mil	2	1	1	0	4
Mike Leake	Cin	2	1	1	0	4
Chris Narveson	Mil	2	2	0	0	4
Nick Blackburn	Min	1	2	1	0	4
Charlie Furbush	2 tms	3	1	0	0	4
Kyle Drabek	Tor	2	1	1	0	4
Dan Haren	LAA	4	-1	0	0	3
Yovani Gallardo	Mil	3	0	0	0	3
Anibal Sanchez	Fla	1	0	1	1	3
Wade Davis	TB	0	2	1	0	3
Livan Hernandez	Was	2	1	0	0	3
John Danks	CWS	-1	2	2	0	3
Paul Maholm	Pit	2	1	0	0	3
Jonathon Niese	NYM	2	0	1	0	3
Johnny Cueto	Cin	1	2	0	0	3
Bruce Chen	KC	2	1	0	0	3
Tim Wakefield	Bos	2	1	0	0	3
Tyler Chatwood	LAA	2	1	0	0	3
Cory Luebke	SD	1	1	1	0	3
Travis Wood	Cin	1	1	1	0	3
Jonny Venters	Atl	2	0	1	0	3
Guillermo Mota	SF	1	1	1	0	3
Wade LeBlanc	SD	1	1	1	0	3
Sam LeCure	Cin	1	0	1	1	3
Jered Weaver	LAA	-1	3	0	0	2
Ian Kennedy	Ari	1	0	1	0	2
Fausto Carmona	Cle	3	-1	0	0	2
Ivan Nova	NYY	2	1	0	-1	2
Jordan Zimmermann	Was	0	3	0	-1	2
Kevin Correia	Pit	2	1	-1	0	2
Jair Jurrjens	Atl	1	0	1	0	2
Carlos Zambrano	ChC	0	1	1	0	2
Francisco Liriano	Min	1	1	0	0	2
Vance Worley	Phi	1	0	0	1	2
Carlos Carrasco	Cle	1	1	0	0	2
Jake Arrieta	Bal	3	-1	0	0	2
Alfredo Simon	Bal	1	0	0	1	2
Danny Duffy	KC	-1	2	1	0	2
Brad Bergesen	Bal	1	1		0	2
Clayton Richard	SD	0	2	0	0	2
Casey Coleman	ChC	1	0	1	0	2
Clay Buchholz	Bos	2	0	0	0	2
Dontrelle Willis	Cin	0	2	0	0	2
Cliff Lee	Phi	0	0	0	1	1
Carl Pavano	Min	2	-1	0	0	1
Matt Cain	SF	2	-1	1	-1	1
Cole Hamels	Phi	4	-2	-1	0	1
Shaun Marcum	Mil	0	1	0	0	1
Jaime Garcia	StL	2	0	-1	0	1
Jon Lester	Bos	-1	2	0	0	1
Kyle Lohse	StL	0	1	0	0	1
Chad Billingsley	LAD	1	0	0	0	1
Chris Capuano	NYM	0	1	0	0	1
Bud Norris	Hou	1	0	0	0	1
Josh Tomlin	Cle	1	1	-1	0	1
Bartolo Colon	NYY	0	1	0	0	1
Jeff Karstens	Pit	1	-1	1	0	1
Dillon Gee	NYM	-1	1	1	0	1
J.A. Happ	Hou	0	1	0	0	1
Josh Collmenter	Ari	0	1	0	0	1
Brandon Beachy	Atl	1	0	0	0	1
Jo-Jo Reyes	2 tms	1	-1	1	0	1
Erik Bedard	2 tms	0	2	-1	0	1
Brett Cecil	Tor	1	0	0	0	1
Anthony Swarzak	Min	0	1	0	0	1
Rodrigo Lopez	ChC	0	1	0	0	1
Jordan Lyles	Hou	1	0	0	0	1
Tyler Clippard	Was	0	1	0	0	1
Tommy Hunter	2 tms	0	1	0	0	1
Brett Anderson	Oak	-1	2	0	0	1

Player	Team	Plus/Minus	SB	Bunts	GFP/DME	Total
Esmil Rogers	Col	-1	1	1	0	1
Cristhian Martinez	Atl	1	0	0	0	1
Craig Kimbrel	Atl	0	1	0	0	1
Edward Mujica	Fla	0	0	1	0	1
Chris Carpenter	StL	-3	2	1	0	0
Tim Lincecum	SF	-1	0	1	0	0
Justin Masterson	Cle	-2	2	0	0	0
Ryan Dempster	ChC	1	0	-1	0	0
Jason Vargas	Sea	1	-1	0	0	0
Colby Lewis	Tex	0	1	-1	0	0
Gavin Floyd	CWS	1	-2	0	1	0
Javier Vazquez	Fla	1	-1	0	0	0
Wandy Rodriguez	Hou	1	-2	1	0	0
Jeremy Hellickson	TB	0	0	0	0	0
Ubaldo Jimenez	2 tms	3	-2	-1	0	0
Ryan Vogelsong	SF	0	0	0	0	0
Charlie Morton	Pit	-1	0	1	0	0
Alexi Ogando	Tex	-2	1	1	0	0
Joel Pineiro	LAA	-1	1	0	0	0
Kyle McClellan	StL	-2	2	0	0	0
Roy Oswalt	Phi	0	-1	1	0	0
Jeff Niemann	TB	0	-1	1	0	0
Dustin Moseley	SD	1	-2	0	1	0
Kyle Kendrick	Phi	0	1	-1	0	0
Phil Coke	Det	-2	1	1	0	0
Jonathan Sanchez	SF	1	0	-1	0	0
Blake Beavan	Sea	0	0	0	0	0
Jim Johnson	Bal	0	0	0	0	0
Daniel McCutchen	Pit	0	0	0	0	0
Mike Minor	Atl	-1	1	0	0	0
Sean Marshall	ChC	0	0	0	0	0
David Price	TB	-1	-1	1	0	-1
Daniel Hudson	Ari	-1	1	-1	0	-1
Randy Wolf	Mil	1	-2	0	0	-1
Luke Hochevar	KC	0	-2	1	0	-1
Mat Latos	SD	1	-2	0	0	-1
Rick Porcello	Det	-1	-1	1	0	-1
Michael Pineda	Sea	-2	1	0	0	-1
Jason Hammel	Col	0	0	-1	0	-1
Brian Duensing	Min	-2	1	-1	1	-1
Marco Estrada	Mil	-1	0	0	0	-1
Rich Harden	Oak	-1	1	0	-1	-1
Zach Duke	Ari	-2	1	0	0	-1
Tim Hudson	Atl	-1	-1	0	0	-2
Madison Bumgarner	SF	-3	2	0	-1	-2
Gio Gonzalez	Oak	-1	-1	0	0	-2
Edwin Jackson	2 tms	1	-2	-1	0	-2
Max Scherzer	Det	-5	2	1	0	-2
Brad Penny	Det	-2	0	0	0	-2
James McDonald	Pit	-2	0	1	-1	-2
Aaron Harang	SD	1	-1	-2	0	-2
Brandon McCarthy	Oak	-1	0	-1	0	-2
Chris Volstad	Fla	-2	0	0	0	-2
Felipe Paulino	2 tms	-1	0	0	-1	-2
Randy Wells	ChC	-1	0	-1	0	-2
Scott Baker	Min	-2	1	-1	0	-2
Homer Bailey	Cin	-1	0	-1	0	-2
Guillermo Moscoso	Oak	0	0	-1	-1	-2
Alfredo Aceves	Bos	-1	-1	0	0	-2
Jake Peavy	CWS	-3	0	1	0	-2
Carlos Villanueva	Tor	2	-2	-2	0	-2
Tom Gorzelanny	Was	-1	0	-1	0	-2
Roy Halladay	Phi	-2	-1	0	0	-3
C.J. Wilson	Tex	0	-2	0	-1	-3
Trevor Cahill	Oak	1	-2	-2	0	-3
Ricky Nolasco	Fla	0	-1	-2	0	-3
Matt Garza	ChC	-2	1	-1	-1	-3
Derek Lowe	Atl	0	-3	0	0	-3
Jason Marquis	2 tms	-3	0	0	0	-3
Jeff Samardzija	ChC	-1	-2	0	0	-3
Aneury Rodriguez	Hou	-1	-2	0	0	-3
Derek Holland	Tex	-6	3	-1	0	-4
A.J. Burnett	NYY	-4	0	0	0	-4
Zach Britton	Bal	-1	0	-3	0	-4
Freddy Garcia	NYY	-1	-2	-1	0	-4
Tommy Hanson	Atl	0	-4	0	0	-4
CC Sabathia	NYY	-6	1	0	0	-5
Felix Hernandez	Sea	-2	-2	-1	0	-5
Brett Myers	Hou	-3	0	-2	0	-5
Josh Beckett	Bos	-1	-4	0	0	-5
Ted Lilly	LAD	2	-5	-1	-1	-5
Matt Harrison	Tex	-4	1	-1	-1	-5
Philip Humber	CWS	-3	-1	-1	0	-5
Edinson Volquez	Cin	-2	-2	-1	0	-5
Ervin Santana	LAA	-2	-3	-2	1	-6
Mike Pelfrey	NYM	-1	-4	-1	0	-6
Brandon Morrow	Tor	-5	-1	1	-1	-6
John Lackey	Bos	-1	-5	0	0	-6

Pitchers - 2010 Runs Saved

Player	Team	Plus/Minus	SB	Bunts	GFP/DME	Total
Mark Buehrle	CWS	6	5	1	0	12
Jake Westbrook	2 tms	11	0	0	1	12
Trevor Cahill	Oak	9	1	0	1	11
Ricky Romero	Tor	6	2	2	0	10
Zack Greinke	KC	3	2	3	1	9
Jon Garland	SD	5	2	2	0	9
Bronson Arroyo	Cin	6	0	1	1	8
R.A. Dickey	NYM	6	0	1	1	8
Javier Vazquez	NYY	5	1	1	0	7
Tim Hudson	Atl	2	2	1	1	6
Bruce Chen	KC	2	3	1	0	6
Chris Carpenter	StL	2	2	0	1	5
Randy Wolf	Mil	4	0	1	0	5
Wade LeBlanc	SD	2	3	0	0	5
Brian Duensing	Min	3	1	1	0	5
Adam Wainwright	StL	2	1	1	0	4
John Danks	CWS	2	2	1	-1	4
Joe Saunders	2 tms	0	3	1	0	4
Johan Santana	NYM	3	0	1	0	4
Wandy Rodriguez	Hou	3	1	0	0	4
Dallas Braden	Oak	1	4	-1	0	4
Kyle Kendrick	Phi	4	1	-1	0	4
Brad Bergesen	Bal	4	0	0	0	4
Bud Norris	Hou	2	0	1	1	4
Jorge de la Rosa	Col	2	0	1	1	4
Ubaldo Jimenez	Col	1	2	0	0	3
Roy Oswalt	2 tms	3	-1	1	0	3
Cole Hamels	Phi	2	1	0	0	3
Clayton Kershaw	LAD	0	3	1	-1	3
Clayton Richard	SD	1	3	-1	0	3
Shaun Marcum	Tor	2	1	0	0	3
Ian Kennedy	Ari	2	0	1	0	3
Mitch Talbot	Cle	1	3	-1	0	3
Scott Kazmir	LAA	1	1	1	0	3
Jeff Karstens	Pit	2	1	0	0	3
Justin Verlander	Det	3	-1	0	0	2
Matt Cain	SF	1	0	1	0	2
Livan Hernandez	Was	-2	3	1	0	2
David Price	TB	-1	1	1	1	2
Jon Lester	Bos	3	0	-1	0	2
Barry Zito	SF	0	1	1	0	2
Derek Lowe	Atl	0	2	0	0	2
Johnny Cueto	Cin	0	2	0	0	2
Jonathon Niese	NYM	2	2	-1	-1	2
Scott Baker	Min	0	2	0	0	2
Nick Blackburn	Min	1	1	0	0	2
Joel Pineiro	LAA	2	0	0	0	2
Mike Leake	Cin	0	1	0	1	2
Jhoulys Chacin	Col	1	0	1	0	2
Brian Bannister	KC	1	0	0	1	2
Hisanori Takahashi	NYM	1	1	0	0	2
Jair Jurrjens	Atl	1	0	1	0	2
Brett Anderson	Oak	0	1	1	0	2
Kris Medlen	Atl	1	1	0	0	2
Jonny Venters	Atl	2	0	0	0	2
Tim Stauffer	SD	1	1	0	0	2
Evan Meek	Pit	3	-1	0	0	2
Brian Burres	Pit	2	0	0	0	2
Felix Hernandez	Sea	1	0	0	0	1
Brett Myers	Hou	0	1	0	0	1
Fausto Carmona	Cle	6	-4	0	-1	1
Jeremy Guthrie	Bal	1	0	0	0	1
Gio Gonzalez	Oak	0	0	1	0	1
Jason Vargas	Sea	1	0	0	0	1
Kevin Millwood	Bal	0	1	0	0	1
Gavin Floyd	CWS	0	1	0	0	1
Paul Maholm	Pit	0	1	0	0	1
Justin Masterson	Cle	0	1	0	0	1
Brett Cecil	Tor	0	1	1	-1	1
Doug Fister	Sea	-2	2	1	0	1
Zach Duke	Pit	1	0	0	0	1
Kevin Slowey	Min	0	1	0	0	1
Brandon Morrow	Tor	-1	1	0	1	1
Scott Feldman	Tex	1	0	0	0	1
Aaron Cook	Col	-1	1	0	1	1
Jeff Francis	Col	1	0	0	0	1
Travis Wood	Cin	1	0	0	0	1
Barry Enright	Ari	1	0	0	0	1
Kyle Lohse	StL	-1	1	1	0	1
Luke French	Sea	-1	2	0	0	1
J.A. Happ	2 tms	0	1	0	0	1
Luis Atilano	Was	1	1	-1	0	1
Brandon League	Sea	-1	1	1	0	1
Roy Halladay	Phi	0	0	0	0	0
Ted Lilly	2 tms	3	-2	-1	0	0
Yovani Gallardo	Mil	0	0	0	0	0
Mat Latos	SD	-1	0	1	0	0
Brian Matusz	Bal	1	0	-1	0	0
Clay Buchholz	Bos	-1	2	0	-1	0
Chris Narveson	Mil	1	1	-2	0	0
Jaime Garcia	StL	-1	1	0	0	0
Kevin Correia	SD	0	0	0	0	0
Armando Galarraga	Det	0	0			0
Carlos Zambrano	ChC	0	0	0	0	0
Craig Stammen	Was	0	0	0	0	0
Tommy Hunter	Tex	-1	0	0	1	0
Madison Bumgarner	SF	0	0			0
Jake Peavy	CWS	0	0	0	0	0
Jeff Suppan	2 tms	-2	2	0	0	0
Jake Arrieta	Bal	1	0	-1	0	0
Daniel Hudson	2 tms	0	0	0	0	0
Nelson Figueroa	2 tms	-1	0	1	0	0
Rich Harden	Tex	-1	1	0	0	0
Blake Hawksworth	StL	-2	1	1	0	0
Kenshin Kawakami	Atl	0	0	0	0	0
Miguel Batista	Was	0	0			0
Scott Olsen	Was	0	0			0
David Huff	Cle	0	0	0	0	0
Mike Pelfrey	NYM	-1	1	-1	0	-1
Max Scherzer	Det	-1	0	0	0	-1
Randy Wells	ChC	0	0	0	-1	-1
Jonathan Sanchez	SF	-2	1	0	0	-1
Josh Johnson	Fla	-1	0	0	0	-1
Phil Hughes	NYY	-1	0	0	0	-1
Dave Bush	Mil	0	-2	1	0	-1
John Lannan	Was	-1	-2	1	1	-1
Tom Gorzelanny	ChC	0	-1	0	0	-1
Vin Mazzaro	Oak	0	0	-1	0	-1
Ben Sheets	Oak	-1	0	0	0	-1
Carlos Silva	ChC	0	0	0	-1	-1
Jamie Moyer	Phi	0	-2	0	1	-1
Aaron Harang	Cin	-2	1	0	0	-1
Ryan Rowland-Smith	Sea	0	0	-1	0	-1
Nate Robertson	2 tms	-2	1	-1	1	-1
Vicente Padilla	LAD	-1	1	-1	0	-1
Matt Belisle	Col	0	0	-1	0	-1
Tyler Clippard	Was	-1	0	0	0	-1
Andy Sonnanstine	TB	0	-1	0	0	-1
David Hernandez	Bal	0	0	-1	0	-1
CC Sabathia	NYY	0	-1	0	-1	-2
Dan Haren	2 tms	-3	0	1	0	-2
Jered Weaver	LAA	0	-2			-2
Ryan Dempster	ChC	1	-1	-1	-1	-2
Matt Garza	TB	-2	0	0	0	-2
C.J. Wilson	Tex	0	-1	-1	0	-2
Hiroki Kuroda	LAD	-1	0	0	-1	-2
Anibal Sanchez	Fla	-4	0	2	0	-2
Chad Billingsley	LAD	0	0	-2	0	-2
Kyle Davies	KC	-1	-1	0	0	-2
Jason Hammel	Col	-1	-1	0	0	-2
Wade Davis	TB	-3	0	1	0	-2
Ricky Nolasco	Fla	-1	1	-2	0	-2
Andy Pettitte	NYY	0	1	-3	0	-2
Josh Beckett	Bos	2	-3	-1	0	-2
Homer Bailey	Cin	-2	0	0	0	-2
Tony Pena	CWS	1	1	-3	-1	-2
John Ely	LAD	-3	1	0	0	-2
Felipe Paulino	Hou	-3	0	1	0	-2
Sean O'Sullivan	2 tms	1	-2	-1	0	-2
Charlie Morton	Pit	-1	-1	0	0	-2
Carl Pavano	Min	0	-3	0	0	-3
Cliff Lee	2 tms	-4	1	0	0	-3
Rodrigo Lopez	Ari	-1	-1	0	-1	-3
Joe Blanton	Phi	-2	0	0	0	-3
Chris Volstad	Fla	0	-3	0	0	-3
Daisuke Matsuzaka	Bos	1	-3	-1	0	-3
Tim Wakefield	Bos	-1	-2	-1	1	-3
David Pauley	Sea	-1	-1	-1	0	-3
Carlos Monasterios	LAD	0	-1	-1	-1	-3
John Lackey	Bos	-2	-2	0	0	-4
Edwin Jackson	2 tms	-2	-1	0	0	-4
James Shields	TB	-4	1	-1	0	-4
Francisco Liriano	Min	-2	0	-1	-1	-4
Rick Porcello	Det	-4	0	0	0	-4
Manny Parra	Mil	-2	-1	0	0	-4
Ross Ohlendorf	Pit	-1	-2	-1	0	-4
Luke Hochevar	KC	-2	-2	0	0	-4
Colby Lewis	Tex	-4	-1	0	0	-5
Jeff Niemann	TB	-3	-2	0	0	-5
Ervin Santana	LAA	-3	-4	1	0	-6
Tim Lincecum	SF	-3	-3	0	0	-6
Tommy Hanson	Atl	-2	-4	0	0	-6
Freddy Garcia	CWS	-4	-2	0	0	-6
A.J. Burnett	NYY	-1	-4	-1	-1	-7
Jeremy Bonderman	Det	-5	0	-2	-1	-8

Pitchers - 2009 Runs Saved

Player	Team	Plus/Minus	SB	Bunts	GFP/DME	Total
Mark Buehrle	CWS	7	3	0	0	10
Zack Greinke	KC	2	3	2	1	8
Brad Bergesen	Bal	5	1	0	0	6
Randy Wolf	LAD	3	1	1	0	5
Jon Garland	2 tms	4	0	0	1	5
Carlos Zambrano	ChC	1	3	1	0	5
Kenshin Kawakami	Atl	2	1	1	1	5
Josh Geer	SD	4	1	0	0	5
D.J. Carrasco	CWS	3	2	0	0	5
Bronson Arroyo	Cin	2	0	1	1	4
Javier Vazquez	Atl	2	1	1	0	4
Jason Marquis	Col	5	-1	-1	1	4
Joel Pineiro	StL	3	1	0	0	4
Zach Duke	Pit	2	2	0	0	4
Jeremy Guthrie	Bal	2	1	1	0	4
Paul Maholm	Pit	2	1	0	1	4
Livan Hernandez	2 tms	2	1	1	0	4
Trevor Cahill	Oak	2	0	1	1	4
Johan Santana	NYM	2	1	0	1	4
Aaron Cook	Col	2	2	0	0	4
Vicente Padilla	2 tms	1	3	0	0	4
Scott Richmond	Tor	1	1	2	0	4
Jeremy Sowers	Cle	2	1	1	0	4
Jason Vargas	Sea	2	2	0	0	4
Brian Bass	Bal	1	2	1	0	4
Justin Verlander	Det	-2	4	1	0	3
Dan Haren	Ari	3	-1	1	0	3
Ubaldo Jimenez	Col	1	0	2	0	3
Jair Jurrjens	Atl	2	0	0	1	3
John Lannan	Was	0	2	1	0	3
Ryan Dempster	ChC	2	0	1	0	3
Barry Zito	SF	3	1	-1	0	3
Roy Oswalt	Hou	1	1	1	0	3
Chad Gaudin	2 tms	1	2	0	0	3
Jordan Zimmermann	Was	2	1	0	0	3
A.J. Burnett	NYY	1	1	0	0	2
Wandy Rodriguez	Hou	1	1	0	0	2
John Danks	CWS	2	1	0	-1	2
Scott Baker	Min	1	0	0	1	2
Andy Pettitte	NYY	-1	2	0	1	2
Ricky Romero	Tor	-1	2	1	0	2
Ross Ohlendorf	Pit	-1	3	0	0	2
Johnny Cueto	Cin	1	2	0	-1	2
Kyle Lohse	StL	2	0	0	0	2
Carlos Villanueva	Mil	1	0	1	0	2
Edward Mujica	SD	1	1	0	0	2
Brett Cecil	Tor	2	1	-1	0	2
Zach Miner	Det	2	0	0	0	2
Bobby Parnell	NYM	0	1	1	0	2
Shairon Martis	Was	2	0	0	0	2
Brian Duensing	Min	2	1	-1	0	2
Chan Ho Park	Phi	1	0	1	0	2
Garrett Olson	Sea	2	0		0	2
Brad Thompson	StL	1	0	0	1	2
Shawn Camp	Tor	1	1	0	0	2
Jamey Wright	KC	1	1	0	0	2
Felix Hernandez	Sea	2	-1	0	0	1
Adam Wainwright	StL	-1	0	1	1	1
Jered Weaver	LAA	1	0	0	0	1
Josh Johnson	Fla	1	-1	0	1	1
Kevin Millwood	Tex	1	0	0	0	1
Chad Billingsley	LAD	-1	2	0	0	1
Gavin Floyd	CWS	2	-1	0	0	1
Joe Saunders	LAA	1	0	0	0	1
Jarrod Washburn	2 tms	2	1	-2	0	1
Clayton Kershaw	LAD	-2	3	0	0	1
J.A. Happ	Phi	-1	1	1	0	1
Aaron Harang	Cin	0	0	1	0	1
Jeff Suppan	Mil	0	1	0	0	1
Ian Snell	2 tms	1	0	0	0	1
Luke Hochevar	KC	1	-1	1	0	1
David Price	TB	0	1	0	0	1
Tim Redding	NYM	1	0	0	0	1
Homer Bailey	Cin	0	0	0	1	1
Jake Peavy	2 tms	1	-1	0	1	1
Russ Ortiz	Hou	0	0	1	0	1
Erik Bedard	Sea	1	0	0	0	1
Cliff Lee	2 tms	-2	1	1	0	0
James Shields	TB	-1	1	0	0	0
Matt Cain	SF	0	1	0	-1	0
Jon Lester	Bos	2	0	-2	0	0
Doug Davis	Ari	-2	3	-1	0	0
Matt Garza	TB	-2	1	1	0	0
Braden Looper	Mil	-2	2	0	0	0
Scott Feldman	Tex	1	-1	0	0	0
John Lackey	LAA	1	-1	0	0	0
Chris Volstad	Fla	1	-1	0	0	0

Player	Team	Plus/Minus	SB	Bunts	GFP/DME	Total
Armando Galarraga	Det	-2	1	1	0	0
Derek Holland	Tex	-2	1	0	1	0
Francisco Liriano	Min	-1	1	0	0	0
David Huff	Cle	0	0	0	0	0
Tommy Hanson	Atl	1	-1	0	0	0
Fausto Carmona	Cle	1	0	0	-1	0
Aaron Laffey	Cle	-1	1	0	0	0
Mike Hampton	Hou	0	0	0	0	0
Gio Gonzalez	Oak	1	1	-1	-1	0
Felipe Paulino	Hou	-2	2	0	0	0
Brandon McCarthy	Tex	0	0	0	0	0
Charlie Morton	Pit	0	0	0	0	0
Ryan Rowland-Smith	Sea	-1	1	0	0	0
Randy Johnson	SF	-1	0	0	1	0
Phil Hughes	NYY	0	0		0	0
Sean Marshall	ChC	0	0	1	-1	0
Alfredo Aceves	NYY	0	-1	1	0	0
Andrew Bailey	Oak	0	0	1	-1	0
Jeff Fulchino	Hou	-1	1	0	0	0
Andrew Miller	Fla	0	-1	1	0	0
Jeff Weaver	LAD	1	-1	0	0	0
CC Sabathia	NYY	0	1	0	-2	-1
Josh Beckett	Bos	0	-1	0	0	-1
Kevin Correia	SD	0	1	-2	0	-1
Joe Blanton	Phi	-1	0	0	0	-1
Jorge de la Rosa	Col	1	-1	-1	0	-1
Jonathan Sanchez	SF	1	-2	0	0	-1
Brian Moehler	Hou	0	-1	-1	1	-1
Brian Bannister	KC	1	-2	0	0	-1
Scott Kazmir	2 tms	-2	1	0	0	-1
Dallas Braden	Oak	-2	2	-1	0	-1
Gil Meche	KC	2	-2	-1	0	-1
Todd Wellemeyer	StL	-2	0	1	0	-1
Matt Palmer	LAA	0	-1	0	0	-1
Micah Owings	Cin	0	0	-1	0	-1
Tommy Hunter	Tex	-2	0	0	1	-1
Craig Stammen	Was	1	-2	0	0	-1
David Hernandez	Bal	-1	0	0	0	-1
Chris Jakubauskas	Sea	-2	1		0	-1
Vin Mazzaro	Oak	-1	0		0	-1
Garrett Mock	Was	-1	1	-1	0	-1
Kevin Slowey	Min	0	-1	0	0	-1
Yusmeiro Petit	Ari	0	-1	0	0	-1
Anibal Sanchez	Fla	1	-1	-1	0	-1
John Maine	NYM	-1	0	0	0	-1
Mark Lowe	Sea	0	0	-1	0	-1
Nick Blackburn	Min	-2	0	0	0	-2
Cole Hamels	Phi	-2	1	0	-1	-2
Yovani Gallardo	Mil	-1	-2	1	0	-2
Ricky Nolasco	Fla	-1	-1	0	0	-2
Mike Pelfrey	NYM	-2	0	-1	1	-2
Ted Lilly	ChC	1	0	-3	0	-2
Jason Hammel	Col	0	-2	0	0	-2
Brett Anderson	Oak	-2	0	0	0	-2
Max Scherzer	Ari	-2	1	-1	0	-2
Jamie Moyer	Phi	-2	0	0	0	-2
Brian Tallet	Tor	-1	1	-2	0	-2
Joba Chamberlain	NYY	-1	-2	1	0	-2
Manny Parra	Mil	-2	0	0	0	-2
Kyle Davies	KC	-1	-1	0	0	-2
Jason Berken	Bal	-1	-1	0	0	-2
Dave Bush	Mil	-2	-1	1	0	-2
Mark Hendrickson	Bal	0	-2	0	0	-2
Andy Sonnanstine	TB	-1	1	-1	-1	-2
Clay Buchholz	Bos	-1	-1	0	0	-2
Todd Coffey	Mil	-1	0	0	-1	-2
Ramon Troncoso	LAD	-2	0	0	0	-2
Kevin Hart	2 tms	0	-2	0	0	-2
Roy Halladay	Tor	-2	-1	0	0	-3
Edwin Jackson	Det	-2	-2	0	1	-3
Carl Pavano	2 tms	1	-4	0	0	-3
Rick Porcello	Det	-2	0	0	-1	-3
Ervin Santana	LAA	-2	-1	0	0	-3
Tim Wakefield	Bos	0	-3	0	0	-3
Hiroki Kuroda	LAD	-2	-1	0	0	-3
Jeff Karstens	Pit	-2	0	-1	0	-3
Glen Perkins	Min	-2	-1	0	0	-3
Chris Carpenter	StL	-5	1	0	0	-4
Jeff Niemann	TB	-2	-2	0	0	-4
Clayton Richard	2 tms	-4	3	-2	-1	-4
Rich Harden	ChC	-2	0	-2	0	-4
Jose Contreras	2 tms	-2	-3	1	0	-4
Justin Masterson	2 tms	-3	-1	0	0	-4
Tim Lincecum	SF	-3	-2	0	0	-5
Derek Lowe	Atl	-5	0	-1	0	-6
Randy Wells	ChC	-4	-1	-1	0	-6
Sean West	Fla	-3	0	-2	-1	-6
Brad Penny	2 tms	-4	-4		-1	-9

Timing Batted Balls:
Improved Plus/Minus System

The split second the batter makes contact with the ball, the timer starts. For a grounder the timer stops when the ball is touched by a fielder or passes the edge of the outfield grass. For a ball in the air the timer stops as soon as the ball hits anything: glove, ground, wall, umpire, bird, . . . We then translate the timer on grounders into average velocity (e.g. 42 MPH) and on balls in the air into hang time (3.1 seconds).

Introducing Timer Plus/Minus

For the past couple of years we have been providing a version of our Timer Plus/Minus System to our team clients. We are introducing the latest update of the new timer system to the public in this book. The new timer system replaces an element of subjectivity in the old system with a more objective element. Under the old system batted balls were categorized into velocity groupings simply as soft, medium or hard, based on the judgment of the video scout. For outfielders, judgment was also necessary to determine if a ball in the air was a flyball, a liner or something in between that we call a fliner. With the new timer system, these judgments are no longer necessary.

Outfield Hang Times

Let's walk through how the timer works and why it's important. For outfielders, the new Timer Plus/Minus System uses hang time. It's straightforward. The longer the ball hangs in the air the easier it is to catch. We have created six hang time groupings (or buckets, as we like to call them). The first grouping (Hang Time Group 1) is for all balls to the outfield that are in the air between 0 and 2.7 seconds. The heat map here shows how often and where balls are caught by outfielders when they are in the air between 0 and 2.7 seconds:

Out Ratio By Batted Ball Location
(Fly Balls 0.0 – 2.7 seconds)

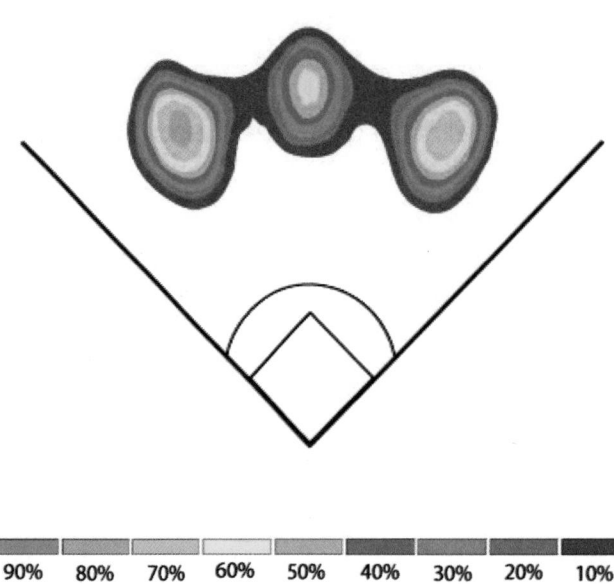

| 90% | 80% | 70% | 60% | 50% | 40% | 30% | 20% | 10% |

We are graphing the Out Ratio of batted balls. That is, the percentage of batted balls in each area that is turned into outs. The heat map shows red if the Out Ratio is over 90 percent. This is an area where balls are almost always caught. An area is colored blue where batted balls in the air are almost never caught. Group 1 here has the hardest hit balls, the ones that get down to the ground the quickest. These balls are caught less frequently. No red areas show up. The areas colored near red are smaller than we'll see in subsequent charts. The areas without color are areas where balls are not caught by outfielders at all.

Here is the chart on Hang Time Group 2, 2.7 to 3.0 seconds.

Out Ratio By Batted Ball Location
(Fly Balls 2.7 – 3.0 seconds)

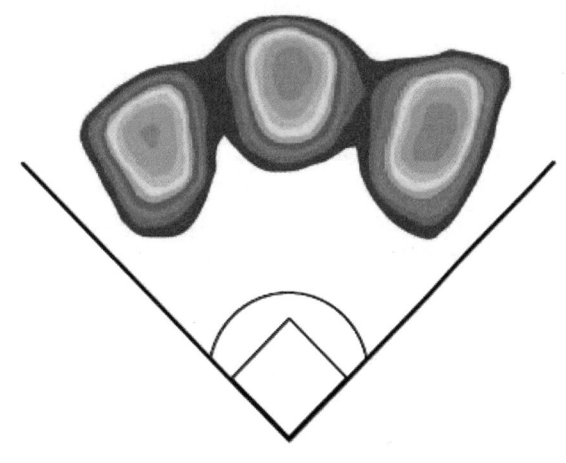

90%	80%	70%	60%	50%	40%	30%	20%	10%

In this chart, more balls are caught. The red areas in the middle of each outfield position are where over 90 percent of balls hit in the air between 2.7 and 3.0 seconds are caught. In the light green and yellow areas balls are caught between 50 and 70 percent of the time. The light blue comes in around 30 percent and the dark blue at 10%. The areas where the blue stops and the field becomes "white" are areas where outfielders catch less than one percent of all batted balls.

The next heat map is for balls hit to outfielders that hang in the air between 3.0 and 3.5 seconds:

Out Ratio By Batted Ball Location
(Fly Balls 3.0 – 3.5 seconds)

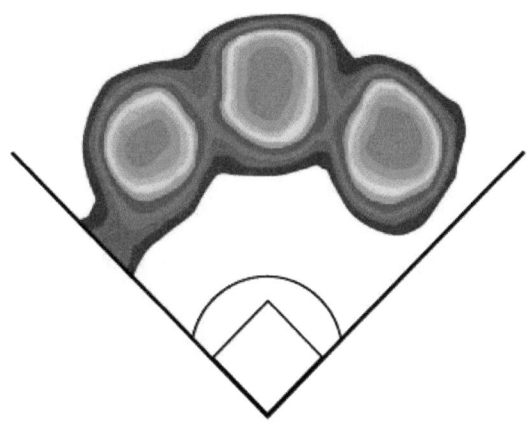

You can see the red area increasing in size. There's even an area that extends towards the left field line where the left fielder has caught some shallow balls. This is the "Juan Pierre" zone. One of his favorite hit locations is shallow down the left field line. Many teams have picked up on this tendency that he and a couple other players have and position their left fielder close to the line and shallow.

The heat map for flyballs between 3.5 and 4.2 seconds shows still larger red zones and an ever expanding area where balls are caught by outfielders:

Out Ratio By Batted Ball Location
(Fly Balls 3.5 – 4.2 seconds)

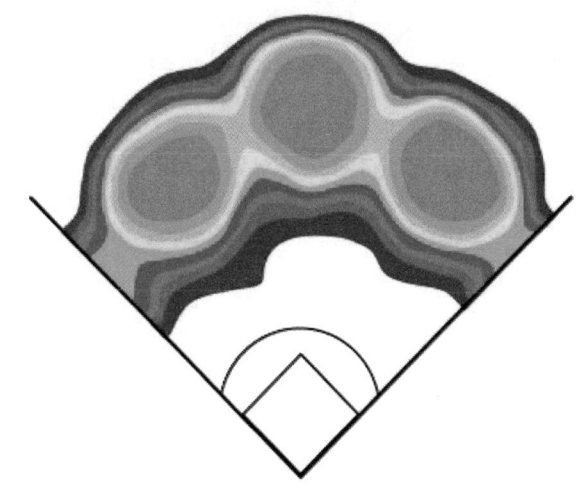

Moving to the map for balls between 4.2 and 5.0 seconds we see the three outfield positions merging together. When a ball hangs up in the air for more than 4.2 seconds, it can be caught over 90 percent of the time anywhere in the outfield from the left field line to the right field line.

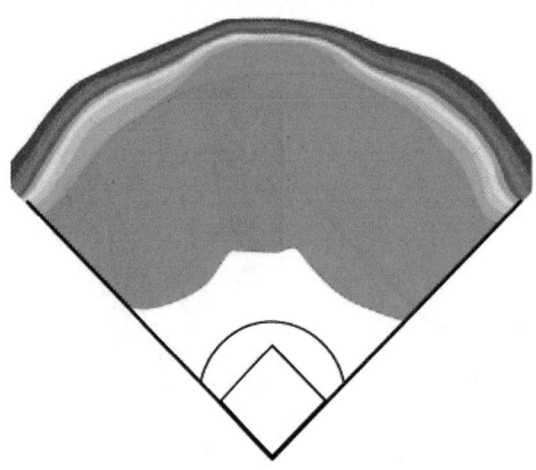

Out Ratio By Batted Ball Location
(Fly Balls 5.0+ seconds)

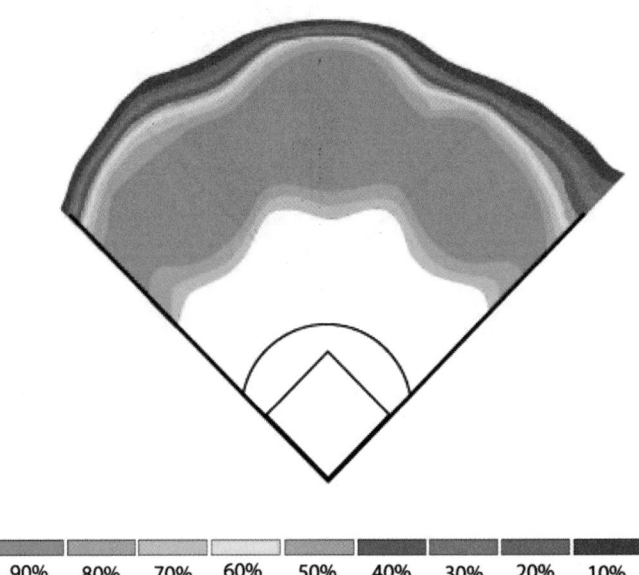

Out Ratio By Batted Ball Location
(Fly Balls 4.2 – 5.0 seconds)

| 90% | 80% | 70% | 60% | 50% | 40% | 30% | 20% | 10% |

Our last chart is for all batted balls hit to outfielders over 5.0 seconds. Just about everything is caught. Now it's not only line to line, it pretty much extends from the shallow outfield to the wall. There's a cut-off in the shallow outfield showing where infielders are making the catches rather than outfielders.

As you progress through longer and longer hang times for balls hit in the air, outfielders catch a higher and higher percentage of them. Each of these hang time groupings that we've gone through has a different level of difficulty. We have organized each of these groupings so that we can compare every outfielder to every other outfielder to see how they each do on plays of varying difficulty.

For a more complete explanation of methodology for the new Timer Plus/Minus System for outfielders, please check out page 441.

Infield Velocities

Similar to outfield batted balls, we break grounders in and through the infield into six groupings as well. However, instead of using hang time, we use velocity. By knowing how long it takes for a grounder to get to a spot and by knowing how far that spot is from home plate, we can calculate the average velocity of the batted ball. (Velocity = Distance divided by Time). Let's walk through our six groupings for infielders using second base as an example. The first grouping has slowly hit grounders, grounders where the velocity is between 0 and 25 miles per hour.

Here is the chart:

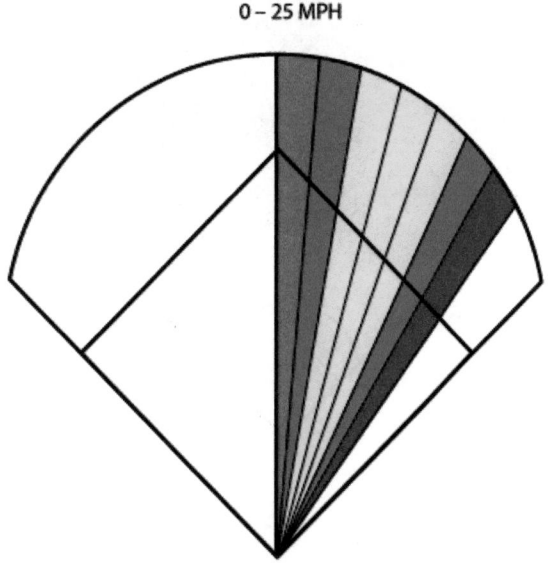

Out Ratio by Batted Ball Location
0 – 25 MPH

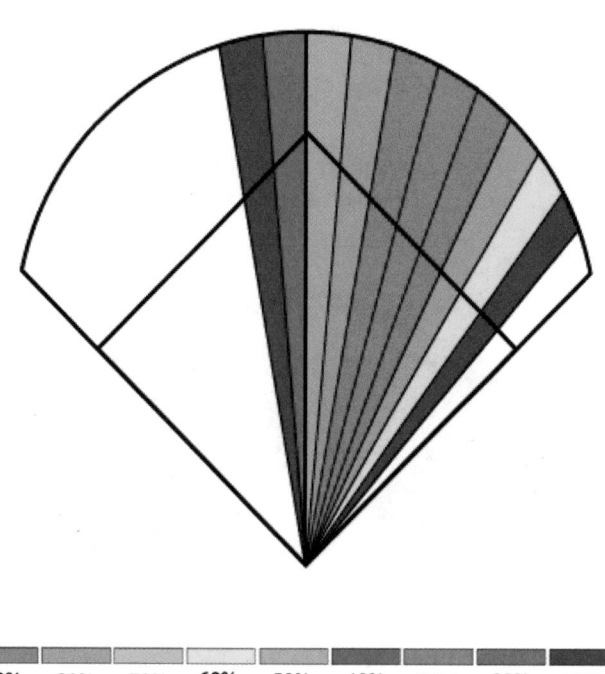

Out Ratio by Batted Ball Location
25 – 45 MPH

90%	80%	70%	60%	50%	40%	30%	20%	10%

These are softly hit groundballs that have an average velocity under 25 miles per hour. They are difficult to turn into outs. In the chart above, there are only three wedges (the yellow ones) where a second baseman can turn as many as 60 percent of batted balls into outs. There is one wedge to each side of those three where he can turn batted balls into outs 30 percent of the time. Then one more wedge on each side, one extending to the second base bag and one extending to the normal first baseman's position, where he can get to 10-20 percent of batted balls.

Here is the chart for Vector Grouping 2, groundballs between 25 and 45 miles per hour:

Balls hit between 25 and 55 miles per hour (this chart and the next one) give second basemen the best chance of turning batted balls into outs. Unlike balls hit under 25 miles per hour, the balls are coming to them, not the other way around. Vector Grouping 2 (25-45 MPH) shows a three-wedge wide area where 90 percent are turned into outs. Second basemen are getting to 50 percent of batted balls at this speed all the way over to the second base bag. They are even ranging beyond second to get to some grounders. On the other side, they are making plays that go through the normal first base position.

Here is Grouping 3, 45 to 55 MPH:

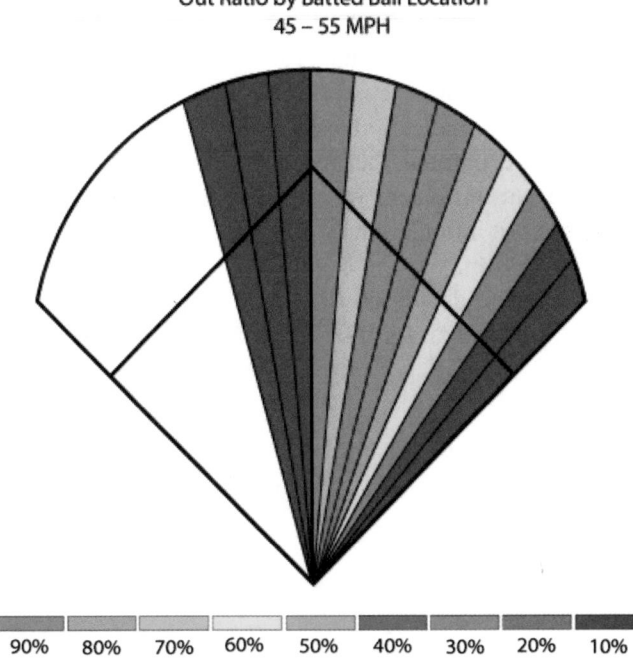

Out Ratio by Batted Ball Location
45 – 55 MPH

| 90% | 80% | 70% | 60% | 50% | 40% | 30% | 20% | 10% |

While the red zone is only two slices wide here, the areas where up to 10 percent of batted balls are fielded by second basemen (dark blue color is an out ratio of 0 to 10 percent) extends into the shortstop position and all the way to the first base line.

Now let's see what happens when groundballs start exceeding the 55 miles per hour speed limit. Here is Grouping 4, batted balls between 55 and 65 miles per hour:

Out Ratio by Batted Ball Location
55 – 65 MPH

The zones are starting to decrease in size. The red zone is now only one slice wide. Second basemen are making some plays one or two steps beyond second base, but not very many.

Speeding up to between 65 and 75 miles per hour:

Out Ratio by Batted Ball Location
65 – 75 MPH

Now we have no red zones. If a ball is hit between 65 and 75 miles per hour right at the normal second base position, it's fielded 80 percent of the time. As we move to either side, the out ratio drops off dramatically. Two slices to the right of the normal second base position we're down to 30 percent. Two slices to the left, we're down to 10 percent.

Our final grouping is for batted balls hit over 75 miles per hour:

Out Ratio by Batted Ball Location
75+ MPH

Now you can really see that the harder hit balls go through for a hit more often. The only way to field a ball over 75 MPH is if it's an at-'em ball.

These charts show that the difficulty of fielding a groundball depends on its velocity. We all knew that instinctively. These charts show how much. The out ratios vary dramatically based on the speed of the batted ball. If we ignored the speed of the ball in trying to evaluate an infielder, we would bias our evaluation against those infielders who had a lot more hard hit balls to contend with.

For more details on the methodology of the Timer Plus/Minus System for infielders, turn to page 441.

Peter Bourjos Has Them Covered

Mark Simon, ESPN Stats & Information

[Editor's note: This article originally ran on ESPNLA.com on August 15, 2011.]

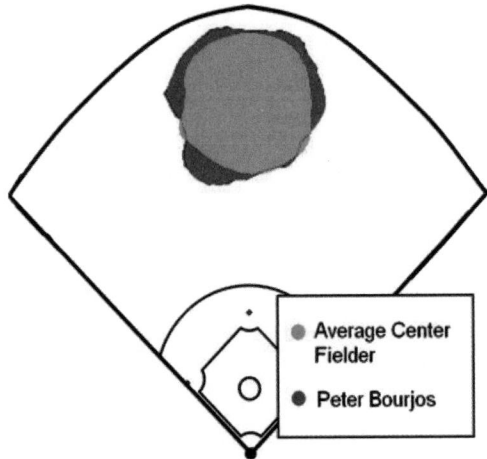

The red shading illustrates the range for a major league center fielder on flyballs with a hang time between 3 and 4 seconds. The blue shading shows the extra ground covered by Peter Bourjos.

It's the fourth inning of last Wednesday's game in Yankee Stadium, with the Angels trailing the hosts 5-0 and Yankees third baseman Eduardo Nunez has just hit a flyball into the vacant right-center field gap.

The Angels have already yielded one triple this inning and it looks as if this has the potential for another, as right fielder Torii Hunter tries to close ground as quickly as his 36-year-old legs can move him.

"Speed kills," Hunter had said a couple hours earlier, and Hunter still has pretty good wheels for a man his age. He launches a head-first dive and watches the ball sail past him.

But behind Hunter is the teammate who he says has wings on his shoes -- like the super-swift mythological figure, Mercury -- center fielder Peter Bourjos. Despite having his vision shielded momentarily by Hunter's flight path, Bourjos is able to reach knee-high with his glove and make the catch, avoiding Hunter, while never breaking stride.

"How did he make that catch?" asked Angels television color commentator Mark Gubicza.

Add it to the list of amazing defensive plays the 24-year-old Bourjos has turned in during his major league career, which is just over a year old.

Breaking Down the Numbers

Baseball Info Solutions (BIS), a company located in Coplay, Penn., is in the business of statistically evaluating baseball, with one emphasis being on looking at defense. Its founder, John Dewan, has written two editions of *The Fielding Bible* on the subject.

**Most Defensive Runs Saved
MLB Teams Entering Saturday**

Team	Runs Saved
Tampa Bay Rays	53
Los Angeles Angels	36
Texas Rangers	31
Cincinnati Reds	26
Seattle Mariners	18

BIS employees do video tracking for every play in every major league game, providing reports and stats to more than half the major league teams. The company has multiple methods of compiling defensive data.

One involves the plotting of points at which plays are made on a computerized baseball diamond, with the ability to denote for an outfielder whether the batted ball was a line drive, flyball or something in-between (they call them "fliners"), and for how long the ball was in the air before either hitting the fielder's glove or the ground.

That allows them to create images such as the one at the top of this article.

The red shading in that picture represents the area in which an average center fielder will catch the ball more often than not, if the ball is in the air for between three and four seconds (that's the hang time for most flyballs). The blue shading represents the extra ground Bourjos covers.

"That right there. . .that's the truth," Hunter said Wednesday after looking at the diagram.

"He's the blue?" asked Angels pitcher Jered Weaver, who has been a major Bourjos beneficiary this season. "That's ridiculous."

When Bourjos saw the image, his first reaction was to smile. It was the same smile he flashed when he made his ridiculous catch later that night.

"That's pretty cool," he said. "They don't usually have those sorts of things for defense."

They didn't, until recently. It's part of the new wave of baseball analysis that has garnered a lot of public attention the last few years.

Evaluating offense is easier for fans, statisticians, and even managers, coaches, and executives than trying to evaluate defense.

When Angels coach Dino Ebel, who positions the team's outfielders, put a value on his team's outfield defense, he used a very basic stat to supplement Mike

Scioscia's comments that this team has the most range of any he has had: triples allowed. The Angels entered Saturday having allowed the third-fewest in the majors: 15, trailing only the Rangers (11) and Red Sox (14).

Baseball Info Solutions has tried to do a more in-depth analysis to compute value on the defensive side.

**Most Defensive Runs Saved
MLB Players (Last 2 Seasons)**

Player	Position	Runs Saved
Brendan Ryan	SS	41
Peter Bourjos	CF	35
Austin Jackson	CF	34
Brett Gardner	LF	33
Alex Gonzalez	SS	31
Note: Bourjos was recalled in August 2010		

BIS uses a plus-minus system to determine how much better or worse a player is than his peers. In Bourjos' case, he rates 15 plays better, meaning he turned 15 more batted balls into outs than the average center fielder would have, had he been in the field for every play that occurred. Those 15 outs were worth 25 bases, based on historical data of base hit types to each spot on the field.

Through a series of calculations, the 15 plays and 25 bases are combined with two other factors -- a throwing arm rating and a home run-robbing rating.

Smush those together and Bourjos' value this season is calculated at 20 Defensive Runs Saved, which as of Saturday matched Yankees left fielder Brett Gardner for the most of any major league outfielder.

There are some things that this system can't take into account, so BIS has another method of evaluation. They have "video scouts" tracking every play of every game, grouping plays into 30-plus categories of Good Fielding Plays (think of those as Web Gem nominees) and 50-plus categories of Defensive Misplays & Errors (things such as slipping and falling, colliding with a teammate, overthrowing a cutoff man).

Since Bourjos played in his first game on Aug. 3, 2010, he has 48 Good Fielding Plays, more than any outfielder in the major leagues. He has 22 Defensive Misplays & Errors, which sounds like a lot, but when you look at the ratio of Good Plays-to-Misplays, only Mariners center fielder Franklin Gutierrez is better among everyday outfielders. A rate of better than 2-to-1 is very good.

The Baseball Perspective

Among the video on a Bourjos highlight reel:

"Home run robberies of Rangers outfielder David Murphy on April 20 and Twins DH Jim Thome on May 27. Those are the two that merit the most mention when teammates are asked to recall their favorite Bourjos plays.

"I'll take Thome's," Angels pitcher Tyler Chatwood said, "because I was pitching for that one."

"A leaping catch at the left-center field fence on July 4 to take an extra-base hit away from Miguel Cabrera.

Angels first baseman Mark Trumbo has been a teammate of Bourjos at multiple minor league stops. He knows the look he saw from Cabrera well.

"Exasperation," Trumbo said.

Trumbo saw Cabrera approach Bourjos the next day. He can take an educated guess on how the conversation went.

"Next time," Trumbo noted the hitter usually says, "I'm hitting the ball to someone else."

"The gap-to-gap sprint from right-center to left-center to rob Cabrera's teammate, Andy Dirks, on July 30. That has become a patented play in the Bourjos arsenal. He could be playing completely opposite where the ball is hit, but can still make the catch.

"He's had balls that he's had no business getting to and he's still gotten them," Angels left fielder Vernon Wells said. "He's improved from a high level to an elite level."

We asked one longtime major league scout to rate Bourjos and give us a comparable player historically. On the scout's 20-to-80 scale, he rated Bourjos' glove an 80 and said Bourjos' skill reminded him of Paul Blair, who won eight Gold Gloves in a nine-year span as a center fielder for the Orioles from 1967 to 1975.

"He has superb instincts," the scout said of Bourjos. "He takes proper angles to where hard-hit flyballs, and deep-and-smoked line drives will land. He lays out to make plays and has no fear of the wall. His footwork and mechanics are sound. He has a quick first step [reacting to the ball] off the bat."

Those who watch him say they think Bourjos can get even better. The scout warns that Bourjos, who spent time on the disabled list earlier this season with a hamstring injury, may end up a DL visitor in the future due to his aggressive style.

"He sacrifices his body all the time," Wells said. "He has one goal in mind: catch the ball no matter what is in his way."

ESPN baseball analyst Chris Singleton, a former center fielder, said he has seen Bourjos a few times and been very impressed, but noted that there's still plenty for a young center fielder to learn. Occasionally, Bourjos will be moving so fast, he'll overrun a ball.

"His feel is still developing," Singleton said.

Hunter has been giving Bourjos advice regularly on things of that nature. To figure out whether to cheat in one direction or another, Bourjos will consider the count and where the catcher sets up.

"It's about being able to see the pitch and be aggressive," Bourjos said.

Hunter's philosophy is to take the situation into account, but he's more cognizant of pitcher and hitter knowledge than what his catcher is doing.

"I had range like [his]," said Hunter, who won nine Gold Gloves from 2001 to 2009 and now leads right fielders in Defensive Runs Saved this season. "But I also positioned myself well. Once he learns the league, he'll be that much better. I can't tell you what I've told him. That knowledge is only for people that I like."

Hunter said he likes Bourjos, a lot, as everyone does. Hunter has been in baseball a long time and he said he has never seen anyone who could make plays quite like Bourjos does.

"With speed like that, you can do anything in this world," Hunter said.

The Ted Williams Shift

THE CLEVELAND INDIANS placed themselves in this unorthodox manner in an attempt to keep Ted Williams from getting another hit and then they walked Williams on four straight balls.

CLEVELAND vs. RED SOX
FENWAY PARK, JULY 14, 1946

One of our readers sent us this photo. It's a picture of what is said to be the very first time the Ted Williams Shift was employed against Williams. It happened on July 14, 1946 in the second game of a double-header.

Indians player-manager Lou Boudreau couldn't take it anymore. The Indians had lost the first game of the double-header at Fenway Park to Boston 11-10, thanks to three home runs and eight RBI by Ted Williams for the Red Sox. In the second game, after Williams doubled down the first base line in his first at-bat, Boudreau decided he was going to do something about it. He invented the "Ted Williams Shift", or the "Boudreau Shift" as it was also called. Boudreau noticed that Williams had an extreme tendency to pull the ball and decided to arrange his fielders to cover the most ground in the areas that Williams hit.

What a cool photo this is, but here's the most interesting thing about it. The Shift is fairly common in today's game, thanks to Boudreau. But Lou did something a little different than what is done today. Take a closer look at the picture. There are *four* infielders to the right of second base, not three as The Shift is employed today. The first baseman is about four feet from the line on the edge of the outfield grass. The second baseman is in short right field quite close to the line, only about 30 feet off the line. The shortstop, Lou himself, is exactly between first and second on the infield edge of the grass. And, amazingly, the third baseman is behind second base but significantly right of the bag, also on the infield edge of the grass. Remarkable.

So where did Teddy Ballgame hit the ball? He didn't. He walked on four pitches.

Is this the first time a shift like this has been employed? It appears not. There's a discussion on www.baseball-fever.com called The Ted Williams Shift. Someone mentioned that Jimmy Dykes may have used a shift against Ted Williams as early as 1941, but it is unconfirmed. The more interesting item in the discussion is about another Williams, Cy Williams, who played for the Cubs and Phillies in the 1910's and 1920's. There's a photocopy of an old newspaper article, apparently written in the 1940's sometime, where the writer interviewed Bill McKechnie. McKechnie played against Cy Williams in the 1910's and relates, "(Cy) Williams was the most consistent dead right field hitter that ever lived. When he came to bat, the team in the field forgot that third base or left field existed."

"The first baseman and right fielder bugged the line. The second baseman moved close to first base and the center fielder pulled over into normal right field. The shortstop played where the second baseman normally stands and the left fielder moved into the center fielder's spot. The third baseman played shortstop like the shortstop usually does for a lefthanded right field hitter."

So, The Shift goes back to at least the 1910's. It was not that common in the old days, apparently only used against players named Williams. But in today's game, it is being used more and more. And rightly so.

The Amazing Carlos Pena

August 25, 2011. The conditions are classic. Day baseball, beautiful bright sun, and perfect temperature at the friendly confines of Wrigley Field. It's the bottom of the fourth. The Braves are leading the Cubs 5-3 in the fourth game of the series. Carlos Pena is leading off the inning. The Shift is on. Three infielders to the right of second base with the second baseman playing in short right field. The third baseman, Martin Prado, is playing in the normal third-base position. Pena takes a ball and a strike and swings through the 1-1 pitch making the count 1 and 2. Now Prado moves. With two strikes he moves a little deeper and to his left. He's pretty much in the normal shortstop position, maybe not quite as deep as a normal shortstop might play.

And Pena bunts. With two strikes. It's a good bunt, not a great one. Pretty much hit to the normal third base position, speed a little faster than the best bunts. Prado races over and fields it about 10 feet into the grass, maybe 12 feet off the line. He has no chance. Pena beats it out by a mile.

It's the third time in the series that Pena has bunted for a hit into The Shift. The Braves thought they were ready for it by keeping Prado at the normal third base position until he got two strikes. They had no clue that Pena would bunt with two strikes. The two previous Pena bunt hits in the series were on the first pitch. Little did they know that Pena, earlier in the season, bunted against The Shift with two strikes on three other occasions and got hits on two of them.

Give credit to the Atlanta announcers for this game, Chip Caray and Joe Simpson. Here are some of their comments while Pena was at the plate:

"He's (Pena) made a believer out of the Braves leading off the inning with that shift. If he tries to bunt they've left Prado over there, pretty much at the normal spot. Everybody else is on the right side. Twice in the series he's bunted against the shift and put down a bunt for a hit."

"Pena is tied for the team lead in bunts. Six of them. Pretty good work for a guy with 23 homers."

After the bunt hit:

"As soon as he saw Martin a little deeper and closer to shortstop, even with two strikes, he was happy to do it." On the replay: "You see that Martin was pushed way over this time, over by shortstop, not expecting this with two strikes."

The most credit goes to Carlos Pena. He sees The Shift a lot. It's not surprising given that he hits 90 percent of his grounders and short liners to the right of second base. But he has a strategy that works. In 2010 he put a bunt in play against The Shift five times. He got four hits. In 2011 he doubled his efforts with 10 bunts against The Shift. He got on base eight times (7 hits, 1 error), got credit for a sacrifice once, and grounded out to the pitcher once. Here is a summary of facts about Pena's amazing bunt performance against The Shift:

- 11 hits, an error and a sacrifice in 15 attempts (.786 batting average)
- 5 of his attempts were with two strikes – 3 hits, an error and a groundout
- 9 on the first pitch and the other with a 1-0 count
- 11 times leading off the inning, plus one other time effectively leading off as the first batter hit a homer

Pena is smart. He is bunting when it makes the most sense. Leading off the inning. With two strikes. Against the Braves, he especially out-smarted them. The first two times in the series he got bunt base hits on the first pitch. On both of those the Braves had The Shift on with Alex Gonzalez, the shortstop, playing in the normal shortstop position. Chipper Jones, the third baseman, was to the right of second base. After Pena got the two bunt hits, the Braves learned their lesson. Or they thought they did. They kept their third baseman at the normal third base position until two strikes. Pena crossed them up and bunted with two strikes.

And Pena is skillful. It is not that easy to bunt as effectively as he has.

Does The Shift Work?

Against Carlos Pena, it doesn't look like The Shift works. Against most everyone else, so far it looks like it does.

We have a couple of years of data to work with. It is not conclusive but we have some pretty strong evidence that we want to present here. Baseball Info Solutions began recording data on the use of shifts in Major League Baseball in 2010. When a hitter puts any ball in play against the shift, our video scouts mark the play as a shift.

This is "the shift", not The Shift. At Baseball Info Solutions we code The Shift and the shift. Anytime a team moves their infielders out of the normal alignment we call it a shift. That includes the Ted Williams Shift, also known as simply The Shift, where three infielders are on one side of the second base bag. But it also includes other similar shifts such as these:

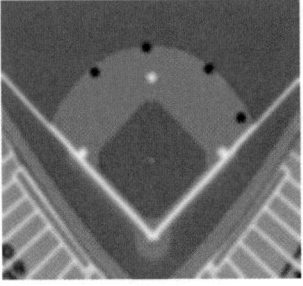

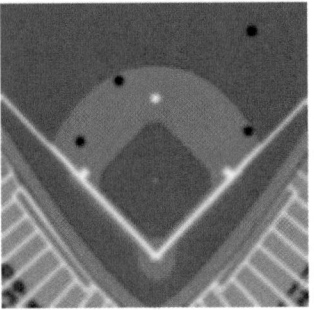

These we code as a generic shift, but we also code The Shift. Three or more infielders to one side. The reason I am emphasizing this is that I owe my readers an apology. In my Stat of the Week of November 30th, 2011 we looked at preliminary data we had at that point. We presented some information on the top five shifted hitters. I thought the data we were using was just The Ted Williams Shift. I later found out that we were using data on all of our shifts, not just The Ted Williams Shift. In this article we will mostly focus on only those plays marked as a true Ted Williams Shift – three or more players to one side of second. The other shifts are important too, but I want to focus more on the Ted Williams Shift.

Over the last two years teams have employed a shift (including Ted Williams Shifts) about 3,800 times. That's out of 370,000 plate appearances, about one percent of the time. The teams that employed a shift most often are:

Teams Employing the Most Shifts on Balls in Play

Team	2010	2011	Total
Tampa Bay Rays	221	216	437
Cleveland Indians	130	148	278
New York Mets	133	75	208
Toronto Blue Jays	79	117	196
Milwaukee Brewers	22	170	192
Note: Includes all shifts, not only Ted Williams Shifts			

The Tampa Bay Rays were the best defensive team in the majors in 2011 based on Defensive Runs Saved. Is it a coincidence that they are also the team that shifted the most? Probably not. The Milwaukee Brewers got some attention last year as they ramped up their shifting from 22 times in 2010 to 170 times in 2011. They even did some shifting on right-handed hitters, 40 times in 2011. The next highest team was the Rays with 15.

Here are the ten hitters who faced a shift most often:

Hitters Facing the Most Shifts

Player	All Shifts
David Ortiz	486
Ryan Howard	461
Carlos Pena	314
Adam Dunn	305
Prince Fielder	253
Jim Thome	223
Adrian Gonzalez	205
Mark Teixeira	180
Brian McCann	118
Jack Cust	115
Note: Includes all shifts, not only Ted Williams Shifts	

We are going to focus on these ten hitters. This chart shows all shifts against these hitters, but we are going to limit our analysis to the times when the Ted Williams Shift (or The Shift) was employed against them. And we are going to further limit our analysis to those at-bats where they put a groundball or short line drive in play. We include the short line drives because they can be fielded by infielders. Here are the batting averages of these ten players when they hit a grounder or short liner with and without The Ted Williams Shift.

Batting Average for the Top Ten Shifted Hitters Against the Ted Williams Shift, 2010-2011 Grounders and Short Liners Only

Player	Ted Williams Shift On	No Ted Williams Shift	Shift Bunt Hits
Ryan Howard	.177	.317	0
David Ortiz	.245	.232	1
Carlos Pena	.243	.191	11
Adam Dunn	.189	.230	0
Prince Fielder	.150	.263	0
Jim Thome	.211	.205	0
Adrian Gonzalez	.186	.251	2
Mark Teixeira	.168	.182	0
Jack Cust	.239	.270	0
Brian McCann	.321	.250	4
Weighted Average	.208	.238	

The shifted hitters here hit 30 points lower, in aggregate, with The Shift on than when it wasn't on. We

also looked at how often these batters got doubles and triples on these groundballs and short line drives. Their modified slugging percentage (no homers on these batted balls through the infield) was .222 against The Shift and .261 with no Shift. That's 39 points lower.

Let's take a closer look.

Six of the ten batters listed here have batting averages that are lower when The Shift is on. Two have batting averages that are about the same (a few points higher for Ortiz and Thome) with The Shift on. Carlos Pena and Brian McCann have higher batting averages with The Shift on.

It turns out, Brian McCann is in the same boat as Carlos Pena. He uses the Bunt Against The Shift strategy. He has bunted five times and gotten four hits. Maybe there is something to this strategy. For the time being, let's assume there is. Let's take Pena and McCann's boat out of the water and focus on the other eight guys. They have only bunted five times total (two for David Ortiz, three for Adrian Gonzalez). Here are the weighted batting averages. (We weight the batting average in a way to equalize their attempts with and without The Shift. For example, Jack Cust faced The Shift on 67 batted balls and 100 without. We adjust his at-bats and hits down by a third for his at-bats without The Shift to get us to an equal number as with The Shift. It's technical. Don't worry if you don't follow this gobbledygook. It works.)

Batting Average for the Eight Shifted Hitters Against the Ted Williams Shift, 2010-2011 Grounders and Short Liners Only

	Ted Williams Shift On	No Ted Williams Shift	Difference
Weighted Batting Average	.194	.245	51 points

When you take out the two guys who bunt a lot, The Shift looks even better with a difference of 51 batting points instead of 30. Modified slugging goes down by 61 points with The Shift on (from .269 to .208).

In Stat of the Week I suggested that a shift only works with the bases empty. Now that we're really studying Ted Williams Shifts only, The Shift also looks effective with men on base.

Batting Average For the Eight Shifted Hitters Against the Ted Williams Shift, 2010-2011 Grounders and Short Liners Only

	Ted Williams Shift On	No Ted Williams Shift	Difference
Bases Empty	.194	.232	38 points
Runners On	.208	.251	43 points

One more adjustment. Baseball Info Solutions has a software product that it provides for its Major League Team customers that helps them with defensive positioning. It's called BIS-D (stands for Baseball Info Solutions—Defense). "BIS-D" uses sophisticated logic to determine and display hit zones for players. It goes well beyond typical spray charts. One example is something we've been doing here – including short liners with grounders for analyzing infield positioning. The software recommends players for whom The Shift should be considered. For left-handed batters, it suggests a Ted Williams Shift for any player who pulls over 80 percent of his grounders and short liners to the right of second base. Interestingly enough, it does not suggest a shift on four of these most-shifted hitters. Let's compare Ryan Howard and Prince Fielder.

Ryan Howard
Last 120 grounders and short liners
Shift candidate (89% right of 2B)

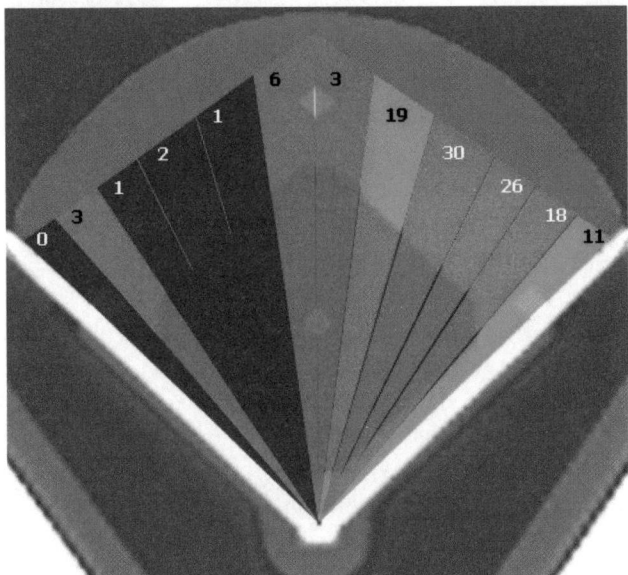

46% of last 250 were grounders and short liners.
0 bunt attempts in last 464 plate appearances

Howard pulls 89 percent of his grounders and short liners to the right of second base. "BIS-D" suggests he is a shift candidate. Looking at the chart, you can immediately see where he's hitting the ball. The darkest red areas are the hot zones. The three zones between first and second are the location of well over 50 percent (74 out 120) of the most recent 120 grounders and short liners that Howard has hit. To the left of second base every area is colored blue, meaning a cold zone. Four of the six zones are dark blue, the coldest zones. Adding up the batted ball counts, Howard has only hit 13 grounders or short liners to the left of second, and 6 of those are in the area closest to second. Looking at the last line of the chart you see that he hasn't attempted a bunt in his last 464 plate appearances. There is no question that the Ted Williams Shift should be used with Howard at the plate.

Prince Fielder
Last 120 grounders and short liners

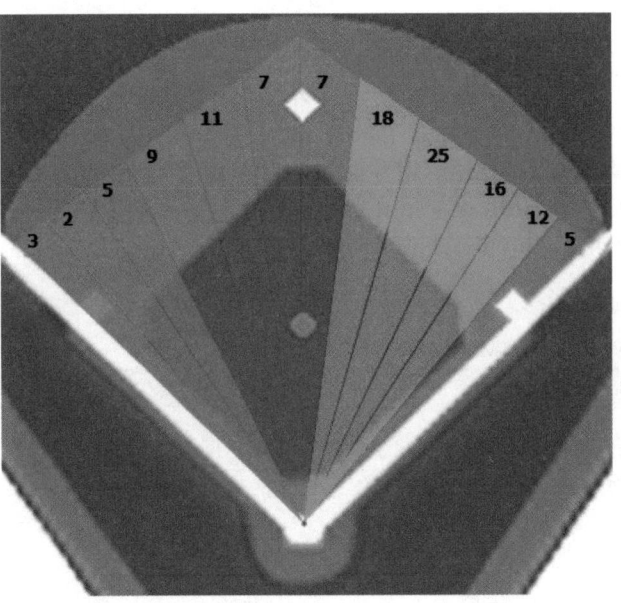

50% of last 250 were grounders and short liners.
0 bunt attempts in last 357 plate appearances

Fielder only pulls 70 percent of his grounders and short liners to the right. "BIS-D" does not suggest a shift. He does have some red zones on the right side of the field, but they are not dark red, the hottest zones. There are three "clear" colored zones in the shortstop position. This means he hits an average number of balls in this area. Applying a full Ted Williams Shift on Fielder may not be the best strategy.

The other two left-handed hitters besides Fielder

that pull less than 80 percent of their grounders and short liners of the remaining eight hitters are David Ortiz and Jim Thome. Ortiz and Thome had slightly higher batting average with The Shift on for them. "BIS-D" does not recommend a shift. Here is how the batting averages for the remaining five guys look with and without The Shift:

Batting Average for the Five Shifted Hitters Against the Ted Williams Shift, 2010-2011 Grounders and Short Liners Only

	Ted Williams Shift On	No Ted Williams Shift	Difference
Weighted Batting Average	.189	.250	61 points

We now have 61 points of batting average differential, instead of 51 like the last chart, when we exclude the two bunting strategists (Pena and McCann) and exclude the three hitters for whom The Shift is not recommended by BIS-D (Fielder, Ortiz and Thome). Granted, we are starting to get down to a limited sample size, but this does provide evidence that The Ted Williams Shift is effective.

BIS-D does not recommend shifting on Fielder, Ortiz and Thome, but it does recommend The Ted Williams shift on 48 other hitters. For example, here's Aubrey Huff. A shift has been employed only 45 times against him in the last two years.

Aubrey Huff
Last 120 grounders and short liners

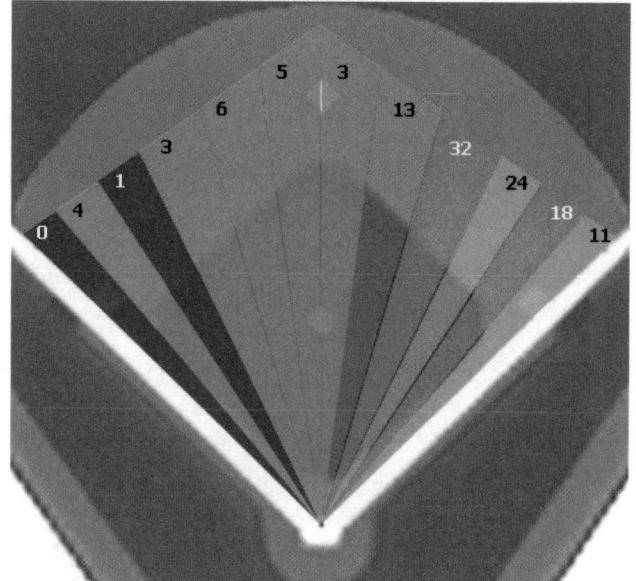

51% of last 250 were grounders and short liners.
1 bunt attempts in last 411 plate appearances

Shifting Against Right-Handed Hitters

Some teams have begun to do a very limited amount of shifting against some right-handed hitters. One of the most prolific right-handed pull hitters in baseball is Atlanta's Dan Uggla, who pulls 91 percent of his groundballs and short liners. He has hit a grounder or short liner against the Ted Williams Shift (mirror image version) eight times with one hit. There are six other guys who have at least two grounder/short liners against the Ted Williams Shift (Jose Bautista, Vladimir Guerrero, Casey McGehee, Marcus Thames, Albert Pujols and Mark Teixeira). Of these, only Thames (94 percent pulled) and Pujols (88 percent) are recommended for The Shift by BIS-D.

Here is Uggla's chart:

Last 120 grounders and short liners
Shift candidate (91% left of 2B)

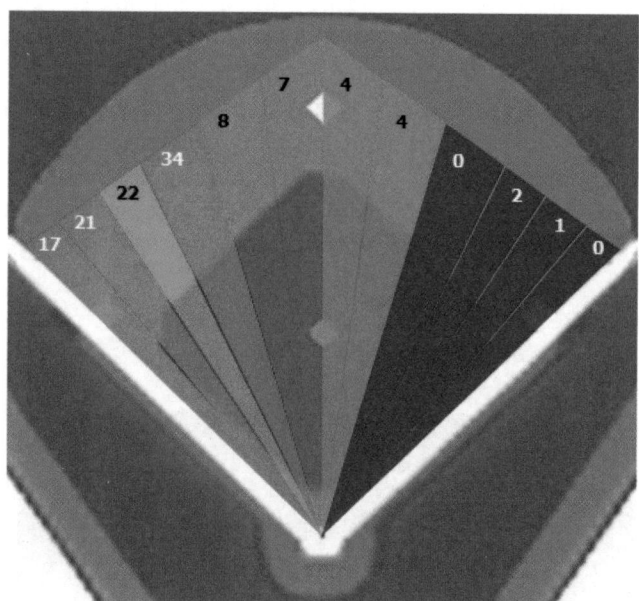

52% of last 250 were grounders and short liners.
0 bunt attempts in last 314 plate appearances

The four zones closest to the third base line are Uggla's four hot zones. He only had 11 of his last 120 grounders/short liners to the right of second. In 2011 Uggla only had eight times when he hit a grounder/short liner against the Ted Williams Shift. Seven of those had the Brewers shifting on him and once it was the Reds. The Brewers had two other shifts where they didn't fully commit. Rickie Weeks was directly behind the bag instead of being left of second. Both times Uggla got a hit. Once Uggla hit it in the zone near the third base position where he hit a ball 22 times, as shown in the chart above. Looking at the video, if they fully committed to the shift with both the second baseman and shortstop closer to third base, I think they would have gotten this one. The other hit went through the area close to second base with 8 Uggla batted balls. It was very hard hit, and unless the second baseman was right in that area (instead of the area with 7 batted balls where they were on the other plays) it still would have been a hit. If they were fully committed to shifting against Uggla, that's probably where the second baseman would be. But you have to give the Brewers credit. At least they aren't too timid to shift dramatically on a right-handed extreme pull hitter. BIS-D recommends shifting be considered whenever a right-handed hitter exceeds 85 percent of his grounders and short liners to the left of second base. There are 56 right-handed hitters recommended for The Shift by BIS-D. Of these, 16 pull over 90 percent of the time.

Bunting Against The Shift

As we saw earlier, Carlos Pena has been quite effective with his Bunt Against The Shift strategy. Brian McCann has done well also. However, it is not likely that bunting will work for everyone. Pena has good speed for a big man. They both can clearly handle the bat when trying to bunt. These two things aren't true for a lot of the major pull hitters in the game today. Plus, you've taken away their power. You can't hit for extra bases on a bunt. Pena employs a good strategy by bunting as a leadoff man to get on base. But a lot of teams wouldn't mind seeing some of these big boppers squaring up to bunt even if they do get a bunt hit once in a while.

Conclusion

If I were running a major league team, I would employ The Shift far more often than teams do currently. If we had more time we'd study the shifts employed by the best defensive team in baseball, the Tampa Bay Rays. They are shifting about three percent of the time compared to under one percent for the rest of the teams in MLB. The Brewers upped how often they shifted last year, but they lost interest as the year went on. After shifting over 130 times in the first three months of the

season, they only shifted 36 times in the last three months. It appears they may have succumbed to the potential embarrassment factor. It is embarrassing when you shift and the hitter gets a hit right in the spot you vacated. But that's short-term thinking. Losing once in a while doesn't invalidate the strategy. The Brewers started the season with just about the worst defensive infield you could assemble. The shifting strategy was working. It showed up in our Defensive Runs Saved numbers. But as the season continued and they shifted less often, their defensive numbers began to drop off. To his credit, however, Ron Roenicke did get fired up about shifting again when the Brewers made the playoffs, even shifting on the right-handed hitting Chris Young during the first playoff series.

But I would go further than the Brewers did early in the season, or even how often the Rays shift. Based on the study above, I'd probably have fewer Ted Williams Shifts on Carlos Pena and Brian McCann because of their bunting ability. But for other lefties who pull 80+ percent of the time and righties who pull 85-90 percent or more, I would increase how often I used The Shift.

There are some questions that require further research:

- Like Pena and McCann, can other hitters improve their bunting skills to attack The Shift?
- Can hitters try to adjust their swing to go the other way if The Shift is on?
- Maybe you want them to try to adjust—are these pull hitters less effective any time The Shift is on? We would have to look at all their plate appearances, not just grounders and short liners to see if there is an overall effect.
- Even if you bunt well, are you still less effective because you've lost your power?
- Does The Shift work against right-handed hitters? Our data is too limited thus far for righties.
- Should pitchers adjust their pitch selection and location with a shift on?
- Hitters don't pull as much with two strikes. Should The Shift be vacated with two strikes? All hitters? Just some?
- Do hitters vary in their pull rates based on pitchers throwing righty or lefty?

Beyond Ted Williams:
Where Do Pulled Groundballs Come From?

While the Ted Williams Shift (dissected on page 43) is a dramatic tactical ploy, not every hitter pulls the ball enough to illicit such a response. However, there are certain factors which can be used to anticipate the batted ball's trajectory and direction.

Let's start with a few basics. Looking at all right-handed batters with at least 250 batted balls over 2010-11, Jason Bay pulled 90 percent of his groundballs while Willie Bloomquist pulled just 57 percent, representing opposite ends of the spectrum. The most extreme left-handers were Carlos Pena (89 percent) and Jonathan Herrera, Brett Gardner and Ichiro Suzuki (54 percent). The average right-handed batter pulled 75 percent of grounders, while the average lefty pulled 72 percent.

By comparison, right-handed batters pulled 62 percent of pure line drives, 54 percent of fliner-liners, 45 percent of fliner-flies and just 42 percent of pure flyballs (for more information on how we define fliners and other batted ball types, see page 435). Lefties show the same trend. The more the hitter gets underneath the ball, the less likely he is to pull it. However, infielders are primarily concerned with groundballs, and that's what we'll focus on in this article.

Pull Percentages by Pitch Type

How does this vary by pitch type? Do hitters pull different pitches at different rates? During a game, you might occasionally notice the shortstop joining a conference between the pitcher and catcher on the mound. Contrary to popular opinion, he's not there to discuss politics or wedding presents. He's often going over the catcher's signs so he knows what pitch is coming and can anticipate accordingly. If the shortstop isn't in sync with the battery, how much does it cost him?

Let's check the data, limiting our sample to right-handed batters facing right-handed pitchers to avoid possible platoon biases:

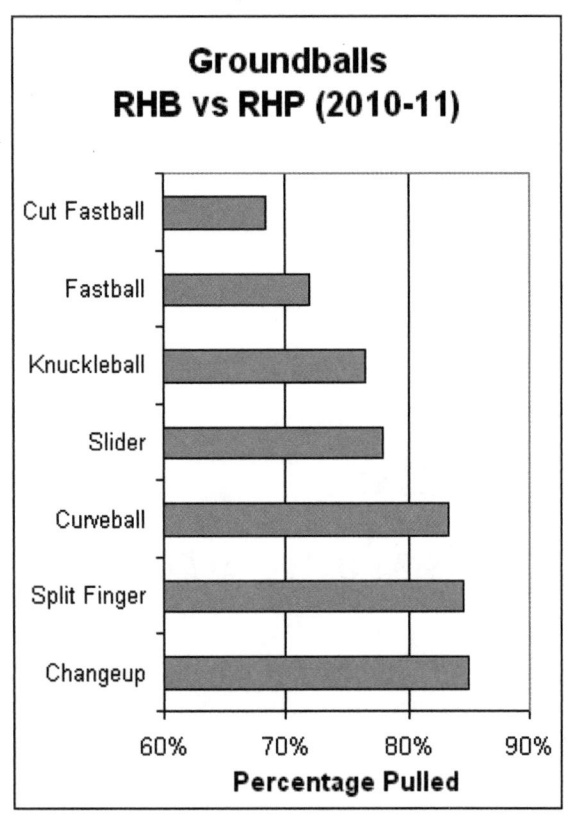

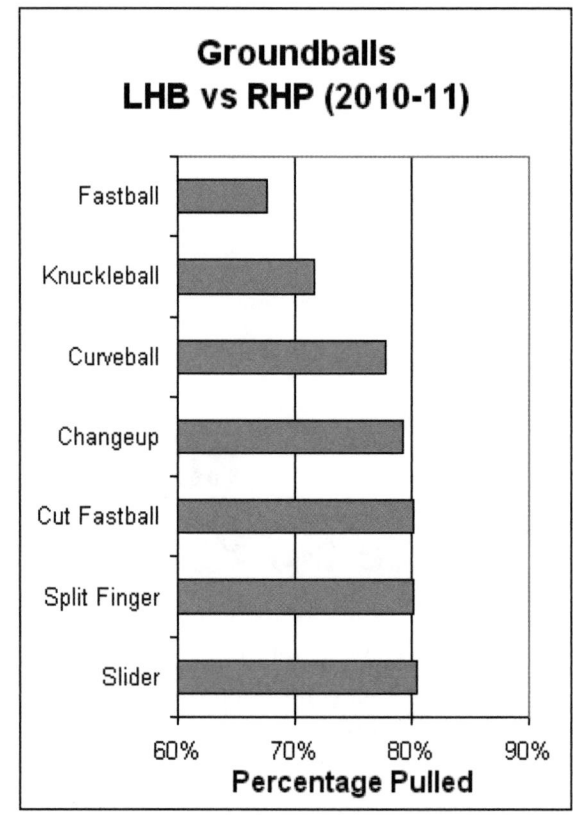

When thrown a curve, splitter or changeup, the average right-handed hitter turns into Jason Bay or Albert Pujols and starts pulling 83-85 percent of grounders. Knowing what pitch is coming would benefit every infielder, allowing them to better position themselves and anticipate the batted ball's ultimate course.

We see a similar effect for left-handed batters facing right-handed pitchers. Pitchers tend to throw more changeups and fewer sliders to opposite-handed hitters, likely causing the reordering of off-speed pitches. However, fastballs are still pulled much less often than breaking balls.

Does this mean defenses should take advantage and start employing the Ted Williams Shift whenever the pitcher is going to throw something off-speed? No, probably not; dramatic pre-pitch movement would likely give away the pitcher's intentions. As a result, the batter would sit on the slow stuff and have a better shot at making good contact. Rather than moving pre-pitch, however, fielders can (and sometimes do) start leaning one way or the other as the pitch is delivered. (Of course, the defense could position themselves for a changeup beforehand then throw him a fastball instead, just to keep him honest. That would develop an interesting mind game between the hitter and the defense.)

Pull Percentages by Count

Speaking of knowing what's coming, what about a 3-0 or 3-1 count? Now looking just at fastballs from righties to righties to avoid a pitch selection bias:

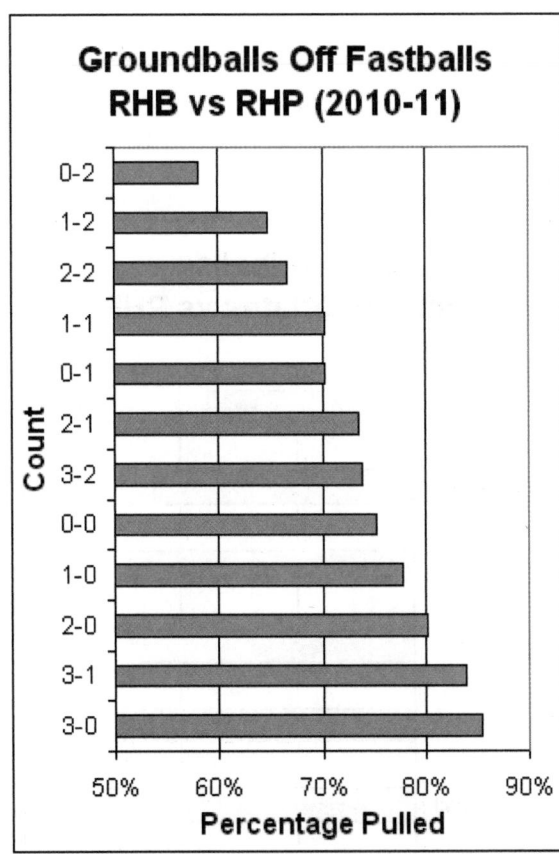

Groundballs Off Fastballs
RHB vs RHP (2010-11)

couldn't handle, well, he was probably going to get on base anyways. And you've taken away the threat of a home run or other extra-base hit in a very dangerous count.

Pull Percentages by Pitch Location

What about pitch location? From an early age, hitters are generally instructed to "go with the pitch," pulling inside pitches and pushing outside pitches to the opposite field. How does that hold up, at least for groundballs? Here's a five-by-five grid of groundball pull percentage by fastball pitch location, with the inner three-by-three representing the strike zone:

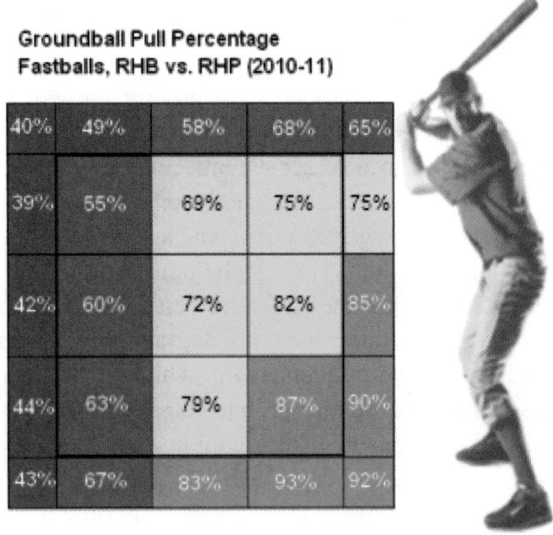

Groundball Pull Percentage
Fastballs, RHB vs. RHP (2010-11)

On 3-0 and 3-1 counts, hitters sit on the fastball and pull around 85 percent of grounders. On the other hand, when behind in the count with no balls and two strikes, hitters turn slap-happy. Getting defensive during the at-bat turns the average hitter into Willie Bloomquist, pulling just 58 percent of grounders.

Let's say you're facing a powerful right-handed hitter like Miguel Cabrera. Your rookie pitcher is terrified of the slugger and has been nibbling at the corners and just missing. Now the count is 3-1, and everyone in the ballpark knows Cabrera is going to get a fastball, belt-high, across the middle of the plate. As awesome as the slugger is, he's even better in 3-1 counts.

What's the harm in moving all three infielders to the left side of second base? If he puts the ball in play, he's almost guaranteed to pull it. With three infielders on his pull side, you might steal a groundball or line drive base hit. Though it's not likely in a hitter's count, there's a slim chance he tries to lay down a bunt; if he does get down a good one that the pitcher, catcher or first baseman

Hitters pull a remarkable 87 percent of pitches in the low, inside corner of the strike zone. Just outside the zone, they pull even more. However, the higher you go or the further you go outside, the more the hitter is likely to hit a grounder the other way. Notice how the height of the pitch makes a large difference on the inner third of the plate (from 93 percent down low to 68 percent above the zone), but outside pitches are rarely pulled regardless of the pitch height.

What about off-speed pitches? Do they demonstrate similar groundball pull percentages by pitch location?

Groundball Pull Percentage
Off-speed, RHB vs. RHP (2010-11)

50%	57%	85%	74%	70%
66%	80%	84%	77%	86%
68%	84%	89%	89%	93%
68%	86%	87%	92%	88%
73%	87%	88%	88%	92%

Let's look at the 48 left-handed batters who are recommended for a shift according to Baseball Info Solutions' Defensive Positioning software (BIS-D). These hitters pull, on average, 81 percent of groundballs. How does that break down by pitch type? (Again, looking at right-handed pitchers only to avoid bias.)

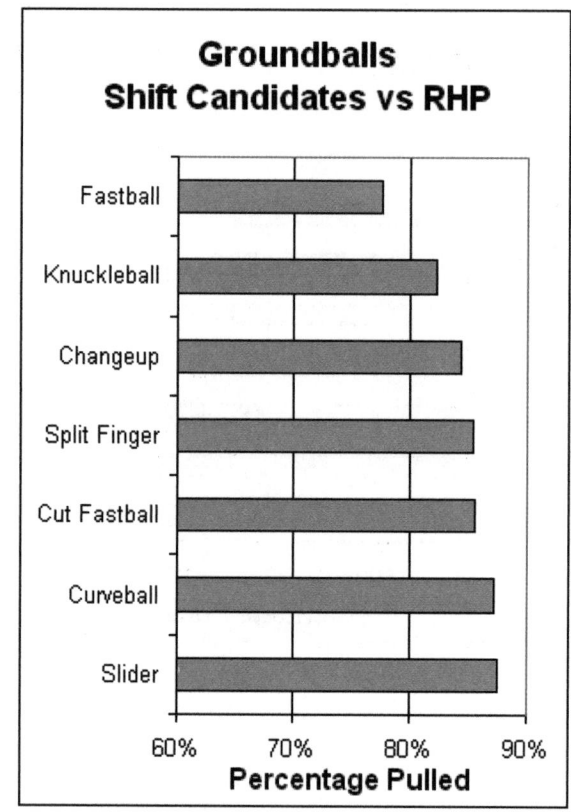

Since these off-speed pitches are pulled more overall, we were expecting to see all that red. The same trend exists, but to a lesser extent: Pitches outside the zone are pulled far less frequently on the ground than inside pitches (though they still manage to pull outside pitches more often than they go the other way).

What does this mean for fielders? As with pitch types, the fielders don't want to telegraph the next pitch. However, given the frequency with which low and inside pitches are pulled on the ground, an intelligent infield defense might want to take a couple steps towards the pull side as the pitch is delivered.

Of course, a defense can't always rely on the pitcher to hit his targets, so there is some risk involved. Behind a control pitcher, however, the defense can comfortably put themselves in position to take away a few hits.

Shift Candidates

What about the flip side of the issue: are there any situations where we should NOT shift against hitters who would normally merit a shift?

Like typical left-handed batters, lefties pull fastballs the least and sliders the most. However, our shift candidates range from 78 percent on fastballs to 87 percent on curves and sliders. For these hitters, the range of pull percentages by pitch type is just 9 percentage points, compared to the 14 for all lefties and 17 points for right-handers. Even on fastballs, these hitters pull 78 percent of grounders, a high enough rate not to question the shift.

What about fastballs in different counts?

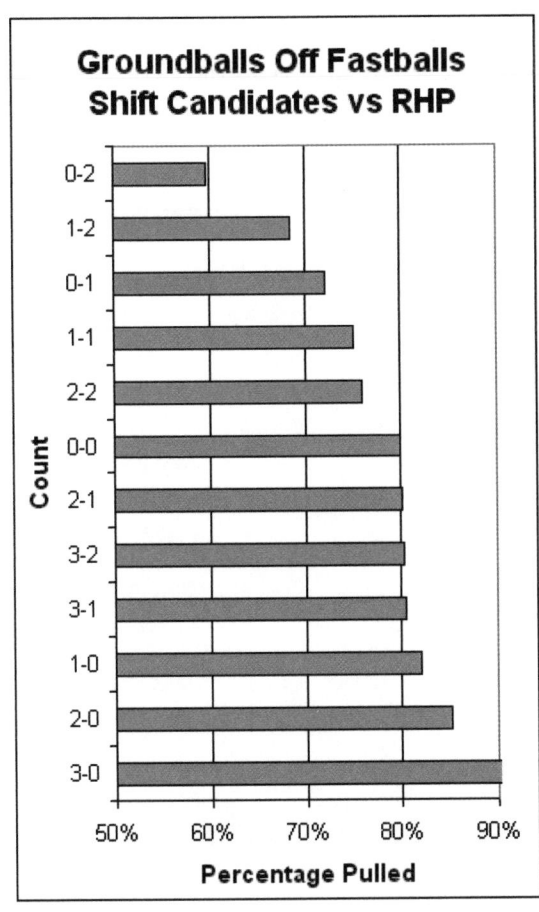

**Groundballs Off Fastballs
Shift Candidates vs RHP**

**Grounball Pull Percentage
Fastballs, Shift Candidates vs. RHP**

83%	71%	80%	58%	36%
83%	87%	84%	73%	55%
93%	84%	90%	81%	54%
88%	93%	88%	81%	58%
100%	88%	90%	83%	50%

Fastballs down and in are pulled around 90 percent of the time. Fewer pitches on the outer third of the plate are pulled, but still in the 70-80 percent range. Pitches off the outside corner are pulled around half the time they're hit on the ground.

Off-speed pitches are pulled even more often, as we would expect from the previous charts. (We've removed the pitch location zones with fewer than 10 groundballs.)

As you can see, when these shift candidates are behind in the count and get a fastball, they pull grounders 75 percent of the time or less. When ahead in the count they predictably sit on the fastball and turn on it, pulling over 80 percent of grounders. A similar count-by-count effect exists for other pitches, albeit in smaller samples.

Lastly, let's look at how our shift candidates pull grounders based on the pitch's location. First, looking at fastballs:

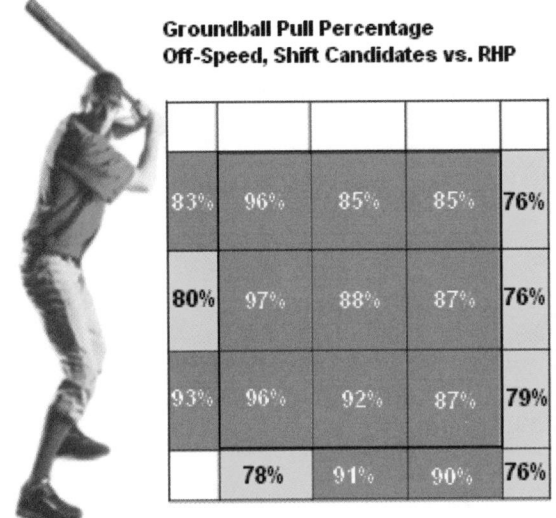

**Groundball Pull Percentage
Off-Speed, Shift Candidates vs. RHP**

83%	96%	85%	85%	76%
80%	97%	88%	87%	76%
93%	96%	92%	87%	79%
	78%	91%	90%	76%

Wow, that's a lot of red. Even off the plate outside, these shift candidates still pull between 75 and 80 percent of groundballs.

If you're playing a shift against these extreme left-handed pull hitters, there are a few variables you should consider. When the count is in the hitter's favor, his groundballs are likely headed to the right side. If you're going to throw an off-speed pitch, he's also likely to pull it no matter where you throw it. However, you may want to shift less aggressively when throwing a fastball ahead in the count 0-2 or 1-2, particularly if you're pitching to the outside corner. In these cases, the shortstop might want to move back to the left side of second base but not completely back to his normal position. In all other cases, shift away!

Jeter vs. Ryan

Six years ago Bill James wrote an article for the first volume of *The Fielding Bible* called "Jeter vs. Everett." At that point Derek Jeter had just won two straight Gold Gloves for his defense at shortstop. One in 2004 and then another one in 2005.

Anyone who read that article came away pretty convinced: there is no way that Jeter should have won either of those Gold Gloves.

So what happened? Jeter won three more Gold Gloves. One happened later in the same year that Bill wrote the article, 2006, and then two more in 2009 and 2010.

Conclusion: there is no way that any one of the voters who voted for Jeter read that article.

They probably won't read this one either. But that won't stop us from trying to prove the same point over and over again. I am going to give it one more try, and this will be short and sweet.

The best shortstop in baseball last year was Brendan Ryan. Ryan saved the Mariners 18 runs with his defense in 2011. The worst shortstop in baseball last year was Derek Jeter. He cost the Yankees 15 runs defensively. That's a 33-run advantage for Ryan. OK, I know. Right there, we've already lost some of you. You don't believe we can measure defense like this. But I'm telling you, we can. So bear with me, and you'll see this more clearly than you ever have.

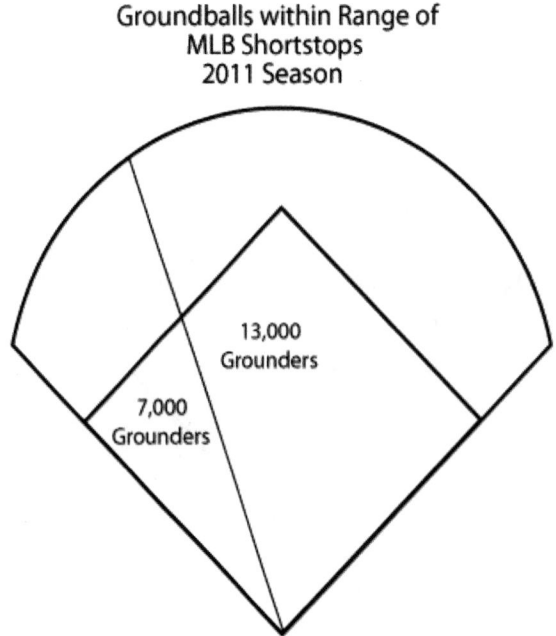

Groundballs within Range of MLB Shortstops 2011 Season

13,000 Grounders

7,000 Grounders

Take a look at this chart. See the line going towards the shortstop position? In 2011 there were 13,000 groundballs to the right of that line within range of major league shortstops to field. They turned 65 percent of those into outs.

When Brendan Ryan was at shortstop last year, there were 336 groundballs hit to the right of that line. What percentage of those did Ryan turn into outs? It must be pretty good, right? After all, he was the "best" shortstop in baseball last year. It turns out he fielded exactly the same percentage, 65 percent.

When Derek Jeter was at shortstop last year, there were 288 groundballs hit to the right of that line. What percentage of those did Jeter turn into outs? It must be pretty bad, right? After all, he was the "worst" shortstop in baseball last year. It turns out he fielded almost exactly the same percentage, 64 percent.

Now let's work our way to the left of that line in increments of about 6-8 feet at a time. Between the line we drew and the third base line there are nine of those areas. Shortstops can turn groundballs into outs in the first four of these areas. In total there were 7,000 groundballs to the left of the line within range of major league shortstops to field, a little more than half the number to the right of the line.

In the first 6-8 feet area to the left of the line, major league shortstops turned groundballs into outs 82 percent of the time in 2011. Brendan Ryan turned 86 percent into outs. Jeter, 73 percent.

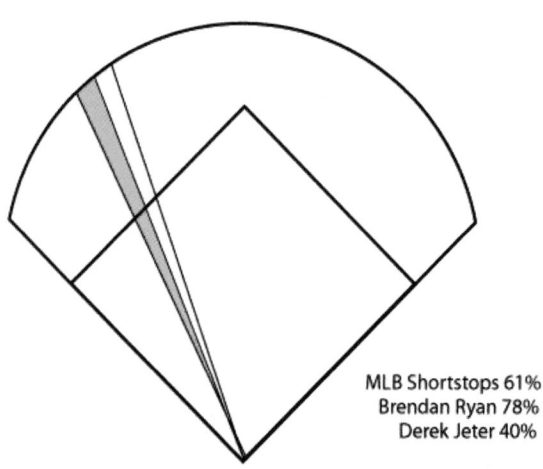

Out Ratio by
Batted Ball Location

MLB Shortstops 61%
Brendan Ryan 78%
Derek Jeter 40%

In the third 6-8 feet area to the left of the line, the major league out ratio for shortstops was 34 percent. Ryan was at 56 percent. That was more than twice as much as Jeter at 26 percent.

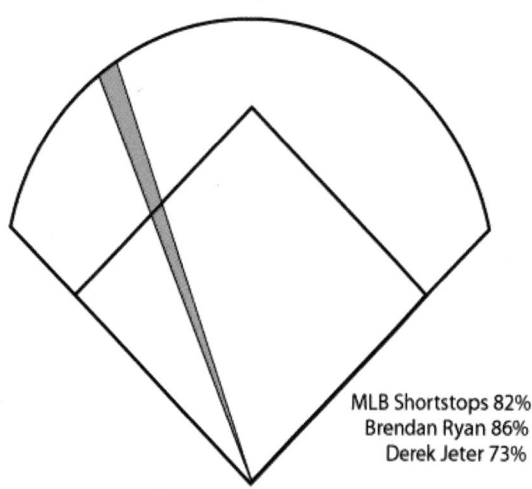

Out Ratio by
Batted Ball Location

MLB Shortstops 82%
Brendan Ryan 86%
Derek Jeter 73%

In the second 6-8 feet area to the left of the line, major league shortstops turned groundballs into outs 61 percent of the time. Ryan turned 78 percent into outs. That was just under twice as much as Jeter at 40 percent.

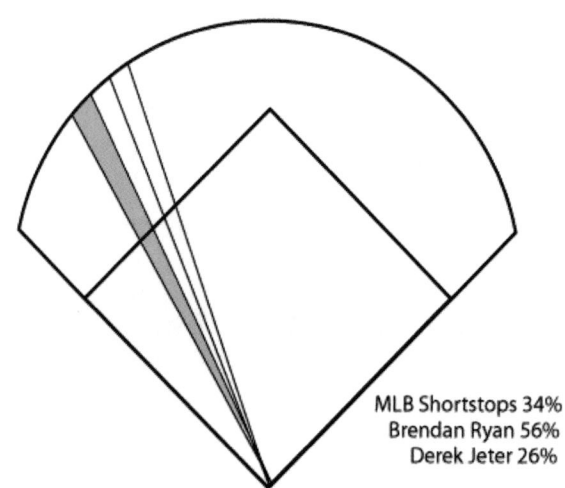

Out Ratio by
Batted Ball Location

MLB Shortstops 34%
Brendan Ryan 56%
Derek Jeter 26%

In the fourth 6-8 feet area to the left of the line, deep into the shortstop hole, the major league out ratio for shortstops was 8 percent. Ryan had a 13 percent out ratio. Jeter had 0. None. Nada.

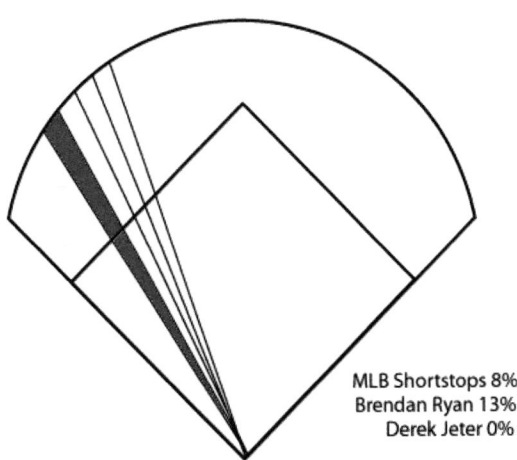

Out Ratio by
Batted Ball Location

MLB Shortstops 8%
Brendan Ryan 13%
Derek Jeter 0%

Here's a chart that summarizes this:

Shortstops Out Ratio by Vector Group

Area	BIS Vectors	MLB Out Ratio	Ryan Out Ratio	Jeter Out Ratio
Right of the Line	199-214	65%	65%	64%
First 6-8 feet Left of Line	200-202	82%	86%	73%
Second 6-8 feet	203-205	61%	78%	40%
Third 6-8 feet	206-208	34%	56%	26%
Fourth 6-8 feet	209-211	8%	13%	0%

Isn't that something? To the right of the line, where most fieldable groundballs by shortstops go, Ryan and Jeter are exactly the same as the average major league shortstop. It's to the left of that line, where fewer fieldable groundballs for shortstops go, that every element of difference between the best shortstop in baseball and the worst shortstop in baseball exists. If Jeter had fielded the same percentage as Ryan in each one of those 6-8 feet areas, he would have turned 38 more hits into outs.

Q.E.D.

By the way, the data presented in this article for Jeter and Ryan is for 2011. If you look at 2010, a Jeter Gold Glove year, you get pretty much the exact same results between Ryan and Jeter. Ryan was the second-best shortstop in 2010 by our measures while Jeter was the fifth-worst.

Good Plays and Misplays

One of the most, if not the most, important breakthroughs we are presenting in this book is the use of Good Plays and Misplays to evaluate defensive performance. Several years ago Bill James devised a technique to categorize plays called Good Fielding Plays and Defensive Misplays. He wrote about this in a chapter from *The Fielding Bible—Volume II* called Defensive Misplays:

"What we are doing here is kind of halfway between sabermetrics and scouting. Scouting is organized observation. Defensive Misplays are very limited but extremely highly organized observations. We watch the games, carefully, repeatedly, and we make "notes" about what happens. These notes are sorted into very narrow categories: Second baseman juggles the ball and loses the opportunity for a Double Play. Two outfielders converge on a pop up and let it drop between them. Fielder pulls his foot off the bag unnecessarily, losing the out. Fielder neglects to cover his base.

"Employing a staff of researchers, we watch every major league game carefully for these plays—and 50 others."

There are 54 separate Defensive Misplays and 28 separate Good Fielding Plays that Baseball Info Solutions has "scouted" going back to 2004. While it may seem that determining whether a play is a misplay is highly subjective, it is not. For example, one of our 54 Misplays is DM38, "Failing to anticipate the wall." The video scout has to decide that a misplay is a DM38 based on three objective elements:

1) Did the outfielder go to the wall in an effort to catch the ball?

2) Did the ball bounce over his head back toward the infield?

3) Did a runner advance an extra base as a result?

If the answer to all three of these questions is yes, it is a DM38. If any one of these answers is no, it is not a DM38. It's that simple. Not a lot of judgment involved. Quite objective.

Runs Saved on Good Plays and Misplays

One of our biggest undertakings in the last three years has been to convert Good Plays and Misplays into Runs Saved. Throughout the charts in this book we abbreviate this as GFP/DME Runs Saved. This stands for Runs Saved on Good Fielding Plays and Runs Saved (or actually, runs lost) on Defensive Misplays and Errors. When a play is ruled an error by the Official Scorer, we take it one step further and categorize the error into one of the 54 Defensive Misplay categories. Errors become part of the equation.

Let's give you some examples involving DM38, Failing to anticipate the wall. Over the last three years a DM38 happened 789 times. The total run value of those plays is -252. That is, we estimate that due to the extra bases allowed on those plays, an extra 252 runs have scored. How do we figure that out? Here's an example. Mark Teixeira hits a flyball towards the Green Monster in Fenway. Carl Crawford runs back to the wall thinking he can make the catch, but the ball hits twenty feet up. Now Crawford is too close to the wall and the ball careens back over his head towards the infield. Teixeira winds up at third base. If Crawford had anticipated the wall properly he would have been able to cleanly field the ball off the wall and hold Teixeira to a double, or possibly even a single. So now we have a man on third rather than a man on first or second. In the long run this costs runs and we're able to estimate those runs using sabermetric techniques.

Here are the players who had the most DM38s in the last three years:

Players with Most DM38s 2009-2011

Player	Failure to Anticipate the Wall	Runs Saved
Jacoby Ellsbury	16	-3
Cody Ross	15	-3
Carl Crawford	14	-3
Nyjer Morgan	14	-2
Chris Young	11	-1

We allocate the 252 runs lost to individual players based on two factors: the number of DM38s they had and how many opportunities they had. One straightforward way to estimate opportunities is to use innings in the field. However, we wanted to go one better. There are many, many innings where an outfielder doesn't have a single ball hit his way. Some pitchers are groundball pitchers and allow fewer balls to reach the outfield. Instead of using innings we decided to use Touches. Touches are an estimate of the number of plays where a fielder touches the ball. It is a better technique to measure opportunities than innings and we use it for most of our GFP/DME Runs Saved calculations.

When adding up all the players in Major League Baseball, our objective is to have Runs Saved total to zero. Therefore, in addition to the players who have cost their team runs on DM38 misplays, we also have players who have positive runs saved values for having made less DM38s per Touch than expected, based on how the average fielder would perform with the same number of touches. The players who have the most runs saved because of having the fewest DM38s relative to Touches are Michael Bourn, Colby Rasmus, Nick Swisher, and Ichiro Suzuki, all of who get credited with two runs saved over the last three years based on this misplay type.

Let's go through some of the key Good Fielding Play and Defensive Misplay types by position.

Catchers

The catching position is the most difficult position to evaluate defensively. In Volume II of *The Fielding Bible* we made good progress by estimating the number of runs a catcher saves (or costs) his team with his ability to control the running game and with his ability to handle pitchers. But what about other areas of catcher defense? What about his ability to block pitches in the dirt to prevent runner advancement? How often does he allow wild pitches, and how often does he prevent them? What about handling difficult throws on plays at the plate? Once he has the throw, how about blocking the plate on the runner trying to score?

Answers to these questions, plus quite a few others, are all things that Baseball Info Solutions is now measuring to evaluate catcher defense. And we've converted all of them into the currency of baseball: runs.

The results are remarkable. If you look at the list of the top catchers in baseball based on Good Plays and Misplays, it matches the perceptions that managers, coaches and scouts have assessed subjectively. Here are the top five catchers over the last three years in Runs Saved on Good Fielding Plays and Defensive Misplays and Errors:

Top Five Catchers 2009-2011
Good Play/Misplay Runs Saved

Player	Runs Saved
Yadier Molina	15
Jeff Mathis	14
Kurt Suzuki	12
Carlos Ruiz	11
Jason Varitek	10

Here are the bottom five:

Bottom Five Catchers 2009-2011
Good Play/Misplay Runs Saved

Player	Runs Saved
A.J. Pierzynski	-16
Miguel Olivo	-14
Jorge Posada	-8
Josh Bard	-8
Jarrod Saltalamacchia	-7
Rob Johnson	-7
Jose Molina	-7

We have developed good plays and misplays that involve every defensive position on the field. We'll be getting to the other positions in more detail later in this article. However, here are two major statements about GFPs and DMEs for catchers relative to the other defensive positions:

1) The run impact of GFP/DMEs for catchers is

higher than any other position. The Runs Saved spread between the 15 runs saved for the three-year leader, Yadier Molina, and the -16 runs saved for the three-year trailer, A.J. Pierzynski, is 31 runs. Only one other position is close, first base. The difference between the best and worst first baseman in the last three years is 29 runs. After that, no other position is over 20 runs.

2) Runs Saved on GFP/DMEs for catchers is higher than any other Runs Saved component for catchers. The spread between the best and worst catchers in Adjusted Earned Runs Saved is 25 runs. The spread for catcher Stolen Base Runs Saved is 23 runs. For catcher Bunt Runs Saved, it's 9 runs.

In short, we have found that measuring Good Fielding Plays and Defensive Misplays and Errors and translating them to Runs Saved is the most significant way to measure catcher defense.

Before we compare the best and the worst, Yadier Molina and A.J. Pierzynski, the second best and second worst catchers in GFP/DME Runs Saved provide some very interesting details. The second best defensive catcher with Good Plays and Misplays over the last three years was Jeff Mathis. The second worst was Miguel Olivo. Here is how they compare:

**Good Play/Misplay Run Impact Chart
2009 - 2011**

Good Play/Misplay Type	Mathis RS	Olivo RS
Preventing WP/PB	10	-8
Catcher Blocks the Plate	3	-2
Handling Throws	1	-2
Slow To Recover	0	-1
Failing to Catch and Tag	0	-1
Total	14	-14

Mathis is better than Olivo at every significant Good Play/Misplay category that involves catchers. Working from the bottom of the chart up:

- In the last three years, Olivo had six plays where he failed to catch and tag the runner on a play. Mathis had three. We estimate those extra misplays have cost Olivo's team about a run.
- The definition for the Slow to Recover misplay is: Fielder slows or stops in an attempt to make a play, allowing a runner to advance (i.e. turn a single into a double) due to the fielder's inattentiveness. Mathis did not have a misplay of this type in the last three years while Olivo had two, costing his team about a run.

- "Handling throws" is a combination of three Good Play/Misplay types: GFP7—Handling difficult throw, GFP8—Catches wild throw, and DM14—Failing to catch the throw. This is a category that mostly involves first basemen, but other players can make good plays and misplays here as well. Olivo had three plays where he failed to catch a throw leading to runners taking extra bases. He had only one good play catching a wild throw. Mathis caught two wild throws and missed one. Olivo cost his team two runs while Mathis saved one.
- Here is the definition of GFP26, Catcher blocks the plate: Catcher blocks the plate to record an out in a situation in which the runner appeared likely to score or in which the catcher and runner collide and the catcher is able to hold onto the ball for the out. Mathis had 16 of these plays in the last three years. Compared to how often other catchers make this play, he saved his team an estimated three runs. Olivo only made five of these plays which, relative to other catchers, cost about two runs.

We estimate that Jeff Mathis saved his team 10 runs preventing wild pitches and passed balls while Olivo cost his team 8.

Preventing Wild Pitches and Passed Balls

The most important defensive impact a catcher can have, that we've found we can measure, involves the ability to prevent runner advancement on wild pitches and passed balls. Nothing separates the better catchers from the worse ones more than this. Like the combined category called "Handling throws", our measurement of a catcher's ability to prevent wild pitches and passed balls involves the combination of three different Good Play/Misplay types plus one regular official statistic. The three plays are:

GFP27. Potential wild pitch catch - Catcher snares a pitch dangerously outside, inside or high to prevent runner or runners from advancing on a pitch that seemed likely to be a wild pitch (Note: the pitch has to be extremely wild in order to reward a catcher with a GFP27).

GFP28. Catcher Blocks - A Catcher's Block only occurs when runners are on base or if the pitch was the third strike. The idea being that a catcher's save must have a positive outcome. If a catcher blocks a ball in the dirt with no one on base, that play in itself does not have a direct positive outcome for the team on defense so long as it wasn't a swinging third strike. There are only two possible positive outcomes, 1) the prevention of the advancement of a base runner or base runners or 2) the recording of an out at first base or on a tag when the failure to block the ball might have resulted in the runner reaching first on a strike out and a wild pitch.

We record a Catcher's Block (CB) when a catcher is able to block a ball in the dirt. Scorers should use their best judgement on balls that are fielded on a short hop by the catcher. Generally balls that barely hit the ground and short hop into the catcher's mitt, where the catcher uses a natural catching motion to receive the pitch, should not be scored as a CB.

DM53. Wild pitch misplay - Catcher gets glove on ball or allows ball to get past him or blocks ball but fails to locate ball quickly resulting in the advancement of a base runner or base runners. (Note: Play would be scored a wild pitch. If a passed ball is scored, you CANNOT also give the catcher a 53 for that play.) There are three ideas associated with the catcher and a wild pitch: 1) the pitch was so wild that there was no possible way a catcher could have prevented the advancement of runners (NOT scored a 53), 2) the pitch should have been blocked preventing the runners from advancing and the catcher failed to do so because he missed the ball, did not react quick enough or did not give a proper effort (scored -53), 3) the pitch in the dirt was blocked or caught by the catcher preventing the advancement of base runners (this should be scored as a CB, a Catcher's Block).

Passed Ball is the official statistic used.

Let's compare Yadier Molina to A.J. Pierzynski over the last three years:

Molina vs. Pierzynski 2009-2011

	Molina	Pierzynski
Catcher Block	1,788	1,075
Potential Wild Pitch Catches	7	4
Passed Balls	17	14
Wild Pitch misplays	87	122
Wild Pitches Impossible to Handle	11	16

Molina and Pierzynski are two of the most durable catchers in baseball over the last three years. Molina has started 398 games at catcher in that time, Pierzynski 359. Each player has handled over 50,000 pitches. Between them, well over 100,000 pitches. Adding all the numbers in this table, there were 3,141 difficult pitches to handle (about 3 percent) for the two catchers. When we count these difficult pitches we are only counting those pitches where runner advancement is possible (either a runner is on base or the batter has a swinging third strike).

That's a lot of difficult pitches to deal with. How catchers handle all these difficult pitches is what separates the best from the worst.

The biggest numbers in this chart are the catcher blocks, pitches in the dirt that the catcher handles preventing runner advancement. Molina has about 4.5 catcher blocks per game he started, Pierzynski about 3.0. This clearly shows that Molina had a more difficult pitching staff to deal with, a staff that throws a lot of pitches in the dirt. But the key is what percentage of the time the catcher prevents wild pitches and passed balls on those difficult pitches. Excluding the wild pitches judged to be impossible to handle, Molina had 1,899 difficult pitches to deal with. He had 104 passed balls or wild pitch misplays. Pierzynski had 1,215 difficult pitches. He had 136 passed balls or wild pitch misplays. Molina allowed about 5.5 percent of difficult pitches to get by him, allowing the runner or the batter to advance. Pierzynski allowed 11.2 percent, more than twice as often.

Let's put this in perspective. If a catcher has about 400 difficult pitches in a season to contend with and he allows runners to advance 5.5 percent of the time, that's 22 times when extra bases are taken. But if he allows 11.2 percent, that's 45 times. Keep in mind that there can be more than one runner on base advancing. And in some of those cases where a swinging third strike is involved, it's not just an extra base, it's an extra base runner. When we analyze the run impact of all those extra bases (and runners), it's significant. Comparing Molina and Pierzynski to all the other catchers in baseball over the last three years, we estimate that Molina saved the Cardinals a total of about 15 runs while A.J. cost the White Sox 14 runs. That's five extra runs per year for the Cardinals and five less runs per year for the White Sox, based solely on Molina's and Pierzynski's abilities to handle difficult pitches.

The top five and bottom five players in Runs Saved by preventing wild pitches and passed balls over the last three years are:

Top Five Players 2009-2011
Preventing Wild Pitches and Passed Balls

Top Five		Bottom Five	
Player	Runs Saved	Player	Runs Saved
Yadier Molina	15	A.J. Pierzynski	-14
Kurt Suzuki	10	Joe Mauer	-9
Jeff Mathis	10	Jose Molina	-8
Jason Varitek	10	Alex Avila	-8
Humberto Quintero	7	Miguel Montero	-8
		Miguel Olivo	-8

Here is the complete Good Play/Misplay Run Impact Chart comparing Yadier and A.J.:

Good Play/Misplay Run Impact Chart
2009 - 2011

Good Play/Misplay Type	Molina Runs Saved	Pierzynski Runs Saved
Preventing WP/PB	15	-14
Catcher Blocks the Plate	1	-2
Handling Throws	0	-1
Failing to let ball roll foul	-1	0
Failing to Catch and Tag	-1	1
Total	14	-16

First Basemen

The second most impactful set of Good Plays and Misplays are primarily used to measure the ability of first basemen to handle throws. We sometimes refer to these as Scoops, but they also include high and wide throws, not just throws in the dirt. There are three Good Play/Misplay types involved:

GFP7, Handling difficult throw – Fielder (normally a first baseman) handles difficult throw from another player and records out. This applies to throws in the dirt or throws wide of the bag. First basemen scoops which are judged to be good scoops should be recorded as GFP7s.

GFP8, Catches wild throw – Fielder catches wild throw preventing the opportunity for the advancement of base runners.

DM 14, Failing to catch the throw – Fielder (most often the First Baseman, and occasionally known as Prince) fails to catch a throw from an **infielder** to complete a play, when the throw was not so bad that the play could not reasonably have been made. (This applies, for example, to a throw in the dirt or a throw wide of the bag, that is still catchable. The play may officially be scored a hit, or as an error on the throw. In either case, it may also be scored as a Defensive Misplay for the failure to catch the throw.)

Like the three categories that get combined to measure the run impact of preventing wild pitches and passed balls, these three categories are combined to measure each fielder's ability to handle throws. Here are the best and worst fielders in handling throws over the last three years:

Top Five Players 2009-2011
Handling Throws

Top Five		Bottom Five	
Player	Runs Saved	Player	Runs Saved
Albert Pujols	5	Garrett Jones	-6
Casey Kotchman	5	Adam Dunn	-5
Todd Helton	4	Billy Butler	-4
James Loney	4	Ryan Howard	-3
Daric Barton	4	Yunel Escobar	-3
Aubrey Huff	4	Lou Marson	-3
		Ryan Theriot	-3
		Geovany Soto	-3

It's interesting to see some non-first basemen on the Bottom Five list. Escobar and Theriot play shortstop while Marson and Soto are catchers. (Theriot also played second base, but we're only counting his shortstop play here.)

Let's compare Albert Pujols and Prince Fielder, the two premier offseason free-agent first basemen. Offensively you can say they are somewhat comparable, but defensively Fielder does not live up to his name. Pujols has been the best first baseman in baseball handling throws over the last three years. The Prince, not so much. He just missed being in the Bottom Five list above. He lost two runs for the Brewers trying to handle difficult throws in the last three years.

Digging a little deeper, Pujols had 121 plays where he handled a difficult throw successfully, 18 plays where he caught a wild throw and 18 plays where he failed to catch the throw. All other throws made to him are considered routine.

Prince Fielder had 78 plays where he handled a difficult throw successfully, 17 plays where he caught a wild throw and 27 plays where he failed to catch the throw. We can quickly see that Pujols had fewer failed catches in a lot more opportunities. By comparing all first basemen to each other, we can determine the run impact of these plays leading us to Pujols being better than Fielder by about seven runs over the three years.

Here is the GFP/DME run impact comparison between Pujols and the worst first baseman in terms of Good Plays and Misplays over the last three years, Garrett Jones.

Good Play/Misplay Run Impact Chart
2009 - 2011

Good Play/Misplay Type	Pujols RS	Jones RS
Handling throws	5	-6
Cutting off runner at home	3	0
Infielder Assist	2	0
Good Force Play	1	0
Losing the Double Play (Lead man)	1	0
Bobbling Ground Out Losing Lead Runner	1	0
Infielder Assist (non-relay)	1	0
Slow to Recover	0	-1
Abandoning the Base	0	-1
Hesitating before throwing	-1	0
Total	13	-8

The big advantage that Pujols has over Jones is handling throws, an 11-run difference. The next three categories on the list, all of them favoring Pujols, involve making throws: Cutting off a runner at home, Infielder Assist, Good Force Play. Pujols is the best throwing first baseman in baseball by a wide margin. He has 37 Good Fielding Plays on throws since 2004, the first year we began recording this stat. That's more than twice as many as the next best player, Todd Helton (16).

Second Basemen

The best second baseman on the planet right now relative to Good Plays and Misplays is Cincinnati's second baseman, Brandon Phillips. He has saved eight runs in the last three years on plays that are recorded as Good Fielding Plays and Defensive Misplays/Errors. That's the best figure among all second basemen in that time. As a result, he has won three National League Gold Gloves in the last four years.

"As a result." That's exactly it. Phillips looks awesome. That's what managers and coaches see on the field and that's why they vote for him for the Gold Glove. That's the kind of thing we are tracking with Good Plays and Misplays. Phillips makes the good plays happen far more often than the misplays and errors. That makes him the best second baseman—on Good Plays and Misplays. And the best second baseman—just watching him play.

But does that make him the best second baseman overall?

Nay, nay, I say. Making good plays is just part of the equation. Making all the plays is the whole equation. Our Defensive Runs Saved system tries to measure the whole equation.

For second basemen, Defensive Runs Saved has three components: runs saved based on the Plus/Minus System, runs saved based on turning Double Plays, and runs saved based on Good Plays and Misplays. Add the three components together and you get Defensive Runs Saved. Other positions have other components, but these are the three for second basemen. Who are the best second basemen in baseball over the last three years based on Defensive Runs Saved? I would normally list the top five, but I'm giving you seven because Phillips comes in seventh:

Defensive Runs Saved Leaders
Second Basemen - 2009 to 2011

Player	Plus/Minus	GDP	GFP/DME	Total
Ian Kinsler	40	5	2	47
Ben Zobrist	46	0	-1	45
Dustin Pedroia	29	2	6	37
Chase Utley	30	3	3	36
Mark Ellis	18	2	7	27
Sean Rodriguez	16	2	2	20
Brandon Phillips	12	-2	8	18

For catchers, GFP/DME Runs Saved is the most significant component of Defensive Runs Saved. That's not true for any other position, and especially not true for second basemen. Our Plus/Minus System is the key for second sackers. It measures how often a given second baseman successfully turns groundballs (and balls in the air) hit to him into outs, compared to all other second basemen in baseball. Phillips is good, having saved 12 runs over the last three years. But he doesn't compare to the top four on the list, all of whom have saved at least 29 runs snaring groundballs at the second base position.

It's not just about looking good. It's about making the plays. Analyzing defense is an ongoing process. We are continually working to improve the system, taking small steps as we go. That's what this book is about, sharing with you the progress that we are making.

There is a player who hasn't won a Gold Glove and hasn't even won a Fielding Bible Award, but he is the best second baseman in baseball, according to Defensive Runs Saved. His name is Ian Kinsler. The other Gold Glove winners besides Phillips in the last three years are Dustin Pedroia (3rd in Defensive Runs Saved), Robinson Cano (7th), Placido Polanco (12th) and Orlando Hudson (15th in Defensive Runs Saved on our list of the 35 players who played the most at second base in the last three years). Fielding Bible Award winners besides Pedroia are Chase Utley (4th) and Aaron Hill (9th).

Ian Kinsler is due.

Shortstops

Troy Tulowitzki and Alex Gonzalez each have eight Runs Saved on Misplays and Good Plays over the last three years, the best shortstop total. The worst total belongs to Starlin Castro who has cost the Cubs nine runs, despite playing only the last two years. Castro had 85 Misplays and Errors in 2011. Ian Desmond was a distant second at shortstop with 58. In 2010, Castro and Desmond tied for the most DMEs in baseball with 67.

How do all those misplays lead to runs lost? Here's a comparison of Tulowitzki and Castro:

Good Play/Misplay Run Impact Chart 2009 - 2011

Good Play/Misplay Type	Tulowitzki RS	Castro RS
Handling throws	2	-1
Losing the double play pivot man	1	-2
Losing the double play lead man	1	0
Started double play quickly	1	0
Infielder Assist	1	0
Good force play	1	0
Quick double play pivot	1	0
Hesitating before throwing	1	-1
Failing to cover the base	1	0
Failing to make the tag	1	-1
Failing to touch the bag	-1	0
Keeping the ball in the infield	-1	1
Wasted throw after hit/error	-1	-1
Juggling relay throw	0	-1
Slow to recover	0	-1
Failing to catch and tag	0	-2
Total	8	-9

Let's go through these in detail.

Castro was a little better in two categories: Keeping the ball in the infield (2 run advantage) and Failing to touch the bag (1 run).

Keeping the ball in the infield: Castro isn't all bad defensively. He makes his share of good fielding plays. He has nine plays where he prevented runner advancement by "stopping a groundball that seemed likely to be heading into the outfield." The phrase in quotes is the wording used in the definition of GFP9, Keeping the ball in the infield. Tulo had fewer (seven) of those plays in far more opportunities than Castro, leading to one run saved for Castro versus one run lost for Tulo.

Failing to touch the bag: There were three times when Tulowitzki "failed to touch the bag or pulled his foot off the bag, resulting in the loss of a force out." Castro only made this misplay once.

Tulowitzki was a better in 13 categories:

Handling throws: This favors Tulowitzki by three runs. Here are the four reasons why:

1) Tulo had seven good fielding plays where he handled a difficult throw. Castro only had one.

2) Tulo caught three wild throws, Castro two.

3) Tulo had four misplays where he failed to catch a throw. Castro had six.

4) There were 15 times where Tulowitzki was helped by his first baseman after he made a bad throw because the first baseman made a good fielding play himself (handling a difficult throw). Castro had 28 occasions where he made a difficult throw and the first baseman bailed him out. In these situations, because the Plus/Minus System gives full credit to the shortstop for the out, we make an adjustment and give some of the credit to the first baseman for making the scoop and we take that exact amount away from the infielder who made the difficult throw. Castro makes more of these difficult throws that still turn into outs than any other infielder in baseball.

Losing the double play (pivot man): Castro had six misplays where he lost a double play because he "juggled, dropped or mishandled a throw from another fielder, or made the play in an exceptionally slow manner." Tulo had one such play.

Losing the double play (lead man): Castro had four of these misplays to only one for Tulowitzki.

Started double play quickly: Troy made a good play by starting a double play quickly 17 times. Starlin, 5 times.

Infielder Assist: This is a relay throw from an outfielder for an out. Tulo 10, Castro 5.

Good force play: "Infielder on a groundball (or,

rarely, an outfielder, usually on a pop-up that falls) forces lead runner with exceptionally quick play when it appeared likely the runner would make it safely to the base." Tulo 15, Castro 7

Quick double play pivot: Troy Tulowitzki 13, Starlin Castro 6.

Hesitating before throwing: The Starman 5, TuloTime 1

Failing to cover the base: "Fielder fails to cover his base, allowing a runner to unnecessarily advance. This applies when the base is not covered due to the fielder's inattentiveness." Starlin fell asleep twice. Tulowitzki was awake 100 percent of the time.

Failing to make the tag: This is where the "fielder fails to apply the tag after a throw is made from an infielder." Castro 3, Tulo 1.

Juggling the relay throw: Castro wins another misplay category, this time with a shutout 3-0.

Slow to recover: This is another "fell asleep" category and another shutout for Castro, 4-0.

Failing to catch and tag: This is like the other missed tag category but involves a throw from an outfielder. Another dubious victory for the Starman, 6-3.

Third Basemen

Good Plays and Misplays make the least difference at third base, compared to the other defensive positions. The range between the best run values in the last three years (Evan Longoria and Scott Rolen, 6) and the worst (many players tied with -3) is only nine runs.

We'll compare Longoria with Mark Reynolds. Reynolds is one of the guys that has cost his team three runs over the last three years on Good Plays and Misplays. He is also one of the worst defenders among third basemen in the game.

Good Play/Misplay Run Impact Chart
2009 - 2011

Good Play/Misplay Type	Longoria RS	Reynolds RS
Started double play quickly	2	-1
Losing the double play lead man	1	-1
Handling throws	1	0
Cutting off a better positioned fielder	1	-1
Cutting off runner at home	1	0
Failing to catch and tag	0	-1
Reaches into stands	0	1
Total	6	-3

Longoria was better in most of these categories. The first two involve double plays. Longoria is very good starting double plays. Reynolds is not. Reynolds is better than Longoria in one area, reaching into the stands to make a catch, which he did five times compared to once for Longoria.

Left Fielders

The lovable Chicago Cubs. Their fans love them. Warts and all. Starlin Castro has a bad case of warts. Lots of misplays. But maybe he is young enough for the wart removal to work. The fans still love him. He is the cornerstone of the franchise. Not Alfonso Soriano. He's now 36 years old. The love affair is over. His 13 runs lost on Good Plays and Misplays in the last three years is the worst among all outfielders. He had 22 Good Plays, 73 Misplays and 25 Errors. That's 76 more misplays and errors than good plays. The next worst left fielder is exactly half as bad. Logan Morrison had 38 more misplays and errors than good plays.

The best left fielder in GPF/DME runs saved is Jason Bay. He had 73 good plays and only 47 misplays and errors in the three years, a net of 26. Compared to Soriano's net of -76. Here is how they compare in runs saved:

Good Play/Misplay Run Impact Chart
2009 - 2011

Good Play/Misplay Type	Bay RS	Soriano RS
Mishandling ball after safe hit	3	-4
Outfield assist after hit or error	2	-1
Holds to single	1	-2
Wasted throw after hit/error	1	0
Cutting off runner at home	0	1
Giving up on a play	0	-1
Hesitating before throwing	0	-1
Slow to recover	0	-1
Robs home run	0	-1
Missing the cutoff man	0	-1
Overrunning the play	0	-1
Slipping	0	-1
Total	7	-13

Mishandling ball after safe hit: This is the single worst problem that Soriano has. In the last three years there have been 19 times where he "misplayed a ball which landed safely for a base hit, but juggled it, dropped it or didn't field it cleanly, allowing a runner or runners to advance to a base he (or they) might otherwise not have been able to reach." This has cost the Cubs four runs. Bay only did this four times, a low total of misplays per opportunity when compared to other outfielders.

Outfield assist after hit or error: Bay had 16 of these good plays while Soriano only had 7.

Holds to single: This is a play where the "fielder holds runner to a single on a ball that seemed more likely to be an extra base hit." Bay makes this good play quite frequently. 13 times in the last three years. Twice for Soriano.

Wasted throw after hit/error: Small advantage to Bay. He made this misplay three times to Soriano's four.

Cutting off runner at home: Bay never made this good play. Soriano did it once. Saved a run.

Giving up on a play: Interesting definition. "Fielder abandons the effort to make a play in the mistaken belief that somebody else will make it." Soriano gave up on a play three times. Bay once.

Hesitating before throwing: He who hesitates is lost. Soriano hesitated three times. Bay never hesitated.

Slow to recover: This is the "fell asleep" play. Four naps on the field for Soriano. Bay dozed off once.

Robs home run: Robbing a home run is the best defensive play a player can make. Do some players have more ability to make this play than others? Probably. In any case, we give major credit when a play like this is made. We give 1.6 runs. However, prior to this year, we didn't "center" this calculation. Our purpose now is to have all of our runs saved numbers add up to zero when totaling all the players. Therefore, we came up with an opportunity element and factored that into the equation. Jason Bay has robbed one home run in the last three years. Based on his estimated opportunities, he nets out to zero runs saved. Soriano hasn't made any of these catches, which results in an estimated one run lost in the three years.

Missing the cutoff man: Soriano missed the cutoff man twice, allowing a runner to take an extra base. Bay never missed.

Overrunning the play: Soriano 2-1 over Bay.

Slipping: Alfonso 2, Jason 0.

Center Fielders

Franklin Gutierrez saved 12 runs on Good Plays and

Misplays in the last three years, the highest total for an outfielder. No other outfielder was in double figures; Jose Bautista was next with 9 GFP/DME runs saved.

The center fielder who had the most trouble with Good Plays and Misplays was B.J. Upton, losing seven runs. Here is a comparison of Gutierrez and B.J.:

Good Play/Misplay Run Impact Chart
2009 - 2011

Good Play/Misplay Type	Gutierrez RS	Upton RS
Robs home run	7	-3
Mishandling ball after safe hit	4	-2
Failing to anticipate the wall	1	0
Wasted throw after hit/error	1	-1
Outfield assist after flyball catch	1	0
Throw toward the wrong base	1	0
Outfield assist after hit or error	-1	-1
Holds to single	-1	0
Hesitating before throwing	-1	0
Total	12	-7

There's a 19 run overall difference between Franklin Gutierrez and B.J. Upton on Good Plays and Misplays. Ten of those come as a result of Gutierrez making six incredible home-run saving catches while B.J made none.

Allow me to take a tangent here. One of my all-time favorite things that Bill James wrote is this: "I will never understand baseball; I will never understand 1 percent of what I need to understand. My view of our work is that we are attacking a mountain range of ignorance with a spoon and a used toothbrush. The things that we do not know are inexhaustible." Sometimes people ask me if I think we've solved the problem with measuring defense. What Bill wrote always comes to mind. Yes, I say things such as "With our tools to measure hitting we can measure maybe 90 percent of a player's batting value, our pitching tools measure 80-90 percent of pitching, with defense we're starting to approach 60 percent." We've made good progress. But the amount we don't know is infinite. Part of my answer is also "We are not done. Not even close. We will keep working to improve, making incrementally subtle improvements in various minutia that when taken all together, will keep moving us forward. In 100 years we will still be doing that. We won't know it all, even then."

We are just beginning to scratch the surface of measuring defense with our used toothbrushes. The surface is the tip of an iceberg and it's a slippery slope. We will make mistakes and we'll have to go back and correct them. But we will inch forward.

Why do I mention this now? Because of our home-run saving catch run value estimates. We have a thousand different little techniques that we've developed over the years to measure defense. OK, maybe not a thousand, but certainly hundreds. But maybe a thousand. Each one of those techniques can be improved, I have no doubt in my mind. And we can develop another thousand to address other issues.

How do we improve our technique for estimating runs saved on home-run saving catches? There's probably another thousand different ways to do this simple thing. One thing we could do is count the exact actual number of runs saved on each catch. If two men were on base, that's three runs saved. That seems logical. But we don't do that. Intentionally. We want to say that all home-run saving catches are the same. The reason is that we don't want to imply a "clutch" nature to saving catches. Can any outfielder rise to the occasion and catch a home run when there's men on base more often than when the bases are empty? Highly unlikely. So we don't want to give more credit based on what is essentially a random number of men on base when he makes that catch.

However, we could study this further and decide there is a good reason to make use of the actual, exact, number of runs saved on each individual play. Mind you, we do this in aggregate. That's why we credit 1.6 runs for each catch. On average there are .6 runners on base. But maybe there's a better way to explicitly use the exact number on each play.

Now back to Gutierrez and Upton. Here is a better way for allocating runs saved on home run catches that we haven't yet factored in. The height of the center field fence in Seattle is 8 feet. The height of the center field fence in Tampa Bay is 9 feet 4 inches. There's no question that it is easier to make a home run saving catch in Seattle where Gutierrez plays half his games than in Tampa Bay where Upton plays half his games. Upton hasn't made this catch yet, but maybe he would have if the fence height was the same as Seattle. Something to work on. But you'll just have to wait for Volume IV for this one.

Right Fielders

What is it with the Upton brothers? Justin also has trouble. Trouble...trouble...trouble. Right here in Norfolk, Virginia. That's where B.J. and Justin were born. Is it nature or nurture? Is it in the genes? In the water in Norfolk? Or was it Cheasapeake, Virginia where they both grew up? Was it the coaching in Cheasepeake? Is it because they both started playing in the majors at an early age? B.J. starting playing at the MLB level in 2004 at the tender age of 19, and then Justin did the same thing three years later. Justin is still only 24 years old. Will he improve? Looking at their career records, there hasn't been a lot of improvement going on. That doesn't bode well for Starlin Castro.

Like his brother, Justin Upton cost his team the most runs on Good Plays and Misplays of any player at his position. He lost 11 runs for the Diamondbacks in the last three years, and he can't find them anywhere.

Well, actually that's not true. He has found them. By covering a ton of ground and making catches in right field. Justin Upton has the second highest total of runs saved (36) in the last three years based on his range in right field (Jason Heyward has 38). That's what puts this in perspective. Justin is a very good outfielder. In fact, he won The Fielding Bible Award in right field this past season. He just happens to make a lot of misplays.

What kind of misplays does he make? How does he compare with his brother? Maybe we can play scientist, detect a similarity, and decide that a player's Good Play/Misplay tendencies are genetic. I doubt it, but here you go:

Good Play/Misplay Run Impact Chart 2009 - 2011

Good Play/Misplay Type	Justin RS	B.J. RS
Robs home run	-1	-3
Mishandling ball after safe hit	-4	-2
Wasted throw after hit/error	-1	-1
Outfield assist after flyball catch	-1	0
Wasted throw after hit/error	-1	-1
Outfield assist after hit or error	-3	-1
Holds to single	-1	0
Total	-11	-7

Looks pretty similar to me. Is it nature or nurture? Both or neither? You make the call.

Pitchers

There are several pitchers who have two runs saved on Good Plays and Misplays in the last three years. And then there's CC Sabathia. He cost his team three runs on

70

these plays. Do ya think his size has anything to do with it? Let's compare him to Zack Grienke, one the best defenders of the area around the pitcher's mound in baseball.

Good Play/Misplay Run Impact Chart
2009 - 2011

Good Play/Misplay Type	Greinke RS	Sabathia RS
Cutting off runner at home	1	0
Good force play	1	0
Giving up on a play	0	-0.5
Losing the double play - bad throw	0	-0.5
Failing to cover first	0	-2
Total	2	-3

Aha! Failing to cover first. CC Sabathia has six of those misplays. Grienke has none. Maybe it is Sabathia's size and he can't get to the bag. Or maybe he just forgets. Here's the definition: "Fielder (normally the pitcher) fails to cover first or is slow to cover first, resulting in the loss of an out or an opportunity to make an out."

Hmm. Slow to cover first...

Size matters.

Matt Kemp and His Two Gold Gloves

Matt Kemp has won two Gold Gloves in the last three years. This article analyzes why Matt Kemp maybe shouldn't have won those Gold Gloves.

Now, before you go on reading, if you haven't read the "Jeter vs. Ryan" article right before this one, go back and do it. It's short, we'll wait. . .

Now, if after reading that article, you still think that Jeter should have won five Gold Gloves, we'll save you some time. Don't bother reading this article.

The Good

As we said, Matt Kemp has won two Gold Gloves in the last three years. There are certainly some good things about his game. He wasn't the National League MVP, but you can sure make a case that he should have been. I won't dwell on this, but our Total Runs system which measures all aspects of a player's game as best we can, including defense, shows Kemp with the most Total Runs in the NL with 158. Ryan Braun was second with 148, and Justin Upton third with 143. Braun won the award.

What was good about Kemp's defense in 2011? We'll compare him to other National League center fielders:

- He led all NL center fielders in games (159).
- He led all NL center fielders in innings (1,380).
- He led in assists (11).
- He started the most double plays (5), tied with the Pirates Andrew McCutchen.
- He had the most Good Fielding Plays (28), also tied with McCutchen.
- He had the most Good Fieldng Plays on throws (8), tied with the Nationals' Rick Ankiel and the Reds' Drew Stubbs.

- He was fifth in putouts (345). McCutchen led with 414.

Looking at all these things, Kemp doesn't seem like a bad choice for the National League Gold Glove in 2011.

The Bad

Here are some other things about Kemp's defense in 2011:

- Kemp was 10th in fielding percentage (.986) among the 15 NL center fielders with 600 or more innings. The Phillies' Shane Victorino was first with 1.000.
- His Revised Zone Rating was .932, 9th out of the 15. He caught 72 balls out of the zone, tied for 8th with this group. But among the nine of those players who played at least 1000 innings, he was tied for last. San Francisco's Andres Torres had the highest zone rating (.950) and Chris Young had the most catches outside the zone (114).
- His UZR was -4.6, 11th out of the 15. Chris Young was first with 14.1.
- Kemp was tied for the third highest total of Defensive Misplays and Errors among NL center fielders (29) with McCutchen and Stubbs. The Mets' Angel Pagan had the most with 36 and Colorado's Dexter Fowler was second with 30.
- According to Defensive Runs Saved, he cost his team five runs defensively overall. Out of the 15 NL center fielders only Pagan (-8 Defensive Runs Saved) and Jordan Schafer with the Braves and Astros (-7) were worse. Arizona's Chris Young saved the most runs, 20.

The Ugly

The most important aspect of center field defense is covering ground. Matt Kemp's range, as measured by Plus/Minus Runs Saved, cost his team 11 runs. That was last out of the 15 NL center fielders with 600 innings. The Marlins' Chris Coghlan lost 12 runs with his lack of range in 568 innings in center field, tied with Baltimore's Adam Jones for the worst CF runs saved total in Major League Baseball.

Is it possible that somehow the Plus/Minus System is not measuring Matt Kemp's range correctly? Let's see if we can go into further detail. Let's take three different approaches to measure Kemp's range against major league averages. The first approach will be based on the hang time of the balls hit to center field. The second approach we'll look at the location of the batted ball and how far center fielders have to range to make the catch. The third approach we'll divide plays into four categories of difficulty.

In the chapter called "Timing Batted Balls" on page 33, we showed how we measure hang time for outfield flyballs. The longer the ball stays in the air the easier it is to catch. Let's use those same six groupings, the same ones we use for the new Plus/Minus System, and compare Kemp to all other MLB center fielders. We will look at what percentage of flyballs (and line drives) that are caught (Out Ratio) by the average center fielder and see what Matt Kemp did on those same types of balls. Here's a chart that summarizes the information for hang time:

Hang Time Analysis
Center Field Out Ratios 2011

Hang Time	All CF	Kemp
Over 5.0 second	95%	92%
4.2 to 5.0 seconds	77%	80%
3.5 to 4.2 seconds	64%	64%
3.0 to 3.5 seconds	54%	45%
2.7 to 3.0 seconds	45%	44%
Under 3.0 seconds	14%	14%

There's one grouping that Matt Kemp was a bit better than the average center fielder in 2011, balls in the air between 4.2 and 5.0 seconds. He caught 80 percent of balls in the air between 4.2 and 5.0 seconds, while the average MLB center fielder caught 77 percent. If he had caught balls at the major league average, he would have had three fewer catches. But there are two groupings where Kemp is significantly worse than the average

center fielder. On balls that hang in the air more than 5.0 seconds, he was at 92 percent while the average was 95 percent. Between 3.0 and 3.5 seconds, he was nine points below the average of 54 percent. If Kemp caught balls at the MLB average, he would have caught 12 more in these two zones.

Summary #1: Based on batted ball hang time analysis, Kemp caught nine fewer balls than the average center fielder in 2011.

Let's look at range another way. Let's look at the location of the batted ball. How far does the center fielder have to range to get the ball? We don't have their starting points, but we can pick the middle point of where all balls are caught in center field and look at distances from that point. Here's a chart that summarizes the out ratios in center field in four different increments from the midpoint:

Distance from Midpoint Analysis
Center Field Out Ratios 2011

Distance from Midpoint	All CF	Kemp
0 to 50 feet	95%	95%
50 to 75 feet	78%	78%
75 to 100 feet	56%	47%
More than 100 feet	50%	38%

This is very telling. On flyballs between 0 and 50 feet from the midpoint, Kemp catches the exact same percentage as the average center fielder. On flyballs between 50 and 75 feet, same thing—Kemp is exactly average. However, as you get further away from the midpoint, Kemp has a harder time making catches. Between 75 and 100 feet, Kemp catches only 47 percent, while the average center fielder catches 56 percent. Over 100 feet it's worse: Kemp catches only 38 percent compared to the 50 percent average. If Kemp were at the major league average in each category, he would have caught 17 more balls.

Summary #2: Based on the distance a center fielder had to range to catch a ball, Kemp caught 17 fewer balls than the average center fielder.

Let's look at range one last way. It's a combination of our first two methods. We look at hang time and location together. This is our Timer Plus/Minus System. We look at the difficulty based on both hang time and location. These are grouped into what we call "buckets." For example, one bucket might be hang time between 2.7 and 3.0 seconds at a distance of 320 feet at vector 175.

Vector 175 is about 25 feet to the right field side of straight-away center field. The out ratio in this bucket might be 73 percent. What we'll do is combine buckets into four groups based on their difficulty. We'll call it a Hard catch if the out ratio is between 0 and 25 percent. For this grouping, the bucket must have an out ratio greater than zero to be included. We'll call a bucket Medium-Hard if the out ratio is between 25 and 50 percent. Medium-Easy are out ratios between 50 and 75 percent. Easy catches are out ratios between 75 and 100 percent (but must be under 100 percent). Here is the summary chart:

Difficulty of Catch Analysis
Center Field Out Ratios 2011

Difficulty of Catch	All CF	Kemp
Easy	96%	95%
Medium-Easy	61%	62%
Medium-Hard	36%	27%
Hard	13%	2%

This one is even more telling. Kemp is making the easy catches like any other center fielder. Both categories of easy: Easy and Medium-Easy. But as the balls get more difficult to catch, he has a harder time making the catch. The balls that are more difficult to catch are not hanging in the air as long and/or they are farther away from him. If Kemp performed at the average level of all other center fielders in each of these difficulty categories, he would have made 14 more catches.

Summary #3: Based on both the hang time of the batted ball and the distance a center fielder had to range to catch a ball, Kemp caught 14 fewer balls than the average center fielder.

Looking at our three summaries, Kemp caught 9, 17 or 14 fewer balls than an average center fielder, depending how you look at it. The third one is the Timer Plus/Minus System. Kemp caught 14 fewer balls than an average center fielder. Digging deeper into these missed catches, the number of bases that were lost as a result of these 14 fewer catches was 20. The extra bases result from missed catches that turn into doubles and triples. This is Kemp's Enhanced Plus/Minus number, -20. He lost 20 bases on 14 fewer plays made in center field than the average center fielder. Those 20 lost bases translate into 11 runs. Kemp's Plus/Minus Runs Saved is -11. Or put another way, based on his range Kemp lost about 11 runs for the Dodgers last year compared to the average center fielder.

To get Kemp's overall performance in center field, we add his Plus/Minus Runs Saved to his OF Arm Runs Saved to his Good Play/Misplay Runs Saved. Kemp has a good arm and saved the Dodgers four runs throwing in 2011. Those Good Fielding Plays also count. He gets another two runs based on his Good Plays and Misplays. In total, Kemp lost five runs for the Dodgers in center field in 2011.

And that, my friends, is not Gold Glove performance.

It's not even an average defensive performance. Average is zero. Kemp is -5.

It is an MVP performance when taking his defense together with his offense and baserunning, but it is not a Gold Glove performance. And it is not a Fielding Bible Award performance. Matt Kemp did not receive a single vote in the voting for The Fielding Bible Awards in 2011.

Conclusion

So why do managers and coaches vote for Kemp for the Gold Glove? Because they only see The Good. They see very little of The Bad. And they don't try to understand The Ugly. The Good showed them:

- Kemp had a tremendous season.
- He played the most games, had the most assists, had a lot of putouts.
- He makes a lot of good to great plays. They don't know about the Good Fielding Plays that we track, but they see them happen on the field. Our tracking confirms that he makes more than his fair share of good plays; he led the league.

Coaches and managers see these things and vote for Kemp in the Gold Glove voting.

Interestingly enough, coaches and managers are the last frontier. The public and the media have begun to accept our advanced defensive analytics. Major league front offices buy into them, for the most part. The coaches and managers are not yet fully on board. Some of them are, but most aren't.

Robinson Cano and Double Plays

Here is the scouting report on Robinson Cano from one of our video scouts:

"Cano's greatest defensive asset is his ability to turn the double play. Robinson has great footwork around the bag when it comes to making the pivot. Cano's quick transfer and throw to first when he receives the ball on the double play are very smooth and have made him one of the best in the game in this area. He is also one of the best at starting the double play. His quick hands and outstanding arm allow him to turn many close plays into outs."

There is no question about it. Cano is excellent on the DP. His quickness is incredible. We have it on record. In the last three years there were 28 times when we recorded Good Fielding Play type 12, "Quick double play pivot," for Cano. That's the most in baseball. Dan Uggla is second with 23, Ian Kinsler third with 20. There were 17 times when we recorded GFP11, "Started double play quickly," for Cano. That's the most in baseball for a second baseman. Ian Kinsler is second with 15. Brandon Phillips had 14.

Here's the problem.

We also keep track of Defensive Misplays. In the last three years we recorded a DM7, "Losing the Double Play (Pivot man)," nine times for Robinson Cano. That's the second-most in baseball. Aaron Hill led second basemen with 10. There were 10 times when we recorded a DM6, "Losing the Double Play (Lead man)," for Cano. That's the most in baseball.

Cano makes the most good plays on double plays and the most misplays on double plays. Maybe he is too quick for his own good. Watching a few of the misplays on video, the biggest problem I saw was Cano trying to move the ball too quickly from his glove to his throwing

hand. Usually he does it so quickly you can't see it, and the net effect is a double play when one might not have occurred. That's how he gets all the Good Plays we give him. But sometimes he is too quick for his own good and misplays the double play into a single out or, on occasion, an outright error with all runners safe.

Runs Saved on GDP Good Plays and Misplays

As shown in our chapter called "Good Plays and Misplays," we have developed a method to estimate the run value of these plays. Here's how this works out for Cano. There are six categories of good plays and misplays for double plays:

- For the 28 times he got a GFP12, Cano gets 1.78 runs.
- For the 17 times he got a GFP11, he gets 0.92 runs.
- GFP13 is "Double play despite aggressive slide." Cano only had four of these good plays in the last three years. That is a below-average performance compared to other second basemen. For example, Brandon Phillips had 21 of these. Howie Kendrick, 15. Skip Schumaker and Dan Uggla, two guys who are not known for their defense at second base, got 14 and 11 respectively. In fact, 22 second basemen have recorded more GFP13s than Cano in the last three years. Cano gets -1.25 runs.
- For the 10 times Cano got a DM6, he gets -1.74 runs.
- For the 9 times he got a DM7, he gets -1.28 runs.

- DM8 is "Losing the Double Play on a bad throw." Cano was better than average with only four of these and gets 0.87 runs.

Add up these runs and you get -0.70 runs, a below-average performance on double plays. Here are the best and worst second basemen in baseball over the last three years on these GDP Good Plays and Misplays:

Double Play Good Plays and Misplays
Best Second Basemen, 2009-11

Player	Runs Saved
Dustin Pedroia	3.90
Chase Utley	3.45
Brandon Phillips	3.26
Ian Kinsler	3.11
Macier Izturis	2.27

Double Play Good Plays and Misplays
Worst Second Basemen, 2009-11

Player	Runs Saved
Aaron Hill	-3.88
Mike Aviles	-3.58
Adam Kennedy	-3.20
Freddy Sanchez	-2.61
Will Rhymes	-2.41

Robinson Cano is not on the leaders list, and he is not on the trailers list. At -0.70 runs, he's a little below the zero mid-point. Cano makes a ton of good plays, but it looks like he loses all the benefit he gains by making the misplays. What we have here, as we watch Cano play and think of him as extraordinarily good on double plays, could be a classic case of perception over reality. The perception, from seeing all those wonderful plays, is that Cano is great on the double play. The reality may be that despite all those plays, the misplays are more detrimental to the team and overshadow the good plays.

Runs Saved on GDPs and Pivots

We have another way that we measure runs saved on double plays. We've been using this technique for a few years and we updated our technique for this book (see page 448). We look at where grounders are hit and how hard they are hit in double play situations to determine the difficulty of the double play attempt. The proper credit or debit is given based on the difficulty of the play. If you look at the three-year chart on page 294 you'll see that Robinson Cano saved one run on GDPs and Pivots in the last three years. That one run is pretty much average. The best were Ian Kinsler with five runs, Kelly Johnson with three and Chase Utley with three as well.

These runs are separate and additional to the runs on GDP Misplays and Good Plays. It doesn't make a strong case for Cano once again. On top of it, if you look at the same chart you'll see that Cano ranked 23rd in the percentage of double plays turned based on GDP opportunites and 30th in Pivot percentage. Those ranks do not suggest an elite double play man.

Adding the one run saved here to the -0.70 for Good Plays/Misplays, you get a net effect of zero runs over the last three years.

What's the Answer?

Observation or Sabermetrics? Is Cano good on the double play or not? Here's how I'll say it. Cano is fantastic on the double play, making play after play, but he may not be helping his team because he makes more than his share of misplays as well. It appears that the net run impact is negligible.

Team Defense

The 2005 Phillies were sort of a transitional team. They spent the entire season between 0 and 10 games out of first, finishing just two back of the Braves. Jon Lieber was the Opening Day starter. Jim Thome was hurt and traded shortly thereafter, and Bobby Abreu was in his last full season in Philadelphia. Placido Polanco was traded to Detroit in June. And Jimmy Rollins and David Bell, already elite defenders on the left side of the infield, were joined by Chase Utley and Ryan Howard to form easily the best defensive infield (85 Runs Saved) over the nine years for which we've calculated Defensive Runs Saved. Carried by their infield defense, this '05 Phillies team saved 95 runs compared to an average defense, the top total of the past nine seasons.

Team Runs Saved: Highest Single Season Totals

Season	Team	Runs Saved
2005	Phillies	95
2011	Rays	85
2009	Mariners	85
2007	Blue Jays	83
2010	Padres	81
2008	Phillies	77
2005	Cardinals	76
2010	Athletics	76
2004	Dodgers	74
2003	Astros	71

Though only one Cardinals team made the top 10 list, they've been the most consistently good defense in the league. With 350 Runs Saved since 2003, they've averaged almost 40 runs better than an average defense per season. Using the common shortcut that 10 runs translates to one win in the standings, that's a four-win advantage per season. Led by Albert Pujols, Scott Rolen, Yadier Molina and Brendan Ryan, they've had only two seasons below zero (2003 and 2011).

Team Runs Saved Leaders Since 2003

Team	Runs Saved
Cardinals	350
Blue Jays	308
Braves	229
Mariners	191
Phillies	178

For whatever reason, that 2005 season featured several of the most extreme defensive teams. The 2005 Royals featured the worst defensive infield (Matt Stairs, Ruben Gotay, Angel Berroa and Mark Teahen), but they weren't the worst defensive team overall. That (dis)honor belongs to the 2005 Yankees, who had three fielders at -20 Runs Saved or worse (Derek Jeter, Robinson Cano and Bernie Williams).

Team Runs Saved: Lowest Single Season Totals

Season	Team	Runs Saved
2005	Yankees	-115
2005	Royals	-112
2009	Royals	-100
2010	Royals	-95
2003	Brewers	-82
2007	Devil Rays	-81
2004	Yankees	-80
2010	Pirates	-77
2011	Marlins	-75
2005	Marlins	-74

The Royals had three of the four worst defensive

teams of the past nine seasons. Oddly, they've also made two of the biggest offseason turnarounds. In 2006, they plugged in free agent signees Mark Grudzielanek and Doug Mientkiewicz and made a number of smaller changes to go from the worst defensive team to an above-average one in just one season. The 2011 team made a similar improvement, with the biggest upgrades coming at shortstop (Alcides Escobar over Yuniesky Betancourt) and left field (Gold Glover Alex Gordon over Scott Podsednik).

The mid-2000's Braves outfields were the best defensive outfields of this time frame. With Andruw Jones in center and Jeff Francoeur in right, the Atlanta outfield saved between 35 and 64 runs per season from 2004 to 2007. The 2011 Diamondbacks outfield ranks right up there with them, at 52 Runs Saved.

The worst defensive outfields in recent history were the 2010 Dodgers and the 2005 Yankees. As illustrated on page 73, Matt Kemp has been at times a terrible defensive center fielder, and the support he got from Andre Ethier and Manny Ramirez in 2010 was abysmal. The 2005 Yankees had a lineup of sluggers, but it cost them in the field. Bernie Williams (-26 Runs Saved) and Gary Sheffield (-14 Runs Saved) were both among the worst at their respective positions.

Description of the Team Defensive Charts

On the following pages, we break down each team's defense by Runs Saved at each position to isolate their strengths and weaknesses for the last three years. For example, in 2011 the best outfield in baseball was the Arizona Diamondbacks. Between the three outfield positions, the team saved 52 runs compared to an average defensive outfield. Fielding Bible Award winner Justin Upton, Gold Glove winner Gerardo Parra and center fielder Chris Young (who might be the best of the three) made sure that nothing fell between them in 2011. Minnesota shortstops, primarily Tsuyoshi Nishioka and Trevor Plouffe, compiled the worst defensive performance of 2011, costing the disappointing Twins 30 runs compared to an average shortstop.

Comparing 2010 to 2011 we find that, out of the 30 teams in baseball, 17 teams improved their defense in 2011 and 13 teams got worse. The 17 teams that improved had an average of 33 more runs saved over the previous year. Those teams increased their win total by an average of 4.2 wins per team. The 13 teams with a fall-off in defense in 2011 fell off by an average of 42 runs, and fell off by 5.5 wins per team. Defense matters.

Team Defensive Runs by Position - 2011

Team	Pitcher	Catcher	First Base	Second Base	Third Base	Shortstop	Left Field	Center Field	Right Field	Total
Tampa Bay Rays	3	2	3	26	25	15	13	-7	5	85
Arizona Diamondbacks	3	5	-7	3	-11	9	18	22	12	54
San Diego Padres	13	6	3	-5	11	-10	5	13	10	46
Cincinnati Reds	13	-6	3	9	13	12	3	-4	1	44
Colorado Rockies	14	9	1	4	2	17	-6	-6	-1	34
Los Angeles Angels	-5	10	11	6	6	-3	-13	12	5	29
Kansas City Royals	6	2	-15	-6	2	10	21	0	5	25
Boston Red Sox	-16	-3	12	17	0	-3	0	7	3	17
Milwaukee Brewers	4	-5	-8	5	4	-8	4	18	2	16
Detroit Tigers	-2	-4	-2	-7	-6	5	17	23	-10	14
Los Angeles Dodgers	9	2	8	-13	4	-5	7	-2	3	13
Houston Astros	-6	9	13	-8	-17	7	9	-13	17	11
Atlanta Braves	-2	-1	-2	-14	6	8	9	-7	13	10
Toronto Blue Jays	6	-7	-7	2	26	16	-9	-12	-9	6
Washington Nationals	1	-3	-5	4	-5	-2	10	6	-2	4
San Francisco Giants	0	12	8	-17	20	1	0	1	-22	3
Texas Rangers	-15	-9	-8	16	8	7	5	2	-4	2
Seattle Mariners	-9	-8	0	13	0	15	-7	-1	-2	1
Cleveland Indians	11	-2	-11	-13	8	4	1	-7	3	-6
New York Yankees	-13	7	1	0	11	-26	21	-7	-3	-9
Chicago White Sox	-3	-6	-8	-1	5	6	-11	-6	8	-16
Baltimore Orioles	-1	19	-5	4	-28	13	-12	-12	1	-21
St Louis Cardinals	10	-8	9	-2	-10	-14	-2	1	-6	-22
Oakland Athletics	-12	2	-1	3	-14	-9	5	-8	7	-27
Pittsburgh Pirates	2	-6	-7	-3	-6	-2	4	3	-14	-29
Chicago Cubs	-7	-1	0	0	-24	-9	-10	0	8	-43
New York Mets	4	-9	18	-20	-9	-15	-8	-6	-13	-58
Philadelphia Phillies	-2	-4	-15	5	3	-5	-26	-2	-13	-59
Minnesota Twins	6	1	1	-10	-13	-30	-10	4	-10	-61
Florida Marlins	-4	-6	4	3	-16	-19	-28	-16	7	-75

Team Defensive Runs by Position - 2010

Team	Pitcher	Catcher	First Base	Second Base	Third Base	Shortstop	Left Field	Center Field	Right Field	Total
San Diego Padres	17	0	-2	8	14	1	11	23	9	81
Oakland Athletics	19	6	18	12	9	9	-10	-2	15	76
St Louis Cardinals	16	19	7	-16	-5	17	8	-8	10	48
Colorado Rockies	12	7	4	5	0	30	0	2	-18	42
Tampa Bay Rays	-12	-5	-2	30	18	5	8	-16	15	41
New York Mets	14	-4	16	3	-13	-7	5	4	22	40
Cincinnati Reds	8	-3	4	10	8	3	-14	1	23	40
New York Yankees	-9	-18	4	16	9	-8	23	21	-3	35
San Francisco Giants	-4	9	3	1	2	-9	10	6	8	26
Atlanta Braves	7	0	-7	5	3	23	-12	-17	16	18
Seattle Mariners	0	-9	-1	-11	8	15	7	3	-1	11
Boston Red Sox	-17	-9	13	8	21	-7	5	-8	4	10
Toronto Blue Jays	10	-7	7	3	-1	16	-5	-7	-7	9
Arizona Diamondbacks	-16	-8	6	-1	-6	-1	12	20	3	9
Milwaukee Brewers	-7	6	-16	-14	-13	10	6	18	11	1
Philadelphia Phillies	6	6	-16	18	2	2	-10	-2	-6	0
Detroit Tigers	-23	-10	0	-2	12	4	20	19	-21	-1
Cleveland Indians	10	-5	-3	10	5	-15	10	-21	1	-8
Washington Nationals	-7	4	-10	-5	20	-7	6	-9	-2	-10
Minnesota Twins	1	7	1	1	11	-5	-14	-4	-13	-15
Los Angeles Angels	-1	-4	6	-6	15	-3	-15	4	-13	-17
Texas Rangers	-11	-11	0	3	-14	-6	10	12	-2	-19
Baltimore Orioles	0	6	-5	-12	-9	5	4	-7	-9	-27
Houston Astros	-1	5	6	-11	-21	-24	-15	30	2	-29
Florida Marlins	-16	6	-12	-10	-17	-20	-2	9	24	-38
Chicago Cubs	-5	-3	4	-3	-15	-6	-17	1	-2	-46
Chicago White Sox	-1	-3	-17	-8	-25	21	-9	-2	-19	-63
Los Angeles Dodgers	-6	1	4	-3	9	4	-15	-43	-18	-67
Pittsburgh Pirates	3	-1	-12	-20	-18	-21	12	-19	-1	-77
Kansas City Royals	7	1	-6	-12	-21	-26	-11	-9	-18	-95

81

Team Defensive Runs by Position - 2009

Team	Pitcher	Catcher	First Base	Second Base	Third Base	Shortstop	Left Field	Center Field	Right Field	Total
Seattle Mariners	9	6	0	-1	27	-7	10	35	6	85
Los Angeles Angels	-1	5	12	13	26	-2	14	4	-1	70
Toronto Blue Jays	3	15	4	15	13	14	4	-7	1	62
St Louis Cardinals	12	10	17	-13	-6	19	-7	5	-2	35
Cincinnati Reds	12	-1	-7	-2	-3	11	9	14	-1	32
Detroit Tigers	-3	2	-2	3	12	6	13	13	-14	30
Tampa Bay Rays	-14	-4	-10	7	16	8	13	-6	20	30
Pittsburgh Pirates	3	4	0	-8	0	19	9	-6	8	29
San Francisco Giants	5	-9	7	2	-9	-8	11	2	13	14
Los Angeles Dodgers	-1	7	4	9	14	5	-11	-9	-5	13
New York Mets	15	-5	13	-12	-12	-2	-1	9	8	13
Colorado Rockies	5	0	-1	9	-1	17	8	-9	-16	12
Philadelphia Phillies	-8	8	-4	13	11	-5	-6	-3	3	9
Texas Rangers	3	0	-4	20	-14	17	-5	-9	0	8
Houston Astros	3	7	0	1	-10	-14	-8	8	15	2
Arizona Diamondbacks	-6	-3	-16	9	-5	11	9	-4	3	-2
Atlanta Braves	5	2	6	-13	2	10	-14	-8	4	-6
Milwaukee Brewers	-10	-5	0	18	-14	-1	-2	5	1	-8
Baltimore Orioles	9	0	-12	-9	-6	17	5	-13	-2	-11
San Diego Padres	2	1	15	-17	-1	-12	-8	17	-9	-12
Chicago White Sox	13	-8	-1	-3	-11	2	-7	7	-4	-12
Cleveland Indians	-2	-14	4	0	-6	1	2	-14	5	-24
New York Yankees	-1	-10	4	-1	-10	3	-3	-1	-6	-25
Chicago Cubs	-3	6	3	3	-9	-3	-16	-6	-1	-26
Oakland Athletics	-2	8	-8	-14	-8	-27	13	1	5	-32
Boston Red Sox	-24	-1	10	12	-15	-23	3	-7	3	-42
Minnesota Twins	-3	-7	2	-19	10	-24	0	1	-8	-48
Washington Nationals	3	-8	-27	1	21	-5	-15	-13	-6	-49
Florida Marlins	-17	-10	-14	-11	-6	1	-22	-2	11	-70
Kansas City Royals	5	-13	-5	-17	-13	-22	6	-6	-35	-100

Defensive Projections

Before the 2011 season, we provided our team clients with projected Defensive Runs Saved. The calculation was relatively simple: prorate each player's three-year Defensive Runs Saved over the number of innings we forecasted them to play at each position. Not to pat ourselves on the back, but we are happy with our first attempt.

For example, at first base, we projected Albert Pujols to lead the league with 10 Runs Saved. As you can see on page 21, he finished with...10 Runs Saved. Not bad. Pujols actually finished third, behind Adrian Gonzalez and James Loney, who we projected for three runs and one run, respectively. We projected Prince Fielder and Ryan Howard to tie as the worst defensive first basemen at -9 Runs Saved; Howard captured the title by costing the Phillies 13 runs and Fielder matched his projection exactly.

At second base, we projected Chase Utley to lead the league with 14 Runs Saved. He actually saved 7 runs, thanks to an injury. Dustin Pedroia and Mark Ellis also finished high in the Runs Saved standings after being among the leaders in our projected Runs Saved. Orlando Hudson was the biggest disappointment, missing his projected total by 18 runs. Overall, seven of our ten projected second base leaders finished in the top ten at the end of the year.

We projected Adrian Beltre, Evan Longoria and Ryan Zimmerman to lead the league in third baseman Runs Saved; Longoria finished first, Pablo Sandoval second and Beltre and Alex Rodriguez tied for third. We projected a bottom five of Chris Johnson, Pedro Alvarez, Aramis Ramirez, Mark Reynolds and Casey McGehee. The actual bottom five was Reynolds, Ramirez, Danny Valencia, Chris Johnson and a fifth-place tie between Pedro Alvarez and Scott Sizemore.

At shortstop, we projected Brendan Ryan to lead the league with 15 Runs Saved; he wound up leading the league with 18. We projected Clint Barmes to tie for third with 9, he finished second with 14. We projected Troy Tulowitzki second with 12, he finished third with 11. We projected Alexei Ramirez to save 9 runs; he actually saved 7.

In the outfield, we projected Brett Gardner, Michael Bourn and Jason Heyward to lead their respective positions in Runs Saved. The actual leaders were Brett Gardner, Austin Jackson and Jason Heyward. Bourn, who we projected for 14 Runs Saved, actually cost the Astros and Braves a combined 3 runs. We projected Gardner for 18; he finished with 23. We projected Heyward for 13; he finished with 15.

Coming off a strong defensive 2010, we projected Jackson for a conservative 9 Runs Saved; he blew right by that with 29 Runs Saved in an excellent sophomore campaign. Speaking of sophomores, we projected Peter Bourjos for 12 Runs Saved and he finished with exactly that.

We didn't know where Lance Berkman was going to play for St. Louis, so we projected him for -5 Runs Saved in left field and an additional -5 in right field. He wound up playing a lot of right field, though not well (-18 Runs Saved).

We projected Matt Wieters, Jeff Mathis and Humberto Quintero among the league leaders at catcher and that's where they finished. We did not do as well with Yadier Molina, Kurt Suzuki and Carlos Ruiz.

We projected Mark Buehrle and Jake Westbrook first and tied for second, respectively, in pitcher Runs Saved. Westbrook finished second and Buehrle tied for third. We projected John Lackey and Ervin Santana among the bottom five pitchers and that's where they finished.

We had three players on whom we missed big. We missed on Orlando Hudson (projected 10 Runs Saved, finished at -8) and Carl Crawford (projected 11 Runs Saved, finished at -2). We didn't see Pablo Sandoval having a good season at third either (projected for -3 Runs Saved, finished with 15).

On the team level, we pegged the Seattle Mariners as the best defensive team heading into the season (69 Runs Saved), but a Franklin Gutierrez lingering intestinal issue and weak offensive production kept other defensive assets off the field. We projected the Rays third with 38 Runs Saved, and they blew away the field with 85.

We projected the Marlins, Brewers and Pirates to tie as the league's worst defensive teams. The Marlins took the crown at -75 Runs Saved thanks to poor play at third base, shortstop, left field and center field. The Jose Reyes signing allows Hanley Ramirez to move from short to third and should improve production on both sides of the ball for 2012. The Brewers actually finished as an above-average defensive team thanks to manager Ron Roenicke's aggressive shifting tactics, which we did not account for.

Listing examples like this is hardly a scientific test, but it suggests we did pretty well for our first try. If we compare each team's projected 2011 Runs Saved to their actual Runs Saved, we get a correlation value of 0.32. Not bad, but we're confident we can do better.

With that in mind, we're trying it again this year. We looked at each player's three-year Defensive Runs Saved, regressed slightly towards the average of zero and penciled in a number of innings played for each player in 2012. We haven't done anything fancy with defensive aging curves. We only have nine years of Runs Saved data, which is not enough to detect smooth aging patterns (trust us, we tried). Additionally, while most defensive skills certainly deteriorate with age, different abilities and skill sets age at different rates.

Your projected 2012 Runs Saved leaders:

Pos	Player
P	Mark Buehrle
C	Matt Wieters
1B	Albert Pujols
2B	Ben Zobrist
3B	Evan Longoria
SS	Brendan Ryan
LF	Brett Gardner
CF	Austin Jackson
RF	Jason Heyward

The projected leaders and trailers are on page 92. You'll notice that the projected Runs Saved leaders are almost always the three-year leaders. Ben Zobrist edges out the three-year leader Ian Kinsler at second base and Franklin Gutierrez tied Austin Jackson as the top center fielder over three seasons.

You might also notice that we project a couple of youngsters to make the top ten at their positions. Both Dustin Ackley (second base) and Brett Lawrie (third) came with questions about their defensive abilities, but we gave them both good projections based on strong showings in the field after their major league call-ups. Last spring, we were similarly aggressive projecting Mike Stanton and Jason Heyward based on their rookie showings and they turned in good and excellent sophomore seasons (respectively). Our projections are not so kind to another youngster, Logan Morrison, forecasting him as the worst defensive outfielder next season.

Listed below are all 30 teams from highest to lowest projected Defensive Runs Saved for 2012. After that, you'll find a position-by-position breakdown of our projections for each team, as well as the individual leaderboards and trailerboards for each position.

Tampa Bay Rays

2012 Projected Runs Saved: 42   Rank: 1
2011 Actual Runs Saved: 85   Rank: 1

The Tampa Bay Rays were the best defensive team in baseball in 2011, and we project them to be the same again in 2012. The strength of their defense is second and third base. Ben Zobrist saved 23 runs in 2011 at second base, and we project him for another 16 runs in 2012. Evan Longoria projects to 15 runs in 2012 after saving 22 in 2011. But it's not just those two positions. We project seven of the nine positions with positive runs saved values. The only two positions below zero are pitchers, where we have them basically average at -1 runs saved and center field, where B.J. Upton has yet to prove himself defensively. In his last two years, Upton has cost the team 26 runs, 19 in 2010 and 7 in 2011.

Seattle Mariners

2012 Projected Runs Saved:	32	Rank:	2
2011 Actual Runs Saved:	1	Rank:	18

The Mariners were baseball's best defensive team in 2009, but their defense has dropped off the last couple of years. We see 2012 as a comeback year for them. A full season of a healthy Franklin Gutierrez, one of the best defensive center fielders in the game, is the key. He saved 10 runs last year playing about half the time due to an injury, but the other Seattle center fielders lost 11 runs playing the rest of the time. We project him for 13 runs saved in 2012 for an improvement of 14 runs in center field, almost half of our projected overall team improvement of 31 runs. Another significant change for Seattle is the addition by subtraction of Milton Bradley, who lost six runs playing in less than 30 games in left field for the 2011 Mariners.

Cincinnati Reds

2012 Projected Runs Saved:	29	Rank:	3
2011 Actual Runs Saved:	44	Rank:	4

Like the Rays, the Reds also have two very strong positions, the two on the left side of the infield. Scott Rolen has turned in double-digit runs saved totals in seven of the last eight years at third base. We project him for nine runs saved in 2012, as his age cuts into his playing time. At shortstop, defensive wizard Paul Janish provides excellent backup for rookie Zack Cozart, who is no defensive slouch himself. Between them we project another nine runs saved. Jay Bruce (five runs projected) is also strong defensively for Cincinnati.

Texas Rangers

2012 Projected Runs Saved:	26	Rank:	4
2011 Actual Runs Saved:	2	Rank:	17

Another team we expect to improve dramatically in the defensive rankings is the Texas Rangers. What a defensive infield they have with Ian Kinsler at second, Elvis Andrus at short and Adrian Beltre at third. They were excellent with 38 runs saved between them in 2011, and we project another 31 from them in 2012. Where is the improvement coming from? Of all places, one area is pitcher defense. In 2011 the Rangers' young pitching staff cost them 15 runs with their lack of defense and lack of holding runners from the pitcher's mound. We see that total dropping 13 runs to a team cost of only two runs.

Los Angeles Angels

2012 Projected Runs Saved:	22	Rank:	5
2011 Actual Runs Saved:	29	Rank:	6

The Angels more than held their own defensively in 2011 and will do so again in 2012. In 2011, they were anchored by strong performances from catcher Jeff Mathis, first baseman Mark Trumbo and center fielder Peter Bourjos. The trio combined for 29 runs saved, but only Bourjos returns in 2012. Trumbo has been replaced defensively by the great Albert Pujols. That's the great defender Albert Pujols, the best defensive first baseman in the game, so the net effect we project between Trumbo's 9 runs saved last season and Pujols' projected 10 runs in 2012 is only one run. While we see the 2012 catching situation headed by Chris Iannetta losing the Angels eight runs compared to 2011, look for improvement from left field. Keeping Howie Kendrick (five runs lost in left in 2011) at his more natural second base position will benefit Los Angeles defensively.

Arizona Diamondbacks

2012 Projected Runs Saved:	21	Rank:	6
2011 Actual Runs Saved:	54	Rank:	2

The Diamondbacks were one of baseball's great surprise stories in 2011, due in large part to their strong defense. Gerardo Parra, Chris Young and Justin Upton formed the best defensive outfield in the game. They combined for 39 runs saved, nearly three quarters of all of Arizona's defensive prowess. We project Young and Upton to take steps back in 2012 and for newcomer Jason Kubel to cut into Parra's playing time. This leaves the outfield still solidly above-average, but no longer other-worldly.

New York Yankees

| 2012 Projected Runs Saved: | 20 | Rank: | 7 |
| 2011 Actual Runs Saved: | -9 | Rank: | 20 |

2011 was a down year defensively in the Bronx, but we expect 2012 will see a comeback for the Yankees. Center fielder Curtis Granderson didn't cover ground in center field as well as he has in the past, costing the team six runs, but we project him to bounce back to the point where he saves four runs, a ten-run improvement. Similarly, we see rebound years coming at shortstop from starter Derek Jeter and backup Eduardo Nunez. Shortstop cost the Yankees 26 runs in 2011, but in 2012 we project just 10 runs being lost for a 16-run improvement. Elsewhere, two-time Fielding Bible Award winner Brett Gardner will continue to wow in left field.

Kansas City Royals

| 2012 Projected Runs Saved: | 18 | Rank: | 8 |
| 2011 Actual Runs Saved: | 25 | Rank: | 7 |

Kansas City has a cornucopia of young talent coming together at the major league level right now, making them the defensive envy of the AL Central. Alex Gordon and his strong right arm burst onto the scene in 2011 with 20 runs saved, but we see him regressing down to "only" 11 runs saved. However, we do expect big things from youngster Lorenzo Cain in center field (projected for six runs saved) and improvement from handing the first base job full-time to Eric Hosmer. First base cost the Royals 15 runs in 2011, but we project Hosmer be only 6 runs below-average in 2012.

Atlanta Braves

| 2012 Projected Runs Saved: | 15 | Rank: | 9 |
| 2011 Actual Runs Saved: | 10 | Rank: | 13 |

The trade deadline deal that brought Michael Bourn to Atlanta looks to be a great boon for the Braves' defense in 2012. Splitting playing time in center field between Nate McLouth, Jordan Schafer and Bourn resulted in a total of seven runs lost. With Bourn there full-time in 2012 we project 0 runs saved, a net improvement of 17 runs. Utility infielder Martin Prado made a strong transition to the starting left field job in 2011 (seven runs saved, with another six as the backup third baseman), but we project some regression in 2012, with only six total runs saved.

Boston Red Sox

| 2012 Projected Runs Saved: | 12 | Rank: | 10 |
| 2011 Actual Runs Saved: | 17 | Rank: | 8 |

Overall, the Red Sox will continue to be a good defensive team, though we project a lot of changes at individual positions. Boston pitchers were the worst fielders in baseball in 2011, costing the Red Sox a total of 16 runs. We expect a lot of improvement coming in 2012, to the point where they will cost the team only one run. Fewer innings to Daisuke Matsuzaka and John Lackey (costing a combined eight runs) is key here. On the negative side, we see regression coming after strong seasons from first baseman Adrian Gonzalez, second baseman Dustin Pedroia and center fielder Jacoby Ellsbury. Those three superstars totalled 37 runs saved in 2011, but we project a total of 18 in 2012.

San Francisco Giants

| 2012 Projected Runs Saved: | 11 | Rank: | 11 |
| 2011 Actual Runs Saved: | 3 | Rank: | 16 |

Like the Red Sox, we project relative consistency for the Giants as a team when comparing 2011 and 2012, but we expect large differences in how they get there. 2011 was a breakout year defensively for third baseman Pablo Sandoval with 15 runs saved, but in 2012, using his three-years numbers for his projections, he becomes an average third baseman. In the outfield we see Nate Schierholtz and Aubrey Huff balancing out Sandoval's drop-off, improving from a combined cost of 14 runs in 2011 to costing the Giants just 1 run in 2012. Second base is another area of improvement for San Francisco, with the free agent departure of Jeff Keppinger, who cost the team 11 runs in 2011.

Philadelphia Phillies

2012 Projected Runs Saved:	6	Rank:	12
2011 Actual Runs Saved:	-59	Rank:	28

We expect the Phillies to easily be the most improved defensive team in the big leagues in 2012. That is as much about the players who won't be playing as it is about any new players. In 2011, Ryan Howard was one of the worst defenders at first base in baseball (-13 runs saved), and Raul Ibanez was one of the worst in left (-23 runs saved). Howard will miss a significant amount of time with an Achilles injury and Ibanez is no longer a Phillie. This leads us to project an improvement of 35 runs saved between first and left alone in 2012. A full season of Hunter Pence in right field will also be beneficial.

Toronto Blue Jays

2012 Projected Runs Saved:	3	Rank:	13
2011 Actual Runs Saved:	6	Rank:	14

Toronto had the best left side of the infield in baseball in 2011, a fact masked by poor defense at nearly every other position. Wunderkind Brett Lawrie burst onto the scene with a whopping 14 runs saved at third base in only a quarter of a season. We can't possibly fathom that pace continuing, but do project Lawrie to save 12 runs over a full season in 2012. At short, Yunel Escobar has been one of the most consistently strong defenders over the past several years, but the trade of backup John McDonald (10 runs saved in 2011) to Arizona hurts the defense overall.

Colorado Rockies

2012 Projected Runs Saved:	2	Rank:	14
2011 Actual Runs Saved:	34	Rank:	5

Four roster moves combine to really hurt our projection of the Rockies' defense in 2012. Longtime Rockie Aaron Cook (six runs saved) led the pitching staff to being the best defensive unit in baseball in 2011, but he is now in Boston. Mark Ellis (17 runs saved) brought his outstanding glove to Colorado in a mid-season trade, but he too has left for free agency. We see the addition of right fielder Michael Cuddyer as a downgrade defensively from Seth Smith. Finally, catcher Chris Iannetta had a tremendous 2011 with eight runs saved, but he has been replaced with Ramon Hernandez, who we project to cost the Rockies four runs in 2012.

San Diego Padres

2012 Projected Runs Saved:	-1	Rank:	15
2011 Actual Runs Saved:	46	Rank:	3

The Padres have a case for being the gold standard for team defense over the past few years, but we don't see that reputation holding up in 2012. New left fielder Carlos Quentin is projected to cost eight runs on defense. More than that, we see a lot of players who had breakout defensive seasons in 2011 regressing in 2012. Cameron Maybin was among the best center fielders in the game with 15 runs saved, but for 2012 we only see him saving 5 runs. Catcher Nick Hundley jumped to the upper tier of the leaderboards in 2011 with a surprising five runs saved, but we expect him to cost one run in 2012. Other players with strong 2011 campaigns that we see regressing in 2012 include outfielders Will Venable and Chris Denorfia, backup infielders Jorge Cantu and Logan Forsythe and pitchers Tim Stauffer and Cory Luebke. In 2011 these players saved 26 runs, but we project them to save just 5 in 2012.

Oakland Athletics

2012 Projected Runs Saved:	-2	Rank:	16
2011 Actual Runs Saved:	-27	Rank:	24

The Athletics are in another rebuilding cycle, having

traded away several key members of their starting rotation before the 2012 season. A's fans can find a silver lining by looking at the defensive projections, which have a strong "addition by subtraction" vibe to them. Oakland pitchers were among the worst defenders in the American League in 2011, costing the team 12 runs. Without Trevor Cahill, Guillermo Moscoso and Gio Gonzalez (costing a total of seven runs between them) we project the Oakland pitchers back to exactly league average defense for 2012. The subtraction of backup corner infielders Kevin Kouzmanoff (-7 runs saved) and Conor Jackson (-5 runs) helps a good amount as well.

Washington Nationals

2012 Projected Runs Saved:	-2	Rank:	16
2011 Actual Runs Saved:	4	Rank:	15

Despite becoming one of the stingier teams in terms of allowing runs, the 2011 Nationals were merely average defensively. We see them continuing to be average in 2012. The return of a healthy Ryan Zimmerman and Adam LaRoche at the infield corners gives the Nats a combined projection of six runs saved, compared to 2011's ten runs lost. However, that boost is counteracted by the departure of the strong defenses of Laynce Nix and Rick Ankiel and their 14 runs saved. New outfield regulars Roger Bernadina and Mike Morse project to lose three runs.

Milwaukee Brewers

2012 Projected Runs Saved:	-3	Rank:	18
2011 Actual Runs Saved:	16	Rank:	9

The Brewers will feature a new-look infield in 2012, but surprisingly we see center field as the reason for a defensive step backward. Holdovers Nyjer Morgan and Carlos Gomez saved an impressive 18 runs in 2011, with Gomez accounting for 15 of the runs. Morgan is projected to continue to be the starter, however, so we only project the duo to save four runs total. We expect to see stark improvement in the infield with the departure of first baseman Prince Fielder (nine runs lost in 2011) and shortstop Yuniesky Betancourt (seven runs lost). The addition of Aramis Ramirez at third looks to hurt, as we project Ramirez to cost the Brewers 14 runs.

Chicago White Sox

2012 Projected Runs Saved:	-9	Rank:	19
2011 Actual Runs Saved:	-16	Rank:	21

The White Sox haven't been known as a strong defensive team recently, but in a defensively weak AL Central they project to be pretty well-off. Shortstop Alexei Ramirez is the stand-out defender in Chicago. Over the past two seasons, Ramirez has been amongst the game's best at short and we project him saving six runs in 2012. More negatively, long-time White Sox first baseman Paul Konerko returns for his 16th season, and we don't see him finding the defensive fountain of youth. He is projected to cost Chicago five runs. The other projected liabilities in the field are catcher A.J. Pierzynski and center fielder Alex Rios at a cost of four runs each.

Cleveland Indians

2012 Projected Runs Saved:	-9	Rank:	19
2011 Actual Runs Saved:	-6	Rank:	19

Cleveland's Jack Hannahan is one of the better defensive third basemen in baseball. He has accumulated 18 runs saved since 2009, eighth most among third basemen, despite spending 2010 in the minor leagues. We see his fancy glovework continuing and his projected six runs saved leads the Indians for 2012. Corner outfielders Shin-Soo Choo and Michael Brantley project well, too, with a combined nine runs saved. We see the Indians' issues to be at first base, where Matt LaPorta has struggled and projects to cost four runs and in center field, where Grady Sizemore's health could press lesser players into service. We project Cleveland center fielders to lose nine runs total.

St. Louis Cardinals

2012 Projected Runs Saved:	-10	Rank:	21
2011 Actual Runs Saved:	-22	Rank:	23

The 2011 Champions didn't win it all based on a strong defense, which perhaps bodes well for them in

2012. We don't foresee much improvement coming in St. Louis, though the Cardinals only have two projected weaknesses in the field. The infield will look odd without the 2011 club's best defender in Albert Pujols, but new first baseman Lance Berkman projects to be average, as does new full-time shortstop Rafael Furcal. Instead it will actually be second baseman Skip Schmaker (projected -7 runs saved) and third baseman David Freese (projected -5 runs saved) that hurt the defense. The one player we see being especially strong in 2012 is catcher Yadier Molina with six runs saved.

Detroit Tigers

| 2012 Projected Runs Saved: | -11 | Rank: | 22 |
| 2011 Actual Runs Saved: | 14 | Rank: | 10 |

The surprise addition of first baseman Prince Fielder, combined with the potent bat of now-third baseman Miguel Cabrera, gives the Tigers an extremely potent one-two offensive punch. However, it also gives Detroit the worst combination of corner infielders in baseball, with a combined projected cost of 21 runs in 2012. Elsewhere, 2011 Fielding Bible Award winner Austin Jackson was phenomenal in center field with 29 runs saved (leading all outfielders), but we have a difficult time seeing that kind of extremely good performance continuing in 2012. We project Jackson to save a still-remarkable 15 runs.

Pittsburgh Pirates

| 2012 Projected Runs Saved: | -13 | Rank: | 23 |
| 2011 Actual Runs Saved: | -29 | Rank: | 25 |

The Pirates share a number of unfortunate similarities with the Orioles. Both are teams without any winning seasons over the past 10-plus years and both are perennial members of the bottom tier of the defensive leaderboards. What's more, like the Orioles, we project the Pirates to have just one above-average defender in new shortstop Clint Barmes (projected for 12 runs saved). Center fielder Andrew McCutchen began to live up to his potential in 2011 with five runs saved, but his three-year numbers suggest that he will slip a little bit in 2012; he's projected at zero runs saved. Pedro Alvarez has been a liability on defense so far in his career and we

see that continuing in 2012 with -8 runs at third base.

Los Angeles Dodgers

| 2012 Projected Runs Saved: | -14 | Rank: | 24 |
| 2011 Actual Runs Saved: | 13 | Rank: | 11 |

No National League team improved defensively between 2010 and 2011 as much as the Dodgers did, picking up a total of an extra 80 runs saved. Center fielder Matt Kemp and right fielder Andre Ethier combined to cost just one run in 2011, improving over 2010 by a whopping 42 runs. But we don't see that much improvement holding up into 2012 and Ethier and Kemp are projected for a total cost of 19 runs on defense. On the plus side, new second baseman Mark Ellis has been one of the five best defenders at second base in recent history and in 2012 we expect him to continue his good performance, saving seven runs.

Houston Astros

| 2012 Projected Runs Saved: | -16 | Rank: | 25 |
| 2011 Actual Runs Saved: | 11 | Rank: | 12 |

Houston's defensive outlook is glum, but it is not all bad. The Astros look strong defensively in right field with Brian Bogusevic. Bogusevic made a strong impression in 2011 with 10 runs saved in limited time. With more playing time coming his way in 2012, we project him to save seven runs. Unfortunately, we see his defensive contributions being overshadowed by the worst left side of the infield in baseball between new shortstop Jed Lowrie and third baseman Chris Johnson. We project them to cost Houston 18 runs. Additionally, we project Jordan Schafer to be one of the worst center fielders in the game, giving up nine runs.

Baltimore Orioles

| 2012 Projected Runs Saved: | -16 | Rank: | 25 |
| 2011 Actual Runs Saved: | -21 | Rank: | 22 |

No team in baseball gave up more runs in 2011 than the Orioles and their poor defense is a core component of that unenviable honor. With few significant roster changes for the 2012 season, we don't see their defensive issues improving. We project just one regular having an above-average year defensively in catcher Matt Wieters. Wieters claimed the 2011 Fielding Bible Award with 17 runs saved and he projects to save another 8 runs in 2012. One place where the Orioles do look improved is in their outfield bench. Backups Felix Pie and Matt Angle cost 20 runs combined, but new fourth outfielder Endy Chavez projects to one run above-average.

Chicago Cubs

2012 Projected Runs Saved:	-25	Rank:	27
2011 Actual Runs Saved:	-43	Rank:	26

2011 was a serious defensive struggle for the Cubs and looks to be again in 2012, but there is good news. Their defensive problems are confined to only a few positions and there is one fewer liability in the field for 2012. New third baseman Ian Stewart is a big upgrade over Aramis Ramirez, who cost the Cubs 18 runs at third in 2011. We project Stewart to save two runs. That upgrade is overshadowed somewhat by our projection for continued poor defense from left fielder Alfonso Soriano and shortstop Starlin Castro. Soriano and Castro were both among the 2011 league leaders in runs lost. In 2012, we see them combining to cost Chicago 18 runs, 10 from Soriano and 8 from Castro.

New York Mets

2012 Projected Runs Saved:	-26	Rank:	28
2011 Actual Runs Saved:	-58	Rank:	27

Things certainly look glum for the Mets' defense yet again in 2012. They are facing some of the worst projections in baseball at three positions. Justin Turner was the worst second baseman in the game in 2011, costing the team 13 runs. This year we project him to cost seven. David Wright has been the second-worst third baseman over the past three seasons. From 2009 through 2011, he has surrendered 34 runs more than the average third baseman. We project him to cost the Mets 11 runs in 2012. Right field will be manned by Lucas Duda. In just a quarter-season's worth of innings in 2011, Duda lost 12 runs in right. As the regular for 2012, we project he will cost the Mets 13 runs.

Minnesota Twins

2012 Projected Runs Saved:	-29	Rank:	29
2011 Actual Runs Saved:	-61	Rank:	29

The Twins look like they will be near the bottom of the defensive continuum among MLB teams again in 2012, but there are some marginal upgrades being made in Minnesota. Right fielder Michael Cuddyer cost 10 runs in 2011, but he has left for free agency. We see new right fielder Josh Willingham only losing one run. Twins shortstops Tsuyoshi Nishioka and Trevor Plouffe lost 26 runs in 2011. The position has been shored up with the addition of Jamey Carroll. We project Carroll and his backups to cost "only" nine runs. Unfortunately, the shortstop position is illustrative of the Twins as a whole: despite having improved, they still remain well below-average.

Miami Marlins

2012 Projected Runs Saved:	-30	Rank:	30
2011 Actual Runs Saved:	-75	Rank:	30

The Marlins were the worst defenders in baseball last year and we don't see that changing in 2012. Five different starters were among the worst—if not the worst—at their positions in 2011: catcher John Buck, shortstop Hanley Ramirez, third baseman Greg Dobbs, left fielder Logan Morrison and center fielder Chris Coghlan. These five players combined to cost the Marlins 66 runs, nearly all of their runs below-average. All five players are returning in 2012 as well, though Dobbs and Coghlan are expected to have reduced roles, and Ramirez has been moved to third base. New shortstop Jose Reyes won't help much; we project him to cost the Marlins seven runs.

Team Defensive Runs by Position - 2012 (Projected)

Team	Pitcher	Catcher	First Base	Second Base	Third Base	Shortstop	Left Field	Center Field	Right Field	Total
Tampa Bay Rays	-1	2	2	20	16	5	4	-9	3	42
Seattle Mariners	-1	-2	-1	4	4	16	0	13	-1	32
Cincinnati Reds	4	0	1	3	9	9	-2	-1	6	29
Texas Rangers	-2	-6	-3	12	12	5	3	6	-1	26
Los Angeles Angels	-3	2	11	1	2	-1	-5	12	3	22
Arizona Diamondbacks	5	2	-2	2	-4	2	4	9	3	21
New York Yankees	-4	5	3	3	2	-10	20	5	-4	20
Kansas City Royals	-1	0	-6	-3	0	2	11	7	8	18
Atlanta Braves	0	-1	-1	-11	0	6	2	10	10	15
Boston Red Sox	-1	-3	7	11	-1	-3	4	0	-2	12
San Francisco Giants	-2	10	3	-3	2	0	-1	3	-1	11
Philadelphia Phillies	0	4	-7	8	3	-4	1	-2	3	6
Toronto Blue Jays	2	1	-3	-2	11	4	-4	-2	-4	3
Colorado Rockies	1	-2	1	-3	6	11	1	-4	-9	2
San Diego Padres	3	-5	1	-1	1	-3	-6	5	4	-1
Washington Nationals	3	-2	1	5	5	-7	0	-5	-2	-2
Oakland Athletics	0	3	4	-6	-7	-3	0	5	2	-2
Milwaukee Brewers	5	-1	2	-6	-14	7	1	4	-1	-3
Chicago White Sox	0	-3	-7	-2	-1	6	0	-3	1	-9
Cleveland Indians	0	-2	-5	-4	7	-3	3	-9	4	-9
St. Louis Cardinals	3	5	0	-9	-6	-1	0	-1	-1	-10
Detroit Tigers	-2	-4	-6	1	-12	0	5	14	-7	-11
Pittsburgh Pirates	-1	1	-4	-6	-10	10	2	-1	-4	-13
Los Angeles Dodgers	0	-6	5	6	-2	-3	4	-13	-5	-14
Houston Astros	1	-1	6	2	-12	-6	-3	-11	8	-16
Baltimore Orioles	2	8	-3	-2	-13	-1	1	-4	-4	-16
Chicago Cubs	-2	-2	1	-1	1	-8	-10	-4	0	-25
New York Mets	3	-3	9	-8	-11	-5	0	2	-13	-26
Minnesota Twins	0	1	-1	-4	-6	-9	-7	-1	-2	-29
Miami Marlins	5	-7	-2	0	-2	-7	-15	-9	7	-30

Infield Runs Saved Leaders

First Basemen Projected 2012 Leaders		Second Basemen Projected 2012 Leaders		Third Basemen Projected 2012 Leaders		Shortstops Projected 2012 Leaders	
Pujols, Albert	10	Zobrist, Ben	16	Longoria, Evan	15	Ryan, Brendan	16
Gonzalez, Adrian	7	Kinsler, Ian	13	Beltre, Adrian	13	Barmes, Clint	12
Barton, Daric	6	Pedroia, Dustin	11	Lawrie, Brett	12	Tulowitzki, Troy	10
Loney, James	5	Utley, Chase	9	Rolen, Scott	9	Wilson, Jack	8
Davis, Ike	5	Ellis, Mark	7	Zimmerman, Ryan	6	Gonzalez, Alex	7
Murphy, Daniel	4	Ackley, Dustin	6	Blake, Casey	6	Ramirez, Alexei	6
Teixeira, Mark	3	Espinosa, Danny	5	Hannahan, Jack	6	Andrus, Elvis	5
Kotchman, Casey	3	Santiago, Ramon	4	Polanco, Placido	5	Cozart, Zack	5
Helton, Todd	3	Rodriguez, Sean	4	Figgins, Chone	4	Escobar, Yunel	4
Wallace, Brett	3	Cano, Robinson	3	Rodriguez, Alex	3	Brignac, Reid	4
		Phillips, Brandon	3				

First Basemen Projected 2012 Trailers		Second Basemen Projected 2012 Trailers		Third Basemen Projected 2012 Trailers		Shortstops Projected 2012 Trailers	
Hosmer, Eric	-6	Uggla, Dan	-11	Cabrera, Miguel	-15	Castro, Starlin	-8
Fielder, Prince	-6	Schumaker, Skip	-7	Ramirez, Aramis	-14	Desmond, Ian	-7
Howard, Ryan	-6	Turner, Justin	-7	Wright, David	-11	Reyes, Jose	-7
Jones, Garrett	-6	Walker, Neil	-6	Johnson, Chris	-11	Lowrie, Jed	-6
Konerko, Paul	-5	Weeks, Jemile	-5	Reynolds, Mark	-9	Jeter, Derek	-6
LaPorta, Matt	-4	Weeks, Rickie	-4	Sizemore, Scorr	-8	Carroll, Jamie	-5
		Nelson, Chris	-4	Alvarez, Pedro	-8		

Outfield Runs Saved Leaders

Left Fielders Projected 2012 Leaders		Center Fielders Projected 2012 Leaders		Right Fielders Projected 2012 Leaders	
Gardner, Brett	20	Jackson, Austin	15	Heyward, Jason	11
Gordon, Alex	11	Gutierrez, Franklin	13	Francoeur, Jeff	8
Raburn, Ryan	7	Bourjos, Peter	12	Bogusevic, Brian	7
Brantley, Michael	5	Bourn, Michael	10	Stanton, Mike	6
Parra, Gerardo	5	Young, Chris	9	Bruce, Jay	5
Gwynn, Tony	4	Cain, Lorenzo	6	Pence, Hunter	4
Crawford, Carl	3	Maybin, Cameron	5	Choo, Shin-Soo	4
Prado, Martin	3	Gentry, Craig	5	Reddick, Josh	4
Hamilton, Josh	3	Gomez, Carlos	5	Upton, Justin	3
Jennings, Desmond	2	Granderson, Curtis	4	Hunter, Torii	3

Left Fielders Projected 2012 Trailers		Center Fielders Projected 2012 Trailers		Right Fielders Projected 2012 Trailers	
Morrison, Logan	-15	Kemp, Matt	-14	Duda, Lucas	-13
Soriano, Alfonso	-10	Upton, B.J.	-9	Cuddyer, Michael	-10
Quentin, Carlos	-8	Schafer, Jordan	-9	Ethier, Andre	-5
Revere, Ben	-5	Coghlan, Chris	-6	Boesch, Brennan	-5
Wells, Vernon	-5	Brantley, Michael	-5	Markakis, Nick	-4
Thames, Eric	-4	Rios, Alex	-4	Swisher, Nick	-4
				Tabata, Jose	-4

Pitcher/Catcher Runs Saved Leaders

Pitchers Projected 2012 Leaders		Catchers Projected 2012 Leaders	
Buehrle, Mark	4	Wieters, Matt	8
Romero, Ricky	3	Molina, Yadier	6
Dickey, R.A.	3	Martin, Russell	5
Westbrook, Jake	3	Posey, Buster	5
Verlander, Justin	2	Stewart, Chris	5
Saunders, Joe	2	Ruiz, Carlos	4
Guthrie, Jeremy	2	Suzuki, Kurt	3
Cahill, Trevor	2	Mathis, Jeff	3
Arroyo, Bronson	2	Montero, Miguel	2
Chacin, Jhoulys	2	Quintero, Humberto	2

Pitchers Projected 2012 Trailers		Catchers Projected 2012 Trailers	
Santana, Ervin	-3	Buck, John	-7
Penny, Brad	-2	Avila, Alex	-4
Lincecum, Tim	-2	Pierzynski, A.J.	-4
36 tied with	-1	Napoli, Mike	-4
		Hernandez, Ramon	-4
		Baker, John	-4

101 Things You Didn't Know about Defense

There are a lot of numbers in this book and even more numbers in the BIS databases that don't fit in these pages. Here are some of the more interesting ones we came across.

Pitcher

1. Top Fielding Relievers

Not only is he one of the best relievers of all-time, Mariano Rivera is also an excellent fielder. Over the last nine years, Rivera has saved the Yankees 13 runs with his glove, five more than the second-best fielding closer (at least 50 saves), Joakim Soria of the Royals.

Player	2003-11 Runs Saved
Mariano Rivera	13
Joakim Soria	8
John Smoltz	7
Six tied with	6

2. Pitchers Who Need a Traffic Light

In many cases, teams prefer to see an infielder or catcher field a ball rather than a pitcher. Since 2009, three pitchers have cost their team a run for "Cutting off a better positioned fielder."

Player	2009-11 Runs Saved
Joe Blanton	-1
Ted Lilly	-1
Joel Pineiro	-1

3. Players Most in Need of Directons to First Base

Someone should introduce CC Sabathia to first base. The Yankee southpaw has failed to cover first base 15 times since 2004, eight times more than the second-biggest culprit, former Yankee David Wells. It's a good thing Miguel Cabrera is moving across the diamond to third base in 2012; he also failed to cover first six times during his short time as a first baseman.

Player	2004-11 Failure to Cover First
CC Sabathia	15
David Wells	7
Brett Myers	6
Derek Lowe	6
Miguel Cabrera	6

4. Pitchers with Most Good Fielding Plays

A pitcher's primary job is run prevention, and usually he seeks to accomplish this with his throwing arm, rather than with his glove. Some pitchers, though, are known for their excellent fielding. Here are the pitchers with the most Good Fielding Plays since 2004.

Player	2004-11 GFP
Livan Hernandez	48
Mark Buehrle	39
Greg Maddux	35
Dontrelle Willis	35
Jake Peavy	32

5. The Bill Buckners of the Mound

Jamie Moyer is the Bill Buckner of the pitcher's mound. Since we began tracking Good Plays and Misplays in 2004, Moyer leads all pitchers with 11 "Groundball through infielder."

Player	2004-11 Groundball Through Infielder
Jamie Moyer	11
A.J. Burnett	10
Jason Marquis	9
Ricky Nolasco	9
Joe Blanton	9

6. Pitchers Who Can Pitch, But Can't Throw

Some pitchers, while they may be able to throw strikes to home plate, have a difficult time throwing strikes to the bases. Matt Garza is the biggest offender. In 2011, he had six Throwing Misplays and Errors, the most of any pitcher.

Player	2011 Throwing DME
Matt Garza	6
Brian Duensing	5
Justin Verlander	5
Aaron Harang	5
James Shields	5

7. Players with the Most Innings without a Defensive Misplay

In 251.0 innings in 2011, Justin Verlander did not record a single Defensive Misplay, making him the player with the most innings in the field without a Defensive Misplay.

Player	2011 Innings
Justin Verlander	251.0
Ervin Santana	228.2
Tim Lincecum	217.0
Yovani Gallardo	207.1
Shaun Marcum	200.2

8. Pitchers with the Most Pickoffs Since 2009

When you think of a pitcher picking off a lot of base runners, usually you think of a lefty like Kenny Rogers or Andy Pettitte. In the last three years, it's actually a righty, James Shields of the Rays, that has the most pickoffs.

Player	2009-11 Pickoffs
James Shields	15
Mark Buehrle	12
Jered Weaver	9
Dallas Braden	9
A.J. Burnett	7

Catcher

9. End of an Era?

Yadier Molina's four-year Fielding Bible Award streak ended this year as the Cardinal backstop had a sub-par season with the glove. He ranked 22nd in Defensive Runs Saved. Since his first season as the Cards' regular catcher in 2005, this is only the second time Molina hasn't ranked in the top three in Runs Saved.

10. Like Running into a Brick Wall

Jeff Mathis is an excellent defensive catcher, and he is willing to put his body in harm's way blocking the plate when a runner is coming home. He's done this 16 times over the last three seasons, good for three Runs Saved. Victor Martinez and Matt Wieters are second, followed by Ryan Doumit and Yadier Molina.

Player	2009-11 Catcher Blocks Home Plate
Jeff Mathis	16
Victor Martinez	13
Matt Wieters	13
Ryan Doumit	12
Yadier Molina	12

11. Maybe He Should Have Blown it Foul

Yadier Molina is a superb fielder, but one area where he could use a little improvement is deciding whether or not to pick up a ball that is heading toward the foul line. Since 2009, Molina is the only player that has cost his team a full run for "Failing to Let the Ball Roll Foul."

12. Not What I Would Want to Be Remembered For

The most Misplays for a single player in a single game is six, accomplished by Eli Whiteside of the Giants on August 29, 2010 against the Diamondbacks, and George Kottaras as a member of the Red Sox, against the Twins on May 27, 2009. 15 players had five in a game.

13. Exceptionally Good at Being Exceptionally Poor

Over the last three years, Miguel Olivo has been flagged for 27 Misplays for "Exceptionally poor play allowing stolen base." This is ten more than the next biggest offenders, Jason Kendall and Brian McCann.

Player	2009-2011 Exceptionally Poor Play Allowing Stolen Base
Miguel Olivo	27
Jason Kendall	17
Brian McCann	17
Ronny Paulino	16
Rod Barajas	14

14. Fielding Percentage is Overrated

Here's a reason why Good Plays and Misplays are such an important way to evaluate a fielder. Miguel Olivo has a sparkling .988 fielding percentage, but the backstop has the most Misplays of any player since we began tracking Good Plays and Misplays in 2004.

Player	2004-2011 Defensive Misplays
Miguel Olivo	351
A.J. Pierzynski	329
Jason Kendall	313
John Buck	285
Miguel Tejada	277

15. His Mother is Just Thankful She Doesn't Do His Laundry Anymore

Yadier Molina is the best catcher at blocking balls in the dirt. Over the last three years, Molina has saved his team 15 runs in Wild Pitch/Passed Ball prevention. He's five runs better than the next-best pitch blocker.

Player	2009-11 Wild Pitch/Passed Ball Prevention Runs Saved
Yadier Molina	15
Kurt Suzuki	10
Jeff Mathis	10
Jason Varitek	10
Humberto Quintero	7

16. Most Innings without a Good Fielding Play in 2011

Player	Innings
Brian Schneider	309.0
Henry Blanco	274.0
Chris Snyder	265.2
CC Sabathia	237.1
Jered Weaver	235.2

17. Rated "Most Likely to Catch Someone Sleeping" in High School

Yadier Molina has picked off 13 base runners since 2009, the highest total among catchers in the last three years.

Player	2009-11 Pickoffs
Yadier Molina	13
Humberto Quintero	11
Rob Johnson	9
Three tied with	6

18. File this Under "He wouldn't make a good goalie"

Over the last three years, Miguel Olivo has allowed 31 passed balls, the most in baseball since 2009, and he hasn't even caught a knuckleballer.

Player	Pickoffs
Miguel Olivo	31
J. Saltalamacchia	28
Rob Johnson	23
Josh Thole	23
Brian McCann	19

First Base

19. There's a Chink in Every Piece of Armor

Mark Teixeira led baseball with 79 Good Fielding Plays in 2011. Of these, 34 were handling difficult throws and 30 were making unlikely outs on groundballs. Teixeira has a terrific reputation on both of these types of plays (despite only three runs saved in 2011), and he was indeed the top first baseman at converting unlikely groundball outs. But Teixeira ranked just fifth among all first basemen handling difficult throws.

Player	2011 Handling Difficult Throws
Carlos Pena	50
Freddie Freeman	44
Eric Hosmer	40
Casey Kotchman	35
Mark Teixeira	34

20. Do They Make Trophies for That?

Adrian Gonzalez is the best first baseman fielding bunts. His 10 Bunt Runs Saved over the course of his career is the highest total of anyone and double the next-best first baseman (Lance Berkman, with 5 Bunt Runs Saved).

21. Baskin Robbins Also Makes Clutch Scoops

Between 2009 and 2011, there have been 19 game-ending scoops on difficult throws in close games. All 19 scoops were made at first base. Only one of these clutch scoops occurred on a play that, if not made, would have blown a lead for the fielding team. This most clutch scoop was made in a Dodgers-Rockies afternoon game on May 27, 2009. Dodgers first baseman James Loney scooped a throw in the dirt from shortstop Juan Castro to retire Brad Hawpe on a slow roller with the bases loaded and the score 8-6.

22. A Man of the People

James Loney must really enjoy interacting with fans because the Dodger first baseman leads all players in Good Fielding Plays for "reaching into the stands." Loney has done this 11 times since 2009, the most in baseball, and has saved the Dodgers two runs reaching into the stands. No word on how many boxes of Cracker Jacks he's spilled doing this.

Player	2011 Reaches into Stands
James Loney	11
Carlos Pena	7
Adam LaRoche	6
Mark Teixeira	6
Ike Davis	5
Justin Smoak	5

23. Earning His Name

Prince Fielder may not be the best fielder in the world, but one thing he's good at is having the awareness to throw home to record an out at the plate. Fielder is one of nine fielders to save his team at least two runs on "Cutting off the runner at home."

Player	2009-11 Cutting off the Runner at Home
Cliff Pennington	3
Albert Pujols	3
Prince Fielder	2
Ian Stewart	2
Jose Lopez	2
Alex Rodriguez	2
Ty Wigginton	2
Brett Wallace	2

24. I'll Take Two Scoops

Over the last three years, Casey Kotchman and Albert Pujols lead all first basemen in Scoop Runs Saved.

Player	2009-11 Scoop Runs Saved
Casey Kotchman	5
Albert Pujols	5
Todd Helton	4
James Loney	4
Daric Barton	4
Aubrey Huff	4

25. Wait...Miguel Cabrera is...Good?

Read this next sentence very slowly and make sure you're sitting down. Miguel Cabrera is a better-than-average first baseman. That's actually true if he's playing away from Comerica Park. Over the last three years, Cabrera has made ten more plays than an average first baseman on the road. Compare that to his home Plus/ Minus of -22, and Cabrera is 32 plays better on the road

than at home, easily the best mark in baseball since 2009.

Player	Home Plus/Minus	Road Plus/Minus	Difference
Miguel Cabrera	-22	+10	32
Adam Jones	-26	-3	23
Placido Polanco	-4	+19	23
Starlin Castro	-17	+5	22
Logan Morrison	-24	-4	20

26. He also enjoys Double Mint Gum

Since 2009, James Loney has been the best first baseman at turning double plays.

Player	2009-11 GDP Runs Saved
James Loney	3
Mark Trumo	2
Albert Pujols	2
Todd Helton	2
10 tied with	1

Second Base

27. Is Poor Fielding Genetic?

Among second basemen in 2011, Rickie Weeks had the highest percentage of Touches turned into DMEs with 8.4 percent. In second place was his brother Jemile with 7.8 percent.

28. All Hail the King of Foul Balls

On foul flyballs behind first base, it's often the second baseman who ranges into foul territory to catch the ball and make the out. Over the last three years, we've awarded Darwin Barney four Good Fielding Plays for "catching difficult foul pop-up" to lead all second basemen.

Player	2009-11 Catching Difficult Foul Pop-up
Darwin Barney	4
Ian Kinsler	3
Six tied with	2

29. The Quickness of Cano

We discuss Robinson Cano's double play abilities on page 77. One of the things Cano gets credit for is his ability to quickly turn double plays. Since we started tracking Good Fielding Plays and Defensive Misplays in 2004, Cano has the most Good Plays for "started double play quickly" with 26.

Player	2004-11 Started Double Play Quickly
Robinson Cano	26
Brandon Phillips	24
Orlando Hudson	21
Ian Kinsler	21
Chase Utley	18

30. The Hitting Coach Says "Just Hit it Right to Him"

Over the past nine years, Rickie Weeks has really struggled at balls hit right to him. He's made 17 fewer plays than the next-worst second baseman at fielding balls straight on.

Player	2004-11 "Straight on" Plus/Minus
Rickie Weeks	-34
Akinori Iwamura	-17
Skip Schumaker	-10
Five tied with	-9

31. These Second Basemen Struggle at Turning Two

Being able to turn the double play is a crucial skill for playing second base, but not all second basemen are adept at turning two. Here are the worst second basemen at turning double plays since 2009.

Player	2009-11 GDP Runs Saved
Orlando Hudson	-5
Luis Castillo	-5
Dan Uggla	-4
Aaron Hill	-4
Mike Aviles	-4

32. The Worst of the Worst

Aaron Hill might be the worst second baseman at turning double plays. In addition to his -4 GDP Runs Saved since 2009, he's also cost his team four runs on Double Play Good Play/Misplays.

Player	2009-11 GFP/DME Runs Saved on Double Plays
Aaron Hill	-4
Mike Aviles	-4
Adam Kennedy	-3
Freddy Sanchez	-3
Five tied with	-2

33. Second Basemen Can Throw, Too!

Even though second baseman don't have to throw the ball too far very often, some second basemen really excel at throwing. Here are the top second basemen on "Throwing" Good Play/Misplay Runs Saved.

Player	2009-11 GFP/DME Runs Saved on Throws
Gordon Beckham	2
Bill Hall	2
Maicer Izturis	2
14 tied with	1

34. Someone Owes their First Baseman a Dinner

A first baseman making a GFP7, "Handling a Difficult Throw," can save another infielder from an error. While shortstops are bailed out more often than other infielders because they field the most groundballs, several second basemen have also benefited from nice plays at first base. Here are the second basemen who have had the most GFP7's on their throws.

Player	2004-11 Difficult Throws Handled by the First Baseman
Dan Uggla	26
Skip Schumaker	22
Robinson Cano	17
Chase Utley	16
Rickie Weeks	16
Brandon Phillips	16
Orlando Hudson	16

Third Base

35. Baseball's Buzzer Beater... If Baseball Used a Clock

There have been 106 good fielding plays (non-scoops) to end close games (within three runs) from 2009 through 2011. Third baseman Brandon Inge has the most close game-ending gems with four, two of which came in one-run games with a runner on first base.

36. The Benefits of Moving

Early in his career, in 2007, Hanley Ramirez was terrible on balls to his right (-21). The very next year, he had a 31-play swing and was +10. Since then, however, Ramirez has gradually gotten worse on balls to his right: +8 in 2009, -14 in 2010, -21 in 2011. His potential move to third base in 2012 will allow him to fine tune his play on balls straight on and to his left as he gets to watch many balls to his right go foul.

37. Most Likely to Succeed

Evan Longoria does basically everything right as a defensive third basemen. In 2011, he led baseball in good fielding plays by a third baseman with 49, GDP runs saved with 1 (tied with several others), GFP/DME Runs Saved with 3, Bunt Runs Saved with 4 and trailed only Pablo Sandoval and Brett Lawrie in Plus/Minus Runs Saved with 14 (compared to Sandoval's and Lawrie's 15).

38. Longoria's Quickness

In this book, we began evaluating the double play abilities of corner infielders to go along with our evaluations of middle infielders. Since 2009, Evan Longoria of the Rays has the most Good Plays for "starting a double play quickly" with 17.

Player	2009-11 Started Double Play Quickly
Evan Longoria	17
Brandon Inge	11
Ryan Zimmerman	11
Pedro Feliz	10
Michael Young	8

39. Please Don't Hit it to Me!

At the hot corner, players really have to be alert; the ball gets to them in a hurry sometimes. In the last nine years, these fielders have had a difficult time on balls hit straight on.

Player	2003-11 "Straight On" Plus/Minus
Garrett Atkins	-43
Edwin Encarnacion	-42
Mark Reynolds	-35
Mike Lowell	-34
Aramis Ramirez	-28

40. Bricks for Hands

Mark Reynolds was charged with a Misplay or an error on 19.1 percent of his touches in 2011, the highest percentage of any position player.

Player	Position	2011 DME per Touch
Mark Reynolds	3B	19.1%
Ronny Paulino	C	17.6%
Kevin Kouzmanoff	3B	16.4%
Aaron Miles	3B	15.4%
Scott Sizemore	3B	15.4%

41. Yes, Catching is Part of the Game

Chone Figgins isn't very good at catching throws. Since 2009, Figgins has been the worst third baseman at catching throws, costing his team two runs on Good Plays and Misplays/Errors for Catching Throws. In fact, he's the only third baseman to cost his team at least two runs on catching throws (16 tied with -1).

42. Bunt Struggles

Over the last three years, Brandon Inge has been the worst third baseman at fielding bunts.

Player	2009-11 Bunt Runs Saved
Brandon Inge	-4
Mark Reynolds	-3
Jose Bautista	-3
11 tied with	-2

43. Repeat After Me...I Appreciate My First Baseman

Here are the third basemen who have been bailed out most often by their first basemen on poor throws.

Player	2004-11 Difficult Throws Handled by the First Baseman
Ryan Zimmerman	36
David Wright	33
Evan Longoria	30
Mark Reynolds	28
Pablo Sandoval	27
Michael Young	27

Shortstop

44. Leaning Left

Shortstops who leaned left in 2011 (15 plays better in Plus/Minus to their left than to their right):

Player	To His Left	To His Right
Hanley Ramirez	+7	-21
Jose Reyes	+4	-19
Edgar Renteria	+13	-7
Ruben Tejada	+8	-7

45. Leaning Right

Shortstops who leaned right in 2011 (15 plays better in Plus/Minus to their right than to their left):

Player	To His Left	To His Right
Yuniesky Betancourt	-14	+18
Alcides Escobar	-5	+19
Elvis Andrus	-10	+13
Brendan Ryan	-2	+18
Alexei Ramirez	-4	+16
J.J. Hardy	-10	+9

46. Hard Slides Don't Scare These Guys

On a double play ball, when the runner on first is rushing toward second, Erick Aybar hangs in there and converts the double play more than any other fielder. Aybar's 15 Good Plays for "Double Play Despite Aggressive Slide" is tops in baseball since 2009.

Player	2009-11 Double Play Despite Aggressive Slide
Erick Aybar	15
Ian Desmond	13
Jason Bartlett	11
Asdrubal Cabrera	11
Five tied with	10

47. He Really is *That Bad*

In case you needed further proof that Derek Jeter is a terrible fielder, the Yankee captain is the only player who has cost his team over 100 runs at one position since 2003. Jeter is 35 runs worse than the next worst fielder.

Player	Position	2003-11 Runs Saved
Derek Jeter	SS	-124
Manny Ramirez	LF	-89
Adam Dunn	LF	-81
Michael Young	SS	-80
Prince Fielder	1B	-75

48. The Castro Promise: The Most Bad Throws in 2/3 the Time or Your Money Back

Starlin Castro leads all players with 39 Misplays and Errors on "bad throws" over the past three seasons despite spending the entire 2009 season in the minors.

Player	2009-11 Bad Throw DME
Starlin Castro	39
Mark Reynolds	37
Ryan Zimmerman	36
Cliff Pennington	35
Hanley Ramirez	35

49. Home is Where the ~~Heart~~ Glove Is

Elvis Andrus must enjoy playing home games. Since 2009, the Rangers' shortstop is an MLB-best 37 plays better at home compared with on the road, according to Basic Plus/Minus.

Player	Home Plus/Minus	Road Plus/Minus	Difference
Elvis Andrus	+22	-15	37
Ryan Braun	+21	-11	32
David Wright	+5	-26	31
Ryan Zimmerman	+35	+5	30
Colby Rasmus	+15	-13	28
Matt Kemp	-12	-40	28

50. The Players Starlin Castro Should Idolize

Alcides Escobar had more Good Fielding Plays on Throwing than any other infielder in 2011.

Player	2011 Throwing GFP
Alcides Escobar	11
Albert Pujols	9
Troy Tulowitzki	8
Robinson Cano	7
Mark Ellis	7

51. Thank You, First Baseman, for Making Me Look Better than I Actually Am

Cliff Pennington has been bailed out by his first basemen the most over the last three years, 49 times altogether. Several other shortstops join Pennington on the list of shortstops that have been saved by their first basemen most often since 2009, as well as shortstop/third baseman Miguel Tejada:

Player	2009-11 Difficult Throws Handled by the First Baseman
Cliff Pennington	49
Alexei Ramirez	45
Miguel Tejada	43
Brendan Ryan	42
Alex Gonzalez	41

Left Field

52. Cannon for an Arm

Alex Gordon led left fielders with 13 runs saved with his arm in 2011. Second place was a tie between Sam Fuld and Laynce Nix with 4 runs saved. The only two outfielders since 2003 to top that score are Alfonso Soriano in 2007 (15) and Richard Hidalgo in 2003 (17).

53. The Biggest Home Run Robbery of Them All

Only once since 2009 has a close game ended with a home run robbing catch, and that was Angels left fielder Juan Rivera taking a potential solo shot away from Tampa Bay's Ben Zobrist to seal a one run victory on August 10, 2009.

54. Ryan Braun Needs a Compass

Someone needs to hand Ryan Braun a compass. Since 2009, Braun has five Misplays for "Throwing toward the wrong base," which is tied with Kosuke Fukudome to lead all players. Carl Crawford and Andrew McCutchen have each been penalized at least three times.

Player	2009-11 Throwing Toward Wrong Base DME
Ryan Braun	5
Kosuke Fukudome	5
Carl Crawford	3
Andrew McCutchen	3
David Murphy	3
Everth Cabrera	3
Colby Rasmus	3

55. Alex Gordon Slipping: Coming to a Blooper Reel Near You

Blooper reels always show players slipping and falling, allowing the ball to drop in for a hit. Since 2009, Alex Gordon leads the majors with five Misplays/Errors for slipping.

Player	2009-11 Slipping DME
Alex Gordon	5
Nyjer Morgan	4
Adrian Beltre	4
Hunter Pence	4

56. Who Needs the DL When You Have an Arm Like This?

Despite missing parts of the last two seasons with injuries, Jason Bay leads all left fielders with four Runs Saved on Good Plays and Misplays involving throwing from 2009-11.

Player	2009-11 GFP/DME Runs Saved on Throwing
Jason Bay	4
Carlos Gonzalez	3
Ryan Braun	3
Four tied with	2

57. Carl Who?

Sam Fuld was credited with a Good Fielding Play on 10 percent of his touches in 2011, the most among outfielders.

Player	2011 GFP per Touch
Sam Fuld	10.1%
Carlos Gonzalez	7.4%
Desmond Jennings	7.0%
Carlos Lee	6.8%
Carlos Gomez	6.7%

58. Oh *that* Carl

When an outfielder fields a batted ball and gets it back to the infield especially quickly, stopping advancing runners in their tracks, we credit him with a Good Fielding Play for Preventing Extra Bases. If the outfielder does this often enough, those plays can save the team runs. Over the last three years, Carl Crawford is the best left fielder on GFP/DME Runs Saved preventing extra bases.

Player	2009-11 Runs Saved on Preventing Extra Bases
Carl Crawford	5
Jason Bay	4
Raul Ibanez	4
Ryan Braun	4
Three tied with	2

59. Deja Vu All Over Again

Friend of *The Fielding Bible*, ESPN Stats & Info's Mark Simon (see his article on Peter Bourjos on page 39), researched the best defensive games of the year. One of the nominees came from an unlikely source: Shelley Duncan. Playing left field for Cleveland on September 14, Duncan made spectacular catches on three straight plays to end the top half of the first inning and to start the second. Even more remarkable, all three balls were hit within a couple feet of each other, about nine feet up the left field wall. Duncan had to jump to make the catch and save all three potential doubles. Later in the game, he also made a diving catch coming in. Ironically, Duncan racked up four Good Fielding Plays in this game alone but only one other GFP in left field all season.

Center Field

60. Going Deep

Chris Young and Austin Jackson tied for the best CF plus/minus score on deep hits at +27 a piece. On the bottom of the leaderboard were Chris Coghlan (-20) and Adam Jones (-19).

61. Thinking Shallow

Cameron Maybin and Shane Victorino led center fielders in Plus/Minus on balls hit in shallow center at +15 and +13 respectively. Michael Bourn was the worst at -15 with Drew Stubbs and Dexter Fowler at -12 each.

62. The Deep End of the Pool

Center fielders that were strong deep but weak shallow (ordered by spread of at least 15).

Player	Shallow Plus/Minus	Deep Plus/Minus	Difference
Dexter Fowler	-12	+23	35
Michael Bourn	-15	+12	27
Austin Jackson	+1	+27	26
Andrew McCutchen	-5	+20	25
Chris Young	+2	+27	25
Nyjer Morgan	-2	+15	17
Franklin Gutierrez	-9	+8	17

63. The Shallow End

Center fielders that were strong shallow but weak deep (ordered by spread of at least 15).

Player	Shallow Plus/Minus	Deep Plus/Minus	Difference
Shane Victorino	+13	-17	30
Adam Jones	+4	-19	23
Chris Coghlan	0	-20	20
Curtis Granderson	+9	-10	19
Andres Torres	+7	-8	15

64. Make Up Your Mind Already

In 2009 and 2010, Andrew McCutchen had a combined shallow +/- of +19 and a deep +/- of -41. In 2011, that average spread of 30 additional bases saved shallow over deep was flipped: he saved 25 more bases deep than shallow.

65. They've Got a Gun

Adam Jones and Rick Ankiel both had eight runs saved with their arms to lead center fielders in 2011.

66. Kick It Like Beckham

In a previous life, Adam Jones might have been a soccer player. Since 2009, Jones leads the majors with three Misplays for "kicking a base hit." Aaron Rowand and Nelson Cruz are the only other players with more than one (they each have two).

Player	2009-11 Kicking a Base Hit
Adam Jones	3
Aaron Rowand	2
Nelson Cruz	2

67. All I Want for Christmas is a Garmin

In addition to his soccer-playing skills, Adam Jones probably could use a map to navigate the outfield. He was flagged with a Misplay 12 times for taking a bad route to the ball.

Player	2009-11 Bad Route to the Ball
Adam Jones	12
Hunter Pence	10
Nick Swisher	9
Five tied with	8

68. Professional Thief

Home run robberies are one of the most exciting defensive play in baseball. Franklin Gutierrez, a two-time Fielding Bible Award winner, has done this six times since 2009.

Player	2009-11 Home Run Robberies
Franklin Gutierrez	6
Adam Jones	5
Carlos Gomez	5
Peter Bourjos	4
Eight tied with	3

69. Where's Spider-Man When You Need Him?

Sometimes, when evaluating Good Play/Misplay data, we organize Good Plays and Misplays into groupings. For instance, all Good Plays and Misplays involving fences and walls are grouped together. Since 2009, Jacoby Ellsbury has cost his team the most runs on Good Plays and Misplays involving the fences and walls. His Red Sox teammate Carl Crawford is also on the list.

Player	2009-11 Runs Saved
Jacoby Ellsbury	-5
Cody Ross	-5
Carl Crawford	-4
Nyjer Morgan	-3
B.J. Upton	-3
Logan Morrison	-3
Matt Kemp	-3

Right Field

70. They've Got a Gun, too

Jeff Francoeur, Torii Hunter, Jason Kubel and Hunter Pence tied with five runs saved with their arms for most by a right fielder in 2011.

71. The Mistakes of Youth

Right field Fielding Bible Award winner Justin Upton and third-place finisher Mike Stanton tied for the most DMEs in right field in 2011 with 49 each.

Player	2011 Misplays + Errors
Justin Upton	49
Mike Stanton	49
Hunter Pence	39
Jayson Werth	37
Jeff Francoeur	34

72. Yeah, But It Looked Good

Spectacular diving catches always make the highlight reels. Of course, not all diving plays result in happy endings. Since 2009, Arizona's Justin Upton and Philadelphia's Hunter Pence each have 10 Misplays on failed dives, the most in MLB.

Player	2009-11 Failed Dives
Justin Upton	10
Hunter Pence	10
Five tied with	9

73. Too Strong for His Own Good

Jeff Francoeur is known for having a strong arm, but since 2004, he's been penalized with eight Misplays for a bad throw to home plate.

Player	2004-11 Bad Throw to Plate
Jeff Francoeur	8
Melky Cabrera	8
Matt Holliday	7
Five tied with	6

74. Overruning the Play

Jayson Werth has cost his team a league-worst two runs over the last three seasons on overrunning the play.

Player	2009-11 Runs Saved on Overrunning the Play
Jayson Werth	-2
Colby Rasmus	-2
Carlos Gomez	-1
12 others with	-1

75. Mishandling Base Hits

Justin Upton is a very good fielder, but one thing he seems to have trouble with is handling base hits. Over the last three years, Upton has cost his team four Runs on "mishandling ball after safe hit" which ties him with Alfonso Soriano for the most runs lost on this Misplay.

Player	2009-11 Runs Saved on Mishandling Ball After Safe Hit
Justin Upton	-4
Alfonso Soriano	-4
Dexter Fowler	-3
Angel Pagan	-3
Shin-Soo Choo	-3

76. Average ~~Joe~~ Jeff

We talk a lot about the "average fielder" but never really put a face on the description. In terms of range, Jeff Francoeur is the definition of average. Over the last three years, over 3,760 innings, Francoeur has a Basic Plus/Minus of zero. He is the player with the most innings and a Basic Plus/Minus of zero since 2009. Here are some other notables.

Player	2009-11 Most Innings with Zero Plus/Minus
Jeff Francoeur	3760.1
Orlando Hudson	3299.0
Felipe Lopez	2361.0
Nate Schierholtz	1843.2
Josh Wilson	1587.0

77. The Perfect Season . . . Sort of

Brandon Guyer, who played 94 innings in the outfield for the Rays (mostly in right field) in 2011, is the position player who played the most innings without a Misplay or an Error.

Player	2011 Innings
Brandon Guyer	94.0
Mike Wilson	59.0
Josh Satin	49.0
Dallas McPherson	36.1
Juan Castro	30.0

78. Defensive Game of the Year

On ESPN.com's "SweetSpot" blog, Mark Simon picked Brent Lillibridge's April 26 as the Defensive Game of the Year, even though the White Sox' utility man only played two innings. Lillibridge came into the game as a pinch runner in the eighth, but he got his moment to shine as the White Sox' right fielder in the ninth. The White Sox had a 3-2 lead, but the Yankees had two runners on with one out. Alex Rodriguez hit a line drive to deep right field; Lillibridge sprinted back, turned around, stretched to his left, and made the catch precisely as he slammed into the wall. Throwing the ball back to the infield, Lillibridge prevented any runners from advancing on what looked to be a game-tying base hit. Two pitches later, Robinson Cano hit a sinking liner toward the right field line. Lillibridge didn't have much time to get to the Rodriguez liner, but he had even less time to get to Cano's rocket. Thanks to a perfectly executed dive, Lillibridge made what Steve Stone termed an "unbelievable catch" to shock the Yankee Stadium crowd and end the ballgame. Without either of these two catches, the Yankees would have tied the game and possibly won it.

79. His Arm Is a Deadly Weapon

Over the past three seasons, Jose Bautista has thrown out more runners without a relay than any other player in baseball.

Player	2009-11 Outfield Kills
Jose Bautista	31
Adam Jones	28
Shin-Soo Choo	26
Jeff Francoeur	26
Nick Markakis	24

General

80. Outfielders with Terrible Arms

Carlos Quentin, Ryan Braun and Seth Smith displayed the weakest outfield arms in 2011, costing their teams six runs apiece compared to average outfielders at their respective positions.

Player	2011 Outfield Arm Runs Saved
Carlos Quentin	-6
Ryan Braun	-6
Seth Smith	-6

81. Who You Gonna Call?

Backing up throws is often mentioned as an overlooked fundamental in the game, so kudos to these four players for going the extra mile and backing up a league-leading three errant throws each over the course of the 2011 season.

Player	2011 Backing up Wild Throws
Gio Gonzalez	3
Dustin Pedroia	3
Danny Espinosa	3
Freddy Sanchez	3

82. We are the 5 percent

Among all 548 outfielders in 2011, 55.5 percent (304) had exactly average arms (runs saved of zero), 23.4 percent (128) were below-average, and 21.2 percent (116) were above-average. 95 percent of all outfielders in 2011 have runs saved between -3 to 3 (standard deviation = 1.51). The 5 percent:

Positive: Alex Gordon, Adam Jones, Rick Ankiel, Torii Hunter, Jason Kubel, Jeff Franceour, Drew Stubbs, Hunter Pence, Sam Fuld, Brian Bogusevic, Matt Kemp, Kosuke Fukudome, Laynce Nix

Negative: Ryan Braun, Carlos Quentin, Justin Upton, Seth Smith, Corey Hart, J.D. Drew, Juan Pierre, Rajai Davis, David Murphy

83. The Home Run Bandits Strike Again

There were 41 home run robbing catches in 2011, maybe the most exciting play in the game. Eighteen went to left field, another 18 to center and 5 to right. These guys did it twice; no one else did it more than once.

Player	2011 Home Run Robberies
Luke Scott	2
Nolan Reimold	2
Austin Jackson	2
Carlos Gomez	2
Peter Bourjos	2

84. An A+ in Run Prevention 101

Two years ago, the 2010 Kansas City Royals were the worst defensive team in the majors, as fielding alone cost the team 95 runs. The 2011 team, on the other hand, featured much-improved fielding as the KC defense saved the team an estimated 25 runs. The 120-run difference was the biggest jump in run prevention in all of baseball.

85. Headed to Summer School

After a stellar season with the gloves in 2010, the Oakland A's forgot how to play defense in 2011. Their 103-run drop-off from 76 Runs Saved in 2010 to -27 Runs Saved in 2011 was the largest defensive decline in the majors.

86. Well that's Embarassing...

One of the more infrequently occurring Good Fielding Plays is "Outfielder Throws Batter Out at First." Basically, a batter hits a ball to right field, jogs to first thinking he has a hit, but an alert right fielder throws him out, robbing the batter of a single. This Good Play has only happened eight times since 2004 and only three times to non-pitchers: Mike Redmond (2010), Daric Barton (2010) and Michael Taylor (2011).

87. Rawlings Manufactures Glove Super Glue, Story at 11

On June 5, 2009, Orlando "El Duque" Hernandez made a memorable play when the ball got stuck in his glove. Alertly, El Duque took off his entire glove and flipped it to first base, with the ball still stuck inside, to record the out. These players weren't as lucky, and were penalized with several Misplays for having the ball stuck in their gloves.

Player	Ball Stuck in Glove 2009-11
Orlando Cabrera	4
Hanley Ramirez	4
Ryan Theriot	3
19 tied with	2

88. Presenting the Runs Saved All-Star Team

Player	Position	Runs Saved Since 2003
Mark Buehrle	P	65
Yadier Molina	C	70
Albert Pujols	1B	126
Chase Utley	2B	130
Adrian Beltre	3B	157
Adam Everett	SS	119
Carl Crawford	LF	68
Andruw Jones	CF	61
Ichiro Suzuki	RF	74

89. The Worst Fielders in Baseball Since 2003. Remember, Kids, Friends Don't Let Friends Play Bad Defense

Player	Position	Runs Saved Since 2003
Daniel Cabrera	P	-34
John Buck	C	-50
Prince Fielder	1B	-75
Rickie Weeks	2B	-52
Ty Wigginton	3B	-75
Derek Jeter	SS	-124
Manny Ramirez	LF	-89
Bernie Williams	CF	-64
Brad Hawpe	RF	-66

90. The Best Throwing Outfield in Baseball Since 2003

Player	Position	Runs Saved Since 2003
Alfonso Soriano	LF	24
Adam Jones	CF	31
Jeff Francoeur	RF	40

91. The Worst Throwing Outfield in Baseball Since 2003

Player	Position	Runs Saved Since 2003
Luis Gonzalez	LF	-24
Juan Pierre	CF	-26
Jermaine Dye/ Brian Giles	RF	-25

92. The Most Good Fielding Plays in a Single Game by a Single Player (or a Married Player)

The most Good Fielding Plays in a single game by a single player is six. Seven players accomplished this feat, including Mark Reynolds, believe it or not.

Player	Game Date
Jason Giambi	April 14, 2009
Everth Cabrera	August 28, 2009
Mark Reynolds	April 14, 2010
David Wright	May 14, 2010
Reid Brignac	June 13, 2010
Gordon Beckham	April 10, 2011
Rafael Furcal	August 31, 2011

93. The Most Good Fielding Plays in a Single Game by a Team

Team	Good Fielding Plays	Game Date
Athletics	13	April 23, 2011
Giants	12	May 25, 2010
Blue Jays	12	June 18, 2010
Tigers	12	September 6, 2010
Tigers	12	September 19, 2010

94. The Most Defensive Misplays/Errors in a Single Game by a Team

Team	Defensive Misplays/ Errors	Game Date
Mariners	16	April 22, 2009
Yankees	14	September 7, 2011
Orioles	13	August 12, 2008
Royals	13	June 18, 2009

95. Introducing Versatility Score

Bill James introduced the Power/Speed Number several years ago as a way of measuring the players with the best combination of power and speed. The formula is 2 * (HR * SB) / (HR + SB). We can use a similar formula to highlight the most versatile players, those who perform well at multiple positions. We'll call this Versatility Number, and the forumula is:

2 * (Runs Saved at Position 1) * (Runs Saved at Position 2) / [(Runs Saved at Position 1) + (Runs Saved at Position 2)]. Ben Zobrist has the highest versatility score of the last three seasons (30.4), thanks to 45 Runs Saved at second base and an additional 23 Runs Saved in right field.

Player	Position 1 (Runs Saved)	Position 2 (Runs Saved)	Versatility Score
Ben Zobrist	2B (45)	RF (23)	30.4
Brett Gardner	LF (49)	CF (16)	19.8
Clint Barmes	2B (15)	SS (29)	19.8
Tony Gwynn	LF (12)	CF (32)	17.5
Jack Wilson	2B (7)	SS (35)	11.7

96. As for the Flip Side...

We can use the same Versatility Score to find the least versatile players since 2009, focusing on the players with negative Runs Saved totals at two positions. By this formula, Adam Dunn is the least versatile player in baseball. In addition to his -38 Runs Saved at first base and -12 Runs Saved in left field, Dunn also cost his team 7 runs in right field. Michael Cuddyer deserves mention as well, thanks to his -8 Runs Saved in a grand total of 19 games and 149 innings at second base.

Player	Position 1 (Runs Saved)	Position 2 (Runs Saved)	Versatility Score
A. Dunn	1B (-38)	LF (-12)	-18.2
C. Quentin	LF (-12)	RF (-24)	-16.0
C. Coghlan	LF (-17)	CF (-13)	-14.7
M.Reynolds	1B (-8)	3B (-33)	-12.9
M. Cuddyer	2B (-8)	RF (-28)	-12.4

97. What About Guys that Played on Multiple Teams?

We can use a similar method to see which players were the most beneficial to two different teams in the same season. We'll call this Split Team Score. Alex Gonzalez has the highest Split Team Score, thanks to his 2010 season split between Atlanta (14 Runs Saved) and Toronto (13 Runs Saved).

Season	Player	Team 1 (Runs Saved)	Team 2 (Runs Saved)	Split Team Score
2010	A. Gonzalez	Atl (14)	Tor (13)	13.5
2008	M. Teixeira	Atl (14)	LAA (7)	9.3
2009	S. Rolen	Tor (10)	Cin (7)	8.2
2004	R. Hidalgo	Hou (7)	NYM (10)	8.2
2009	J. Wilson	Pit (23)	Sea (5)	8.2

98. Who Were the Worst?

Season	Player	Team 1 (Runs Saved)	Team 2 (Runs Saved)	Split Team Score
2009	O. Cabrera	Oak (-16)	Min (-13)	-14.3
2006	F. Lopez	Cin (-11)	Was (-12)	-11.5
2009	Y. Betancourt	Sea (-7)	KC (-11)	-8.6
2005	B. Boone	Sea (-16)	Min (-5)	-7.6
2008	J. Edmonds	SD (-5)	ChC (-10)	-6.7

99. The Youngest Players Ever to Record a Good Fielding Play

Player	Age
Mike Trout	19 years, 11 months, 1 day
B.J. Upton	19 years , 11 months, 14 days
Justin Upton	19 years, 11 months, 25 days
Andres Blanco	20 years, 0 months, 6 days
Madison Bumgarner	20 years, 1 month, 7 days

100. Fielding's AARP: The Oldest Players Ever to Record a Good Fielding Play

Player	Age
Julio Franco	48 years, 10 months, 27 days
Jamie Moyer	47 years, 7 months, 9 days
Randy Johnson	45 years, 9 months, 9 days
Roger Clemens	45 years, 1 month, 12 days
Omar Vizquel	44 years, 4 months, 13 days

101. The Longest Streaks of Good Fielding Plays Without Defensive Misplays

Alex Gonzalez and Dustin Pedroia both had streaks of 22 consecutive Good Fielding Plays without a Defensive Misplay or Error, the longest such streaks in the majors in 2011.

Player	Start of Streak	Next DME	GFP
Alex Gonzalez	April 8, 2011	May 12, 2011	22
Dustin Pedroia	July 7, 2011	September 4, 2011	22
Todd Helton	May 6, 2011	July 16, 2011	19
Casey Kotchman	June 6, 2011	July 16, 2011	18
James Loney	April 1, 2011	April 22, 2011	15

Top Ten List of
Best Defensive Evaluation Methods

Maybe this flies under David Letterman's radar but it is big time on mine. Do our methods for evaluating defense work? If they do, they should be reflecting the skills of individual players compared to others. If a player has certain skills, he will repeat them from season to season. For example, if a player is a home run hitter, he generally continues to be a home run hitter from season to season. Similarly with defense. If a player has a good throwing arm, he will generally have a good throwing arm from season to season. If our methods reflect this skill, it should show in the numbers and should generally repeat from season to season.

Jeff Francouer has a good throwing arm. By our methods, he has the best throwing arm among all right fielders in baseball. If our methods work, and Francouer is generally consistent, we should see a pattern of positive numbers in his OF Arm Runs Saved from year to year. In fact we do. His annual totals of runs saved due to his throwing arm from 2006 to 2011 are: 3, 10, 2, 4, 8, 5. Every year he has a positive number of runs saved. That's a total of 32 runs saved in the last six years, the best in baseball.

Showing that the best player is consistent is nice, but it's not enough. We need to see consistency when looking at all players. How do we do this? We can use a mathematical technique called correlation coefficients. Correlation coefficients run from 0.00 to 1.00 with 0.00 being no correlation and 1.00 be a perfect correlation. (Actually, they run from -1.00 to 1.00 with -1.00 being an exact opposite correlation, but we're not really going to have many of those here.) Using just one player, Jeff Francouer, if he had totals of 5, 5, 5, 5, 5, 5 for the six seasons, that would be a 1.00 correlation. But no one does that. No one is that consistent.

In short, we are looking for coefficients above zero to determine correlation, the more above zero the better. We made our standard a bit higher because we decided to do even-odd correlations. Sounds like even more complication, but it's easier than it sounds. Because a given factor like an injury between two consecutive seasons or reduced playing team between two consecutive seasons can artificially improve the correlation, we are going to only compare totals from even-numbered years with totals from odd-numbered years. For Francouer, we are comparing his OF Arm Runs Saved total in his even-numbered seasons to his total in odd-numbered seasons:

2006	3 runs
2008	2 runs
2010	8 runs
Even Season Total:	13 runs
2007	10 runs
2009	4 runs
2011	5 runs
Odd Season Total:	19 runs

For each of our methods we take about 50-100 regular players over the past six seasons and look for correlation. We expect that the players who have high totals in even seasons will also have high totals in odd seasons; similarly, players with negative totals in even seasons are expected to repeat their poor defense in odd seasons. The correlation coefficient tells us how well the two sets match up.

Now that I've set the stage for you with this introduction, let me waste no more of your time and get to the list.

The Top Ten List of our Best Defensive Evaluation Methods are:

Number Ten

Air Plus/Minus for Infielders – Correlation 0.31

In his old abstracts Bill James used to rave about Kansas City second baseman Frank White. At the time he had no way of measuring it, but he assured us that no other infielder covered more ground tracking down balls hit in the air than White. Today's counterpart to White is Ian Kinsler. He is the best second baseman in baseball tracking down balls hit in the air. His season by season Air Plus/Minus totals are +6, +3, -2, +7, +10, and +7.

The correlation coefficient for this, our 10th best method (or the worst method, depending on how you want to say it) is 0.31. That's not bad. I'm a bit surprised it came out that well. Here it is by position:

Air Plus/Minus Correlation Coefficients

Position	Correlation
First Base	-0.07
Second Base	0.50
Third Base	0.11
Shortstop	0.18

The correlation for second basemen jumps up to 0.50. It really appears that we're measuring a skill here. Not so much for first basemen. It's even negative. We'll need to see more data over the years to see if this gets any better. Our third base and shortstop correlations are pretty low as well.

Number Nine

Bunt Runs Saved – Correlation 0.31

How well are we doing on measuring a defender's ability to handle bunts? About the same as evaluating their ability to handle pop-ups. A 0.31 correlation coefficient. Once again, not bad. Here it is by position:

Bunt Runs Saved Correlation Coefficients

Position	Correlation
Pitcher	0.45
Catcher	0.40
First Base	0.41
Third Base	0.11

I'm a bit surprised by how low the correlation coefficient is for third basemen fielding bunts (0.11). I would have expected that one to be the highest.

The best player fielding bunts has been Adrian Gonzalez with a total of 10 Bunt Runs Saved in the last five years.

Number Eight

GDP Runs Saved – Correlation 0.35

The two positions break out like this:

GDP Runs Saved Correlation Coefficients

Position	Correlation
Second Base	0.42
Shortstop	0.36

Second basemen are showing a bit more consistency. While this may simply be a statistical variation, it does make sense because making a pivot is a harder play for a second baseman than a shortstop. The second base pivot is something we measure and is a skill that certain players exhibit more than others.

The best player over the last six years on the double play is Ian Kinsler. He has saved his teams 14 runs with his ability to both start and turn the double play.

Number Seven

Catcher Stolen Base Runs Saved – Correlation 0.37

This is a stat that we are confident we are measuring well. As we show the correlation of each method, we are really measuring two things: 1) how well the stat works, and 2) how consistent the players are at that skill from year to year. In this case where we think we are measuring well, the reason the correlation isn't higher is simply that catchers vary quite a bit from year to year. For example, the most consistent catcher throwing out runners in the last several years has been Yadier Molina. Yet, in 2011 he was below average and had his worst season with a 25 percent caught stealing rate. Nevertheless, Yadier remains the best catcher throwing out baserunners (and the best at holding more than his share of runners at first base due to their fear of his arm). His throwing has saved the Cardinals 42 runs over his eight-year career.

Number Six

Catcher Adjusted Earned Runs Saved – Correlation 0.43

Can you measure how well a catcher calls a game? Can one catcher help save runs in this area compared to another catcher? Can he help a pitcher have a lower ERA when he's catching than when another catcher is catching?

I am so excited about this one. The correlation of 0.43 really means we're measuring something real here. The correlation shows that good catchers are generally good from year to year in terms of how many runs they saved for their pitchers. And the bad catchers are bad. One thing that really stands out is that this correlation is higher than the correlation for catcher throwing arms (0.43 vs. 0.37). That's an implication that we are doing better measuring a catcher's ability to call a game than we are measuring his ability to throw out baserunners. Even if this is not quite true, the fact that we're anywhere close is fantastic.

Here is a list of all the catchers we studied to come up with this correlation:

Player	Odd Years	Even Years	Total Adjusted Earned Runs Saved
Jason Kendall	8	6	14
Joe Mauer	10	4	14
Jose Molina	4	9	13
Jason Varitek	8	4	12
Ronny Paulino	3	9	12
Jeff Mathis	7	4	11
A.J. Pierzynski	6	4	10
Matt Wieters	10	0	10
Ryan Hanigan	4	6	10

Player	Odd Years	Even Years	Total Adjusted Earned Runs Saved
Brad Ausmus	4	5	9
Carlos Ruiz	3	5	8
Russell Martin	8	0	8
David Ross	4	2	6
Matt Treanor	4	2	6
Miguel Montero	7	-1	6
Rod Barajas	0	5	5
Gerald Laird	-2	7	5
Jesus Flores	3	2	5
Chris Snyder	3	2	5
Yadier Molina	0	5	5
Yorvit Torrealba	1	2	3
Humberto Quintero	2	1	3
Chris Iannetta	3	0	3
Jason LaRue	0	1	1
Ramon Castro	0	1	1
Johnny Estrada	0	1	1
Wil Nieves	0	1	1
Geovany Soto	-3	4	1
Paul Bako	0	0	0
Ivan Rodriguez	0	0	0
Ryan Doumit	-1	1	0
Alex Avila	2	-2	0
Dioner Navarro	1	-2	-1
Lou Marson	0	-1	-1
Kurt Suzuki	-10	9	-1
Josh Bard	2	-4	-2
Miguel Olivo	-4	2	-2
Nick Hundley	4	-6	-2
Brian McCann	-5	3	-2
Gregg Zaun	3	-6	-3
Bengie Molina	-3	-1	-4
Mike Redmond	-3	-1	-4
Michael Barrett	-5	1	-4
Kelly Shoppach	0	-4	-4
John Baker	-3	-1	-4
Paul LoDuca	0	-5	-5
Henry Blanco	-6	-2	-8
John Buck	-4	-5	-9
Mike Napoli	-2	-9	-11
Ramon Hernandez	-4	-10	-14
Brian Schneider	-6	-10	-16
Jorge Posada	-11	-6	-17
Victor Martinez	-11	-11	-22
Kenji Johjima	-14	-9	-23

Look at the names at the top of the list. These are the guys who are really helping their pitchers by calling a good game. If you gave this list to major league managers and coaches I think they would tell you that it really looks reasonable. Jason Varitek, Jose Molina, Joe Mauer, A.J. Pierzynski, Jeff Mathis – they have all been known for calling good games. The bottom of the list: a lot of these guys are no surprise – like Kenji Johjima,

Victor Martinez, Jorge Posada. Henry Blanco might be a surprise, but that's what makes this interesting and informative. The numbers are showing that he has not done well calling games.

Number Five

Good Plays/Misplays Runs Saved – Correlation 0.48

This is our newest method. We calculated this for every player going back to 2003. We're very happy with the 0.48 correlation for a new method. There are so many elements involved it's good to see it come out well. This is the only method we use that applies to all nine positions. Here are the correlations by position:

Good Play/Misplay Runs Saved Correlation Coefficients

Position	Correlation
Pitcher	0.22
Catcher	0.65
First Base	0.64
Second Base	0.42
Third Base	0.23
Shortstop	0.33
Left Field	0.30
Center Field	0.08
Right Field	0.61

I was excited about Catcher Adjusted ERA Runs Saved. I'm even more excited with how this comes out for measuring catchers and their run impact on Good Plays and Misplays. Six years ago we had no clue how to measure catchers. Now we've made a lot of progress. For the very first time, by combining our various measures for catchers, we can measure catcher defense. Very, very cool.

The correlation for center fielders didn't come out very good (0.08). Surprising. We'll have to look further into this one.

Overall, the best player on Misplays/Good Plays is Jeff Mathis with 23 runs saved in the last six years.

Number Four

Outfield Arm Runs Saved – Correlation 0.57

I expected this one to come out pretty good. An outfielder's ability to throw out runners and the fear he induces in them preventing them from trying is a real thing. I think our method to measure this is good, and we improved on it for this volume. Here it is by position:

Outfield Arm Runs Saved Correlation Coefficients

Position	Correlation
Left Field	0.33
Center Field	0.57
Right Field	0.80

Our technique for right fielders really comes out well. As mentioned above, Jeff Francouer is the best we've measured.

Number Three

Basic Plus/Minus – Correlation 0.61

This is the method we first introduced and remains the most comprehensive and the most important method we have. We updated it this year incorporating our batted ball timer. The correlation of 0.61 is good. Here it is by position:

Basic Plus/Minus Correlation Coefficients

Position	Correlation
Pitcher	0.57
First Base	0.65
Second Base	0.52
Third Base	0.76
Shortstop	0.63
Left Field	0.60
Center Field	0.48
Right Field	0.67

The best player has been Adrian Beltre at +122 since 2006. He has made 122 more plays than the average third baseman in that time. Wow.

Number Two

Plus/Minus Runs Saved – Correlation 0.61

This is very similar to Number Three but we gave it two places on this list because it's so important. Here is the correlation for Plus/Minus Runs Saved by position:

Plus/Minus Runs Saved Correlation Coefficients

Position	Correlation
Pitcher	0.58
First Base	0.61
Second Base	0.58
Third Base	0.79
Shortstop	0.64
Left Field	0.54
Center Field	0.51
Right Field	0.64

As with Basic Plus/Minus, the best player has been Adrian Beltre at 96 Plus/Minus Runs Saved.

And the Number One Method for Evaluating Defense is:

Pitchers Stolen Base Runs Saved – Correlation 0.68

The best method we have measures a pitcher's control of the running game. Three years ago we introduced this method saying that the pitcher has more control of the running game than the catcher. This method is the best method while the catcher method regarding the catcher's control of the running game comes in sixth. While that may mean we're not measuring catchers very well, I don't think so. I think we are measuring catchers well. The variation in catchers, as I mentioned above, is their own variation. The fact that the pitchers' method comes in better is encouraging.

The pitcher with the best control of the running game over the last six years has been Mark Buehrle at 24 Runs Saved.

Adding all eight Runs Saved components together, Defensive Runs Saved as a whole correlates at .59 across all positions. The strongest correlations are in the infield, while the weakest correlations are at center field and catcher.

Defensive Runs Saved Correlation Coefficients

Position	Correlation
Pitcher	0.74
Catcher	0.45
First Base	0.68
Second Base	0.58
Third Base	0.78
Shortstop	0.65
Left Field	0.50
Center Field	0.29
Right Field	0.63

Do We Need Defensive Park Factors?

Many Orioles fans have been puzzled by the lack of love defensive metrics show outfielders Adam Jones and Nick Markakis. After all, both have won Gold Gloves in the past three years, though they've never finished higher than 15th and 7th, respectively, in Fielding Bible Award voting during that time frame.

When digging deeper, some have wondered if defensive metrics have some sort of park bias that works against Jones and Markakis. Let's look at their basic Plus/Minus numbers (plays made above or below-average) at home and on the road:

Basic Plus/Minus
Home and Road

Year	Nick Markakis, RF		Adam Jones, CF	
	Home	Road	Home	Road
2006	-1	+2	-	-
2007	-9	+3	-	-
2008	+1	+6	+6	-1
2009	-7	+1	-11	-2
2010	-9	-3	-8	-1
2011	-4	-2	-7	0
Total	-29	+7	-20	-4

Both players have regularly performed worse at home than on the road. Jones and Markakis have combined to be 49 plays below-average at home but 3 plays above-average on the road. The Ultimate Zone Rating system (UZR), which also relies on the detailed batted ball tracking information from Baseball Info Solutions, shows similar results.

Do we have some form of measurement bias in the works, or have Jones and Markakis legitimately performed better on the road?

Baseball Info Solutions addresses many forms of potential bias by rotating scorers through different parks. While some data collection efforts rely on stringers located at the park, BIS records data from video streams and rotates scorers daily. As a result, any slight tendencies of individual video scouts are evened out across all teams and ballparks over the course of the season. (BIS data collection is discussed in greater detail on page 435.)

The most unique trait about the playing field at Camden Yards is the 25-foot wall featuring the out-of-town scoreboard in right field. That park effect is eliminated in the Plus/Minus System (and the UZR system, as we understand it) by excluding any batted ball that is unfieldable because it hit high off the wall. Additionally, the UZR system has explicit park factors applied on groundballs and flyballs. We would expect these park factors to handle potential data biases; however, UZR shows similar home/road splits for Jones and Markakis.

This could simply be a statistical anomaly indicative of nothing more than random variation. For example, take David Ortiz from 2004 through 2006. He led Major League Baseball in road home runs every one of those years, hitting 24 more home runs on the road than at home. For the rest of his career in Boston, his home-road totals are basically even.

Let's look further.

Other Oriole Outfielders in Camden

Jones and Markakis have played a substantial number of innings at Camden Yards (about 6,700). Having made 52 more plays on the road than at home is significant. But if you look at all other Orioles outfielders who have played in Camden, in about twice as many innings, you don't have the same effect. All other Orioles outfielders in Camden Yards since 2003 have actually been a little better at home than on the road, opposite of what Jones and Markakis have done. They have made one fewer play than average at home, and eight fewer plays on the road. It's as we would expect for outfielders in general: they are about the same at home as on the road.

Opponent Outfielders in Camden

Jones and Markakis have played together since 2008. Let's look at all Orioles opponents since then, specifically comparing how their outfielders fare at Camden and at their home ballpark.

Orioles Opponents Outfield Plus/Minus

	Camden Yards	Other
2008	-9	-3
2009	-9	-2
2010	-8	-1
2011	-9	+1
Total	-35	-4

We do see a fairly consistent gap of 6-10 plays per season and a 31-play gap over four seasons.

However, it's interesting to note that teams appear to play better defense at home than on the road. Since 2005, teams have been about +900 plays above expected on groundballs at home and -900 on groundballs on the road. This difference amounts to about +4 plays per team per season at home and -4 plays on the road. Split among four infielders plus the pitcher, this is not quite +1 play per season. On outfield flyballs, teams average about +1 at home and -1 on the road, per season. Call it a home-field advantage, sleeping in your own bed, eating home-cooked meals or whatever you like.

We would expect Orioles opponents to play about eight plays worse over four seasons at Camden Yards compared to their home ballparks. However, this doesn't explain the 31-play gap seen by Oriole opponents. Plus, the concept that players play better defense at home is foreign to Markakis and Jones. They've done the opposite. Is this all a statistical fluke or is there something specific going on at Camden Yards?

For me personally, I have a hard time believing numbers unless there is a good underlying reason for what those numbers are saying. These numbers, though not a large sample size, are suggesting that batted balls in Camden Yards are more difficult to handle than those in other parks, even after taking into account where the ball is hit, how hard it was hit, the trajectory of the ball and whether it hit the wall. We are holding all these things constant. So is it real, or is it sample size? I can't think of an underlying reason for it to be real, but that doesn't mean it's not.

Groundball and Flyball Park Factors

We can go one step further by calculating actual groundball and flyball park factors. To do so, we added together the total number of plays made by the Orioles and their opponents at Camden Yards, then divided by the expected number of plays made by both teams at Camden Yards. We repeat the calculation for both teams in Orioles road games, then divide the former by the latter. Let's walk through this example with the actual numbers.

In 2011, the Plus/Minus System estimated that the Orioles were expected to make 767 plays on balls in the air (line drives, fliners and flyballs, both infield and outfield) at Camden Yards. They actually made 755 plays (-12 Plus/Minus rating). During Orioles road games, Baltimore defenders made 672 plays compared to an expected 686 (-14). The Orioles were two plays better at Camden. That makes the park factor for just the Orioles' players 1.004 (rounded to 1.00). The calculation is:

Oriole Player Park Factor = Actual to Expected at Home Divided by Actual to Expected on the Road

Actual to Expected at Home is 755/767 = .984

Actual to Expected on the Road is 672/686 = .980

Oriole Player Park Factor = .984/.980=1.004

Going back to games at Camden, Orioles opponents caught 676 flies and liners compared to an expected 686 (-10). During Orioles road games, their opponents made 723 plays, one more than expected (+1 plus/minus). Oriole opponent outfielders were 11 plays worse at Camden. The park factor for just the Orioles' opponents in Camden is .984 (rounded to .98).

We combine these two park factors of 1.00 and .98.

We could just average them, but we want to take into account the fact that one team may have more balls in the air to handle. Here is how the calculation works to get the complete park factor:

$$[(755 + 676)/(767 + 686)] / [(672 + 723)/(686 + 722)] = 0.99 \text{ (rounded)}$$

The 2011 Camden Yards Plus/Minus park factor on line drives and flyballs was 0.99. In other words, the Orioles and their opponents made about 1 percent fewer plays at home than on the road. At most, this amounts to about a couple of plays per season per position.

We can repeat this process for groundballs, as well as for every team for every season. We went back to 2005 (seven seasons) for this study.

There were 25 ballparks which were active all seven seasons. Out of those 25 parks, Camden Yards had the fifth-lowest flyball park factor. The lowest was Boston's Fenway Park.

**Five Lowest Flyball Plus/Minus Park Factors
2005-11**

Team	Flyball Park Factor
Red Sox	0.98
Cubs	0.98
Royals	0.99
Reds	0.99
Orioles	0.99

As we mentioned earlier, the Plus/Minus System removes all flyballs which bounce unreachably high off the outfield wall. We began recording this "wall ball" information in 2007. Here's the year-by-year park factors for Fenway:

Fenway Park Flyball Plus/Minus Park Factor

Season	Flyball Park Factor
2005	0.96
2006	0.96
2007	0.96
2008	1.00
2009	0.98
2010	1.00
2011	1.00

As you can see, the park factor almost disappears shortly after we began removing unreachable wall balls

from the Plus/Minus System.

At the other end of the spectrum, we see Milwaukee's Miller Park with the largest flyball Plus/Minus park effect:

**Five Lowest Flyball Plus/Minus Park Factors
2005-11**

Team	Flyball Park Factor
Brewers	1.02
Padres	1.02
Blue Jays	1.02
Indians	1.01
Athletics	1.01

Split between outfielders and infielders, this largest park effect may amount to just a couple plays per season. However, as we saw with Adam Jones and Nick Markakis, playing better or worse at home, even over several seasons, doesn't necessarily mean there's something to it.

We noticed that the more seasons we included, the smaller the range from the highest to lowest park factors. We initially studied 2008-11, and the range was about twice what it is going back to 2005. This suggests that the more years we use, the less statistical fluctuation there is. In other words, there is a lot of random variation in the numbers that doesn't even out over four seasons. Even including seven seasons as we've done here won't eliminate all of the variation. More than likely, true park factors are less extreme than suggested by seven years of data.

With that in mind, let's take a look at the groundball park factors:

**Five Highest Groundball Plus/Minus Park Factors
2005-11**

Team	Groundball Park Factor
Padres	1.02
Athletics	1.02
Dodgers	1.01
Blue Jays	1.01
Red Sox	1.01

We were wondering if the two remaining parks with artificial surfaces would show up at the top. Only the Blue Jays made the top five. Tampa's Tropicana Field, home of the Rays, ranked 18th out of 25 parks at 0.99.

**Five Lowest Groundball Plus/Minus Park Factors
2005-11**

Team	Groundball Park Factor
Marlins	0.97
Tigers	0.98
Brewers	0.98
Mariners	0.99
Phillies	0.99

For these seven years, the Marlins shared a park with the Miami Dolphins; perhaps the field conditions were poor year-round and affected their play. If this is true, that would suggest this is a true park factor, not a random variation—that it is harder to make plays despite the fact that we already account for the speed and direction of the groundball. But this could still be random variation.

Splitting these affected plays across five infielders (including the pitcher) suggests an impact of four plays per position per season. Of course, the Marlins are moving to a new, baseball-only stadium in 2012; perhaps their defensive numbers going forward will tell us how much their previous park was hurting them, if at all.

Conclusions

We've investigated differences in defensive play between parks and found them to be relatively small. With the most extreme parks, the observed effect amounts to at most five plays per season; Orioles outfielders Jones and Markakis are affected even less, demonstrating that their home/road splits are largely due to legitimately weaker play at Camden Yards. We also found that other inexplicable and unpredictable factors are greatly obscuring true park effects, making it difficult to tell exactly how much each ballpark affects defensive play.

Nevertheless, we did find a couple of things that could justify using adjustments to our defensive analytics:

1) There is some indication that players play better defense at home than on the road. A home/road adjustment might be worth considering.

2) From the Marlins' park factor, it is possible to speculate that the condition of the playing surface can affect how difficult it is to make a play at a given park. Some parks might justify a park factor.

This study suggests that further research will be needed to determine whether these observed effects are true differences or random variation due to sample-size. But even if they are true differences, we have seen that the effects are small, especially after we've reviewed more and more seasons of data to minimize the sample-size problem.

To answer the title question of this article: No, we don't *need* defensive park factors. If we research it further, it is possible that properly applied park factors might affect a player's plus/minus number by one or two plays. But for now we are content with our conclusion that our "Manny Adjustment" for wall balls accounts for the most important element and that otherwise the effect is minimal.

Defensive Sabermetrics vs. Conventional Wisdom

There are players whose advanced statistical numbers don't match even the most trained eyes. While coaches, scouts, the media and/or fans might have one opinion of a player, the numbers don't always agree. Sometimes, the numbers are missing something; we'll be the first to admit that. As much progress as we like to think we've made in the past decade with defensive statistics, we have a long way to go before we're satisfied. However, the numbers can frequently tell us things that our eyes don't always catch.

In this section, we're tackling some of the most controversial defenders in baseball. We're going to break down each one to give you our best explanations for the contrasting opinions. We aren't expecting to convince every one of you that our numbers are right; we do hope that by the time you finish this article you will have learned something.

We'll go down the defensive spectrum one position at a time, starting with catchers and finishing with first basemen. We also tacked a couple pitchers on at the end for good measure.

Catchers

Jason Varitek gets a lot of negative publicity for his glass arm, especially in recent years, and many people, Red Sox fans included, are ready to see him retire. However, the numbers show us that the veteran backstop has more than compensated for his poor arm with his handling of the pitching staff and pitch blocking abilities.

His catcher-block percentage [catcher blocks / (catcher blocks + wild pitch misplays)] over 2009-11 was fourth among regular catchers, and he saved the second-most runs as a result of saving wild pitches and passed balls.

A.J. Pierzynski is one of those polarizing players that you love if he's on your team and hate if he's not. Chances are, your opinion of his defense is probably the same. Many people cite his superb pitcher-handling skills, but our Adjusted Earned Runs system gives him just three runs of credit in that department. He's been inconsistent deterring the opposing running game, and his agility on bunts is nothing newsworthy. However, our Good Plays/Misplays data shows us that Pierzynski has cost the White Sox more runs on wild pitches than any other catcher in baseball over the last three seasons, and his catcher-block percentage tops only Alex Avila's. His overall defensive value is firmly in the below-average range, according to our numbers.

Shortstops

Derek Jeter has been the favorite whipping boy of defensive metrics for the past decade, but we can't resist. For more beating of a dead horse, check out the comparison of Jeter and Brendan Ryan on page 57.

Erick Aybar emerged as the new American League Gold Glove winner at the position in 2011, though he's never finished above fourth in the Fielding Bible Award voting. Aybar doesn't make a lot of errors, turns a lot of double plays, and makes a lot of Good Fielding Plays according to BIS Video Scouts. The Plus/Minus System, however, sees him as an average shortstop, saving seven runs in 2010 but losing four in 2011.

Center Fielders

Matt Kemp has won two Gold Gloves in the past three seasons. The case against him is made on page 73.

Adam Jones is similarly controversial. Our Outfield Arms Runs Saved agrees that Jones has a fantastic arm and excels throwing out baserunners. However, the Plus/Minus System is not at all fond of his range in the outfield. Jones has done well on shallow-hit balls. He has saved about 10 bases above average on shallow catches over his career. But he's lost an estimated 50 bases on deeply hit balls.

Adam Jones Shallow, Medium and Deep Plus/Minus

Season	Innings	Shallow	Medium	Deep
2006	193	-2	0	1
2007	34	0	0	3
2008	1102	5	7	-5
2009	1005	4	-4	-25
2010	1298	-1	-16	-5
2011	1281	4	-6	-19
Total	4913	10	-19	-50

According to the numbers, Chris Young is one of the more underrated center fielders in the game. He doesn't have a good arm and consequently doesn't gun down opposing baserunners, which costs him a couple runs each year. However, his 41 Plus/Minus Runs Saved over the past three seasons tops all center fielders. The polar opposite of Adam Jones, Young is willing to sacrifice a few shallow-hit singles for a few catches in the deep gaps.

Chris Young Shallow, Medium and Deep Plus/Minus

Season	Innings	Shallow	Medium	Deep
2006	149	1	1	3
2007	1263	2	6	-10
2008	1390	-5	9	15
2009	1020	-4	-2	12
2010	1350	0	-1	29
2011	1373	2	10	27
Total	6546	-4	23	76

Second Basemen

In *The Fielding Bible—Volume II*, we compared the flashy style of Brandon Phillips with the ultra-positioning of Chase Utley. Three years and two more Phillips Gold Gloves later, the comparison is still valid.

Phillips certainly catches your attention; he leads all second basemen with 185 Good Fielding Plays over the past three years. The Plus/Minus System agrees, to an extent, with 12 Plus/Minus Runs Saved over the last three seasons. We gave him eight additional runs for his Good Fielding Plays and (lack of) Defensive Misplays. After subtracting two runs for a below-average performance turning double plays, Phillips winds up with 18 Runs Saved from 2009-11.

Utley, however, bests him in the Plus/Minus System. Both have higher Plus/Minus scores to their right (Utley's total is a little better), they make the plays straight on (Utley is a little better), and relatively struggle to their left in the hole (Phillips is a little better). Outside of groundballs, Utley fields more line drives and flyballs. The Plus/Minus System estimated Phillips made three fewer plays than an average second baseman on balls in the air, while Utley made ten more plays than average. Utley's positioning leaves him in the right place to snag line drives that others would have no shot at.

A small edge on groundballs and double plays, along with a decent edge on line drives and flies, gives Utley an 18-run advantage on Phillips over the past three seasons.

Third Basemen

David Wright won Gold Gloves in 2007 and 2008 though his advanced defensive numbers never quite supported the claim. In his best Defensive Runs Saved season, his 13 Runs Saved tied him with Scott Rolen for third in the National League, trailing both Ryan Zimmerman and Pedro Feliz, that season's Fielding Bible Award winner. Hampered by injuries in recent years, Wright has fallen off a cliff defensively, and the 34 runs he has cost the Mets compared to an average third baseman over 2009-11 was the second-lowest in baseball.

Breaking down his Plus/Minus numbers, we see a relative strength towards the hole but a glaring weakness toward Wright's right. The Plus/Minus System estimates he's made 65 fewer plays on grounders to his right compared to an average third baseman. Unfortunately, these grounders down the line often go into the corner for doubles, as opposed to the singles he saves going to his left.

David Wright's Plus/Minus Breakdown

Season	Innings	Left	Middle	Right
2004	604	-2	14	-2
2005	1404	0	2	-14
2006	1365	8	-6	-10
2007	1418	18	9	-11
2008	1433	1	6	-2
2009	1232	-2	0	-6
2010	1373	-1	0	-15
2011	894	8	-3	-5
Total	9724	30	22	-65

After Pablo Sandoval's rookie season, many wondered if he'd be able to hit well enough to stay in the majors after an inevitable move to first base. The Kung Fu Panda, as he is affectionately known, never struggled as badly according to Defensive Runs Saved. We estimate that he cost the Giants 11 runs defensively in 2009—certainly not what you hope for but not quite as bad as the worst defenders in the league. We estimate that he improved to the average third baseman level with one Run Saved in his offensively disappointing 2010 season.

Much was made of his weight loss and better conditioning heading into 2011, and the Panda took his defensive game to another level. We estimate that he saved the Giants 15 runs with his glove, most of it going to his right towards the third base foul line. If the offensive and defensive improvement is legitimate, the still-young Sandoval could have many productive years remaining at the hot corner.

Right Fielders

Justin Upton doesn't have a good arm (-11 Runs Saved since 2009) and makes more Defensive Misplays and Errors than any other right fielder (costing him 11 more runs since 2009); however, like his teammate Chris Young, he more than compensates by robbing extra base hits on deep-hit balls. His 36 Plus/Minus Runs Saved since 2009 trails only Jason Heyward among right fielders. In fact, Fielding Bible Award voters were willing to overlook his shortcomings and elect him the best defensive right fielder in baseball in 2011.

Nick Markakis and Andre Ethier won the right field Gold Glove in 2011, presumably because they were the only regular right fielders who didn't make an error all season. Unfortunately, there's more to good defense than avoiding errors, especially in the outfield. While Ethier rates below-average according to Runs Saved in every aspect of outfield defense, Markakis has thrown out the third-most baserunners over the past three seasons. He's also played more innings in the field than any other right fielder during that span. While durability is a good thing, it also means that we have to put his baserunner kills into perspective. His above-average arm doesn't make up for the estimated 24 runs he's cost the Orioles with his lack of range since 2009.

Left Fielders

When Alex Gordon was handed the 2011 Gold Glove over Brett Gardner, we were pretty upset. In retrospect, the Royals' converted third baseman did have a pretty good season. Gordon had 20 outfield assists, 12 of them unassisted kills, leading the American League by a wide margin: Gardner's 7 assists and 5 kills were second. We estimate this gap as about 10 runs.

However, Gardner's range overcomes Gordon's 10-run head start. We estimate that Gardner saved 35 runs with his range in left field (20 in 2011 alone). Gordon's range looked a little better when we implemented the new Timer Plus/Minus System, but his eight runs (five in 2011) just can't touch Gardner's. Gardner, a two-time Fielding Bible Award winner, was likely the best choice.

First Basemen

Four-time Gold Glove winner Mark Teixeira trails only Albert Pujols in Good Fielding Plays over the past three seasons. Many have cited his ability to scoop low throws in the dirt as a vital part of the Yankees' defensive improvement in recent seasons. While Teixeira was regarded as a much better handler of throws than his predecessor Jason Giambi, we debunked that myth in a Stat of the Week. Teixeira is at least an average scooper, but Giambi actually scooped a higher percentage of bad throws with the Yankees.

Additionally, while the Plus/Minus System estimates that he makes more plays than the average first baseman (it especially likes his range to his right), it doesn't see him as other-wordly as his reputation would suggest. The Defensive Runs Saved System estimates he's saved the Yankees 11 runs during his three years in New York, good for tenth among first basemen.

Daric Barton, on the other hand, is the only first baseman to unseat Albert Pujols' grasp on the Fielding Bible Award, albeit for one season only (2010). The Plus/Minus System likes Barton's range in all directions. The only thing holding him back is his bat; he hasn't hit well enough to stay in the lineup and on the field.

Pitchers

Pitchers don't usually earn a bad defensive reputation, but there are a few who deserve it. John Lackey and Tommy Hanson can't control the running game, while Tim Lincecum and Brad Penny can't field the position. Ervin Santana is the king, however, since he can't do either. This has cost him an estimated five runs per season since 2009.

Here's a fun game you can play once the World Series is over and you're waiting for the awards announcements.

Go to your favorite baseball statistics website. I'd recommend Fangraphs or Baseball-Reference. Find the National League pitcher fielding statistics section for the most-recent season. Sort the list of pitchers according to innings in descending order. Now, go down the list until you find one with a perfect 1.000 fielding percentage.

There's your new NL Gold Glove winner.

We tried this during the week of the Gold Glove announcements in 2009. When Adam Wainwright took home the trophy later that week, we laughed a little but didn't think much about it.

In 2010, we tried the same trick but faced a dilemma. Both Bronson Arroyo and Randy Wolf had 1.000 fielding percentages in the same number of innings. Arroyo seemed like the more popular guy, so we went with him. Sure enough, Arroyo won the award. Two for two.

In 2011, the technique pointed to Clayton Kershaw. Three for three.

Not that any of these are bad selections; they're perfectly fine, maybe even good choices. Our Defensive Runs Saved System likes how Clayton Kershaw shuts down the running game, but it likes how Zack Greinke holds baserunners and fields his position. We like how Arroyo fields his position, but we really like how Jake Westbrook generates groundballs and gobbles them up with relative ease.

In the American League, Mark Buehrle's reputation as a highlight-reel fielder (how often do you get to say that?!?) and pickoff champion has locked up the Gold Glove since Kenny Rogers retired. With Buehrle moving to the National League, however, the AL award is up for grabs. I bet we can predict how that's going to turn out.

Why We Need Advanced Defensive Metrics

Mitchel Lichtman

Why do we need advanced defensive metrics, and how do we know that they "work?" Scouts, managers, coaches, and even fans and the media, have been evaluating defensive skills and performance for over 100 years. Presumably, they've been doing a pretty good job of it. Is there any doubt that players like Willie Mays, Bill Mazeroski, Brooks Robinson, Ozzie Smith, and more recently Peter Bourjos and Adrian Beltre (among others of course) were or are defensive wizards, and that the likes of Harmon Killebrew, "Marvelous" Marv Throneberry, Manny Ramirez, and Adam Dunn (at least in the outfield) were or are severe defensive liabilities? What can Ultimate Zone Rating (UZR) and Defensive Runs Saved offer that baseball insiders, from scouting and observation, cannot?

Bill James once said (I am loosely paraphrasing) that a good baseball statistic should surprise you some significant (but not too great) percentage of the time, otherwise, "What's the point?" In other words, while to some extent a quality metric should confirm what you already know, it also should be able to "see" that which the human eye and brain cannot, as well as correct the biases and subjectivities that limit human beings in their ability to make accurate judgments and evaluations.

In that respect, Derek Jeter wins multiple Gold Gloves while advanced defensive metrics consistently rate him as a poor defender. In fact, if you Google "undeserved gold gloves" and "Jeter," you get 30,300 hits. On the flip side, Adam Everett in his prime was a darling of advanced defensive metrics, yet he's won exactly zero Gold Glove awards (although admittedly he is considered a good defensive shortstop—he must be, considering his poor offensive skills). He was recognized by a panel of numbers-savvy experts with the inagural shortstop Fielding Bible Award in 2006.

Similarly, players like Ken Griffey, Jr., Bernie Williams, and Steve Finley were traditionally considered to be good to excellent defenders, yet UZR rated them as bad to awful for at least several years before their retirements.

Then there are players who, for various reasons, were generally not considered plus defenders by MLB insiders, yet were rated highly by advanced metrics. Among these were David Eckstein, Matt Holliday, Austin Kearns, and J.D. Drew. Interestingly, with more and more teams and the media accepting and embracing these new, advanced defensive stats, it is becoming more difficult to find large rifts between conventional and sabermetric defensive evaluation.

Advanced defensive metrics serve three important purposes besides highlighting potential "mistakes" in traditional defensive evaluation (in all fairness to scouts and their ilk, when an objective metric differs from a scout in its assessment of defense, the "truth" is likely somewhere in the middle—close to which end is a matter of an unresolved debate, and is largely player-dependent). One, they enable us to accurately quantify the run or win value of good or bad defense; two, they allow us to distinguish fielders on a more accurate and granular level than traditional defensive evaluation; and three, they provide a framework for comparing fielders at different positions.

If you were to ask an old-time scout or even a manager how many wins a particular defensive wizard saves over the course of a season, it wouldn't be unusual for their enthusiastic response to be, "five or six," or perhaps even "10." I'm sure it seems that way, with no real analytical framework to go by. One thing that play-by-play defensive analyses have taught us is that the range of theoretical wins (a theoretical win is around 10 theoretical runs, and a theoretical run is equal to a little over one successful fielding play that would normally be a hit) along the spectrum of a poor to a great fielder is only around two to four wins, depending on the position (more up the middle and less at the corners). In other words, a great shortstop like Adam Everett or Ozzie Smith in their prime can save a team 1.5 to 2 wins as compared to an average shortstop. A poorly skilled shortstop, like the current version of Yuniesky Betancourt, can cost his team on the order of 1 to 1.5 wins a season. In any given season, where a few great or terrible plays (essentially a "lucky" or "unlucky" performance) can make a large difference, those numbers may increase by 50 percent or so. A defensive wizard saving his team five or ten wins per season is both an illusion and a pipedream.

Basically, UZR, Defensive Runs Saved, and similar metrics can tell us (approximately, but more accurately than the human eye alone) not only whether a player is a good, great, poor or mediocre defender, but how much, in actual runs and wins, that player's performance was worth in any given time period, and how much we think that player's performance will be worth in the future. For example, most people would agree that Adam Dunn, Carlos Lee, Hideki Matsui, Bobby Abreu and Magglio Ordonez have little defensive value at a corner outfield position. But what does that mean in terms of runs and wins? How much offense would you have to gain or lose in order to put one or the other in left field or right field? I don't think a scout can answer that question very well. According to UZR, going into 2011, the respective corner outfield projections per 150 games for these five players were -14 runs (Dunn), -4 runs (Lee), -10 runs (Matsui), -14 runs (Abreu) and -8 runs (Ordonez). While all of these players have seen better days in the field (or never had a better day!), clearly, at least according to UZR, Lee is a much better defender, compared to Dunn, Matsui and Abreu, with Magglio somewhere in between. A 10 run, or one win, difference, as between Lee and Dunn or Abreu, is nothing to sneeze at!

On the plus side, what about highly touted defenders like Ian Kinsler, Chase Utley, Brandon Phillips, Mark Ellis and Dustin Pedroia at second base? Again, most MLB insiders would rate these players as "plus" fielders, however, if you asked 10 scouts to rank them, you would probably get 10 different lists. What did UZR say about their expected defensive value going into 2011? Kinsler was projected at +2 runs, Utley +10, Phillips +4, Ellis +1 and Pedroia +5. Defensive Runs Saved projected a similar range for these four players, from Utley at 14 Runs Saved to Kinsler and Phillips with 5. Again, while both systems like all of these players, the difference between Utley and Kinsler or Ellis is almost one win. Teams pay around five million dollars for a win on the free-agent market!

Finally, using the framework of advanced metrics and analyzing players who have played multiple positions at around the same time in their careers, we are able to fairly compare and quantify the relative value of two (or more) players at two different defensive positions or the same player at multiple positions. For example, let's say that we project Jason Werth as an average defender in right field. What would he be worth in center fielder? How would he compare, value-wise, to a center fielder like Shane Victorino, his former teammate, who was projected at -5 runs going into 2011? Using "positional adjustments" garnered from the aforementioned analyses of players who played multiple positions, we find that there is about a 10 run (per 150 games) difference between center field and either right field or left field. That is not to say that center fielder is inherently more "difficult" (some MLB players would say the opposite in fact). It is that the average center fielder is faster (in 2010, 12 of the 14 fastest players in MLB patrolled center fielder) and a more skillful fielder than the typical corner outfielder. That means that a league average right fielder, like Werth, would likely be 10 runs worse than average in center fielder, or 5 runs worse than Victorino. Similarly, we can use the following positional adjustments, per 150 games, to compare any fielder at any position, to any other fielder (or the same player) at any other position.

Catcher	+12.5 runs
Shortstop	+7.5 runs
Second Base	+2.5 runs
Third Base	+2.5 runs
Center Field	+2.5 runs
Left Field	-7.5 runs
Right Field	-7.5 runs
First Base	-12.5 runs
Designated Hitter	-17.5 runs

Of course, each position requires a certain set of unique skills, such that these "translations" do not apply to all players at all positions. The way to interpret the numbers is this: if a shortstop (+7.5) moves to third base, second base or even center field (all +2.5 runs), he is expected to gain 5 runs, 7.5 minus 2.5, in defensive value per 150 games—i.e. his UZR is expected to increase by 5. (Again, that number going from the IF to the OF, or vice versa, is not nearly as reliable as it is going from the infield to the infield or the outfield to the outfield.) Similarly, if a third baseman (+2.5), like Miguel Cabrera or Albert Pujols, moves to first base (-12.5), he is expected to gain a whopping 15 runs, at least after gaining some experience at the new position.

While catcher is a unique and difficult position, thus it is given a +12.5 "adjustment," it does not easily or frequently translate into another position and vice versa (just ask Mike Piazza). Similarly, the designated hitter is a "phantom" position, although typically it is occupied by a player with poor defensive skills at any position (think Jim Thome, David Ortiz or Frank Thomas). However, in order to be able to compare players at any and all defensive positions, every position must be assigned a reasonably accurate "positional adjustment," one of the many benefits of utilizing the framework of advanced defensive metrics.

Now we come to that final, all-important question: Since advanced defensive metrics are often "black boxes" (they use a methodology that is complex and difficult to understand), how do we know that they work? How do we know that Elvis Andrus is likely to provide almost a win per season worth of defensive value to the Rangers, or that Jeter is indeed worth almost a win less than the average MLB shortstop (and that they are two wins apart)?

There is a way that we can actually test the UZR values, using real, live runs, and not theoretical ones, as calculated by the complex and opaque UZR engine. Several years ago, my colleague and co-author Tom Tango invented a unique method of analysis called "Without and With You" (WOWY). Basically, he looks at the relevant results (for example, defense, as measured by the percentage of batted balls turned into outs) for a player when he is on the field versus when he is not on the field, controlling for things that likely influence those results, like the park, the pitcher, the batter and the base runners. In other words, if we want to evaluate someone's fielding, the most realistic and transparent way to do that is to compare what percentage of balls in play (in any part of the field) were fielded by that player as compared to all other players at the same position, given the same pitchers, batters, base runners and parks.

For example, in the *2008 Hardball Times Annual*, Tango computed a WOWY for Derek Jeter and other shortstops in order to "verify" whether Jeter was indeed a much below average shortstop as metrics like UZR and Defensive Runs Saved suggested. What Tango found was that when he controlled for the pitcher on the mound, the batter at the plate, the runners on base and the park, Jeter

consistently came out in the bottom of the pack, while shortstops like Rey Sanchez and Adam Everett typically came out on top. The only context in which Jeter fared "better than awful" (somewhere in the "bottom-middle" of the pack) was the park. In that case, Jeter checked in at "only" 18 plays per season worse than average (from 1993 to 2007).

When controlling for pitcher, batter, and base runners, Jeter fielded 38, 25 and 11 fewer plays per season than the average shortstop. Granted, Derek may have saved a few runs here and there from heads-up relay throws and the like, but it is clear from Tango's WOWY analysis that he simply makes many fewer plays than the average shortstop. From 2003 to 2007 UZR rated Jeter at around 12 plays per season below average, while the Plus/Minus system pegged him at about 24 plays below average. WOWY is a very nice method of analysis which suffers from few biases and is transparent and easy to understand—and it completely validates the advanced metrics' assessment of Jeter! Of course one accurate player evaluation does not a great system make!

In order to validate UZR across many players, I one-upped Tango's WOWY system. Rather than tracking the fraction of batted balls fielded by a particular position with and without a certain player on the field (at that position of course), I looked at the number of runs scored while a certain player was on the field and while he was not, also controlling for other relevant factors, like the opposing batters, the pitcher and the park. While runs scored per game is influenced by a lot more variables than percentage of balls fielded, and it is a much coarser measure that requires a larger sample size, it is also the ultimate in fielder evaluation. After all, when it comes to defensive evaluation, the one and only thing that most people care about is how many runs did such-and-such fielder cost or save his team when he was on the field as compared to when another player filled his shoes at the same position, given the same pitcher, batters and park. This kind of WOWY is similar to the *plus-minus* evaluation systems used in the NHL and more recently in the NBA.

So what does this kind of WOWY tell us about UZR? In other words, does UZR give us an accurate representation of how many actual runs a player saves or costs his team on a per game basis? For example, if a player is rated as a +8 defender per 150 games, does his team truly allow .05 (8/150) fewer runs per game than with an average fielder taking his place, everything else being equal?

In order to answer these questions, I looked at all

games from 2004 to 2010 and did a "runs allowed" WOWY controlling for pitcher, batter, park and home/away status for all players that fell into one of five categories:

1) Very good (>2 standard deviations (SD) in UZR rating—an average of +21 per 150 games)

2) Good (>1 SD and < 2 SD— an average of +15 per 150)

3) Neutral (Within plus or minus .5 SD—0 UZR)

4) Poor (>1 SD and < 2 SD—an average of -15 per 150)

5) Very poor (>2 SD—an average of -24 per 150)

Here are the expected runs allowed per game based on the average UZR of each group as compared to the actual runs allowed WOWY difference:

UZR Rating	Runs Allowed WOWY Difference	Average UZR for that Bucket per Game (per 150 games)
Good (>1 SD)	.14 per game	.10 (+15 UZR)
Bad (<1 SD)	-.09	-.10 (-15 UZR)
Neutral (+/- .5 SD)	.03	0
Very Good (>2 SD)	.43	.14 (+21)
Very Bad (<2 SD)	-.15	-.16 (-24)

As you can see, when UZR identified an excellent defender (0.14 fewer runs allowed per game), they did in fact save almost half a run per game, quite a bit more than UZR suggests. When UZR classified a fielder as good (saving 0.10 runs per game), that group allowed 0.14 runs per game less than the average fielder—a pretty good match. If anything, UZR is a conservative estimator of good or great fielders (perhaps due to something called "range bias"). For the other buckets, UZR and actual runs saved/cost are almost identical.

From this kind of WOWY analysis, it is clear that UZR and presumably other advanced metrics are very good approximations of how many runs/wins a particular fielder saves or costs his team on a per game or per season basis, based on the complex methodology and the batted ball and play-by-play data that fuels their calculations. Accurately quantifying a player's defensive value is an extremely important piece of information as it enables us to include defense in the total package of a player's value on the field. Without the "runs saved/cost" framework, it is difficult if not impossible to add together a player's defensive, offensive and base running value in order to get a complete picture of that player's worth. UZR or Defensive Runs Saved along with positional adjustments also allow us to compare the defensive value of players across the fielding spectrum as well as the total offensive, defensive and base running value of all players, whether they play a mean shortstop or a statuesque first base. In other words, advanced defensive metrics work!

Infield Defense on Groundballs

Chris Dial

There are always lots of questions concerning how things happen in baseball—how often does small ball pay off? Do runners move up on groundballs very often? Should a right-handed batter "take two and hit to right?" Is the groundball-in-play performance the same for left-handed batters and right-handed batters?

About twenty years ago I read a piece in the *Elias Baseball Analyst* about whether or not David Justice would ever learn to hit left-handers. The conclusion of their analysis on left-handed hitters' development over their careers was that he could improve his batting average, but he'll do so at the expense of power (slugging percentage). So what happens when left-handed batters face left-handed pitchers? We know left-handed batters struggle against left-handed pitchers, but can we learn more from play-by-play (PBP) data about how much a left-hander's batting performance is impacted just by pulling the ball on the ground?

The following information is from 2011, and one season isn't conclusive, but the sample size is significant (58,000 groundballs). It covers information such as batter and pitcher handedness, batted ball direction (vector), the fielding team and the ballpark, and an approximate batted ball speed (slow, medium, fast). It includes the first fielder that touched it. Errors are not identified as errors, simply "Not Out," but handled by an infielder. As a point of reference, the number of groundballs is approximately the same as the number on Baseball-Reference's 2011 MLB splits page.

Now let's get down to business.

Left Side Groundballs

We are going to look at a couple of questions specifically. What happens when a groundball is hit across the spectrum of the infield?

It is well documented that more errors occur on the left side of the infield (third base and shortstop). The shortstop and third baseman have longer throws and thus less time to recover from a bobble. The second baseman can drop it once or twice and still get the runner. As such, right-handed batters reach on error more than left-handed batters, because they hit more groundballs to the left side. How big is the effect?

In the mid-1980s, John Dewan developed Zone Rating for STATS. The definition is "if a ball to a zone resulted in an out more than 50 percent of the time, then that was in the player's zone of responsibility." This led to intensive tracking of every ball in play, and where on the field it was hit.

Groundballs by Batter Side (2011)

Batting Side	Reached	Total	Reached Base Avg.
Left	6083	24952	.244
Right	8825	33239	.266

That's right—when right-handed batters hit groundballs, they reach base twenty-two points higher. Most of that is attributable to Derek Jeter. Not really. It isn't just errors, though. There is some error effect, but when we consider only balls that go through cleanly, right-handed batters maintain a significant advantage: 0.205 to 0.219. One of the all-time greats, Tony Gwynn, loved the "5-6" hole. It is fertile ground. Mesopotamia fertile.

So what is the split on groundballs to either side of the infield?

Groundballs by Batter Hand and Side of Infield (2011)

Side of the Infield	Bat Side	Reached	Total	Batting Average
Left	Left	2011	6734	.299
Right	Left	4072	18218	.224
Left	Right	6899	25061	.275
Right	Right	1926	8178	.236

Seventy-five points for lefties? Take two and hit to the left. So what you see is that when a left-hander pulls the ball on the ground, he's going to be out. Remember, as we take finer slices, the sample size shrinks, meaning this analysis will have to be repeated with more data, but the early returns confirm that there's an advantage to going the other way for left-handed hitters. Yes, it means more singles, and sacrificing power isn't always the best option.

Groundballs by Batter/Pitcher Hand and Side of Infield (2011)

Batter Hand Side of Infield	Left Left	Left Right	Left Overall	Right Left	Right Right	Right Overall
vs. LHP	.262	.220	.232	.277	.262	.273
vs. RHP	.308	.224	.246	.275	.224	.262
AL	.298	.226	.245	.277	.229	.266
NL	.300	.221	.244	.274	.240	.266

As you can see, you can cut the data other ways—by right/left-handed batters, right/left-handed pitchers, or league—and you get the same result. Hitting to the left side provides a significant advantage.

The question then becomes is it because of the distance from first, or are there vector differences? How does the out percentage look across the field? Is there a lower gradient as you move across the diamond regardless of the handedness of the batter?

Baseball today is tracked in depth, and Baseball Info Solutions uses more granular vectors to indicate ball direction. There are 90 vectors in fair territory, with second base representing Vector 180. The third base line is Vector 225, and the first base line is Vector 135. Since groundballs are plotted where a fielder first touches the ball, there are groundballs that are marked in foul territory, but they are few and have minimal impact on the data.

Here is the distribution of all groundballs, as though you were looking from home plate (third base is on the left; first base on the right), with groundouts to the pitcher removed for the time being:

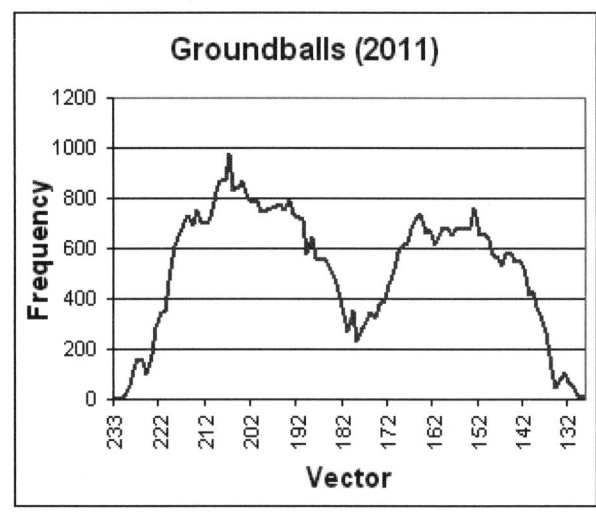

These are hits, outs and errors (Balls In Play). A moderately even and expected distribution, with a noticeable bulge in the 5-6 hole.

How often are those balls turned into outs? As you can see from the above numbers, left-handers out percentage is going to increase as we move across the infield. One of the key questions is where?

The infield can be seen as a spectrum, going from the left side (3B) to the right (1B). In order to analyze this spectrum, we utilize each vector as tracked. Here is the continuum of out percentage by handedness of the batter:

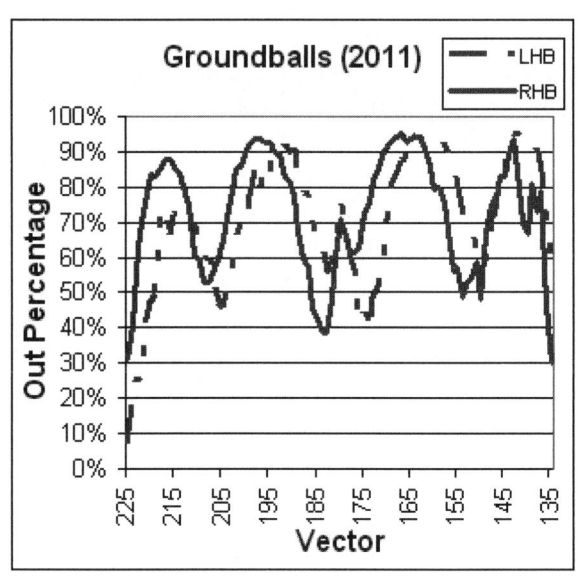

This graph is illustrative of several observable behaviors in the major leagues. For left-handed hitters (the dotted line) the infield, except the first baseman, shifts toward first, playing the pulled grounder. For right-handed hitters, first basemen struggle with the shot down the line. Balls hit to the right side are outs 77 percent of the time, and balls hit to the left are outs 72 percent of the time.

And does it mean less power, as Elias said all those years ago? These are all groundballs, mind you, and what we see is 5 percent more "slow" groundballs when the ball in play is to the opposite field.

Do Infielders Overlap?

The other question we want to know is whether or not a rangy third baseman is stealing from his shortstop.

You can see that at every vector between the infielders, the out percentage is nearly 50 percent regardless of the vector, with the exception of up the middle past the pitcher. Those vectors will have some fielded by the player on either side (3B/SS or 2B/1B). The division between the positions is clear.

Let's take an in-depth look by vector at the left side of the infield. Starting at the third base line and moving towards the middle:

Ball in Play Vector	Third Baseman Out Pct	Shortstop Out Pct	Hit Pct
225	27%	0%	73%
224	43%	0%	57%

Along the third base line, grounders make it through for base hits more often than not. As we move off the line and closer to the third baseman, however, the hit percentage declines, and the third baseman out percentage rises. The third baseman converts balls into outs greater than 50 percent of the time from Vector 223 (about 5 feet off the line) to Vector 209.

Ball in Play Vector	Third Baseman Out Pct	Shortstop Out Pct	Hit Pct
223	67%	0%	33%
222	75%	0%	25%
221	83%	0%	17%
220	89%	0%	11%
219	87%	0%	13%
218	92%	0%	8%
217	92%	0%	8%
216	91%	0%	9%
215	91%	0%	9%
214	89%	0%	11%
213	83%	0%	17%
212	79%	0%	21%
211	67%	1%	32%
210	63%	3%	35%
209	51%	7%	42%

By Vector 209, the third baseman has dropped to 51 percent outs, and the shortstop has picked up a small handful as well. Then we see a four vector gap where the play is typically made successfully, but neither the third baseman nor the shortstop claims a majority.

Ball in Play Vector	Third Baseman Out Pct	Shortstop Out Pct	Hit Pct
208	45%	13%	42%
207	25%	23%	42%
206	26%	35%	39%
205	21%	43%	35%

At Vector 210, the SS converts just 3 percent into outs. At 209, the SS pulls in 7 percent, then 13 percent in Vector 208. By the time the shortstop begins to convert 50 percent or more, the third baseman can now only reach 18 percent at Vector 204. The overlap is not a bunch, but this could be significant.

Ball in Play Vector	Third Baseman Out Pct	Shortstop Out Pct	Hit Pct
204	18%	54%	28%
203	14%	65%	21%
202	13%	73%	15%
201	7%	80%	13%
200	7%	84%	9%
199	6%	87%	8%
198	3%	92%	5%
197	4%	90%	6%
196	4%	91%	5%
195	2%	93%	5%
194	2%	92%	5%
193	1%	92%	7%
192	0%	89%	10%
191	1%	87%	13%
190	1%	83%	17%
189	0%	75%	24%
188	1%	67%	33%
187	1%	65%	34%
186	0%	53%	47%

Under the Zone Rating definitions, a third baseman's zone would include Vectors from 223 to 209, and the shortstop's zone would extend from 204 to 186, with four degrees of separation between them. The third baseman does field a small percentage of balls just inside the shortstop's zone, however.

Is the batted ball speed the key variable here? When "slow" is removed from the dataset, the third baseman can only get there about 8 percent of the time.

Ball in Play Vector	Third Baseman Out Pct	Shortstop Out Pct	Hit Pct
204	8%	60%	33%
203	5%	70%	25%
202	3%	80%	18%
201	2%	86%	12%
200	1%	90%	9%

So, no, a third baseman doesn't "steal" from a shortstop. Slow-hit balls would result in a hit if the shortstop had to come in for them.

For both questions, as the data is for a single year, a larger sample size will strengthen these results. The data has many more uses—how does Jeter's performance overlay with Elvis Andrus'? Where does any shortstop excel or need to improve? Stay tuned.

Expected Batting Average on Balls in Play

We've spent countless hours on the Plus/Minus System and Defensive Runs Saved numbers, doing our darnedest to estimate what an average fielder would have done on each play, then comparing each fielder to the average. Somewhere along the way, it occurred to us that our work doubles as a pretty good way to answer one of the toughest challenges in baseball analytics: separating pitching from fielding.

For example, let's say CC Sabathia gets Kevin Youkilis to ground a ball a few steps to the right of the shortstop. If Derek Jeter makes the play and throws out Youkilis, it's going down in the scorebook as a groundout for Sabathia, an 0-for-1 for Youkilis, and an assist for Jeter. On the other hand, if the ball sneaks through the infield for a hit, it will count against Sabathia and for Youkilis, even though they didn't do anything differently. Once the ball is in play, the fielder (in this case Derek Jeter) is in control of the play's destiny, and everyone else has to live with the consequences.

Batting Average on Balls In Play

Given the pitcher's lack of control over the outcome of the play, sabermetricians have studied pitchers' Batting Average on Balls In Play (BABIP). Some analysts, beginning with Voros McCracken, have asserted that pitchers have little or no control over their BABIP, and that any BABIP above or below the league average can be written off as "luck." If this assumption were entirely valid, we would be able to evaluate pitchers entirely based on their events that don't involve balls in play, primarily strikeouts, walks and home runs.

Further study has qualified this original hypothesis, observing that certain pitchers have a limited ability to allow fewer hits on balls in play. However, even these pitchers can have large swings from year to year, suggesting that there are larger factors at work.

We calculate Batting Average on Balls In Play as the number of hits allowed (excluding home runs and bunts) divided by the number of outs and hits on balls in play (again, excluding home runs and bunts). One technicality: when we say "outs" and "hits," we actually mean "plays made" and "plays not made," per the Plus/Minus System's definition. Errors are grouped with hits in "plays not made," while groundouts, fielder's choice outs and double plays all count as one "play made." As a result, our Batting Average on Balls In Play is not technically batting average; it's more like "Play Not Made Percentage."

The league average BABIP, as we've defined it here, was .308 in 2011. Here are the lowest BABIP numbers for 2011 (for the 100 pitchers who faced at least 660 batters):

Lowest BABIP in 2011

Pitcher	BABIP
Jeremy Hellickson	.231
Justin Verlander	.247
Josh Beckett	.254
Jered Weaver	.258
Josh Tomlin	.259

Jeremy Hellickson certainly had a fantastic rookie season, nabbing Rookie of the Year honors thanks to an ERA under 3.00. He also allowed the lowest Batting Average on Balls In Play of any regular starter last season. Justin Verlander had an even better season, winning both the Cy Young and MVP awards, while Jered Weaver finished runner-up in the Cy Young voting.

Highest BABIP in 2011

Pitcher	BABIP
Jonathan Niese	.369
Ricky Nolasco	.351
Derek Lowe	.348
John Lackey	.348
Madison Bumgarner	.348

Jonathon Niese actually had a decent season, posting the best strikeout and walk rates of his career, but his strength was not in preventing hits on balls in play. Ricky Nolasco, Derek Lowe and John Lackey all had very disappointing seasons thanks in part to balls in play, though Nolasco and Lackey both had noticeable declines in peripheral walk and strikeout rates. Edwin Jackson would have made this list too (a BABIP of .349 for the White Sox and .354 for the Cardinals) except that we've split out each pitcher's stints with different teams.

Expected Batting Average on Balls In Play

After the pitcher releases the pitch, he obviously won't touch the ball again unless it is hit in his general direction; however, based on the location and movement of the pitch, the pitcher can, to some extent, control where the batter hits the ball. As we see in the article "Beyond Ted Williams" on page 51, different pitch types in different locations are pulled at different rates. Additionally, pitches up in the zone are more likely to be hit in the air, while pitches down in the zone are more likely to be hit on the ground. So, a pitcher certainly does have some control over balls in play against him.

There are a number of factors beyond the pitcher's control, however, which affect the outcome of the play. The batter, for one. The defense, for another. Did the fielder make the play which was expected of him? We've certainly put a lot of effort into evaluating fielders. If we were to remove the effect of the defense, what would a pitcher's BABIP look like?

Let's go back to the groundball to Derek Jeter's right. The Plus/Minus System will estimate how often the average shortstop makes that play, let's say 76 percent of the time. We'll call that the "Out Ratio." Rather than giving the pitcher Sabathia full credit for an out (or full penalty for a hit), we can give him a more appropriate

0.76 outs (and 0.24 hits) for the groundball. Similarly, we can estimate the "Out Ratio" of every ball in play during the 2011 season. Adding them up over the entire season, we can calculate Expected Batting Average on Balls In Play for each pitcher.

After neutralizing the effect of the defense, here are the lowest and highest Expected BABIP rates for 2011:

Lowest Expected BABIP in 2011

Pitcher	BABIP	ExpBABIP
Jered Weaver	.258	.258
Jeremy Hellickson	.231	.269
Michael Pineda	.274	.273
Justin Verlander	.247	.274
Josh Beckett	.254	.277

It's possible that Jered Weaver and Jeremy Hellickson, with the lowest Expected BABIP figures in 2011, were fortunate beneficiaries of hitters who got themselves out. Grooving a fastball down the middle of the plate can be dangerous, but sometimes the hitter doesn't take advantage and pops the ball up instead of driving it deep in the gap. In that case, the pitcher lucked out.

You'll notice that four of the five names on this list match the lowest BABIP list. The pitchers who gave up the fewest hits on balls in play tended to be the same pitchers who induced the easiest plays. The same is true at the other end of the spectrum.

Highest Expected BABIP in 2011

Pitcher	BABIP	ExpBABIP
Jonathan Niese	.368	.362
Zack Greinke	.344	.355
John Lackey	.348	.354
Jake Westbrook	.329	.351
Derek Lowe	.348	.346

Three of the five on this list are repeats. Niese gave up a lot of hits on balls in play because he gave up a lot of hard-to-field balls. Perhaps they were perfectly placed hits, or maybe he gave up a lot of solid contact. Derek Lowe and Jake Westbrook are both heavily reliant on groundballs to get outs.

BABIP Outliers

Comparing each pitcher's BABIP to what we'd

expect from the characteristics of the balls in play allowed will allow us to strip out the impact of the fielders behind him. Here are the pitchers whose BABIP exceeded their Expected BABIP the most (their defense hurt them the more than other pitchers):

Highest BABIP Minus Expected BABIP in 2011

Pitcher	BABIP	ExpBABIP	Difference
Roy Halladay	.313	.284	29 points
Matt Garza	.337	.309	28
Anibal Sanchez	.329	.303	26
Derek Holland	.321	.297	24
Matt Harrison	.314	.291	22

Roy Halladay, Matt Garza and Anibal Sanchez pitched for teams (the Phillies, Cubs and Marlins) which finished 28th, 26th and 30th, respectively, in Team Defensive Runs Saved. Derek Holland and Matt Harrison pitched for the 17th-ranked Rangers.

Here are the pitchers whose BABIP's were much better than they should have been, thanks to the defense behind them:

Lowest BABIP Minus Expected BABIP in 2011

Pitcher	BABIP	ExpBABIP	Difference
Jeremy Hellickson	.231	.269	-38 points
James Shields	.266	.304	-37
Joe Saunders	.285	.316	-31
Ivan Nova	.303	.333	-30
Alexi Ogando	.281	.309	-28

Jeremy Hellickson had the lowest BABIP and the lowest Expected BABIP, but the Rays' defense helped him become the biggest "overachiever" in baseball. To give you an idea, Hellickson allowed 554 balls in play last season. That 38-point BABIP gap, multiplied by 554, tells you that the AL Rookie of the Year allowed 21 fewer hits than expected based on the batted balls allowed. Hellickson's teammate, James Shields, was also a beneficiary of the Rays' defense. Shields allowed 638 balls in play and beat his Expected BABIP by 37 points. Those 37 points amount to 24 fewer hits and errors, the most in all of baseball. Joe Saunders, the third-biggest overachiever, pitched for the National League's best defensive team in Arizona.

Impact of BABIP

It's important to note that a low BABIP, or even a low Expected BABIP, does not make someone a good pitcher. First of all, not every hit is the same. Soft singles through the infield are much less damaging than extra-base hits in the gap. Additionally, not every out is the same. Groundballs can be converted for double plays, while flyball double plays are extremely rare. Lastly, there are non-ball in play events which can significantly help or hurt a pitcher, such as strikeouts, walks and home runs. Ideally, we would build on Expected BABIP, factoring in the impact of extra-base hits, strikeouts, walks and home runs to better assess the pitcher's overall role in run prevention.

With that being said, inducing outs on balls in play is one piece of the greater puzzle. What kind of pitchers tend to have lower Expected Batting Averages on Balls In Play? While looking at the top and bottom five extremes can be interesting, it's not nearly enough to draw any firm conclusions. Instead, we can measure the correlation coefficient of two variables to measure the strength of the relationship. Correlation values range from -1.0 to 1.0. The closer the correlation value is to 1.0, the closer the two variables are related; if one goes up, the other usually also goes up. If the correlation value is negative, that indicates an inverse relationship (if one goes up, the other usually goes down). A correlation value near zero implies a minimal or non-existent relationship.

	Correlation with ExpBABIP
BABIP	0.83
Strikeouts per Batter Faced	-0.21
Walks per Batted Faced	0.26

In the chart above, we see that Expected BABIP is strongly linked to actual BABIP, as we'd probably expect. The defense can only help or hurt so much.

Strikeout rate is negatively correlated with Expected BABIP, meaning that pitchers who strike out more batters tend to have lower Expected BABIP. Walks, on the other hand, are positively correlated with Expected BABIP. Pitchers who walk more hitters tend to allow more hits on balls in play. Pitchers with poor control tend to walk more hitters, but they're also more likely to miss over the middle of the plate. Hitters are more likely to drive pitches hanging over the middle of the plate, and when they hit the ball hard, fielders usually have a harder time making the play.

Where does this leave us? We've learned that pitchers don't all allow equally difficult balls in play. Some pitchers induce easier-to-field balls in play than others over the course of the season. We have yet to determine if this skill persists from season to season and how well Expected BABIP relates to run prevention as a whole. After all, the pitcher's primary objective isn't to prevent hitters from reaching base—it's to prevent them from scoring runs.

ERA vs. PRA:
Team Defensive Independent Pitching

The purpose of ERA is to try to measure what a pitcher's true performance is without the failings of the defense. ERA is an attempt to create a Defensive Independent Pitching statistic. It is a good attempt and we've been using it for years.

We now have a better way to do this at the team level. Thanks to Defensive Runs Saved we can get a better estimate of how good a team's pitching is, independent of its defense. We do this by asking the question, "How many runs would the pitching staff have allowed if they had an average defense?" In each of the last two years we have published articles in *The Hardball Times Baseball Annual* about this topic. Since publishing the latest article this past fall, we have updated our Defensive Runs Saved system (DRS) for this book. Below, we reprint the article called "Separating the Pitching from the Fielding" from *The Hardball Times Baseball Annual 2012* with our brand new Defensive Runs Saved numbers.

Separating the Pitching from the Fielding (Updated)

Who were the best pitching staffs in baseball in 2011? The standard answer is: In the American League, the Los Angeles Angels led with a 3.57 team ERA, with the Tampa Bay Rays a point behind at 3.58; in the National League, the Philadelphia Phillies were at the top with a 3.02 ERA, while the San Francisco Giants weren't too far behind at 3.20.

But that's not really just pitching. When you look at a team ERA, it's about how well the pitchers pitched, but it's also about how well the defenders defended. Last year in *The Hardball Times Baseball Annual* we came up with a technique to factor out the defense. This gave us a fielding independent pitching stat called Pitching Runs Allowed, or just Pitching Runs.

Here's the shocker: The best pitching staff in the American League in 2011 was . . .cough, cough. . .The New York Yankees!

Are you kidding me? This blows me away. At the beginning of the year I was taunting our die-hard Yankee fan in the Baseball Info Solutions office, Rob Burckhard, about how bad the Yankee pitching was looking. Rob wasn't too optimistic about it either, but he was confident that the offense would easily carry the day. For pitching, it was Sabathia and Rivera, and that's it. Phil Hughes was a maybe at best. A.J. Burnett was more than questionable. And Ivan Nova was an unknown commodity. The Yanks were planning to see if they could work in a couple of old has-beens named Freddy Garcia and Bartolo Colon.

Sabathia (19-8, 3.00 ERA) and Rivera (1.91, 44 saves) did their usual thing during the year. But the next two hopefuls, Hughes and Burnett, turned in 5.79 and 5.15 ERAs. So then, how did the Yankees do it? How did they have the fewest Pitching Runs in the American League? It had to be smoke and mirrors, I'm thinking. But it was the Retreads and The Rookie who came through in the rotation. Garcia and Colon posted 3.62 and 4.00 ERAs in 51 starts between them, while Ivan Nova was a Rookie of the Year candidate with his 16-4 record and 3.70 ERA. In the bullpen, Mariano received massive assistance from David Robertson with a 1.08 ERA in 70 games. Overall, the bullpen ERA of 3.12 was the best in the American League.

Using the Pitching Runs technique, we showed that it was the Chicago White Sox who had the best pitching staff in the American League in 2010. In 2011, they fared well again, coming in sixth. Pitching Runs uses Team Runs Saved (as presented beginning on page 79) to remove the defensive component out of team runs allowed. In short, Pitching Runs are an estimate of the number of runs the team would have allowed with an average defense.

The best defensive team in the American League in 2011 was the Tampa Bay Rays. Their defense saved them 85 runs. Overall, the team allowed 614 runs. If they had an average defense (0 runs saved), they would have allowed 85 more runs. For 2011, Tampa Bay had 699 Pitching Runs (614 plus 85). The Yankees had 648 Pitching Runs (657 Runs Allowed plus -9 Runs Saved).

Thus, in our opinion, the top pitching staffs in the American League during 2011 were:

Top American League Pitching Staffs in 2011

Team	Runs Allowed	Runs Saved	Pitching Runs
Yankees	657	-9	648
Athletics	679	-27	652
Angels	633	29	662
Mariners	675	1	676
Rangers	677	2	679
White Sox	706	-16	690
Rays	614	85	699
Tigers	711	14	725

The Rays and the Angels allowed the fewest runs in the AL. They had formidable defenses, finishing No. 1 and No. 2 in the AL in Defensive Runs Saved. The Yankees had a slightly below-average defense and, as a result, rise to the top on the Pitching Runs list.

The Seattle Mariners are fourth on this list, which reminds us of park effects. The Mariners' pitching is good, but their park also helped save a lot of runs. As did Tropicana Field for Tampa Bay and the Big A for Anaheim.

Over in the National League, the Philadelphia Phillies lapped the field. And then some. Their defense in 2011 was, shall we say, not so good. It cost the team 59 runs. The pitching was overwhelmingly good. They only allowed 470 Pitching Runs. The next-best team was San Francisco, way behind at 581. Here are the best NL

pitching staffs of 2011:

Top National League Pitching Staffs in 2011

Team	Runs Allowed	Runs Saved	Pitching Runs
Phillies	529	-59	470
Giants	578	3	581
Braves	605	10	615
Dodgers	612	13	625
Marlins	702	-75	627
Nationals	643	4	647
Brewers	638	16	654
Padres	611	46	657

Going Back to 2003

ERA says the league-leading teams in 2011 were the Los Angeles Angels and the Philadelphia Phillies, but when we equalize defense among the teams, the Yankees take the top pitching spot from the Angels. The Yankees had 657 runs allowed, but only 648 when you remove the defense. Using this number, we have a better way to estimate how good a team's pitching staff is. It's an upgrade from ERA. Let's state this in the same format as ERA. We'll use the same calculation as ERA and take 648, multiply by nine and divide by innings. For the Yankees we get 4.00. This is the number of runs per nine innings the pitching, independent of defense, allowed. Let's call it PRA, Pitching Run Average. Here is a summary of 2011:

2011 ERA vs. PRA

League	Best Team ERA		Best Team PRA	
AL	Angels	3.57	Yankees	4.00
NL	Phillies	3.02	Phillies	2.86

The Phillies have a PRA lower than their ERA. That's going to be pretty rare as we look back. ERA is a defense independent statistic that removes the error component. But it does so by taking those runs associated with errors out of the calculation. PRA doesn't remove the defensive runs. It uses Defensive Runs Saved which averages to zero for all teams. What we see here, with the Phillies' PRA lower than their ERA, is a defense that was really poor.

Here are the annual team ERA and PRA leaders going back to 2003:

2010 ERA vs. PRA

League	Best Team ERA		Best Team PRA	
AL	Athletics	3.56	White Sox	3.99
NL	Giants	3.36	Giants	3.75

2009 ERA vs. PRA

League	Best Team ERA		Best Team PRA	
AL	Mariners	3.87	Red Sox	4.35
NL	Dodgers	3.41	Dodgers	3.81

2008 ERA vs. PRA

League	Best Team ERA		Best Team PRA	
AL	Blue Jays	3.49	Blue Jays	4.11
NL	Dodgers	3.68	Dodgers	3.96

2007 ERA vs. PRA

League	Best Team ERA		Best Team PRA	
AL	Red Sox	3.87	Red Sox	4.09
NL	Padres	3.70	Padres	4.02

2006 ERA vs. PRA

League	Best Team ERA		Best Team PRA	
AL	Tigers	3.84	Twins	4.35
NL	Padres	3.87	Padres	4.37

2005 ERA vs. PRA

League	Best Team ERA		Best Team PRA	
AL	Twins	4.03	Twins	4.27
NL	Cardinals	3.49	Mets	3.91

2004 ERA vs. PRA

League	Best Team ERA		Best Team PRA	
AL	Twins	4.03	Twins	4.27
NL	Braves	3.74	Cubs	3.97

2003 ERA vs. PRA

League	Best Team ERA		Best Team PRA	
AL	Athletics	3.63	Athletics	4.08
NL	Dodgers	3.16	Dodgers	3.85

We can see quite a few times where the best pitching staff is not the team with the lowest ERA. PRA gives a team front office a better way to assess their pitching.

We also see here again how good the Phillies' pitching staff was in 2011. Not only was their PRA of 2.86 below 3.00, the next-best league-leading team, going all the way back to 2003, was 89 points away at 3.75 (Giants 2010). The 2011 Giants were even better, however. They had a PRA of 3.56. Part of what we have here is a reflection of the lower scoring that took place MLB-wide in 2011. The 2011 Braves also had a lower PRA (3.74) than the 2010 Giants' 3.75.

A Fresh Take on Replacement Level Valuation

Our Defensive Runs Saved system featured throughout this book is centered with the league average at zero, as are many other defensive metrics. Good players save runs compared to average fielders and naturally have positive Runs Saved; bad players cost their team runs and have Runs Saved totals below zero.

However, there are times when it's advantageous to utilize a different baseline.

By definition, when we compare to the league average, somebody has to be below it. Below-average players aren't *bad*, exactly; they're just not as good as the above-average ones. They're certainly not worthless players. Major league teams have to stick nine guys out there every game, and they could do far worse than slightly below average players.

Let's say a major league team loses their shortstop due to sudden injury or trade. They could promote a shortstop from their own minor league system to fill the void. They could shop around, checking with other teams for major or minor league shortstops who could be acquired at the low cost of a bag of baseballs. Alternatively, they could explore the free agent market, looking for shortstops who were recently released or weren't offered a contract for the season.

Of course, none of these options is likely to become a long-term solution. They're looking for the best shortstop they can find at a minimum cost. Because he can theoretically be replaced at little or no cost, a shortstop of this caliber is considered "replacement level."

Many baseball analysts, including Keith Woolner, Tom Tango, and Dave Studenmund, have advocated the concept of a replacement level baseline when evaluating baseball players. Woolner, a former Baseball Prospectus writer now working for the Cleveland Indians, created VORP (Value Over Replacement Player) as a method of measuring a player's offensive production (in runs) compared to a replacement level player at his position. Tom Tango, a consultant to various MLB teams, outlined a framework for WAR (Wins Above Replacement), combining measures of each player's offensive, defensive, and positional value to estimate how many wins he contributed to his team's efforts. WAR is featured on the websites FanGraphs.com and Baseball-Reference.com. Studenmund took Bill James' Wins Shares system and translated it to a replacement level baseline. On the Hardball Times website, he termed his new statistic Win Shares Above Bench.

In theory, no team should have to settle for less production than a replacement level player at each position. In practice, however, teams may settle for a lower level of production in the short-term. Both Adam Dunn and Alex Rios significantly underperformed and rated below replacement level in 2011; neither was expected to be *that* bad, but if they continue to struggle, the White Sox will fill their spots with cheaper and more productive players. Similarly, the Pirates will continue to give Pedro Alvarez chances at the major league level because his upside is so high, despite his sub-replacement level production in the meantime.

A hypothetical replacement level might make sense, but how do we establish its definition in practice? Several analysts have developed techniques with varying results, and in this article we present ours.

In *The Fielding Bible—Volume II*, we introduced "Total Runs" as a method of incorporating hitting, baserunning, and defense into one all-inclusive number. (For more information on Total Runs, check out page

167.) In this study, we have omitted the positional adjustment so we can isolate hitting, baserunning, and defense.

Each season, our Baserunning Runs metric centers roughly at zero across the whole league, while our Defensive Runs Saved evaluations center at zero for each position. Bill James' Runs Created was established such that the total number of Runs Created is roughly equal to the league's number of runs scored. Unfortunately, the league's offensive level rises and falls over time. The average team scored fewer runs in 2011 than they did five years previously. As a result, 80 Runs Created in 2011 is more impressive than 80 Runs Created in 2006.

Since we want a common baseline for each season, we will need to convert Runs Created to Runs Created Above Average (RCAA). For each season, we took the entire league's Runs Created and divided by the total number of plate appearances to set the league average Runs Created per plate appearance. We then multiply each player's total plate appearances by the league's Runs Created per plate appearance for that season to estimate how many runs the average hitter would have created in the same opportunities. Lastly, we subtract this total from the hitter's actual Runs Created to arrive at Runs Created Above Average.

Combining these three pieces (Baserunning Runs, Runs Saved, and Runs Created Above Average), we can calculate the offensive and defensive contributions each team received from each position. For example, Twins shortstops combined for -19 Runs Created Above Average, 2 Baserunning Runs, and -30 Runs Saved in 2011. This sum of -47 runs amounted to the least productive season any team got out of any one position (excluding pitchers). National League Most Valuable Player Ryan Braun headed the most productive position; Brewers left fielders combined for 59 Runs Created Above Average, 3 Baserunning Runs, 4 Runs Saved: a total of 66 Runs Above Average. The difference between the most and least productive positions was 113 runs.

Next, let's look at the average production from each position over the past nine seasons.

Average Production by Position (2003-2011)

Pos	Runs Created Above Average	Baserunning Runs	Runs Saved	Runs Above Average
C	-8	-2	0	-10
1B	14	-1	0	12
2B	-1	2	0	1
3B	3	0	0	2
SS	-5	2	0	-4
LF	9	0	0	10
CF	3	2	0	5
RF	10	0	0	10

Note that Runs Created Above Average skews positive for position players because pitchers are usually terrible hitters and absorb a large portion of the negative Runs Created Above Average.

Placing the positions in order from highest to lowest average level of production, we have:

1B (12), LF/RF (10), CF (5), 3B (2), 2B (1), SS (-4), C (-10).

As we would expect, this average player ordering mimics the defensive spectrum Bill James introduced in his 1980s *Baseball Abstracts*. Starting from the left, the defensive demands of each position increase as you move right.

Many statistics compare players to the average, and we could use that same baseline here to evaluate players' overall value. However, there are a few reasons this may not be ideal.

For example, Yankees shortstop Derek Jeter is roughly an average shortstop at this point in his career. As a shortstop, he created seven runs above average at the plate, ran for three more on the basepaths, but surrendered -15 runs in the field, for a total of -5 Runs Above Average, just one run below the level of an average shortstop.

However, a shortstop who played just one inning would rate at 0 runs above average—higher than Jeter. Ramiro Pena, for instance, played 25 innings as a shortstop, totaling -3 Runs Above Average. According to Runs Above Average, Jeter appears the lesser contributor.

Obviously, this is screwy. Jeter was more valuable to the Yankees, but our average baseline isn't clearly showing us what we know intuitively. Had Ramiro Pena played as often as Jeter, he would have finished far below Jeter's -5 Runs Above Average.

We turn to replacement level to resolve this issue. Because Jeter is much better than a replacement level shortstop, his Runs Above Replacement grows the more he plays. Pena, on the other hand, is roughly a replacement level player and would have little or no value above replacement, no matter how much he plays.

But exactly how bad is replacement level? How low should we set the replacement level baseline?

We can approximate replacement level for each position by measuring the least amount of production any team got from those players in a given season. With that in mind, here is the 2011 Replacement Level Team:

Replacement Level Team (2011)

Team	Pos	Runs Created Above Average	Baserunning Runs	Runs Saved	Runs Above Average
MIN	C	-38	0	1	-37
OAK	1B	-22	-2	-1	-25
NYM	2B	-11	-1	-20	-32
SEA	3B	-38	-2	0	-40
MIN	SS	-19	2	-30	-47
MIN	LF	-19	-3	-10	-32
TOR	CF	-25	1	-12	-36
PIT	RF	-1	-6	-14	-21

As you can see, the Twins "earned" three spots on the replacement level team. None of the represented teams made the playoffs or contended deep into the season. In two cases (Twins SS, Twins C) the starter missed significant time due to injury and performed below expectations when he was on the field.

In two instances (Mariners 3B, Pirates RF), teams were hoping for a player to return to previous levels of performance. In another case (Twins LF), a trade opened up a hole with no clear replacement.

And in three cases (Mets 2B, Athletics 1B, Blue Jays CF) teams tried multiple players in the starting lineup, though none played well enough to stick. The Blue Jays have addressed their weakness in center field with the mid-season acquisition of Colby Rasmus, while the A's and Mets have entered full rebuilding mode and will likely continue to experiment with cheap solutions for the short-term.

There are reasons to think this replacement level is too low. In some of the above cases, a cellar-dwelling team wanted to give a young player a shot to fulfill his potential (at the risk of sub-par performance in the short-

term). In the case of Mariners third basemen, Seattle signed Chone Figgins to a long-term contract with the expectation he'd be far above replacement level. He's been a complete disappointment, but because they made such a large financial commitment to him, they have continued to give him chances to return to a respectable level of production. That being said, if the Mariners found themselves in a competitive pennant race, they could likely find a superior third base option in the minors or externally at little cost.

There are also reasons to believe this replacement level is too high. Most of the eight cases mentioned above were filled by backup players already on the roster. Presumably, the freely available external players were generally inferior to the in-house options. If we want to establish the level of freely available external options, we might have to go lower.

This calculation differs somewhat from the estimation of previous "replacement" and "bench" baselines. However, we're building off of the same concept and, rather than introducing a new acronym to the sabermetric lexicon, we will borrow the same replacement level terminology. For this article, our approximation of replacement level is sufficient if not ideal.

We can similarly look at the replacement level teams for previous seasons, dating back to 2003. Here is the average production from the replacement level at each position over the past nine years:

Pos	Runs Created Above Average	Baserunning Runs	Runs Saved	Runs Above Average
C	-32	-2	-3	-38
1B	-13	-3	-9	-25
2B	-21	1	-18	-38
3B	-19	0	-14	-33
SS	-28	1	-19	-46
LF	-16	-1	-7	-24
CF	-20	1	-16	-35
RF	-9	-1	-17	-27

Implied Defensive Spectrum: LF (-24), 1B (-25), RF (-27), 3B (-33), CF (-35), 2B/C (-38), SS (-46).

The defensive spectrum lines up pretty well here, with the exception of catchers.

Before we go any further, let's compare the average and replacement levels at each position:

Replacement Level vs. Average Position (2003-2011)

Pos	Replacement Runs	Average Runs	Difference
C	-38	-10	28
1B	-25	12	37
2B	-38	1	39
3B	-33	2	35
SS	-46	-4	42
LF	-24	10	34
CF	-35	5	40
RF	-27	10	37

Curiously, shortstops show the largest gap between average and replacement level, while catchers exhibit the smallest. It's possible, even likely, that we're not fully measuring the defensive impact of catchers *despite* all of our advancements introduced elsewhere in this book. For example, we're using a 33 percent credibility factor in Adjusted Earned Runs Saved due to the volume of random noise in the data. It's possible that we'll develop more direct ways to measure specific skills, such as pitch calling and/or framing, which will improve our understanding of catcher defense.

Exactly how bad is a replacement level player? Aside from catchers, we have an answer to our question: every other position demonstrates a 34 to 42 run gap between average and replacement level over a full season.

Wins Above Replacement

We can use this new approximation of replacement level to create a Wins Above Replacement (WAR) metric. First, we need to clear up the technical details. For this calculation, we are awarding offensive and defensive replacement level separately. For example, replacement level shortstops averaged -28 Runs Created Above Average and +1 Baserunning Runs in 636 plate appearances, or -0.0437 runs per plate appearance. On defense, they averaged -19 Runs Saved in 1,436 innings, or -0.0133 runs per inning.

In 2011, Troy Tulowitzki spent 1,208 innings and 603 plate appearances as a shortstop (plus 3 at-bats as a pinch hitter, which we'll come back to later), totaling 34 Runs Created Above Average, -2 Baserunning Runs, and 11 Runs Saved. In 603 plate appearances, a replacement level shortstop would have accumulated 603 * -0.0437 = -26 runs at-bat and 1,208 * -0.0133 = -16 runs in the field, a total of -42 runs above average. Tulo's 43 runs above average minus the -42 runs of a replacement shortstop amounts to 85 runs above replacement, the highest for any shortstop in 2011.

Splitting the offensive and defensive replacement level allows us to appropriately value players who are leveraged by their managers as defensive replacements or pinch hitters. For instance, the 2010 World Champion San Francisco Giants had a couple of defensive liabilities in the outfield, most notably Pat Burrell. Manager Bruce Bochy would regularly wait until Burrell's spot in the lineup came up between the sixth and eighth innings, let him hit, then insert a pinch runner or defensive substitute for the rest of the game. By doing so, the Giants got the most out of Burrell's bat while minimizing his innings in the field. Conversely, Bochy minimized the substitute's at-bats and maximized his time in left field.

Total Runs and other Wins Above Replacement methods have a separate positional adjustment, adding or subtracting runs based on the relative difficulty of the position. By calculating replacement level separately for offense and defense as we've done here, we've eliminated the need for an additional adjustment based on defensive position.

We treat pinch hitters, pinch runners, and designated hitters as 11th and 12th offensive positions and calculate offensive replacement level in the same manner. These positions have no defensive contributions, obviously, so there is no defensive replacement level to account for.

Previous studies have shown that every ten runs translates to roughly one win in the standings; therefore, we can estimate that Tulowitzki's 85 runs above replacement was worth 8.5 wins for the Rockies above a replacement level shortstop.

And with that, on to the results! Here are the top twenty seasons since 2003:

Top Wins Above Replacement Seasons (2003-11)

Season	Player	WAR
2004	Barry Bonds	10.8
2009	Albert Pujols	10.8
2008	Chase Utley	10.8
2008	Albert Pujols	10.7
2004	Scott Rolen	10.7
2003	Alex Rodriguez	10.7
2004	Adrian Beltre	10.3
2004	Todd Helton	10.3
2003	Albert Pujols	10.3
2006	Albert Pujols	10.0
2005	Albert Pujols	9.9
2003	Barry Bonds	9.8
2005	Derrek Lee	9.7
2007	Alex Rodriguez	9.7
2007	Jimmy Rollins	9.7
2006	Chase Utley	9.7
2007	Chase Utley	9.6
2007	Albert Pujols	9.6
2007	Troy Tulowitzki	9.6
2011	Jacoby Ellsbury	9.5

We have a three-way tie: Bonds' 172 Runs Created (95 Runs Created Above Average) far surpass any other total during the time period, Utley's 31 Runs Saved in 2008 is among the best defensive seasons, and Pujols' 2009 is probably the best combination of the two. Bonds places two seasons on the list, Utley three, A-Rod two, and Pujols an astounding six!

Three of these names are no surprise among the greatest players of the last decade, but Utley's 2006-08 seasons are criminally underrated. More on that in a minute.

Let's go position by position and look at the top seasons since 2003. Note: for each position, we're only considering the time spent at that position. Any innings or plate appearances spent at other positions, including pinch hit appearances, are not included.

Top Catcher Wins Above Replacement Seasons (2003-11)

Season	Player	WAR
2003	Javy Lopez	7.7
2009	Joe Mauer	7.4
2007	Russell Martin	7.1
2003	Jason Kendall	6.1
2010	Joe Mauer	6.0

Javy Lopez (remember him?) had a career year with 43 home runs in 2003, earning him All-Star and Silver Slugger honors. Joe Mauer won the 2009 AL MVP award. The top 2011 catchers were Fielding Bible Award winner Matt Wieters (5.6 WAR) and Alex Avila (5.3 WAR).

Top First Baseman Wins Above Replacement Seasons (2003-11)

Season	Player	WAR
2004	Todd Helton	10.3
2009	Albert Pujols	10.2
2008	Albert Pujols	10.2
2006	Albert Pujols	10.0
2005	Albert Pujols	9.8

Pujols had seven straight seasons (2004-10) in the top ten at the position, putting him on another planet. His 2003 doesn't make this list because he spent most of the season in left field. His 2011 total of "only" 6.1 Wins Above Replacement came after missing a few weeks with an elbow injury.

This seems like a good time to bring up one factor we haven't addressed here—park effects. Todd Helton put up 149 Runs Created (65 RCAA) in the friendly Coors Field air in 2004. On top of that, Helton's been a pretty good defensive first baseman. Perhaps we'll work in park adjustments next time around.

With Pujols having a down year, the top first basemen of 2011 were Miguel Cabrera (8.1 WAR) and Adrian Gonzalez (7.9 WAR).

Top Second Baseman Wins Above Replacement Seasons (2003-11)

Season	Player	WAR
2008	Chase Utley	10.8
2007	Chase Utley	9.7
2010	Robinson Cano	9.5
2006	Chase Utley	9.4
2009	Chase Utley	9.2

Similar to Pujols' dominance at first base, Utley has had most of the best second base seasons in recent history. We wrote about the Phillies' second baseman in some detail when introducing Total Runs in Volume II, citing the two MVP awards given to teammates Ryan Howard (2006) and Jimmy Rollins (2007) while Utley has never finished higher than seventh in the voting.

Utley has been overlooked for a couple of reasons. First of all, he had a hard time earning regular playing time after reaching the majors. His minor league numbers were just like his eventual major league numbers—good, with a decent batting average, high on-base percentage, and some power—but there was little that screamed "I'm a future MVP candidate." The Phillies had David Bell and Placido Polanco at third and second, respectively, both very good defenders in their own right.

By 2005, the Phillies couldn't ignore him any longer and traded Placido Polanco to Detroit and handed Utley the everyday second base job. Then entering his prime at 26, Utley posted five straight seasons where he averaged 40 doubles, 30 homers, and a .300 batting average—all very good numbers but not league-leading in any department. He knew how to draw a walk, and also led the league three times in being hit by pitch, further boosting his on-base percentage.

Utley also happens to be one of the most efficient base stealers of the era. Over the past three years, he has swiped 50 bases and has been caught only *twice*. In 2009, he stole 23 bases without being caught even once.

Lastly, Utley's defense is among the best in the game. Not a flashy fielder like some of his second base counterparts, Utley plays smart defense, adjusting his positioning before the pitch based on the hitter, count, and situation. As a result, he makes plays all over the field that others can't reach with sheer athleticism. His 2011 injuries broke an unmatched streak of seven consecutive seasons of double-digit Defensive Runs Saved.

Altogether, Utley totals 63 Wins Above Replacement. Since 2003, only Albert Pujols has been more valuable. Most of the best players, not surprisingly, are good hitters, baserunners, and fielders.

Most Wins Above Replacement (2003-11)

Player	Runs Created Above Average	Baserunning Runs	Runs Saved	WAR
Albert Pujols	594	21	121	86
Chase Utley	212	26	137	63
Alex Rodriguez	320	1	21	62
Jimmy Rollins	85	26	67	59
Mark Teixeira	265	-3	73	56
Carlos Beltran	217	25	39	53
Adrian Beltre	102	2	157	52
Ichiro Suzuki	156	20	77	51
Todd Helton	278	0	30	50
Rafael Furcal	56	21	55	48

Not only has Utley been worth 375 runs above average during his career, but a replacement level player would have been worth -254 runs above average in the same playing time. This 629-run difference converts to 63 Wins Above Replacement.

As with Pujols, Utley's down year (due to injury) allowed Dustin Pedroia (8.8 WAR) and Ian Kinsler (8.2 WAR) to take the top spots at the position in 2011.

Top Third Baseman Wins Above Replacement Seasons (2003-11)

Season	Player	WAR
2004	Scott Rolen	10.7
2004	Adrian Beltre	10.3
2007	Alex Rodriguez	9.4
2007	David Wright	9.4
2005	Alex Rodriguez	9.1

Scott Rolen and Adrian Beltre both had fantastic 2004 seasons. Beltre was a slightly better hitter, but Rolen (historically a fantastic baserunner) had a seven-run baserunning advantage and an eight run defensive edge to claim the top spot. Evan Longoria led 2011 third basemen at 6.8 WAR.

Top Shortstop Wins Above Replacement Seasons (2003-11)

Season	Player	WAR
2003	Alex Rodriguez	10.5
2007	Jimmy Rollins	9.7
2007	Troy Tulowitzki	9.6
2008	Hanley Ramirez	9.1
2010	Troy Tulowitzki	9.1

Remember when A-Rod was a shortstop? Yeah, he was pretty good: 133 Runs Created (47 RCAA) and 8 Runs Saved as a shortstop, and you have an MVP on a last-place team. Tulowitzki makes the top 5 twice and top 11 four times, including a league-leading 8.5 WAR in 2011, largely on the strength of his outstanding glove work. Or, more accurately, his rocket arm.

Top Left Fielder Wins Above Replacement Seasons (2003-11)

Season	Player	WAR
2004	Barry Bonds	10.3
2003	Barry Bonds	9.3
2011	Alex Gordon	8.6
2007	Matt Holliday	8.3
2011	Ryan Braun	8.1

Two seasons of Barry Bonds, but I'd bet you didn't see Alex Gordon coming, did you? Not only did Gordon have a breakout year at the plate and a league-leading Outfield Arm Runs Saved total, but the new Timer Plus/Minus system likes Gordon's flyball coverage as well.

Top Center Fielder Wins Above Replacement Seasons (2003-11)

Season	Player	WAR
2011	Jacoby Ellsbury	9.4
2006	Carlos Beltran	8.6
2004	Carlos Beltran	8.5
2007	Curtis Granderson	8.4
2011	Matt Kemp	8.4

For whatever reason, 2011 saw a number of fantastic seasons from outfielders. Alex Gordon set the non-Bonds record for left fielder WAR since 2003, and Ellsbury joins him with a 9.4 WAR figure that topped every player at every position last year. NL MVP runner-up Matt Kemp joins him in the top-five, along with two seasons of Carlos Beltran.

Top Right Fielder Wins Above Replacement Seasons (2003-11)

Season	Player	WAR
2004	Ichiro Suzuki	9.1
2004	J.D. Drew	8.5
2004	Bobby Abreu	8.0
2003	Gary Sheffield	7.9
2008	Nick Markakis	7.7

A nice selection of five different right fielders wraps up our tour across the diamond. Justin Upton topped all right fielders in 2011 with 7.4 WAR.

Lastly, let's look at the top-five designated hitter seasons:

Top Designated Hitter Wins Above Replacement Seasons (2003-11)

Season	Player	WAR
2007	David Ortiz	7.7
2006	David Ortiz	6.5
2005	David Ortiz	6.3
2006	Travis Hafner	6.1
2005	Travis Hafner	6.1

David Ortiz is no surprise as the best designated hitter of the era. It's interesting to note that the top designated hitters generally have lower Wins Above Replacement marks than the top players at other positions, with the possible exception of catchers. Obviously, designated hitters don't have a defensive component, so their impact is limited. Catchers, on the other hand, need more days off and don't play every day, so their impact is also limited.

Runs Saved Against Zero

Bill James

[Editor's note: This article originally ran on BillJamesOnline.com on August 18, 2011.]

Let us suppose that a team scores 750 runs. Of those 750 runs, we are able to say with a fair degree of confidence who created how many; the starting catcher created 56, the starting first baseman created 91, the backup catcher created 22, the third catcher created 8 and the fourth catcher created 1, etc. etc. We know how to do this; we have known how to do this for thirty years, although we can do it a little better now than we did 30 years ago.

But let us ask this question instead: How many runs did each fielder save? I don't mean how many runs each fielder saved against average; I am asking how many runs he saved in total, as compared to a player making zero defensive contributions.

I have a theory of how that number can be reached, and I am going to explain that theory in this article. I will use National League shortstops of the 1980s to illustrate the process; at the end of this process we will have an estimate of the runs saved by every National League shortstop of the 1980s. But this process is not limited or specific to shortstops, the 1980s, or the National League; it could be used for any fielder. Some elements outlined today are specific to shortstops, but there are parallel systems for other positions.

We work toward the answer we need by asking a series of four questions. Those four questions are:

1) How many runs were saved by the team?

2) Of those runs that were saved by the team, how many were saved by the fielders and how many by the pitchers?

3) Of those runs that were saved by the fielders, how many were saved by the shortstops?

4) Of those runs that were saved by the shortstops on the team, how many were saved by this shortstop as opposed to the team's other shortstops?

To answer any of those four questions will require us to pose and answer another set of questions. At points that will require us to do some comically convoluted mathematics which will, at times, disorient us and leave us uncertain as to why exactly we need to know this, but it's essentially a logical process.

I. How Many Runs Were Saved by the Team?

This actually is easy. Let us suppose that
a) the team scored 750 runs,
b) the team allowed 750 runs,
c) the league run average was 750 runs per team,
d) the team played .500 ball, and
e) the park factor was 1.000 (meaning that the park neither increased nor decreased scoring).

How many runs did the team "save", against zero? Obviously, 750. If this team's offense and defense are equal (O=D) and the runs scored equal 750 (O=750) then obviously D=750.

As runs scored rise from zero, runs saved must fall the same distance in order for offense and defense to be equal; therefore, they must fall from twice the league average (2Lg). Twice the league average, park adjusted, is 2Lgp.

We can answer this question (How many runs were saved by the team) by asking seven simple questions:

1) What was the league average of runs scored per inning?

2) How many innings did the team pitch?

3) How many runs could the team have expected to

allow in those innings?

4) What was the park factor?

5) Adjusting for the park factor, how many runs could the team have been expected to allow if they were average? (Lgp)

6) How many runs could the team have been expected to allow at the zero point? (2Lgp)

7) How many runs fewer than that did they allow?

Let us take the 1988 Los Angeles Dodgers, champions of the World. The National League in 1988 scored 7,522 runs in 17,481 innings, or .4303 runs per inning. The Dodgers pitched 1,463 innings. They could have been expected to allow 630 runs, if they had average pitching and defense and were in an average park.

Surprisingly, Dodger Stadium in 1988 functioned as a hitter's park, increasing offense by 8%, an adjusted park factor of 1.042. Adjusting for the park, the Dodgers could have been expected to allow 656 runs.

Twice that number (the zero point for runs allowed) would be 1,312 runs. If the Dodgers had zero pitching and defense, they would have allowed 1,312 runs.

They actually allowed 544 runs. Therefore, the team's pitching and defense saved 768 runs.

I will post, simultaneous with this article, a spreadsheet named 1980s RS SS 1.wk1 (1980s Runs Saved Shortstops 1), which gives the number of runs saved by every National League team in the 1980s. These were the top ten run-saving teams of the decade:

Year	City	Team	Runs Saved
1985	Chicago	Cubs	838
1987	Montreal	Expos	832
1984	Atlanta	Braves	792
1986	Houston	Astros	791
1982	Pittsburgh	Pirates	790
1980	Philadelphia	Phillies	788
1987	Pittsburgh	Pirates	784
1987	Philadelphia	Phillies	781
1986	St. Louis	Cardinals	781
1984	Chicago	Cubs	780

All ten of these teams played in hitter's parks. As a hitter's park expands the number of runs that are scored, it also expands the number of runs saved. The ten teams that saved the fewest runs in a year, in the 1980s, were all teams from 1981, when a strike wiped out a third of the schedule. But setting aside 1981, the teams saving the fewest runs were:

Year	City	Team	Runs Saved
1984	San Francisco	Giants	497
1989	Pittsburgh	Pirates	531
1988	Houston	Astros	546
1983	Houston	Astros	548
1988	San Francisco	Giants	549
1985	San Francisco	Giants	550
1988	Philadelphia	Phillies	551
1982	San Francisco	Giants	551
1988	New York	Mets	554
1980	New York	Mets	555

All of these teams except the 1988 Phillies played in pitchers' parks.

Most of these were not very good teams. A list of teams saving the most runs is generally a list of pretty good teams; a list of teams saving the fewest runs is generally a list of not-very-good teams.

The notable exception on this list is the 1988 Mets, a team that won 100 games (100-60) with the formidable starting rotation of Dwight Gooden, Ron Darling, David Cone, Bobby Ojeda and Sid Fernandez. Surely that collection of pitchers must have saved a large number of runs, no?

No. The National League ERA in 1988 was the lowest of the decade, 3.45; thus, the runs scored per inning for the league were very low. Four of the ten teams on the list above were from 1988.

The 1988 Mets scored and allowed 704 runs on the road but only 531 at home, creating an extremely low park factor (raw park factor of .75, park adjustment factor of .877). This was the second-lowest park factor for any National League team in the 1980s.

The Mets missed a couple of games, so their innings pitched for the season was a little low. Combining these factors, the Mets faced the potential of allowing only 1,086 runs even if they had zero pitching and defense value—easily the lowest number for any National League team in the 1980s, other than the strike-shortened 1981 season. They actually allowed only 532 runs—also the fewest of any National League team during the 1980s, other than 1981—but the number saved (554) was still relatively low.

2. Of those runs that were saved by the team, how many were saved by the fielders and how many by the pitchers?

We cannot answer this question with great confidence. I have a theory, I have a formula; I have a process for answering this question. You may be able to come up with a better theory, a better formula, a better process. I hope you can. Until you do, however, my theory is what we have.

I operate on the following assumptions:

1) About two-thirds of the work of run prevention is done by pitchers; about one-third is done by fielders.

2) If the pitchers' strikeouts are high, this number is higher, because strikeouts take defensive responsibility away from the fielders and give it to the pitchers. If the pitchers' strikeouts are low, the defensive responsibility is higher.

3) If the pitchers' walks are high, this number is higher, because there is nothing a fielder can do about walks. If the pitchers' walks are low, the defensive responsibility is higher. (The same with hit batsmen, of course.)

4) If the pitchers' home runs allowed are high, this number is higher, because, again, there is nothing a fielder can do about home runs allowed.

5) If the teams' errors are high, this number is lower, because errors are the responsibility of fielders, rather than pitchers.

6) If the teams' double play total is high, this number is lower, because double plays also are the responsibility of fielders.

7) If the team has a good Defensive Efficiency Record (DER), this number is lower, because DER is the responsibility of fielders. DER is an answer to this question: Of all balls put in play against this team, what percentage were turned into outs?

Regarding point 6, double plays are also adjusted for the team's expected double plays. Expected double plays are based on the league double play average, adjusted for the ground ball rate of the team, and adjusted for the number of runners on first base against the team. If a team has a lot of runners on base and their pitchers get ground balls, obviously we expect them to turn more double plays. The 1985 Atlanta Braves, because they had a ground-ball staff that led the National League in walks, had an expectation of turning 193 double plays. They actually turned 197, so they exceeded expectations,

but only by four. The 1988 Mets, because they had a strikeout staff with relatively few runners on base, had an expectation of turning only 105 double plays. They actually turned 127, exceeding expectations by 22. We adjust the defense's responsibility for runs saved based not only on double plays, but also on double plays versus expectation. A fuller explanation of how we figure expected double plays will be given in section III of this article (below).

Based on these six factors, we estimate what percentage of the team's defensive success—what percentage of their runs saved—should be credited to the team's fielders. This is done in the following way.

Figure 1 (F1) is the batters faced by the team's pitchers.

Figure 2 (F2) is figured as follows:
Strikeouts,
Plus 1.25 * Walks,
Plus 1.25 * Hit Batsmen,
Plus 6 * Home Runs Allowed.

F2 is a summary of the events for which we hold the pitcher responsible. We start with the strikeouts, which figure into the end game as a simple percentage of batter's faced; the higher the percentage of strikeouts by the pitchers, the higher the share of pitcher responsibility. Walks and Hit Batsmen are multiplied by 1.25 because one walk or hit batsman has more impact on the game than one strikeout. Home Runs allowed are weighted at 6.00 because these events have an immense impact on the outcomes of games, compared one to one with strikeouts.

Figure 3 (F3) is team's Defensive Efficiency Record, minus .625, times the number of balls in play against the team. (As a team's pitchers get credit for every strikeout, their fielders get credit for every out recorded above a level of zero competence. A defensive efficiency record of .625 is considered to be a zero-competence level for a team's fielders. The team's fielders get a "point" for every out recorded above that level.)

Figure 4 (F4) is the team's double plays, times 2, plus 3 times (Double Plays Minus Expected Double Plays), plus two times errors, plus F3.

Figure 5 (F5) is F1, minus F2, minus F4, times 2/3, plus F2.

Figure 6 (F6) is F1 minus F5.

The percentage of the team's runs saved which are attributed to the team's fielders, rather than their pitchers, is F6/F1.

Let's run through that for the 1988 Dodgers. Dodger pitchers in 1988 faced 6050 batters; that would be our F1.

Of those 6050 batters, Dodger pitchers struck out 1,029, walked 473, and hit 22. They gave up 84 home runs. That makes their "F2" score 2152 (1029, + 495*1.25, + 84*6).

Their fielders had a Defensive Efficiency record of .713 (.71316), which is very good, and there were 4,442 balls in play against the team. That makes an F3 score of 385, meaning that the Dodger fielders recorded 385 outs above a team of zero-competence fielders.

The Dodgers turned 126 double plays against an expectation of 128. They committed 142 errors. That makes an F4 score of 915 (2*126 + (3* (126-128)) + (2 * 142) + 385).

Dodger pitchers faced 6050 batters, and we have attributed sole responsibility for 2,152 of those to the pitchers, and 915 to the fielders. That makes 3,067 "attributed" batters, which leaves 2,933 "un-attributed" batters. Two-thirds of those we now assign to the pitchers, and one-third to the fielders. That makes 4,141 batters attributed to the pitchers, which leaves 1,909 to be attributed to the fielders. Thus, 31.6% of the fielding success of the 1988 Dodgers is attributed to their fielders (1909/6050); 68.4% is attributed to their pitchers.

(At this point I can foresee a long line of misunderstanding and argument which will flow from this, so let me spend a minute to try to stave that off. People will try to tell me that Vorosian analysis has demonstrated that all a pitcher really does is give up home runs, strike out batters and issue walks; otherwise, one pitcher is the same as another. Therefore, since one pitcher is the same as another when the ball is in play, the lion's share of the credit for recording outs on balls in play—if not, indeed, ALL of the credit for recording outs on balls in play—should go to the fielders, not the pitchers.

The first problem with that analysis is that it would lead to absurdly low run-prevention values for pitchers. An attribution system that proceeded on those assumptions would lead to a Cy Young pitcher being credited with preventing an unrealistically low number of runs, and would imply that major league teams were behaving unreasonably in paying pitchers what they pay them and in carrying 12 or 13 pitchers on the roster, since these players would appear to have very little value.

What that approach essentially fails to recognize is that a pitcher succeeds when he gets a ball in play. Balls in play generally become outs. If you visualize sub-major league pitchers on the same scale as major league pitchers, the sub-major league pitchers would issue vast numbers of walks and would give up huge numbers of home runs, leaving very little room for the defense to save the game. Major league pitchers succeed because they avoid those outcomes, getting balls in play—and Vorosian analysis shows that one ball in play is very much like another one.

Stated another way, the batter is two-thirds out when he puts the ball in play. Stated in a third way, Vorosian analysis shows that a very large percentage of the composite material of an offense is essentially inert, inactive material. The fact that a very large percentage of the game is not a variable makes the "Active" or variable component of the equation much more important.

Two pitchers each have 900 balls in play, but one of them has 100 strikeouts, 80 walks and 25 homers allowed; the other has 200 strikeouts, 50 walks and 10 home runs allowed. Stated relative to the batters faced, the differences of 100 strikeouts, 30 walks and 15 home runs are small distinctions—yet because of the interactive nature of offense, which works on long sequences, these are (as we know) huge differences in practice. This is why we attribute the outcomes of balls in play primarily to pitchers, rather than to fielders.)

Anyway, 31.6% of the run-prevention success of the 1988 Dodgers is attributed to their fielders. This is a mid-range number, a normal number; the average for all National League teams throughout the 1980s was 31.4%. The highest figures of the decade, ranging from 36.2% to 34.2%, were by the St. Louis Cardinals of 1981, 1980, 1982, 1986 and 1985, in that order. The lowest figures were 27.2%, by the 1987 Houston Astros and by the 1987 Chicago Cubs, and 28.2%, by the 1986 Chicago Cubs.

At the time I publish this article I will also post a spreadsheet, 1980s Pitcher v Defense Percentages, which is intended to enable you to follow the math for all 1980s NL teams to whatever extent you might wish to do.

Combining Steps One and Two

Once we have determined how many Runs were Saved by each team and what percentage of those should be attributed to the defense, we can combine those to calculate how many Runs were Saved by each team's defense. These numbers are also in the file, 1980s Pitcher v Defense Percentages.

These are the ten National League teams of the 1980s which we credit with saving the most runs by defensive play:

Year	City	Team	Runs Saved
1986	St. Louis	Cardinals	268
1982	St. Louis	Cardinals	261
1980	Philadelphia	Phillies	249
1985	Chicago	Cubs	249
1984	Atlanta	Braves	249
1987	Montreal	Expos	245
1982	Atlanta	Braves	244
1988	Montreal	Expos	244
1988	Los Angeles	Dodgers	242
1984	Los Angeles	Dodgers	242

And these are the ten teams that we credit with Saving the fewest Runs by defense, not counting the strike-blighted 1981 season:

Year	City	Team	Runs Saved
1984	San Francisco	Giants	148
1986	San Diego	Padres	162
1985	San Francisco	Giants	164
1988	Houston	Astros	165
1988	Philadelphia	Phillies	166
1989	Philadelphia	Phillies	167
1980	New York	Mets	168
1986	Los Angeles	Dodgers	171
1989	Pittsburgh	Pirates	172
1982	San Francisco	Giants	175

III. Attributing Runs Saved to the Shortstop Position

We now begin the third stage of our four-stage process, which is dividing those runs saved by the team up among the non-pitching fielding positions.

Again, we have to make assumptions that we cannot absolutely verify. Future research may find ways to verify these assumptions or to replace them, but. . .we have to start somewhere.

Our system begins with the assumption that 15.4% of the Runs Saved by a team's fielders are credited to the shortstops, stressing of course that it will not be 15.4% in all cases. 15.4% is a starting point, not an ending point. The starting percentages we use are:

15.4% for catchers
9.9% for first basemen
13.6% for second basemen
12.4% for third basemen

15.4% for shortstops
33.3% for the three outfielders

Prior to 1920 the percentages at second base and third base are reversed (13.6% for third basemen, 12.4% for second basemen) and from 1920-1939 second base and third base are credited with 13% each.

We start with 15.4% for shortstops, and we adjust this for:

1) Assists versus expected assists,
2) Putouts versus expected putouts,
3) Errors versus expected errors, and
4) Double Plays versus expected Double Plays.

Assists. To figure expected assists, we take the league percentage of assists that are recorded by shortstops, apply that to the team, and increase that by one assist for every 100 balls put in play by left-handed pitchers, above or below the league average. Let's stick with the 1988 Dodgers for illustration.

In the National League in 1988 there were 21,246 assists, of which 5,877 were by shortstops (I hope. These are the numbers I have in my file, and at the moment I am too lazy to double-check them.) Anyway, that's 27.66%, so we expect 27.66% of the assists by the Dodgers to be recorded by their shortstops.

The 1988 Dodgers had 1,746 assists. We expect 27.66% of those to be made by their shortstops, so that's 483 expected assists by Dodger shortstops.

You will note here that we have adjusted for the Ground Ball tendency of the pitching staff. The vast majority of ground ball outs result in assists, and the vast majority of assists result from ground balls. If the team's pitching staff throws ground balls the team will have a high assists totals, always and absolutely; therefore, we will expect the team's infielders to have more assists. Thus we are not misled by the ground ball tendency of the pitching staff.

However, the 1988 Dodgers had only 875 balls put in play against left-handed pitching, which is a very low number—lowest in the National League. Balls put in play against left-handed pitching tend disproportionately to go to the left side of the infield (third base and shortstop). Since the Dodgers had few left-handed pitchers, that reduces somewhat the number of expected assists by their shortstops.

(You actually can ignore this effect with regard to shortstops, with minimal consequence. It makes a real difference with regard to third basemen and first basemen, basically a negligible difference with regard to shortstops and second basemen. But since we have to figure it with regard to the corner infielders, we have the data we need and we'll factor it in with regard to the middle infielders as well.)

Anyway, the average National League team in 1988 had 1,526 balls put in play against left-handed pitching. The Dodgers had only 875. That's -651. For every extra 100 balls put in play against lefties there is an expected increase of one assist by the shortstops, so that's -6.51 for the Dodgers. This reduces the expected assists by Dodger shortstops to 476.

Dodger shortstops in 1988 actually had 497 assists. That's 21 more than expected. For every assist above expectations, we will credit them with an additional .13 runs saved. Put that number aside, and we'll use it later in summing up.

Now let's deal with **Putouts**. We begin by figuring the league's shortstop putouts as a percentage of league putouts, minus strikeouts, minus assists. Strikeouts are not balls in play, and assisted putouts are ground balls, so we eliminate those as potential shortstop putouts. The result we can call the League Shortstop Unassisted Putout Percentage.

League SS PO divided by League PO minus Strikeouts minus Assists

We multiply the league shortstop unassisted putout percentage times the team putouts, minus putouts, minus assists. This is the expected number of putouts by the team's shortstops.

Except that, again, we have to adjust for the left-handed/right-handed bias of the team. There is an increase of one assist by shortstops for every one hundred balls in play against left-handed pitchers; there is a decrease of one putout by shortstops for every 110 balls in play. That's why you can kind of ignore the left-handed/right-handed bias for shortstops; it pretty much evens out.

Anyway, let's do the 1988 Dodgers for illustration. In the National League in 1988 there were 52,442 putouts (I hope. I'm not double-checking this data as I work.) Of those, 11,032 were strikeouts (that leaves 41,410), and 21,246 were assisted. That leaves 20,164 un-assisted putouts for the league, a high percentage of which are balls caught in the air. Of those 20,164 un-assisted putouts, 3,112 were by shortstops. That's 15.4%-- coincidentally the same percentage of the run prevention value that we are attributing to shortstops.

Anyway, the 1988 Dodgers had 4,390 putouts, of which 1,029 were strikeouts (leaving 3,361) and 1,746 were assisted (leaving 1,615). We expect Dodger shortstops to record 15.4% of those 1,615 putouts. That's 249. We expect Dodger shortstops to have 249 putouts.

Except that batters tend to pop out the ball to the opposite field, so this figure should be higher for the Dodgers, because they have little left-handed pitching (which means that they have lots of right-handed pitching, which means that they faced lots of opposition left-handed batters, who tend to pop out to shortstop and third base.) The Dodgers, as we established earlier, had 651 fewer balls in play against left-handed pitchers than average, and there will be an increase of shortstop putouts of one for every 110 of those. That's an increase of...well, let's call it six. So we expect Dodger shortstops (1988) to have 255 putouts, rather than 249.

Dodger shortstops actually had 277 putouts, 22 more than expected. For each one putout over expectation, we credit the shortstop with .04 runs saved. Again, we will put this figure aside, and come back to it when we are summing up.

Errors. The error percentage is the complement of the fielding percentage. If the league fielding percentage at a position is .900, the error percentage is .100; if the fielding percentage is .950, the error percentage is .050.

We figure the number of expected errors for the team at the position, based on the league error percentage at the position. The fielding percentage of National League shortstops in 1988 was .967; therefore, the error percentage was .033 (.0326).

Dodger shortstops in 1988 had 794 total chances. We expect them, then, to have 26 errors. They actually had only 20 errors.

For each 4 errors less than the league norm, we credit the shortstops with one extra run saved. Again, set this number aside, and we will come back to it in summing up.

Double Plays. We have to start by estimating the number of runners on first base against each team. We have to start there because, to interpret the double play data, we have to calculate expected double plays, and, to estimate expected double plays, we have to consider how many runners are on first base against each team.

The formula for estimated runners on first base (ERO1B) is Hits minus Home Runs, times .781, plus walks, plus hit batsmen, minus wild pitches, minus balks, minus passed balls, minus stolen bases allowed, minus runners caught stealing.

$$ERO1B = (H-HR)*.781 + BB + HBP - WP - BK - PB - SB - CS$$

I would explain how we derived that formula, but you'd never get that hour of your life back. We figure the number of estimated runners on first base against the team, and against the league. Find the percentage, team divided by league. Multiply the league double plays by that percentage. That's ExpDP1, expected Double Plays, stage 1.

This we have to modify by the team's number of assists per inning pitched. Figure the team's assists per inning pitched, and divide by the league norm. Multiply ExpDP1 by that figure, and the result is expected Double Plays.

Subtract expected from actual Double Plays for the team. For each 10 double plays above or below expectation, credit the shortstop with one run saved.

One Run Saved for each ten Double Plays (I can hear you asking). Why so few?

For shortstops and second basemen, we don't look at the individual double play total; we look at the team number. It just works better; the individual double play totals are subject to a variety of biases, and they're difficult to work with. Unlike almost every other offensive and defensive stat, they don't even add up to the team total. It's much cleaner to ask the question, did the team turn more double plays than we would expect them to turn? If the team turned more double plays than expected, we can assume that that reflects well on the second basemen and shortstops for the team.

But on the individual level, there are a number of issues. First, when shortstops and second basemen participate in a double play, they are credited with putouts and assists. We have already given them credit for those putouts and assists. We are now double-counting the credits.

Second, we are evaluating team double plays here. Some of the double plays that we are crediting here go 5-4-3, 1-4-3, or. ..well, 3 un-assisted, or 4 un-assisted. Some of them didn't have anything to do with the shortstop. We are not crediting specific double plays; we are crediting the shortstop for his presumed contribution to the double play excellence of the team, which sometimes involves plays that he didn't have anything to do with.

What happens if the team's second baseman is superb at turning the double play, but their shortstop is lousy? What happens is, you're going to have one hell of a time sorting that one out, no matter how you approach it. My approach is to credit the team with the team's ability to turn double plays, and then to presume that the shortstop is a contributor to that. I doubt that you can do much better, but feel free to try.

Anyway, that's why the ratio of runs saved to double plays is so low; there are issues of attribution.

Let's do the 1988 Dodgers. In the National League in 1988 there were 14,293 estimated runners on first base, of which 1,158 were against the Dodgers. That's 8.1%.

There were 1,609 double plays in the league. 8.1% of that would be 130. We expect the Dodgers to turn 130 double plays, but now let's look at the ground ball rate.

In the National League in 1988 there were 21,246 assists (ground balls) in 17,480.2 innings, or 1.215 assists per inning. For the Dodgers, there were 1,746 assists in 1463.1 innings, or 1.193 assists per inning. The Dodgers' ground ball rate was 1.8% below the league norm. We thus have to reduce their expected double plays by 1.8%.

OK, that cuts the Dodgers' expected double plays from 130 to 128. The Dodgers in 1988 actually turned 126 double plays, two less than expected. Put this number aside, and we'll pull it into the overall estimate of the team's defensive performance at the position, which begins now.

OK, the Runs Saved by Dodger Shortstops in 1988 are:

37 as a base number (242 * .154),

plus 3 because the team exceeded its expected shortstop assists,

plus 1 because the team exceeded its expected shortstop putouts,

plus 1 because the team had fewer shortstop errors than expected,

minus zero (minus 2/10) because the team turned two fewer double plays than expected.

Altogether that makes 42 Runs Saved by Dodger shortstops in 1988—the highest total in the National League in 1988.

I have posted the file 1980s RS SS 2, which contains all of the information necessary to figure these estimates for every National League team in the 1980s.

Since we have come this far, we might now observe the year-by-year team leaders:

Year	City	Team	Runs Saved
1980	St. Louis	Cardinals	45
1981	St. Louis	Cardinals	27
1982	St. Louis	Cardinals	53
1983	Pittsburgh	Pirates	40
1984	St. Louis	Cardinals	44
1985	St. Louis	Cardinals	44
1986	St. Louis	Cardinals	46
1987	St. Louis	Cardinals	46
1988	Los Angeles	Dodgers	42
1989	Chicago	Cubs	40

IV. Assigning Credit to the Individual Shortstop

Finally, we have to move the credit for preventing runs from the position to the individual shortstop.

This is work, but it's conceptually simple. I can explain it in one paragraph, two sentences. We take the defensive statistics of the team at the position, and pro-rate those to the innings played by each shortstop, thus creating an "expected putouts", "expected assists", "expected errors" and "expected double plays" by each individual shortstop. We credit the shortstop with his share of the Runs Saved by the team at the position, based on innings, but modified by the same rates used on the team level—.04 for each putout, .13 for each assist, .25 for each error, and .10 for each double play.

These are the defensive statistics for the Los Angeles Dodger shortstops in 1988, aggregate:

G	DI	DI3	PO	A	Err	DP
181	1463.1	4390	277	497	20	94

DI is "defensive innings"; DI3 is "thirds of a defensive inning", also known as "Outs". Of the 4,390 DI3, Alfredo Griffin was in the field for 2,378, and Dave Anderson for 1,947:

	G	DI	DI3	PO	A	Err	DP
	181	1463.1	4390	277	497	20	94
Alfredo Griffin	93	792.2	2378				
Dave Anderson	82	649	1947				
Mike Sharperson	4	18.2	56				
Jeff Hamilton	2	2	3				

Based on the defensive innings, then, we could expect Alfredo Griffin to have recorded 150 putouts and 269 assists, Dave Anderson 123 putouts and 220 assists, Mike Sharperson 4 and 6, and Jeff Hamilton one of each:

	G	DI	DI3	PO	A	Err	DP
	181	1463.1	4390	277	497	20	94
Alfredo Griffin	93	792.2	2378	**150**	**269**	11	51
Dave Anderson	82	649	1947	**123**	**220**	9	42
Mike Sharperson	4	18.2	56	**4**	**6**	0	1
Jeff Hamilton	2	3	9	**1**	**1**	0	0

In fact, though, Griffin recorded only 145 putouts, and only 264 assists. These are the actual defensive statistics of the four Dodger shortstops:

	G	DI	DI3	PO	A	Err	DP
	181	1463.1	4390	277	497	20	94
Alfredo Griffin	93	792.2	2378	**145**	**264**	15	44
Dave Anderson	82	649	1947	**128**	**225**	5	49
Mike Sharperson	4	18.2	56	**4**	**5**	0	0
Jeff Hamilton	2	3	9	**0**	**3**	0	1

On a per-inning basis, Anderson did better than Griffin in all four categories—more putouts, more assists, fewer errors and more double plays. This chart compares the actual to the expected data:

	G	DI	DI3	PO	A	Err	DP
	181	1463.1	4390	277	497	20	94
Alfredo Griffin	93	792.2	2378	-5	-5	4	-7
Dave Anderson	82	649	1947	5	5	-4	7
Mike Sharperson	4	18.2	56	0	-1	0	-1
Jeff Hamilton	2	3	9	-1	2	0	1

The Dodger shortstops in 1988 were credited with saving 42.13 runs. When we apportion those based on innings in the field, we get 22.82 Runs Saved for Griffin, 18.68 for Anderson, and 0.54 for Mike Sharperson:

City	DI3	Runs
	4390	42.13
Alfredo Griffin	2378	22.82
Dave Anderson	1947	18.68
Mike Sharperson	56	0.54
Jeff Hamilton	9	0.09

However, when we subtract .2 runs from Griffin for Putouts (-5 * .04), .65 runs for Assists (-5 * .13), 1 for Errors (4 * .25) and .7 for Double Plays (-7 * .10), Griffin drops to 20 Runs Saved, and Anderson goes up to 21:

	DI3	Runs	PO	A	Err	DP	Total
	4390	42.13	0	0	0	0	42.13
Alfredo Griffin	2378	22.82	-0.2	-0.65	-1	-0.7	20.27
Dave Anderson	1947	18.68	0.2	0.65	1	0.7	21.23
Mike Sharperson	56	0.54	0	-0.13	0	-0.1	0.31
Jeff Hamilton	9	0.09	-0.05	0.26	0	0.1	0.40

Noting for the record that Griffin does not have bad defensive stats in 1988; he merely has bad defensive stats compared to Anderson. The Dodgers, after all, have the best defensive stats in the league at the position.

The Results

Make That

*** The Results!! ***

By the process outlined here, the top three Run-Saving shortstops for each year in the 1980s were as follows:

Year	Player	Team	Runs Saved
1980	Ozzie Smith	SD	38
1980	Gary Concepcion	Cin	33
1980	Garry Templeton	StL	32
1981	Ozzie Smith	SD	26
1981	Dave Concepcion	Cin	23
1981	Chris Speier	Mon	21
1982	Ozzie Smith	StL	46
1982	Rafael Ramirez	Atl	40
1982	Dave Concepcion	Cin	36
1983	Dale Berra	Pit	40
1983	Ozzie Smith	StL	36
1983	Dickie Thon	Hou	34
1984	Ozzie Smith	StL	34
1984	Craig Reynolds	Hou	29
1984	Rafael Ramirez	Atl	29
1985	Ozzie Smith	StL	44
1985	Garry Templeton	SD	38
1985	Rafael Santana	NY	29
1986	Ozzie Smith	StL	41
1986	Jose Uribe	SF	33
1986	Shawon Dunston	Chi	31
1987	Ozzie Smith	StL	43
1987	Rafael Santana	NY	29
1987	Garry Templeton	SD	27
1988	Ozzie Smith	StL	34
1988	Barry Larkin	Cin	32
1988	Shawon Dunston	Chi	27
1989	Ozzie Smith	StL	34
1989	Jose Uribe	SF	34
1989	Shawon Dunston	Chi	33

Apparently Ozzie Smith was pretty good; I'll put out a news release. There are no actual ties in this data, of course; the appearance of ties is due to rounding off to the nearest run.

Simultaneous with the publication of this, I will publish the spreadsheet 1980s RS SS 3, which will have full data for every National League shortstop of the 1980s.

This is the career data for those players who had 900 or more innings at shortstop during the decade, plus Luis Gomez, who had 898:

Player	G	DI	PO	A	E	DP	FPct	Runs Saved
Luis Aguayo	238	1273.1	224	413	24	81	.964	24
Dave Anderson	403	3008.1	572	1044	47	197	.972	75
Bob Bailor	178	996.1	184	385	14	70	.976	22
Rafael Belliard	355	2433	425	834	35	142	.973	46
Dale Berra	542	4584.1	824	1651	106	277	.959	108
Larry Bowa	741	6112.2	1099	2199	83	387	.975	131
Hubie Brooks	371	3191.2	483	1008	70	190	.955	49
Dave Concepcion	875	7444	1414	2468	113	477	.972	166
Ivan DeJesus	737	6238	1061	2209	125	384	.963	112
Mariano Duncan	356	2984.1	520	1028	84	165	.949	47
Kevin Elster	320	2417.1	451	760	31	130	.975	56
Tom Foley	328	2168.1	435	693	33	141	.972	51
Tim Foli	219	1845	368	683	27	145	.975	48
Ron Gardenhire	230	1642	360	596	45	97	.955	31
Luis Gomez	140	898	150	338	19	57	.963	18
Alfredo Griffin	224	1921	353	597	29	113	.970	45
Steve Jeltz	581	4366.2	832	1476	68	270	.971	95
Howard Johnson	162	947	154	278	23	60	.949	16
Sammy Khalifa	160	1311	246	485	27	71	.964	26
Barry Larkin	385	3287	588	1214	62	191	.967	84
Johnnie LeMaster	666	5463.1	1081	1921	115	315	.963	92
Jose Oquendo	259	1817.2	350	644	38	127	.963	42
Spike Owen	142	1212.1	232	388	13	65	.979	26
Al Pedrique	126	930	181	314	15	66	.971	21
Rafael Ramirez	1155	9883.2	1858	3473	263	755	.953	206
Craig Reynolds	783	5965.2	1048	2110	97	369	.970	140
Luis Rivera	186	1409.1	233	447	30	97	.958	29
Bill Russell	606	4913.1	859	1835	105	284	.962	109
Rafael Santana	484	3894.2	810	1267	65	266	.970	98
Ozzie Smith	1452	12759.1	2505	5054	164	950	.979	378
Chris Speier	623	4772.2	946	1666	79	315	.971	115
Kurt Stillwell	131	1026	181	322	34	62	.937	20
Frank Taveras	245	1870	377	565	51	112	.949	24
Garry Templeton	1279	10921.1	2152	3897	222	723	.965	252
Andres Thomas	476	4002	738	1439	99	291	.957	81
Derrel Thomas	177	1166.2	234	369	37	82	.942	24
Dickie Thon	704	5554.1	980	1991	100	384	.967	131
Jose Uribe	691	5784.1	1047	2022	93	400	.971	136

On a per-inning basis, we estimate that Ozzie saved 30 runs per 1,000 innings. These are the shortstops, rated on a per-inning basis:

	G	DI	Runs Saved	RS/ 1000 DI
Ozzie Smith	1452	12759.1	378	30
Tim Foli	219	1845	48	26
Barry Larkin	385	3287	84	25
Rafael Santana	484	3894.2	98	25
Dave Anderson	403	3008.1	75	25
Shawon Dunston	605	5165.1	125	24
Chris Speier	623	4772.2	115	24
Tom Foley	328	2168.1	51	24
Dale Berra	542	4584.1	108	24
Craig Reynolds	783	5965.2	140	24
Alfredo Griffin	224	1921	45	24
Dickie Thon	704	5554.1	131	24
Jose Uribe	691	5784.1	136	23
Kevin Elster	320	2417.1	56	23
Jose Oquendo	259	1817.2	42	23
Garry Templeton	1279	10921.1	252	23
Al Pedrique	126	930	21	23
Dave Concepcion	875	7444	166	22
Bill Russell	606	4913.1	109	22
Bob Bailor	178	996.1	22	22
Steve Jeltz	581	4366.2	95	22
Larry Bowa	741	6112.2	131	21
Spike Owen	142	1212.1	26	21
Rafael Ramirez	1155	9883.2	206	21
Luis Rivera	186	1409.1	29	21
Luis Gomez	140	898	18	20
Andres Thomas	476	4002	81	20
Derrel Thomas	177	1166.2	24	20
Sammy Khalifa	160	1311	26	20
Kurt Stillwell	131	1026	20	19
Rafael Belliard	355	2433	46	19
Luis Aguayo	238	1273.1	24	19
Ron Gardenhire	230	1642	31	19
Ivan DeJesus	737	6238	112	18
Howard Johnson	162	947	16	17
Johnnie LeMaster	666	5463.1	92	17
Mariano Duncan	356	2984.1	47	16
Hubie Brooks	371	3191.2	49	15
Frank Taveras	245	1870	24	13

Tomorrow, I'll debate myself about some of the choices I have made here, and talk a little bit about how else this might have been done.

Runs Saved Against Zero Afterthoughts

[Editor's note: This follow-up article to "Runs Saved Against Zero" originally ran on BillJamesOnline.com on August 19, 2011.]

Yesterday I introduced a method to estimate the number of Runs Saved by a shortstop, as opposed to a zero-value defensive player. I believe there is merit in the method. I believe that it reliably identifies the best defensive players, not 100% of the time, and it creates a context in which to compare and contrast offensive and defensive values. I think it is worth having.

However, there were choices to be made in constructing that system, and it's not absolutely clear that all of the choices I made were the right ones. The number of runs that we are estimating a defender to save seems unrealistically low. It is low compared to other types of defensive analysis, and it is low compared to intuitive observation. Anyone can look at a good defensive shortstop, playing short, and realize that the difference between him and a complete oaf at shortstop must be more than 30 or 40 runs a year.

What we are calling the zero-point in this analysis is not truly the zero point. This is true for two reasons. First, one cannot score fewer runs in a ballgame or in a season than zero. If my wife and sons and I were to play against a major league baseball team, we might score zero runs in a season, but we could not score fewer than zero—thus, could not miss the league average by more than 750 runs, assuming that 750 runs is the average.

We could and would, however, allow more than 1500 runs, or 750 more than average. 1500 runs allowed (2Lg, or twice the league norm) is not a true zero-point; it is merely a point which is equidistant from true zero on the opposite end of the scale.

Also, if a team scored zero runs in a season and allowed 750, their winning percentage would be zero, but if they scored 750 and allowed 1500, it would not be zero. It would be about .200. In order to have no expectation of ever winning a game, you would have to allow an infinite number of runs.

Of course one cannot work very well with infinite numbers, but one could make the system more realistic by moving the theoretical zero-point further away from the league norm. Let us suppose that the theoretical zero point was not 2Lg, but 3Lg (three times the league norm). That would be treating a .100 winning percentage as

.000, rather than treating .200 as .000, a smaller distortion. That system would portray the defenders on a team as preventing 1500 runs, if the league norm was 750 runs scored, rather than preventing 750 runs (including those prevented by the pitcher).

In the system as I outlined it, if one pitcher allows 80 runs and a teammate pitches the same number of innings and allows 60 runs, this system doesn't show a 20-run difference between them, since it will credit part of the separation to the fielders. If we changed the zero point to 3Lg, then we could restore the pitchers to full credit for runs saved, and still greatly increase the percentage of success that was credited to the defensive players. This would increase the runs saved against zero estimate for Ozzie Smith in a typical season from about 35-40 to something more than 100.

This would imply that the runs saved were much greater than the runs allowed, but we can still make offense equal defense by assigning less Win Value to one run saved than to one run scored. This is realistic. If a team is average defensively, if they allow 750 runs, then to go from 400 runs scored to 500 increases their expected wins by 14. But if a team is average offensively—that is, if the team scores 750 runs—then to go from 1100 runs allowed down to 1000, although it is a parallel step on the other side of the spectrum, increases their expected wins by less than 7. One run scored is more valuable than one run saved, since runs scored rise from zero and runs saved fall from an infinite sky.

But there are problems with that theory, too, among those that that theory reduces the Win Value of pitchers so low that teams appear to be behaving very irrationally in terms of the resources that they devote to pitching—resources being roster space, salary costs, and player development costs.

We could solve these problems by going back to a primitive assertion: baseball is 75% pitching. The argument isn't as irrational as I once argued that it is. What is meant by saying that baseball is 75% pitching is this.

Offense is bounded by zero; a team cannot score fewer than zero runs, therefore wins result from scoring more runs than zero.

Defense, on the other hand, is unbounded; a team can allow any number of runs—let us say four times the league average. From a defensive standpoint, wins result from allowing fewer runs than four times the league average. Therefore, the number of runs that must be prevented to win the pennant is much larger than the number of runs that must be scored.

But there are problems with that theory, too. If this theory were meaningfully true in major league baseball, then the standard deviation of runs allowed would have to be higher than the standard deviation of runs scored, which is not true. The theory could be true in a theoretical universe involving players at widely different skill levels, but irrelevant in a real universe in which only players comparable in skill level are competing with one another.

All mathematical models represent the baseball universe as being more simple than it actually is. This is a limitation that we live with. Because the mathematical models are always simplifications, they are always untrue if looked at from one angle or another.

Runs Created for Pitchers

Many years ago, back in the 1980's when his *Baseball Abstracts* were the bestselling baseball books on the market, Bill James invented Runs Created. Runs Created is a formula that measures the total offensive performance of a hitter, including such things as hitting for average, hitting for power, getting on base and stealing bases. One of the best things about the design of the formula is that if you total it up for all players and teams, it adds up to the number of runs scored in the league. Bill has made tweaks to his formula over the years and, to this day, it remains one of the best, if not the best, methods for measuring a hitter's output.

In Volume II of *The Fielding Bible*, we went one step further. We wanted to be able to measure not just the offensive contribution of a player but his defensive contribution as well. To do this, we needed to add three things to Runs Created to come up with what we called Total Runs:

1) Baserunning Runs—Bill's formula accounts for a player's base stealing contributions, but not what he does on the bases other than that. For example, how often does he go first to third on a single, score from first on a double, score from third on a flyball to the outfield, get thrown out on the bases, etc. Baserunning Runs estimates that contribution. When added to Runs Created, we now have a slightly better estimate of a player's total offense. Runs Created plus Baserunning Runs still adds up to the league total runs because Baserunning Runs total up to zero for the league. A player has positive Baserunning Runs if he is above average on the basepaths and negative Baserunning Runs if he is below average.

2) Defensive Runs Saved—Like Baserunning Runs, DRS totals to zero across the league. It raises or lowers the hitter's total based on whether his defensive contributions are above or below average.

3) Positional Adjustment—Shortstops are more valuable defensively than left fielders. Catchers are more valuable than first basemen. The Positional Adjustment estimates the defensive value of each position relative to each other. For example, we say that a player has a value of 36 runs if he plays shortstop for a full season. A first baseman gets 13 runs for a full season.

Breaking Defense into Pitching and Fielding

Now we want to take a third step. We want to bring pitchers into our Total Runs calculation so that we can compare every player in baseball to each other. To do that we need to come up with a way to convert a pitcher's actions into runs. We are going to call this Pitching Runs Created. The way we do that is by looking at total defense (which includes pitching) and then breaking that down between pitching and fielding.

Traditionally, defensive metrics (in this case referring to fielding) have been based around zero, with above-average players in the positives, below-average players in the negatives, and league-average players right at zero. Our own Plus/Minus and Defensive Runs Saved systems are two examples. When we want to compare defense to offense, however, we need to unite the two on a common baseline.

In the article "Runs Saved Against Zero" (page 151), Bill James introduces a system for measuring defensive contributions (including pitching) on the same scale as Runs Created. While Bill's article focuses primarily on evaluating fielders, we already have our own system for that. Instead, we're interested in splitting the credit between fielders and pitchers, then appropriately evaluating each pitcher's contribution.

We've come up with a method to calculate Pitching Runs Created. It starts with the same premise as Bill's article, that offense equals defense. Pitching Runs Created plus Defensive Runs equals Hitting Runs Created. To get there, we have a lot of math we are going to walk you through, but if you'd like to skip that and take our word for it that we've figured out how to do Pitching Runs Created, skip "The Calculation" section here and go right to "The Math Is Over Now."

The Calculation

First, we calculate Pitching & Defense Runs Created for each pitcher. We follow a calculation similar to the one laid out in Bill's article. Splitting the National and American Leagues, we multiply the league average number of runs allowed per inning by the pitcher's number of innings pitched, then multiply that by two. From that, we subtract the number of runs allowed by the given pitcher. This result represents the number of runs "created" by the combination of the pitcher and the fielders in those innings. (Of course, pitchers and fielders don't create runs, they attempt to prevent them; we only use the term "runs created" here because we've converted to the same scale as offensive runs.)

We'll use James Shields' 2011 season with Tampa Bay as an example. He threw a career-high 249 1/3 innings, allowing 83 runs. The American League allowed 0.4948 runs per inning last season, roughly half a run per inning. The Pitching & Defense Runs Created with James Shields on the mound was 0.4948 * 249 1/3 * 2 - 83 = 163.7 runs.

Next, we have to split the pitcher credit from the fielder credit. We again borrow some pieces from Bill's formulas, but since we have Defensive Runs Saved for each team, we make a few adjustments to use our defensive measures. We calculate each team's Defensive Runs Saved per inning, and multiply by the number of innings thrown by the given pitcher. In theory, this roughly approximates the number of runs his defense helped or hurt him over the course of the season. We subtract this from the pitcher's Pitching & Defense Runs Created to get a new value; let's call that "A." Shields pitched for baseball's best defensive team, at 85 Runs Saved (in 1,449 innings). For Shields, who pitched 249

1/3 innings, we have his Pitching & Defense Runs Created, 163.7, minus (85 / 1449 * 249 1/3), or "A" = 163.7 - 14.6 = 149.1 runs. This represents the number of Pitching & Defense Runs Created Shields would have amassed with an average defense behind him.

We then estimate what percentage of the team's runs are attributable to the fielders, rather than the pitcher. If a pitcher gets a lot of strikeouts and gives up a lot of walks and home runs, there's nothing the fielders can do about that. We'll give the pitcher more of the credit (or blame). If instead he pitches to contact, the seven guys behind him are doing a larger share of the work and deserve credit. We add the pitcher's Strikeouts + 1.25 * Walks + 1.25 * HBP + 6 * Home Runs, and we subtract this sum from the total number of batters faced. We divide this number by three, then by the total number of batters faced. This is the proportion of the runs we will attribute to the fielders, based on the pitcher's reliance on them. Let's call this quantity "B."

Shields had 225 strikeouts, 65 walks, 5 hit batsmen and a relatively high 26 home runs, 249 + 1.25 * 65 + 1.25 * 5 + 6 * 26 = 468.5. Subtract that from the 975 batters faced by Shields in 2011, then divide by three: (975 - 468.5) / 3 = 168.8. Divide that quotient by the same 975, and we get B = 168.8 / 975 = 0.173. We're attributing 17.3 percent of the runs to the fielders, and the rest to the pitchers. This is a relatively low percentage, since Shields had a high number of strikeouts and gave up a lot of home runs.

Next, we multiply "A," the number of Pitching & Defense Runs Created the pitcher would have amassed with an average defense behind him, by "B," the proportion of the runs we will attribute to the fielders. We then add the team's total Defensive Runs Saved to arrive at Fielding Runs Created, the number of runs attributable to the fielders. Lastly, if we subtract out the Fielding Runs Created from the Pitching & Defense Runs Created, we arrive at the individual pitcher's Pitching Runs Created.

For Shields, A is 149.1 and B is 0.173. The product, 149.1 * 0.173 = 123.3, means that we're crediting Shields with 123.3 Pitching Runs Created. This was the fifth-highest total of 2011, behind a Tiger, an Angel and two Phillies.

The Math Is Over Now

We now have Pitching Runs Created. Our first

question was, does it pass the reasonability test? For example, where does Justin Verlander come out?

Pitching Runs Created Leaders (2011)

Pitcher	Pitching Runs Created
Justin Verlander	143
Jered Weaver	132
Cliff Lee	129
Roy Halladay	126
James Shields	123

Justin Verlander, your 2011 AL Cy Young and MVP winner, tops the list. No surprise there. Three Phillies in the top ten (Cole Hamels tied for eighth). I think we've got something that works.

What about relievers?

Top Pitching Runs Created Relievers (2011)

Pitcher	Pitching Runs Created
Tyler Clippard	55
Jonny Venters	51
David Robertson	49
Jim Johnson	47
Eric O'Flaherty	46

Not who you were expecting? Well, Pitching Runs Created doesn't know if the reliever faced the bottom of the order in the sixth inning of a blowout or if he pitched the ninth against the middle of the Yankees' lineup in a close game. PRC only cares if you threw a lot of innings without allowing many runs. No reliever did that better than Tyler Clippard, who threw 88 1/3 innings with an ERA under 2.00. Jonny Venters had similar numbers but was a little more reliant on the defense behind him.

What about the best pitching seasons of the past nine years?

Top Individual Pitching Runs Created Seasons (2003-11)

Season	Pitcher	Pitching Runs Created
2004	Johan Santana	159
2009	Zack Greinke	159
2003	Roy Halladay	150
2006	Johan Santana	146
2011	Justin Verlander	143
2004	Curt Schilling	140
2004	Randy Johnson	140
2006	Bronson Arroyo	140
2007	Jake Peavy	140
2008	CC Sabathia	140

The 2004 Johan Santana and 2009 Zack Greinke tie atop the Pitching Runs Created leaderboard. Both led the American League in ERA (2.61 vs. 2.16), threw almost the same number of innings (228 vs. 229 1/3) and won the Cy Young Award. Despite facing 35 more batters, Greinke in 2009 had fewer strikeouts, walks, hit batters and home runs allowed than Santana in 2004; therefore, Santana earned a larger percentage of the defensive runs. However, Greinke pitched for one of the worst defenses in the nine-year history of Defensive Runs Saved. The 2009 Kansas City Royals were an estimated 100 runs worse than an average defense, and Greinke relied on them a lot. Once we give back some of those runs, Greinke finishes in a virtual tie with Santana for the top spot.

You might be asking yourself "Bronson Arroyo?!?" Yes, that's not a typo. How did he get here? Arroyo threw a career-high 240 2/3 innings with a career-high 184 strikeouts and a career-low 3.29 ERA. He did all this in front of one of the league's worst defenses, featuring a 36-year-old Ken Griffey, Jr. in center, Adam Dunn in left, Edwin Encarnacion at third and Felipe Lopez at short. To top it off, Brandon Phillips had the only below-average defensive season of his career at second base. Despite all of this, Arroyo had the best season of his career. His ERA would have looked even better with a better defense behind him.

Were the 2011 Phillies the best pitching staff in recent memory? PRC says no:

Top Team Pitching Runs Created Seasons
(2003-11)

Season	Team	Pitching Runs Created
2004	Twins	770
2004	Athletics	747
2004	Angels	746
2003	Athletics	745
2007	Red Sox	739
2003	Yankees	737
2007	Padres	735
2004	Cubs	734
2003	Mariners	732
2011	Phillies	727

The 2011 Phillies finish tenth largely because the offensive levels were lower in 2011 than any other season in our time frame. The 2004 Twins, led by Johan Santana, lead the field with 770 Pitching Runs Created.

Now that we have Pitching Runs Created, we can put all the pitchers on the same footing with the hitters. We do that in the next article called "Total Runs."

Total Runs

A baseball player isn't just a hitter or a pitcher or a fielder or a baserunner. He's all of these things. We introduced Total Runs in *The Fielding Bible—Volume II* to determine a player's complete value to his team in the currency of the game: runs. Total Runs factors in a player's contributions in all aspects of the game to paint a complete picture of his talent in the form of one number. With Total Runs, we're trying to find the best all around players in the game.

Since Volume II, we've made a few upgrades to Total Runs. The enhancements to our Runs Saved metrics presented in the pages of this book are only one improvement to the Total Runs formula. We also added Pitching Runs Created (see page 163) to better evaluate a player's contribution on the mound.

Here's the new and improved formula:

Runs Created +
Baserunning Runs +
Runs Saved +
Positional Adjustment +
Pitching Runs Created

Let's review each component of Total Runs.

Runs Created

Runs Created, a formula invented by Bill James, is an estimate of the number of a team's runs that an individual hitter is responsible for. We're using the version printed in the *Bill James Handbook 2012*, without the clutch adjustment at the end. Take Jose Bautista and the Blue Jays, for example. The Jays scored 743 runs in 2011, and based on his offensive contribution to the team through his hits, home runs, walks, sacrifice flies, etc., Bautista's contribution is calculated to be 134 runs.

Baserunning Runs

Running the bases is about choices and risk. A ball is hit, and a runner's mind has to decide many things in a short amount of time. Has the ball been caught? Do I stay or try to advance? How far do I try to advance? How do I get the phone number of the girl sitting in the third row? We can't really evaluate that last choice, but we can assess the others with a technique similar to our Outfield Arms metric (page 445). With the assistance of our handy-dandy Run Matrix (see page 439), we are able to determine the run expectancy change of one of three outcomes: advancing, getting thrown out and staying at a base. We sum all the expectancy changes for each outcome and calculate the average run expectancy change for the league. With this information, we can compare a player's individual performance to the league average to get the player's baserunning runs above or below average. Rangers double play duo Elvis Andrus (11 baserunning runs) and Ian Kinsler (9) were the best baserunners in 2011, while Paul Konerko (-9) was the worst.

Runs Saved

Let's call this your final exam. You've come this far. You define Runs Saved for me. Here's some space (if you need some help, refer to page 17!)

Pitching Runs Created

The biggest addition to the Total Runs formula is Pitching Runs Created. We received a lot of hate mail over the last three years from pitchers who wanted to be evaluated alongside their teammates through Total Runs. Guys, we got your letters, and your wish is our command.

For more a detailed explanation of Pitching Runs Created, see page 163.

Positional Adjustment

In January 2012, when the Mariners acquired catching prospect Jesus Montero from the Yankees, many pundits were hesitant to determine a winner or a loser in the trade because a lot was riding on whether Montero would remain at catcher for the foreseeable future. They get it; not all positions are the same. There's a reason why teams like to put big immobile players at first base— that's where they can do the least damage in the field. However, anybody can play first base (well, almost anybody), but not everyone can handle shortstop without costing the team oodles of runs. Since we want to compare players across positions, we have to adjust for the relative difficulty of each position. That's why we have a Positional Adjustment.

Here are the Positional Adjustment values for a fielder who plays a full season of 1,440 innings at the position:

Positional Adjustment Values

Position	Adjustment (in Runs)
Pitcher	15
Catcher	42
First Base	13
Second Base	32
Third Base	25
Shortstop	36
Left Field	19
Center Field	29
Right Field	20

For fielders who play multiple positions, we pro-rate their Positional Adjustment based on innings at each spot on the diamond. The Positional Adjustment is also dependent on the number of innings played in the field, so, for instance, no catcher will get the full 42 run adjustment unless he caught a full season of innings behind the plate.

Total Runs

Those are the five components to Total Runs. Before we show you the individual record of all players with at least 50 Total Runs in 2011, let's have some fun.

Over the next few pages, you'll notice that most hitters have a big, fat zero in their Pitching Runs Created column. The key word, of course, is *most*. Some position players help their team by taking the mound to throw an inning or two to aid an overworked bullpen. Wilson Valdez of the Phillies did this in 2011 and actually recorded a win. He was also credited with one Pitching Run Created. Let's look at some other position players who have taken the mound recently:

Notable Pitching Runs Created Performances by Hitters

Player	Season	Runs Created
Wilson Valdez	2011	1
Michael Cuddyer	2011	1
Darnell McDonald	2011	-1
Aaron Miles	2010	1
Nick Swisher	2009	1

Aside from Darnell McDonald's disastrous inning in 2011, each player on this list actually helped their team when called upon to pitch.

Of course, we also measure a pitcher's contributions on offense. Here are some notable offensive performances from pitchers:

Notable Offensive Runs Created Performances by Pitchers

Player	Season	Runs Created
Matt Garza	2011	-3
Hiroki Kuroda	2010	-4
Carlos Zambrano	2008	13
Micah Owings	2007	14
Carlos Zambrano	2005	10

Ah, so that's why Hiroki Kuroda wanted to pitch for an American League team this year.

Okay, but this is a Total Runs article, not a Runs Created article, let's see some Total Runs! Here are the top five pitchers in 2011:

Top Pitchers in 2011

Player	Runs Created	BR Runs	Runs Saved	Pos. Adj.	Pitching Runs Created	Total
J. Verlander	0	0	5	3	143	151
J. Weaver	0	0	2	2	132	136
C. Lee	4	0	1	2	129	136
C. Kershaw	4	1	5	2	121	133
J. Shields	-1	0	7	3	123	132

Kudos to Clayton Kershaw for being the most well-rounded pitcher of 2011! Of the American League pitchers on this list, James Shields is the only one who did his team damage in the limited number of at-bats AL pitchers get.

In the next several pages, we're going to list all of the players with at least 50 Total Runs in 2011, and we'll let you peruse that list on your own. Here are your Total Runs leaders for 2009 and 2010:

2009 Total Runs Leaders

Player	Runs Created	BR Runs	Runs Saved	Pos. Adj.	Pitching Runs Created	Total
A. Pujols	149	1	17	12	0	179
Z. Greinke	0	0	8	2	159	169
C. Utley	120	6	12	30	0	168
C. Figgins	101	8	29	24	0	162
B. Zobrist	108	2	25	24	0	159

Greinke won the Cy Young in 2009, thanks to a minuscule 2.16 ERA in 229 1/3 innings. The addition of our new Pitching Runs Created metric captures just how good Greinke was that season...and it was certainly better than a 17th-place finish in AL MVP voting. According to Total Runs, he had the best season of any player in the American League in 2009.

2010 Total Runs Leaders

Player	Runs Created	BR Runs	Runs Saved	Pos. Adj.	Pitching Runs Created	Total
R. Cano	117	4	16	31	0	168
A. Pujols	132	4	8	12	0	156
E. Longoria	104	6	20	23	0	153
C. Gonzalez	123	8	2	20	0	153
J. Hamilton	122	4	11	15	0	152

Despite a breakout season in 2010 in which he hit 54 home runs and drove in 124 runs, Joey Bats (AKA Jose Bautista) doesn't make the top five. His lackluster defense (-3 Runs Saved) and baserunning (-3 runs) helps him fall to number eight. The Yankees' Robinson Cano had a terrific all-around season and played many innings at a position that requires tremendous skill. He had the best season of anyone in 2011.

We've looked at the leaders in Total Runs for 2009 and 2010. Your turn. Flip the page and explore the numbers for 2011.

2011 Total Runs

| Player | Team | OFFENSIVE | | DEFENSIVE | | TOTAL |
		Runs Created	Baserunning Runs	Pitching Runs Created	Positional Average	Runs Saved	Runs
Jacoby Ellsbury	Bos	131	4	0	27	7	169
Dustin Pedroia	Bos	116	-2	0	31	18	163
Ian Kinsler	Tex	106	9	0	28	18	161
Matt Kemp	LAD	131	4	0	28	-5	158
Ben Zobrist	TB	98	2	0	28	29	157
Jose Bautista	Tor	134	5	0	18	-2	155
Alex Gordon	KC	112	6	0	17	19	154
Justin Verlander	Det	0	0	143	3	5	151
Ryan Braun	Mil	127	2	0	16	3	148
Adrian Gonzalez	Bos	127	-5	0	12	12	146
Miguel Cabrera	Det	136	-1	0	12	-3	144
Justin Upton	Ari	112	4	0	19	8	143
Robinson Cano	NYY	109	2	0	30	1	142
Troy Tulowitzki	Col	102	-2	0	30	11	141
Joey Votto	Cin	124	-1	0	13	4	140
Curtis Granderson	NYY	114	4	0	27	-6	139
Jered Weaver	LAA	0	0	132	2	2	136
Cliff Lee	Phi	4	0	129	2	1	136
Chris Young	Ari	82	4	0	28	20	134
Clayton Kershaw	LAD	4	1	121	2	5	133
James Shields	TB	-1	0	123	3	7	132
Hunter Pence	2 Tms	107	4	0	19	1	131
Brandon Phillips	Cin	93	2	0	29	6	130
Andrew McCutchen	Pit	97	1	0	27	5	130
Asdrubal Cabrera	Cle	91	2	0	33	3	129
Evan Longoria	TB	84	1	0	20	22	127
Austin Jackson	Det	70	1	0	25	29	125
Prince Fielder	Mil	126	-5	0	13	-9	125
Michael Bourn	2 Tms	93	7	0	27	-3	124
Elvis Andrus	Tex	73	11	0	32	7	123
Roy Halladay	Phi	-1	-1	126	2	-3	123
Melky Cabrera	KC	99	3	0	26	-5	123
Albert Pujols	StL	104	-3	0	12	9	122
Alexei Ramirez	CWS	76	4	0	35	7	122
Matt Wieters	Bal	70	0	0	34	17	121
Ricky Romero	Tor	0	0	114	2	5	121
Shane Victorino	Phi	92	4	0	23	2	121
Jose Reyes	NYM	102	5	0	27	-13	121
Alex Avila	Det	90	-2	0	34	-3	119
Adrian Beltre	Tex	86	2	0	17	13	118
CC Sabathia	NYY	0	0	121	2	-5	118
Cole Hamels	Phi	0	0	114	2	1	117
Miguel Montero	Ari	77	0	0	34	5	116
Dan Haren	LAA	0	0	111	2	3	116
Starlin Castro	ChC	92	-1	0	35	-10	116
Mark Teixeira	NYY	99	1	0	12	3	115
J.J. Hardy	Bal	78	0	0	28	8	114
Carlos Gonzalez	Col	89	1	0	16	8	114
Yunel Escobar	Tor	77	2	0	28	7	114
Doug Fister	2 Tms	1	0	106	3	4	114
Mike Stanton	Fla	94	0	0	17	3	114
Nick Markakis	Bal	90	2	0	19	3	114
Danny Espinosa	Was	78	-1	0	31	5	113
Brett Gardner	NYY	70	2	0	17	23	112
Carlos Beltran	2 Tms	98	1	0	16	-3	112
Cameron Maybin	SD	68	4	0	24	15	111
Peter Bourjos	LAA	70	3	0	26	12	111
Jhonny Peralta	Det	81	-3	0	31	2	111
Michael Young	Tex	108	2	0	12	-12	110
Carlos Lee	Hou	88	-7	0	14	14	109
Jay Bruce	Cin	91	1	0	19	-2	109
Neil Walker	Pit	78	3	0	31	-3	109
Howie Kendrick	LAA	77	1	0	24	6	108
Erick Aybar	LAA	75	2	0	32	-1	108
Pablo Sandoval	SF	77	-1	0	16	15	107
Jeff Francoeur	KC	89	-2	0	19	1	107
C.J. Wilson	Tex	1	0	107	2	-3	107
Carlos Santana	Cle	88	-3	0	28	-6	107
Ian Kennedy	Ari	1	0	101	2	2	106
Josh Hamilton	Tex	88	0	0	15	2	105
Adam Jones	Bal	81	2	0	26	-4	105
Felix Hernandez	Sea	0	0	108	2	-5	105

| | | OFFENSIVE | | DEFENSIVE | | | TOTAL |
Player	Team	Runs Created	Baserunning Runs	Pitching Runs Created	Positional Average	Runs Saved	Runs
Jimmy Rollins	Phi	78	4	0	30	-7	105
Lance Berkman	StL	105	2	0	15	-17	105
Torii Hunter	LAA	76	2	0	17	9	104
Tim Lincecum	SF	-2	0	104	2	0	104
Dan Uggla	Atl	83	2	0	32	-13	104
R.A. Dickey	NYM	-1	0	92	2	10	103
Mike Napoli	Tex	88	-2	0	17	0	103
Gaby Sanchez	Fla	84	1	0	12	5	102
Chris Carpenter	StL	1	0	99	2	0	102
Gio Gonzalez	Oak	0	0	102	2	-2	102
Drew Stubbs	Cin	75	4	0	27	-4	102
Michael Morse	Was	97	0	0	12	-7	102
Matt Cain	SF	1	0	97	2	1	101
Dexter Fowler	Col	75	7	0	22	-3	101
Paul Konerko	CWS	105	-9	0	9	-4	101
Omar Infante	Fla	68	-1	0	29	4	100
Justin Masterson	Cle	0	0	98	2	0	100
Ervin Santana	LAA	0	0	104	2	-6	100
Emilio Bonifacio	Fla	84	-2	0	25	-7	100
Josh Beckett	Bos	-1	0	103	2	-5	99
Aramis Ramirez	ChC	100	-5	0	22	-18	99
James Loney	LAD	75	1	0	11	11	98
Mark Buehrle	CWS	1	0	88	2	7	98
David Ortiz	Bos	104	-6	0	0	0	98
Corey Hart	Mil	84	0	0	15	-1	98
Gerardo Parra	Ari	68	0	0	15	14	97
Alcides Escobar	KC	53	-1	0	35	10	97
Kelly Johnson	2 Tms	70	-1	0	27	1	97
David Price	TB	0	0	96	2	-1	97
Ian Desmond	Was	61	6	0	33	-3	97
Brian McCann	Atl	73	-5	0	32	-4	96
B.J. Upton	TB	77	-1	0	27	-7	96
Brendan Ryan	Sea	46	4	0	27	18	95
Hiroki Kuroda	LAD	-1	-1	88	2	7	95
Matt Holliday	StL	83	0	0	13	-1	95
Carlos Pena	ChC	84	1	0	11	-1	95
Yadier Molina	StL	69	-4	0	34	-4	95
Todd Helton	Col	76	2	0	9	7	94
Chase Utley	Phi	62	5	0	20	7	94
Anibal Sanchez	Fla	0	0	89	2	3	94
Jon Lester	Bos	-1	0	92	2	1	94
Yovani Gallardo	Mil	6	0	82	2	3	93
Kevin Youkilis	Bos	73	2	0	17	1	93
Jeremy Hellickson	TB	0	0	91	2	0	93
Nick Swisher	NYY	87	-5	0	17	-6	93
Mark Ellis	2 Tms	46	4	0	24	18	92
Alex Gonzalez	Atl	50	0	0	33	9	92
Alberto Callaspo	LAA	66	2	0	20	4	92
Coco Crisp	Oak	66	2	0	23	1	92
Victor Martinez	Det	90	-4	0	7	-1	92
Jayson Werth	Was	74	2	0	19	-3	92
Clint Barmes	Hou	53	-2	0	26	14	91
Chris Iannetta	Col	54	1	0	28	8	91
Casey Kotchman	TB	78	-1	0	11	3	91
Matt Joyce	TB	77	3	0	15	-4	91
Jon Jay	StL	62	2	0	17	9	90
Andre Ethier	LAD	75	-4	0	15	4	90
Carlos Ruiz	Phi	60	-1	0	31	0	90
Freddie Freeman	Atl	84	-4	0	12	-2	90
Billy Butler	KC	95	-4	0	1	-2	90
Ichiro Suzuki	Sea	71	3	0	19	-3	90
Rickie Weeks	Mil	74	-1	0	22	-5	90
Martin Prado	Atl	58	1	0	17	13	89
Mark Trumbo	LAA	69	0	0	12	8	89
Russell Martin	NYY	52	-1	0	31	7	89
Ryan Vogelsong	SF	3	0	84	2	0	89
Ryan Roberts	Ari	71	3	0	21	-6	89
Derek Jeter	NYY	76	2	0	26	-15	89
Josh Willingham	Oak	78	-1	0	11	0	88
Tim Hudson	Atl	0	0	88	2	-2	88
Joe Saunders	Ari	2	0	76	2	7	87
Alex Rodriguez	NYY	60	0	0	13	13	86
Robert Andino	Bal	50	2	0	25	9	86
Jeremy Guthrie	Bal	0	0	78	2	6	86

		OFFENSIVE		DEFENSIVE			TOTAL
Player	Team	Runs Created	Baserunning Runs	Pitching Runs Created	Positional Average	Runs Saved	Runs
Darwin Barney	ChC	56	2	0	26	2	86
Shaun Marcum	Mil	3	-1	81	2	1	86
Daniel Hudson	Ari	7	-1	79	2	-1	86
Madison Bumgarner	SF	1	0	85	2	-2	86
Seth Smith	Col	79	0	0	15	-8	86
Nyjer Morgan	Mil	57	5	0	16	7	85
Ryan Howard	Phi	92	-6	0	12	-13	85
Gordon Beckham	CWS	50	2	0	29	3	84
Aaron Hill	2 Tms	55	0	0	27	2	84
Carl Pavano	Min	-1	0	82	2	1	84
Edwin Jackson	2 Tms	2	0	82	2	-2	84
Trevor Cahill	Oak	-1	0	86	2	-3	84
Juan Pierre	CWS	69	8	0	18	-11	84
Brennan Boesch	Det	65	3	0	11	4	83
Marco Scutaro	Bos	58	0	0	24	1	83
Colby Lewis	Tex	0	0	81	2	0	83
Kurt Suzuki	Oak	51	0	0	33	-1	83
Chipper Jones	Atl	71	-2	0	17	-3	83
Cliff Pennington	Oak	60	0	0	32	-9	83
Jhoulys Chacin	Col	1	0	72	2	7	82
Wandy Rodriguez	Hou	2	-1	79	2	0	82
Randy Wolf	Mil	1	0	80	2	-1	82
Placido Polanco	Phi	53	1	0	18	9	81
Javier Vazquez	Fla	1	-1	79	2	0	81
Gavin Floyd	CWS	0	0	79	2	0	81
Carlos Quentin	CWS	71	-2	0	12	0	81
Nelson Cruz	Tex	73	-1	0	14	-5	81
Jason Heyward	Atl	50	1	0	14	15	80
Kyle Lohse	StL	1	0	76	2	1	80
Eric Hosmer	KC	77	2	0	10	-9	80
Michael Cuddyer	Min	80	0	1	15	-16	80
Michael Pineda	Sea	0	0	78	2	-1	79
Geovany Soto	ChC	51	-1	0	30	-1	79
Johnny Damon	TB	81	0	0	1	-3	79
Derek Holland	Tex	0	0	81	2	-4	79
Tim Stauffer	SD	0	0	69	2	7	78
Alexi Ogando	Tex	0	0	76	2	0	78
Matt Harrison	Tex	-1	0	82	2	-5	78
Mark Reynolds	Bal	81	0	0	20	-23	78
Dustin Ackley	Sea	50	0	0	17	10	77
Daniel Murphy	NYM	57	1	0	11	8	77
Jason Vargas	Sea	0	0	75	2	0	77
Brandon McCarthy	Oak	0	0	77	2	-2	77
Matt Garza	ChC	-3	0	81	2	-3	77
John Buck	Fla	52	-3	0	33	-5	77
J.P. Arencibia	Tor	54	-3	0	31	-5	77
Yuniesky Betancourt	Mil	52	0	0	32	-7	77
Jason Bartlett	SD	51	5	0	30	-9	77
Michael Brantley	Cle	53	1	0	16	6	76
Marlon Byrd	ChC	53	3	0	20	0	76
Kosuke Fukudome	2 Tms	67	-5	0	17	-3	76
Jonathan Lucroy	Mil	51	0	0	30	-5	76
Angel Pagan	NYM	61	2	0	21	-8	76
Ivan Nova	NYY	0	0	71	2	2	75
Jordan Zimmermann	Was	2	0	69	2	2	75
Max Scherzer	Det	0	0	75	2	-2	75
Chase Headley	SD	59	-2	0	16	1	74
Sean Rodriguez	TB	42	3	0	22	6	73
Johnny Cueto	Cin	-2	0	70	2	3	73
Mat Latos	SD	-3	0	75	2	-1	73
Scott Baker	Min	1	0	73	1	-2	73
Wilson Ramos	Was	51	-1	0	28	-5	73
A.J. Pierzynski	CWS	56	-3	0	29	-9	73
Jair Jurrjens	Atl	-2	0	70	2	2	72
Carl Crawford	Bos	58	2	0	14	-2	72
Maicer Izturis	LAA	58	-1	0	18	-3	72
John Danks	CWS	0	0	66	2	3	71
Josh Tomlin	Cle	1	0	67	2	1	71
Nick Hundley	SD	45	1	0	19	5	70
Zack Greinke	Mil	1	0	63	2	4	70
Vance Worley	Phi	2	0	65	1	2	70
Jeff Karstens	Pit	-1	0	68	2	1	70
David DeJesus	Oak	52	2	0	15	1	70
Colby Rasmus	2 Tms	53	-1	0	22	-4	70

172

		OFFENSIVE		DEFENSIVE			TOTAL
Player	Team	Runs Created	Baserunning Runs	Pitching Runs Created	Positional Average	Runs Saved	Runs
Philip Humber	CWS	0	0	73	2	-5	70
John Lannan	Was	-1	-1	64	2	5	69
Ronny Cedeno	Pit	37	1	0	26	5	69
Mike Leake	Cin	1	0	62	2	4	69
Bruce Chen	KC	0	0	64	2	3	69
Hideki Matsui	Oak	63	2	0	3	1	69
Bud Norris	Hou	0	0	66	2	1	69
Ryan Dempster	ChC	-2	0	69	2	0	69
Jemile Weeks	Oak	57	-1	0	19	-6	69
Miguel Olivo	Sea	44	3	0	31	-9	69
Jamey Carroll	LAD	61	-2	0	25	-15	69
Will Venable	SD	49	1	0	12	6	68
David Murphy	Tex	50	1	0	13	4	68
Paul Maholm	Pit	-1	0	64	2	3	68
Casey McGehee	Mil	47	-3	0	21	3	68
Luke Hochevar	KC	0	0	67	2	-1	68
Ryan Zimmerman	Was	58	0	0	15	-5	68
Ted Lilly	LAD	-2	-1	74	2	-5	68
David Wright	NYM	59	-1	0	16	-6	68
Rick Ankiel	Was	40	1	0	17	9	67
Wade Davis	TB	1	0	61	2	3	67
Bartolo Colon	NYY	0	0	64	2	1	67
Chris Capuano	NYM	-3	0	67	2	1	67
Jaime Garcia	StL	-2	0	66	2	1	67
Vladimir Guerrero	Bal	66	1	0	0	0	67
Jason Bay	NYM	57	-1	0	14	-3	67
Jarrod Saltalamacchia	Bos	45	1	0	25	-4	67
Edwin Encarnacion	Tor	69	-1	0	6	-7	67
Jake Westbrook	StL	1	0	55	2	8	66
Chad Billingsley	LAD	3	0	60	2	1	66
Jeff Francis	KC	0	0	59	2	4	65
Cory Luebke	SD	2	0	59	1	3	65
Juan Rivera	2 Tms	54	-1	0	10	2	65
Ben Revere	Min	44	6	0	18	-3	65
Ricky Nolasco	Fla	-1	0	67	2	-3	65
Freddy Garcia	NYY	0	0	67	2	-4	65
Mitch Moreland	Tex	59	-1	0	11	-4	65
Brett Myers	Hou	1	-1	68	2	-5	65
Josh Collmenter	Ari	1	-1	61	2	1	64
Charlie Morton	Pit	-1	0	63	2	0	64
Bobby Abreu	LAA	68	-4	0	3	-3	64
Derrek Lee	2 Tms	59	-1	0	9	-3	64
Adam Lind	Tor	62	-3	0	9	-4	64
Danny Valencia	Min	58	-3	0	22	-13	64
Aaron Harang	SD	-2	0	65	2	-2	63
Aaron Miles	LAD	47	3	0	20	-7	63
Jack Hannahan	Cle	41	-1	0	15	7	62
Chris Narveson	Mil	2	0	54	2	4	62
Stephen Drew	Ari	40	1	0	18	3	62
Brent Morel	CWS	41	1	0	18	2	62
Ruben Tejada	NYM	42	1	0	19	0	62
Delmon Young	2 Tms	51	1	0	13	-3	62
A.J. Burnett	NYY	0	0	64	2	-4	62
Ryan Theriot	StL	44	1	0	23	-6	62
Tony Gwynn	LAD	35	2	0	9	15	61
Jerry Hairston	2 Tms	44	-3	0	15	5	61
James McDonald	Pit	-2	-1	64	2	-2	61
Ryan Ludwick	2 Tms	55	-1	0	15	-8	61
Denard Span	Min	35	4	0	12	9	60
Carlos Zambrano	ChC	8	-1	49	2	2	60
Dillon Gee	NYM	-1	0	58	2	1	60
Rick Porcello	Det	0	0	59	2	-1	60
Aubrey Huff	SF	58	-3	0	11	-6	60
Orlando Hudson	SD	49	-2	0	21	-8	60
Scott Sizemore	2 Tms	50	2	0	17	-9	60
Alfonso Soriano	ChC	60	-4	0	13	-9	60
Alex Rios	CWS	42	2	0	25	-9	60
Shin-Soo Choo	Cle	42	4	0	10	3	59
Alfredo Aceves	Bos	0	0	60	1	-2	59
Laynce Nix	Was	44	1	0	8	5	58
Rod Barajas	LAD	37	-2	0	21	2	58
Brandon Beachy	Atl	-2	0	58	1	1	58
Roy Oswalt	Phi	-1	0	58	1	0	58
Justin Smoak	Sea	54	-3	0	8	-1	58

173

| Player | Team | OFFENSIVE | | DEFENSIVE | | | TOTAL |
		Runs Created	Baserunning Runs	Pitching Runs Created	Positional Average	Runs Saved	Runs
Skip Schumaker	StL	41	1	-1	18	-1	58
Brandon Morrow	Tor	-1	0	63	2	-6	58
Sam Fuld	TB	36	2	0	9	10	57
Tyler Clippard	Was	0	0	55	1	1	57
Ryan Hanigan	Cin	36	1	0	20	0	57
Chris Getz	KC	36	1	0	21	-1	57
Josh Thole	NYM	40	-2	0	23	-4	57
Ty Wigginton	Col	51	-2	0	13	-5	57
Garrett Jones	Pit	58	-6	0	12	-7	57
Ryan Raburn	Det	49	2	0	15	-9	57
Logan Morrison	Fla	70	-1	0	14	-26	57
Josh Reddick	Bos	38	0	0	8	10	56
Nick Blackburn	Min	0	0	50	2	4	56
Livan Hernandez	Was	2	-1	50	2	3	56
David Freese	StL	46	-1	0	12	-1	56
Alexi Casilla	Min	40	0	0	18	-2	56
Chris Volstad	Fla	2	0	54	2	-2	56
Mike Pelfrey	NYM	0	0	60	2	-6	56
Cody Ross	SF	52	1	0	14	-11	56
Ramon Santiago	Det	31	1	0	15	8	55
Bronson Arroyo	Cin	-1	0	50	2	4	55
Jonny Venters	Atl	0	0	51	1	3	55
Erik Bedard	2 Tms	0	0	53	1	1	55
Ubaldo Jimenez	2 Tms	-1	0	54	2	0	55
Andres Torres	SF	38	3	0	16	-2	55
Guillermo Moscoso	Oak	0	0	56	1	-2	55
Carlos Gomez	Mil	27	1	0	11	15	54
Brett Lawrie	Tor	32	1	0	7	14	54
Jonathon Niese	NYM	-1	-1	51	2	3	54
Fausto Carmona	Cle	0	0	50	2	2	54
Willie Bloomquist	Ari	37	1	0	15	1	54
Chris Heisey	Cin	43	1	0	9	1	54
Brian Duensing	Min	0	0	53	2	-1	54
Orlando Cabrera	2 Tms	32	1	0	24	-3	54
Ramon Hernandez	Cin	42	-3	0	19	-4	54
Justin Turner	NYM	52	-2	0	19	-15	54
Joe Mauer	Min	38	1	0	13	1	53
Eric Thames	Tor	50	6	0	9	-12	53
Desmond Jennings	TB	41	2	0	7	2	52
Francisco Liriano	Min	1	0	48	1	2	52
Kyle McClellan	StL	0	0	51	1	0	52
Jose Tabata	Pit	42	1	0	10	-1	52
Jason Kubel	Min	51	-3	0	7	-3	52
Nate Schierholtz	SF	45	2	0	11	-6	52
Raul Ibanez	Phi	62	-3	0	16	-23	52
Travis Hafner	Cle	51	0	0	0	0	51
Kyle Kendrick	Phi	1	0	49	1	0	51
Jeff Niemann	TB	0	0	50	1	0	51
Jed Lowrie	Bos	35	3	0	15	-2	51
Derek Lowe	Atl	4	-1	49	2	-3	51
John Mayberry	Phi	45	0	0	9	-3	51
Zach Britton	Bal	4	0	49	2	-4	51
Greg Dobbs	Fla	46	0	0	14	-9	51
Vernon Wells	LAA	50	-3	0	15	-11	51
Yorvit Torrealba	Tex	44	-5	0	24	-12	51
Chris Denorfia	SD	37	-1	0	10	4	50
Tyler Chatwood	LAA	1	0	45	1	3	50
Mike Moustakas	KC	38	-4	0	14	2	50
Edgar Renteria	Cin	31	2	0	16	1	50
Rafael Furcal	2 Tms	35	2	0	18	-5	50
Wilson Betemit	2 Tms	48	-1	0	12	-9	50
Hanley Ramirez	Fla	42	2	0	19	-13	50

Albert Pujols   Brett Gardner
Dustin Pedroia   Austin Jackson
Adrian Beltre   Justin Upton
Troy Tulowitzki
                    Matt Wieters
                    Mark Buehrle

THE FIELDING BIBLE AWARDS 2011

The Fielding Bible Awards 2011

Chase Utley, baseball's best base runner, is on first base with nobody out in the top of the sixth in the 2011 NLDS. Utley and his fellow Phillies are one win away from advancing to the league championship series, leading the five-game series two games to one, but they are down in the game 3-2. If they can score, it's a tie game.

Hunter Pence hits a groundball to shortstop Rafael Furcal. Since Utley is running with the pitch there's no chance to get him on a force at second, so Furcal throws to first.

Utley knows baserunning, down to the split second. He has a full head of steam rounding second base and he knows that, as the Cards make the out at first, he'll have just enough time, even with a throw, to make it safely into third.

Except that Albert Pujols decides to skip the out at first. He comes off the bag early to intercept the throw. His momentum takes him about ten to fifteen feet closer to third base and his perfectly accurate throw nabs Utley despite his head-first slide. Instead of having the tying run on third with one out, there's just a runner on first.

A brilliant play by a brilliant defender taking out a brilliant base runner in an extremely crucial situation. Plays like this are the reason that Albert Pujols has won his fifth Fielding Bible Award for defensive excellence in the six seasons that the award has been in existence.

Joining Pujols as repeat winners in 2011 are: Mark Buehrle (his third in a row), Troy Tulowitzki (three), Adrian Beltre (three), and Brett Gardner (two). First-time Fielding Bible Award winners this year are Dustin Pedroia, Austin Jackson, Justin Upton, and Matt Wieters.

Here's a short refresher course on how the awards are determined: We ask our panel of ten experts to rank 10 players at each position on a scale from one to ten. We then use the same voting technique as the Major League Baseball MVP voting. A first place vote gets 10 points, second place 9 points, third place 8 points, etc. Total up the points for each player, and the player with the most points wins the award. A perfect score is 100.

One important distinction that differentiates our award from most other baseball awards, including the Gold Gloves, is that we only have one winner for all of Major League Baseball, instead of separate winners for each league. Our intention is to continue to stand up and say, "This is the best fielder at this position in the major leagues last season."

Oh, and one more distinction from the Gold Gloves that isn't a distinction anymore. They have finally agreed with us this year that separate awards should be given for left fielders, center fielders, and right fielders. They are different positions, folks, and now even the Gold Glove award establishment admits it.

Here are the Fielding Bible Awards for the 2011 season:

First Base – Albert Pujols, St. Louis

Albert Pujols reclaims his award after a one-year hiatus (Daric Barton). The Throw in the NLDS was no fluke. Since Baseball Info Solutions started tracking Good Fielding Plays (GFP) in 2004, Albert Pujols has 37 GFPs on throws. The next best first basemen are Todd Helton with 16, and three others with 15, Mark Teixeira, Prince Fielder, and Lyle Overbay.

Previous Winners:

2010	Daric Barton
2009	Albert Pujols
2008	Albert Pujols
2007	Albert Pujols
2006	Albert Pujols

Second Base – Dustin Pedroia, Boston

Dustin Pedroia wins his first Fielding Bible Award with 97 of a possible 100 points. He took seven first-place votes and was voted second by the other three panelists. Pedroia has done well in voting in each of the last four years. He lost in a tie-breaker to Aaron Hill in 2009 (each had 76 points), placed fourth in 2008, and seventh in 2010.

Previous Winners:

2010	Chase Utley
2009	Aaron Hill
2008	Brandon Phillips
2007	Aaron Hill
2006	Orlando Hudson

Third Base – Adrian Beltre, Texas

Adrian Beltre received eight first-place votes beating last year's winner, Evan Longoria, 98 to 90. It doesn't matter where he plays. Los Angeles, Seattle, Boston, and now Texas. Beltre excels year after year. He has saved an estimated 156 runs defensively for his teams since 2003, an average of 17 runs prevented per year. That was his exact total for the Rangers in 2011, which translates into about two extra wins per year for his clubs, just on defense.

Previous Winners:

2010	Evan Longoria
2009	Ryan Zimmerman
2008	Adrian Beltre
2007	Pedro Feliz
2006	Adrian Beltre

Shortstop – Troy Tulowitzki, Colorado

Troy Tulowitzki goes back-to-back, two Fielding Bible Awards in two years, and his third award of his five-year MLB career. Tulo is especially adept at making plays to his right. The Plus/Minus System credits him with 45 more plays in the shortstop hole compared to an average MLB shortstop over his five seasons. Tulowitzki also excels in another area. He had 67 Good Fielding Plays in 2011 compared to only 29 Defensive Misplays or Errors. That +38 figure was tops in baseball. (Alcides Escobar was second at shortstop with +30.) Dustin Pedroia was tops among second basemen in 2011 with +44, so he and Tulowitzki make a truly spectacular double play combination as Fielding Bible Award winners.

Previous Winners:

2010   Troy Tulowitzki
2009   Jack Wilson
2008   Jimmy Rollins
2007   Troy Tulowitzki
2006   Adam Everett

Left Field – Brett Gardner, New York Yankees

Brett Gardner is the new Carl Crawford. Gardner repeats as the Fielding Bible Award winner in left field after Crawford won three of the four previous years. It was nearly unanimous as Gardner took nine first-place votes and one second. Gardner's 22 Defensive Runs Saved tied him with center field winner Austin Jackson for the most runs saved by an outfielder in 2011. That's an extraordinary total for a left fielder. Normally the best center fielders save significantly more runs defensively than the best left fielders. For Gardner, having a center fielder's range gives him a tremendous advantage, but he has an excellent throwing arm as well. He has saved the Yankees 13 runs (out of his 35 total) with his arm over the last two years.

Previous Winners:

2010   Brett Gardner
2009   Carl Crawford
2008   Carl Crawford
2007   Eric Byrnes
2006   Carl Crawford

Center Field – Austin Jackson, Detroit

He topped all center fielders with 21 Runs Saved in 2010, but Austin Jackson had to do it even better (with 22 Runs Saved) in 2011 to earn his first Fielding Bible Award. Jackson has made 63 more plays than an average center fielder over the last two years. That's an incredible total. It's on the plays over his head that AJ really excels (43 of the 63). Making 43 more catches than an average center fielder on balls hit deep is where those lofty Runs Saved totals come in, as he is saving doubles and triples when he makes these catches.

Previous Winners:

2010   Michael Bourn
2009   Franklin Gutierrez
2008   Carlos Beltran
2007   Andruw Jones
2006   Carlos Beltran

Right Field – Justin Upton, Arizona

Justin Upton wins his first Fielding Bible Award in 2011, unseating three-time winner Ichiro Suzuki. With Ichiro's down year defensively (he finished tenth in the voting), panelists were divided in their balloting with seven different right fielders receiving first-place votes. Upton received three first-place votes, Jason Heyward two, with one apiece for Mike Stanton, Torii Hunter, Andre Ethier, Jay Bruce, and Nate Schierholtz. Like Austin Jackson in center field, Upton excels on deeply hit balls, where he fielded 18 more balls in 2011 than the average right fielder would have, based on the depth, angle, and velocity of those hit to him.

Previous Winners:

2010   Ichiro Suzuki
2009   Ichiro Suzuki
2008   Franklin Gutierrez
2007   Alex Rios
2006   Ichiro Suzuki

Catcher – Matt Wieters, Baltimore

After Yadier Molina won the previous four Fielding Bible Awards, Matt Wieters wins his first. And it wasn't even close in the voting, Wieters 97 to Molina 74. When you look at the numbers, it wasn't close there either. Prior to 2011, Molina has thrown out 42 percent of base runners. On top of that, he has picked off an average of six base runners per year. In 2011, Yadier dropped to 25 percent caught stealing and only picked two runners off. Wieters threw out 36 percent of basestealers in 2011. But it was the pitcher handling department where Wieters really excelled. Nine of his 14 runs saved are estimated for his pitcher handling, while Molina also had a down year in this area, costing the Cardinals six runs.

Previous Winners:

2010   Yadier Molina
2009   Yadier Molina
2008   Yadier Molina
2007   Yadier Molina
2006   Ivan Rodriguez

Pitcher – Mark Buehrle, Chicago White Sox

It's a third consecutive Fielding Bible Award for Mark Buehrle. It is remarkable how Buehrle puts up excellent Defensive Runs Saved numbers year after year. He saved an estimated nine runs defensively for the White Sox in 2011, tops among all pitchers in baseball. He had eight saved runs in 2010, 11 in 2009, and has averaged about eight per year going back to 2004. His control of the running game is uncanny. Only three base runners were successful stealing bases in 2011 with Buehrle on the mound, while nine of them were caught stealing or picked off by Buehrle. He covers his position as well, with 15 of his Runs Saved guarding the territory around the mound over the last three years.

Previous Winners:

2010   Mark Buehrle
2009   Mark Buehrle
2008   Kenny Rogers
2007   Johan Santana
2006   Greg Maddux

Background of the Fielding Bible Awards

While *The Fielding Bible* and *The Fielding Bible— Volume II* (and this book) put a lot of emphasis on the numbers, especially Defensive Runs Saved and the Plus-Minus System, I feel that visual observation and subjective judgment are still very important parts of determining the best defensive players. Also, I think people have a right to know who is voting and all the players they are voting for. Therefore, in setting up the Fielding Bible Awards, we took the following steps:

1. ***We appointed a panel of experts to vote.*** We have a panel of ten experts plus three "tie-breaker" ballots. (See below.)

2. ***We rate everybody in one group.*** The Gold Glove vote is divided into National League and American League. We make ours different by putting everybody together. Besides, is playing shortstop in the American League one thing and playing shortstop in the National League a different thing, or are they really very much the same thing? Two years ago we had a great example of this rule. Without the Fielding Bible Award, Jack Wilson wins nada, because he switched teams in mid-year. According to our panelists (and unlike the Gold Glove voters), Jack was the best fielding shortstop in baseball in 2009. Period. He deserved to be recognized for that.

3. ***We use a ten-man ballot and a ten-point scale.*** We use a ten-man ballot (I'm referring to the players listed, not the panel of experts). Then we give ten points for first place, nine points for second place, etc., down to one point for tenth place. We feel strongly that a ten-man ballot with weighted positions leads to more accurate outcomes.

4. ***We define the list of candidates.*** Only players who actually were regulars at the position are candidates. This eliminates the possibility of a vote going to somebody who wasn't really playing the position.

5. ***We are publishing the balloting.*** We summarize

the voting at each position, clearly identifying whom everybody voted for. Publishing the actual vote totals encourages the voters to take their votes more seriously. Also, we feel the public will have more respect for the voting if they have more insight into the process.

There is something cool about having ten experts and a ten-man ballot and a ten-point scale, because that gives each position 100 possible points. If all ten voters place one player first on their ballot, he scores 100. This year it was close for Brett Gardner as he scored 99.

Here are the tie-breaker rules (which came into play in our very first year and did so again in 2010). They are applied one at a time until we have a winner:

      1. Most first-place votes wins.

      2. Count the tie-breaker ballots, highest point tally wins.

      3. Award goes to player with the higher plus/minus rating.

Ballots were due two days after the end of the regular season. Here is this year's panel:

You probably know **Bill James**, a baseball writer and analyst published for more than thirty years. Bill is the Senior Baseball Operations Advisor for the Boston Red Sox.

The **BIS Video Scouts** at Baseball Info Solutions (BIS) study every game of the season, multiple times, charting a huge list of valuable game details.

The man who created Strat-O-Matic Baseball, **Hal Richman**, continues to lead his company's annual in-depth analysis of each player's season. Hal cautions SOM players that his voting on this ballot may or may not reflect the eventual fielding ratings for players in his game. Ballots were due prior to the completion of his annual research effort to evaluate player defense.

Named the best sports columnist in America by the Associated Press Sports Editors in 2003 and 2005, **Joe Posnanski** is a Senior Writer at Sports Illustrated and occasional columnist for the Kansas City *Star*. His website is www.joeposnanski.com

For over twenty-five years, BIS owner **John Dewan** has collected, analyzed, and published in-depth baseball statistics and analysis. He wrote *The Fielding Bible* in 2006 and *The Fielding Bible—Volume II* in 2009. *The Fielding Bible—Volume III* is in your hand.

Peter Gammons serves as an on-air and online analyst for MLB Network, MLB.com, and NESN (New England Sports Network). He is the 56th recipient of the J. G. Taylor Spink Award for outstanding baseball writing given by the BBWAA (Baseball Writers Association of America).

Doug Glanville played nine seasons in Major League Baseball and was well known for his excellent outfield defense. Currently, he is a baseball analyst at ESPN, primarily on *Baseball Tonight*, ESPN.com, and ESPN *The Magazine.*

After nearly fifteen years with ESPN.com, **Rob Neyer** joined SB Nation as National Baseball Editor in 2011. He has written six books about baseball.

Todd Radcliffe is Lead Video Scout at Baseball Info Solutions and brings fifteen years of Major League Baseball scouting experience to the panel.

The **Tom Tango Fan Poll** represents the results of a poll taken at the website, Tango on Baseball (www.tangotiger.net). Besides hosting the website, Tom writes research articles devoted to sabermetrics.

Our three tie-breakers are **Steve Moyer**, president of Baseball Info Solutions, **Dan Casey**, veteran Video Scout at BIS, and **Dave Studenmund**, one of the founders of www.hardballtimes.com and *The Hardball Times Baseball Annual.*

Defensive Scouting Reports

Each March about 20 individuals walk through the doors of Baseball Info Solutions World Headquarters in Coplay, Pennsylvania, to begin the annual process of scouting every pitch and every play of the Major League Baseball season. They are the Baseball Info Solutions Video Scouts. These individuals have already passed a rigorous screening process in which their baseball acumen was tested, their pitch-charting ability evaluated and their knowledge of the game determined. Over the course of the next several months, no one will watch more baseball than the BIS Video Scouts. And no one will visually understand the strengths and weaknesses of MLB players better.

As in past volumes of *The Fielding Bible*, we've invited the Video Scouts to share their expertise about the defensive prowess of hundreds of MLB players for the book. This time around, we even added a few pitchers. The Video Scouts who evaluated the players and wrote the preliminary reports are: Dan Casey, Tani Cohen, Will Cohen, Maxwell Cook, Jason Eisele, Mike Fecteau, Adam Hayes, Andy Johnson, Brady Johnston, Christian Karayannides, Ian Kenyon, Mike Piekarski, Craig Vanderkam and Jon Vrecsics. The reports went through a rigorous review process by John Dewan, Ben Jedlovec, Steve Moyer, Mike Piekarski, Jon Vrecsics and Dan Casey to form the Defensive Scouting Reports you see in this book. The reports appear with the players' "data blocks."

Player Data Blocks

You must be thinking, "what is a data block?" We thought it would be helpful to include some numbers with the scouting reports, and we organized this data in rectangles, or blocks, above the scouting report. Think of them as data Legos.

We display a player's innings played and Defensive Runs Saved for 2011, as well as his total for each over the past three years. Since Good Fielding Plays along with Defensive Misplays and Errors have become a staple of our player evaluations, we also include a player's total Good Plays and Misplays/Errors for the 2011 season. Based on the number of touches the player had, we tell you how many the average player at his position would have had with the same number of touches.

The last item in the data Legos is the player's Good Play/Misplay Percentage. An average player has a Good Play/Misplay Percentage of .500. Houston's Brett Wallace is the definition of an average fielder when considering good plays and misplays. At first base in 2011, he had 34 GFPs and 18 DMEs. We'd expect the average first baseman, with the same number of touches, to have 33 GFPs and 18 DMEs. That's a .502 Good Play/Misplay Percentage. On the other hand, Dustin Pedroia has a sparkling .701 Good Play/Misplay Percentage, which means his combination of Good Plays, Misplays and Errors is better than the average second baseman with the same number of touches. His 66 GFPs are 15 more than we would expect the average fielder to have, and he had 18 fewer Misplays and Errors than the average fielder. (By the way, both Wallace and Pedroia were above-average fielders overall in 2011: Wallace had five runs saved in just 96 games at first base, and Pedroia saved 18 runs at second base in 159 games.)

Gold Gloves That Should Have Been

Along with the scouting reports by position, we also show the Gold Gloves That Should Have Been as the lead-in to every position's scouting reports. In each of the first two *Fielding Bibles* we used the numbers in the book to help us reevaluate the Gold Glove selections, and we're excited to review the Gold Glove winners with our new methodologies.

The Gold Glove Awards made a significant improvement in 2011 by handing out position-specific Gold Gloves for outfielders rather than three generic "outfield" Gold Gloves. We still have some disagreement with their winners, but it's nice to see the Gold Glove Awards recognizing that there are three distinct outfield positions.

For all of the criticism the Gold Glove voters receive, we actually agree with 46 percent of their choices over the nine years of this book. Here's a year-by-year chart that shows where we agree and disagree with the Gold Glove winners:

Year	Gold Glove Winners Reviewed	Agree	Disagree
2003	14	9	5
2004	14	11	3
2005	14	6	8
2006	18	10	8
2007	19	6	13
2008	18	7	11
2009	18	5	13
2010	18	9	9
2011	18	7	11
Total	151	70	81

My Personal Ratings

In addition to reconsidering the recent Gold Glove winners, I provide my personal ratings at each position. These ratings show the top-five and bottom-five fielders based on players who set foot on the field in 2011. While it's easy to look at the Runs Saved numbers at each position and choose the players with the highest totals, I value visual observation and took into consideration the scouting reports in the following pages.

Without further ado, let's look at the first position.

Catchers Evaluations

Year	League	Gold Glove Winners	Should Have Been
2006	AL	Ivan Rodriguez	Ivan Rodriguez
	NL	Brad Ausmus	Yadier Molina
2007	AL	Ivan Rodriguez	Joe Mauer
	NL	Russell Martin	Yadier Molina
2008	AL	Joe Mauer	Jose Molina
	NL	Yadier Molina	Bengie Molina
2009	AL	Joe Mauer	Gerald Laird
	NL	Yadier Molina	Yadier Molina
2010	AL	Joe Mauer	Kurt Suzuki
	NL	Yadier Molina	Yadier Molina
2011	AL	Matt Wieters	Matt Wieters
	NL	Yadier Molina	Yadier Molina

My Personal Ratings

Top Five

1 Yadier Molina, StL
2 Jeff Mathis, Tor
3 Matt Wieters, Bal
4 Humberto Quintero, Hou
5 Russell Martin, NYY

Bottom Five

26 Alex Avila, Det
27 Ramon Hernandez, Col
28 J.P. Arencibia, Tor
29 John Buck, Fla
30 Victor Martinez, Det

Player teams based on transactions through February 1, 2012

Catchers

Matt Wieters

	Innings	Runs Saved
2011	1150	17
2009-2011	2948.2	26

	Good Plays	Misplays and Errors
Wieters 2011	12	40
Avg Catcher	11	47
Good Play/Misplay Pct		.553

Wieters had a breakout year defensively in 2011 and was rewarded with his first career Fielding Bible Award. He is deceptively quick behind the plate, despite his 6'5" frame, utilizing his length when snagging wild pitches and blocking wide balls in the dirt. His crouch and size can create difficulties when blocking wild pitches under him, but Matt's quick hands and peerless instincts counterbalance any issues with his height. Wieters possesses world-class arm strength, a smooth exchange, and excellent throwing mechanics. His long legs slow his release, but help produce power while transitioning through the throwing motion.

Yadier Molina

	Innings	Runs Saved
2011	1150	-4
2009-2011	3464.2	25

	Good Plays	Misplays and Errors
Molina 2011	11	53
Avg Catcher	11	45
Good Play/Misplay Pct		.461

Molina saw his streak of four consecutive Fielding Bible Awards come to an end in 2011 with the breakout defensive season of award winner Matt Wieters. Despite a down season in which he had his lowest caught-stealing percentage of his career (25 percent), Yadier continues to be one of the game's elite catchers. Over his eight-year career, his greatest asset has been his ability to shut down the running game. While this isn't always seen in his caught-stealing percentages, baserunners are hesitant to take that extra half-step because they know Molina will throw behind them. Molina also led Major League Baseball in blocking balls in the dirt with 657 during the 2011 season. He is constantly stopping balls in the dirt. He continues to be everything you could ask for in a defensive catcher.

Jeff Mathis

	Innings	Runs Saved
2011	698	8
2009-2011	1908.2	22

	Good Plays	Misplays and Errors
Mathis 2011	13	31
Avg Catcher	10	39
Good Play/Misplay Pct		.633

Mathis is one the best defensive catchers in baseball. Last season he shared the catching duties for the Los Angeles Angels, thanks entirely to his catching skills. Mathis is an athletic catcher with a strong fundamental foundation. He only moves his glove when receiving a pitch and has very soft hands for a catcher. Mathis often helps his pitchers with his ability to frame pitches. He is as good as they get moving behind the plate and using his athleticism to block balls in the dirt to keep runners from advancing. As good as he is at blocking pitches, he may be even better at blocking runners from scoring. Baseball Info Solutions has credited Mathis with a Good Fielding Play blocking runners 16 times in the last three years, more than any other catcher in the game. Mathis has plus arm strength and accuracy on his throws. He has the ability to get his body into throwing position quickly. All this has resulted in him saving 22 runs for the Angels over the last three years. Mathis' bat might keep him from earning a starting role, but at age 29 he should be able to help a major league club with his superb defense for at least a few more years.

Russell Martin

	Innings	Runs Saved
2011	1044.1	7
2009-2011	3036.2	19

	Good Plays	Misplays and Errors
Martin 2011	18	61
Avg Catcher	15	63
Good Play/Misplay Pct		.548

Martin rebounded nicely from an injury-plagued 2010 campaign to have a good season defensively. He showed no ill effects from the hip injury that hampered him in 2010, as he also saw a couple of innings at second and third base in addition to catching. Martin's catching mechanics are very good. He has little movement in his body as he catches a pitch. This allows him to catch the ball in a manner that makes it easy for him to frame pitches. He is very good at blocking balls in the dirt. Martin has above-average arm strength and is generally accurate with his throws. He has quick feet, which

Catchers

allows him to get his body into position to throw quickly. Martin should continue to be an above-average defensive catcher over the next couple of years.

Humberto Quintero

	Innings	Runs Saved
2011	642	6
2009-2011	1722.2	17

	Good Plays	Misplays and Errors
Quintero 2011	7	18
Avg Catcher	8	31
Good Play/Misplay Pct		.616

Quintero never had more than 200 at-bats until 2010, but he has nine years of major league experience (including seven with the Houston Astros) thanks to his outstanding defensive ability. He excels at blocking balls in the dirt and uses his chest to keep balls in front of him. Quintero possesses a strong arm and will throw behind runners at any base. He had eight catcher pickoffs in 2010 and added four more the following season. Quintero does a nice job handling the Astros' pitching staff, and became the personal catcher to Brett Myers prior to the 2010 season, which saw Myers post solid numbers across the board. Quintero is a keeper in a backup role, evidenced by his longevity despite being just a career .234 hitter.

Carlos Ruiz

	Innings	Runs Saved
2011	1051	0
2009-2011	2907.2	17

	Good Plays	Misplays and Errors
Ruiz 2011	15	20
Avg Catcher	12	51
Good Play/Misplay Pct		.755

Carlos Ruiz has ranked among the top defensive catchers in the majors in recent years due in large part to his astounding ability to avoid mistakes. He has committed far fewer defensive misplays than the average catcher and is one of the best in the business at preventing wild pitches. Ruiz also excels at handling plays at the plate. He is terrific at catching throws off of difficult hops and displays textbook form blocking off runners from home plate. However, Ruiz turned in his worst defensive season thus far in 2011. A big part of his drop-off was due to his caught-stealing percentage, which dipped from 26 percent in 2010 to only 19 percent in 2011. Ruiz also displayed poor framing ability as he tended to move his shoulders too much and as a result he

lost some close strike calls for his pitching staff. Ruiz will be 33 years old entering the 2012 season, and it's possible that wear and tear is catching up to him and beginning to diminish his defensive skills.

Kurt Suzuki

	Innings	Runs Saved
2011	1132.1	-1
2009-2011	3364	13

	Good Plays	Misplays and Errors
Suzuki 2011	20	55
Avg Catcher	13	54
Good Play/Misplay Pct		.600

Suzuki is a valuable defensive catcher who calls a smart game and handles the staff well. Suzuki finished third among catchers in the 2010 Fielding Bible Award voting, and he had one of his finer seasons throwing out would-be basestealers in 2011. Though he doesn't have great arm strength, he is accurate with his throws and rarely overthrows the base on stolen base attempts. As with most catchers, Suzuki earns his paycheck defensively and not with the bat. Suzuki had been in the positive in Defensive Runs Saved for three straight seasons before taking a step back this year and dipping into the red at -1. However, his leadership is extremely valuable to the Athletics' young pitching staff. Suzuki is one of the most durable and athletic catchers in baseball, and is tremendous at blocking balls in the dirt. He led the majors with 12 potential wild pitch Good Fielding Plays, four more than the next closest catcher (Russell Martin, 8).

Chris Stewart

	Innings	Runs Saved
2011	460.1	12
2009-2011	461.1	12

	Good Plays	Misplays and Errors
Stewart 2011	9	28
Avg Catcher	6	27
Good Play/Misplay Pct		.570

Catchers

Buster Posey

	Innings	Runs Saved
2011	361	3
2009-2011	1063	11

	Good Plays	Misplays and Errors
Posey 2011	1	15
Avg Catcher	5	19
Good Play/Misplay Pct		.215

It's difficult to think about Posey's defense without recalling the brutal collision that ended his 2011 season in late May. That single unfortunate play caused many fans and analysts to advocate a position change to keep the budding superstar out of harm's way when his career resumes, but it is the defensive talent he demonstrated before that play that may ultimately encourage the Giants to let Posey maintain his natural position. In 1,063 career innings behind the plate through 2011 (that's the equivalent of about a full season worth of catching), Posey saved his team 11 runs. That rate of performance, if sustained, would make him a top-5 catcher defensively. Posey derives most of his value from solid control of the running game, showcasing a faster-than-average pop time and a strong arm. His throws are usually well-placed on stolen base attempts, but he'll sometimes rush a barehanded pickup and throw wildly when fielding a soft grounder or attempting to prevent advancement on a pitch in the dirt. In addition to limiting base-stealing opportunities, Posey does a decent job at keeping the ball in front of him with men on base. Hopefully baseball fans will get an opportunity to see if Posey can continue to supplement his hitting skills with good defense behind the plate.

David Ross

	Innings	Runs Saved
2011	378.2	3
2009-2011	1061.1	11

	Good Plays	Misplays and Errors
Ross 2011	5	18
Avg Catcher	4	17
Good Play/Misplay Pct		.533

Jason Varitek

	Innings	Runs Saved
2011	574.2	-1
2009-2011	1774	9

	Good Plays	Misplays and Errors
Varitek 2011	2	28
Avg Catcher	8	35
Good Play/Misplay Pct		.227

Jason Varitek will turn 40 years old early in the 2012 season, yet he's still an above-average defensive catcher. First, though, let's acknowledge his one glaring weakness. Varitek has a well-below-average throwing arm, which makes running on him all too easy. He's caught a measly 12 percent of basestealers over the last three years. This is reflected in his -13 stolen base runs saved during that time period, which ranks last in all of baseball. That out of the way, Varitek is still a good defensive catcher because he pretty much does everything else well. Specifically, Varitek is excellent at handling his pitching staff, as evidenced by his 11 adjusted earned runs saved, tied for first in baseball from 2009-2011. Also, Varitek excels at preventing wild pitches and passed balls, as indicated by his 10 runs saved in that category (tied for second in all of baseball over the last three years). Despite Varitek's well publicized shortcomings in controlling the running game, he remains a solid option behind the plate.

Chris Iannetta

	Innings	Runs Saved
2011	943.2	8
2009-2011	2150.1	8

	Good Plays	Misplays and Errors
Iannetta 2011	10	43
Avg Catcher	13	51
Good Play/Misplay Pct		.489

Chris Iannetta has worked himself into a terrific defensive catcher, rating as one of the top receivers in 2011. Beginning with his handling of the pitching staff, a perennially young group in Colorado, he has shown his ability to call a good game in a ballpark suited for lots of offense. As for the running game, he has an accurate arm and quick release, and he comes out of his crouch quickly to fire the throw to second base. He had the highest caught-stealing percentage of his career this year, dramatically improving from his poor performance in 2010.

Catchers

Miguel Montero

	Innings	Runs Saved
2011	1169.1	5
2009-2011	2752.1	8

	Good Plays	Misplays and Errors
Montero 2011	21	46
Avg Catcher	12	49
Good Play/Misplay Pct		.653

Armed with an improved pitching staff, Montero matured as a catcher last year. Aside from his improvement as a receiver, he also made steady progress at preventing possible wild pitches on balls in the dirt, previously a huge weakness. While preventing many mistakes by his pitchers, he also was extremely successful at throwing out base runners attempting to steal. This is mostly due to his very strong and accurate throwing arm and quick transfer behind the plate. Not only does he throw out runners stealing, but he also affects the running game since he is very capable of picking runners off first base if they wander too far. Coming off a season of playing almost twice as many innings as he had before, he definitely has made the Diamondbacks comfortable making him the catcher of the future.

Koyie Hill

	Innings	Runs Saved
2011	349	0
2009-2011	1521.2	7

	Good Plays	Misplays and Errors
Hill 2011	4	23
Avg Catcher	4	16
Good Play/Misplay Pct		.417

Rod Barajas

	Innings	Runs Saved
2011	733.1	2
2009-2011	2483.2	5

	Good Plays	Misplays and Errors
Barajas 2011	9	27
Avg Catcher	9	38
Good Play/Misplay Pct		.578

Rod Barajas is an average defensive catcher whose abilities on offense have made him a starter for multiple teams. He rarely commits a misplay, and he is quite reliable on balls in play. Behind the plate, he is a solid backstop. He will occasionally stab at low pitches to his right, but he often makes an effort to use his whole body to block balls. On stolen base attempts, he is fundamentally sound, but average at best as he moves a little slow at times. He has a strong arm, and is relatively accurate with it, but he will occasionally bounce throws to second on stolen base attempts. He is not particularly good on tag plays at the plate.

Ryan Hanigan

	Innings	Runs Saved
2011	687.1	0
2009-2011	1883.1	5

	Good Plays	Misplays and Errors
Hanigan 2011	8	27
Avg Catcher	6	25
Good Play/Misplay Pct		.549

At the start of the season Hanigan was the backup catcher. Not only did it turn out that he played as much as Ramon Hernandez, he also performed better. He did a much better job working with the Reds' staff than Hernandez. Ryan also did a fine job controlling the running game. He was not very good at blocking balls in the dirt, but the wildness of his pitching staff may have something to do with that. Hanigan is a gritty player, never giving up ground at the plate, while also receiving the ball very well when there is a play at the plate.

Joe Mauer

	Innings	Runs Saved
2011	408.2	0
2009-2011	2299.1	5

	Good Plays	Misplays and Errors
Mauer 2011	2	23
Avg Catcher	4	17
Good Play/Misplay Pct		.264

Joe Mauer remains one of the better catchers in the majors. However, his history of injuries does not help his chances to remain at that level for the remainder of his career. Because of this, he played some first base for the first time in 2011. Nonetheless, Mauer has all the tools you look for in a catcher. He has an excellent base and foundation, and has great footwork. He receives the ball well and has a quick catch and release, which helps control the running game, along with his accurate and strong arm. His staff seems comfortable with him, which is just as important as his ability to call a good game. The only weakness in his game has been some difficulty blocking pitches in the dirt. Squatting down on his 6'5" frame may have something to do with that.

Catchers

Rob Johnson

	Innings	Runs Saved
2011	475	3
2009-2011	1670	4

	Good Plays	Misplays and Errors
Johnson 2011	8	23
Avg Catcher	9	37
Good Play/Misplay Pct		.589

Tyler Flowers

	Innings	Runs Saved
2011	256.2	3
2009-2011	315.1	3

	Good Plays	Misplays and Errors
Flowers 2011	1	12
Avg Catcher	4	15
Good Play/Misplay Pct		.255

Bobby Wilson

	Innings	Runs Saved
2011	317	3
2009-2011	601.2	3

	Good Plays	Misplays and Errors
Wilson 2011	4	15
Avg Catcher	4	17
Good Play/Misplay Pct		.523

Rene Rivera

	Innings	Runs Saved
2011	299.1	3
2009-2011	299.1	3

	Good Plays	Misplays and Errors
Rivera 2011	4	12
Avg Catcher	3	11
Good Play/Misplay Pct		.578

Ivan Rodriguez

	Innings	Runs Saved
2011	304.2	2
2009-2011	2150.2	3

	Good Plays	Misplays and Errors
Rodriguez 2011	5	16
Avg Catcher	3	13
Good Play/Misplay Pct		.563

In his prime, the 2006 Fielding Bible Award winner was one of the most feared defensive catchers in baseball history. However, in an injury-plagued 2011 season, Rodriguez only caught a little over 300 innings. While he began the year splitting starting catcher duties with Wilson Ramos, he was injured through most of July and August, and then only entered into five games in September as the Nationals appeared to be grooming Ramos for the starting job. In the short time he did play, he showed that he still was a solid choice at catcher. His arm strength still gives basestealers nightmares, and he obviously knows how to handle a rotation that is not always overpowering and a bullpen that is very young. The one area in which his age is evident is his lateral movement and ability to block balls in the dirt. He is by no means awful, but he is not where he once was when he was the best catcher in the game. While he probably will never assume a starting role again, he still can serve as a useful option and teacher, especially on an inexperienced team.

Jose Molina

	Innings	Runs Saved
2011	399	-2
2009-2011	1200.1	3

	Good Plays	Misplays and Errors
Molina 2011	5	22
Avg Catcher	4	17
Good Play/Misplay Pct		.483

Landon Powell

	Innings	Runs Saved
2011	273.1	2
2009-2011	814.1	2

	Good Plays	Misplays and Errors
Powell 2011	3	12
Avg Catcher	3	11
Good Play/Misplay Pct		.507

Catchers

Carlos Corporan

	Innings	Runs Saved
2011	411.1	2
2009-2011	413.1	2

	Good Plays	Misplays and Errors
Corporan 2011	5	26
Avg Catcher	6	26
Good Play/Misplay Pct		.442

Lou Marson

	Innings	Runs Saved
2011	667	2
2009-2011	1567	1

	Good Plays	Misplays and Errors
Marson 2011	9	27
Avg Catcher	8	34
Good Play/Misplay Pct		.578

Dioner Navarro

	Innings	Runs Saved
2011	428	1
2009-2011	1680.1	2

	Good Plays	Misplays and Errors
Navarro 2011	14	27
Avg Catcher	6	25
Good Play/Misplay Pct		.681

J.R. Towles

	Innings	Runs Saved
2011	365.2	1
2009-2011	596.1	1

	Good Plays	Misplays and Errors
Towles 2011	4	12
Avg Catcher	5	20
Good Play/Misplay Pct		.578

Towles had a season to forget in 2011. Although he started the season splitting time as Houston's starting catcher, his performance got him demoted to the minor leagues by early July. His arm strength and accuracy are not good at all, and he therefore struggled to throw out basestealers. While he did well at blocking balls in the dirt, he looked overwhelmed at times when handling pitchers. Overall, he needs to work tirelessly to improve his catch and release behind the plate or else he will not be a suitable big league catcher.

Drew Butera

	Innings	Runs Saved
2011	670.2	-1
2009-2011	1065.1	2

	Good Plays	Misplays and Errors
Butera 2011	8	31
Avg Catcher	7	30
Good Play/Misplay Pct		.515

An extremely gifted defensive player, Butera earned himself more playing time in 2011 while Joe Mauer was on the disabled list. He has a strong, accurate arm, which is why base runners rarely attempt to steal when Butera is behind the plate. He also does a good job blocking the plate on tag plays and has become Carl Pavano's personal catcher, catching every one of his starts. His primary role for the Twins has been as a defensive specialist who earns spot starts to give Joe Mauer's knees a rest. He doesn't yet have Mauer's acumen in handling the staff, but that will come with more experience. He may never be an everyday starter at catcher due to his offensive deficiencies, but he should have a long major league career as a defensive oriented catcher.

Michael McKenry

	Innings	Runs Saved
2011	485	1
2009-2011	494	1

	Good Plays	Misplays and Errors
McKenry 2011	6	25
Avg Catcher	6	23
Good Play/Misplay Pct		.497

Salvador Perez

	Innings	Runs Saved
2011	338.2	1
2009-2011	338.2	1

	Good Plays	Misplays and Errors
Perez 2011	10	24
Avg Catcher	5	19
Good Play/Misplay Pct		.632

Catchers

Brayan Pena

	Innings	Runs Saved
2011	537	3
2009-2011	1088	0

	Good Plays	Misplays and Errors
Pena 2011	14	24
Avg Catcher	7	28
Good Play/Misplay Pct		.706

Brett Hayes

	Innings	Runs Saved
2011	312.2	-1
2009-2011	503.1	0

	Good Plays	Misplays and Errors
Hayes 2011	5	13
Avg Catcher	3	14
Good Play/Misplay Pct		.613

Francisco Cervelli

	Innings	Runs Saved
2011	316.1	-1
2009-2011	1281.2	0

	Good Plays	Misplays and Errors
Cervelli 2011	5	19
Avg Catcher	3	14
Good Play/Misplay Pct		.520

Cervelli was touted as a great defensive catcher in the minor leagues, but he's been plagued by inconsistency and prone to mental mistakes as a backup for the Yankees. In fact, over the last two seasons Cervelli has committed the second-most errors (19 in 1,040 innings) at the catcher position, despite being relegated to backup duty. During that span, only Miguel Olivo (20 in 1,999 innings) and Russell Martin (20 in 1,835 innings) have more, albeit in nearly twice as much playing time. Cervelli was thrust into action in 2010 following a foot injury to Jorge Posada, but saw less action in 2011 with Russell Martin serving as the primary catcher for the Yankees. Despite a 36 percent caught stealing percentage in the minors, Cervelli has a career rate of just 18 percent in the majors, including 4 for 28 in 2011. This is partly due to inaccuracy and a slow release, but the Yankee pitchers also deserve some of the blame. Cervelli also struggles to block balls in the dirt and has

shown a tendency to reach for the ball rather than shift in front of it to block it with his chest. The good news is that Cervelli is still just 25 years old, with room to improve, and his defensive misplay rate was lower in 2011 than it was in 2010. However, given his current defensive limitations and New York's organizational depth at the position, Cervelli may not figure into the Yankees' future plans.

Henry Blanco

	Innings	Runs Saved
2011	274	0
2009-2011	1143	-1

	Good Plays	Misplays and Errors
Blanco 2011	0	11
Avg Catcher	2	10
Good Play/Misplay Pct		.000

Eli Whiteside

	Innings	Runs Saved
2011	583.2	-2
2009-2011	1238.1	-1

	Good Plays	Misplays and Errors
Whiteside 2011	9	28
Avg Catcher	8	32
Good Play/Misplay Pct		.570

Jonathan Lucroy

	Innings	Runs Saved
2011	1043.2	-5
2009-2011	1698.2	-1

	Good Plays	Misplays and Errors
Lucroy 2011	10	72
Avg Catcher	12	49
Good Play/Misplay Pct		.364

Jonathan Lucroy was given full-time catching duties in just his second year in the bigs, and he inherited a very talented pitching staff with which to work. He did an admirable job with them, particularly with two newcomers to the starting rotation. He is very good at framing pitches and is also one of the best in the league at blocking balls in the dirt with runners on base. His biggest shortcoming is in limiting the running game. As of yet he does not consistently throw strikes to second base, and he can stand to quicken his release of the throw. Until then, runners will continue to take advantage of this weakness.

Catchers

Hank Conger

	Innings	Runs Saved
2011	450	-1
2009-2011	530	-2

	Good Plays	Misplays and Errors
Conger 2011	7	26
Avg Catcher	7	29
Good Play/Misplay Pct		.526

Hank Conger is a solid defensive backup catcher who can struggle to control the running game. It is rare for him to make a mistake on balls in play. Behind the plate, he frames pitches well, which benefits his pitchers. He does use his body to block low pitches, but will try and stab at balls on occasion. A few wild pitches will get away from him, but passed balls are a rarity. His caught stealing rate is low, but everything seems fundamentally sound on stolen base attempts; he has good footwork and he transfers the ball well. Conger has average to good arm strength, but his accuracy can be inconsistent on stolen base and pickoff attempts. When his throws are offline on stolen base attempts, they tend to drift to the first base side of second.

Jarrod Saltalamacchia

	Innings	Runs Saved
2011	856	-4
2009-2011	1622.2	-2

	Good Plays	Misplays and Errors
Saltalamacchia 2011	9	56
Avg Catcher	13	53
Good Play/Misplay Pct		.398

Jarrod Saltalamacchia has improved defensively with additional playing time at the catcher position with the Red Sox, but other than his throwing arm, you still can't say he is a good defensive catcher. Saltalamacchia's passed ball numbers will be exaggerated because of all the innings spent catching knuckleballer Tim Wakefield, but he still does not exhibit excellent reactions behind the plate. Saltamacchia utilizes his large 6'4" frame by throwing his body in front of every wild pitch, but does not have the finesse and coordination to corral the difficult throws in the dirt. Saltalamacchia's arm strength is average for his position, but he did a good job with a pitching staff that is horrible at holding runners. His defensive issues can be remedied with experience, and Saltalamacchia has the athleticism to find success behind the plate.

Ronny Paulino

	Innings	Runs Saved
2011	511	-6
2009-2011	1833.2	-2

	Good Plays	Misplays and Errors
Paulino 2011	3	33
Avg Catcher	6	24
Good Play/Misplay Pct		.272

Ronny Paulino rated as a below-average defensive catcher this year, costing the Mets approximately six runs in just over 500 innings. At the crux of that was an inability to put a stop to the opponents' stealing. He can be particularly slow in making the throw to second base, and several times he lost the chance at the baserunner before a throw was even attempted. He fared about as well as the Mets' primary catcher, Josh Thole, in handling the pitching staff.

Brian Schneider

	Innings	Runs Saved
2011	309	-3
2009-2011	1079.1	-3

	Good Plays	Misplays and Errors
Schneider 2011	0	9
Avg Catcher	3	11
Good Play/Misplay Pct		.000

Nick Hundley

	Innings	Runs Saved
2011	654.1	5
2009-2011	1957.1	-4

	Good Plays	Misplays and Errors
Hundley 2011	10	28
Avg Catcher	9	38
Good Play/Misplay Pct		.595

On the surface, Nick Hundley appears to be a solid, potentially above-average starting catcher on defense. Hundley is an adept pitch blocker. He is quick off his feet and gets his body into good position to limit wild pitches. He is equally skilled at limiting stolen bases with good footwork and a strong arm. However, his receiving skills leave much to be desired. Hundley sets a high target, and sits high with runners on base, which lets him get better throws off to second base, but it makes getting low strike calls nearly impossible for his pitchers. He also has a tendency to set up too directly over the plate, meaning he has to reach for balls on the corners, making the pitch seem more like a ball. His good

Catchers

blocking instincts hurt him here as he can be jumpy behind the plate, again costing his pitchers valuable strike calls.

George Kottaras

	Innings	Runs Saved
2011	253	-1
2009-2011	1038.1	-4

	Good Plays	Misplays and Errors
Kottaras 2011	1	5
Avg Catcher	3	10
Good Play/Misplay Pct		.452

Wilson Ramos

	Innings	Runs Saved
2011	951.2	-5
2009-2011	1144	-4

	Good Plays	Misplays and Errors
Ramos 2011	6	47
Avg Catcher	9	38
Good Play/Misplay Pct		.344

2011 was the first full year for Ramos to show off his abilities as a catcher. His greatest defensive asset is his strong throwing arm. His strong and accurate throwing arm helped him to throw out runners at a rate of 28 percent this year, which ranked 3rd in baseball among catchers who started at least 100 games. He has very quick feet and excellent footwork when he is getting ready to release a throw to second base. This allows him to consistently throw the ball where the infielder can catch it and apply a quick tag. Ramos does struggle with handling pitches in the dirt. He is below average at blocking balls and could really develop into a great defensive catcher with improvement in this area.

Ryan Doumit

	Innings	Runs Saved
2011	461.1	-6
2009-2011	1867	-4

	Good Plays	Misplays and Errors
Doumit 2011	5	27
Avg Catcher	6	24
Good Play/Misplay Pct		.433

Miguel Olivo

	Innings	Runs Saved
2011	1064.1	-9
2009-2011	2845	-4

	Good Plays	Misplays and Errors
Olivo 2011	14	85
Avg Catcher	14	57
Good Play/Misplay Pct		.404

Olivo has never been the type to impress on the offensive side of the ball, but the journeyman catcher has earned playing time for the past decade with his excellent throwing skills behind the plate. This asset sets him apart from many of his contemporaries, but especially from his predecessor in Seattle, Kenji Johjima. But Olivo has a huge hole in his game. He struggles with balls in the dirt and allows too many balls to roll to the backstop. Despite his arm, Olivo is an average catcher at best.

Geovany Soto

	Innings	Runs Saved
2011	1041.2	-1
2009-2011	2700	-5

	Good Plays	Misplays and Errors
Soto 2011	13	49
Avg Catcher	14	56
Good Play/Misplay Pct		.522

Historically Soto has not had a good arm behind the plate, but he did a suitable job in 2011 and threw out 26 percent of the runners who tried to steal. However, his arm also got him into trouble. He had almost as many errors in 2011 as his last three seasons combined, most of them on wild throws on stolen base attempts (allowing the runner to take an extra base).

Carlos Santana

	Innings	Runs Saved
2011	786.1	-4
2009-2011	1126.1	-5

	Good Plays	Misplays and Errors
Santana 2011	7	43
Avg Catcher	9	36
Good Play/Misplay Pct		.401

Behind the plate, Santana is a below average defender, ranking in the lower third of all catchers in runs saved in 2011. In his first full season last year, he had some trouble throwing out runners. He has average arm strength, but many times he bobbles the transfer from the glove to his throwing hand, allowing the easy stolen base.

Catchers

He also has some difficulty at blocking pitches in the dirt. Surprisingly, when he's stationed at first base, scooping up bad throws is one of his strong points. He saw a considerable amount of time over there in 2011, but is still a work in progress overall.

as he is prone to misplaying wild pitches and allowing base runners to advance. He has above-average arm strength and a quick release. His accuracy on throws is average. Treanor is an average defensive catcher who should continue to find a role in the majors as a backup.

J.P. Arencibia

	Innings	Runs Saved
2011	1059.2	-5
2009-2011	1122.2	-5

	Good Plays	Misplays and Errors
Arencibia 2011	11	75
Avg Catcher	14	59
Good Play/Misplay Pct		.376

Arencibia made a name for himself in his rookie season, displaying impressive home run power for a catcher. If he'd like to hold on to that positional qualifier for long, he would help his cause by reducing the number of bases he gives away from behind the dish. Arencibia tied for last with -5 Stolen Base Runs Saved in 2011, and he put extra pressure on an average arm by struggling to handle difficult pitches. Even more apparent was his inability to block wild pitches that bounced right in front of him. Arencibia showed a tendency to rely heavily on his glove to stab low breaking balls, when going to his knees and using his body would have allowed him to block several of the pitches that ultimately got by. Moreover, Arencibia's 12 passed balls in 2011 had him trail only a pair of knuckleball-handlers, Jarrod Saltalamacchia and Josh Thole. While either his poor running game management or his limited blocking skills might be tolerable individually, it is the combination of the two that makes Arencibia one of the weakest defensive catchers in the game.

Matt Treanor

	Innings	Runs Saved
2011	565.2	-2
2009-2011	1212.1	-6

	Good Plays	Misplays and Errors
Treanor 2011	9	40
Avg Catcher	6	26
Good Play/Misplay Pct		.481

Treanor had an average season defensively in limited action. The veteran catcher is fundamentally sound when it comes to his receiving skills. There is very little movement as he catches the ball. He helps his pitchers get strike calls with his ability to frame pitches. However, Treanor can improve his pitch blocking skills,

John Jaso

	Innings	Runs Saved
2011	603.1	-3
2009-2011	1322.1	-6

	Good Plays	Misplays and Errors
Jaso 2011	6	34
Avg Catcher	7	28
Good Play/Misplay Pct		.421

John Jaso's defense behind the plate could be defined as "serviceable." He is a decent enough receiver and has done a nice job handling the young Rays pitching staff the past few seasons. However, Jaso lacks arm strength and has below-average footwork on throws to second. Teams will continue to run on him until he shows improvement. He was also below-average blocking pitches in the dirt.

Yorvit Torrealba

	Innings	Runs Saved
2011	823.2	-12
2009-2011	2164.2	-6

	Good Plays	Misplays and Errors
Torrealba 2011	8	37
Avg Catcher	9	38
Good Play/Misplay Pct		.471

Signed to split time with Mike Napoli as the Rangers' backstop in 2011, Torrealba was thought to be the superior defensive option. Torrealba broke the 100 game plateau in 2011 for just the second time in his career, and developed a good rapport with the pitching staff. He had been inconsistent in the last handful of seasons throwing out basestealers, but his 27 percent success rate in 2011 was better than his career average. He has a strong arm and good footwork but still has a bit of a quirky throwing motion. However, while he ranked third among catchers saving eight runs defensively in 2010, he fell to -12 in 2011. Given Napoli's surprisingly decent defensive season and hot second-half bat, Torrealba saw his playing time diminish late in the season. With a potent Rangers lineup, Torrealba should continue to see playing time next year as a defensive catcher as long as he can show that his 2011 season was an anomaly.

Catchers

Kelly Shoppach

	Innings	Runs Saved
2011	625.2	3
2009-2011	1701.1	-7

	Good Plays	Misplays and Errors
Shoppach 2011	5	22
Avg Catcher	6	26
Good Play/Misplay Pct		.483

Since the beginning of the 2008 season, Shoppach had not been very valuable defensively, but he seemed to have turned it around in 2011. Sharing time with John Jaso, Shoppach ranked in the top ten among catchers in runs saved and posted the best caught stealing numbers of his career. In fact, among all players who caught over 600 innings, Shoppach was second in all of baseball, throwing out 37 percent of basestealers. While the Rays' pitching staff deserves some of the credit, Shoppach does have a very good arm and extremely quick feet. Additionally, Shoppach has the perfect build for a catcher —he does a decent job blocking pitches in the dirt and allowed just one passed ball all season. He calls a good game and gives his pitchers the confidence to throw any pitch in any situation. Shoppach's defense kept the Rays' brass satisfied, even at the expense of hitting below the Mendoza Line.

Chris Snyder

	Innings	Runs Saved
2011	265.2	-1
2009-2011	1541	-8

	Good Plays	Misplays and Errors
Snyder 2011	0	10
Avg Catcher	3	12
Good Play/Misplay Pct		.000

Josh Thole

	Innings	Runs Saved
2011	793.1	-4
2009-2011	1388	-8

	Good Plays	Misplays and Errors
Thole 2011	9	33
Avg Catcher	10	42
Good Play/Misplay Pct		.529

Josh Thole is a below-average catcher. He is reliable on balls in play, but will have the occasional miscue. However, behind the plate, he has his struggles. He has a tendency to stab at balls low and in the dirt, rather than block them with his body. This leads to misplays on wild pitches, and a high number of passed balls. However, it should be noted that Thole was the backstop for a majority of R.A. Dickey's starts, and he clearly struggled catching the knuckleball as he acquired over half of his passed balls in those games. He is fundamentally sound on stolen base attempts, though he will fly open on his throws, causing them to drift to the first base side of second. As a result, he only threw out 18 percent of would-be basestealers in 2011. Both his arm strength and accuracy are decent, but can be inconsistent.

Brian McCann

	Innings	Runs Saved
2011	1083	-4
2009-2011	3271.1	-10

	Good Plays	Misplays and Errors
McCann 2011	8	53
Avg Catcher	14	57
Good Play/Misplay Pct		.383

Brian McCann made some strides in cutting down would-be basestealers in 2010, but struggled to keep that going for a second consecutive year as his caught-stealing rate fell back in line with his career norms. On steal attempts, he transfers the ball very quickly out of the glove, but when he gets up it is perhaps too much of a hop rather than a step and plant with his back foot, preventing him from getting as much on the throw as he could. Though he throws accurately, the ball can hang up in the air a bit too long. He may have an average arm, but he is well above average handling plays around the plate, especially bunts. Overall McCann is fine defensively, but it's his bat that keeps him among the top catchers in the game.

Mike Napoli

	Innings	Runs Saved
2011	506.1	1
2009-2011	1789.1	-11

	Good Plays	Misplays and Errors
Napoli 2011	5	19
Avg Catcher	5	19
Good Play/Misplay Pct		.520

Despite having a reputation as a poor defensive catcher, Napoli turned in the best defensive season of his career. Napoli has consistently struggled throwing out runners, but in 2011 he improved in this department, throwing out 10 runners on 31 stolen base attempts, good for 32 percent, compared to his career rate of 21 percent. Napoli remains a below-average defensive catcher when

Catchers

it comes to blocking balls in the dirt. It appears Napoli made some improvements defensively last year, and it remains to be seen if he can continue to improve.

Alex Avila

	Innings	Runs Saved
2011	1157	-2
2009-2011	2067	-11

	Good Plays	Misplays and Errors
Avila 2011	20	64
Avg Catcher	13	54
Good Play/Misplay Pct		.563

Avila took some positive steps forward with his defense behind the plate last year, however there are still areas with room for improvement. Blocking balls in the dirt was particularly a problem for Avila last year, coming in second-worst in the league in this category with 54 misplays throughout the season. Baserunners weren't afraid to run on Avila last year. His caught-stealing percentage is shown as 32 percent, an excellent rate, on many websites, but that includes 14 times where the pitcher threw to first and the runner was caught-stealing. His real caught-stealing percentage excludes pitcher CS and is published in this book as 23 percent, which is the league average.

A.J. Pierzynski

	Innings	Runs Saved
2011	1008	-9
2009-2011	3204.2	-14

	Good Plays	Misplays and Errors
Pierzynski 2011	7	52
Avg Catcher	12	50
Good Play/Misplay Pct		.357

A.J. Pierzynski deserves a lot of credit for having played 11 straight full seasons at catcher, averaging over 130 games played per season. He is incredibly consistent if nothing else. Fortunately he is something else: very average…and not in a negative way. There's a lot of value in having an everyday catcher who is incredibly durable and who will bring league-average production every season. On defense, Pierzynski's age is beginning to show in more ways than one. His feet have slowed over the years, negatively impacting his ability to quickly block pitches in the dirt and to get into position to gun down runners. He is slightly below-average controlling the running game but significantly below-average blocking pitches. However his age is an asset as well. Pierzynski has learned over time how to steal a call here

and there by employing excellent framing skills. He sets a good low target and shifts his body quietly to stay in position as he receives pitches. But most importantly his experience behind the plate every day for years has given him a great understanding of opposing hitters and how to pitch them. There are very few catchers better at handling their pitchers than A.J., both calling for the right pitches at the right time and keeping his pitchers in the right frame of mind.

Ramon Hernandez

	Innings	Runs Saved
2011	658	-4
2009-2011	1841	-17

	Good Plays	Misplays and Errors
Hernandez 2011	4	30
Avg Catcher	7	28
Good Play/Misplay Pct		.354

Ramon Hernandez is an older catcher, and his age seems to be getting the best of him. His mobility is declining significantly, and he struggles with balls in the dirt from time to time. His base is solid, but he seems to be on his heels more than he should with runners on. He receives and frames the ball well. His arm is still above-average but seems to be fading ever so slightly. He still threw out 32 percent of would-be basestealers in 2011, which ranks towards the top in all of baseball. Some question his ability to call a good game, but his staff seems comfortable with him.

John Buck

	Innings	Runs Saved
2011	1144	-5
2009-2011	2443.2	-19

	Good Plays	Misplays and Errors
Buck 2011	5	42
Avg Catcher	12	50
Good Play/Misplay Pct		.329

John Buck set a new career high for innings caught in 2011. He struggles with balls in the dirt, as he seems to get lazy from time to time, resulting in a high number of wild pitch misplays. A poor foundation and a lack of mobility play into his struggles with these pitches, as well as his difficulties in throwing out basestealers. He has a slightly below-average to average arm and teams have taken notice.

First Basemen Evaluations

Year	League	Gold Glove Winners	Should Have Been
2003	AL	John Olerud	John Olerud
	NL	Derrek Lee	J.T. Snow
2004	AL	Darin Erstad	Darin Erstad
	NL	Todd Helton	Todd Helton
2005	AL	Mark Teixeira	Mark Teixeira
	NL	Derrek Lee	Albert Pujols
2006	AL	Mark Teixeira	Doug Mientkiewicz
	NL	Albert Pujols	Albert Pujols
2007	AL	Kevin Youkilis	Casey Kotchman
	NL	Derrek Lee	Albert Pujols
2008	AL	Carlos Pena	Carlos Pena
	NL	Adrian Gonzalez	Albert Pujols
2009	AL	Mark Teixeira	Casey Kotchman
	NL	Adrian Gonzalez	Albert Pujols
2010	AL	Mark Teixeira	Daric Barton
	NL	Albert Pujols	Albert Pujols
2011	AL	Adrian Gonzalez	Adrian Gonzalez
	NL	Joey Votto	Albert Pujols

My Personal Ratings

Top Five

1 Albert Pujols, LAA
2 Adrian Gonzalez, Bos
3 James Loney, LAD
4 Daric Barton, Oak
5 Todd Helton, Col

Bottom Five

26 Miguel Cabrera, Det
27 Matt LaPorta, Cle
28 Prince Fielder, Det
29 Ryan Howard, Phi
30 Adam Dunn, CWS

Player teams based on transactions through February 1, 2012.

First Basemen

Albert Pujols

	Innings	Runs Saved
2011	1260.1	10
2009-2011	4017.2	35

	Good Plays	Misplays and Errors
Pujols 2011	67	29
Avg First Baseman	62	33
Good Play/Misplay Pct		.553

Pujols, the only five-time Fielding Bible Award winner, had a good year defensively at first base for the Cardinals. When injuries struck, Pujols volunteered to move back to third base for a few games and was creditable if not spectacular. At first base, he shows a quick first step from the low, athletic position he assumes as the pitch is thrown. This allows him to have good range on balls hit to his left and his right. Pujols has soft hands for a first basemen. If he can get to a ball he makes the play. He is one of the best in baseball at helping his fellow infielders out with his ability to handle difficult throws. Pujols' arm is tremendous. Since he started playing first full-time in 2004, he has more than doubled the next-best throwing first baseman with 37 Good Fielding Plays on throws (Todd Helton is second with 16). Pujols has been the best first baseman in baseball for years and shows no signs of anything different moving forward.

Daric Barton

	Innings	Runs Saved
2011	568.1	4
2009-2011	2318.2	25

	Good Plays	Misplays and Errors
Barton 2011	40	19
Avg First Baseman	28	15
Good Play/Misplay Pct		.530

In 2010 Daric Barton won the only Fielding Bible Award since the awards began six years ago that doesn't have Albert Pujols' name on it. That year Barton saved the A's a staggering 18 runs with his defense, a mark six runs higher than his closest competition. In fact, over the last nine years the only first basemen with better seasons than Barton's 2010 were Mark Texeira's 2003 and 2008 (19 and 21 runs saved, respectively) and Albert Pujols' 2007 (31 runs saved). Barton struggled with the bat in 2011 and was optioned to Triple-A Sacramento in June, but his defense remained above-average at the major league level. Barton was drafted as a catcher by the St. Louis Cardinals out of high school in 2003, and transitioned very well from behind the plate to first base when Oakland acquired him in the Mark Mulder trade in late 2004. Barton has incredible range when fielding groundballs and catching pop-ups, and ranked third among first basemen in 2011 with a Good Fielding Play on 6.1 percent of his Touches.

Adrian Gonzalez

	Innings	Runs Saved
2011	1352.2	12
2009-2011	4109.2	24

	Good Plays	Misplays and Errors
Gonzalez 2011	56	20
Avg First Baseman	59	32
Good Play/Misplay Pct		.599

Adrian Gonzalez is one of the premier defensive first basemen in baseball. He possesses a combination of soft hands and sensible, quick judgment that few in baseball can match. He is especially strong on balls toward the line, while balls to his right have a better chance of getting through the infield. On throws to first, he is a sure-handed receiver and does a good job on balls in the dirt. He handles bunts better than any other first baseman, both playing them well, and more importantly, being smart with what he does with the ball when he fields it. Gonzalez does not make unnecessary throws, which makes him especially good on relay plays. He does have a strong, accurate arm that he is not afraid to show off on force attempts across the diamond.

James Loney

	Innings	Runs Saved
2011	1203.2	11
2009-2011	3883.1	20

	Good Plays	Misplays and Errors
Loney 2011	71	26
Avg First Baseman	53	28
Good Play/Misplay Pct		.593

Loney has long been known as a defensive stopper at first base. His glove-work is stellar, as he routinely helps out his teammates by scooping balls out of the dirt at first base. His tall frame makes him a solid target, and he has good flexibility to get extension off the base. Loney is not a great athlete, but he does a good job covering the area around first base on groundballs. He is excellent chasing down pop fouls and has reached into the stands to record an out 11 times in the last three years. Carlos Pena is second with 7.

First Basemen

Daniel Murphy

	Innings	Runs Saved
2011	419	8
2009-2011	1268.1	19

	Good Plays	Misplays and Errors
Murphy 2011	31	13
Avg First Baseman	20	11
Good Play/Misplay Pct		.560

Over his young career, Daniel Murphy has spent a fair amount of time playing first, second, third and left. He played mostly first base last season out of necessity following Ike Davis' season-ending injury, but it doesn't mean he will be limited to playing there in the future. Despite the brand that utility players like Murphy usually get, that "he just isn't good enough at one position," Murphy has shown in limited time that he's at least average if not quite good at all of them. He has been excellent at first base. Murphy doesn't have a tremendous skill set, but he manages to consistently convert outs. In about one full season of defensive play at first base over the last two years he has saved the Mets an estimated 19 runs with his defense. He has soft hands, receiving the ball well at first base and has aggressive instincts to make tough plays. He also boasts a strong and accurate throwing arm, especially for a first baseman.

Todd Helton

	Innings	Runs Saved
2011	987.2	7
2009-2011	3210.1	15

	Good Plays	Misplays and Errors
Helton 2011	35	14
Avg First Baseman	47	25
Good Play/Misplay Pct		.572

Todd Helton's defensive prowess has hardly regressed with age. He has remained a slick fielding first baseman with limited misplays. Helton no longer possesses the superhuman range to his right, but reacts well to sharply hit balls and is very smooth around the bag. He is one of the best at saving errors for his fellow infielders scooping and snaring difficult throws.

Casey Kotchman

	Innings	Runs Saved
2011	1222.1	3
2009-2011	3082.1	13

	Good Plays	Misplays and Errors
Kotchman 2011	53	20
Avg First Baseman	53	28
Good Play/Misplay Pct		.586

Although Kotchman doesn't get to quite as many balls as he used to, he is still an elite first baseman. He has a strong, accurate arm that can gun down a runner trying to advance to any base. He never gives up on pop-ups and often reaches balls that others would not. Kotchman's ability to handle difficult throws is what stands out the most. He led all of baseball with five runs saved on scoop plays over the past three years. He can also handle the difficult throws on turf, where bounces are usually straight but unpredictable in height.

Ike Davis

	Innings	Runs Saved
2011	317	1
2009-2011	1580	13

	Good Plays	Misplays and Errors
Davis 2011	8	13
Avg First Baseman	15	8
Good Play/Misplay Pct		.248

Davis played in just 36 games in 2011 before an ankle injury ended his season, but his defensive ability was on display the previous season—his first as the Mets' starting first baseman. In 2010, Davis ranked second among first baseman in plus/minus (+14) and second in runs saved (12), en route to a third-place finish in the Fielding Bible Award voting. A left-handed thrower, his greatest asset on groundballs is his range to his right, but he does an adequate job handling most everything hit at him. Though he only has one full season to his name and fielding metrics fluctuate from year-to-year, Davis is still just 24 years old, so the Mets appear set defensively at first base for several seasons.

First Basemen

Mark Teixeira

	Innings	Runs Saved
2011	1274	3
2009-2011	3869.1	11

	Good Plays	Misplays and Errors
Teixeira 2011	79	29
Avg First Baseman	58	31
Good Play/Misplay Pct		.593

Teixeira is one of the best first basemen in the league at ranging to his right. He is able to react very quickly on balls hit in that direction and turn them into outs. Teixeira's instincts and quick reactions at first base allowed him to lead all first basemen this past season in groundball-out Good Fielding Plays by a wide margin with 30, while the next-best first baseman had 18. Despite these things, he has only averaged about four runs saved per year over the last three, after saving 21 runs defensively during the 2008 season. Four runs per year is above-average play at first base, but not Gold Glove or Fielding Bible Award calibre (despite the fact that he won Gold Gloves in 2009 and 2010). In those years, the winners should have been Casey Kotchman and Daric Barton, not Teixeira. As an example, one area where Kotchman and Barton are better is their ability to handle difficult throws. By our metrics, Kotchman has saved five runs on scoops in the last three years and Barton four. Teixeira has been exactly average with zero runs saved.

Mark Trumbo

	Innings	Runs Saved
2011	1257.1	9
2009-2011	1290.1	10

	Good Plays	Misplays and Errors
Trumbo 2011	48	29
Avg First Baseman	61	32
Good Play/Misplay Pct		.469

Trumbo isn't what Angels fans are used to at first base after experiencing the glove work of Casey Kotchman and Mark Texiera over the past few years, but he proved he is a more-than capable defender. Overall he saved nine runs for the Angels defending his position at first base. He has good range, especially on balls to his right. He has been very effective with a strong arm when throws are needed, espcially on double plays. Trumbo's downfall is his inability to scoop difficult throws out of the dirt. He has a tough time with all poorly thrown balls, and they often end up either in the stands or in right field.

Nick Evans

	Innings	Runs Saved
2011	337.2	9
2009-2011	375.2	9

	Good Plays	Misplays and Errors
Evans 2011	24	5
Avg First Baseman	17	9
Good Play/Misplay Pct		.720

Adam LaRoche

	Innings	Runs Saved
2011	375	5
2009-2011	2923	9

	Good Plays	Misplays and Errors
LaRoche 2011	17	5
Avg First Baseman	18	10
Good Play/Misplay Pct		.645

Adam LaRoche saw his 2011 season come to an end rather quickly due to injuries. He struggled early in his career defensively at first base as he posted runs saved totals of -13 and -11 in 2005 and 2006. But he has gotten the feel for the position the last couple of years with 11 runs saved, combining 2010 and his partial season of 2011. His range is decent to his left and even better to his right. He is very good at scooping difficult throws. He won't wow you with his abilities, but he is now a more-than reliable first baseman.

Lyle Overbay

	Innings	Runs Saved
2011	917	-4
2009-2011	3293	9

	Good Plays	Misplays and Errors
Overbay 2011	34	21
Avg First Baseman	43	23
Good Play/Misplay Pct		.464

Overbay built an excellent defensive reputation during his five seasons with the Blue Jays. He's an aggressive fielder who will capitalize on a great arm to cut off the lead runner whenever possible. These skills could not save him in 2011, when another very important aspect of his game abandoned him. Overbay's defense was hurt by a severe drop-off in his range, most notably on groundballs to his right. Considering his age (34 in 2011), a decline in range is not surprising. Overbay was slightly below average at handling difficult throws over the past three years.

First Basemen

Carlos Lee

	Innings	Runs Saved
2011	624.1	7
2009-2011	768.1	8

	Good Plays	Misplays and Errors
Lee 2011	33	20
Avg First Baseman	29	15
Good Play/Misplay Pct		.469

Brett Wallace

	Innings	Runs Saved
2011	768.2	5
2009-2011	1144	8

	Good Plays	Misplays and Errors
Wallace 2011	34	18
Avg First Baseman	33	18
Good Play/Misplay Pct		.502

The 25-year-old Brett Wallace is still working on his offensive game, but he has shown some defensive ability at first base in about a season's worth of games the last two years. He has good reactions and can range to his right to make a play, though he has less success with balls hit to his left. He fields the bunt well, charging and fielding cleanly and throwing accurately to the base. If his hitting comes around as expected, Wallace could be a valuable overall player.

Justin Morneau

	Innings	Runs Saved
2011	479.1	-3
2009-2011	2239.1	7

	Good Plays	Misplays and Errors
Morneau 2011	21	10
Avg First Baseman	21	11
Good Play/Misplay Pct		.529

Morneau has averaged just 95 games played over the past three seasons due to a myriad of injuries. He overcame a lower back stress fracture suffered near the end of 2009 to return to MVP form in the first half of 2010. Complementing his outstanding offensive performance, Morneau was putting together the best defensive season of his career, saving an estimated eight runs for the Twins before the All-Star break. He was nearly mistake-free at first base, fielding hard grounders with ease as well as showcasing superb scooping ability. Morneau likely would have been a contender for a Fielding Bible Award, but his stellar season ended prematurely when he slid into the knee of Toronto's John McDonald in early July. Morneau experienced symptoms of the resultant post-concussion syndrome through 2011 and had occasional lapses in coordination. His defense suffered, although not as much as his offense. Hopefully he can re-emerge as a good fielder with a full recovery.

Joey Votto

	Innings	Runs Saved
2011	1427.2	4
2009-2011	3807.2	5

	Good Plays	Misplays and Errors
Votto 2011	61	34
Avg First Baseman	67	36
Good Play/Misplay Pct		.490

Joey Votto has good footwork around the first base bag and moves well for his size. He is not afraid to sprawl out for a ball out of his reach, and he does particularly well ranging to his right. He throws accurately to pitchers covering the bag, and he does a nice job saving his infielders from throwing errors by scooping the ball out of the dirt. He struggles with balls hit sharply down the line, but overall he has a nice presence in the field to complement his big stick. He won a Gold Glove in 2011, but that overrates his abilities. Albert Pujols, the Fielding Bible Award winner, would have been the better choice. James Loney rates defensively above Votto in the National League as well.

Aubrey Huff

	Innings	Runs Saved
2011	1032.2	2
2009-2011	2680	4

	Good Plays	Misplays and Errors
Huff 2011	43	23
Avg First Baseman	47	25
Good Play/Misplay Pct		.500

Huff has made the move from the outfield to first base, and has been a much more adept defender in the infield. At 35 years old, his range is limited, and he is rather slow to react to the ball. However, he has been an adequate fielder at first base by doing two things well: he has an excellent ability to scoop balls in the dirt, and he does a good job limiting the number of errors he makes. Long known for his offensive abilities, Huff has settled in to be an average defensive first baseman for the Giants.

First Basemen

Xavier Nady

	Innings	Runs Saved
2011	391.1	0
2009-2011	814.1	3

	Good Plays	Misplays and Errors
Nady 2011	21	7
Avg First Baseman	18	10
Good Play/Misplay Pct		.616

Anthony Rizzo

	Innings	Runs Saved
2011	341.2	2
2009-2011	341.2	2

	Good Plays	Misplays and Errors
Rizzo 2011	13	8
Avg First Baseman	15	8
Good Play/Misplay Pct		.465

Juan Rivera

	Innings	Runs Saved
2011	303.2	0
2009-2011	410.2	2

	Good Plays	Misplays and Errors
Rivera 2011	11	5
Avg First Baseman	13	7
Good Play/Misplay Pct		.540

Derrek Lee

	Innings	Runs Saved
2011	984	-3
2009-2011	3422.2	2

	Good Plays	Misplays and Errors
Lee 2011	45	28
Avg First Baseman	45	24
Good Play/Misplay Pct		.462

The strength of Lee has always been his ability to scoop up errant throws by infielders and either record the out or prevent the advancement of runners. He was consistent in this area of his defensive game once again, but his reaction time and sure-handedness on balls in play was not what it once was. In 2011, Lee cost one of his teams runs defensively (-3 runs saved) for the first time since he had -8 runs saved in 2003.

Brad Hawpe

	Innings	Runs Saved
2011	383	-1
2009-2011	455	1

	Good Plays	Misplays and Errors
Hawpe 2011	18	10
Avg First Baseman	18	10
Good Play/Misplay Pct		.490

After many miserable years patrolling right field, Brad Hawpe was finally given a shot to play first base, where his lack of foot speed and inability to read flyballs might be better hidden. Surprisingly, Hawpe played quite competently during his time in the infield, but sadly, his lack of performance with the bat led to decreased playing time and eventually, Hawpe had season-ending surgery. What Hawpe did display in his limited time was soft hands receiving throws and fielding balls. He read grounders well and got decent jumps, especially moving right to his glove side. He hasn't yet mastered the art of the scoop. Hawpe has only had limited time playing first base. It remains to be seen if he can continue to handle the position adequately. He has room for improvement, but it wouldn't be surprising to see him regress.

Mike Carp

	Innings	Runs Saved
2011	263.2	-1
2009-2011	457	1

	Good Plays	Misplays and Errors
Carp 2011	13	9
Avg First Baseman	12	6
Good Play/Misplay Pct		.436

Luke Hughes

	Innings	Runs Saved
2011	274	0
2009-2011	274	0

	Good Plays	Misplays and Errors
Hughes 2011	17	9
Avg First Baseman	13	7
Good Play/Misplay Pct		.502

First Basemen

Lucas Duda

	Innings	Runs Saved
2011	323.1	0
2009-2011	323.1	0

	Good Plays	Misplays and Errors
Duda 2011	15	10
Avg First Baseman	16	9
Good Play/Misplay Pct		.445

Jesus Guzman

	Innings	Runs Saved
2011	434	0
2009-2011	448	0

	Good Plays	Misplays and Errors
Guzman 2011	15	15
Avg First Baseman	19	10
Good Play/Misplay Pct		.348

Chris Marrero

	Innings	Runs Saved
2011	264.1	-1
2009-2011	264.1	-1

	Good Plays	Misplays and Errors
Marrero 2011	10	6
Avg First Baseman	12	6
Good Play/Misplay Pct		.471

Freddie Freeman

	Innings	Runs Saved
2011	1370.1	-2
2009-2011	1409.1	-2

	Good Plays	Misplays and Errors
Freeman 2011	70	30
Avg First Baseman	62	33
Good Play/Misplay Pct		.555

Freddie Freeman showed good mobility at first base for the Braves in 2011. The talented rookie reacted well on line drives and had tremendous range into the outfield and foul territory. His large 6'5" frame was a consistent target at first base and Freeman did a very good job at picking balls out of the dirt and stretching to corral wild throws. His defensive difficulties stemmed from groundballs as he sometimes misplayed grounders hit directly to him. Freeman needs to improve his hands and lateral range to his right on grounders in order to elevate his defense to the next level.

Mitch Moreland

	Innings	Runs Saved
2011	799	-2
2009-2011	1119.2	-2

	Good Plays	Misplays and Errors
Moreland 2011	30	16
Avg First Baseman	35	19
Good Play/Misplay Pct		.501

Moreland possesses the basic skills necessary to play a solid first base. He is above-average with his glove when it comes to fielding grounders, and he holds his own picking throws out of the dirt. The main limitation early in his career has been poor awareness. In particular, Moreland will abandon first base too often when the second baseman or pitcher is capable of getting to the ball. Moreland spent most of his playing time at right field while he was in the high minors and should pick up on the subtleties of first base with more experience. Since he doesn't get good jumps on flyballs, first base is likely the best fit for him long-term.

Carlos Santana

	Innings	Runs Saved
2011	565	-2
2009-2011	565	-2

	Good Plays	Misplays and Errors
Santana 2011	37	17
Avg First Baseman	29	16
Good Play/Misplay Pct		.538

Paul Goldschmidt

	Innings	Runs Saved
2011	368	-3
2009-2011	368	-3

	Good Plays	Misplays and Errors
Goldschmidt 2011	29	7
Avg First Baseman	17	9
Good Play/Misplay Pct		.689

First Basemen

Juan Miranda

	Innings	Runs Saved
2011	401	-4
2009-2011	474.1	-3

	Good Plays	Misplays and Errors
Miranda 2011	7	10
Avg First Baseman	17	9
Good Play/Misplay Pct		.272

It's tough to get a real gauge on Juan Miranda in the field because he's seen so little time over the past years. In the little time he has seen, he hasn't been great. There's not a whole lot of quickness or athleticism in his muscular frame, meaning his range is average at best. He doesn't have great speed in general, and this hurt him most when he needed to quickly charge bunt attempts. His hands are probably the best part of his game, and he showed that he is more comfortable fielding a ball to his glove-side, as many players are. Overall, Juan Miranda is best described as a below-average first baseman who is still learning how to defend the position.

Justin Smoak

	Innings	Runs Saved
2011	926.2	-1
2009-2011	1734.1	-4

	Good Plays	Misplays and Errors
Smoak 2011	36	18
Avg First Baseman	42	22
Good Play/Misplay Pct		.517

Smoak displayed adequate defense at first base in his second season in the majors. Smoak's range at first base is slightly below-average. His best asset at first base is his ability to pick wild throws out of the dirt when needed. Smoak has not handled bunt attempts well, costing his team a run in each of his two years.

Carlos Pena

	Innings	Runs Saved
2011	1258.1	-1
2009-2011	3627	-4

	Good Plays	Misplays and Errors
Pena 2011	77	35
Avg First Baseman	54	29
Good Play/Misplay Pct		.540

Pena had a decent defensive year in his one-year fling with the Chicago Cubs. He has plus range on balls to his right and slightly below-average range to his left. However, he can be prone to an occasional misplay on groundballs or line drives right to him. Pena reacts well to sharply hit balls. He has the ability to get his body into a good fielding position even after holding a runner on first. Although he will occasionally drop a catchable throw, he is good at turning bad throws from other infielders into outs. At age 34, Pena is not as good defensively as he once was, but he still gets the job done.

Adam Lind

	Innings	Runs Saved
2011	965.1	-4
2009-2011	1041.1	-4

	Good Plays	Misplays and Errors
Lind 2011	48	22
Avg First Baseman	45	24
Good Play/Misplay Pct		.538

Though he is a below-average first baseman, Adam Lind was moved to the position from a crowded Toronto outfield. His outfield experience has proven beneficial at first base as he plays balls hit in the air well, especially difficult foul flies. He can look very stiff in the field, and his poor range on groundballs reflects that. Grounders that Lind misplays are usually the result of a failed dive or trying to play a ball to his side, rather than getting his body behind the ball. He does scoop a lot of balls at first, saving his fellow infielders from committing costly defensive miscues, but he drops the occasional throw, costing his team near-certain outs. His arm is average at best, though at first base it is rarely challenged.

Gaby Sanchez

	Innings	Runs Saved
2011	1354	5
2009-2011	2615.1	-5

	Good Plays	Misplays and Errors
Sanchez 2011	50	29
Avg First Baseman	60	32
Good Play/Misplay Pct		.480

Sanchez's defense at first base was good in 2011; it forced the Marlins to move prospect Logan Morrison away from his natural position and into left field. During the 2011 season, Sanchez was one of the lone defensive bright spots on a team that ranked last in the major leagues in defensive runs saved. Sanchez doesn't have great range to his left, and did make a fair number of misplays on grounders, but overall his defense was above-average. Sanchez was below-average handling throws that were in the dirt or that pulled him off the base, according to our runs saved data on scoop plays.

First Basemen

Among the traditional fielding statistics, Sanchez's .996 fielding percentage was fifth in the majors at the position, as he committed just five errors all season.

Conor Jackson

	Innings	Runs Saved
2011	392	-5
2009-2011	461	-5

	Good Plays	Misplays and Errors
Jackson 2011	14	7
Avg First Baseman	17	9
Good Play/Misplay Pct		.517

Michael Young

	Innings	Runs Saved
2011	302	-5
2009-2011	302	-5

	Good Plays	Misplays and Errors
Young 2011	8	11
Avg First Baseman	13	7
Good Play/Misplay Pct		.280

Michael Morse

	Innings	Runs Saved
2011	723.1	-7
2009-2011	829.1	-5

	Good Plays	Misplays and Errors
Morse 2011	35	16
Avg First Baseman	35	19
Good Play/Misplay Pct		.539

Morse has spent the past couple of years primarily in the outfield, but moved to first base in 2011 after Adam LaRoche went on the disabled list. A converted shortstop, fielding groundballs is nothing new to Morse, who simply outgrew the position with his 6'5, 230-pound frame. Morse has always had a strong arm going back to his days as a shortstop. He's a solid athlete for a first baseman, but he has had trouble on plays to his left. In the outfield, he lacked range, but at first base, where he's not asked to run as much, he should have more than enough athletic ability to be an average defender, though it hasn't been reflected in his runs saved numbers yet. He does a good job of scooping balls in the dirt. Overall his play at first base in 2011 was a bit below-average.

Brandon Allen

	Innings	Runs Saved
2011	440.1	-1
2009-2011	712.1	-6

	Good Plays	Misplays and Errors
Allen 2011	19	17
Avg First Baseman	19	10
Good Play/Misplay Pct		.374

Michael Cuddyer

	Innings	Runs Saved
2011	352.2	1
2009-2011	1370	-7

	Good Plays	Misplays and Errors
Cuddyer 2011	11	4
Avg First Baseman	17	9
Good Play/Misplay Pct		.595

Mark Reynolds

	Innings	Runs Saved
2011	375.2	-1
2009-2011	602.2	-8

	Good Plays	Misplays and Errors
Reynolds 2011	31	13
Avg First Baseman	17	9
Good Play/Misplay Pct		.560

Miguel Cabrera

	Innings	Runs Saved
2011	1322	-3
2009-2011	3922.1	-9

	Good Plays	Misplays and Errors
Cabrera 2011	52	28
Avg First Baseman	60	32
Good Play/Misplay Pct		.498

Miguel Cabrera is a first baseman because there's nowhere else to hide him. As one of the slower players in the league, and not particularly athletic, his range is almost as bad at first base as it was at other positions he's played. In the past, he had a terrible habit of abandoning first base and cutting off the second baseman to play balls in the hole. Most notably, in the ninth inning of Armando Galarraga's 2010 near-perfecto, most viewers focused on the blown call; however, had Cabrera not overestimated his own range and abandoned first base, Galarraga would never have had to cover first, and the play would have been a semi-routine 4-3 groundout. He corrected that behavior in 2011, but at the cost of

First Basemen

becoming maybe a little too shy going to his right. Cabrera has good hands when the ball is hit to him, but he is one of the worst in baseball handling difficult throws from his infielders. His arm is good for a first baseman. As of press time the Tigers are planning on trying Cabrera at third base after signing Prince Fielder. Miggy last played third in early 2008, but that experiment lasted just 14 games after he accumulated five errors and cost the Tigers three runs. This was coming off of -19 runs saved season playing third base full-time in 2007. Trying him again at third base is the same train wreck waiting to happen.

Eric Hosmer

	Innings	Runs Saved
2011	1135.2	-9
2009-2011	1135.2	-9

	Good Plays	Misplays and Errors
Hosmer 2011	69	34
Avg First Baseman	52	28
Good Play/Misplay Pct		.520

The rookie made his debut in 2011 and made an immediate impact at the plate, but his defense at first base has plenty of room for improvement. His range is well below-average, and his execution on bunts is poor. It seems on the surface that his problems stem from his psyche, and he doesn't allow his instincts to take control. He needs to learn to trust his abilities and not over-think things. He is still very young, and his defense can absolutely improve. Look for Hosmer to put in the work in the off-season and in Spring Training, and have a better defensive campaign in 2012.

Matt LaPorta

	Innings	Runs Saved
2011	802.2	-11
2009-2011	1672	-13

	Good Plays	Misplays and Errors
LaPorta 2011	32	23
Avg First Baseman	38	20
Good Play/Misplay Pct		.427

Matt LaPorta leaves something to be desired at first base. He has poor range and is also below-average at handling bad throws. He makes more misplays and errors than the average first baseman, and he makes fewer good plays as well. He is also a liability when fielding bunts.

Garrett Jones

	Innings	Runs Saved
2011	260.1	-3
2009-2011	1440.2	-15

	Good Plays	Misplays and Errors
Jones 2011	11	14
Avg First Baseman	13	7
Good Play/Misplay Pct		.296

Paul Konerko

	Innings	Runs Saved
2011	963.1	-4
2009-2011	3206.2	-16

	Good Plays	Misplays and Errors
Konerko 2011	32	20
Avg First Baseman	46	25
Good Play/Misplay Pct		.461

Paul Konerko is playing first base because he is big and slow. At this point in his career, in his mid-thirties, no one is expecting much from Konerko on the defensive end of the field. What you can expect from him are decent hands, he won't drop too many throws, and when a ball is hit at him, he converts outs at a good rate. His range will never impress, and he lacks the athleticism required to make diving plays consistently. One aspect of his game is quite good, however. He handles difficult throws quite well, making nice scoops and other catches to save errors from his infield teammates.

Prince Fielder

	Innings	Runs Saved
2011	1394.2	-9
2009-2011	4236.2	-26

	Good Plays	Misplays and Errors
Fielder 2011	48	42
Avg First Baseman	63	34
Good Play/Misplay Pct		.379

It's no secret that Fielder's name fails to reflect his strength as a player; baseball's favorite misnomer has been a defensive liability for his entire career. Since the beginning of 2006 (his first full season), no first baseman has lost more potential outs by failing to catch a throw than Fielder. He doesn't scoop balls in the dirt well at all, and he will occasionally take a low throw off the heel of his glove. Fielder is notorious for his limited range, a claim that has been supported by years worth of ugly plus/minus ratings. Although he still lets more grounders

First Basemen

get through/by him than his counterparts do, Fielder's numbers improved slightly in 2011, and he showed an ability to make some nice diving stops.

Ryan Howard

	Innings	Runs Saved
2011	1309	-13
2009-2011	3926.1	-30

	Good Plays	Misplays and Errors
Howard 2011	58	33
Avg First Baseman	60	32
Good Play/Misplay Pct		.484

Howard was a below-average first baseman in 2011, as he has been each season since accumulating 11 runs saved in part-time play in 2005. He has the physical tools to be an average defender, it just has not happened for him. Howard has limited range to both his right and left, but has the ability to make difficult plays moving either way if he can get to the ball. Howard provides his infielders a large target to throw to at first, but he does not have great hands as evidenced by his poor numbers on scoop plays (fourth-worst in baseball from 2009-2011, costing the Phillies three runs). He is able to get himself into a good fielding position after holding a base runner on first. Howard has a below-average arm, but is generally accurate when he does throw. He will also make mental mistakes like taking steps to his right toward a ball he has no chance of getting, and then not being able to cover first base, costing his team an out if his pitcher fails to get over in time. Despite being a bit below-average, Howard was an adequate defender for the majority of his first four full seasons in the bigs, but has regressed considerably the last two.

Adam Dunn

	Innings	Runs Saved
2011	284.2	-4
2009-2011	2070.2	-38

	Good Plays	Misplays and Errors
Dunn 2011	9	11
Avg First Baseman	13	7
Good Play/Misplay Pct		.304

Second Basemen Evaluations

Year	League	Gold Glove Winners	Should Have Been
2003	AL	Bret Boone	Orlando Hudson
	NL	Luis Castillo	Luis Castillo
2004	AL	Bret Boone	Orlando Hudson
	NL	Luis Castillo	Luis Castillo
2005	AL	Orlando Hudson	Orlando Hudson
	NL	Luis Castillo	Craig Counsell
2006	AL	Mark Grudzielanek	Mark Ellis
	NL	Orlando Hudson	Orlando Hudson
2007	AL	Placido Polanco	Aaron Hill
	NL	Orlando Hudson	Orlando Hudson
2008	AL	Dustin Pedroia	Mark Ellis
	NL	Brandon Phillips	Chase Utley
2009	AL	Placido Polanco	Ian Kinsler
	NL	Orlando Hudson	Chase Utley
2010	AL	Robinson Cano	Robinson Cano
	NL	Brandon Phillips	Chase Utley
2011	AL	Dustin Pedroia	Ben Zobrist
	NL	Brandon Phillips	Brandon Phillips

My Personal Ratings

Top Five

1 Ian Kinsler
2 Ben Zobrist
3 Dustin Pedroia
4 Chase Utley
5 Brandon Phillips

Bottom Five

26 Skip Schumaker
27 Rickie Weeks
28 Justin Turner
29 Dan Uggla
30 Jeff Keppinger

Player teams based on transactions through February 1, 2012

Second Basemen

Ian Kinsler

	Innings	Runs Saved
2011	1269	18
2009-2011	3432.1	47

	Good Plays	Misplays and Errors
Kinsler 2011	54	38
Avg Second Baseman	48	38
Good Play/Misplay Pct		.526

Ian Kinsler is simply a beast of a second baseman. He's the total defensive package—great speed and a lighting-fast first step to cover a ton of ground, especially up the middle. He has a strong enough arm at second, and he rarely makes a poor throw. He displays tremendous athleticism and makes diving plays with ease. Perhaps the best part of his game is his double play ability. Kinsler is incredibly quick around the bag with his hands and uses excellent footwork to avoid the baserunner and make accurate throws. He has saved more runs than anybody else in baseball playing defense at second base with 47.

Ben Zobrist

	Innings	Runs Saved
2011	1058.1	23
2009-2011	2144	45

	Good Plays	Misplays and Errors
Zobrist 2011	39	28
Avg Second Baseman	39	30
Good Play/Misplay Pct		.521

Zobrist has played every position, with the exception of pitcher and catcher, at various points in his Rays career. With Tampa Bay in 2011, he started 118 games at second base and 33 games in right field and was excellent defensively at both positions. Zobrist ranked first in the majors with 23 runs saved at second base and also saved an impressive 6 runs in right field. Over the last three seasons, Zobrist ranks first in basic plus/minus (+61) and second in runs saved (45 runs) at second base. A former shortstop, Zobrist has a strong arm and above-average range. He made 19 more plays on groundballs and 10 more plays on pop-ups and liners than the average second baseman. As a corner outfielder, Zobrist's strong arm often comes into play by holding batters to singles or preventing the advancement of runners. The Rays were the best defensive team in the majors and Zobrist's defensive abilities at both second base and right field were key contributing factors.

Dustin Pedroia

	Innings	Runs Saved
2011	1392.1	18
2009-2011	3406.1	37

	Good Plays	Misplays and Errors
Pedroia 2011	66	22
Avg Second Baseman	51	40
Good Play/Misplay Pct		.701

Pedroia's reputation as a small, scrappy, intelligent player applies to more than his hitting—it can be used to describe his defense, too. Pedroia ranked second in runs saved (18 runs) and third in basic plus/minus (+19) among second baseman in 2011 and his three-year totals rank in the top five in both categories at the position, as well. In addition to his excellent range, Pedroia's combination of instincts, footwork, agility and throwing accuracy make him one of the top defensive second basemen in the majors. The former Arizona State shortstop makes a habit of turning tough plays into outs; he ranked first among second baseman with 35 groundball-out Good Fielding Plays. He's one of the best at his position in turning the double play, be it as the lead man with a good feed, or pivot man, hanging in there despite an aggressive slide. While Pedroia's bat gets a lot of attention, his glove is equally impressive. For his efforts he was rewarded with his first career Fielding Bible Award in 2011.

Chase Utley

	Innings	Runs Saved
2011	887.2	7
2009-2011	3251.2	36

	Good Plays	Misplays and Errors
Utley 2011	28	23
Avg Second Baseman	37	29
Good Play/Misplay Pct		.487

Injury and probably aging affected Utley's fielding in 2011. The 2010 Fielding Bible Award winner at second base has always been strong at fielding balls up the middle. However, fielding balls to his left has become a challenge over the last few seasons. In 2008, Utley was doing what we called ultra positioning. (See the article "What Makes Chase Utley So Good" in *The Fielding Bible—Volume II*.) He played left-handed hitters even further into the first base-second base hole than normal. It enabled him to make 32 more plays to his left than an average second baseman that year. Before that year, he was also excellent to his left. But since then, it appears that he has abandoned the ultra positioning that

Second Basemen

we saw in 2008. He has made 13 fewer plays to his left the last three years. This decrease in range and a drop in his double play success rate really hurt his overall defensive value in 2011. While the 2011 Chase Utley was not the elite fielder he has been in recent years, he remains a dependable, above-average second baseman. It will be interesting to see if a healhty Utley can return to elite status.

Mark Ellis

	Innings	Runs Saved
2011	1054.2	17
2009-2011	2947.2	27

	Good Plays	Misplays and Errors
Ellis 2011	46	16
Avg Second Baseman	45	35
Good Play/Misplay Pct		.692

Mark Ellis is likely the most dependable infielder in baseball. He isn't flashy, nor is he the fleetest of foot, but he makes every play one can expect from a second baseman. He moves well to both his left and right. groundballs can eat him up from time to time, but it is rare for Ellis not to recover and make a play somewhere when this happens. He excels on plays where his range is tested, in part because he throws so well on the run. Ellis possesses average throwing strength, but he is extremely accurate. He is excellent on the double play, very quick with only a very rare misplay or error.

Sean Rodriguez

	Innings	Runs Saved
2011	352.2	3
2009-2011	1067	20

	Good Plays	Misplays and Errors
Rodriguez 2011	25	11
Avg Second Baseman	13	10
Good Play/Misplay Pct		.640

Rodriguez has compiled a nice portfolio of impressive plays while manning seven defensive positions over the past two years. A benefactor of Tampa Bay's intelligent defensive positioning, Rodriguez has been in the right places to make several great snares on hard grounders and line drives. His strong arm helps him make tough plays, but he'll sometimes let the ball sail over the first baseman's head when he doesn't take time to plant his feet. As good as his best work has been, Rodriguez misplayed a surprising number of easy grounders in 2011, mostly when he was playing on the left side of the infield. Perhaps he was more comfortable

spending most of his time at second base before Ben Zobrist nudged him into a utility fielder role.

Brandon Phillips

	Innings	Runs Saved
2011	1324	6
2009-2011	3967.1	18

	Good Plays	Misplays and Errors
Phillips 2011	57	34
Avg Second Baseman	51	40
Good Play/Misplay Pct		.567

Phillips is an incredibly athletic infielder known for his flashy, between-the-legs and behind-the-back plays. The numbers support his strong track record as an above-average second baseman; he's even won a Fielding Bible Award (2008). He's quick, demonstrates good reactions and can make the off-balance throw and quick release when the play calls for it. What's not to like? Well, the Plus/Minus System likes him, but not enough to put him at the top of the league. When we compared Phillips and Chase Utley in *The Fielding Bible—Volume II*, we found that Utley is much better than Phillips at positioning himself pre-pitch. Phillips stands in roughly the same spot regardless of who's at the plate. On groundballs, he's often able to make up for it with his speed and athleticism. However, there are hard grounders and line drives he just can't reach because he's not positioned properly.

Robinson Cano

	Innings	Runs Saved
2011	1340	1
2009-2011	4133	17

	Good Plays	Misplays and Errors
Cano 2011	68	50
Avg Second Baseman	56	44
Good Play/Misplay Pct		.515

Cano really excels at ranging to his right, where he made 11 more plays than an average second baseman based on the Plus/Minus System in 2011. While he was below-average going to his left in 2011, he has posted positive numbers in that category in previous seasons. Cano has quick hands and an outstanding arm which allow him to turn many close plays into outs. On double plays, Cano is a magician, both starting them and on the pivot. However, the magician is dropping cards too frequently, and the net effect may not be a positive. (See the article called "Robinson Cano and Double Plays" on

Second Basemen

page 77). Cano's defensive abilities really complement Mark Teixeira's on the right side of the Yankee infield.

Aaron Hill

	Innings	Runs Saved
2011	1198.1	2
2009-2011	3758.1	13

	Good Plays	Misplays and Errors
Hill 2011	40	28
Avg Second Baseman	45	35
Good Play/Misplay Pct		.527

Last summer the D'Backs eschewed a power-hitting second baseman in Kelly Johnson for Aaron Hill's proven top glove. Hill has been a stellar fielder during his career and is a two-time Fielding Bible Award winner at second base. He displays excellent instincts for reading balls off the bat and great quickness to cover large amounts of ground with his small frame. Hill is very athletic when he needs to be, making diving plays with incredibly soft hands. His arm isn't particularly strong, which is why he's at second to begin with, but he is highly accurate and rarely makes mistakes. One area Hill struggles with is on double plays. Far too often only one out is made on likely double play balls, both when he's the initial fielder and when he's the pivot man. Hill makes a lot of misplays on double plays and has lost more runs on Good Plays/Misplays involving double plays over the last three years (four runs) than any other player in baseball.

Howie Kendrick

	Innings	Runs Saved
2011	937.2	10
2009-2011	2994.1	10

	Good Plays	Misplays and Errors
Kendrick 2011	35	20
Avg Second Baseman	34	27
Good Play/Misplay Pct		.577

Kendrick was one of the best defensive second basemen in 2011. He showed his athleticism by appearing in games at first base and left field along with his customary position as the starting second baseman for the Angels. Kendrick is especially good on balls hit to his left, where he has made 35 more plays than an average second baseman in the last three years. He is able to read a ball quickly off the bat, which enhances his range. Kendrick has above-average arm strength and accuracy throwing from his normal ¾ arm angle. He is able to throw accurately while on the run as well. He

could work on releasing the ball quicker on his throws. Kendrick is competent on the double play, but it is not his strength. He makes more than his share of misplays on throws as the lead man on the double play. But his footwork around the bag allows him to make the turn in a timely manner, and he is especially good getting his throws off on the aggressively sliding runner. Another weakness he showed in 2011 was getting to soft flies in the outfield.

Dustin Ackley

	Innings	Runs Saved
2011	741	10
2009-2011	741	10

	Good Plays	Misplays and Errors
Ackley 2011	25	18
Avg Second Baseman	27	21
Good Play/Misplay Pct		.520

Danny Espinosa

	Innings	Runs Saved
2011	1393	5
2009-2011	1604.1	10

	Good Plays	Misplays and Errors
Espinosa 2011	65	47
Avg Second Baseman	58	45
Good Play/Misplay Pct		.519

Espinosa had a very good defensive season for the Nationals. The former college shortstop brings many of the same skills to second base in the majors. He has plus range when moving to his right and left. He can also go get a flyball hit softly to the outfield. He is able to get back to his feet very quickly when attempting a diving play. Espinosa has plus arm strength and accuracy with a quick release on his throws. These tools help Espinosa make a lot of difficult plays that other second basemen might struggle with. Espinosa has very soft hands. As the season progressed, he improved his footwork on double play pivots and he is not afraid to stand his ground to complete a double play. He has also improved his feeds to shortstop on double plays. Espinosa is a smart defensive player who knows where he should be on the field at all times. In his first full season in the majors, Espinosa showed all the tools of a potential Fielding Bible Award winner.

Second Basemen

Jack Wilson

	Innings	Runs Saved
2011	342.1	7
2009-2011	342.1	7

	Good Plays	Misplays and Errors
Wilson 2011	15	7
Avg Second Baseman	13	11
Good Play/Misplay Pct		.626

Injuries and the Brendan Ryan acquisition forced this former Fielding Bible Award winner at shortstop to move to second base in 2011. Dating back to his days in Pittsburgh, Wilson has always had great range to his right, enabling him to utilize his strong and accurate arm. This strength to his right held up at the new position as well. His effort on defense is always at full throttle, which contributed to a number of spectacular plays, but also led to some mental mistakes as you might expect from a player learning a new position.

Ramon Santiago

	Innings	Runs Saved
2011	434.2	4
2009-2011	718.1	6

	Good Plays	Misplays and Errors
Santiago 2011	12	7
Avg Second Baseman	17	13
Good Play/Misplay Pct		.572

Jonathan Herrera

	Innings	Runs Saved
2011	499	0
2009-2011	924.1	6

	Good Plays	Misplays and Errors
Herrera 2011	19	11
Avg Second Baseman	19	14
Good Play/Misplay Pct		.574

Herrera was an average defensive second baseman this past season for the Rockies in a utility role. While the majority of his playing time came at second base, he also saw time at third base and shortstop. Herrera has above-average range moving to both his right and his left. He also has the ability to cover ground catching balls in the air that reach the outfield. He is good at reading the ball off the bat and has a quick first step, which helps his range. Herrera has below-average arm strength, making him best suited for second base. He showed the ability to start and turn double plays quickly.

He is a smart defensive player and is rarely caught out of position on a play on which he should be backing up. With his ability to play average or better defense at three infield positions, Herrera should not have difficulty finding at least a big league utility job in coming years.

Robert Andino

	Innings	Runs Saved
2011	724.1	5
2009-2011	813.1	5

	Good Plays	Misplays and Errors
Andino 2011	28	20
Avg Second Baseman	28	22
Good Play/Misplay Pct		.522

Andino is a versatile utility player who splits time at second base, third base and shortstop. He has good range and a plus arm to throw out base runners. Andino is a smart player who rarely makes mistakes. Unfortunately his sub-par bat has kept him from earning a daily starting role, but his main value is as a versatile player who can be a defensive specialist. He is comfortable at both second base and short, but shortstop is his natural position.

Luke Hughes

	Innings	Runs Saved
2011	301.1	5
2009-2011	301.1	5

	Good Plays	Misplays and Errors
Hughes 2011	11	4
Avg Second Baseman	13	10
Good Play/Misplay Pct		.682

Jose Altuve

	Innings	Runs Saved
2011	460.2	3
2009-2011	460.2	3

	Good Plays	Misplays and Errors
Altuve 2011	22	7
Avg Second Baseman	16	12
Good Play/Misplay Pct		.710

Second Basemen

Maicer Izturis

	Innings	Runs Saved
2011	422.2	-5
2009-2011	1166.1	3

	Good Plays	Misplays and Errors
Izturis 2011	19	12
Avg Second Baseman	17	14
Good Play/Misplay Pct		.553

Though he also spent time at short and third, Izturis was a below-average defensive second baseman for the Angels in 2011. Izturis has slightly below-average range moving both to his right and left. He does not have the best instincts when reading the ball off the bat. He has average arm strength and accuracy. Izturis is good at deciding when is the right time to charge or sit back on a ball. He has shown the ability to throw accurately while on the run. He throws more over the top when throwing on the run than he does with his feet set. Izturis does not have the soft hands that many middle infielders possess and will occasionally misplay a grounder or drop a catchable throw because of it. He is quick at starting and turning double plays from second base. At age 31 and with a career OPS of .728 to go with adequate defense at three infield positions, Izturis should continue to be in the major leagues in at least a utility role for the next few years.

Omar Infante

	Innings	Runs Saved
2011	1283.1	4
2009-2011	2038	2

	Good Plays	Misplays and Errors
Infante 2011	54	36
Avg Second Baseman	54	42
Good Play/Misplay Pct		.539

Infante has some physical limitations that put him at a natural disadvantage. First, he is on the slow side, so his pure ability to get to the ball is below-average. He also demonstrates a preference to remain on his feet more than most middle infielders do, so he is unlikely to make spectacular plays on well-hit balls. Even by second baseman standards, Infante's arm is weak, so he has particular trouble gunning down faster runners at first on groundballs up the middle. Despite these weaknesses, Infante's sound fundamentals allow him to do a serviceable job in the field. His greatest asset is the preparedness and fluidity of his throwing motion; he is ready to throw immediately even when he needs to spin, slide, charge or turn the double play. He does know how to bare-hand a chopper when charging, providing valuable compensation for the low velocity of his throws.

Orlando Hudson

	Innings	Runs Saved
2011	959.2	-8
2009-2011	3299	2

	Good Plays	Misplays and Errors
Hudson 2011	30	27
Avg Second Baseman	40	32
Good Play/Misplay Pct		.464

Orlando Hudson has a reputation for excellent defensive play at second base, but his ability has diminished since his heyday as one of the top defensive options at his position. Advanced age and a number of wrist and groin injuries have limited Hudson's range and fielding ability. He does not possess an above-average arm and therefore cannot always finish plays when deep in the hole to his right. He is below-average on double plays. Hudson can still flash signs of his 2006 Fielding Bible Award-winning form, with sure-handed fielding and smooth exchanges, but his award-winning days are over.

Darwin Barney

	Innings	Runs Saved
2011	1110.1	1
2009-2011	1164.2	1

	Good Plays	Misplays and Errors
Barney 2011	47	42
Avg Second Baseman	46	36
Good Play/Misplay Pct		.466

Anyone who followed Dan Uggla's improbable 33-game hitting streak in 2011 got an intriguing peek at Darwin Barney's defensive skill. Ranging well into right field, Barney made a spectacular lunging catch to rob a hit from Uggla and ultimately prevent the streak from continuing. That play was no fluke, as Barney made a handful of other great grabs near the right field foul line in his first full season. Barney also does a pretty good job at getting to groundballs, but on difficult plays he'll often rush and bounce his throw to first; he was fortunate to have a scooper like Carlos Pena to keep his error count down. One of Barney's bigger weaknesses has been converting double plays, particularly when he's the lead man and this task is especially challenging with Starlin Castro as his partner.

Second Basemen

Ruben Tejada

	Innings	Runs Saved
2011	457.1	1
2009-2011	845.1	0

	Good Plays	Misplays and Errors
Tejada 2011	29	13
Avg Second Baseman	18	14
Good Play/Misplay Pct		.635

Johnny Giavotella

	Innings	Runs Saved
2011	385.1	-1
2009-2011	385.1	-1

	Good Plays	Misplays and Errors
Giavotella 2011	23	17
Avg Second Baseman	14	11
Good Play/Misplay Pct		.514

Jason Kipnis

	Innings	Runs Saved
2011	305	-2
2009-2011	305	-2

	Good Plays	Misplays and Errors
Kipnis 2011	11	16
Avg Second Baseman	12	10
Good Play/Misplay Pct		.349

Jamey Carroll

	Innings	Runs Saved
2011	549.1	-10
2009-2011	1235.1	-2

	Good Plays	Misplays and Errors
Carroll 2011	16	18
Avg Second Baseman	19	15
Good Play/Misplay Pct		.410

Carroll made 57 starts at second base and 54 starts at shortstop for the Dodgers in 2011. Previously in his career, Carroll had a reputation as an above-average defender, but he's trending in the wrong direction at both positions. Coming off his age-37 season, Carroll now has a weak arm and below-average range, but relies on positioning—playing the percentages, depending on the pitcher and the batter—to remain effective. His footwork, hands, first step quickness and throwing accuracy are all just average. Carroll's nine errors in 2011 matched a career high and he made an additional nine defensive misplays on groundballs. He's no longer the defensive player he used to be, but his ability to play multiple infield positions makes him a valuable utility player.

Kelly Johnson

	Innings	Runs Saved
2011	1224	1
2009-2011	3150.1	-3

	Good Plays	Misplays and Errors
Johnson 2011	33	28
Avg Second Baseman	45	35
Good Play/Misplay Pct		.479

Kelly Johnson is an average second baseman. His runs saved totals have centered around zero the past few seasons mainly due to his lack of range. Johnson has an average arm, but he is very good at turning the double play—ranking near the top in all of baseball in 2011.

Gordon Beckham

	Innings	Runs Saved
2011	1307.2	3
2009-2011	2419	-4

	Good Plays	Misplays and Errors
Beckham 2011	64	34
Avg Second Baseman	53	41
Good Play/Misplay Pct		.595

Beckham is a good defensive middle infielder who has a penchant for highlight-reel plays. He has solid range for a second baseman and moves exceptionally well to his left. His lateral movement is smooth, and he rarely takes himself out of plays or throws the ball away. Most of his errors come from mishandling groundballs. Beckham is a converted shortstop who moved to second base because of the presence of Alexei Ramirez, but he has the versatility to play either position if needed. The former top prospect hasn't produced at the plate the way the White Sox were hoping, but his glove work has been solid and should continue to earn him playing time in the future.

Second Basemen

Aaron Miles

	Innings	Runs Saved
2011	519	-2
2009-2011	987.1	-4

	Good Plays	Misplays and Errors
Miles 2011	15	17
Avg Second Baseman	20	15
Good Play/Misplay Pct		.408

The journeyman infielder started 61 games at second base and 49 games at third for the Los Angeles Dodgers in 2011. Miles is an average second baseman and consistently average with runs saved totals around zero every year for the past six. His only real defensive strength is his versatility. In his career, he has experience playing every position except first base and catcher. Given that Miles had only made nine career starts at third base prior to last season it was no surprise his defense at third was shaky. His lack of range and poor arm strength were really exploited at the hot corner. A Dodgers non-roster invitee to spring training who ended up playing in 136 total games, the 2011 season was yet another reminder that Miles is a backup utility infielder and nothing more.

Orlando Cabrera

	Innings	Runs Saved
2011	709.1	-4
2009-2011	709.1	-4

	Good Plays	Misplays and Errors
Cabrera 2011	21	28
Avg Second Baseman	29	23
Good Play/Misplay Pct		.369

Orlando Cabrera saw action at second base for the first time since the 2000 season and even had a handful of games at third base for the first time in his career. He is no longer the fielder he once was, but he handled the switch well enough and has proven his terrible defensive 2009 season to be an outlier. As a shortstop he had consistently better range to his left than his right, but that was flipped as a second baseman, as he fared better up the middle of the field than to his right. He is still prone to some mistakes, giving back a number of the runs he takes away. After a mid-season trade to San Francisco in 2011 he mainly played shortstop again. Cabrera announced his retirement during the offseason.

Jemile Weeks

	Innings	Runs Saved
2011	849.1	-6
2009-2011	849.1	-6

	Good Plays	Misplays and Errors
Weeks 2011	28	33
Avg Second Baseman	31	25
Good Play/Misplay Pct		.398

Jemile Weeks is a fast youngster capable of doing very exciting things with his speed. At this stage in his career, though, he's a reckless defensive player needing to reign in some of his wild play. Given his speed, Weeks should have tremendous range, but his glove can prove a hindrance to whatever he is able to get to. He has a tendency to try to field balls to his sides, rather than getting his body behind grounders. This makes him more susceptible to having playable balls get past him. Weeks is also prone to making careless mistakes. Giving up on plays, not covering bases and cutting off other fielders are all tendencies typical of a player needing to mature. Weeks has a strong arm for a second baseman, but tends to sidearm his throws. He can get sloppy with his accuracy when he lets his arm drop too much.

Freddy Sanchez

	Innings	Runs Saved
2011	514.1	-6
2009-2011	2407	-6

	Good Plays	Misplays and Errors
Sanchez 2011	15	16
Avg Second Baseman	18	14
Good Play/Misplay Pct		.423

Sanchez's defense has been trending downward in recent seasons, which shouldn't be a surprise given that he's playing into his mid-30s. Though he gets a lot of praise for his hustle, at this point in his career Sanchez is average at best at second base. That being said, he's still a passable defender, albeit a little limited on range. He makes all the routine plays and has an accurate arm, though he has had trouble on double plays the last couple of years. Sanchez is still a heady defender with good instincts and gets good jumps on balls in the air. Sanchez has been hampered by injuries the past two seasons, playing some of 2010 on a knee that was less than 100 percent and missing the final four months of 2011 with a shoulder injury. Limited range, age and recent injury history are the biggest flaws for Sanchez going forward.

Second Basemen

Wilson Valdez

	Innings	Runs Saved
2011	316.2	-6
2009-2011	634	-7

	Good Plays	Misplays and Errors
Valdez 2011	12	11
Avg Second Baseman	13	10
Good Play/Misplay Pct		.460

Brian Roberts

	Innings	Runs Saved
2011	347	1
2009-2011	2186	-8

	Good Plays	Misplays and Errors
Roberts 2011	17	8
Avg Second Baseman	13	11
Good Play/Misplay Pct		.624

Injuries have sidelined Roberts for much of the last two seasons, but in the innings he has been on the field he has performed adequately. While his value is based on his offensive abilities, he is still serviceable defensively. His speed has slipped a bit, but his range is still average. He also has a good arm, and he turns the double play quickly. However, the effect that his numerous recent injuries have on his quickness and agility will determine whether he remains a worthwhile defender.

Ryan Raburn

	Innings	Runs Saved
2011	401	-8
2009-2011	521	-8

	Good Plays	Misplays and Errors
Raburn 2011	13	20
Avg Second Baseman	15	11
Good Play/Misplay Pct		.337

Bill Hall

	Innings	Runs Saved
2011	387.2	-8
2009-2011	760	-8

	Good Plays	Misplays and Errors
Hall 2011	15	20
Avg Second Baseman	15	12
Good Play/Misplay Pct		.369

It's fair to say that Bill Hall's best days are behind him. Hall was once a quick-footed and sure-handed shortstop, but those skills have faded with age and injury. What's left is a player who doesn't have the speed or athletic ability to cover enough ground at any non-first base position and Hall doesn't have the bat to command first base. Hall was let go twice in 2011: first by the Astros and later by the Giants. He'll need to improve his footwork and agility if he wants to continue his career as a utility infielder.

Alexi Casilla

	Innings	Runs Saved
2011	470.2	1
2009-2011	1201	-11

	Good Plays	Misplays and Errors
Casilla 2011	25	14
Avg Second Baseman	19	15
Good Play/Misplay Pct		.582

Alexi Casilla is a decent defensive middle infielder, though better suited to play second base. He is a speedy player capable of looking very smooth in the field. He has good range going toward the foul lines when positioned on either side of second base. He struggles defending up the middle, despite flashing the ability to range that far. Casilla's glove fails him at times, and grounders will get past him, often as a result of trying to field balls to his side or aggressively charging balls. He can provide a quick pivot on double play attempts, but does drop balls and make poor throws preventing the completion of double plays. He possesses average arm strength and accuracy, but he bounces a lot of throws to first base, even from the right side of the infield.

Second Basemen

Neil Walker

	Innings	Runs Saved
2011	1382.1	-3
2009-2011	2277	-11

	Good Plays	Misplays and Errors
Walker 2011	58	37
Avg Second Baseman	56	44
Good Play/Misplay Pct		.550

Although he is a good athlete, Walker lacks the speed required to impress with his range. While he was outstanding on balls to his right in 2011, he must improve substantially on grounders to his left in order to keep his defensive detriment to a minimum. Walker does excel in two areas of defense, however. He is one of the top second basemen in the game at both handling difficult throws and catching tough line drives. His 15 Good Fielding Plays for infielder line drive outs ranks third among all second basemen over the past two seasons.

Rickie Weeks

	Innings	Runs Saved
2011	974	-5
2009-2011	2667	-14

	Good Plays	Misplays and Errors
Weeks 2011	31	40
Avg Second Baseman	35	27
Good Play/Misplay Pct		.377

Rickie Weeks is a unique second baseman. He has very good range to both his left and right, which makes him a very aggressive infielder. He struggles most on balls hit straight on. He gets to a lot of balls, but this leads him to being in position to make a lot of Defensive Misplays. He can make a great play, then turn around and butcher the next routine one. He struggles with throws from time to time and is most inconsistent on throws trying to turn a double play. He also allows too many balls to slip past him. His runs saved totals continue to be below-average. His athleticism is a good asset for him, but he leans on it too much. If he would work on the finer mechanics, he could improve as a second baseman.

Chris Getz

	Innings	Runs Saved
2011	894.1	-2
2009-2011	2325.2	-15

	Good Plays	Misplays and Errors
Getz 2011	23	25
Avg Second Baseman	36	28
Good Play/Misplay Pct		.418

Getz is a speedy second baseman who can't seem to put it all together defensively. He has above-average range to the left, but struggles with balls to his right and straight on. Getz has a strong arm for a second baseman and does a good job of keeping his throws out of the dirt, making only two throwing errors in 894 innings at second base in 2011. For as dependable as Getz is on throws, the rest of his defensive game is a bit sloppy. Getz lacks consistency when fielding grounders and also makes more mental mistakes than he should. Perhaps with more regular playing time Getz could clean up his defensive issues, but given his track record at the plate, that seems unlikely to happen.

Adam Kennedy

	Innings	Runs Saved
2011	293.2	-2
2009-2011	1343	-15

	Good Plays	Misplays and Errors
Kennedy 2011	10	7
Avg Second Baseman	11	8
Good Play/Misplay Pct		.527

Kennedy's main value comes in his versatility, as he can defend at three positions: second base, first base and third base. He started 2011 playing primarily at second base, his most natural position, but was switched to a utility/designated hitter role after top-prospect Dustin Ackley was called up in June. Kennedy has decent range at second and does a nice job of fielding routine groundballs. He's a solid all-around defender who doesn't do anything spectacular, but doesn't do anything horribly either.

Second Basemen

Justin Turner

	Innings	Runs Saved
2011	642.1	-13
2009-2011	679.1	-15

	Good Plays	Misplays and Errors
Turner 2011	26	23
Avg Second Baseman	27	21
Good Play/Misplay Pct		.469

Turner became the surprise everyday second baseman for the Mets in 2011 after starting the season in Triple-A. His hot hitting early on earned him the job, though he cooled off significantly in the later months. While his bat impressed, his defense certainly did not. Turner finished tied for last in Defensive Runs Saved among regular second basemen, costing the Mets 13 runs. Turner is slow for a middle infielder and displayed below-average range in all directions. He also played some third base and shortstop, showing good hands when fielding the balls he did get to, as he rarely misplayed a grounder. He struggled with double play opportunities and with his throwing in general, especially at third base. If Turner hopes to earn more playing time going forward, he's going to need to hit like he did in April and May unless he can improve his defense dramatically.

Jeff Keppinger

	Innings	Runs Saved
2011	791	-11
2009-2011	2000.1	-23

	Good Plays	Misplays and Errors
Keppinger 2011	18	20
Avg Second Baseman	29	23
Good Play/Misplay Pct		.413

A career utility infielder, Jeff Keppinger has found a home at second base in recent years. If his body of work has proven anything, it is that he is quite a below-average fielder. He has reliable hands and doesn't make a whole lot of errors, but his strengths as a defender end there. His lateral range is very limited due to a slow first step and very low top speed. This is where he hurts a team most on defense. He just can't convert groundballs into outs at a league-average rate. He lacks arm strength, which has pushed him over to second base as his only real option as an infielder.

Skip Schumaker

	Innings	Runs Saved
2011	739	-3
2009-2011	2742.2	-30

	Good Plays	Misplays and Errors
Schumaker 2011	29	22
Avg Second Baseman	29	23
Good Play/Misplay Pct		.507

In three seasons at second base, Skip Schumaker has shown marked defensive improvement, going from being one of the worst fielders to a slightly below-average fielder. He plays balls hit to his right better than to his left, but that may be a result of often being positioned up the middle. Skip has some difficulty with groundballs, knocking down many that average fielders would field cleanly. However, he recovers well from booted balls to throw runners out at first. His arm can be wildly inconsistent. As an outfielder, his arm has been an asset, both for its strength and accuracy, but as an infielder, throwing accuracy has proven difficult. Skip's off-target throws, even on routine plays that end in outs, tend to overshadow the arm strength he possesses, which he displays pivoting on double plays. As he is a capable outfielder, Schumaker is good at tracking down pop-ups, especially balls that drift beyond the infield.

Dan Uggla

	Innings	Runs Saved
2011	1431.2	-13
2009-2011	4225.1	-34

	Good Plays	Misplays and Errors
Uggla 2011	45	53
Avg Second Baseman	55	43
Good Play/Misplay Pct		.399

Dan Uggla will always be the type of player from whom you happily take the offensive production and live with the defensive shortcomings. He just doesn't move particularly well and his short strides rarely allow him to reach anything other than routine groundballs. He is also prone to bobbling and/or throwing away the ball once he reaches it and subsequently he led all second basemen with 53 Defensive Misplays Plus Errors in 2011.

Third Basemen Evaluations

Year	League	Gold Glove Winners	Should Have Been
2003	AL	Eric Chavez	Eric Chavez
	NL	Scott Rolen	Adrian Beltre
2004	AL	Eric Chavez	Eric Chavez
	NL	Scott Rolen	Scott Rolen
2005	AL	Eric Chavez	Eric Chavez
	NL	Mike Lowell	David Bell
2006	AL	Eric Chavez	Adrian Beltre
	NL	Scott Rolen	Scott Rolen
2007	AL	Adrian Beltre	Brandon Inge
	NL	David Wright	Pedro Feliz
2008	AL	Adrian Beltre	Adrian Beltre
	NL	David Wright	David Wright
2009	AL	Evan Longoria	Adrian Beltre
	NL	Ryan Zimmerman	Ryan Zimmerman
2010	AL	Evan Longoria	Evan Longoria
	NL	Scott Rolen	Scott Rolen
2011	AL	Adrian Beltre	Adrian Betlre
	NL	Placido Polanco	Pablo Sandoval

My Personal Ratings

Top Five

1 Evan Longoria, TB
2 Adrian Beltre, Tex
3 Scott Rolen, Cin
4 Jack Hannahan, Cle
5 Casey Blake, Col

Bottom Five

26 Chris Johnson, Hou
27 Pedro Alvarez, Pit
28 Edwin Encarnacion
29 Aramis Ramirez, Mil
30 Mark Reynolds, Bal

Player teams based on transactions through February 1, 2012

Third Basemen

Evan Longoria

	Innings	Runs Saved
2011	1124.2	22
2009-2011	3758	61

	Good Plays	Misplays and Errors
Longoria 2011	49	30
Avg Third Baseman	38	40
Good Play/Misplay Pct		.636

Evan Longoria ranks as one of the top defensive third baseman in the game today and was recognized in 2010 with a Fielding Bible Award. He sports excellent lateral movement, especially when ranging to his right. He has good footwork and can make strong off-balance throws from deep in foul territory. He is not as good at fielding balls right at him. His quick first step and soft hands are big helps when fielding soft grounders and bunts. Longoria possesses a very strong arm, but occasionally delivers wide throws and struggles with accuracy. While it's not the main responsibility of a third baseman, Longoria is excellent at starting the double play. Like Troy Tulowitzki who is head and shoulders above all other shortstops on double plays, Longoria stars at double plays at third. His five runs saved in that category the past three years is more than twice as much as any other third baseman. On top of that, he has the most runs saved on double play good plays and misplays in that timeframe (2.4 runs).

Adrian Beltre

	Innings	Runs Saved
2011	980.1	13
2009-2011	3311.1	52

	Good Plays	Misplays and Errors
Beltre 2011	35	32
Avg Third Baseman	31	33
Good Play/Misplay Pct		.539

Beltre, a three-time Fielding Bible Award winner, was the best defensive third baseman in baseball in 2011, according to our panel of voters. Beltre has above-average range moving to both his right and his left. He is able to react quickly to sharply hit balls. He is good at keeping the ball on the infield, preventing the potential advancement of base runners. He has great hands for a third baseman, and has done well on making catches on difficult throws, though they don't come up as often for third basemen. However, he will occasionally misplay an apparently routine grounder or line drive. He has one of the best arms in the game for a third baseman, throwing from his usual side-arm angle. Despite throwing side-arm, Beltre has above-average accuracy both with his feet set and on the run. Beltre has consistently been one of the top defensive third baseman in the big leagues since becoming a full-time major leaguer in 1999 at the age of 20. However, he missed 35+ games in both 2009 and 2011 with injuries, whereas from 2002 to 2006 he played in at least 156 games every year. Barring something unforeseen, he will be in the running for his fourth Fielding Bible Award this year and should continue to be a contender for the next few years at least.

Scott Rolen

	Innings	Runs Saved
2011	547.1	10
2009-2011	2739.2	37

	Good Plays	Misplays and Errors
Rolen 2011	15	14
Avg Third Baseman	17	18
Good Play/Misplay Pct		.534

Rolen is among a small group of active players who have continued to play excellent defense through their mid-thirties. His intelligent play has helped him age well; he rarely makes a mental error and knows when to go for the tough fielder's choice, ranking first in runs saved since 2009 in this Good Play category. He doesn't have the exceptional range that he used to, but he can still make the highlight-reel play every now and then. Rolen's incredible reflexes have made him one of the best in the business for years at snagging sharp grounders and liners hit straight on. He also has pinpoint throwing accuracy and might make a bad toss only on the toughest of plays. Rolen's across-the-board strength in our good plays/misplays data is quite impressive, as he shows a positive runs saved rating in 29 of the 33 categories that apply to third basemen.

Chone Figgins

	Innings	Runs Saved
2011	679.2	-1
2009-2011	2018.2	28

	Good Plays	Misplays and Errors
Figgins 2011	22	32
Avg Third Baseman	20	22
Good Play/Misplay Pct		.423

Chone Figgins was ultimately removed from his starting job at third base due to his brutal offensive performance, but his defense was nothing to write home about either, at least in 2011. In 2009, Figgins actually had a fantastic defensive season, leading all third

Third Basemen

basemen with 29 runs saved and finishing 3rd in the Fielding Bible Awards voting. Since then, Figgins was moved to second base in 2010, where he really struggled defensively, and then moved back to third base in 2011. He remains a good athlete, but his hands are not as good as they once were. He seemed to have trouble consistently seeing the tough grounders into his glove. He was still an average defender overall, but one expects more from a guy who's hitting as poorly as Figgins was. The problem is that outside of 2009, which looks like an outlier, his performance at third base has been right around average during his career, so average is a reasonable expectation for him. Moving forward, Figgins' bat will determine if he can stay on the field.

Ryan Zimmerman

	Innings	Runs Saved
2011	866.2	-5
2009-2011	3393.2	28

	Good Plays	Misplays and Errors
Zimmerman 2011	29	24
Avg Third Baseman	28	30
Good Play/Misplay Pct		.563

Zimmerman has gained a reputation as one of the best defensive third basemen in baseball. The 2009 Fielding Bible Award winner has made 35 more plays than an average third baseman and has saved 28 runs for the Nationals over the past three years. He has quick, soft hands, great range and a cannon for an arm. Our good play/misplay data rates him as the best 3B since 2009 on throws, and the second-best at saving extra bases (normally by keeping a ball in the infield that would have been a double or scored a runner from second base had it reached the outfield). However, Zimmerman took a step back defensively in 2011. He was placed on the disabled list toward the beginning of the season with an abdominal strain and missed about two months following surgery. It remains to be seen if the injury had any correlation to Zimmerman's defensive regression last season, but the smart money has him returning to form as one of the best defensive third basemen in 2012.

Martin Prado

	Innings	Runs Saved
2011	297	6
2009-2011	932.2	20

	Good Plays	Misplays and Errors
Prado 2011	9	10
Avg Third Baseman	11	11
Good Play/Misplay Pct		.490

Casey Blake

	Innings	Runs Saved
2011	383.2	4
2009-2011	2748.2	20

	Good Plays	Misplays and Errors
Blake 2011	7	6
Avg Third Baseman	11	12
Good Play/Misplay Pct		.555

Although he played very few games in 2011, Casey Blake has played a very solid third base over the past three years. He has shown above-average range for a third baseman, and has always been great at getting to balls hit down the line. Blake's arm accuracy is a big contributor to his defensive success at third base. He has been very accurate with his throws, and his fellow infielders can usually count on Blake to deliver the throw on target.

Brandon Inge

	Innings	Runs Saved
2011	730.2	-2
2009-2011	3344.1	20

	Good Plays	Misplays and Errors
Inge 2011	16	24
Avg Third Baseman	26	28
Good Play/Misplay Pct		.416

Brandon Inge saw his career take a hit in 2011, as at one point he was designated for assignment by the Detroit Tigers. Inge's defense at third has always been a strong point in his game. His range has diminished in recent years, but he still has very good hands and will make spectacular plays on occasion. As a former catcher, he has a strong arm, though he can struggle with his accuracy at times. And he also struggles on bunts; he has cost the Tigers more runs (four) on bunts in the last three years than any other third baseman in baseball. He shows flashes of his old self, but it is evident that he is on the downside of his career.

Jack Hannahan

	Innings	Runs Saved
2011	819	6
2009-2011	1432	18

	Good Plays	Misplays and Errors
Hannahan 2011	30	19
Avg Third Baseman	31	33
Good Play/Misplay Pct		.628

Though he does not garner much attention, Hannahan has quietly become one of the best third

Third Basemen

basemen in the league. He has very smooth hands. He will occasionally fail to charge choppers aggressively enough and is forced to try to field the ball on tough short hops. Other than those, he normally puts himself in the right place to make the plays. He gets the ball out of his glove very quickly in order to get the speediest baserunners, and there is nobody better at charging slow grounders and completing the barehanded throw to first. Hannahan is best reacting to hard shots near him, and he also does quite well on balls toward the foul line.

Placido Polanco

	Innings	Runs Saved
2011	1044.2	9
2009-2011	2120	16

	Good Plays	Misplays and Errors
Polanco 2011	33	25
Avg Third Baseman	36	38
Good Play/Misplay Pct		.585

Polanco was a plus defender last season for the Phillies. Polanco has very good range when moving to his right but does have some difficulty on balls hit to his left, where he is only average. He is able to react quickly to sharply hit balls, which makes him an ideal fit for third base while also positioning himself well to field the ball on a good hop. Polanco has average arm strength for a third baseman. He is accurate with his throws both on the run and with his feet set. Polanco consistently puts a good charge on choppers or softly hit grounders. Polanco has missed a significant number of games the past two seasons with various ailments, which at age 36 is a concern. Nevertheless, he will remain in contention for a Fielding Bible Award this year and over the next couple of seasons if he can stay healthy.

Chase Headley

	Innings	Runs Saved
2011	895.1	1
2009-2011	2528.2	15

	Good Plays	Misplays and Errors
Headley 2011	33	25
Avg Third Baseman	28	30
Good Play/Misplay Pct		.585

After returning to his natural position at the hot corner and leading all National League third basemen in Defensive Runs Saved in 2010, Chase Headley took a step back during an injury-filled 2011 campaign. Headley suffered a sprained ankle, a calf sprain and shoulder soreness in his throwing arm at various times throughout the year, all of which contributed to his decline in

defensive production. This is not to say that Headley was bad in the field in 2011, only that he declined from elite to average. He still ranges very well to his left, but his former quick first step slowed down, hurting his ability to cover the line and to charge bunts. His arm accuracy was also affected by the sore shoulder he suffered in a collision. Based on our good play/misplay data, Headley was worse on throws in 2011 than he was in 2010. A bounce-back is likely for Mr. Headley in 2012, as long as he's healthy.

Brett Lawrie

	Innings	Runs Saved
2011	380.1	14
2009-2011	380.1	14

	Good Plays	Misplays and Errors
Lawrie 2011	19	18
Avg Third Baseman	17	18
Good Play/Misplay Pct		.530

Originally a catcher, Milwaukee converted Brett Lawrie into a second baseman for his first two minor league seasons. Worried about his defense, the Blue Jays moved him to third after acquiring him in the Shaun Marcum trade before the 2011 season. Before his major league promotion, scouts doubted he would stick long-term at second or third, predicting an eventual move to the outfield or first base. Of course, as soon as Lawrie reached Toronto he turned into a defensive highlight reel. He displayed great reactions in both directions and made several athletic plays. As you would expect from a former catcher, Lawrie has a fantastic arm; the biggest problem is its accuracy, which led to high error totals in the minors. He needs to learn to get the ball to the pivot man quicker on double play attempts, but his timing should improve with experience at the position. As Lawrie showed after his promotion, he has the athletic potential to hold down third base long-term; the challenge will be learning the position and refining his game on the job at the major league level.

Alex Rodriguez

	Innings	Runs Saved
2011	762	13
2009-2011	2782.2	11

	Good Plays	Misplays and Errors
Rodriguez 2011	26	17
Avg Third Baseman	24	26
Good Play/Misplay Pct		.620

Rodriguez was an excellent defender for the Yankees in 2011. He got better as the season progressed,

Third Basemen

showing much more mobility once he returned from the disabled list in August following surgery on his right knee. Rodriguez had above-average range when moving to his right, but average range to his left in 2011. However, after his knee surgery he began to do better moving to his left as well. The former shortstop has soft hands for a third baseman. Rodriguez has plus arm strength throwing from a 3/4 arm angle. He is normally accurate with his throws, but occasionally they can sail on him due to that arm angle. Another area he can improve is throwing on the run. One way to do this would be quickening his release. Rodriguez has had mixed results defensively since permanently moving to third base in 2004, but in 2011 he was at the top of his game. If his knee does not prove to be a long-term problem, he still has the physical tools to put together a few more consistent defensive seasons like he did in 2011.

Josh Harrison

	Innings	Runs Saved
2011	363.1	9
2009-2011	363.1	9

	Good Plays	Misplays and Errors
Harrison 2011	15	13
Avg Third Baseman	14	15
Good Play/Misplay Pct		.552

Don Kelly

	Innings	Runs Saved
2011	325	4
2009-2011	444	9

	Good Plays	Misplays and Errors
Kelly 2011	8	9
Avg Third Baseman	11	11
Good Play/Misplay Pct		.487

Jose Lopez

	Innings	Runs Saved
2011	288.1	-1
2009-2011	1541	9

	Good Plays	Misplays and Errors
Lopez 2011	4	7
Avg Third Baseman	8	8
Good Play/Misplay Pct		.379

A former second baseman, Lopez has seen the bulk of his time at third base over the past two years. Lopez moves well in both directions but looks more comfortable when ranging to his left. He has a strong arm and has no problem making a crisp throw from the hot corner. Lopez saw his playing time as a third baseman decrease in 2011, as he played some second base and first base and also spent time in the minors after being signed by the Marlins shortly after he was released by Colorado. As a third baseman, he posted average runs saved numbers. After bouncing around the infield last season and playing well everywhere, Lopez may be nicely suited as a utility man as his career goes forward.

Alberto Callaspo

	Innings	Runs Saved
2011	1139.1	4
2009-2011	2372.1	8

	Good Plays	Misplays and Errors
Callaspo 2011	37	36
Avg Third Baseman	38	41
Good Play/Misplay Pct		.523

Alberto Callaspo settled in nicely at third base during his second full season there, his first with the Angels. Coming up as a middle infielder, Callaspo does lack the traditional skill set of a third baseman, mainly because he doesn't have a strong throwing arm. Our good play/misplay data shows Callaspo as having surrendered two runs misplaying throws in the last three years. He makes up for this with strong athletic ability, good quickness and accurate throws. Callaspo excels at backhanding grounders down the line, and his hands are generally reliable, particularly on bunt plays.

Ian Stewart

	Innings	Runs Saved
2011	284	3
2009-2011	2040.1	8

	Good Plays	Misplays and Errors
Stewart 2011	8	9
Avg Third Baseman	8	9
Good Play/Misplay Pct		.487

Ian Stewart continues to be plagued by injuries in his young, disappointing career as he missed significant time in 2011 due to a damaged wrist. With an agile build and good hands, Stewart has saved 16 runs at third base over his career. Unfortunately, we still have not seen what he can do at the position in a full season thanks to injuries and struggles at the plate. Stewart handles balls hit at him well, with quick reactions on hard-hit balls, while he struggles most going toward the line. Our good play/misplay data places Stewart third in runs saved among all third basemen on throwing plays since 2009

Third Basemen

despite having less playing time than other third basemen.

Juan Uribe

	Innings	Runs Saved
2011	462.2	5
2009-2011	978.2	7

	Good Plays	Misplays and Errors
Uribe 2011	23	9
Avg Third Baseman	14	14
Good Play/Misplay Pct		.732

Uribe keeps his cool at the hot corner. He's not the flashiest defender, but he is excellent at handling hard grounders and liners. Uribe has one of the most accurate infield arms in all of baseball; his five defensive misplays and errors related to poor throws over the past three years (at all positions) are a very low total. Uribe's reflexes make it easy for him to guard the line, where he can plant his feet and make a strong throw without a bounce to first. Third base is a natural fit for Uribe's skill set, but he makes plays with enough consistency to remain capable at second base. At this point in his career, the shortstop position might be a bit of a stretch for him.

Maicer Izturis

	Innings	Runs Saved
2011	301.2	2
2009-2011	550.1	6

	Good Plays	Misplays and Errors
Izturis 2011	10	6
Avg Third Baseman	8	9
Good Play/Misplay Pct		.640

Kevin Kouzmanoff

	Innings	Runs Saved
2011	576.1	-7
2009-2011	2994.2	6

	Good Plays	Misplays and Errors
Kouzmanoff 2011	33	34
Avg Third Baseman	20	21
Good Play/Misplay Pct		.509

Kevin Kouzmanoff has been an inconsistent defender from year to year throughout his career. Kouzmanoff produced at a high level in the field in 2010 but dropped off last season. The main problem for him was an increase in errors. Kouzmanoff's 13 errors in only 66 games started exceeded his total from 2010 when he had full-time play. Simply handling grounders was the key problem. Kouzmanoff had more misplays and errors on grounders in 2011 (17) than he did in 2010 (11) in, once again, half the playing time.

Pablo Sandoval

	Innings	Runs Saved
2011	904.2	15
2009-2011	3157.1	5

	Good Plays	Misplays and Errors
Sandoval 2011	42	27
Avg Third Baseman	29	31
Good Play/Misplay Pct		.624

Sandoval lost 38 pounds prior to the 2011 season, and not only did he bounce back offensively, his defense improved dramatically as well. Despite being a catcher originally, Sandoval has been stationed at the hot corner and first base since 2010. He caught a total of 113.1 innings in his first two years with San Francisco, and while the front office flirted with the possibility of Sandoval doing some catching when Buster Posey was lost for the season, that never came to fruition. Even prior to the 2011 season, the out-of-shape Sandoval was a decent third baseman with a strong arm and surprising agility. In 2011, with his improved physical condition, Sandoval's defense at third was nothing less than superb, with much more range than he had before. The hard work Sandoval put in during the offseason led to his finishing second among third baseman in plus/minus (+19) and second in runs saved (15). He is a very polished third baseman, exhibiting good footwork, and he does a nice job charging bunt grounders. Kung Fu Panda ranked highly among third baseman in many good fielding play subsets, and his 42 total Good Fielding Plays were third-most at the position. For his outstanding defensive campaign, Sandoval finished third in the Fielding Bible Award voting. Still young, if The Panda can stay in shape, he could not only hold down the third base job but could also factor into future Fielding Bible Award voting.

Jayson Nix

	Innings	Runs Saved
2011	334.2	9
2009-2011	857.2	5

	Good Plays	Misplays and Errors
Nix 2011	12	10
Avg Third Baseman	12	13
Good Play/Misplay Pct		.562

Third Basemen

Lonnie Chisenhall

	Innings	Runs Saved
2011	461	3
2009-2011	461	3

	Good Plays	Misplays and Errors
Chisenhall 2011	12	20
Avg Third Baseman	17	18
Good Play/Misplay Pct		.390

Eric Chavez

	Innings	Runs Saved
2011	305.2	3
2009-2011	372.2	2

	Good Plays	Misplays and Errors
Chavez 2011	12	3
Avg Third Baseman	9	10
Good Play/Misplay Pct		.810

Jed Lowrie

	Innings	Runs Saved
2011	268.1	2
2009-2011	281.1	2

	Good Plays	Misplays and Errors
Lowrie 2011	5	9
Avg Third Baseman	10	11
Good Play/Misplay Pct		.372

Mike Moustakas

	Innings	Runs Saved
2011	778	2
2009-2011	778	2

	Good Plays	Misplays and Errors
Moustakas 2011	19	26
Avg Third Baseman	25	27
Good Play/Misplay Pct		.438

In his first half-season in the majors, not much was expected out of Moustakas defensively. Moose has a thick build and doesn't have the range to be a plus defender at third base according to scouting reports, but he posted positive plus/minus numbers in a small sample last season. He does have above-average arm strength and quick reflexes which enable him to handle the hard-hit balls right at him. He struggled on bunts, which is not surprising given his build. His footwork is poor and his throwing accuracy needs to improve, but he has a good work ethic and should get better in these areas. Given that Moustakas is a below-average athlete, it's hard to envision him ever being better than major league average at third base, and it would probably be best to trust the scouting reports until we have more defensive data on him. Eventually, considering his body type and lack of quickness, he may be forced to move from the hot corner, either to right field, where he could still utilize his strong arm, or across the diamond to first base. Expect him to stay at third base through his twenties, but don't rule out a possible position change in the future.

Kyle Seager

	Innings	Runs Saved
2011	335.2	2
2009-2011	335.2	2

	Good Plays	Misplays and Errors
Seager 2011	10	10
Avg Third Baseman	12	13
Good Play/Misplay Pct		.516

Jerry Hairston

	Innings	Runs Saved
2011	370	-2
2009-2011	740.2	2

	Good Plays	Misplays and Errors
Hairston 2011	8	14
Avg Third Baseman	11	12
Good Play/Misplay Pct		.379

In 2011, Hairston was a slightly below-average defensive third baseman. As he has done throughout his career, Hairston showed great versatility for the Brewers and Nationals. He made appearances at second base, shortstop, left field and center field in addition to third base. Hairston has average range for a third baseman. He is slightly better moving to his left than he is to his right. Hairston did have some occasional misplays on groundballs and line drives. He has average arm strength for a third baseman, and his accuracy on throws is also average; on occasion a throw will get away from him. Throughout his career, Hairston has added to his value by playing multiple positions, and he should continue to have an important utility role for at least a couple more seasons.

Third Basemen

Brent Morel

	Innings	Runs Saved
2011	1058	2
2009-2011	1222	1

	Good Plays	Misplays and Errors
Morel 2011	44	28
Avg Third Baseman	32	34
Good Play/Misplay Pct		.627

The more he plays the better he gets, and he was already known as a good third baseman when he came up from the minors. Brent Morel still has some problems with throws, and balls will eat him up from time to time, but he has not yet reached his potential. His range to his left is solid, but he needs work to his right. He rushes throws and doesn't have the best footwork all the time. He rates very well preventing extra bases, mostly because he does a good job of at least knocking down balls that are hit near him. Even though no out was recorded on these plays, they did at least keep the batter at first base or a runner on second from scoring. As Morel gets more playing time, he could morph into one of the better third basemen in the league.

Brandon Wood

	Innings	Runs Saved
2011	377.2	-6
2009-2011	831.1	1

	Good Plays	Misplays and Errors
Wood 2011	10	17
Avg Third Baseman	12	13
Good Play/Misplay Pct		.386

Miguel Cairo

	Innings	Runs Saved
2011	432.1	3
2009-2011	683	0

	Good Plays	Misplays and Errors
Cairo 2011	7	16
Avg Third Baseman	15	16
Good Play/Misplay Pct		.318

Kevin Youkilis

	Innings	Runs Saved
2011	948.2	0
2009-2011	1458	0

	Good Plays	Misplays and Errors
Youkilis 2011	29	24
Avg Third Baseman	28	30
Good Play/Misplay Pct		.563

Youkilis shifted back across the diamond to third base in 2011 to accommodate Adrian Gonzalez taking over at first base. Third base is the weaker of Youk's two positions, and this year his mobility was further limited due to a hip injury. In spite of that, his range numbers were not noticeably different from what he's done at third base previously. Youk's strongest asset as a third baseman is his arm, while he's weakest on groundballs. Overall, he is an average third baseman defensively, which when coupled with his explosive bat, makes for an excellent asset at the hot corner.

Justin Turner

	Innings	Runs Saved
2011	277.2	-1
2009-2011	313.2	0

	Good Plays	Misplays and Errors
Turner 2011	8	12
Avg Third Baseman	8	9
Good Play/Misplay Pct		.416

Jimmy Paredes

	Innings	Runs Saved
2011	390.2	-1
2009-2011	390.2	-1

	Good Plays	Misplays and Errors
Paredes 2011	15	22
Avg Third Baseman	12	13
Good Play/Misplay Pct		.421

Miguel Tejada

	Innings	Runs Saved
2011	372.1	7
2009-2011	1195.2	-2

	Good Plays	Misplays and Errors
Tejada 2011	18	8
Avg Third Baseman	13	14
Good Play/Misplay Pct		.706

Third Basemen

Tejada's age and declining production at the plate have pushed him out of the league, as he was released last September by the Giants. He split his time between shortstop and third base in 2011, with a handful of games at second. He no longer has the range to play shortstop, but he held his own at third base in 2011, where he showed great improvement from his poor 2010 campaign, his first year at the hot corner. Both seasons were small samples, and when combined are equivalent to about a full season of play. A fair assessment is that he's a slightly below-average third baseman, mainly because he struggles with balls hit near him due to poor initial reactions.

Mike Aviles

	Innings	Runs Saved
2011	347.2	-1
2009-2011	392.2	-2

	Good Plays	Misplays and Errors
Aviles 2011	11	16
Avg Third Baseman	12	12
Good Play/Misplay Pct		.423

In addition to 20 starts at second base and eight at shortstop, the utility infielder made 36 starts at third base between the Royals and Red Sox in 2011. Aviles' defense has slipped noticeably since the 2008 season following a recovery from reconstructive elbow surgery performed in July 2009. Since then, Aviles went from a combined 12 runs saved at the infield positions in 2008 to -8 in 2010 and -2 in 2011. His footwork isn't very good regardless of position, but his range is adequate, and he does have the arm strength necessary to make all the throws from third base or shortstop. However, Aviles is a tentative defender even on routine plays, and he made a lot of defensive miscues, both of the mental and physical variety. He did not appear to take well to the role of a utility man. Overall, his net -11 Good Fielding Play minus Defensive Misplays and Errors was worse than all but eight infielders in the league, regardless of position. If Aviles ever hopes to be looked upon as more than a backup infielder, his glove work needs to improve.

Eduardo Nunez

	Innings	Runs Saved
2011	285.1	-2
2009-2011	368.1	-3

	Good Plays	Misplays and Errors
Nunez 2011	6	11
Avg Third Baseman	8	8
Good Play/Misplay Pct		.368

Daniel Descalso

	Innings	Runs Saved
2011	666	-6
2009-2011	739	-5

	Good Plays	Misplays and Errors
Descalso 2011	22	19
Avg Third Baseman	19	20
Good Play/Misplay Pct		.553

Descalso was a below-average defensive third baseman in 2011, his first full season in the majors. Despite that, he was viewed by manager Tony La Russa as the better defensive option at third base, as he frequently came in as a late-inning defensive replacement for David Freese. He was a versatile defensive player for the Cardinals, as he also saw action at second base and shortstop. Descalso has plus range moving both to his left and his right. Descalso does not have the best hands for third base. He will have difficulty with some groundballs on occasion, particularly sharply hit balls near him, as he needs to react quicker. He also does not have the best instincts at the position. Occasionally he will cut off a fielder in better position to make the play or turn the wrong way on a ball, potentially costing the team an out. Descalso's biggest asset on defense is his plus arm strength, which is why throwing plays rate as his best category based on our good plays/misplays runs saved data. He is generally accurate with his throws, however, one will occasionally get away from him. Descalso has the ability to become an average or better defensive third baseman in the coming years, but his hands probably limit his ceiling.

Ryan Roberts

	Innings	Runs Saved
2011	902.1	-7
2009-2011	1042.1	-6

	Good Plays	Misplays and Errors
Roberts 2011	30	30
Avg Third Baseman	30	32
Good Play/Misplay Pct		.516

Ryan Roberts emerged as the starting third baseman for the D'Backs in 2011, and he did so largely because of his bat. Not to say that Roberts is horrible in the field, but he won't be taking home any Fielding Bible Awards any time soon either. Roberts' best attribute is his ability to chase down pop-ups that other third basemen wouldn't get to; he ranked second among all third basemen with a plus/minus of +4 on balls in the air. Roberts covers the line well, and is quick to make a diving stop, but he's not

Third Basemen

quick enough to cover ground in the hole. The biggest area he needs to improve in is the consistency of his hands. Roberts came up as a second baseman and still needs to adjust to fielding hard-hit balls at the hot corner.

plays/misplays data. A manager could plug him in at third and not feel overly worried about it, though he may be looking for a defensive replacement come the late innings.

David Freese

	Innings	Runs Saved
2011	674	-1
2009-2011	1272.1	-7

	Good Plays	Misplays and Errors
Freese 2011	24	26
Avg Third Baseman	21	23
Good Play/Misplay Pct		.496

Freese came onto the scene in a big way during the Cardinals' magical run through the playoffs, but his defense remains a step behind his clutch hitting at the moment. Daniel Descalso was assigned to be Freese's defensive caddy by manager Tony La Russa, replacing Freese late in the game on a regular basis last year. Freese has good hands and an accurate arm, but his reactions are often a bit slow. He struggles with balls that he has to move quickly to field, particularly balls hit sharply down the line. He is also prone to the occasional slip-up, such as the dropped pop-up we saw in the World Series. In limited time Freese has performed well on the double play, converting 81.8 percent of his opportunities (by comparison Evan Longoria, the three-year leader in GDP runs saved, converted 72.7 percent of his opportunities). Freese has yet to play a full season in the big leagues and should see some steady improvement as he gets more comfortable.

Ty Wigginton

	Innings	Runs Saved
2011	520.1	-1
2009-2011	1004	-7

	Good Plays	Misplays and Errors
Wigginton 2011	15	15
Avg Third Baseman	14	15
Good Play/Misplay Pct		.516

Ty Wigginton is a utility player. He played first base, third base, left field and right field in 2011, but registered the most time at the hot corner. His stats won't pop out as being great, nor will they show him being completely terrible. He is a somewhat serviceable third baseman. He has limited range, and he is average at covering bunts. Wigginton struggles going towards the foul line, but does a better job ranging to his left. His arm is solid, as he ranks second among all third basemen the past three years in runs saved on throws based on good

Aaron Miles

	Innings	Runs Saved
2011	459.2	-5
2009-2011	496.2	-7

	Good Plays	Misplays and Errors
Miles 2011	13	19
Avg Third Baseman	12	13
Good Play/Misplay Pct		.422

Melvin Mora

	Innings	Runs Saved
2011	270.1	-3
2009-2011	1760.2	-8

	Good Plays	Misplays and Errors
Mora 2011	6	9
Avg Third Baseman	9	9
Good Play/Misplay Pct		.416

Chipper Jones

	Innings	Runs Saved
2011	1006.1	-3
2009-2011	2839.2	-9

	Good Plays	Misplays and Errors
Jones 2011	21	24
Avg Third Baseman	26	28
Good Play/Misplay Pct		.483

Much like his career overall, Chipper Jones' defensive value has gone up and down depending on his health in a given season. Overall, he has counteracted the effects of aging by playing within his ability defensively. Due to slower reactions, Chipper has trouble handling many hard-hit balls hit straight on, but he rarely misplays hits when he has enough time to react. He can no longer effectively play soft-hit balls or bunts down the third base line, and therefore must position himself in off the dirt when speedy hitters are in the batter's box to guard against that. Chipper's arm accuracy has remained consistently excellent, and he will seldom bounce throws to first base when he has time to set his feet.

Third Basemen

Danny Valencia

	Innings	Runs Saved
2011	1280.2	-13
2009-2011	1990	-10

	Good Plays	Misplays and Errors
Valencia 2011	28	44
Avg Third Baseman	39	41
Good Play/Misplay Pct		.405

Danny Valencia rates as a below-average third baseman. His glove is inconsistent, and his range is limited. He seems comfortable backhanding balls, but he struggles on balls hit to his left or straight on. Valencia possesses a strong throwing arm, but lacks consistent accuracy. His throws tend to get wide when he is rushed, usually when charging bunts or recovering on deflected balls. Valencia does a good job keeping the ball in the infield, saving extra bases, but he struggles starting double plays.

Greg Dobbs

	Innings	Runs Saved
2011	755	-9
2009-2011	1073.2	-12

	Good Plays	Misplays and Errors
Dobbs 2011	15	28
Avg Third Baseman	21	22
Good Play/Misplay Pct		.364

Greg Dobbs is a valuable utility bat who can fill in at any corner infield or outfield position. His defense, however, is not a valued commodity. Most often used at third, Dobbs generally makes routine plays, though he can look quite stiff while doing so. His range to his left is limited, and grounders hit directly at him can prove challenging. His decision to throw on tough plays sometimes proves to be reckless, but occasionally he does turn in a good play. His arm strength is average at best, while his throwing accuracy is lacking.

Scott Sizemore

	Innings	Runs Saved
2011	782	-11
2009-2011	820	-12

	Good Plays	Misplays and Errors
Sizemore 2011	24	35
Avg Third Baseman	22	23
Good Play/Misplay Pct		.423

Edwin Encarnacion

	Innings	Runs Saved
2011	273.2	-4
2009-2011	1841.2	-14

	Good Plays	Misplays and Errors
Encarnacion 2011	4	13
Avg Third Baseman	8	8
Good Play/Misplay Pct		.247

Encarnacion's propensity for errors has earned him the nickname "E5" from baseball fans, which is, of course, how you score an error at third base. While he does struggle at the hot corner, his defense has improved a bit from earlier in his career with the Cincinnati Reds. Encarnacion can make the routine fielding plays, but his erratic arm has kept him from being a legitimate option at third base. Of his 111 career errors at third base, 71 have been of the throwing variety. He can make routine plays, but Encarnacion's range is well below-average in all directions. A good part of his defensive shortcomings at third base have been due to lack of effort and a plethora of mental mistakes. Toronto eventually realized all this and started playing Encarnacion at designated hitter in 2011.

Casey McGehee

	Innings	Runs Saved
2011	1233.1	3
2009-2011	3089.2	-21

	Good Plays	Misplays and Errors
McGehee 2011	32	40
Avg Third Baseman	37	39
Good Play/Misplay Pct		.461

McGehee has more trouble fielding grounders than a third baseman should. While his difficulty with fielding hot shots is forgivable, his frequency of botching routine plays is not. McGehee has a bad habit of lifting his glove prematurely to let the ball sneak by, especially when he ranges to his left. He doesn't move well laterally, so he'll often go to the ground when other third basemen wouldn't have to, making some plays appear more difficult than they actually are. McGehee had a spike in throwing errors in 2011 (9 of the 17 for his career came that year) but most of those were close enough to have been handled better by Prince Fielder; with a little luck, his throwing error count should come back down to a respectable level in future seasons. McGehee's best strength as a fielder is getting rid of the ball quickly, which helps him start double plays and also stands out when he charges soft grounders and bunts. Nevertheless,

Third Basemen

McGehee improved defensively in 2011. After two seasons where he cost the Brewers 10 and 14 runs defensively, he actually saved three runs for them in 2011. Part of this improvement is attributable to manager Ron Roenicke's aggressive shifting, saving a number of plays that would not otherwise have been made.

Pedro Alvarez

	Innings	Runs Saved
2011	549	-11
2009-2011	1363.2	-21

	Good Plays	Misplays and Errors
Alvarez 2011	24	31
Avg Third Baseman	23	24
Good Play/Misplay Pct		.453

Alvarez has always been heralded more for his bat than his glove. His glove has been well below-average in his short time in the majors thus far with Pittsburgh. Despite having only played about 50 percent of the games at third base over the past two years, he has made the sixth-most Defensive Misplays and Errors on grounders at the position over that time. He just doesn't have the soft hands or the quick reflexes needed to man the hot corner effectively. He has also struggled with the accuracy on his throws and lacks the fielding skill and quickness to be effective at fielding bunts. Alvarez has a large frame for a third baseman at 6'3" and 235 pounds, and the Pirates may look to move him to first base in the future, where he can use that frame as a target, and where he will not be asked to throw the ball across the field as much.

Wilson Betemit

	Innings	Runs Saved
2011	696	-7
2009-2011	1194.1	-22

	Good Plays	Misplays and Errors
Betemit 2011	13	26
Avg Third Baseman	22	24
Good Play/Misplay Pct		.348

Betemit leaves a lot to be desired with the glove at third base. He doesn't play balls well in either direction and struggles when he needs to make throws on the run. Betemit possesses a strong arm, but poor accuracy has always been an issue for him. His range is very limited, and he often has to rush his throws on slow rollers and grounders in the hole which can lead to wildness. After being used as a utility infielder earlier in his career, teams have wised up recently and have kept him mainly at

third. As poor as his defensive performance has been as a third baseman, Betemit was even more abysmal as a shortstop and second baseman.

Michael Young

	Innings	Runs Saved
2011	342	-3
2009-2011	2878	-29

	Good Plays	Misplays and Errors
Young 2011	12	10
Avg Third Baseman	11	11
Good Play/Misplay Pct		.562

Young played four positions in 2011—first base, second base, third base and shortstop, and he was sub-par at all of them. His lack of range has always been his biggest issue defensively. Even at first base, the least-demanding infield position in terms of range, Young was below-average. He struggled to adjust to the finer points of the position as well, doing a poor job of handling difficult throws in the dirt or wide of the bag. Young does have an above-average arm for a third baseman, which can help him to start double plays quickly. Young won a Gold Glove at shortstop in 2008, an award which looked dubious at the time and now looks more and more so as time goes on. At age 35, Young appears be on the verge of being forced into a designated hitter role exclusively.

Chris Johnson

	Innings	Runs Saved
2011	841.1	-12
2009-2011	1679.1	-30

	Good Plays	Misplays and Errors
Johnson 2011	18	28
Avg Third Baseman	25	26
Good Play/Misplay Pct		.407

Johnson has marginal speed and can look awkward manning the hot corner. His range is quite limited, especially to his left; so many balls that could be outs will shoot through the hole on the left side of the infield when Johnson is at third. He gets into trouble when he gets ahead of himself, trying to make a play before securing the ball. This leads to a lot of bobbled grounders and rushed, wild throws. Johnson has been fairly effective at fielding bunts so far in his career. He won't turn many sacrifice attempts into force outs, but he does a nice job of always getting an out on the play. He also has a strong throwing arm, but his accuracy is an issue.

Third Basemen

Mark Reynolds

	Innings	Runs Saved
2011	984.1	-22
2009-2011	3324	-33

	Good Plays	Misplays and Errors
Reynolds 2011	29	57
Avg Third Baseman	29	30
Good Play/Misplay Pct		.352

It is well documented that Mark Reynolds has been a defensive liability throughout his career, but in 2011 he brought it to another level of ineptitude. Not only does he have terrible range, he also misses plays that are right at him. He handles plays to his left adequately, but balls hit to his right elude him regularly. He lacks the sure-handedness and fluidity that it takes to cleanly gobble up groundballs, and even when he makes the occasional flashy play, he cannot consistently throw accurately without coming to a normal throwing position and setting his feet. This shows itself in his struggles starting double plays. It is a different story when considering his performance on balls in the air. He has surprisingly quick reaction time on line drives compared to his futility with groundballs, and always seems to make numerous plays on pop-ups near or in the stands. Reynolds was a bit better in his short time at first base, as you might expect, though still below-average. First base is a better place to hide Reynolds defensively.

David Wright

	Innings	Runs Saved
2011	893.2	-6
2009-2011	3498.2	-34

	Good Plays	Misplays and Errors
Wright 2011	31	32
Avg Third Baseman	28	30
Good Play/Misplay Pct		.508

Wright has won two Gold Gloves but no Fielding Bible Awards in his career, and that's not an oversight from our voting panel. Of his 19 errors and 13 additional defensive misplays in the 2011 season, 10 came on bad throws and 12 came on mishandled groundballs. He has a tendency to rush throws and throw side-arm, which explains why he rated among the trailers in our good plays/misplays runs saved on throwing plays. While his range to the left is above-average, he's made 26 fewer plays to his right than the average third baseman in the last three years. It may not be the main responsibility of a third baseman, but Wright ranked as the worst third baseman in double play runs saved over the past three

years and also rated poorly in that category based on good plays/misplays runs saved. Over the last three seasons, Wright's runs saved total of -34 ranks near the bottom of all regular major league third basemen. The key, though, is that he does a lot of good things as well. He led all major league third baseman with 76 good fielding plays in 2010, 17 more than the next closest player. Despite a trip to the disabled list in 2011, Wright ranked in the top ten at the position in good fielding plays per touch (11.5 percent). It seems that Wright has the physical tools to make highlight-reel plays; if his range to his right improved and he limited the misplays on throws, he could possibly work his way into the Fielding Bible Award discussion in the future.

Aramis Ramirez

	Innings	Runs Saved
2011	1241.1	-18
2009-2011	2928.1	-38

	Good Plays	Misplays and Errors
Ramirez 2011	38	48
Avg Third Baseman	33	35
Good Play/Misplay Pct		.458

Ramirez has been on a steady decline over the past three years, bottoming out in 2011 with the worst defensive season of his career. He was second-to-last among third basemen in Runs Saved with -18, and had the second-most Defensive Misplays and Errors with 48. He trailed only Mark Reynolds in both of those categories. A look at his error totals would indicate that poor throws are his main problem, but the Defensive Misplay data tells another story. Ramirez was only credited with four fielding errors this year, but our numbers show he made 21 Defensive Misplays on grounders, not including those four errors. He made only three misplays on throws that were not counted as one of his nine throwing errors. Ramirez has limited range and poor mobility, which at least prevents him from misplaying even more grounders than he already does. His unsteady glove and wild arm hurt him especially in double play situations. Ramirez does do one thing well: fielding bunts with above-average success. He possesses a strong throwing arm and can gun down speedy runners on bunt attempts despite his own lack of mobility.

Shortstops Evaluations

Year	League	Gold Glove Winners	Should Have Been
2003	AL	Alex Rodriguez	Alex Rodriguez
	NL	Edgar Renteria	Adam Everett
2004	AL	Derek Jeter	Miguel Tejada
	NL	Cesar Izturis	Cesar Izturis
2005	AL	Derek Jeter	Juan Uribe
	NL	Omar Vizquel	Adam Everett
2006	AL	Derek Jeter	Alex Gonzalez
	NL	Omar Vizquel	Adam Everett
2007	AL	Orlando Cabrera	John McDonald
	NL	Jimmy Rollins	Troy Tulowitzki
2008	AL	Michael Young	Erick Aybar
	NL	Jimmy Rollins	Jimmy Rollins
2009	AL	Derek Jeter	Elvis Andrus
	NL	Jimmy Rollins	Troy Tulowitzki
2010	AL	Derek Jeter	Alexei Ramirez
	NL	Troy Tulowitzki	Brendan Ryan
2011	AL	Erick Aybar	Brendan Ryan
	NL	Troy Tulowitzki	Troy Tulowitzki

My Personal Ratings

Top Five

1 Brendan Ryan, Sea
2 Troy Tulowitzki, Col
3 John McDonald, Ari
4 Clint Barmes, Pit
5 Alexei Ramirez, CWS

Bottom Five

26 Starlin Castro, ChC
27 Ryan Theriot, SF
28 Derek Jeter, NYY
29 Hanley Ramirez, Mia
30 Yuniesky Betancourt, KC

Player teams based on transactions through February 1, 2012

Shortstops

Brendan Ryan

	Innings	Runs Saved
2011	1060.2	18
2009-2011	3018.2	62

	Good Plays	Misplays and Errors
Ryan 2011	59	41
Avg Shortstop	48	41
Good Play/Misplay Pct		.553

Brendan Ryan fit right in with the defensive-minded Mariners in his first year with the club, again rating as one of the top defensive shortstops in the league. His 62 Runs Saved at shortstop over the past three seasons are 19 more than any other shortstop over that time. Ryan possesses great footwork and a strong arm, allowing him to complete the play no matter which way his momentum is carrying him. His signature play involves grabbing a ball in the hole and throwing across his body while moving toward third for the out at first. He is also great at charging the ball and fielding it barehanded when necessary. Additionally, he turns the double play well and has quick reactions on line drives. At shortstop, Ryan does it all. For more about how good Ryan is going to his right, see "Jeter vs. Ryan" on page 57.

Troy Tulowitzki

	Innings	Runs Saved
2011	1208.1	11
2009-2011	3567.1	43

	Good Plays	Misplays and Errors
Tulowitzki 2011	67	29
Avg Shortstop	55	47
Good Play/Misplay Pct		.665

Tulo is an elite defensive shortstop, having taken home three Fielding Bible Awards in only five full seasons in the majors. He is a very good all-around shortstop, but because of his arm strength he really stands out on plays to his right. In the last five years, he has made about 10 plays per year more than the average shortstop going to his right. Only Brendan Ryan is better. Even plays from deep in the hole seem routine, since he can gun a runner down from anywhere on the diamond. Tulowitzki also rarely makes a bad throw, recording only two throwing errors and just three Defensive Misplays on bad throws while playing over 1,200 innings at shortstop in 2011. But there is one area where no other shortstop comes close. Turning double plays. Look at these double play stats for Tulowitzki:

Tulo on the Double Play - Compared to all MLB shortstops (2009 through 2001):

Highest percentage of GDPs Started per Opportunity: Troy Tulowitzki, 72.4%

Highest percentage of GDPs Turned as the middle man per Opp: Troy Tulowitzki, 70.5%

Most Good Play/Misplay Runs Saved on Double Plays: Troy Tulowitzki, 4

Most Runs Saved on GDPs and Pivots: Troy Tulowitzki, 8

In all of baseball, no player dominates all the defensive statistics like Tulo does on double plays. Very amazing.

Alex Gonzalez

	Innings	Runs Saved
2011	1316	9
2009-2011	3633	31

	Good Plays	Misplays and Errors
Gonzalez 2011	62	37
Avg Shortstop	53	46
Good Play/Misplay Pct		.590

Gonzalez turned in a second-consecutive stellar season at shortstop in 2011, finishing fifth at the position with nine Defensive Runs Saved. He is very fluid moving left and right, and his quick release helps to record outs on many close plays. Gonzalez is one of the best fielders at any position at catching difficult throws. He is also a Web Gem machine, turning in highlight-reel plays on a regular basis. Gonzalez's 41 Good Fielding Plays on groundballs were the most by any shortstop this season.

Clint Barmes

	Innings	Runs Saved
2011	1058.1	14
2009-2011	1522.2	29

	Good Plays	Misplays and Errors
Barmes 2011	44	31
Avg Shortstop	45	39
Good Play/Misplay Pct		.550

Playing shortstop full-time for the first time since 2006, Clint Barmes really shined defensively for the Astros in 2011. Barmes does not have as strong an arm

Shortstops

as some other shortstops, but he makes up for it with terrific footwork and a quick release. He has excellent range (especially up the middle), and when he dives to snag a ball, he gets back to his feet so quickly that it is almost all in one motion. For four years, from 2007 through 2010, Barmes had to take a back seat in Colorado to the best defensive shortstop in the game during that time, Troy Tulowitzki. That was unfortunate because Barmes is also one of the best defensive shortstops in the game. Now that he's with another team, he has his opportunity to shine.

Alexei Ramirez

	Innings	Runs Saved
2011	1382	7
2009-2011	4052.1	29

	Good Plays	Misplays and Errors
Ramirez 2011	64	46
Avg Shortstop	57	49
Good Play/Misplay Pct		.545

When the White Sox signed Ramirez prior to the 2008 season, manager Ozzie Guillen was insistent that one day he could be the best defensive shortstop in the majors. Ramirez didn't live up to his defensive billing at the start of his major league career, playing second base his first year, but in the last two seasons he has developed into one of the finer defensive shortstops in baseball. Since moving to short permanently in 2009, Ramirez has saved 29 runs for the Sox. He has tremendous range, especially to his right, great first-step quickness and a good arm, and his instincts keep getting better as he grows more accustomed to the position. Over the previous three years, he's made 32 more plays than the average shortstop, a testament to his raw athleticism that has turned him into a defensive star. He still makes a fair number of errors, but his range is so good that he turns more hits into outs than outs into errors. For example, Ramirez tied for second among shortstops with 36 Good Fielding Plays on grounders, but also ranked third with 23 Defensive Misplays and Errors on grounders. He also tied for second among shortstops in Good Fielding Plays on flies and liners but also had the most Defensive Misplays and Errors in that category. He has struggled with consistency and has occasional lapses in concentration, holding him back from even better defensive numbers. Ozzie's original prediction now looks pretty smart, but Ramirez remains one of the more underrated defensive shortstops in baseball.

Yunel Escobar

	Innings	Runs Saved
2011	1121	7
2009-2011	3509	23

	Good Plays	Misplays and Errors
Escobar 2011	35	39
Avg Shortstop	44	38
Good Play/Misplay Pct		.436

Prior to 2011, Yunel Escobar looked poised to join the small group of elite defensive shortstops in the game. He did not take that next step, however, but still produced at a well above-average level. Escobar is nearly the whole package: he reads the ball well off the bat and has quick feet. In Atlanta, he especially excelled going to his left on plays up the middle, but fared better going to his right in his first full season in Toronto. He has soft hands and uses good footwork to set up his throws, which he makes with superb strength. Escobar can take that next step and become one of the elite defensive shortstops if he can clean up his throwing mistakes. He has recorded more Defensive Misplays and Errors on throws than any shortstop not named Starlin over the past three years.

Paul Janish

	Innings	Runs Saved
2011	743.1	6
2009-2011	1752	20

	Good Plays	Misplays and Errors
Janish 2011	36	22
Avg Shortstop	32	27
Good Play/Misplay Pct		.585

In 2011, Janish played the most innings of his career and confirmed the belief that he is a top-flight defensive shortstop. Janish has made 46 more Good Fielding Plays than Defensive Misplays and errors over the past three seasons, good for sixth-best among shortstops despite playing only about half the time. He reacts to every type of groundball correctly, and moves very deliberately to the ball while keeping his movements controlled. He boasts great range to his left and easily makes throws on the run or while charging slow grounders. If he has a weakness, it's double plays. He struggles at times to execute a clean turn to complete double plays and also ranks as below-average at starting double plays.

Shortstops

John McDonald

	Innings	Runs Saved
2011	264.2	10
2009-2011	578	17

	Good Plays	Misplays and Errors
McDonald 2011	16	9
Avg Shortstop	13	11
Good Play/Misplay Pct		.605

When the Diamondbacks traded for the versatile McDonald, they obviously noticed how extraordinarily good he was at shortstop because he stopped playing other positions after the move. While he has been consistently good at his other positions throughout his career, he is off the charts at shortstop despite playing mostly on turf. With tremendous range (especially to his right), soft hands and a flair for the dramatic, he is always dependable. He does not have the strongest arm in the league, but it is very accurate. He rarely throws the ball away even when throwing from his knees. Since we started tracking our advanced defensive analytics in 2003, McDonald has 45 runs saved in 3,254 innings at shortstop, an average of well over 20 runs saved per season if he played full-time. That's Brendan Ryan and Troy Tulowitzki territory.

Elvis Andrus

	Innings	Runs Saved
2011	1261.1	7
2009-2011	3790.2	15

	Good Plays	Misplays and Errors
Andrus 2011	54	40
Avg Shortstop	54	47
Good Play/Misplay Pct		.537

Elvis Andrus is one of the best young shortstops in baseball. He's fast, fluid and capable of making spectacular plays look mundane. His range is very good, but in the past two seasons he has struggled with balls hit to his left. He is fantastic moving to his right and making plays deep in the hole. He's great on double play pivots as well, helped in large part by his absolute cannon for an arm. His accuracy can betray him, though, which can negate the positives his arm strength provides. What can really be disturbing about Andrus are his bouts of lackadaisical play. Waiting back on some slower grounders or hesitating before throwing can be compensated for by a strong arm, but they are still mental errors with the potential to be costly.

Alcides Escobar

	Innings	Runs Saved
2011	1387.1	10
2009-2011	2838.2	14

	Good Plays	Misplays and Errors
Escobar 2011	77	47
Avg Shortstop	61	53
Good Play/Misplay Pct		.585

Alcides Escobar is a spectacular defensive shortstop. He was merely good in 2010, his first full major league season, but lived up to the scouting reports in 2011 by leading all shortstops with 77 Good Fielding Plays. He features top-tier range (especially to his right), and displays impressive body control when picking up tough grounders and throwing off-balance. Escobar has a very strong arm that is complemented by a quick exchange and release, but he sometimes struggles with accuracy, especially in double play situations. He ranks well below-average in all of our double play metrics. As Escobar matures, he should reduce his number of mistakes and have a chance to be one of the game's best defenders at the position.

Reid Brignac

	Innings	Runs Saved
2011	680.2	7
2009-2011	1233	14

	Good Plays	Misplays and Errors
Brignac 2011	32	21
Avg Shortstop	28	24
Good Play/Misplay Pct		.567

Brignac ranked in the top ten in both Plus/Minus and Runs Saved among shortstops in 2011. He has a strong arm with a quick release, and he throws accurately. He has great range to his right and good range to his left, though he can struggle with balls hit straight on. Brignac is a reliable shortstop who could get looks as a full-time starter in the future if his hitting can catch up to his defense.

Shortstops

Marco Scutaro

	Innings	Runs Saved
2011	928.2	1
2009-2011	3347.1	13

	Good Plays	Misplays and Errors
Scutaro 2011	28	35
Avg Shortstop	36	31
Good Play/Misplay Pct		.408

Marco Scutaro has seen his Runs Saved totals at shortstop plummet since joining the Red Sox in 2010. With the Blue Jays in 2008-2009 he totaled 18 Runs Saved, but has only saved two runs for the Red Sox in his two seasons with the team. He has an average arm for the shortstop position and ranks in the middle of the pack as far as turning double plays. He remains a solid middle infielder, but at this point in his career he probably will never regain the defensive prowess he displayed across the Canadian border.

Stephen Drew

	Innings	Runs Saved
2011	731.1	3
2009-2011	3132.2	12

	Good Plays	Misplays and Errors
Drew 2011	38	18
Avg Shortstop	29	25
Good Play/Misplay Pct		.645

Stephen Drew, the anchor of Arizona's infield defense, saw his 2011 season come to an unfortunate end with a fractured right ankle in mid-July. Drew's glovework isn't as flashy as others across the league, but he gets the job done. His defense is best described as quietly efficient, as he makes even difficult plays look routine. He is very good at making plays deep in the hole thanks to his strong arm. Though he lacks the overall great range you would want in a shortstop, Drew makes up for it by limiting his mistakes. Drew had 20 more Good Fielding Plays than Defensive Misplays and Errors, a figure that ranked sixth among shortstops in 2011.

Elliot Johnson

	Innings	Runs Saved
2011	337.2	8
2009-2011	337.2	8

	Good Plays	Misplays and Errors
Johnson 2011	14	6
Avg Shortstop	13	11
Good Play/Misplay Pct		.667

Rafael Furcal

	Innings	Runs Saved
2011	726.2	-5
2009-2011	2809.2	6

	Good Plays	Misplays and Errors
Furcal 2011	40	32
Avg Shortstop	32	28
Good Play/Misplay Pct		.518

Age and a plethora of injuries all contributed to Furcal's poor play at shortstop in 2011. Furcal has struggled with balls in the hole for a few years now as his range has decreased, but this past year he struggled even more with balls that were hit straight on. His arm remains his best tool and helps him continue to be successful on some of the balls that he is able to get to up the middle behind the second base bag. Furcal can still be a capable defender, but as he gets on in years, he will have to learn to play smarter and position himself better. As a young, wildly athletic player, Furcal made a lot of errors and misplays. As that athleticism fades each year, those kinds of mistakes are no longer as forgivable.

J.J. Hardy

	Innings	Runs Saved
2011	1133	8
2009-2011	2940.2	5

	Good Plays	Misplays and Errors
Hardy 2011	46	23
Avg Shortstop	51	43
Good Play/Misplay Pct		.632

J.J. Hardy could be the most underrated shortstop in baseball. He makes all the plays he should and can make the exceptional play on occasion. In the last couple of years, he has made more plays to his right than to his left. That's opposite of what he did in Milwaukee before that. He is a bigger guy, so he looks like he doesn't move well, but in fact he has great reactions. Hardy has a very strong and accurate arm which helps him make plays in the hole. He did a great job in 2011 of avoiding mistakes in the field. He made 20 fewer misplays and errors than the average shortstop would have made given his number of touches. Hardy's career looked like it was in a tailspin coming into 2011, but he recovered in a big way both at the plate and in the field.

Shortstops

Jhonny Peralta

	Innings	Runs Saved
2011	1245	2
2009-2011	1971.1	5

	Good Plays	Misplays and Errors
Peralta 2011	26	33
Avg Shortstop	50	43
Good Play/Misplay Pct		.404

Peralta played a decent defensive shortstop in 2011 after spending most of his time at third base the previous two seasons. Peralta has plus range moving to his left and below-average range moving to his right. He is also very good at charging soft groundballs. Peralta has average arm strength for a shortstop. He is able to get rid of the ball quickly when throwing with his feet set or on the run. He occasionally will throw from a side-arm angle when he is throwing on the run. While Peralta ranks as about average at turning double plays, he could improve his footwork around the bag and his accuracy on his feeds. Peralta is not much fun to watch in the field, as his unusually low number of Good Fielding Plays indicates, but he makes enough plays to be serviceable at the position.

Erick Aybar

	Innings	Runs Saved
2011	1262	-1
2009-2011	3631	4

	Good Plays	Misplays and Errors
Aybar 2011	56	43
Avg Shortstop	55	47
Good Play/Misplay Pct		.528

Aybar has been an effective defender at shortstop throughout his career, but does not deserve to be listed among the best in the game. He does not have the strongest arm to complete the play even if he fields the ball cleanly when moving towards the hole. While his athleticism allows him to get to more balls than most shortstops, he often has sloppy and erratic footwork that can take the velocity off his throws and slows down his ball transfer. Other times, he displays poor judgment by making throws when it is clear he has no play. On the other hand, he is very quick at getting off the ground and setting his feet when he dives for a ball. Aybar also excels at leaping over aggressively sliding runners on the pivot and completing tough double plays. He did win the 2011 Gold Glove Award thanks to his flashy and athletic play, but according to the Runs Saved system, this was a down-year defensively for Aybar, and even in his best defensive seasons he has not played at an award-winning level.

Brandon Crawford

	Innings	Runs Saved
2011	507.1	3
2009-2011	507.1	3

	Good Plays	Misplays and Errors
Crawford 2011	24	19
Avg Shortstop	20	17
Good Play/Misplay Pct		.521

Crawford impressed with his play at shortstop for the Giants in 2011. Called up in late May all the way from High-A San Jose, he struggled to adjust to major league pitching, but his defense did not suffer. He displayed above-average range to his left and showed a knack for charging difficult slow grounders. Crawford has soft hands for a shortstop and is excellent at both picking tough hops on grounders and scooping up difficult throws. He also was good at turning the double play. He has the kind of footwork around the bag that allows him to get the throw off quickly and accurately to first. He made many of the rookie mistakes you would expect from a young shortstop, but definitely displayed a skill set that could allow him to become one of the better defenders at the position in the future.

Asdrubal Cabrera

	Innings	Runs Saved
2011	1326.2	3
2009-2011	3022	2

	Good Plays	Misplays and Errors
Cabrera 2011	62	40
Avg Shortstop	52	45
Good Play/Misplay Pct		.571

Cabrera was only a slightly above-average defender for the Indians despite making some of the most memorable defensive plays of 2011. He had above-average range to his left and below-average range to his right, although in past seasons when he has played some second base this was reversed. Cabrera has plus arm strength. He is able to get rid of the ball quickly with above-average accuracy throwing from a 3/4 arm angle. Cabrera can get lazy on routine plays and his throws can sail because of this. In the last three years, he has done a very nice job on the double play, saving two runs on GDPs and Pivots and three more runs making more GDP Good Plays than Misplays. Cabrera is still just 26 years old, and this was his first full season at shortstop. If

Shortstops

Cabrera can maintain his ability to make the amazing play while improving his consistency on the more routine plays, he could become a true defensive standout.

Sean Rodriguez

	Innings	Runs Saved
2011	430.2	0
2009-2011	439.2	0

	Good Plays	Misplays and Errors
Rodriguez 2011	16	15
Avg Shortstop	14	12
Good Play/Misplay Pct		.478

Mike Fontenot

	Innings	Runs Saved
2011	284	1
2009-2011	345	-1

	Good Plays	Misplays and Errors
Fontenot 2011	10	11
Avg Shortstop	10	9
Good Play/Misplay Pct		.439

Mike Fontenot primarily played second base earlier in his career but saw the most action at shortstop this past year. Still, as a part-time player with little offensive value, he will benefit his team the most by bouncing around the infield as his manager sees fit. As a shortstop in 2011, he demonstrated much better range up the middle than to his right. As a late-inning defensive replacement, you could certainly do worse.

Alexi Casilla

	Innings	Runs Saved
2011	306.2	-3
2009-2011	498	-1

	Good Plays	Misplays and Errors
Casilla 2011	8	13
Avg Shortstop	14	12
Good Play/Misplay Pct		.346

Ruben Tejada

	Innings	Runs Saved
2011	353	-1
2009-2011	574.2	-2

	Good Plays	Misplays and Errors
Tejada 2011	30	18
Avg Shortstop	15	13
Good Play/Misplay Pct		.589

Willie Bloomquist

	Innings	Runs Saved
2011	501	1
2009-2011	739.2	-3

	Good Plays	Misplays and Errors
Bloomquist 2011	21	11
Avg Shortstop	19	16
Good Play/Misplay Pct		.621

Dee Gordon

	Innings	Runs Saved
2011	446.1	-3
2009-2011	446.1	-3

	Good Plays	Misplays and Errors
Gordon 2011	28	23
Avg Shortstop	19	16
Good Play/Misplay Pct		.511

Jason Bartlett

	Innings	Runs Saved
2011	1211	-9
2009-2011	3468.2	-5

	Good Plays	Misplays and Errors
Bartlett 2011	39	44
Avg Shortstop	51	44
Good Play/Misplay Pct		.432

Bartlett's range fell off dramatically in 2011 after leaving Tampa Bay to join the Padres. Bartlett's age and decreasing athleticism likely played a part, but it also may have had something to do with the sophisticated positioning schemes that the Rays use. Without that advantage on his side, Bartlett's already decreasing range was completely exposed. He still possesses one powerful weapon at short: his strong arm puts him on the winning side of plenty of close plays when he has to range to his right. However, Bartlett tends to get too aggressive with throws on relay plays, failing to get the runner he was targeting while allowing a trailing runner to advance. He has never been particularly good at turning or starting double plays, but did an acceptable job in that area in 2011.

Shortstops

Cliff Pennington

	Innings	Runs Saved
2011	1272.1	-9
2009-2011	3110.2	-5

	Good Plays	Misplays and Errors
Pennington 2011	50	48
Avg Shortstop	50	43
Good Play/Misplay Pct		.472

Pennington has sandwiched two very poor defensive seasons around one sparkling one in 2010. His numbers fell off considerably in almost every category in 2011 and resembled the poor performance he put up over 60 games in 2009. Pennington has one of the wildest throwing arms of any shortstop in baseball. His 18 Defensive Misplays and Errors on throws in 2011 ranked third-most among shortstops. Pennington went through bouts when seemingly every throw he made to first base bounced in the dirt, and he was only saved from having many more errors by the sure hands of his first basemen. Despite the inaccuracy, the strength of Pennington's throwing arm is arguably his best defensive asset. He is able to make plays deep in the hole by planting and throwing off of his back foot rather than having to make a jump-throw. His arm strength helps him do a great job cutting off runners at home, and it also plays a part in his being one of the best shortstops in the game at both starting and turning double plays, along with quick technical footwork around the bag.

Jamey Carroll

	Innings	Runs Saved
2011	504.2	-5
2009-2011	1077.2	-6

	Good Plays	Misplays and Errors
Carroll 2011	10	11
Avg Shortstop	17	15
Good Play/Misplay Pct		.439

Jimmy Rollins

	Innings	Runs Saved
2011	1207	-7
2009-2011	3316	-6

	Good Plays	Misplays and Errors
Rollins 2011	38	23
Avg Shortstop	48	42
Good Play/Misplay Pct		.587

Jimmy Rollins, the 2008 Fielding Bible Award winner at shortstop, has seen his defensive abilities take a hit after he was hit by injuries. He is no longer at the top of the list of the best shortstops in the game. He still has a nose for the ball, allowing him to make some great plays, and his arm is still above-average. But it's his range that has taken the biggest hit, as he just doesn't get to the balls he used to. Rollins is one of the better shortstops in the league at turning the double play. If he can stay healthy and rediscover some of the athleticism he's lost over the years, he can continue to be a serviceable shortstop for a few more years.

Jed Lowrie

	Innings	Runs Saved
2011	398	-3
2009-2011	738.1	-7

	Good Plays	Misplays and Errors
Lowrie 2011	14	16
Avg Shortstop	15	13
Good Play/Misplay Pct		.429

Lowrie will generally go unnoticed when he's playing his best defense. He has only modest range and hasn't demonstrated the skill to make spectacular plays, but his strength through 2010 was in his apparent ability to limit mistakes. Lowrie made a good first impression by playing 386 error-free innings at shortstop during his 2008 rookie season, and followed that up with just a pair of errors through 340 1/3 innings at short over the following two years. Our data indicates that his defense was far from perfect during that time, but his gaffes became more obvious and frequent in 2011. His 15 total errors between short and third along with another 10 misplays combined to form a subpar year in the field characterized mainly by awkward handling of groundballs. Lowrie's only consistent demonstration of skill involves him ranging to his right and making mini jump-throws to first. He seems to do this out of habit rather than necessity, but his motion is quick and his throws are strong enough that it appears to help him on close plays.

Emilio Bonifacio

	Innings	Runs Saved
2011	543.2	-5
2009-2011	750.2	-7

	Good Plays	Misplays and Errors
Bonifacio 2011	19	21
Avg Shortstop	22	19
Good Play/Misplay Pct		.438

Bonifacio unexpectedly logged the majority of his defensive innings at shortstop in 2011 due to the health issues of Hanley Ramirez. Bonifacio is used at every

Shortstops

position outside of first base and catcher. He is above-average defensively at second and third base, and can do the job adequately at shortstop and in the outfield. Shortstop is not his best position, since he lacks the arm strength to convert on balls fielded far to his right and the wingspan to even reach others. In the outfield, he lacks natural instincts and only is useful there because of his great speed. So far his weak arm strength has not hindered his performance, as baserunners have not taken many extra bases on balls hit to him. Bonifacio fills in where needed for the Marlins, and with Jose Reyes and Hanley Ramirez now manning the left side of the infield, it is likely that Bonifacio is headed back to the outfield.

Ronny Cedeno

	Innings	Runs Saved
2011	1050.1	5
2009-2011	2911	-8

	Good Plays	Misplays and Errors
Cedeno 2011	39	39
Avg Shortstop	50	43
Good Play/Misplay Pct		.462

Ronny Cedeno has been a bit of an enigma defensively thus far in his career. In 2010 he ranked among the worst shortstops in baseball in Runs Saved due in large part to a terrible performance on balls hit to his right. In 2011, he improved dramatically on balls to both his right and left, and raised his plus/minus total on groundballs from -13 to +12, a 25-play swing. At the same time, his performance on double plays swooned. Cedeno's glovework can let him down at times, often on plays up the middle. He will give away outs with rare lapses in concentration, dropping easy grounders or completely misjudging how to play a ball. He has a strong arm and decent accuracy. At times he seems to attempt to guide the ball when he has time to throw, which can lead to throws that short-hop the first baseman.

Eduardo Nunez

	Innings	Runs Saved
2011	386.1	-9
2009-2011	425.2	-10

	Good Plays	Misplays and Errors
Nunez 2011	7	25
Avg Shortstop	14	12
Good Play/Misplay Pct		.194

Edgar Renteria

	Innings	Runs Saved
2011	628	1
2009-2011	2252.2	-11

	Good Plays	Misplays and Errors
Renteria 2011	19	26
Avg Shortstop	26	23
Good Play/Misplay Pct		.386

Edgar Renteria's days as a slick fielder are long gone, and at the age of 35 his already modest defensive skills are likely to start eroding at a quicker pace. Renteria has seen his playing time cut heavily in the last two seasons, with good reason. He doesn't have the foot speed required to cover an average amount of ground, and his arm strength doesn't allow him to get away with getting to balls late. Renteria is much more comfortable moving to his left on plays up the middle, but he struggles to convert grounders in the hole into outs. His hands have become increasingly unreliable recently, and his arm accuracy has decreased, leading to a rise in throwing errors. Despite all this, in terms of runs saved, his defense has been average in part-time play the last two years costing his teams only one run defensively overall.

Ryan Theriot

	Innings	Runs Saved
2011	755	-8
2009-2011	2312	-11

	Good Plays	Misplays and Errors
Theriot 2011	22	37
Avg Shortstop	33	28
Good Play/Misplay Pct		.338

Theriot has earned playing time due to his ability to hit for average, but leaves much to be desired in the field. He does not get to nearly as many groundball outs as he should, often failing to reach balls that most shortstops in baseball would get to rather easily. He also has a fairly weak arm and has trouble throwing the ball on a line from deep in the hole at short. Theriot is a converted second baseman who seems to be a more natural fit at second than at short.

Shortstops

Tsuyoshi Nishioka

	Innings	Runs Saved
2011	508.1	-12
2009-2011	508.1	-12

	Good Plays	Misplays and Errors
Nishioka 2011	22	31
Avg Shortstop	24	21
Good Play/Misplay Pct		.379

In Japan, Nishioka was a batting champion, two-time stolen base champion and three-time Gold Glove winner. Across the Pacific, Nishioka has struggled at the plate, on the base paths and in the field. Nishioka has played only 68 games so far with the Twins, and those giving him the benefit of the doubt could attribute some of his rookie struggles to lingering effects of the broken fibula injury he suffered in his first week. We've seen nothing more than hints of his ability so far. One of the repeated defensive difficulties for Nishioka has been taking groundballs off his glove, especially those hit hard right at him. Another is holding onto the ball too long by double-clutching or spinning unnecessarily. The third is a variety of communication issues: letting a popup drop between him and a teammate, failing to cover second base on a double play up the middle and losing awareness of baserunners when he positions himself to receive a throw from the outfield. A full healthy season could help Nishioka's chemistry with his teammates and ease his jitters, but he'll have to get off to a good start in 2012 to avoid the pressures of further scrutiny.

Ian Desmond

	Innings	Runs Saved
2011	1317.2	-3
2009-2011	2662	-13

	Good Plays	Misplays and Errors
Desmond 2011	48	58
Avg Shortstop	57	49
Good Play/Misplay Pct		.416

Desmond was able to rebound from a slow start defensively to have a reasonably solid defensive season for the Nationals. Early in the season Desmond was battling himself in the field, misplaying routine groundballs and dropping catchable throws. These issues subsided as the season went on. In 2011, Desmond showed improved range to his left after a poor showing in 2010, though he still was slightly below-average on balls in that direction. On balls to his right, it was another story. He was well below-average after excelling on those plays in 2010. As the season progressed, he got

better at making plays on the run and charging softly hit groundballs. Desmond has plus arm strength with a quick release, though he must continue to improve his throwing accuracy. One of Desmond's greatest strengths is his athleticism, which allows him to excel at tracking down tough short flies and liners. This athleticism, combined with his physical toughness, makes Desmond one of the best shortstops in the game at turning double plays with aggressive baserunners bearing down on him. If he can maintain his concentration, Desmond has the tools to become an above-average defensive shortstop. But he's not there yet.

Starlin Castro

	Innings	Runs Saved
2011	1398.2	-10
2009-2011	2472.1	-14

	Good Plays	Misplays and Errors
Castro 2011	69	85
Avg Shortstop	66	56
Good Play/Misplay Pct		.411

Castro's skills at shortstop are very unrefined. In his first two seasons, he has made a staggering total of 152 Defensive Misplays and Errors, the most by any shortstop by a wide margin. (For more on this, see page 67.) He has shown the ability to make great plays at times, but far too often he makes bad misplays on routine groundballs that can cost his team severely. Starlin's main weakness is his arm accuracy. He made many wild throws this year on routine plays that shortstops are expected to make, leading all shortstops in Defensive Misplays on throws. Double plays are another area of concern, as his footwork around the bag is still a work in progress. Playing the 2011 season at only 21 years old, Castro possesses great athleticism and has the potential to round out some of the rough edges of his defense with more experience.

Trevor Plouffe

	Innings	Runs Saved
2011	396.2	-14
2009-2011	464.2	-15

	Good Plays	Misplays and Errors
Plouffe 2011	9	21
Avg Shortstop	17	15
Good Play/Misplay Pct		.269

240

Shortstops

Jose Reyes

	Innings	Runs Saved
2011	1087	-13
2009-2011	2563.2	-18

	Good Plays	Misplays and Errors
Reyes 2011	45	39
Avg Shortstop	45	39
Good Play/Misplay Pct		.498

Jose Reyes is a real mixed bag at short. If he played up to his athletic ability, he would be one of the better fielders in the league, but for some reason, he is wildly inconsistent. In one play he can show off his blinding speed, quick hands and cannon arm, while finishing the play by making an inaccurate throw because he didn't set his feet. This is pretty much the story of Reyes in the field: moments of ineptitude with flashes of greatness sprinkled in. At his worst, he struggles moving to his right to make the stop and long throw from the hole. The raw ability is there for Reyes, but he needs to learn to slow his game down to see the ball into the glove every time and to utilize proper footwork to set his body and make accurate throws. His seemingly perennial injuries certainly haven't helped.

Angel Sanchez

	Innings	Runs Saved
2011	366.2	-7
2009-2011	859.2	-20

	Good Plays	Misplays and Errors
Sanchez 2011	9	17
Avg Shortstop	16	14
Good Play/Misplay Pct		.313

Sanchez was a below-average defensive shortstop in 2011. He served as a utility infielder for the Astros, as he also saw time at second and third base. At shortstop, Sanchez has average range moving to his left and well below-average range moving to his right. The biggest problem Sanchez has at shortstop is his inability to consistently field groundballs cleanly. He has average arm strength for a shortstop with a quick release and is usually pretty accurate with his throws. Sanchez is better suited for second base, where his lack of range would be less exposed, and he could recover more easily when he mishandles grounders. In 366 innings at shortstop, Sanchez made 10 misplays and 7 errors, but only made one misplay in his 134 innings at second base.

Derek Jeter

	Innings	Runs Saved
2011	1047.1	-15
2009-2011	3611.2	-21

	Good Plays	Misplays and Errors
Jeter 2011	31	31
Avg Shortstop	36	31
Good Play/Misplay Pct		.462

Derek Jeter has many special talents, but turning likely hits into outs is not among his best. In fact, Jeter's struggles to make plays had him ranked dead last among shortstops in Runs Saved in 2011. This should come as no surprise to readers of prior *Fielding Bible* editions, as he has now ranked near or at the bottom of the position for eight of the nine years BIS has been tracking balls in play. To many baseball fans, however, Jeter's poor defensive performance reaching balls goes unnoticed. He almost never makes an error fielding groundballs or line drives he can get to, and the bulk of his rarely committed errors are of the throwing variety. His patented jump-throw showcases his two key weaknesses: limited mobility and a relatively weak arm. These two weaknesses make fielding grounders to his right look challenging and sometimes downright spectacular, when in reality, most shortstops are able to plant their feet and deliver a stronger and more accurate throw to first without theatrics. For more on plays to Jeter's right, see "Jeter vs. Ryan" on page 57.

Miguel Tejada

	Innings	Runs Saved
2011	334.1	-5
2009-2011	2202.1	-22

	Good Plays	Misplays and Errors
Tejada 2011	14	17
Avg Shortstop	14	12
Good Play/Misplay Pct		.415

Orlando Cabrera

	Innings	Runs Saved
2011	309.1	3
2009-2011	2728.2	-26

	Good Plays	Misplays and Errors
Cabrera 2011	18	17
Avg Shortstop	14	12
Good Play/Misplay Pct		.477

Shortstops

Hanley Ramirez

	Innings	Runs Saved
2011	754.2	-13
2009-2011	3230.2	-30

	Good Plays	Misplays and Errors
Ramirez 2011	35	33
Avg Shortstop	28	24
Good Play/Misplay Pct		.477

Earlier in his career, Hanley Ramirez was prone to simple mistakes and did not always set himself in order to make the easy throw. He's cut down on the Defensive Misplays and Errors since 2007, when he led all shortstops with 70. However, he hasn't covered as much ground in recent seasons, particularly in the 3B/SS hole. Previous managers have questioned his effort on a regular basis, and we have to wonder if his range suffers as a result. He's also inconsistent in double play situations, often bobbling balls in an effort to make a quick play. Even before the Jose Reyes signing forced Miami's hand, Ramirez was due for a position change.

Yuniesky Betancourt

	Innings	Runs Saved
2011	1278.2	-7
2009-2011	3769.1	-52

	Good Plays	Misplays and Errors
Betancourt 2011	47	40
Avg Shortstop	50	43
Good Play/Misplay Pct		.503

Betancourt bounced back a bit this year from a horrendous three-year stretch when he was arguably the worst defensive player in the game at any position. In 2011, he improved from wretched to merely poor. Part of the improvement has to do with his manager, Ron Roenicke. Roenicke entered the 2011 season with the worst set of four infielders in baseball by far. However, he was able to get the most out of them by using extensive positioning (see "The Ted Williams Shift" on page 43). All four of them (Betancourt, Prince Fielder at first, Rickie Weeks at second and Casey McGehee at third) went from double-digit negative plus/minus numbers to single digits. (McGehee even crossed over into the positive numbers at +3.) Betancourt has a quick first step and a strong arm, but not much in the way of solid footwork. He has consistently struggled with balls hit to his left, lacking the range and speed to stop most grounders up the middle from becoming base hits. Betancourt does have one defensive attribute: equally distributing his errors. He has made 28 throwing errors and 29 fielding errors over the past three seasons.

Left Fielders Evaluations

Year	League	Gold Glove Winners	Should Have Been
2003	AL	none	none
	NL	none	none
2004	AL	none	none
	NL	none	none
2005	AL	none	almost: Carl Crawford
	NL	none	none
2006	AL	none	none
	NL	none	none
2007	AL	none	none
	NL	none	none
2008	AL	none	none
	NL	none	Willie Harris
2009	AL	none	Carl Crawford
	NL	none	Nyjer Morgan
2010	AL	Carl Crawford	Brett Gardner
	NL	none	Gerardo Parra
2011	AL	Alex Gordon	Brett Gardner
	NL	Gerardo Parra	Tony Gwynn

My Personal Ratings

Top Five

1 Brett Gardner, NYY
2 Gerardo Parra, Ari
3 Tony Gwynn, LAD
4 Alex Gordon, KC
5 Sam Fuld, TB

Bottom Five

26 Delmon Young, Det
27 Juan Pierre, Phi
28 Logan Morrison, Mia
29 Alfonso Soriano, Chi
30 Raul Ibanez, FA

Player teams based on transactions through February 1, 2012

Left Fielders

Brett Gardner

	Innings	Runs Saved
2011	1158.2	23
2009-2011	2064.2	49

	Good Plays	Misplays and Errors
Gardner 2011	33	23
Avg Left Fielder	24	26
Good Play/Misplay Pct		.615

Gardner, the 2010 Fielding Bible Award winner, was recognized a second time in 2011 as the top defensive left fielder in baseball. He is a converted center fielder who still sees a few innings at the position when needed. Gardner has phenomenal range for a left fielder. He will only occasionally misread a ball off the bat or take a bad route to the ball. However, he has the speed to make up for those rare mistakes and still gives himself a chance to make a play. His greatest strength is ranging deep into the left center field gap and making the catch. Gardner has average arm strength but is very accurate with his throws. He gets his body behind the ball when he goes to throw after fielding a grounder or catching a flyball. This helps him prevent the potential advancement of base runners by getting rid of the ball quickly. Gardner on occasion can be overaggressive, leading to a failed dive attempt, an overrun of the play, or a wasted throw after a hit or flyball catch. Gardner should continue to be a perennial Fielding Bible Award contender.

Alex Gordon

	Innings	Runs Saved
2011	1309	20
2009-2011	1795.1	23

	Good Plays	Misplays and Errors
Gordon 2011	31	26
Avg Left Fielder	27	30
Good Play/Misplay Pct		.570

Formerly a below-average fielder at third base, Gordon transitioned to left field in 2010. Much like he did as a hitter, Gordon enjoyed a true breakthrough in 2011 as a fielder to finish among the leaders in Defensive Runs Saved at his position. Gordon's most impressive skill is throwing out base runners, especially those attempting to score from second on a single. One might assume that his arm strength is primarily responsible for his success, but Gordon's skills in recovering shallow hits and quickly releasing accurate throws are even more noteworthy. These abilities allowed Gordon to record 12 base runner kills (assists without a relay), more than twice as many as any other American League left fielder in 2011. Alfonso Soriano had similar success after moving from the infield to left field and his quick release and accurate throws gave him league-leading kills totals for a couple seasons. Let's hope Gordon ages more gracefully than the Cubs' outfielder, on both sides of the ball.

Gerardo Parra

	Innings	Runs Saved
2011	1018	11
2009-2011	2164.1	23

	Good Plays	Misplays and Errors
Parra 2011	31	27
Avg Left Fielder	23	26
Good Play/Misplay Pct		.561

Gerardo Parra is one of the best outfielders that the average fan may not be familiar with. He gets great jumps on the ball and takes great routes on nearly every ball hit to him, which shows in his Defensive Runs Saved. The combination of above-average footspeed and excellent route-running allows Parra to play the huge outfields in the NL West very well. Parra has a strong arm and recorded 10 base runner kills in 2011, leading all National League left fielders.

Carl Crawford

	Innings	Runs Saved
2011	1098.1	-2
2009-2011	3641.1	18

	Good Plays	Misplays and Errors
Crawford 2011	17	22
Avg Left Fielder	22	24
Good Play/Misplay Pct		.462

Crawford, a three-time Fielding Bible Award winner while with Tampa Bay, parlayed his on-base abilities and defensive reputation into a seven-year, $142 million contract with the Boston Red Sox prior to the 2011 season. Crawford makes good reads, has phenomenal range and takes good routes on flyballs. Why, then, did his defense suffer in 2011? In short, he struggled adapting to Fenway's unique left field. The greatest component of Crawford's defensive value is his range, yet much of this factor is taken away playing in front of the Green Monster barely over 300 feet from home. He was visibly intimidated by the wall at times when heading back for flyballs. Crawford still graded above-average on shallow and medium flies, but was -21 on deep balls, -16 of that at Fenway. With time, he will improve his reads and know when to play the ball off the

Left Fielders

wall and when to go for it. Crawford possesses an average throwing arm, ranking in the middle of the pack in OF Arms Runs Saved for left fielders; fortunately he doesn't have to throw very far in such a shallow left field. Now into his thirties and limited by a short left field, it's likely his best defensive seasons are behind him.

Laynce Nix

	Innings	Runs Saved
2011	504.1	6
2009-2011	1331.1	17

	Good Plays	Misplays and Errors
Nix 2011	8	10
Avg Left Fielder	10	11
Good Play/Misplay Pct		.471

Nix was an above-average defensive left fielder for the Nationals in 2011. He also saw time at first base, center field and right field. Nix has decent overall range in left field but really excels at tracking down deep flies. Nix is able to get good jumps on balls due to his ability to read the ball off of the bat. He has above-average arm strength and average accuracy and was one of the best left fielders in baseball at preventing runners from taking the extra base in 2011. Nix has been a solid defender in left field throughout his career, and at age 31, should be able to maintain this performance level for several more seasons at least.

Ryan Raburn

	Innings	Runs Saved
2011	335.2	4
2009-2011	1282	14

	Good Plays	Misplays and Errors
Raburn 2011	11	12
Avg Left Fielder	7	7
Good Play/Misplay Pct		.505

Perhaps it is best to start with Raburn's best defensive trait: his versatility. He is a max-effort player willing to play anywhere in the field. He possesses decent outfield range and average speed. However, he seems to be out of place no matter what his position is. His infield range is below-average, but his defense is hurt most by bobbled and missed grounders. Though better suited as an outfielder, he will occasionally drop a flyball or boot a safe hit. Raburn shows flashes of arm strength, but is plagued by inconsistent throwing accuracy, particularly at second base. In the outfield, his arm has been an asset overall, saving six runs over the past three

seasons. He can be overaggressive at times, however, allowing runners to advance on throws he never should have made.

Tony Gwynn

	Innings	Runs Saved
2011	624.1	12
2009-2011	624.1	12

	Good Plays	Misplays and Errors
Gwynn 2011	17	10
Avg Left Fielder	12	13
Good Play/Misplay Pct		.654

Gwynn has always been an excellent defensive center fielder. It comes as no surprise that he was also excellent in left field in his first year at that position for the Dodgers in 2011. He has great speed and plays deep in the outfield, allowing him to make a number of outstanding plays on the run that would otherwise end up as doubles or triples. He retreats well and is always aware of where the wall is when making the play. Gwynn's ability to track down shallow flies and liners is hurt a bit by playing deep, but his great speed minimizes the damage. And the net effect is positive, as he is giving up a few singles to save extra-base hits. Gwynn's throwing arm plays better in left field than in center, but he has the range, speed and overall skills to be an excellent defender at any outfield position.

Brennan Boesch

	Innings	Runs Saved
2011	424	5
2009-2011	774.1	12

	Good Plays	Misplays and Errors
Boesch 2011	11	11
Avg Left Fielder	10	11
Good Play/Misplay Pct		.526

Boesch was an above-average left fielder this past season. He also saw time in right field for the Tigers. Boesch has average range for a left fielder. He gets good jumps on the ball due to his ability to read the ball off of the bat. As a right fielder, however, he tends to have more difficulty with deep balls. Boesch was able to prevent the advancement of base runners with his above-average arm strength and average accuracy. Boesch can improve the release on his throws, as it can be long at times. He also could work on his footwork when charging groundballs or catching flyballs to get in better position to throw more quickly. Thus far in his career, Boesch has been a much better defender in left field than in right field. With some improvements and more

Left Fielders

playing time, he should be able to become an above-average defender at both corner outfield positions.

Sam Fuld

	Innings	Runs Saved
2011	604.2	9
2009-2011	694	11

	Good Plays	Misplays and Errors
Fuld 2011	30	19
Avg Left Fielder	13	14
Good Play/Misplay Pct		.637

Sam Fuld impressed with his fielding in his first full season in the majors. Fuld covers a great deal of ground with top-tier speed that compensates for his short legs. He is generously listed at 5'10", but has excellent leaping ability and good body control while airborne. Fuld generally takes very good routes to balls, especially those hit to either side of him and reads hits off the wall very instinctively. He does struggle with balls hit over his head, at times turning the wrong way on the ball and losing any chance of making the play. On occasion, Fuld can also be overly overaggressive diving for balls he should play more conservatively. Fuld possesses an average arm, but has excellent footwork which allows him to get into his throwing position very quickly. His throws are accurate, and he has been very effective at preventing runners from taking the extra base. He can field and release the ball very quickly by using a spin move when ranging to his left. He will sometimes misplay hard groundballs when rushing to make a strong throw. Fuld has superior acceleration and timing and often makes plays with his legs and his hustle, rather than his glove and his arm.

Josh Hamilton

	Innings	Runs Saved
2011	709	4
2009-2011	1481.2	11

	Good Plays	Misplays and Errors
Hamilton 2011	19	12
Avg Left Fielder	13	15
Good Play/Misplay Pct		.638

Hamilton has been quoted as saying he loves and prefers center field, but the Rangers believe playing him in left will keep him healthy and save wear and tear on his body. It will probably also save the Rangers some runs. Over the last two seasons, almost 75 percent of his innings defensively came in left field with the rest in center. In that time, he has saved 11 runs defensively in left and 2 in center. He reads the ball off the bat well and takes good routes. He also has a very strong and accurate arm and is aggressive coming in on grounders to make throws. Hamilton gives a great effort and is known for courageous defense. However, he has missed a number of games in the outfield as a result of three separate injuries from crashing into a wall while making a catch. Much of his defensive value is dependent upon his health. When at full strength, Hamilton can be a serviceable center fielder or an outstanding left fielder. However, when he is limping around the field dealing with injuries, Hamilton can still be an asset in left field but is a liability in center. Hamilton is a legit five-tool player and hopefully in the future he can avoid injury while continuing to show off his defensive ability.

Michael Brantley

	Innings	Runs Saved
2011	558.1	8
2009-2011	684.2	10

	Good Plays	Misplays and Errors
Brantley 2011	10	10
Avg Left Fielder	11	12
Good Play/Misplay Pct		.526

Brantley played the majority of his innings in left field instead of center field for the first time in his career and seemed better suited for the less-demanding defensive position. Brantley plays the ball well off the bat and takes excellent routes, especially laterally, giving him an advantage on balls hit at a lower trajectory. On tougher plays, Brantley prefers sliding to diving; he usually won't let the ball get by him when he does this, but he's not going to make as many spectacular catches as some of his counterparts. Brantley hasn't been able to cover the deep outfield well, especially in center field and will often let the ball get over his head for extra bases. Since he's proven to be more capable of charging and sliding than making an over-the-shoulder grab, he may benefit from playing deeper. In 2011, Brantley showed off his accurate arm, saving two runs on throws playing left.

Kyle Blanks

	Innings	Runs Saved
2011	300	7
2009-2011	663	10

	Good Plays	Misplays and Errors
Blanks 2011	5	5
Avg Left Fielder	6	7
Good Play/Misplay Pct		.526

Left Fielders

Travis Snider

	Innings	Runs Saved
2011	367	3
2009-2011	1236	10

	Good Plays	Misplays and Errors
Snider 2011	8	8
Avg Left Fielder	7	8
Good Play/Misplay Pct		.526

Despite limited playing time in 2011, Travis Snider has shown that he can be at least a league-average left fielder if not slightly better than average. Snider has good enough speed for a left fielder and generally takes good routes on flyballs. He struggled with fielding base hits cleanly and with flyball routes in the first few weeks of the season, but his defense was much improved after he was recalled from the minors in July. Overall, he won't thrill with his range, but his best attribute is his throwing arm. Snider has done a good job improving his overall arm strength and accuracy and in the past three years he has been one of baseball's best left fielders at preventing runners from taking the extra base.

Matt Holliday

	Innings	Runs Saved
2011	990.2	-1
2009-2011	3685.2	9

	Good Plays	Misplays and Errors
Holliday 2011	10	16
Avg Left Fielder	19	21
Good Play/Misplay Pct		.410

Matt Holliday had a down year in left field in 2011 after three straight years of solid defensive numbers. He cost the Cardinals one run defensively in 2011 after having saved 15 runs over the previous three seasons. base runners were not afraid to test Holliday's arm, as teams took extra bases without fear and were usually successful. Holliday's arm has never been his calling card, as he has lost his teams 21 runs on throws over the course of his career. Holliday's best attribute this year was his ability to track down balls hit over his head, which also was his biggest strength in 2010. However, his overall range this year was lacking compared to past seasons, possibly due in part to a nagging quad injury which plagued Holliday for part of the season.

Ryan Braun

	Innings	Runs Saved
2011	1250	3
2009-2011	3940	8

	Good Plays	Misplays and Errors
Braun 2011	17	21
Avg Left Fielder	24	27
Good Play/Misplay Pct		.474

Ryan Braun exhibited a strong arm and above-average range in left field for the Brewers in 2011, but struggled mightily to prevent the advancement of base runners. Originally a third baseman, Braun struggles going back on balls over his head in left field. As a result, he plays deeper than most left fielders. Consequently, he saves many potential extra-base hits at the expense of a few singles which fall in front of him. Thanks to the former third baseman's reactions, he does get great jumps off the bat. Braun also impressed with his arm, throwing out five base runners from left field with surprising arm strength and excellent accuracy. Braun's deep positioning may have been part of the reason base runners ran all over him in 2011. He did record five base runner kills, but allowed runners to take the extra base over 45 percent of the time, one of the worst rates among all left fielders in 2011. It was not a one-year phenomenon, as Braun has cost his team runs on throws for each of the past three seasons, totaling 12 runs lost overall.

Jose Tabata

	Innings	Runs Saved
2011	626	3
2009-2011	1397.1	8

	Good Plays	Misplays and Errors
Tabata 2011	8	12
Avg Left Fielder	12	14
Good Play/Misplay Pct		.426

Jose Tabata was limited due to injuries in 2011, but he still showed above-average range in left field. Tabata has the speed to chase down hard-hit balls and balls in the gap. His weaknesses are his arm accuracy and decision-making. Teams were not afraid to run against him and Tabata too often would make overaggressive throws, allowing base runners to advance unnecessarily.

Left Fielders

Martin Prado

	Innings	Runs Saved
2011	854	7
2009-2011	854	7

	Good Plays	Misplays and Errors
Prado 2011	15	13
Avg Left Fielder	16	18
Good Play/Misplay Pct		.562

Patrolling left field regularly for the first time, Prado definitely showed he could transition seamlessly. He played an above-average left field this past season despite having only played 23 innings there prior to 2011. He easily handled medium flyballs and excelled on reaching deeper flies. With a strong third baseman's arm, Prado was able to prevent runners from advancing and also threw a good number of them out, recording six base runner kills. Prado has proven to be a solid defender at both left field and third base.

Juan Rivera

	Innings	Runs Saved
2011	414.2	3
2009-2011	2139.2	7

	Good Plays	Misplays and Errors
Rivera 2011	4	7
Avg Left Fielder	7	8
Good Play/Misplay Pct		.388

Rivera was an average defensive left fielder in 2011. He also saw time at both first base and right field for the Dodgers and Blue Jays. Rivera has below-average range for a left fielder, but he was above-average going back on the ball despite not having great speed or quickness. He does this by getting good reads on the ball off of the bat. Rivera has average arm strength and accuracy. Rivera could improve his hands and his effort. There were a couple instances on which a flyball hit off of his glove, and he was unable to make the play. Also, he let a couple of balls fall in for hits when he might have had a chance at making a play with a stronger effort. Rivera has been inconsistent defensively throughout his career and had a particularly bad year in left field in 2010 (-12 runs saved). But he came back in 2011, and at age 33 he should be able to continue as an average defender for at least the near future.

Fred Lewis

	Innings	Runs Saved
2011	315.2	7
2009-2011	1631.2	5

	Good Plays	Misplays and Errors
Lewis 2011	8	3
Avg Left Fielder	7	8
Good Play/Misplay Pct		.748

Lewis is prone to taking some bad routes causing the occasional missed catch, so he certainly doesn't pass the eye test defensively in left field. He's had a tendency throughout his career of muffing easy plays, leading to the common misconception that he's a poor fielder. However, he uses his speed and athleticism to make up for his deficiencies. Lewis tracks down a lot of balls that other corner outfielders would not get to, making him a plus defender in left field. Lewis ranks in the top ten among left fielders in Plus/Minus Runs Saved over the past three seasons. Given his plus speed and range, Lewis has seen some action in center and right field previously in his career, but his lack of a strong throwing arm make him best suited to left field. Though Lewis often makes it adventurous, his speed makes up for some mistakes and the bottom line is he usually gets the job done.

Carlos Gonzalez

	Innings	Runs Saved
2011	518	2
2009-2011	1284.2	5

	Good Plays	Misplays and Errors
Gonzalez 2011	17	9
Avg Left Fielder	10	11
Good Play/Misplay Pct		.677

Gonzalez can play all three outfield spots, but the Rockies play him primarily in left field. He is a fluid athlete who can range to either side and will give up his body to make the tough catch. Gonzalez saved eight runs in the outfield for the Rockies in 2011: two in left field, two in center and four in right. He has a rocket for an arm and runners rarely test him on the base paths. Despite having the physical ability to play center field, the Rockies have played him mostly in left field because they have another very capable center fielder in Dexter Fowler. His main issue at this point is that he tries to gamble too often, which nets him some spectacular plays, but also results in a bunch of defensive misplays. This is especially evident in plays at the wall, where he recorded six defensive misplays in 2011 for failing to anticipate

Left Fielders

the wall, meaning he went to the wall trying to make a catch but failed, allowing the ball to bounce back past him and giving away extra bases.

arm strength leaves a lot to be desired. Coaches and batters know this about Murphy, often test him and rarely regret it.

Desmond Jennings

	Innings	Runs Saved
2011	467	3
2009-2011	482	4

	Good Plays	Misplays and Errors
Jennings 2011	13	9
Avg Left Fielder	8	9
Good Play/Misplay Pct		.616

Nolan Reimold

	Innings	Runs Saved
2011	593.2	-2
2009-2011	1501	4

	Good Plays	Misplays and Errors
Reimold 2011	10	17
Avg Left Fielder	14	15
Good Play/Misplay Pct		.395

Carlos Peguero

	Innings	Runs Saved
2011	325.2	3
2009-2011	325.2	3

	Good Plays	Misplays and Errors
Peguero 2011	9	8
Avg Left Fielder	6	7
Good Play/Misplay Pct		.556

David Murphy

	Innings	Runs Saved
2011	556.1	1
2009-2011	1947.2	3

	Good Plays	Misplays and Errors
Murphy 2011	8	8
Avg Left Fielder	11	12
Good Play/Misplay Pct		.526

Much of Murphy's ability in left field can be attributed to his positioning. Because he has some trouble retreating on deep flyballs, backpedaling instead of running in full stride, Murphy tends to play a little deeper than other left fielders. However, the result is that he saves some doubles and triples at the cost of some short flies and liners dropping in front of him. The net effect is positive. Murphy has saved an estimated 20 bases making catches on deep balls at the cost of about 4 bases missing shallow ones over the last three years. His

Alex Presley

	Innings	Runs Saved
2011	406	2
2009-2011	417	2

	Good Plays	Misplays and Errors
Presley 2011	7	9
Avg Left Fielder	8	9
Good Play/Misplay Pct		.464

J.D. Martinez

	Innings	Runs Saved
2011	436.1	2
2009-2011	436.1	2

	Good Plays	Misplays and Errors
Martinez 2011	13	8
Avg Left Fielder	9	10
Good Play/Misplay Pct		.644

Jason Bay

	Innings	Runs Saved
2011	1053.1	-3
2009-2011	3153.1	2

	Good Plays	Misplays and Errors
Bay 2011	26	16
Avg Left Fielder	21	23
Good Play/Misplay Pct		.644

Jason Bay is best summed up as a technically solid fielder who is past his physical prime. Bay has not often rated as a plus fielder, but he hasn't hurt the Mets too much in the last two years. His best asset is his hands; he rarely makes mistakes on routine plays, which keeps his error total very low. On flyballs, Bay has limited range. He is at his best moving laterally and charging the ball, but in 2011 he tended to struggle on deep flies in the expansive Citi Field. His range is hurt mostly by his lack of athleticism which has waned with age, leaving him with a slower than average first step and top speed. Bay's arm is also nothing to write home about, as he throws with below-average strength and has a slow release.

Left Fielders

Luke Scott

	Innings	Runs Saved
2011	330.2	3
2009-2011	632.2	1

	Good Plays	Misplays and Errors
Scott 2011	5	5
Avg Left Fielder	7	8
Good Play/Misplay Pct		.526

Used primarily as a designated hitter the last several years, Luke Scott was forced back into a regular role in the outfield in 2011 with the arrival of Vladimir Guerrero. However, he only saw 64 games of action before shoulder surgery caused him to miss the rest of the season. Nevertheless, Scott showed that he can still be a serviceable left fielder when healthy. He appears to read the ball well off the bat, giving him a good first step that helps offset his below-average speed. His arm, though not a strength, is fairly accurate. Scott flashed the leather on deep flyballs several times this year, even taking away a couple home runs from opposing batters.

Michael Morse

	Innings	Runs Saved
2011	421	0
2009-2011	430.2	0

	Good Plays	Misplays and Errors
Morse 2011	7	8
Avg Left Fielder	8	9
Good Play/Misplay Pct		.493

Pat Burrell

	Innings	Runs Saved
2011	349.2	0
2009-2011	983.2	0

	Good Plays	Misplays and Errors
Burrell 2011	3	7
Avg Left Fielder	5	5
Good Play/Misplay Pct		.323

Burrell didn't earn the nickname "Pat the Bat" just by his play at the plate. He also earned it because that's the only area of his game that truly shines. Burrell is incredibly slow for an outfielder and has next to no range in left field. In fact, during a game in 2011, Tim Lincecum had a no-hitter through six innings, and Burrell asked to be taken out of the game for a defensive replacement, acknowledging his defensive shortcomings. On the plus side, Burrell has a strong arm and can make a crisp accurate throw to the bases without exerting himself too much. He also does a nice job of taking efficient routes to flyballs.

Shelley Duncan

	Innings	Runs Saved
2011	253.1	-6
2009-2011	562.1	0

	Good Plays	Misplays and Errors
Duncan 2011	4	8
Avg Left Fielder	5	6
Good Play/Misplay Pct		.357

Chris Heisey

	Innings	Runs Saved
2011	393	-2
2009-2011	489.2	-1

	Good Plays	Misplays and Errors
Heisey 2011	3	11
Avg Left Fielder	7	8
Good Play/Misplay Pct		.233

Jerry Sands

	Innings	Runs Saved
2011	288	-2
2009-2011	288	-2

	Good Plays	Misplays and Errors
Sands 2011	5	9
Avg Left Fielder	6	7
Good Play/Misplay Pct		.382

Jerry Sands is a young, adequate corner outfielder. He possesses only average speed, which contributes to his overall subpar range. He can struggle to get good reads and jumps on balls, resulting in poor routes and missed catches. However, Sands can cover for some of his defensive shortcomings with his impressive arm strength. He wields a cannon arm with solid accuracy that would be a plus in right field and should give runners pause when Sands has it loaded up in left.

Left Fielders

Corey Patterson

	Innings	Runs Saved
2011	396.2	-4
2009-2011	863.1	-2

	Good Plays	Misplays and Errors
Patterson 2011	10	7
Avg Left Fielder	8	9
Good Play/Misplay Pct		.614

Patterson was an average defensive outfielder, playing all three positions, in a part-time role for the Cardinals and Blue Jays in 2011. He reads the ball well off the bat and consequently gets a good jump on most hits in his direction. On occasion he will miss a dive attempt, mishandle a ball after a hit, or overrun a play due to his overaggressiveness. Patterson's throwing arm is nothing special but will neither hurt nor help his team much. He will continue to provide value to a club with his ability to play all of the outfield positions.

Cody Ross

	Innings	Runs Saved
2011	530	-5
2009-2011	620.1	-2

	Good Plays	Misplays and Errors
Ross 2011	8	11
Avg Left Fielder	10	11
Good Play/Misplay Pct		.447

Ross was once a reliable option in center field, but in 2011 he was below-average at every outfield position. He is not a good fit for right field because he has a below-average arm. He does have a dependable glove and rarely mishandles the ball. He is probably best suited for left field, where his subpar throwing arm and limited range are not as detrimental as they would be in the other outfield spots. Ross has struggled with the difficult, high outfield walls in his home parks throughout his career. In Florida he had to deal with the "Teal Monster" in left field, and in San Francisco he had to handle the 24-foot high wall in right field, made up of a mixture of brick and chain-link fencing. His 15 defensive misplays over the past three seasons for "failing to anticipate the wall" ranks second in all of baseball. Ross signed with the Red Sox in the offseason and is expected to see time in left field, where he will have to deal with his ultimate nightmare: the Green Monster.

Josh Willingham

	Innings	Runs Saved
2011	829.1	0
2009-2011	2401.1	-3

	Good Plays	Misplays and Errors
Willingham 2011	14	11
Avg Left Fielder	16	18
Good Play/Misplay Pct		.586

The former catcher moved to left field prior to the 2006 season, but his defense out there is passable at best. His range and arm strength are below par and Willingham's already limited mobility continues to decrease with age. He has a middling throwing arm for a left fielder, consistently ranking around the middle of the pack in runs saved on throws. As he is not a natural outfielder, Willingham has been known to make some mental mistakes in the field, allowing runners to advance due to his inattentiveness. Willingham has also spent time on the disabled list in three of the last four seasons, making durability a real question mark.

Rene Tosoni

	Innings	Runs Saved
2011	321	-4
2009-2011	321	-4

	Good Plays	Misplays and Errors
Tosoni 2011	9	7
Avg Left Fielder	8	9
Good Play/Misplay Pct		.588

Ryan Ludwick

	Innings	Runs Saved
2011	1005	-5
2009-2011	1018	-4

	Good Plays	Misplays and Errors
Ludwick 2011	22	18
Avg Left Fielder	18	20
Good Play/Misplay Pct		.576

Ryan Ludwick doesn't excel enough in any one area to set himself apart, but he also doesn't lack enough anywhere to be heavily criticized. Ludwick will never be known for his acceleration or top speed, but he possesses good enough instincts to get good reads on flyballs. He positions himself well and excels at taking direct routes to the ball. Recently, Ludwick has done his best work on shallow flyballs on which he has displayed decent athleticism in making diving catches. He rounds out his game with decent arm strength and good accuracy; though he lacks the footwork to quickly get into throwing

Left Fielders

position. 2011 was a down year defensively for Ludwick, but he has bounced back from tough years in the past and performed much better the following seasons.

Eric Young

	Innings	Runs Saved
2011	269.1	-4
2009-2011	334.1	-6

	Good Plays	Misplays and Errors
Young 2011	4	6
Avg Left Fielder	5	6
Good Play/Misplay Pct		.426

Austin Kearns

	Innings	Runs Saved
2011	264.1	-4
2009-2011	966.1	-8

	Good Plays	Misplays and Errors
Kearns 2011	6	6
Avg Left Fielder	5	6
Good Play/Misplay Pct		.526

Kearns was a below-average defensive left fielder in 2011. He also played some right field for the Indians this past season, a position where Kearns once excelled. Now into his thirties, Kearns has below-average range for either position. He has difficulty with flyballs that are hit deep. Kearns can struggle at times with his reads of the ball off of the bat. He can also improve the routes he takes to the ball, as they occasionally will cost him an opportunity at making a play. Kearns was average throwing the baseball this past season. Kearns can improve his throwing by working on getting his body in better position when he goes to throw. Kearns' biggest problem the last two years has been his hitting, which has been way below what is normally acceptable for a corner outfielder. Now that his defense has slipped as well, Kearns may be on his way out of the league.

Vernon Wells

	Innings	Runs Saved
2011	930.2	-8
2009-2011	930.2	-8

	Good Plays	Misplays and Errors
Wells 2011	14	20
Avg Left Fielder	20	22
Good Play/Misplay Pct		.438

Vernon Wells manned left field with the Angels in 2011 for the first time in his career. After performing at a below-average level in center the three previous years,

Wells did not fare any better in left. Wells tends to get pretty good reads on flies and takes direct routes, excelling especially at chasing down deep-hit balls. His range extends furthest on those balls hit over his head, but he's not quick enough to have plus range in the gaps. Wells' biggest downfall is shaky hands—he is too often unable to cleanly field both flies and grounders, leading to extra bases and runs given away. Wells is also a bit overaggressive with his throws, often unsuccessfully trying to cut down a lead runner while the trailer advances.

Eric Thames

	Innings	Runs Saved
2011	456.1	-9
2009-2011	456.1	-9

	Good Plays	Misplays and Errors
Thames 2011	10	14
Avg Left Fielder	8	9
Good Play/Misplay Pct		.443

Felix Pie

	Innings	Runs Saved
2011	349.2	-11
2009-2011	1202	-12

	Good Plays	Misplays and Errors
Pie 2011	7	14
Avg Left Fielder	9	10
Good Play/Misplay Pct		.357

Carlos Lee

	Innings	Runs Saved
2011	645.1	7
2009-2011	3014	-17

	Good Plays	Misplays and Errors
Lee 2011	20	11
Avg Left Fielder	12	14
Good Play/Misplay Pct		.669

From 2005-2010, Lee cost his teams a total of 45 runs with his poor defensive play in left field. In 2011, the Astros finally moved him out of a full-time role there, and he split time between left field and first base. As he transitioned into becoming a full-time first baseman, something surprising happened: according to our numbers, Lee played his best outfield defense since 2004. How did this happen? Most likely it has something to do with his smaller sample size of innings in left field and the possibility that Lee's legs were kept fresher throughout the year by not facing the rigors of playing the outfield every day. Lee also made more Good

Left Fielders

Fielding Plays (20) in his 645 innings in left field than he did in 1,096 innings (15) there last year. Given his veteran status and advancing age, Lee knows his capabilities and does not over-exert himself in the field. He will catch what he gets to. The combination of Houston's small left field and Lee's reduced range really limits his opportunities for mistakes. He possesses a below-average arm, in terms of both strength and accuracy, but did manage to record six base runner kills during his limited time in the outfield in 2011. Lee spent a substantial amount of time at first base in 2011. His gracelessness in the outfield carried over to his play at first. Lee can look overmatched at times at first base, but overall the early returns were positive. Time will tell if Lee can maintain that level of performance.

Juan Pierre

	Innings	Runs Saved
2011	1365	-11
2009-2011	3348.2	-19

	Good Plays	Misplays and Errors
Pierre 2011	23	29
Avg Left Fielder	26	29
Good Play/Misplay Pct		.468

As he has aged, Juan Pierre has become one of the worst left fielders in the game. He has no throwing arm to speak of, and base runners take advantage at will. He routinely takes bad routes to the baseball, and he doesn't seem to see the ball well off the bat. He gets to the shallow balls okay, but struggles tremendously tracking deep balls. Speed is the only aspect of his game that keeps him in left field, but as he ages he gets worse. Though Pierre was once a good center fielder, he now lacks a nose for the ball and the instincts it takes to play even an average left field.

Jonny Gomes

	Innings	Runs Saved
2011	550.1	0
2009-2011	1840.1	-22

	Good Plays	Misplays and Errors
Gomes 2011	7	10
Avg Left Fielder	11	12
Good Play/Misplay Pct		.438

Between his 2005 debut and 2010, Gomes did almost nothing well defensively; he never finished a season with positive runs saved in left field or right field during that span. In 2010, Dusty Baker and the Reds looked past Gomes' defensive shortcomings and allowed him to play the majority of his team's games in the field for the first time in his career. With the increased playing time, Gomes cost the Reds 21 runs in left field and established his candidacy as one of the worst outfielders in baseball. Since then, Gomes turned 30 and: a) found inspiration to tidy the appearance of his Bill James Online profile, b) visited his local library for references on defensive fundamentals and/or c) had enough good fortune over about 600 innings to fool us into thinking that he might not be so bad after all. If we are going to consider the possibility that he has what it takes to follow up on his improved defensive performance of 2011, we'll first have to buy into his reduction of misplays. Gomes had all sorts of problems in 2010: bad routes, wild throws, missed catches, fear of walls, etc. He managed to do away with most of that last season, rarely embarrassing himself for reasons other than his own aggressiveness. (He still has the propensities to dive for anything close and ignore the cutoff man.) Furthermore, we'd have to trust his decision to play deep even against hitters of modest power. Gomes was able to cut down on extra-base hits and make some great catches deep in left field last year, which went a long way in his plus/minus makeover. All things considered, Gomes looked respectable enough in 2011 to provide counterpoint to a disastrous 2010. We don't have enough evidence yet to be confident that he's become truly adequate in the field, but he's at least given critics a reason to quiet down.

Delmon Young

	Innings	Runs Saved
2011	994.1	-3
2009-2011	3078.2	-24

	Good Plays	Misplays and Errors
Young 2011	12	20
Avg Left Fielder	20	22
Good Play/Misplay Pct		.400

Delmon Young improved in our ratings from 2010 to 2011, but you wouldn't necessarily be able to tell from watching him play. His short strides make it difficult to cover a lot of ground and he doesn't always take the most direct path to the ball. He has the ability to make plays look tougher than they really are as a result. He will often reach the ball just in time, either capping off a catch with a little hop, or alternatively having it drop right off his glove. He plays deep to make tracking down these hard flyballs easier, but it opens the door for hits to fall in front of him. Despite the improvement, he remains a below-average left fielder.

Left Fielders

Logan Morrison

	Innings	Runs Saved
2011	1021.1	-26
2009-2011	1565.1	-31

	Good Plays	Misplays and Errors
Morrison 2011	17	47
Avg Left Fielder	20	22
Good Play/Misplay Pct		.287

Morrison's first full season in the outfield was a struggle, to put it mildly. The converted first baseman had to learn on the job and the evidence is clear in his defensive performance this year, as he cost the Marlins 26 runs defensively, the worst total among all left fielders in baseball. Morrison's wide range of misplays and indecisiveness this year were evidence of a player who didn't have outfield experience. He also doesn't get great reads off the bat due to inexperience and this leads to many other difficulties outfielders can encounter when chasing down balls in the air.

Raul Ibanez

	Innings	Runs Saved
2011	1196.2	-23
2009-2011	3614.1	-36

	Good Plays	Misplays and Errors
Ibanez 2011	17	23
Avg Left Fielder	21	23
Good Play/Misplay Pct		.451

Ibanez has been a well below-average left fielder for half a decade now. He has cost the Mariners and Phillies 62 runs with his defensive play in those five years. Prior to that, he wasn't bad with 24 runs saved in the previous four years. Ibanez has well below-average range, and he can struggle at times reading the ball off of the bat. This will cause him to break the wrong way or take a bad route to the ball, potentially costing his team an out. His lack of athleticism is especially evident when he is tracking deep flies, as he often cannot reach them or is only able to get a piece of his glove on balls most left fielders would catch. Ibanez has below-average arm strength and his accuracy is average. He gets his body in a good position to throw when charging groundballs or catching flyballs. However, Ibanez's decision-making has cost him, as far too often he has attempted to throw runners out at home or third in vain, allowing the trail runners to advance. Ibanez would be better suited for a DH role at this point in his career.

Alfonso Soriano

	Innings	Runs Saved
2011	1007	-9
2009-2011	3122.2	-37

	Good Plays	Misplays and Errors
Soriano 2011	6	29
Avg Left Fielder	18	20
Good Play/Misplay Pct		.187

Following a move from second base to the outfield, Soriano rated above-average in his first three seasons in left field. As an outfielder, Soriano was among the best defenders in baseball when it came to throwing out runners. In his first three seasons in the outfield, Soriano recorded 42 base runner kills. Since 2009, though, Soriano's defense overall has been poor, and the 37 runs he's lost defensively for the Cubs over the last three seasons ranks last among left fielders. He has extremely limited range, struggles with hard-hit balls and tends to take poor routes. Soriano was known early in his outfield career for a trademark hop upon catching flyballs, which often caused lapses in concentration and led to errors. He's all but eliminated this in the past few seasons, however. base runners have become less apt to run on Soriano after his early success throwing them out and he has only recorded 13 kills in the past three seasons. Soriano still provides some defensive value by preventing baserunners from advancing, but not hearly as much as when he was throwing out runners left and right. Soriano had an unwarranted reputation as a poor left fielder following the initial move from second base, but he has definitely begun to fit that description in recent seasons.

Center Fielders Evaluations

Year	League	Gold Glove Winners	Should Have Been
2003	AL	Mike Cameron Torii Hunter	Mike Cameron Torii Hunter
	NL	Andruw Jones Jim Edmonds	Andruw Jones Jim Edmonds
2004	AL	Torii Hunter Vernon Wells	Torii Hunter Vernon Wells
	NL	Andruw Jones Steve Finley Jim Edmonds	Andruw Jones Steve Finley
2005	AL	Torii Hunter Vernon Wells	Torii Hunter Aaron Rowand
	NL	Andruw Jones Jim Edmonds	Andruw Jones Willy Taveras
2006	AL	Torii Hunter Vernon Wells	Vernon Wells
	NL	Andruw Jones Carlos Beltran Mike Cameron	Andruw Jones Carlos Beltran Willy Taveras
2007	AL	Torii Hunter Grady Sizemore Ichiro Suzuki	Ichiro Suzuki Coco Crisp
	NL	Andruw Jones Carlos Beltran Aaron Rowand	Andruw Jones Carlos Beltran
2008	AL	Torii Hunter Grady Sizemore	Carlos Gomez
	NL	Carlos Beltran Shane Victorino Nate McLouth	Carlos Beltran Shane Victorino
2009	AL	Torii Hunter Adam Jones	Franklin Gutierrez

	NL	Michael Bourn Shane Victorino Matt Kemp	Michael Bourn
2010	AL	Franklin Gutierrez	Austin Jackson
	NL	Michael Bourn Carlos Gonzalez Shane Victorino	Michael Bourn
2011	AL	Jacoby Ellsbury	Austin Jackson
	NL	Matt Kemp	Chris Young

My Personal Ratings

Top Ten

1 Austin Jackson, Det
2 Franklin Gutierrez, Sea
3 Peter Bourjos, LAA
4 Carlos Gomez, Mil
5 Chris Young, Ari

Bottom Five

26 Melky Cabrera, SF
27 Grady Sizemore, Cle
28 Jordan Schafer, Atl
29 Nate McLouth, Atl
30 Chris Coghlan, Mia

Player teams based on transactions through February 1, 2012

Center Fielders

Austin Jackson

	Innings	Runs Saved
2011	1264	29
2009-2011	2520.1	42

	Good Plays	Misplays and Errors
Jackson 2011	20	17
Avg Center Fielder	24	27
Good Play/Misplay Pct		.575

Austin Jackson has proven to be an absolute vacuum in Comerica Park's expansive outfield. His outstanding fielding ability was recognized by the Fielding Bible Award voting panel, as Jackson won the award for the first time in his career in 2011. Jackson possesses top speed and acceleration that are matched by few others in MLB. He combines his speed with excellent instincts and flyball recognition to display elite range in center, tracking down numerous balls that would likely otherwise end up as extra-base hits. Jackson doesn't have the strongest arm, but he uses his speed and good footwork to get into ideal throwing position quickly, lining up accurate throws. Jackson's only real weakness is that he'll occasionally turn a single into a double by overrunning the play or not fielding a batted ball cleanly. This is likely a concentration issue that he should eliminate as he continues to grow as an elite fielder.

Franklin Gutierrez

	Innings	Runs Saved
2011	763	10
2009-2011	3393.2	42

	Good Plays	Misplays and Errors
Gutierrez 2011	20	6
Avg Center Fielder	15	17
Good Play/Misplay Pct		.793

Franklin Gutierrez is the only player in the history of the Fielding Bible Awards to win at two different positions. He was awarded in 2008 for his defense in right field, and then took home another award in 2009 after moving over to center field. He is not incredibly quick, but has elite range because of his tremendous instincts in center field. He takes great routes to balls in the air and has an excellent understanding of defensive positioning. He has good wall awareness, with an innate ability to discern when to attempt a catch and when to play it off the wall. Gutierrez has perfect timing and above-average leaping ability, which makes for a deadly combination when diving for balls or leaping at the wall. Throwing-wise, he is about average. Runners took more liberties with Franklin last year, but he nailed five of

them on kills. He is very good about not wasting a throw when there's no play to be made.

Michael Bourn

	Innings	Runs Saved
2011	1359	-3
2009-2011	3874.1	38

	Good Plays	Misplays and Errors
Bourn 2011	16	26
Avg Center Fielder	25	29
Good Play/Misplay Pct		.415

In 2010 Bourn took home a Fielding Bible Award for his efforts patrolling the spacious center field at Minute Maid Park. However, he saw his numbers drop significantly in 2011. Bourn did well tracking down balls hit hard to the deep part of the park, but less so on balls to shallow center field where a more immediate reaction is required. Obviously blessed with great speed, Bourn was caught a few times breaking in the wrong direction off contact, allowing those balls to drop for hits. Still, he has shown an ability to make all of those plays in the past, and takes clear direct paths to his spot once he gets going. He also had a few instances when he slipped or overran the ball, situations that aren't necessarily predictive but affected his ratings nonetheless. Players can have down years defensively just like they do at the plate. Based on his track record of success and strong abilities, a resurgence would appear to be likely for the speedster.

Chris Young

	Innings	Runs Saved
2011	1373.1	20
2009-2011	3743.2	32

	Good Plays	Misplays and Errors
Young 2011	23	18
Avg Center Fielder	26	29
Good Play/Misplay Pct		.595

Who are the best center fielders in the game? Chris Young has firmly put himself in the conversation. Showing outstanding range to all fields, Young is excellent in getting to the deep ball. He has great footwork, allowing him to get great jumps on the ball and to take good routes. He was second among all center fielders with 20 runs saved in 2011. The one thing lacking with Young is his arm, as he had only one baserunner kill in 2011. However, he compensates for this by making smart throws, not recklessly throwing behind runners or having many wasted throws. Young

Center Fielders

has put himself on the map, and a future Fielding Bible Award could be in the cards.

Bourjos' immediate impact on the game, check out Mark Simon's article reprinted on page 39.

Carlos Gomez

	Innings	Runs Saved
2011	569	15
2009-2011	2012.1	25

	Good Plays	Misplays and Errors
Gomez 2011	22	16
Avg Center Fielder	11	13
Good Play/Misplay Pct		.613

Gomez was a tremendous defensive center fielder for the Brewers in 2011 despite sharing playing time. Gomez is a big, athletic outfielder with big-time speed, both contributing to his great range in center field. He reads the ball well off of the bat and therefore gets a good jump on the ball. At times he will miss an opportunity to make a play because of a bad route. Gomez also can improve his decision-making on balls hit to the wall. There were instances in which he would be too aggressive and allow the ball to get by him, costing his team an extra base. He features plus arm strength for a center fielder. Over the past two seasons, Gomez has really done a good job of preventing runners from taking the extra base, getting his body behind every throw. Gomez has been one of the best defensive center fielders in baseball over his career. If his bat could keep him in the lineup, he'd be a perennial contender for the Fielding Bible Award.

Peter Bourjos

	Innings	Runs Saved
2011	1269.1	12
2009-2011	1719	25

	Good Plays	Misplays and Errors
Bourjos 2011	29	23
Avg Center Fielder	22	26
Good Play/Misplay Pct		.592

Bourjos has quickly evolved into one of the game's best center fielders. He has good range, gets an amazing first step at the crack of the bat and handles balls all over the outfield, shallow, medium and deep. His speed plays a big role in his success and allows him to make up for any missteps he might make. In addition to good range, Bourjos increases his defensive value with a great arm. Bourjos has been particularly adept at preventing runners from taking the extra base. His arm strength, combined with the baseball IQ to make smart throws to the proper bases, make him a complete outfielder. For more on

Curtis Granderson

	Innings	Runs Saved
2011	1348	-6
2009-2011	3852.1	17

	Good Plays	Misplays and Errors
Granderson 2011	30	22
Avg Center Fielder	24	28
Good Play/Misplay Pct	·	.611

Curtis Granderson had a down year in the field in 2011 after establishing himself as an above-average fielder in previous years. For some reason, despite elite speed and athleticism, Granderson struggled to make good reads on balls in 2011. He took an abnormally high number of bad routes on flyballs in addition to breaking in the wrong direction on numerous occasions, costing him several opportunities to convert outs. On the plus side, Granderson, who has never had a very strong arm, tends to make good decisions with his throws. He was very accurate and kept runners at bay at an above-average rate. Look for Granderson to bounce back in 2012 because he still has the physical skill set to perform at a high level.

Cameron Maybin

	Innings	Runs Saved
2011	1173	15
2009-2011	2223.1	15

	Good Plays	Misplays and Errors
Maybin 2011	27	26
Avg Center Fielder	22	25
Good Play/Misplay Pct		.545

Cameron Maybin is capable of making any play, regardless of difficulty, and making it look easy. His speed is the source of his fantastic range, which makes him a natural fit for Petco Park. He moves fluidly and breaks well on flyballs. He has strong natural instincts and is not afraid to be aggressive going after a ball. This aggressiveness will occasionally get the better of him. The result is that he'll misplay balls hit to the wall more than most, aggressively ranging back, thinking he can make the play. By the time he realizes he can't get there the ball then bounds back towards the infield allowing runners to advance. Another consequence of his aggressiveness is that he'll often misplay a hit charging in on a ball he hopes to catch, but if he doesn't get there it turns a single into a double. He can occasionally cover for these miscues with highlight-reel plays, but these must be remedied for him to continue to mature into an outstanding center fielder. Maybin has a strong arm, but not the results that come with that. His accuracy betrays him at times, and because of that runners will challenge him on the basepaths. However, if this skill is fully honed, he will be a threat to advancing runners for many years.

Angel Pagan

	Innings	Runs Saved
2011	1045	-8
2009-2011	2343.2	15

	Good Plays	Misplays and Errors
Pagan 2011	17	36
Avg Center Fielder	21	25
Good Play/Misplay Pct		.352

Pagan seemed to take a step back defensively in 2011 after two very good years in center field with the Mets. He really struggled with balls hit to medium depth this past year, as he had difficulty taking the correct routes on balls. He showed flashes of his former self by occasionally taking good angles to cut off extra bases and making great catches on shallow flyballs. Pagan's biggest weakness, though, is his tendency to misplay hits, thus allowing runners to take extra bases. He ranked near the bottom in runs saved among center fielders in this category over the past three years. With his speed and history of success, there is no reason why Pagan cannot rebound in the future.

Coco Crisp

	Innings	Runs Saved
2011	1134.1	1
2009-2011	2171.1	13

	Good Plays	Misplays and Errors
Crisp 2011	26	17
Avg Center Fielder	21	24
Good Play/Misplay Pct		.638

As he creeps up in age, Crisp is becoming an average defensive center fielder. Crisp is a speedy outfielder who can cover a lot of ground with his above-average range. He is able to get a good jump on the ball because of his ability to read the ball off of the bat. Last season, Crisp had some difficulty with balls that he was able to get a glove on but was unable to catch, allowing the ball to fall; he was tied for the second-most of this type of misplay among center fielders. Crisp has below-average arm strength for a center fielder. His accuracy on throws is average. Crisp does a good job of getting his body in a position to throw quickly, but even so,

runners take the extra base at a well above-average rate against him while not being thrown out often. Crisp has been an above-average defensive center fielder for several seasons of his career, but it remains to be seen if he can get back there going forward.

Craig Gentry

	Innings	Runs Saved
2011	313.2	8
2009-2011	390.2	10

	Good Plays	Misplays and Errors
Gentry 2011	6	3
Avg Center Fielder	6	7
Good Play/Misplay Pct		.697

Rick Ankiel

	Innings	Runs Saved
2011	785.1	8
2009-2011	1778.1	7

	Good Plays	Misplays and Errors
Ankiel 2011	19	15
Avg Center Fielder	15	17
Good Play/Misplay Pct		.593

Ankiel ditched pitching in 2005 because of control issues, but there's nothing wrong with his arm from the center field position. He still possesses the arm strength of a pitcher, and he has no problem throwing strikes from the outfield. Baserunners rarely test what is arguably the best outfield arm in baseball; when they do, Ankiel effortlessly delivers a laser, with pinpoint accuracy, for an easy catch and tag by the infielder. Ankiel's total of eight runs saved with his arm in 2011 led major league center fielders. He is a very impressive athlete, gets good jumps and has good foot speed with average range in center. His biggest weakness is going back on well-hit balls. He will often compound the problem by charging into the wall while not making the catch, allowing the runners to take additional bases. He has the versatility to play any of the three outfield positions, though left field would be a waste of his unbelievable arm. Considering the struggles Ankiel faced with the Cardinals as a pitcher, the move to the outfield has certainly helped prolong his career.

Center Fielders

Jacoby Ellsbury

	Innings	Runs Saved
2011	1358.1	7
2009-2011	2765.2	4

	Good Plays	Misplays and Errors
Ellsbury 2011	19	25
Avg Center Fielder	26	29
Good Play/Misplay Pct		.467

Finally healthy, Jacoby Ellsbury displayed excellent range in center field in 2011, with quick foot speed, fast jumps and tremendous confidence and timing. Having tremendous range is the number one responsibility of a great defensive center fielder. But Ellsbury has two gaping holes in his game. First, he has a ton of trouble playing the ball off the Green Monster and other outfield fences. He ranks last in runs saved in all of baseball over the last three years by a considerable margin on plays involving fences and walls. He recorded 16 Defensive Misplays for failing to anticipate the wall over the past three seasons, including 7 in 2011 alone. Second, Ellsbury has below-average arm strength and accuracy. Baserunners have not been shy about challenging him, taking the extra base at a rate well above-average.

Michael Saunders

	Innings	Runs Saved
2011	376.1	3
2009-2011	484.1	4

	Good Plays	Misplays and Errors
Saunders 2011	7	5
Avg Center Fielder	7	8
Good Play/Misplay Pct		.617

When Franklin Gutierrez started the season on the disabled list, Saunders filled in as the Mariners' everyday center fielder. His defense was good, but his offensive production was below-average, so Saunders spent much of the season shuttling back and forth between Seattle and Triple-A Tacoma. The best defensive fit for Saunders with the Mariners would likely be left field. He is athletic and covers a lot of ground in the outfield, with a good corner arm. From a baseball perspective, Saunders' defense hardly outweighs his offensive deficiencies, but his bat becomes more tolerable as a center fielder. Saunders played more center field than left throughout his minor league career. Although he plays shallow, he has the range to track down well-hit balls. Saunders earned the nickname "The Condor" from play-by-play announcer Dave Sims for his speed and glove in the outfield. While his versatility is an asset moving forward, Saunders has to start hitting at the major league level to figure into Seattle's future plans.

Andres Torres

	Innings	Runs Saved
2011	776	-3
2009-2011	1584	4

	Good Plays	Misplays and Errors
Torres 2011	11	12
Avg Center Fielder	12	14
Good Play/Misplay Pct		.514

Andres Torres is a sure-handed, speedy outfielder. He gets solid jumps, moves smoothly and takes good routes on flyballs. Most of his troubles come from runners taking the extra base on him. He possesses a very average arm, both in terms of strength and accuracy, which does little to deter advancing runners. He may be trying too hard to compensate for this, as one of his weaknesses is a tendency to mishandle base hits. Torres wants to get to the ball quicker trying to prevent a runner from advancing, but the result has been compounding the problem. Given his tremendous speed, Torres showed some expansive range during a defensive breakout season in 2010. Due to leg injuries, however, his range was reduced in 2011. At his worst, Torres was still a good defensive option at all three outfield positions.

Aaron Rowand

	Innings	Runs Saved
2011	413.2	2
2009-2011	2235.2	3

	Good Plays	Misplays and Errors
Rowand 2011	7	4
Avg Center Fielder	8	9
Good Play/Misplay Pct		.668

While Aaron Rowand has certainly lost a step from his prime days roaming center field, he still remains capable of fielding the position. He doesn't have the speed to cover as much ground as he once did, but he still makes good reads and usually gets quick jumps on balls. He also has reliable hands, as he rarely drops balls he can get a glove on, even if it means slamming face-first into a fence. Rowand has been known for his fearlessness in the outfield, but he sometimes can turn that into over-aggressiveness by slipping or even kicking a base hit he was chasing. His throwing arm is neither strong nor particularly accurate.

Center Fielders

Corey Patterson

	Innings	Runs Saved
2011	287.2	0
2009-2011	392.2	3

	Good Plays	Misplays and Errors
Patterson 2011	5	7
Avg Center Fielder	5	6
Good Play/Misplay Pct		.451

Shane Victorino

	Innings	Runs Saved
2011	1150.2	2
2009-2011	3746.1	2

	Good Plays	Misplays and Errors
Victorino 2011	10	15
Avg Center Fielder	18	21
Good Play/Misplay Pct		.434

Victorino plays a shallow center field, which accounts for his extremely above-average performance on shallow flyballs and extremely below-average rating on deep flyballs. Despite this, he is very good at going back on flyballs over his head. He takes full strides, and more often than not takes good routes. He just doesn't get to as many deep balls as others because of where he plays, not because he's slow in recognizing the flight path of the ball. He goes all out on every play and is never deterred by the wall or oncoming teammates when going after a ball. His shallow play and his great arm make him one of the best center fielders in the game at preventing advancement of runners. The league now knows better than to challenge Victorino.

Jason Pridie

	Innings	Runs Saved
2011	312.2	2
2009-2011	312.2	2

	Good Plays	Misplays and Errors
Pridie 2011	2	9
Avg Center Fielder	6	7
Good Play/Misplay Pct		.204

Josh Hamilton

	Innings	Runs Saved
2011	259	-2
2009-2011	993.2	2

	Good Plays	Misplays and Errors
Hamilton 2011	6	5
Avg Center Fielder	4	5
Good Play/Misplay Pct		.580

Jon Jay

	Innings	Runs Saved
2011	570	4
2009-2011	765	1

	Good Plays	Misplays and Errors
Jay 2011	19	11
Avg Center Fielder	11	13
Good Play/Misplay Pct		.665

Jon Jay played a little bit of everything in the outfield in 2011, but following Colby Rasmus' departure from the Cardinals, Jay saw most of his time in center field. He proved that he is more than capable of playing an effective major league center field. Jay's strongest attributes are his quick acceleration and top speed, leading to good range especially on shallow-hit balls. Jay shows good athleticism and isn't afraid to lay out to make a catch. He has reliable hands, as he rarely fails to catch a ball he gets his glove on and generally fields hits cleanly, as opposed to fumbling the ball and allowing runners to move up. His throwing arm is nothing special—decent strength, slightly below-average accuracy. Jay could stand to improve his overall route running and initial reads on flies, as his weaknesses in these areas keep him from being an elite fielder.

Ezequiel Carrera

	Innings	Runs Saved
2011	426	1
2009-2011	426	1

	Good Plays	Misplays and Errors
Carrera 2011	8	17
Avg Center Fielder	8	9
Good Play/Misplay Pct		.351

Center Fielders

Endy Chavez

	Innings	Runs Saved
2011	514.1	0
2009-2011	581.1	1

	Good Plays	Misplays and Errors
Chavez 2011	11	4
Avg Center Fielder	8	9
Good Play/Misplay Pct		.760

Bryan Petersen

	Innings	Runs Saved
2011	316.2	0
2009-2011	316.2	0

	Good Plays	Misplays and Errors
Petersen 2011	6	8
Avg Center Fielder	5	6
Good Play/Misplay Pct		.463

Denard Span

	Innings	Runs Saved
2011	585.1	9
2009-2011	2522.1	-1

	Good Plays	Misplays and Errors
Span 2011	12	10
Avg Center Fielder	12	14
Good Play/Misplay Pct		.580

Span lives up to his name by reaching balls that seem certain to drop. He has always been good at covering the deep outfield, but there's a hidden reason why he can make it to the wall with ease: Span can afford to position himself deeper than most center fielders because he is excellent at charging flares in front of him. Span's relentless pursuit will occasionally reveal its downside, as he'll sprint past a rebound off the wall or slide for a ball out of reach. A May 2011 article by Tyler Mason of Fox Sports North documented recent adjustments made by Span to support his plus/minus breakthrough: "I know where to play certain guys on certain counts and situations. Just a year better and a year older at that position," Span said, adding, "I'm just learning to position myself better and position my corner guys a little better." His arm is below-average, as baserunners take the extra base at a higher-than-average rate while not being thrown out often.

Nyjer Morgan

	Innings	Runs Saved
2011	724.2	3
2009-2011	2311.2	-1

	Good Plays	Misplays and Errors
Morgan 2011	15	16
Avg Center Fielder	14	16
Good Play/Misplay Pct		.519

Nyjer Morgan played a solid center field in 2011. His best defensive tool was his range in center, particularly his ability to range for balls hit deep. One of the reasons Morgan excels at balls hit deep is his ability to play balls near the wall. Morgan, also known as Tony Plush, doesn't shy away from contact with the wall and made many great catches on the warning track or against the wall this past season. This aggressiveness can cost him at times too, as he has had 14 Defensive Misplays in the last three years for failing to anticipate the wall and allowing the ball to bounce back past him, giving away extra bases. This gave him the second-worst runs saved of all centerfielders from 2009-2011 in this category. Morgan's arm has always been his weakness, and opponents can take extra bases without fear of being thrown out. He has had no baserunner kills in the last two years in center field after recording five in 2009.

Ben Revere

	Innings	Runs Saved
2011	776.1	-1
2009-2011	814.1	-1

	Good Plays	Misplays and Errors
Revere 2011	14	22
Avg Center Fielder	17	19
Good Play/Misplay Pct		.423

Revere saw most of his playing time in center field in 2011, but got occasional time in left. His speed is his best asset, allowing him to make some nice highlight-reel catches. His biggest weak spot is arm strength, as he possesses one of the worst outfield throwing arms in baseball. On more than one occasion a runner at first tagged up and safely advanced to second on a lazy flyball to deep center field. Revere can take some bad routes to the ball, but more times than not his speed makes up for it. Given his speed, Revere should be able to develop into a solid center fielder long-term.

Center Fielders

Drew Stubbs

	Innings	Runs Saved
2011	1329	-4
2009-2011	2927.1	-1

	Good Plays	Misplays and Errors
Stubbs 2011	15	29
Avg Center Fielder	24	28
Good Play/Misplay Pct		.373

Stubbs has all the tools to be an above-average defensive center fielder, but not everything has clicked for him yet in his three-year career. He has good speed to cover a lot of ground in center and has above-average arm strength for the position. His five runs saved with his arm tied for fourth among major league outfielders in 2011. However, he can be overly aggressive with his arm at times, and made some poor throwing decisions rather than simply hitting the cut-off man. Stubbs plays a very shallow center field, and ranked tied for fourth among all center fielders in Defensive Misplays (26). Breaking in the wrong direction, failed dives for flyballs and misplaying balls off the wall were recurring misplays for Stubbs in 2011. Stubbs has the underlying physical skills to become a very good defensive center fielder, but his defensive numbers have moved in the wrong direction since he entered the majors.

Colby Rasmus

	Innings	Runs Saved
2011	1092.2	-4
2009-2011	3143.2	-2

	Good Plays	Misplays and Errors
Rasmus 2011	12	26
Avg Center Fielder	21	24
Good Play/Misplay Pct		.347

Rasmus is a very aggressive center fielder, and his aggressiveness led to many misplays in 2011. He doesn't always get great reads on flyballs that could be caught if he were to get a quick first step. This led him to really struggle on deep flyballs this year. Rasmus would often have to overcompensate for his reads resulting in failed dives or overrunning the play. He allowed runners to take the extra base far more often in 2011 than he has in the past, so that is something to keep an eye on going forward.

Mike Cameron

	Innings	Runs Saved
2011	350	1
2009-2011	2009.2	-4

	Good Plays	Misplays and Errors
Cameron 2011	8	13
Avg Center Fielder	7	8
Good Play/Misplay Pct		.415

Now at 39 years of age, Mike Cameron has certainly lost a step, but he still played some solid defense for the Marlins after they picked him up mid-year. He can no longer range to snag all the deep flies, but his experience shows in his quick reads and direct routes to the balls in the middle of the field. His arm strength is also no longer what it was, and baserunners were aggressive against him. One of his biggest weaknesses was a tendency to mishandle hits, resulting in runners gaining additional bases. You get the feeling Cameron is the type of guy who will keep playing as long as his body (and bat) allows, and his defense appears that it will hold up a bit longer.

Roger Bernadina

	Innings	Runs Saved
2011	420.2	-2
2009-2011	606	-5

	Good Plays	Misplays and Errors
Bernadina 2011	10	11
Avg Center Fielder	7	9
Good Play/Misplay Pct		.511

Marlon Byrd

	Innings	Runs Saved
2011	998	0
2009-2011	3148.2	-6

	Good Plays	Misplays and Errors
Byrd 2011	18	15
Avg Center Fielder	18	21
Good Play/Misplay Pct		.580

Marlon Byrd is a consistent, reliable, if unspectacular, center fielder. His speed and range are a little below-average, but he is able to get a good read on most balls. He will make all the routine catches, and it is rare for him not to make a catch when he gets to a ball in the air. When he misses a catchable ball, it is usually the result of a failed dive or aggressive play. Byrd's arm strength is average at best, but he has held his own

Center Fielders

keeping runners honest. His arm is fairly accurate, and because he gets to the ball quickly he'll often hold a batter to a single instead of a double despite his middling arm strength.

Rajai Davis

	Innings	Runs Saved
2011	652	-9
2009-2011	2185.2	-8

	Good Plays	Misplays and Errors
Davis 2011	11	11
Avg Center Fielder	12	14
Good Play/Misplay Pct		.535

Anyone who has seen Rajai Davis can tell that he has incredible, top-of-the-league speed. Why then over the last year has he struggled to post decent defensive numbers? The answer lies in a number of factors led by his trouble with initial reads. Davis too often relies on his high speed to make up for poor initial judgment of flyballs. When he fails to reach a flyball at home playing in the Rogers Centre, the penalty is severe because the ball bounces so high. Davis really struggles on plays near the wall, as he was near the bottom of the league on these types of plays. He has also had communication issues in the outfield leading to some plays not being made that could've been had he not given up on the play, figuring someone else would make it. Finally, Davis possesses a weak throwing arm of which runners take constant advantage.

Alex Rios

	Innings	Runs Saved
2011	1230	-9
2009-2011	2822.2	-8

	Good Plays	Misplays and Errors
Rios 2011	17	30
Avg Center Fielder	25	29
Good Play/Misplay Pct		.395

The former Blue Jays' right fielder was claimed off waivers in August 2009 by the White Sox and immediately became their everyday center fielder. Rios was once looked at as a top defensive outfielder, taking home a Fielding Bible Award in 2007 for his defense in right field. In the past few seasons, in conjunction with the move to center field, Rios' defense has been on a steady decline. Over the entire course of the 2011 season, Rios' defense and hustle were questioned, as he misjudged or took lazy routes to flyballs and failed to cut balls off in the gap. Rios does have good speed, but doesn't have the range in center to show for it. He was

once known for an excellent throwing arm, but his performance in recent years holding runners and throwing them out has been below-average. Overall, Rios has been a huge disappointment for the White Sox, especially offensively but also defensively, and they're stuck with his bloated contract through 2014.

Adam Jones

	Innings	Runs Saved
2011	1281	-4
2009-2011	3584.1	-10

	Good Plays	Misplays and Errors
Jones 2011	24	35
Avg Center Fielder	26	30
Good Play/Misplay Pct		.441

Adam Jones is a bundle of defensive extremes. He has saved more runs with his arm over the last three years than any other center fielder, and he's done it by a wide margin. He's also made some spectacular catches, including five robbed home runs since the start of 2009. (Only Franklin Gutierrez has more among all outfielders during that span, with six). He can also play center field and chew gum at the same time, blowing bubbles for the TV cameras. Unfortunately for Jones, this hasn't been enough to compensate for his weaknesses. Jones isn't very fast for a center fielder, and he often complicates this problem by taking a bad route or breaking in the wrong direction, leading MLB in each of these misplays over the past three years. This has been a particular problem on fliners (trajectory between liner and fly) toward the gaps that get past him for extra bases. He also gives more bases away than he should by mishandling balls after they land for hits; he is among the trailers in runs saved in this category over the last three years. Given his skill set, Jones seems like a logical candidate for a shift to right field, but that's unlikely to happen as long as he and Nick Markakis are in the same lineup.

Dexter Fowler

	Innings	Runs Saved
2011	1072.2	-3
2009-2011	2998.2	-12

	Good Plays	Misplays and Errors
Fowler 2011	13	30
Avg Center Fielder	20	23
Good Play/Misplay Pct		.333

Dexter Fowler shows promise in the field, but has room for improvement. He covers a lot of ground (the center fielder in Colorado has to), but he has trouble with shallow balls. This could be because of the huge center

Center Fielders

field in Colorado and not wanting to get burned deep. Nonetheless, it is something that he must work on. He occasionally takes bad routes, and has mishandled balls after a hit more than one would want (ranking as the worst center fielder the past three years in this category). Fowler has allowed baserunners to take the extra base on his arm at a significantly higher-than-average rate.

Andrew McCutchen

	Innings	Runs Saved
2011	1353.2	5
2009-2011	3596.2	-13

	Good Plays	Misplays and Errors
McCutchen 2011	28	29
Avg Center Fielder	26	30
Good Play/Misplay Pct		.527

In 2011, McCutchen's Defensive Runs Saved total was positive for the first time in his career. His greatest improvement was on deep flies, where he rated as -21 in 2009 and -20 in 2010. He improved dramatically to +20 in 2011. He has great speed that allows him to range for flyballs that most center fielders cannot reach. Improved positioning and routes allowed him to fully utilize that speed for the first time this past season. He has an above-average arm as well to gun down runners on the base paths. Despite this, runners have challenged him and taken the extra base slightly more than average, suggesting that he may need to work on his accuracy a bit. This past year McCutchen did a much better job of keeping his throws down, and he made much better throws into the infield compared to years past.

Melky Cabrera

	Innings	Runs Saved
2011	1265.2	-6
2009-2011	2457	-13

	Good Plays	Misplays and Errors
Cabrera 2011	26	30
Avg Center Fielder	23	26
Good Play/Misplay Pct		.500

Cabrera found a home last season in center field. However, his skill set on defense would be better suited to one of the corner outfield positions. He has a strong, accurate arm and has no problem throwing out runners from the outfield. This year, though, runners took the extra base on him at a much higher rate than they have in previous years, so this bears watching. Cabrera does not possess the necessary speed to stand out in center field. He's been known to make spectacular leaping and diving plays in the outfield, but some of this can be attributed to

Cabrera consistently taking bad routes to flyballs which puts him out of position to make routine catches.

Chris Coghlan

	Innings	Runs Saved
2011	568.1	-13
2009-2011	568.1	-13

	Good Plays	Misplays and Errors
Coghlan 2011	9	11
Avg Center Fielder	10	12
Good Play/Misplay Pct		.485

Coghlan had a bad first year in center field in 2011, as he struggled to patrol the cavernous outfield in Florida. His range was one of the worst in the league, and he was truly awful on deep balls. He also struggled throwing the ball, as baserunners ran all over him, though he did have two baserunner kills. Coghlan has never been a great defender since coming to the majors, but he had shown some signs of improvement in 2010. A positive is that Coghlan was average on his GFP/DME runs saved, so at least he's not messing up routine plays out there. Still, Coghlan seems miscast as a center fielder, and unless he shows marked improvement, he should be moved back to where he played in 2010: left field.

Grady Sizemore

	Innings	Runs Saved
2011	479.1	-6
2009-2011	1555.1	-14

	Good Plays	Misplays and Errors
Sizemore 2011	8	9
Avg Center Fielder	9	10
Good Play/Misplay Pct		.506

Sizemore was a below-average defensive center fielder in 2011, as he suffered through another injury-plagued season. He is an athletic player who has seen some of both his offensive and defensive tools diminish due to injuries over the past couple of seasons. Sizemore's once terrific range has now been greatly reduced, and he has lost runs defensively in center field in each of the last five seasons. His best defensive attribute early in his career was running down deep flies and making acrobatic catches near the wall. Now, that part of his defensive game might be his biggest weakness. Sizemore is still not afraid to sacrifice his body in an attempt to make a play, though he may regret some of those past sacrifices now. He has below-average arm strength and average accuracy. He hasn't recorded a baserunner kill since 2008. Sizemore is able to get his

Center Fielders

body behind the throw and get rid of the ball quickly. Sizemore is closing in on age 30, and if his injury issues continue to plague him, he may be ticketed for left field in the near future.

Jordan Schafer

	Innings	Runs Saved
2011	672	-7
2009-2011	1104	-18

	Good Plays	Misplays and Errors
Schafer 2011	9	15
Avg Center Fielder	13	15
Good Play/Misplay Pct		.409

Schafer was a below-average center fielder for the Astros and Braves in 2011, which, combined with his weak hitting, leaves his major league career in jeopardy. His biggest defensive asset is his speed. He is a speedy outfielder, which you would think would translate into good range, but he simply hasn't made the catches other center fielders make. Schafer has slightly below-average range on balls classified as shallow or medium, and has posted his worst numbers on deep balls. Schafer has below-average arm strength and accuracy. He had a number of misplays in categories like throwing to the wrong base, wasted throws after a hit or fly out, and missing the cutoff man. He also can be over-aggressive at times, which leads to him having issues near walls and fences or mishandling a ball after a hit because he was trying to throw it too quickly. All of these events cost his team bases. With his speed, if Schafer can improve his throwing accuracy and decision-making, he has the ability to become at least an average defensive center fielder despite the lack of a plus arm.

Michael Brantley

	Innings	Runs Saved
2011	412.2	-2
2009-2011	1141.1	-20

	Good Plays	Misplays and Errors
Brantley 2011	3	8
Avg Center Fielder	8	9
Good Play/Misplay Pct		.302

Nate McLouth

	Innings	Runs Saved
2011	498	-7
2009-2011	2179.1	-23

	Good Plays	Misplays and Errors
McLouth 2011	13	15
Avg Center Fielder	8	9
Good Play/Misplay Pct		.500

Simply put, Nate McLouth is a below-average center fielder. In 55 games played in center in 2011, McLouth mishandled eight balls off his glove, either flyballs or grounders, roughly one every seven games. It's safe to say that he has fairly shaky hands. He tends to play shallow and struggles reading deep flyballs, resulting in costly extra-base hits. The really startling thing is that he also struggles on shallow-hit balls despite his positioning. His arm isn't strong enough to dissuade runners from taking extra bases, and he hasn't had a baserunner kill from any of the three outfield positions that he's played since 2009. On the positive side, McLouth does still show strong athleticism, putting his body on the line to make diving plays (especially coming in), and he has a good sense for playing balls off the wall.

B.J. Upton

	Innings	Runs Saved
2011	1326.1	-7
2009-2011	3856.2	-26

	Good Plays	Misplays and Errors
Upton 2011	26	27
Avg Center Fielder	23	27
Good Play/Misplay Pct		.526

Upton was a below-average defensive center fielder in 2011. He is notorious for playing a very shallow center field and trying to use his speed to get to balls hit over his head. However, he has consistently posted negative numbers on balls classified as "deep." Upton has great speed and athleticism, yet his range numbers have been trending negative. Upton has had a tendency to mix in spectacular plays along with misplays. This is evidenced by him ranking among the leaders in both good fielding plays and defensive misplays between 2009 and 2011. Upton has plus arm strength for a center fielder. His accuracy on throws is average. Upton can get too aggressive at times leading to him mishandling the ball after a hit, wasting throws, throwing towards the wrong base or missing the cut-off man. All of these mistakes can potentially lead to his team losing bases, and subsequently runs. Upton has all of the physical

Center Fielders

tools to be an above-average defensive center fielder, but so far it hasn't happened for him.

Matt Kemp

	Innings	Runs Saved
2011	1380	-5
2009-2011	4081.1	-46

	Good Plays	Misplays and Errors
Kemp 2011	28	28
Avg Center Fielder	23	26
Good Play/Misplay Pct		.535

Matt Kemp has all the physical tools of a great athlete, but he remains a poor defender in center field due to his inability to consistently take good routes on balls. He can come up short on catchable flyballs because of a late break off the bat; the result is his range numbers are well below-average, particularly on deep balls, despite having the athleticism to do better. Still, because of his sheer athletic ability, Kemp is fully capable of making his share of highlight plays. This is reflected in the fact that he has more good fielding plays than any other center fielder over the past three years (he also had the most misplays). Kemp did win the Gold Glove in 2011, most likely because people remember all those highlight-reel plays, similar to when Nate McLouth won in 2008. (To be fair, Kemp's runs saved in 2011 were moderately below-average, while McLouth in 2008 was the trailer by a significant margin.) Posting MVP-caliber numbers with the bat also didn't hurt. He has a very strong and accurate arm that causes baserunners to think twice before challenging him. His eight baserunner kills this season were among the leaders in the outfield. Perhaps his instincts will get better over time, and given his huge offensive outburst in 2011, improvement on the defensive end is not out of the question. See "Matt Kemp and His Two Gold Gloves" on page 73.

Right Fielders Evaluations

Year	League	Gold Glove Winners	Should Have Been
2003	AL	Ichiro Suzuki	Ichiro Suzuki
	NL	Jose Cruz	Richard Hidalgo
2004	AL	Ichiro Suzuki	Ichiro Suzuki
	NL	none	Richard Hidalgo
2005	AL	Ichiro Suzuki	Ichiro Suzuki
	NL	Bobby Abreu	Geoff Jenkins
2006	AL	Ichiro Suzuki	Ichiro Suzuki
			Alex Rios
	NL	none	none
2007	AL	none	Alex Rios
	NL	Jeff Francoeur	Jeff Francoeur
2008	AL	Ichiro Suzuki	Franklin Gutierrez
			Nick Markakis
	NL	none	none
2009	AL	Ichiro Suzuki	Ichiro Suzuki
	NL	none	Hunter Pence
2010	AL	Ichiro Suzuki	Ichiro Suzuki
	NL	none	Jay Bruce
2011	AL	Nick Markakis	Torii Hunter
	NL	Andre Ethier	Jason Heyward

My Personal Ratings

Top Ten

1 Jason Heyward, Atl
2 Torii Hunter, LAA
3 Justin Upton, Ari
4 Will Venable, SD
5 Shin-Soo Choo, Cle

Bottom Five

26 Carlos Quentin, SD
27 Jason Kubel, Ari
28 Michael Cuddyer, Col
29 Magglio Ordonez, FA
30 Lance Berkman, StL

Player teams based on transactions through February 1, 2012

Right Fielders

Jason Heyward

	Innings	Runs Saved
2011	990.1	15
2009-2011	2186.2	30

	Good Plays	Misplays and Errors
Heyward 2011	12	20
Avg Right Fielder	18	21
Good Play/Misplay Pct		.416

Heyward gained notoriety during his rookie year for his offensive prowess, but he is also an outstanding defensive outfielder. He led all right fielders in Runs Saved in 2011 with 15. He has a strong arm, but it hasn't proven effective yet as he's lost seven runs on baserunner advancements the last two years. He does a great job of reading the ball off the bat, which compensates for his lack of foot speed and range in right field. Heyward runs efficient routes to the ball while it is in the air and plays deep enough to not allow balls to get over his head. His main problem at this point is staying on the field, as he continues to make frequent trips to the disabled list.

Jeff Francoeur

	Innings	Runs Saved
2011	1352	1
2009-2011	3760.1	29

	Good Plays	Misplays and Errors
Francoeur 2011	28	34
Avg Right Fielder	29	34
Good Play/Misplay Pct		.495

Historically an above-average fielder, 2011 was somewhat of a down year for Francoeur, his first in Kansas City. His strength? A rocket arm. He led all major league right fielders in assists with 16. It was the other areas of his defense that were lacking. His outfield range is average, and he had an especially poor showing in 2011. He tends to take poor routes to hard-hit balls, despite good jumps off balls in play. Francoeur has below-average wall awareness and does not always play hard hits off the wall to hold baserunners. He must improve his routes and wall awareness to bring his defense in right field back to the upper tier.

Ben Zobrist

	Innings	Runs Saved
2011	289.2	6
2009-2011	1368.1	23

	Good Plays	Misplays and Errors
Zobrist 2011	9	5
Avg Right Fielder	6	7
Good Play/Misplay Pct		.681

Hunter Pence

	Innings	Runs Saved
2011	1342.2	1
2009-2011	4088.2	20

	Good Plays	Misplays and Errors
Pence 2011	28	39
Avg Right Fielder	26	31
Good Play/Misplay Pct		.460

In the last two years, Pence has put up two average defensive seasons after having two excellent seasons in 2008 and 2009, when he finished runner-up in Fielding Bible Award voting. Like his unorthodox swing, Pence has an unconventional throwing motion which tempts opposing baserunners. Unfortunately for them, he gets to the ball quickly, and his throws are impressively accurate. After leading the National League in assists and kills in 2008-09, Pence has cooled off a bit the past two seasons. His range has also dropped off to roughly league-average territory, though he's continued his tendency of being much better on shallow-hit balls rather than deep ones. Despite the slight drop-off, Pence rarely misses an inning in the field. Now playing for a contender for the first time in his career, Pence should be motivated to regain that lost step and compete for the title of best defensive right fielder once again.

Jay Bruce

	Innings	Runs Saved
2011	1371	-2
2009-2011	3380.2	20

	Good Plays	Misplays and Errors
Bruce 2011	16	26
Avg Right Fielder	27	32
Good Play/Misplay Pct		.422

Bruce does an excellent job at getting to flyballs. In 2010, he did so well at this that he finished second among right fielders in both Plus/Minus Runs Saved and the Fielding Bible Award voting. Bruce couldn't repeat his dominance in 2011, as he saw a significant transition away from great catches and toward near misses. Even

Right Fielders

though he continued to get good jumps and run straight paths, Bruce had a surprising number of balls sneak by him or bounce off his glove last season. Bruce's consistently aggressive play will allow extra bases in other areas too, as he'll occasionally overrun balls near the wall or waste a throw after a base hit. Despite the mishaps, Bruce has enough skill to make plenty of outs and be a defensive asset. If he can execute on tough plays more consistently (or practice better judgment when he cannot), Bruce has a chance to re-establish himself as one of the better right fielders in baseball.

Mike Stanton

	Innings	Runs Saved
2011	1219	3
2009-2011	2073.2	16

	Good Plays	Misplays and Errors
Stanton 2011	25	49
Avg Right Fielder	24	29
Good Play/Misplay Pct		.377

Mike Stanton has proven himself to be more than capable with the glove early in his career. Stanton's 16 runs saved was sixth among all right fielders over the last three years, despite having only played the last two. For a big guy, Stanton has great range in right field. Stanton currently owns a career +26 in the Plus/Minus System for his first two seasons in the major leagues. When he gets a good jump on the ball and takes a good route, he is able to chase down as many flyballs as any right fielder. He showcases one of the game's strongest arms in right field and is very aggressive when using it. One of Mike's weaknesses in 2011 was his routes to the ball, as he led all major league outfielders in "bad route" misplays. This weakness is an issue that playing time and experience can cure, which should help him continue to improve.

Will Venable

	Innings	Runs Saved
2011	662.2	5
2009-2011	1756.2	15

	Good Plays	Misplays and Errors
Venable 2011	10	11
Avg Right Fielder	12	14
Good Play/Misplay Pct		.519

Venable has great speed for a right fielder, and it shows. His range is among the best of all MLB right fielders. While he is prone to mishandling the ball once it arrives when pressured by base runners, he has the potential to be an elite defender. His arm is a little weak

compared to the prototypical right fielder. With so much ground to cover, the Padres are lucky to have a guy who can chase down most flyballs and maneuver around the uniquely configured wall in right field of PETCO Park.

Justin Upton

	Innings	Runs Saved
2011	1366.2	8
2009-2011	3663.2	14

	Good Plays	Misplays and Errors
Upton 2011	23	49
Avg Right Fielder	28	33
Good Play/Misplay Pct		.358

Justin Upton turned in another fantastic season in right field in 2011 and was recognized with his first Fielding Bible Award. Justin is unquestionably one of the best right fielders at playing balls hit deep. He saved 34 more bases on plays hit deep than an average right fielder this year, a figure that was second in the majors among right fielders. Upton is fearless and goes back very hard on balls hit over his head. His speed allows him the chance to make plays that many right fielders don't even get close to. His aggressiveness and quick instincts in the field help him to cut off seemingly sure doubles and turn them into singles. He does have two flaws: He makes too many little misplays, and his arm is weak enough that baserunners run wild. Both have cost the Diamondbacks double-digit runs over the past three years. If he can learn to throw to the right base and play balls off the wall better, both problems will be alleviated. Just entering his prime, he still has time to correct his mistakes and become one of the most well-rounded players in the game.

J.D. Drew

	Innings	Runs Saved
2011	587.1	-2
2009-2011	2773.1	13

	Good Plays	Misplays and Errors
Drew 2011	4	9
Avg Right Fielder	11	13
Good Play/Misplay Pct		.346

J.D. Drew is one of those stealthy good fielders. It's hard to tell from the way he moves in the field how much ground he really covers, especially in the vast right field of Fenway Park. In 2009 and 2010, Drew may have been one of the most underrated right fielders, ranking in the top five in Runs Saved both years. He is a smart fielder who makes great initial reads on balls and always takes direct routes. He excelled especially at tracking down

Right Fielders

flies in the deepest parts of the park with sure hands. His biggest flaw is a weak arm, which costs the team a few runs per year. Drew has battled several hamstring injuries recently, slowing his already less than stellar speed, and his range took a hit in 2011 as well. It's unlikely that Drew will regain the range he once had, but if he continues to play, he will still have value because of his intelligence.

Shin-Soo Choo

	Innings	Runs Saved
2011	735.1	3
2009-2011	3069.2	12

	Good Plays	Misplays and Errors
Choo 2011	15	24
Avg Right Fielder	16	19
Good Play/Misplay Pct		.426

Choo was limited by injuries to 85 games in 2011 but provided an impact defensively when he was healthy. Choo features one of the best arms in right field in baseball, and despite an injury-shortened 2011 season, was tied for second among all outfielders in kills (direct outfield assists) over the last three seasons (26). In fact, he was drafted as a pitcher with a 97-mph fastball by the Seattle Mariners in 2000. He's never pitched in the majors, but Choo, despite Tommy John surgery in 2007, still insists he can hit 94 mph on the radar gun. He looked better in right field before his injury. Choo still had good range but seemed to make recurring fielding misplays this past season. He didn't get good reads off the bat, took some bad routes, booted balls hit in his direction and lost balls in the sun. That being said, Choo's prior history suggests he's one of the better right fielders in the game, and he'll remain an asset defensively as he enters the 2012 season 100 percent healthy.

Brian Bogusevic

	Innings	Runs Saved
2011	277	10
2009-2011	286	10

	Good Plays	Misplays and Errors
Bogusevic 2011	13	5
Avg Right Fielder	6	7
Good Play/Misplay Pct		.755

Torii Hunter

	Innings	Runs Saved
2011	1179.1	9
2009-2011	1589.1	8

	Good Plays	Misplays and Errors
Hunter 2011	36	26
Avg Right Fielder	24	28
Good Play/Misplay Pct		.622

Hunter has long been known for the way he can track down deep flyballs hit over his head. This continued to be the case in 2011, even though he moved to right field on a full-time basis. However, he did have some trouble adjusting to the high wall in right field of Angel Stadium. Occasionally, Hunter attempted to make a spectacular catch but ended up getting burned, as the ball bounced back onto the field for additional bases. As a right fielder, runners challenged his arm much more than they had for years. He responded with an impressive 14 baserunner kills, leading all outfielders in 2011. While his position has changed and his skills have diminished slightly, Hunter is still a very good outfielder and never hesitant to make a flashy play.

Josh Reddick

	Innings	Runs Saved
2011	432.2	7
2009-2011	534.1	7

	Good Plays	Misplays and Errors
Reddick 2011	5	13
Avg Right Fielder	8	9
Good Play/Misplay Pct		.314

Garrett Jones

	Innings	Runs Saved
2011	659	-4
2009-2011	1400	7

	Good Plays	Misplays and Errors
Jones 2011	11	13
Avg Right Fielder	14	17
Good Play/Misplay Pct		.501

Garrett Jones is a big guy and has bounced around a few different positions for the Pirates the last several years. He spent much of 2011 in right field, and was a little bit below-average for the position. He has decent speed for his size, but his range is rather limited in the outfield nonetheless. He has an average arm for a right fielder. At first base, he has limited mobility and is very poor at handling difficult throws.

Right Fielders

Chris Denorfia

	Innings	Runs Saved
2011	445	3
2009-2011	563	6

	Good Plays	Misplays and Errors
Denorfia 2011	10	11
Avg Right Fielder	9	10
Good Play/Misplay Pct		.519

Chris Denorfia is quietly a good fielder. He has seen time in all three outfield positions over the past two seasons in San Diego. Denorfia isn't skilled enough at this point in his career (he's already in his thirties) to play a plus center field, but his skills translate well to the corners, where he makes his best defensive contributions. His range is strongest in front of him and moving laterally, while he doesn't do as well on deep flies. His hands are right around average; he makes some mistakes, but not many. He excels at making quick, accurate reads in order to get good jumps on balls. He is a good athlete with plus speed and the propensity to make nice diving plays. His throwing arm doesn't stand out as a positive or negative part of his game.

Jon Jay

	Innings	Runs Saved
2011	303.2	7
2009-2011	685.1	5

	Good Plays	Misplays and Errors
Jay 2011	10	7
Avg Right Fielder	7	8
Good Play/Misplay Pct		.629

Tyler Colvin

	Innings	Runs Saved
2011	314.2	4
2009-2011	703	5

	Good Plays	Misplays and Errors
Colvin 2011	6	6
Avg Right Fielder	7	8
Good Play/Misplay Pct		.543

Cody Ross

	Innings	Runs Saved
2011	268	-4
2009-2011	1150.2	5

	Good Plays	Misplays and Errors
Ross 2011	4	9
Avg Right Fielder	4	5
Good Play/Misplay Pct		.346

David DeJesus

	Innings	Runs Saved
2011	992.2	5
2009-2011	1600	4

	Good Plays	Misplays and Errors
DeJesus 2011	29	15
Avg Right Fielder	19	23
Good Play/Misplay Pct		.697

DeJesus, a former center fielder, turned in one of the best seasons of his career with the glove playing right field in 2011. He is very sure-handed and makes very few mistakes. DeJesus isn't flashy, but he is very fundamentally sound and smart. David rarely costs his team extra bases by making errant throws or poor decisions after fielding the ball. His ability to constantly be aware of his surroundings and game situations allowed him to put together a terrific season in 2011, and put him amongst the right field league leaders in runs saved with five.

Carlos Gonzalez

	Innings	Runs Saved
2011	295.1	4
2009-2011	623.2	4

	Good Plays	Misplays and Errors
Gonzalez 2011	9	7
Avg Right Fielder	6	7
Good Play/Misplay Pct		.604

Casper Wells

	Innings	Runs Saved
2011	274.1	1
2009-2011	425.2	3

	Good Plays	Misplays and Errors
Wells 2011	4	4
Avg Right Fielder	5	6
Good Play/Misplay Pct		.543

Right Fielders

Matt Joyce

	Innings	Runs Saved
2011	1006.1	-2
2009-2011	1439.1	3

	Good Plays	Misplays and Errors
Joyce 2011	22	21
Avg Right Fielder	18	22
Good Play/Misplay Pct		.555

Joyce has all the tools to be a good right fielder despite a slightly below-average season in 2011. Capable of playing either corner outfield position, Joyce has solid defensive instincts with good range and a strong, accurate arm. He charges groundballs aggressively and does a nice job preventing runners from taking extra bases on balls hit down the line. In total, Joyce has saved three runs in four seasons at the corner outfield positions, despite being at -4 runs saved for 2011. The eye test says he's not a below-average fielder, and his career numbers indicate that in spite of a slightly below-average runs saved figure this past season.

Nate Schierholtz

	Innings	Runs Saved
2011	703.2	-8
2009-2011	1843.2	3

	Good Plays	Misplays and Errors
Schierholtz 2011	13	15
Avg Right Fielder	13	16
Good Play/Misplay Pct		.507

Schierholtz was a below-average defensive right fielder this past season. He also saw limited time in left field for the Giants in 2011. He showed below-average range, although he was better on shallow hit flyballs than ones hit deeper. The overwhelming majority of Schierholtz's mistakes in the field came from mishandling and misjudging the ball. Once he had it, he rarely made bad throws or had mental errors like throwing to the wrong base. He has above-average arm strength and accuracy, along with a quick release on his throws. Prior to this past season, Schierholtz had been an above-average right fielder. Unless there are unknown physical issues, chances are he just had a defensive "slump" last year and in 2012 will return more to what he had been before.

Kosuke Fukudome

	Innings	Runs Saved
2011	1061	-2
2009-2011	2141	2

	Good Plays	Misplays and Errors
Fukudome 2011	20	26
Avg Right Fielder	23	27
Good Play/Misplay Pct		.478

In his four seasons in the United States, Kosuke Fukudome has shown range that rates below-average in center but about average in right field. He reads flyballs well and always puts himself in a good position to catch the ball and make a quick throw. He has difficulty with hard-hit balls and sometimes misplays hits to the wall. Though he's occasionally prone to throwing mistakes, allowing the runner to take an additional base, his arm is strong and rates among the top half of all right fielders.

Corey Hart

	Innings	Runs Saved
2011	1087.2	-1
2009-2011	3217	0

	Good Plays	Misplays and Errors
Hart 2011	20	24
Avg Right Fielder	21	25
Good Play/Misplay Pct		.498

Overall, Hart was about average in 2011, as he's been for most of his career. He has shown above-average range on deep-hit balls in recent years, but hasn't really excelled in other areas of his defense. His arm costs the Brewers a few runs each year. He makes his fair share of good catches, but occasionally bobbles base hits, allowing runners to take an extra base.

Xavier Paul

	Innings	Runs Saved
2011	274.1	-2
2009-2011	387.1	-1

	Good Plays	Misplays and Errors
Paul 2011	5	8
Avg Right Fielder	6	7
Good Play/Misplay Pct		.426

Right Fielders

Ichiro Suzuki

	Innings	Runs Saved
2011	1333	-3
2009-2011	4036	-1

	Good Plays	Misplays and Errors
Suzuki 2011	23	14
Avg Right Fielder	23	27
Good Play/Misplay Pct		.661

At age 37, Ichiro saw his performance decline across the board, rating as an average defender in the last three years. While he rarely made any mistakes in right field, he appears to have lost a step tracking down flyballs, particularly those hit over his head. Though he still gunned down a handful of runners on the bases, his once terrific arm is no longer a strength. Opposing baserunners took notice, advancing at the highest rate against him in his career. It remains to be seen if Ichiro will bounce back from a down year as other veterans have, or if this is the beginning of the end for the future Hall of Famer and three-time Fielding Bible Award winner.

Jayson Werth

	Innings	Runs Saved
2011	1172.2	-4
2009-2011	3632.1	-2

	Good Plays	Misplays and Errors
Werth 2011	31	37
Avg Right Fielder	24	29
Good Play/Misplay Pct		.499

Overall, Werth was a below-average outfielder in 2011. He possesses decent athleticism, and good speed and acceleration, but has difficulty ranging back on deeply hit flyballs. The Nationals also gave Werth some time in center in 2011, where he did well in limited innings. The strongest part of his defensive game is by far his arm. He also has good footwork he learned as a former catcher. He uses both to make strong, accurate throws to cut down runners and make them think twice about taking an extra base. Jayson plays an aggressive game which sometimes means wasting throws, and he too frequently makes the mistake of thinking about making a throw before actually fielding a ball cleanly. His hands are definitely his biggest weakness as he has had a well above-average number of balls bounce off his glove in one way or another.

Carlos Beltran

	Innings	Runs Saved
2011	1153.2	-3
2009-2011	1153.2	-3

	Good Plays	Misplays and Errors
Beltran 2011	22	27
Avg Right Fielder	20	24
Good Play/Misplay Pct		.492

Beltran was a slightly below-average right fielder for the Giants and Mets in 2011. This was his first full season playing right after playing center field for the majority of his career. Beltran was a two-time Fielding Bible Award winner in center field (2006 and 2008), but injuries and age have sapped him of his defensive prowess. The present-day Beltran has average range for a right fielder. Reading the ball off of the bat is something Beltran can work on, as he continues his transition to the corner outfield. He occasionally takes a bad route to the ball, but he is very good at going back on hard-hit flyballs. He also did a good job of preventing the advancement of base runners with his arm. Beltran has above-average arm strength and accuracy with a quick release. He has the tools to become a good defensive right fielder as he continues to learn the position.

Nelson Cruz

	Innings	Runs Saved
2011	863.2	-6
2009-2011	2698.2	-3

	Good Plays	Misplays and Errors
Cruz 2011	16	19
Avg Right Fielder	18	21
Good Play/Misplay Pct		.500

Cruz got a lot of negative attention for misplaying a David Freese flyball in the World Series which left the door open for the Cardinals' remarkable comeback. Though his 2011 season was his worst defensive season by the numbers, he's not all that bad. He'll throw out a handful of base runners per year—about what you expect from a right fielder. Cruz is good at moving to both his left and his right, and until last year he had never had a below-average season according to the Plus/Minus System. He can occasionally give up the extra base on failed diving attempts or just plain mishandling base hits.

Right Fielders

Jose Bautista

	Innings	Runs Saved
2011	1014	-7
2009-2011	2283	-5

	Good Plays	Misplays and Errors
Bautista 2011	21	32
Avg Right Fielder	19	23
Good Play/Misplay Pct		.438

Jose Bautista put up another terrific year with the bat, but he has yet to show that he can be a great outfielder. Occasionally getting late jumps and taking poor routes, he struggles getting to balls hit deep and over his head. In fact, he graded out worst among all right fielders on deep flyballs in 2011, according to the Plus/Minus System. As you might expect from a former third baseman, his greatest asset defensively is his arm strength, and he racked up ten unassisted kills in the outfield and kept other runners from advancing. Even though he still makes the occasional appearance at third base, it appears that the Blue Jays will keep Bautista primarily in right field, moving forward.

Reed Johnson

	Innings	Runs Saved
2011	266	0
2009-2011	444	-6

	Good Plays	Misplays and Errors
Johnson 2011	3	5
Avg Right Fielder	5	6
Good Play/Misplay Pct		.416

Matt Diaz

	Innings	Runs Saved
2011	335.2	-2
2009-2011	876.1	-8

	Good Plays	Misplays and Errors
Diaz 2011	5	10
Avg Right Fielder	6	7
Good Play/Misplay Pct		.373

Seth Smith

	Innings	Runs Saved
2011	867.1	-6
2009-2011	1091	-9

	Good Plays	Misplays and Errors
Smith 2011	13	26
Avg Right Fielder	17	20
Good Play/Misplay Pct		.373

Seth Smith spent some time in left field in 2011 but logged the most innings in right. He only had one assist in right field and runners took the extra base on 61 percent of opportunities to do so against him, which was among the highest of all right fielders. He sees the ball well off the bat, but does struggle occasionally with shallow hit balls. The bulk of his errors and misplays have come from mishandling or misplaying balls that have landed for hits, allowing baserunners to advance unnecessarily.

Brennan Boesch

	Innings	Runs Saved
2011	366.2	-1
2009-2011	954	-10

	Good Plays	Misplays and Errors
Boesch 2011	8	5
Avg Right Fielder	7	9
Good Play/Misplay Pct		.655

Jason Kubel

	Innings	Runs Saved
2011	413.2	-3
2009-2011	1303	-11

	Good Plays	Misplays and Errors
Kubel 2011	11	8
Avg Right Fielder	9	11
Good Play/Misplay Pct		.620

Kubel has the bat to be an everyday player in the majors, but his defense has relegated him to more of a platoon outfield and designated hitter role. He has a strong, accurate arm that helps keep base runners honest, but his lack of range has become a problem in the outfield. Kubel lacks athleticism and has below-average foot speed, which makes him a liability in right field. His lack of athleticism can partly be attributed to a knee injury he suffered in 2004 that required major reconstructive surgery. Deep-hit balls have never been his strength, and occasionally the problem is compounded when an extra base is taken due to misplaying the ball off the wall.

Right Fielders

Ben Francisco

	Innings	Runs Saved
2011	445	-7
2009-2011	680.2	-11

	Good Plays	Misplays and Errors
Francisco 2011	5	13
Avg Right Fielder	9	10
Good Play/Misplay Pct		.314

Francisco is a fairly versatile defensive outfielder, starting at all three spots over the last three seasons. He didn't see any action in center in 2011, but he did start 13 games in left and 49 games in right. He's only an adequate corner outfielder. His range is below-average, and he takes questionable routes to some balls and misplays others completely. His arm strength and accuracy aren't terrible, but occasionally he tries to throw out the lead runner after a base hit, allowing another runner to take an extra base. In short, Francisco is no more than a journeyman utility outfielder with below-average fielding skills.

Domonic Brown

	Innings	Runs Saved
2011	451	-9
2009-2011	563	-11

	Good Plays	Misplays and Errors
Brown 2011	3	13
Avg Right Fielder	7	8
Good Play/Misplay Pct		.215

Nick Markakis

	Innings	Runs Saved
2011	1389.2	2
2009-2011	4194	-12

	Good Plays	Misplays and Errors
Markakis 2011	38	18
Avg Right Fielder	27	33
Good Play/Misplay Pct		.715

Nick Markakis is an acceptable defensive right fielder, although his 2011 Gold Glove Award might lead you to think he's better than that. He's dependable in that he makes all the routine plays, as he demonstrated in 2011 by making no errors. However, his lack of speed prevents him from reaching anything more than that, though not from a lack of effort. Balls he gets to in the air that are not caught are usually accompanied by a jumping or diving effort. He has solid speed and moves smoothly in the field. Markakis has a strong, accurate arm which makes runners cautious when trying to advance. Despite widespread knowledge of his throwing ability, he consistently compiles high assist totals. It doesn't hurt that he rarely misses a game, and that Orioles pitchers put gobs of runners on base, resulting in a lot of opportunities to throw guys out.

Nick Swisher

	Innings	Runs Saved
2011	1190.1	-4
2009-2011	3345	-12

	Good Plays	Misplays and Errors
Swisher 2011	28	23
Avg Right Fielder	25	30
Good Play/Misplay Pct		.591

Swisher was a below-average right fielder in 2011, also playing 44 innings at first base for the Yankees this past season. He has slightly below-average range for a right fielder, and occasionally he will struggle on balls that are hit over his head. He is much better coming in on shallow-hit balls. Swisher is good at reading the ball off of the bat, but at times he will take a bad route to the ball preventing him from making a play. Swisher has average arm strength and accuracy and is an aggressive outfielder. This season he had some instances of mishandling the ball after a hit. He was good at preventing the potential advancement of base runners with his ability to get to and get rid of the ball quickly. Swisher still has the ability to be an average defensive corner outfielder, and for most of his eight-year career that is close to what he has been.

Lucas Duda

	Innings	Runs Saved
2011	335.1	-12
2009-2011	335.1	-12

	Good Plays	Misplays and Errors
Duda 2011	2	16
Avg Right Fielder	7	8
Good Play/Misplay Pct		.129

Right Fielders

Andre Ethier

	Innings	Runs Saved
2011	1091.1	4
2009-2011	3608	-18

	Good Plays	Misplays and Errors
Ethier 2011	20	14
Avg Right Fielder	21	25
Good Play/Misplay Pct		.629

Ethier was hampered by a nagging knee injury throughout his 2011 campaign. He has only average speed for an outfielder but makes up for it with efficient routes. He plays conservatively, getting to the deep ball very well but struggling to come up with catches on shallow-hit liners. He has a below-average throwing arm, and although he recorded six baserunner kills in 2011, he has cost the Dodgers 12 runs with his arm over the past three years. He doesn't make many fielding mistakes, though, finishing as the only regular National League right fielder with a 1.000 fielding percentage.

Lance Berkman

	Innings	Runs Saved
2011	865.1	-18
2009-2011	865.1	-18

	Good Plays	Misplays and Errors
Berkman 2011	12	24
Avg Right Fielder	16	19
Good Play/Misplay Pct		.373

The days of Lance Berkman being an effective outfielder are behind him. At this point in his career, there is little positive to say about his game in the outfield. A 2010 knee surgery combined with his veteran status in his mid-thirties has left Lance without a whole lot of mobility. Simply put, he is slow. He doesn't get good-enough jumps or reads on balls to make up for this lack of speed, which means he is responsible for a number of extra hits. One positive is that he is quite sure-handed and doesn't tend to mishandle balls often. His arm strength and accuracy are at best league-average.

Carlos Quentin

	Innings	Runs Saved
2011	854.2	0
2009-2011	1751.2	-24

	Good Plays	Misplays and Errors
Quentin 2011	13	12
Avg Right Fielder	15	18
Good Play/Misplay Pct		.563

After a dreadful defensive 2010 season, Carlos Quentin rebounded in 2011 to play average defense. The veteran Quentin is reliable in making all the routine plays. He is particularly sure-handed on flyballs, and his range is decent enough, but his speed is average at best. Quentin is a plus fielder coming in on a ball, whether it is shallow or medium depth. He is below-average on deep flyballs, and, though it does not occur often, he can have trouble with balls off or near the wall. Quentin's glove-related difficulties occur frequently once balls are down for hits. His glaring defensive shortcoming, though, is his poor throwing arm. In terms of both strength and accuracy, his arm is simply lacking.

Michael Cuddyer

	Innings	Runs Saved
2011	639.1	-10
2009-2011	2170.1	-28

	Good Plays	Misplays and Errors
Cuddyer 2011	15	12
Avg Right Fielder	12	15
Good Play/Misplay Pct		.598

Cuddyer posted time at three different positions in 2011, not including the pitching appearance he made in a blowout game. He logged the most innings in right field. The veteran does not have the speed to play the outfield at even an average level at this stage of his career. He just does not get to balls most other major league players would, especially on deep flyballs. He does have a nose for the ball and can make a great play from time to time. His best asset is his arm, but it isn't plus enough to merit any more time in the outfield going forward. At this point in his career, Cuddyer really belongs at first base.

Right Fielders

Magglio Ordonez

	Innings	Runs Saved
2011	471.2	-9
2009-2011	1876.2	-29

	Good Plays	Misplays and Errors
Ordonez 2011	8	13
Avg Right Fielder	9	11
Good Play/Misplay Pct		.422

Ordonez has never been a standout with the glove, and his defense has declined significantly over the past four seasons as he's played into his late thirties. He really shouldn't be playing much right field anymore at this point in his career, but the Tigers couldn't put him at designated hitter in 2011 because that'd take the bat out of the hands of either Alex Avila or Victor Martinez. Ordonez has clearly lost a step defensively; he has below-average to poor range, especially on deep balls. He has a weak arm that is tested often, so all things considered Ordonez is one of the worst defensive right fielders in the major leagues. Ordonez played just 24 complete games in right in 2011 (out of the 68 games he started), as he was regularly taken out for a defensive replacement, sometimes as soon as the fifth inning.

Pitchers Evaluations

Year	League	Gold Glove Winners	Should Have Been
2006	AL	Kenny Rogers	Kenny Rogers
	NL	Greg Maddux	Greg Maddux
2007	AL	Johan Santana	Johan Santana
	NL	Greg Maddux	Tim Hudson
2008	AL	Mike Mussina	Kenny Rogers
	NL	Greg Maddux	Greg Maddux
2009	AL	Mark Buehrle	Mark Buehrle
	NL	Adam Wainwright	Jon Garland
2010	AL	Mark Buehrle	Mark Buehrle
	NL	Bronson Arroyo	Bronson Arroyo
2011	AL	Mark Buehrle	Mark Buehrle
	NL	Clayton Kershaw	Jake Westbrook

My Personal Ratings

Top Five

1 Mark Buehrle, Mia
2 Zack Greinke, Mil
3 Jake Westbrook, Stl
4 R.A. Dickey, NYM
5 Bronson Arroyo, Cin

Bottom Five

171 Tommy Hanson, Atl
172 John Lackey, Bos
173 A.J. Burnett, NYY
174 Brad Penny, FA
175 Ervin Santana, LAA

Player teams based on transactions through February 1, 2012

Pitchers

Mark Buehrle

	Innings	Runs Saved
2011	205.1	7
2009-2011	629	29

	Good Plays	Misplays and Errors
Buehrle 2011	1	3
Avg Pitcher	3	6
Good Play/Misplay Pct		.379

Buehrle does all the things you want out of a pitcher defensively, and he has consistently rated as one of the best in the league as a result. Buehrle works extremely quickly on the mound and likewise has a quick move to home plate. This and his incredibly deceptive pick off move to first base effectively shut down the running game. Few baserunners attempt to steal, and when they do they are usually caught. In each of the past six years, runners have been caught with Buehrle on the mound more than 50 percent of the time. In 200+ innings in 2011, only three runners successfully stole a base with Buehrle on the mound, while six runners were either picked off or caught stealing by his own throw to first. Buehrle gets himself into great fielding position after each pitch and reacts quickly to field the ball. Buehrle was rewarded with his third-consecutive Fielding Bible Award in 2011. He is, without question, the best defender of his position in the game.

Zack Greinke

	Innings	Runs Saved
2011	171.2	4
2009-2011	621	21

	Good Plays	Misplays and Errors
Greinke 2011	4	2
Avg Pitcher	2	3
Good Play/Misplay Pct		.785

Zack Greinke's excellent fielding ability is an often-overlooked part of his game. Greinke has pitching mechanics that put him in a balanced fielding position upon follow-through. He is a great athlete and quick off the mound to field anything in his area. His arm is obviously quite strong and laser accurate. Perhaps the best part of his defensive game, however, comes in his ability to hold runners. Greinke consistently allows a low number of stolen base attempts and a low success rate, especially for a right-hander.

Bronson Arroyo

	Innings	Runs Saved
2011	199	4
2009-2011	635	16

	Good Plays	Misplays and Errors
Arroyo 2011	3	7
Avg Pitcher	3	6
Good Play/Misplay Pct		.440

While Arroyo couldn't match his stellar 2010 season defensively (8 Runs Saved, perfect fielding percentage and zero misplays), he still put together an excellent year in 2011. He has decent range on slow groundballs and bunts to all sides, but he sometimes has difficulty when he is rushed to make the play or he fails to set his feet. When this happens, he drops to a side-arm throw and consistently sends the throw to the right of the first baseman. The same flaw can be seen when he rushes his pick off throws. Since he often changes his arm slot when he pitches, he sometimes falls into the side-arm slot when he throws, decreasing his accuracy and adding movement to the ball on its way to the expecting fielder. Runners rarely attempt to steal on Arroyo and over his career they have been thrown out at almost a 40 percent clip.

Justin Verlander

	Innings	Runs Saved
2011	251	5
2009-2011	715.1	10

	Good Plays	Misplays and Errors
Verlander 2011	2	5
Avg Pitcher	3	5
Good Play/Misplay Pct		.423

Verlander finishes his delivery with a big pivot that causes him to face first base and displace his body to that side of the mound; this becomes exaggerated when he famously turns up the heat in the later innings. Because of this, Verlander has virtually no chance of fielding most balls hit with decent velocity toward the third base side of the mound. Even soft tappers to that side result in hurried throws due to the change of direction and elongated route. On the other hand, Verlander's momentum allows him to make more plays to the first base side of the field, somewhat compensating for the deficiency toward third. Overall, this has worked out for him, as he has posted above-average plus/minus numbers. Even though Verlander utilizes a high kick when delivering from the stretch, his pick off move is so quick to first base and his fastball is so quick to the plate

Pitchers

that he keeps the running game at bay.

Cliff Lee

	Innings	Runs Saved
2011	232.2	1
2009-2011	676.2	-2

	Good Plays	Misplays and Errors
Lee 2011	5	3
Avg Pitcher	2	4
Good Play/Misplay Pct		.753

Lee improved his defense from recent years, but still only had an average year in 2011 according to our metrics. One of Lee's strengths defensively is controlling the running game, but he gave up the most stolen bases in his career in 2011 with 11, as many as his previous two seasons combined. Still, that was better than the major league average of between 14 and 15 for starting pitchers with over 200 innings. As far as defending the area around the mound is concerned, Lee has had negative plus/minus numbers in each of the last eight years. The only season where he didn't make fewer plays than the average pitcher was his rookie year, when he was exactly at a zero plus/minus figure.

Tim Wakefield

	Innings	Runs Saved
2011	154.2	3
2009-2011	424.1	-3

	Good Plays	Misplays and Errors
Wakefield 2011	0	1
Avg Pitcher	2	3
Good Play/Misplay Pct		.000

Ever the wily knuckleballer, Tim Wakefield has shown he still has some defensive prowess. He moves well off the mound, though speed is not his strength. He is particularly good covering the first base side of the infield. As a result of veteran experience, he wastes no time moving to cover first on balls hit to the right side and knows when to back up throws to third and home. Wakefield did a decent job of holding runners in check last season, as well, which in recent seasons hasn't been a strong point for him. A full 43 percent of the runners attempting to steal on him were caught in 2011, his highest percentage since his rookie year, way back in 1992. His pick off move is still capable of catching runners (three last year), while his slide step from the stretch helps to get his slow knuckleball to the plate a little quicker.

Edwin Jackson

	Innings	Runs Saved
2011	199.2	-2
2009-2011	623	-9

	Good Plays	Misplays and Errors
Jackson 2011	1	6
Avg Pitcher	2	4
Good Play/Misplay Pct		.234

Jackson cost his teams two runs defensively in 2011 giving him -15 Runs Saved combined over the previous four seasons. This puts him significantly below-average among pitchers. Jackson really struggled to hold runners on in 2011. Of the 23 stolen bases attempted with Jackson on the mound, only one was caught stealing (4 percent). His career numbers are better, but still below-average for a pitcher, at 21 percent. Over the past three seasons, Jackson's fielding percentage is just .892, with 11 of his 12 errors of the throwing variety. He's also committed five additional defensive misplays during that span.

A.J. Burnett

	Innings	Runs Saved
2011	190.1	-4
2009-2011	584	-9

	Good Plays	Misplays and Errors
Burnett 2011	0	7
Avg Pitcher	2	4
Good Play/Misplay Pct		.000

Burnett has never been the fleetest of foot defensively, partly because his large, 6'4", 230-pound frame takes a little longer to get going off the mound. When he does go after groundballs, he's better to his left than to his right, mainly because his follow-through on his pitches naturally takes his momentum over to that side. He has a long motion to the plate, which historically has resulted in a high number of stolen bases against him. Burnett did improve in that area from 2010's whopping 37 stolen bases against him down to a somewhat more respectable, but still high, 24 in 2011. Overall, Burnett is a poor defender and has cost the Yankees (and himself) 11 runs in this area over the last two years.

Pitchers

John Lackey

	Innings	Runs Saved
2011	160	-6
2009-2011	551.1	-10

	Good Plays	Misplays and Errors
Lackey 2011	2	5
Avg Pitcher	2	4
Good Play/Misplay Pct		.423

Very little went right for John Lackey this year, and even his normally below-average defense took a step back as well. Lackey is not particularly good at fielding his position. He will occasionally uncork a wild throw or fail to cover first base. But his real problem comes with limiting the opponents' running game. While Lackey has never been good at holding runners, men on base ran wild against him in 2011, as his caught-stealing percentage plummeted to a career-low 8 percent. In fact, he allowed the most stolen bases of his career (and second-most in baseball in 2011 with 33), despite pitching the fewest number of innings since his rookie year in 2002.

Tim Lincecum

	Innings	Runs Saved
2011	217	0
2009-2011	654.2	-11

	Good Plays	Misplays and Errors
Lincecum 2011	3	1
Avg Pitcher	2	4
Good Play/Misplay Pct		.846

Prior to 2011, fielding was the one aspect of Lincecum's game that was lacking. However, Lincecum took a huge step forward with his defense in 2011. An inability to hold runners was one of Lincecum's weaknesses, but he has made major improvements in that category. Runners attempted more steals against Lincecum than ever before in 2011, but were caught at a career-high rate of 38 percent of the time. He also caught two runners stealing without delivering a pitch, the first two Pitcher Caught Stealing plays of his career. Lincecum experimented pitching exclusively from the stretch at times, and his ability to hold runners has really benefited from his quicker delivery to home plate.

Ervin Santana

	Innings	Runs Saved
2011	228.2	-6
2009-2011	591	-15

	Good Plays	Misplays and Errors
Santana 2011	3	5
Avg Pitcher	2	4
Good Play/Misplay Pct		.523

Ervin Santana is not a good defensive pitcher, but it's not a question of athleticism. His delivery leaves him almost completely facing towards first base and falling off the mound in that direction. This motion only worsens when throwing from the stretch. Not surprisingly, he doesn't field the balls up the middle that pitchers can ordinarily handle. Additionally, Santana can't hold opposing baserunners, and the league has started to notice. Over 2010-11, Santana allowed 65 successful stolen bases in 78 attempts, not a good ratio. In his younger days, Santana could throw 200 innings and limit the opposition to 10 or fewer successful stolen base attempts. Those days are gone, however, and Santana is one of the worst defensive pitchers in the league.

Defensive Replacements

One way of getting factual information about a player's defense is simply to look at how many times he was put into the game for defense, and how many times he was taken out of the game for defense.

We limit the definition of defensive replacements to certain situations to better capture the intent of the substitutions. For our purposes, a substitute is a defensive replacement if he enters the game in the seventh inning or later while his team is in the field or before that half inning. His team can be down by one run, tied, or winning by at most two plus the number of runners on base. For example, if the fielding team is winning by three runs and a sub enters the game at the start of the inning, we don't consider it a defensive replacement; however, if the defensive team is leading by four but the bases are loaded, any subs would be considered defensive replacements.

The chart below gives all players who were used as defensive substitutes five or more times in 2011, or who were removed for substitutes five or more times.

Team	Position	Player	Def In	Def Out
Atlanta Braves	Left Field	Eric Hinske	2	8
Atlanta Braves	Right Field	Jason Heyward	7	1
Atlanta Braves	Right Field	Eric Hinske	1	5
Atlanta Braves	Third Base	Martin Prado	6	1
Baltimore Orioles	Left Field	Matt Angle	6	0
Baltimore Orioles	Left Field	Felix Pie	5	0
Baltimore Orioles	Left Field	Nolan Reimold	1	7
Baltimore Orioles	Left Field	Luke Scott	0	5
Baltimore Orioles	Second Base	Robert Andino	6	0
Chicago Cubs	Catcher	Koyie Hill	5	0
Chicago Cubs	Left Field	Reed Johnson	12	1
Chicago Cubs	Left Field	Tony Campana	9	0
Chicago Cubs	Left Field	Blake DeWitt	1	5
Chicago Cubs	Left Field	Alfonso Soriano	1	21
Chicago Cubs	Right Field	Reed Johnson	8	3
Chicago White Sox	Right Field	Brent Lillibridge	6	0
Cincinnati Reds	Catcher	Ryan Hanigan	12	0
Cincinnati Reds	Catcher	Ramon Hernandez	3	5
Cincinnati Reds	Center Field	Drew Stubbs	6	0
Cincinnati Reds	Center Field	Chris Heisey	0	6
Cincinnati Reds	Left Field	Chris Heisey	23	1
Cincinnati Reds	Left Field	Fred Lewis	1	9
Cincinnati Reds	Left Field	Jonny Gomes	0	9
Cincinnati Reds	Shortstop	Paul Janish	9	2
Cincinnati Reds	Shortstop	Edgar Renteria	4	9
Cincinnati Reds	Third Base	Miguel Cairo	5	2
Cleveland Indians	Catcher	Carlos Santana	5	1
Cleveland Indians	Left Field	Shelley Duncan	0	8
Cleveland Indians	Third Base	Jack Hannahan	8	0
Cleveland Indians	Third Base	Lonnie Chisenhall	1	5
Colorado Rockies	Left Field	Ryan Spilborghs	7	0
Colorado Rockies	Left Field	Ty Wigginton	0	5
Detroit Tigers	Left Field	Ryan Raburn	5	1
Detroit Tigers	Left Field	Andy Dirks	5	0
Detroit Tigers	Left Field	Brennan Boesch	1	10
Detroit Tigers	Right Field	Don Kelly	13	1
Detroit Tigers	Right Field	Casper Wells	10	0
Detroit Tigers	Right Field	Brennan Boesch	2	11
Detroit Tigers	Right Field	Magglio Ordonez	0	12
Detroit Tigers	Second Base	Ramon Santiago	14	0
Detroit Tigers	Second Base	Ryan Raburn	0	14
Detroit Tigers	Third Base	Brandon Inge	14	0
Detroit Tigers	Third Base	Don Kelly	1	6
Detroit Tigers	Third Base	Wilson Betemit	0	9
Florida Marlins	Left Field	Logan Morrison	0	5

Team	Position	Player	Def In	Def Out
Florida Marlins	Third Base	Greg Dobbs	5	4
Houston Astros	Catcher	J.R. Towles	6	0
Houston Astros	First Base	Carlos Lee	6	3
Houston Astros	Left Field	Jason Bourgeois	9	0
Houston Astros	Left Field	Carlos Lee	0	8
Kansas City Royals	Catcher	Brayan Pena	6	0
Kansas City Royals	Second Base	Chris Getz	8	0
Kansas City Royals	Second Base	Johnny Giavotella	0	7
Los Angeles Angels	Catcher	Jeff Mathis	8	0
Los Angeles Angels	Catcher	Bobby Wilson	7	0
Los Angeles Angels	Left Field	Reggie Willits	7	0
Los Angeles Angels	Left Field	Vernon Wells	6	0
Los Angeles Angels	Left Field	Bobby Abreu	0	8
Los Angeles Dodgers	Catcher	Dioner Navarro	5	0
Los Angeles Dodgers	First Base	James Loney	7	2
Los Angeles Dodgers	Left Field	Tony Gwynn	13	2
Los Angeles Dodgers	Second Base	Jamey Carroll	10	0
Milwaukee Brewers	Center Field	Carlos Gomez	5	0
Milwaukee Brewers	Center Field	Nyjer Morgan	2	5
Minnesota Twins	Catcher	Drew Butera	8	0
Minnesota Twins	Catcher	Rene Rivera	6	0
Minnesota Twins	Second Base	Matt Tolbert	5	0
New York Mets	Right Field	Jason Pridie	5	1
New York Yankees	Left Field	Brett Gardner	10	0
New York Yankees	Left Field	Andruw Jones	0	7
New York Yankees	Right Field	Chris Dickerson	14	0
New York Yankees	Right Field	Nick Swisher	0	13
Oakland Athletics	Left Field	Ryan Sweeney	6	0
Oakland Athletics	Third Base	Andy LaRoche	8	1
Pittsburgh Pirates	First Base	Lyle Overbay	5	2
Pittsburgh Pirates	Left Field	Jose Tabata	6	3
Pittsburgh Pirates	Right Field	Xavier Paul	19	0
Pittsburgh Pirates	Right Field	Garrett Jones	1	11
Pittsburgh Pirates	Right Field	Matt Diaz	1	9
Pittsburgh Pirates	Third Base	Brandon Wood	11	0
Pittsburgh Pirates	Third Base	Josh Harrison	0	9
San Diego Padres	First Base	Anthony Rizzo	6	0
San Diego Padres	First Base	Jesus Guzman	0	6
San Diego Padres	Left Field	Chris Denorfia	13	0
San Diego Padres	Left Field	Ryan Ludwick	0	7
San Diego Padres	Right Field	Chris Denorfia	2	5
San Francisco Giants	Catcher	Eli Whiteside	7	0
San Francisco Giants	Center Field	Andres Torres	7	3
San Francisco Giants	Center Field	Aaron Rowand	3	9
San Francisco Giants	Left Field	Aaron Rowand	19	3
San Francisco Giants	Left Field	Cody Ross	14	4
San Francisco Giants	Left Field	Pat Burrell	1	13
San Francisco Giants	Left Field	Brandon Belt	1	5
San Francisco Giants	Shortstop	Brandon Crawford	6	0
San Francisco Giants	Shortstop	Mike Fontenot	2	5
Seattle Mariners	Left Field	Greg Halman	6	0
Seattle Mariners	Left Field	Carlos Peguero	0	6
St Louis Cardinals	Right Field	Skip Schumaker	10	0
St Louis Cardinals	Right Field	Jon Jay	6	4
St Louis Cardinals	Right Field	Lance Berkman	2	17
St Louis Cardinals	Second Base	Daniel Descalso	7	3
St Louis Cardinals	Second Base	Nick Punto	6	2
St Louis Cardinals	Second Base	Ryan Theriot	5	0
St Louis Cardinals	Second Base	Skip Schumaker	0	14
St Louis Cardinals	Third Base	Daniel Descalso	17	4
St Louis Cardinals	Third Base	David Freese	0	14
Tampa Bay Rays	Catcher	Kelly Shoppach	7	1
Tampa Bay Rays	First Base	Casey Kotchman	5	0
Tampa Bay Rays	Second Base	Ben Zobrist	6	1
Tampa Bay Rays	Second Base	Sean Rodriguez	1	5
Tampa Bay Rays	Shortstop	Reid Brignac	9	0
Tampa Bay Rays	Shortstop	Sean Rodriguez	5	3
Texas Rangers	First Base	Mitch Moreland	5	1
Texas Rangers	First Base	Michael Young	0	7
Texas Rangers	Left Field	David Murphy	6	2
Texas Rangers	Left Field	Nelson Cruz	1	6
Texas Rangers	Right Field	Nelson Cruz	5	2
Texas Rangers	Right Field	Mitch Moreland	3	5
Washington Nationals	Center Field	Rick Ankiel	10	2
Washington Nationals	Center Field	Roger Bernadina	2	7
Washington Nationals	Left Field	Roger Bernadina	13	1
Washington Nationals	Left Field	Brian Bixler	8	1
Washington Nationals	Left Field	Laynce Nix	3	13
Washington Nationals	Left Field	Michael Morse	0	8
Washington Nationals	Third Base	Alex Cora	8	1
Washington Nationals	Third Base	Jerry Hairston	1	7

Evaluating Outfielder Throwing Arms

How often does a runner score from second on a single to center field?

Answer: 78 percent of the time (in 2011)

How often does a runner get thrown out trying to score on a single to center?

Answer: 2 percent of the time

These questions and answers are the keys to evaluating the quality of an outfielder's throwing arm. In this case we're looking at one position (center field) and one situation (runner on second, single to center). It's just one component of Outfield Arms Runs Saved, which in turn is just one component of the overall system, Defensive Runs Saved.

If a center fielder allows runners to score from second 90 percent of the time on singles to center and never throws a runner out, that's not good when compared to the overall averages (or, stated another way, compared to the average center fielder). But if he keeps the runner from scoring, say, 50 percent of the time and throws out 5 percent, that is good.

Let's take two players from the 2011 season as examples: former pitcher Rick Ankiel, center fielder for the Washington Nationals, and Ben Revere of the Minnesota Twins. There were 34 times in 2011 when Ankiel was patrolling center field for the Nationals when a batter hit a single to center with a man on second. There were 33 such occasions for Revere. But Ankiel only allowed 21 runners to score and threw out two others, while Revere allowed 29 to score and threw out none. That's a big difference.

As a result, Ankiel was better than the average center fielder, and using our method for estimating how many runs his performance saved the team, we estimate he saved the Nationals four runs compared to the average center fielder. On the other hand, we estimate that Revere cost his team two runs in these situations where there was a single with a runner on second base.

That's a six-run difference between Ankiel and Revere based on just over 30 plays for each of them.

Let's summarize this in a chart:

Runner on Second, Single to Center

	Runner Scores	Stays at Third	Thrown Out	Runs Saved
Avg. CF in 2011	78%	20%	2%	0
Rick Ankiel	62%	32%	6%	4
Ben Revere	88%	12%	0%	-2

The New System

Now let's look at the same chart for a couple of other players, Shane Victorino of the Phillies and B.J. Upton of the Rays. Victorino had 32 plays and Upton 39.

Runner on Second, Single to Center
Old Outfield Arm Runs Saved

	Runner Scores	Stays at Third	Thrown Out	Runs Saved
Avg. CF in 2011	78%	20%	2%	0
Shane Victorino	63%	37%	0%	2.44
B.J. Upton	74%	23%	3%	0.34

We'll use more significant digits to measure Runs Saved for these two players. Upton's performance is about average (0.34 runs saved) while Victorino appears to have been above average with 2.44 runs saved in these situations.

However, this is based on our old system for determining Outfield Arms Runs Saved. Mind you, the old system was very good. When comparing players season-to-season (see chapter on correlations on page 113) it had one of the highest correlation coefficients (0.57) of any of our systems. Nevertheless, we felt we could improve on it and have implemented a new technique for the 2010 and 2011 season. We'll use Victorino and Upton to give you an example of how we've changed the system.

Not all singles to center field are created equal. It is much more difficult for a center fielder to hold or throw out a runner trying to score from second on some types of hits than others. Here are some examples of plays that are more difficult for the fielder to prevent runner advancement, based on data from the 2011 season:

1) Singles with two outs on balls hit in the air – With less than two outs, a runner on second base has to hold up on a single hit in the air. With two outs, he can take off with abandon. The data shows this. With two outs, a runner scores from second 94 percent of the time, but with less than two outs that drops to about half the time (52%).

2) Groundball singles – Runners score from second 91 percent of the time on groundball singles compared to 70 percent for flyball singles.

3) Groundball singles not hit to straight-away center field – If a base hit goes to the edges of the center field area rather than to straight-away center field, it's easier for the baserunner to advance. Not much easier—runners score 95 percent of the time on balls hit to the edges compared to 88 percent on straight-away hits—but easier.

4) Softly hit groundball singles – If a groundball gets through the infield to center field for a hit but it's softly hit, it's a bit easier for baserunners to advance than on harder hit balls (93 percent for a ball hit below the speed limit of 55 miles per hour, 90 percent for those hit harder than the speed limit).

Let's compare Upton and Victorino again. While Victorino was in center field, batters hit 11 flyballs with less than two outs to straight-away center field. The old system gave too much credit for holding runners in these situations. Runners advance less often on flyballs with less than two outs. The old system gave Victorino 3.91 runs of credit. Under the new system, which recognizes that holding runners on flies with less than two outs is not as difficult of a play, Victorino only gets 1.20 runs of credit. Upton had fewer of these types of hits with 6. The old system gave Upton 2.19 runs of credit and the new system gives him about 0.70 runs. Victorino gets

2.71 fewer runs in the new system; Upton gets 1.49 fewer runs. Switching to the new system Upton improves by 1.22 runs compared to Victorino (subtracting Upton's 1.49 from Victorino's 2.71).

Upton also fares better because more groundball singles were allowed with a man on second when he was in the field than Victorino. There were 19 grounders for Upton compared to only 11 for Victorino. The old system didn't give enough credit for holding runners on groundball singles and Upton gains 2.39 runs compared to only .93 runs for Victorino. Upton improves more than Victorino by 1.46 runs.

As a result, when we add up all the plays for both players, the new system now actually shows Upton's performance to be slightly better than Victorino's, despite the fact that a lower percentage of runners scored on Victorino. Upton gets 1.50 defensive runs for his work on singles with a runner on second while Victorino only gets 0.86 runs of credit.

Runner on Second, Single to Center
New Outfield Arm Runs Saved

	Runner Scores	Stays at Third	Thrown Out	Runs Saved
Avg. CF in 2011	78%	20%	2%	0
Shane Victorino	63%	37%	0%	0.86
B.J. Upton	74%	23%	3%	1.50

Looking at all components of the Outfield Arms Runs Saved system, the old system put Shane Victorino at two Defensive Runs Saved while B.J. Upton had one. The new, more sophisticated system keeps Upton at one Defensive Run Saved while Victorino drops three runs to minus-one.

As you can see, these changes are small. But because we are measuring the outcomes at a much deeper level, the system is improved. The old system suggested that Victorino was one run better than Upton in 2011, but the new system shows Upton's performance to be about two runs better than Victorino's.

One final note. Let's keep this in perspective. B.J. Upton's arm was a bit better than Victorino's in 2011, but overall Victorino was a better defensive center fielder. In comparison to other center fielders, Upton had trouble handling an outfielder's main job, covering ground to catch batted balls, and as a result his overall defense cost the Rays about seven runs. Victorino was an average center fielder in 2011 saving one run overall with his defense.

The Best and Worst Throwing Arms

With our new system in place let's take a look at some of the more interesting results:

- Adam Jones, center fielder for the Baltimore Orioles, has had the best throwing arm in baseball over the last three years. Over that span he has saved the Orioles 23 runs with his arm with 30 baserunner kills. (A kill is a direct throw by an outfielder to a base to nab the baserunner.) The next best center fielder in that time span only had nine runs saved with his arm (Rick Ankiel). Unfortunately, despite having the best arm in baseball, Jones is a below average defensive center fielder overall. In that same time frame he has *cost* the Orioles 38 runs with his inability to cover ground and make catches that other center fielders make.

- The best right field arm of the last three years belongs to Jeff Francouer, who played for the Royals in 2011. He has saved 17 runs with 29 kills. Four other right fielders have accumulated double-digit runs saved in the last three years: Jose Bautista (13), Shin-Soo Choo (12), Jayson Werth (11) and Hunter Pence (10). The other Hunter, Torii Hunter, tied Pence, Jason Kubel, and Francoeur for the lead among right fielders in 2011 with five runs saved with his arm.

- The best left field throwing arm in 2011 was Alex Gordon, also with the Royals. Gordon's one-year total of 13 runs saved was the best single season mark in the last three years. Gordon moved from third base to left field in late 2010. His total of 14 runs saved with his arm is the best three-year total for any left fielder despite playing less than a year and a half. The only other double-digit left fielder is Brett Gardner with 10 runs saved with his arm in the three years.

- Gordon's performance is impressive for being new to the outfield, but it is not unprecedented. Alfonso Soriano moved from second base to left field and saved 7 runs in his first year with his arm (2006) and 15 in his second. Soriano had 15 kills in 2006 and 19 in 2007. Gordon had 12 kills in 2011 among his 20 assists. The other eight assists involved relays.

- The single best throwing year we have recorded since we started tracking this was Richard Hidalgo's 17 runs saved playing right field for Houston in 2003. He also had 19 kills that year, tying him with Alfonso Soriano's kill total in 2007 for the most we've recorded for a single season. Alfonso Soriano's 15 runs saved in 2007 is the second highest total on record, and Alex Gordon's 13 runs saved with his arm last year is third.

Best Outfield Throwing Seasons Since 2003

Player	Pos	Year	Runs Saved
Richard Hidalgo	RF	2003	17
Alfonso Soriano	LF	2007	15
Alex Gordon	LF	2011	13
Shane Victorino	RF	2007	11
Richard Hidalgo	RF	2004	11
Jim Edmonds	CF	2004	11
Michael Cuddyer	RF	2007	10
Jeff Francoeur	RF	2007	10
Nick Markakis	RF	2008	10
Adam Jones	CF	2009	10
Shin-Soo Choo	RF	2010	10

- With two of the best throwing outfielders in baseball over the last three years in Gordon and Francoeur, the Kansas City Royals had the best throwing outfield in baseball last year. Tied with the Washington Nationals. Both had 19 runs saved from their outfielders' throwing arms. The Nationals had the best center field arm in Rick Ankiel (8 outfield arm runs saved in center field, tied for most in 2011 with Adam Jones).

Best Outfield Arms - 2011

Team	Runs Saved
Kansas City Royals	19
Washington Nationals	19
Chicago Cubs	9
Los Angeles Angels	7
Houston Astros	7

Worst Outfield Arms - 2011

Team	Runs Saved
Chicago White Sox	-12
Pittsburgh Pirates	-9
Milwaukee Brewers	-8
Atlanta Braves	-8
Colorado Rockies	-7
Boston Red Sox	-7
St. Louis Cardinals	-7

- The 2007 Philadelphia Phillies had the best throwing arms on record with 26 outfield arm runs saved. That year Aaron Rowand saved 8 runs with his arm in center field while in right field Shane Victorino (11) and Jayson Werth (5) combined for 16.

- The worst throwing arm over the last three years is Carlos Quentin, who has cost the White Sox about 13 runs with his arm in right field. There are a bunch of guys tied with -12: in left, Ryan Braun. In center, Denard Span. In right, J.D. Drew, Ichiro Suzuki, and Andre Ethier.

- Ichiro Suzuki? One of the worst throwing outfielders over the last three years? That's a surprise. From 2003 to 2008 in right field Ichiro had 15 runs saved with his arm, including 31 kills. Runners didn't test his arm very often. They had 666 opportunities to advance while Ichiro was in right field during those years and 290 advanced. That's a 43.5 percent advance rate, above average for a right fielder. The average right fielder allows about a 48 percent advance rate. But in the last three years, runners have advanced 51 percent of the time, including a career worst 56 percent in 2011. Ichiro's kill rate is also down from about six per year playing right field between 2003 and 2008 to about four per year in the last three.

The "Centering" Change in the New System

Readers and analysts who follow this data closely may have already noticed. Effective with the release of this book, runs saved figures based on outfielder arms have been restated going back to 2003. For example, based on the old system, Nick Markakis had 14 outfield arm runs saved in 2008. Under the new system he has 10 for that year.

In the old system we gave credit of .75 runs for what we call Miscellaneous Kills. These are Kills (outfield assists without a relay) that occur in situations other than our main three: 1) First to Third on a Single, 2) Second to Home on a Single, and 3) First to Home on a Double. A simple example of a Miscellaneous Kill is an outfielder throwing a runner out at third trying to tag up on a flyball. Giving a .75 run credit was a good estimate of the value of those plays, but it led to league totals that were greater than zero when totaling all players. The totals for the three main situations totaled to zero, but Miscellaneous Kill runs saved pushed totals above zero.

In the new system, we still credit each Miscellaneous Kill as .75 runs, but we created a "centering" technique with Miscellaneous Kills to bring the league totals to zero. We do this by adding up all Miscellaneous Kill runs saved and pro-rating them back to all outfielders (by position) based on the number of opportunities they had to make those kills, as best we can estimate. These are his Expected Miscellaneous Kill runs.

For example, B.J. Upton had four Miscellaneous Kills in 2011 adding 3.00 (4 x 0.75) to his runs saved total. His pro-rated share of all Miscellaneous Kill runs based on his opportunities is 2.28 runs. We subtract his expected runs of 2.28 from his actual runs of 3.00 to give him 0.72 runs in the new Outfield Arms Runs Saved system compared to the old amount of 3.00.

If you compare old system Outfield Arm Runs Saved numbers with new ones, you'll see that most players have dropped a couple runs or so. That's because of this new centering technique.

Left Fielders - 3-Year Throwing

Player	Opps	Extra Bases	Pct	Kills	Runs Saved
Alex Gordon	195	55	.282	14	15
Brett Gardner	156	43	.276	13	10
Laynce Nix	123	26	.211	6	8
Ryan Raburn	118	39	.331	12	6
Juan Rivera	214	76	.355	12	6
David DeJesus	144	53	.368	11	5
Travis Snider	131	40	.305	6	4
Felix Pie	157	49	.312	7	4
Logan Morrison	157	50	.318	7	4
Carl Crawford	315	102	.324	8	4
Carlos Gonzalez	108	35	.324	10	3
Gerardo Parra	212	70	.330	15	2
Chris Coghlan	177	62	.350	9	2
Nolan Reimold	187	66	.353	8	2
Johnny Damon	142	46	.324	6	1
Lastings Milledge	127	46	.362	7	1
Jason Bay	352	128	.364	15	1
Josh Willingham	240	92	.383	9	1
Jonny Gomes	218	70	.321	8	0
Josh Hamilton	136	46	.338	4	0
Michael Saunders	108	41	.380	6	0
Carlos Lee	376	138	.367	14	-2
Raul Ibanez	322	119	.370	13	-2
Alfonso Soriano	277	104	.375	13	-2
Fred Lewis	178	64	.360	4	-3
Scott Hairston	110	42	.382	2	-3
Ryan Ludwick	85	36	.424	4	-3
Matt Holliday	338	129	.382	12	-4
Seth Smith	117	47	.402	5	-4
Delmon Young	332	133	.401	15	-5
Jose Tabata	154	61	.396	3	-6
David Murphy	200	86	.430	6	-7
Manny Ramirez	109	52	.477	4	-7
Juan Pierre	296	105	.355	4	-10
Ryan Braun	418	159	.380	14	-12
MLB Totals	13124	4674	.356	531	

Left Fielders - 2010 Throwing

Player	Tm	Opps	Extra Bases	Pct	Kills	Runs Saved
Brett Gardner	NYY	67	16	.239	8	7
Felix Pie	Bal	63	13	.206	5	5
Pat Burrell	SF	59	11	.186	1	3
Logan Morrison	Fla	62	20	.323	3	3
Chris Coghlan	Fla	83	29	.349	7	3
Melky Cabrera	Atl	48	14	.292	3	2
Alex Gordon	KC	69	21	.304	2	2
Michael Saunders	Sea	77	29	.377	6	2
Delmon Young	Min	139	53	.381	9	2
Josh Willingham	Was	93	39	.419	5	2
Gerardo Parra	Ari	50	14	.280	3	1
Ryan Raburn	Det	44	13	.295	3	1
Lastings Milledge	Pit	59	20	.339	4	1
Austin Kearns	2 tms	65	21	.323	2	0
Josh Hamilton	Tex	71	24	.338	2	0
Seth Smith	Col	52	18	.346	2	0
Carl Crawford	TB	85	31	.365	3	0
Jason Bay	NYM	86	32	.372	4	0
Corey Patterson	Bal	59	23	.390	2	0
Juan Rivera	LAA	81	35	.432	4	0
Carlos Gonzalez	Col	37	17	.459	4	0
Travis Snider	Tor	41	13	.317	1	-1
Fred Lewis	Tor	86	30	.349	1	-1
Matt Holliday	StL	117	44	.376	4	-1
David Murphy	Tex	58	26	.448	3	-1
Jonny Gomes	Cin	126	47	.373	4	-2
Matt Diaz	Atl	34	13	.382	0	-2
Raul Ibanez	Phi	112	45	.402	3	-3
Jose Tabata	Pit	85	36	.424	3	-3
Juan Pierre	CWS	138	45	.326	2	-4
Ryan Braun	Mil	153	56	.366	5	-4
Alfonso Soriano	ChC	103	40	.388	3	-4
Scott Hairston	SD	48	24	.500	0	-5
Carlos Lee	Hou	139	60	.432	4	-6
Scott Podsednik	2 tms	132	52	.394	0	-7
MLB Totals		4399	1586	.361	188	

Left Fielders - 2011 Throwing

Player	Tm	Opps	Extra Bases	Pct	Kills	Runs Saved
Alex Gordon	KC	126	34	.270	12	13
Laynce Nix	Was	47	12	.255	4	4
Sam Fuld	TB	48	14	.292	4	4
Juan Rivera	2 tms	33	10	.303	2	3
Brett Gardner	NYY	89	27	.303	5	3
Carlos Lee	Hou	74	24	.324	6	3
Carlos Gonzalez	Col	48	12	.250	4	2
Michael Brantley	Cle	52	14	.269	3	2
J.D. Martinez	Hou	45	14	.311	4	2
Gerardo Parra	Ari	106	35	.330	10	2
Cody Ross	SF	54	18	.333	4	2
Martin Prado	Atl	74	26	.351	6	2
Brennan Boesch	Det	58	23	.397	4	2
Jonny Gomes	2 tms	63	16	.254	1	1
Logan Morrison	Fla	95	30	.316	4	1
Michael Morse	Was	37	12	.324	2	1
Alfonso Soriano	ChC	93	32	.344	5	1
Carl Crawford	Bos	112	35	.313	0	0
Josh Willingham	Oak	80	25	.313	3	0
Alex Presley	Pit	64	21	.328	0	0
Josh Hamilton	Tex	65	22	.338	2	0
Jason Bay	NYM	102	36	.353	3	0
Desmond Jennings	TB	31	12	.387	2	0
Tony Gwynn	LAD	58	25	.431	3	0
Nolan Reimold	Bal	70	27	.386	3	-1
Vernon Wells	LAA	86	32	.372	2	-2
Matt Holliday	StL	97	42	.433	4	-2
Eric Thames	Tor	37	19	.514	1	-2
Jose Tabata	Pit	69	25	.362	0	-3
Raul Ibanez	Phi	107	41	.383	2	-3
Delmon Young	2 tms	101	39	.386	4	-3
Ryan Ludwick	2 tms	85	36	.424	4	-3
Juan Pierre	CWS	113	44	.389	2	-4
David Murphy	Tex	61	31	.508	0	-4
Ryan Braun	Mil	106	48	.453	5	-6
MLB Totals		4230	1523	.360	182	

Left Fielders - 2009 Throwing

Player	Tm	Opps	Extra Bases	Pct	Kills	Runs Saved
Wladimir Balentien	2 tms	45	10	.222	5	5
Ryan Raburn	Det	44	14	.318	7	5
David DeJesus	KC	141	51	.362	11	5
Carl Crawford	TB	118	36	.305	5	4
Raul Ibanez	Phi	103	33	.320	8	4
Juan Rivera	LAA	100	31	.310	6	3
Scott Hairston	2 tms	54	15	.278	2	2
Nolan Reimold	Bal	98	33	.337	4	2
Laynce Nix	Cin	47	10	.213	1	1
Ben Francisco	2 tms	56	15	.268	0	1
Denard Span	Min	45	14	.311	2	1
Carlos Lee	Hou	163	54	.331	4	1
Lastings Milledge	Pit	63	22	.349	3	1
Jason Bay	Bos	164	60	.366	8	1
Alfonso Soriano	ChC	81	32	.395	5	1
Fred Lewis	SF	54	17	.315	1	0
Johnny Damon	NYY	109	35	.321	4	0
Nyjer Morgan	Pit	45	15	.333	2	0
Carlos Quentin	CWS	97	34	.351	3	0
Scott Podsednik	CWS	55	20	.364	2	0
Matt Holliday	2 tms	124	43	.347	4	-1
Chris Coghlan	Fla	94	33	.351	2	-1
Gerardo Parra	Ari	56	21	.375	2	-1
Josh Willingham	Was	67	28	.418	1	-1
Ryan Braun	Mil	159	55	.346	4	-2
Juan Pierre	LAD	45	16	.356	0	-2
David Murphy	Tex	81	29	.358	3	-2
Adam Lind	Tor	53	19	.358	0	-2
Chris Duncan	StL	37	16	.432	1	-2
Seth Smith	Col	46	19	.413	1	-3
Adam Dunn	Was	51	24	.471	1	-3
Garret Anderson	Atl	81	29	.358	2	-4
Delmon Young	Min	92	41	.446	2	-4
Manny Ramirez	LAD	73	31	.425	2	-5
Chase Headley	SD	90	45	.500	2	-7
MLB Totals		4495	1565	.348	161	

Center Fielders - 3-Year Throwing

Player	Opps	Extra Bases	Pct	Kills	Runs Saved
Adam Jones	359	178	.496	28	23
Rick Ankiel	180	85	.472	12	9
Shane Victorino	307	147	.479	15	7
Matt Kemp	343	184	.536	19	7
Peter Bourjos	139	65	.468	8	6
Drew Stubbs	265	131	.494	13	6
Angel Pagan	270	142	.526	8	6
Curtis Granderson	341	172	.504	12	5
Marlon Byrd	310	174	.561	12	4
Michael Bourn	383	212	.554	14	2
Colby Rasmus	280	142	.507	4	1
Carlos Gomez	205	104	.507	7	1
B.J. Upton	319	170	.533	11	1
Austin Jackson	227	124	.546	10	1
Franklin Gutierrez	285	154	.540	10	0
Andrew McCutchen	356	206	.579	13	-1
Melky Cabrera	255	153	.600	13	-1
Nyjer Morgan	264	136	.515	5	-2
Vernon Wells	273	145	.531	4	-2
Aaron Rowand	180	107	.594	7	-2
Andres Torres	118	73	.619	4	-2
Tony Gwynn	159	100	.629	8	-2
Cody Ross	158	88	.557	4	-3
Torii Hunter	174	97	.557	2	-3
Nate McLouth	198	119	.601	5	-4
Rajai Davis	188	113	.601	7	-4
Chris Young	375	212	.565	9	-5
Mike Cameron	202	120	.594	4	-5
Cameron Maybin	213	128	.601	6	-6
Coco Crisp	187	116	.620	2	-6
Alex Rios	311	165	.531	3	-7
Jacoby Ellsbury	263	159	.605	4	-7
Grady Sizemore	186	110	.591	0	-8
Dexter Fowler	305	187	.613	9	-8
Denard Span	243	153	.630	5	-12
MLB Totals	12449	6882	.553	444	

Center Fielders - 2010 Throwing

Player	Tm	Opps	Extra Bases	Pct	Kills	Runs Saved
Marlon Byrd	ChC	135	67	.496	5	5
Adam Jones	Bal	113	60	.531	10	5
Angel Pagan	NYM	94	44	.468	4	4
Shane Victorino	Phi	108	50	.463	8	3
Chris Young	Ari	144	75	.521	7	3
Carlos Beltran	NYM	51	25	.490	4	2
Michael Bourn	Hou	105	55	.524	5	2
Curtis Granderson	NYY	96	51	.531	4	2
Mitch Maier	KC	47	22	.468	3	1
Carlos Gomez	Mil	70	33	.471	2	1
Rick Ankiel	2 tms	54	29	.537	4	1
Andrew McCutchen	Pit	133	84	.632	8	1
Drew Stubbs	Cin	108	51	.472	4	0
Trevor Crowe	Cle	62	37	.597	3	0
Tony Gwynn	SD	63	38	.603	4	0
Aaron Rowand	SF	48	32	.667	4	0
B.J. Upton	TB	97	46	.474	1	-1
Colby Rasmus	StL	101	49	.485	0	-1
Austin Jackson	Det	123	68	.553	5	-1
Coco Crisp	Oak	46	28	.609	1	-1
Cameron Maybin	Fla	62	38	.613	3	-1
Cody Ross	2 tms	66	37	.561	1	-2
Torii Hunter	LAA	83	47	.566	0	-2
Andres Torres	SF	52	32	.615	1	-2
Nate McLouth	Atl	44	28	.636	0	-2
Alex Rios	CWS	140	69	.493	1	-3
Franklin Gutierrez	Sea	108	57	.528	0	-3
Julio Borbon	Tex	95	52	.547	2	-3
Vernon Wells	Tor	124	71	.573	2	-3
Denard Span	Min	136	79	.581	4	-3
Michael Brantley	Cle	55	34	.618	0	-3
Rajai Davis	Oak	55	37	.673	1	-3
Matt Kemp	LAD	120	70	.583	3	-4
Dexter Fowler	Col	105	63	.600	1	-4
Nyjer Morgan	Was	132	71	.538	0	-6
MLB Totals		4129	2244	.543	158	

Center Fielders - 2011 Throwing

Player	Tm	Opps	Extra Bases	Pct	Kills	Runs Saved
Rick Ankiel	Was	72	30	.417	7	8
Adam Jones	Bal	141	78	.553	13	8
Drew Stubbs	Cin	124	66	.532	8	5
Matt Kemp	LAD	109	59	.541	8	4
Carlos Gomez	Mil	49	19	.388	3	3
Peter Bourjos	LAA	98	45	.459	4	3
Curtis Granderson	NYY	122	60	.492	5	2
Austin Jackson	Det	104	56	.538	5	2
Marlon Byrd	ChC	93	56	.602	4	2
B.J. Upton	TB	114	63	.553	5	1
Franklin Gutierrez	Sea	69	44	.638	5	1
Ezequiel Carrera	Cle	45	26	.578	1	0
Jon Jay	StL	41	25	.610	3	0
Andres Torres	SF	54	35	.648	2	0
Shane Victorino	Phi	71	32	.451	0	-1
Grady Sizemore	Cle	54	27	.500	0	-1
Endy Chavez	Tex	33	17	.515	1	-1
Alex Rios	CWS	144	79	.549	2	-1
Angel Pagan	NYM	128	74	.578	1	-1
Jordan Schafer	2 tms	68	40	.588	1	-1
Melky Cabrera	KC	139	90	.647	8	-1
Chris Coghlan	Fla	44	30	.682	2	-1
Nyjer Morgan	Mil	82	46	.561	0	-2
Nate McLouth	Atl	37	21	.568	0	-2
Cameron Maybin	SD	108	62	.574	2	-2
Colby Rasmus	2 tms	85	52	.612	1	-2
Jacoby Ellsbury	Bos	125	78	.624	3	-2
Dexter Fowler	Col	83	55	.663	3	-2
Andrew McCutchen	Pit	132	73	.553	3	-3
Chris Young	Ari	123	69	.561	1	-3
Michael Bourn	2 tms	131	75	.573	2	-3
Denard Span	Min	51	32	.627	0	-3
Ben Revere	Min	89	56	.629	3	-3
Coco Crisp	Oak	96	62	.646	1	-3
Rajai Davis	Tor	53	33	.623	0	-4
MLB Totals		4022	2268	.564	139	

Center Fielders - 2009 Throwing

Player	Tm	Opps	Extra Bases	Pct	Kills	Runs Saved
Adam Jones	Bal	105	40	.381	5	10
Matt Kemp	LAD	114	55	.482	8	7
Nyjer Morgan	2 tms	50	19	.380	5	6
Shane Victorino	Phi	128	65	.508	7	5
Colby Rasmus	StL	94	41	.436	3	4
Willy Taveras	Cin	65	32	.492	4	3
Angel Pagan	NYM	48	24	.500	3	3
Rajai Davis	Oak	80	43	.538	6	3
Michael Bourn	Hou	147	82	.558	7	3
Mitch Maier	KC	63	37	.587	6	3
Kosuke Fukudome	ChC	89	43	.483	3	2
Franklin Gutierrez	Sea	108	53	.491	5	2
Brett Gardner	NYY	74	39	.527	2	2
Curtis Granderson	Det	123	61	.496	3	1
Vernon Wells	Tor	137	68	.496	2	1
Josh Hamilton	Tex	44	22	.500	2	1
Andrew McCutchen	Pit	91	49	.538	2	1
B.J. Upton	TB	108	61	.565	5	1
Rick Ankiel	StL	54	26	.481	1	0
Nate McLouth	2 tms	117	70	.598	5	0
Cody Ross	Fla	81	43	.531	2	-1
Carlos Beltran	NYM	74	40	.541	1	-1
Torii Hunter	LAA	91	50	.549	2	-1
Melky Cabrera	NYY	66	37	.561	2	-1
Aaron Rowand	SF	91	53	.582	2	-2
Dexter Fowler	Col	117	69	.590	5	-2
Carlos Gomez	Min	86	52	.605	2	-3
Marlon Byrd	Tex	82	51	.622	3	-3
Tony Gwynn	SD	93	61	.656	3	-3
Jacoby Ellsbury	Bos	129	75	.581	1	-4
Willie Harris	Was	54	33	.611	0	-4
Mike Cameron	Mil	134	78	.582	1	-5
Chris Young	Ari	108	68	.630	1	-5
Grady Sizemore	Cle	101	64	.634	0	-5
Denard Span	Min	56	42	.750	1	-6
MLB Totals		4298	2370	.551	147	

Right Fielders - 3-Year Throwing

Player		Opps	Extra Bases	Pct	Kills	Runs Saved
Jeff Francoeur		364	150	.412	26	17
Jose Bautista		229	102	.445	24	13
Shin-Soo Choo		345	167	.484	26	12
Jayson Werth		356	143	.402	19	11
Hunter Pence		410	176	.429	21	10
Ben Zobrist		128	46	.359	10	8
Bobby Abreu		193	84	.435	11	7
Nate Schierholtz		165	76	.461	17	7
Torii Hunter		155	84	.542	16	5
Mike Stanton		222	99	.446	13	4
Nick Markakis		424	200	.472	24	4
Jason Kubel		127	66	.520	12	4
Nick Swisher		327	145	.443	11	3
Garrett Jones		142	59	.415	4	2
Michael Cuddyer		199	89	.447	9	2
Matt Joyce		129	58	.450	9	2
Kosuke Fukudome		202	93	.460	9	2
Ryan Sweeney		124	59	.476	7	2
Jay Bruce		324	152	.469	19	1
Will Venable		154	66	.429	5	0
Carlos Beltran		114	56	.491	4	0
Magglio Ordonez		214	104	.486	10	-1
Cody Ross		95	51	.537	6	-1
Ryan Ludwick		224	106	.473	6	-2
Nelson Cruz		255	122	.478	10	-3
David DeJesus		157	88	.561	8	-5
Corey Hart		254	126	.496	8	-7
Brad Hawpe		180	91	.506	2	-7
Jason Heyward		190	103	.542	6	-7
Seth Smith		107	64	.598	0	-7
Justin Upton		366	172	.470	5	-11
J.D. Drew		259	131	.506	5	-11
Andre Ethier		316	170	.538	13	-12
Ichiro Suzuki		395	203	.514	11	-13
Carlos Quentin		168	103	.613	2	-13
MLB Totals		12650	6042	.478	612	

Right Fielders - 2010 Throwing

Player	Tm	Opps	Extra Bases	Pct	Kills	Runs Saved
Shin-Soo Choo	Cle	138	59	.428	12	10
Jeff Francoeur	2 tms	100	30	.300	7	8
Jose Bautista	Tor	99	43	.434	11	6
Jayson Werth	Phi	96	32	.333	5	5
Nate Schierholtz	SF	46	20	.435	6	4
Ben Zobrist	TB	60	24	.400	5	3
Brennan Boesch	Det	46	18	.391	3	2
Michael Cuddyer	Min	41	18	.439	4	2
Mike Stanton	Fla	102	48	.471	8	2
Nick Swisher	NYY	105	53	.505	6	2
Michael Morse	Was	41	18	.439	2	1
Roger Bernadina	Was	56	27	.482	5	1
Nick Markakis	Bal	151	66	.437	5	0
Will Venable	SD	54	24	.444	1	0
Cody Ross	2 tms	29	13	.448	2	0
Bobby Abreu	LAA	67	35	.522	4	0
Torii Hunter	LAA	30	16	.533	2	0
Magglio Ordonez	Det	75	34	.453	3	-1
Hunter Pence	Hou	141	64	.454	5	-1
Nelson Cruz	Tex	74	35	.473	2	-1
Corey Hart	Mil	111	53	.477	4	-1
Kosuke Fukudome	ChC	73	37	.507	3	-1
Ryan Sweeney	Oak	45	23	.511	2	-1
Jason Kubel	Min	63	38	.603	5	-1
J.D. Drew	Bos	95	43	.453	1	-2
Jay Bruce	Cin	108	53	.491	5	-2
Brad Hawpe	2 tms	53	27	.509	0	-2
Jose Guillen	2 tms	39	22	.564	1	-2
David DeJesus	KC	52	31	.596	2	-2
Ryan Ludwick	2 tms	88	47	.534	2	-3
Justin Upton	Ari	118	58	.492	0	-5
Ichiro Suzuki	Sea	144	74	.514	4	-5
Andre Ethier	LAD	112	59	.527	2	-5
Jason Heyward	Atl	104	56	.538	4	-5
Carlos Quentin	CWS	91	58	.637	2	-7
MLB Totals		4164	1988	.477	202	

Right Fielders - 2011 Throwing

Player	Tm	Opps	Extra Bases	Pct	Kills	Runs Saved
Hunter Pence	2 tms	137	59	.431	7	5
Jason Kubel	Min	46	21	.457	7	5
Jeff Francoeur	KC	144	68	.472	11	5
Torii Hunter	LAA	125	68	.544	14	5
Nick Swisher	NYY	131	53	.405	3	3
Kosuke Fukudome	2 tms	120	52	.433	5	3
Jayson Werth	Was	141	62	.440	8	3
Jose Bautista	Tor	97	49	.505	10	3
Mike Stanton	Fla	120	51	.425	5	2
Nick Markakis	Bal	137	68	.496	9	2
Shin-Soo Choo	Cle	78	39	.500	6	2
Nate Schierholtz	SF	64	30	.469	4	1
Ben Francisco	Phi	43	22	.512	2	1
Magglio Ordonez	Det	54	28	.519	5	1
Will Venable	SD	44	21	.477	2	0
Matt Joyce	TB	89	43	.483	5	0
Carlos Beltran	2 tms	114	56	.491	4	0
Chris Denorfia	SD	46	23	.500	4	0
Michael Cuddyer	Min	63	32	.508	3	0
Garrett Jones	Pit	70	32	.457	2	-1
Brennan Boesch	Det	32	19	.594	1	-1
Josh Reddick	Bos	35	22	.629	3	-1
Jay Bruce	Cin	128	62	.484	5	-2
Lance Berkman	StL	80	41	.513	1	-2
Domonic Brown	Phi	33	17	.515	0	-2
Jason Heyward	Atl	86	47	.547	2	-2
Andre Ethier	LAD	93	53	.570	6	-2
Nelson Cruz	Tex	71	37	.521	3	-3
David DeJesus	Oak	102	55	.539	4	-3
Ichiro Suzuki	Sea	127	71	.559	5	-3
Corey Hart	Mil	82	43	.524	2	-4
J.D. Drew	Bos	52	28	.538	1	-4
Justin Upton	Ari	128	62	.484	3	-5
Seth Smith	Col	80	49	.613	0	-5
Carlos Quentin	CWS	77	45	.584	0	-6
MLB Totals		4180	2065	.494	209	

Right Fielders - 2009 Throwing

Player	Tm	Opps	Extra Bases	Pct	Kills	Runs Saved
Bobby Abreu	LAA	120	47	.392	7	7
Hunter Pence	Hou	132	53	.402	9	6
Jay Bruce	Cin	88	37	.420	9	5
Alex Rios	2 tms	101	33	.327	1	4
Ryan Church	2 tms	55	21	.382	6	4
Jeff Francoeur	2 tms	120	52	.433	8	4
Jayson Werth	Phi	119	49	.412	6	3
Randy Winn	SF	53	19	.358	3	2
Brandon Moss	Pit	72	30	.417	6	2
Clete Thomas	Det	55	23	.418	4	2
Ryan Ludwick	StL	119	51	.429	4	2
Gabe Gross	TB	64	28	.438	6	2
Ryan Sweeney	Oak	62	29	.468	4	2
Nate Schierholtz	SF	55	26	.473	7	2
Nick Markakis	Bal	136	66	.485	10	2
Nelson Cruz	Tex	110	50	.455	5	1
Elijah Dukes	Was	63	32	.508	3	1
Will Venable	SD	56	21	.375	2	0
Jeremy Hermida	Fla	56	22	.393	2	0
Michael Cuddyer	Min	95	39	.411	2	0
Cody Ross	Fla	49	26	.531	2	0
Shin-Soo Choo	Cle	129	69	.535	8	0
Justin Upton	Ari	120	52	.433	2	-1
Matt Diaz	Atl	63	28	.444	0	-1
Magglio Ordonez	Det	85	42	.494	2	-1
Nick Swisher	NYY	91	39	.429	2	-2
Corey Hart	Mil	61	30	.492	2	-2
Milton Bradley	ChC	72	36	.500	2	-2
Jermaine Dye	CWS	99	55	.556	6	-4
Ichiro Suzuki	Sea	124	58	.468	2	-5
Brad Hawpe	Col	124	62	.500	2	-5
Andre Ethier	LAD	111	58	.523	5	-5
J.D. Drew	Bos	112	60	.536	3	-5
Jose Guillen	KC	57	37	.649	2	-5
Brian Giles	SD	63	42	.667	2	-6
MLB Totals		4306	1989	.462	201	

Groundball Double Plays and Pivots

In the Plus/Minus System, we credit an infielder for making an out on a play. We do not, however, penalize or reward the fielder for his ability to get more than one out when the situation calls for it. We developed a separate Runs Saved component to account for infielders' double play skills.

Our original GDP system measured double play conversion rates, compared each player to the average, and converted to Runs Saved. Utilizing our batted ball timer data, we developed a new system for evaluating double play groundballs. In addition to middle infielders, the new methodology also accounts for corner infielders. We implemented this new double plays system for seasons where BIS batted ball timer data is available (2009 to the present); for previous seasons, we continue to use the original GDP Runs Saved system.

The columns in the charts are defined as follows:

GDPs: How many times the player was involved in a groundball double play, either starting the double play or as the "pivot" man.

GDP Opps: How many times the player was involved in a fielding play on a groundball in a double play situation (man on first with less than two outs). This includes DPs, force outs, errors, etc.

Pivots: How many times the player made the double play pivot (for second basemen: 6-4-3 DP or 5-4-3 DP or 1-4-3 or 3-4-3 or 2-4-3).

Pivot Opps: How many times the player accepted a force out at second in a situation that could have been a double play (for second basemen: 6-4, 5-4, 1-4 or 3-4).

Overall, the difference between the best and worst infielders on double play opportunities is relatively small—usually ranging only six to ten runs in a given

season. However, there are certain curiosities on the following pages which pique our interest.

The Rangers' middle infield duo of Ian Kinsler and Elvis Andrus stands out; Kinsler rates as the top second baseman over the past three years, and Andrus sits third among shortstops. Both led or tied for the major league lead in both 2009 and 2011; interestingly, both dropped off in 2010 to the middle of the pack. Perhaps because Kinsler missed two months due to injury, the duo didn't handle the opportunities quite as skillfully that year but bounced right back the next.

Orlando Hudson is the three-year trailer at second. Somewhat impressively, Hudson rated below average on three different teams during those three years: the 2009 Dodgers, 2010 Twins and 2011 Padres. His 2009 partner, Rafael Furcal, rated above average on double plays that season, both starting and turning double plays at an above average rate. The 2010 Twins shortstop, J.J. Hardy, was below average all three years, also for three different teams.

Hudson's 2011 counterpart in San Diego, Jason Bartlett, also rates as the worst double play turner over the past three years.

Baseball people often cite a middle infield's need to get in a rhythm together, a la Alan Trammell and Lou Whitaker of the 1980's Detroit Tigers. With a league-leading eight Double Play Runs Saved over three years, Troy Tulowitzki is the most recent counter example. The Rockies haven't found a long-term second base solution, trying fourteen different players at the position over the past three years. However, the three-time Fielding Bible Award winner hasn't missed a beat, both starting and turning double plays more often than any other shortstop.

Second Basemen - 3-Year GDPs & Pivots

Player	GDP Opps	GDP	GDP Pct	Rank	Pivot Opps	Pivots	Pivot Pct	Rank	Runs Saved
Ian Kinsler	377	258	.684	7	232	160	.690	10	5
Kelly Johnson	344	236	.686	6	238	166	.697	7	3
Chase Utley	323	223	.690	5	199	137	.688	11	3
Mark Ellis	327	217	.664	19	207	129	.623	27	2
Dustin Pedroia	312	212	.679	10	194	133	.686	12	2
Freddy Sanchez	215	146	.679	12	148	97	.655	18	2
Clint Barmes	191	135	.707	2	124	83	.669	16	2
Robinson Cano	463	300	.648	23	308	189	.614	30	1
Rickie Weeks	259	176	.680	9	179	124	.693	8	1
Gordon Beckham	265	173	.653	22	176	111	.631	23	1
Neil Walker	255	168	.659	20	173	113	.653	19	1
Brian Roberts	230	159	.691	4	143	105	.734	2	1
Luis Valbuena	190	128	.674	16	129	90	.698	6	1
Omar Infante	183	124	.678	14	104	77	.740	1	1
Placido Polanco	152	110	.724	1	100	67	.670	15	1
Danny Espinosa	161	109	.677	15	102	73	.716	3	1
Chone Figgins	159	108	.679	11	99	66	.667	17	1
Jose Lopez	141	99	.702	3	92	62	.674	14	1
Jamey Carroll	105	68	.648	24	69	42	.609	31	1
Ben Zobrist	208	131	.630	27	141	91	.645	21	0
Felipe Lopez	177	120	.678	13	104	74	.712	4	0
Martin Prado	148	99	.669	18	102	66	.647	20	0
Ryan Theriot	119	81	.681	8	80	54	.675	13	0
Howie Kendrick	303	198	.653	21	182	126	.692	9	-1
Chris Getz	280	175	.625	30	178	112	.629	24	-1
Jeff Keppinger	169	106	.627	28	111	69	.622	28	-1
Alexi Casilla	126	77	.611	33	79	50	.633	22	-1
Brandon Phillips	441	284	.644	25	309	191	.618	29	-2
Skip Schumaker	287	192	.669	17	193	137	.710	5	-2
Alberto Callaspo	165	105	.636	26	102	60	.588	33	-2
Adam Kennedy	148	90	.608	34	84	46	.548	35	-2
Blake DeWitt	125	75	.600	35	89	52	.584	34	-3
Aaron Hill	452	282	.624	31	309	187	.605	32	-4
Dan Uggla	414	256	.618	32	272	171	.629	25	-4
Orlando Hudson	342	214	.626	29	226	142	.628	26	-5
MLB Totals	13628	8938	.656		8869	5766	.650		

Second Basemen - 2011 GDPs & Pivots

Player	Tm	GDP Opps	GDP	GDP Pct	Rank	Pivot Opps	Pivots	Pivot Pct	Rank	Runs Saved
Ian Kinsler	Tex	142	102	.718	2	80	56	.700	7	3
Robinson Cano	NYY	139	96	.691	9	96	61	.635	19	2
Kelly Johnson	2 tms	118	82	.695	8	82	56	.683	12	2
Mark Ellis	2 tms	129	84	.651	16	83	50	.602	24	1
Ben Zobrist	TB	98	65	.663	13	66	47	.712	4	1
Rickie Weeks	Mil	93	63	.677	12	61	41	.672	13	1
Robert Andino	Bal	90	58	.644	18	62	40	.645	15	1
Dustin Ackley	Sea	70	48	.686	10	37	22	.595	29	1
Maicer Izturis	LAA	49	35	.714	5	31	22	.710	5	1
Jamey Carroll	LAD	46	33	.717	4	26	19	.731	2	1
Freddy Sanchez	SF	39	30	.769	1	27	19	.704	6	1
Jose Altuve	Hou	37	26	.703	6	23	14	.609	23	1
Danny Espinosa	Was	136	89	.654	15	83	57	.687	10	0
Gordon Beckham	CWS	130	80	.615	23	89	52	.584	31	0
Aaron Hill	2 tms	130	80	.615	23	83	50	.602	24	0
Omar Infante	Fla	111	72	.649	17	59	41	.695	9	0
Chris Getz	KC	108	65	.602	27	60	36	.600	26	0
Howie Kendrick	LAA	89	59	.663	14	54	39	.722	3	0
Jemile Weeks	Oak	70	45	.643	19	39	25	.641	17	0
Orlando Cabrera	2 tms	67	42	.627	20	43	28	.651	14	0
Alexi Casilla	Min	53	36	.679	11	30	19	.633	20	0
Ruben Tejada	NYM	47	33	.702	7	30	21	.700	7	0
Jonathan Herrera	Col	39	28	.718	3	19	13	.684	11	0
Ramon Santiago	Det	46	26	.565	32	31	20	.645	15	0
Aaron Miles	LAD	41	24	.585	30	27	15	.556	33	0
Neil Walker	Pit	172	106	.616	22	119	74	.622	22	-1
Brandon Phillips	Cin	153	94	.614	25	110	66	.600	26	-1
Dan Uggla	Atl	140	82	.586	28	96	60	.625	21	-1
Dustin Pedroia	Bos	131	82	.626	21	84	50	.595	28	-1
Chase Utley	Phi	86	50	.581	31	52	28	.538	34	-1
Skip Schumaker	StL	71	43	.606	26	40	30	.750	1	-1
Darwin Barney	ChC	100	56	.560	33	65	38	.585	30	-2
Jeff Keppinger	2 tms	60	31	.517	35	41	23	.561	32	-2
Orlando Hudson	SD	111	65	.586	29	66	42	.636	18	-3
Justin Turner	NYM	66	35	.530	34	44	20	.455	35	-3
MLB Totals		4395	2808	.639		2818	1786	.634		

Second Basemen - 2010 GDPs & Pivots

Player	Tm	GDP Opps	GDP	GDP Pct	Rank	Pivot Opps	Pivots	Pivot Pct	Rank	Runs Saved
Chase Utley	Phi	106	81	.764	1	58	45	.776	2	3
Robinson Cano	NYY	171	113	.661	19	109	70	.642	16	2
Neil Walker	Pit	83	62	.747	3	54	39	.722	5	2
Chone Figgins	Sea	159	108	.679	14	99	66	.667	13	1
Kelly Johnson	Ari	144	99	.688	13	100	69	.690	10	1
Gordon Beckham	CWS	135	93	.689	12	87	59	.678	11	1
Rickie Weeks	Mil	131	92	.702	8	95	69	.726	3	1
Mark Ellis	Oak	107	74	.692	10	71	47	.662	14	1
Jeff Keppinger	Hou	96	65	.677	15	62	39	.629	19	1
Luis Valbuena	Cle	92	61	.663	18	56	39	.696	8	1
Sean Rodriguez	TB	72	51	.708	7	46	33	.717	6	1
Dustin Pedroia	Bos	69	50	.725	5	52	37	.712	7	1
Omar Infante	Atl	57	41	.719	6	37	29	.784	1	1
Brian Roberts	Bal	49	37	.755	2	29	21	.724	4	1
David Eckstein	SD	99	67	.677	16	64	40	.625	21	0
Martin Prado	Atl	100	64	.640	22	66	40	.606	25	0
Clint Barmes	Col	79	55	.696	9	52	34	.654	15	0
Chris Getz	KC	67	44	.657	20	52	33	.635	17	0
Jonathan Herrera	Col	41	30	.732	4	26	18	.692	9	0
Julio Lugo	Bal	40	25	.625	25	29	17	.586	30	0
Brandon Phillips	Cin	138	89	.645	21	95	58	.611	24	-1
Dan Uggla	Fla	131	83	.634	23	88	53	.602	26	-1
Orlando Hudson	Min	125	76	.608	30	86	53	.616	23	-1
Skip Schumaker	StL	103	71	.689	11	74	50	.676	12	-1
Ian Kinsler	Tex	110	67	.609	29	76	48	.632	18	-1
Ryan Theriot	2 tms	92	57	.620	26	62	37	.597	28	-1
Freddy Sanchez	SF	75	47	.627	24	47	27	.574	31	-1
Luis Castillo	NYM	61	36	.590	32	35	20	.571	32	-1
Will Rhymes	Det	52	35	.673	17	35	22	.629	20	-1
Aaron Hill	Tor	141	86	.610	28	105	63	.600	27	-2
Howie Kendrick	LAA	116	70	.603	31	73	45	.616	22	-2
Blake DeWitt	2 tms	109	67	.615	27	76	45	.592	29	-2
Adam Kennedy	Was	68	40	.588	33	37	19	.514	33	-2
Cristian Guzman	2 tms	59	32	.542	34	42	21	.500	34	-2
Mike Aviles	KC	81	41	.506	35	53	26	.491	35	-3
MLB Totals		4593	3016	.657		3034	1949	.642		

Second Basemen - 2009 GDPs & Pivots

Player	Tm	GDP Opps	GDP	GDP Pct	Rank	Pivot Opps	Pivots	Pivot Pct	Rank	Runs Saved
Ian Kinsler	Tex	125	89	.712	9	76	56	.737	4	3
Kaz Matsui	Hou	133	97	.729	2	85	61	.718	11	2
Dustin Pedroia	Bos	112	80	.714	7	58	46	.793	1	2
Clint Barmes	Col	112	80	.714	7	72	49	.681	17	2
Freddy Sanchez	2 tms	101	69	.683	17	74	51	.689	16	2
Maicer Izturis	LAA	64	50	.781	1	41	29	.707	12	2
Placido Polanco	Det	143	103	.720	4	97	65	.670	19	1
Chase Utley	Phi	131	92	.702	11	89	64	.719	9	1
Jose Lopez	Sea	123	88	.715	6	81	56	.691	15	1
Howie Kendrick	LAA	98	69	.704	10	55	42	.764	2	1
Felipe Lopez	2 tms	148	102	.689	14	85	60	.706	13	0
Brandon Phillips	Cin	150	101	.673	18	104	67	.644	23	0
Brian Roberts	Bal	144	99	.688	16	92	68	.739	3	0
Skip Schumaker	StL	113	78	.690	12	79	57	.722	8	0
David Eckstein	SD	99	71	.717	5	74	54	.730	6	0
Luis Valbuena	Cle	87	60	.690	13	64	46	.719	10	0
Mark Ellis	Oak	91	59	.648	21	53	32	.604	28	0
Kelly Johnson	Atl	82	55	.671	19	56	41	.732	5	0
Ben Zobrist	TB	68	41	.603	30	44	26	.591	30	0
Martin Prado	Atl	48	35	.729	3	36	26	.722	7	0
Anderson Hernandez	2 tms	51	34	.667	20	34	24	.706	13	0
Nick Punto	Min	51	33	.647	22	35	22	.629	25	0
Alexi Casilla	Min	55	33	.600	31	38	25	.658	21	0
Mike Fontenot	ChC	48	31	.646	23	31	21	.677	18	0
Jamey Carroll	Cle	38	24	.632	27	27	15	.556	34	0
Orlando Hudson	LAD	106	73	.689	15	74	47	.635	24	-1
Chris Getz	CWS	105	66	.629	28	66	43	.652	22	-1
Akinori Iwamura	TB	63	38	.603	29	40	25	.625	26	-1
Delwyn Young	Pit	57	32	.561	34	43	23	.535	35	-1
Aaron Hill	Tor	181	116	.641	25	121	74	.612	27	-2
Alberto Callaspo	KC	151	97	.642	24	94	56	.596	29	-2
Dan Uggla	Fla	143	91	.636	26	88	58	.659	20	-2
Manny Burriss	SF	53	29	.547	35	34	20	.588	31	-2
Robinson Cano	NYY	153	91	.595	32	103	58	.563	33	-3
Luis Castillo	NYM	108	64	.593	33	65	38	.585	32	-4
MLB Totals		4640	3114	.671		3017	2031	.673		

Shortstops - 3-Year GDPs & Pivots

Player	GDP Opps	GDP	GDP Pct	Rank	Pivot Opps	Pivots	Pivot Pct	Rank	Runs Saved
Troy Tulowitzki	409	296	.724	1	251	177	.705	1	8
Brendan Ryan	364	260	.714	2	211	142	.673	6	6
Elvis Andrus	425	297	.699	6	262	174	.664	7	5
Alexei Ramirez	427	289	.677	13	256	164	.641	10	4
Cliff Pennington	343	239	.697	8	206	140	.680	5	4
Jimmy Rollins	308	216	.701	4	166	114	.687	3	4
Stephen Drew	294	198	.673	14	168	105	.625	14	3
Yunel Escobar	421	290	.689	10	253	159	.628	13	2
Erick Aybar	404	270	.668	15	253	160	.632	12	2
Asdrubal Cabrera	330	231	.700	5	187	120	.642	9	2
Jack Wilson	184	125	.679	11	109	69	.633	11	2
Alex Gonzalez	362	255	.704	3	171	105	.614	19	1
Jose Reyes	271	177	.653	19	167	102	.611	20	1
Cesar Izturis	255	169	.663	16	150	91	.607	21	1
Jhonny Peralta	214	145	.678	12	131	81	.618	16	1
Rafael Furcal	280	193	.689	9	170	111	.653	8	0
Ronny Cedeno	289	182	.630	24	166	100	.602	22	0
Everth Cabrera	136	90	.662	17	76	43	.566	29	0
Josh Wilson	138	86	.623	28	77	44	.571	28	0
Yuniesky Betancourt	385	243	.631	23	213	131	.615	18	-1
Orlando Cabrera	287	180	.627	25	171	102	.596	24	-1
Miguel Tejada	248	162	.653	18	142	88	.620	15	-1
Clint Barmes	149	104	.698	7	87	60	.690	2	-1
Ramon Santiago	161	103	.640	21	95	65	.684	4	-1
Marco Scutaro	331	212	.640	20	178	110	.618	17	-2
Ian Desmond	296	187	.632	22	182	109	.599	23	-2
Starlin Castro	261	155	.594	33	143	79	.552	31	-2
Ryan Theriot	248	151	.609	30	158	83	.525	35	-2
Paul Janish	213	133	.624	27	117	67	.573	27	-2
J.J. Hardy	321	190	.592	34	194	106	.546	32	-3
Alcides Escobar	299	186	.622	29	181	98	.541	33	-3
Edgar Renteria	220	132	.600	32	121	67	.554	30	-3
Derek Jeter	384	232	.604	31	220	128	.582	26	-4
Hanley Ramirez	311	195	.627	26	192	114	.594	25	-4
Jason Bartlett	340	189	.556	35	185	99	.535	34	-7
MLB Totals	13680	8902	.651		7984	4871	.610		

Shortstops - 2011 GDPs & Pivots

Player	Tm	GDP Opps	GDP	GDP Pct	Rank	Pivot Opps	Pivots	Pivot Pct	Rank	Runs Saved
Elvis Andrus	Tex	148	109	.736	1	95	67	.705	3	3
Alexei Ramirez	CWS	136	95	.699	5	75	53	.707	2	3
Erick Aybar	LAA	154	107	.695	6	94	63	.670	7	2
Troy Tulowitzki	Col	146	104	.712	3	94	65	.691	5	2
Jimmy Rollins	Phi	122	88	.721	2	69	50	.725	1	2
Yuniesky Betancourt	Mil	124	83	.669	9	62	39	.629	10	2
Cliff Pennington	Oak	138	97	.703	4	83	57	.687	6	1
Brendan Ryan	Sea	122	81	.664	10	76	46	.605	13	1
Stephen Drew	Ari	71	46	.648	16	37	22	.595	17	1
Jose Reyes	NYM	131	84	.641	18	82	51	.622	11	0
Jason Bartlett	SD	131	83	.634	20	74	42	.568	21	0
Jhonny Peralta	Det	125	81	.648	15	76	46	.605	13	0
Yunel Escobar	Tor	121	77	.636	19	78	45	.577	20	0
Rafael Furcal	2 tms	92	62	.674	8	64	38	.594	18	0
Marco Scutaro	Bos	94	59	.628	21	53	32	.604	15	0
Ryan Theriot	StL	84	54	.643	17	60	35	.583	19	0
Reid Brignac	TB	62	41	.661	12	37	21	.568	21	0
Willie Bloomquist	Ari	54	32	.593	27	29	15	.517	30	0
Emilio Bonifacio	Fla	51	31	.608	24	35	19	.543	27	0
Brandon Crawford	SF	43	29	.674	7	23	16	.696	4	0
Jamey Carroll	LAD	40	26	.650	14	25	16	.640	9	0
Ian Desmond	Was	140	84	.600	25	89	49	.551	26	-1
Alex Gonzalez	Atl	116	76	.655	13	59	33	.559	25	-1
J.J. Hardy	Bal	123	73	.593	26	76	43	.566	23	-1
Asdrubal Cabrera	Cle	117	73	.624	22	72	43	.597	16	-1
Clint Barmes	Hou	98	65	.663	11	60	39	.650	8	-1
Derek Jeter	NYY	103	63	.612	23	59	36	.610	12	-1
Hanley Ramirez	Fla	73	42	.575	29	47	24	.511	32	-1
Edgar Renteria	Cin	64	37	.578	28	29	15	.517	30	-1
Dee Gordon	LAD	37	21	.568	32	22	9	.409	35	-1
Starlin Castro	ChC	139	78	.561	33	79	42	.532	28	-2
Ronny Cedeno	Pit	114	65	.570	31	64	36	.563	24	-2
Paul Janish	Cin	84	46	.548	34	49	26	.531	29	-2
Tsuyoshi Nishioka	Min	64	34	.531	35	41	20	.488	34	-2
Alcides Escobar	KC	169	97	.574	30	107	54	.505	33	-3
MLB Totals		4545	2893	.637		2691	1614	.600		

Shortstops - 2010 GDPs & Pivots

Player	Tm	GDP Opps	GDP	GDP Pct	Rank	Pivot Opps	Pivots	Pivot Pct	Rank	Runs Saved
Troy Tulowitzki	Col	144	107	.743	5	88	64	.727	3	4
Yunel Escobar	2 tms	170	127	.747	3	102	72	.706	4	3
Brendan Ryan	StL	138	102	.739	6	81	60	.741	2	3
Alex Gonzalez	2 tms	154	115	.747	4	57	39	.684	6	2
Cliff Pennington	Oak	139	97	.698	8	84	56	.667	12	2
Stephen Drew	Ari	120	83	.692	9	67	43	.642	16	2
Jose Reyes	NYM	117	82	.701	7	72	45	.625	18	2
Jimmy Rollins	Phi	71	56	.789	1	35	28	.800	1	2
Alexei Ramirez	CWS	158	105	.665	16	97	62	.639	17	1
Cesar Izturis	Bal	123	81	.659	17	72	44	.611	21	1
Asdrubal Cabrera	Cle	104	79	.760	2	65	44	.677	8	1
Alcides Escobar	Mil	96	66	.688	10	53	31	.585	24	1
Ronny Cedeno	Pit	101	65	.644	23	62	35	.565	28	1
Derek Jeter	NYY	150	95	.633	25	87	52	.598	23	0
Elvis Andrus	Tex	145	94	.648	20	85	51	.600	22	0
Starlin Castro	ChC	122	77	.631	26	64	37	.578	27	0
Orlando Cabrera	Cin	93	61	.656	19	55	37	.673	11	0
Josh Wilson	Sea	89	56	.629	28	52	29	.558	30	0
Ramon Santiago	Det	85	55	.647	21	54	35	.648	15	0
Tommy Manzella	Hou	69	44	.638	24	41	23	.561	29	0
Jack Wilson	Sea	55	37	.673	13	32	21	.656	14	0
Juan Uribe	SF	64	37	.578	30	43	25	.581	25	0
Edgar Renteria	SF	41	28	.683	11	24	15	.625	18	0
Ian Desmond	Was	134	88	.657	18	76	50	.658	13	-1
Hanley Ramirez	Fla	115	77	.670	14	68	46	.676	9	-1
Marco Scutaro	Bos	90	58	.644	22	43	29	.674	10	-1
J.J. Hardy	Min	101	57	.564	31	59	32	.542	32	-1
Rafael Furcal	LAD	75	51	.680	12	41	28	.683	7	-1
Miguel Tejada	SD	65	41	.631	27	38	21	.553	31	-1
Angel Sanchez	2 tms	48	32	.667	15	27	19	.704	5	-1
Jerry Hairston	SD	45	25	.556	32	29	18	.621	20	-1
Erick Aybar	LAA	105	64	.610	29	62	36	.581	26	-2
Jamey Carroll	LAD	56	31	.554	33	31	16	.516	34	-2
Jason Bartlett	TB	101	52	.515	35	49	26	.531	33	-3
Yuniesky Betancourt	KC	145	77	.531	34	81	40	.494	35	-4
MLB Totals		4537	2992	.659		2605	1636	.628		

Shortstops - 2009 GDPs & Pivots

Player	Tm	GDP Opps	GDP	GDP Pct	Rank	Pivot Opps	Pivots	Pivot Pct	Rank	Runs Saved
Erick Aybar	LAA	145	99	.683	15	97	61	.629	13	2
Elvis Andrus	Tex	132	94	.712	8	82	56	.683	7	2
Troy Tulowitzki	Col	119	85	.714	7	69	48	.696	4	2
Asdrubal Cabrera	Cle	109	79	.725	4	50	33	.660	11	2
Brendan Ryan	StL	104	77	.740	2	54	36	.667	9	2
Jack Wilson	2 tms	107	74	.692	12	61	37	.607	17	2
Yuniesky Betancourt	2 tms	116	83	.716	6	70	52	.743	2	1
Rafael Furcal	LAD	113	80	.708	9	65	45	.692	5	1
Ronny Cedeno	2 tms	74	52	.703	10	40	29	.725	3	1
Cliff Pennington	Oak	66	45	.682	16	39	27	.692	5	1
Nick Green	Bos	60	41	.683	14	38	23	.605	18	1
Robert Andino	Bal	56	41	.732	3	27	14	.519	32	1
Alex Cora	NYM	54	39	.722	5	37	25	.676	8	1
Nick Punto	Min	40	30	.750	1	23	15	.652	12	1
Miguel Tejada	Hou	165	108	.655	23	96	59	.615	16	0
Alexei Ramirez	CWS	133	89	.669	20	84	49	.583	22	0
Adam Everett	Det	112	74	.661	22	65	37	.569	27	0
Cesar Izturis	Bal	112	73	.652	24	68	40	.588	21	0
Jimmy Rollins	Phi	115	72	.626	27	62	36	.581	23	0
Stephen Drew	Ari	103	69	.670	19	64	40	.625	14	0
Cristian Guzman	Was	101	68	.673	18	54	36	.667	9	0
Alex Gonzalez	2 tms	92	64	.696	11	55	33	.600	19	0
Everth Cabrera	SD	92	63	.685	13	51	29	.569	28	0
Paul Janish	Cin	83	56	.675	17	42	26	.619	15	0
Orlando Cabrera	2 tms	157	97	.618	30	97	56	.577	24	-1
Marco Scutaro	Tor	147	95	.646	25	82	49	.598	20	-1
Yunel Escobar	Atl	130	86	.662	21	73	42	.575	25	-1
Ryan Theriot	ChC	143	85	.594	31	85	41	.482	34	-1
J.J. Hardy	Mil	97	60	.619	28	59	31	.525	31	-1
Ramon Santiago	Det	54	34	.630	26	26	20	.769	1	-1
Brendan Harris	Min	37	21	.568	33	18	8	.444	35	-1
Hanley Ramirez	Fla	123	76	.618	29	77	44	.571	26	-2
Edgar Renteria	SF	115	67	.583	32	68	37	.544	29	-2
Derek Jeter	NYY	131	74	.565	34	74	40	.541	30	-3
Jason Bartlett	TB	108	54	.500	35	62	31	.500	33	-4
MLB Totals		4598	3017	.656		2688	1621	.603		

Fielding Bunts

Bunts might be the toughest aspect of defensive play to evaluate. Hitters bunt for different reasons, teams use different bunt coverages, and fielders react differently depending on the situation, baserunners, etc. Additionally, there are countless different outcomes to accommodate, especially in sacrifice situations. But none of this stops us from trying.

We devised a new method for evaluating fielders on bunted balls. Our new system looks at the defensive position of the player who fields the ball, the situation (sacrifice or non-sacrifice), the location (one of six zones, three on each side of the mound) and whether a pitcher or non-pitcher laid down the bunt. While the old Bunt Runs Saved system was limited to corner infielders, the new system rates pitchers and catchers as well as first and third basemen. The full Bunt Runs Saved methodology is explained on page 450. We've restated all nine seasons since the first *Fielding Bible* according to the new system.

On the following pages, we present new bunt fielding charts with a breakdown of the bunt outcomes. Here is a brief description of each column:

Sacrifice Bunts

Attempts–A sacrifice bunt attempt is defined by the situation. If the bunt came with at least one runner on base and less than two outs, we consider it a sacrifice attempt.

Sac Hits–A sacrifice hit is any bunt where the batter is credited with a sacrifice and fielded by the player in question.

Hits–A hit is any bunt hit in a sacrifice situation.

Sac Hit Average–(Sac Hits + Hits) / Attempts. For the fielder, a lower sac hit average is better.

Bunt Hits

Attempts–A bunt hit attempt is defined as any bunt with no runners on base OR two outs.

Bunt Hits–A bunt hit is any hit in a bunt hit (non-sacrifice) situation.

Bunt Hit Average–Bunt Hits / Attempts. As with sacrifice bunts, a lower Bunt Hit Average is better.

The best defensive player fielding bunts over the last three years is Evan Longoria, third baseman for the Tampa Bay Rays. He has saved seven runs based on our new bunt runs saved method. The next best player over that time is Adrian Gonzalez with five bunt runs saved. Let's walk through the data in the charts for Longoria and a few other players.

Evan Longoria fielded 71 bunt attempts over the last three years, 40 of those in sacrifice situations. Of the 40, 23 went down as sacrifice bunts for the batter, and the batter reached safely on a single 6 other times. Out of the remaining 11 bunts in sacrifice situations, 3 were scored as groundouts, 3 were fielder's choice plays (where Longoria threw out a lead runner instead of going for the sacrifice), 2 were bunt flyouts, 2 were turned into double plays and 1 was credited as an assist to Longoria but an error on first baseman Carlos Pena for dropping the throw. Longoria didn't make a single error on any of his bunt attempts.

Batters are fairly successful bunting for a hit to Alex Rodriguez. Out of the 17 bunts fielded by A-Rod in non-sacrifice situations, 12 have been beaten out for hits. By contrast, Adrian Beltre allowed only 3 hits in 12 bunt hit attempts he has fielded.

Brandon Inge turned 12 sacrifice bunts into hits, 4 more than any other third baseman in baseball. While he fielded bunt hits more adequately, it's no surprise he comes in last on the three-year Bunt Runs Saved leaderboard.

Miguel Montero is a beast when it comes to fielding bunt hit attempts. He fielded more bunt hit attempts than any other catcher over the last three years (23), and he threw out a league-leading 19 of them. Note to opposing hitters: if you're going to lay down a bunt against the Diamondbacks, push it far away from Montero. Similarly, Miguel Olivo threw out 13 of the 14 bunt hit attempts he fielded, including all 8 in 2011.

Ryan Howard (7) and Miguel Cabrera (6) turned more sacrifice bunts into hits over the three-year period of 2009-11 than any other first baseman. This is especially disappointing for Cabrera, who as an American League first baseman has fielded fewer than half as many sacrifice bunt attempts (23 compared to Howard's 54). Cabrera turned more than one-quarter of the sacrifice bunts he fielded into base hits.

Between Cabrera, Inge and catcher Alex Avila, the Tigers have put together the worst bunt-fielding unit in the majors over the past three years. Of course, the impact has been relatively modest (-10 Bunt Runs Saved combined) compared to the offensive production Detroit gets from Cabrera and Avila.

Catchers - 3-Year Bunt Defense

Player	SAC BUNTS				BUNT HITS			Runs Saved
	Attempts	Sac Hits	Hits	Sac Hit Average	Attempts	Bunt Hits	Bunt Hit Average	
Rob Johnson	18	8	2	.556	9	1	.111	4
Brian McCann	41	29	0	.707	12	3	.250	4
Ramon Hernandez	26	13	0	.500	4	2	.500	3
Ronny Paulino	22	13	0	.591	6	2	.333	3
Chris Iannetta	31	22	0	.710	3	1	.333	3
Matt Wieters	24	18	0	.750	16	3	.188	3
Joe Mauer	12	6	0	.500	6	0	.000	2
Humberto Quintero	27	14	2	.593	5	0	.000	2
Chris Snyder	20	15	1	.800	9	2	.222	2
Jason Varitek	7	4	0	.571	7	2	.286	1
Ivan Rodriguez	28	18	0	.643	9	2	.222	1
Carlos Ruiz	33	20	2	.667	6	1	.167	1
Kurt Suzuki	14	10	0	.714	8	3	.375	1
Geovany Soto	34	26	0	.765	5	0	.000	1
Lou Marson	13	6	1	.538	4	1	.250	0
Ryan Doumit	22	14	1	.682	10	3	.300	0
Yadier Molina	52	33	3	.692	8	4	.500	0
Miguel Montero	27	17	3	.741	23	4	.174	0
Ryan Hanigan	17	12	1	.765	2	0	.000	0
Jonathan Lucroy	9	7	0	.778	4	1	.250	0
Jarrod Saltalamacchia	13	6	1	.538	4	2	.500	-1
Russell Martin	30	17	0	.567	7	3	.429	-1
Dioner Navarro	7	4	0	.571	3	0	.000	-1
Nick Hundley	22	12	1	.591	6	4	.667	-1
Miguel Olivo	22	13	2	.682	14	1	.071	-1
Jeff Mathis	20	12	2	.700	11	4	.364	-1
John Buck	13	9	1	.769	5	3	.600	-1
A.J. Pierzynski	19	12	3	.789	10	3	.300	-1
Gerald Laird	20	12	2	.700	4	1	.250	-2
Mike Napoli	11	8	1	.818	4	2	.500	-2
Victor Martinez	13	8	3	.846	1	0	.000	-2
Rod Barajas	23	17	3	.870	5	1	.200	-2
Kelly Shoppach	10	6	3	.900	2	1	.500	-2
Alex Avila	12	9	2	.917	5	3	.600	-3
Yorvit Torrealba	24	16	1	.708	8	3	.375	-5
MLB Totals	1179	749	76	.700	352	92	.261	

Catchers - 2011 Bunt Defense

Player	Team	SAC BUNTS				BUNT HITS			Runs Saved
		Attempts	Sac Hits	Hits	Sac Hit Average	Attempts	Bunt Hits	Bunt Hit Average	
Ramon Hernandez	Cin	10	4	0	.400	1	1	1.000	2
Ronny Paulino	NYM	8	4	0	.500	1	0	.000	2
Drew Butera	Min	5	3	0	.600	3	0	.000	2
Brian McCann	Atl	17	11	0	.647	6	3	.500	2
Eli Whiteside	SF	4	1	0	.250	0	0		1
Lou Marson	Cle	6	2	0	.333	3	1	.333	1
Chris Iannetta	Col	9	6	0	.667	0	0		1
J.P. Arencibia	Tor	6	3	1	.667	5	1	.200	1
Carlos Ruiz	Phi	16	10	1	.688	3	0	.000	1
Geovany Soto	ChC	18	13	0	.722	2	0	.000	1
Matt Wieters	Bal	10	9	0	.900	4	1	.250	1
Jason Varitek	Bos	1	0	0	.000	2	1	.500	0
Humberto Quintero	Hou	9	3	2	.556	1	0	.000	0
Nick Hundley	SD	7	4	0	.571	2	2	1.000	0
Kurt Suzuki	Oak	5	3	0	.600	3	2	.667	0
Carlos Santana	Cle	3	2	0	.667	2	0	.000	0
Jonathan Lucroy	Mil	3	2	0	.667	4	1	.250	0
Ryan Hanigan	Cin	4	3	0	.750	0	0		0
Miguel Montero	Ari	13	9	1	.769	12	2	.167	0
John Buck	Fla	10	7	1	.800	2	2	1.000	0
Miguel Olivo	Sea	7	4	2	.857	8	0	.000	0
Alex Avila	Det	7	6	0	.857	4	2	.500	0
Josh Thole	NYM	15	13	0	.867	1	0	.000	0
Jarrod Saltalamacchia	Bos	7	3	0	.429	3	2	.667	-1
Russell Martin	NYY	5	3	0	.600	2	2	1.000	-1
Wilson Ramos	Was	13	8	1	.692	1	0	.000	-1
Kelly Shoppach	TB	4	2	1	.750	0	0		-1
Brayan Pena	KC	5	2	2	.800	2	0	.000	-1
Yadier Molina	StL	17	13	1	.824	3	0	.000	-1
A.J. Pierzynski	CWS	9	6	2	.889	3	2	.667	-1
Jeff Mathis	LAA	7	5	2	1.000	5	0	.000	-1
John Jaso	TB	4	3	1	1.000	1	1	1.000	-1
Rod Barajas	LAD	11	10	1	1.000	1	0	.000	-1
Matt Treanor	2 tms	4	2	2	1.000	1	0	.000	-2
Yorvit Torrealba	Tex	8	6	0	.750	5	2	.400	-4
MLB Totals		401	265	24	.721	115	30	.261	

301

Catchers - 2010 Bunt Defense

Player	Team	SAC BUNTS				BUNT HITS			Runs Saved
		Attempts	Sac Hits	Hits	Sac Hit Average	Attempts	Bunt Hits	Bunt Hit Average	
Humberto Quintero	Hou	11	5	0	.455	3	0	.000	2
Ramon Hernandez	Cin	11	7	0	.636	2	1	.500	2
Matt Wieters	Bal	9	6	0	.667	8	0	.000	2
Chris Snyder	2 tms	13	9	1	.769	4	0	.000	2
Koyie Hill	ChC	11	4	0	.364	0	0		1
Ronny Paulino	Fla	7	3	0	.429	2	1	.500	1
Kurt Suzuki	Oak	4	2	0	.500	4	1	.250	1
Jason Kendall	KC	8	3	1	.500	2	1	.500	1
Joe Mauer	Min	6	3	0	.500	4	0	.000	1
Miguel Montero	Ari	5	3	0	.600	7	1	.143	1
Yadier Molina	StL	17	10	1	.647	2	2	1.000	1
Buster Posey	SF	3	2	0	.667	0	0		1
Brian McCann	Atl	14	11	0	.786	2	0	.000	1
Francisco Cervelli	NYY	3	3	0	1.000	4	1	.250	1
John Jaso	TB	1	0	0	.000	3	1	.333	0
Nick Hundley	SD	3	1	0	.333	2	1	.500	0
Jeff Mathis	LAA	5	2	0	.400	2	2	1.000	0
Ivan Rodriguez	Was	12	8	0	.667	3	0	.000	0
Bengie Molina	2 tms	10	5	2	.700	3	2	.667	0
Ryan Doumit	Pit	14	9	1	.714	7	3	.429	0
A.J. Pierzynski	CWS	5	3	1	.800	7	1	.143	0
Jonathan Lucroy	Mil	6	5	0	.833	0	0		0
Geovany Soto	ChC	3	3	0	1.000	1	0	.000	0
Yorvit Torrealba	SD	7	3	1	.571	1	0	.000	-1
John Buck	Tor	3	2	0	.667	2	1	.500	-1
Gerald Laird	Det	6	3	1	.667	2	1	.500	-1
Miguel Olivo	Col	10	7	0	.700	1	0	.000	-1
Carlos Ruiz	Phi	10	6	1	.700	2	1	.500	-1
Rod Barajas	2 tms	8	5	1	.750	2	1	.500	-1
Lou Marson	Cle	5	3	1	.800	0	0		-1
Jorge Posada	NYY	2	2	0	1.000	1	0	.000	-1
Matt Treanor	Tex	2	1	1	1.000	3	1	.333	-1
Russell Martin	LAD	9	7	0	.778	2	1	.500	-2
Victor Martinez	Bos	9	5	3	.889	1	0	.000	-2
Alex Avila	Det	3	2	1	1.000	1	1	1.000	-2
MLB Totals		390	238	29	.685	131	38	.290	

Catchers - 2009 Bunt Defense

Player	Team	SAC BUNTS				BUNT HITS			Runs Saved
		Attempts	Sac Hits	Hits	Sac Hit Average	Attempts	Bunt Hits	Bunt Hit Average	
Russell Martin	LAD	16	7	0	.438	3	0	.000	2
Ivan Rodriguez	2 tms	12	6	0	.500	5	1	.200	2
Ryan Doumit	Pit	6	3	0	.500	2	0	.000	1
Carlos Ruiz	Phi	7	4	0	.571	1	0	.000	1
Chris Iannetta	Col	12	8	0	.667	1	0	.000	1
Brian McCann	Atl	10	7	0	.700	4	0	.000	1
Jason Varitek	Bos	4	3	0	.750	4	1	.250	1
Rob Johnson	Sea	3	3	0	1.000	3	0	.000	1
Miguel Olivo	KC	5	2	0	.400	5	1	.200	0
Joe Mauer	Min	2	1	0	.500	1	0	.000	0
Matt Wieters	Bal	5	3	0	.600	4	2	.500	0
Jarrod Saltalamacchia	Tex	5	2	1	.600	1	0	.000	0
A.J. Pierzynski	CWS	5	3	0	.600	0	0		0
Koyie Hill	ChC	5	3	0	.600	1	0	.000	0
Yadier Molina	StL	18	10	1	.611	3	2	.667	0
Jeff Mathis	LAA	8	5	0	.625	4	2	.500	0
Ryan Hanigan	Cin	10	6	1	.700	2	0	.000	0
Omir Santos	NYM	7	5	0	.714	0	0		0
Victor Martinez	2 tms	4	3	0	.750	0	0		0
Gerald Laird	Det	8	5	1	.750	1	0	.000	0
Rod Barajas	Tor	4	2	1	.750	2	0	.000	0
Geovany Soto	ChC	13	10	0	.769	2	0	.000	0
Ronny Paulino	Fla	7	6	0	.857	3	1	.333	0
Kelly Shoppach	Cle	4	3	1	1.000	1	0	.000	0
Gregg Zaun	2 tms	2	2	0	1.000	1	0	.000	0
Kurt Suzuki	Oak	5	5	0	1.000	1	0	.000	0
Jorge Posada	NYY	2	2	0	1.000	2	0	.000	0
Jason Kendall	Mil	13	4	1	.385	2	1	.500	-1
John Baker	Fla	8	3	1	.500	2	1	.500	-1
Bengie Molina	SF	12	5	2	.583	4	0	.000	-1
Dioner Navarro	TB	3	2	0	.667	2	0	.000	-1
Nick Hundley	SD	12	7	1	.667	2	1	.500	-1
Josh Bard	Was	8	5	1	.750	2	0	.000	-1
Miguel Montero	Ari	9	5	2	.778	4	1	.250	-1
Mike Napoli	LAA	6	5	1	1.000	2	0	.000	-1
MLB Totals		388	246	23	.693	106	24	.226	

First Basemen - 3-Year Bunt Defense

	SAC BUNTS				BUNT HITS			Runs
Player	Attempts	Sac Hits	Hits	Sac Hit Average	Attempts	Bunt Hits	Bunt Hit Average	Saved
Adrian Gonzalez	54	39	2	.759	15	4	.267	5
Lance Berkman	30	19	2	.700	6	3	.500	3
Daniel Murphy	21	12	0	.571	5	2	.400	2
Todd Helton	47	37	2	.830	3	0	.000	2
Paul Konerko	21	13	2	.714	11	5	.455	1
Adam LaRoche	32	23	1	.750	7	2	.286	1
Chris Davis	4	3	0	.750	2	1	.500	1
Ike Davis	28	20	2	.786	4	1	.250	1
Daric Barton	20	16	0	.800	5	2	.400	1
Aubrey Huff	40	35	0	.875	8	3	.375	1
Jorge Cantu	11	10	0	.909	2	1	.500	1
Justin Morneau	10	10	0	1.000	2	1	.500	1
Michael Cuddyer	6	3	1	.667	7	4	.571	0
Albert Pujols	35	22	2	.686	8	5	.625	0
James Loney	37	25	3	.757	10	5	.500	0
Gaby Sanchez	26	18	2	.769	4	2	.500	0
Mark Teixeira	20	14	3	.850	8	3	.375	0
Freddie Freeman	14	10	2	.857	1	1	1.000	0
Carlos Pena	32	25	3	.875	5	2	.400	0
Mark Trumbo	8	7	0	.875	2	2	1.000	0
Russell Branyan	10	7	2	.900	6	0	.000	0
Billy Butler	10	9	0	.900	5	3	.600	0
Ty Wigginton	6	3	1	.667	1	1	1.000	-1
Kevin Youkilis	15	9	2	.733	4	2	.500	-1
Joey Votto	47	33	3	.766	5	2	.400	-1
Prince Fielder	33	23	3	.788	11	5	.455	-1
Casey Kotchman	18	14	2	.889	6	4	.667	-1
Adam Dunn	30	25	2	.900	6	3	.500	-1
Ryan Howard	54	43	7	.926	14	3	.214	-1
Lyle Overbay	20	12	1	.650	3	1	.333	-2
Justin Smoak	11	5	4	.818	4	1	.250	-2
Derrek Lee	49	39	4	.878	6	3	.500	-2
Matt LaPorta	8	4	3	.875	2	1	.500	-3
Miguel Cabrera	23	16	6	.957	11	4	.364	-3
Garrett Jones	8	5	3	1.000	3	3	1.000	-3
MLB Totals	1188	858	103	.809	293	123	.420	

First Basemen - 2011 Bunt Defense

		SAC BUNTS				BUNT HITS			Runs
Player	Team	Attempts	Sac Hits	Hits	Sac Hit Average	Attempts	Bunt Hits	Bunt Hit Average	Saved
Adrian Gonzalez	Bos	12	8	0	.667	2	1	.500	3
Carlos Santana	Cle	2	1	0	.500	3	2	.667	1
Daniel Murphy	NYM	13	8	0	.615	0	0		1
Xavier Nady	Ari	3	2	0	.667	1	0	.000	1
Mitch Moreland	Tex	3	2	0	.667	3	0	.000	1
Derrek Lee	2 tms	10	6	1	.700	2	0	.000	1
Lyle Overbay	2 tms	10	7	0	.700	1	0	.000	1
Carlos Lee	Hou	7	5	0	.714	0	0		1
Ryan Howard	Phi	22	19	2	.955	6	1	.167	1
Conor Jackson	2 tms	0	0	0		1	0	.000	0
Brett Wallace	Hou	11	5	2	.636	2	0	.000	0
James Loney	LAD	9	5	1	.667	5	4	.800	0
Albert Pujols	StL	13	8	1	.692	3	3	1.000	0
Daric Barton	Oak	7	5	0	.714	1	0	.000	0
Jesus Guzman	SD	7	4	1	.714	0	0		0
Adam Lind	Tor	4	2	1	.750	0	0		0
Gaby Sanchez	Fla	16	13	0	.812	3	2	.667	0
Freddie Freeman	Atl	14	10	2	.857	1	1	1.000	0
Mark Trumbo	LAA	7	6	0	.857	2	2	1.000	0
Prince Fielder	Mil	8	7	0	.875	4	1	.250	0
Mark Teixeira	NYY	9	6	2	.889	3	1	.333	0
Carlos Pena	ChC	28	22	3	.893	4	1	.250	0
Brandon Allen	2 tms	4	4	0	1.000	1	1	1.000	0
Justin Morneau	Min	2	2	0	1.000	0	0		0
Eric Hosmer	KC	12	6	2	.667	1	1	1.000	-1
Joey Votto	Cin	20	14	2	.800	2	1	.500	-1
Aubrey Huff	SF	21	17	0	.810	2	1	.500	-1
Michael Morse	Was	12	9	2	.917	0	0		-1
Todd Helton	Col	13	11	2	1.000	0	0		-1
Miguel Cabrera	Det	7	5	2	1.000	4	2	.500	-1
Casey Kotchman	TB	2	1	1	1.000	4	3	.750	-1
Paul Konerko	CWS	5	3	2	1.000	3	1	.333	-1
Justin Smoak	Sea	2	1	1	1.000	3	1	.333	-1
Juan Miranda	Ari	6	3	0	.500	0	0		-2
Matt LaPorta	Cle	7	3	3	.857	1	1	1.000	-3
MLB Totals		418	300	41	.816	98	42	.429	

First Basemen - 2010 Bunt Defense

Player	Team	SAC BUNTS				BUNT HITS			Runs Saved
		Attempts	Sac Hits	Hits	Sac Hit Average	Attempts	Bunt Hits	Bunt Hit Average	
Lance Berkman	2 tms	9	5	0	.556	3	2	.667	2
Todd Helton	Col	16	11	0	.688	3	0	.000	2
Paul Konerko	CWS	7	2	0	.286	4	1	.250	1
Casey Kotchman	Sea	7	5	0	.714	0	0		1
Ike Davis	NYM	24	16	2	.750	4	1	.250	1
James Loney	LAD	13	10	0	.769	3	1	.333	1
Daric Barton	Oak	10	8	0	.800	3	2	.667	1
Adam Dunn	Was	18	15	0	.833	5	2	.400	1
Aubrey Huff	SF	15	15	0	1.000	5	2	.400	1
Brett Wallace	Hou	8	3	0	.500	1	0	.000	0
Prince Fielder	Mil	13	7	1	.615	3	2	.667	0
Kendrys Morales	LAA	3	1	1	.667	1	1	1.000	0
Michael Cuddyer	Min	3	1	1	.667	2	0	.000	0
Gaby Sanchez	Fla	10	5	2	.700	1	0	.000	0
Adam LaRoche	Ari	14	10	1	.786	3	0	.000	0
Adrian Gonzalez	SD	25	18	2	.800	5	2	.400	0
Joey Votto	Cin	17	14	0	.824	0	0		0
Justin Morneau	Min	3	3	0	1.000	0	0		0
Mark Teixeira	NYY	8	7	1	1.000	3	1	.333	0
Carlos Pena	TB	1	1	0	1.000	1	1	1.000	0
Russell Branyan	2 tms	3	3	0	1.000	0	0		0
Mike Napoli	LAA	1	1	0	1.000	0	0		0
Billy Butler	KC	6	6	0	1.000	1	1	1.000	0
Matt LaPorta	Cle	1	1	0	1.000	1	0	.000	0
Lyle Overbay	Tor	6	3	0	.500	0	0		-1
Albert Pujols	StL	10	7	0	.700	2	2	1.000	-1
Kevin Youkilis	Bos	7	3	2	.714	2	1	.500	-1
Ty Wigginton	Bal	4	2	1	.750	1	1	1.000	-1
Justin Smoak	2 tms	9	4	3	.778	1	0	.000	-1
Xavier Nady	ChC	6	4	1	.833	0	0		-1
Ryan Howard	Phi	16	12	2	.875	3	1	.333	-1
Derrek Lee	2 tms	14	13	0	.929	2	2	1.000	-1
Miguel Cabrera	Det	9	6	3	1.000	4	0	.000	-1
Troy Glaus	Atl	3	3	0	1.000	3	1	.333	-1
Garrett Jones	Pit	4	3	1	1.000	3	3	1.000	-2
MLB Totals		391	280	30	.793	85	33	.388	

First Basemen - 2009 Bunt Defense

Player	Team	SAC BUNTS				BUNT HITS			Runs Saved
		Attempts	Sac Hits	Hits	Sac Hit Average	Attempts	Bunt Hits	Bunt Hit Average	
Adrian Gonzalez	SD	17	13	0	.765	8	1	.125	2
Daniel Murphy	NYM	8	4	0	.500	5	2	.400	1
Victor Martinez	2 tms	7	4	0	.571	1	1	1.000	1
Adam LaRoche	3 tms	14	9	0	.643	4	2	.500	1
Albert Pujols	StL	12	7	1	.667	3	0	.000	1
Aubrey Huff	Bal	4	3	0	.750	1	0	.000	1
Lance Berkman	Hou	17	12	1	.765	3	1	.333	1
Nick Johnson	2 tms	14	11	0	.786	1	0	.000	1
Todd Helton	Col	18	15	0	.833	0	0		1
Jorge Cantu	Fla	6	5	0	.833	2	1	.500	1
Paul Konerko	CWS	9	8	0	.889	4	3	.750	1
Justin Morneau	Min	5	5	0	1.000	2	1	.500	1
Jason Giambi	2 tms	4	4	0	1.000	2	0	.000	1
Mark Teixeira	NYY	3	1	0	.333	2	1	.500	0
Ryan Garko	2 tms	5	3	0	.600	2	1	.500	0
Joey Votto	Cin	10	5	1	.600	3	1	.333	0
Carlos Pena	TB	3	2	0	.667	0	0		0
Kevin Youkilis	Bos	6	4	0	.667	2	1	.500	0
Billy Butler	KC	4	3	0	.750	3	2	.667	0
Kendrys Morales	LAA	9	6	1	.778	2	2	1.000	0
Travis Ishikawa	SF	11	8	1	.818	2	0	.000	0
Russell Branyan	Sea	7	4	2	.857	6	0	.000	0
Daric Barton	Oak	3	3	0	1.000	1	0	.000	0
Chad Tracy	Ari	3	3	0	1.000	3	2	.667	0
Chris Davis	Tex	1	1	0	1.000	1	1	1.000	0
Andy Marte	Cle	4	2	1	.750	2	2	1.000	-1
James Loney	LAD	15	10	2	.800	2	0	.000	-1
Miguel Cabrera	Det	7	5	1	.857	3	2	.667	-1
Prince Fielder	Mil	12	9	2	.917	4	2	.500	-1
Ryan Howard	Phi	16	12	3	.938	5	1	.200	-1
Adam Dunn	Was	10	9	1	1.000	1	1	1.000	-1
Hank Blalock	Tex	6	4	2	1.000	0	0		-1
Casey Kotchman	2 tms	9	8	1	1.000	2	1	.500	-1
Lyle Overbay	Tor	4	2	1	.750	2	1	.500	-2
Derrek Lee	ChC	25	20	3	.920	2	1	.500	-2
MLB Totals		379	278	32	.818	110	48	.436	

Third Basemen - 3-Year Bunt Defense

	SAC BUNTS				BUNT HITS			
Player	Attempts	Sac Hits	Hits	Sac Hit Average	Attempts	Bunt Hits	Bunt Hit Average	Runs Saved
Evan Longoria	40	23	6	.725	31	15	.484	7
Adrian Beltre	26	15	5	.769	12	3	.250	3
Alberto Callaspo	23	18	2	.870	20	13	.650	3
Pablo Sandoval	27	21	3	.889	10	5	.500	2
Miguel Tejada	20	14	2	.800	8	6	.750	1
David Freese	12	10	0	.833	4	3	.750	1
Aramis Ramirez	35	26	4	.857	20	12	.600	1
Ian Stewart	22	14	5	.864	6	3	.500	1
Chone Figgins	16	13	1	.875	9	7	.778	1
Andy LaRoche	24	20	1	.875	9	5	.556	1
Casey Blake	21	16	3	.905	11	6	.545	1
Chris Johnson	12	11	0	.917	5	3	.600	1
Jhonny Peralta	20	15	4	.950	12	5	.417	1
Scott Rolen	15	11	1	.800	6	6	1.000	0
Chase Headley	21	16	1	.810	6	5	.833	0
Casey McGehee	29	18	6	.828	9	4	.444	0
Alex Rodriguez	19	14	2	.842	17	12	.706	0
Kevin Youkilis	15	9	4	.867	6	3	.500	0
Ryan Zimmerman	52	42	5	.904	13	9	.692	0
Edwin Encarnacion	11	8	2	.909	6	2	.333	0
Placido Polanco	22	19	3	1.000	12	8	.667	0
Brent Morel	10	8	2	1.000	9	6	.667	0
Michael Young	13	8	3	.846	13	10	.769	-1
Wilson Betemit	15	8	5	.867	10	6	.600	-1
Mark Teahen	15	7	6	.867	17	10	.588	-1
Pedro Alvarez	14	11	2	.929	8	7	.875	-1
Danny Valencia	20	15	5	1.000	10	8	.800	-1
Jose Lopez	18	14	4	1.000	8	6	.750	-1
Jack Hannahan	5	3	1	.800	10	9	.900	-2
David Wright	32	22	5	.844	17	11	.647	-2
Chipper Jones	25	20	3	.920	13	8	.615	-2
Melvin Mora	16	10	5	.938	8	5	.625	-2
Kevin Kouzmanoff	34	24	8	.941	24	14	.583	-2
Mark Reynolds	31	25	5	.968	19	12	.632	-3
Brandon Inge	28	16	12	1.000	14	7	.500	-4
MLB Totals	1199	862	202	.887	666	406	.610	

Third Basemen - 2011 Bunt Defense

		SAC BUNTS				BUNT HITS			
Player	Team	Attempts	Sac Hits	Hits	Sac Hit Average	Attempts	Bunt Hits	Bunt Hit Average	Runs Saved
Evan Longoria	TB	12	6	1	.583	5	1	.200	4
Aramis Ramirez	ChC	12	11	0	.917	9	5	.556	2
Alex Rodriguez	NYY	4	3	0	.750	9	5	.556	1
Ryan Zimmerman	Was	15	12	0	.800	6	5	.833	1
Pablo Sandoval	SF	6	5	0	.833	2	0	.000	1
Juan Uribe	LAD	7	6	0	.857	1	1	1.000	1
Chris Johnson	Hou	7	6	0	.857	2	2	1.000	1
Aaron Miles	LAD	6	5	1	1.000	3	2	.667	1
Lonnie Chisenhall	Cle	4	3	1	1.000	3	0	.000	1
Chone Figgins	Sea	5	5	0	1.000	4	2	.500	1
Scott Rolen	Cin	3	1	0	.333	1	1	1.000	0
Jack Hannahan	Cle	3	2	0	.667	6	5	.833	0
Ty Wigginton	Col	3	1	1	.667	5	4	.800	0
Adrian Beltre	Tex	7	4	1	.714	2	1	.500	0
Kevin Youkilis	Bos	10	5	3	.800	4	2	.500	0
Wilson Betemit	2 tms	11	6	3	.818	6	3	.500	0
Chipper Jones	Atl	6	5	0	.833	3	2	.667	0
Kevin Kouzmanoff	2 tms	7	4	2	.857	4	2	.500	0
Casey McGehee	Mil	8	5	2	.875	1	0	.000	0
Alberto Callaspo	LAA	12	10	1	.917	9	8	.889	0
Miguel Cairo	Cin	2	2	0	1.000	0	0		0
David Freese	StL	5	5	0	1.000	3	3	1.000	0
Placido Polanco	Phi	13	11	2	1.000	5	3	.600	0
Brent Morel	CWS	9	7	2	1.000	7	5	.714	0
Ryan Roberts	Ari	8	5	1	.750	4	4	1.000	-1
David Wright	NYM	9	5	2	.778	4	2	.500	-1
Pedro Alvarez	Pit	6	4	1	.833	5	4	.800	-1
Chase Headley	SD	8	7	1	1.000	1	1	1.000	-1
Danny Valencia	Min	11	8	3	1.000	9	7	.778	-1
Daniel Descalso	StL	4	3	1	1.000	2	1	.500	-1
Scott Sizemore	Oak	7	5	2	1.000	6	6	1.000	-1
Greg Dobbs	Fla	12	10	2	1.000	5	4	.800	-2
Mike Moustakas	KC	5	2	3	1.000	5	4	.800	-2
Brandon Inge	Det	7	2	5	1.000	4	2	.500	-2
Mark Reynolds	Bal	7	5	2	1.000	5	5	1.000	-3
MLB Totals		402	287	69	.886	246	153	.622	

Third Basemen - 2010 Bunt Defense

Player	Team	SAC BUNTS				BUNT HITS			Runs Saved
		Attempts	Sac Hits	Hits	Sac Hit Average	Attempts	Bunt Hits	Bunt Hit Average	
Alberto Callaspo	2 tms	11	8	1	.818	11	5	.455	3
Evan Longoria	TB	12	9	1	.833	18	9	.500	3
Adrian Beltre	Bos	13	7	3	.769	5	1	.200	2
Ian Stewart	Col	10	6	1	.700	1	1	1.000	1
David Freese	StL	7	5	0	.714	1	0	.000	1
Chase Headley	SD	12	9	0	.750	4	3	.750	1
Casey McGehee	Mil	17	11	2	.765	4	2	.500	1
Scott Rolen	Cin	6	5	0	.833	1	1	1.000	1
Jorge Cantu	2 tms	14	9	2	.786	5	3	.600	0
Pablo Sandoval	SF	5	3	1	.800	2	2	1.000	0
David Wright	NYM	11	7	2	.818	6	3	.500	0
Andy LaRoche	Pit	7	6	0	.857	3	2	.667	0
Pedro Feliz	2 tms	9	7	1	.889	2	1	.500	0
Miguel Tejada	2 tms	10	7	2	.900	7	5	.714	0
Casey Blake	LAD	10	7	2	.900	6	4	.667	0
Wilson Betemit	KC	3	2	1	1.000	4	3	.750	0
Brandon Inge	Det	12	9	3	1.000	5	1	.200	0
Omar Vizquel	CWS	4	4	0	1.000	2	2	1.000	0
Placido Polanco	Phi	9	8	1	1.000	7	5	.714	0
Chris Johnson	Hou	5	5	0	1.000	3	1	.333	0
Wes Helms	Fla	5	5	0	1.000	3	1	.333	0
Felipe Lopez	2 tms	2	2	0	1.000	0	0		0
Pedro Alvarez	Pit	8	7	1	1.000	3	3	1.000	0
Danny Valencia	Min	9	7	2	1.000	1	1	1.000	0
Mark Reynolds	Ari	13	12	1	1.000	5	3	.600	0
Jhonny Peralta	2 tms	4	4	0	1.000	5	4	.800	0
Alex Rodriguez	NYY	12	9	2	.917	5	4	.800	-1
Ryan Zimmerman	Was	20	16	3	.950	2	1	.500	-1
Michael Young	Tex	9	6	3	1.000	2	2	1.000	-1
Edwin Encarnacion	Tor	4	2	2	1.000	3	1	.333	-1
Jose Lopez	Sea	16	12	4	1.000	8	6	.750	-1
Kevin Kouzmanoff	Oak	16	13	3	1.000	10	7	.700	-1
Melvin Mora	Col	4	2	2	1.000	4	2	.500	-1
Chipper Jones	Atl	7	4	2	.857	4	2	.500	-2
Aramis Ramirez	ChC	12	8	3	.917	7	5	.714	-2
MLB Totals		418	306	67	.892	202	120	.594	

Third Basemen - 2009 Bunt Defense

Player	Team	SAC BUNTS				BUNT HITS			Runs Saved
		Attempts	Sac Hits	Hits	Sac Hit Average	Attempts	Bunt Hits	Bunt Hit Average	
Mark DeRosa	2 tms	9	7	0	.778	4	3	.750	2
Gordon Beckham	CWS	9	5	1	.667	5	4	.800	1
Aramis Ramirez	ChC	11	7	1	.727	4	2	.500	1
Pedro Feliz	Phi	14	11	0	.786	6	5	.833	1
Adrian Beltre	Sea	6	4	1	.833	5	1	.200	1
Edwin Encarnacion	2 tms	7	6	0	.857	3	1	.333	1
Emilio Bonifacio	Fla	7	4	2	.857	5	1	.200	1
Jeff Keppinger	Hou	7	5	1	.857	3	1	.333	1
Casey Blake	LAD	10	8	1	.900	4	1	.250	1
Jhonny Peralta	Cle	16	11	4	.938	7	1	.143	1
Pablo Sandoval	SF	16	13	2	.938	6	3	.500	1
Alex Rodriguez	NYY	3	2	0	.667	3	3	1.000	0
Michael Young	Tex	3	2	0	.667	5	4	.800	0
Evan Longoria	TB	16	8	4	.750	8	5	.625	0
Chone Figgins	LAA	11	8	1	.818	5	5	1.000	0
Andy LaRoche	Pit	14	11	1	.857	6	3	.500	0
Garrett Atkins	Col	7	4	2	.857	5	3	.600	0
Adam Kennedy	Oak	8	5	2	.875	3	1	.333	0
Bill Hall	2 tms	9	7	1	.889	2	1	.500	0
Mark Reynolds	Ari	11	8	2	.909	9	4	.444	0
Ryan Zimmerman	Was	17	14	2	.941	5	3	.600	0
Kevin Youkilis	Bos	4	3	1	1.000	2	1	.500	0
Chipper Jones	Atl	12	11	1	1.000	6	4	.667	0
Joe Crede	Min	2	2	0	1.000	4	3	.750	0
Mike Lowell	Bos	2	2	0	1.000	3	2	.667	0
Geoff Blum	Hou	3	2	1	1.000	0	0		0
Mark Teahen	KC	8	3	4	.875	9	5	.556	-1
Melvin Mora	Bal	10	6	3	.900	3	2	.667	-1
Kevin Kouzmanoff	SD	11	7	3	.909	10	5	.500	-1
David Wright	NYM	12	10	1	.917	7	6	.857	-1
Casey McGehee	Mil	4	2	2	1.000	4	2	.500	-1
Ian Stewart	Col	11	7	4	1.000	4	2	.500	-1
Scott Rolen	2 tms	6	5	1	1.000	4	4	1.000	-1
Brandon Inge	Det	9	5	4	1.000	5	4	.800	-2
Jack Hannahan	2 tms	2	1	1	1.000	4	4	1.000	-2
MLB Totals		379	269	66	.884	218	133	.610	

Revised Zone Ratings

The original Zone Ratings were developed by this book's co-author John Dewan 20 years ago while at STATS, Inc. The basic concept was to define an area for each position (called a zone) where the fielder should be expected to make plays. Utilizing the new batted ball locations recorded by STATS, Inc. scorers, he defined each position's zone as the area where at least 50 percent of batted balls are handled successfully. Count all the balls that a player successfully fields, divide by the number of batted balls recorded in his zone, and you have his Zone Rating.

Later with Baseball Info Solutions, John revised his original methodology and published the new system in *The Fielding Bible*. The revisions included the separation of plays made out of the fielder's zone from the in-zone plays. Under the original system, all plays made (in the zone or out of the zone) were included in the Zone Rating numerator plus double plays were counted twice. Under the revised system, the out of zone plays were removed from the numerator and included separately as plays made "Out Of Zone" (OOZ). Double plays are not counted

The new system also has separate zones for outfield line drives, fliners, and flyballs. Since outfielders don't have time to range as far on line drives, the line drive zones are much smaller than the fliner and flyball zones.

Let's walk through an example. In 2011, Clint Barmes made 261 in zone plays out of 300 batted balls in the shortstop's zone. On top of that, the Astros' shortstop made 48 out of zone plays and had 65 double plays. Under the old calculation, his zone rating would be (261 + 48 + 65)/(300 + 48) = 1.075. Under the new calculation, his zone rating is 261/300 = 0.870, and we separately list the 48 out of zone plays. In the new system, zone ratings cannot be greater than 1.000.

Zone Ratings have a lot of similarities to the Plus/Minus System. Both systems rate fielders on their ability to make plays on batted balls. Both systems look at the same plays, using much of the same data. The Plus/Minus System, however, divides the field into hundreds of smaller zones and estimates the difficulty of each play between 0 and 1, rather than simply separating in zone and out of zone. Zone Ratings are admittedly less sophisticated than the Plus/Minus System, but there's value in having more than one set of numbers to evaluate a player.

On the following pages, the charts are fairly simple:

Balls In Zone - Number of batted balls marked inside the position's pre-determined zone while the player was on the field. The zones are determined based on areas where 50 percent of plays are made for outs.

Plays Made - A play is considered "made" by the fielder if he gets a putout or assist on the batted ball in his position's zone. This includes catching the ball on the fly, throwing out the batter at first, or retiring a runner via force out (among other things).

Zone Rating - Plays Made divided by Balls In Zone.

Plays Out of Zone - Number of plays made out of the position's zone.

First Basemen - 3-Year Zone Ratings

Player	Balls In Zone	Plays Made	Zone Rating	Plays Out Of Zone
Kevin Youkilis	186	159	.855	52
Daric Barton	308	255	.828	106
Justin Morneau	296	244	.824	60
Casey Kotchman	434	356	.820	81
Daniel Murphy	170	139	.818	57
Lyle Overbay	465	376	.809	87
Aubrey Huff	339	274	.808	74
Adrian Gonzalez	654	526	.804	103
James Loney	477	383	.803	95
Todd Helton	506	406	.802	80
Russell Branyan	241	192	.797	74
Ike Davis	196	156	.796	66
Derrek Lee	453	359	.792	84
Albert Pujols	714	564	.790	164
Joey Votto	523	412	.788	130
Matt LaPorta	277	218	.787	37
Mark Trumbo	230	181	.787	45
Justin Smoak	252	198	.786	34
Mark Teixeira	619	478	.772	117
Gaby Sanchez	428	330	.771	64
Lance Berkman	301	231	.767	79
Michael Cuddyer	189	145	.767	35
Ryan Howard	582	446	.766	73
Adam LaRoche	459	351	.765	116
Miguel Cabrera	598	453	.758	106
Jorge Cantu	210	158	.752	42
Paul Konerko	464	347	.748	75
Ty Wigginton	186	139	.747	47
Garrett Jones	215	160	.744	41
Freddie Freeman	194	143	.737	33
Billy Butler	368	271	.736	84
Chris Davis	192	141	.734	35
Carlos Pena	443	324	.731	106
Prince Fielder	584	427	.731	97
Adam Dunn	309	220	.712	36

First Basemen - 2010 Zone Ratings

Player	Tm	Balls In Zone	Plays Made	Zone Rating	Plays Out Of Zone
Justin Morneau	Min	98	86	.878	16
Kevin Youkilis	Bos	103	88	.854	26
Kendrys Morales	LAA	60	51	.850	12
Daric Barton	Oak	153	127	.830	69
Lance Berkman	2 tms	93	76	.817	28
Adrian Gonzalez	SD	207	169	.816	36
Brett Wallace	Hou	38	31	.816	14
Russell Branyan	2 tms	89	72	.809	28
Mike Napoli	LAA	90	72	.800	27
Lyle Overbay	Tor	173	138	.798	40
Derrek Lee	2 tms	161	128	.795	37
Ike Davis	NYM	140	111	.793	58
Ty Wigginton	Bal	107	84	.785	33
Casey Kotchman	Sea	129	101	.783	27
Xavier Nady	ChC	45	35	.778	15
Matt LaPorta	Cle	110	85	.773	20
James Loney	LAD	165	127	.770	41
Aubrey Huff	SF	95	73	.768	28
Justin Smoak	2 tms	110	84	.764	23
Adam LaRoche	Ari	202	154	.762	46
Carlos Pena	TB	149	113	.758	43
Joey Votto	Cin	155	117	.755	51
Mark Teixeira	NYY	228	172	.754	43
Adam Dunn	Was	180	135	.750	28
Billy Butler	KC	183	137	.749	35
Albert Pujols	StL	222	166	.748	60
Miguel Cabrera	Det	198	148	.747	37
Michael Cuddyer	Min	101	75	.743	18
Garrett Jones	Pit	145	107	.738	29
Todd Helton	Col	116	84	.724	31
Gaby Sanchez	Fla	199	141	.709	38
Troy Glaus	Atl	120	85	.708	16
Ryan Howard	Phi	183	128	.699	29
Prince Fielder	Mil	172	114	.663	48
Paul Konerko	CWS	184	119	.647	29

First Basemen - 2011 Zone Ratings

Player	Tm	Balls In Zone	Plays Made	Zone Rating	Plays Out Of Zone
Todd Helton	Col	199	171	.859	15
Aubrey Huff	SF	126	108	.857	26
Daric Barton	Oak	94	80	.851	13
Casey Kotchman	TB	167	141	.844	18
James Loney	LAD	158	131	.829	26
Gaby Sanchez	Fla	228	188	.825	26
Xavier Nady	Ari	45	37	.822	5
Carlos Lee	Hou	109	89	.817	14
Adrian Gonzalez	Bos	234	191	.816	17
Brandon Allen	2 tms	76	62	.816	6
Albert Pujols	StL	222	181	.815	28
Juan Miranda	Ari	57	46	.807	3
Jesus Guzman	SD	61	49	.803	12
Justin Smoak	Sea	142	114	.803	11
Joey Votto	Cin	225	180	.800	38
Daniel Murphy	NYM	50	40	.800	13
Adam Lind	Tor	149	119	.799	12
Carlos Santana	Cle	113	90	.796	10
Brett Wallace	Hou	115	91	.791	18
Conor Jackson	2 tms	62	49	.790	7
Lyle Overbay	2 tms	128	101	.789	13
Matt LaPorta	Cle	155	122	.787	13
Mark Trumbo	LAA	227	178	.784	41
Justin Morneau	Min	74	58	.784	7
Paul Konerko	CWS	147	115	.782	10
Ryan Howard	Phi	193	150	.777	13
Derrek Lee	2 tms	139	108	.777	20
Prince Fielder	Mil	210	163	.776	21
Mark Teixeira	NYY	213	164	.770	37
Miguel Cabrera	Det	203	156	.768	17
Eric Hosmer	KC	176	134	.761	6
Mitch Moreland	Tex	107	80	.748	17
Michael Morse	Was	124	92	.742	4
Freddie Freeman	Atl	188	138	.734	32
Carlos Pena	ChC	153	111	.725	27

First Basemen - 2009 Zone Ratings

Player	Tm	Balls In Zone	Plays Made	Zone Rating	Plays Out Of Zone
Kevin Youkilis	Bos	75	64	.853	25
Paul Konerko	CWS	133	113	.850	36
Travis Ishikawa	SF	106	89	.840	26
Lyle Overbay	Tor	164	137	.835	34
Casey Kotchman	2 tms	138	114	.826	36
Daniel Murphy	NYM	120	99	.825	44
Ryan Garko	2 tms	82	67	.817	23
Ryan Howard	Phi	206	168	.816	31
James Loney	LAD	154	125	.812	28
Justin Morneau	Min	124	100	.806	37
Kendrys Morales	LAA	184	148	.804	50
Joey Votto	Cin	143	115	.804	41
Derrek Lee	ChC	153	123	.804	27
Albert Pujols	StL	270	217	.804	76
Mark Teixeira	NYY	178	142	.798	37
Chad Tracy	Ari	64	51	.797	19
Todd Helton	Col	191	151	.791	34
Aubrey Huff	Bal	118	93	.788	20
Daric Barton	Oak	61	48	.787	24
Russell Branyan	Sea	133	104	.782	44
Adrian Gonzalez	SD	213	166	.779	50
Hank Blalock	Tex	86	67	.779	14
Jorge Cantu	Fla	146	111	.760	24
Victor Martinez	2 tms	62	47	.758	20
Miguel Cabrera	Det	197	149	.756	52
Lance Berkman	Hou	180	136	.756	46
Nick Johnson	2 tms	161	121	.752	40
Chris Davis	Tex	127	95	.748	21
Prince Fielder	Mil	202	150	.743	28
Adam LaRoche	3 tms	194	143	.737	61
Billy Butler	KC	174	128	.736	49
Andy Marte	Cle	58	42	.724	15
Carlos Pena	TB	141	100	.709	36
Jason Giambi	2 tms	66	46	.697	9
Adam Dunn	Was	83	54	.651	7

Second Basemen - 3-Year Zone Ratings

Player	Balls In Zone	Plays Made	Zone Rating	Plays Out Of Zone
Chase Utley	914	784	.858	95
Ian Kinsler	977	833	.853	108
Dustin Pedroia	917	779	.850	97
Mark Ellis	889	752	.846	82
Clint Barmes	569	479	.842	39
Ben Zobrist	547	460	.841	95
Placido Polanco	419	350	.835	44
Jeff Keppinger	615	511	.831	29
Aaron Hill	1067	886	.830	130
Howie Kendrick	859	713	.830	90
Rickie Weeks	689	571	.829	66
Chris Getz	690	568	.823	59
Jamey Carroll	359	295	.822	25
Brandon Phillips	1120	919	.821	106
Danny Espinosa	479	393	.820	61
Felipe Lopez	452	370	.819	42
Martin Prado	396	324	.818	41
Robinson Cano	1149	940	.818	148
Orlando Hudson	960	785	.818	91
Omar Infante	702	574	.818	51
Blake DeWitt	305	248	.813	29
Ryan Theriot	304	247	.813	40
Chone Figgins	389	316	.812	28
Freddy Sanchez	623	505	.811	52
Alberto Callaspo	390	315	.808	29
Luis Valbuena	429	346	.807	40
Gordon Beckham	738	595	.806	73
Kelly Johnson	892	718	.805	69
Dan Uggla	1213	976	.805	101
Alexi Casilla	389	311	.799	27
Brian Roberts	630	502	.797	71
Jose Lopez	354	282	.797	40
Adam Kennedy	430	342	.795	29
Skip Schumaker	919	723	.787	71
Neil Walker	637	497	.780	64

Second Basemen - 2010 Zone Ratings

Player	Tm	Balls In Zone	Plays Made	Zone Rating	Plays Out Of Zone
Dustin Pedroia	Bos	187	161	.861	13
Mark Ellis	Oak	297	255	.859	18
Ian Kinsler	Tex	246	210	.854	23
Luis Valbuena	Cle	208	177	.851	15
Jeff Keppinger	Hou	345	292	.846	13
Freddy Sanchez	SF	242	204	.843	17
Chase Utley	Phi	306	257	.840	36
Aaron Hill	Tor	334	280	.838	35
Clint Barmes	Col	182	152	.835	9
Jonathan Herrera	Col	137	114	.832	14
Will Rhymes	Det	131	109	.832	16
David Eckstein	SD	273	227	.832	15
Omar Infante	Atl	182	151	.830	12
Adam Kennedy	Was	204	169	.828	14
Rickie Weeks	Mil	353	292	.827	19
Robinson Cano	NYY	373	308	.826	45
Kelly Johnson	Ari	367	303	.826	22
Orlando Hudson	Min	335	276	.824	36
Luis Castillo	NYM	170	140	.824	13
Martin Prado	Atl	249	205	.823	33
Dan Uggla	Fla	396	326	.823	23
Sean Rodriguez	TB	179	147	.821	33
Mike Aviles	KC	251	205	.817	23
Blake DeWitt	2 tms	270	220	.815	27
Chone Figgins	Sea	387	315	.814	27
Julio Lugo	Bal	118	96	.814	15
Cristian Guzman	2 tms	179	144	.804	19
Brian Roberts	Bal	138	111	.804	11
Brandon Phillips	Cin	386	310	.803	36
Ryan Theriot	2 tms	248	199	.802	34
Howie Kendrick	LAA	354	281	.794	29
Gordon Beckham	CWS	334	263	.787	31
Chris Getz	KC	142	111	.782	16
Skip Schumaker	StL	342	263	.769	33
Neil Walker	Pit	243	182	.749	11

Second Basemen - 2011 Zone Ratings

Player	Tm	Balls In Zone	Plays Made	Zone Rating	Plays Out Of Zone
Howie Kendrick	LAA	273	247	.905	25
Chase Utley	Phi	251	225	.896	24
Ian Kinsler	Tex	343	299	.872	38
Aaron Miles	LAD	138	119	.862	6
Dustin Ackley	Sea	199	170	.854	29
Dustin Pedroia	Bos	363	309	.851	50
Mark Ellis	2 tms	321	272	.847	45
Chris Getz	KC	267	225	.843	28
Darwin Barney	ChC	321	269	.838	32
Orlando Hudson	SD	286	239	.836	15
Orlando Cabrera	2 tms	238	198	.832	29
Brandon Phillips	Cin	372	309	.831	32
Danny Espinosa	Was	419	347	.828	51
Rickie Weeks	Mil	261	215	.824	30
Jeff Keppinger	2 tms	220	181	.823	14
Alexi Casilla	Min	169	139	.822	14
Gordon Beckham	CWS	404	332	.822	42
Ben Zobrist	TB	262	215	.821	48
Dan Uggla	Atl	405	331	.817	39
Omar Infante	Fla	455	371	.815	37
Ruben Tejada	NYM	140	114	.814	11
Robert Andino	Bal	215	175	.814	16
Ramon Santiago	Det	129	105	.814	11
Jose Altuve	Hou	127	103	.811	14
Aaron Hill	2 tms	326	264	.810	44
Robinson Cano	NYY	397	318	.801	59
Neil Walker	Pit	394	315	.799	53
Jemile Weeks	Oak	257	204	.794	27
Skip Schumaker	StL	252	200	.794	17
Jonathan Herrera	Col	148	117	.791	19
Maicer Izturis	LAA	154	121	.786	11
Jamey Carroll	LAD	160	125	.781	9
Kelly Johnson	2 tms	319	247	.774	34
Justin Turner	NYM	210	162	.771	17
Freddy Sanchez	SF	134	102	.761	10

Second Basemen - 2009 Zone Ratings

Player	Tm	Balls In Zone	Plays Made	Zone Rating	Plays Out Of Zone
Maicer Izturis	LAA	161	139	.863	14
Ben Zobrist	TB	193	166	.860	31
Mike Fontenot	ChC	126	108	.857	12
Jamey Carroll	Cle	122	104	.852	14
Anderson Hernandez	2 tms	168	143	.851	10
Chase Utley	Phi	357	302	.846	35
Clint Barmes	Col	387	327	.845	30
Dustin Pedroia	Bos	367	309	.842	34
Aaron Hill	Tor	407	342	.840	51
Ian Kinsler	Tex	388	324	.835	47
Mark Ellis	Oak	271	225	.830	19
Brandon Phillips	Cin	362	300	.829	38
Robinson Cano	NYY	379	314	.828	44
Chris Getz	CWS	281	232	.826	15
Placido Polanco	Det	389	321	.825	39
Felipe Lopez	2 tms	376	308	.819	38
Kaz Matsui	Hou	342	279	.816	23
Kelly Johnson	Atl	206	168	.816	13
Delwyn Young	Pit	121	98	.810	6
Martin Prado	Atl	147	119	.810	8
Alberto Callaspo	KC	361	291	.806	27
Freddy Sanchez	2 tms	247	199	.806	25
Nick Punto	Min	141	113	.801	9
Skip Schumaker	StL	325	260	.800	21
Howie Kendrick	LAA	232	185	.797	36
Orlando Hudson	LAD	339	270	.796	40
Jose Lopez	Sea	323	256	.793	36
Manny Burriss	SF	120	95	.792	12
Brian Roberts	Bal	383	302	.789	45
Luis Castillo	NYM	344	271	.788	26
David Eckstein	SD	298	231	.775	33
Dan Uggla	Fla	412	319	.774	39
Akinori Iwamura	TB	145	110	.759	28
Alexi Casilla	Min	174	132	.759	10
Luis Valbuena	Cle	201	152	.756	24

Third Basemen - 3-Year Zone Ratings

Player	Balls In Zone	Plays Made	Zone Rating	Plays Out Of Zone
Jack Hannahan	360	286	.794	64
Scott Rolen	616	469	.761	119
Alex Rodriguez	638	485	.760	88
Casey Blake	622	471	.757	96
Jose Lopez	401	303	.756	61
Alberto Callaspo	549	412	.750	70
Placido Polanco	573	426	.743	71
Kevin Kouzmanoff	645	479	.743	95
Adrian Beltre	722	535	.741	169
Brandon Inge	784	579	.739	110
Ian Stewart	458	336	.734	83
Evan Longoria	820	599	.730	140
Chone Figgins	442	322	.729	110
Pablo Sandoval	671	488	.727	125
Melvin Mora	461	331	.718	58
Ryan Zimmerman	747	534	.715	182
Andy LaRoche	511	365	.714	63
Chase Headley	520	369	.710	102
Danny Valencia	506	358	.708	49
David Freese	349	244	.699	43
Miguel Tejada	331	231	.698	46
Kevin Youkilis	321	223	.695	42
Michael Young	628	436	.694	83
Casey McGehee	754	523	.694	83
Jhonny Peralta	451	311	.690	71
Edwin Encarnacion	418	288	.689	67
Brent Morel	286	197	.689	30
Pedro Alvarez	406	279	.687	53
David Wright	799	549	.687	142
Mark Teahen	353	240	.680	44
Chipper Jones	572	386	.675	128
Wilson Betemit	283	190	.671	22
Chris Johnson	365	245	.671	38
Mark Reynolds	781	510	.653	108
Aramis Ramirez	642	419	.653	82

Third Basemen - 2010 Zone Ratings

Player	Tm	Balls In Zone	Plays Made	Zone Rating	Plays Out Of Zone
Jose Lopez	Sea	329	252	.766	56
Danny Valencia	Min	179	137	.765	22
Kevin Kouzmanoff	Oak	278	212	.763	49
Casey Blake	LAD	264	199	.754	47
Scott Rolen	Cin	276	207	.750	41
Alex Rodriguez	NYY	248	185	.746	28
Evan Longoria	TB	271	201	.742	43
Alberto Callaspo	2 tms	259	192	.741	33
Adrian Beltre	Bos	284	210	.739	74
Ryan Zimmerman	Was	234	173	.739	57
Chipper Jones	Atl	150	110	.733	43
Brandon Inge	Det	303	222	.733	30
Ian Stewart	Col	230	167	.726	39
Chase Headley	SD	291	211	.725	67
Pablo Sandoval	SF	244	176	.721	51
Placido Polanco	Phi	297	212	.714	33
Jhonny Peralta	2 tms	229	163	.712	32
Andy LaRoche	Pit	138	98	.710	12
Edwin Encarnacion	Tor	200	142	.710	34
Michael Young	Tex	308	218	.708	36
Casey McGehee	Mil	326	227	.696	26
David Freese	StL	162	112	.691	18
David Wright	NYM	365	251	.688	52
Mark Reynolds	Ari	284	195	.687	33
Pedro Feliz	2 tms	195	133	.682	31
Chris Johnson	Hou	157	107	.682	24
Felipe Lopez	2 tms	134	91	.679	9
Wes Helms	Fla	108	73	.676	23
Miguel Tejada	2 tms	229	154	.672	30
Melvin Mora	Col	105	70	.667	11
Wilson Betemit	KC	94	62	.660	9
Jorge Cantu	2 tms	128	84	.656	25
Pedro Alvarez	Pit	237	155	.654	34
Aramis Ramirez	ChC	229	148	.646	35
Omar Vizquel	CWS	132	85	.644	19

Third Basemen - 2011 Zone Ratings

Player	Tm	Balls In Zone	Plays Made	Zone Rating	Plays Out Of Zone
Alex Rodriguez	NYY	165	137	.830	23
Jack Hannahan	Cle	224	179	.799	24
Pablo Sandoval	SF	214	167	.780	42
Juan Uribe	LAD	103	80	.777	7
Placido Polanco	Phi	276	214	.775	38
Scott Rolen	Cin	120	92	.767	20
Alberto Callaspo	LAA	278	211	.759	33
Adrian Beltre	Tex	221	167	.756	34
Mike Moustakas	KC	185	137	.741	27
Pedro Alvarez	Pit	169	124	.734	19
Brandon Inge	Det	196	140	.714	25
Ryan Roberts	Ari	230	164	.713	23
Casey McGehee	Mil	297	211	.710	36
Evan Longoria	TB	254	180	.709	33
Lonnie Chisenhall	Cle	130	92	.708	15
David Freese	StL	183	129	.705	24
Miguel Cairo	Cin	122	85	.697	21
Chone Figgins	Sea	163	113	.693	14
Brent Morel	CWS	243	168	.691	28
Greg Dobbs	Fla	152	105	.691	17
Kevin Kouzmanoff	2 tms	144	99	.688	12
Ty Wigginton	Col	115	79	.687	14
Chase Headley	SD	181	124	.685	31
Wilson Betemit	2 tms	181	124	.685	13
Kevin Youkilis	Bos	219	149	.680	17
Aaron Miles	LAD	96	65	.677	9
Ryan Zimmerman	Was	232	157	.677	23
Danny Valencia	Min	327	221	.676	27
David Wright	NYM	199	134	.673	40
Daniel Descalso	StL	145	97	.669	21
Chris Johnson	Hou	199	133	.668	14
Chipper Jones	Atl	202	135	.668	35
Aramis Ramirez	ChC	268	175	.653	22
Scott Sizemore	Oak	167	104	.623	16
Mark Reynolds	Bal	231	139	.602	22

Third Basemen - 2009 Zone Ratings

Player	Tm	Balls In Zone	Plays Made	Zone Rating	Plays Out Of Zone
Joe Crede	Min	165	131	.794	39
Jack Hannahan	2 tms	136	107	.787	40
Scott Rolen	2 tms	220	170	.773	58
Casey Blake	LAD	275	211	.767	41
Brandon Inge	Det	285	217	.761	55
Ian Stewart	Col	165	125	.758	36
Kevin Kouzmanoff	SD	223	168	.753	34
Chone Figgins	LAA	279	209	.749	96
Bill Hall	2 tms	123	92	.748	26
Pedro Feliz	Phi	354	262	.740	32
Kevin Youkilis	Bos	96	71	.740	24
Geoff Blum	Hou	188	139	.739	20
Evan Longoria	TB	295	218	.739	64
Andy LaRoche	Pit	333	245	.736	48
Melvin Mora	Bal	284	208	.732	40
Adrian Beltre	Sea	217	158	.728	61
Ryan Zimmerman	Was	281	204	.726	102
Alex Rodriguez	NYY	225	163	.724	37
Garrett Atkins	Col	151	109	.722	24
Gordon Beckham	CWS	217	156	.719	39
Mike Lowell	Bos	221	155	.701	17
David Wright	NYM	235	164	.698	50
Adam Kennedy	Oak	171	119	.696	26
Edwin Encarnacion	2 tms	157	109	.694	26
Jeff Keppinger	Hou	120	83	.692	18
Pablo Sandoval	SF	213	145	.681	32
Emilio Bonifacio	Fla	173	117	.676	28
Mark Teahen	KC	195	131	.672	28
Michael Young	Tex	239	160	.669	40
Mark DeRosa	2 tms	199	133	.668	30
Jhonny Peralta	Cle	222	148	.667	39
Aramis Ramirez	ChC	145	96	.662	25
Mark Reynolds	Ari	266	176	.662	53
Casey McGehee	Mil	131	85	.649	21
Chipper Jones	Atl	220	141	.641	50

Shortstops - 3-Year Zone Ratings

Player	Balls In Zone	Plays Made	Zone Rating	Plays Out Of Zone
Clint Barmes	462	401	.868	78
Paul Janish	537	459	.855	72
J.J. Hardy	911	774	.850	114
Brendan Ryan	983	834	.848	191
Ramon Santiago	394	331	.840	63
Edgar Renteria	635	532	.838	66
Jimmy Rollins	947	792	.836	109
Elvis Andrus	1078	898	.833	158
Jhonny Peralta	550	456	.829	89
Yunel Escobar	1035	857	.828	179
Alex Gonzalez	1101	909	.826	174
Jose Reyes	773	635	.821	92
Troy Tulowitzki	1089	894	.821	158
Alexei Ramirez	1205	989	.821	201
Alcides Escobar	818	670	.819	147
Erick Aybar	992	811	.818	163
Cesar Izturis	681	556	.816	104
Jack Wilson	499	407	.816	94
Rafael Furcal	875	712	.814	140
Ronny Cedeno	958	779	.813	141
Derek Jeter	951	763	.802	103
Cliff Pennington	967	774	.800	124
Stephen Drew	895	716	.800	142
Jason Bartlett	973	777	.799	153
Ryan Theriot	689	549	.797	95
Marco Scutaro	961	764	.795	164
Orlando Cabrera	808	641	.793	79
Josh Wilson	443	351	.792	45
Asdrubal Cabrera	856	674	.787	145
Starlin Castro	730	574	.786	115
Miguel Tejada	730	574	.786	77
Ian Desmond	806	633	.785	119
Hanley Ramirez	843	653	.775	124
Yuniesky Betancourt	1143	865	.757	169
Everth Cabrera	447	337	.754	60

Shortstops - 2010 Zone Ratings

Player	Tm	Balls In Zone	Plays Made	Zone Rating	Plays Out Of Zone
Jimmy Rollins	Phi	218	188	.862	17
Edgar Renteria	SF	146	125	.856	8
J.J. Hardy	Min	263	224	.852	34
Jamey Carroll	LAD	189	160	.847	21
Ramon Santiago	Det	181	153	.845	36
Brendan Ryan	StL	366	309	.844	69
Rafael Furcal	LAD	257	216	.840	35
Troy Tulowitzki	Col	324	270	.833	51
Jack Wilson	Sea	167	138	.826	32
Orlando Cabrera	Cin	282	232	.823	29
Elvis Andrus	Tex	377	308	.817	46
Jerry Hairston	SD	141	115	.816	30
Cliff Pennington	Oak	454	370	.815	53
Alex Gonzalez	2 tms	462	375	.812	74
Alexei Ramirez	CWS	450	365	.811	67
Josh Wilson	Sea	296	239	.807	31
Alcides Escobar	Mil	331	267	.807	55
Erick Aybar	LAA	310	250	.806	61
Miguel Tejada	SD	158	127	.804	15
Jose Reyes	NYM	346	277	.801	43
Yunel Escobar	2 tms	367	293	.798	72
Cesar Izturis	Bal	349	277	.794	56
Stephen Drew	Ari	357	282	.790	58
Juan Uribe	SF	227	179	.789	30
Ronny Cedeno	Pit	372	292	.785	48
Yuniesky Betancourt	KC	420	328	.781	49
Jason Bartlett	TB	301	235	.781	45
Derek Jeter	NYY	356	277	.778	38
Ian Desmond	Was	369	287	.778	47
Angel Sanchez	2 tms	126	98	.778	14
Marco Scutaro	Bos	346	268	.775	50
Tommy Manzella	Hou	207	160	.773	29
Starlin Castro	ChC	307	236	.769	60
Asdrubal Cabrera	Cle	242	186	.769	42
Hanley Ramirez	Fla	334	251	.751	45

Shortstops - 2011 Zone Ratings

Player	Tm	Balls In Zone	Plays Made	Zone Rating	Plays Out Of Zone
Brandon Crawford	SF	143	128	.895	24
Clint Barmes	Hou	300	261	.870	48
Brendan Ryan	Sea	299	259	.866	68
Paul Janish	Cin	230	199	.865	37
Willie Bloomquist	Ari	137	118	.861	20
Jimmy Rollins	Phi	350	300	.857	48
Yunel Escobar	Tor	292	249	.853	55
J.J. Hardy	Bal	352	300	.852	50
Ronny Cedeno	Pit	343	292	.851	66
Alex Gonzalez	Atl	389	330	.848	69
Jhonny Peralta	Det	338	286	.846	55
Jose Reyes	NYM	339	286	.844	37
Alexei Ramirez	CWS	377	316	.838	78
Troy Tulowitzki	Col	340	284	.835	65
Elvis Andrus	Tex	339	283	.835	67
Alcides Escobar	KC	391	326	.834	82
Erick Aybar	LAA	343	284	.828	65
Jason Bartlett	SD	363	300	.826	44
Edgar Renteria	Cin	195	161	.826	30
Marco Scutaro	Bos	232	190	.819	53
Stephen Drew	Ari	196	157	.801	40
Starlin Castro	ChC	423	338	.799	55
Ian Desmond	Was	395	315	.797	69
Rafael Furcal	2 tms	226	180	.796	40
Reid Brignac	TB	191	151	.791	46
Asdrubal Cabrera	Cle	335	264	.788	74
Cliff Pennington	Oak	329	258	.784	61
Derek Jeter	NYY	269	210	.781	40
Yuniesky Betancourt	Mil	376	292	.777	81
Dee Gordon	LAD	116	90	.776	21
Ryan Theriot	StL	242	186	.769	38
Jamey Carroll	LAD	120	92	.767	25
Tsuyoshi Nishioka	Min	154	118	.766	32
Emilio Bonifacio	Fla	138	105	.761	26
Hanley Ramirez	Fla	181	137	.757	33

Shortstops - 2009 Zone Ratings

Player	Tm	Balls In Zone	Plays Made	Zone Rating	Plays Out Of Zone
Paul Janish	Cin	194	167	.861	20
Elvis Andrus	Tex	362	307	.848	45
Derek Jeter	NYY	326	276	.847	25
J.J. Hardy	Mil	296	250	.845	30
Adam Everett	Det	253	212	.838	39
Yunel Escobar	Atl	376	315	.838	52
Edgar Renteria	SF	294	246	.837	28
Brendan Ryan	StL	318	266	.836	54
Ramon Santiago	Det	149	124	.832	12
Cesar Izturis	Bal	312	259	.830	39
Ryan Theriot	ChC	373	309	.828	46
Jack Wilson	2 tms	271	223	.823	48
Erick Aybar	LAA	339	277	.817	37
Alex Gonzalez	2 tms	250	204	.816	31
Alexei Ramirez	CWS	378	308	.815	56
Stephen Drew	Ari	342	277	.810	44
Brendan Harris	Min	152	123	.809	14
Hanley Ramirez	Fla	328	265	.808	46
Robert Andino	Bal	161	130	.807	20
Rafael Furcal	LAD	392	316	.806	65
Asdrubal Cabrera	Cle	279	224	.803	29
Ronny Cedeno	2 tms	243	195	.802	27
Jimmy Rollins	Phi	379	304	.802	44
Nick Punto	Min	141	113	.801	20
Troy Tulowitzki	Col	425	340	.800	42
Marco Scutaro	Tor	383	306	.799	61
Cliff Pennington	Oak	184	146	.793	10
Cristian Guzman	Was	340	267	.785	43
Jason Bartlett	TB	309	242	.783	64
Nick Green	Bos	188	147	.782	32
Miguel Tejada	Hou	469	362	.772	51
Orlando Cabrera	2 tms	439	335	.763	35
Everth Cabrera	SD	307	229	.746	42
Alex Cora	NYM	132	97	.735	18
Yuniesky Betancourt	2 tms	347	245	.706	39

Left Fielders - 3-Year Zone Ratings

Player	Balls In Zone	Plays Made	Zone Rating	Plays Out Of Zone
Laynce Nix	213	202	.948	70
David DeJesus	234	217	.927	78
Matt Holliday	597	551	.923	182
Alex Gordon	380	350	.921	95
Brett Gardner	361	332	.920	162
Carlos Gonzalez	182	166	.912	71
Ryan Braun	723	659	.911	184
Josh Hamilton	245	223	.910	109
Scott Hairston	193	175	.907	55
Travis Snider	212	192	.906	60
Juan Pierre	593	537	.906	176
Carl Crawford	688	622	.904	247
David Murphy	362	326	.901	105
Johnny Damon	252	226	.897	64
Seth Smith	221	198	.896	78
Gerardo Parra	417	372	.892	170
Ryan Raburn	250	223	.892	95
Josh Willingham	395	352	.891	136
Delmon Young	561	498	.888	130
Ryan Ludwick	138	122	.884	69
Michael Saunders	243	214	.881	61
Nolan Reimold	309	272	.880	89
Jason Bay	592	521	.880	150
Chris Coghlan	348	306	.879	64
Fred Lewis	275	241	.876	96
Raul Ibanez	570	497	.872	135
Manny Ramirez	191	166	.869	41
Juan Rivera	404	351	.869	124
Alfonso Soriano	529	459	.868	134
Jonny Gomes	329	285	.866	72
Logan Morrison	284	245	.863	78
Felix Pie	282	243	.862	78
Lastings Milledge	184	158	.859	70
Jose Tabata	267	229	.858	100
Carlos Lee	450	380	.844	133

Left Fielders - 2010 Zone Ratings

Player	Tm	Balls In Zone	Plays Made	Zone Rating	Plays Out Of Zone
Travis Snider	Tor	67	64	.955	24
Austin Kearns	2 tms	146	135	.925	35
Alfonso Soriano	ChC	182	167	.918	37
Alex Gordon	KC	121	111	.917	21
Ryan Raburn	Det	91	83	.912	34
Carlos Gonzalez	Col	68	62	.912	15
Carl Crawford	TB	263	238	.905	68
Ryan Braun	Mil	250	226	.904	53
Pat Burrell	SF	114	103	.904	18
Raul Ibanez	Phi	188	169	.899	43
Matt Diaz	Atl	77	69	.896	24
Josh Hamilton	Tex	141	126	.894	53
Brett Gardner	NYY	169	151	.893	49
Matt Holliday	StL	220	196	.891	65
Scott Podsednik	2 tms	245	217	.886	47
Josh Willingham	Was	138	122	.884	42
Chris Coghlan	Fla	146	129	.884	31
Juan Pierre	CWS	264	233	.883	74
Carlos Lee	Hou	156	136	.872	47
Gerardo Parra	Ari	117	102	.872	44
Felix Pie	Bal	130	113	.869	34
David Murphy	Tex	98	85	.867	28
Delmon Young	Min	221	191	.864	48
Michael Saunders	Sea	145	125	.862	40
Scott Hairston	SD	82	70	.854	24
Logan Morrison	Fla	107	91	.850	25
Jonny Gomes	Cin	187	159	.850	38
Seth Smith	Col	86	73	.849	34
Melky Cabrera	Atl	80	67	.838	15
Lastings Milledge	Pit	92	77	.837	33
Jason Bay	NYM	128	107	.836	34
Jose Tabata	Pit	157	131	.834	58
Corey Patterson	Bal	101	84	.832	32
Fred Lewis	Tor	121	100	.826	34
Juan Rivera	LAA	149	120	.805	47

Left Fielders - 2011 Zone Ratings

Player	Tm	Balls In Zone	Plays Made	Zone Rating	Plays Out Of Zone
Brett Gardner	NYY	192	181	.943	113
Delmon Young	2 tms	181	170	.939	44
Michael Brantley	Cle	82	77	.939	41
Alex Presley	Pit	48	45	.938	26
Jonny Gomes	2 tms	92	86	.935	28
Tony Gwynn	LAD	91	85	.934	39
Josh Hamilton	Tex	104	97	.933	56
Juan Pierre	CWS	218	203	.931	75
Laynce Nix	Was	85	79	.929	23
Matt Holliday	StL	158	146	.924	51
Alex Gordon	KC	259	239	.923	74
Juan Rivera	2 tms	64	59	.922	18
Vernon Wells	LAA	173	159	.919	82
Martin Prado	Atl	138	126	.913	45
David Murphy	Tex	92	84	.913	39
Ryan Braun	Mil	204	186	.912	73
Eric Thames	Tor	68	62	.912	29
Carlos Gonzalez	Col	67	61	.910	32
Desmond Jennings	TB	73	66	.904	34
Jason Bay	NYM	170	153	.900	67
Brennan Boesch	Det	79	71	.899	31
Michael Morse	Was	68	61	.897	28
Nolan Reimold	Bal	115	103	.896	44
Jose Tabata	Pit	110	98	.891	42
Carl Crawford	Bos	181	161	.890	74
Gerardo Parra	Ari	190	169	.889	98
Ryan Ludwick	2 tms	137	121	.883	69
Logan Morrison	Fla	177	154	.870	53
Alfonso Soriano	ChC	158	137	.867	50
Carlos Lee	Hou	97	84	.866	35
Josh Willingham	Oak	123	106	.862	53
Cody Ross	SF	79	68	.861	41
Raul Ibanez	Phi	183	157	.858	51
Sam Fuld	TB	115	97	.843	65
J.D. Martinez	Hou	74	61	.824	31

Left Fielders - 2009 Zone Ratings

Player	Tm	Balls In Zone	Plays Made	Zone Rating	Plays Out Of Zone
Laynce Nix	Cin	86	85	.988	33
Matt Holliday	2 tms	219	209	.954	66
Scott Hairston	2 tms	100	95	.950	31
Scott Podsednik	CWS	127	119	.937	20
David DeJesus	KC	233	216	.927	77
Denard Span	Min	95	88	.926	27
Josh Willingham	Was	134	124	.925	41
Ryan Braun	Mil	269	247	.918	58
Gerardo Parra	Ari	110	101	.918	28
Seth Smith	Col	109	100	.917	35
Johnny Damon	NYY	191	175	.916	45
Carl Crawford	TB	244	223	.914	105
David Murphy	Tex	172	157	.913	38
Juan Pierre	LAD	111	101	.910	27
Wladimir Balentien	2 tms	105	95	.905	27
Juan Rivera	LAA	191	172	.901	59
Chase Headley	SD	184	165	.897	50
Manny Ramirez	LAD	123	110	.894	29
Ben Francisco	2 tms	113	101	.894	15
Jason Bay	Bos	294	261	.888	49
Fred Lewis	SF	105	93	.886	34
Lastings Milledge	Pit	85	75	.882	36
Chris Coghlan	Fla	202	177	.876	33
Chris Duncan	StL	68	59	.868	20
Nyjer Morgan	Pit	104	90	.865	51
Delmon Young	Min	159	137	.862	38
Nolan Reimold	Bal	159	137	.862	35
Raul Ibanez	Phi	199	171	.859	41
Carlos Quentin	CWS	147	126	.857	32
Garret Anderson	Atl	179	153	.855	41
Ryan Raburn	Det	94	79	.840	33
Adam Lind	Tor	84	70	.833	10
Adam Dunn	Was	95	79	.832	20
Alfonso Soriano	ChC	189	155	.820	47
Carlos Lee	Hou	197	160	.812	51

Center Fielders - 3-Year Zone Ratings

Player	Balls In Zone	Plays Made	Zone Rating	Plays Out Of Zone
Andres Torres	350	336	.960	106
Denard Span	663	627	.946	166
Franklin Gutierrez	916	866	.945	230
Austin Jackson	568	534	.940	230
Coco Crisp	538	505	.939	119
Carlos Gomez	505	474	.939	160
Aaron Rowand	504	473	.938	141
Peter Bourjos	405	379	.936	121
Shane Victorino	837	783	.935	210
Mike Cameron	524	489	.933	120
Chris Young	892	832	.933	266
B.J. Upton	989	921	.931	233
Rick Ankiel	413	384	.930	125
Michael Bourn	877	814	.928	284
Cameron Maybin	528	490	.928	191
Tony Gwynn	350	324	.926	121
Colby Rasmus	685	634	.926	186
Jacoby Ellsbury	662	612	.924	166
Dexter Fowler	674	623	.924	173
Drew Stubbs	756	698	.923	159
Angel Pagan	575	530	.922	163
Nyjer Morgan	549	506	.922	207
Nate McLouth	484	446	.921	134
Marlon Byrd	738	680	.921	206
Adam Jones	999	918	.919	233
Cody Ross	383	351	.916	89
Rajai Davis	526	482	.916	142
Grady Sizemore	367	336	.916	110
Curtis Granderson	907	830	.915	240
Matt Kemp	932	848	.910	195
Alex Rios	713	648	.909	186
Melky Cabrera	569	515	.905	122
Torii Hunter	488	440	.902	125
Vernon Wells	650	584	.898	146
Andrew McCutchen	885	794	.897	256

Center Fielders - 2010 Zone Ratings

Player	Tm	Balls In Zone	Plays Made	Zone Rating	Plays Out Of Zone
Andres Torres	SF	167	161	.964	32
Aaron Rowand	SF	164	156	.951	36
Coco Crisp	Oak	170	161	.947	22
Denard Span	Min	357	333	.933	75
Mitch Maier	KC	158	147	.930	26
Austin Jackson	Det	297	276	.929	109
Michael Bourn	Hou	296	274	.926	86
Franklin Gutierrez	Sea	375	347	.925	66
Chris Young	Ari	360	332	.922	86
Shane Victorino	Phi	318	293	.921	67
B.J. Upton	TB	358	329	.919	67
Marlon Byrd	ChC	317	291	.918	80
Julio Borbon	Tex	288	264	.917	71
Adam Jones	Bal	395	362	.916	60
Cameron Maybin	Fla	179	164	.916	51
Carlos Gomez	Mil	139	127	.914	25
Curtis Granderson	NYY	285	260	.912	55
Cody Ross	2 tms	165	150	.909	30
Rick Ankiel	2 tms	120	109	.908	32
Rajai Davis	Oak	173	157	.908	33
Drew Stubbs	Cin	356	323	.907	57
Dexter Fowler	Col	221	200	.905	39
Angel Pagan	NYM	218	197	.904	62
Tony Gwynn	SD	124	112	.903	48
Alex Rios	CWS	316	285	.902	99
Colby Rasmus	StL	233	210	.901	50
Vernon Wells	Tor	313	282	.901	72
Nyjer Morgan	Was	280	252	.900	87
Matt Kemp	LAD	320	287	.897	43
Torii Hunter	LAA	220	196	.891	56
Carlos Beltran	NYM	143	127	.888	19
Nate McLouth	Atl	123	109	.886	28
Andrew McCutchen	Pit	337	295	.875	78
Trevor Crowe	Cle	161	140	.870	36
Michael Brantley	Cle	150	130	.867	26

Center Fielders - 2011 Zone Ratings

Player	Tm	Balls In Zone	Plays Made	Zone Rating	Plays Out Of Zone
Denard Span	Min	160	155	.969	51
Jon Jay	StL	128	123	.961	44
Austin Jackson	Det	271	258	.952	121
Andres Torres	SF	141	134	.950	62
Franklin Gutierrez	Sea	196	186	.949	51
Jacoby Ellsbury	Bos	313	297	.949	91
Ben Revere	Min	172	163	.948	81
Shane Victorino	Phi	229	217	.948	79
Drew Stubbs	Cin	311	294	.945	72
Dexter Fowler	Col	251	237	.944	72
Rick Ankiel	Was	184	173	.940	61
B.J. Upton	TB	315	296	.940	86
Peter Bourjos	LAA	276	259	.938	92
Cameron Maybin	SD	257	241	.938	101
Nyjer Morgan	Mil	153	143	.935	73
Endy Chavez	Tex	91	85	.934	41
Coco Crisp	Oak	272	254	.934	67
Chris Young	Ari	299	279	.933	114
Matt Kemp	LAD	294	274	.932	72
Ezequiel Carrera	Cle	88	82	.932	30
Colby Rasmus	2 tms	235	218	.928	84
Andrew McCutchen	Pit	331	307	.927	107
Nate McLouth	Atl	109	101	.927	28
Marlon Byrd	ChC	219	202	.922	71
Grady Sizemore	Cle	98	90	.918	33
Carlos Gomez	Mil	134	123	.918	61
Adam Jones	Bal	325	298	.917	82
Chris Coghlan	Fla	132	121	.917	36
Angel Pagan	NYM	247	226	.915	76
Michael Bourn	2 tms	310	283	.913	84
Jordan Schafer	2 tms	143	130	.909	61
Rajai Davis	Tor	140	127	.907	47
Alex Rios	CWS	307	277	.902	72
Melky Cabrera	KC	276	249	.902	67
Curtis Granderson	NYY	310	278	.897	77

Center Fielders - 2009 Zone Ratings

Player	Tm	Balls In Zone	Plays Made	Zone Rating	Plays Out Of Zone
Angel Pagan	NYM	110	107	.973	25
Carlos Gomez	Min	232	224	.966	74
Franklin Gutierrez	Sea	345	333	.965	113
Josh Hamilton	Tex	103	99	.961	33
Mike Cameron	Mil	351	337	.960	67
Nyjer Morgan	2 tms	116	111	.957	47
Kosuke Fukudome	ChC	190	181	.953	45
Denard Span	Min	146	139	.952	40
Colby Rasmus	StL	217	206	.949	52
Chris Young	Ari	233	221	.948	66
Michael Bourn	Hou	271	257	.948	114
Melky Cabrera	NYY	203	192	.946	34
Shane Victorino	Phi	290	273	.941	64
Tony Gwynn	SD	217	204	.940	65
B.J. Upton	TB	316	296	.937	80
Nate McLouth	2 tms	252	236	.937	78
Curtis Granderson	Det	312	292	.936	108
Rick Ankiel	StL	109	102	.936	32
Willie Harris	Was	123	115	.935	28
Carlos Beltran	NYM	180	168	.933	40
Aaron Rowand	SF	237	221	.932	78
Rajai Davis	Oak	213	198	.930	62
Willy Taveras	Cin	217	201	.926	65
Mitch Maier	KC	162	150	.926	31
Marlon Byrd	Tex	202	187	.926	55
Adam Jones	Bal	279	258	.925	91
Cody Ross	Fla	195	180	.923	53
Dexter Fowler	Col	202	186	.921	62
Brett Gardner	NYY	149	137	.919	49
Grady Sizemore	Cle	219	200	.913	59
Torii Hunter	LAA	263	240	.913	69
Matt Kemp	LAD	318	287	.903	80
Jacoby Ellsbury	Bos	319	287	.900	70
Vernon Wells	Tor	313	280	.895	72
Andrew McCutchen	Pit	217	192	.885	71

Right Fielders - 3-Year Zone Ratings

Player		Balls In Zone	Plays Made	Zone Rating	Plays Out Of Zone
Matt Joyce		254	240	.945	77
Ichiro Suzuki		717	672	.937	263
Cody Ross		198	184	.929	77
Ben Zobrist		240	223	.929	113
J.D. Drew		494	459	.929	164
Ryan Sweeney		275	255	.927	92
Justin Upton		701	650	.927	249
Andre Ethier		617	571	.925	174
Jason Heyward		359	332	.925	122
Corey Hart		585	541	.925	172
Jay Bruce		697	642	.921	207
David DeJesus		284	261	.919	109
Will Venable		320	294	.919	120
Nick Swisher		639	584	.914	193
Nelson Cruz		587	536	.913	203
Nate Schierholtz		310	283	.913	113
Jose Bautista		390	356	.913	125
Mike Stanton		387	353	.912	146
Kosuke Fukudome		454	414	.912	120
Hunter Pence		764	695	.910	248
Carlos Beltran		171	155	.906	75
Jayson Werth		707	640	.905	224
Shin-Soo Choo		594	537	.904	181
Torii Hunter		291	263	.904	102
Nick Markakis		848	766	.903	177
Michael Cuddyer		416	373	.897	85
Ryan Ludwick		415	371	.894	116
Jeff Francoeur		733	655	.894	209
Magglio Ordonez		329	293	.891	78
Carlos Quentin		327	291	.890	69
Garrett Jones		266	235	.883	94
Seth Smith		184	162	.880	68
Bobby Abreu		406	357	.879	72
Brad Hawpe		302	264	.874	58
Jason Kubel		250	217	.868	72

Right Fielders - 2010 Zone Ratings

Player	Tm	Balls In Zone	Plays Made	Zone Rating	Plays Out Of Zone
Cody Ross	2 tms	81	77	.951	33
Jay Bruce	Cin	275	259	.942	84
Nate Schierholtz	SF	93	87	.935	31
Michael Morse	Was	107	100	.935	23
Nelson Cruz	Tex	180	168	.933	60
Justin Upton	Ari	220	204	.927	61
Hunter Pence	Hou	284	263	.926	78
Ichiro Suzuki	Sea	281	260	.925	95
Kosuke Fukudome	ChC	167	154	.922	36
Andre Ethier	LAD	189	173	.915	50
Jason Heyward	Atl	188	172	.915	64
Ben Zobrist	TB	136	124	.912	58
Corey Hart	Mil	227	206	.907	66
Ryan Ludwick	2 tms	204	185	.907	65
Will Venable	SD	118	107	.907	37
Ryan Sweeney	Oak	123	111	.902	37
Nick Markakis	Bal	306	275	.899	57
Mike Stanton	Fla	174	156	.897	63
Jose Bautista	Tor	145	130	.897	49
Torii Hunter	LAA	96	86	.896	20
J.D. Drew	Bos	200	179	.895	55
Bobby Abreu	LAA	151	135	.894	36
David DeJesus	KC	118	105	.890	28
Michael Cuddyer	Min	115	102	.887	15
Jayson Werth	Phi	208	184	.885	65
Roger Bernadina	Was	94	83	.883	22
Nick Swisher	NYY	228	201	.882	64
Jason Kubel	Min	126	110	.873	32
Brennan Boesch	Det	126	110	.873	23
Jose Guillen	2 tms	86	75	.872	23
Shin-Soo Choo	Cle	236	205	.869	62
Brad Hawpe	2 tms	97	84	.866	14
Jeff Francoeur	2 tms	207	177	.855	63
Magglio Ordonez	Det	128	109	.852	26
Carlos Quentin	CWS	181	153	.845	30

Right Fielders - 2011 Zone Ratings

Player	Tm	Balls In Zone	Plays Made	Zone Rating	Plays Out Of Zone
Will Venable	SD	106	103	.972	44
Chris Denorfia	SD	81	78	.963	23
Matt Joyce	TB	163	156	.957	55
Corey Hart	Mil	192	183	.953	69
J.D. Drew	Bos	106	101	.953	45
Domonic Brown	Phi	63	60	.952	18
Carlos Quentin	CWS	146	138	.945	39
Andre Ethier	LAD	184	173	.940	70
David DeJesus	Oak	160	150	.938	81
Ichiro Suzuki	Sea	190	178	.937	85
Jason Heyward	Atl	171	160	.936	58
Justin Upton	Ari	233	218	.936	122
Michael Cuddyer	Min	108	101	.935	41
Nick Swisher	NYY	213	199	.934	74
Josh Reddick	Bos	75	70	.933	33
Mike Stanton	Fla	213	197	.925	83
Lance Berkman	StL	143	132	.923	41
Ben Francisco	Phi	78	72	.923	14
Shin-Soo Choo	Cle	142	131	.923	41
Jeff Francoeur	KC	270	249	.922	79
Jose Bautista	Tor	192	177	.922	56
Jay Bruce	Cin	252	230	.913	76
Torii Hunter	LAA	195	177	.908	82
Nick Markakis	Bal	249	226	.908	86
Carlos Beltran	2 tms	171	155	.906	75
Jayson Werth	Was	229	206	.900	82
Brennan Boesch	Det	79	71	.899	17
Magglio Ordonez	Det	68	61	.897	26
Seth Smith	Col	143	128	.895	54
Hunter Pence	2 tms	219	196	.895	89
Nate Schierholtz	SF	116	103	.888	39
Kosuke Fukudome	2 tms	223	198	.888	67
Garrett Jones	Pit	130	115	.885	40
Nelson Cruz	Tex	169	149	.882	67
Jason Kubel	Min	77	67	.870	28

Right Fielders - 2009 Zone Ratings

Player	Tm	Balls In Zone	Plays Made	Zone Rating	Plays Out Of Zone
Ryan Church	2 tms	103	99	.961	42
Randy Winn	SF	145	139	.959	48
Ryan Sweeney	Oak	128	122	.953	43
J.D. Drew	Bos	188	179	.952	64
Ichiro Suzuki	Sea	246	234	.951	83
Gabe Gross	TB	120	113	.942	36
Shin-Soo Choo	Cle	216	201	.931	78
Nick Swisher	NYY	198	184	.929	55
Jayson Werth	Phi	270	250	.926	77
Magglio Ordonez	Det	133	123	.925	26
Andre Ethier	LAD	244	225	.922	54
Nate Schierholtz	SF	101	93	.921	43
Nelson Cruz	Tex	238	219	.920	76
Justin Upton	Ari	248	228	.919	66
Milton Bradley	ChC	169	155	.917	42
Corey Hart	Mil	166	152	.916	37
Cody Ross	Fla	81	74	.914	30
Alex Rios	2 tms	199	181	.910	47
Nick Markakis	Bal	293	265	.904	34
Hunter Pence	Hou	261	236	.904	81
Jeremy Hermida	Fla	113	102	.903	38
Jay Bruce	Cin	170	153	.900	47
Jeff Francoeur	2 tms	256	229	.895	67
Elijah Dukes	Was	112	100	.893	30
Clete Thomas	Det	108	96	.889	31
Brandon Moss	Pit	131	116	.885	55
Matt Diaz	Atl	77	68	.883	21
Michael Cuddyer	Min	193	170	.881	29
Jermaine Dye	CWS	219	192	.877	46
Brian Giles	SD	105	92	.876	21
Will Venable	SD	96	84	.875	39
Bobby Abreu	LAA	244	213	.873	36
Brad Hawpe	Col	195	170	.872	43
Ryan Ludwick	StL	192	167	.870	43
Jose Guillen	KC	102	80	.784	16

Nine-Year Register

Don't you just love the smell of fresh stats in the morning? In the pages that follow are the most comprehensive fielding evaluations we've ever produced. These pages detail the last nine years of fielding data for every position player that spent 200 innings in the field in 2011 and every pitcher that spent 50 innings on the mound.

With these charts, we can recognize Adrian Beltre as the best defensive third baseman in baseball over the last nine years. The 157 runs he's saved his team defensively in that time dwarfs Scott Rolen's second highest total of 114. On the other side of the spectrum, Ty Wigginton has cost his team an estimated 74 runs. That's a 231-run difference between the best and worst third basemen over the last nine years. Since we estimate that 10 runs equate to one win, it's also a 23 win difference between the two players just because of defensive ability. This is why defensive evaluations are so critical. One glove could be the difference between spending October on the golf course or participating in playoff baseball.

In this book, we introduce some wonderful new techniques and metrics for our evaluations. Many of these new techniques are enhancements on our old techniques but utilize new data, such as our ball in play timer data. We only starting timing balls in play in 2009, so the charts that follow feature a mix of our old systems

that were introduced in Volume I and Volume II and the new systems we explain in this book. Here's a rundown of what you're looking at:

Plus/Minus – New system for infielders for 2010 and 2011 using timer-based velocities. For outfielders, we use the timer-based hang times for 2009, 2010, and 2011.

Bunts – New system for all players and all years.

Double Plays – Old system through 2008. New system for 2009 and beyond. Corner infielders are only considered by the new system. We'll display a dash for corner infielders for any season prior to 2009.

Outfield Arms – Old system through 2009. New system for 2010 and beyond.

Good Plays/Misplays – We don't have 2003 data, so we'll display a dash for all players for this season.

The methodology section at the end of the book is a great resource for those who are interested in the mathematics behind each of our systems. For a more detailed explanation of the column headings, take a look at the One-Year Register introduction on page 407.

Catchers

J.P. Arencibia

		BASIC						BUNTS			PITCHER HANDLING						STOLEN BASES						RUNS SAVED					
Year	Team	G	Inn	TC	E	Pct	GFP	DM	Opps	Sac Hits	Bunt Hits	W	L	Pct	ER	CERA	Pitch Block	SB	CCS	PCS	CPO	CS%	SB Saved	Adj ER	SB	Bunt	GFP/ DME	Total	Rank
2010	Tor	8	63.0	51	0	1.000	0	2				4	3	.571	31	4.43	29	3	2	0	0	.40	1	0	0		0	0	
2011	Tor	122	1059.2	900	6	.993	11	69	11	3	2	55	63	.466	507	4.31	517	87	18	10	1	.17	-9	1	-5	1	-2	-5	28
		130	1122.2	951	6	.994	11	71	11	3	2	59	66	.472	538	4.31	546	90	20	10	1	.18	-8	1	-5	1	-2	-5	-

Alex Avila

		BASIC						BUNTS			PITCHER HANDLING						STOLEN BASES						RUNS SAVED					
Year	Team	G	Inn	TC	E	Pct	GFP	DM	Opps	Sac Hits	Bunt Hits	W	L	Pct	ER	CERA	Pitch Block	SB	CCS	PCS	CPO	CS%	SB Saved	Adj ER	SB	Bunt	GFP/ DME	Total	Rank
2009	Det	25	153.1	108	0	1.000	0	4	2	1	1	8	9	.471	94	5.52	53	11	4	0	0	.27	0	-1	0	-1	0	-2	-
2010	Det	98	756.2	594	4	.993	15	33	4	2	2	41	43	.488	376	4.47	253	43	20	0	0	.32	-2	-2	-2	-2	-1	-7	30
2011	Det	133	1157.0	1018	5	.995	20	59	11	6	2	78	52	.600	499	3.88	462	85	26	14	0	.23	-2	3	-2	0	-3	-2	18
		256	2067.0	1720	9	.995	35	96	17	9	5	127	104	.550	969	4.22	768	139	50	14	0	.26	-5	0	-4	-3	-4	-11	-

Rod Barajas

		BASIC						BUNTS			PITCHER HANDLING						STOLEN BASES						RUNS SAVED					
Year	Team	G	Inn	TC	E	Pct	GFP	DM	Opps	Sac Hits	Bunt Hits	W	L	Pct	ER	CERA	Pitch Block	SB	CCS	PCS	CPO	CS%	SB Saved	Adj ER	SB	Bunt	GFP/ DME	Total	Rank
2003	Ari	79	595.0	583	0	1.000	-	-	10	6	1	36	29	.554	239	3.62	-	26	16	1	1	.38	2	0	2	1	-	3	11
2004	Tex	105	908.2	686	7	.990	4	21	3	1	0	61	41	.598	454	4.50	118	42	16	6	0	.28	-1	0	-1	0	-2	-3	23
2005	Tex	119	1025.1	739	9	.988	10	32	7	3	2	57	60	.487	567	4.98	147	44	21	2	0	.32	2	-2	1	-1	-3	-5	26
2006	Tex	94	825.0	636	10	.984	5	21	6	3	1	48	46	.511	434	4.73	181	38	15	4	1	.28	2	-1	2	-1	0	0	14
2007	Phi	38	303.0	266	0	1.000	1	17	4	4	0	17	20	.459	174	5.17	70	12	6	1	0	.33	1	0	1	0	-4	-3	-
2008	Tor	98	785.1	725	4	.994	17	23	6	2	0	54	36	.600	290	3.32	270	42	17	5	1	.29	2	4	2	-1	3	8	5
2009	Tor	120	974.1	869	8	.991	8	35	6	2	1	52	58	.473	461	4.26	374	53	22	5	1	.29	2	1	2	0	3	6	7
2010	2 tms	96	776.0	711	3	.996	4	20	10	5	2	46	41	.529	334	3.87	268	34	5	1	0	.13	-6	2	-4	-1	0	-3	21
2011	LAD	88	733.1	701	2	.997	9	25	12	10	1	44	41	.518	291	3.57	371	60	14	6	0	.19	-1	-1	-1	-1	5	2	10
		837	6926.0	5916	43	.993	58	194	64	36	10	415	372	.527	3244	4.22	1799	351	132	31	4	.27	3	3	4	-4	2	5	13

Josh Bard

		BASIC						BUNTS			PITCHER HANDLING						STOLEN BASES						RUNS SAVED					
Year	Team	G	Inn	TC	E	Pct	GFP	DM	Opps	Sac Hits	Bunt Hits	W	L	Pct	ER	CERA	Pitch Block	SB	CCS	PCS	CPO	CS%	SB Saved	Adj ER	SB	Bunt	GFP/ DME	Total	Rank
2003	Cle	87	715.2	546	5	.991	-	-	6	0	0	35	45	.438	343	4.31	-	41	19	4	0	.32	5	-2	3	1	-	2	15
2004	Cle	7	53.0	51	0	1.000	0	6				4	2	.667	23	3.91	11	4	2	0	0	.33	0	0	0	0	-1	-1	-
2005	Cle	31	219.2	177	3	.983	1	4	1	0	1	15	8	.652	78	3.20	17	7	2	2	1	.22	0	1	0	-1	-1	-1	-
2006	2 tms	78	547.2	457	3	.993	8	15	5	2	1	26	30	.464	266	4.37	132	53	9	2	2	.15	-3	-4	-1	1	3	-1	19
2007	SD	108	927.1	793	3	.996	3	31	11	5	2	62	41	.602	354	3.44	264	121	8	2	0	.06	-12	2	-9	-1	-1	-9	32
2008	SD	49	416.2	352	3	.991	6	9	10	2	1	16	31	.340	197	4.26	109	53	9	1	1	.15	-2	0	-1	0	0	-1	-
2009	Was	79	630.2	429	5	.988	8	45	10	5	1	23	48	.324	347	4.95	222	43	7	9	0	.14	-2	0	-1	-1	-7	-9	31
2010	Sea	39	304.0	216	2	.991	5	12	2	0	1	10	25	.286	145	4.29	100	12	3	3	1	.20	-2	0	-1	-1	-1	-3	-
2011	Sea	25	201.0	170	2	.988	2	6				8	15	.348	88	3.94	78	15	7	2	0	.32	0	0	0	0	0	0	-
		503	4015.2	3191	26	.992	33	128	45	14	7	199	245	.448	1841	4.13	933	349	66	25	5	.16	-16	-3	-10	-2	-8	-23	32

Henry Blanco

		BASIC						BUNTS			PITCHER HANDLING						STOLEN BASES						RUNS SAVED					
Year	Team	G	Inn	TC	E	Pct	GFP	DM	Opps	Sac Hits	Bunt Hits	W	L	Pct	ER	CERA	Pitch Block	SB	CCS	PCS	CPO	CS%	SB Saved	Adj ER	SB	Bunt	GFP/ DME	Total	Rank
2003	Atl	52	388.0	281	1	.996	-	-	3	1	0	23	19	.548	193	4.48	-	33	10	1	0	.23	-1	-1	-1	0	-	-2	-
2004	Min	114	872.1	737	7	.991	5	28	2	1	0	52	43	.547	412	4.25	186	31	25	5	0	.45	7	-6	5	0	-1	-2	17
2005	ChC	54	422.1	439	1	.998	5	11	5	1	1	27	21	.563	168	3.58	93	20	19	0	0	.49	6	1	4	0	0	5	-
2006	ChC	69	526.0	502	1	.998	2	20	4	3	0	24	35	.407	289	4.94	181	24	15	3	0	.38	5	-2	3	0	-1	0	14
2007	ChC	14	109.0	106	0	1.000	0	8	1	0	0	3	10	.231	58	4.79	56	8	2	1	0	.20	-1	0	-1	0	0	-1	-
2008	ChC	45	257.2	252	2	.992	2	8	4	2	0	16	12	.571	112	3.91	73	12	9	1	0	.43	2	2	0	-1	1	-
2009	SD	60	508.0	472	0	1.000	4	17	4	1	0	29	29	.500	265	4.69	175	27	14	4	0	.34	3	-5	2	0	0	-3	-
2010	NYM	46	361.0	312	1	.997	3	13	4	3	1	22	19	.537	136	3.39	120	11	11	0	1	.50	3	0	3	0	-1	2	-
2011	Ari	37	274.0	192	1	.995	0	10	2	1	0	12	19	.387	141	4.63	113	13	8	3	0	.38	2	-1	2	0	-1	0	-
		491	3718.1	3293	14	.996	21	115	29	13	4	208	207	.501	1774	4.29	997	179	113	18	1	.39	27	-14	19	0	-5	0	18

John Buck

		BASIC						BUNTS			PITCHER HANDLING						STOLEN BASES						RUNS SAVED					
Year	Team	G	Inn	TC	E	Pct	GFP	DM	Opps	Sac Hits	Bunt Hits	W	L	Pct	ER	CERA	Pitch Block	SB	CCS	PCS	CPO	CS%	SB Saved	Adj ER	SB	Bunt	GFP/ DME	Total	Rank
2004	KC	68	575.0	393	3	.992	5	26	4	0	0	24	42	.364	339	5.31	150	30	7	7	0	.19	-1	-2	0	0	-2	-4	27
2005	KC	117	976.2	698	3	.996	15	48	9	5	2	36	76	.321	615	5.67	149	60	27	4	3	.31	-2	-2	0	0	-3	-5	26
2006	KC	112	930.1	658	6	.991	7	47	5	3	0	41	66	.383	590	5.71	413	33	13	4	1	.28	0	1	0	-1	-1	-1	19
2007	KC	112	924.1	734	8	.989	17	39	9	6	1	43	61	.413	455	4.43	303	44	9	3	0	.17	-5	-4	-4	0	-1	-9	32
2008	KC	107	950.1	783	8	.990	3	41	4	2	1	49	57	.462	480	4.55	315	59	7	5	0	.11	-10	-1	-7	0	-4	-12	35
2009	KC	46	366.2	331	8	.976	3	14	1	0	0	18	23	.439	211	5.18	151	41	8	0	1	.16	-6	0	-4	0	1	-3	-
2010	Tor	112	933.0	778	5	.994	5	43	5	2	1	52	52	.500	462	4.46	392	47	15	3	1	.24	-5	-5	-3	-1	-2	-11	34
2011	Fla	135	1144.0	1055	5	.995	5	37	12	7	3	60	69	.465	496	3.90	357	83	15	2	1	.15	-5	0	-3	0	-2	-5	28
		809	6800.1	5430	46	.992	60	285	49	25	9	323	446	.420	3648	4.83	2230	397	101	28	7	.20	-34	-13	-21	-2	-14	-50	34

Catchers

Drew Butera

		BASIC							BUNTS			PITCHER HANDLING						STOLEN BASES						RUNS SAVED					
Year	Team	G	Inn	TC	E	Pct	GFP	DM	Opps	Sac Hits	Bunt Hits	W	L	Pct	ER	CERA	Pitch Block	SB	CCS	PCS	CPO	CS%	SB Saved	Adj ER	SB	Bunt	GFP/DME	Total	Rank
2010	Min	47	394.2	332	5	.985	4	15	1	0	0	22	22	.500	180	4.10	135	21	14	2	0	.40	6	-1	4	0	0	3	-
2011	Min	93	670.2	461	5	.989	8	26	8	3	0	27	48	.360	369	4.95	272	48	20	2	2	.29	3	-6	3	2	0	-1	14
		140	1065.1	793	10	.987	12	41	9	3	0	49	70	.412	549	4.64	407	69	34	4	2	.33	9	-7	7	2	0	2	-

Francisco Cervelli

		BASIC							BUNTS			PITCHER HANDLING						STOLEN BASES						RUNS SAVED					
Year	Team	G	Inn	TC	E	Pct	GFP	DM	Opps	Sac Hits	Bunt Hits	W	L	Pct	ER	CERA	Pitch Block	SB	CCS	PCS	CPO	CS%	SB Saved	Adj ER	SB	Bunt	GFP/DME	Total	Rank
2008	NYY	3	13.2	11	0	1.000	0	0				0	1	.000	12	7.90	7	1	0	0	0	.00	0	0	0		0	0	-
2009	NYY	40	241.1	222	1	.995	4	6	2	1	0	17	8	.680	92	3.43	61	13	8	2	0	.38	3	1	2	0	1	4	-
2010	NYY	90	724.0	637	13	.980	9	39	7	3	1	44	36	.550	325	4.04	270	55	8	1	1	.13	-6	3	-4	1	-3	-3	21
2011	NYY	41	316.1	302	6	.980	5	13				25	10	.714	123	3.50	155	24	4	0	0	.14	-5	1	-3		1	-1	-
		174	1295.1	1172	20	.983	18	58	9	4	1	86	55	.610	552	3.84	493	93	20	3	1	.18	-8	5	-5	1	-1	0	-

Hank Conger

		BASIC							BUNTS			PITCHER HANDLING						STOLEN BASES						RUNS SAVED					
Year	Team	G	Inn	TC	E	Pct	GFP	DM	Opps	Sac Hits	Bunt Hits	W	L	Pct	ER	CERA	Pitch Block	SB	CCS	PCS	CPO	CS%	SB Saved	Adj ER	SB	Bunt	GFP/DME	Total	Rank
2010	LAA	10	80.0	69	3	.957	1	1				7	2	.778	17	1.91	22	7	1	1	0	.13	-1	0	-1		0	-1	-
2011	LAA	56	450.0	355	6	.983	7	20	5	3	0	24	24	.500	192	3.84	233	53	10	2	1	.16	-5	-1	-3	0	3	-1	-
		66	530.0	424	9	.979	8	21	5	3	0	31	26	.544	209	3.55	255	60	11	3	1	.15	-6	-1	-4	0	3	-2	-

Carlos Corporan

		BASIC							BUNTS			PITCHER HANDLING						STOLEN BASES						RUNS SAVED					
Year	Team	G	Inn	TC	E	Pct	GFP	DM	Opps	Sac Hits	Bunt Hits	W	L	Pct	ER	CERA	Pitch Block	SB	CCS	PCS	CPO	CS%	SB Saved	Adj ER	SB	Bunt	GFP/DME	Total	Rank
2009	Mil	1	2.0	3	0	1.000	0	0				0	0	-	0	0.00	1	0	0	0	0	-	0	0	0		0	0	-
2011	Hou	50	411.1	407	6	.985	5	20	4	4	0	14	32	.304	183	4.00	245	43	9	0	0	.17	-2	1	-1	-1	3	2	-
		51	413.1	410	6	.985	5	20	4	4	0	14	32	.304	183	3.98	246	43	9	0	0	.17	-2	1	-1	-1	3	2	-

Ryan Doumit

		BASIC							BUNTS			PITCHER HANDLING						STOLEN BASES						RUNS SAVED					
Year	Team	G	Inn	TC	E	Pct	GFP	DM	Opps	Sac Hits	Bunt Hits	W	L	Pct	ER	CERA	Pitch Block	SB	CCS	PCS	CPO	CS%	SB Saved	Adj ER	SB	Bunt	GFP/DME	Total	Rank
2005	Pit	50	422.0	323	8	.975	3	14	9	2	3	19	29	.396	217	4.63	89	21	10	4	0	.32		-1	0	0	-2	-3	-
2006	Pit	11	91.2	79	1	.987	4	3	5	3	1	4	6	.400	62	6.09	38	11	2	2	0	.15	-1	0	-1	-1	1	-1	-
2007	Pit	28	223.2	158	2	.987	3	7	3	0	0	6	22	.214	137	5.51	77	21	4	2	0	.16	0	0	0	0	1	1	-
2008	Pit	106	909.0	663	8	.988	6	38	14	5	0	45	58	.437	512	5.07	346	68	15	10	0	.18	-3	0	-2	1	0	-1	19
2009	Pit	71	615.1	477	6	.987	11	25	8	3	0	27	43	.386	306	4.48	293	44	11	9	0	.20	0	2	0	1	3	6	7
2010	Pit	100	790.1	594	6	.990	12	39	21	9	4	38	53	.418	435	4.95	342	79	6	5	1	.07	-12	1	-8	0	3	-4	29
2011	Pit	60	461.1	353	6	.983	5	21	3	2	0	21	32	.396	245	4.78	183	41	11	2	0	.21	-1	-3	-1	-1	-1	-6	-
		426	3513.1	2647	37	.986	44	147	63	24	8	160	243	.397	1914	4.90	1362	285	59	34	1	.17	-17	-1	-12	0	5	-8	26

A.J. Ellis

		BASIC							BUNTS			PITCHER HANDLING						STOLEN BASES						RUNS SAVED					
Year	Team	G	Inn	TC	E	Pct	GFP	DM	Opps	Sac Hits	Bunt Hits	W	L	Pct	ER	CERA	Pitch Block	SB	CCS	PCS	CPO	CS%	SB Saved	Adj ER	SB	Bunt	GFP/DME	Total	Rank
2008	LAD	3	10.0	8	0	1.000	1	0				0	1	.000	5	4.50	7	0	0	0	0	-	0	0	0		0	0	-
2009	LAD	7	27.2	38	0	1.000	0	1				1	1	.500	11	3.58	15	1	0	0	0	.00	0	0	0		0	0	-
2010	LAD	43	308.2	286	1	.997	1	16	2	2	0	14	20	.412	142	4.14	95	26	8	2	0	.24	-1	0	0	0	-2	-2	-
2011	LAD	29	221.2	178	0	1.000	0	10	1	0	0	14	11	.560	89	3.61	75	11	2	2	0	.15	-1	0	-1	0	-2	-3	-
		82	568.0	510	1	.998	2	27	3	2	0	29	33	.468	246	3.90	192	38	10	4	0	.21	-2	0	-1	0	-4	-5	-

Tyler Flowers

		BASIC							BUNTS			PITCHER HANDLING						STOLEN BASES						RUNS SAVED					
Year	Team	G	Inn	TC	E	Pct	GFP	DM	Opps	Sac Hits	Bunt Hits	W	L	Pct	ER	CERA	Pitch Block	SB	CCS	PCS	CPO	CS%	SB Saved	Adj ER	SB	Bunt	GFP/DME	Total	Rank
2009	CWS	6	27.0	20	0	1.000	0	1				1	2	.333	17	5.67	11	2	0	0	0	.00	0	0	0		0	0	-
2010	CWS	7	31.2	31	0	1.000	0	3				2	1	.667	15	4.26	11	2	1	0	0	.33	0	0	0		0	0	-
2011	CWS	31	256.2	260	2	.992	1	10				16	12	.571	113	3.96	120	25	6	2	0	.19	1	1	1		1	3	-
		44	315.1	311	2	.994	1	14				19	15	.559	145	4.14	142	29	7	2	0	.19	1	1	1		1	3	-

Ryan Hanigan

		BASIC							BUNTS			PITCHER HANDLING						STOLEN BASES						RUNS SAVED					
Year	Team	G	Inn	TC	E	Pct	GFP	DM	Opps	Sac Hits	Bunt Hits	W	L	Pct	ER	CERA	Pitch Block	SB	CCS	PCS	CPO	CS%	SB Saved	Adj ER	SB	Bunt	GFP/DME	Total	Rank
2007	Cin	3	20.0	16	0	1.000	0	0				2	0	1.000	9	4.05	9	1	0	0	0	.00	0	0	0		0	0	-
2008	Cin	30	229.1	206	1	.995	2	7	4	3	0	14	11	.560	106	4.16	80	15	8	0	0	.35	-1	1	-1	0	0	0	-
2009	Cin	88	670.1	539	1	.998	10	24	12	6	1	34	38	.472	318	4.27	183	28	19	2	2	.40	2	0	2	0	-1	1	17
2010	Cin	68	525.2	461	4	.991	2	10	3	3	0	38	20	.655	196	3.36	132	28	12	1	0	.30	0	5	0	0	-1	4	-
2011	Cin	89	687.1	574	4	.993	8	23	4	3	0	38	35	.521	303	3.97	209	34	13	5	0	.28	-1	4	-1	0	-3	0	12
		278	2132.2	1796	10	.994	22	64	23	15	1	126	104	.548	932	3.93	613	106	52	8	2	.33	-1	10	0	0	-5	5	-

Catchers

Brett Hayes

Year	Team	G	Inn	TC	E	Pct	GFP	DM	Opps	Sac Hits	Bunt Hits	W	L	Pct	ER	CERA	Pitch Block	SB	CCS	PCS	CPO	CS%	SB Saved	Adj ER	SB	Bunt	GFP/DME	Total	Rank
2010	Fla	24	190.2	155	0	1.000	4	7	6	2	1	9	12	.429	85	4.01	60	13	5	1	0	.28	0	0	0	0	1	1	-
2011	Fla	50	312.2	274	0	1.000	5	13	5	3	0	12	21	.364	144	4.14	97	20	5	2	1	.20	-1	0	0	0	-1	-1	-
		74	503.1	429	0	1.000	9	20	11	5	1	21	33	.389	229	4.09	157	33	10	3	1	.23	-1	0	0	0	0	0	-

Ramon Hernandez

Year	Team	G	Inn	TC	E	Pct	GFP	DM	Opps	Sac Hits	Bunt Hits	W	L	Pct	ER	CERA	Pitch Block	SB	CCS	PCS	CPO	CS%	SB Saved	Adj ER	SB	Bunt	GFP/DME	Total	Rank
2003	Oak	139	1172.2	926	8	.991	-	-	4	2	1	84	49	.632	453	3.48	-	73	24	12	0	.25	3	1	2	-1		2	15
2004	SD	108	925.1	794	6	.992	8	26	10	5	0	51	55	.481	412	4.01	142	53	18	3	0	.25	2	-2	1	0	1	0	11
2005	SD	97	806.0	684	8	.988	7	22	3	0	0	52	42	.553	362	4.04	88	52	18	0	0	.26	1	6	1	1	-1	7	6
2006	Bal	135	1094.1	875	13	.985	9	49	5	2	1	58	68	.460	637	5.24	344	55	35	7	4	.39	10	-3	9	0	-1	5	5
2007	Bal	104	855.0	687	7	.990	8	31	7	1	0	43	54	.443	494	5.20	378	68	17	3	0	.20	-5	0	-3	2	3	2	12
2008	Bal	127	1039.1	768	9	.988	11	49	9	2	0	57	62	.479	579	5.01	345	99	21	3	1	.18	-3	3	-2	2	-1	2	14
2009	Cin	55	451.0	380	1	.997	3	15	6	2	0	23	30	.434	221	4.41	143	33	11	7	2	.25	-4	-1	-2	-1	-2	-6	-
2010	Cin	91	732.0	647	4	.994	5	21	13	7	1	45	40	.529	390	4.80	319	35	14	4	3	.29	-2	-10	0	2	1	-7	30
2011	Cin	82	658.0	549	1	.998	4	29	11	4	1	34	42	.447	310	4.24	249	39	18	5	0	.32	0	-3	0	2	-3	-4	22
		938	7733.2	6310	57	.991	55	242	68	25	4	447	442	.503	3858	4.49	2008	507	176	44	10	.26	3	-9	6	7	-3	1	17

Koyie Hill

Year	Team	G	Inn	TC	E	Pct	GFP	DM	Opps	Sac Hits	Bunt Hits	W	L	Pct	ER	CERA	Pitch Block	SB	CCS	PCS	CPO	CS%	SB Saved	Adj ER	SB	Bunt	GFP/DME	Total	Rank
2004	Ari	11	83.0	63	1	.984	0	10				1	9	.100	74	8.02	26	8	3	1	0	.27	0	0	0		-2	-2	-
2005	Ari	32	211.1	157	0	1.000	1	9	3	2	0	9	14	.391	128	5.45	47	12	2	2	0	.14	0	0	0	1	-1	0	-
2007	ChC	31	232.1	202	1	.995	2	1	2	1	1	17	8	.680	77	2.98	73	10	4	0	0	.29	1	1	1	-1	1	2	-
2008	ChC	9	42.2	42	1	.976	0	2	1	0	1	1	1	.500	26	5.48	28	6	1	0	0	.14	-1	0	-1	-1	1	-1	-
2009	ChC	79	627.1	622	3	.995	8	22	6	3	0	42	27	.609	257	3.69	243	30	20	0	2	.40	6	2	5	0	0	7	4
2010	ChC	72	545.1	526	4	.992	7	20	11	4	0	24	36	.400	252	4.16	244	37	5	3	0	.12	-4	0	-3	1	2	0	17
2011	ChC	45	349.0	340	6	.982	4	17	2	1	0	22	16	.579	166	4.28	154	25	7	1	0	.22	-1	1	-1	0	0	0	-
		279	2091.0	1952	16	.992	22	81	25	11	2	116	111	.511	980	4.22	815	128	42	7	2	.25	1	4	1	0	1	6	-

Nick Hundley

Year	Team	G	Inn	TC	E	Pct	GFP	DM	Opps	Sac Hits	Bunt Hits	W	L	Pct	ER	CERA	Pitch Block	SB	CCS	PCS	CPO	CS%	SB Saved	Adj ER	SB	Bunt	GFP/DME	Total	Rank
2008	SD	59	486.1	402	4	.990	10	18	8	3	0	21	34	.382	257	4.76	166	42	13	1	0	.24	3	-1	2	-1	2	2	-
2009	SD	74	643.1	556	6	.989	8	36	14	7	2	38	33	.535	286	4.00	214	56	10	4	0	.15	-4	-5	-3	-1	-2	-1	19
2010	SD	76	659.2	664	4	.994	8	17	5	1	1	37	36	.507	273	3.72	164	41	11	6	0	.21	-1	-5	-1	0	-2	-8	32
2011	SD	76	654.1	567	6	.989	10	22	9	4	2	30	43	.411	257	3.53	258	57	24	8	1	.30	3	-1	2	0	4	5	6
		285	2443.2	2189	20	.991	36	93	36	15	5	126	146	.463	1073	3.95	802	196	58	19	1	.23	0	-2	0	-2	2	-2	-

Chris Iannetta

Year	Team	G	Inn	TC	E	Pct	GFP	DM	Opps	Sac Hits	Bunt Hits	W	L	Pct	ER	CERA	Pitch Block	SB	CCS	PCS	CPO	CS%	SB Saved	Adj ER	SB	Bunt	GFP/DME	Total	Rank
2006	Col	21	191.2	147	0	1.000	2	10	1	1	0	12	8	.600	130	6.10	44	18	3	0	0	.14	-1	-1	-1	0	-1	-3	-
2007	Col	60	496.2	329	1	.997	7	7	4	2	0	31	23	.574	260	4.71	151	33	8	2	1	.20	-1	-2	0	0	2	0	14
2008	Col	100	837.0	657	0	1.000	9	34	10	6	0	46	50	.479	429	4.61	246	41	8	4	1	.16	-2	2	-1	1	-2	0	18
2009	Col	89	763.2	606	5	.992	13	29	13	8	0	46	41	.529	357	4.21	252	50	15	3	1	.23	1	1	1	1	0	3	12
2010	Col	52	443.0	411	6	.985	5	21	12	8	1	23	26	.469	228	4.63	180	35	6	4	1	.15	-4	-1	-2	1	-1	-3	-
2011	Col	105	943.2	817	2	.998	10	41	9	6	0	51	54	.486	442	4.22	417	70	26	4	1	.27	4	4	3	1	0	8	2
		427	3675.2	2967	14	.995	46	142	49	31	1	209	202	.509	1846	4.52	1290	247	66	17	5	.21	-3	3	0	4	-2	5	13

John Jaso

Year	Team	G	Inn	TC	E	Pct	GFP	DM	Opps	Sac Hits	Bunt Hits	W	L	Pct	ER	CERA	Pitch Block	SB	CCS	PCS	CPO	CS%	SB Saved	Adj ER	SB	Bunt	GFP/DME	Total	Rank
2008	TB	3	16.0	12	0	1.000	0	1				1	0	1.000	8	4.50	9	0	0	0	0	-	0	0	0	0		0	-
2010	TB	96	719.0	646	5	.992	5	28	4	0	1	43	37	.538	309	3.87	290	41	9	3	0	.18	-3	-1	-2	0	0	-3	21
2011	TB	82	603.1	509	4	.992	6	30	5	3	2	39	28	.582	226	3.37	240	50	8	2	0	.14	-4	2	-3	-1	-1	-3	21
		181	1338.1	1167	9	.992	11	59	9	3	3	83	65	.561	543	3.65	539	91	17	5	0	.16	-7	1	-5	-1	-1	-6	-

Rob Johnson

Year	Team	G	Inn	TC	E	Pct	GFP	DM	Opps	Sac Hits	Bunt Hits	W	L	Pct	ER	CERA	Pitch Block	SB	CCS	PCS	CPO	CS%	SB Saved	Adj ER	SB	Bunt	GFP/DME	Total	Rank
2007	Sea	4	6.0	2	0	1.000	0	0				0	0		2	3.00	1	0	0	0	0	-	0	0	0			0	-
2008	Sea	10	64.0	51	0	1.000	1	4				1	6	.143	36	5.06	36	10	1	1	0	.09	-2	0	-1		0	-1	-
2009	Sea	80	684.1	557	4	.993	14	36	6	3	0	46	29	.613	245	3.22	158	41	17	1	4	.29	3	4	4	1	-5	4	11
2010	Sea	61	510.2	386	4	.990	5	25	7	0	2	23	30	.434	227	4.00	130	22	12	0	2	.35	2	-2	-2	1	-4	-3	-
2011	SD	63	475.0	429	2	.995	8	21	14	5	1	22	32	.407	173	3.28	196	49	11	4	3	.18	-4	1	-2	2	2	3	-
		218	1740.0	1425	10	.993	28	86	27	8	3	92	101	.477	683	3.53	521	122	41	6	9	.25	0	3	3	4	-7	3	-

Catchers

George Kottaras

	BASIC							BUNTS			PITCHER HANDLING						STOLEN BASES						RUNS SAVED					
Year Team	G	Inn	TC	E	Pct	GFP	DM	Opps	Sac Hits	Bunt Hits	W	L	Pct	ER	CERA	Pitch Block	SB	CCS	PCS	CPO	CS%	SB Saved	Adj ER	SB	Bunt	GFP/DME	Total	Rank
2008 Bos	2	8.0	5	0	1.000	0	0	-	-		0	0	-	7	7.88	1	0	0	0	0	-	0	0	0			0	-
2009 Bos	39	243.2	205	1	.995	4	17	1	1	0	14	11	.560	145	5.36	76	26	4	1	0	.13	-2	-2	-1	0	-1	-4	-
2010 Mil	61	541.2	458	4	.991	4	13	8	3	0	30	30	.500	268	4.45	309	44	4	4	0	.08	-8	1	-5	0	5	1	-
2011 Mil	36	253.0	179	0	1.000	1	5	1	1	0	20	11	.645	102	3.63	101	18	3	0	0	.14	-2	0	-2	0	1	-1	-
	138	1046.1	847	5	.994	9	35	10	5	0	64	52	.552	522	4.49	487	88	11	5	0	.11	-11	-1	-8	0	5	-4	-

Gerald Laird

	BASIC							BUNTS			PITCHER HANDLING						STOLEN BASES						RUNS SAVED					
Year Team	G	Inn	TC	E	Pct	GFP	DM	Opps	Sac Hits	Bunt Hits	W	L	Pct	ER	CERA	Pitch Block	SB	CCS	PCS	CPO	CS%	SB Saved	Adj ER	SB	Bunt	GFP/DME	Total	Rank
2003 Tex	16	111.0	74	1	.986	-	-	1	1	0	5	7	.417	71	5.76	-	4	3	0	0	.43	0	0	0	0		0	-
2004 Tex	49	397.0	299	5	.983	8	12	3	1	0	23	23	.500	194	4.40	120	17	12	2	0	.41	3	2	2	0	2	6	-
2005 Tex	13	99.0	69	3	.957	0	4	1	1	0	5	6	.455	55	5.00	19	8	3	0	0	.27	-1	0	-1	0	0	-1	-
2006 Tex	71	578.1	427	5	.988	4	18	4	1	1	31	34	.477	282	4.39	108	25	19	2	1	.43	5	0	4	0	-2	2	8
2007 Tex	119	987.1	762	12	.984	15	30	8	2	1	53	61	.465	524	4.78	414	59	39	1	1	.40	9	0	7	1	5	13	3
2008 Tex	88	753.0	566	8	.986	2	29	2	2	0	43	43	.500	436	5.21	258	53	20	1	0	.27	2	5	1	0	-3	3	7
2009 Det	135	1090.1	925	3	.997	14	36	9	5	1	65	58	.528	513	4.23	374	59	40	2	2	.40	9	-2	7	0	1	6	7
2010 Det	87	670.2	573	5	.991	8	34	8	3	2	39	37	.513	306	4.11	218	58	24	6	0	.29	-2	2	-2	-1	-2	-3	21
2011 StL	31	213.0	197	3	.985	1	10	7	4	0	13	9	.591	83	3.51	102	16	3	1	0	.16	-1	0	-1	-1	0	-2	-
	609	4899.2	3892	45	.988	48	173	43	20	5	277	278	.499	2464	4.53	1613	299	163	14	4	.35	22	7	17	-1	1	24	7

Jonathan Lucroy

	BASIC							BUNTS			PITCHER HANDLING						STOLEN BASES						RUNS SAVED					
Year Team	G	Inn	TC	E	Pct	GFP	DM	Opps	Sac Hits	Bunt Hits	W	L	Pct	ER	CERA	Pitch Block	SB	CCS	PCS	CPO	CS%	SB Saved	Adj ER	SB	Bunt	GFP/DME	Total	Rank
2010 Mil	75	655.0	663	5	.992	4	37	6	5	0	36	38	.486	320	4.40	521	37	15	2	0	.29	3	-1	2	0	3	4	10
2011 Mil	132	1043.2	1046	7	.993	10	65	7	2	1	68	46	.596	421	3.63	647	77	21	9	0	.21	-5	0	-4	0	-1	-5	28
	207	1698.2	1709	12	.993	14	102	13	7	1	104	84	.553	741	3.93	1168	114	36	11	0	.24	-2	-1	-2	0	2	-1	-

Lou Marson

	BASIC							BUNTS			PITCHER HANDLING						STOLEN BASES						RUNS SAVED					
Year Team	G	Inn	TC	E	Pct	GFP	DM	Opps	Sac Hits	Bunt Hits	W	L	Pct	ER	CERA	Pitch Block	SB	CCS	PCS	CPO	CS%	SB Saved	Adj ER	SB	Bunt	GFP/DME	Total	Rank
2008 Phi	1	9.0	10	0	1.000	0	0				1	0	1.000	3	3.00	6	0	1	0	0	1.00	0	0	0			0	-
2009 2 tms	21	175.0	158	1	.994	0	6	3	1	0	6	14	.300	105	5.40	57	11	8	2	0	.42	2	0	2	0	-1	1	-
2010 Cle	87	725.0	552	4	.993	8	26	5	3	1	38	43	.469	349	4.33	209	51	26	5	0	.34	2	-1	1	-1	-1	-2	20
2011 Cle	78	667.0	524	5	.990	9	22	9	2	1	36	38	.486	319	4.30	185	48	24	6	0	.33	5	0	3	1	-2	2	10
	187	1576.0	1244	10	.992	17	54	17	6	2	81	95	.460	776	4.43	457	110	59	13	0	.35	10	-1	6	0	-4	1	-

Russell Martin

	BASIC							BUNTS			PITCHER HANDLING						STOLEN BASES						RUNS SAVED					
Year Team	G	Inn	TC	E	Pct	GFP	DM	Opps	Sac Hits	Bunt Hits	W	L	Pct	ER	CERA	Pitch Block	SB	CCS	PCS	CPO	CS%	SB Saved	Adj ER	SB	Bunt	GFP/DME	Total	Rank
2006 LAD	117	1015.0	856	6	.993	6	34	15	8	1	71	43	.623	443	3.93	216	71	25	7	0	.26	1	2	0	0	-2	0	14
2007 LAD	145	1254.0	1164	14	.988	25	35	27	14	2	78	65	.545	550	3.95	386	82	33	8	4	.29	7	4	7	1	6	18	1
2008 LAD	149	1238.0	1118	11	.990	15	37	13	7	0	76	62	.551	499	3.63	418	70	17	6	1	.20	-2	-2	-1	-1	3	-1	19
2009 LAD	137	1201.0	1133	7	.994	19	58	19	7	0	78	55	.586	450	3.37	483	74	25	8	2	.25	0	4	1	2	0	7	4
2010 LAD	93	791.1	750	10	.987	19	29	11	7	1	47	42	.528	354	4.03	342	43	19	8	4	.31	3	0	4	-2	3	5	9
2011 NYY	125	1044.1	972	10	.990	18	51	7	3	2	67	51	.568	429	3.70	618	95	35	5	0	.27	3	0	2	-1	6	7	4
	766	6543.2	5993	58	.990	102	244	92	46	6	417	318	.567	2725	3.75	2463	435	154	42	11	.26	11	8	13	-1	16	36	2

Victor Martinez

	BASIC							BUNTS			PITCHER HANDLING						STOLEN BASES						RUNS SAVED					
Year Team	G	Inn	TC	E	Pct	GFP	DM	Opps	Sac Hits	Bunt Hits	W	L	Pct	ER	CERA	Pitch Block	SB	CCS	PCS	CPO	CS%	SB Saved	Adj ER	SB	Bunt	GFP/DME	Total	Rank
2003 Cle	40	342.0	255	1	.996	-	-	4	1	2	14	26	.350	160	4.21		20	8	1	0	.29	0	0	0	-1		-1	-
2004 Cle	132	1108.0	933	6	.994	5	39	8	5	1	59	65	.476	614	4.99	297	89	26	4	0	.23	-4	-7	-3	0	2	-8	31
2005 Cle	142	1233.0	967	5	.995	5	21	4	4	0	78	61	.561	504	3.68	132	96	25	4	2	.21	-2	-3	-1	0	4	0	16
2006 Cle	133	1110.0	806	8	.990	12	37	10	4	3	65	62	.512	546	4.51	224	100	16	6	1	.14	-12	-6	-9	-1	0	-16	35
2007 Cle	121	1042.0	836	4	.995	13	31	8	1	1	70	48	.593	465	4.01	286	70	30	3	1	.30	2	-2	2	-1	-1	-2	21
2008 Cle	55	447.1	347	3	.991	7	9	3	0	1	24	30	.444	214	4.31	79	22	10	3	0	.31	1	0	1	-1	0	0	-
2009 2 tms	85	687.0	526	4	.992	8	24	4	3	0	41	41	.500	425	5.57	237	56	8	1	0	.13	-7	-8	-4	0	0	-12	34
2010 Bos	110	904.0	828	6	.993	13	43	10	5	3	62	44	.585	430	4.28	329	99	17	10	2	.15	-5	-5	-2	-2	1	-8	32
2011 Det	26	219.0	160	2	.988	3	11				13	13	.500	128	5.26	94	29	7	1	0	.19	-1	-1	-1	0		-2	-
	844	7093.0	5658	39	.993	66	215	51	23	11	426	390	.522	3496	4.44	1678	581	147	33	5	.20	-28	-32	-17	-6	6	-49	33

Catchers

Jeff Mathis

	BASIC							BUNTS			PITCHER HANDLING						STOLEN BASES						RUNS SAVED					
Year Team	G	Inn	TC	E	Pct	GFP	DM	Opps	Sac Hits	Bunt Hits	W	L	Pct	ER	CERA	Pitch Block	SB	CCS	PCS	CPO	CS%	SB Saved	Adj ER	SB	Bunt	GFP/DME	Total	Rank
2005 LAA	3	5.0	4	0	1.000	0	0				0	0	-	0	0.00	2	0	0	0	0	-	0	0	0		0	0	-
2006 LAA	20	133.0	101	3	.970	0	6	1	0	0	4	10	.286	86	5.82	58	12	2	1	0	.14	-1	-1	-1		0	-2	-
2007 LAA	57	467.0	429	4	.991	12	24	4	0	0	34	18	.654	202	3.89	261	40	8	0	7	.17	-4	0	1	0	2	3	-
2008 LAA	94	793.1	694	13	.981	12	17	11	6	1	58	32	.644	323	3.66	395	57	16	4	3	.22	-4	3	-1	0	7	9	4
2009 LAA	79	657.0	572	7	.988	13	24	12	5	2	46	32	.590	291	3.99	340	52	17	1	1	.25	0	4	0	0	6	10	1
2010 LAA	67	553.2	476	7	.985	21	37	7	2	2	29	33	.468	226	3.67	317	43	7	4	3	.14	-4	2	-1	0	3	4	10
2011 LAA	91	698.0	568	3	.995	13	28	12	5	2	45	34	.570	252	3.25	405	48	12	6	1	.20	0	3	1	-1	5	8	2
	411	3307.0	2844	37	.987	71	136	47	18	7	216	159	.576	1380	3.76	1778	252	62	16	15	.20	-13	11	-1	-1	23	32	3

Joe Mauer

	BASIC							BUNTS			PITCHER HANDLING						STOLEN BASES						RUNS SAVED					
Year Team	G	Inn	TC	E	Pct	GFP	DM	Opps	Sac Hits	Bunt Hits	W	L	Pct	ER	CERA	Pitch Block	SB	CCS	PCS	CPO	CS%	SB Saved	Adj ER	SB	Bunt	GFP/DME	Total	Rank
2004 Min	32	257.0	224	2	.991	0	2	1	1	0	19	10	.655	97	3.40	45	11	5	2	0	.31	0	1	0	0	0	1	-
2005 Min	116	999.2	743	5	.993	5	24	4	0	1	53	57	.482	410	3.69	117	31	18	5	0	.37	0	-1	0	0	-2	-3	21
2006 Min	120	1059.1	914	4	.996	4	28	6	3	0	71	48	.597	461	3.92	214	36	17	5	0	.32	-1	-1	-1	1	-3	-4	29
2007 Min	91	777.2	634	1	.998	5	29	2	0	0	44	44	.500	327	3.78	188	21	19	5	0	.48	4	5	3		-5	3	11
2008 Min	139	1203.0	886	3	.997	7	43	4	1	0	73	62	.541	564	4.22	280	51	18	11	1	.26	-2	1	-1	0	-7	-7	32
2009 Min	109	939.0	758	3	.996	7	24	3	1	0	62	43	.590	448	4.29	269	54	17	2	0	.24	-1	4	-1	0	-1	2	14
2010 Min	112	951.2	733	3	.996	13	25	10	3	0	66	41	.617	404	3.82	228	53	15	4	0	.22	-1	4	-1	1	-1	3	12
2011 Min	52	408.2	313	4	.987	2	19	5	2	0	21	26	.447	201	4.43	146	28	10	2	0	.26	-1	1	0	1	-2	0	-
	771	6596.0	5205	25	.995	43	194	35	11	1	409	331	.553	2912	3.97	1487	285	119	36	1	.29	-1	14	-1	3	-21	-5	22

Brian McCann

	BASIC							BUNTS			PITCHER HANDLING						STOLEN BASES						RUNS SAVED					
Year Team	G	Inn	TC	E	Pct	GFP	DM	Opps	Sac Hits	Bunt Hits	W	L	Pct	ER	CERA	Pitch Block	SB	CCS	PCS	CPO	CS%	SB Saved	Adj ER	SB	Bunt	GFP/DME	Total	Rank
2005 Atl	57	449.1	334	3	.991	4	8	10	6	0	33	16	.673	195	3.91	72	22	5	0	1	.19	-2	-1	-1	1	-1	-2	-
2006 Atl	124	1016.1	826	9	.989	2	26	8	2	1	62	56	.525	498	4.41	234	70	20	1	0	.22	-1	2	-1	0	-2	-1	19
2007 Atl	132	1139.0	973	13	.987	10	37	22	11	2	70	60	.538	492	3.89	288	70	17	2	0	.20	-3	1	-2	0	-4	-5	24
2008 Atl	138	1143.1	958	9	.991	11	38	26	17	0	61	71	.462	540	4.25	300	93	21	6	2	.18	-1	7	0	2	-1	8	5
2009 Atl	127	1078.2	994	12	.988	14	39	14	7	0	69	55	.556	438	3.65	297	76	21	3	1	.22	0	-4	0	1	-2	-5	25
2010 Atl	136	1109.2	1050	14	.987	14	36	16	11	0	74	55	.574	456	3.70	339	84	31	5	0	.27	5	-6	4	1	0	-1	19
2011 Atl	126	1083.0	1061	5	.995	8	48	23	11	3	60	58	.508	434	3.61	463	104	22	7	0	.17	-4	-2	-3	2	-1	-4	22
	840	7019.1	6196	65	.990	63	232	119	65	6	429	371	.536	3053	3.91	1993	519	137	24	4	.21	-6	-3	-3	7	-11	-10	29

Michael McKenry

	BASIC							BUNTS			PITCHER HANDLING						STOLEN BASES						RUNS SAVED					
Year Team	G	Inn	TC	E	Pct	GFP	DM	Opps	Sac Hits	Bunt Hits	W	L	Pct	ER	CERA	Pitch Block	SB	CCS	PCS	CPO	CS%	SB Saved	Adj ER	SB	Bunt	GFP/DME	Total	Rank
2010 Col	2	9.0	6	0	1.000	0	0				0	1	.000	6	6.00	7	0	0	0	0	-	0	0	0	0	0	0	-
2011 Pit	58	485.0	388	5	.987	6	20	2	1	0	26	28	.481	201	3.73	199	39	10	3	0	.20	0	0	0		1	1	-
	60	494.0	394	5	.987	6	20	2	1	0	26	29	.473	207	3.77	206	39	10	3	0	.20	0	0	0		1	1	-

Jose Molina

	BASIC							BUNTS			PITCHER HANDLING						STOLEN BASES						RUNS SAVED					
Year Team	G	Inn	TC	E	Pct	GFP	DM	Opps	Sac Hits	Bunt Hits	W	L	Pct	ER	CERA	Pitch Block	SB	CCS	PCS	CPO	CS%	SB Saved	Adj ER	SB	Bunt	GFP/DME	Total	Rank
2003 Ana	53	332.0	239	1	.996	-		2	2	0	17	22	.436	150	4.07	-	18	6	1	1	.25	-2	1	-1	0		0	-
2004 Ana	70	524.1	481	3	.994	7	20	2	0	1	34	23	.596	251	4.31	84	23	19	3	5	.45	5	1	6	0	-3	4	5
2005 LAA	65	480.1	452	3	.993	5	21	3	2	0	33	20	.623	195	3.65	98	19	18	2	3	.49	8	0	7	0	-1	6	-
2006 LAA	76	603.1	560	8	.986	12	36	2	1	0	38	33	.535	267	3.98	206	27	19	1	4	.41	5	1	5	0	-4	2	8
2007 2 tms	69	492.1	470	4	.991	8	20	3	2	0	31	22	.585	252	4.61	157	31	12	1	1	.28	0	1	-1	0	0	0	14
2008 NYY	97	737.0	689	3	.996	6	29	7	3	1	43	38	.531	302	3.69	197	42	32	1	1	.43	11	5	8	0	-2	11	2
2009 NYY	49	356.2	388	1	.997	8	18	2	2	0	24	18	.571	131	3.31	105	23	5	4	2	.18	-2	3	-1	0	-1	1	-
2010 Tor	56	444.2	456	2	.996	6	26	1	0	0	29	22	.569	184	3.72	163	19	13	2	2	.41	3	3	3	0	-2	4	-
2011 Tor	48	399.0	367	1	.997	5	21				26	18	.591	194	4.38	108	24	12	0	2	.33	0	1	1	0	-4	-2	-
	583	4369.2	4102	26	.994	57	191	22	12	2	275	216	.560	1926	3.97	1118	226	136	15	21	.38	27	15	29	-1	-17	26	4

Yadier Molina

	BASIC							BUNTS			PITCHER HANDLING						STOLEN BASES						RUNS SAVED					
Year Team	G	Inn	TC	E	Pct	GFP	DM	Opps	Sac Hits	Bunt Hits	W	L	Pct	ER	CERA	Pitch Block	SB	CCS	PCS	CPO	CS%	SB Saved	Adj ER	SB	Bunt	GFP/DME	Total	Rank
2004 StL	51	344.0	274	2	.993	4	12	2	1	1	24	15	.615	139	3.64	83	9	8	0	1	.47	3	1	2	-1		0	2	-
2005 StL	114	959.1	757	7	.991	14	25	14	8	1	73	38	.658	361	3.39	239	14	17	8	9	.55	7	3	9	0	-1	11	3
2006 StL	127	1037.1	817	4	.995	13	21	12	8	2	61	57	.517	522	4.53	431	37	26	3	7	.41	6	1	7	-1	7	14	1
2007 StL	107	861.1	651	6	.991	7	28	9	5	0	46	55	.455	414	4.33	408	23	23	4	2	.50	10	6	8	1	0	15	2
2008 StL	119	1002.0	733	10	.986	21	40	10	4	2	61	53	.535	470	4.22	377	34	16	2	7	.32	4	-2	6	0	-1	3	7
2009 StL	138	1176.2	971	5	.995	19	37	21	10	3	79	57	.581	455	3.48	564	32	16	6	8	.33	1	0	4	0	5	9	3
2010 StL	135	1138.0	979	5	.995	14	27	19	10	3	72	58	.554	409	3.23	567	35	28	5	3	.44	6	6	1	7	20	1
2011 StL	138	1150.0	929	5	.995	11	48	20	13	1	72	60	.545	499	3.91	657	46	15	4	2	.25	-1	-6	0	-1	3	-4	22
	929	7668.2	6111	44	.993	103	238	107	59	13	488	393	.554	3269	3.84	3326	230	149	32	39	.39	36	9	42	-1	20	70	1

Catchers

Miguel Montero

		BASIC							BUNTS			PITCHER HANDLING						STOLEN BASES						RUNS SAVED					
Year	Team	G	Inn	TC	E	Pct	GFP	DM	Opps	Sac Hits	Bunt Hits	W	L	Pct	ER	CERA	Pitch Block	SB	CCS	PCS	CPO	CS%	SB Saved	Adj ER	SB	Bunt	GFP/DME	Total	Rank
2006	Ari	5	40.0	40	0	1.000	0	1	2	1	0	1	3	.250	21	4.73	11	3	1	0	0	.25	0	0	0	0	0	0	-
2007	Ari	73	510.2	376	6	.984	10	17	7	3	0	26	31	.456	273	4.81	142	35	9	1	0	.20	-5	-3	-4	2	-1	-6	27
2008	Ari	53	404.2	379	4	.989	4	23	8	4	2	17	28	.378	206	4.58	121	27	6	1	0	.18	-3	-2	-2	-1	-4	-9	-
2009	Ari	111	924.2	802	9	.989	10	49	13	5	3	48	53	.475	422	4.11	338	67	18	5	0	.21	-1	7	-1	-1	-3	2	14
2010	Ari	79	658.1	522	2	.996	9	31	12	3	1	30	45	.400	314	4.29	226	47	16	5	1	.25	0	1	1	1	-2	1	15
2011	Ari	134	1169.1	997	11	.989	21	35	25	9	3	82	49	.626	468	3.60	356	48	28	4	2	.37	3	3	3	0	-1	5	6
		455	3707.2	3116	32	.990	54	156	67	25	9	204	209	.494	1704	4.14	1194	227	78	16	3	.26	-7	6	-3	1	-11	-7	25

Mike Napoli

		BASIC							BUNTS			PITCHER HANDLING						STOLEN BASES						RUNS SAVED					
Year	Team	G	Inn	TC	E	Pct	GFP	DM	Opps	Sac Hits	Bunt Hits	W	L	Pct	ER	CERA	Pitch Block	SB	CCS	PCS	CPO	CS%	SB Saved	Adj ER	SB	Bunt	GFP/DME	Total	Rank
2006	LAA	94	716.1	631	8	.987	5	30	4	2	1	47	30	.610	299	3.76	262	38	16	1	0	.30	1	1	1	0	0	2	8
2007	LAA	75	598.2	499	7	.986	5	28	3	3	0	38	30	.559	285	4.28	239	49	13	2	1	.21	-3	-1	-2	-1	-1	-5	24
2008	LAA	75	625.0	493	3	.994	4	27	4	1	1	42	29	.592	309	4.45	218	52	9	2	0	.15	-5	-3	-3	0	-1	-7	32
2009	LAA	96	758.0	582	8	.986	10	35	8	5	1	51	33	.607	409	4.86	385	74	13	8	0	.15	-5	-3	-4	-1	3	-5	25
2010	LAA	66	525.0	443	6	.986	8	31	4	2	1	24	35	.407	299	5.13	252	52	13	6	1	.20	0	-7	0	-1	1	-7	-
2011	Tex	61	506.1	458	2	.996	5	17	3	1	1	42	15	.737	178	3.16	153	21	10	2	1	.32	1	2	1	0	-2	1	-
		467	3729.1	3106	34	.989	36	168	26	14	5	244	172	.587	1779	4.29	1509	286	74	21	3	.21	-12	-11	-7	-3	0	-21	31

Dioner Navarro

		BASIC							BUNTS			PITCHER HANDLING						STOLEN BASES						RUNS SAVED					
Year	Team	G	Inn	TC	E	Pct	GFP	DM	Opps	Sac Hits	Bunt Hits	W	L	Pct	ER	CERA	Pitch Block	SB	CCS	PCS	CPO	CS%	SB Saved	Adj ER	SB	Bunt	GFP/DME	Total	Rank
2004	NYY	4	13.0	9	0	1.000	0	0				1	0	1.000	2	1.38	8	0	0	0	0	-	0	0	0		0	0	-
2005	LAD	50	435.2	367	2	.995	6	8	14	10	0	24	25	.490	210	4.34	41	33	8	1	0	.20	-1	0	-1	0	-1	-2	-
2006	2 tms	78	653.2	524	8	.985	3	33	7	1	2	28	47	.373	355	4.89	172	48	18	2	0	.27	-2	0	-1	-1	-3	-5	31
2007	TB	112	956.1	895	14	.984	12	39	10	2	2	47	63	.427	584	5.50	367	71	24	6	0	.25	-4	0	-3	0	1	-2	21
2008	TB	117	1011.1	897	5	.994	10	33	7	2	1	70	43	.619	438	3.90	279	45	25	3	0	.36	6	-5	4	0	-1	-2	22
2009	TB	113	921.1	784	5	.994	8	39	5	2	0	56	49	.533	433	4.23	313	61	19	3	1	.24	0	0	-1	-1	-2	-2	22
2010	TB	46	331.0	296	4	.986	4	10	1	0	0	25	11	.694	107	2.91	106	19	7	5	0	.27	0	3	0	0	0	3	-
2011	LAD	54	428.0	455	7	.985	14	20	4	2	0	22	24	.478	163	3.43	165	41	10	4	5	.20	-3	1	0	0	0	1	-
		574	4750.1	4227	45	.989	57	182	48	19	5	273	262	.510	2292	4.34	1451	318	111	24	6	.26	-4	-1	-1	-2	-5	-9	28

Miguel Olivo

		BASIC							BUNTS			PITCHER HANDLING						STOLEN BASES						RUNS SAVED					
Year	Team	G	Inn	TC	E	Pct	GFP	DM	Opps	Sac Hits	Bunt Hits	W	L	Pct	ER	CERA	Pitch Block	SB	CCS	PCS	CPO	CS%	SB Saved	Adj ER	SB	Bunt	GFP/DME	Total	Rank
2003	CWS	113	848.0	740	9	.988	-	-	6	1	2	54	44	.551	358	3.80	-	34	19	0	3	.36	2	1	3	-1	-	3	11
2004	2 tms	95	760.1	544	5	.991	12	33	3	1	0	42	41	.506	383	4.53	137	32	11	6	3	.26	-3	4	-1	0	-3	0	11
2005	2 tms	91	690.0	543	9	.983	10	24	9	2	3	34	43	.442	326	4.25	118	32	12	2	2	.27	-1	1	1	0	-2	0	16
2006	Fla	124	971.1	804	7	.991	10	42	14	10	1	52	57	.477	476	4.41	296	48	25	5	2	.34	3	-1	3	1	-1	2	8
2007	Fla	119	990.1	863	12	.986	21	45	15	7	2	47	64	.423	555	5.04	352	51	20	5	8	.28	1	-5	5	-1	-4	-5	24
2008	TB	58	494.1	415	5	.988	4	29	4	1	1	26	30	.464	243	4.42	152	19	12	2	1	.39	4	0	3	0	-5	-2	22
2009	KC	103	845.2	773	8	.990	5	61	10	2	1	38	59	.392	422	4.49	360	56	17	4	0	.23	-2	1	-1	0	-6	-6	29
2010	Col	111	935.0	892	9	.990	10	42	11	7	0	56	51	.523	405	3.90	432	45	30	3	3	.40	14	3	11	-1	-2	11	2
2011	Sea	127	1064.1	917	11	.988	14	74	15	4	2	54	66	.450	446	3.77	427	79	25	6	1	.24	-4	0	-3	0	-6	-9	33
		941	7599.1	6491	75	.988	86	350	87	35	12	403	455	.470	3614	4.28	2274	396	171	33	23	.30	14	4	21	-2	-29	-6	23

Ronny Paulino

		BASIC							BUNTS			PITCHER HANDLING						STOLEN BASES						RUNS SAVED					
Year	Team	G	Inn	TC	E	Pct	GFP	DM	Opps	Sac Hits	Bunt Hits	W	L	Pct	ER	CERA	Pitch Block	SB	CCS	PCS	CPO	CS%	SB Saved	Adj ER	SB	Bunt	GFP/DME	Total	Rank
2005	Pit	2	11.0	10	0	1.000	0	1				1	0	1.000	2	1.64	1	1	0	0	0	.00	0	0	0		0	0	-
2006	Pit	124	1047.0	882	11	.988	12	46	21	12	2	53	64	.453	488	4.19	310	67	24	14	3	.26	2	9	2	0	0	11	2
2007	Pit	129	1088.0	849	7	.992	6	35	13	8	0	58	61	.487	557	4.61	344	74	19	8	1	.20	-2	2	-1	0	-1	0	14
2008	Pit	32	260.0	216	2	.991	3	8	3	2	0	8	19	.296	157	5.43	95	23	8	0	0	.26	1	0	1	0	1	2	-
2009	Fla	77	582.1	559	2	.996	2	28	10	6	1	33	30	.524	269	4.16	164	50	19	3	1	.28	2	2	2	0	-3	1	17
2010	Fla	85	740.1	697	6	.991	6	29	9	3	1	43	41	.512	331	4.02	271	53	21	3	1	.28	1	0	1	1	1	3	12
2011	NYM	68	511.0	412	7	.983	3	26	9	4	0	22	34	.393	254	4.47	147	47	10	2	0	.18	-4	-1	-3	2	-4	-6	32
		517	4239.2	3625	35	.990	32	173	65	35	4	218	249	.467	2058	4.37	1332	315	101	30	6	.24	0	12	2	3	-6	11	12

Brayan Pena

		BASIC							BUNTS			PITCHER HANDLING						STOLEN BASES						RUNS SAVED					
Year	Team	G	Inn	TC	E	Pct	GFP	DM	Opps	Sac Hits	Bunt Hits	W	L	Pct	ER	CERA	Pitch Block	SB	CCS	PCS	CPO	CS%	SB Saved	Adj ER	SB	Bunt	GFP/DME	Total	Rank
2005	Atl	15	81.0	51	0	1.000	1	4	2	1	1	2	5	.286	57	6.33	18	8	1	1	0	.11	-1	0	-1	-1	-1	-3	-
2006	Atl	15	71.0	32	0	1.000	0	0	2	1	1	2	3	.400	34	4.31	25	3	0	0	0	.00	-1	0	0	0	0	0	-
2007	Atl	10	59.1	54	0	1.000	1	2				0	5	.000	40	6.07	38	4	2	2	0	.33	0	0	0	0	1	1	-
2009	KC	30	213.2	175	0	1.000	3	16	1	1	0	9	15	.375	132	5.56	82	17	4	5	0	.19	-1	0	-1	0	-3	-4	-
2010	KC	47	337.1	296	3	.990	3	13	5	0	0	13	22	.371	178	4.75	111	29	11	1	0	.28	1	0	0	1	0	1	-
2011	KC	69	537.0	444	2	.995	14	22	7	2	2	22	35	.386	268	4.49	215	48	16	11	0	.25	2	-1	2	-1	3	3	8
		186	1299.1	1052	5	.995	22	57	17	5	4	48	85	.361	709	4.91	489	109	34	20	0	.24	0	-1	0	-1	0	-2	

Catchers

Salvador Perez

	BASIC								BUNTS			PITCHER HANDLING						STOLEN BASES						RUNS SAVED					
Year	Team	G	Inn	TC	E	Pct	GFP	DM	Opps	Sac Hits	Bunt Hits	W	L	Pct	ER	CERA	Pitch Block	SB	CCS	PCS	CPO	CS%	SB Saved	Adj ER	SB	Bunt	GFP/DME	Total	Rank
2011	KC	39	338.2	314	3	.990	10	21	4	2	0	19	20	.487	159	4.23	187	26	5	2	3	.16	0	-1	1	0	1	1	-

A.J. Pierzynski

	BASIC								BUNTS			PITCHER HANDLING						STOLEN BASES						RUNS SAVED					
Year	Team	G	Inn	TC	E	Pct	GFP	DM	Opps	Sac Hits	Bunt Hits	W	L	Pct	ER	CERA	Pitch Block	SB	CCS	PCS	CPO	CS%	SB Saved	Adj ER	SB	Bunt	GFP/DME	Total	Rank
2003	Min	135	1165.2	895	6	.993	-	-	8	3	0	75	56	.573	537	4.15	-	46	17	3	0	.27	-2	6	-1	1	-	6	4
2004	SF	118	1022.0	754	1	.999	9	40	13	7	1	65	52	.556	488	4.30	200	51	11	4	0	.18	-5	2	-3	0	-1	-2	17
2005	CWS	128	1117.2	852	1	.999	6	30	8	3	1	77	47	.621	464	3.74	109	79	20	3	1	.20	-1	-5	0	1	7	3	10
2006	CWS	132	1125.0	860	3	.997	1	47	4	1	0	74	52	.587	559	4.47	231	90	21	4	0	.19	-2	5	-2	0	-6	-3	27
2007	CWS	130	1058.0	844	2	.998	11	35	4	4	0	54	62	.466	519	4.41	234	62	12	8	0	.16	1	7	0	0	-3	4	9
2008	CWS	131	1134.1	976	9	.991	7	35	6	2	0	67	60	.528	533	4.23	269	96	11	10	0	.10	-4	-5	-3	1	-2	-9	34
2009	CWS	131	1104.0	934	5	.995	5	47	5	3	0	63	61	.508	503	4.10	314	99	20	10	1	.17	1	1	1	0	-7	-5	25
2010	CWS	127	1092.2	931	5	.995	5	47	12	3	2	68	55	.553	479	3.95	356	75	16	11	2	.18	2	4	2	0	-6	0	17
2011	CWS	120	1008.0	886	4	.995	7	48	12	6	4	54	58	.482	453	4.04	405	94	14	10	0	.13	-4	-2	-3	-1	-9	-9	33
		1152	9827.1	7932	36	.995	51	329	72	32	8	597	503	.543	4535	4.15	2118	692	142	63	4	.17	-14	13	-9	2	-21	-15	30

Buster Posey

	BASIC								BUNTS			PITCHER HANDLING						STOLEN BASES						RUNS SAVED					
Year	Team	G	Inn	TC	E	Pct	GFP	DM	Opps	Sac Hits	Bunt Hits	W	L	Pct	ER	CERA	Pitch Block	SB	CCS	PCS	CPO	CS%	SB Saved	Adj ER	SB	Bunt	GFP/DME	Total	Rank
2009	SF	7	40.0	36	0	1.000	0	2				1	3	.250	16	3.60	13	1	1	0	0	.50	0	0	0		0	0	-
2010	SF	76	662.0	662	6	.991	8	23	3	2	0	46	29	.613	234	3.18	250	39	18	5	0	.32	6	1	4	1	2	8	3
2011	SF	41	361.0	359	2	.994	1	13	1	1	0	23	18	.561	134	3.34	133	27	11	4	0	.29	3	0	2	0	1	3	-
		124	1063.0	1057	8	.992	9	38	4	3	0	70	50	.583	384	3.25	396	67	30	9	0	.31	10	1	6	1	3	11	-

Landon Powell

	BASIC								BUNTS			PITCHER HANDLING						STOLEN BASES						RUNS SAVED					
Year	Team	G	Inn	TC	E	Pct	GFP	DM	Opps	Sac Hits	Bunt Hits	W	L	Pct	ER	CERA	Pitch Block	SB	CCS	PCS	CPO	CS%	SB Saved	Adj ER	SB	Bunt	GFP/DME	Total	Rank
2009	Oak	36	274.0	230	3	.987	3	8	1	1	0	14	16	.467	137	4.50	90	11	9	2	1	.45	3	0	3	0	-1	2	-
2010	Oak	38	267.0	212	6	.972	5	5	2	1	1	12	17	.414	132	4.45	76	17	4	5	0	.19	0	-1	0	-2	1	-2	-
2011	Oak	33	273.1	254	2	.992	3	10	1	1	0	18	12	.600	82	2.70	76	16	6	3	0	.27	2	2	1	0	-1	2	-
		107	814.1	696	11	.984	11	23	4	3	1	44	45	.494	351	3.88	242	44	19	10	1	.30	5	1	4	-2	-1	2	-

Humberto Quintero

	BASIC								BUNTS			PITCHER HANDLING						STOLEN BASES						RUNS SAVED					
Year	Team	G	Inn	TC	E	Pct	GFP	DM	Opps	Sac Hits	Bunt Hits	W	L	Pct	ER	CERA	Pitch Block	SB	CCS	PCS	CPO	CS%	SB Saved	Adj ER	SB	Bunt	GFP/DME	Total	Rank
2003	SD	11	58.1	55	1	.982	-	-	2	0	0	0	7	.000	42	6.48	-	2	0	1	1	.00	0	0	0	0	-	0	-
2004	SD	21	171.2	140	0	1.000	2	3	1	0	0	14	5	.737	70	3.67	31	8	1	0	0	.11	-1	0	0	0	1	1	-
2005	Hou	16	124.0	92	1	.989	2	2	1	0	0	9	6	.600	54	3.92	41	7	1	1	1	.13	-3	0	-1	0	1	0	-
2006	Hou	10	56.2	48	0	1.000	0	1				2	5	.286	35	5.56	17	2	3	0	1	.60	2	0	2		0	2	-
2007	Hou	26	151.2	112	2	.982	1	2	2	2	0	5	10	.333	86	5.10	45	8	5	0	0	.38	2	0	1	0	1	2	-
2008	Hou	59	447.0	400	1	.998	5	6	7	3	0	30	22	.577	243	4.89	136	15	7	2	1	.32	1	0	1	0	2	3	-
2009	Hou	59	427.0	399	5	.987	3	15	8	6	0	21	30	.412	206	4.34	209	14	9	3	0	.39	3	1	2	0	1	4	-
2010	Hou	87	653.2	615	5	.992	12	14	14	5	0	41	33	.554	290	3.99	204	35	17	2	7	.33	1	1	4	2	0	7	6
2011	Hou	77	642.0	589	5	.992	7	13	10	3	2	25	48	.342	329	4.61	293	48	11	3	4	.19	-1	1	1	0	4	6	5
		366	2732.0	2450	20	.992	32	56	45	19	2	147	166	.470	1355	4.46	976	139	54	12	15	.28	4	3	10	2	10	25	-

Wilson Ramos

	BASIC								BUNTS			PITCHER HANDLING						STOLEN BASES						RUNS SAVED					
Year	Team	G	Inn	TC	E	Pct	GFP	DM	Opps	Sac Hits	Bunt Hits	W	L	Pct	ER	CERA	Pitch Block	SB	CCS	PCS	CPO	CS%	SB Saved	Adj ER	SB	Bunt	GFP/DME	Total	Rank
2010	2 tms	22	192.1	147	0	1.000	8	5	3	2	0	9	12	.429	79	3.70	78	10	1	0	0	.09	0	0	0	0	1	1	-
2011	Was	108	951.2	744	5	.993	6	42	14	8	1	54	52	.509	394	3.73	386	48	19	4	0	.28	2	-2	1	-1	-3	-5	28
		130	1144.0	891	5	.994	14	47	17	10	1	63	64	.496	473	3.72	464	58	20	4	0	.26	2	-2	1	-1	-2	-4	-

Rene Rivera

	BASIC								BUNTS			PITCHER HANDLING						STOLEN BASES						RUNS SAVED					
Year	Team	G	Inn	TC	E	Pct	GFP	DM	Opps	Sac Hits	Bunt Hits	W	L	Pct	ER	CERA	Pitch Block	SB	CCS	PCS	CPO	CS%	SB Saved	Adj ER	SB	Bunt	GFP/DME	Total	Rank
2004	Sea	2	3.0	4	0	1.000	0	0				0	0	-	0	0.00	-	0	0	0	0	-	0	0	0			0	-
2005	Sea	15	111.0	76	3	.961	1	5	2	1	0	4	8	.333	54	4.38	20	4	1	1	0	.20	0	0	0	0	-1	-1	-
2006	Sea	35	266.0	237	3	.987	2	9	3	2	0	14	16	.467	107	3.62	65	15	5	4	0	.25	0	2	0	-1	0	1	-
2011	Min	44	299.1	250	3	.988	4	9	4	2	0	14	21	.400	130	3.91	126	15	6	4	0	.29	0	2	0	1	0	3	-
		96	679.1	567	9	.984	7	23	9	5	1	32	45	.416	291	3.86	211	34	12	9	0	.26	0	4	0	0	-1	3	-

Catchers

Ivan Rodriguez

		BASIC							BUNTS			PITCHER HANDLING						STOLEN BASES						RUNS SAVED					
Year	Team	G	Inn	TC	E	Pct	GFP	DM	Opps	Sac Hits	Bunt Hits	W	L	Pct	ER	CERA	Pitch Block	SB	CCS	PCS	CPO	CS%	SB Saved	Adj ER	SB	Bunt	GFP/DME	Total	Rank
2003	Fla	138	1132.1	969	8	.992	-	-	11	4	1	80	54	.597	483	3.84	-	40	19	1	2	.32	0	5	1	0	-	6	4
2004	Det	125	1051.0	833	11	.987	12	49	13	6	2	58	66	.468	568	4.86	143	40	16	3	1	.29	-2	2	-1	-1	-7	-7	30
2005	Det	123	1032.2	766	4	.995	11	37	13	3	2	56	65	.463	511	4.45	84	33	26	9	6	.44	11	1	10	0	-5	6	7
2006	Det	123	1054.1	801	2	.998	6	34	7	4	0	73	48	.603	449	3.83	195	25	21	5	1	.46	6	1	5	1	-4	3	6
2007	Det	127	1052.2	890	6	.993	18	53	7	3	0	67	52	.563	515	4.40	246	47	19	2	2	.29	3	5	3	-1	-8	-1	19
2008	2 tms	112	930.0	683	5	.993	7	31	11	4	1	52	53	.495	473	4.58	235	52	23	2	0	.31	0	3	0	1	-1	3	7
2009	2 tms	115	962.0	845	7	.992	24	32	17	6	1	54	54	.500	488	4.57	271	41	19	3	1	.32	5	-6	4	2	-1	-1	19
2010	Was	102	884.0	768	4	.995	10	16	15	8	0	46	56	.451	417	4.25	298	42	19	3	1	.31	3	-4	2	0	4	2	14
2011	Was	37	304.2	266	3	.989	5	13	5	4	1	16	18	.471	111	3.28	106	12	12	1	0	.50	4	1	3	-1	-1	2	-
		1002	8403.2	6821	50	.993	93	265	99	42	8	502	466	.519	4015	4.30	1578	332	174	29	14	.34	29	8	27	1	-23	13	10

David Ross

		BASIC							BUNTS			PITCHER HANDLING						STOLEN BASES						RUNS SAVED					
Year	Team	G	Inn	TC	E	Pct	GFP	DM	Opps	Sac Hits	Bunt Hits	W	L	Pct	ER	CERA	Pitch Block	SB	CCS	PCS	CPO	CS%	SB Saved	Adj ER	SB	Bunt	GFP/DME	Total	Rank
2003	LA	38	314.0	289	4	.986	-	-	2	2	0	16	19	.457	160	4.59	-	29	13	3	0	.31	4	-3	3	-1	-	-1	-
2004	LA	67	451.2	379	3	.992	4	19	7	3	0	25	26	.490	213	4.24	68	27	11	1	2	.29	-1	-1	0	1	-2	-2	-
2005	2 tms	42	304.0	237	3	.987	0	10	10	8	0	14	19	.424	140	4.14	40	6	7	2	0	.54	3	1	2	0	-2	1	-
2006	Cin	75	620.2	521	8	.985	2	22	12	10	1	34	39	.466	294	4.26	96	17	12	2	1	.41	2	2	2	1	-5	0	14
2007	Cin	108	837.1	717	5	.993	10	31	14	5	2	38	60	.388	425	4.57	182	36	23	2	1	.39	6	2	5	-1	-4	2	12
2008	2 tms	54	399.2	378	3	.992	7	17	7	4	0	16	27	.372	227	5.11	128	26	10	0	0	.28	1	-1	1	1	1	2	-
2009	Atl	52	354.0	352	1	.997	4	8	4	2	0	16	20	.444	135	3.43	77	21	16	3	0	.43	6	1	4	1	1	7	-
2010	Atl	57	328.2	302	4	.987	3	12	5	2	1	17	16	.515	115	3.15	89	18	7	1	0	.28	1	1	1	0	-1	1	-
2011	Atl	49	378.2	372	3	.992	5	15	7	7	0	28	14	.667	131	3.11	133	22	10	1	1	.31	3	1	3	0	-1	3	-
		542	3988.2	3547	34	.990	35	134	68	43	4	204	240	.459	1840	4.15	813	202	109	15	5	.35	26	3	21	2	-13	13	10

Carlos Ruiz

		BASIC							BUNTS			PITCHER HANDLING						STOLEN BASES						RUNS SAVED					
Year	Team	G	Inn	TC	E	Pct	GFP	DM	Opps	Sac Hits	Bunt Hits	W	L	Pct	ER	CERA	Pitch Block	SB	CCS	PCS	CPO	CS%	SB Saved	Adj ER	SB	Bunt	GFP/DME	Total	Rank
2006	Phi	24	176.1	161	3	.981	1	9	4	3	0	9	9	.500	81	4.13	52	11	2	1	1	.15	-1	0	0	-1	-1	-2	-
2007	Phi	111	912.2	744	2	.997	16	25	16	10	0	58	42	.580	465	4.59	270	57	19	7	4	.25	1	3	2	1	2	8	6
2008	Phi	110	828.0	686	5	.993	11	24	20	11	1	55	37	.598	354	3.85	310	65	14	6	2	.18	-3	0	-1	1	3	3	7
2009	Phi	107	882.1	759	3	.996	13	20	8	4	0	57	43	.570	392	4.00	271	61	15	8	0	.20	0	4	0	1	5	10	1
2010	Phi	118	974.1	880	6	.993	7	15	12	6	2	70	39	.642	360	3.33	275	50	18	2	1	.26	2	5	2	-1	1	7	6
2011	Phi	128	1051.0	1022	4	.996	15	16	19	10	1	70	43	.619	357	3.06	351	77	18	5	1	.19	-3	-4	-2	1	5	0	12
		598	4824.2	4252	23	.995	63	109	79	44	4	319	213	.600	2009	3.75	1529	321	86	29	9	.21	-4	8	1	2	15	26	4

Jarrod Saltalamacchia

		BASIC							BUNTS			PITCHER HANDLING						STOLEN BASES						RUNS SAVED					
Year	Team	G	Inn	TC	E	Pct	GFP	DM	Opps	Sac Hits	Bunt Hits	W	L	Pct	ER	CERA	Pitch Block	SB	CCS	PCS	CPO	CS%	SB Saved	Adj ER	SB	Bunt	GFP/DME	Total	Rank
2007	2 tms	47	372.2	285	3	.989	7	23	3	2	0	19	23	.452	197	4.76	139	37	6	2	0	.14	-3	-1	-2	0	0	-3	-
2008	Tex	54	464.1	371	9	.976	5	21	4	0	2	26	26	.500	265	5.14	146	40	7	2	0	.15	-6	0	-5	-1	0	-6	-
2009	Tex	83	714.0	537	7	.987	4	27	6	2	1	46	36	.561	324	4.08	231	61	17	2	0	.22	-1	5	-1	0	-1	3	12
2010	2 tms	7	52.2	49	1	.980	0	0	1	1	0	1	5	.167	25	4.27	11	6	1	0	0	.14	0	0	0	0	-1	-1	-
2011	Bos	101	856.0	740	6	.992	9	50	10	3	2	47	49	.490	439	4.62	274	83	28	9	0	.25	6	-2	4	-1	-5	-4	22
		292	2459.2	1982	26	.987	25	121	24	8	5	139	139	.500	1250	4.57	801	227	59	15	0	.21	-5	2	-4	-2	-7	-11	

Carlos Santana

		BASIC							BUNTS			PITCHER HANDLING						STOLEN BASES						RUNS SAVED					
Year	Team	G	Inn	TC	E	Pct	GFP	DM	Opps	Sac Hits	Bunt Hits	W	L	Pct	ER	CERA	Pitch Block	SB	CCS	PCS	CPO	CS%	SB Saved	Adj ER	SB	Bunt	GFP/DME	Total	Rank
2010	Cle	40	340.0	270	3	.989	5	16	5	2	1	19	21	.475	167	4.42	120	22	9	3	0	.29	2	-1	1	0	-1	-1	-
2011	Cle	95	786.1	630	7	.989	7	36	5	2	0	44	44	.500	366	4.19	239	56	15	3	1	.21	-2	0	-1	0	-3	-4	22
		135	1126.1	900	10	.989	12	52	10	4	1	63	65	.492	533	4.26	359	78	24	6	1	.24	0	-1	0	0	-4	-5	-

Brian Schneider

		BASIC							BUNTS			PITCHER HANDLING						STOLEN BASES						RUNS SAVED					
Year	Team	G	Inn	TC	E	Pct	GFP	DM	Opps	Sac Hits	Bunt Hits	W	L	Pct	ER	CERA	Pitch Block	SB	CCS	PCS	CPO	CS%	SB Saved	Adj ER	SB	Bunt	GFP/DME	Total	Rank
2003	Mon	98	841.0	709	3	.996	-	-	3	0	0	49	46	.516	351	3.76	-	24	21	6	0	.47	3	2	2	0	-	4	9
2004	Mon	133	1114.0	875	2	.998	14	24	6	4	0	52	73	.416	478	3.86	159	36	33	3	4	.48	10	11	9	1	3	24	1
2005	Was	113	926.2	711	5	.993	17	27	11	7	1	52	53	.495	400	3.88	118	48	29	3	4	.38	5	3	6	0	-5	4	9
2006	Was	123	990.1	752	5	.993	13	26	12	3	2	45	66	.405	581	5.28	235	58	21	4	0	.27	1	-7	1	1	3	-2	24
2007	Was	122	1051.1	761	6	.992	12	38	6	2	0	52	68	.433	560	4.79	404	53	22	2	0	.29	2	-7	1	0	0	-6	27
2008	NYM	109	881.0	787	5	.994	15	35	6	3	2	53	45	.541	402	4.11	246	42	16	5	0	.28	0	-2	0	-1	-3	-6	30
2009	NYM	57	437.1	355	1	.997	5	14	7	5	0	19	33	.365	225	4.63	121	19	9	1	0	.32	1	0	1	0	-1	0	-
2010	Phi	46	333.0	276	2	.993	5	11	2	1	0	18	20	.474	169	4.57	109	30	8	0	0	.21	-2	-1	-1	0	2	0	-
2011	Phi	40	309.0	287	1	.997	0	8	4	4	0	28	8	.778	99	2.88	97	20	3	0	0	.13	-4	1	-3	0	-1	-3	-
		841	6883.2	5513	30	.995	81	183	57	29	5	368	412	.472	3265	4.27	1489	330	162	24	8	.33	16	0	16	1	-2	15	9

Catchers

Kelly Shoppach

Year Team	G	Inn	TC	E	Pct	GFP	DM	Opps	Sac Hits	Bunt Hits	W	L	Pct	ER	CERA	Pitch Block	SB	CCS	PCS	CPO	CS%	SB Saved	Adj ER	SB	Bunt	GFP/DME	Total	Rank
2005 Bos	7	29.0	14	0	1.000		1	2			1	1	.500	16	4.97	1	2	0	0	0	.00	0	0	0		0	0	-
2006 Cle	40	280.1	230	2	.991	6	15	1	0	0	12	19	.387	128	4.11	91	19	10	1	1	.34	3	1	2	0	1	4	-
2007 Cle	58	420.0	319	4	.987	4	21	4	2	0	26	18	.591	194	4.16	115	23	13	0	0	.36	3	2	2	1	-2	3	-
2008 Cle	110	872.2	627	7	.989	9	27	9	3	1	50	44	.532	424	4.37	278	37	10	0	0	.21	-3	-2	-2	1	1	-2	22
2009 Cle	81	672.0	511	4	.992	5	26	5	3	1	32	42	.432	349	4.67	205	49	13	2	0	.21	-4	0	-2	0	-3	-5	25
2010 TB	56	403.2	344	2	.994	8	13	3	1	2	28	18	.609	195	4.35	149	29	6	0	0	.17	-3	-3	-2	-1	1	-5	-
2011 TB	86	625.2	525	3	.994	5	19	4	2	1	39	32	.549	262	3.77	266	26	15	3	1	.37	6	-2	5	-1	1	3	8
	438	3303.1	2570	22	.991	38	123	26	11	5	188	174	.519	1568	4.27	1105	185	67	6	2	.27	1	-4	3	0	-1	-2	20

Chris Snyder

Year Team	G	Inn	TC	E	Pct	GFP	DM	Opps	Sac Hits	Bunt Hits	W	L	Pct	ER	CERA	Pitch Block	SB	CCS	PCS	CPO	CS%	SB Saved	Adj ER	SB	Bunt	GFP/DME	Total	Rank
2004 Ari	29	247.1	232	0	1.000	1	12	2	1	0	11	16	.407	119	4.33	85	13	6	0	0	.32	1	1	1	0	0	2	-
2005 Ari	113	915.2	725	2	.997	11	36	13	5	2	50	55	.476	462	4.54	134	46	12	5	0	.21	1	6	1	0	-4	3	10
2006 Ari	60	495.0	431	2	.995	1	24	6	5	1	24	31	.436	250	4.55	95	21	13	4	0	.38	2	0	1	-1	-3	-3	-
2007 Ari	106	891.1	781	1	.999	8	27	11	7	1	63	40	.612	369	3.73	343	52	18	11	1	.26	2	3	2	0	3	8	6
2008 Ari	112	922.2	846	0	1.000	3	29	13	8	2	59	47	.557	393	3.83	331	49	20	2	0	.29	2	2	1	-1	1	3	7
2009 Ari	56	436.0	384	0	1.000	6	21	8	4	2	19	32	.373	224	4.62	157	26	5	3	1	.16	-2	-1	-1	0	-2	-4	-
2010 2 tms	101	839.1	741	4	.995	3	38	17	9	1	35	61	.365	481	5.16	441	63	14	5	0	.18	-5	0	-3	2	-2	-3	21
2011 Pit	33	265.2	218	0	1.000	0	10	4	2	0	16	14	.533	100	3.39	97	17	5	1	0	.23	-1	1	-1	0	-1	-1	-
	610	5013.0	4358	9	.998	33	197	74	41	9	277	296	.483	2398	4.31	1683	287	93	31	2	.24	1	12	1	0	-8	5	13

Geovany Soto

Year Team	G	Inn	TC	E	Pct	GFP	DM	Opps	Sac Hits	Bunt Hits	W	L	Pct	ER	CERA	Pitch Block	SB	CCS	PCS	CPO	CS%	SB Saved	Adj ER	SB	Bunt	GFP/DME	Total	Rank
2006 ChC	7	55.0	71	1	.986	1	2				2	5	.286	32	5.24	19	5	0	0	0	.00	-1	0	0	0	0	0	-
2007 ChC	16	122.0	119	0	1.000	1	3				10	3	.769	49	3.61	39	10	4	0	0	.29	0	0	0	1	1	1	-
2008 ChC	136	1150.1	1071	5	.995	10	33	6	1	1	80	51	.611	486	3.80	370	69	18	7	0	.21	-6	3	-4	-1	0	-2	22
2009 ChC	96	811.0	775	5	.994	6	29	15	10	0	41	51	.446	360	4.00	265	59	23	0	0	.28	1	-1	1	0	-1	-1	19
2010 ChC	104	847.1	811	4	.995	6	31	4	3	0	49	48	.505	404	4.29	324	74	18	3	0	.20	-6	1	-4	0	0	-3	21
2011 ChC	122	1041.2	994	13	.987	13	36	20	13	0	49	70	.412	499	4.31	371	85	30	6	0	.26	2	-2	1	1	-1	-1	14
	481	4027.1	3841	28	.993	37	134	45	27	1	231	228	.503	1830	4.09	1388	302	93	16	0	.24	-9	1	-6	0	-1	-6	23

Chris Stewart

Year Team	G	Inn	TC	E	Pct	GFP	DM	Opps	Sac Hits	Bunt Hits	W	L	Pct	ER	CERA	Pitch Block	SB	CCS	PCS	CPO	CS%	SB Saved	Adj ER	SB	Bunt	GFP/DME	Total	Rank
2006 CWS	5	15.0	19	0	1.000	0	0				1	0	1.000	8	4.80	1	1	2	0	0	.67	1	0	1		0	1	-
2007 Tex	17	105.1	106	2	.981	0	10				5	6	.455	58	4.96	28	8	4	0	0	.33	0	0	0		-2	-2	-
2008 NYY	1	8.0	8	0	1.000	0	2				0	1	.000	6	6.75	3	1	0	0	0	.00	0	0	0		-1	-1	-
2010 SD	1	1.0	1	0	1.000	0	0				0	0	-	0	0.00	-	0	0	0	0	-	0					0	-
2011 SF	63	460.1	485	7	.986	9	21	6	5	0	27	24	.529	138	2.70	205	34	19	3	2	.36	7	3	6	1	2	12	-
	87	589.2	619	9	.985	9	33	6	5	0	33	31	.516	210	3.21	237	44	25	3	2	.36	8	3	7	1	-1	10	-

Kurt Suzuki

Year Team	G	Inn	TC	E	Pct	GFP	DM	Opps	Sac Hits	Bunt Hits	W	L	Pct	ER	CERA	Pitch Block	SB	CCS	PCS	CPO	CS%	SB Saved	Adj ER	SB	Bunt	GFP/DME	Total	Rank
2007 Oak	66	539.0	465	2	.996	4	20	6	4	2	27	34	.443	318	5.31	261	29	7	0	0	.19	0	-7	0	-1	1	-7	30
2008 Oak	141	1215.0	986	6	.994	18	21	3	0	0	64	72	.471	521	3.86	425	55	16	16	0	.23	3	3	2	0	5	10	3
2009 Oak	135	1173.1	996	5	.995	27	39	6	5	0	61	71	.462	553	4.24	507	81	17	10	0	.17	-3	1	-2	0	7	6	7
2010 Oak	123	1058.1	868	8	.991	17	32	8	2	1	65	56	.537	387	3.29	389	66	10	9	0	.13	-3	6	-2	1	3	8	3
2011 Oak	129	1132.1	976	7	.993	20	48	8	3	2	55	72	.433	476	3.78	471	98	23	15	1	.19	0	-4	1	0	2	-1	14
	594	5118.0	4291	28	.993	86	160	31	14	5	272	305	.471	2255	3.97	2053	329	73	50	1	.18	-3	-1	-1	0	18	16	8

Craig Tatum

Year Team	G	Inn	TC	E	Pct	GFP	DM	Opps	Sac Hits	Bunt Hits	W	L	Pct	ER	CERA	Pitch Block	SB	CCS	PCS	CPO	CS%	SB Saved	Adj ER	SB	Bunt	GFP/DME	Total	Rank
2009 Cin	26	173.0	148	1	.993	2	3	4	3	0	8	11	.421	83	4.32	52	7	3	1	0	.30	1	0	0	0	1	1	-
2010 Bal	42	310.2	242	3	.988	3	9	5	3	0	17	17	.500	157	4.55	140	25	2	0	0	.07	-3	0	-2	1	1	0	-
2011 Bal	30	239.2	226	3	.987	6	6	4	1	0	10	17	.370	159	5.97	121	20	8	0	0	.29	-1	-1	0	3	3	3	-
	98	723.1	616	7	.989	11	18	13	7	0	35	45	.438	399	4.96	313	52	13	1	0	.20	-1	-1	-1	1	5	4	-

Josh Thole

Year Team	G	Inn	TC	E	Pct	GFP	DM	Opps	Sac Hits	Bunt Hits	W	L	Pct	ER	CERA	Pitch Block	SB	CCS	PCS	CPO	CS%	SB Saved	Adj ER	SB	Bunt	GFP/DME	Total	Rank
2009 NYM	16	127.1	76	1	.987	0	6				7	8	.467	60	4.24	24	4	1	1	0	.20	0	0	0	0	-1	-1	-
2010 NYM	61	467.1	373	3	.992	6	17	14	6	3	21	30	.412	185	3.56	118	14	8	3	0	.36	1	-1	0	0	-2	-3	-
2011 NYM	102	793.1	703	2	.997	9	31	16	13	0	45	46	.495	373	4.23	284	65	14	3	0	.18	-6	-1	-4	0	1	-4	22
	179	1388.0	1152	6	.995	15	54	30	19	3	73	84	.465	618	4.01	426	83	23	7	0	.22	-5	-2	-4	0	-2	-8	-

Catchers

Yorvit Torrealba

Year Team	G	Inn	TC	E	Pct	GFP	DM	Opps	Sac Hits	Bunt Hits	W	L	Pct	ER	CERA	Pitch Block	SB	CCS	PCS	CPO	CS%	SB Saved	Adj ER	SB	Bunt	GFP/DME	Total	Rank
2003 SF	66	495.2	395	1	.997	-	-	9	5	1	31	21	.596	228	4.14	-	22	14	5	1	.39	3	-2	2	0	-	0	-
2004 SF	59	433.0	369	2	.995	6	22	9	4	0	26	19	.578	215	4.47	130	21	6	3	0	.22	-1	-1	-1	2	0	0	-
2005 2 tms	68	536.2	406	0	1.000	7	12	6	3	0	25	35	.417	271	4.54	65	36	15	5	0	.29	-1	-1	-1	1	1	0	16
2006 Col	63	530.0	376	5	.987	4	10	9	8	0	20	41	.328	277	4.70	89	31	16	5	0	.34	6	-2	4	0	0	2	8
2007 Col	112	935.1	742	7	.991	14	24	33	16	2	56	49	.533	428	4.12	252	61	13	2	1	.18	0	6	0	2	0	8	6
2008 Col	67	581.0	461	2	.996	0	21	6	3	1	27	37	.422	331	5.13	170	45	12	4	0	.21	1	-2	1	-2	-2	-5	29
2009 Col	64	545.1	532	0	1.000	8	19	11	7	1	36	25	.590	265	4.37	208	49	4	4	1	.08	-6	0	-3	0	1	-2	-
2010 SD	92	795.2	729	3	.996	7	15	8	3	1	53	36	.596	278	3.14	252	38	13	9	0	.25	1	6	1	-1	2	8	3
2011 Tex	98	823.2	732	9	.988	8	28	13	6	2	49	46	.516	394	4.31	251	56	21	6	0	.27	-1	-5	-1	-4	-2	-12	35
	689	5676.1	4742	29	.994	54	151	104	55	8	323	309	.511	2687	4.26	1417	359	114	43	3	.24	2	-1	2	-2	0	-1	19

J.R. Towles

Year Team	G	Inn	TC	E	Pct	GFP	DM	Opps	Sac Hits	Bunt Hits	W	L	Pct	ER	CERA	Pitch Block	SB	CCS	PCS	CPO	CS%	SB Saved	Adj ER	SB	Bunt	GFP/DME	Total	Rank
2007 Hou	14	95.0	71	0	1.000	2	3				7	2	.778	45	4.26	42	3	3	0	0	.50	1	0	1			1	-
2008 Hou	53	408.2	327	2	.994	3	10	1	0	0	24	23	.511	217	4.78	162	13	5	2	0	.28	-1	0	-1	0	0	-1	
2009 Hou	15	114.0	91	0	1.000	2	1	2	2	0	5	9	.357	71	5.61	45	10	1	0	0	.09	-2	0	-1	0	1	0	
2010 Hou	15	116.2	100	1	.990	0	3	1	1	0	4	9	.308	58	4.47	48	8	3	0	0	.27	0	0	0	0	0	0	
2011 Hou	51	365.2	312	6	.981	4	6	5	4	0	16	25	.390	198	4.87	165	38	6	2	0	.14	-3	-1	-2	1	3	1	
	148	1100.0	901	9	.990	11	23	9	7	0	56	68	.452	589	4.82	462	72	18	4	0	.20	-5	-1	-3	1	4	1	-

Matt Treanor

Year Team	G	Inn	TC	E	Pct	GFP	DM	Opps	Sac Hits	Bunt Hits	W	L	Pct	ER	CERA	Pitch Block	SB	CCS	PCS	CPO	CS%	SB Saved	Adj ER	SB	Bunt	GFP/DME	Total	Rank
2004 Fla	27	147.2	126	3	.976	0	4	2	1	1	6	8	.429	72	4.39	21	11	3	0	0	.21	-1	0	0	-1	-1	-2	-
2005 Fla	55	366.2	328	5	.985	4	10	6	1	1	21	20	.512	195	4.79	62	24	9	0	0	.27	2	-1	1	0	1	1	-
2006 Fla	61	439.2	403	3	.993	4	6	4	3	0	26	24	.520	205	4.20	158	18	13	3	0	.42	-3	4	0	3	4	7	-
2007 Fla	53	440.2	404	3	.993	9	19	7	3	1	23	27	.460	230	4.70	150	42	6	1	1	.13	2	-2	0	1	1	1	-
2008 Fla	65	524.2	490	8	.984	7	15	8	4	2	31	29	.517	269	4.61	203	44	12	3	0	.21	-1	1	-1	-2	3	1	16
2009 Det	4	32.0	28	0	1.000	1	2				1	3	.250	14	5.91	19	4	0	0	0	.00	-1	0	-1		0	-1	-
2010 Tex	81	614.2	536	3	.994	5	23	5	1	2	42	25	.627	268	3.92	170	44	11	6	0	.20	-2	1	-1	-1	-2	-3	21
2011 2 tms	72	565.2	447	4	.991	9	36	5	2	2	30	34	.469	284	4.52	220	42	11	3	0	.21	0	2	0	-2	-2	-2	18
	418	3131.2	2762	29	.990	38	115	37	15	9	180	170	.514	1544	4.44	1003	229	65	16	1	.22	-2	5	-1	-6	4	2	16

Jason Varitek

Year Team	G	Inn	TC	E	Pct	GFP	DM	Opps	Sac Hits	Bunt Hits	W	L	Pct	ER	CERA	Pitch Block	SB	CCS	PCS	CPO	CS%	SB Saved	Adj ER	SB	Bunt	GFP/DME	Total	Rank
2003 Bos	137	1075.1	906	9	.990	-	-	3	1	0	73	46	.613	539	4.51	-	61	19	4	0	.24	1	-5	-1	0	-	-4	31
2004 Bos	130	1062.2	931	2	.998	10	16	6	3	1	73	48	.603	494	4.18	227	77	20	3	2	.21	-3	-3	-1	0	4	0	11
2005 Bos	130	1089.0	824	8	.990	19	38	4	1	0	73	54	.575	609	5.03	265	65	16	5	1	.20	-9	-10	-6	0	8	-8	30
2006 Bos	99	822.1	679	4	.994	5	20	3	0	1	58	36	.617	442	4.84	289	46	10	3	0	.18	-4	0	-3	0	2	-1	19
2007 Bos	125	1064.0	982	6	.994	5	10	7	0	2	73	48	.603	449	3.80	367	63	19	1	0	.23	-3	-2	-2	-1	4	-1	19
2008 Bos	131	1041.1	949	4	.996	6	24	7	5	0	73	47	.608	424	3.66	356	56	13	3	0	.19	-3	3	-2	0	1	2	14
2009 Bos	108	924.0	896	3	.997	7	22	8	3	1	61	45	.575	397	3.87	374	108	10	6	0	.08	-12	8	-8	1	6	7	4
2010 Bos	39	275.1	255	0	1.000	1	5	3	1	0	18	9	.667	124	4.05	90	34	8	1	0	.19	0	1	0	0	2	3	-
2011 Bos	68	574.2	551	4	.993	2	24	3	0	1	42	22	.656	228	3.57	283	73	10	2	0	.12	-7	2	-5	0	2	-1	14
	967	7928.2	6973	40	.994	55	159	44	14	6	544	355	.605	3706	4.21	2251	583	125	28	3	.18	-40	-6	-26	0	29	-3	21

Eli Whiteside

Year Team	G	Inn	TC	E	Pct	GFP	DM	Opps	Sac Hits	Bunt Hits	W	L	Pct	ER	CERA	Pitch Block	SB	CCS	PCS	CPO	CS%	SB Saved	Adj ER	SB	Bunt	GFP/DME	Total	Rank
2005 Bal	9	32.2	27	2	.926	0	1				2	1	.667	14	3.86	7	3	1	0	0	.25	0	0	0	0	-	0	-
2009 SF	47	314.0	316	5	.984	4	14	6	3	1	21	12	.636	105	3.01	111	20	8	5	1	.29	2	2	2	-1	-2	1	-
2010 SF	55	340.2	362	6	.994	4	25	4	2	0	18	14	.563	134	3.54	157	29	9	3	0	.24	1	0	1	1	-2	0	-
2011 SF	81	583.2	541	5	.991	9	23	4	1	0	33	31	.516	214	3.30	203	53	13	5	0	.20	-2	-2	-1	1	0	-2	18
	192	1271.0	1246	14	.989	16	63	14	6	1	74	58	.561	467	3.31	478	105	31	13	1	.23	2	0	2	1	-4	-1	-

Matt Wieters

Year Team	G	Inn	TC	E	Pct	GFP	DM	Opps	Sac Hits	Bunt Hits	W	L	Pct	ER	CERA	Pitch Block	SB	CCS	PCS	CPO	CS%	SB Saved	Adj ER	SB	Bunt	GFP/DME	Total	Rank
2009 Bal	86	738.1	529	5	.991	10	25	9	3	2	27	57	.321	413	5.03	242	65	18	3	0	.22	-3	1	-2	0	3	2	14
2010 Bal	126	1060.1	831	5	.994	9	29	17	6	0	48	73	.397	537	4.56	333	53	21	3	2	.28	6	0	5	2	0	7	6
2011 Bal	132	1150.0	930	5	.995	12	35	14	9	1	57	72	.442	583	4.56	435	58	32	2	0	.36	7	9	5	1	2	17	1
	344	2948.2	2290	15	.993	31	89	40	18	3	132	202	.395	1533	4.68	1010	176	71	8	2	.29	10	10	8	3	5	26	4

Catchers

Bobby Wilson

		BASIC							BUNTS			PITCHER HANDLING						STOLEN BASES						RUNS SAVED					
Year	Team	G	Inn	TC	E	Pct	GFP	DM	Opps	Sac Hits	Bunt Hits	W	L	Pct	ER	CERA	Pitch Block	SB	CCS	PCS	CPO	CS%	SB Saved	Adj ER	SB	Bunt	GFP/ DME	Total	Rank
2008	LAA	7	16.0	16	0	1.000	0	0				0	0	-	6	3.38	8	0	0	0	0	-	0	0	0		0	0	-
2009	LAA	11	24.0	20	0	1.000	0	1				0	0	-	8	3.00	15	1	0	0	0	.00	0	0	0		0	0	-
2010	LAA	38	260.2	230	1	.996	0	9	2	1	0	18	11	.621	105	3.63	105	26	6	2	0	.19	-1	1	-1	0	0	0	-
2011	LAA	47	317.0	266	1	.996	4	14	3	1	0	17	18	.486	137	3.89	195	25	8	2	1	.24	0	-1	1	1	2	3	-
		103	617.2	532	2	.996	4	24	5	2	0	35	29	.547	256	3.73	323	52	14	4	1	.21	-1	0	0	1	2	3	-

First Basemen

Brandon Allen

		BASIC							BUNTS			GDP			PLUS/MINUS								RUNS SAVED					
Year	Team	G	Inn	TC	E	Pct	GFP	DM	Opp	Sac Hits	Bunt Hits	Opp	GDP	Pct	Outs Made	To His Right	Straight On	To His Left	GB	Air	Total	Enhanced	+/-	Bunt	GDP	GFP/DME	Total	Rank
2009	Ari	32	254.2	273	2	.993	7	9	3	3	0	2	0	.000	45	0	-3	-2	-5	0	-5	-6	-4	0		-1	-5	-
2010	Ari	4	17.1	14	0	1.000	0	0				0	0		3	0	0	0	0	0	0	0	0			0	0	-
2011	2 tms	51	440.1	439	4	.991	19	13	5	4	1	5	3	.600	100	-1	+2	-1	0	0	0	0	0	0	0	-1	-1	17
		87	712.1	726	6	.992	26	22	8	7	1	7	3	.429	148	-1	-1	-3	-5	0	-5	-6	-4	0	0	-2	-6	

Daric Barton

		BASIC							BUNTS			GDP			PLUS/MINUS								RUNS SAVED					
Year	Team	G	Inn	TC	E	Pct	GFP	DM	Opp	Sac Hits	Bunt Hits	Opp	GDP	Pct	Outs Made	To His Right	Straight On	To His Left	GB	Air	Total	Enhanced	+/-	Bunt	GDP	GFP/DME	Total	Rank
2007	Oak	18	157.2	160	0	1.000	2	4	1	1	0	-	-	-	30	+2	+1	+1	+4	+1	+5	+5	4	0	-	-1	3	-
2008	Oak	134	1121.2	1107	13	.988	51	20	7	3	2	-	-	-	206	0	+2	+5	+7	-2	+5	+7	5	0	-	-1	4	11
2009	Oak	51	416.2	444	1	.998	25	8	4	3	0	8	4	.500	94	+1	0	+1	+2	0	+2	+3	2	0	0	1	3	11
2010	Oak	157	1333.2	1492	10	.993	85	19	13	8	2	23	9	.391	269	+9	+7	+6	+20	0	+20	+22	16	1	0	1	18	1
2011	Oak	65	568.1	643	8	.988	40	11	8	5	0	6	3	.500	141	-2	+4	+3	+2	0	+2	+5	4	0	0	0	4	11
		425	3598.0	3846	32	.992	203	62	33	20	4	37	16	.432	740	+10	+14	+16	+35	-1	+34	+42	31	1	0	0	32	5

Brandon Belt

		BASIC							BUNTS			GDP			PLUS/MINUS								RUNS SAVED					
Year	Team	G	Inn	TC	E	Pct	GFP	DM	Opp	Sac Hits	Bunt Hits	Opp	GDP	Pct	Outs Made	To His Right	Straight On	To His Left	GB	Air	Total	Enhanced	+/-	Bunt	GDP	GFP/DME	Total	Rank
2011	SF	31	203.0	214	1	.995	9	3	1	0	0	1	1	1.000	32	0	+1	+1	+1	0	+1	+1	1	0	0	1	2	-

Miguel Cabrera

		BASIC							BUNTS			GDP			PLUS/MINUS								RUNS SAVED					
Year	Team	G	Inn	TC	E	Pct	GFP	DM	Opp	Sac Hits	Bunt Hits	Opp	GDP	Pct	Outs Made	To His Right	Straight On	To His Left	GB	Air	Total	Enhanced	+/-	Bunt	GDP	GFP/DME	Total	Rank
2008	Det	143	1204.0	1199	9	.992	38	24	3	1	1	-	-	-	219	-4	-5	+3	-7	1	-8	-6	-4	0	-	-3	-7	30
2009	Det	153	1315.0	1327	7	.995	68	26	10	5	3	26	8	.308	280	+1	-4	+4	+1	-1	0	+2	1	-1	0	-1	-1	21
2010	Det	148	1285.1	1327	13	.990	52	17	13	6	3	22	8	.364	245	-10	+3	0	-6	+1	-5	-6	-4	-1	0	0	-5	27
2011	Det	152	1322.0	1379	13	.991	52	15	11	5	4	23	13	.565	226	-7	0	+1	-7	-2	-9	-7	-5	-1	1	2	-3	25
		596	5126.1	5232	42	.992	210	82	37	17	11	71	29	.408	970	-20	-6	+8	-19	-3	-22	-17	-12	-3	1	-2	-16	28

Mike Carp

		BASIC							BUNTS			GDP			PLUS/MINUS								RUNS SAVED					
Year	Team	G	Inn	TC	E	Pct	GFP	DM	Opp	Sac Hits	Bunt Hits	Opp	GDP	Pct	Outs Made	To His Right	Straight On	To His Left	GB	Air	Total	Enhanced	+/-	Bunt	GDP	GFP/DME	Total	Rank
2009	Sea	16	127.1	130	0	1.000	6	1	1	0	1	4	2	.500	36	0	+1	+1	+2	0	+2	+2	1	0	0	1	2	-
2010	Sea	9	66.0	69	0	1.000	3	0				0	0		10	0	0	0	0	0	0	+1	0	0	0	0	0	-
2011	Sea	34	263.2	269	2	.993	13	7	3	1	0	3	1	.333	47	+2	-3	0	-1	-1	-2	-2	-1	0	0	0	-1	-
		59	457.0	468	2	.996	22	8	4	1	1	7	3	.429	93	+2	-2	+1	+1	-1	0	+1	0	0	0	1	1	-

Michael Cuddyer

		BASIC							BUNTS			GDP			PLUS/MINUS								RUNS SAVED					
Year	Team	G	Inn	TC	E	Pct	GFP	DM	Opp	Sac Hits	Bunt Hits	Opp	GDP	Pct	Outs Made	To His Right	Straight On	To His Left	GB	Air	Total	Enhanced	+/-	Bunt	GDP	GFP/DME	Total	Rank
2003	Min	5	27.0	32	1	.969	-	-	2	0	1	-	-	-	5				-2	0	-2	-3	-2	0	-	-	-2	-
2004	Min	10	35.0	36	0	1.000	0	0				-	-	-	9	+1	-1	0	+1	0	+1	+1	1		-	0	1	-
2005	Min	8	33.0	37	0	1.000	1	0				-	-	-	7	0	0	0	0	0	0	0	0		-	0	0	-
2006	Min	6	52.0	51	0	1.000	0	3				-	-	-	11	-1	+1	-1	-1	0	-1	-1	-1		-	0	-1	-
2007	Min	4	39.0	34	0	1.000	1	0	2	2	0	-	-	-	5	0	+1	0	+2	0	+2	+2	1	0	-	0	1	-
2008	Min	2	18.0	24	1	.958	0	0				-	-	-	3	-1	+1	0	0	0	0	0	0		-	0	1	-
2009	Min	34	296.0	296	4	.986	14	8	5	0	3	2	0	.000	50	+1	0	0	+2	0	+2	+1	1	0	0	-1	0	-
2010	Min	84	721.1	802	3	.996	34	22	5	1	1	4	1	.250	121	-5	+1	-3	-7	0	-7	-7	-5	0	0	-3	-8	28
2011	Min	46	352.2	380	2	.995	11	2	3	2	1	3	0	.000	72	0	+2	-1	+1	-1	0	+1	1	0	0	1	1	-
		199	1574.0	1692	11	.993	61	35	17	5	6	9	1	.111	283	-5	+5	-5	-4	-1	-5	-6	-5	0	0	-3	-8	

Chris Davis

		BASIC							BUNTS			GDP			PLUS/MINUS								RUNS SAVED					
Year	Team	G	Inn	TC	E	Pct	GFP	DM	Opp	Sac Hits	Bunt Hits	Opp	GDP	Pct	Outs Made	To His Right	Straight On	To His Left	GB	Air	Total	Enhanced	+/-	Bunt	GDP	GFP/DME	Total	Rank
2008	Tex	51	404.0	393	1	.997	22	10	3	2	0	-	-	-	78	-2	0	-2	-3	+1	-2	-3	-2	0	-	1	-1	18
2009	Tex	100	825.1	895	3	.997	55	18	2	1	1	8	3	.375	166	-2	-3	+1	-5	-1	-6	-6	-4	0	0	1	-3	27
2010	Tex	41	298.2	293	2	.993	17	4	2	2	0	4	0	.000	53	+1	0	0	+1	+1	+2	+3	2	0	0	0	2	-
2011	2 tms	31	221.2	240	0	1.000	7	5	2	0	0	2	1	.500	36	0	-2	-2	-3	0	-3	-4	-3	1	0	0	-2	-
		223	1749.2	1821	6	.997	101	37	9	5	1	14	4	.286	333	-3	-5	-3	-10	+1	-9	-10	-7	1	0	2	-4	19

Ike Davis

		BASIC							BUNTS			GDP			PLUS/MINUS								RUNS SAVED					
Year	Team	G	Inn	TC	E	Pct	GFP	DM	Opp	Sac Hits	Bunt Hits	Opp	GDP	Pct	Outs Made	To His Right	Straight On	To His Left	GB	Air	Total	Enhanced	+/-	Bunt	GDP	GFP/DME	Total	Rank
2010	NYM	146	1263.0	1353	9	.993	44	16	28	16	3	16	11	.688	234	+5	+7	+1	+13	+1	+14	+14	10	1	1	0	12	2
2011	NYM	36	317.0	322	1	.997	8	12	4	4	0	5	0	.000	74	+2	+1	0	+1	+1	+2	+3	2	0	0	-1	1	-
		182	1580.0	1675	10	.994	52	28	32	20	3	21	11	.524	308	+7	+8	+1	+14	+2	+16	+17	12	1	1	-1	13	

First Basemen

Lucas Duda

Year	Team	G	Inn	TC	E	Pct	GFP	DM	Opp	Sac Hits	Bunt Hits	Opp GDP	GDP	Pct	Outs Made	To His Right	Straight On	To His Left	GB	Air	Total	Enhanced	+/-	Bunt	GDP	GFP/DME	Total	Rank
2011	NYM	43	323.1	367	2	.995	15	8	6	3	1	4	2	.500	69	-1	+1	-1	-1	0	-1	-1	0	1	0	-1	0	

Adam Dunn

Year	Team	G	Inn	TC	E	Pct	GFP	DM	Opp	Sac Hits	Bunt Hits	Opp GDP	GDP	Pct	Outs Made	To His Right	Straight On	To His Left	GB	Air	Total	Enhanced	+/-	Bunt	GDP	GFP/DME	Total	Rank
2003	Cin	19	84.2	90	1	.989	-	-	2	1	1	-	-	-	21	-1	+1	0	0	0	0	0	0	0	-	-	0	-
2004	Cin	10	58.2	80	0	1.000	2	1				-	-	-	14	0	+1	0	0	0	0	0	0	0	-	0	0	-
2005	Cin	33	251.1	259	4	.985	9	4	3	1	1	-	-	-	40	0	-2	-2	-4	0	-4	-4	-3	0	-	-1	-4	
2006	Cin	2	17.0	17	1	.941	1	1				-	-	-	4				-1	0	-1	-1	-1		-	0	-1	
2008	Ari	19	128.0	133	3	.977	3	3	4	3	1	-	-	-	20	-2	-2	0	-4	0	-4	-4	-3	-1	-	-1	-5	-
2009	Was	67	540.0	576	8	.986	18	22	11	9	2	1	1	1.000	95	-8	-11	-3	-22	-2	-24	-24	-18	-1	0	-4	-23	35
2010	Was	153	1246.0	1309	13	.990	38	17	23	15	2	11	4	.364	213	-5	-3	-4	-12	0	-12	-12	-9	1	-1	-2	-11	31
2011	CWS	35	284.2	287	4	.986	9	7	2	1	1	3	3	1.000	39	-1	0	-1	-3	0	-3	-3	-2	-1	0	-1	-4	
		338	2610.1	2751	34	.988	80	55	45	30	8	15	8	.533	446	-17	-16	-10	-46	-2	-48	-48	-36	-2	-1	-9	-48	34

Nick Evans

Year	Team	G	Inn	TC	E	Pct	GFP	DM	Opp	Sac Hits	Bunt Hits	Opp GDP	GDP	Pct	Outs Made	To His Right	Straight On	To His Left	GB	Air	Total	Enhanced	+/-	Bunt	GDP	GFP/DME	Total	Rank
2008	NYM	3	12.0	7	0	1.000	1	1				-	-	-	1				0	0	0	0	0		-	0	0	-
2009	NYM	5	38.0	39	1	.974	2	2	1	1	0	1	0	.000	8	+1	-1	0	0	0	0	0	0	0	0	0	0	-
2011	NYM	45	337.2	398	2	.992	24	2	12	9	0	5	0	.000	71	+1	+5	0	+7	+2	+9	+8	7	1	-1	2	9	
		53	387.2	444	4	.991	27	5	13	10	0	6	0	.000	80	+2	+4	0	+7	+2	+9	+8	7	1	-1	2	9	-

Prince Fielder

Year	Team	G	Inn	TC	E	Pct	GFP	DM	Opp	Sac Hits	Bunt Hits	Opp GDP	GDP	Pct	Outs Made	To His Right	Straight On	To His Left	GB	Air	Total	Enhanced	+/-	Bunt	GDP	GFP/DME	Total	Rank
2005	Mil	7	34.0	30	0	1.000	2	0	1	1	0	-	-	-	6				0	0	0	0	0	0	-	0	0	-
2006	Mil	152	1319.1	1358	11	.992	28	34	37	20	8	-	-	-	241	0	-6	-8	-15	-2	-17	-18	-13	-3	-	-6	-22	35
2007	Mil	153	1338.0	1276	14	.989	43	30	19	10	4	-	-	-	252	-4	-8	-4	-16	+1	-15	-15	-11	-3	-	-1	-15	34
2008	Mil	155	1383.2	1475	17	.988	54	30	26	15	2	-	-	-	257	-1	-4	-7	-12	-1	-13	-12	-9	1	-	-4	-12	34
2009	Mil	162	1431.0	1460	7	.995	64	23	16	9	4	12	6	.500	260	0	-4	0	-5	+2	-3	-3	-2	-1	0	2	0	20
2010	Mil	160	1411.0	1341	4	.997	46	22	16	7	3	16	4	.250	235	+4	-9	-9	-14	-5	-19	-20	-15	0	0	-2	-17	35
2011	Mil	159	1394.2	1431	15	.990	48	27	12	7	1	17	7	.412	253	-3	-5	-2	-9	0	-9	-9	-7	0	0	-2	-9	32
		948	8311.2	8371	68	.992	285	166	127	69	22	45	17	.378	1504	-4	-36	-31	-71	-5	-76	-76	-56	-6	0	-13	-75	35

Freddie Freeman

Year	Team	G	Inn	TC	E	Pct	GFP	DM	Opp	Sac Hits	Bunt Hits	Opp GDP	GDP	Pct	Outs Made	To His Right	Straight On	To His Left	GB	Air	Total	Enhanced	+/-	Bunt	GDP	GFP/DME	Total	Rank
2010	Atl	12	39.0	41	0	1.000	4	0				0	0	-	8	0	+1	0	0	0	0	0	0		0	0	0	-
2011	Atl	156	1370.1	1415	6	.996	70	24	15	10	3	8	1	.125	234	-2	-4	+1	-6	+1	-5	-5	-3	0	0	1	-2	21
		168	1409.1	1456	6	.996	74	24	15	10	3	8	1	.125	242	-2	-3	+1	-6	+1	-5	-5	-3	0	0	1	-2	

Paul Goldschmidt

Year	Team	G	Inn	TC	E	Pct	GFP	DM	Opp	Sac Hits	Bunt Hits	Opp GDP	GDP	Pct	Outs Made	To His Right	Straight On	To His Left	GB	Air	Total	Enhanced	+/-	Bunt	GDP	GFP/DME	Total	Rank
2011	Ari	43	368.0	373	0	1.000	29	7	2	0	2	6	2	.333	60	-2	-1	-1	-4	-2	-6	-6	-5	-1	0	3	-3	-

Adrian Gonzalez

Year	Team	G	Inn	TC	E	Pct	GFP	DM	Opp	Sac Hits	Bunt Hits	Opp GDP	GDP	Pct	Outs Made	To His Right	Straight On	To His Left	GB	Air	Total	Enhanced	+/-	Bunt	GDP	GFP/DME	Total	Rank
2004	Tex	11	89.0	100	1	.990	2	1	1	0	0	-	-	-	15	0	+1	0	+1	0	+1	+1	1	0	-	-1	0	-
2005	Tex	10	71.0	93	2	.978	2	1	1	1	0	-	-	-	15	+1	-1	-1	-1	0	-1	-1	-1	0	-	0	-1	-
2006	SD	155	1341.0	1365	7	.995	47	22	23	15	3	-	-	-	286	-3	+4	0	+1	-1	0	0	0	0	-	3	3	14
2007	SD	161	1462.2	1620	10	.994	39	31	26	14	1	-	-	-	284	0	-5	0	-5	-1	-6	-7	-5	2	-	-5	-8	29
2008	SD	161	1417.1	1442	6	.996	53	21	26	14	1	-	-	-	282	-1	-7	-1	-8	+2	-6	-6	-4	3	-	1	0	16
2009	SD	156	1359.2	1367	7	.995	69	19	25	13	1	23	9	.391	303	+1	-2	+8	+7	+2	+9	+12	9	2	0	4	15	2
2010	SD	159	1397.1	1459	8	.995	58	29	30	18	4	24	9	.375	269	-6	+1	+3	-1	-2	-3	-4	-3	0	0	0	-3	25
2011	Bos	156	1352.2	1351	4	.997	56	16	14	8	1	18	8	.444	287	+2	-2	+9	+6	+1	+7	+9	7	3	0	2	12	1
		969	8490.2	8797	45	.995	325	141	146	83	11	65	26	.400	1741	-6	-11	+18	0	+1	+1	+4	4	10	0	4	18	10

Jesus Guzman

Year	Team	G	Inn	TC	E	Pct	GFP	DM	Opp	Sac Hits	Bunt Hits	Opp GDP	GDP	Pct	Outs Made	To His Right	Straight On	To His Left	GB	Air	Total	Enhanced	+/-	Bunt	GDP	GFP/DME	Total	Rank
2009	SF	3	14.0	10	0	1.000	1	2				0	0	-	3	0	0	0	0	0	0	0	0		0	0	0	-
2011	SD	53	434.0	419	4	.990	15	11	7	4	1	5	2	.400	73	+1	+3	-1	+3	-2	+1	+1	1	0	0	-1	0	15
		56	448.0	429	4	.991	16	13	7	4	1	5	2	.400	76	+1	+3	-1	+3	-2	+1	+1	1	0	0	-1	0	-

First Basemen

Brad Hawpe

	BASIC							BUNTS			GDP			PLUS/MINUS								RUNS SAVED					
Year	Team	G	Inn	TC	E	Pct	GFP	DM	Opp	Sac Hits	Bunt Hits	Opp	GDP	Pct	Outs Made	To His Right	Straight On	To His Left	GB	Air	Total	Enhanced	+/-	Bunt	GDP	GFP/DME	Total	Rank
2010	2 tms	9	72.0	58	0	1.000	2	0	1	1	0	0	0	-	12	+1	+1	+1	+2	0	+2	+2	2	0	0	0	2	
2011	SD	44	383.0	404	4	.990	18	6	8	5	1	8	3	.375	72	+1	0	-2	0	0	0	-1	-1	0	0	0	-1	
		53	455.0	462	4	.991	20	6	9	6	1	8	3	.375	84	+2	+1	-1	+2	0	+2	+1	1	0	0	0	1	

Todd Helton

	BASIC							BUNTS			GDP			PLUS/MINUS								RUNS SAVED					
Year	Team	G	Inn	TC	E	Pct	GFP	DM	Opp	Sac Hits	Bunt Hits	Opp	GDP	Pct	Outs Made	To His Right	Straight On	To His Left	GB	Air	Total	Enhanced	+/-	Bunt	GDP	GFP/DME	Total	Rank
2003	Col	159	1369.0	1586	11	.993	-	-	33	21	5	-	-	-	307	+1	-3	-2	-4	-5	-9	-11	-8	0	-	-	-8	32
2004	Col	153	1320.2	1503	4	.997	41	24	36	28	1	-	-	-	262	+10	+1	-2	+9	0	+9	+11	8	1	-	3	12	1
2005	Col	144	1229.2	1359	5	.996	51	25	23	16	2	-	-	-	272	-3	+2	0	-1	+1	0	-1	-1	1	-	0	0	21
2006	Col	145	1272.1	1456	4	.997	34	17	18	10	4	-	-	-	256	-5	0	-2	-7	+1	-6	-7	-5	-2	-	3	-4	26
2007	Col	153	1337.0	1545	2	.999	47	24	19	12	0	-	-	-	287	-1	+3	+5	+7	0	+7	+9	7	1	-	0	8	5
2008	Col	81	715.1	890	3	.997	60	7	9	7	1	-	-	-	156	-3	+7	+2	+7	0	+7	+6	4	0	-	3	7	7
2009	Col	149	1275.0	1448	3	.998	70	23	18	15	0	8	3	.375	242	-2	+4	-3	-2	+1	-1	-1	-1	1	0	2	2	15
2010	Col	115	947.2	1017	8	.992	45	8	19	11	0	19	12	.632	152	+3	-4	+3	0	+1	+1	+2	1	2	1	2	6	10
2011	Col	119	987.2	1092	3	.997	35	11	13	11	2	18	12	.667	222	-4	+4	+7	+8	-1	+7	+6	5	-1	1	2	7	6
		1218	10454.1	11896	43	.996	383	139	188	131	15	45	27	.600	2156	-4	+14	+8	+17	-2	+15	+14	10	3	2	15	30	7

Eric Hosmer

	BASIC							BUNTS			GDP			PLUS/MINUS								RUNS SAVED					
Year	Team	G	Inn	TC	E	Pct	GFP	DM	Opp	Sac Hits	Bunt Hits	Opp	GDP	Pct	Outs Made	To His Right	Straight On	To His Left	GB	Air	Total	Enhanced	+/-	Bunt	GDP	GFP/DME	Total	Rank
2011	KC	127	1135.2	1182	8	.993	69	26	13	6	3	17	3	.176	205	-4	-2	-3	-7	0	-7	-9	-7	-1	-1	0	-9	32

Ryan Howard

	BASIC							BUNTS			GDP			PLUS/MINUS								RUNS SAVED					
Year	Team	G	Inn	TC	E	Pct	GFP	DM	Opp	Sac Hits	Bunt Hits	Opp	GDP	Pct	Outs Made	To His Right	Straight On	To His Left	GB	Air	Total	Enhanced	+/-	Bunt	GDP	GFP/DME	Total	Rank
2004	Phi	8	60.2	65	0	1.000	-	1	-	-	-	-	-	-	9	+1	+1	0	+2	0	+2	+2	1	-	-	0	1	-
2005	Phi	84	706.1	752	5	.993	19	20	5	5	0	-	-	-	149	+15	+6	-2	+19	0	+19	+16	12	0	-	-1	11	3
2006	Phi	159	1412.0	1478	14	.991	34	33	20	13	2	-	-	-	257	-5	+2	-3	-6	-3	-9	-9	-7	0	-	-2	-9	30
2007	Phi	140	1241.0	1306	12	.991	39	27	24	15	0	-	-	-	240	-2	-2	-3	-8	0	-8	-5	-4	1	-	-1	-4	24
2008	Phi	159	1402.2	1528	19	.988	64	37	13	8	1	-	-	-	309	+1	-10	+5	-4	+2	-2	0	0	1	-	-5	-4	25
2009	Phi	156	1388.1	1409	14	.990	61	22	21	12	4	11	3	.273	301	-2	+2	-3	-3	0	-3	-1	-1	-1	0	-2	-4	29
2010	Phi	139	1229.0	1339	14	.990	51	27	19	12	3	9	4	.444	209	-7	-4	-5	-19	+1	-18	-14	-11	-1	0	-1	-13	33
2011	Phi	149	1309.0	1361	9	.993	58	24	28	19	3	12	7	.583	234	-8	-10	+2	-16	-2	-18	-17	-12	1	0	-2	-13	35
		994	8749.0	9238	87	.991	326	191	130	84	13	32	14	.438	1708	-7	-15	-9	-35	-2	-37	-28	-22	1	0	-14	-35	32

Aubrey Huff

	BASIC							BUNTS			GDP			PLUS/MINUS								RUNS SAVED					
Year	Team	G	Inn	TC	E	Pct	GFP	DM	Opp	Sac Hits	Bunt Hits	Opp	GDP	Pct	Outs Made	To His Right	Straight On	To His Left	GB	Air	Total	Enhanced	+/-	Bunt	GDP	GFP/DME	Total	Rank
2003	TB	22	181.1	178	0	1.000	-	-	-	-	-	-	-	-	35	0	-1	0	-1	0	-1	-2	-1	-	-	-	-1	-
2004	TB	38	274.1	290	1	.997	6	7	1	0	0	-	-	-	60	0	+3	-3	0	-1	-1	-2	-1	0	-	0	-1	-
2005	TB	25	161.1	139	0	1.000	2	1	2	0	2	-	-	-	22	0	-2	0	-2	0	-2	-2	-1	-1	-	0	-2	-
2006	Hou	3	8.0	9	0	1.000	0	0	-	-	-	-	-	-	3	+1	0	0	+2	0	+2	+2	1	-	-	0	1	-
2007	Bal	51	421.0	451	3	.993	16	13	7	6	1	-	-	-	61	+1	0	-1	-1	0	-1	-2	-1	-1	-	-2	-4	-
2008	Bal	24	194.1	193	0	1.000	8	4	5	2	2	-	-	-	39	-4	0	0	-4	+1	-3	-2	-1	0	-	0	-1	-
2009	Bal	93	826.0	885	4	.995	42	13	5	3	0	11	5	.455	164	-8	-1	+1	-9	-1	-10	-10	-7	1	0	1	-5	30
2010	SF	100	821.1	813	3	.996	41	3	20	15	2	6	1	.167	146	+3	-1	+1	+5	+1	+6	+4	3	1	0	3	7	7
2011	SF	120	1032.2	1067	5	.995	43	18	23	17	1	4	1	.250	187	-3	+3	+4	+1	-1	0	+3	2	-1	0	1	2	14
		476	3920.1	4025	16	.996	158	59	63	43	8	21	7	.333	717	-10	+1	+2	-9	-1	-10	-11	-6	-1	0	3	-4	18

Luke Hughes

	BASIC							BUNTS			GDP			PLUS/MINUS								RUNS SAVED					
Year	Team	G	Inn	TC	E	Pct	GFP	DM	Opp	Sac Hits	Bunt Hits	Opp	GDP	Pct	Outs Made	To His Right	Straight On	To His Left	GB	Air	Total	Enhanced	+/-	Bunt	GDP	GFP/DME	Total	Rank
2011	Min	36	274.0	292	1	.997	17	8				3	1	.333	51	-1	+2	+1	+1	0	+1	+1	1	0	0	-1	0	-

Conor Jackson

	BASIC							BUNTS			GDP			PLUS/MINUS								RUNS SAVED					
Year	Team	G	Inn	TC	E	Pct	GFP	DM	Opp	Sac Hits	Bunt Hits	Opp	GDP	Pct	Outs Made	To His Right	Straight On	To His Left	GB	Air	Total	Enhanced	+/-	Bunt	GDP	GFP/DME	Total	Rank
2005	Ari	20	161.0	187	5	.973	5	3	6	5	1	-	-	-	29	0	0	-2	-2	-1	-3	-4	-3	-1	-	-1	-5	-
2006	Ari	129	1078.2	1202	12	.990	25	26	23	18	2	-	-	-	210	-7	-9	+4	-11	0	-11	-11	-8	0	-	-4	-12	33
2007	Ari	108	867.2	918	11	.988	25	19	10	7	0	-	-	-	164	-4	+7	-8	-4	0	-4	-6	-4	0	-	-1	-5	26
2008	Ari	68	571.2	567	4	.993	18	16	8	5	1	-	-	-	102	-1	-2	0	-3	-1	-4	-5	-4	0	-	-1	-5	27
2009	Ari	6	43.0	44	1	.977	4	1				0	0	-	5	0	0	0	0	0	0	0	0		0	0	0	-
2010	Ari	3	26.0	29	0	1.000	1	0				1	0	.000	5	-1	+1	0	0	0	0	0	0		0	0	0	-
2011	2 tms	53	392.0	372	1	.997	14	6	1	0	0	3	1	.333	74	-3	-1	-3	-5	-1	-6	-7	-5	0	0	-2	-7	30
		387	3140.0	3319	34	.990	92	71	48	35	4	4	1	.250	589	-16	-4	-9	-25	-3	-28	-33	-24	-1	0	-7	-32	31

First Basemen

Garrett Jones

Year	Team	G	Inn	TC	E	Pct	GFP	DM	Opp	Sac Hits	Bunt Hits	Opp GDP	Pct	Outs Made	To His Right	Straight On	To His Left	GB	Air	Total	Enhanced	+/-	Bunt	GDP	GFP/DME	Total	Rank
2007	Min	8	63.0	61	0	1.000	1	1				-	-	12				-2	0	-2	-2	-1				-1	-
2009	Pit	30	255.2	284	1	.996	10	4	2	2	0	4	2	.500	61	0	-1	+1	0	+1	+1	+2	1	0	0	-1	0	-
2010	Pit	112	924.1	990	9	.991	48	27	7	3	4	13	4	.308	195	-4	-2	-1	-8	+3	-5	-5	-4	-2	-1	-5	-12	32
2011	Pit	34	260.1	277	3	.989	11	11	2	0	2	1	0	.000	39	0	-1	0	-1	+1	0	0	0	-1	0	-2	-3	-
		184	1503.2	1612	13	.992	70	43	11	5	6	18	6	.333	307	-4	-4	0	-11	+5	-6	-5	-4	-3	-1	-8	-16	

Adam Kennedy

Year	Team	G	Inn	TC	E	Pct	GFP	DM	Opp	Sac Hits	Bunt Hits	Opp GDP	Pct	Outs Made	To His Right	Straight On	To His Left	GB	Air	Total	Enhanced	+/-	Bunt	GDP	GFP/DME	Total	Rank
2008	StL	3	18.0	27	1	.963	1	1				-	-	4	+1			0	0	0	0	0		-	0	0	-
2009	Oak	1	3.0	1	0	1.000	0	0						0								0			0	0	-
2010	Was	51	113.0	113	1	.991	3	3	4	4	0	0	0	-	15	+1	-1	0	+2	0	+2	+1	1	0	0	0	1	-
2011	Sea	36	218.0	243	2	.992	15	6	3	2	0	3	0	.000	49	+4	-1	-1	+2	0	+2	+2	2	0	0	1	3	-
		91	352.0	384	4	.990	19	10	7	6	0	3	0	.000	68	+6	-2	-1	+4	0	+4	+3	3	0	0	1	4	

Paul Konerko

Year	Team	G	Inn	TC	E	Pct	GFP	DM	Opp	Sac Hits	Bunt Hits	Opp GDP	Pct	Outs Made	To His Right	Straight On	To His Left	GB	Air	Total	Enhanced	+/-	Bunt	GDP	GFP/DME	Total	Rank
2003	CWS	119	938.2	971	2	.998	-	-	15	7	3	-	-	204	-1	-3	+2	-2	+2	0	+4	3	0		-	3	11
2004	CWS	139	1177.2	1235	6	.995	40	12	12	4	3	-	-	208	-8	-6	+3	-11	-2	-13	-12	-9	-1	-	3	-7	31
2005	CWS	146	1272.2	1407	6	.996	34	12	16	10	2	-	-	275	-1	-1	+1	-1	-1	-2	-2	-1	0	-	2	1	19
2006	CWS	140	1181.2	1244	6	.995	38	23	11	4	3	-	-	208	-6	-1	0	-4	-1	-5	-5	-4	0	-	1	-3	24
2007	CWS	141	1227.2	1256	5	.996	45	18	12	4	1	-	-	245	+1	-7	+2	-3	0	-3	-3	-2	2	-	0	0	18
2008	CWS	116	995.2	1092	7	.994	54	15	5	2	2	-	-	209	+3	-2	+1	+2	0	+2	-2	-1	-1	-	1	-1	17
2009	CWS	134	1141.0	1242	4	.997	70	13	13	8	3	12	4	.333	230	-2	+6	0	+4	0	+4	+2	1	1	-1	0	1	16
2010	CWS	125	1102.1	1159	7	.994	48	10	11	2	1	27	15	.556	191	-5	-10	-7	-23	-1	-24	-23	-17	1	1	2	-13	34
2011	CWS	111	963.1	1048	5	.995	32	15	8	3	3	16	12	.750	170	-4	+1	-3	-7	+1	-6	-5	-4	-1	1	0	-4	28
		1171	10000.2	10654	47	.996	361	118	103	44	21	55	31	.564	1940	-23	-23	+1	-45	-2	-47	-46	-34	1	1	9	-23	30

Casey Kotchman

Year	Team	G	Inn	TC	E	Pct	GFP	DM	Opp	Sac Hits	Bunt Hits	Opp GDP	Pct	Outs Made	To His Right	Straight On	To His Left	GB	Air	Total	Enhanced	+/-	Bunt	GDP	GFP/DME	Total	Rank
2004	Ana	34	270.1	249	3	.988	17	7	2	2	0	-	-	45	0	-3	0	-2	0	-2	-2	-1	0	-	1	0	-
2005	LAA	20	131.0	118	0	1.000	1	3				-	-	24	0	0	-3	-2	0	-2	-5	-4		-	1	-4	-
2006	LAA	26	197.0	195	0	1.000	8	2	1	1	0	-	-	44	+4	+1	+1	+5	0	+5	+5	4	0	-	1	5	-
2007	LAA	130	1033.0	1049	3	.997	53	21	3	1	1	-	-	223	+9	+4	+7	+20	+1	+21	+24	18	0	-	0	18	2
2008	2 tms	141	1210.1	1303	2	.998	76	16	8	5	3	-	-	263	+2	+10	0	+11	+1	+12	+14	10	-1	-	3	12	5
2009	2 tms	114	893.1	939	0	1.000	43	14	11	8	2	11	3	.273	193	+4	+2	+4	+10	0	+10	+10	7	-1	0	1	7	7
2010	Sea	116	966.2	1021	1	.999	48	16	7	5	0	14	3	.214	183	0	+1	+4	+5	-1	+4	+4	3	1	-1	0	3	13
2011	TB	146	1222.1	1201	2	.998	53	18	6	1	4	13	7	.538	215	0	-2	+5	+1	-1	0	+2	1	-1	0	3	3	13
		727	5924.0	6075	11	.998	299	97	38	23	10	38	13	.342	1190	+19	+13	+18	+48	0	+48	+52	38	-2	-1	9	44	3

Matt LaPorta

Year	Team	G	Inn	TC	E	Pct	GFP	DM	Opp	Sac Hits	Bunt Hits	Opp GDP	Pct	Outs Made	To His Right	Straight On	To His Left	GB	Air	Total	Enhanced	+/-	Bunt	GDP	GFP/DME	Total	Rank
2009	Cle	10	78.0	84	2	.976	2	2				1	0	.000	18	0	+1	0	+1	0	+1	+1	1			-1	0	-
2010	Cle	93	791.1	876	3	.997	38	18	2	1	0	9	4	.444	132	+1	0	0	+1	+1	+2	+1	1	0	0	-3	-2	23
2011	Cle	97	802.2	855	7	.992	32	16	8	3	4	11	6	.545	170	-5	-2	-5	-12	+2	-10	-10	-7	-3	0	-1	-11	34
		200	1672.0	1815	12	.993	72	36	10	4	4	21	10	.476	320	-4	-1	-5	-10	+3	-7	-8	-5	-3	0	-5	-13	26

Adam LaRoche

Year	Team	G	Inn	TC	E	Pct	GFP	DM	Opp	Sac Hits	Bunt Hits	Opp GDP	Pct	Outs Made	To His Right	Straight On	To His Left	GB	Air	Total	Enhanced	+/-	Bunt	GDP	GFP/DME	Total	Rank
2004	Atl	98	720.0	784	5	.994	17	9	8	6	0	-	-	123	+2	-2	+1	+1	0	+1	+1	1	0	-	1	2	17
2005	Atl	125	1019.1	1154	7	.994	28	27	11	7	2	-	-	232	0	-15	-3	-18	0	-18	-17	-12	-1	-	0	-13	34
2006	Atl	142	1153.1	1218	5	.996	31	26	24	16	4	-	-	243	-10	-2	-3	-14	-1	-15	-14	-10	0	-	-1	-11	32
2007	Pit	151	1301.1	1383	6	.996	31	16	20	9	5	-	-	269	-4	+6	+1	+3	-1	+2	+3	2	0	-	0	2	11
2008	Pit	129	1135.2	1219	8	.993	39	14	23	10	5	-	-	206	0	-1	-6	-7	+2	-5	-8	-6	1	-	1	-5	28
2009	3 tms	148	1308.1	1435	2	.999	55	24	18	9	2	22	8	.364	279	+1	+3	-3	0	-1	-1	-5	-4	1	0	1	-2	26
2010	Ari	146	1239.2	1272	11	.991	55	22	17	10	1	19	12	.632	260	+6	0	-1	+6	+1	+7	+5	4	0	1	1	6	9
2011	Was	43	375.0	412	0	1.000	17	5	4	4	0	9	3	.333	90	+2	+1	+3	+6	+1	+7	+7	5	0	0	0	5	-
		982	8252.2	8877	44	.995	273	143	125	71	19	50	23	.460	1702	-3	-10	-11	-23	+1	-22	-28	-20	1	1	2	-16	29

First Basemen

Carlos Lee

Year	Team	G	Inn	TC	E	Pct	GFP	DM	Opp	Sac Hits	Bunt Hits	Opp	GDP	Pct	Outs Made	To His Right	Straight On	To His Left	GB	Air	Total	Enhanced	+/-	Bunt	GDP	GFP/DME	Total	Rank
2009	Hou	1	1.0	2	0	1.000	1	0							0							0					0	-
2010	Hou	20	143.0	128	1	.992	14	4				2	0	.000	27	0	+2	-1	+1	0	+1	+1	1			0	1	-
2011	Hou	79	624.1	658	5	.992	33	15	7	5	0	13	8	.615	130	+4	+2	+1	+6	-1	+5	+6	5	1	1	0	7	6
		100	768.1	788	6	.992	48	19	7	5	0	15	8	.533	157	+4	+4	0	+7	-1	+6	+7	6	1	1	0	8	

Derrek Lee

Year	Team	G	Inn	TC	E	Pct	GFP	DM	Opp	Sac Hits	Bunt Hits	Opp	GDP	Pct	Outs Made	To His Right	Straight On	To His Left	GB	Air	Total	Enhanced	+/-	Bunt	GDP	GFP/DME	Total	Rank
2003	Fla	155	1353.2	1382	5	.996	-	-	21	14	2	-	-	-	259	-4	-8	-3	-15	+2	-13	-13	-9	1	-	-	-8	33
2004	ChC	161	1432.0	1393	6	.996	55	24	29	22	0	-	-	-	269	0	-4	+1	-3	0	-3	-2	-1	1	-	1	1	19
2005	ChC	158	1386.0	1451	6	.996	57	18	36	22	2	-	-	-	256	0	-7	+6	-2	+2	0	+2	1	1	-	3	5	13
2006	ChC	47	393.2	401	5	.988	22	7	12	10	0	-	-	-	73	0	-1	+2	+1	+1	+2	+3	2	1	-	1	4	-
2007	ChC	147	1274.1	1259	7	.994	63	21	23	15	3	-	-	-	234	0	+1	-3	-3	-2	-5	-4	-3	-1	-	4	0	19
2008	ChC	153	1339.1	1312	9	.993	55	12	19	13	0	-	-	-	304	+1	-6	+8	+3	0	+3	+6	4	1	-	1	6	9
2009	ChC	139	1231.1	1188	6	.995	57	19	27	20	4	16	5	.313	233	-2	0	+3	+1	+1	+2	+4	3	-2	-1	3	3	10
2010	2 tms	144	1207.1	1190	7	.994	43	10	16	13	2	12	4	.333	229	-3	+1	+5	+1	+1	+2	+4	3	-1	0	0	2	17
2011	2 tms	113	984.0	1021	8	.992	45	20	12	6	1	14	4	.286	170	+2	-2	-1	-1	-3	-4	-4	-3	1	0	-1	-3	24
		1217	10601.2	10597	59	.994	397	131	195	135	14	42	13	.310	2027	-6	-26	+18	-18	+2	-16	-4	-3	2	-1	12	10	14

Adam Lind

Year	Team	G	Inn	TC	E	Pct	GFP	DM	Opp	Sac Hits	Bunt Hits	Opp	GDP	Pct	Outs Made	To His Right	Straight On	To His Left	GB	Air	Total	Enhanced	+/-	Bunt	GDP	GFP/DME	Total	Rank
2010	Tor	11	76.0	79	0	1.000	4	2				3	0	.000	16	0	+1	0	+1	0	+1	+1	1		0	-1	0	-
2011	Tor	109	965.1	1020	4	.996	48	18	4	2	1	13	4	.308	166	-2	-2	+1	-4	0	-4	-3	-2	0	-1	-1	-4	27
		120	1041.1	1099	4	.996	52	20	4	2	1	16	4	.250	182	-2	-1	+1	-3	0	-3	-2	-1	0	-1	-2	-4	-

James Loney

Year	Team	G	Inn	TC	E	Pct	GFP	DM	Opp	Sac Hits	Bunt Hits	Opp	GDP	Pct	Outs Made	To His Right	Straight On	To His Left	GB	Air	Total	Enhanced	+/-	Bunt	GDP	GFP/DME	Total	Rank
2006	LAD	39	228.2	228	1	.996	5	2	2	1	0	-	-	-	36	-2	+3	+3	+4	-1	+3	+5	4	0	-	0	4	-
2007	LAD	93	774.2	795	9	.989	33	16	11	7	1	-	-	-	159	+5	-1	-1	+2	0	+2	+2	1	0	-	1	2	12
2008	LAD	158	1362.2	1498	13	.991	69	17	21	12	1	-	-	-	248	+2	-6	+2	-2	0	-2	-1	-1	1	-	1	1	13
2009	LAD	155	1341.0	1361	7	.995	70	18	17	10	2	18	10	.556	254	-4	-1	+5	0	+2	+2	+4	3	-1	1	2	5	9
2010	LAD	160	1338.2	1368	4	.997	66	16	16	10	1	14	10	.714	230	0	+3	-4	+2	-1	+1	-1	-1	1	1	3	4	11
2011	LAD	150	1203.2	1208	5	.996	71	21	14	5	5	16	9	.563	242	+2	+5	+1	+8	+2	+10	+10	7	0	1	3	11	2
		755	6249.1	6458	39	.994	314	90	81	45	10	48	29	.604	1169	+3	+3	+6	+14	+2	+16	+19	13	1	3	10	27	8

Chris Marrero

Year	Team	G	Inn	TC	E	Pct	GFP	DM	Opp	Sac Hits	Bunt Hits	Opp	GDP	Pct	Outs Made	To His Right	Straight On	To His Left	GB	Air	Total	Enhanced	+/-	Bunt	GDP	GFP/DME	Total	Rank
2011	Was	31	264.1	270	2	.993	10	4	7	5	1	1	1	1.000	46	-1	0	+1	-1	+1	0	0	0	0	0	-1	-1	-

Juan Miranda

Year	Team	G	Inn	TC	E	Pct	GFP	DM	Opp	Sac Hits	Bunt Hits	Opp	GDP	Pct	Outs Made	To His Right	Straight On	To His Left	GB	Air	Total	Enhanced	+/-	Bunt	GDP	GFP/DME	Total	Rank
2008	NYY	5	32.2	32	0	1.000	2	2				-	-	-	8	+1	0	0	+1	0	+1	+1	1		-	0	1	-
2009	NYY	8	23.0	20	0	1.000	1	0				0	0	-	4	0	-1	0	0	0	0	0	0		0	0	0	-
2010	NYY	13	50.1	58	0	1.000	3	0				0	0	-	13	0	0	0	0	+1	+1	+1	1		0	0	1	-
2011	Ari	46	401.0	395	4	.990	7	6	6	3	0	4	3	.750	65	-1	-1	0	-2	0	-2	-2	-1	-2	0	-1	-4	26
		72	507.0	505	4	.992	13	8	6	3	0	4	3	.750	90	0	-2	0	-1	+1	0	0	1	-2	0	-1	-2	-

Mitch Moreland

Year	Team	G	Inn	TC	E	Pct	GFP	DM	Opp	Sac Hits	Bunt Hits	Opp	GDP	Pct	Outs Made	To His Right	Straight On	To His Left	GB	Air	Total	Enhanced	+/-	Bunt	GDP	GFP/DME	Total	Rank
2010	Tex	40	320.2	307	2	.993	10	3	2	0	2	1	1	1.000	47	0	+1	-1	0	0	0	0	0	-1	0	1	0	-
2011	Tex	99	799.0	789	4	.995	30	12	6	2	0	5	2	.400	129	0	-6	+2	-4	0	-4	-4	-3	1	0	0	-2	21
		139	1119.2	1096	6	.995	40	15	8	2	2	6	3	.500	176	0	-5	+1	-4	0	-4	-4	-3	0	0	1	-2	-

First Basemen

Justin Morneau

Year	Team	G	Inn	TC	E	Pct	GFP	DM	Opp	Sac Hits	Bunt Hits	Opp	GDP	Pct	Outs Made	To His Right	Straight On	To His Left	GB	Air	Total	Enhanced	+/-	Bunt	GDP	GFP/DME	Total	Rank
				BASIC						BUNTS			GDP					PLUS/MINUS							RUNS SAVED			
2003	Min	7	34.2	34	1	.971	-		1	0	0	-	-		9	-1	-1	0	-2	0	-2	-3	-2	0	-	-	-2	-
2004	Min	61	538.1	567	3	.995	22	15	2	1	1	-	-		90	-2	+1	-2	-2	-1	-3	-3	-2	0	-	1	-1	23
2005	Min	138	1166.1	1290	8	.994	41	18	11	4	1	-	-		246	-2	+7	+6	+11	0	+11	+13	9	1	-	-1	9	5
2006	Min	153	1346.1	1415	8	.994	38	24	12	8	0	-	-		254	+1	-1	-1	0	+1	+1	+1	1	2	-	-1	2	17
2007	Min	143	1259.1	1296	5	.996	52	16	9	8	1	-	-		274	-6	+2	+1	-3	+3	0	0	0	-1	-	1	0	16
2008	Min	155	1363.2	1409	4	.997	70	25	5	4	1	-	-		239	+1	-3	0	-2	0	-2	-1	-1	0	-	-1	-2	20
2009	Min	123	1071.2	1045	3	.997	50	13	7	5	1	11	3	.273	198	+1	+2	+2	+3	+1	+4	+3	2	1	-1	0	2	13
2010	Min	77	688.1	734	1	.999	28	6	3	3	0	14	10	.714	130	-1	+4	+4	+6	0	+6	+7	5	0	1	2	8	3
2011	Min	56	479.1	485	1	.998	21	9	2	2	0	7	4	.571	83	-3	-1	+1	-3	+1	-2	-2	-2	0	0	-1	-3	23
		913	7948.0	8275	34	.996	322	126	52	35	5	32	17	.531	1523	-14	+10	+11	+8	+5	+13	+15	10	3	0	0	13	12

Michael Morse

Year	Team	G	Inn	TC	E	Pct	GFP	DM	Opp	Sac Hits	Bunt Hits	Opp	GDP	Pct	Outs Made	To His Right	Straight On	To His Left	GB	Air	Total	Enhanced	+/-	Bunt	GDP	GFP/DME	Total	Rank
				BASIC						BUNTS			GDP					PLUS/MINUS							RUNS SAVED			
2006	Sea	2	10.0	11	0	1.000	1	0				-	-		1	0			0	0	0	0	0	-	0	0	-
2007	Sea	5	28.0	36	0	1.000	0	0				-	-		10	0	0	0	0	0	0	0	0	-	0	0	-
2009	Was	11	46.0	52	0	1.000	2	0	1	1	0	0	0	-	14	+1	0	+1	+2	0	+2	+2	1	0	0	0	1	-
2010	Was	19	60.0	63	0	1.000		1				1	0	.000	13	-1	+1	0	+1	0	+1	0	1	0	0	0	1	-
2011	Was	85	723.1	793	6	.992	35	10	12	9	2	11	5	.455	135	-1	-4	-5	-8	+1	-7	-9	-7	-1	0	1	-7	31
		122	867.1	955	6	.994	38	11	13	10	2	12	5	.417	173	-1	-3	-4	-5	+1	-4	-7	-5	-1	0	1	-5	-

Daniel Murphy

Year	Team	G	Inn	TC	E	Pct	GFP	DM	Opp	Sac Hits	Bunt Hits	Opp	GDP	Pct	Outs Made	To His Right	Straight On	To His Left	GB	Air	Total	Enhanced	+/-	Bunt	GDP	GFP/DME	Total	Rank
				BASIC						BUNTS			GDP					PLUS/MINUS							RUNS SAVED			
2009	NYM	101	849.1	874	10	.989	44	22	13	4	2	18	8	.444	201	+7	+5	+1	+13	+1	+14	+14	10	1	1	-1	11	3
2011	NYM	52	419.0	459	4	.991	31	9	13	8	0	10	6	.600	74	+4	+2	0	+6	+2	+8	+8	6	1	0	1	8	5
		153	1268.1	1333	14	.989	75	31	26	12	2	28	14	.500	275	+11	+7	+1	+19	+3	+22	+22	16	2	1	0	19	-

Xavier Nady

Year	Team	G	Inn	TC	E	Pct	GFP	DM	Opp	Sac Hits	Bunt Hits	Opp	GDP	Pct	Outs Made	To His Right	Straight On	To His Left	GB	Air	Total	Enhanced	+/-	Bunt	GDP	GFP/DME	Total	Rank
				BASIC						BUNTS			GDP					PLUS/MINUS							RUNS SAVED			
2005	SD	44	299.1	292	4	.986	14	9	4	1	2	-	-		69	0	+2	+2	+4	0	+4	+5	4	-1	-	-1	2	-
2006	2 tms	35	240.1	284	2	.993	8	6	10	5	0	-	-		57	+1	+2	-1	+2	0	+2	+2	1	1	-	0	2	-
2008	NYY	3	4.0	4	0	1.000	0	0				-	-		0	0	0	0	0	0	0	0	0	-	0	0	-
2010	ChC	52	423.0	426	1	.998	18	5	6	4	1	10	4	.400	71	+3	+1	+1	+5	0	+5	+5	4	-1	0	-1	3	12
2011	Ari	52	391.1	407	3	.993	21	4	4	2	0	2	0	.000	61	-2	-3	+2	-2	-1	-3	-3	-3	1	0	2	0	16
		186	1358.0	1413	10	.993	61	24	24	12	3	12	4	.333	260	+2	+2	+4	+9	-1	+8	+9	6	0	0	1	7	-

Mike Napoli

Year	Team	G	Inn	TC	E	Pct	GFP	DM	Opp	Sac Hits	Bunt Hits	Opp	GDP	Pct	Outs Made	To His Right	Straight On	To His Left	GB	Air	Total	Enhanced	+/-	Bunt	GDP	GFP/DME	Total	Rank
				BASIC						BUNTS			GDP					PLUS/MINUS							RUNS SAVED			
2010	LAA	70	586.1	552	6	.989	30	10	1	1	0	4	2	.500	124	+3	+1	-2	+3	-1	+2	+1	1	0	0	0	1	19
2011	Tex	35	246.1	243	1	.996	9	7				2	1	.500	38	+2	0	-2	+1	-1	0	-1	0	0	0	-1	-1	-
		105	832.2	795	7	.991	39	17	1	1	0	6	3	.500	162	+5	+1	-4	+4	-2	+2	0	1	0	0	-1	0	-

Lyle Overbay

Year	Team	G	Inn	TC	E	Pct	GFP	DM	Opp	Sac Hits	Bunt Hits	Opp	GDP	Pct	Outs Made	To His Right	Straight On	To His Left	GB	Air	Total	Enhanced	+/-	Bunt	GDP	GFP/DME	Total	Rank
				BASIC						BUNTS			GDP					PLUS/MINUS							RUNS SAVED			
2003	Ari	75	604.0	703	2	.997	-		9	5	1	-	-		154	0	+4	+4	+8	-1	+7	+9	7	0	-	-	7	6
2004	Mil	158	1360.1	1434	11	.992	26	25	28	13	4	-	-		246	+2	-2	-9	-9	0	-9	-14	-10	1	-	-3	-12	35
2005	Mil	154	1265.0	1240	10	.992	37	19	23	15	1	-	-		247	+2	+6	-3	+5	0	+5	+4	3	1	-	1	5	11
2006	Tor	145	1233.0	1459	9	.994	41	22	4	0	2	-	-		305	+3	+3	-1	+5	+2	+7	+7	5	-1	-	0	4	10
2007	Tor	119	972.1	1166	5	.996	41	17	4	2	0	-	-		218	+3	+5	+4	+12	-1	+11	+13	9	1	-	1	11	3
2008	Tor	156	1354.2	1476	5	.997	38	21	9	3	3	-	-		324	+7	+7	-1	+13	0	+13	+11	8	-1	-	-1	6	8
2009	Tor	130	1055.1	1132	2	.998	38	16	6	2	2	26	10	.385	230	+1	+2	+5	+8	+2	+10	+10	7	-2	0	1	6	8
2010	Tor	153	1320.2	1416	6	.996	41	14	6	3	0	24	11	.458	244	+3	+3	+3	+8	0	+8	+9	7	-1	1	0	7	5
2011	2 tms	109	917.0	994	8	.992	34	13	11	7	0	18	9	.500	153	-7	0	-1	-9	+2	-7	-7	-5	1	0	0	-4	29
		1199	10082.1	11020	58	.995	296	147	100	50	13	68	30	.441	2121	+14	+28	+1	+41	+4	+45	+42	31	-1	1	-1	30	6

First Basemen

Carlos Pena

		BASIC							BUNTS			GDP		PLUS/MINUS								RUNS SAVED					
Year	Team	G	Inn	TC	E	Pct	GFP	DM	Opp	Sac Hits	Bunt Hits	Opp GDP	Pct	Outs Made	To His Right	Straight On	To His Left	GB	Air	Total	Enhanced	+/-	Bunt	GDP	GFP/DME	Total	Rank
2003	Det	128	1094.2	1240	13	.990	-	-	11	5	2	-	-	206	+1	-3	-1	-3	0	-3	-5	-4	-2	-	-	-6	27
2004	Det	135	1159.1	1226	6	.995	49	12	11	6	2	-	-	182	+4	+7	-2	+9	-1	+8	+4	3	0	-	3	6	7
2005	Det	51	429.1	456	3	.993	13	11	6	2	3	-	-	94	-4	+1	-1	-3	0	-3	-5	-4	-1	-	-2	-7	-
2006	Bos	17	80.0	87	1	.989	2	2	-	-		-	-	14	0	+1	0	+1	0	+1	+1	1	-	-	0	1	-
2007	TB	144	1221.0	1192	8	.993	47	21	16	8	3	-	-	264	+8	+8	-5	+10	-1	+9	+4	3	1	-	4	8	6
2008	TB	132	1168.2	1099	2	.998	64	22	12	6	1	-	-	262	+11	+8	-5	+14	+1	+15	+14	10	2	-	3	15	4
2009	TB	133	1155.0	1136	10	.991	52	17	3	2	0	12	3	.250	215	+3	+1	-9	-4	-2	-6	-5	-4	0	0	1	-3	27
2010	TB	142	1213.2	1163	6	.995	53	21	2	1	1	16	8	.500	228	+4	+4	-8	+1	+1	+2	+1	0	0	0	0	0	21
2011	ChC	153	1258.1	1212	8	.993	77	27	32	22	4	15	5	.333	200	+6	-4	-3	0	0	0	-1	-1	0	0	0	-1	18
		1035	8780.0	8811	57	.994	357	133	93	52	16	43	16	.372	1665	+33	+23	-34	+25	-2	+23	+8	4	0	0	9	13	13

Albert Pujols

Year	Team	G	Inn	TC	E	Pct	GFP	DM	Opp	Sac Hits	Bunt Hits	Opp GDP	Pct	Outs Made	To His Right	Straight On	To His Left	GB	Air	Total	Enhanced	+/-	Bunt	GDP	GFP/DME	Total	Rank
2003	StL	62	369.2	374	1	.997	-	-	2	2	0	-	-	76	+3	-1	+3	+5	+1	+6	+7	5	0	-	-	5	-
2004	StL	150	1338.2	1582	10	.994	51	19	10	7	0	-	-	300	-1	+1	+6	+6	-1	+5	+8	6	1	-	0	7	4
2005	StL	158	1358.2	1707	14	.992	67	21	17	3	4	-	-	304	+6	0	+3	+9	0	+9	+10	7	2	-	4	13	2
2006	StL	143	1244.1	1463	6	.996	45	22	26	16	5	-	-	287	+18	+5	+3	+26	+2	+28	+25	18	-1	-	0	17	1
2007	StL	154	1324.2	1457	8	.995	68	23	17	9	1	-	-	334	+13	+14	+6	+33	+1	+34	+37	27	0	-	4	31	1
2008	StL	144	1215.0	1438	6	.996	62	16	10	4	2	-	-	303	+9	+8	+4	+20	+1	+21	+20	15	0	-	3	18	2
2009	StL	159	1376.2	1671	13	.992	97	16	15	7	1	32	13	.406	364	+11	+5	-3	+14	+1	+15	+14	10	1	0	6	17	1
2010	StL	157	1380.2	1619	4	.998	93	18	12	7	2	25	17	.680	286	-2	-4	+6	0	+4	+4	+5	3	-1	1	5	8	4
2011	StL	146	1260.1	1430	11	.992	67	18	16	8	4	21	11	.524	271	0	+5	+2	+7	+3	+10	+9	7	0	1	2	10	3
		1273	10868.2	12741	73	.994	550	153	125	63	19	78	41	.526	2525	+57	+33	+30	+120	+12	+132	+135	98	2	2	24	126	1

Mark Reynolds

Year	Team	G	Inn	TC	E	Pct	GFP	DM	Opp	Sac Hits	Bunt Hits	Opp GDP	Pct	Outs Made	To His Right	Straight On	To His Left	GB	Air	Total	Enhanced	+/-	Bunt	GDP	GFP/DME	Total	Rank
2008	Ari	1	2.0	2	1	.500	0	0				-	-	0				-1	0	-1	-1	-1	-		0	-1	-
2009	Ari	28	218.0	202	5	.975	14	8				2	1	.500	30	-2	-3	-1	-6	0	-6	-6	-4		0	-2	-6	-
2010	Ari	5	9.0	8	0	1.000	0	0				0	0	-	2	-1	0	0	-1	0	-1	-1	-1		0	0	-1	-
2011	Bal	44	375.2	392	5	.987	31	8	2	1	0	3	1	.333	69	-2	0	-1	-4	0	-4	-3	-2	0	0	1	-1	-
		78	604.2	604	11	.982	45	16	2	1	0	5	2	.400	101	-5	-3	-2	-12	0	-12	-11	-8	0	0	-1	-9	-

Juan Rivera

Year	Team	G	Inn	TC	E	Pct	GFP	DM	Opp	Sac Hits	Bunt Hits	Opp GDP	Pct	Outs Made	To His Right	Straight On	To His Left	GB	Air	Total	Enhanced	+/-	Bunt	GDP	GFP/DME	Total	Rank
2008	LAA	1	2.0	5	0	1.000	0	0				-	-	1	0	0	0	0	0	0	0	0	-		0	0	-
2010	LAA	13	107.0	111	1	.991	5	2				1	1	1.000	27	+1	+1	+1	+2	0	+2	+2	2	0	0	2	-
2011	2 tms	38	303.2	305	3	.990	11	2	2	0	1	3	1	.333	54	0	-1	+1	0	0	0	0	0	0	0	0	-
		52	412.2	421	4	.990	16	4	2	0	1	4	2	.500	82	+1	0	+2	+2	0	+2	+2	2	0	0	2	-

Anthony Rizzo

Year	Team	G	Inn	TC	E	Pct	GFP	DM	Opp	Sac Hits	Bunt Hits	Opp GDP	Pct	Outs Made	To His Right	Straight On	To His Left	GB	Air	Total	Enhanced	+/-	Bunt	GDP	GFP/DME	Total	Rank
2011	SD	45	341.2	344	2	.994	13	6	5	4	0	5	1	.200	62	+1	-1	+2	+3	-1	+2	+2	2	0	0	0	2	-

Gaby Sanchez

Year	Team	G	Inn	TC	E	Pct	GFP	DM	Opp	Sac Hits	Bunt Hits	Opp GDP	Pct	Outs Made	To His Right	Straight On	To His Left	GB	Air	Total	Enhanced	+/-	Bunt	GDP	GFP/DME	Total	Rank
2008	Fla	3	11.0	14	0	1.000	1	1				-	-	1	-1	+1	0	0	0	0	0	0	-		0	0	-
2009	Fla	1	8.0	12	0	1.000	0	0				0	0	-	1				0	0	0	0	0			0	0	-
2010	Fla	149	1253.1	1196	11	.991	64	18	11	5	2	11	5	.455	235	0	-11	+4	-9	-3	-12	-11	-8	0	0	-2	-10	30
2011	Fla	153	1354.0	1368	5	.996	50	24	19	13	2	17	5	.294	263	+2	+5	-2	+5	+2	+7	+6	5	0	0	0	5	8
		306	2626.1	2590	16	.994	115	43	30	18	4	28	10	.357	500	+1	-5	+2	-4	-1	-5	-5	-3	0	0	-2	-5	22

Carlos Santana

Year	Team	G	Inn	TC	E	Pct	GFP	DM	Opp	Sac Hits	Bunt Hits	Opp GDP	Pct	Outs Made	To His Right	Straight On	To His Left	GB	Air	Total	Enhanced	+/-	Bunt	GDP	GFP/DME	Total	Rank
2011	Cle	66	565.0	669	4	.994	37	13	5	1	2	11	5	.455	125	-3	0	+2	-2	-1	-3	-2	-2	1	0	-1	-2	20

First Basemen

Justin Smoak

		BASIC							BUNTS			GDP			PLUS/MINUS								RUNS SAVED					
										Sac	Bunt				Outs	To His	Straight	To His									GFP/		
Year	Team	G	Inn	TC	E	Pct	GFP	DM	Opp	Hits	Hits	Opp	GDP	Pct	Made	Right	On	Left	GB	Air	Total	Enhanced	+/-	Bunt	GDP	DME	Total	Rank
2010	2 tms	94	807.2	833	5	.994	37	14	10	4	3	7	1	.143	158	+1	-3	+1	-1	-2	-3	-3	-2	-1	0	0	-3	24
2011	Sea	108	926.2	950	7	.993	36	11	5	1	2	13	5	.385	165	+1	+1	0	-1	-3	-4	-2	-1	-1	0	1	-1	18
		202	1734.1	1783	12	.993	73	25	15	5	5	20	6	.300	323	+2	-2	+1	-2	-5	-7	-5	-3	-2	0	1	-4	17

Mark Teixeira

		BASIC							BUNTS			GDP			PLUS/MINUS								RUNS SAVED					
										Sac	Bunt				Outs	To His	Straight	To His									GFP/		
Year	Team	G	Inn	TC	E	Pct	GFP	DM	Opp	Hits	Hits	Opp	GDP	Pct	Made	Right	On	Left	GB	Air	Total	Enhanced	+/-	Bunt	GDP	DME	Total	Rank
2003	Tex	116	932.2	1006	4	.996	-	-	13	6	6	-	-	-	208	+11	+16	+2	+29	+2	+31	+29	21	-2	-	-	19	1
2004	Tex	142	1223.0	1317	10	.992	37	18	13	8	2	-	-	-	320	0	-1	+5	+4	-1	+3	+7	5	0	-	0	5	9
2005	Tex	155	1358.0	1482	3	.998	66	23	10	6	0	-	-	-	337	+8	+2	+3	+13	+1	+14	+17	12	1	-	0	13	1
2006	Tex	159	1399.0	1572	4	.997	55	17	6	1	1	-	-	-	307	0	+2	+3	+5	-1	+4	+2	1	1	-	6	8	5
2007	2 tms	128	1098.0	1190	5	.996	50	15	14	13	1	-	-	-	228	-2	-2	+2	-3	+1	-2	-4	-3	0	-	3	0	19
2008	2 tms	153	1335.0	1498	5	.997	93	17	10	9	0	-	-	-	312	+5	+11	+7	+23	+1	+24	+23	17	0	-	4	21	1
2009	NYY	152	1303.2	1275	4	.997	78	26	5	1	1	13	3	.231	249	+4	-1	0	+3	-2	+1	0	0	0	-1	3	2	14
2010	NYY	149	1291.2	1310	3	.998	79	18	11	7	2	26	11	.423	298	+5	+1	+1	+6	+2	+8	+8	5	0	0	1	6	8
2011	NYY	147	1274.0	1306	4	.997	79	25	12	6	3	15	4	.267	251	+9	-2	-1	+9	-1	+8	+5	4	0	-1	0	3	12
		1301	11215.0	11956	42	.996	537	159	94	57	16	54	18	.333	2510	+40	+26	+22	+89	+2	+91	+87	62	0	-2	17	77	2

Mark Trumbo

		BASIC							BUNTS			GDP			PLUS/MINUS								RUNS SAVED					
										Sac	Bunt				Outs	To His	Straight	To His									GFP/		
Year	Team	G	Inn	TC	E	Pct	GFP	DM	Opp	Hits	Hits	Opp	GDP	Pct	Made	Right	On	Left	GB	Air	Total	Enhanced	+/-	Bunt	GDP	DME	Total	Rank
2010	LAA	6	33.0	42	0	1.000	1	0	1	1	0	0	0	-	7	+1	0	0	+2	0	+2	+2	1	0	0	0	1	-
2011	LAA	149	1257.1	1384	10	.993	48	19	9	6	2	18	14	.778	281	+6	+4	0	+10	0	+10	+10	7	0	2	0	9	4
		155	1290.1	1426	10	.993	49	19	10	7	2	18	14	.778	288	+7	+4	0	+12	0	+12	+12	8	0	2	0	10	-

Joey Votto

		BASIC							BUNTS			GDP			PLUS/MINUS								RUNS SAVED					
										Sac	Bunt				Outs	To His	Straight	To His									GFP/		
Year	Team	G	Inn	TC	E	Pct	GFP	DM	Opp	Hits	Hits	Opp	GDP	Pct	Made	Right	On	Left	GB	Air	Total	Enhanced	+/-	Bunt	GDP	DME	Total	Rank
2007	Cin	17	137.0	118	0	1.000	9	1	2	1	1	-	-	-	26	+2	-4	+1	-1	+1	0	0	0	0	-	1	1	-
2008	Cin	144	1223.2	1197	11	.991	57	33	27	16	5	-	-	-	282	+6	+4	+7	+17	+1	+18	+18	13	-2	-	-4	7	6
2009	Cin	130	1097.0	1071	10	.991	55	23	13	5	2	18	4	.222	222	0	+5	-5	-1	+1	0	0	0	0	-1	-1	-2	22
2010	Cin	148	1283.0	1265	5	.996	75	19	17	14	0	14	9	.643	240	+5	-2	-5	+1	+2	+3	-1	-1	0	1	3	3	16
2011	Cin	160	1427.2	1520	6	.996	61	28	22	14	3	21	5	.238	292	+12	+3	-4	+14	0	+14	+11	8	-1	-1	-2	4	10
		599	5168.1	5171	32	.994	257	104	81	50	11	53	18	.340	1062	+25	+6	-6	+30	+5	+35	+28	20	-3	-1	-3	13	11

Brett Wallace

		BASIC							BUNTS			GDP			PLUS/MINUS								RUNS SAVED					
										Sac	Bunt				Outs	To His	Straight	To His									GFP/		
Year	Team	G	Inn	TC	E	Pct	GFP	DM	Opp	Hits	Hits	Opp	GDP	Pct	Made	Right	On	Left	GB	Air	Total	Enhanced	+/-	Bunt	GDP	DME	Total	Rank
2010	Hou	48	375.1	362	3	.992	21	5	9	3	1	5	2	.400	55	+2	+1	+1	+4	-2	+2	+2	2	0	0	1	3	14
2011	Hou	96	768.2	742	6	.992	34	12	13	5	2	7	0	.000	140	+2	+4	-4	+2	+2	+4	+5	4	0	-1	2	5	9
		144	1144.0	1104	9	.992	55	17	22	8	3	12	2	.167	195	+4	+5	-3	+6	0	+6	+7	6	0	-1	3	8	-

Michael Young

		BASIC							BUNTS			GDP			PLUS/MINUS								RUNS SAVED					
										Sac	Bunt				Outs	To His	Straight	To His									GFP/		
Year	Team	G	Inn	TC	E	Pct	GFP	DM	Opp	Hits	Hits	Opp	GDP	Pct	Made	Right	On	Left	GB	Air	Total	Enhanced	+/-	Bunt	GDP	DME	Total	Rank
2011	Tex	36	302.0	283	3	.989	8	8	2	1	1	4	3	.750	33	-1	-1	-3	-4	+1	-3	-4	-3	0	0	-2	-5	-

Second Basemen

Dustin Ackley

Year	Team	G	Inn	TC	E	Pct	GFP	DM	Opps	GDP	Pct	Outs Made	To His Right	Straight On	To His Left	GB	Air	Total	+/-	GDP	GFP/ DME	Total	Rank
2011	Sea	86	741.0	375	6	.984	25	12	70	48	.686	251	0	+2	+12	+13	-2	+11	9	1	0	10	6

Ryan Adams

Year	Team	G	Inn	TC	E	Pct	GFP	DM	Opps	GDP	Pct	Outs Made	To His Right	Straight On	To His Left	GB	Air	Total	+/-	GDP	GFP/ DME	Total	Rank
2011	Bal	26	213.0	111	2	.982	10	7	22	14	.636	63	-3	-2	0	-5	+1	-4	-3	0	0	-3	

Jose Altuve

Year	Team	G	Inn	TC	E	Pct	GFP	DM	Opps	GDP	Pct	Outs Made	To His Right	Straight On	To His Left	GB	Air	Total	+/-	GDP	GFP/ DME	Total	Rank
2011	Hou	55	460.2	217	2	.991	22	5	37	26	.703	145	-1	0	+2	+1	0	+1	1	1	1	3	14

Robert Andino

Year	Team	G	Inn	TC	E	Pct	GFP	DM	Opps	GDP	Pct	Outs Made	To His Right	Straight On	To His Left	GB	Air	Total	+/-	GDP	GFP/ DME	Total	Rank
2008	Fla	15	89.2	63	2	.968	3	1	15	7	.467	39	+2	+1	0	+3	+1	+4	3	0	0	3	-
2009	Bal	8	39.0	20	0	1.000	0	0	4	4	1.000	12	0	+1	-1	0	-1	-1	-1	0	0	-1	-
2010	Bal	8	50.0	16	0	1.000	1	0	1	1	1.000	14	0	0	+1	+1	0	+1	1	0	0	1	-
2011	Bal	94	724.1	402	4	.990	28	16	90	58	.644	242	-4	+4	+3	+3	+2	+5	4	1	0	5	10
		125	903.0	501	6	.988	32	17	110	70	.636	307	-2	+6	+3	+7	+2	+9	7	1	0	8	-

Darwin Barney

Year	Team	G	Inn	TC	E	Pct	GFP	DM	Opps	GDP	Pct	Outs Made	To His Right	Straight On	To His Left	GB	Air	Total	+/-	GDP	GFP/ DME	Total	Rank
2010	ChC	10	54.1	32	2	.938	4	0	9	5	.556	14	-1	+1	0	-1	0	-1	-1	0	1	0	-
2011	ChC	135	1110.1	619	12	.981	47	30	100	56	.560	373	-3	+1	+3	+1	+3	+4	3	-2	0	1	16
		145	1164.2	651	14	.978	51	30	109	61	.560	387	-4	+2	+3	0	+3	+3	2	-2	1	1	-

Gordon Beckham

Year	Team	G	Inn	TC	E	Pct	GFP	DM	Opps	GDP	Pct	Outs Made	To His Right	Straight On	To His Left	GB	Air	Total	+/-	GDP	GFP/ DME	Total	Rank
2010	CWS	126	1111.1	632	12	.981	49	25	135	93	.689	372	-8	-4	0	-12	0	-12	-9	1	1	-7	27
2011	CWS	149	1307.2	723	8	.989	64	26	130	80	.615	463	-8	+3	+12	+6	0	+6	4	0	-1	3	13
		275	2419.0	1355	20	.985	113	51	265	173	.653	835	-16	-1	+12	-6	0	-6	-5	1	0	-4	23

Manny Burriss

Year	Team	G	Inn	TC	E	Pct	GFP	DM	Opps	GDP	Pct	Outs Made	To His Right	Straight On	To His Left	GB	Air	Total	+/-	GDP	GFP/ DME	Total	Rank
2008	SF	41	282.0	150	4	.973	15	5	30	13	.433	90	+1	+2	+3	+5	0	+5	4	-1	0	3	-
2009	SF	61	494.0	253	7	.972	24	16	53	29	.547	148	0	-2	-2	-4	-1	-5	-4	-2	0	-6	28
2010	SF	5	12.0	4	0	1.000	0	0	0	0	-	2	0	0	0	0	0	0	0	0	0	0	-
2011	SF	39	230.0	142	3	.979	15	4	33	23	.697	75	0	-4	+2	-2	+1	-1	-1	1	0	0	-
		146	1018.0	549	14	.974	54	25	116	65	.560	315	+1	-4	+3	-1	0	-1	-1	-2	0	-3	-

Orlando Cabrera

Year	Team	G	Inn	TC	E	Pct	GFP	DM	Opps	GDP	Pct	Outs Made	To His Right	Straight On	To His Left	GB	Air	Total	+/-	GDP	GFP/ DME	Total	Rank
2011	2 tms	85	709.1	400	6	.985	21	22	67	42	.627	264	+4	+1	-3	+3	-5	-2	-2	0	-2	-4	26

Robinson Cano

Year	Team	G	Inn	TC	E	Pct	GFP	DM	Opps	GDP	Pct	Outs Made	To His Right	Straight On	To His Left	GB	Air	Total	+/-	GDP	GFP/ DME	Total	Rank
2005	NYY	131	1142.2	666	17	.974	40	19	152	70	.461	441	-16	-2	-15	-33	+6	-27	-21	-2	1	-22	34
2006	NYY	118	1009.0	572	9	.984	24	25	137	69	.504	387	-2	-3	-1	-5	+1	-4	-3	0	-1	-4	24
2007	NYY	159	1408.2	830	13	.984	47	25	187	122	.652	530	+6	+2	+9	+16	+1	+17	13	9	1	23	1
2008	NYY	159	1376.2	800	13	.984	69	29	178	88	.494	530	-6	+1	-8	-13	-4	-17	-13	0	1	-12	33
2009	NYY	161	1399.2	744	12	.984	60	39	153	91	.595	485	+1	-1	+8	+8	0	+8	6	-3	-3	0	18
2010	NYY	158	1393.1	776	3	.996	45	29	171	113	.661	454	+3	+1	+9	+14	+6	+20	15	2	-1	16	3
2011	NYY	157	1340.0	777	10	.987	68	40	139	96	.691	461	+11	-5	-5	+1	-1	0	0	2	-1	1	17
		1043	9070.0	5165	77	.985	353	206	1117	649	.581	3288	-3	-7	-3	-12	+9	-3	-3	8	-3	2	20

Second Basemen

Jamey Carroll

		BASIC							GDP			PLUS/MINUS							RUNS SAVED				
Year	Team	G	Inn	TC	E	Pct	GFP	DM	Opps	GDP	Pct	Outs Made	To His Right	Straight On	To His Left	GB	Air	Total	+/-	GDP	GFP/DME	Total	Rank
2003	Mon	11	51.1	27	0	1.000	-	-	11	5	.455	12	0	-2	0	-1	-1	-2	-2	0	-	-2	-
2004	Mon	51	344.2	182	1	.995	8	5	45	28	.622	82	-2	+1	-7	-8	-1	-9	-7	2	2	-3	-
2005	Was	63	427.2	246	5	.980	16	8	63	27	.429	151	-4	-1	+10	+6	-1	+5	4	-1	0	3	-
2006	Col	109	894.2	586	3	.995	36	13	139	91	.655	396	+4	+4	+8	+16	-3	+13	10	6	2	18	3
2007	Col	60	431.1	247	2	.992	15	6	68	35	.515	165	0	+1	+2	+2	-3	-1	-1	0	1	0	20
2008	Cle	74	580.1	300	3	.990	23	12	73	42	.575	203	+1	0	-1	0	-4	-4	-3	2	0	-1	20
2009	Cle	56	467.0	227	1	.996	19	5	38	24	.632	149	+1	+3	+4	+8	-2	+6	5	0	1	6	9
2010	LAD	48	219.0	126	0	1.000	13	4	21	11	.524	79	+2	+4	-3	+3	-2	+1	1	0	1	2	-
2011	LAD	81	549.1	256	5	.980	16	13	46	33	.717	161	-9	-5	+2	-12	-4	-16	-12	1	1	-10	32
		553	3965.1	2197	20	.991	146	66	504	296	.587	1398	-7	+5	+15	+14	-21	-7	-5	10	8	13	15

Alexi Casilla

		BASIC							GDP			PLUS/MINUS							RUNS SAVED				
Year	Team	G	Inn	TC	E	Pct	GFP	DM	Opps	GDP	Pct	Outs Made	To His Right	Straight On	To His Left	GB	Air	Total	+/-	GDP	GFP/DME	Total	Rank
2006	Min	4	13.0	13	0	1.000	0	0	5	4	.800	7				0	+1	+1	1	0	0	1	-
2007	Min	52	421.0	237	10	.958	21	10	67	36	.537	145	-5	-2	+4	-4	0	-4	-3	1	-1	-3	25
2008	Min	95	833.2	455	12	.974	47	15	125	66	.528	288	-11	-3	+9	-5	+1	-4	-3	1	-1	-3	23
2009	Min	72	571.1	316	5	.984	21	17	55	33	.600	214	-11	-5	+3	-13	-3	-16	-12	0	-1	-13	34
2010	Min	24	159.0	86	1	.988	12	4	18	8	.444	53	-2	0	+3	+1	+1	+2	2	-1	0	1	-
2011	Min	56	470.2	265	6	.977	25	8	53	36	.679	186	-2	+2	-1	-1	0	-1	-1	0	2	1	18
		303	2468.2	1372	34	.975	126	54	323	183	.567	893	-31	-8	+18	-22	0	-22	-16	1	-1	-16	30

Mark Ellis

		BASIC							GDP			PLUS/MINUS							RUNS SAVED				
Year	Team	G	Inn	TC	E	Pct	GFP	DM	Opps	GDP	Pct	Outs Made	To His Right	Straight On	To His Left	GB	Air	Total	+/-	GDP	GFP/DME	Total	Rank
2003	Oak	153	1297.2	793	14	.982	-	-	174	87	.500	535	-1	+1	+16	+17	+6	+23	17	0	-	17	3
2005	Oak	115	972.0	543	6	.989	19	20	134	74	.552	373	+2	+1	+5	+9	+2	+11	8	2	-2	8	11
2006	Oak	123	1070.0	632	2	.997	17	24	152	89	.586	390	-3	+8	+5	+10	+3	+13	10	4	1	15	5
2007	Oak	150	1322.0	806	5	.994	40	31	177	95	.537	560	0	+5	+11	+16	+3	+19	14	2	-3	13	6
2008	Oak	115	1011.2	568	4	.993	29	18	131	81	.618	373	+9	+7	+5	+22	+3	+25	19	5	-1	23	2
2009	Oak	105	906.2	487	5	.990	32	10	91	59	.648	335	+3	+3	-3	+3	-3	0	0	0	2	2	14
2010	Oak	116	986.1	549	3	.995	31	16	107	74	.692	340	+1	+3	+2	+6	+1	+7	6	1	1	8	5
2011	2 tms	123	1054.2	636	3	.995	46	13	129	84	.651	390	+6	+5	-1	+11	+5	+16	12	1	4	17	4
		1000	8621.0	5014	42	.992	214	132	1095	643	.587	3296	+17	+33	+40	+94	+20	+114	86	15	2	103	2

Danny Espinosa

		BASIC							GDP			PLUS/MINUS							RUNS SAVED				
Year	Team	G	Inn	TC	E	Pct	GFP	DM	Opps	GDP	Pct	Outs Made	To His Right	Straight On	To His Left	GB	Air	Total	+/-	GDP	GFP/DME	Total	Rank
2010	Was	25	211.1	131	0	1.000	14	3	25	20	.800	75	-4	-2	+8	+2	+1	+3	3	1	1	5	-
2011	Was	158	1393.0	784	14	.982	65	33	136	89	.654	488	+5	+2	+1	+8	-1	+7	5	0	0	5	9
		183	1604.1	915	14	.985	79	36	161	109	.677	563	+1	0	+9	+10	0	+10	8	1	1	10	-

Chris Getz

		BASIC							GDP			PLUS/MINUS							RUNS SAVED				
Year	Team	G	Inn	TC	E	Pct	GFP	DM	Opps	GDP	Pct	Outs Made	To His Right	Straight On	To His Left	GB	Air	Total	+/-	GDP	GFP/DME	Total	Rank
2008	CWS	7	23.0	15	0	1.000	1	0	3	1	.333	11				0	0	0	0	0	0	0	-
2009	CWS	106	896.1	501	7	.986	24	18	105	66	.629	323	-7	0	0	-7	-3	-10	-8	-1	-2	-11	31
2010	KC	64	535.0	280	3	.989	14	8	67	44	.657	155	+4	-4	-2	-2	-2	-4	-3	0	1	-2	23
2011	KC	110	894.1	494	6	.988	23	19	108	65	.602	297	-3	-1	+5	+2	-3	-1	-1	0	-1	-2	22
		287	2348.2	1290	16	.988	62	45	283	176	.622	786	-6	-5	+3	-7	-8	-15	-12	-1	-2	-15	29

Johnny Giavotella

		BASIC							GDP			PLUS/MINUS							RUNS SAVED				
Year	Team	G	Inn	TC	E	Pct	GFP	DM	Opps	GDP	Pct	Outs Made	To His Right	Straight On	To His Left	GB	Air	Total	+/-	GDP	GFP/DME	Total	Rank
2011	KC	46	385.1	177	5	.972	23	12	27	16	.593	119	0	-3	+2	-1	-1	-2	-1	-1	1	-1	-

Alberto Gonzalez

		BASIC							GDP			PLUS/MINUS							RUNS SAVED				
Year	Team	G	Inn	TC	E	Pct	GFP	DM	Opps	GDP	Pct	Outs Made	To His Right	Straight On	To His Left	GB	Air	Total	+/-	GDP	GFP/DME	Total	Rank
2008	NYY	4	28.0	11	0	1.000	2	0	1	1	1.000	9	0	0	+1	+1	0	+1	1	0	0	1	-
2009	Was	55	363.0	208	1	.995	11	3	46	33	.717	129	-9	-1	+4	-6	-2	-8	-6	1	2	-3	-
2010	Was	38	120.1	78	1	.987	5	1	23	17	.739	40	+1	-1	+1	0	+1	+1	1	0	0	1	-
2011	SD	41	243.1	116	2	.983	11	3	17	13	.765	65	-1	-4	+4	0	0	0	0	1	0	1	-
		138	754.2	413	4	.990	29	7	87	64	.736	243	-9	-6	+10	-5	-1	-6	-4	2	2	0	-

Second Basemen

Carlos Guillen

		BASIC							GDP			PLUS/MINUS							RUNS SAVED				
Year	Team	G	Inn	TC	E	Pct	GFP	DM	Opps	GDP	Pct	Outs Made	To His Right	Straight On	To His Left	GB	Air	Total	+/-	GDP	GFP/DME	Total	Rank
2010	Det	47	393.1	227	3	.987	11	8	47	33	.702	141	+5	+1	-8	-2	0	-2	-1	1	0	0	
2011	Det	25	215.2	119	2	.983	3	6	22	18	.818	71	-1	-1	-2	-4	0	-4	-2	1	0	-1	-
		72	609.0	346	5	.986	14	14	69	51	.739	212	+4	0	-10	-6	0	-6	-3	2	0	-1	

Bill Hall

		BASIC							GDP			PLUS/MINUS							RUNS SAVED				
Year	Team	G	Inn	TC	E	Pct	GFP	DM	Opps	GDP	Pct	Outs Made	To His Right	Straight On	To His Left	GB	Air	Total	+/-	GDP	GFP/DME	Total	Rank
2003	Mil	18	134.2	91	4	.956	-	-	22	12	.545	52	0	-1	-3	-4	0	-4	-3	0	-	-3	-
2004	Mil	50	418.1	217	9	.959	11	10	48	25	.521	118	+6	-2	0	+4	+2	+6	5	0	0	5	10
2005	Mil	23	185.0	101	4	.960	7	3	24	5	.208	66	0	+2	+1	+2	0	+2	2	-2	1	1	-
2006	Mil	4	34.0	15	0	1.000	0	0	1	1	1.000	14	+1	0	0	+1	+1	+2	2	0	0	2	-
2008	Mil	6	32.0	21	2	.905	0	1	5	1	.200	17	+1	0	-1	0	0	0	0	0	0	0	-
2009	Sea	3	19.0	6	0	1.000	0	1	1	0	.000	5	0	0	0	0	0	0	0	0	0	0	-
2010	Bos	51	353.1	178	6	.966	10	10	34	20	.588	104	+2	+1	-1	+2	-1	+1	1	0	-1	0	-
2011	2 tms	51	387.2	197	6	.970	15	14	42	18	.429	101	-4	0	-6	-11	+4	-7	-5	-3	0	-8	-
		206	1564.0	826	31	.962	44	39	177	82	.463	477	+6	0	-10	-6	+6	0	2	-5	0	-3	-

Jonathan Herrera

		BASIC							GDP			PLUS/MINUS							RUNS SAVED				
Year	Team	G	Inn	TC	E	Pct	GFP	DM	Opps	GDP	Pct	Outs Made	To His Right	Straight On	To His Left	GB	Air	Total	+/-	GDP	GFP/DME	Total	Rank
2008	Col	21	122.0	84	2	.976	9	0	20	13	.650	53	+6	-2	-2	+2	0	+2	2	1	2	5	-
2010	Col	57	425.1	244	4	.984	14	3	41	30	.732	159	+1	0	+4	+5	+2	+7	5	0	1	6	8
2011	Col	62	499.0	247	2	.992	19	9	39	28	.718	173	+1	-3	0	-2	+2	0	0	0	0	0	21
		140	1046.1	575	8	.986	42	12	100	71	.710	385	+8	-5	+2	+5	+4	+9	7	1	3	11	-

Aaron Hill

		BASIC							GDP			PLUS/MINUS							RUNS SAVED				
Year	Team	G	Inn	TC	E	Pct	GFP	DM	Opps	GDP	Pct	Outs Made	To His Right	Straight On	To His Left	GB	Air	Total	+/-	GDP	GFP/DME	Total	Rank
2005	Tor	22	177.2	111	1	.991	9	6	34	14	.412	78	0	+1	+2	+3	-2	+1	1	-1	0	0	-
2006	Tor	112	914.1	526	7	.987	34	19	132	86	.652	355	+15	+2	+11	+28	-3	+25	19	6	1	26	1
2007	Tor	160	1410.0	818	14	.983	76	26	193	110	.570	575	+7	+9	+7	+23	-1	+22	17	4	1	22	2
2008	Tor	55	479.0	238	1	.996	17	8	50	25	.500	164	-2	+2	0	0	-2	-2	-2	0	1	-1	-
2009	Tor	156	1372.0	798	7	.991	65	31	181	116	.641	480	+8	+5	+10	+23	-3	+20	15	-2	0	13	4
2010	Tor	137	1188.0	629	10	.984	45	26	141	86	.610	369	+4	-7	+8	+5	-5	0	0	-2	0	-2	21
2011	2 tms	137	1198.1	635	7	.989	40	21	130	80	.615	392	+2	-2	+5	+5	-2	+3	3	0	-1	2	15
		779	6739.1	3755	47	.987	286	137	861	517	.600	2413	+34	+10	+43	+87	-18	+69	53	5	2	60	5

Orlando Hudson

		BASIC							GDP			PLUS/MINUS							RUNS SAVED				
Year	Team	G	Inn	TC	E	Pct	GFP	DM	Opps	GDP	Pct	Outs Made	To His Right	Straight On	To His Left	GB	Air	Total	+/-	GDP	GFP/DME	Total	Rank
2003	Tor	139	1146.2	756	12	.984	-	-	180	93	.517	513	-7	0	+24	+17	+5	+22	17	1	-	18	2
2004	Tor	133	1124.2	736	12	.984	43	22	162	79	.488	486	+4	+7	+16	+26	+9	+35	27	-1	-1	25	1
2005	Tor	130	1067.2	698	6	.991	66	19	143	77	.538	487	-1	+1	+18	+17	+3	+20	15	2	2	19	4
2006	Ari	157	1349.0	834	13	.984	53	25	195	101	.518	550	-3	-11	+23	+8	+5	+13	10	1	2	13	7
2007	Ari	137	1183.1	655	10	.985	50	33	166	89	.536	433	-8	-5	+25	+11	+9	+20	15	2	0	17	4
2008	Ari	105	904.2	493	9	.982	48	9	106	53	.500	345	-11	0	+4	-7	+3	-4	-3	0	3	0	18
2009	LAD	145	1272.1	692	8	.988	71	21	106	73	.689	465	-10	-5	+13	-1	+9	+8	6	-1	1	6	8
2010	Min	123	1067.0	637	8	.987	46	17	125	76	.608	401	-1	+2	+6	+8	0	+8	6	-1	-1	4	10
2011	SD	114	959.2	550	4	.993	30	23	111	65	.586	323	-7	+2	-2	-7	0	-7	-5	-3	0	-8	31
		1183	10075.0	6051	82	.986	407	169	1294	706	.546	4003	-44	-9	+127	+72	+43	+115	88	0	6	94	3

Luke Hughes

		BASIC							GDP			PLUS/MINUS							RUNS SAVED				
Year	Team	G	Inn	TC	E	Pct	GFP	DM	Opps	GDP	Pct	Outs Made	To His Right	Straight On	To His Left	GB	Air	Total	+/-	GDP	GFP/DME	Total	Rank
2011	Min	37	301.1	189	2	.989	11	2	36	25	.694	111	-2	+2	+1	+1	+2	+3	3	1	1	5	-

Omar Infante

		BASIC							GDP			PLUS/MINUS							RUNS SAVED				
Year	Team	G	Inn	TC	E	Pct	GFP	DM	Opps	GDP	Pct	Outs Made	To His Right	Straight On	To His Left	GB	Air	Total	+/-	GDP	GFP/DME	Total	Rank
2003	Det	2	13.0	6	0	1.000	-	-	2	2	1.000	3				0	0	0	0	0	-	0	-
2004	Det	105	874.2	499	12	.976	16	20	124	71	.573	270	-6	-5	+3	-8	-1	-9	-7	3	-1	-5	28
2005	Det	69	591.2	343	4	.988	10	8	88	47	.534	190	-5	-2	0	-6	-1	-7	-5	1	-1	-5	23
2006	Det	37	307.1	177	4	.977	3	3	41	26	.634	110	+4	-1	+2	+5	0	+5	4	2	0	6	-
2007	Det	20	124.1	69	1	.986	3	2	15	6	.400	44	-1	0	+2	+1	0	+1	1	0	0	1	-
2008	Atl	10	74.0	33	0	1.000	2	0	13	6	.462	19	+1	+1	0	+2	0	+2	2	0	0	2	-
2009	Atl	30	199.0	106	2	.981	6	2	15	11	.733	72	+1	+3	-6	-3	-2	-5	-4	0	-1	-5	-
2010	Atl	65	555.2	312	7	.978	19	14	57	41	.719	201	+1	+1	0	+3	+3	+6	4	1	-2	3	12
2011	Fla	146	1283.1	734	8	.989	54	28	111	72	.649	514	+1	+4	0	+6	0	+6	4	0	0	4	11
		484	4023.0	2279	38	.983	113	77	466	282	.605	1423	-4	+1	+1	0	-1	-1	-1	7	-5	1	21

Second Basemen

Maicer Izturis

		BASIC							GDP			PLUS/MINUS							RUNS SAVED				
Year	Team	G	Inn	TC	E	Pct	GFP	DM	Opps	GDP	Pct	Outs Made	To His Right	Straight On	To His Left	GB	Air	Total	+/-	GDP	GFP/DME	Total	Rank
2004	Mon	10	88.0	44	1	.977	1	1	7	4	.571	31	+1	-1	-1	-1	0	-1	-1	0	0	-1	-
2005	LAA	1	8.0	8	0	1.000	0	0	1			6	0			0	-1	-1	-1	0	0	-1	-
2006	LAA	4	24.0	11	0	1.000	1	1	3	2	.667	7	0	0	+1	+1	0	+1	1	0	0	1	-
2007	LAA	40	305.1	141	0	1.000	3	8	35	23	.657	97	-3	0	0	-3	-1	-4	-3	2	0	-1	-
2008	LAA	23	183.2	112	2	.982	6	4	26	13	.500	65	0	-1	+2	0	+1	+1	1	0	0	1	-
2009	LAA	68	567.1	296	2	.993	25	11	64	50	.781	193	-1	+5	+3	+7	-3	+4	3	2	2	7	7
2010	LAA	22	176.1	83	1	.988	10	1	10	5	.500	55	+2	+1	-3	-1	0	-1	0	0	1	1	-
2011	LAA	49	422.2	249	4	.984	19	8	49	35	.714	158	-3	-2	-7	-11	+1	-10	-8	1	2	-5	28
		217	1775.1	944	10	.989	65	34	195	132	.677	612	-4	+2	-5	-8	-3	-11	-8	5	5	2	-

Kelly Johnson

		BASIC							GDP			PLUS/MINUS							RUNS SAVED				
Year	Team	G	Inn	TC	E	Pct	GFP	DM	Opps	GDP	Pct	Outs Made	To His Right	Straight On	To His Left	GB	Air	Total	+/-	GDP	GFP/DME	Total	Rank
2007	Atl	133	1153.1	624	14	.978	38	30	153	79	.516	412	+5	-4	-6	-5	+5	0	0	1	-2	-1	21
2008	Atl	144	1198.2	701	14	.980	37	31	182	83	.456	441	-3	-2	+5	0	-1	-1	-1	-2	-4	-7	26
2009	Ari	84	655.2	367	10	.973	19	16	82	55	.671	211	+4	0	-4	0	-2	-2	-2	0	-2	-4	25
2010	Ari	149	1270.2	677	8	.988	39	18	144	99	.688	388	-4	+6	0	+3	-6	-3	-3	1	2	0	17
2011	2 tms	141	1224.0	627	10	.984	33	18	118	82	.695	358	-2	-1	-1	-4	+1	-3	-3	2	2	1	20
		651	5502.1	2996	56	.981	166	113	679	398	.586	1810	0	-1	-6	-6	-3	-9	-9	2	-4	-11	25

Howie Kendrick

		BASIC							GDP			PLUS/MINUS							RUNS SAVED				
Year	Team	G	Inn	TC	E	Pct	GFP	DM	Opps	GDP	Pct	Outs Made	To His Right	Straight On	To His Left	GB	Air	Total	+/-	GDP	GFP/DME	Total	Rank
2006	LAA	28	220.0	115	0	1.000	6	4	33	23	.697	75	-4	+2	+4	+2	0	+3	2	2	0	4	-
2007	LAA	86	751.1	409	4	.978	22	18	91	49	.538	275	-2	0	+9	+7	0	+7	5	1	0	6	10
2008	LAA	92	776.0	446	4	.991	28	7	99	61	.616	308	-13	-4	+13	-5	+1	-4	-3	3	3	3	14
2009	LAA	95	805.2	431	4	.991	35	16	98	69	.704	293	-7	-1	+13	+4	+1	+5	4	1	0	5	10
2010	LAA	143	1251.0	634	9	.986	47	29	116	70	.603	396	-11	-5	+13	-3	-1	-4	-4	-2	1	-5	26
2011	LAA	108	937.2	483	4	.992	35	16	89	59	.663	318	+5	+7	+9	+21	-7	+14	10	0	0	10	5
		552	4741.2	2518	30	.988	173	90	526	331	.629	1665	-32	-1	+61	+26	-5	+21	14	5	4	23	14

Adam Kennedy

		BASIC							GDP			PLUS/MINUS							RUNS SAVED				
Year	Team	G	Inn	TC	E	Pct	GFP	DM	Opps	GDP	Pct	Outs Made	To His Right	Straight On	To His Left	GB	Air	Total	+/-	GDP	GFP/DME	Total	Rank
2003	Ana	140	1119.2	612	6	.990	-	-	131	70	.534	445	+6	0	+8	+15	0	+15	11	1	-	12	6
2004	Ana	144	1225.0	654	12	.982	39	25	133	62	.466	438	+2	0	-3	-1	+8	+7	5	-1	2	6	8
2005	LAA	127	1107.2	569	5	.991	28	22	110	65	.591	401	+11	-1	+8	+18	-2	+16	12	3	1	16	6
2006	LAA	133	1140.2	575	9	.984	25	27	127	70	.551	405	+3	-5	0	-3	+4	+1	1	2	-1	2	15
2007	StL	79	630.1	374	7	.981	25	15	95	42	.442	250	+2	-1	-1	+1	-2	-1	-1	-2	0	-3	24
2008	StL	84	635.2	375	7	.981	27	3	85	53	.624	245	+15	-1	+5	+18	0	+18	14	3	1	18	3
2009	Oak	50	421.0	215	7	.967	19	17	55	30	.545	137	-2	+2	-8	-7	-3	-10	-8	-1	-2	-11	-
2010	Was	86	628.1	357	7	.980	20	11	68	40	.588	222	-2	+2	+6	+6	-4	+2	1	-2	-1	-2	20
2011	Sea	34	293.2	148	1	.993	10	6	25	20	.800	100	-4	0	+1	-3	0	-3	-2	1	-1	-2	-
		877	7202.0	3879	61	.984	193	126	829	452	.545	2643	+31	-4	+16	+44	+1	+45	33	4	-1	36	11

Jeff Keppinger

		BASIC							GDP			PLUS/MINUS							RUNS SAVED				
Year	Team	G	Inn	TC	E	Pct	GFP	DM	Opps	GDP	Pct	Outs Made	To His Right	Straight On	To His Left	GB	Air	Total	+/-	GDP	GFP/DME	Total	Rank
2004	NYM	32	257.2	149	2	.987	5	1	38	19	.500	89	-1	-1	+1	-2	0	-2	-2	0	1	-1	-
2006	KC	1	8.0	6	0	1.000	0	0	2	2	1.000	4				+1	+1	+2	2	0	0	2	-
2007	Cin	3	26.0	17	0	1.000	1	0	4	2	.500	13	+1	-1	-1	+1	+1	0	0	0	0	0	-
2008	Cin	3	23.0	10	0	1.000	0	1	2	1	.500	3	-1	0		-1	0	-1	-1	0	0	-1	-
2009	Hou	22	138.2	82	1	.988	5	2	13	10	.769	50	0	0	-2	-2	0	-2	-2	0	0	-2	-
2010	Hou	126	1070.2	574	6	.990	31	15	96	65	.677	369	-9	+5	-7	-11	-3	-14	-10	1	-1	-10	32
2011	2 tms	93	791.0	390	5	.987	18	15	60	31	.517	252	-7	-2	-5	-14	+4	-10	-7	-2	-2	-11	33
		280	2315.0	1228	14	.989	60	34	215	130	.605	780	-17	+1	-14	-30	+3	-27	-20	-1	-2	-23	31

Ian Kinsler

		BASIC							GDP			PLUS/MINUS							RUNS SAVED				
Year	Team	G	Inn	TC	E	Pct	GFP	DM	Opps	GDP	Pct	Outs Made	To His Right	Straight On	To His Left	GB	Air	Total	+/-	GDP	GFP/DME	Total	Rank
2006	Tex	119	1032.0	658	18	.973	28	31	153	86	.562	424	-3	+1	-8	-10	+6	-4	-3	3	-3	-3	22
2007	Tex	130	1136.2	736	17	.977	43	26	163	88	.540	459	+7	-4	+1	+4	+3	+7	5	2	-3	4	11
2008	Tex	121	1064.0	700	18	.974	38	15	201	113	.562	412	-1	+2	-15	-13	-2	-15	-11	4	-2	-9	30
2009	Tex	144	1258.0	711	11	.985	63	22	125	89	.712	495	+6	-1	+10	+16	+7	+23	17	3	2	22	1
2010	Tex	103	905.1	475	7	.985	38	15	110	67	.609	297	-2	+1	+3	+1	+10	+11	8	-1	0	7	7
2011	Tex	144	1269.0	677	11	.984	54	27	142	102	.718	442	+9	+3	+2	+13	+7	+20	15	3	0	18	2
		761	6665.0	3957	82	.979	264	136	894	545	.610	2529	+16	+2	-7	+11	+31	+42	31	14	-6	39	9

Second Basemen

Jason Kipnis

Year	Team	G	Inn	TC	E	Pct	GFP	DM	Opps	GDP	Pct	Outs Made	To His Right	Straight On	To His Left	GB	Air	Total	+/-	GDP	GFP/DME	Total	Rank
2011	Cle	36	305.0	164	6	.963	11	10	29	13	.448	112	-1	+1	-1	-1	-1	-2	-1	-1	0	-2	-

Aaron Miles

Year	Team	G	Inn	TC	E	Pct	GFP	DM	Opps	GDP	Pct	Outs Made	To His Right	Straight On	To His Left	GB	Air	Total	+/-	GDP	GFP/DME	Total	Rank
2003	CWS	3	14.0	7	0	1.000	-	-	0			6	0	+1	0	0	0	0	0		-	0	-
2004	Col	128	1029.0	636	10	.984	27	16	169	63	.373	371	-1	+5	+14	+18	+3	+21	16	-6	2	12	3
2005	Col	79	602.0	367	6	.984	21	13	100	45	.450	229	-6	0	+1	-5	-3	-8	-6	-2	1	-7	29
2006	StL	88	649.2	407	10	.975	11	8	109	55	.505	238	+1	-1	+2	+2	-2	0	0	0	2	2	16
2007	StL	85	590.2	317	5	.984	17	10	70	36	.514	184	+5	+2	-5	+1	-2	-1	-1	0	-1	-2	22
2008	StL	85	499.2	259	3	.988	17	13	68	41	.603	171	+2	-1	-5	-4	+5	+1	1	2	-2	1	16
2009	ChC	35	253.2	142	2	.986	10	8	31	18	.581	71	0	-1	0	-1	-1	-2	-2	0	-1	-3	-
2010	StL	50	214.2	123	2	.984	8	6	22	13	.591	86	+2	+1	-2	+1	+2	+3	2	0	-1	1	-
2011	LAD	72	519.0	260	2	.992	15	15	41	24	.585	161	-4	+2	-1	-3	0	-3	-2	0	0	-2	23
		625	4372.1	2518	40	.984	126	89	610	295	.484	1517	-1	+8	+4	+9	+2	+11	8	-6	0	2	19

Chris Nelson

Year	Team	G	Inn	TC	E	Pct	GFP	DM	Opps	GDP	Pct	Outs Made	To His Right	Straight On	To His Left	GB	Air	Total	+/-	GDP	GFP/DME	Total	Rank
2010	Col	4	26.0	17	2	.882	1	0	2	0	.000	11	-1	+1	-2	-3	0	-3	-2	0	0	-2	-
2011	Col	29	208.2	97	3	.969	6	6	24	16	.667	59	-2	-4	-2	-7	-1	-8	-6	0	0	-6	-
		33	234.2	114	5	.956	7	6	26	16	.615	70	-3	-3	-4	-10	-1	-11	-8	0	0	-8	-

Dustin Pedroia

Year	Team	G	Inn	TC	E	Pct	GFP	DM	Opps	GDP	Pct	Outs Made	To His Right	Straight On	To His Left	GB	Air	Total	+/-	GDP	GFP/DME	Total	Rank
2006	Bos	27	172.0	121	3	.975	5	6	28	15	.536	82	-1	0	-2	-2	+1	-1	-1	0	0	-1	-
2007	Bos	137	1141.1	625	6	.990	68	18	126	71	.563	417	-1	+3	-5	-4	-1	-5	-4	2	4	2	15
2008	Bos	157	1376.1	733	6	.992	66	25	176	90	.511	477	+1	+4	+9	+13	+2	+15	11	1	1	13	5
2009	Bos	154	1346.2	663	6	.991	50	11	112	80	.714	458	-3	+5	+7	+10	+4	+14	11	2	1	14	3
2010	Bos	75	667.1	352	3	.991	32	4	69	50	.725	208	+1	+4	+2	+8	-3	+5	3	1	1	5	9
2011	Bos	159	1392.1	722	7	.990	66	15	131	82	.626	456	+7	+7	+9	+23	-4	+19	15	-1	4	18	2
		709	6096.0	3216	31	.990	287	79	642	388	.604	2098	+4	+23	+20	+48	-1	+47	35	5	11	51	6

Brandon Phillips

Year	Team	G	Inn	TC	E	Pct	GFP	DM	Opps	GDP	Pct	Outs Made	To His Right	Straight On	To His Left	GB	Air	Total	+/-	GDP	GFP/DME	Total	Rank
2003	Cle	109	925.1	572	11	.981	-	-	144	73	.507	345	+8	+4	-5	+7	-1	+6	5	0	-	5	14
2004	Cle	6	56.2	37	1	.973	5	2	10	4	.400	16	0	-1	+1	0	0	0	0	0	0	0	-
2005	Cle	2	18.0	9	0	1.000	0	0	2	2	1.000	6	0	0	0	0	0	0	0	0	0	0	-
2006	Cin	142	1216.1	681	16	.977	41	29	170	76	.447	403	+2	-5	-2	-5	+1	-4	-3	-3	-1	-7	27
2007	Cin	156	1371.0	782	8	.990	76	35	198	101	.510	491	+3	+7	-2	+8	+3	+11	8	1	0	9	8
2008	Cin	140	1237.2	706	7	.990	66	27	183	80	.437	429	+17	+4	0	+21	-4	+17	13	-3	3	13	4
2009	Cin	151	1332.1	725	9	.988	65	29	150	101	.673	444	+5	+1	-6	0	-1	-1	-1	0	3	2	15
2010	Cin	152	1311.0	703	3	.996	63	19	138	89	.645	430	+9	+5	-5	+9	0	+9	6	-1	5	10	4
2011	Cin	148	1324.0	721	6	.992	57	28	153	94	.614	428	+6	+2	+4	+11	-2	+9	7	-1	0	6	8
		1006	8792.1	4936	61	.988	373	169	1148	620	.540	2992	+50	+17	-15	+51	-4	+47	35	-7	10	38	10

Nick Punto

Year	Team	G	Inn	TC	E	Pct	GFP	DM	Opps	GDP	Pct	Outs Made	To His Right	Straight On	To His Left	GB	Air	Total	+/-	GDP	GFP/DME	Total	Rank
2003	Phi	16	83.0	65	1	.985	-	-	17	5	.294	38	-1	0	+2	+1	+1	+2	2	-1	-	1	-
2004	Min	19	111.1	55	1	.982	3	5	19	10	.526	35	+2	+2	-2	+2	0	+2	2	0	0	2	-
2005	Min	73	564.1	331	7	.979	17	7	70	42	.600	226	-3	+1	+14	+12	0	+12	9	2	0	11	9
2006	Min	17	114.2	73	2	.973	3	9	18	9	.500	50	-2	+1	0	-1	+1	0	0	0	-1	-1	-
2007	Min	25	172.1	112	3	.973	13	3	26	9	.346	73	+1	-2	-2	-3	+2	-1	-1	-1	0	-2	-
2008	Min	26	215.2	135	2	.985	9	5	30	16	.533	88	-1	-2	+4	+2	-1	+1	1	0	0	1	-
2009	Min	63	510.1	269	0	1.000	29	5	51	33	.647	180	-8	0	+7	-1	0	-1	-1	0	3	2	15
2010	Min	12	77.0	47	3	.936	3	2	6	5	.833	36	0	+1	-1	0	+1	+1	0	0	0	0	-
2011	StL	45	243.0	151	2	.987	9	6	34	24	.706	95	0	0	+3	+2	+1	+3	2	0	1	3	-
		296	2091.2	1238	21	.983	86	42	271	153	.565	821	-12	+1	+25	+14	+5	+19	14	0	3	17	-

Second Basemen

Ryan Raburn

Year Team	G	Inn	TC	E	Pct	GFP	DM	Opps	GDP	Pct	Outs Made	To His Right	Straight On	To His Left	GB	Air	Total	+/-	GDP	GFP/DME	Total	Rank
2004 Det	11	64.2	32	1	.969	1	3	9	4	.444	21	0	0	+1	+1	0	+1	1	0	-1	0	-
2007 Det	10	74.0	37	1	.973	1	1	7	5	.714	25	-3	-1	-1	-4	-1	-5	-4	0	0	-4	-
2008 Det	16	118.0	66	5	.924	4	6	17	12	.706	40	+2	-3	-1	-3	-1	-4	-3	1	-1	-3	-
2010 Det	18	120.0	71	1	.986	5	2	16	10	.625	40	-3	0	0	-2	0	-2	-2	1	1	0	-
2011 Det	56	401.0	201	10	.950	13	10	34	20	.588	123	0	-1	-5	-6	-3	-9	-7	0	-1	-8	-
	111	777.2	407	18	.956	24	22	83	51	.614	249	-4	-5	-6	-14	-5	-19	-15	2	-2	-15	-

Brian Roberts

Year Team	G	Inn	TC	E	Pct	GFP	DM	Opps	GDP	Pct	Outs Made	To His Right	Straight On	To His Left	GB	Air	Total	+/-	GDP	GFP/DME	Total	Rank
2003 Bal	107	925.0	529	7	.987	-	-	120	63	.525	353	-3	+3	+13	+12	+4	+16	12	1	-	13	5
2004 Bal	150	1322.1	669	8	.988	28	40	167	89	.533	448	-1	-4	+3	-2	0	-2	-2	2	-3	-3	21
2005 Bal	141	1208.0	659	8	.988	35	20	152	84	.553	453	+8	+2	+6	+16	+2	+18	14	2	-1	15	8
2006 Bal	137	1167.2	598	9	.985	31	20	156	85	.545	397	-4	+8	+4	+8	-1	+7	5	2	1	8	11
2007 Bal	154	1329.2	742	7	.991	56	24	205	101	.493	488	+1	+3	-2	+1	-1	0	0	0	0	0	19
2008 Bal	154	1320.0	738	8	.989	57	29	211	105	.498	474	+13	+2	-15	-1	-3	-4	-3	0	3	0	18
2009 Bal	158	1340.2	692	11	.984	38	21	144	99	.688	435	-5	-4	+2	-7	-3	-10	-8	0	0	-8	29
2010 Bal	59	498.1	235	3	.987	14	7	49	37	.755	144	+1	+3	-7	-2	-1	-3	-2	1	0	-1	18
2011 Bal	39	347.0	191	3	.984	17	5	37	23	.622	125	0	-2	+1	-1	+1	0	0	0	1	1	-
	1099	9458.2	5053	64	.987	276	166	1241	686	.553	3317	+10	+11	+5	+24	-2	+22	16	8	1	25	12

Ryan Roberts

Year Team	G	Inn	TC	E	Pct	GFP	DM	Opps	GDP	Pct	Outs Made	To His Right	Straight On	To His Left	GB	Air	Total	+/-	GDP	GFP/DME	Total	Rank
2006 Tor	7	31.2	19	0	1.000	0	1	3	1	.333	12	0	0	+1	+1	0	+1	1	0	0	1	-
2007 Tor	1	2.2	1	0	1.000	0	0	0		-	1				0	0	0	0		0	0	-
2009 Ari	57	407.1	218	2	.991	17	12	35	18	.514	146	-4	+1	+6	+3	+5	+8	6	-2	-2	2	-
2010 Ari	1	8.0	7	0	1.000	1	0	1	1	1.000	2	-1	0	0	-1	0	-1	0	0	0	0	-
2011 Ari	28	212.2	125	4	.968	6	2	27	17	.630	72	+1	0	0	+1	-1	0	0	0	0	0	-
	94	662.1	370	6	.984	24	15	66	37	.561	233	-4	+1	+7	+4	+4	+8	7	-2	-2	3	-

Sean Rodriguez

Year Team	G	Inn	TC	E	Pct	GFP	DM	Opps	GDP	Pct	Outs Made	To His Right	Straight On	To His Left	GB	Air	Total	+/-	GDP	GFP/DME	Total	Rank
2008 LAA	51	423.2	226	2	.991	14	7	58	36	.621	149	-4	+1	+1	-2	0	-2	-2	2	0	0	-
2009 LAA	5	36.0	11	0	1.000	2	1	5	4	.800	6	-1	0	0	-1	0	-1	-1	0	0	-1	-
2010 TB	92	678.1	366	6	.984	37	10	72	51	.708	225	+1	+4	+7	+13	+7	+20	15	1	2	18	1
2011 TB	48	352.2	180	2	.989	25	9	30	23	.767	113	+2	-2	+1	+1	+1	+2	2	1	0	3	-
	196	1490.2	783	10	.987	78	27	165	114	.691	493	-2	+3	+9	+11	+8	+19	14	4	2	20	-

Freddy Sanchez

Year Team	G	Inn	TC	E	Pct	GFP	DM	Opps	GDP	Pct	Outs Made	To His Right	Straight On	To His Left	GB	Air	Total	+/-	GDP	GFP/DME	Total	Rank
2003 Bos	3	20.0	11	0	1.000	-	-	4	1	.250	4				0	0	0	0	0	-	0	-
2004 Pit	3	25.0	7	0	1.000	0	0	1	1	1.000	2	0	0		0	0	0	0	0	0	0	-
2005 Pit	58	387.1	227	2	.991	16	6	65	38	.585	125	-1	0	-3	-4	-2	-6	-5	2	1	-2	-
2006 Pit	23	165.1	80	0	1.000	4	2	27	13	.481	46	-1	0	+1	-1	-1	-2	-2	0	0	-2	-
2007 Pit	146	1272.2	701	9	.987	50	17	205	112	.546	378	+2	+2	-7	-3	-2	-5	-4	3	2	1	18
2008 Pit	131	1135.2	653	7	.989	37	23	190	96	.505	369	+2	-2	+5	+5	-3	+2	2	0	2	4	12
2009 2 tms	110	949.2	522	5	.990	44	27	101	69	.683	304	+8	+1	-7	+2	+2	+4	3	2	-2	3	12
2010 SF	109	943.0	458	4	.991	44	17	75	47	.627	283	-1	0	+1	0	-3	-3	-2	-1	0	-3	24
2011 SF	58	514.1	244	3	.988	15	13	39	30	.769	143	-3	-1	-8	-12	+3	-9	-7	1	0	-6	30
	641	5413.0	2903	30	.990	210	105	707	407	.576	1654	+6	0	-18	-13	-6	-19	-15	7	3	-5	24

Ramon Santiago

Year Team	G	Inn	TC	E	Pct	GFP	DM	Opps	GDP	Pct	Outs Made	To His Right	Straight On	To His Left	GB	Air	Total	+/-	GDP	GFP/DME	Total	Rank
2003 Det	53	461.0	268	10	.963	-	-	73	40	.548	165	-5	-1	-3	-9	+1	-8	-6	1	-	-5	25
2005 Sea	2	17.0	4	0	1.000	0	0	1	1	1.000	4	+1	0	0	+1	0	+1	1	0	0	1	-
2006 Det	12	70.2	33	0	1.000	0	1	6	4	.667	22	+1	0	+2	+3	+1	+4	3	0	0	3	-
2008 Det	21	117.2	66	0	1.000	6	5	20	13	.650	37	-1	0	-1	-2	+1	-1	-1	1	0	0	-
2009 Det	29	156.2	85	0	1.000	3	2	22	14	.636	50	+1	-2	-2	-3	+1	-2	-2	0	0	-2	-
2010 Det	25	127.0	69	1	.986	4	0	12	11	.917	45	0	+2	+1	+3	+1	+4	3	1	0	4	-
2011 Det	75	434.2	237	1	.996	12	6	46	26	.565	143	-1	+3	0	+2	+3	+5	4	0	0	4	11
	217	1384.2	762	12	.984	25	14	180	109	.606	466	-4	+2	-3	-5	+8	+3	2	3	0	5	-

Second Basemen

Skip Schumaker

		BASIC							GDP			PLUS/MINUS							RUNS SAVED				
Year	Team	G	Inn	TC	E	Pct	GFP	DM	Opps	GDP	Pct	Outs Made	To His Right	Straight On	To His Left	GB	Air	Total	+/-	GDP	GFP/ DME	Total	Rank
2009	StL	133	989.1	544	9	.983	49	14	113	78	.690	337	+3	+1	-16	-12	-2	-14	-11	0	1	-10	30
2010	StL	123	1014.1	585	16	.973	30	12	103	71	.689	340	-1	-11	-6	-18	-3	-21	-16	-1	0	-17	35
2011	StL	95	739.0	397	7	.982	29	15	71	43	.606	273	-3	0	-5	-8	+6	-2	-2	-1	0	-3	24
		351	2742.2	1526	32	.979	108	41	287	192	.669	950	-1	-10	-27	-38	+1	-37	-29	-2	1	-30	32

Ruben Tejada

		BASIC							GDP			PLUS/MINUS							RUNS SAVED				
Year	Team	G	Inn	TC	E	Pct	GFP	DM	Opps	GDP	Pct	Outs Made	To His Right	Straight On	To His Left	GB	Air	Total	+/-	GDP	GFP/ DME	Total	Rank
2010	NYM	50	388.0	211	6	.972	14	8	40	30	.750	119	-3	-5	+2	-5	+4	-1	-1	1	-1	-1	-
2011	NYM	55	457.1	245	4	.984	29	9	47	33	.702	150	-5	+1	0	-3	+2	-1	-1	0	2	1	18
		105	845.1	456	10	.978	43	17	87	63	.724	269	-8	-4	+2	-8	+6	-2	-2	1	1	0	-

Matt Tolbert

		BASIC							GDP			PLUS/MINUS							RUNS SAVED				
Year	Team	G	Inn	TC	E	Pct	GFP	DM	Opps	GDP	Pct	Outs Made	To His Right	Straight On	To His Left	GB	Air	Total	+/-	GDP	GFP/ DME	Total	Rank
2008	Min	11	75.0	46	1	.978	3	2	10	6	.600	30	-4	0	+2	-2	0	-2	-2	0	0	-2	-
2009	Min	36	285.0	186	2	.989	16	5	44	30	.682	118	-8	0	+2	-6	0	-6	-5	0	1	-4	-
2010	Min	20	131.2	63	1	.984	3	3	11	7	.636	43	-2	+1	-1	-3	0	-3	-2	0	0	-2	-
2011	Min	36	244.0	142	3	.979	14	3	24	20	.833	78	-2	0	+2	+1	+3	+4	3	1	1	5	-
		103	735.2	437	7	.984	36	13	89	63	.708	269	-16	+1	+5	-10	+3	-7	-6	1	2	-3	-

Justin Turner

		BASIC							GDP			PLUS/MINUS							RUNS SAVED				
Year	Team	G	Inn	TC	E	Pct	GFP	DM	Opps	GDP	Pct	Outs Made	To His Right	Straight On	To His Left	GB	Air	Total	+/-	GDP	GFP/ DME	Total	Rank
2009	Bal	3	6.0	6	0	1.000	1	0	2	1	.500	3				0	0	0	0	0	0	0	-
2010	2 tms	6	31.0	15	0	1.000	2	3	5	3	.600	4	-1	0	-2	-3	-1	-4	-2	0	0	-2	-
2011	NYM	78	642.1	358	8	.978	26	15	66	35	.530	219	-6	-2	-3	-10	0	-10	-8	-3	-2	-13	34
		87	679.1	379	8	.979	29	18	73	39	.534	226	-7	-2	-5	-13	-1	-14	-10	-3	-2	-15	-

Dan Uggla

		BASIC							GDP			PLUS/MINUS							RUNS SAVED				
Year	Team	G	Inn	TC	E	Pct	GFP	DM	Opps	GDP	Pct	Outs Made	To His Right	Straight On	To His Left	GB	Air	Total	+/-	GDP	GFP/ DME	Total	Rank
2006	Fla	151	1304.1	752	15	.980	26	43	206	107	.519	486	-6	+3	+5	+2	-2	0	0	1	-4	-3	21
2007	Fla	158	1383.2	736	11	.985	30	40	196	102	.520	438	-7	+4	-15	-18	-1	-19	-14	1	-2	-15	34
2008	Fla	144	1272.2	700	13	.981	62	27	154	74	.481	464	+9	-5	0	+3	+1	+4	3	-1	2	4	11
2009	Fla	158	1401.1	706	16	.977	52	35	143	91	.636	469	+1	-4	-12	-16	+3	-13	-10	-2	0	-12	33
2010	Fla	158	1392.1	745	18	.976	50	21	131	83	.634	441	-2	0	-7	-9	-1	-10	-8	-1	0	-9	30
2011	Atl	159	1431.2	749	15	.980	45	38	140	82	.586	448	-2	+4	-10	-8	-5	-13	-10	-1	-2	-13	35
		928	8186.0	4388	88	.980	265	204	970	539	.556	2746	-7	+2	-39	-46	-5	-51	-39	-3	-6	-48	34

Chase Utley

		BASIC							GDP			PLUS/MINUS							RUNS SAVED				
Year	Team	G	Inn	TC	E	Pct	GFP	DM	Opps	GDP	Pct	Outs Made	To His Right	Straight On	To His Left	GB	Air	Total	+/-	GDP	GFP/ DME	Total	Rank
2003	Phi	37	302.0	175	3	.983	-	0	47	29	.617	105	+6	0	-6	0	-1	-1	-1	2	-	1	-
2004	Phi	50	410.1	227	4	.982	17	7	54	26	.481	136	+6	-3	+2	+4	+3	+7	5	0	2	7	-
2005	Phi	135	1195.1	687	15	.978	45	17	144	64	.444	456	+20	+1	+3	+23	+3	+26	20	-2	2	20	3
2006	Phi	156	1367.1	800	18	.978	47	29	194	106	.546	474	+5	0	+9	+14	+2	+16	12	3	3	18	2
2007	Phi	132	1167.0	671	10	.985	46	27	172	80	.465	407	+17	0	+4	+21	+1	+22	17	-2	3	18	3
2008	Phi	159	1395.2	816	13	.984	57	35	204	96	.471	513	+8	+6	+32	+46	0	+46	35	-2	-3	30	1
2009	Phi	155	1357.0	774	12	.984	42	25	131	92	.702	482	+10	+7	-6	+12	+2	+14	11	1	0	12	6
2010	Phi	114	1007.0	586	11	.981	49	9	106	81	.764	370	+12	+2	-7	+7	+8	+15	11	3	3	17	2
2011	Phi	100	887.2	488	5	.990	28	18	86	50	.581	315	+5	+5	0	+10	0	+10	8	-1	0	7	7
		1038	9089.1	5224	91	.983	331	167	1138	624	.548	3258	+89	+18	+31	+137	+18	+155	118	2	10	130	1

Wilson Valdez

		BASIC							GDP			PLUS/MINUS							RUNS SAVED				
Year	Team	G	Inn	TC	E	Pct	GFP	DM	Opps	GDP	Pct	Outs Made	To His Right	Straight On	To His Left	GB	Air	Total	+/-	GDP	GFP/ DME	Total	Rank
2004	CWS	5	30.0	13	0	1.000	0	3	3	2	.667	8	0	0	-1	0	0	0	0	0	0	0	-
2007	LAD	12	59.0	41	0	1.000	4	3	7	4	.571	29	+1	+1	0	+1	0	+1	1	0	0	1	-
2009	NYM	1	3.0	0	0	-	0	0	0	0	-	0				0	0	0	0	0		0	-
2010	Phi	42	314.1	149	1	.993	10	3	26	21	.808	91	+5	+1	-8	-2	-3	-5	-3	1	1	-1	-
2011	Phi	45	316.2	175	2	.989	12	9	33	19	.576	106	+1	+3	-7	-3	-3	-6	-5	0	-1	-6	-
		105	723.0	378	3	.992	26	18	69	46	.667	234	+7	+5	-16	-4	-6	-10	-7	1	0	-6	-

Second Basemen

Neil Walker

Year	Team	G	Inn	TC	E	Pct	GFP	DM	Opps	GDP	Pct	Outs Made	To His Right	Straight On	To His Left	GB	Air	Total	+/-	GDP	GFP/DME	Total	Rank
				BASIC					GDP					PLUS/MINUS							RUNS SAVED		
2010	Pit	105	894.2	463	7	.985	27	12	83	62	.747	274	-3	-3	-13	-19	+5	-14	-10	2	0	-8	29
2011	Pit	159	1382.1	781	6	.992	58	31	172	106	.616	448	+20	0	-18	+3	-10	-7	-5	-1	3	-3	25
		264	2277.0	1244	13	.990	85	43	255	168	.659	722	+17	-3	-31	-16	-5	-21	-15	1	3	-11	27

Jemile Weeks

Year	Team	G	Inn	TC	E	Pct	GFP	DM	Opps	GDP	Pct	Outs Made	To His Right	Straight On	To His Left	GB	Air	Total	+/-	GDP	GFP/DME	Total	Rank
				BASIC					GDP					PLUS/MINUS							RUNS SAVED		
2011	Oak	96	849.1	422	13	.969	28	20	70	45	.643	286	-3	-2	+1	-5	-4	-9	-6	0	0	-6	29

Rickie Weeks

Year	Team	G	Inn	TC	E	Pct	GFP	DM	Opps	GDP	Pct	Outs Made	To His Right	Straight On	To His Left	GB	Air	Total	+/-	GDP	GFP/DME	Total	Rank
				BASIC					GDP					PLUS/MINUS							RUNS SAVED		
2003	Mil	4	21.0	3	1	.667	-	-	1			1	-1			0		0	0		-	0	-
2005	Mil	95	837.1	432	21	.951	25	38	109	52	.477	273	-3	-9	+4	-8	-3	-11	-8	-1	-1	-10	31
2006	Mil	92	794.0	460	22	.952	19	34	141	65	.461	265	-1	-8	-2	-10	-3	-13	-10	-2	-2	-14	32
2007	Mil	115	984.0	531	13	.976	38	33	129	67	.519	301	-1	-5	-5	-12	-5	-17	-13	1	2	-10	32
2008	Mil	120	1056.0	604	15	.975	36	44	163	75	.460	356	+3	-7	+4	+1	+1	+2	2	-2	-4	-4	24
2009	Mil	35	303.2	167	6	.964	11	4	35	21	.600	98	+5		+3	+9	+1	+10	8	-1	0	7	-
2010	Mil	159	1389.1	736	15	.980	44	38	131	92	.702	409	+4	+3	-14	-7	-8	-15	-12	1	-5	-16	34
2011	Mil	115	974.0	481	15	.969	31	25	93	63	.677	286	+4	-8	+7	+3	-7	-4	-3	1	-3	-5	27
		735	6359.1	3414	108	.968	204	216	802	435	.542	1989	+10	-34	-3	-24	-24	-48	-36	-3	-13	-52	35

Jack Wilson

Year	Team	G	Inn	TC	E	Pct	GFP	DM	Opps	GDP	Pct	Outs Made	To His Right	Straight On	To His Left	GB	Air	Total	+/-	GDP	GFP/DME	Total	Rank
				BASIC					GDP					PLUS/MINUS							RUNS SAVED		
2011	Sea	45	342.1	192	2	.990	15	5	37	25	.676	114	+2	+2	+2	+5	+3	+8	7	0	0	7	-

Ben Zobrist

Year	Team	G	Inn	TC	E	Pct	GFP	DM	Opps	GDP	Pct	Outs Made	To His Right	Straight On	To His Left	GB	Air	Total	+/-	GDP	GFP/DME	Total	Rank
				BASIC					GDP					PLUS/MINUS							RUNS SAVED		
2008	TB	8	41.0	22	0	1.000	2	1	8	3	.375	11	+1	0	+1	+2	0	+2	2	0	0	2	-
2009	TB	91	714.2	372	4	.989	19	7	68	41	.603	253	+8	+4	+8	+20	+3	+23	17	0	-1	16	2
2010	TB	55	371.0	193	3	.984	18	6	42	25	.595	115	+3	-1	+5	+8	+1	+9	7	-1	0	6	-
2011	TB	131	1058.1	535	6	.989	39	22	98	65	.663	330	+15	0	+5	+19	+10	+29	22	1	0	23	1
		285	2185.0	1122	13	.988	78	36	216	134	.620	709	+27	+3	+19	+49	+14	+63	48	0	-1	47	7

Third Basemen

Pedro Alvarez

		BASIC							BUNTS			GDP			PLUS/MINUS								RUNS SAVED					
Year	Team	G	Inn	TC	E	Pct	GFP	DM	Opp	Sac Hits	Bunt Hits	Opp	GDP	Pct	Outs Made	To His Right	Straight On	To His Left	GB	Air	Total	Enhanced	+/-	Bunt	GDP	GFP/ DME	Total	Rank
2010	Pit	94	814.2	276	17	.938	35	19	11	7	4	19	13	.684	229	+1	-10	-4	-12	-1	-13	-13	-10	0	0		-10	28
2011	Pit	66	549.0	214	14	.935	24	17	11	4	5	22	10	.455	167	-3	-3	-4	-8	0	-8	-10	-8	-1	-1	-1	-11	30
		160	1363.2	490	31	.937	59	36	22	11	9	41	23	.561	396	-2	-13	-8	-20	-1	-21	-23	-18	-1	-1	-1	-21	-

Mike Aviles

		BASIC							BUNTS			GDP			PLUS/MINUS								RUNS SAVED					
Year	Team	G	Inn	TC	E	Pct	GFP	DM	Opp	Sac Hits	Bunt Hits	Opp	GDP	Pct	Outs Made	To His Right	Straight On	To His Left	GB	Air	Total	Enhanced	+/-	Bunt	GDP	GFP/ DME	Total	Rank
2008	KC	7	29.2	6	0	1.000	1	0	-	-	-	-	-	-	5	-2	-1	+2	-1	0	-1	-1	-1			0	-1	-
2009	KC	2	10.0	0	0	-	0	0				0	0	-	0				0	0	0	0	0			0	0	-
2010	KC	5	35.0	4	1	.750	0	0				0	0	-	2	-1	0	0	-1	0	-1	-1	-1		0	0	-1	-
2011	2 tms	46	347.2	106	8	.925	11	8	9	4	4	12	4	.333	87	-2	0	0	-2	+1	-1	-1	-1	0	0	0	-1	-
		60	422.1	116	9	.922	12	8	9	4	4	12	4	.333	94	-5	-1	+2	-4	+1	-3	-3	-3	0	0	0	-3	-

Jose Bautista

		BASIC							BUNTS			GDP			PLUS/MINUS								RUNS SAVED					
Year	Team	G	Inn	TC	E	Pct	GFP	DM	Opp	Sac Hits	Bunt Hits	Opp	GDP	Pct	Outs Made	To His Right	Straight On	To His Left	GB	Air	Total	Enhanced	+/-	Bunt	GDP	GFP/ DME	Total	Rank
2004	3 tms	17	67.0	25	1	.960	2	1	2	0	2	-	-	-	19	-1	0	0	+1	0	+1	0	0	0		0	0	-
2005	Pit	8	58.2	21	1	.952	0	1	2	2	0	-	-	-	16	0	+1	0	+1	0	+1	0	0	0		0	0	-
2006	Pit	33	267.1	82	6	.927	6	6	6	2	1	-	-	-	65	+1	-8	-4	-11	0	-11	-11	-8	0		0	-8	-
2007	Pit	126	1064.2	361	15	.958	57	25	16	11	3	-	-	-	306	-2	-14	-7	-23	0	-23	-23	-17	0		-1	-18	32
2008	2 tms	99	766.1	268	11	.959	39	21	14	7	7	-	-	-	235	-2	-1	+1	-2	0	-2	-3	-2	-2		0	-4	24
2009	Tor	26	209.0	69	3	.957	14	8	3	0	2	6	2	.333	58	+1	+3	-1	+3	0	+3	+4	3	0	0	0	3	-
2010	Tor	48	393.0	130	4	.969	17	11	8	1	6	6	3	.500	108	0	-1	0	-2	+3	+1	+2	1	-2	0	1	0	-
2011	Tor	25	205.0	81	2	.975	7	4	1	0	1	5	1	.200	74	+3	+2	+2	+6	+2	+8	+8	6	-1	0	0	5	-
		382	3031.0	1037	43	.959	142	77	52	23	22	17	6	.353	881	0	-18	-9	-27	+5	-22	-23	-17	-5	0	0	-22	23

Adrian Beltre

		BASIC							BUNTS			GDP			PLUS/MINUS								RUNS SAVED					
Year	Team	G	Inn	TC	E	Pct	GFP	DM	Opp	Sac Hits	Bunt Hits	Opp	GDP	Pct	Outs Made	To His Right	Straight On	To His Left	GB	Air	Total	Enhanced	+/-	Bunt	GDP	GFP/ DME	Total	Rank
2003	LA	157	1346.0	439	19	.957	-	-	15	3	2	-	-	-	350	+13	+11	+2	+26	-1	+25	+30	23	2	-	-	25	2
2004	LA	155	1340.1	452	10	.978	35	39	34	18	9	-	-	-	381	+10	+18	+1	+30	-1	+29	+30	23	-1	-	0	22	2
2005	Sea	155	1325.2	425	14	.967	38	34	18	4	6	-	-	-	364	+5	-3	+5	+7	+1	+8	+11	8	0	-	0	8	9
2006	Sea	155	1358.0	474	15	.968	54	27	16	8	4	-	-	-	404	+22	-7	+9	+23	-2	+21	+24	18	1	-	0	19	4
2007	Sea	147	1279.1	426	18	.958	45	26	10	5	3	-	-	-	370	+3	-2	+4	+4	-1	+3	+7	5	-1	-	0	4	13
2008	Sea	139	1208.1	386	14	.964	62	15	13	6	4	-	-	-	328	+6	+3	+21	+30	+1	+31	+32	24	1	-	2	27	1
2009	Sea	111	988.1	341	14	.959	45	21	11	4	2	19	13	.684	302	+9	+1	+11	+21	+1	+22	+26	20	1	0	-1	20	3
2010	Bos	154	1342.2	442	19	.957	46	30	18	7	4	42	27	.643	364	+1	+8	+14	+25	-4	+21	+20	15	2	1	1	19	2
2011	Tex	112	980.1	312	11	.965	35	21	9	4	2	30	19	.633	260	+6	+6	+7	+19	-1	+18	+18	14	0	0	-1	13	3
		1285	11169.0	3697	134	.964	360	213	144	59	36	91	59	.648	3123	+75	+35	+74	+185	-7	+178	+198	150	5	1	1	157	1

Wilson Betemit

		BASIC							BUNTS			GDP			PLUS/MINUS								RUNS SAVED					
Year	Team	G	Inn	TC	E	Pct	GFP	DM	Opp	Sac Hits	Bunt Hits	Opp	GDP	Pct	Outs Made	To His Right	Straight On	To His Left	GB	Air	Total	Enhanced	+/-	Bunt	GDP	GFP/ DME	Total	Rank
2004	Atl	7	39.0	8	0	1.000	1	1	-	-	-	-	-	-	8	+1	0	+1	+1	0	+1	+1	1		-	0	1	-
2005	Atl	63	431.0	126	6	.952	14	3	9	4	5	-	-	-	114	0	+3	+3	+7	0	+7	+7	5	-2	-	1	4	-
2006	2 tms	79	602.0	164	7	.957	10	15	10	6	2	-	-	-	135	-1	-5	+1	-5	0	-5	-7	-6	1	-	-1	-6	26
2007	2 tms	67	408.2	101	6	.941	7	8	8	2	5	-	-	-	91	+2	0	-3	-1	-1	-2	-4	-3	0	-	-1	-4	-
2008	NYY	21	100.0	28	3	.893	2	4				-	-	-	24	-3	-1	0	-4	0	-4	-6	-5		-	0	-5	-
2009	CWS	6	43.0	8	4	.500	1	2	1	0	1	1	0	.000	4	-1	-1	-1	-3	0	-3	-3	-2	-1	0	0	-3	-
2010	KC	53	455.1	113	8	.929	11	12	7	2	4	17	6	.353	89	-6	-2	-6	-15	+2	-13	-13	-10	0	-1	-1	-12	30
2011	2 tms	87	696.0	208	11	.947	13	15	17	6	6	20	9	.450	170	+1	-5	-5	-10	+2	-8	-8	-6	0	0	-1	-7	26
		383	2775.0	756	45	.940	59	60	52	20	23	38	15	.395	635	-7	-11	-10	-30	+3	-27	-33	-26	-2	-1	-3	-32	27

Casey Blake

		BASIC							BUNTS			GDP			PLUS/MINUS								RUNS SAVED					
Year	Team	G	Inn	TC	E	Pct	GFP	DM	Opp	Sac Hits	Bunt Hits	Opp	GDP	Pct	Outs Made	To His Right	Straight On	To His Left	GB	Air	Total	Enhanced	+/-	Bunt	GDP	GFP/ DME	Total	Rank
2003	Cle	140	1184.0	400	19	.953	-	-	19	6	10	-	-	-	343	+8	+5	-1	+11	+5	+16	+18	14	-1	-	-	13	4
2004	Cle	152	1352.1	422	26	.938	35	37	11	6	5	-	-	-	345	-3	-7	-2	-10	+1	-9	-7	-5	0	-	0	-5	23
2005	Cle	6	40.0	14	1	.929	2	0				-	-	-	13	+1	0	0	+1	0	+1	+1	1		-	0	1	-
2007	Cle	145	1209.0	371	14	.962	42	25	14	6	5	-	-	-	316	+9	-4	-13	-8	0	-8	-5	-4	0	-	1	-3	24
2008	2 tms	133	1104.2	325	14	.957	45	16	13	6	5	-	-	-	280	+7	-10	-3	-6	+1	-5	-4	-3	1	-	0	-2	22
2009	LAD	134	1161.0	372	10	.973	46	12	14	8	2	34	23	.676	314	+9	+4	-7	+6	0	+6	+8	6	1	0	2	9	9
2010	LAD	139	1204.0	352	15	.957	34	7	16	7	6	33	14	.424	291	+12	-2	0	+8	+2	+10	+12	9	0	-1	-1	7	9
2011	LAD	45	383.2	112	6	.946	7	0	2	1	1	8	4	.500	85	+2	+3	-2	+3	0	+3	+4	3	0	0	1	4	-
		894	7638.2	2368	105	.956	211	97	89	40	34	75	41	.547	1987	+45	-11	-28	+5	+9	+14	+27	21	1	-1	3	24	9

Third Basemen

Emilio Bonifacio

Year	Team	G	Inn	TC	E	Pct	GFP	DM	Opp	Sac Hits	Bunt Hits	Opp	GDP	Pct	Outs Made	To His Right	Straight On	To His Left	GB	Air	Total	Enhanced	+/-	Bunt	GDP	GFP/ DME	Total	Rank
2009	Fla	86	717.2	213	14	.934	21	13	12	4	3	20	10	.500	179	-1	-3	+6	+2	-1	+1	+1	1	1	-1	-1	0	17
2010	Fla	6	37.0	13	0	1.000	0	1				1	1	1.000	12	0	0	+1	+2	-1	+1	+1	1		0	0	1	-
2011	Fla	36	245.2	67	3	.955	5	5	7	5	1	9	8	.889	51	-3	+4	+1	+1	+1	+2	+3	2	0	0	-2	0	-
		128	1000.1	293	17	.942	26	19	19	9	4	30	19	.633	242	-4	+1	+8	+5	-1	+4	+5	4	1	-1	-3	1	-

Miguel Cairo

Year	Team	G	Inn	TC	E	Pct	GFP	DM	Opp	Sac Hits	Bunt Hits	Opp	GDP	Pct	Outs Made	To His Right	Straight On	To His Left	GB	Air	Total	Enhanced	+/-	Bunt	GDP	GFP/ DME	Total	Rank
2003	StL	12	33.0	11	2	.818	-	-				-	-	-	5	-2	0	0	-2	0	-2	-1	-1				-1	-
2004	NYY	8	54.1	19	2	.895	1	1				-	-	-	17	-3	+2	-1	-1	0	-1	-2	-2			0	-2	-
2005	NYM	3	6.0	2	0	1.000	0	1				-	-	-	2	0	0	0			0	0	0			0	0	-
2006	NYY	8	41.0	11	0	1.000	0	1	2	0	1	-	-	-	10	0	+1	0	+1	0	+1	+1	1	0		0	1	-
2007	2 tms	22	124.0	39	2	.949	4	1	1	1	0	-	-	-	33	-1	+4	0	+4	0	+4	+3	3	0	-	0	3	-
2008	Sea	19	112.0	35	1	.971	8	2	1	1	0	-	-	-	32	+2	-1	0	+1	0	+1	+1	1	0	-	0	1	-
2009	Phi	1	9.0	2	0	1.000	0	0				0	0	-	2				0	0	0	0	0		0	0	0	-
2010	Cin	37	241.2	48	2	.958	5	6	3	0	1	1	1	1.000	33	-2	-1	0	-2	-2	-4	-5	-4	1	0	0	-3	-
2011	Cin	58	432.1	143	4	.972	7	12	2	2	0	15	9	.600	121	-2	0	+5	+3	+1	+4	+4	3	0	0	0	3	10
		168	1053.1	310	13	.958	25	24	9	4	2	16	10	.625	255	-8	+5	+4	+4	-1	+3	+1	1	1	0	0	2	-

Alberto Callaspo

Year	Team	G	Inn	TC	E	Pct	GFP	DM	Opp	Sac Hits	Bunt Hits	Opp	GDP	Pct	Outs Made	To His Right	Straight On	To His Left	GB	Air	Total	Enhanced	+/-	Bunt	GDP	GFP/ DME	Total	Rank
2006	Ari	2	5.0	2	0	1.000	0	0				-	-	-	2				+1	0	+1	+1	1		-	0	1	-
2007	Ari	18	119.1	35	1	.971	4	2	1	0	1	-	-	-	30	0	+1	0	0	0	0	0	0	0	-	0	0	-
2008	KC	1	8.0	6	0	1.000	0	0				-	-	-	5	0	+1	0	+1	0	+1	+1	1		-	0	1	-
2009	KC	14	99.0	24	0	1.000	3	2				3	1	.333	21	0	0	+1	+2	0	+2	+2	2		0	0	2	-
2010	2 tms	130	1134.0	333	10	.970	40	18	22	8	6	33	21	.636	272	+6	+2	-7	+2	0	+2	+2	1	3	0	-2	2	15
2011	LAA	129	1139.1	365	15	.959	37	21	21	10	9	33	22	.667	303	+5	+7	-5	+7	-3	+4	+4	4	0	1	-1	4	9
		294	2504.2	765	26	.966	84	43	44	18	16	69	44	.638	633	+11	+11	-11	+13	-3	+10	+10	9	3	1	-3	10	-

Eric Chavez

Year	Team	G	Inn	TC	E	Pct	GFP	DM	Opp	Sac Hits	Bunt Hits	Opp	GDP	Pct	Outs Made	To His Right	Straight On	To His Left	GB	Air	Total	Enhanced	+/-	Bunt	GDP	GFP/ DME	Total	Rank
2003	Oak	154	1333.1	482	14	.971			19	9	7	-	-	-	379	+3	-1	+3	+5	0	+5	+9	7	0	-	-	7	7
2004	Oak	125	1129.0	401	13	.968	31	27	18	10	5	-	-	-	314	+8	0	+2	+10	-1	+9	+13	10	0	-	1	11	6
2005	Oak	153	1348.1	437	15	.966	54	22	12	5	2	-	-	-	381	+16	-5	-1	+10	0	+10	+15	11	1	-	0	12	5
2006	Oak	134	1165.2	391	5	.987	34	30	9	6	1	-	-	-	354	+16	-9	-9	-2	-1	-3	+2	2	1	-	0	3	13
2007	Oak	88	774.2	241	6	.975	22	15	8	3	4	-	-	-	213	+6	-2	+3	+7	+1	+8	+10	8	0	-	0	8	8
2008	Oak	15	130.0	45	1	.978	8	4	1	1	0	-	-	-	42	0	0	-2	-1	+1	0	0	0	0	-	0	0	-
2009	Oak	8	67.0	20	0	1.000	4	4				2	2	1.000	17	0	+1	-2	-1	0	-1	-1	-1		0	0	-1	-
2011	NYY	42	305.2	86	0	1.000	12	3	8	3	2	7	6	.857	73	+3	0	-2	0	+1	+1	+2	2	0	1	0	3	-
		719	6253.2	2103	54	.974	165	105	75	37	21	9	8	.889	1773	+52	-16	-8	+28	+1	+29	+50	39	2	1	1	43	6

Lonnie Chisenhall

Year	Team	G	Inn	TC	E	Pct	GFP	DM	Opp	Sac Hits	Bunt Hits	Opp	GDP	Pct	Outs Made	To His Right	Straight On	To His Left	GB	Air	Total	Enhanced	+/-	Bunt	GDP	GFP/ DME	Total	Rank
2011	Cle	58	461.0	168	10	.940	12	10	7	3	1	14	6	.429	141	-4	+4	+2	+1	0	+1	+2	2	1	0	0	3	11

Chris Davis

Year	Team	G	Inn	TC	E	Pct	GFP	DM	Opp	Sac Hits	Bunt Hits	Opp	GDP	Pct	Outs Made	To His Right	Straight On	To His Left	GB	Air	Total	Enhanced	+/-	Bunt	GDP	GFP/ DME	Total	Rank
2008	Tex	32	276.0	78	3	.962	5	9	2	0	0	-	-	-	66	-1	-3	-5	-9	0	-9	-9	-7	0	-	-1	-8	-
2009	Tex	11	85.0	19	2	.895	2	3	1	0	1	1	1	1.000	16	-3	0	0	-3	0	-3	-3	-2	-1	0	0	-3	-
2010	Tex	1	2.0	1	0	1.000	0	0				0	0	-	1	0	0	0	0	0	0	0	0		0	0	0	-
2011	2 tms	26	222.1	57	8	.860	2	1	2	0	2	5	4	.800	44	-4	+1	-2	-5	0	-5	-6	-3	-1	0	1	-3	-
		70	585.1	155	13	.916	9	13	5	0	3	6	5	.833	127	-8	-2	-7	-17	0	-17	-18	-12	-2	0	0	-14	-

Daniel Descalso

Year	Team	G	Inn	TC	E	Pct	GFP	DM	Opp	Sac Hits	Bunt Hits	Opp	GDP	Pct	Outs Made	To His Right	Straight On	To His Left	GB	Air	Total	Enhanced	+/-	Bunt	GDP	GFP/ DME	Total	Rank
2010	StL	9	73.0	17	0	1.000	2	0	2	1	1	4	4	1.000	16	0	+1	+1	+2	0	+2	+2	1	0	0	0	1	-
2011	StL	117	666.0	182	6	.967	22	13	6	3	2	19	13	.684	145	+2	-6	+1	-3	-4	-7	-7	-5	-1	0	0	-6	25
		126	739.0	199	6	.970	24	13	8	4	3	23	17	.739	161	+2	-5	+2	-1	-4	-5	-5	-4	-1	0	0	-5	-

Third Basemen

Greg Dobbs

		BASIC							BUNTS			GDP			PLUS/MINUS								RUNS SAVED					
Year	Team	G	Inn	TC	E	Pct	GFP	DM	Opp	Sac Hits	Bunt Hits	Opp	GDP	Pct	Outs Made	To His Right	Straight On	To His Left	GB	Air	Total	Enhanced	+/-	Bunt	GDP	GFP/DME	Total	Rank
2004	Sea	14	108.2	28	2	.929	1	1				-	-	-	25	+1	-2	+1	0	0	0	0	0		-	0	0	-
2005	Sea	2	11.0	9	0	1.000	0	1				-	-	-	8	0	+1	-1	0	0	0	0	0		-	0	0	-
2006	Sea	2	2.0	1	0	1.000	1	0				-	-	-	1				0	0	0	0	0		-	0	0	-
2007	Phi	68	418.0	128	7	.945	13	9	7	4	2	-	-	-	106	0	0	-4	-4	0	-4	-4	-3	0	-	0	-3	23
2008	Phi	52	327.1	104	3	.971	18	13	7	0	3	-	-	-	88	+1	-4	-2	-5	0	-5	-5	-4	0	-	1	-3	
2009	Phi	16	88.2	28	0	1.000	3	1				2	1	.500	28	+1	+2	-2	+2	0	+2	+2	2		0	0	2	
2010	Phi	36	230.0	59	6	.898	4	2	3	2	1	1	1	1.000	44	0	-3	-1	-4	-1	-5	-5	-4	0	0	-1	-5	
2011	Fla	100	755.0	192	11	.943	15	17	17	10	6	12	7	.583	154	-1	-2	-6	-9	-1	-10	-9	-7	-2	0	0	-9	29
		290	1940.2	549	29	.947	55	44	34	16	12	15	9	.600	454	+2	-8	-15	-20	-2	-22	-21	-16	-2	0	0	-18	-

Edwin Encarnacion

		BASIC							BUNTS			GDP			PLUS/MINUS								RUNS SAVED					
Year	Team	G	Inn	TC	E	Pct	GFP	DM	Opp	Sac Hits	Bunt Hits	Opp	GDP	Pct	Outs Made	To His Right	Straight On	To His Left	GB	Air	Total	Enhanced	+/-	Bunt	GDP	GFP/DME	Total	Rank
2005	Cin	56	478.0	180	10	.944	20	9	5	3	1	-	-	-	154	+4	-1	0	+2	0	+2	+5	4	-	0	4	16	
2006	Cin	111	931.1	295	25	.915	29	26	14	5	7	-	-	-	244	-1	-6	-10	-18	+2	-16	-15	-11	-2	-	0	-13	34
2007	Cin	137	1168.0	340	16	.953	47	18	17	5	8	-	-	-	298	+1	-21	+4	-16	+3	-13	-15	-11	-1	-	1	-11	30
2008	Cin	143	1237.0	330	23	.930	37	24	13	7	3	-	-	-	278	-7	-6	-7	-20	-1	-21	-21	-16	0	-	-1	-17	35
2009	2 tms	85	726.1	209	11	.947	19	19	10	6	1	22	10	.455	176	-4	-1	-3	-9	-1	-10	-10	-8	1	0	0	-7	29
2010	Tor	95	841.2	263	18	.932	25	16	7	2	3	18	9	.500	217	+4	-3	-4	-4	+2	-2	-1	-1	-1	0	-1	-3	19
2011	Tor	36	273.2	74	8	.892	4	5				4	1	.250	57	-2	-4	+1	-6	-1	-7	-5	-4		0	0	-4	
		663	5656.0	1691	111	.934	181	117	66	28	23	44	20	.455	1424	-5	-42	-19	-71	+4	-67	-62	-47	-3	0	-1	-51	34

Chone Figgins

		BASIC							BUNTS			GDP			PLUS/MINUS								RUNS SAVED					
Year	Team	G	Inn	TC	E	Pct	GFP	DM	Opp	Sac Hits	Bunt Hits	Opp	GDP	Pct	Outs Made	To His Right	Straight On	To His Left	GB	Air	Total	Enhanced	+/-	Bunt	GDP	GFP/DME	Total	Rank
2004	Ana	92	705.1	197	11	.944	21	20	12	5	3	-	-	-	161	-3	+1	+6	+4	-1	+3	+1	1	1	-	1	3	14
2005	LAA	56	437.2	132	3	.977	10	11	10	3	5	-	-	-	116	+3	+6	-5	+3	+1	+2	+4	3	0	-	0	3	
2006	LAA	34	280.1	82	10	.878	11	12	5	3	2	-	-	-	65	-4	-4	-2	-10	0	-10	-9	-7	-1	-	1	-7	
2007	LAA	99	836.2	230	13	.943	30	18	10	5	3	-	-	-	193	-4	+2	-1	-3	-1	-4	-3	-2	1	-	0	-1	21
2008	LAA	105	914.1	275	6	.978	32	27	7	3	2	-	-	-	243	+4	+6	-1	+9	0	+9	+11	8	0	-	-3	5	11
2009	LAA	154	1339.0	437	14	.968	71	31	16	8	6	39	26	.667	382	+2	+15	+23	+40	-1	+39	+40	30	0	0	-1	29	1
2011	Sea	80	679.2	185	11	.941	22	21	9	5	2	10	7	.700	148	-4	+1	+2	-5	0	-5	-2	-1	1	0	-1	-1	17
		620	5193.0	1538	68	.956	197	140	69	32	23	49	33	.673	1308	-6	+27	+22	+38	-4	+34	+42	32	2	0	-3	31	8

Todd Frazier

		BASIC							BUNTS			GDP			PLUS/MINUS								RUNS SAVED					
Year	Team	G	Inn	TC	E	Pct	GFP	DM	Opp	Sac Hits	Bunt Hits	Opp	GDP	Pct	Outs Made	To His Right	Straight On	To His Left	GB	Air	Total	Enhanced	+/-	Bunt	GDP	GFP/DME	Total	Rank
2011	Cin	27	207.2	64	2	.969	7	3	3	1	1	4	1	.250	49	0	+1	+2	+3	-1	+2	+2	1	0	0	0	1	-

David Freese

		BASIC							BUNTS			GDP			PLUS/MINUS								RUNS SAVED					
Year	Team	G	Inn	TC	E	Pct	GFP	DM	Opp	Sac Hits	Bunt Hits	Opp	GDP	Pct	Outs Made	To His Right	Straight On	To His Left	GB	Air	Total	Enhanced	+/-	Bunt	GDP	GFP/DME	Total	Rank
2009	StL	7	41.1	11	0	1.000	1	0				1	1	1.000	9	-1			-1	0	-1	-1	-1		0	0	-1	-
2010	StL	66	557.0	179	9	.950	22	9	8	5	0	19	16	.842	144	-3	-3	0	-6	-2	-8	-8	-6	1	1	-1	-5	22
2011	StL	88	674.0	204	12	.941	24	14	8	5	3	24	19	.792	170	-3	+1	-1	-1	-1	-2	-3	-2	0	1	0	-1	18
		161	1272.1	394	21	.947	47	23	16	10	3	44	36	.818	323	-7	-2	-1	-8	-3	-11	-12	-9	1	2	-1	-7	-

Jerry Hairston

		BASIC							BUNTS			GDP			PLUS/MINUS								RUNS SAVED					
Year	Team	G	Inn	TC	E	Pct	GFP	DM	Opp	Sac Hits	Bunt Hits	Opp	GDP	Pct	Outs Made	To His Right	Straight On	To His Left	GB	Air	Total	Enhanced	+/-	Bunt	GDP	GFP/DME	Total	Rank
2004	Bal	1	3.0	1	0	1.000	0	0				-	-	-	1	0			0			0	0		-	0	0	-
2006	Tex	1	8.0	2	0	1.000	0	0				-	-	-	2				0	0	0	0	0		-	0	0	-
2007	Tex	10	44.2	17	1	.941	3	1	1	1	0	-	-	-	14	+1	0	0	+1	0	+1	+1	1		-	0	1	-
2008	Cin	1	2.0	0	0		0	0				-	-	-					0	0	0	0	0		-	0	0	-
2009	2 tms	49	351.1	105	6	.914	12	6	3	1	0	9	6	.667	87	-6	+3	+4	+1	+2	+3	+3	2	1	0	1	4	
2010	SD	3	19.1	4	0	1.000	0	0	1	1	0	0	0	-	2	0	0	0	+1	0	+1	+1	0	0	0	0	0	
2011	2 tms	49	370.0	102	6	.941	8	8	5	3	2	7	3	.429	80	0	-4	+1	-3	0	-3	-3	-2	-1	0	1	-2	
		114	798.1	231	16	.931	23	15	10	6	2	16	9	.563	186	-5	-1	+5	0	+2	+2	+2	1	0	0	2	3	

Jack Hannahan

		BASIC							BUNTS			GDP			PLUS/MINUS								RUNS SAVED					
Year	Team	G	Inn	TC	E	Pct	GFP	DM	Opp	Sac Hits	Bunt Hits	Opp	GDP	Pct	Outs Made	To His Right	Straight On	To His Left	GB	Air	Total	Enhanced	+/-	Bunt	GDP	GFP/DME	Total	Rank
2007	Oak	41	361.2	100	3	.970	12	4	9	5	2	-	-	-	87	+2	0	0	+2	-2	0	0	0	1	-	0	1	-
2008	Oak	126	983.2	297	9	.970	53	24	12	4	4	-	-	-	261	+3	+10	+5	+18	+1	+19	+21	16	0	-	-1	15	2
2009	2 tms	84	613.0	209	7	.967	24	16	6	1	5	22	14	.636	188	+6	+5	+8	+18	-1	+17	+18	14	-2	0	0	12	7
2011	Cle	104	819.0	296	5	.983	30	14	9	2	5	29	13	.448	247	+7	+6	-4	+10	-1	+9	+9	7	0	-1	0	6	7
		355	2777.1	902	24	.973	120	56	36	12	16	51	27	.529	783	+18	+21	+9	+48	-3	+45	+48	37	-1	-1	-1	34	7

345

Third Basemen

Josh Harrison

Year	Team	G	Inn	TC	E	Pct	GFP	DM	Opp	Sac Hits	Bunt Hits	Opp	GDP	Pct	Outs Made	To His Right	Straight On	To His Left	GB	Air	Total	Enhanced	+/-	Bunt	GDP	GFP/DME	Total	Rank
2011	Pit	50	363.1	137	6	.956	15	7	5	3	0	9	6	.667	114	+7	+1	+1	+9	+1	+10	+10	8	1	0	0	9	-

Chase Headley

Year	Team	G	Inn	TC	E	Pct	GFP	DM	Opp	Sac Hits	Bunt Hits	Opp	GDP	Pct	Outs Made	To His Right	Straight On	To His Left	GB	Air	Total	Enhanced	+/-	Bunt	GDP	GFP/DME	Total	Rank
2007	SD	5	38.1	6	1	.833	1	0				-	-	-	5	0	-2	0	-2	-1	-3	-3	-2	-		0	-2	-
2008	SD	7	55.0	13	1	.923	2	0				-	-	-	11	+1	0	0	+1	0	+1	+1	1	-		0	1	-
2009	SD	28	225.2	54	5	.907	7	2	2	0	1	3	1	.333	46	-2	+3	-1	0	0	0	0	0	0	0	0	0	-
2010	SD	158	1407.2	388	13	.966	35	9	16	9	3	35	19	.543	331	0	+9	+8	+18	+1	+19	+18	14	1	-1	0	14	3
2011	SD	107	895.1	272	11	.960	33	14	9	7	2	15	10	.667	213	-7	+2	+4	0	+2	+2	0	0	-1	0	2	1	15
		305	2622.0	733	31	.958	78	25	27	16	6	53	30	.566	606	-8	+12	+11	+17	+2	+19	+16	13	0	-1	2	14	12

Brandon Inge

Year	Team	G	Inn	TC	E	Pct	GFP	DM	Opp	Sac Hits	Bunt Hits	Opp	GDP	Pct	Outs Made	To His Right	Straight On	To His Left	GB	Air	Total	Enhanced	+/-	Bunt	GDP	GFP/DME	Total	Rank
2004	Det	73	524.2	185	12	.935	10	15	10	3	3	-	-	-	140	-4	-7	+6	-5	-1	-6	-8	-6	1	-	-1	-6	27
2005	Det	160	1399.2	529	23	.957	34	29	18	10	6	-	-	-	462	+16	-6	-3	+7	-2	+5	+12	9	-1	-	1	9	7
2006	Det	159	1392.0	555	22	.960	35	27	10	2	4	-	-	-	501	+14	+15	-7	+23	+1	+24	+27	21	0	-	3	24	1
2007	Det	150	1309.2	434	18	.959	46	27	10	4	5	-	-	-	395	+9	+6	+5	+20	-2	+18	+22	17	0	-	-1	16	3
2008	Det	51	324.1	119	1	.992	18	6	1	0	1	-	-	-	112	+4	+1	-3	+2	-1	+1	+1	1	-1	-	1	1	-
2009	Det	161	1387.0	444	20	.955	59	21	14	5	8	45	32	.711	389	+2	+12	-3	+11	+2	+13	+13	10	-2	1	3	12	8
2010	Det	144	1226.2	395	9	.977	43	20	17	9	4	31	20	.645	326	+7	+6	-3	+10	+1	+11	+11	8	0	1	1	10	7
2011	Det	99	730.2	248	9	.964	16	15	11	2	7	17	11	.647	209	-3	+4	+2	+3	-1	+2	+1	1	-2	0	-1	-2	20
		997	8294.2	2909	114	.961	261	160	91	35	38	93	63	.677	2534	+45	+31	-6	+71	-3	+68	+79	61	-5	2	6	64	4

Maicer Izturis

Year	Team	G	Inn	TC	E	Pct	GFP	DM	Opp	Sac Hits	Bunt Hits	Opp	GDP	Pct	Outs Made	To His Right	Straight On	To His Left	GB	Air	Total	Enhanced	+/-	Bunt	GDP	GFP/DME	Total	Rank
2005	LAA	45	275.2	90	8	.911	9	4	9	3	5	-	-	-	75	-4	+1	+6	+3	0	+3	+3	2	-1	-	0	1	-
2006	LAA	87	707.1	203	13	.936	17	15	7	5	2	-	-	-	176	+2	-5	-3	-6	0	-6	-6	-5	0	-	0	-5	24
2007	LAA	53	447.0	115	3	.974	12	7	4	2	2	-	-	-	100	-1	+6	0	+5	-1	+4	+4	3	0	-	0	3	16
2008	LAA	5	34.1	8	0	1.000	1	0				-	-	-	8	0	0	0	0	0	0	0	0	-		0	0	-
2009	LAA	5	25.0	7	0	1.000	1	0				0	0	-	7	0	+1	0	0	0	0	0	0		0	0	0	-
2010	LAA	28	223.2	62	1	.984	9	0	4	1	1	9	6	.667	49	+4	-2	+2	+5	0	+5	+5	4	0	0	0	4	-
2011	LAA	37	301.2	84	3	.964	10	3	4	2	1	2	1	.500	68	-1	+3	+1	+3	0	+3	+3	2	0	0	0	2	-
		260	2014.2	569	28	.951	59	29	28	13	11	11	7	.636	483	0	+4	+6	+10	-1	+9	+9	6	-1	0	0	5	-

Chris Johnson

Year	Team	G	Inn	TC	E	Pct	GFP	DM	Opp	Sac Hits	Bunt Hits	Opp	GDP	Pct	Outs Made	To His Right	Straight On	To His Left	GB	Air	Total	Enhanced	+/-	Bunt	GDP	GFP/DME	Total	Rank
2009	Hou	7	48.0	7	0	1.000	0	0				1	0	.000	7	-1	0	0	-1	0	-1	-2	-2		0	0	-2	-
2010	Hou	90	790.0	195	18	.908	13	6	8	5	1	20	11	.550	155	+1	-11	-8	-18	-2	-20	-20	-15	0	0	-1	-16	35
2011	Hou	101	841.1	237	15	.937	18	13	9	6	2	23	14	.609	184	-4	-5	-8	-15	-2	-17	-18	-14	1	0	1	-12	32
		198	1679.1	439	33	.925	31	19	17	11	3	44	25	.568	346	-4	-16	-16	-34	-4	-38	-40	-31	1	0	0	-30	-

Chipper Jones

Year	Team	G	Inn	TC	E	Pct	GFP	DM	Opp	Sac Hits	Bunt Hits	Opp	GDP	Pct	Outs Made	To His Right	Straight On	To His Left	GB	Air	Total	Enhanced	+/-	Bunt	GDP	GFP/DME	Total	Rank
2004	Atl	96	802.0	241	6	.975	22	13	13	7	3	-	-	-	211	+2	-4	+10	+8	0	+8	+8	6	0	-	1	7	9
2005	Atl	101	830.1	254	5	.980	25	12	16	9	4	-	-	-	209	+1	+1	-3	-1	0	-1	-2	-2	-1	-	0	-3	24
2006	Atl	105	888.1	282	18	.936	21	14	14	6	2	-	-	-	234	-1	-12	-5	-18	-1	-19	-20	-15	1	-	0	-14	35
2007	Atl	126	1080.2	310	9	.971	38	16	19	12	3	-	-	-	262	+2	+4	-1	+4	-1	+3	+3	2	1	-	1	4	15
2008	Atl	115	987.1	312	13	.958	29	14	13	8	2	-	-	-	264	+5	-3	+9	+11	-1	+10	+10	8	1	-	1	10	4
2009	Atl	133	1136.2	315	22	.930	36	18	18	11	5	30	22	.733	245	-4	-8	+1	-11	+1	-10	-11	-8	0	1	1	-6	26
2010	Atl	89	696.2	209	10	.952	15	10	11	4	4	20	9	.450	169	+1	-2	+5	+6	-1	+5	+3	2	-2	0	0	0	17
2011	Atl	116	1006.1	248	6	.976	21	18	9	5	2	20	11	.550	211	-5	-2	+3	-2	-1	-3	-5	-3	0	0	0	-3	21
		881	7428.1	2171	89	.959	207	115	113	62	25	70	42	.600	1805	+1	-26	+19	-3	-4	-7	-14	-10	0	1	4	-5	19

Don Kelly

Year	Team	G	Inn	TC	E	Pct	GFP	DM	Opp	Sac Hits	Bunt Hits	Opp	GDP	Pct	Outs Made	To His Right	Straight On	To His Left	GB	Air	Total	Enhanced	+/-	Bunt	GDP	GFP/DME	Total	Rank
2009	Det	4	14.0	7	0	1.000	0	0				1	1	1.000	7	0	0	+1	0	0	0	0	0		0	0	0	-
2010	Det	15	105.0	41	3	.927	8	0	2	0	1	6	4	.667	34	+1	+3	+1	+4	0	+4	+5	4	0	0	1	5	-
2011	Det	45	325.0	103	4	.961	8	5	4	0	2	12	5	.417	82	0	-1	+5	+2	+1	+3	+5	4	0	0	0	4	-
		64	444.0	151	7	.954	16	5	6	0	3	19	10	.526	123	+1	+2	+7	+6	+1	+7	+10	8	0	0	1	9	-

Third Basemen

Adam Kennedy

Year	Team	G	Inn	TC	E	Pct	GFP	DM	Opp	Sac Hits	Bunt Hits	Opp GDP	Pct	Outs Made	To His Right	Straight On	To His Left	GB	Air	Total	Enhanced	+/-	Bunt	GDP	GFP/DME	Total	Rank
2009	Oak	82	691.2	219	13	.941	26	11	11	5	3	16	6	.375	185	+1	-3	-5	-6	-1	-7	-6	-5	0	-1	0	-6	25
2010	Was	8	45.1	9	1	.889	1	1				1	0	.000	7	+1	0	0	+1	0	+1	+1	1		0	0	1	-
2011	Sea	27	210.2	57	2	.965	5	6	2	0	0	3	2	.667	46	0	-1	-1	-1	-1	-2	-3	-2	1	0	0	-1	-
		117	947.2	285	16	.944	32	18	13	5	3	20	8	.400	238	+2	-4	-6	-6	-2	-8	-8	-6	1	-1	0	-6	

Kevin Kouzmanoff

Year	Team	G	Inn	TC	E	Pct	GFP	DM	Opp	Sac Hits	Bunt Hits	Opp GDP	Pct	Outs Made	To His Right	Straight On	To His Left	GB	Air	Total	Enhanced	+/-	Bunt	GDP	GFP/DME	Total	Rank
2006	Cle	2	16.0	7	1	.857	0	1				-	-	-	6	0	-1	0	-1	0	-1	0	0		-	0	0	-
2007	SD	136	1135.1	322	22	.932	34	22	19	4	7	-	-	-	267	-3	+4	-5	-4	+1	-3	-4	-3	0	-	-1	-4	26
2008	SD	154	1379.0	416	11	.974	49	26	18	5	7	-	-	-	358	+8	-8	-5	-5	+1	-4	-2	-2	0	-	2	0	20
2009	SD	139	1186.2	311	3	.990	44	16	21	7	8	35	18	.514	276	+6	+4	-6	+4	+3	+7	+7	5	-1	-1	-1	2	12
2010	Oak	142	1231.2	380	12	.968	43	29	26	13	10	34	23	.676	309	+7	+7	+3	+14	0	+14	+17	13	-1	1	-2	11	4
2011	2 tms	71	576.1	181	13	.928	33	21	11	4	4	15	9	.600	141	0	-1	-7	-9	-1	-10	-10	-7	0	0	0	-7	28
		644	5525.0	1617	62	.962	203	115	95	33	36	84	50	.595	1357	+18	+5	-20	-1	+4	+3	+8	6	-2	0	-2	2	17

Brett Lawrie

Year	Team	G	Inn	TC	E	Pct	GFP	DM	Opp	Sac Hits	Bunt Hits	Opp GDP	Pct	Outs Made	To His Right	Straight On	To His Left	GB	Air	Total	Enhanced	+/-	Bunt	GDP	GFP/DME	Total	Rank
2011	Tor	43	380.1	164	6	.963	19	12	4	2	1	12	5	.417	138	+3	+7	+9	+18	+1	+19	+20	15	0	-1	0	14	-

Evan Longoria

Year	Team	G	Inn	TC	E	Pct	GFP	DM	Opp	Sac Hits	Bunt Hits	Opp GDP	Pct	Outs Made	To His Right	Straight On	To His Left	GB	Air	Total	Enhanced	+/-	Bunt	GDP	GFP/DME	Total	Rank
2008	TB	119	1045.2	328	12	.963	49	15	20	8	8	-	-	-	292	0	+5	+4	+10	-1	+9	+11	8	0	-	2	10	4
2009	TB	151	1302.2	427	13	.970	63	18	24	8	9	44	35	.795	371	+3	+5	+10	+18	+1	+19	+21	16	0	2	1	19	4
2010	TB	151	1330.2	417	14	.966	59	19	30	9	10	42	30	.714	319	+14	-1	+5	+13	0	+13	+17	13	3	2	2	20	1
2011	TB	130	1124.2	367	14	.962	49	16	17	6	2	42	28	.667	296	+15	-5	+3	+8	+5	+13	+19	14	4	1	3	22	1
		551	4803.2	1539	53	.966	220	68	91	31	29	128	93	.727	1278	+32	+4	+22	+49	+5	+54	+68	51	7	5	8	71	3

Jose Lopez

Year	Team	G	Inn	TC	E	Pct	GFP	DM	Opp	Sac Hits	Bunt Hits	Opp GDP	Pct	Outs Made	To His Right	Straight On	To His Left	GB	Air	Total	Enhanced	+/-	Bunt	GDP	GFP/DME	Total	Rank
2004	Sea	1	1.0	0	0	-	0	0				-	-	-	0				0	0	0	0	0	-		0	0	-
2005	Sea	1	9.0	5	1	.800	1	0				-	-	-	3	+1			0	0	0	+1	1			0	1	-
2007	Sea	3	15.0	8	1	.875	1	1				-	-	-	6	+1	0	0	+1	0	+1	+1	1	-		0	1	-
2010	Sea	142	1252.2	447	18	.960	32	30	24	12	10	31	21	.677	375	-1	+7	+7	+14	+2	+16	+15	11	-1	0	0	10	6
2011	2 tms	39	288.1	78	5	.936	4	2	2	2	0	7	3	.429	67	0	0	-1	-1	0	-1	-1	0	0	-1	0	-1	-
		186	1566.0	538	25	.954	38	33	26	14	10	38	24	.632	451	+1	+7	+6	+14	+2	+16	+16	13	-1	-1	0	11	-

Jed Lowrie

Year	Team	G	Inn	TC	E	Pct	GFP	DM	Opp	Sac Hits	Bunt Hits	Opp GDP	Pct	Outs Made	To His Right	Straight On	To His Left	GB	Air	Total	Enhanced	+/-	Bunt	GDP	GFP/DME	Total	Rank
2008	Bos	45	243.2	77	2	.974	4	2	6	1	3	-	-	-	66	0	+1	0	+1	0	+1	0	0	1	-	0	1	-
2009	Bos	4	10.0	5	0	1.000	1	1	0	0		0	0	-	5	0	+1	0	-1	0	-1	0	0	0	-	0	0	-
2010	Bos	1	3.0	1	0	1.000	0	0	0	0		0	0	-	1	0	+1	0	0	0	0	0	0	0	0	0	0	-
2011	Bos	33	268.1	97	5	.948	5	4	5	2	2	8	5	.625	77	+5	-1	0	+3	-1	+2	+2	2	0	0	0	2	-
		83	525.0	180	7	.961	10	7	11	3	5	8	5	.625	149	+5	0	0	+3	-1	+2	+2	2	1	0	0	3	-

Michael Martinez

Year	Team	G	Inn	TC	E	Pct	GFP	DM	Opp	Sac Hits	Bunt Hits	Opp GDP	Pct	Outs Made	To His Right	Straight On	To His Left	GB	Air	Total	Enhanced	+/-	Bunt	GDP	GFP/DME	Total	Rank
2011	Phi	26	218.2	63	2	.968	10	5				1	1	1.000	56	0	-3	-1	-4	+1	-3	-3	-3	0	0	0	-3	-

Casey McGehee

Year	Team	G	Inn	TC	E	Pct	GFP	DM	Opp	Sac Hits	Bunt Hits	Opp GDP	Pct	Outs Made	To His Right	Straight On	To His Left	GB	Air	Total	Enhanced	+/-	Bunt	GDP	GFP/DME	Total	Rank
2008	ChC	6	41.2	16	0	1.000	1	0				-	-	-	16	+1	0	+1	+3	0	+3	+3	2		-	0	2	-
2009	Mil	71	530.1	155	13	.916	14	15	8	2	4	16	10	.625	128	-4	-2	-4	-9	-3	-12	-11	-8	-1	0	-1	-10	30
2010	Mil	153	1326.0	366	17	.954	36	20	21	11	4	40	25	.625	298	+1	-11	-5	-15	-3	-18	-18	-14	1	0	-1	-14	33
2011	Mil	147	1233.1	347	20	.942	32	20	9	5	2	22	15	.682	289	-2	0	+2	+2	0	+2	-1	0	0	1	2	3	12
		377	3131.1	884	50	.943	83	55	38	18	10	78	50	.641	731	-4	-13	-6	-19	-6	-25	-27	-20	0	1	0	-19	22

Third Basemen

Aaron Miles

		BASIC							BUNTS			GDP			PLUS/MINUS								RUNS SAVED					
Year	Team	G	Inn	TC	E	Pct	GFP	DM	Opp	Sac Hits	Bunt Hits	Opp	GDP	Pct	Outs Made	To His Right	Straight On	To His Left	GB	Air	Total	Enhanced	+/-	Bunt	GDP	GFP/DME	Total	Rank
2006	StL	1	2.1	0	0	-	0	0				-	-	-	0							0			-		0	-
2007	StL	3	19.0	8	0	1.000	0	0				-	-	-	7	+1	0	0	+1	-1	0	+1	1		-	0	1	-
2008	StL	11	61.0	18	0	1.000	1	2				-	-	-	16	0	+1	+1	+2	0	+2	+1	1		-	0	1	-
2009	ChC	4	12.0	2	0	1.000	0	0				0	0	-	2	0			0	0	0	0	0		0	0	0	-
2010	StL	5	25.0	9	2	.778	0	0	1	1	0	0	0	-	3	0	-2	0	-3	0	-3	-2	-2	0	0	0	-2	-
2011	LAD	61	459.2	111	8	.928	13	11	9	5	3	9	5	.556	87	-5	0	-1	-5	-1	-6	-7	-5	1	0	-1	-5	22
		85	579.0	148	10	.932	14	13	10	6	3	9	5	.556	115	-4	-1	0	-5	-2	-7	-7	-5	1	0	-1	-5	-

Melvin Mora

		BASIC							BUNTS			GDP			PLUS/MINUS								RUNS SAVED					
Year	Team	G	Inn	TC	E	Pct	GFP	DM	Opp	Sac Hits	Bunt Hits	Opp	GDP	Pct	Outs Made	To His Right	Straight On	To His Left	GB	Air	Total	Enhanced	+/-	Bunt	GDP	GFP/DME	Total	Rank
2004	Bal	138	1210.1	401	21	.948	31	23	14	5	6	-	-	-	334	-4	-12	-1	-16	+2	-14	-15	-11	-1	-	0	-12	33
2005	Bal	148	1289.2	415	18	.957	50	16	11	3	6	-	-	-	375	+2	+4	-2	+4	+1	+5	+6	5	0	-	1	6	14
2006	Bal	154	1323.0	413	17	.959	22	28	13	5	7	-	-	-	367	+1	-5	0	-4	+1	-3	-2	-2	-3	-	0	-5	22
2007	Bal	120	1051.1	349	10	.971	45	30	18	11	5	-	-	-	306	+5	-1	-1	+3	+1	+4	+6	5	1	-	0	6	10
2008	Bal	124	1059.2	351	14	.960	39	20	12	5	4	-	-	-	312	+7	-9	-12	-15	0	-15	-13	-10	0	-	-1	-11	34
2009	Bal	124	1050.1	378	11	.971	41	20	13	6	5	25	17	.680	337	+2	+4	-6	+1	-1	0	+2	2	-1	0	-1	0	16
2010	Col	63	440.0	115	5	.957	11	9	8	2	4	10	4	.400	94	+3	-4	-2	-5	0	-5	-3	-2	-1	-1	-1	-5	20
2011	Ari	31	270.1	86	3	.965	6	6	3	2	1	5	1	.200	73	+1	-1	-1	-1	0	-1	-2	-1	0	-1	-1	-3	-
		902	7694.2	2508	99	.961	245	152	92	39	38	40	22	.550	2198	+17	-24	-25	-33	+4	-29	-21	-14	-5	-2	-3	-24	24

Brent Morel

		BASIC							BUNTS			GDP			PLUS/MINUS								RUNS SAVED					
Year	Team	G	Inn	TC	E	Pct	GFP	DM	Opp	Sac Hits	Bunt Hits	Opp	GDP	Pct	Outs Made	To His Right	Straight On	To His Left	GB	Air	Total	Enhanced	+/-	Bunt	GDP	GFP/DME	Total	Rank
2010	CWS	20	164.0	38	1	.974	14	2	3	1	1	2	1	.500	34	0	+2	-3	-2	0	-2	-2	-1	0	0	0	-1	-
2011	CWS	125	1058.0	297	14	.953	44	14	16	7	7	24	9	.375	247	-4	+1	+4	+2	+1	+3	+2	1	0	-1	2	2	14
		145	1222.0	335	15	.955	58	16	19	8	8	26	10	.385	281	-4	+3	+1	0	+1	+1	0	0	0	-1	2	1	-

Mike Moustakas

		BASIC							BUNTS			GDP			PLUS/MINUS								RUNS SAVED					
Year	Team	G	Inn	TC	E	Pct	GFP	DM	Opp	Sac Hits	Bunt Hits	Opp	GDP	Pct	Outs Made	To His Right	Straight On	To His Left	GB	Air	Total	Enhanced	+/-	Bunt	GDP	GFP/DME	Total	Rank
2011	KC	89	778.0	240	11	.954	19	15	10	2	7	16	10	.625	198	0	+6	-2	+4	+1	+5	+5	4	-2	0	0	2	13

Daniel Murphy

		BASIC							BUNTS			GDP			PLUS/MINUS								RUNS SAVED					
Year	Team	G	Inn	TC	E	Pct	GFP	DM	Opp	Sac Hits	Bunt Hits	Opp	GDP	Pct	Outs Made	To His Right	Straight On	To His Left	GB	Air	Total	Enhanced	+/-	Bunt	GDP	GFP/DME	Total	Rank
2011	NYM	28	220.2	60	4	.933	7	1	4	2	1	4	4	1.000	48	-2	+1	+3	+1	0	+1	+2	2	0	0	0	2	-

Jayson Nix

		BASIC							BUNTS			GDP			PLUS/MINUS								RUNS SAVED					
Year	Team	G	Inn	TC	E	Pct	GFP	DM	Opp	Sac Hits	Bunt Hits	Opp	GDP	Pct	Outs Made	To His Right	Straight On	To His Left	GB	Air	Total	Enhanced	+/-	Bunt	GDP	GFP/DME	Total	Rank
2009	CWS	12	89.0	23	1	.957	0	1	1	0	0	4	2	.500	20	0	+1	+1	+1	0	+1	+1	1	0	0	0	1	-
2010	2 tms	56	434.0	139	16	.885	7	6	6	4	1	7	5	.714	102	-1	-1	-2	-6	0	-6	-4	-4	0	0	-1	-5	-
2011	Tor	41	334.2	118	3	.975	12	7	2	0	0	10	6	.600	99	+2	+2	+7	+11	+2	+13	+13	9	0	0	0	9	-
		109	857.2	280	20	.929	19	14	9	4	1	21	13	.619	221	+1	+2	+6	+6	+2	+8	+10	6	0	0	-1	5	-

Eduardo Nunez

		BASIC							BUNTS			GDP			PLUS/MINUS								RUNS SAVED					
Year	Team	G	Inn	TC	E	Pct	GFP	DM	Opp	Sac Hits	Bunt Hits	Opp	GDP	Pct	Outs Made	To His Right	Straight On	To His Left	GB	Air	Total	Enhanced	+/-	Bunt	GDP	GFP/DME	Total	Rank
2010	NYY	15	83.0	18	1	.944	1	2				4	1	.250	17	-1	0	0	-2	+1	-1	-1	-1		0	0	-1	-
2011	NYY	40	285.1	74	6	.919	6	5	2	1	0	7	5	.714	59	0	-3	0	-5	0	-5	-3	-2	0	0	0	-2	-
		55	368.1	92	7	.924	7	7	2	1	0	11	6	.545	76	-1	-3	0	-7	+1	-6	-4	-3	0	0	0	-3	-

Jimmy Paredes

		BASIC							BUNTS			GDP			PLUS/MINUS								RUNS SAVED					
Year	Team	G	Inn	TC	E	Pct	GFP	DM	Opp	Sac Hits	Bunt Hits	Opp	GDP	Pct	Outs Made	To His Right	Straight On	To His Left	GB	Air	Total	Enhanced	+/-	Bunt	GDP	GFP/DME	Total	Rank
2011	Hou	46	390.2	107	5	.953	15	17	9	6	3	4	3	.750	79	-3	-1	+3	-1	-1	-2	-2	-2	-1	0	2	-1	-

Third Basemen

Placido Polanco

	BASIC							BUNTS			GDP			PLUS/MINUS								RUNS SAVED					
Year Team	G	Inn	TC	E	Pct	GFP	DM	Opp	Sac Hits	Bunt Hits	Opp	GDP	Pct	Outs Made	To His Right	Straight On	To His Left	GB	Air	Total	Enhanced	+/-	Bunt	GDP	GFP/DME	Total	Rank
2003 Phi	21	179.0	49	2	.959	-	-	6	3	2	-	-	-	42	-1	0	+1	+1	0	+1	0	0	0	-	-	0	-
2004 Phi	13	96.0	41	0	1.000	4	2	2	1	0	-	-	-	33	0	+2	+1	+3	+1	+4	+4	3	0	-	0	3	-
2005 2 tms	9	57.1	27	0	1.000	3	0				-	-	-	26	+3	+1	+1	+5	0	+5	+5	4		-	0	4	-
2010 Phi	123	1075.1	351	5	.986	41	12	16	8	6	31	27	.871	297	+15	-8	-5	+1	+2	+3	+5	4	0	2	1	7	10
2011 Phi	118	1044.2	345	8	.977	33	17	18	11	5	32	13	.406	295	+14	+4	-3	+14	-1	+13	+13	10	0	-1	0	9	6
	284	2452.1	813	15	.982	81	31	42	23	13	63	40	.635	693	+31	-1	-5	+24	+2	+26	+27	21	0	1	1	23	-

Martin Prado

	BASIC							BUNTS			GDP			PLUS/MINUS								RUNS SAVED					
Year Team	G	Inn	TC	E	Pct	GFP	DM	Opp	Sac Hits	Bunt Hits	Opp	GDP	Pct	Outs Made	To His Right	Straight On	To His Left	GB	Air	Total	Enhanced	+/-	Bunt	GDP	GFP/DME	Total	Rank
2006 Atl	8	38.0	7	1	.857	0	1	1	0	1	-	-	-	6	-2	0	-1	-2	0	-2	-2	-2	-1	-	0	-3	-
2007 Atl	9	44.0	11	0	1.000	1	1	2	1	1	-	-	-	10	0	-1	+2	+1	0	+1	+1	1	0	-	0	1	-
2008 Atl	24	158.2	56	1	.982	9	7	3	1	1	-	-	-	52	0	+2	+2	+4	0	+4	+4	3	0	-	0	3	-
2009 Atl	41	266.0	81	2	.975	12	3	3	2	1	8	5	.625	72	+2	+1	+4	+8	0	+8	+8	6	0	0	0	6	-
2010 Atl	43	369.2	118	5	.958	15	8	5	2	1	8	8	1.000	90	-6	+7	+5	+8	+1	+9	+8	6	1	1	0	8	-
2011 Atl	41	297.0	101	5	.950	9	5	8	4	2	10	6	.600	85	-1	+6	+2	+7	-2	+5	+5	4	1	0	1	6	-
	166	1173.1	374	14	.963	46	25	22	10	7	26	19	.731	315	-7	+15	+14	+26	-1	+25	+24	18	1	1	1	21	-

Aramis Ramirez

	BASIC							BUNTS			GDP			PLUS/MINUS								RUNS SAVED					
Year Team	G	Inn	TC	E	Pct	GFP	DM	Opp	Sac Hits	Bunt Hits	Opp	GDP	Pct	Outs Made	To His Right	Straight On	To His Left	GB	Air	Total	Enhanced	+/-	Bunt	GDP	GFP/DME	Total	Rank
2003 2 tms	159	1397.2	466	33	.929			18	10	5	-	-	-	377	+1	-1	-4	-4	-3	-7	-4	-3	1	-	-	-2	24
2004 ChC	144	1245.1	323	10	.969	36	29	17	9	4	-	-	-	272	+2	-9	-3	-10	-1	-11	-8	-6	1	-	1	-4	22
2005 ChC	119	1020.1	304	16	.947	26	23	13	10	3	-	-	-	257	-2	0	+3	+1	0	+1	0	0	0	-	-1	-1	22
2006 ChC	156	1353.0	375	13	.965	28	39	16	12	3	-	-	-	321	-5	+3	-5	-7	0	-7	-6	-5	0	-	-2	-7	27
2007 ChC	126	1091.1	358	10	.972	41	28	16	9	3	-	-	-	316	+4	+8	+4	+16	-2	+14	+15	11	1	-	-1	11	6
2008 ChC	147	1282.2	326	18	.945	39	21	15	8	4	-	-	-	279	-8	-2	-1	-11	-1	-12	-12	-9	1	-	-1	-9	31
2009 ChC	79	683.2	192	10	.948	20	17	15	7	3	20	10	.500	152	-3	-4	-1	-8	+1	-7	-8	-6	1	0	0	-5	22
2010 ChC	118	1003.1	262	16	.939	26	26	19	8	8	20	7	.350	207	-5	-10	+2	-16	+3	-13	-13	-10	-2	-1	-2	-15	34
2011 ChC	145	1241.1	298	14	.953	38	34	21	11	5	24	12	.500	249	-8	-13	-5	-25	+2	-23	-24	-18	2	-1	-1	-18	34
	1193	10318.2	2904	140	.952	254	217	150	84	38	64	29	.453	2430	-24	-28	-12	-64	-1	-65	-60	-46	5	-2	-7	-50	33

Mark Reynolds

	BASIC							BUNTS			GDP			PLUS/MINUS								RUNS SAVED					
Year Team	G	Inn	TC	E	Pct	GFP	DM	Opp	Sac Hits	Bunt Hits	Opp	GDP	Pct	Outs Made	To His Right	Straight On	To His Left	GB	Air	Total	Enhanced	+/-	Bunt	GDP	GFP/DME	Total	Rank
2007 Ari	104	842.1	223	11	.951	29	18	11	7	2	-	-	-	188	-6	-5	+3	-9	-1	-10	-8	-6	2	-	1	-3	25
2008 Ari	150	1288.1	356	34	.904	46	33	16	9	5	-	-	-	293	-4	-6	-3	-13	0	-13	-11	-8	-2	-	-1	-11	33
2009 Ari	130	1125.2	347	19	.945	55	33	20	8	6	35	23	.657	294	0	-10	+4	-6	-1	-7	-6	-5	0	0	0	-5	21
2010 Ari	142	1214.0	369	18	.951	56	20	18	12	4	31	17	.548	295	-4	-1	-3	-6	+3	-3	-5	-4	0	-1	-1	-6	23
2011 Bal	114	984.1	253	26	.897	29	31	12	5	7	25	16	.640	198	-8	-13	-2	-21	-1	-22	-23	-18	-3	1	-2	-22	35
	640	5454.2	1548	108	.930	215	135	77	41	24	91	56	.615	1268	-22	-35	-1	-55	0	-55	-53	-41	-3	0	-3	-47	32

Ryan Roberts

	BASIC							BUNTS			GDP			PLUS/MINUS								RUNS SAVED					
Year Team	G	Inn	TC	E	Pct	GFP	DM	Opp	Sac Hits	Bunt Hits	Opp	GDP	Pct	Outs Made	To His Right	Straight On	To His Left	GB	Air	Total	Enhanced	+/-	Bunt	GDP	GFP/DME	Total	Rank
2007 Tor	3	22.0	3	1	.667	1	0	-	-	-	-	-	-	2				0	0	0	0	0		0	0	0	-
2009 Ari	19	132.0	41	3	.927	3	0	1	0	1	3	3	1.000	36	-1	+1	+1	+2	0	+2	+2	2	-1	0	0	1	-
2010 Ari	1	8.0	2	0	1.000	0	0	0	0		0	0		2	0	0	0	0	0	0	0	0	0	0	0	0	-
2011 Ari	107	902.1	281	10	.964	30	20	12	5	5	19	12	.632	242	+3	-11	-3	-9	+4	-5	-7	-6	-1	0	0	-7	26
	130	1064.1	327	14	.957	34	20	13	5	6	22	15	.682	282	+2	-10	-2	-7	+4	-3	-5	-4	-2	0	0	-6	-

Alex Rodriguez

	BASIC							BUNTS			GDP			PLUS/MINUS								RUNS SAVED					
Year Team	G	Inn	TC	E	Pct	GFP	DM	Opp	Sac Hits	Bunt Hits	Opp	GDP	Pct	Outs Made	To His Right	Straight On	To His Left	GB	Air	Total	Enhanced	+/-	Bunt	GDP	GFP/DME	Total	Rank
2004 NYY	155	1364.1	375	13	.965	37	23	10	3	6	-	-	-	317	-1	+19	+2	+21	+1	+22	+17	13	-1	-	2	14	4
2005 NYY	161	1384.2	415	12	.971	41	26	9	3	6	-	-	-	371	-7	+13	-3	+2	+4	+6	+2	2	-2	-	0	0	20
2006 NYY	151	1287.2	382	24	.937	23	22	8	2	5	-	-	-	327	+3	-7	-7	-11	-2	-13	-12	-9	-3	-	-1	-13	33
2007 NYY	154	1330.0	370	13	.965	40	22	16	9	6	-	-	-	330	+3	+3	-4	+2	0	+2	+3	2	-1	-	-2	-1	20
2008 NYY	131	1126.1	334	10	.970	39	13	11	4	6	-	-	-	292	-5	+6	+1	+2	+1	+3	+1	1	-2	-	3	2	17
2009 NYY	116	974.1	275	9	.967	36	18	6	2	3	28	13	.464	250	-8	+2	+2	-5	0	-5	-8	-6	0	-1	-2	-5	22
2010 NYY	124	1046.1	292	7	.976	29	11	17	9	6	28	20	.714	252	-5	+14	-4	+7	0	+7	+5	3	-1	1	0	3	12
2011 NYY	89	762.0	225	6	.973	26	11	13	3	5	18	10	.556	190	+6	+11	-1	+15	-3	+12	+14	11	1	0	1	13	4
	1081	9275.2	2668	94	.965	271	146	90	35	43	74	43	.581	2329	-14	+61	-14	+33	+1	+34	+22	17	-9	0	5	13	13

Third Basemen

Scott Rolen

Year	Team	G	Inn	TC	E	Pct	GFP	DM	Opp	Sac Hits	Bunt Hits	Opp GDP	GDP	Pct	Outs Made	To His Right	Straight On	To His Left	GB	Air	Total	Enhanced	+/-	Bunt	GDP	GFP/DME	Total	Rank
2003	StL	153	1339.0	420	13	.969	-	-	13	9	2	-	-	-	332	-2	+4	-4	-2	0	-2	-7	-5	1	-	-	-4	27
2004	StL	142	1228.0	428	10	.977	41	19	15	8	6	-	-	-	375	+6	+13	+13	+32	+2	+34	+37	28	0	-	2	30	1
2005	StL	56	486.0	179	6	.966	29	4	6	3	1	-	-	-	156	+3	+3	+9	+15	0	+15	+16	12	1	-	1	14	3
2006	StL	142	1215.2	426	15	.965	41	23	19	16	3	-	-	-	376	-7	+25	+4	+22	+1	+23	+19	14	1	-	1	16	5
2007	StL	112	935.0	321	10	.969	30	15	12	6	3	-	-	-	286	+7	+3	+6	+16	-2	+14	+15	11	0	-	1	12	4
2008	Tor	115	1006.2	302	11	.964	32	11	10	7	2	-	-	-	266	-7	+12	+8	+13	0	+13	+13	10	0	-	-1	9	6
2009	2 tms	127	1118.1	328	5	.985	38	16	10	5	5	29	12	.414	294	+7	+6	+8	+21	+1	+22	+23	17	-1	-1	2	17	5
2010	Cin	130	1074.0	350	8	.977	54	13	7	5	1	44	25	.568	297	+2	+11	-5	+10	+1	+11	+9	7	1	0	2	10	8
2011	Cin	63	547.1	161	4	.975	15	10	4	1	1	12	8	.667	133	-4	+11	+3	+10	-1	+9	+9	7	0	1	2	10	5
		1040	8950.0	2915	82	.972	280	111	96	60	24	85	45	.529	2515	+5	+88	+42	+137	+2	+139	+134	101	3	0	10	114	2

Pablo Sandoval

Year	Team	G	Inn	TC	E	Pct	GFP	DM	Opp	Sac Hits	Bunt Hits	Opp GDP	GDP	Pct	Outs Made	To His Right	Straight On	To His Left	GB	Air	Total	Enhanced	+/-	Bunt	GDP	GFP/DME	Total	Rank
2008	SF	12	85.0	17	0	1.000	1	2	1	1	0	-	-	-	16	+2	+1	-1	-2	0	+1	+1	1	0	-	0	1	-
2009	SF	120	1028.0	276	11	.960	31	17	22	13	5	24	10	.417	233	0	-7	-6	-12	-1	-13	-13	-10	1	-1	-1	-11	31
2010	SF	143	1224.2	334	13	.961	44	17	7	3	3	33	20	.606	272	+4	-5	-2	-2	-2	-4	-5	-3	0	1	3	1	16
2011	SF	106	904.2	295	10	.966	42	17	8	5	0	24	11	.458	246	+12	+8	+1	+20	-1	+19	+20	15	1	0	-1	15	2
		381	3242.1	922	34	.963	118	53	38	22	8	81	41	.506	767	+18	-3	-8	+8	-5	+3	+3	3	2	0	1	6	16

Kyle Seager

Year	Team	G	Inn	TC	E	Pct	GFP	DM	Opp	Sac Hits	Bunt Hits	Opp GDP	GDP	Pct	Outs Made	To His Right	Straight On	To His Left	GB	Air	Total	Enhanced	+/-	Bunt	GDP	GFP/DME	Total	Rank
2011	Sea	42	335.2	120	4	.967	10	6	5	2	2	8	2	.250	104	+2	-3	+2	0	+2	+2	+3	2	0	0	0	2	-

Scott Sizemore

Year	Team	G	Inn	TC	E	Pct	GFP	DM	Opp	Sac Hits	Bunt Hits	Opp GDP	GDP	Pct	Outs Made	To His Right	Straight On	To His Left	GB	Air	Total	Enhanced	+/-	Bunt	GDP	GFP/DME	Total	Rank
2010	Det	6	38.0	15	1	.933	1	1	2	0	2	1	1	1.000	9	-2	+1	+1	0	0	0	0	0	-1	0		-1	-
2011	Oak	91	782.0	196	13	.934	24	22	13	5	8	13	8	.615	157	-7	-4	-2	-11	+1	-10	-11	-9	-1	0	-1	-11	31
		97	820.0	211	14	.934	25	23	15	5	10	14	9	.643	166	-9	-3	-1	-11	+1	-10	-11	-9	-2	0	-1	-12	-

Ian Stewart

Year	Team	G	Inn	TC	E	Pct	GFP	DM	Opp	Sac Hits	Bunt Hits	Opp GDP	GDP	Pct	Outs Made	To His Right	Straight On	To His Left	GB	Air	Total	Enhanced	+/-	Bunt	GDP	GFP/DME	Total	Rank
2007	Col	11	41.1	21	0	1.000	3	0	-	-	-	-	-	-	20	+1	+2	+2	+4	+1	+5	+5	4	-	-		4	-
2008	Col	65	531.1	177	10	.944	27	8	10	4	3	-	-	-	153	+1	+3	0	+4	0	+4	+4	3	0	-	1	4	14
2009	Col	121	831.0	226	7	.969	39	22	15	7	6	20	9	.450	194	+3	+2	-1	+4	-1	+3	+5	4	-1	-1	-2	0	15
2010	Col	115	925.1	281	10	.964	37	20	11	6	2	27	14	.519	244	-11	+6	+6	+3	+1	+4	+2	2	1	0	2	5	11
2011	Col	42	284.0	85	6	.929	8	3	2	1	0	5	2	.400	65	-2	+1	+1	+1	+1	+2	+1	1	1	0	1	3	-
		354	2613.0	790	33	.958	114	53	38	18	11	52	25	.481	676	-8	+14	+8	+16	+2	+18	+17	14	1	-1	2	16	11

Mark Teahen

Year	Team	G	Inn	TC	E	Pct	GFP	DM	Opp	Sac Hits	Bunt Hits	Opp GDP	GDP	Pct	Outs Made	To His Right	Straight On	To His Left	GB	Air	Total	Enhanced	+/-	Bunt	GDP	GFP/DME	Total	Rank
2005	KC	128	1068.1	377	20	.947	49	27	14	4	5	-	-	-	311	-9	-6	-11	-25	+1	-24	-30	-23	1	-	1	-21	35
2006	KC	109	923.2	330	14	.958	32	24	11	4	5	-	-	-	280	-11	+5	+8	+2	+2	+4	0	0	-1	-	0	-1	15
2008	KC	19	166.0	45	3	.933	5	1	2	0	1	-	-	-	36	0	0	-2	-1	0	-1	-2	-2	-1	-	0	-3	-
2009	KC	107	869.0	248	11	.956	28	13	17	3	9	20	9	.450	208	-8	-1	-5	-14	+1	-13	-12	-9	-1	-1	-1	-12	32
2010	CWS	52	411.0	124	10	.919	14	10	6	3	3	12	6	.500	96	-8	-3	-1	-10	-1	-11	-12	-10	0	0	-1	-11	-
2011	2 tms	32	219.2	68	0	1.000	11	3	9	1	4	5	2	.400	57	+1	+2	0	+3	+1	+4	+4	3	0	0	0	3	-
		447	3657.2	1192	58	.951	139	78	59	15	27	37	17	.459	988	-35	-3	-11	-45	+4	-41	-52	-41	-2	-1	-1	-45	31

Miguel Tejada

Year	Team	G	Inn	TC	E	Pct	GFP	DM	Opp	Sac Hits	Bunt Hits	Opp GDP	GDP	Pct	Outs Made	To His Right	Straight On	To His Left	GB	Air	Total	Enhanced	+/-	Bunt	GDP	GFP/DME	Total	Rank
2010	2 tms	97	823.1	284	15	.947	39	24	17	7	7	30	17	.567	228	-3	-7	-4	-12	+2	-10	-10	-8	0	0	-1	-9	27
2011	SF	44	372.1	130	2	.985	18	6	11	7	1	15	9	.600	105	+2	+1	+3	+6	+1	+7	+7	5	1	0	1	7	-
		141	1195.2	414	17	.959	57	30	28	14	8	45	26	.578	333	-1	-6	-1	-6	+3	-3	-3	-3	1	0	0	-2	-

Third Basemen

Justin Turner

		BASIC							BUNTS			GDP			PLUS/MINUS								RUNS SAVED					
Year	Team	G	Inn	TC	E	Pct	GFP	DM	Opp	Sac Hits	Bunt Hits	Opp	GDP	Pct	Outs Made	To His Right	Straight On	To His Left	GB	Air	Total	Enhanced	+/-	Bunt	GDP	GFP/DME	Total	Rank
2009	Bal	7	34.0	10	0	1.000	0	1				2	1	.500	10	0	+1	+1	+2	0	+2	+2	2		0	0	2	-
2010	NYM	1	2.0	2	0	1.000	0	0				1	1	1.000	2	0	-1	0	-1	0	-1	-1	-1		0	0	-1	-
2011	NYM	36	277.2	79	4	.949	8	8	5	2	2	5	3	.600	61	-2	+3	-3	-1	+1	0	-1	-1	0	0	0	-1	-
		44	313.2	91	4	.956	8	9	5	2	2	8	5	.625	73	-2	+3	-2	0	+1	+1	0	0	0	0	0	0	-

Juan Uribe

		BASIC							BUNTS			GDP			PLUS/MINUS								RUNS SAVED					
Year	Team	G	Inn	TC	E	Pct	GFP	DM	Opp	Sac Hits	Bunt Hits	Opp	GDP	Pct	Outs Made	To His Right	Straight On	To His Left	GB	Air	Total	Enhanced	+/-	Bunt	GDP	GFP/DME	Total	Rank
2004	CWS	27	181.1	57	2	.965	3	0	3	1	2	-	-	-	48	0	+3	+1	+3	0	+3	+3	2	-1	-		1	2
2008	CWS	57	460.1	173	7	.960	18	14	8	4	4	9	7	.778	152	+6	-7	-2	-3	0	-3	-3	-2	-1	-	-1	-4	-
2009	SF	44	323.1	99	4	.960	13	5	9	6	2				80	+1	-1	0	0	0	0	+1	1	0	1	0	2	-
2010	SF	26	192.2	69	3	.957	8	4	5	4	0	3	1	.333	54	-1	+2	0	+1	0	+1	+1	1	-1	0	0	0	-
2011	LAD	59	462.2	136	3	.978	23	6	8	6	1	8	2	.250	111	+4	+3	-1	+5	+1	+6	+7	5	1	0	-1	5	8
		213	1620.1	534	19	.964	65	29	33	21	9	20	10	.500	445	+10	0	-2	+6	+1	+7	+9	7	-2	1	-1	5	-

Danny Valencia

		BASIC							BUNTS			GDP			PLUS/MINUS								RUNS SAVED					
Year	Team	G	Inn	TC	E	Pct	GFP	DM	Opp	Sac Hits	Bunt Hits	Opp	GDP	Pct	Outs Made	To His Right	Straight On	To His Left	GB	Air	Total	Enhanced	+/-	Bunt	GDP	GFP/DME	Total	Rank
2010	Min	81	709.1	223	6	.973	23	11	10	7	3	19	12	.632	193	+5	-1	0	+5	0	+5	+4	3	0	0	0	3	12
2011	Min	147	1280.2	351	18	.949	28	26	20	8	10	34	20	.588	300	-2	-7	-7	-14	0	-14	-15	-11	-1	0	-1	-13	33
		228	1990.0	574	24	.958	51	37	30	15	13	53	32	.604	493	+3	-8	-7	-9	0	-9	-11	-8	-1	0	-1	-10	

Ty Wigginton

		BASIC							BUNTS			GDP			PLUS/MINUS								RUNS SAVED					
Year	Team	G	Inn	TC	E	Pct	GFP	DM	Opp	Sac Hits	Bunt Hits	Opp	GDP	Pct	Outs Made	To His Right	Straight On	To His Left	GB	Air	Total	Enhanced	+/-	Bunt	GDP	GFP/DME	Total	Rank
2003	NYM	155	1329.0	426	16	.962	-	-	23	6	7	-	-	-	360	-14	-8	+1	-21	-2	-23	-26	-20	1	-	-	-19	35
2004	2 tms	122	931.1	289	18	.938	13	20	20	11	8	-	-	-	236	-5	-1	+5	-1	-1	-2	-4	-4	-3	-	0	-7	28
2005	Pit	40	305.0	85	9	.894	6	9	5	2	3	-	-	-	65	-11	-5	+1	-15	0	-15	-18	-14	-1	-	0	-15	-
2006	TB	34	274.1	84	5	.940	6	8	4	0	3	-	-	-	73	-2	-7	-1	-9	-1	-10	-11	-8	-1	-	0	-9	-
2007	2 tms	80	647.1	205	8	.961	18	16	11	9	2	-	-	-	177	-6	-2	-1	-8	+1	-7	-11	-8	-1	-	-1	-10	29
2008	Hou	82	652.0	196	6	.969	22	15	9	2	6	-	-	-	172	-3	+2	+1	0	-1	-1	-5	-4	-2	-	-1	-7	26
2009	Bal	39	317.2	82	4	.951	7	4	2	1	1	7	4	.571	70	-6	-1	-2	-9	0	-9	-9	-7	0	0	1	-6	-
2010	Bal	22	166.0	51	5	.902	7	3	3	2	0	3	2	.667	37	-3	+1	+1	-1	-1	-2	-2	-1	1	0	0	0	-
2011	Col	68	520.1	133	4	.970	15	11	8	1	5	18	11	.611	109	-2	0	-2	-4	+1	-3	-3	-2	0	0	1	-1	18
		642	5143.0	1551	75	.952	94	86	85	34	35	28	17	.607	1299	-52	-21	+3	-68	-4	-72	-89	-68	-6	0	0	-74	35

Brandon Wood

		BASIC							BUNTS			GDP			PLUS/MINUS								RUNS SAVED					
Year	Team	G	Inn	TC	E	Pct	GFP	DM	Opp	Sac Hits	Bunt Hits	Opp	GDP	Pct	Outs Made	To His Right	Straight On	To His Left	GB	Air	Total	Enhanced	+/-	Bunt	GDP	GFP/DME	Total	Rank
2007	LAA	10	75.0	27	1	.963	0	2	5	3	2	-	-	-	22	0	-1	+1	0	0	0	-1	-1	0	-	0	-1	-
2008	LAA	32	188.0	60	2	.948	5	3	6	3	1	-	-	-	50	0	0	0	0	0	0	0	0	1	-	0	1	-
2009	LAA	9	41.0	7	0	1.000	1	0				0	0	-	7				-1	0	-1	-1	-1		0		0	-1	-
2010	LAA	56	412.2	114	5	.956	17	4	3	2	0	6	3	.500	93	+1	+6	+2	+10	0	+10	+10	7	1	0	0	8	-
2011	Pit	61	377.2	113	3	.973	10	14	8	3	5	12	6	.500	97	0	+1	-1	0	-2	-2	-2	-2	-2	-1	-1	-6	-
		168	1094.1	321	11	.966	33	23	22	11	8	18	9	.500	269	+1	+6	+2	+9	-2	+7	+6	3	0	-1	-1	1	-

David Wright

		BASIC							BUNTS			GDP			PLUS/MINUS								RUNS SAVED					
Year	Team	G	Inn	TC	E	Pct	GFP	DM	Opp	Sac Hits	Bunt Hits	Opp	GDP	Pct	Outs Made	To His Right	Straight On	To His Left	GB	Air	Total	Enhanced	+/-	Bunt	GDP	GFP/DME	Total	Rank
2004	NYM	69	603.2	189	11	.942	11	10	7	1	3	-	-	-	155	-2	+14	-2	+10	-3	+7	+6	5	0	-	-1	4	13
2005	NYM	160	1404.1	462	24	.948	56	38	24	11	7	-	-	-	396	-14	+2	0	-12	-2	-14	-17	-13	2	-	0	-11	32
2006	NYM	153	1365.1	414	19	.954	38	34	18	13	2	-	-	-	339	-10	-6	+8	-8	-2	-10	-11	-8	2	-	-2	-8	28
2007	NYM	159	1418.1	452	21	.954	56	26	25	13	6	-	-	-	384	-11	+9	+18	+16	0	+16	+13	10	1	-	1	12	5
2008	NYM	159	1433.1	416	16	.962	78	24	13	7	1	-	-	-	356	-2	+6	+1	+5	-2	+3	+2	2	1	-	2	5	12
2009	NYM	142	1232.0	361	19	.950	44	25	19	10	7	28	14	.500	302	-6	0	-2	-8	-1	-9	-15	-11	-1	-1	-1	-14	33
2010	NYM	155	1373.0	451	20	.956	76	28	17	7	5	43	23	.535	365	-15	0	-1	-13	-1	-14	-17	-13	0	-1	0	-14	31
2011	NYM	101	893.2	267	19	.929	31	13	13	5	4	15	6	.400	202	-5	-3	+8	0	-4	-4	-4	-3	-1	-1	-1	-6	24
		1098	9723.2	3012	148	.951	390	198	136	67	35	86	43	.500	2499	-65	+22	+30	-10	-15	-25	-43	-31	4	-3	-2	-32	28

351

Third Basemen

Kevin Youkilis

		BASIC							BUNTS			GDP			PLUS/MINUS								RUNS SAVED					
Year	Team	G	Inn	TC	E	Pct	GFP	DM	Opp	Sac Hits	Bunt Hits	Opp	GDP	Pct	Outs Made	To His Right	Straight On	To His Left	GB	Air	Total	Enhanced	+/-	Bunt	GDP	GFP/DME	Total	Rank
2004	Bos	65	506.0	158	5	.968	7	11	4	3	0	-	-	-	145	-1	+6	+4	+8	-1	+7	+7	5	1	-	-1	5	12
2005	Bos	24	139.0	39	0	1.000	4	1	1	1	0	-	-	-	37	-1	0	-1	-3	0	-3	-5	-4	0	-	0	-4	-
2006	Bos	16	92.0	41	3	.927	2	1	1	0	0	-	-	-	37	+2	-1	-2	-2	+1	-1	-1	-1		-	0	-1	-
2007	Bos	13	108.0	38	3	.921	3	3	1	0	1	-	-	-	33	-1	+1	0	0	0	0	+1	1	0	-	0	1	-
2008	Bos	36	252.0	96	3	.969	5	5	4	4	0	-	-	-	86	+1	+3	+4	+7	0	+7	+8	6	0	-	0	6	-
2009	Bos	63	494.1	155	4	.974	16	4	6	3	2	7	4	.571	141	-3	+1	+1	-1	0	-1	0	0	0	0	1	1	14
2010	Bos	2	15.0	8	0	1.000	1	1	1	1	0	0	0	-	6	0	-1	-1	-2	+1	-1	-1	-1	0	0	0	-1	-
2011	Bos	112	948.2	273	9	.967	29	15	14	5	5	15	7	.467	224	+8	-7	+1	0	0	0	+2	2	0	-1	-1	0	16
		331	2555.0	808	27	.967	67	41	32	17	8	22	11	.500	709	+5	+2	+6	+7	+1	+8	+11	8	1	-1	-1	7	15

Michael Young

		BASIC							BUNTS			GDP			PLUS/MINUS								RUNS SAVED					
Year	Team	G	Inn	TC	E	Pct	GFP	DM	Opp	Sac Hits	Bunt Hits	Opp	GDP	Pct	Outs Made	To His Right	Straight On	To His Left	GB	Air	Total	Enhanced	+/-	Bunt	GDP	GFP/DME	Total	Rank
2009	Tex	134	1165.2	289	9	.969	39	23	8	2	4	26	20	.769	255	-5	-10	-6	-21	0	-21	-23	-17	0	1	1	-15	34
2010	Tex	155	1370.1	379	19	.950	42	15	11	6	5	37	23	.622	312	-13	+2	-5	-12	0	-12	-16	-12	-1	0	2	-11	29
2011	Tex	40	342.0	101	5	.950	12	5	7	0	4	11	7	.636	81	-3	+1	-1	-2	-1	-3	-5	-4	0	0	1	-3	-
		329	2878.0	769	33	.957	93	43	26	8	13	74	50	.676	648	-21	-7	-12	-35	-1	-36	-44	-33	-1	1	4	-29	26

Ryan Zimmerman

		BASIC							BUNTS			GDP			PLUS/MINUS								RUNS SAVED					
Year	Team	G	Inn	TC	E	Pct	GFP	DM	Opp	Sac Hits	Bunt Hits	Opp	GDP	Pct	Outs Made	To His Right	Straight On	To His Left	GB	Air	Total	Enhanced	+/-	Bunt	GDP	GFP/DME	Total	Rank
2005	Was	14	111.0	32	0	1.000	1	3	4	2	1	-	-	-	26	+1	-1	0	0	0	0	+1	1	0	-	0	1	-
2006	Was	157	1368.1	427	15	.965	57	41	22	9	7	-	-	-	368	+3	-1	0	+1	-1	0	+2	2	-1	-	-2	-1	14
2007	Was	161	1431.2	511	23	.955	75	35	32	16	8	-	-	-	419	-4	+21	+2	+20	+4	+24	+21	16	1	-	1	18	2
2008	Was	104	910.2	304	10	.967	48	22	13	10	0	-	-	-	263	-7	+10	+5	+8	+2	+10	+10	8	2	-	-1	9	7
2009	Was	154	1337.2	459	17	.963	81	32	22	14	5	34	18	.529	391	-4	+15	+25	+36	-5	+31	+28	21	0	0	1	22	2
2010	Was	137	1189.1	344	17	.951	55	17	22	16	4	31	18	.581	278	-6	+13	+9	+16	0	+16	+16	12	-1	-1	1	11	5
2011	Was	97	866.2	278	12	.957	29	12	21	12	5	19	11	.579	214	-5	-4	-2	-12	0	-12	-10	-8	1	0	2	-5	23
		824	7215.1	2355	94	.960	346	162	136	79	30	84	47	.560	1959	-22	+53	+39	+69	0	+69	+68	52	2	-1	2	55	5

Shortstops

Robert Andino

	BASIC							GDP			PLUS/MINUS							RUNS SAVED				
Year	Team	G	Inn	TC	E	Pct	GFP	DM	Opps	GDP	Pct	Outs Made	To His Right	Straight On	To His Left	GB	Air	Total	+/-	GDP	GFP/DME	Total	Rank
2005	Fla	17	120.0	45	2	.956	2	2	14	7	.500	30	-2	-1	-2	-5	0	-5	-4	0	-1	-5	-
2006	Fla	9	55.2	28	1	.964	1	1	6	2	.333	22	-1	+1	-1	-1	0	-1	-1	0	0	-1	-
2007	Fla	3	20.0	7	0	1.000	0	3	2	1	.500	6	-1	0	0	-1	0	-1	-1	0	0	-1	-
2008	Fla	4	8.0	2	0	1.000	0	0	0		-	2	+1			+1	0	+1	1		0	1	-
2009	Bal	62	478.1	247	8	.968	17	12	56	41	.732	188	+2	+1	+1	+5	-2	+3	2	1	0	3	14
2010	Bal	7	42.0	20	1	.950	0	2	4	3	.750	14	+1	-1	0	0	-1	-1	0	0	0	0	-
2011	Bal	30	223.1	133	5	.962	16	6	25	17	.680	104	+4	+2	-4	+2	+2	+4	3	0	0	3	-
		132	947.1	482	17	.965	36	26	107	71	.664	366	+4	+2	-6	+1	-1	0	0	1	-1	0	-

Elvis Andrus

	BASIC							GDP			PLUS/MINUS							RUNS SAVED				
Year	Team	G	Inn	TC	E	Pct	GFP	DM	Opps	GDP	Pct	Outs Made	To His Right	Straight On	To His Left	GB	Air	Total	+/-	GDP	GFP/DME	Total	Rank
2009	Tex	145	1238.0	690	22	.968	60	25	132	94	.712	472	+2	+4	+6	+12	+3	+15	11	2	2	15	3
2010	Tex	148	1291.1	659	16	.976	40	27	145	94	.648	444	-2	+1	-8	-9	+3	-6	-4	0	-3	-7	30
2011	Tex	147	1261.1	677	25	.963	54	15	148	109	.736	434	+13	+1	-10	+4	+3	+7	5	3	-1	7	9
		440	3790.2	2026	63	.969	154	67	425	297	.699	1350	+13	+6	-12	+7	+9	+16	12	5	-2	15	16

Erick Aybar

	BASIC							GDP			PLUS/MINUS							RUNS SAVED				
Year	Team	G	Inn	TC	E	Pct	GFP	DM	Opps	GDP	Pct	Outs Made	To His Right	Straight On	To His Left	GB	Air	Total	+/-	GDP	GFP/DME	Total	Rank
2006	LAA	19	76.0	39	4	.897	4	0	8	6	.750	23	-3	0	+2	-1	0	-1	-1	0	0	-1	-
2007	LAA	20	79.0	41	3	.927	3	1	9	2	.222	31	-1	-1	+2	0	-1	-1	-1	-1	0	-2	-
2008	LAA	96	784.2	434	18	.959	55	17	101	60	.594	304	+6	+3	-6	+3	+5	+8	6	0	4	10	7
2009	LAA	136	1189.1	629	11	.983	60	25	145	99	.683	422	-4	+2	-2	-4	0	-4	-3	2	2	1	19
2010	LAA	135	1179.2	563	21	.963	44	36	105	64	.610	386	+6	-4	+4	+6	+3	+9	7	-2	-1	4	12
2011	LAA	142	1262.0	658	13	.980	56	30	154	107	.695	437	-4	-1	-2	-7	+1	-6	-4	2	1	-1	20
		548	4570.2	2364	70	.970	222	109	522	338	.648	1603	0	-1	-2	-3	+8	+5	4	1	6	11	18

Clint Barmes

	BASIC							GDP			PLUS/MINUS							RUNS SAVED				
Year	Team	G	Inn	TC	E	Pct	GFP	DM	Opps	GDP	Pct	Outs Made	To His Right	Straight On	To His Left	GB	Air	Total	+/-	GDP	GFP/DME	Total	Rank
2003	Col	12	75.0	48	2	.958	-	-	6	4	.667	24	-1	-1	-2	-4	0	-4	-3	0	-	-3	-
2004	Col	9	76.0	54	1	.981	1	1	9	6	.667	20	+1	0	+2	+3	-1	+2	2	0	0	2	-
2005	Col	80	681.2	403	17	.958	22	19	105	59	.562	277	+12	-5	+10	+17	0	+17	13	-1	0	12	7
2006	Col	125	1072.2	582	18	.969	26	27	127	85	.669	405	+22	+2	+3	+27	0	+27	21	3	1	25	2
2007	Col	8	35.0	21	1	.952	1	0	4	3	.750	14	-1	+1	0	-1	0	-1	-1	0	0	-1	-
2008	Col	36	285.0	173	3	.983	12	4	41	25	.610	119	+2	-1	-1	0	0	0	0	0	0	0	-
2009	Col	16	103.1	63	1	.984	4	0	10	7	.700	51	+5	0	-1	+5	0	+5	4	0	0	4	-
2010	Col	47	361.0	196	5	.974	17	10	41	32	.780	141	+5	+1	+8	+15	-1	+14	11	0	0	11	-
2011	Hou	122	1058.1	539	12	.978	44	19	98	65	.663	369	0	+12	+5	+18	+1	+19	14	-1	1	14	2
		455	3748.0	2079	60	.971	127	80	441	286	.649	1420	+45	+9	+24	+80	-1	+79	61	1	2	64	5

Jason Bartlett

	BASIC							GDP			PLUS/MINUS							RUNS SAVED				
Year	Team	G	Inn	TC	E	Pct	GFP	DM	Opps	GDP	Pct	Outs Made	To His Right	Straight On	To His Left	GB	Air	Total	+/-	GDP	GFP/DME	Total	Rank
2004	Min	5	22.0	18	2	.889	0	1	5	3	.600	11	+1	0	-1	0	+1	+1	1	0	0	1	-
2005	Min	68	585.2	329	7	.979	22	12	62	42	.677	257	+1	+3	+9	+12	+2	+14	11	2	0	13	6
2006	Min	99	879.2	442	13	.971	29	20	97	45	.464	349	+1	+9	0	+9	+4	+13	10	-3	0	7	8
2007	Min	138	1194.0	646	26	.960	60	31	136	83	.610	467	+11	-2	+4	+13	+5	+18	14	1	0	15	5
2008	TB	125	1097.0	529	16	.970	43	26	113	62	.549	381	+11	-4	-11	-4	+3	-1	-1	-1	1	-1	18
2009	TB	134	1153.2	529	20	.962	40	25	108	54	.500	391	+8	-5	+6	+10	0	+10	8	-4	1	5	12
2010	TB	131	1104.0	472	11	.977	31	23	101	52	.515	340	-3	-3	+4	-2	+4	+2	2	-3	0	-1	19
2011	SD	138	1211.0	612	18	.971	39	26	131	83	.634	417	+3	-2	-10	-10	-1	-11	-8	0	-1	-9	29
		838	7247.0	3577	113	.968	264	164	753	424	.563	2613	+33	-4	+1	+28	+18	+46	37	-8	1	30	14

Yuniesky Betancourt

	BASIC							GDP			PLUS/MINUS							RUNS SAVED				
Year	Team	G	Inn	TC	E	Pct	GFP	DM	Opps	GDP	Pct	Outs Made	To His Right	Straight On	To His Left	GB	Air	Total	+/-	GDP	GFP/DME	Total	Rank
2005	Sea	53	454.0	223	5	.978	22	9	50	32	.640	161	-2	0	+1	-1	0	-1	-1	1	-1	-1	19
2006	Sea	157	1374.1	702	20	.972	39	33	141	88	.624	502	+4	0	-4	0	-3	-3	-2	2	-1	-1	21
2007	Sea	152	1302.1	697	23	.967	68	37	174	104	.598	463	-11	+6	-5	-10	0	-10	-8	1	2	-5	23
2008	Sea	153	1325.1	659	21	.968	49	25	150	93	.620	446	+7	-7	-21	-21	+2	-19	-14	1	-1	-14	35
2009	2 tms	133	1159.0	570	18	.968	52	24	116	83	.716	400	+1	-10	-21	-30	+3	-27	-20	1	1	-18	34
2010	KC	151	1331.2	692	18	.974	39	21	145	77	.531	464	+2	-5	-21	-25	-2	-27	-20	-4	-3	-27	35
2011	Mil	149	1278.2	606	21	.965	47	19	124	83	.669	426	+18	-14	-14	-10	-1	-11	-9	2	0	-7	26
		948	8225.1	4149	126	.970	316	168	900	560	.622	2862	+19	-30	-85	-97	-1	-98	-74	4	-3	-73	33

Shortstops

Willie Bloomquist

Year	Team	BASIC							GDP			PLUS/MINUS							RUNS SAVED				
		G	Inn	TC	E	Pct	GFP	DM	Opps	GDP	Pct	Outs Made	To His Right	Straight On	To His Left	GB	Air	Total	+/-	GDP	GFP/DME	Total	Rank
2003	Sea	18	123.2	63	2	.968	-		17	8	.471	41	0	+1	+1	+2	0	+2	2	-1	-	1	-
2004	Sea	20	139.1	66	3	.955	0	2	14	11	.786	38	-1	-1	-2	-5	0	-5	-4	1	0	-3	-
2005	Sea	24	180.0	86	3	.965	7	5	13	7	.538	73	+5	-1	-4	0	+1	+1	1	0	0	1	-
2006	Sea	17	65.1	32	0	1.000	4	2	5	3	.600	27	+4	-1	-2	+2	+1	+3	2	0	0	2	-
2007	Sea	20	124.0	63	1	.984	4	4	11	4	.364	51	+2	0	0	+1	-1	0	0	-1	0	-1	-
2008	Sea	12	93.0	40	0	1.000	4	1	7	1	.143	29	+2	-1	0	+1	+1	+2	2	-1	0	1	-
2009	KC	38	237.2	137	6	.956	7	7	31	21	.677	94	0	-2	-1	-3	-1	-4	-3	0	-1	-4	-
2010	KC	1	1.0	0	0	-	0	0	0	0	-	0	0	0	0	0	0	0	0	0		0	-
2011	Ari	59	501.0	235	5	.979	21	6	54	32	.593	169	-2	+2	-1	-1	+1	0	0	0	1	1	19
		209	1465.0	722	20	.972	47	27	152	87	.572	522	+10	-3	-9	-3	+2	-1	0	-2	0	-2	

Emilio Bonifacio

Year	Team	BASIC							GDP			PLUS/MINUS							RUNS SAVED				
		G	Inn	TC	E	Pct	GFP	DM	Opps	GDP	Pct	Outs Made	To His Right	Straight On	To His Left	GB	Air	Total	+/-	GDP	GFP/DME	Total	Rank
2009	Fla	20	135.1	46	3	.935	7	4	7	5	.714	36	-2	0	+1	-1	-1	-2	-2	0	-1	-3	-
2010	Fla	9	71.2	22	0	1.000	1	0	1	0	.000	19	+1	0	0	+1	0	+1	1	0	0	1	-
2011	Fla	67	543.2	261	9	.966	19	12	51	31	.608	177	-10	-5	+3	-12	+5	-7	-5	0	0	-5	24
		96	750.2	329	12	.964	27	16	59	36	.610	232	-11	-5	+4	-12	+4	-8	-6	0	-1	-7	

Reid Brignac

Year	Team	BASIC							GDP			PLUS/MINUS							RUNS SAVED				
		G	Inn	TC	E	Pct	GFP	DM	Opps	GDP	Pct	Outs Made	To His Right	Straight On	To His Left	GB	Air	Total	+/-	GDP	GFP/DME	Total	Rank
2008	TB	4	21.1	13	2	.846	0	0	3	3	1.000	5	0	-1	-2	-2	-1	-3	-2	0	0	-2	-
2009	TB	28	211.2	90	2	.978	16	3	17	8	.471	63	+1	0	-1	0	0	0	0	-1	2	1	-
2010	TB	50	340.2	168	4	.976	20	4	34	21	.618	116	+5	+1	0	+6	+1	+7	5	0	1	6	-
2011	TB	91	680.2	328	7	.979	32	14	62	41	.661	239	+12	-9	+3	+6	+3	+9	7	0	0	7	8
		173	1254.1	599	15	.975	68	21	116	73	.629	423	+18	-9	0	+10	+3	+13	10	-1	3	12	

Asdrubal Cabrera

Year	Team	BASIC							GDP			PLUS/MINUS							RUNS SAVED				
		G	Inn	TC	E	Pct	GFP	DM	Opps	GDP	Pct	Outs Made	To His Right	Straight On	To His Left	GB	Air	Total	+/-	GDP	GFP/DME	Total	Rank
2007	Cle	7	42.0	29	0	1.000	4	1	9	5	.556	23	0	+1	+1	+2	0	+2	2	0	0	2	-
2008	Cle	20	154.2	102	5	.951	10	6	22	16	.727	68	+1	-3	+1	-1	+2	+1	1	1	0	2	-
2009	Cle	100	870.0	440	9	.980	44	17	109	79	.725	326	-5	+1	-4	-7	+5	-2	-2	2	0	0	22
2010	Cle	95	825.1	431	12	.972	41	15	104	79	.760	270	+3	-2	-5	-3	-3	-6	-5	1	3	-1	21
2011	Cle	151	1326.2	617	15	.976	62	25	117	73	.624	416	-1	-5	+7	+2	+1	+3	2	-1	2	3	14
		373	3218.2	1619	41	.975	161	64	361	252	.698	1103	-2	-8	0	-7	+5	-2	-2	3	5	6	20

Orlando Cabrera

Year	Team	BASIC							GDP			PLUS/MINUS							RUNS SAVED				
		G	Inn	TC	E	Pct	GFP	DM	Opps	GDP	Pct	Outs Made	To His Right	Straight On	To His Left	GB	Air	Total	+/-	GDP	GFP/DME	Total	Rank
2003	Mon	162	1385.2	732	18	.975			157	90	.573	414	-1	+1	+7	+7	-2	+5	4	-1	-	3	15
2004	2 tms	159	1358.2	678	15	.978	23	31	152	83	.546	427	+2	+3	+4	+10	+3	+13	10	-2	-1	7	7
2005	LAA	141	1240.2	583	7	.988	44	24	128	75	.586	425	-8	0	+16	+7	0	+7	5	0	1	6	12
2006	LAA	152	1320.2	646	16	.975	46	36	150	91	.607	434	-18	-6	+13	-10	-2	-12	-9	1	-2	-10	30
2007	LAA	153	1330.2	665	11	.983	61	36	153	99	.647	462	-8	+4	+4	0	+2	+2	2	3	0	5	15
2008	CWS	161	1389.2	730	16	.978	55	40	146	93	.637	528	-3	-2	+8	+2	-1	+1	1	2	-1	2	16
2009	2 tms	158	1388.2	711	25	.965	68	38	157	97	.618	492	-26	-4	-11	-42	+2	-40	-30	-1	2	-29	35
2010	Cin	121	1030.2	476	11	.977	37	21	93	61	.656	314	-4	+4	0	+1	0	+1	1	0	-1	0	17
2011	2 tms	39	309.1	155	5	.968	18	12	37	22	.595	110	-2	+1	+4	+3	0	+3	2	0	1	3	-
		1246	10754.2	5376	124	.977	352	238	1173	711	.606	3606	-68	+1	+45	-22	+2	-20	-14	2	-1	-13	25

Jamey Carroll

Year	Team	BASIC							GDP			PLUS/MINUS							RUNS SAVED				
		G	Inn	TC	E	Pct	GFP	DM	Opps	GDP	Pct	Outs Made	To His Right	Straight On	To His Left	GB	Air	Total	+/-	GDP	GFP/DME	Total	Rank
2003	Mon	14	50.0	22	0	1.000	-		3	3	1.000	11	0	0	0	-1	0	-1	-1	0	-	-1	-
2004	Mon	10	59.0	27	0	1.000	2	1	8	4	.500	14	0	-1	0	-1	0	-1	-1	0	0	-1	-
2005	Was	41	241.0	118	0	1.000	8	1	23	16	.696	78	-1	0	-3	-4	0	-4	-3	1	0	-2	-
2006	Col	10	62.0	34	1	.971	0	1	8	6	.750	25	+2	-1	0	+1	+1	+2	2	0	0	2	-
2007	Col	11	57.0	32	0	1.000	1	0	7	5	.714	25	+1	0	0	+1	+1	+2	2	0	0	2	-
2010	LAD	69	573.0	279	4	.986	11	4	56	31	.554	211	-2	+4	+2	+4	-2	+2	1	-2	0	-1	20
2011	LAD	66	504.2	214	4	.981	10	7	40	26	.650	149	-3	0	-1	-4	-3	-7	-5	0	0	-5	24
		221	1546.2	726	9	.988	32	14	145	91	.628	513	-3	+2	-2	-4	-3	-7	-5	-1	0	-6	

Shortstops

Alexi Casilla

		BASIC							GDP			PLUS/MINUS							RUNS SAVED				
Year	Team	G	Inn	TC	E	Pct	GFP	DM	Opps	GDP	Pct	Outs Made	To His Right	Straight On	To His Left	GB	Air	Total	+/-	GDP	GFP/DME	Total	Rank
2006	Min	2	2.0	3	0	1.000	0	0	2	2	1.000	1	0			0	0	0	0	0	0	0	-
2007	Min	5	30.0	12	0	1.000	1	2	4	1	.250	9	0	+1	-1	0	0	0	0	0	0	0	-
2008	Min	2	10.0	5	0	1.000	0	1	0		-	5	0	0	0	0	0	0	0	0	0	0	-
2009	Min	2	2.0	1	0	1.000	0	0	1	1	1.000	1				+1	0	+1	1	0	0	1	-
2010	Min	30	189.1	103	4	.961	11	4	16	14	.875	70	+6	-2	-2	+2	-3	-1	-1	1	1	1	-
2011	Min	36	306.2	162	5	.969	8	8	31	22	.710	112	+6	-4	-4	-2	-2	-4	-3	0	0	-3	-
		77	540.0	286	9	.969	20	15	54	40	.741	198	+12	-5	-7	+1	-5	-4	-3	1	1	-1	

Starlin Castro

		BASIC							GDP			PLUS/MINUS							RUNS SAVED				
Year	Team	G	Inn	TC	E	Pct	GFP	DM	Opps	GDP	Pct	Outs Made	To His Right	Straight On	To His Left	GB	Air	Total	+/-	GDP	GFP/DME	Total	Rank
2010	ChC	123	1073.2	544	27	.950	45	40	122	77	.631	361	+3	-7	+4	+1	+3	+4	3	0	-7	-4	24
2011	ChC	158	1398.2	742	29	.961	69	56	139	78	.561	505	-7	-6	-1	-13	+5	-8	-6	-2	-2	-10	31
		281	2472.1	1286	56	.956	114	96	261	155	.594	866	-4	-13	+3	-12	+8	-4	-3	-2	-9	-14	

Ronny Cedeno

		BASIC							GDP			PLUS/MINUS							RUNS SAVED				
Year	Team	G	Inn	TC	E	Pct	GFP	DM	Opps	GDP	Pct	Outs Made	To His Right	Straight On	To His Left	GB	Air	Total	+/-	GDP	GFP/DME	Total	Rank
2005	ChC	29	158.2	70	1	.986	5	2	14	6	.429	47	-2	+1	0	-1	+1	0	0	-1	0	-1	-
2006	ChC	134	1129.2	528	23	.956	31	31	95	55	.579	399	+10	-6	+2	+5	0	+5	4	0	-1	3	17
2007	ChC	15	110.0	49	2	.959	5	1	6	5	.833	38	+2	0	-2	0	0	0	0	0	0	0	-
2008	ChC	27	182.2	94	3	.968	10	8	16	8	.500	72	0	+1	-3	-2	+1	-1	-1	0	-1	-2	-
2009	2 tms	82	711.2	366	9	.975	26	13	74	52	.703	272	0	+3	-5	-1	-4	-5	-4	1	-1	-4	26
2010	Pit	136	1149.0	583	18	.969	44	15	101	65	.644	406	-19	+6	0	-13	-1	-14	-11	1	1	-9	32
2011	Pit	125	1050.1	601	13	.978	39	26	114	65	.570	432	0	0	+12	+12	0	+12	9	-2	-2	5	12
		548	4492.0	2291	69	.970	160	96	420	256	.610	1666	-9	+5	+4	0	-3	-3	-3	-1	-4	-8	23

Brandon Crawford

		BASIC							GDP			PLUS/MINUS							RUNS SAVED				
Year	Team	G	Inn	TC	E	Pct	GFP	DM	Opps	GDP	Pct	Outs Made	To His Right	Straight On	To His Left	GB	Air	Total	+/-	GDP	GFP/DME	Total	Rank
2011	SF	65	507.1	248	7	.972	24	12	43	29	.674	184	-3	+3	+4	+5	0	+5	3	0	0	3	13

Chase d'Arnaud

		BASIC							GDP			PLUS/MINUS							RUNS SAVED				
Year	Team	G	Inn	TC	E	Pct	GFP	DM	Opps	GDP	Pct	Outs Made	To His Right	Straight On	To His Left	GB	Air	Total	+/-	GDP	GFP/DME	Total	Rank
2011	Pit	29	206.2	94	6	.936	13	6	22	12	.545	68	-1	-3	-2	-6	+1	-5	-4	-1	0	-5	-

Ian Desmond

		BASIC							GDP			PLUS/MINUS							RUNS SAVED				
Year	Team	G	Inn	TC	E	Pct	GFP	DM	Opps	GDP	Pct	Outs Made	To His Right	Straight On	To His Left	GB	Air	Total	+/-	GDP	GFP/DME	Total	Rank
2009	Was	17	136.1	84	4	.952	9	7	22	15	.682	50	-1	-1	-1	-3	+1	-2	-2	0	-1	-3	-
2010	Was	149	1208.0	637	34	.947	46	33	134	88	.657	413	+8	-1	-13	-6	+3	-3	-3	-1	-3	-7	29
2011	Was	152	1317.2	686	23	.966	48	35	140	84	.600	474	-13	+3	-1	-10	+7	-3	-2	-1	0	-3	21
		318	2662.0	1407	61	.957	103	75	296	187	.632	937	-6	+1	-15	-19	+11	-8	-7	-2	-4	-13	

Stephen Drew

		BASIC							GDP			PLUS/MINUS							RUNS SAVED				
Year	Team	G	Inn	TC	E	Pct	GFP	DM	Opps	GDP	Pct	Outs Made	To His Right	Straight On	To His Left	GB	Air	Total	+/-	GDP	GFP/DME	Total	Rank
2006	Ari	56	480.1	228	5	.978	16	9	55	32	.582	161	+5	0	-5	0	+2	+2	2	0	0	2	18
2007	Ari	147	1283.1	638	17	.973	41	34	145	90	.621	434	+17	-10	-15	-7	+6	-1	-1	1	-1	-1	20
2008	Ari	151	1294.1	582	14	.976	40	23	128	78	.609	422	+6	-8	-7	-8	+3	-5	-4	1	1	-2	23
2009	Ari	132	1142.0	546	11	.980	45	14	103	69	.670	404	+14	-6	-2	+6	+4	+10	8	0	1	9	8
2010	Ari	147	1259.1	607	10	.984	35	13	120	83	.692	411	+6	+8	-10	+4	-9	-5	-3	2	1	0	18
2011	Ari	84	731.1	345	7	.980	38	11	71	46	.648	245	+1	0	-3	-1	+2	+1	0	1	2	3	15
		717	6190.2	2946	64	.978	215	104	622	398	.640	2077	+49	-16	-42	-6	+8	+2	2	5	4	11	19

Alcides Escobar

		BASIC							GDP			PLUS/MINUS							RUNS SAVED				
Year	Team	G	Inn	TC	E	Pct	GFP	DM	Opps	GDP	Pct	Outs Made	To His Right	Straight On	To His Left	GB	Air	Total	+/-	GDP	GFP/DME	Total	Rank
2008	Mil	2	2.0	0	0	-	0	0	0		-	0				0	0	0	0			0	-
2009	Mil	37	300.0	159	6	.962	15	11	34	23	.676	112	-5	+2	0	-2	+2	0	0	-1	-1	-2	-
2010	Mil	138	1151.1	552	20	.964	31	19	96	66	.688	394	+6	-6	+4	+6	+4	+10	5	1	0	6	11
2011	KC	158	1387.1	745	15	.980	77	32	169	97	.574	492	+19	+5	-5	+19	-4	+15	11	-3	2	10	4
		335	2840.2	1456	41	.972	123	62	299	186	.622	998	+20	+1	-1	+21	+1	+22	16	-3	1	14	

Shortstops

Yunel Escobar

Year	Team	G	Inn	TC	E	Pct	GFP	DM	Opps	GDP	Pct	Outs Made	To His Right	Straight On	To His Left	GB	Air	Total	+/-	GDP	GFP/DME	Total	Rank
		BASIC							**GDP**			**PLUS/MINUS**							**RUNS SAVED**				
2007	Atl	53	363.0	176	4	.977	13	8	29	21	.724	135	-2	+3	+1	+2	-2	0	0	1	0	1	-
2008	Atl	126	1105.2	605	16	.974	44	27	145	74	.510	439	0	+19	+22	-2	+20	15	-3	-4	8	9	
2009	Atl	139	1208.2	613	13	.979	52	32	130	86	.662	451	-5	+9	+14	+18	-1	+17	13	-1	-5	7	10
2010	2 tms	134	1179.1	645	18	.972	58	28	170	127	.747	424	+2	-1	+11	+13	-3	+10	7	3	-1	9	6
2011	Tor	132	1121.0	539	14	.974	35	25	121	77	.636	363	+8	0	+2	+12	-2	+10	8	0	-1	7	7
		584	4977.2	2578	65	.975	202	120	595	385	.647	1812	+3	+14	+47	+67	-10	+57	43	0	-11	32	13

Mike Fontenot

Year	Team	G	Inn	TC	E	Pct	GFP	DM	Opps	GDP	Pct	Outs Made	To His Right	Straight On	To His Left	GB	Air	Total	+/-	GDP	GFP/DME	Total	Rank
		BASIC							**GDP**			**PLUS/MINUS**							**RUNS SAVED**				
2007	ChC	3	19.0	4	2	.500	0	0	0		-	2	-2	0		-2	0	-2	-2		0	-2	-
2008	ChC	1	1.0	0	0	-	0	0	0			0							0			0	
2010	2 tms	9	61.0	28	1	.964	1	2	4	3	.750	23	-1	-2	-2	-4	+2	-2	-2	0	0	-2	
2011	SF	37	284.0	126	4	.968	10	7	22	16	.727	87	-6	+3	+2	0	+2	+2	1	1	-1	1	-
		50	365.0	158	7	.956	11	9	26	19	.731	112	-9	+1	0	-6	+4	-2	-3	1	-1	-3	

Rafael Furcal

Year	Team	G	Inn	TC	E	Pct	GFP	DM	Opps	GDP	Pct	Outs Made	To His Right	Straight On	To His Left	GB	Air	Total	+/-	GDP	GFP/DME	Total	Rank
		BASIC							**GDP**			**PLUS/MINUS**							**RUNS SAVED**				
2003	Atl	155	1350.0	749	31	.959	-	-	174	103	.592	510	+6	-8	+12	+10	0	+10	8		-	8	5
2004	Atl	131	1134.0	627	24	.962	45	24	160	95	.594	413	-1	-2	+5	+1	+1	+2	2	0	2	4	13
2005	Atl	152	1306.1	775	15	.981	59	39	172	110	.640	539	+14	0	+8	+22	+4	+26	20	3	1	24	3
2006	LAD	156	1371.0	788	27	.966	44	22	198	114	.576	539	+6	+1	-4	+3	+1	+4	3	-1	2	4	14
2007	LAD	138	1210.0	686	19	.972	64	25	151	94	.623	474	-8	+3	+12	+7	-1	+6	5	2	2	9	9
2008	LAD	36	296.0	142	4	.972	12	2	27	17	.630	102	+1	+2	-2	0	0	0	0	0	0	0	-
2009	LAD	149	1282.1	626	20	.968	54	27	113	80	.708	472	-3	+3	+10	+11	-3	+8	6	1	0	7	11
2010	LAD	93	800.2	421	19	.955	28	13	75	51	.680	297	-3	+4	+7	+8	-2	+6	5	-1	0	4	13
2011	2 tms	85	726.2	394	14	.964	40	18	92	62	.674	261	-3	-6	+6	-2	-2	-4	-4	0	-1	-5	23
		1095	9477.0	5208	173	.967	346	170	1162	726	.625	3607	+9	-3	+54	+60	-2	+58	45	4	6	55	8

Alex Gonzalez

Year	Team	G	Inn	TC	E	Pct	GFP	DM	Opps	GDP	Pct	Outs Made	To His Right	Straight On	To His Left	GB	Air	Total	+/-	GDP	GFP/DME	Total	Rank
		BASIC							**GDP**			**PLUS/MINUS**							**RUNS SAVED**				
2003	Fla	150	1315.2	678	16	.976	-	-	143	99	.692	466	-6	0	-3	-8	-1	-9	-7	4		-3	26
2004	Fla	158	1351.2	666	16	.976	51	32	144	88	.611	459	+8	-1	+3	+10	-1	+9	7	1	1	9	5
2005	Fla	124	1087.1	604	16	.974	48	18	138	90	.652	406	+2	0	-1	+1	-2	-1	-1	3	1	3	15
2006	Bos	111	966.1	475	7	.985	29	18	106	62	.585	352	-11	+3	+12	+5	-1	+4	3	0	1	4	14
2007	Cin	103	872.2	427	16	.963	37	15	98	66	.673	306	-4	+4	+1	+2	+2	+4	3	2	0	5	14
2009	2 tms	112	948.1	425	7	.984	42	14	92	64	.696	307	-6	+5	-2	-3	-4	-7	-6	0	1	-5	27
2010	2 tms	157	1368.2	700	19	.973	79	22	154	115	.747	519	-2	-1	+23	+21	+3	+24	19	2	6	27	1
2011	Atl	149	1316.0	633	12	.981	62	25	116	76	.655	465	+3	+3	+3	+10	+2	+12	9	-1	1	9	5
		1064	9226.2	4608	109	.976	348	144	991	660	.666	3280	-16	+13	+36	+38	-2	+36	27	11	11	49	9

Dee Gordon

Year	Team	G	Inn	TC	E	Pct	GFP	DM	Opps	GDP	Pct	Outs Made	To His Right	Straight On	To His Left	GB	Air	Total	+/-	GDP	GFP/DME	Total	Rank
		BASIC							**GDP**			**PLUS/MINUS**							**RUNS SAVED**				
2011	LAD	54	446.1	218	10	.954	28	13	37	21	.568	149	-7	0	+2	-5	+3	-2	-2	-1	0	-3	21

J.J. Hardy

Year	Team	G	Inn	TC	E	Pct	GFP	DM	Opps	GDP	Pct	Outs Made	To His Right	Straight On	To His Left	GB	Air	Total	+/-	GDP	GFP/DME	Total	Rank
		BASIC							**GDP**			**PLUS/MINUS**							**RUNS SAVED**				
2005	Mil	119	937.2	402	10	.975	14	21	78	46	.590	316	+13	0	-4	+9	+1	+10	8	0	0	8	10
2006	Mil	32	257.2	143	2	.986	4	6	39	25	.641	93	+5	0	+3	+8	-1	+7	5	1	1	7	-
2007	Mil	149	1271.2	578	13	.978	48	19	122	76	.623	443	-14	+4	+16	+6	+1	+7	5	1	3	9	9
2008	Mil	145	1268.1	647	15	.977	52	19	147	79	.537	477	-1	-1	+18	+16	+3	+19	14	-2	1	13	3
2009	Mil	112	949.1	472	8	.983	38	23	97	60	.619	351	-1	-2	+8	+5	-1	+4	3	-1	0	2	16
2010	Min	100	858.1	450	11	.976	22	14	101	57	.564	310	+2	+2	-6	-2	-3	-5	-3	-1	-1	-5	27
2011	Bal	129	1133.0	620	6	.990	46	17	123	73	.593	429	+9	+8	-10	+6	+4	+10	8	-1	1	8	6
		786	6676.0	3312	65	.980	224	119	707	416	.588	2419	+13	+11	+25	+48	+4	+52	40	-3	5	42	12

Paul Janish

Year	Team	G	Inn	TC	E	Pct	GFP	DM	Opps	GDP	Pct	Outs Made	To His Right	Straight On	To His Left	GB	Air	Total	+/-	GDP	GFP/DME	Total	Rank
		BASIC							**GDP**			**PLUS/MINUS**							**RUNS SAVED**				
2008	Cin	36	204.1	112	3	.973	15	2	16	8	.500	84	-3	+2	0	-1	0	-1	-1	0	1	0	-
2009	Cin	82	592.1	325	3	.991	33	9	83	56	.675	233	-1	+7	+8	+13	0	+13	10	0	1	11	7
2010	Cin	62	416.1	211	4	.981	16	1	46	31	.674	141	-3	-1	+5	+1	0	+1	1	0	2	3	-
2011	Cin	103	743.1	392	10	.974	36	12	84	46	.548	270	+1	+9	+4	+15	-4	+11	8	-2	0	6	11
		283	1956.1	1040	20	.981	100	24	229	141	.616	728	-6	+17	+17	+28	-4	+24	18	-2	4	20	-

Shortstops

Derek Jeter *4-0-at* (handwritten)

		BASIC							GDP			PLUS/MINUS							RUNS SAVED				
Year	Team	G	Inn	TC	E	Pct	GFP	DM	Opps	GDP	Pct	Outs Made	To His Right	Straight On	To His Left	GB	Air	Total	+/-	GDP	GFP/ DME	Total	Rank
2003	NYY	118	1033.2	444	14	.968	-	-	88	46	.523	336	-12	+3	-6	-15	+1	-14	-11	-2	-	-13	34
2004	NYY	154	1341.2	678	13	.981	28	20	146	85	.582	456	-24	+5	-25	-25	+9	-16	-12	0	-1	-13	33
2005	NYY	157	1352.2	731	15	.979	42	20	156	84	.538	526	-18	+3	-25	-39	+5	-34	-26	-2	1	-27	34
2006	NYY	150	1292.1	610	15	.975	32	15	131	75	.573	450	-10	+1	-10	-19	-3	-22	-17	-1	2	-16	33
2007	NYY	155	1318.1	607	18	.970	45	15	152	98	.645	420	-14	-6	+6	-33	-1	-34	-26	3	-1	-24	34
2008	NYY	148	1258.2	579	12	.979	35	17	106	58	.547	430	-18	+9	-1	-10	-1	-11	-8	-1	-1	-10	32
2009	NYY	150	1260.2	554	8	.986	39	16	131	74	.565	398	-3	+6	+2	+5	+1	+6	5	-3	1	3	13
2010	NYY	151	1303.2	553	6	.989	29	33	150	95	.633	374	-11	+10	-7	-8	-3	-11	-8	0	-1	-9	31
2011	NYY	122	1047.1	432	12	.972	31	19	103	63	.612	291	-15	+3	-5	-17	0	-17	-13	-1	-1	-15	35
		1305	11209.0	5188	113	.978	281	155	1163	678	.583	3681	-125	+34	-71	-161	+8	-153	-116	-7	-1	-124	35

Elliot Johnson

		BASIC							GDP			PLUS/MINUS							RUNS SAVED				
Year	Team	G	Inn	TC	E	Pct	GFP	DM	Opps	GDP	Pct	Outs Made	To His Right	Straight On	To His Left	GB	Air	Total	+/-	GDP	GFP/ DME	Total	Rank
2008	TB	2	18.0	11	1	.909	0	1	3	3	1.000	8	0	0	-1	-1	0	-1	-1	0	0	-1	-
2011	TB	52	337.2	149	1	.993	14	5	24	17	.708	110	+5	-2	+4	+7	+2	+9	7	1	0	8	-
		54	355.2	160	2	.988	14	6	27	20	.741	118	+5	-2	+3	+6	+2	+8	6	1	0	7	-

Jed Lowrie

		BASIC							GDP			PLUS/MINUS							RUNS SAVED				
Year	Team	G	Inn	TC	E	Pct	GFP	DM	Opps	GDP	Pct	Outs Made	To His Right	Straight On	To His Left	GB	Air	Total	+/-	GDP	GFP/ DME	Total	Rank
2008	Bos	49	386.0	155	0	1.000	9	6	35	21	.600	123	+3	+2	0	+6	+2	+8	6	0	0	6	-
2009	Bos	26	163.2	75	1	.987	7	5	21	15	.714	49	-2	+2	+1	+1	-2	-1	-1	0	0	-1	-
2010	Bos	23	176.2	73	1	.986	2	4	23	17	.739	48	-2	0	0	-3	-1	-4	-3	0	0	-3	-
2011	Bos	49	398.0	181	10	.945	14	6	34	21	.618	123	+6	0	-6	-1	-3	-4	-3	0	0	-3	-
		147	1124.1	484	12	.975	32	21	113	74	.655	343	+5	+4	-5	+3	-4	-1	-1	0	0	-1	-

Mike McCoy

		BASIC							GDP			PLUS/MINUS							RUNS SAVED				
Year	Team	G	Inn	TC	E	Pct	GFP	DM	Opps	GDP	Pct	Outs Made	To His Right	Straight On	To His Left	GB	Air	Total	+/-	GDP	GFP/ DME	Total	Rank
2010	Tor	7	43.0	21	1	.952	2	1	1	0	.000	17	-1	-2	+1	-2	0	-2	-1	0	0	-1	-
2011	Tor	26	211.0	118	4	.966	7	4	21	12	.571	79	-2	+2	+5	+5	-1	+4	3	0	0	3	-
		33	254.0	139	5	.964	9	5	22	12	.545	96	-3	0	+6	+3	-1	+2	2	0	0	2	-

John McDonald

		BASIC							GDP			PLUS/MINUS							RUNS SAVED				
Year	Team	G	Inn	TC	E	Pct	GFP	DM	Opps	GDP	Pct	Outs Made	To His Right	Straight On	To His Left	GB	Air	Total	+/-	GDP	GFP/ DME	Total	Rank
2003	Cle	27	195.0	97	4	.959	-	-	22	15	.682	57	-3	0	0	-4	+1	-3	-2	1	-	-1	-
2004	Cle	30	166.2	95	5	.947	9	3	20	15	.750	60	-1	-2	-1	-3	0	-3	-2	1	1	0	-
2005	2 tms	54	375.1	232	8	.966	12	9	49	32	.653	163	+3	+3	+1	+7	-1	+6	4	1	1	6	-
2006	Tor	90	661.2	350	14	.960	21	18	77	52	.675	238	+9	-2	-5	+1	0	+1	1	2	-1	2	19
2007	Tor	102	799.1	450	8	.982	57	14	110	63	.573	312	+6	+6	+12	+25	+1	+26	20	0	3	23	2
2008	Tor	67	478.0	223	9	.960	21	7	55	30	.545	149	-2	+1	-1	-2	+1	-1	-1	-1	0	-2	19
2009	Tor	31	198.1	105	1	.990	8	3	36	22	.611	69	0	-1	+4	+4	-1	+3	2	0	1	3	-
2010	Tor	19	115.0	67	1	.985	9	4	21	13	.619	42	+2	+1	+1	+4	+1	+5	4	0	0	4	-
2011	2 tms	38	264.2	150	2	.987	16	7	31	19	.613	107	+5	+1	+3	+10	0	+10	8	0	2	10	-
		458	3254.0	1769	52	.971	153	65	421	261	.620	1197	+19	+7	+14	+42	+2	+44	34	4	7	45	11

Tsuyoshi Nishioka

		BASIC							GDP			PLUS/MINUS							RUNS SAVED				
Year	Team	G	Inn	TC	E	Pct	GFP	DM	Opps	GDP	Pct	Outs Made	To His Right	Straight On	To His Left	GB	Air	Total	+/-	GDP	GFP/ DME	Total	Rank
2011	Min	60	508.1	278	10	.964	22	21	64	34	.531	180	-3	-3	-1	-7	-2	-9	-7	-2	-3	-12	32

Eduardo Nunez

		BASIC							GDP			PLUS/MINUS							RUNS SAVED				
Year	Team	G	Inn	TC	E	Pct	GFP	DM	Opps	GDP	Pct	Outs Made	To His Right	Straight On	To His Left	GB	Air	Total	+/-	GDP	GFP/ DME	Total	Rank
2010	NYY	11	39.1	23	0	1.000	3	5	8	6	.750	19	0	-1	0	-1	+1	0	0	0	-1	-1	-
2011	NYY	50	386.1	161	14	.913	7	11	30	14	.467	109	-2	-5	-2	-9	0	-9	-7	-1	-1	-9	-
		61	425.2	184	14	.924	10	16	38	20	.526	128	-2	-6	-2	-10	+1	-9	-7	-1	-2	-10	-

Shortstops

Cliff Pennington

	BASIC							GDP			PLUS/MINUS							RUNS SAVED				
Year Team	G	Inn	TC	E	Pct	GFP	DM	Opps	GDP	Pct	Outs Made	To His Right	Straight On	To His Left	GB	Air	Total	+/-	GDP	GFP/DME	Total	Rank
2008 Oak	10	56.0	30	4	.867	2	1	4	4	1.000	17	-4	-2	-1	-6	0	-6	-5	0	0	-5	-
2009 Oak	60	533.2	279	8	.971	26	13	66	45	.682	188	-9	+1	-6	-14	0	-14	-11	1	1	-9	31
2010 Oak	156	1304.2	739	25	.966	71	21	139	97	.698	503	-1	+3	+5	+7	+2	+9	7	2	4	13	5
2011 Oak	147	1272.1	612	22	.964	50	26	138	97	.703	394	+5	-11	-7	-13	-1	-14	-10	1	0	-9	30
	373	3166.2	1660	59	.964	149	61	347	243	.700	1102	-9	-9	-9	-26	+1	-25	-19	4	5	-10	-

Jhonny Peralta

	BASIC							GDP			PLUS/MINUS							RUNS SAVED				
Year Team	G	Inn	TC	E	Pct	GFP	DM	Opps	GDP	Pct	Outs Made	To His Right	Straight On	To His Left	GB	Air	Total	+/-	GDP	GFP/DME	Total	Rank
2003 Cle	72	624.0	334	8	.976	-	-	67	38	.567	222	+4	+2	-8	-1	+1	0	0	0	-	0	18
2004 Cle	7	55.0	27	3	.889	0	1	4	2	.500	15	0	-2	0	-2	+1	-1	-1	0	0	-1	-
2005 Cle	141	1232.1	638	19	.970	35	20	132	94	.712	465	-5	-3	-10	-12	-2	-14	-11	5	1	-5	26
2006 Cle	147	1275.1	710	16	.977	22	40	152	93	.612	535	+3	-1	-15	-13	+4	-9	-7	1	-1	-7	28
2007 Cle	152	1348.0	720	19	.974	39	33	164	95	.579	511	+12	-7	-8	-3	0	-3	-2	0	0	-2	22
2008 Cle	146	1271.1	658	14	.979	34	20	153	97	.634	469	0	-6	-2	-7	-3	-10	-8	2	1	-5	29
2009 Cle	41	334.0	189	4	.979	15	6	51	39	.765	128	+4	-2	+1	+2	+2	+4	3	1	-2	2	-
2010 Det	46	392.1	191	3	.984	15	3	38	25	.658	131	-4	+3	+3	+2	0	+2	1	0	0	1	-
2011 Det	145	1245.0	608	7	.988	26	26	125	81	.648	409	-6	+8	+8	+10	-4	+6	4	0	-2	2	16
	897	7777.1	4075	93	.977	186	149	886	564	.637	2885	+8	-2	-31	-24	-1	-25	-21	9	-3	-15	26

Trevor Plouffe

	BASIC							GDP			PLUS/MINUS							RUNS SAVED				
Year Team	G	Inn	TC	E	Pct	GFP	DM	Opps	GDP	Pct	Outs Made	To His Right	Straight On	To His Left	GB	Air	Total	+/-	GDP	GFP/DME	Total	Rank
2010 Min	9	68.0	34	1	.971	0	2	7	5	.714	21	0	-1	0	-1	-1	-2	-1	0	0	-1	-
2011 Min	45	396.2	195	11	.944	9	10	51	31	.608	125	-5	0	-11	-15	-2	-17	-13	0	-1	-14	-
	54	464.2	229	12	.948	9	12	58	36	.621	146	-5	-1	-11	-16	-3	-19	-14	0	-1	-15	-

Alexei Ramirez

	BASIC							GDP			PLUS/MINUS							RUNS SAVED				
Year Team	G	Inn	TC	E	Pct	GFP	DM	Opps	GDP	Pct	Outs Made	To His Right	Straight On	To His Left	GB	Air	Total	+/-	GDP	GFP/DME	Total	Rank
2008 CWS	16	53.0	24	1	.958	3	1	6	4	.667	18	-3	0	0	-2	-1	-3	-2	0	0	-2	-
2009 CWS	148	1293.2	650	20	.969	51	26	133	89	.669	453	+9	-4	+3	+7	-4	+3	2	0	0	2	17
2010 CWS	156	1376.2	768	20	.974	56	22	158	105	.665	519	+19	+4	-6	+18	+6	+24	18	1	1	20	3
2011 CWS	155	1382.0	690	16	.977	64	30	136	95	.699	481	+16	-3	-4	+9	-4	+5	4	3	0	7	10
	475	4105.1	2132	57	.973	174	79	433	293	.677	1471	+41	-3	-7	+32	-3	+29	22	4	1	27	15

Hanley Ramirez

	BASIC							GDP			PLUS/MINUS							RUNS SAVED				
Year Team	G	Inn	TC	E	Pct	GFP	DM	Opps	GDP	Pct	Outs Made	To His Right	Straight On	To His Left	GB	Air	Total	+/-	GDP	GFP/DME	Total	Rank
2005 Bos	2	6.0	1	0	1.000	0	0	0		-	1				0		0	0			0	-
2006 Fla	154	1323.1	694	26	.963	42	36	163	103	.632	467	0	-4	+2	-3	-3	-6	-5	2	0	-3	24
2007 Fla	151	1301.2	641	24	.963	54	46	150	90	.600	462	-21	-8	-6	-34	-3	-37	-28	1	-1	-28	35
2008 Fla	150	1302.0	659	22	.967	48	25	139	79	.568	473	+10	-4	-1	+6	-1	+5	2	-1	-4	-3	24
2009 Fla	146	1259.0	580	10	.983	38	27	123	76	.618	412	+8	+1	-2	+7	-2	+5	4	-2	0	2	15
2010 Fla	140	1217.0	558	16	.971	47	35	115	77	.670	364	-14	-2	+1	-15	-6	-21	-16	-1	-2	-19	34
2011 Fla	86	754.2	329	14	.957	35	19	73	42	.575	211	-21	+2	+7	-12	-4	-16	-12	-1	0	-13	33
	829	7163.2	3462	112	.968	264	188	763	467	.612	2390	-38	-15	+1	-52	-20	-72	-55	-2	-7	-64	32

Edgar Renteria

	BASIC							GDP			PLUS/MINUS							RUNS SAVED				
Year Team	G	Inn	TC	E	Pct	GFP	DM	Opps	GDP	Pct	Outs Made	To His Right	Straight On	To His Left	GB	Air	Total	+/-	GDP	GFP/DME	Total	Rank
2003 StL	156	1367.1	646	16	.975	-	-	124	76	.613	435	-6	+3	+5	+1	-3	-2	-2	1	-	-1	21
2004 StL	149	1307.1	650	11	.983	16	31	147	83	.565	436	-2	-1	+12	+9	0	+9	7	-1	-3	3	14
2005 Bos	153	1293.0	655	30	.954	38	35	154	82	.532	451	+3	-14	+2	-9	-2	-11	-8	-2	-3	-13	30
2006 Atl	146	1265.1	597	13	.978	33	25	128	73	.570	447	-17	0	+18	+1	+5	+6	5	-1	0	4	13
2007 Atl	121	1019.1	480	11	.977	37	26	111	70	.631	361	-19	-1	+18	-2	+1	-1	-1	1	-2	-2	21
2008 Det	138	1173.1	578	16	.972	38	25	150	88	.587	427	-11	-6	+7	-11	+2	-9	-7	0	1	-6	31
2009 SF	123	1071.2	474	14	.970	26	19	115	67	.583	339	-12	+3	+1	-8	-2	-10	-8	-2	0	-10	32
2010 SF	68	553.0	233	4	.983	12	13	41	28	.683	167	-9	+6	+2	-2	0	-2	-1	0	-1	-2	23
2011 Cin	86	628.0	316	13	.959	19	13	64	37	.578	231	-7	0	+13	+6	-2	+4	3	-1	-1	1	17
	1140	9678.1	4629	128	.972	219	187	1034	604	.584	3294	-80	-10	+78	-15	-1	-16	-12	-5	-9	-26	27

Shortstops

Jose Reyes

		BASIC							GDP			PLUS/MINUS							RUNS SAVED				
Year	Team	G	Inn	TC	E	Pct	GFP	DM	Opps	GDP	Pct	Outs Made	To His Right	Straight On	To His Left	GB	Air	Total	+/-	GDP	GFP/DME	Total	Rank
2003	NYM	69	596.1	329	9	.973	-	-	73	39	.534	248	+9	+3	-2	+9	+1	+10	8	-1	-	7	8
2004	NYM	10	72.2	46	2	.957	2	1	9	5	.556	34	0	0	+1	+1	-3	-2	-2	0	0	-2	-
2005	NYM	161	1398.1	682	18	.974	47	35	148	97	.655	481	-14	-1	+3	-13	+3	-10	-8	3	-1	-6	27
2006	NYM	149	1320.1	583	17	.971	29	36	121	68	.562	444	+2	+10	+1	+14	+2	+16	12	-1	-2	9	6
2007	NYM	160	1431.1	660	12	.982	54	29	134	82	.612	500	+5	+5	+7	+16	-3	+13	10	1	0	11	8
2008	NYM	158	1420.1	660	17	.974	51	23	149	86	.577	481	-3	+4	-1	0	-2	-2	-2	0	0	-2	20
2009	NYM	35	305.1	145	5	.966	6	5	23	11	.478	110	+5	-1	-2	+2	-2	0	0	-1	0	-1	-
2010	NYM	133	1171.1	556	15	.973	38	26	117	82	.701	386	-5	-1	0	-6	+1	-5	-4	2	-2	-4	26
2011	NYM	124	1087.0	554	18	.968	45	21	131	84	.641	365	-19	+4	+4	-11	-7	-18	-14	0	1	-13	34
		999	8803.0	4215	113	.973	272	176	905	554	.612	3049	-20	+23	+11	+12	-10	+2	0	3	-4	-1	21

Sean Rodriguez

		BASIC							GDP			PLUS/MINUS							RUNS SAVED				
Year	Team	G	Inn	TC	E	Pct	GFP	DM	Opps	GDP	Pct	Outs Made	To His Right	Straight On	To His Left	GB	Air	Total	+/-	GDP	GFP/DME	Total	Rank
2008	LAA	4	20.0	17	0	1.000	0	0	4	2	.500	12	0	0	+1	+2	0	+2	2	0	0	2	-
2010	TB	5	9.0	3	0	1.000	0	0	0	0	-	2	0	0	0	0	0	0	0	0	0	0	-
2011	TB	60	430.2	169	9	.947	16	6	36	22	.611	116	0	-2	+1	-1	+1	0	0	0	0	0	-
		69	459.2	189	9	.952	16	6	40	24	.600	130	0	-2	+2	+1	+1	+2	2	0	0	2	-

Jimmy Rollins

		BASIC							GDP			PLUS/MINUS							RUNS SAVED				
Year	Team	G	Inn	TC	E	Pct	GFP	DM	Opps	GDP	Pct	Outs Made	To His Right	Straight On	To His Left	GB	Air	Total	+/-	GDP	GFP/DME	Total	Rank
2003	Phi	154	1357.2	680	14	.979	-	-	140	89	.636	511	+6	+5	0	+11	+1	+12	9	2	-	11	2
2004	Phi	154	1376.2	621	9	.986	39	20	130	82	.631	442	+2	+4	-1	+5	0	+5	4	2	3	9	6
2005	Phi	157	1356.0	631	12	.981	35	26	127	76	.598	473	+3	-2	+17	+19	+4	+23	17	0	1	18	4
2006	Phi	157	1378.0	670	11	.984	44	37	135	90	.667	500	-3	+4	+7	+8	+4	+12	9	3	0	12	5
2007	Phi	162	1441.1	717	11	.985	55	21	164	101	.616	529	+12	-6	-1	+5	+2	+7	5	1	-1	5	13
2008	Phi	132	1168.0	593	7	.988	65	26	127	69	.543	455	+2	+2	+16	+20	+3	+23	17	-2	3	18	1
2009	Phi	155	1364.2	607	6	.990	55	36	115	72	.626	469	-1	+4	-5	-2	-1	-3	-2	0	0	-2	24
2010	Phi	88	744.1	335	6	.982	29	11	71	56	.789	242	-9	+4	+3	-1	+2	+1	0	2	1	3	14
2011	Phi	138	1207.0	581	7	.988	38	16	122	88	.721	426	-15	+9	-6	-13	+1	-12	-9	2	0	-7	26
		1297	11393.2	5435	83	.985	360	193	1131	723	.639	4047	-3	+24	+30	+52	+16	+68	50	10	7	67	4

Brendan Ryan

		BASIC							GDP			PLUS/MINUS							RUNS SAVED				
Year	Team	G	Inn	TC	E	Pct	GFP	DM	Opps	GDP	Pct	Outs Made	To His Right	Straight On	To His Left	GB	Air	Total	+/-	GDP	GFP/DME	Total	Rank
2007	StL	28	163.2	99	3	.970	5	8	22	15	.682	71	+2	-3	+3	+3	0	+3	2	1	-2	1	-
2008	StL	40	255.1	134	1	.993	6	4	30	17	.567	98	+1	+2	+1	+4	-1	+3	2	0	-1	1	-
2009	StL	105	830.2	507	8	.984	55	20	104	77	.740	389	+20	-3	+3	+20	+5	+25	19	2	1	22	2
2010	StL	139	1127.1	644	17	.974	48	20	138	102	.739	433	+26	-1	0	+25	0	+25	19	3	0	22	2
2011	Sea	123	1060.2	572	15	.974	59	26	122	81	.664	386	+18	+5	-2	+21	0	+21	16	1	1	18	1
		435	3437.2	1956	44	.978	173	78	416	292	.702	1377	+67	0	+5	+73	+4	+77	58	7	-1	64	6

Angel Sanchez

		BASIC							GDP			PLUS/MINUS							RUNS SAVED				
Year	Team	G	Inn	TC	E	Pct	GFP	DM	Opps	GDP	Pct	Outs Made	To His Right	Straight On	To His Left	GB	Air	Total	+/-	GDP	GFP/DME	Total	Rank
2006	KC	4	20.1	11	0	1.000	0	1	3	2	.667	9	+1	+1	0	+1	0	+1	1	0	0	1	-
2010	2 tms	58	493.0	216	5	.977	19	14	48	32	.667	141	-10	-5	-1	-16	0	-16	-12	-1	0	-13	33
2011	Hou	46	366.2	194	7	.964	9	10	40	22	.550	130	-9	+2	0	-7	0	-7	-6	-1	0	-7	-
		108	880.0	421	12	.971	28	25	91	56	.615	280	-18	-2	-1	-22	0	-22	-17	-2	0	-19	-

Marco Scutaro

		BASIC							GDP			PLUS/MINUS							RUNS SAVED				
Year	Team	G	Inn	TC	E	Pct	GFP	DM	Opps	GDP	Pct	Outs Made	To His Right	Straight On	To His Left	GB	Air	Total	+/-	GDP	GFP/DME	Total	Rank
2003	NYM	1	2.0	2	0	1.000	-	-	0			2				0	0	0	0			0	-
2004	Oak	16	113.1	69	2	.971	2	3	16	8	.500	46	-1	0	-1	-3	0	-3	-2	0	0	-2	-
2005	Oak	81	663.0	336	8	.976	13	16	76	46	.605	239	-7	+2	-2	-8	0	-8	-6	0	-1	-7	28
2006	Oak	69	572.2	264	9	.966	15	21	57	35	.614	207	-10	-3	-10	-23	-3	-26	-20	0	-2	-22	34
2007	Oak	43	348.0	168	5	.970	14	7	36	22	.611	122	+1	-1	0	0	+1	+1	1	0	1	2	-
2008	Tor	56	472.1	241	5	.979	20	9	46	25	.543	174	+1	+4	+6	+12	0	+12	9	-1	-1	7	10
2009	Tor	143	1252.2	621	10	.984	45	15	147	95	.646	453	-1	+2	+14	+15	+1	+16	12	-1	0	11	6
2010	Bos	132	1166.0	514	18	.965	24	17	90	58	.644	391	+2	-6	+5	+1	+3	+4	3	-1	-1	1	15
2011	Bos	109	928.2	428	12	.972	28	23	94	59	.628	299	+6	-1	-2	+3	-1	+2	2	0	-1	1	18
		650	5518.2	2643	69	.974	161	111	562	348	.619	1933	-9	-3	+10	-3	+1	-2	-1	-3	-5	-9	24

Shortstops

Miguel Tejada

Year	Team	G	Inn	TC	E	Pct	GFP	DM	Opps	GDP	Pct	Outs Made	To His Right	Straight On	To His Left	GB	Air	Total	+/-	GDP	GFP/DME	Total	Rank
2003	Oak	162	1417.2	751	21	.972	-	-	151	85	.563	481	-5	+2	-4	-7	+3	-4	-3	-1	-	-4	27
2004	Bal	162	1421.2	813	24	.970	53	45	191	105	.550	561	+6	+7	+2	+15	-1	+14	11	-2	-4	5	9
2005	Bal	160	1394.2	754	22	.971	43	36	166	95	.572	526	+25	-4	-17	+4	+1	+5	4	-1	1	4	13
2006	Bal	150	1293.2	674	19	.972	31	37	158	96	.608	466	+1	0	-13	-12	-2	-14	-11	1	-1	-11	32
2007	Bal	124	1068.2	522	15	.971	39	38	135	73	.541	362	+5	-4	-3	-2	-2	-4	-3	-2	-1	-6	24
2008	Hou	157	1354.1	640	11	.983	49	30	144	90	.625	472	+5	+7	-4	+7	0	+7	5	2	-1	6	12
2009	Hou	158	1371.1	710	21	.970	57	38	165	108	.655	504	-7	-7	-5	-19	-2	-21	-16	0	1	-15	33
2010	SD	58	496.2	233	3	.987	14	12	65	41	.631	153	0	+2	+1	+3	-2	+1	0	-1	-1	-2	22
2011	SF	42	334.1	162	8	.951	14	9	18	13	.722	111	-3	0	-3	-6	0	-6	-4	0	-1	-5	-
		1173	10153.0	5259	144	.973	300	245	1193	706	.592	3636	+27	+3	-46	-17	-5	-22	-17	-4	-7	-28	28

Ruben Tejada

Year	Team	G	Inn	TC	E	Pct	GFP	DM	Opps	GDP	Pct	Outs Made	To His Right	Straight On	To His Left	GB	Air	Total	+/-	GDP	GFP/DME	Total	Rank
2010	NYM	28	221.2	110	2	.982			28	15	.536	76	-2	0	+5	+2	-2	0	0	-1	0	-1	-
2011	NYM	41	353.0	181	8	.956	30	10	43	19	.442	126	-7	+1	+8	+1	+2	+3	2	-3	0	-1	-
		69	574.2	291	10	.966	41	14	71	34	.479	202	-9	+1	+13	+3	0	+3	2	-4	0	-2	-

Ryan Theriot

Year	Team	G	Inn	TC	E	Pct	GFP	DM	Opps	GDP	Pct	Outs Made	To His Right	Straight On	To His Left	GB	Air	Total	+/-	GDP	GFP/DME	Total	Rank
2006	ChC	2	17.0	8	1	.875	1	1	2	1	.500	5	-1	0	-1	-1	-1	-2	-2	0	0	-2	-
2007	ChC	108	859.0	394	8	.980	33	16	79	52	.658	301	+1	+2	+4	+6	-1	+5	4	2	0	6	12
2008	ChC	149	1266.0	562	14	.975	48	30	107	64	.598	425	+2	-3	+1	+1	+5	+6	5	0	-3	2	15
2009	ChC	151	1311.0	632	15	.976	35	34	143	85	.594	444	0	+8	+2	+10	-3	+7	5	-1	-4	0	20
2010	ChC	29	246.0	115	3	.974	9	9	21	12	.571	79	-3	+1	-3	-4	+1	-3	-3	-1	1	-3	-
2011	StL	91	755.0	388	17	.956	22	20	84	54	.643	262	+3	-7	-5	-9	-1	-10	-8	0	0	-8	28
		530	4454.0	2099	58	.972	148	110	436	268	.615	1516	+2	+1	-1	+3	0	+3	1	0	-6	-5	22

Matt Tolbert

Year	Team	G	Inn	TC	E	Pct	GFP	DM	Opps	GDP	Pct	Outs Made	To His Right	Straight On	To His Left	GB	Air	Total	+/-	GDP	GFP/DME	Total	Rank
2008	Min	14	90.0	41	1	.976	0	1	8	4	.500	31	-1	0	-1	-2	0	-2	-2	0	0	-2	-
2009	Min	3	8.0	6	0	1.000	0	0	2	2	1.000	3	0	0	-1	0	0	0	0	0	0	0	-
2010	Min	3	4.0	4	0	1.000	0	0	1	1	1.000	1	0	0	0	0	0	0	0	0	0	0	-
2011	Min	31	210.0	110	3	.973	3	2	24	18	.750	72	-4	+1	-1	-4	+1	-3	-2	1	0	-1	-
		51	312.0	161	4	.975	3	3	35	25	.714	107	-5	+1	-3	-6	+1	-5	-4	1	0	-3	-

Troy Tulowitzki

Year	Team	G	Inn	TC	E	Pct	GFP	DM	Opps	GDP	Pct	Outs Made	To His Right	Straight On	To His Left	GB	Air	Total	+/-	GDP	GFP/DME	Total	Rank
2006	Col	25	220.1	118	2	.983	11	9	34	23	.676	71	-1	-2	-3	+2	-2	0	-4	1	0	-3	-
2007	Col	155	1375.0	834	11	.987	77	45	167	108	.647	614	+24	+5	+6	+35	0	+35	27	3	1	31	1
2008	Col	101	863.1	509	8	.984	39	18	114	62	.544	355	-4	+4	+1	+1	+3	+4	3	-1	1	3	14
2009	Col	151	1294.0	657	9	.986	75	23	119	85	.714	485	+11	0	-2	+9	+2	+11	8	2	3	13	5
2010	Col	122	1065.0	610	10	.984	58	23	144	107	.743	383	+5	+5	+4	+14	+3	+17	13	4	2	19	4
2011	Col	140	1208.1	684	6	.991	67	23	146	104	.712	434	+12	+1	-2	+11	-3	+8	6	2	3	11	3
		694	6026.0	3412	46	.987	327	145	724	489	.675	2342	+47	+12	+6	+64	+6	+70	53	11	10	74	3

Jack Wilson

Year	Team	G	Inn	TC	E	Pct	GFP	DM	Opps	GDP	Pct	Outs Made	To His Right	Straight On	To His Left	GB	Air	Total	+/-	GDP	GFP/DME	Total	Rank
2003	Pit	149	1294.2	689	17	.975	-	-	161	96	.596	434	+3	0	+2	+5	+3	+8	6	0	-	6	10
2004	Pit	156	1355.2	743	17	.977	41	27	177	118	.667	491	+14	0	-6	+9	+2	+11	8	4	-1	11	4
2005	Pit	157	1360.0	782	14	.982	75	28	184	120	.652	544	+27	+8	-9	+26	+5	+31	24	4	4	32	1
2006	Pit	131	1130.0	641	18	.972	44	20	132	82	.621	454	+8	-3	-8	-3	+3	0	0	1	4	5	12
2007	Pit	131	1142.0	640	11	.983	69	30	162	109	.673	470	+28	-5	-14	+9	+1	+10	8	4	2	14	7
2008	Pit	80	696.1	397	5	.987	41	17	83	50	.602	285	+15	-1	+2	+16	0	+16	12	0	1	13	4
2009	2 tms	105	917.1	481	12	.975	45	20	107	74	.692	334	+22	+3	+2	+28	+4	+32	25	2	1	28	1
2010	Sea	60	518.1	287	8	.972	37	8	55	37	.673	205	+13	0	-10	+3	+5	+8	6	0	2	8	7
2011	2 tms	26	204.0	116	2	.983	8	4	22	14	.636	72	+1	-2	-1	-2	+1	-1	0	0	-1	-1	-
		995	8618.1	4776	104	.978	360	154	1083	700	.646	3289	+131	0	-42	+91	+24	+115	89	15	12	116	2

Left Fielders

Jason Bay

Year	Team	G	Inn	TC	E	Pct	GFP	DM	Opps to Advance	Extra Bases	Pct	Kills	Outs Made	Basic	Shallow	Medium	Deep	Enhanced	+/-	Throws	GFP/DME	Total	Rank
2003	Pit	24	180.1	35	1	.971	-	-	16	7	.438	0	29	0	-1	0	+1		0	-1		-1	
2004	Pit	116	959.0	213	2	.991	10	11	101	40	.396	2	179	+1	-2	-3	-4	+3	2	-2	1	1	13
2005	Pit	146	1185.2	268	1	.996	17	8	121	49	.405	3	266	-2	-5	-4	+9	-1	-1	-7	4	-4	23
2006	Pit	157	1373.0	329	3	.991	12	17	176	72	.409	4	316	+4	-5	0	+19	+12	7	-8	-1	-2	24
2007	Pit	142	1237.0	286	8	.972	23	16	172	63	.366	7	266	-14	-8	-14	+4	-19	-11	-2	2	-11	31
2008	2 tms	154	1344.2	266	4	.985	23	9	169	72	.426	5	254	-11	-8	-7	+3	-12	-7	-4	4	-7	28
2009	Bos	150	1279.1	325	0	1.000	32	21	164	60	.366	8	310	-2	+2	+2	-10	-6	-3	1	4	2	16
2010	NYM	93	820.2	148	1	.993	15	9	86	32	.372	4	141	-1	-5	-3	+11	+4	2	0	1	3	12
2011	NYM	122	1053.1	226	2	.991	26	14	102	36	.353	3	220	-4	-2	+4	-11	-9	-5	0	2	-3	27
		1104	9433.0	2096	22	.990	158	105	1107	431	.389	36	1981	-29	-34	-25	+22	-28	-16	-23	17	-22	29

Brandon Belt

Year	Team	G	Inn	TC	E	Pct	GFP	DM	Opps to Advance	Extra Bases	Pct	Kills	Outs Made	Basic	Shallow	Medium	Deep	Enhanced	+/-	Throws	GFP/DME	Total	Rank
2011	SF	31	231.0	50	3	.940	2	2	22	8	.364	1	46	+3	+3	+2	-4	+1	1	0	0	1	-

Kyle Blanks

Year	Team	G	Inn	TC	E	Pct	GFP	DM	Opps to Advance	Extra Bases	Pct	Kills	Outs Made	Basic	Shallow	Medium	Deep	Enhanced	+/-	Throws	GFP/DME	Total	Rank
2009	SD	18	110.0	27	0	1.000	2	3	7	2	.286	0	26	+2	+2	+1	+1	+3	2	0	0	2	-
2010	SD	30	253.0	48	0	1.000	3	5	24	10	.417	2	45	0	-1	-2	+4	+1	1	0	0	1	-
2011	SD	37	300.0	66	1	.985	5	4	37	10	.270	3	63	+2	+3	-3	+6	+6	3	2	2	7	-
		85	663.0	141	1	.993	10	12	68	22	.324	5	134	+4	+4	-4	+11	+10	6	2	2	10	-

Brennan Boesch

Year	Team	G	Inn	TC	E	Pct	GFP	DM	Opps to Advance	Extra Bases	Pct	Kills	Outs Made	Basic	Shallow	Medium	Deep	Enhanced	+/-	Throws	GFP/DME	Total	Rank
2010	Det	44	350.1	93	4	.957	9	7	47	14	.298	1	86	+2	-2	-1	+15	+12	7	0	0	7	-
2011	Det	57	424.0	108	2	.981	11	9	58	23	.397	4	102	+1	0	-5	+7	+3	1	2	2	5	10
		101	774.1	201	6	.970	20	16	105	37	.352	5	188	+3	-2	-6	+22	+15	8	2	2	12	-

Emilio Bonifacio

Year	Team	G	Inn	TC	E	Pct	GFP	DM	Opps to Advance	Extra Bases	Pct	Kills	Outs Made	Basic	Shallow	Medium	Deep	Enhanced	+/-	Throws	GFP/DME	Total	Rank
2008	Ari	1	2.0	0	0	-	0	0				0	0	0						0			0	-
2009	Fla	6	21.1	3	0	1.000	0	0	4	1	.250	0	3	0	0	0	0	0	0	0	0	0	-
2010	Fla	7	48.1	9	0	1.000	3	1	5	1	.200	1	8	-1	-1	+1	-1	-1	-1	1	1	1	-
2011	Fla	32	247.1	57	1	.982	3	6	19	5	.263	1	54	-1	-1	0	-4	-5	-3	2	0	-1	-
		46	319.0	69	1	.986	6	7	28	7	.250	2	65	-2	-2	+1	-5	-6	-4	3	1	0	-

Milton Bradley

Year	Team	G	Inn	TC	E	Pct	GFP	DM	Opps to Advance	Extra Bases	Pct	Kills	Outs Made	Basic	Shallow	Medium	Deep	Enhanced	+/-	Throws	GFP/DME	Total	Rank
2004	LA	17	128.0	35	0	1.000	2	2	12	5	.417	1	34	+1	-1	+1	+4	+2	1	1	0	2	-
2007	SD	40	326.1	77	2	.974	9	4	27	9	.333	1	72	+3	-1	0	+5	+5	3	-1	1	3	-
2008	Tex	1	8.0	1	0	1.000	0	1	3	1	.333	0	1	-1			-2		-2	-1	0	0	-1	-
2010	Sea	39	323.1	91	1	.989	9	8	32	13	.406	3	87	+2	+4	-2	0	+2	1	0	-1	0	-
2011	Sea	26	213.0	55	2	.964	6	6	25	10	.400	0	53	-3	+1	+1	-8	-7	-4	-1	-1	-6	-
		123	998.2	259	5	.981	26	21	99	38	.384	5	247	+2	+3	-2	+1		0	-1	-1	-2	-

Michael Brantley

Year	Team	G	Inn	TC	E	Pct	GFP	DM	Opps to Advance	Extra Bases	Pct	Kills	Outs Made	Basic	Shallow	Medium	Deep	Enhanced	+/-	Throws	GFP/DME	Total	Rank
2009	Cle	8	63.1	13	0	1.000	0	0	11	1	.091	0	13	+1	+2	0	+1	+3	2	1	0	3	-
2010	Cle	7	63.0	5	0	1.000	0	0	7	0	.000	0	5	-1	+1	0	-4	-3	-2	1	0	-1	-
2011	Cle	66	558.1	125	2	.984	10	8	52	14	.269	3	118	+8	+2	+8	0	+10	6	2	0	8	6
		81	684.2	143	2	.986	10	8	70	15	.214	3	136	+8	+5	+8	-3	+10	6	4	0	10	-

Ryan Braun

Year	Team	G	Inn	TC	E	Pct	GFP	DM	Opps to Advance	Extra Bases	Pct	Kills	Outs Made	Basic	Shallow	Medium	Deep	Enhanced	+/-	Throws	GFP/DME	Total	Rank
2008	Mil	149	1310.1	284	0	1.000	24	25	123	46	.374	6	275	+4	+1	0	+5	+7	4	1	2	7	5
2009	Mil	158	1364.0	314	2	.994	27	29	159	55	.346	4	305	-3	-6	+4	-7	-9	-5	-2	3	-4	25
2010	Mil	153	1326.0	288	3	.990	23	16	153	56	.366	5	279	+6	-8	+2	+25	+19	11	-4	2	9	3
2011	Mil	147	1250.0	268	1	.996	17	20	106	48	.453	5	259	+7	+2	+4	+7	+14	8	-6	1	3	12
		607	5250.1	1154	6	.995	91	90	541	205	.379	20	1118	+14	-11	+10	+30	+31	18	-11	8	15	10

Left Fielders

Pat Burrell

		BASIC							THROWING				PLUS/MINUS						RUNS SAVED				
Year	Team	G	Inn	TC	E	Pct	GFP	DM	Opps to Advance	Extra Bases	Pct	Kills	Outs Made	Basic	Shallow	Medium	Deep	Enhanced	+/-	Throws	GFP/DME	Total	Rank
2003	Phi	140	1186.2	247	6	.976	-	-	113	37	.327	4	229	+7	+6	+4	-3	+7	4	3	-	7	3
2004	Phi	122	1060.0	230	4	.983	21	20	104	29	.279	7	207	-3	-5	+8	0	-7	-4	4	1	1	16
2005	Phi	153	1296.2	253	7	.972	29	17	149	50	.336	9	236	+3	+3	+6	-15	0	4	2		6	8
2006	Phi	126	987.2	215	3	.986	14	23	100	40	.400	6	205	-14	-2	-6	-18	-26	-15	1	-1	-15	34
2007	Phi	138	1028.1	194	10	.948	12	22	112	42	.375	6	176	-14	+3	-4	-26	-27	-15	0	-2	-17	34
2008	Phi	155	1198.1	216	2	.991	32	21	133	40	.301	7	201	-10	+7	-3	-22	-19	-11	4	4	-3	25
2009	TB	1	2.0	0	0	-	0	0				0	0	0				0	0			0	22
2010	SF	87	632.0	127	2	.984	6	10	59	11	.186	1	121	-4	0	-1	-6	-8	-4	3	1	0	22
2011	SF	54	349.2	59	4	.932	3	3	22	9	.409	1	53	+1	+1	-2	+2	+2	1	0	-1	0	-
		976	7741.1	1541	38	.975	117	116	792	258	.326	41	1428	-34	+13	+2	-88	-78	-44	19	4	-21	28

Mike Carp

		BASIC							THROWING				PLUS/MINUS						RUNS SAVED				
Year	Team	G	Inn	TC	E	Pct	GFP	DM	Opps to Advance	Extra Bases	Pct	Kills	Outs Made	Basic	Shallow	Medium	Deep	Enhanced	+/-	Throws	GFP/DME	Total	Rank
2010	Sea	1	4.0	0	0	-	0	0	1	0	.000	0	0	-1	-1	0	0	-1	0	0	0	0	-
2011	Sea	27	216.2	55	4	.927	9	5	22	9	.409	0	49	-4	-1	-4	-5	-10	-5	-1	-1	-7	-
		28	220.2	55	4	.927	9	5	23	9	.391	0	49	-5	-2	-4	-5	-11	-5	-1	-1	-7	-

Carl Crawford

		BASIC							THROWING				PLUS/MINUS						RUNS SAVED				
Year	Team	G	Inn	TC	E	Pct	GFP	DM	Opps to Advance	Extra Bases	Pct	Kills	Outs Made	Basic	Shallow	Medium	Deep	Enhanced	+/-	Throws	GFP/DME	Total	Rank
2003	TB	137	1159.1	330	3	.991	-	-	134	47	.351	5	294	+9	+5	+1	+8	+14	8	2	-	10	1
2004	TB	123	1010.0	280	1	.996	14	21	107	30	.280	3	270	+14	+9	+5	+8	+22	12	3	-1	14	1
2005	TB	147	1246.2	346	2	.994	29	20	159	38	.239	3	341	+15	+6	+3	+14	+19	11	4	-3	12	3
2006	TB	148	1252.1	314	3	.990	14	28	156	60	.385	7	302	+6	+2	+3	+4	+10	6	-1	0	5	9
2007	TB	139	1186.1	293	4	.986	18	16	143	45	.315	2	286	0	+1	+2	-3	0	0	-1	-1	-2	22
2008	TB	108	920.2	237	4	.983	20	11	69	23	.333	0	231	+16	+10	+7	+6	+23	13	-1	-1	11	2
2009	TB	154	1282.2	337	4	.988	29	24	118	36	.305	5	327	+16	+12	+8	-5	+16	9	4	-1	12	2
2010	TB	147	1260.1	315	2	.994	32	15	85	31	.365	3	306	+10	+10	+8	-6	+12	7	0	1	8	4
2011	Bos	127	1098.1	239	3	.987	17	19	112	35	.313	0	235	-1	+3	+14	-21	-4	-2	0	0	-2	24
		1230	10416.2	2691	26	.990	173	154	1083	345	.319	28	2592	+85	+58	+51	+5	+112	64	10	-6	68	1

Andy Dirks

		BASIC							THROWING				PLUS/MINUS						RUNS SAVED				
Year	Team	G	Inn	TC	E	Pct	GFP	DM	Opps to Advance	Extra Bases	Pct	Kills	Outs Made	Basic	Shallow	Medium	Deep	Enhanced	+/-	Throws	GFP/DME	Total	Rank
2011	Det	38	236.2	67	1	.985	4	6	24	12	.500	1	66	+5	-1	-4	+17	+12	7	0	0	7	-

Shelley Duncan

		BASIC							THROWING				PLUS/MINUS						RUNS SAVED				
Year	Team	G	Inn	TC	E	Pct	GFP	DM	Opps to Advance	Extra Bases	Pct	Kills	Outs Made	Basic	Shallow	Medium	Deep	Enhanced	+/-	Throws	GFP/DME	Total	Rank
2007	NYY	4	12.0	3	0	1.000	0	0	3	1	.333	0	3	-1		0	-1	-1	-1	0	0	-1	-
2010	Cle	41	309.0	72	0	1.000	14	8	38	8	.211	4	66	-1	+2	+5	-9	-1	0	5	1	6	-
2011	Cle	37	253.1	61	1	.984	4	7	29	7	.241	1	58	-8	-4	-4	-6	-14	-8	2	0	-6	-
		82	574.1	136	1	.993	18	15	70	16	.229	5	127	-10	-2	+1	-16	-16	-9	7	1	-1	-

Sam Fuld

		BASIC							THROWING				PLUS/MINUS						RUNS SAVED				
Year	Team	G	Inn	TC	E	Pct	GFP	DM	Opps to Advance	Extra Bases	Pct	Kills	Outs Made	Basic	Shallow	Medium	Deep	Enhanced	+/-	Throws	GFP/DME	Total	Rank
2007	ChC	1	1.0	0	0	-	0	0				0									0		-
2009	ChC	29	79.1	26	1	.962	5	1	9	2	.222	1	24	+2	+2	+1	+1	+3	2	1	0	3	-
2010	ChC	8	10.0	1	0	1.000	0	1				0	1	-1	0	0	-2	-1	-1	0	0	-1	-
2011	TB	75	604.2	170	3	.982	30	16	48	14	.292	4	162	+4	+5	+5	-7	+4	2	4	3	9	5
		113	695.0	197	4	.980	35	18	57	16	.281	5	187	+5	+7	+6	-8	+6	3	5	3	11	-

Brett Gardner

		BASIC							THROWING				PLUS/MINUS						RUNS SAVED				
Year	Team	G	Inn	TC	E	Pct	GFP	DM	Opps to Advance	Extra Bases	Pct	Kills	Outs Made	Basic	Shallow	Medium	Deep	Enhanced	+/-	Throws	GFP/DME	Total	Rank
2008	NYY	17	145.1	26	0	1.000	2	2	11	2	.182	1	25	-1	0	-2	0	-2	-1	1	0	0	-
2010	NYY	123	906.0	210	1	.995	17	8	67	16	.239	8	200	+16	+5	+7	+14	+27	15	7	4	26	1
2011	NYY	149	1158.2	305	4	.987	33	19	89	27	.303	5	294	+26	+19	+11	+7	+36	20	3	0	23	1
		289	2210.0	541	5	.991	52	29	167	45	.269	14	519	+41	+24	+16	+21	+61	34	11	4	49	2

Left Fielders

Jonny Gomes

Year	Team	G	Inn	TC	E	Pct	GFP	DM	Opps to Advance	Extra Bases	Pct	Kills	Outs Made	Basic	Shallow	Medium	Deep	Enhanced	+/-	Throws	GFP/ DME	Total	Rank
2005	TB	14	110.0	31	0	1.000	3	2	13	2	.154	1	30	-4	0	+2	-6	-9	-5	1	0	-4	-
2007	TB	26	186.1	44	0	1.000	1	7	22	8	.364	1	42	-7	-3	-2	-5	-10	-6	1	0	-5	-
2008	TB	9	40.0	13	0	1.000	1	0	6	5	.833	0	13	-1	0	-1	-1	-2	-1	-1	0	-2	-
2009	Cin	37	253.0	50	1	.980	5	8	29	7	.241	3	46	-2	-1	0	-3	-4	-2	1	0	-1	-
2010	Cin	129	1037.0	207	4	.981	18	26	126	47	.373	4	196	-17	-8	-2	-19	-30	-17	-2	-2	-21	35
2011	2 tms	73	550.1	117	2	.983	7	8	63	16	.254	1	114	-1	-6	+1	+6	+1	1	1	-2	0	20
		288	2176.2	462	7	.985	35	51	259	85	.328	10	441	-32	-18	-2	-28	-54	-30	1	-4	-33	31

Carlos Gonzalez

Year	Team	G	Inn	TC	E	Pct	GFP	DM	Opps to Advance	Extra Bases	Pct	Kills	Outs Made	Basic	Shallow	Medium	Deep	Enhanced	+/-	Throws	GFP/ DME	Total	Rank
2009	Col	47	294.1	69	0	1.000	9	6	23	6	.261	2	67	+1	0	-1	-1	-2	-1	1	0	0	-
2010	Col	63	472.1	83	1	.988	10	6	37	17	.459	4	77	+2	-1	0	+3	+2	1	0	2	3	13
2011	Col	61	518.0	99	1	.990	17	8	48	12	.250	4	93	-2	0	-5	+3	-2	-1	2	1	2	17
		171	1284.2	251	2	.992	36	20	108	35	.324	10	237	+1	-1	-6	+5	-2	-1	3	3	5	-

Alex Gordon

Year	Team	G	Inn	TC	E	Pct	GFP	DM	Opps to Advance	Extra Bases	Pct	Kills	Outs Made	Basic	Shallow	Medium	Deep	Enhanced	+/-	Throws	GFP/ DME	Total	Rank
2010	KC	55	486.1	136	2	.985	17	13	69	21	.304	2	132	+3	0	+3	+3	+5	3	2	-2	3	11
2011	KC	148	1309.0	335	3	.991	31	23	126	34	.270	12	313	+5	+4	+7	-1	+10	5	13	2	20	2
		203	1795.1	471	5	.989	48	36	195	55	.282	14	445	+8	+4	+10	+2	+15	8	15	0	23	-

Tony Gwynn

Year	Team	G	Inn	TC	E	Pct	GFP	DM	Opps to Advance	Extra Bases	Pct	Kills	Outs Made	Basic	Shallow	Medium	Deep	Enhanced	+/-	Throws	GFP/ DME	Total	Rank
2007	Mil	4	6.0	1	0	1.000	0	0	0	0	-	0	1	0		0		0	0	0	0	0	-
2008	Mil	1	4.0	1	0	1.000	0	0	1	0	.000	0	1	0			+1	+1	1	0	0	1	-
2011	LAD	110	624.1	132	1	.992	17	9	58	25	.431	3	124	+5	-7	+5	+20	+18	10	0	2	12	3
		115	634.1	134	1	.993	17	9	59	25	.424	3	126	+5	-7	+5	+21	+19	11	0	2	13	-

Josh Hamilton

Year	Team	G	Inn	TC	E	Pct	GFP	DM	Opps to Advance	Extra Bases	Pct	Kills	Outs Made	Basic	Shallow	Medium	Deep	Enhanced	+/-	Throws	GFP/ DME	Total	Rank
2007	Cin	9	27.0	5	0	1.000			6	1	.167	0	5	0	0	0	-1	-1	-1	0	0	-1	-
2010	Tex	92	772.2	190	4	.979	14	11	71	24	.338	2	179	+10	+9	-4	+8	+13	7	0	0	7	6
2011	Tex	85	709.0	161	4	.975	19	8	65	22	.338	2	153	+5	+4	+1	+1	+7	4	0	0	4	11
		186	1508.2	356	8	.978	34	19	142	47	.331	4	337	+15	+13	-3	+8	+19	10	0	0	10	-

Willie Harris

Year	Team	G	Inn	TC	E	Pct	GFP	DM	Opps to Advance	Extra Bases	Pct	Kills	Outs Made	Basic	Shallow	Medium	Deep	Enhanced	+/-	Throws	GFP/ DME	Total	Rank
2004	CWS	1	2.0	2	0	1.000	0	0	0	0	-	0	2	-1	0		0	-1	-1	0	0	-1	-
2006	Bos	11	33.0	11	0	1.000	1	2	3	1	.333	1	10	-3	0	-1	-4	-5	-3	1	0	-2	-
2007	Atl	85	620.1	145	3	.979	17	13	71	27	.380	4	138	+10	+1	+4	+14	+18	10	-1	1	10	3
2008	Was	86	562.0	151	2	.987	16	10	63	21	.333	2	145	+12	0	+5	+14	+20	11	1	1	13	1
2009	Was	45	175.2	34	0	1.000	6	3	21	7	.333	0	34	+1	0	0	+2	+2	1	-1	1	1	-
2010	Was	46	200.1	39	1	.974	2	3	14	5	.357	0	38	+2	+1	-1	+4	+4	2	-1	0	1	-
2011	NYM	33	241.1	48	0	1.000	1	8	31	12	.387	0	48	-4	-4	-1	0	-5	-3	-1	-1	-5	-
		307	1834.2	430	6	.986	43	39	203	73	.360	7	415	+17	-2	+6	+30	+33	17	-2	2	17	-

Chris Heisey

Year	Team	G	Inn	TC	E	Pct	GFP	DM	Opps to Advance	Extra Bases	Pct	Kills	Outs Made	Basic	Shallow	Medium	Deep	Enhanced	+/-	Throws	GFP/ DME	Total	Rank
2010	Cin	38	96.2	25	0	1.000	2	1	12	1	.083	0	24	+1	0	-1	+2	+1	1	0	0	1	-
2011	Cin	88	393.0	88	2	.977	3	9	29	15	.517	1	85	+3	+4	+4	-6	+1	1	-2	-1	-2	-
		126	489.2	113	2	.982	5	10	41	16	.390	1	109	+4	+4	+3	-4	+2	2	-2	-1	-1	-

Left Fielders

Eric Hinske

		BASIC							THROWING				PLUS/MINUS						RUNS SAVED				
Year	Team	G	Inn	TC	E	Pct	GFP	DM	Opps to Advance	Extra Bases	Pct	Kills	Outs Made	Basic	Shallow	Medium	Deep	Enhanced	+/-	Throws	GFP/ DME	Total	Rank
2006	2 tms	6	24.0	5	0	1.000	1	0	2	0	.000	0	5	0	+1	-1	-1	-1	-1	0	0	-1	-
2007	Bos	24	101.0	27	0	1.000	3	3	10	1	.100	0	26	-1	0	+1	-2	-1	-1	1	1	1	-
2008	TB	40	265.0	48	1	.979	4	3	26	10	.385	0	45	+1	-1	+3	0	+2	1	-1	0	0	-
2009	NYY	2	17.0	7	0	1.000	0	4	4	3	.750	0	7	-1	0	-2		-2	-1	-1	-1	-3	-
2010	Atl	50	360.0	66	1	.985	2	4	24	14	.583	0	65	-3	-3	0	-1	-3	-2	-3	-1	-6	-
2011	Atl	32	211.0	42	0	1.000	3	2	17	5	.294	0	41	0	-2	-1	+4	+1	0	0	1	1	-
		154	978.0	195	2	.990	13	16	83	33	.398	0	189	-4	-5	0	0	-4	-4	-4	0	-8	-

Matt Holliday

		BASIC							THROWING				PLUS/MINUS						RUNS SAVED				
Year	Team	G	Inn	TC	E	Pct	GFP	DM	Opps to Advance	Extra Bases	Pct	Kills	Outs Made	Basic	Shallow	Medium	Deep	Enhanced	+/-	Throws	GFP/ DME	Total	Rank
2004	Col	115	917.0	188	7	.963	10	18	110	42	.382	1	168	0	+4	-2	+2	-2	-1	-6	-2	-9	31
2005	Col	123	1049.2	248	7	.972	12	15	117	40	.342	3	236	+8	+9	+1	+6	+12	7	-3	-1	3	11
2006	Col	153	1334.1	291	6	.979	12	30	138	60	.435	3	277	-3	+2	+2	-17	-12	-7	-5	0	-12	32
2007	Col	157	1383.2	306	3	.990	22	17	144	46	.319	3	296	+3	-3	+2	+5	+4	2	-1	-1	0	18
2008	Col	139	1229.0	252	3	.988	24	16	163	54	.331	3	240	+3	-2	+5	+5	+9	5	-2	2	5	7
2009	2 tms	155	1353.1	287	5	.983	18	20	124	43	.347	4	275	+3	+1	+6	+1	+7	4	-1	0	3	14
2010	StL	155	1341.2	272	3	.989	13	16	117	44	.376	4	260	+7	-3	-2	+23	+18	10	-1	-2	7	5
2011	StL	115	990.2	203	3	.985	10	13	97	42	.433	4	197	-4	-11	-2	+13	+1	0	-2	1	-1	23
		1112	9599.2	2047	37	.982	121	145	1010	371	.367	25	1949	+17	-3	+10	+38	+37	20	-21	-3	-4	22

Raul Ibanez

		BASIC							THROWING				PLUS/MINUS						RUNS SAVED				
Year	Team	G	Inn	TC	E	Pct	GFP	DM	Opps to Advance	Extra Bases	Pct	Kills	Outs Made	Basic	Shallow	Medium	Deep	Enhanced	+/-	Throws	GFP/ DME	Total	Rank
2003	KC	128	1042.0	242	3	.988	-	-	104	34	.327	6	215	-5	-14	-1	+14	-2	-1	2	-	1	18
2004	Sea	110	949.1	241	4	.983	12	20	93	31	.333	6	216	+6	+7	+1	+3	+8	4	3	-1	6	8
2005	Sea	55	463.2	113	2	.982	8	7	59	18	.305	5	106	+3	-3	+1	+6	+8	4	4	0	8	7
2006	Sea	157	1396.2	314	2	.994	24	20	171	52	.304	9	301	-1	-3	-4	+8	+2	1	4	4	9	4
2007	Sea	131	1114.1	240	6	.975	25	28	143	56	.392	4	224	-13	-3	-5	-16	-25	-14	-2	-1	-17	33
2008	Sea	153	1340.0	316	5	.984	30	28	160	54	.338	6	303	-10	-8	-8	-3	-19	-11	3	-1	-9	33
2009	Phi	129	1123.2	224	2	.991	30	17	103	33	.320	8	212	-9	-2	-6	-8	-16	-9	4	3	-2	21
2010	Phi	145	1294.0	218	2	.991	18	18	112	45	.402	3	212	-5	+3	+4	-21	-15	-8	-3	0	-11	29
2011	Phi	134	1196.2	214	1	.995	17	22	107	41	.383	2	208	-18	-5	-10	-17	-32	-18	-3	-2	-23	34
		1142	9920.1	2122	27	.987	164	160	1052	364	.346	49	1997	-52	-28	-28	-34	-91	-52	12	2	-38	33

Desmond Jennings

		BASIC							THROWING				PLUS/MINUS						RUNS SAVED				
Year	Team	G	Inn	TC	E	Pct	GFP	DM	Opps to Advance	Extra Bases	Pct	Kills	Outs Made	Basic	Shallow	Medium	Deep	Enhanced	+/-	Throws	GFP/ DME	Total	Rank
2010	TB	2	15.0	5	0	1.000	0	1	1	1	1.000	0	5	0	0	+2	-1	+1	1	0	0	1	-
2011	TB	53	467.0	104	1	.990	13	8	31	12	.387	2	100	+6	+5	0	+2	+7	4	0	-1	3	14
		55	482.0	109	1	.991	13	9	32	13	.406	2	105	+6	+5	+2	+1	+8	5	0	-1	4	-

Andruw Jones

		BASIC							THROWING				PLUS/MINUS						RUNS SAVED				
Year	Team	G	Inn	TC	E	Pct	GFP	DM	Opps to Advance	Extra Bases	Pct	Kills	Outs Made	Basic	Shallow	Medium	Deep	Enhanced	+/-	Throws	GFP/ DME	Total	Rank
2009	Tex	12	98.2	24	0	1.000		2	12	2	.167	0	24	0	0	-2	+1	-1	-1	0	0	-1	-
2010	CWS	12	101.0	23	0	1.000	2	0	13	5	.385	1	21	-2	+1	-2	-1	-2	-1	1	0	0	-
2011	NYY	39	247.0	60	1	.983	3	1	16	4	.250	0	59	+1	+1	-3	+3	+1	1	-1	0	0	-
		63	446.2	107	1	.991	5	3	41	11	.268	1	104	-1	+2	-7	+3	-2	-1	0	0	-1	-

Austin Kearns

		BASIC							THROWING				PLUS/MINUS						RUNS SAVED				
Year	Team	G	Inn	TC	E	Pct	GFP	DM	Opps to Advance	Extra Bases	Pct	Kills	Outs Made	Basic	Shallow	Medium	Deep	Enhanced	+/-	Throws	GFP/ DME	Total	Rank
2003	Cin	1	1.2	0	0	-	-	-				0										0	-
2010	2 tms	91	702.0	176	4	.977	11	9	65	21	.323	2	170	0	+4	0	-9	-6	-3	0	-1	-4	25
2011	Cle	36	264.1	70	0	1.000	6	6	27	8	.296	0	70	-3	+4	0	-12	-8	-4	1	-1	-4	-
		128	968.0	246	4	.984	17	15	92	29	.315	2	240	-3	+8	0	-21	-14	-7	1	-2	-8	-

Left Fielders

Carlos Lee

	BASIC							THROWING				PLUS/MINUS						RUNS SAVED				
Year Team	G	Inn	TC	E	Pct	GFP	DM	Opps to Advance	Extra Bases	Pct	Kills	Outs Made	Basic	Shallow	Medium	Deep	Enhanced	+/-	Throws	GFP/ DME	Total	Rank
2003 CWS	156	1328.2	322	7	.978	-	-	129	57	.442	4	303	+6	+4	+2	+9	+15	8	-7	-	1	13
2004 CWS	148	1277.2	293	0	1.000	24	17	118	43	.364	8	277	-1	-1	+1	+12	+6	3	3	4	10	3
2005 Mil	162	1404.0	321	6	.981	18	13	138	48	.348	5	307	-8	-15	+2	+6	-9	-5	-2	-1	-8	33
2006 2 tms	149	1259.1	238	6	.975	8	19	138	48	.348	2	227	-11	-7	-9	+5	-8	-4	-4	1	-7	30
2007 Hou	157	1369.1	273	4	.985	30	22	151	59	.391	6	261	+2	0	-1	+3	+2	1	-3	2	0	19
2008 Hou	110	915.1	192	1	.995	9	20	87	34	.391	1	187	+4	+3	+3	-6	0	0	-4	-2	-6	27
2009 Hou	154	1272.1	222	2	.991	17	27	163	54	.331	4	211	-6	-1	+3	-13	-11	-6	1	-1	-6	27
2010 Hou	133	1096.1	195	6	.969	15	22	139	60	.432	4	183	-9	-9	-5	-2	-16	-9	-6	-3	-18	34
2011 Hou	80	645.1	131	2	.985	20	9	74	24	.324	6	118	+2	+4	0	-1	+3	2	3	2	7	8
	1249	10568.1	2187	34	.984	141	149	1137	427	.376	40	2074	-21	-22	-4	+13	-18	-10	-19	2	-27	30

Fred Lewis

	BASIC							THROWING				PLUS/MINUS						RUNS SAVED				
Year Team	G	Inn	TC	E	Pct	GFP	DM	Opps to Advance	Extra Bases	Pct	Kills	Outs Made	Basic	Shallow	Medium	Deep	Enhanced	+/-	Throws	GFP/ DME	Total	Rank
2006 SF	6	18.0	8	1	.875	0	0	3	1	.333	0	7	0		0	0	0	0	0	0	0	
2007 SF	24	115.0	33	1	.970	0	4	18	4	.222	0	32	+3	+2	+1	+1	+4	2	0	-1	1	-
2008 SF	112	905.2	195	6	.969	21	20	88	33	.375	3	177	+4	+6	+1	-4	+4	2	1	-2	1	16
2009 SF	83	589.2	133	3	.977	8	21	54	17	.315	1	127	+5	+2	+7	-1	+8	4	0	-1	3	14
2010 Tor	84	726.1	138	3	.978	10	16	86	30	.349	1	134	-3	-4	-7	+8	-3	-2	-1	-2	-5	26
2011 Cin	45	315.2	79	0	1.000	8	3	38	17	.447	2	76	+7	+1	+4	+9	+14	8	-2	1	7	-
	354	2670.1	586	14	.976	47	64	287	102	.355	7	553	+16	+7	+6	+13	+27	14	-2	-5	7	12

Ryan Ludwick

	BASIC							THROWING				PLUS/MINUS						RUNS SAVED				
Year Team	G	Inn	TC	E	Pct	GFP	DM	Opps to Advance	Extra Bases	Pct	Kills	Outs Made	Basic	Shallow	Medium	Deep	Enhanced	+/-	Throws	GFP/ DME	Total	Rank
2003 2 tms	17	132.0	35	0	1.000	-	-	10	3	.300	0	34	+3	+1	+1	+4	+6	4	-1	-	3	-
2005 Cle	9	59.0	17	1	.941	0	2	9	3	.333	0	16	-2	-3	+1	+1	-2	-1	0	-1	-2	-
2007 StL	49	324.0	87	0	1.000	14	5	25	9	.360	1	86	+6	+2	+3	+4	+9	5	-1	1	5	-
2008 StL	29	169.2	44	0	1.000	3	3	21	14	.667	0	42	-3	-1	-2	-1	-5	-3	-4	1	-7	-
2009 StL	1	8.0	1	0	1.000	0	1	0	0	-	0	1	0		0	0	0	0	0	0	0	
2010 StL	1	5.0	2	0	1.000	0	0				0	2	+1	0	0	+3	+3	1	0	0	1	-
2011 2 tms	117	1005.0	200	1	.995	22	17	85	36	.424	4	190	0	+4	-9	+1	-4	-3	-3	1	-5	28
	223	1702.2	386	2	.995	39	28	150	65	.433	5	371	+5	+3	-6	+12	+7	3	-9	1	-5	-

J.D. Martinez

	BASIC							THROWING				PLUS/MINUS						RUNS SAVED				
Year Team	G	Inn	TC	E	Pct	GFP	DM	Opps to Advance	Extra Bases	Pct	Kills	Outs Made	Basic	Shallow	Medium	Deep	Enhanced	+/-	Throws	GFP/ DME	Total	Rank
2011 Hou	51	436.1	98	1	.990	13	7	45	14	.311	4	92	-2	+3	-1	-7	-4	-2	2	2	2	18

Hideki Matsui

	BASIC							THROWING				PLUS/MINUS						RUNS SAVED				
Year Team	G	Inn	TC	E	Pct	GFP	DM	Opps to Advance	Extra Bases	Pct	Kills	Outs Made	Basic	Shallow	Medium	Deep	Enhanced	+/-	Throws	GFP/ DME	Total	Rank
2003 NYY	118	997.1	228	7	.969	-	-	121	47	.388	4	210	-10	-12	-4	+3	-12	-7	-2	-	-9	31
2004 NYY	162	1388.0	318	7	.978	13	23	136	36	.265	5	289	-15	-15	-11	-5	-20	-11	5	1	-5	27
2005 NYY	115	977.1	229	3	.987	22	14	119	41	.345	4	219	-2	-8	-2	+10	+4	2	0	2	4	10
2006 NYY	36	289.0	84	1	.988	3	6	43	19	.442	1	82	0	+3	0	-4	-1	-1	-3	0	-4	-
2007 NYY	112	980.0	222	3	.986	12	15	105	33	.314	5	214	0	+4	-2	-11	-9	-5	5	-1	-1	21
2008 NYY	21	176.1	43	1	.977	2	5	21	11	.524	2	40	0	+1	-1	-1	-1	-1	-1	1	-1	-
2010 LAA	18	123.0	17	0	1.000	3	3	21	7	.333	1	16	-5	-1	-1	-7	-8	-5	0	0	-5	-
2011 Oak	27	232.1	57	1	.982	8	2	22	4	.182	2	53	-5	-4	+2	-4	-6	-3	2	2	1	-
	609	5163.1	1198	23	.981	63	68	588	198	.337	24	1123	-37	-32	-19	-19	-53	-31	6	5	-20	27

Nate McLouth

	BASIC							THROWING				PLUS/MINUS						RUNS SAVED				
Year Team	G	Inn	TC	E	Pct	GFP	DM	Opps to Advance	Extra Bases	Pct	Kills	Outs Made	Basic	Shallow	Medium	Deep	Enhanced	+/-	Throws	GFP/ DME	Total	Rank
2006 Pit	3	8.0	2	0	1.000	1	0	0	0	-	0	2	0		0	0	0	0	0	0	0	
2007 Pit	24	110.1	19	0	1.000	4	2	16	4	.250	0	19	-1	-1	0	0	0	0	1	0	1	-
2008 Pit	4	18.0	2	0	1.000	0	0	0	0	-	0	2	0		0	0	0	0	0	0	0	
2010 Atl	8	52.0	8	0	1.000	1	5	5	3	.600	0	8	-3	-1	-1	-2	-5	-3	0	0	-3	
2011 Atl	26	202.0	38	0	1.000	6	0	14	7	.500	0	38	+3	+2	-1	+2	+4	2	-1	0	1	-
	65	390.1	69	0	1.000	12	7	35	14	.400	0	69	-1	0	-2	0	-1	-1	0	0	-1	

Logan Morrison

	BASIC							THROWING				PLUS/MINUS						RUNS SAVED				
Year Team	G	Inn	TC	E	Pct	GFP	DM	Opps to Advance	Extra Bases	Pct	Kills	Outs Made	Basic	Shallow	Medium	Deep	Enhanced	+/-	Throws	GFP/ DME	Total	Rank
2010 Fla	62	544.0	123	3	.976	13	18	62	20	.323	3	116	-7	-4	-5	-4	-12	-7	3	-1	-5	27
2011 Fla	119	1021.1	218	5	.977	17	42	95	30	.316	4	207	-21	-9	-10	-22	-40	-23	1	-4	-26	35
	181	1565.1	341	8	.977	30	60	157	50	.318	7	323	-28	-13	-15	-26	-52	-30	4	-5	-31	

Left Fielders

Michael Morse

		BASIC							THROWING				PLUS/MINUS						RUNS SAVED				
Year	Team	G	Inn	TC	E	Pct	GFP	DM	Opps to Advance	Extra Bases	Pct	Kills	Outs Made	Basic	Shallow	Medium	Deep	Enhanced	+/-	Throws	GFP/DME	Total	Rank
2005	Sea	8	55.0	11	0	1.000	1	2	6	2	.333	0	10	0		0	+1	0	0	-1	0	-1	-
2006	Sea	2	10.0	1	0	1.000	0	0	1	1	1.000	0	1	0		-1	+1	0	0	0	0	0	-
2009	Was	2	9.2	4	0	1.000	1	0	0	0	-	0	4	0	0		0	0	0	0	0	0	-
2011	Was	55	421.0	94	1	.989	7	7	37	12	.324	2	89	-4	0	-1	-5	-5	-3	1	2	0	21
		67	495.2	110	1	.991	9	9	44	15	.341	2	104	-4	0	-2	-3	-5	-3	0	2	-1	-

David Murphy

		BASIC							THROWING				PLUS/MINUS						RUNS SAVED				
Year	Team	G	Inn	TC	E	Pct	GFP	DM	Opps to Advance	Extra Bases	Pct	Kills	Outs Made	Basic	Shallow	Medium	Deep	Enhanced	+/-	Throws	GFP/DME	Total	Rank
2006	Bos	6	20.0	1	0	1.000	0	1	2	1	.500	0	1	-1	-1	0	-1	-2	-1	0	0	-1	-
2007	2 tms	32	95.1	27	1	.963	0	1	13	4	.308	0	26	0	0	-1	+2	+1	1	-1	-1	-1	-
2008	Tex	54	404.2	90	1	.989	6	6	48	14	.292	2	86	-4	0	-1	-5	-6	-3	2	0	-1	20
2009	Tex	104	858.1	200	1	.995	9	16	81	29	.358	3	195	-2	0	-5	+4	0	0	-2	-1	-3	22
2010	Tex	74	533.0	120	1	.992	9	6	58	26	.448	3	113	+3	-1	+4	+5	+8	4	-1	2	5	9
2011	Tex	78	556.1	129	4	.969	8	4	61	31	.508	0	123	+2	-3	+3	+11	+10	6	-4	-1	1	19
		348	2467.2	567	8	.986	32	34	263	105	.399	8	544	-2	-5	0	+16	+11	7	-6	-1	0	19

Laynce Nix

		BASIC							THROWING				PLUS/MINUS						RUNS SAVED				
Year	Team	G	Inn	TC	E	Pct	GFP	DM	Opps to Advance	Extra Bases	Pct	Kills	Outs Made	Basic	Shallow	Medium	Deep	Enhanced	+/-	Throws	GFP/DME	Total	Rank
2003	Tex	5	28.0	16	2	.875	-	-	4	2	.500	0	14	-1	0	0	-2	-2	-1	0	-	-1	-
2007	Mil	1	1.1	0	0	-	0	0				0	0									0	-
2008	Mil	2	10.0	4	0	1.000	1	0	1	0	.000	0	4	0	0	+1	0	0	0	0	0	0	-
2009	Cin	72	558.0	121	1	.992	12	14	47	10	.213	1	118	+8	+5	+1	+6	+11	6	1	-2	5	9
2010	Cin	50	269.0	54	0	1.000	6	3	29	4	.138	1	52	+5	+1	+5	0	+6	3	3	0	6	-
2011	Was	73	504.1	110	2	.982	8	8	47	12	.255	4	102	-1	-2	-2	+8	+4	2	4	0	6	9
		203	1370.2	305	5	.984	27	25	128	28	.219	6	290	+11	+4	+5	+12	+19	10	8	-2	16	-

Gerardo Parra

		BASIC							THROWING				PLUS/MINUS						RUNS SAVED				
Year	Team	G	Inn	TC	E	Pct	GFP	DM	Opps to Advance	Extra Bases	Pct	Kills	Outs Made	Basic	Shallow	Medium	Deep	Enhanced	+/-	Throws	GFP/DME	Total	Rank
2009	Ari	75	577.0	136	3	.978	12	6	56	21	.375	2	129	0	0	+4	-4	+1	1	-1	1	1	18
2010	Ari	76	569.1	155	3	.981	17	9	50	14	.280	3	146	+10	-2	+5	+14	+17	10	1	0	11	2
2011	Ari	125	1018.0	281	2	.993	31	25	106	35	.330	10	267	+11	+1	+6	+10	+17	9	2	0	11	4
		276	2164.1	572	8	.986	60	40	212	70	.330	15	542	+21	-1	+15	+20	+35	20	2	1	23	5

Corey Patterson

		BASIC							THROWING				PLUS/MINUS						RUNS SAVED				
Year	Team	G	Inn	TC	E	Pct	GFP	DM	Opps to Advance	Extra Bases	Pct	Kills	Outs Made	Basic	Shallow	Medium	Deep	Enhanced	+/-	Throws	GFP/DME	Total	Rank
2010	Bal	56	466.2	125	5	.960	13	10	59	23	.390	2	116	+2	+1	+1	0	+3	2	0	0	2	15
2011	2 tms	56	396.2	96	0	1.000	10	7	37	12	.324	2	93	-2	-2	0	-5	-6	-4	0	0	-4	-
		112	863.1	221	5	.977	23	17	96	35	.365	4	209	0	-1	+1	-5	-3	-2	0	0	-2	-

Carlos Peguero

		BASIC							THROWING				PLUS/MINUS						RUNS SAVED				
Year	Team	G	Inn	TC	E	Pct	GFP	DM	Opps to Advance	Extra Bases	Pct	Kills	Outs Made	Basic	Shallow	Medium	Deep	Enhanced	+/-	Throws	GFP/DME	Total	Rank
2011	Sea	40	325.2	83	1	.988	9	7	25	11	.440	2	79	0	-3	+2	+3	+3	1	0	2	3	-

Felix Pie

		BASIC							THROWING				PLUS/MINUS						RUNS SAVED				
Year	Team	G	Inn	TC	E	Pct	GFP	DM	Opps to Advance	Extra Bases	Pct	Kills	Outs Made	Basic	Shallow	Medium	Deep	Enhanced	+/-	Throws	GFP/DME	Total	Rank
2007	ChC	2	5.0	1	0	1.000	0	0	0	0	-	0	1	0	0	0	0	0	0	0	0	0	-
2008	ChC	1	8.2	3	0	1.000	0	1	2	0	.000	0	3	-1	0	-1	0	-1	-1	0	0	-1	-
2009	Bal	44	272.0	89	1	.989	5	9	42	15	.357	1	85	-2	+3	-2	-4	-4	-2	1	0	-1	-
2010	Bal	70	580.1	155	1	.994	18	15	63	13	.206	5	147	-4	-3	-4	-2	-9	-5	5	0	0	23
2011	Bal	67	349.2	90	0	1.000	7	14	52	21	.404	1	89	-10	-8	-9	+1	-16	-9	-2	0	-11	-
		184	1215.2	338	2	.994	30	39	159	49	.308	7	325	-17	-8	-16	-5	-30	-17	4	0	-13	-

Juan Pierre

		BASIC							THROWING				PLUS/MINUS						RUNS SAVED				
Year	Team	G	Inn	TC	E	Pct	GFP	DM	Opps to Advance	Extra Bases	Pct	Kills	Outs Made	Basic	Shallow	Medium	Deep	Enhanced	+/-	Throws	GFP/DME	Total	Rank
2008	LAD	84	622.2	128	0	1.000	11	9	71	27	.380	0	125	+3	+2	+1	+2	+5	3	-4	1	0	17
2009	LAD	94	653.1	129	0	1.000	7	8	45	16	.356	0	128	+3	-1	+2	+6	+6	3	-2	0	1	17
2010	CWS	149	1330.1	312	1	.997	28	18	138	45	.326	2	306	-2	+5	-2	-15	-12	-7	-4	2	-9	28
2011	CWS	155	1365.0	290	7	.976	23	22	113	44	.389	2	278	-7	-1	+9	-19	-11	-6	-4	-1	-11	33
		482	3971.1	859	11	.987	69	57	367	132	.360	4	837	-3	+5	+10	-26	-12	-7	-14	2	-19	26

Left Fielders

Martin Prado

Year	Team	G	Inn	TC	E	Pct	GFP	DM	Opps to Advance	Extra Bases	Pct	Kills	Outs Made	Basic	Shallow	Medium	Deep	Enhanced	+/-	Throws	GFP/ DME	Total	Rank
2008	Atl	3	23.0	7	0	1.000	0	0	1	0	.000	0	7	+1	+1	0	-1	+1	1	0	0	1	-
2011	Atl	100	854.0	180	3	.983	15	10	74	26	.351	6	171	+1	-3	+5	+5	+6	4	2	1	7	7
		103	877.0	187	3	.984	15	10	75	26	.347	6	178	+2	-2	+5	+4	+7	5	2	1	8	-

Alex Presley

Year	Team	G	Inn	TC	E	Pct	GFP	DM	Opps to Advance	Extra Bases	Pct	Kills	Outs Made	Basic	Shallow	Medium	Deep	Enhanced	+/-	Throws	GFP/ DME	Total	Rank
2010	Pit	2	11.0	0	0	-	0	0				0	0	0	0	0	0	0	0	0	0	0	-
2011	Pit	48	406.0	74	1	.986	7	8	64	21	.328	0	71	+2	-2	0	+9	+6	3	0	-1	2	16
		50	417.0	74	1	.986	7	8	64	21	.328	0	71	+2	-2	0	+9	+6	3	0	-1	2	-

Ryan Raburn

Year	Team	G	Inn	TC	E	Pct	GFP	DM	Opps to Advance	Extra Bases	Pct	Kills	Outs Made	Basic	Shallow	Medium	Deep	Enhanced	+/-	Throws	GFP/ DME	Total	Rank
2007	Det	10	58.0	17	0	1.000	0	2	7	2	.286	1	16	-3	-2	-1	0	-4	-2	1	0	-1	-
2008	Det	30	127.2	32	1	.969	5	4	13	5	.385	1	29	0	0	-1	+2	+1	1	1	0	2	-
2009	Det	70	437.2	126	5	.960	14	17	44	14	.318	7	112	0	-3	-3	+10	+4	2	5	1	8	4
2010	Det	73	508.2	124	4	.968	16	8	44	13	.295	3	116	0	0	0	+2	+3	1	1	0	2	16
2011	Det	52	335.2	95	3	.968	11	9	30	12	.400	2	89	+3	+4	0	+1	+5	3	0	1	4	-
		235	1467.2	394	13	.967	46	40	138	46	.333	14	362	0	-1	-5	+15	+9	5	8	2	15	-

Nolan Reimold

Year	Team	G	Inn	TC	E	Pct	GFP	DM	Opps to Advance	Extra Bases	Pct	Kills	Outs Made	Basic	Shallow	Medium	Deep	Enhanced	+/-	Throws	GFP/ DME	Total	Rank
2009	Bal	88	732.1	184	5	.973	12	11	98	33	.337	4	172	+1	+1	0	0	+1	1	2	2	5	10
2010	Bal	22	175.0	44	1	.977	3	5	19	6	.316	1	42	+2	+1	+1	+1	+2	1	1	-1	1	-
2011	Bal	73	593.2	155	3	.981	10	14	70	27	.386	3	147	0	+3	-6	-1	-5	-3	-1	2	-2	25
		183	1501.0	383	9	.977	25	30	187	66	.353	8	361	+3	+5	-5	0	-2	-1	2	3	4	-

Juan Rivera

Year	Team	G	Inn	TC	E	Pct	GFP	DM	Opps to Advance	Extra Bases	Pct	Kills	Outs Made	Basic	Shallow	Medium	Deep	Enhanced	+/-	Throws	GFP/ DME	Total	Rank
2003	NYY	34	289.2	67	2	.970	-	-	30	11	.367	0	58	+2	+3	-2	+1	+2	1	-1	-	0	-
2004	Mon	10	71.0	18	0	1.000	0	3	11	6	.545	1	14	+1	-1	0	+5	+1	1	0	-1	0	-
2005	LAA	33	297.2	75	0	1.000	7	4	28	10	.357	3	72	+5	+5	0	+6	+9	5	0	1	6	-
2006	LAA	56	478.1	136	3	.978	10	5	37	10	.270	5	126	-1	-5	+1	-1	-5	-3	5	2	4	12
2007	LAA	2	15.0	0	0	-	0	0	1	0	.000	0	0	0				0	0	0	0	0	-
2008	LAA	41	307.0	64	2	.969	3	5	20	7	.350	3	59	-2	-3	0	-1	-3	-2	1	1	0	-
2009	LAA	124	1032.1	243	2	.992	24	10	100	31	.310	6	231	+7	0	+3	+11	+14	8	3	5	16	1
2010	LAA	83	692.2	177	5	.972	12	24	81	35	.432	4	167	-12	-5	-7	-6	-18	-10	0	-2	-12	30
2011	2 tms	56	414.2	80	0	1.000	4	7	33	10	.303	2	77	-2	0	-4	+4	0	0	3	0	3	15
		439	3598.1	860	14	.984	60	58	341	120	.352	24	804	-2	-6	-9	+19	0	0	11	6	17	9

Trayvon Robinson

Year	Team	G	Inn	TC	E	Pct	GFP	DM	Opps to Advance	Extra Bases	Pct	Kills	Outs Made	Basic	Shallow	Medium	Deep	Enhanced	+/-	Throws	GFP/ DME	Total	Rank
2011	Sea	30	230.0	60	3	.950	10	7	31	16	.516	2	55	-1	-1	+1	-1	-1	0	-1	2	1	-

Cody Ross

Year	Team	G	Inn	TC	E	Pct	GFP	DM	Opps to Advance	Extra Bases	Pct	Kills	Outs Made	Basic	Shallow	Medium	Deep	Enhanced	+/-	Throws	GFP/ DME	Total	Rank
2006	3 tms	41	214.2	41	0	1.000	4	3	12	3	.250	0	41	0	+1	0	-3	-2	-2	0	0	-2	-
2007	Fla	8	47.0	18	1	.944	2	0	8	2	.250	0	16	+1	0	+1	0	+1	1	1	0	2	-
2008	Fla	17	45.0	11	0	1.000	4	0	8	1	.125	1	10	+1	+1	+1	0	+1	1	1	1	3	-
2010	2 tms	23	90.1	14	1	.929	3	2	6	2	.333	2	11	0	+1	-1	+1	+1	1	2	0	3	-
2011	SF	83	530.0	114	1	.991	8	10	54	18	.333	4	109	-4	+5	-8	-10	-13	-7	2	0	-5	29
		172	927.0	198	3	.985	21	15	88	26	.295	7	187	-2	+8	-7	-12	-12	-6	6	1	1	-

Aaron Rowand

Year	Team	G	Inn	TC	E	Pct	GFP	DM	Opps to Advance	Extra Bases	Pct	Kills	Outs Made	Basic	Shallow	Medium	Deep	Enhanced	+/-	Throws	GFP/ DME	Total	Rank
2003	CWS	24	25.1	6	0	1.000	-	-	3	2	.667	0	6	0	-1	0	0	-1	-1	0	-	-1	-
2011	SF	46	219.2	34	1	.971	7	5	19	6	.316	0	32	-1	0	0	-1	-2	-1	0	1	0	-
		70	245.0	40	1	.975	7	5	22	8	.364	0	38	-1	-1	0	-1	-3	-2	0	1	-1	-

Left Fielders

Jerry Sands

		BASIC							THROWING				PLUS/MINUS						RUNS SAVED				
Year	Team	G	Inn	TC	E	Pct	GFP	DM	Opps to Advance	Extra Bases	Pct	Kills	Outs Made	Basic	Shallow	Medium	Deep	Enhanced	+/-	Throws	GFP/DME	Total	Rank
2011	LAD	41	288.0	65	0	1.000	5	9	29	12	.414	3	61	-3	-2	-3	-1	-7	-4	1	1	-2	-

Luke Scott

		BASIC							THROWING				PLUS/MINUS						RUNS SAVED				
Year	Team	G	Inn	TC	E	Pct	GFP	DM	Opps to Advance	Extra Bases	Pct	Kills	Outs Made	Basic	Shallow	Medium	Deep	Enhanced	+/-	Throws	GFP/DME	Total	Rank
2005	Hou	21	151.1	25	1	.960	6	4	13	3	.231	2	22	+1	-2	+1	0	+2	1	1	0	2	-
2006	Hou	50	417.0	82	0	1.000	7	8	37	12	.324	1	81	+5	+3	+3	+2	+8	4	0	0	4	11
2007	Hou	5	18.0	4	0	1.000	0	0	1	0	.000	0	4	0	0	0		+1	1	0	0	1	-
2008	Bal	106	840.1	205	2	.990	9	10	105	37	.352	2	200	+3	0	+3	+7	+10	6	-2	-1	3	11
2009	Bal	26	199.0	53	0	1.000	5	4	31	12	.387	0	53	-2	0	0	-3	-3	-2	-1	1	-2	-
2010	Bal	14	103.0	22	0	1.000	0	0	10	3	.300	0	22	-1	0	-1	+1	0	0	0	0	0	-
2011	Bal	45	330.2	83	1	.988	5	4	36	14	.389	0	82	+1	-4	0	+7	+3	2	-2	3	3	-
		267	2059.1	474	4	.992	32	30	233	81	.348	5	464	+7	-3	+6	+14	+21	12	-4	3	11	11

Travis Snider

		BASIC							THROWING				PLUS/MINUS						RUNS SAVED				
Year	Team	G	Inn	TC	E	Pct	GFP	DM	Opps to Advance	Extra Bases	Pct	Kills	Outs Made	Basic	Shallow	Medium	Deep	Enhanced	+/-	Throws	GFP/DME	Total	Rank
2008	Tor	13	99.0	16	0	1.000	3	3	5	2	.400	2	14	-2	0	-1	-2	-3	-2	1	0	-1	-
2009	Tor	56	435.1	91	1	.989	8	8	47	16	.340	3	90	+1	+1	+1	-1	+1	1	2	-1	2	-
2010	Tor	53	433.2	93	3	.968	9	6	41	13	.317	1	87	+7	+3	0	+8	+11	6	-1	0	5	8
2011	Tor	44	367.0	83	3	.964	8	5	43	11	.256	2	77	-1	0	+2	-1	0	0	3	0	3	-
		166	1335.0	283	7	.975	28	22	136	42	.309	8	268	+5	+4	+2	+4	+9	5	5	-1	9	-

Alfonso Soriano

		BASIC							THROWING				PLUS/MINUS						RUNS SAVED				
Year	Team	G	Inn	TC	E	Pct	GFP	DM	Opps to Advance	Extra Bases	Pct	Kills	Outs Made	Basic	Shallow	Medium	Deep	Enhanced	+/-	Throws	GFP/DME	Total	Rank
2006	Was	158	1373.2	359	11	.969	26	25	154	59	.383	15	326	+6	-10	+3	+26	+19	11	7	0	18	1
2007	ChC	122	1064.0	269	6	.978	25	22	124	41	.331	19	245	-2	-4	+2	0	-2	-1	15	3	17	1
2008	ChC	108	937.1	201	5	.975	14	24	63	19	.302	8	186	-1	0	+1	-2	-1	-1	4	-1	2	14
2009	ChC	116	1004.1	219	11	.950	6	29	81	32	.395	5	202	-9	-4	-1	-9	-14	-8	1	-7	-14	34
2010	ChC	134	1111.1	217	7	.968	10	22	103	40	.388	3	201	-8	0	-1	-13	-15	-8	-4	-2	-14	32
2011	ChC	128	1007.0	202	7	.965	6	22	93	32	.344	5	187	-2	+3	-1	-13	-11	-6	1	-4	-9	32
		766	6497.2	1467	47	.968	87	144	618	223	.361	55	1347	-16	-15	+3	-11	-24	-13	24	-11	0	20

Ryan Sweeney

		BASIC							THROWING				PLUS/MINUS						RUNS SAVED				
Year	Team	G	Inn	TC	E	Pct	GFP	DM	Opps to Advance	Extra Bases	Pct	Kills	Outs Made	Basic	Shallow	Medium	Deep	Enhanced	+/-	Throws	GFP/DME	Total	Rank
2006	CWS	6	12.0	2	0	1.000		1	4	2	.500	0	2	0	0	0		0	0	0	0	0	-
2007	CWS	11	92.2	20	0	1.000	2	1	13	5	.385	1	19	-1	0	+1	-2	-1	-1	0	0	-1	-
2008	Oak	13	43.0	12	0	1.000	2	0	6	3	.500	0	12	0	0	0	-1	-1	-1	-1	0	-2	-
2009	Oak	7	44.0	10	0	1.000	1	0	4	1	.250	1	8	0	0	0	0	0	0	1	0	1	-
2011	Oak	41	219.0	42	0	1.000	3	1	6	3	.500	1	41	+7	+3	+4	+3	+9	5	0	0	5	-
		78	410.2	86	0	1.000	8	3	33	14	.424	3	82	+6	+3	+5	0	+7	3	0	0	3	-

Jose Tabata

		BASIC							THROWING				PLUS/MINUS						RUNS SAVED				
Year	Team	G	Inn	TC	E	Pct	GFP	DM	Opps to Advance	Extra Bases	Pct	Kills	Outs Made	Basic	Shallow	Medium	Deep	Enhanced	+/-	Throws	GFP/DME	Total	Rank
2010	Pit	93	771.1	195	1	.995	12	10	85	36	.424	3	189	+9	+4	-1	+9	+12	7	-3	1	5	7
2011	Pit	76	626.0	145	1	.993	8	11	69	25	.362	0	140	+6	0	+4	+7	+12	7	-3	-1	3	13
		169	1397.1	340	2	.994	20	21	154	61	.396	3	329	+15	+4	+3	+16	+24	14	-6	0	8	-

Eric Thames

		BASIC							THROWING				PLUS/MINUS						RUNS SAVED				
Year	Team	G	Inn	TC	E	Pct	GFP	DM	Opps to Advance	Extra Bases	Pct	Kills	Outs Made	Basic	Shallow	Medium	Deep	Enhanced	+/-	Throws	GFP/DME	Total	Rank
2011	Tor	52	456.1	93	1	.989	10	13	37	19	.514	1	91	-2	0	+1	-10	-9	-5	-2	-2	-9	31

Rene Tosoni

		BASIC							THROWING				PLUS/MINUS						RUNS SAVED				
Year	Team	G	Inn	TC	E	Pct	GFP	DM	Opps to Advance	Extra Bases	Pct	Kills	Outs Made	Basic	Shallow	Medium	Deep	Enhanced	+/-	Throws	GFP/DME	Total	Rank
2011	Min	38	321.0	92	3	.967	9	4	49	19	.388	3	85	-2	+1	-2	-7	-7	-4	0	0	-4	-

Left Fielders

Vernon Wells

		BASIC						THROWING					PLUS/MINUS					RUNS SAVED				
								Opps to	Extra				Outs								GFP/		
Year	Team	G	Inn	TC	E	Pct	GFP	DM	Advance	Bases	Pct	Kills	Made	Basic	Shallow	Medium	Deep	Enhanced	+/-	Throws	DME	Total	Rank
2011	LAA	111	930.2	248	3	.988	14	17	86	32	.372	2	241	-5	-4	-12	+11	-5	-3	-2	-3	-8	30

Josh Willingham

		BASIC						THROWING					PLUS/MINUS					RUNS SAVED				
								Opps to	Extra				Outs								GFP/		
Year	Team	G	Inn	TC	E	Pct	GFP	DM	Advance	Bases	Pct	Kills	Made	Basic	Shallow	Medium	Deep	Enhanced	+/-	Throws	DME	Total	Rank
2004	Fla	3	21.0	6	0	1.000	0	1	1	0	.000	0	6	-1	0	0	-1	-1	-1	0	0	-1	-
2005	Fla	1	1.0	0	0	-	0	0				0										0	-
2006	Fla	132	1069.2	218	7	.968	13	18	107	33	.308	3	206	-2	+1	-2	-5	-6	-3	2	-2	-3	27
2007	Fla	137	1176.1	223	3	.987	14	16	151	40	.265	5	211	-14	-7	+5	-16	-18	-10	4	-1	-7	26
2008	Fla	98	855.1	173	0	1.000	18	17	93	30	.323	7	166	+5	+3	+1	+4	+8	4	4	3	11	3
2009	Was	87	691.2	172	5	.971	13	15	67	28	.418	1	165	+1	+2	+2	-6	-2	-1	-1	-2	-4	23
2010	Was	108	880.1	172	1	.994	18	12	93	39	.419	5	164	0	+3	-2	-5	-4	-2	2	1	1	19
2011	Oak	96	829.1	164	2	.988	14	9	80	25	.313	3	159	-6	-1	-1	-4	-6	-3	0	3	0	21
		662	5524.2	1128	18	.984	90	88	592	195	.329	24	1077	-17	+1	+3	-33	-29	-16	11	2	-3	21

Delmon Young

		BASIC						THROWING					PLUS/MINUS					RUNS SAVED				
								Opps to	Extra				Outs								GFP/		
Year	Team	G	Inn	TC	E	Pct	GFP	DM	Advance	Bases	Pct	Kills	Made	Basic	Shallow	Medium	Deep	Enhanced	+/-	Throws	DME	Total	Rank
2008	Min	151	1324.0	301	8	.973	27	29	145	52	.359	7	282	-17	-11	+5	-20	-25	-14	1	-1	-14	35
2009	Min	98	806.2	184	5	.973	12	12	92	41	.446	2	175	-7	-6	-1	-2	-8	-4	-4	0	-8	28
2010	Min	149	1277.2	255	4	.984	22	27	139	53	.381	9	239	-16	-3	-8	-17	-28	-16	2	1	-13	31
2011	2 tms	115	994.1	228	7	.969	12	13	101	39	.386	4	214	-2	-6	0	+7	+1	1	-3	-1	-3	26
		513	4402.2	968	24	.975	73	81	477	185	.388	22	910	-42	-26	-4	-32	-60	-33	-4	-1	-38	32

Eric Young

		BASIC						THROWING					PLUS/MINUS					RUNS SAVED				
								Opps to	Extra				Outs								GFP/		
Year	Team	G	Inn	TC	E	Pct	GFP	DM	Advance	Bases	Pct	Kills	Made	Basic	Shallow	Medium	Deep	Enhanced	+/-	Throws	DME	Total	Rank
2010	Col	10	65.0	12	1	.917	3	5	7	4	.571	0	11	0	-1	0	0	0	0	-1	-1	-2	-
2011	Col	35	269.1	51	1	.980	4	5	34	15	.441	0	50	-1	0	+1	-2	-1	0	-3	-1	-4	-
		45	334.1	63	2	.968	7	10	41	19	.463	0	61	-1	-1	+1	-2	-1	0	-4	-2	-6	-

Center Fielders

Rick Ankiel

		BASIC							THROWING				PLUS/MINUS						RUNS SAVED				
Year	Team	G	Inn	TC	E	Pct	GFP	DM	Opps to Advance	Extra Bases	Pct	Kills	Outs Made	Basic	Shallow	Medium	Deep	Enhanced	+/-	Throws	GFP/DME	Total	Rank
2007	StL	22	137.0	27	0	1.000	2	4	9	5	.556	0	27	-1	-1	-2	+1	-1	-1	0		-1	
2008	StL	89	766.1	222	5	.977	20	21	76	33	.434	4	213	-10	-5	-5	-9	-19	-11	5	1	-5	25
2009	StL	66	458.2	139	4	.971	17	18	54	26	.481	1	134	+3	+3	+1	-1	+2	1	0	-1	0	18
2010	2 tms	70	534.1	150	4	.973	12	6	54	29	.537	4	141	-1	+4	-4	-2	-2	-1	1	-1	-1	18
2011	Was	105	785.1	243	1	.996	19	14	72	30	.417	7	234	0	+5	0	-7	-2	-1	8	1	8	8
		352	2681.2	781	14	.982	70	63	265	123	.464	16	749	-8	+6	-10	-18	-22	-13	14	0	1	19

Roger Bernadina

		BASIC							THROWING				PLUS/MINUS						RUNS SAVED				
Year	Team	G	Inn	TC	E	Pct	GFP	DM	Opps to Advance	Extra Bases	Pct	Kills	Outs Made	Basic	Shallow	Medium	Deep	Enhanced	+/-	Throws	GFP/DME	Total	Rank
2008	Was	14	108.0	28	1	.964	3	3	15	10	.667	0	27	+1	+1	+1	0	+1	1	-1	0	0	-
2009	Was	1	7.2	3	0	1.000	1	0	0	0	-	0	3	0	0	0	-1	0	0	0	0	0	-
2010	Was	26	177.2	48	1	.979	5	2	27	15	.556	2	45	-5	-2	-2	-2	-6	-3	0	0	-3	-
2011	Was	56	420.2	107	0	1.000	10	11	42	22	.524	3	103	-8	-4	+1	-9	-12	-7	2	3	-2	-
		97	714.0	186	2	.989	19	16	84	47	.560	5	178	-12	-5	0	-12	-17	-9	1	3	-5	

Julio Borbon

		BASIC							THROWING				PLUS/MINUS						RUNS SAVED				
Year	Team	G	Inn	TC	E	Pct	GFP	DM	Opps to Advance	Extra Bases	Pct	Kills	Outs Made	Basic	Shallow	Medium	Deep	Enhanced	+/-	Throws	GFP/DME	Total	Rank
2009	Tex	4	26.0	7	0	1.000	0	0	4	2	.500	0	7	+1	+1	0	0	0	0	0	0	0	-
2010	Tex	133	1095.2	341	4	.988	19	18	95	52	.547	2	335	+11	-4	+16	+14	+25	14	-3	0	11	7
2011	Tex	32	243.1	72	1	.986	6	9	24	9	.375	1	70	-3	+1	-3	-5	-7	-4	1	0	-3	-
		169	1365.0	420	5	.988	25	27	123	63	.512	3	412	+9	-2	+13	+9	+18	10	-2	0	8	

Jason Bourgeois

		BASIC							THROWING				PLUS/MINUS						RUNS SAVED				
Year	Team	G	Inn	TC	E	Pct	GFP	DM	Opps to Advance	Extra Bases	Pct	Kills	Outs Made	Basic	Shallow	Medium	Deep	Enhanced	+/-	Throws	GFP/DME	Total	Rank
2010	Hou	24	162.0	50	0	1.000	4	3	16	11	.688	0	50	+2	+3	+2	-4	0	0	-2	0	-2	-
2011	Hou	34	244.0	63	0	1.000	0	3	21	14	.667	0	63	+2	+2	-1	0	+1	0	-2	0	-2	-
		58	406.0	113	0	1.000	4	6	37	25	.676	0	113	+4	+5	+1	-4	+1	0	-4	0	-4	

Peter Bourjos

		BASIC							THROWING				PLUS/MINUS						RUNS SAVED				
Year	Team	G	Inn	TC	E	Pct	GFP	DM	Opps to Advance	Extra Bases	Pct	Kills	Outs Made	Basic	Shallow	Medium	Deep	Enhanced	+/-	Throws	GFP/DME	Total	Rank
2010	LAA	51	449.2	160	1	.994	22	7	41	20	.488	4	149	+8	+7	-1	+3	+8	5	3	5	13	-
2011	LAA	147	1269.1	361	4	.989	29	19	98	45	.459	4	351	+3	+4	+4	+2	+10	6	3	3	12	5
		198	1719.0	521	5	.990	51	26	139	65	.468	8	500	+11	+11	+3	+5	+18	11	6	8	25	

Michael Bourn

		BASIC							THROWING				PLUS/MINUS						RUNS SAVED				
Year	Team	G	Inn	TC	E	Pct	GFP	DM	Opps to Advance	Extra Bases	Pct	Kills	Outs Made	Basic	Shallow	Medium	Deep	Enhanced	+/-	Throws	GFP/DME	Total	Rank
2007	Phi	12	56.2	16	0	1.000	1	2	7	4	.571	0	16	+3	+2	0	+4	+6	3	0	0	3	-
2008	Hou	130	1009.0	305	5	.984	24	19	100	59	.590	4	291	-1	-9	+10	+4	+3	2	-2	1	1	15
2009	Hou	154	1326.0	385	3	.992	29	23	147	82	.558	7	371	+10	+7	-2	+7	+12	7	3	1	11	5
2010	Hou	138	1189.1	370	3	.992	34	11	105	55	.524	5	359	+26	+11	+3	+34	+49	27	2	1	30	1
2011	2 tms	156	1359.0	376	3	.992	16	23	131	75	.573	2	367	-4	-15	-3	+22	+5	2	-3	-2	-3	20
		590	4940.0	1452	14	.990	104	78	490	275	.561	18	1404	+34	-4	+8	+71	+75	41	0	1	42	3

Michael Brantley

		BASIC							THROWING				PLUS/MINUS						RUNS SAVED				
Year	Team	G	Inn	TC	E	Pct	GFP	DM	Opps to Advance	Extra Bases	Pct	Kills	Outs Made	Basic	Shallow	Medium	Deep	Enhanced	+/-	Throws	GFP/DME	Total	Rank
2009	Cle	20	166.0	47	1	.979	1	4	22	14	.636	0	46	-1	-1	-1	0	-3	-2	-1	-1	-4	-
2010	Cle	65	562.2	158	2	.987	9	8	55	34	.618	0	156	-11	+1	-1	-22	-22	-12	-3	1	-14	32
2011	Cle	52	412.2	119	1	.992	3	7	40	23	.575	0	118	+2	+2	+2	-4	-1	0	-1	-1	-2	-
		137	1141.1	324	4	.988	13	19	117	71	.607	0	320	-10	+2	0	-26	-26	-14	-5	-1	-20	

Center Fielders

Marlon Byrd

	BASIC							THROWING				PLUS/MINUS						RUNS SAVED				
Year Team	G	Inn	TC	E	Pct	GFP	DM	Opps to Advance	Extra Bases	Pct	Kills	Outs Made	Basic	Shallow	Medium	Deep	Enhanced	+/-	Throws	GFP/DME	Total	Rank
2003 Phi	131	1100.1	305	5	.984	-	-	99	53	.535	3	288	+1	+2	-2	0	0	0	1	-	1	17
2004 Phi	92	753.1	201	2	.990	13	18	62	37	.597	1	181	-7	+1	+4	-29	-19	-11	-2	-2	-15	34
2005 2 tms	16	95.0	20	0	1.000	0	2	3	1	.333	0	20	-1	-1	0	-3	-1	-1	1	0	0	-
2006 Was	57	393.1	127	1	.992	8	7	58	29	.500	1	125	+3	-3	+3	+7	+8	4	1	4	9	-
2007 Tex	63	496.1	120	2	.983	6	7	44	29	.659	2	114	-3	-3	-2	+2	-3	-2	1	-1	-2	24
2008 Tex	57	433.0	156	3	.981	9	9	48	24	.500	3	149	0	-2	-1	+4	+1	1	2	1	4	-
2009 Tex	104	889.0	250	3	.988	20	14	82	51	.622	3	242	-4	+7	-1	-18	-12	-7	-3	0	-10	31
2010 ChC	151	1261.2	380	3	.992	39	13	135	67	.496	5	369	0	+1	-4	-1	-4	-2	5	1	4	12
2011 ChC	118	998.0	284	3	.989	18	12	93	56	.602	4	273	-4	-7	+4	-4	-8	-4	2	2	0	17
	789	6420.0	1843	22	.988	113	82	624	347	.556	22	1761	-15	-5	+1	-42	-38	-22	8	5	-9	26

Melky Cabrera

	BASIC							THROWING				PLUS/MINUS						RUNS SAVED				
Year Team	G	Inn	TC	E	Pct	GFP	DM	Opps to Advance	Extra Bases	Pct	Kills	Outs Made	Basic	Shallow	Medium	Deep	Enhanced	+/-	Throws	GFP/DME	Total	Rank
2005 NYY	6	49.0	9	0	1.000	0	5	8	5	.625	0	9	-3	+1	-4	-4	-7	-4	0	0	-4	-
2006 NYY	4	23.0	8	0	1.000	1	1	3	2	.667	0	8	-2	-1	0	-3	-4	-2	0	0	-2	-
2007 NYY	131	1072.2	364	4	.989	23	30	132	72	.545	13	347	-10	-2	-7	-12	-21	-12	7	1	-4	31
2008 NYY	117	973.2	283	4	.986	22	13	88	46	.523	4	272	+1	-2	+7	-2	+3	2	1	1	4	12
2009 NYY	103	806.1	228	0	1.000	7	18	66	37	.561	2	226	-7	-4	-9	+4	-9	-5	-1	-1	-7	29
2010 Atl	55	385.0	102	3	.971	9	8	50	26	.520	3	95	-2	+2	0	-6	-4	-2	1	1	0	-
2011 KC	144	1265.2	332	3	.991	26	27	139	90	.647	8	316	-10	-4	0	-9	-13	-7	-1	2	-6	27
	560	4575.1	1326	14	.989	88	102	486	278	.572	30	1273	-33	-10	-13	-32	-55	-30	7	4	-19	31

Mike Cameron

	BASIC							THROWING				PLUS/MINUS						RUNS SAVED				
Year Team	G	Inn	TC	E	Pct	GFP	DM	Opps to Advance	Extra Bases	Pct	Kills	Outs Made	Basic	Shallow	Medium	Deep	Enhanced	+/-	Throws	GFP/DME	Total	Rank
2003 Sea	147	1284.0	492	4	.992	-	-	119	73	.613	2	475	+13	+5	+1	+17	+23	13	-2	-	11	3
2004 NYM	135	1184.0	369	8	.978	18	30	135	68	.504	0	349	0	+7	+3	-13	-8	-4	0	-4	-8	28
2005 NYM	10	79.0	16	0	1.000	0	1	7	5	.714	0	15	0	-1	0	0	+1	1	-1	0	0	-
2006 SD	141	1244.0	379	6	.984	20	31	106	68	.642	3	367	+5	-4	+7	+5	+9	5	-3	-2	0	19
2007 SD	150	1329.0	377	5	.987	24	16	144	83	.576	4	365	-2	-7	+1	+7	+2	1	-1	3	3	12
2008 Mil	119	1057.0	297	1	.997	26	21	86	42	.488	2	293	+7	+1	+5	+7	+12	7	-2	-1	4	11
2009 Mil	147	1267.2	412	4	.990	15	31	134	78	.582	1	404	+8	-1	+17	+3	+18	10	-5	-4	1	17
2010 Bos	46	392.0	116	2	.983	12	8	34	18	.529	1	111	-7	-1	-1	-10	-12	-7	1	0	-6	-
2011 2 tms	42	350.0	97	0	1.000	8	13	34	24	.706	2	94	+5	+6	+3	-4	+5	3	-1	-1	1	-
	937	8186.2	2555	30	.988	123	151	799	459	.574	15	2473	+29	+5	+36	+12	+50	29	-14	-9	6	14

Tony Campana

	BASIC							THROWING				PLUS/MINUS						RUNS SAVED				
Year Team	G	Inn	TC	E	Pct	GFP	DM	Opps to Advance	Extra Bases	Pct	Kills	Outs Made	Basic	Shallow	Medium	Deep	Enhanced	+/-	Throws	GFP/DME	Total	Rank
2011 ChC	29	208.2	54	0	1.000	5	8	18	10	.556	0	54	+3	+2	-2	+2	+2	1	0	-1	0	-

Ezequiel Carrera

	BASIC							THROWING				PLUS/MINUS						RUNS SAVED				
Year Team	G	Inn	TC	E	Pct	GFP	DM	Opps to Advance	Extra Bases	Pct	Kills	Outs Made	Basic	Shallow	Medium	Deep	Enhanced	+/-	Throws	GFP/DME	Total	Rank
2011 Cle	55	426.0	117	3	.974	8	14	45	26	.578	1	112	-1	-1	0	+7	+6	3	0	-2	1	14

Endy Chavez

	BASIC							THROWING				PLUS/MINUS						RUNS SAVED				
Year Team	G	Inn	TC	E	Pct	GFP	DM	Opps to Advance	Extra Bases	Pct	Kills	Outs Made	Basic	Shallow	Medium	Deep	Enhanced	+/-	Throws	GFP/DME	Total	Rank
2003 Mon	135	1033.1	291	3	.990	-	-	85	34	.400	6	214	-4	0	+2	-13	-12	-7	8	-	1	21
2004 Mon	127	1081.2	315	5	.984	16	13	96	54	.563	6	258	+12	+6	+1	-1	+15	8	3	1	12	3
2005 2 tms	34	137.0	36	1	.972	4	0	8	3	.375	1	32	+1	+2	-1	+1	-1	-1	2	0	1	-
2006 NYM	39	264.1	85	0	1.000	2	2	15	8	.533	1	83	+5	+4	+1	+1	+6	3	1	0	4	-
2007 NYM	10	58.0	24	0	1.000	0	0	3	3	1.000	0	24	+3	+1	+1	+3	+5	3	-1	0	2	-
2008 NYM	10	38.1	10	0	1.000	1	0	7	5	.714	0	9	0	0	0	+1	+1	1	-1	0	0	-
2009 Sea	8	67.0	18	0	1.000	1	3	11	6	.545	0	17	0	0	+1	0	+1	1	0	0	1	-
2011 Tex	66	514.1	130	1	.992	11	3	33	17	.515	1	126	0	-2	+4	+1	+2	1	-1	0	0	16
	429	3194.0	909	10	.989	35	21	258	130	.504	15	763	+17	+11	+9	-7	+17	9	11	1	21	10

Chris Coghlan

	BASIC							THROWING				PLUS/MINUS						RUNS SAVED				
Year Team	G	Inn	TC	E	Pct	GFP	DM	Opps to Advance	Extra Bases	Pct	Kills	Outs Made	Basic	Shallow	Medium	Deep	Enhanced	+/-	Throws	GFP/DME	Total	Rank
2011 Fla	65	568.1	160	0	1.000	9	11	44	30	.682	2	157	-10	0	-2	-20	-22	-12	-1	0	-13	35

Center Fielders

Coco Crisp

	BASIC							THROWING				PLUS/MINUS						RUNS SAVED				
Year Team	G	Inn	TC	E	Pct	GFP	DM	Opps to Advance	Extra Bases	Pct	Kills	Outs Made	Basic	Shallow	Medium	Deep	Enhanced	+/-	Throws	GFP/ DME	Total	Rank
2003 Cle	53	462.0	126	0	1.000	-	-	34	18	.529	1	112	+1	0	0	+3	+3	2	-1	-	1	16
2004 Cle	94	807.1	212	4	.981	13	19	85	48	.565	1	199	+2	-2	0	+8	+3	2	-2	-1	-1	19
2005 Cle	10	79.2	22	1	.955	0	2	5	3	.600	0	21	-1	-1	0	-2	-3	-2	0	-1	-3	-
2006 Bos	103	900.2	250	1	.996	18	18	98	55	.561	1	246	-5	+1	-2	-5	-7	-4	-2	0	-6	29
2007 Bos	144	1216.1	416	1	.998	26	17	108	55	.509	4	408	+18	+9	+1	+16	+26	15	-1	1	15	2
2008 Bos	114	886.0	240	2	.992	9	14	74	44	.595	1	234	-2	-4	+1	+1	-2	-1	-4	0	-5	23
2009 KC	49	412.0	123	3	.976	6	6	45	26	.578	0	120	+7	+2	+1	+10	+13	7	-2	0	5	-
2010 Oak	73	625.0	186	2	.989	19	5	46	28	.609	1	182	+3	-4	+2	+11	+9	5	-1	3	7	8
2011 Oak	133	1134.1	324	1	.997	26	16	96	62	.646	1	321	-4	-4	-2	+10	+4	2	-3	2	1	15
	773	6523.1	1899	15	.992	117	97	591	339	.574	9	1843	+19	-3	+1	+52	+46	26	-16	4	14	13

Rajai Davis

	BASIC							THROWING				PLUS/MINUS						RUNS SAVED				
Year Team	G	Inn	TC	E	Pct	GFP	DM	Opps to Advance	Extra Bases	Pct	Kills	Outs Made	Basic	Shallow	Medium	Deep	Enhanced	+/-	Throws	GFP/ DME	Total	Rank
2007 2 tms	58	379.1	127	0	1.000	13	10	44	23	.523	2	124	-1	+2	+10	-15	-4	-2	2	-1	-1	-
2008 2 tms	88	487.2	158	1	.994	12	8	61	29	.475	2	153	+5	+3	0	+5	+7	4	1	1	6	-
2009 Oak	113	856.1	271	4	.985	23	18	80	43	.538	6	260	+3	0	+3	+3	+5	3	3	0	6	10
2010 Oak	83	677.1	194	2	.990	7	11	55	37	.673	1	190	-3	-1	+4	-4	0	0	-3	-2	-5	23
2011 Tor	79	652.0	178	2	.989	11	9	53	33	.623	0	174	-7	-9	+4	-6	-11	-6	-4	1	-9	33
	421	3052.2	928	9	.990	66	56	293	165	.563	11	901	-3	-5	+21	-17	-3	-1	-1	-1	-3	23

Jacoby Ellsbury

	BASIC							THROWING				PLUS/MINUS						RUNS SAVED				
Year Team	G	Inn	TC	E	Pct	GFP	DM	Opps to Advance	Extra Bases	Pct	Kills	Outs Made	Basic	Shallow	Medium	Deep	Enhanced	+/-	Throws	GFP/ DME	Total	Rank
2007 Bos	16	107.0	38	0	1.000	2	3	9	4	.444	0	38	-1	0	0	-1	-2	-1	0		-2	-
2008 Bos	66	546.2	174	0	1.000	19	9	62	34	.548	1	171	+4	-2	+7	+3	+8	4	-2	1	3	13
2009 Bos	153	1302.2	364	2	.995	20	28	129	75	.581	1	357	-5	-5	-1	+6	+1	1	-4	-2	-5	25
2010 Bos	13	104.2	33	0	1.000	4	1	9	6	.667	0	33	+2	+1	0	+4	+5	3	-1	0	2	-
2011 Bos	154	1358.1	394	0	1.000	19	25	125	78	.624	3	388	+12	+3	+3	+11	+17	9	-2	0	7	9
	402	3419.1	1003	2	.998	64	66	334	197	.590	5	987	+12	-3	+9	+23	+29	16	-9	-2	5	16

Dexter Fowler

	BASIC							THROWING				PLUS/MINUS						RUNS SAVED				
Year Team	G	Inn	TC	E	Pct	GFP	DM	Opps to Advance	Extra Bases	Pct	Kills	Outs Made	Basic	Shallow	Medium	Deep	Enhanced	+/-	Throws	GFP/ DME	Total	Rank
2008 Col	9	49.2	13	0	1.000	2	1	4	4	1.000	1	12	+1	0	0	+2	+2	1	0	0	1	-
2009 Col	127	977.2	256	4	.984	13	26	117	69	.590	5	248	-5	0	-8	-2	-10	-6	0	-3	-11	34
2010 Col	120	948.1	242	1	.996	22	6	105	63	.600	1	239	-3	-6	-3	+11	+3	2	-4	4	2	14
2011 Col	122	1072.2	323	8	.975	13	22	83	55	.663	3	309	0	-12	-4	+23	+6	3	-2	-4	-3	19
	378	3048.1	834	13	.984	49	55	309	191	.618	10	808	-7	-18	-15	+34	+1	0	-8	-3	-11	28

Craig Gentry

	BASIC							THROWING				PLUS/MINUS						RUNS SAVED				
Year Team	G	Inn	TC	E	Pct	GFP	DM	Opps to Advance	Extra Bases	Pct	Kills	Outs Made	Basic	Shallow	Medium	Deep	Enhanced	+/-	Throws	GFP/ DME	Total	Rank
2009 Tex	7	33.0	9	0	1.000	1	2	5	3	.600	1	8	+1	0	+2	-1	+1	1	0	0	1	-
2010 Tex	7	44.0	9	0	1.000	0	0	3	1	.333	0	9	0	+1	0	0	+1	1	0	0	1	-
2011 Tex	55	313.2	104	1	.990	6	2	33	18	.545	0	103	+9	+3	+4	+9	+16	9	-1	0	8	-
	69	390.2	122	1	.992	7	4	41	22	.537	1	120	+10	+4	+6	+8	+18	11	-1	0	10	-

Carlos Gomez

	BASIC							THROWING				PLUS/MINUS						RUNS SAVED				
Year Team	G	Inn	TC	E	Pct	GFP	DM	Opps to Advance	Extra Bases	Pct	Kills	Outs Made	Basic	Shallow	Medium	Deep	Enhanced	+/-	Throws	GFP/ DME	Total	Rank
2007 NYM	4	12.0	4	0	1.000	-	-	0	0	-	0	4	+1	0	0	+3	+3	2	0	0	2	-
2008 Min	151	1271.2	453	8	.982	34	32	135	73	.541	4	437	+14	-2	+8	+24	+29	16	-2	-2	12	2
2009 Min	132	848.2	301	1	.997	16	14	86	52	.605	2	298	+6	0	+3	+7	+10	6	-3	2	5	11
2010 Mil	75	594.2	159	5	.969	13	9	70	33	.471	2	152	+3	-2	+10	+1	+10	5	1	-1	5	10
2011 Mil	87	569.0	188	0	1.000	22	16	49	19	.388	3	184	+13	+9	+3	+4	+17	9	3	3	15	4
	449	3296.0	1105	14	.987	86	71	340	177	.521	11	1075	+37	+5	+24	+39	+69	38	-1	2	39	5

Carlos Gonzalez

	BASIC							THROWING				PLUS/MINUS						RUNS SAVED				
Year Team	G	Inn	TC	E	Pct	GFP	DM	Opps to Advance	Extra Bases	Pct	Kills	Outs Made	Basic	Shallow	Medium	Deep	Enhanced	+/-	Throws	GFP/ DME	Total	Rank
2008	69	528.2	183	2	.989	11	12	50	26	.520	4	176	+4	+1	+1	+4	+6	3	3	0	6	9
2009 Col	43	309.2	87	2	.977	9	3	24	12	.500	2	83	+1	+1	-3	+2	0	0	1	1	2	-
2010 Col	58	452.2	127	0	1.000	12	9	39	23	.590	1	126	0	-3	-4	+8	0	0	-1	0	-1	-
2011 Col	30	248.1	66	0	1.000	8	7	32	16	.500	3	63	0	0	+2	-2	-1	0	2	0	2	-
	200	1539.1	463	4	.991	40	31	145	77	.531	10	448	+5	-1	-4	+12	+5	3	5	1	9	-

Center Fielders

Curtis Granderson

		BASIC							THROWING				PLUS/MINUS						RUNS SAVED				
Year	Team	G	Inn	TC	E	Pct	GFP	DM	Opps to Advance	Extra Bases	Pct	Kills	Outs Made	Basic	Shallow	Medium	Deep	Enhanced	+/-	Throws	GFP/ DME	Total	Rank
2004	Det	8	61.0	17	0	1.000	1	0	7	5	.714	1	16	-1	0	0	-1	-2	-1	0	0	-1	-
2005	Det	41	320.0	121	0	1.000	5	6	34	17	.500	1	119	+7	+2	+4	+9	+12	7	1	4	12	-
2006	Det	157	1312.0	389	1	.997	16	13	120	64	.533	0	385	+8	+6	+3	+4	+12	7	-3	-1	3	11
2007	Det	157	1285.0	439	5	.989	26	25	154	82	.532	8	424	+11	+2	+6	+12	+20	11	1	2	14	3
2008	Det	140	1188.0	375	4	.989	22	14	123	67	.545	3	366	-8	-6	0	-6	-11	-6	-4	0	-10	28
2009	Det	160	1384.0	407	3	.993	18	20	123	61	.496	3	400	+6	-2	-2	+19	+14	8	1	2	11	4
2010	NYY	134	1120.1	323	2	.994	20	17	96	51	.531	4	315	+6	-5	+8	+16	+18	10	2	0	12	6
2011	NYY	155	1348.0	368	3	.992	30	19	122	60	.492	5	355	-5	+9	-18	-10	-19	-11	2	3	-6	28
		952	8018.1	2439	18	.993	138	114	779	407	.522	25	2380	+24	+6	+1	+43	+44	25	0	10	35	8

Franklin Gutierrez

		BASIC							THROWING				PLUS/MINUS						RUNS SAVED				
Year	Team	G	Inn	TC	E	Pct	GFP	DM	Opps to Advance	Extra Bases	Pct	Kills	Outs Made	Basic	Shallow	Medium	Deep	Enhanced	+/-	Throws	GFP/ DME	Total	Rank
2005	Cle	2	3.0	1	0	1.000	0	0	0	0		0	1	0				0	0	0	0	0	-
2006	Cle	7	27.0	14	0	1.000	1	2	1	0	.000	0	14	+2	0	+1	+4	+5	3	0	0	3	-
2007	Cle	8	32.0	11	0	1.000	1	0	2	1	.500	0	11	0		-1	+3	+1	1	0	0	1	-
2008	Cle	12	97.0	32	1	.969	2	1	8	3	.375	1	30	-2	-2	-1	0	-3	-2	1	1	0	-
2009	Sea	153	1353.1	458	7	.985	30	14	108	53	.491	0	446	+22	-1	+13	+34	+46	26	2	4	32	1
2010	Sea	146	1277.1	415	0	1.000	28	24	108	57	.528	0	413	-3	-5	-4	+7	-1	-1	-3	4	0	16
2011	Sea	92	763.0	244	0	1.000	20	6	69	44	.638	5	237	0	-9	+9	+8	+9	5	1	4	10	6
		420	3552.2	1175	8	.993	82	47	296	158	.534	11	1152	+19	-17	+17	+56	+57	32	1	13	46	2

Josh Hamilton

		BASIC							THROWING				PLUS/MINUS						RUNS SAVED				
Year	Team	G	Inn	TC	E	Pct	GFP	DM	Opps to Advance	Extra Bases	Pct	Kills	Outs Made	Basic	Shallow	Medium	Deep	Enhanced	+/-	Throws	GFP/ DME	Total	Rank
2007	Cin	71	555.2	178	4	.978	12	7	50	28	.560	4	168	+1	+1	+1	-4	-2	-1	1	1	1	19
2008	Tex	111	912.0	276	5	.982	21	19	112	67	.598	1	268	-5	+5	-10	-8	-13	-7	-2	-1	-10	30
2009	Tex	56	472.2	134	0	1.000	12	7	44	22	.500	2	132	-1	0	-1	0	-1	-1	1	0	0	19
2010	Tex	40	262.0	77	0	1.000	7	3	27	10	.370	2	74	+2	+3	+2	0	+4	2	2	0	4	-
2011	Tex	35	259.0	73	1	.986	6	4	19	9	.474	0	71	0	+2	+3	-9	-3	-2	0	0	-2	-
		313	2461.1	738	10	.986	58	40	252	136	.540	9	713	-3	+11	-5	-21	-15	-9	2	0	-7	-

Austin Jackson

		BASIC							THROWING				PLUS/MINUS						RUNS SAVED				
Year	Team	G	Inn	TC	E	Pct	GFP	DM	Opps to Advance	Extra Bases	Pct	Kills	Outs Made	Basic	Shallow	Medium	Deep	Enhanced	+/-	Throws	GFP/ DME	Total	Rank
2010	Det	149	1256.1	398	6	.985	29	22	123	68	.553	5	385	+18	+9	-3	+24	+30	17	-1	-3	13	4
2011	Det	152	1264.0	390	3	.992	20	14	104	56	.538	5	379	+20	+1	+12	+27	+40	23	2	4	29	1
		301	2520.1	788	9	.989	49	36	227	124	.546	10	764	+38	+10	+9	+51	+70	40	1	1	42	-

Jon Jay

		BASIC							THROWING				PLUS/MINUS						RUNS SAVED				
Year	Team	G	Inn	TC	E	Pct	GFP	DM	Opps to Advance	Extra Bases	Pct	Kills	Outs Made	Basic	Shallow	Medium	Deep	Enhanced	+/-	Throws	GFP/ DME	Total	Rank
2010	StL	27	195.0	65	0	1.000	4	7	18	9	.500	2	63	-2	+3	-1	-10	-8	-4	1	0	-3	-
2011	StL	75	570.0	174	3	.983	19	8	41	25	.610	3	167	+8	+7	+2	-1	+8	4	0	0	4	11
		102	765.0	239	3	.987	23	15	59	34	.576	5	230	+6	+10	+1	-11	0	0	1	0	1	-

Adam Jones

		BASIC							THROWING				PLUS/MINUS						RUNS SAVED				
Year	Team	G	Inn	TC	E	Pct	GFP	DM	Opps to Advance	Extra Bases	Pct	Kills	Outs Made	Basic	Shallow	Medium	Deep	Enhanced	+/-	Throws	GFP/ DME	Total	Rank
2006	Sea	26	193.0	75	3	.960	3	3	20	10	.500	3	67	-1	-2	0	+1	0	0	3	0	3	-
2007	Sea	7	34.0	11	1	.909	0	0	0	0		0	10	+2	0	0	+3	+3	2	0	0	2	-
2008	Bal	129	1102.0	343	3	.991	18	20	115	49	.426	4	337	+5	+5	+7	-5	+7	4	5	-3	6	8
2009	Bal	118	1005.0	363	5	.986	26	28	105	40	.381	5	349	-13	+4	-4	-25	-25	-14	10	6	2	16
2010	Bal	149	1298.1	441	7	.984	23	28	113	60	.531	10	422	-9	-1	-16	-5	-22	-12	5	-1	-8	30
2011	Bal	148	1281.0	403	8	.980	24	27	141	78	.553	13	380	-7	+4	-6	-19	-21	-12	8	0	-4	24
		577	4913.1	1636	27	.983	94	106	494	237	.480	35	1565	-23	+10	-19	-50	-58	-32	31	2	1	20

Matt Kemp

		BASIC							THROWING				PLUS/MINUS						RUNS SAVED				
Year	Team	G	Inn	TC	E	Pct	GFP	DM	Opps to Advance	Extra Bases	Pct	Kills	Outs Made	Basic	Shallow	Medium	Deep	Enhanced	+/-	Throws	GFP/ DME	Total	Rank
2006	LAD	29	189.2	40	3	.925	3	9	21	13	.619	0	37	-2	-1	-3	-1	-4	-2	0	-1	-3	-
2007	LAD	6	17.1	8	0	1.000	2	0	1	0	.000	0	8	0	0	0	+1	+1	1	0	2	3	-
2008	LAD	101	825.2	220	1	.995	22	13	76	40	.526	8	209	0	+7	-3	-6	-2	-1	5	1	5	10
2009	LAD	158	1355.1	383	2	.995	48	33	114	55	.482	8	367	-10	-2	-7	-13	-22	-12	7	1	-4	24
2010	LAD	158	1346.0	338	5	.985	26	28	120	70	.583	3	330	-28	-3	-23	-27	-53	-30	-4	-3	-37	35
2011	LAD	159	1380.0	361	5	.986	28	23	109	59	.541	8	346	-14	-9	+2	-13	-20	-11	4	2	-5	25
		611	5114.0	1350	16	.988	129	106	441	237	.537	27	1297	-54	-8	-34	-59	-100	-55	12	2	-41	34

Center Fielders

John Mayberry

	BASIC							THROWING				PLUS/MINUS						RUNS SAVED				
Year Team	G	Inn	TC	E	Pct	GFP	DM	Opps to Advance	Extra Bases	Pct	Kills	Outs Made	Basic	Shallow	Medium	Deep	Enhanced	+/-	Throws	GFP/DME	Total	Rank
2010 Phi	2	7.0	2	0	1.000	0	0	1	1	1.000	0	2	0	0	0	0	0	0	0	0	0	-
2011 Phi	32	246.2	64	2	.969	2	7	18	9	.500	0	62	-3	-2	-2	+2	-2	-1	-1	-2	-4	-
	34	253.2	66	2	.970	2	7	19	10	.526	0	64	-3	-2	-2	+2	-2	-1	-1	-2	-4	-

Cameron Maybin

	BASIC							THROWING				PLUS/MINUS						RUNS SAVED				
Year Team	G	Inn	TC	E	Pct	GFP	DM	Opps to Advance	Extra Bases	Pct	Kills	Outs Made	Basic	Shallow	Medium	Deep	Enhanced	+/-	Throws	GFP/DME	Total	Rank
2007 Det	5	25.0	10	0	1.000	2	2	3	2	.667	0	10	0	0	0	+1	+1	1	0	0	1	-
2008 Fla	8	63.0	23	0	1.000	1	1	3	2	.667	0	23	+1	0	+1	0	+2	1	0	0	1	-
2009 Fla	52	416.0	126	1	.992	7	13	43	28	.651	1	124	-1	-3	+2	-2	-3	-2	-3	-1	-6	-
2010 Fla	77	634.1	223	4	.982	20	13	62	38	.613	2	214	+7	+1	+4	+8	+13	7	-1	0	6	9
2011 SD	136	1173.0	349	5	.986	27	21	108	62	.574	3	342	+18	+15	+3	+14	+32	18	-2	-1	15	3
	278	2311.1	731	10	.986	57	50	219	132	.603	6	713	+25	+13	+10	+21	+45	25	-6	-2	17	-

Andrew McCutchen

	BASIC							THROWING				PLUS/MINUS						RUNS SAVED				
Year Team	G	Inn	TC	E	Pct	GFP	DM	Opps to Advance	Extra Bases	Pct	Kills	Outs Made	Basic	Shallow	Medium	Deep	Enhanced	+/-	Throws	GFP/DME	Total	Rank
2009 Pit	108	952.2	275	2	.993	18	21	91	49	.538	1	263	-2	+11	-10	-21	-20	-11	1	0	-10	32
2010 Pit	152	1290.1	386	5	.987	36	27	133	84	.632	8	373	-6	+8	-6	-20	-18	-10	1	1	-8	29
2011 Pit	155	1353.2	430	7	.984	28	22	132	73	.553	3	414	+3	-5	0	+20	+14	8	-3	0	5	10
	415	3596.2	1091	14	.987	82	70	356	206	.579	13	1050	-5	+14	-16	-21	-24	-13	-1	1	-13	30

Nate McLouth

	BASIC							THROWING				PLUS/MINUS						RUNS SAVED				
Year Team	G	Inn	TC	E	Pct	GFP	DM	Opps to Advance	Extra Bases	Pct	Kills	Outs Made	Basic	Shallow	Medium	Deep	Enhanced	+/-	Throws	GFP/DME	Total	Rank
2005 Pit	21	166.0	36	0	1.000	2	0	14	8	.571	0	36	0	+1	+1	-2	-2	-1	0	0	-1	-
2006 Pit	42	345.0	86	1	.988	7	7	45	24	.533	1	84	0	-1	+3	-2	0	0	0	-1	-1	-
2007 Pit	66	495.1	146	2	.986	11	9	69	39	.565	2	142	-6	-4	+1	-7	-9	-5	-2	-1	-8	32
2008 Pit	149	1300.1	386	1	.997	31	24	144	74	.514	5	380	-20	-5	+4	-34	-37	-21	-1	-1	-23	35
2009 2 tms	129	1120.1	323	1	.997	27	15	117	70	.598	5	314	+4	+1	+6	-2	+6	3	0	2	5	12
2010 Atl	71	561.0	140	2	.986	8	13	44	28	.636	0	137	-13	-3	-7	-21	-30	-17	-2	-2	-21	34
2011 Atl	55	498.0	131	2	.985	13	13	37	21	.568	0	129	-2	-1	-2	-3	-6	-3	-2	-2	-7	29
	533	4486.0	1248	9	.993	99	81	470	264	.562	10	1222	-37	-12	+6	-71	-78	-44	-7	-5	-56	35

Nyjer Morgan

	BASIC							THROWING				PLUS/MINUS						RUNS SAVED				
Year Team	G	Inn	TC	E	Pct	GFP	DM	Opps to Advance	Extra Bases	Pct	Kills	Outs Made	Basic	Shallow	Medium	Deep	Enhanced	+/-	Throws	GFP/DME	Total	Rank
2007 Pit	28	221.2	87	1	.989	6	4	27	16	.593	2	84	+4	+1	+3	+2	+6	3	0	0	3	-
2008 Pit	17	97.1	31	0	1.000	2	2	8	5	.625	0	31	+3	+2	-1	+2	+3	2	-1	0	1	-
2009 2 tms	56	462.2	168	3	.982	14	14	50	19	.380	5	158	+1	0	+1	-2	-1	-1	6	-1	4	13
2010 Was	134	1124.1	346	5	.986	20	31	132	71	.538	0	339	+5	0	+9	-7	+3	1	-6	-3	-8	28
2011 Mil	95	724.2	222	2	.991	15	14	82	46	.561	0	216	+17	-2	-1	+15	+13	7	-2	-2	3	12
	330	2630.2	854	11	.987	57	65	299	157	.525	7	828	+17	+1	+11	+10	+24	12	-3	-6	3	-

Angel Pagan

	BASIC							THROWING				PLUS/MINUS						RUNS SAVED				
Year Team	G	Inn	TC	E	Pct	GFP	DM	Opps to Advance	Extra Bases	Pct	Kills	Outs Made	Basic	Shallow	Medium	Deep	Enhanced	+/-	Throws	GFP/DME	Total	Rank
2006 ChC	1	3.0	1	0	1.000	1	0	0	0		0	1	+1		+1		+1	1	0	0	1	-
2007 ChC	34	236.0	60	0	1.000	1	8	29	13	.448	0	60	+1	+1	-1	+2	+2	1	1	0	2	-
2008 NYM	2	18.2	8	0	1.000	0	0	1	1	1.000	0	8	0	-1	+1	0	0	0	0	0	0	-
2009 NYM	61	506.1	138	2	.986	12	12	48	24	.500	3	132	+2	-2	0	+12	+10	6	3	1	10	6
2010 NYM	94	792.1	270	4	.985	15	16	94	44	.468	4	258	+10	+4	+13	+4	+20	11	4	-2	13	5
2011 NYM	121	1045.0	317	10	.968	17	26	128	74	.578	1	302	-10	-2	-12	+4	-9	-5	-1	-2	-8	32
	313	2601.1	794	16	.980	46	62	300	156	.520	8	761	+4	0	+2	+22	+24	14	7	-3	18	-

Corey Patterson

	BASIC							THROWING				PLUS/MINUS						RUNS SAVED				
Year Team	G	Inn	TC	E	Pct	GFP	DM	Opps to Advance	Extra Bases	Pct	Kills	Outs Made	Basic	Shallow	Medium	Deep	Enhanced	+/-	Throws	GFP/DME	Total	Rank
2003 ChC	82	710.1	159	4	.975	-	-	71	48	.676	1	150	0	0	-3	+3	0	0	-3		-3	26
2004 ChC	157	1367.2	333	1	.997	18	21	104	54	.519	6	321	+6	+8	+6	+3	+7	4	4	0	8	6
2005 ChC	122	986.2	250	5	.980	15	14	88	50	.568	5	240	0	+1	+9	-5	+4	2	0	-1	1	19
2006 Bal	133	1076.2	356	4	.989	16	15	111	63	.568	5	345	+13	+3	+5	+15	+27	15	1	-1	15	2
2007 Bal	132	1057.1	292	3	.990	19	18	102	56	.549	3	281	-3	-6	-7	+15	+2	1	0	2	3	12
2008 Cin	124	798.0	248	3	.988	17	12	63	29	.460	3	242	+4	-1	0	+11	+10	6	0	3	9	6
2009 2 tms	6	39.0	9	0	1.000	0	1	3	1	.333	0	9	+2	+2	0	+1	+3	2	0	0	2	-
2010 Bal	10	66.0	21	0	1.000	2	2	1	0	.000	0	21	+2	+3	+1	-1	+2	1	0	0	1	-
2011 2 tms	40	287.2	74	0	1.000	5	7	25	16	.640	0	74	+2	+3	+5	-5	+2	1	0	-1	0	-
	806	6389.1	1742	20	.989	92	90	568	317	.558	23	1683	+26	+13	+16	+41	+57	32	2	2	36	7

Center Fielders

Bryan Petersen

Year	Team	G	Inn	TC	E	Pct	GFP	DM	Opps to Advance	Extra Bases	Pct	Kills	Outs Made	Basic	Shallow	Medium	Deep	Enhanced	+/-	Throws	GFP/DME	Total	Rank
2011	Fla	42	316.2	76	2	.974	6	6	27	17	.630	3	71	-1	0	-2	-1	-3	-2	2	0	0	-

Jason Pridie

Year	Team	G	Inn	TC	E	Pct	GFP	DM	Opps to Advance	Extra Bases	Pct	Kills	Outs Made	Basic	Shallow	Medium	Deep	Enhanced	+/-	Throws	GFP/DME	Total	Rank
2011	NYM	43	312.2	88	2	.977	2	7	38	23	.605	1	85	+4	+1	+3	+5	+9	5	-1	-2	2	-

Colby Rasmus

Year	Team	G	Inn	TC	E	Pct	GFP	DM	Opps to Advance	Extra Bases	Pct	Kills	Outs Made	Basic	Shallow	Medium	Deep	Enhanced	+/-	Throws	GFP/DME	Total	Rank
2009	StL	124	945.2	266	5	.981	9	16	94	41	.436	3	258	+6	+4	+2	+6	+11	6	4	-2	8	7
2010	StL	134	1105.1	266	5	.981	12	16	101	49	.485	0	256	-3	+1	+2	-14	-11	-6	-1	1	-6	27
2011	2 tms	127	1092.2	312	6	.981	12	20	85	52	.612	1	302	-1	+3	+3	-8	-2	-1	-2	-1	-4	22
		385	3143.2	844	16	.981	33	52	280	142	.507	4	816	+2	+8	+7	-16	-2	-1	1	-2	-2	22

Ben Revere

Year	Team	G	Inn	TC	E	Pct	GFP	DM	Opps to Advance	Extra Bases	Pct	Kills	Outs Made	Basic	Shallow	Medium	Deep	Enhanced	+/-	Throws	GFP/DME	Total	Rank
2010	Min	6	38.0	10	1	.900	0	0	4	3	.750	0	9	0	0	0	0	0	0	0	0	0	-
2011	Min	89	776.1	252	6	.976	14	16	89	56	.629	3	244	+3	0	-6	+13	+7	4	-3	-2	-1	18
		95	814.1	262	7	.973	14	16	93	59	.634	3	253	+3	0	-6	+13	+7	4	-3	-2	-1	

Alex Rios

Year	Team	G	Inn	TC	E	Pct	GFP	DM	Opps to Advance	Extra Bases	Pct	Kills	Outs Made	Basic	Shallow	Medium	Deep	Enhanced	+/-	Throws	GFP/DME	Total	Rank
2004	Tor	3	21.0	1	0	1.000	0	0	3	3	1.000	0	1	-1	-1	-1	-1	-3	-2	0	0	-2	-
2005	Tor	5	36.0	12	0	1.000	0	1	2	0	.000	0	12	+1	0	0	-1	+2	1	0	0	1	-
2006	Tor	6	32.0	7	0	1.000	0	1	3	2	.667	0	6	+1	+1	0	-1	0	0	0	0	0	-
2007	Tor	22	161.2	47	2	.957	2	2	18	8	.444	0	44	-1	0	-2	-1	-2	-1	1	0	0	-
2008	Tor	62	522.2	169	3	.982	11	6	46	25	.543	7	156	+4	+1	+4	+5	+8	4	5	1	10	5
2009	2 tms	42	346.0	103	2	.981	2	7	27	17	.630	0	101	+4	+1	+3	+6	+9	5	-3	0	2	-
2010	CWS	143	1246.2	395	5	.987	21	22	140	69	.493	1	384	+3	-2	+8	-5	+1	1	-3	1	-1	17
2011	CWS	143	1230.0	357	3	.992	17	27	144	79	.549	2	349	-6	-3	-5	-3	-11	-6	-1	-2	-9	33
		426	3596.0	1091	15	.986	53	66	383	203	.530	10	1053	+5	-3	+7	-1	+4	2	-1	0	1	18

Aaron Rowand

Year	Team	G	Inn	TC	E	Pct	GFP	DM	Opps to Advance	Extra Bases	Pct	Kills	Outs Made	Basic	Shallow	Medium	Deep	Enhanced	+/-	Throws	GFP/DME	Total	Rank
2003	CWS	65	378.2	107	0	1.000	-	-	32	18	.563	3	98	-2	-2	-2	+2	-3	-2	3	-	1	19
2004	CWS	126	1018.2	304	6	.980	12	21	100	53	.530	6	289	-2	-2	+10	+14	+5	3	2	0	5	11
2005	CWS	157	1367.2	394	3	.992	27	18	113	56	.496	1	388	+19	+3	+15	+27	+34	19	-3	-1	15	3
2006	Phi	107	900.2	262	5	.981	20	22	94	54	.574	2	250	-4	+4	+5	-19	-11	-6	0	-1	-7	30
2007	Phi	161	1373.2	405	2	.995	37	40	153	81	.529	9	392	+1	+4	-5	-3	-4	-2	8	-2	4	10
2008	SF	149	1275.1	422	4	.991	19	34	140	69	.493	4	411	-4	0	-3	-5	-8	-4	2	-3	-5	24
2009	SF	137	1127.0	307	3	.990	21	22	91	53	.582	2	299	0	0	+6	-5	+1	1	-2	-1	-2	23
2010	SF	85	695.0	196	0	1.000	18	14	48	32	.667	4	192	+2	0	+4	-1	+3	2	0	1	3	13
2011	SF	60	413.2	125	0	1.000	7	4	41	22	.537	1	123	+3	+5	-8	+5	+2	1	0	1	2	-
		1047	8550.1	2522	23	.991	161	175	812	438	.539	32	2442	+13	+12	+22	+15	+19	12	10	-6	16	12

Michael Saunders

Year	Team	G	Inn	TC	E	Pct	GFP	DM	Opps to Advance	Extra Bases	Pct	Kills	Outs Made	Basic	Shallow	Medium	Deep	Enhanced	+/-	Throws	GFP/DME	Total	Rank
2010	Sea	14	108.0	32	0	1.000	2	1	7	4	.571	0	32	+1	+1	0	+1	+2	1	0	0	1	-
2011	Sea	46	376.1	119	0	1.000	7	5	37	22	.595	0	118	+1	0	+3	0	+3	2	-1	2	3	-
		60	484.1	151	0	1.000	9	6	44	26	.591	0	150	+2	+1	+3	+1	+5	3	-1	2	4	

Jordan Schafer

Year	Team	G	Inn	TC	E	Pct	GFP	DM	Opps to Advance	Extra Bases	Pct	Kills	Outs Made	Basic	Shallow	Medium	Deep	Enhanced	+/-	Throws	GFP/DME	Total	Rank
2009	Atl	50	432.0	131	0	1.000	11	11	56	33	.589	2	127	-8	-3	-1	-12	-17	-10	-1	0	-11	-
2011	2 tms	79	672.0	194	2	.990	9	13	68	40	.588	1	191	-2	-1	-2	-3	-6	-4	-1	-2	-7	30
		129	1104.0	325	2	.994	20	24	124	73	.589	3	318	-10	-4	-3	-15	-23	-14	-2	-2	-18	

Center Fielders

Grady Sizemore

		BASIC							THROWING				PLUS/MINUS						RUNS SAVED				
Year	Team	G	Inn	TC	E	Pct	GFP	DM	Opps to Advance	Extra Bases	Pct	Kills	Outs Made	Basic	Shallow	Medium	Deep	Enhanced	+/-	Throws	GFP/DME	Total	Rank
2004	Cle	42	348.1	106	1	.991	5	6	34	14	.412	0	95	+1	+4	+2	+10	+2	1	2	1	4	-
2005	Cle	155	1370.0	379	3	.992	21	11	113	53	.469	2	373	+5	+2	+7	+11	+14	8	0	2	10	6
2006	Cle	160	1379.1	419	3	.993	21	20	170	93	.547	2	409	-1	-4	+4	+5	+4	2	-3	1	0	20
2007	Cle	160	1408.2	405	2	.995	23	22	138	80	.580	2	399	-2	-6	0	+6	0	0	-4	0	-4	29
2008	Cle	151	1338.0	386	2	.995	28	22	131	68	.519	2	382	-3	-8	+2	+9	+2	1	-2	-2	-3	17
2009	Cle	92	806.1	260	0	1.000	19	19	101	64	.634	0	259	-2	-2	+4	-1	+1	1	-5	-1	-5	25
2010	Cle	32	269.2	65	1	.985	9	5	31	19	.613	0	64	0	0	0	-1	-1	0	-2	-1	-3	-
2011	Cle	56	479.1	126	2	.984	8	7	54	27	.500	0	123	-4	+1	-5	-5	-9	-5	-1	0	-6	26
		848	7399.2	2146	14	.993	134	112	772	418	.541	8	2104	-6	-13	+14	+34	+13	8	-15	0	-7	24

Denard Span

		BASIC							THROWING				PLUS/MINUS						RUNS SAVED				
Year	Team	G	Inn	TC	E	Pct	GFP	DM	Opps to Advance	Extra Bases	Pct	Kills	Outs Made	Basic	Shallow	Medium	Deep	Enhanced	+/-	Throws	GFP/DME	Total	Rank
2008	Min	19	116.2	36	1	.972	5	3	22	12	.545	1	34	-2	-2	0	0	-2	-1	1	0	0	-
2009	Min	84	587.1	181	1	.994	8	7	56	42	.750	0	179	+2	+1	-1	0	0	0	-6	1	-5	27
2010	Min	153	1349.2	416	4	.990	27	25	136	79	.581	4	408	0	+6	-17	+5	-6	-3	-3	1	-5	25
2011	Min	67	585.1	208	1	.995	12	9	51	32	.627	0	206	+15	+8	+5	+11	+24	13	-3	-1	9	7
		323	2639.0	841	7	.992	52	44	265	165	.623	6	827	+15	+13	-13	+16	+16	9	-11	1	-1	-

Drew Stubbs

		BASIC							THROWING				PLUS/MINUS						RUNS SAVED				
Year	Team	G	Inn	TC	E	Pct	GFP	DM	Opps to Advance	Extra Bases	Pct	Kills	Outs Made	Basic	Shallow	Medium	Deep	Enhanced	+/-	Throws	GFP/DME	Total	Rank
2009	Cin	42	368.2	115	0	1.000	8	9	33	14	.424	1	111	+5	+4	+2	+1	+7	4	1	-1	4	-
2010	Cin	147	1229.2	392	5	.987	13	20	108	51	.472	4	376	-8	-12	+1	+7	-4	-2	0	1	-1	19
2011	Cin	157	1329.0	377	3	.992	15	26	124	66	.532	8	365	-9	-12	+8	-10	-14	-8	5	-1	-4	23
		346	2927.1	884	8	.991	36	55	265	131	.494	13	852	-12	-20	+11	-2	-11	-6	6	-1	-1	21

Ryan Sweeney

		BASIC							THROWING				PLUS/MINUS						RUNS SAVED				
Year	Team	G	Inn	TC	E	Pct	GFP	DM	Opps to Advance	Extra Bases	Pct	Kills	Outs Made	Basic	Shallow	Medium	Deep	Enhanced	+/-	Throws	GFP/DME	Total	Rank
2006	CWS	7	35.0	8	0	1.000	-	2	2	2	1.000	0	8	-1	-2	-1	0	-3	-2	0	0	-2	-
2007	CWS	3	26.0	6	0	1.000	1	0	1	0	.000	0	6	+1	+1	0	+1	+2	1	0	0	1	-
2008	Oak	51	362.2	95	0	1.000	2	9	27	17	.630	0	95	-3	-3	-2	+3	-2	-1	-2	-1	-4	-
2009	Oak	57	452.2	151	1	.993	11	6	58	33	.569	1	146	-2	-4	-3	+6	0	0	-2	2	0	-
2010	Oak	1	8.0	2	0	1.000	0	1	2	0	.000	0	2	+1	+1	0	0	+1	0	0	0	0	-
2011	Oak	34	245.2	75	0	1.000	5	2	25	14	.560	0	75	-4	-2	0	-5	-7	-4	-1	0	-5	-
		153	1130.0	337	1	.997	19	20	115	66	.574	1	332	-8	-9	-6	+5	-9	-6	-5	1	-10	-

Andres Torres

		BASIC							THROWING				PLUS/MINUS						RUNS SAVED				
Year	Team	G	Inn	TC	E	Pct	GFP	DM	Opps to Advance	Extra Bases	Pct	Kills	Outs Made	Basic	Shallow	Medium	Deep	Enhanced	+/-	Throws	GFP/DME	Total	Rank
2003	Det	36	269.0	82	1	.988	-	-	28	21	.750	0	76	0	-4	0	+6	+2	1	-3	-	-2	-
2004	Det	1	1.0	0	0	-	0	0				0										0	-
2005	Tex	4	30.0	11	0	1.000	0	1	3	3	1.000	0	11	+1	0	0	+3	+3	2	-1	0	1	-
2009	SF	37	152.1	54	0	1.000	2	2	12	6	.500	1	53	+4	+2	+3	+1	+6	3	0	0	3	-
2010	SF	84	655.2	195	1	.995	11	10	52	32	.615	0	193	+6	-3	+6	+10	+13	8	-2	-2	4	11
2011	SF	106	776.0	205	3	.985	11	9	54	35	.648	2	196	0	+7	-3	-8	-4	-2	0	-1	-3	21
		268	1884.0	547	5	.991	24	22	149	97	.651	4	529	+11	+2	+6	+12	+20	12	-6	-3	3	-

B.J. Upton

		BASIC							THROWING				PLUS/MINUS						RUNS SAVED				
Year	Team	G	Inn	TC	E	Pct	GFP	DM	Opps to Advance	Extra Bases	Pct	Kills	Outs Made	Basic	Shallow	Medium	Deep	Enhanced	+/-	Throws	GFP/DME	Total	Rank
2007	TB	78	664.2	217	2	.991	14	29	84	48	.571	7	204	+1	-1	+3	-1	+1	1	3	-3	1	18
2008	TB	143	1248.2	401	7	.983	32	34	121	72	.595	13	378	+3	+14	-7	-18	-10	-6	6	-3	-3	19
2009	TB	144	1228.2	385	6	.990	26	22	108	61	.565	5	376	+2	+7	+4	-12	-1	0	0	0	0	19
2010	TB	154	1301.2	405	5	.988	20	29	97	46	.474	1	396	-7	+3	-7	-17	-22	-12	-1	-6	-19	33
2011	TB	151	1326.1	391	3	.992	26	24	114	63	.553	5	381	-4	+6	-11	-7	-12	-7	1	-1	-7	31
		670	5770.0	1799	21	.988	118	138	524	290	.553	31	1735	-5	+29	-18	-55	-44	-25	10	-13	-28	33

Center Fielders

Shane Victorino

		BASIC						THROWING				PLUS/MINUS						RUNS SAVED				
								Opps to	Extra			Outs								GFP/		
Year	Team	G	Inn	TC	E	Pct	GFP	DM	Advance	Bases	Pct	Kills	Made	Basic	Shallow	Medium	Deep	Enhanced	+/-	Throws	DME	Total	Rank
2003	SD	16	110.0	23	0	1.000	-	-	15	5	.333	1	20	-1	-2	0	-1	-3	-2	2	-	0	-
2005	Phi	5	7.0	0	0	-	0	0				0						0	0			0	-
2006	Phi	67	557.2	167	0	1.000	14	12	58	32	.552	4	161	+8	+11	-2	-2	+6	3	2	2	7	8
2007	Phi	4	16.0	3	0	1.000	1	4	4	2	.500	0	3	-1	-1	0	-1	-2	-1	0	-1	-2	-
2008	Phi	139	1195.1	323	2	.994	21	27	109	56	.514	6	314	+12	+14	-2	+1	+14	8	4	-2	10	3
2009	Phi	149	1330.1	345	1	.997	26	24	128	65	.508	7	337	-7	0	-4	-7	-11	-6	5	0	-1	22
2010	Phi	143	1265.1	373	2	.995	24	20	108	50	.463	8	360	-6	-3	+7	-13	-9	-5	3	3	1	15
2011	Phi	130	1150.2	296	0	1.000	10	15	71	32	.451	0	296	+8	+13	+8	-17	+5	3	-1	0	2	13
		653	5632.1	1530	5	.997	96	102	493	242	.491	26	1491	+13	+32	+7	-40	0	0	15	2	17	11

Chris Young

		BASIC						THROWING				PLUS/MINUS						RUNS SAVED				
								Opps to	Extra			Outs								GFP/		
Year	Team	G	Inn	TC	E	Pct	GFP	DM	Advance	Bases	Pct	Kills	Made	Basic	Shallow	Medium	Deep	Enhanced	+/-	Throws	DME	Total	Rank
2006	Ari	24	149.1	51	0	1.000	4	2	16	11	.688	0	50	+3	+1	+1	+3	+5	3	-1	0	2	-
2007	Ari	146	1263.0	366	6	.984	16	29	123	70	.569	2	354	-1	+2	+6	-10	-3	-2	-2	0	-4	30
2008	Ari	159	1390.0	401	3	.993	9	31	126	71	.563	2	393	+6	-5	+9	+15	+21	12	-6	-5	1	14
2009	Ari	124	1020.1	292	2	.993	9	21	108	68	.630	1	287	+2	-4	-2	+12	+5	3	-5	-4	-6	28
2010	Ari	156	1350.0	435	7	.984	33	15	144	75	.521	7	417	+12	0	-1	+29	+29	16	3	-1	18	2
2011	Ari	155	1373.1	401	3	.993	23	15	123	69	.561	1	393	+19	+2	+10	+27	+39	22	-3	1	20	2
		764	6546.0	1946	21	.989	94	113	640	364	.569	13	1894	+41	-4	+23	+76	+96	54	-14	-9	31	9

Right Fielders

Jose Bautista

		BASIC							THROWING				PLUS/MINUS						RUNS SAVED				
Year	Team	G	Inn	TC	E	Pct	GFP	DM	Opps to Advance	Extra Bases	Pct	Kills	Outs Made	Basic	Shallow	Medium	Deep	Enhanced	+/-	Throws	GFP/ DME	Total	Rank
2004	4 tms	19	89.1	19	1	.947	1	2	10	3	.300	1	15	-1	-1	0	-1	-2	-1	0	0	-1	-
2006	Pit	25	172.2	32	0	1.000	1	2	13	4	.308		31	0	-2	+2	+1	+2	1	0	-1	0	-
2007	Pit	16	130.0	26	2	.923	2	1	10	5	.500	1	23	0	0	0	0	-1	-1	1	0	0	-
2009	Tor	36	286.1	72	0	1.000	7	7	33	10	.303	3	71	+2	+1	+1	0	+2	1	4	0	5	-
2010	Tor	113	982.2	194	3	.985	25	13	99	43	.434	11	179	-14	-3	-5	-14	-23	-13	6	4	-3	24
2011	Tor	116	1014.0	252	6	.976	21	26	97	49	.505	10	233	-8	0	-3	-20	-23	-13	3	3	-7	30
		325	2675.0	595	12	.980	57	51	262	114	.435	26	552	-21	-5	-5	-34	-45	-26	14	6	-6	24

Carlos Beltran

		BASIC							THROWING				PLUS/MINUS						RUNS SAVED				
Year	Team	G	Inn	TC	E	Pct	GFP	DM	Opps to Advance	Extra Bases	Pct	Kills	Outs Made	Basic	Shallow	Medium	Deep	Enhanced	+/-	Throws	GFP/ DME	Total	Rank
2011	2 tms	134	1153.2	241	1	.996	22	26	114	56	.491	4	230	-3	-1	-8	+6	-3	-2	0	-1	-3	21

Lance Berkman

		BASIC							THROWING				PLUS/MINUS						RUNS SAVED				
Year	Team	G	Inn	TC	E	Pct	GFP	DM	Opps to Advance	Extra Bases	Pct	Kills	Outs Made	Basic	Shallow	Medium	Deep	Enhanced	+/-	Throws	GFP/ DME	Total	Rank
2004	Hou	90	780.1	157	0	1.000	10	13	64	29	.453	7	127	-3	-5	-5	-13	-6	-3	4	2	3	12
2005	Hou	11	78.0	16	0	1.000		3	5	3	.600	0	16	0	-1	+1	0	-1	-1	0	0	-1	-
2006	Hou	42	305.2	62	3	.952	7	7	31	16	.516	2	56	-2	0	+1	-4	-3	-2	1	-1	-2	-
2007	Hou	31	229.2	52	2	.962	4	3	27	20	.741	0	49	-4	0	-7	-1	-9	-5	-3	-1	-9	-
2011	StL	110	865.1	180	4	.978	12	20	80	41	.513	1	173	-10	-2	-8	-14	-24	-14	-2	-2	-18	35
		284	2259.0	467	9	.981	33	46	207	109	.527	11	421	-19	-8	-18	-32	-43	-25	0	-2	-27	31

Brennan Boesch

		BASIC							THROWING				PLUS/MINUS						RUNS SAVED				
Year	Team	G	Inn	TC	E	Pct	GFP	DM	Opps to Advance	Extra Bases	Pct	Kills	Outs Made	Basic	Shallow	Medium	Deep	Enhanced	+/-	Throws	GFP/ DME	Total	Rank
2010	Det	79	587.1	142	6	.958	9	14	46	18	.391	3	133	-10	0	-1	-15	-16	-9	2	-2	-9	29
2011	Det	51	366.2	92	1	.989	8	4	32	19	.594	1	88	-1	+2	0	-2	0	0	-1	0	-1	16
		130	954.0	234	7	.970	17	18	78	37	.474	4	221	-11	+2	-1	-17	-16	-9	1	-2	-10	-

Brian Bogusevic

		BASIC							THROWING				PLUS/MINUS						RUNS SAVED				
Year	Team	G	Inn	TC	E	Pct	GFP	DM	Opps to Advance	Extra Bases	Pct	Kills	Outs Made	Basic	Shallow	Medium	Deep	Enhanced	+/-	Throws	GFP/ DME	Total	Rank
2010	Hou	2	9.0	3	0	1.000	1	0	3	2	.667	0	3	-1	0	-1	+1	-1	0	0	0	0	-
2011	Hou	40	277.0	79	2	.975	13	3	31	18	.581	6	67	+1	-1	0	+3	+3	2	4	4	10	-
		42	286.0	82	2	.976	14	3	34	20	.588	6	70	0	-1	-1	+4	+2	2	4	4	10	-

Domonic Brown

		BASIC							THROWING				PLUS/MINUS						RUNS SAVED				
Year	Team	G	Inn	TC	E	Pct	GFP	DM	Opps to Advance	Extra Bases	Pct	Kills	Outs Made	Basic	Shallow	Medium	Deep	Enhanced	+/-	Throws	GFP/ DME	Total	Rank
2010	Phi	15	112.0	30	1	.967	3	6	18	8	.444	1	28	-2	-1	-1	-3	-4	-2	0	0	-2	-
2011	Phi	52	451.0	82	4	.951	3	9	33	17	.515	0	78	-5	-4	-2	-3	-8	-5	-2	-2	-9	32
		67	563.0	112	5	.955	6	15	51	25	.490	1	106	-7	-5	-3	-6	-12	-7	-2	-2	-11	-

Jay Bruce

		BASIC							THROWING				PLUS/MINUS						RUNS SAVED				
Year	Team	G	Inn	TC	E	Pct	GFP	DM	Opps to Advance	Extra Bases	Pct	Kills	Outs Made	Basic	Shallow	Medium	Deep	Enhanced	+/-	Throws	GFP/ DME	Total	Rank
2008	Cin	78	590.0	157	9	.943	15	12	57	27	.474	5	143	+1	+3	+4	-11	-4	-2	1	-1	-2	20
2009	Cin	98	810.1	213	2	.991	19	22	88	37	.420	9	200	-3	-3	+1	-1	-3	-2	5	2	5	10
2010	Cin	146	1199.1	353	3	.992	27	14	108	53	.491	5	343	+20	+8	+10	+13	+31	18	-2	1	17	1
2011	Cin	155	1371.0	320	4	.988	16	22	128	62	.484	5	306	+4	+6	+1	-7	+1	0	-2	0	-2	18
		477	3970.2	1043	18	.983	77	70	381	179	.470	24	992	+22	+14	+16	-6	+25	14	2	2	18	10

Shin-Soo Choo

		BASIC							THROWING				PLUS/MINUS						RUNS SAVED				
Year	Team	G	Inn	TC	E	Pct	GFP	DM	Opps to Advance	Extra Bases	Pct	Kills	Outs Made	Basic	Shallow	Medium	Deep	Enhanced	+/-	Throws	GFP/ DME	Total	Rank
2006	Cle	30	256.2	70	1	.986	6	4	22	7	.318	1	67	+3	+2	-1	+6	+7	4	1	1	6	-
2007	Cle	2	11.0	0	0	-	0	0					0	0					0			0	-
2008	Cle	51	398.1	90	1	.989	5	13	44	22	.500	1	89	0	-7	0	+7	0	0	-2	-2	-4	-
2009	Cle	124	1084.2	297	7	.976	23	23	129	69	.535	8	279	+4	+5	+3	-2	+5	3	0	1	4	13
2010	Cle	142	1249.2	285	4	.986	35	18	138	59	.428	12	267	-7	+7	-5	-19	-17	-10	10	5	5	11
2011	Cle	85	735.1	185	4	.978	15	20	78	39	.500	6	172	0	+1	+1	+1	+3	2	2	-1	3	9
		434	3735.2	927	17	.982	84	78	411	196	.477	28	874	0	+8	-2	-7	-2	-1	11	4	14	14

Right Fielders

Tyler Colvin

		BASIC							THROWING					PLUS/MINUS					RUNS SAVED				
								Opps to	Extra				Outs								GFP/		
Year	Team	G	Inn	TC	E	Pct	GFP	DM	Advance	Bases	Pct	Kills	Made	Basic	Shallow	Medium	Deep	Enhanced	+/-	Throws	DME	Total	Rank
2010	ChC	59	388.1	104	5	.952	9	6	50	20	.400	2	93	+1	+3	+1	-5	0	0	2	-1	1	-
2011	ChC	44	314.2	79	1	.987	6	5	35	12	.343	2	76	0	-1	0	+3	+2	1	2	1	4	-
		103	703.0	183	6	.967	15	11	85	32	.376	4	169	+1	+2	+1	-2	+2	1	4	0	5	-

Nelson Cruz

		BASIC							THROWING					PLUS/MINUS					RUNS SAVED				
								Opps to	Extra				Outs								GFP/		
Year	Team	G	Inn	TC	E	Pct	GFP	DM	Advance	Bases	Pct	Kills	Made	Basic	Shallow	Medium	Deep	Enhanced	+/-	Throws	DME	Total	Rank
2005	Mil	6	16.0	4	0	1.000	0	0	3	1	.333	0	4	0	0	0	+1	0	0	0	0	0	-
2006	Tex	38	307.1	73	0	1.000	6	3	33	14	.424	3	69	+2	-1	0	+5	+4	2	2	0	4	-
2007	Tex	82	604.1	158	5	.968	11	13	73	38	.521	1	148	+3	-3	+4	+6	+7	4	-2	-2	0	17
2008	Tex	31	274.0	75	2	.973	5	5	42	17	.405	1	72	+2	+4	+1	-2	+4	2	-1	0	1	-
2009	Tex	120	1035.2	308	3	.990	18	23	110	50	.455	5	295	-2	-3	-6	+8	0	0	1	-1	0	19
2010	Tex	94	799.1	236	5	.979	15	17	74	35	.473	2	228	-2	-4	-3	+12	+6	3	-1	1	3	13
2011	Tex	109	863.2	225	5	.978	16	14	71	37	.521	3	216	-1	+3	-3	-5	-5	-3	-3	0	-6	28
		480	3900.1	1079	20	.981	71	75	406	192	.473	15	1032	+2	-4	-7	+25	+16	8	-4	-2	2	20

Michael Cuddyer

		BASIC							THROWING					PLUS/MINUS					RUNS SAVED				
								Opps to	Extra				Outs								GFP/		
Year	Team	G	Inn	TC	E	Pct	GFP	DM	Advance	Bases	Pct	Kills	Made	Basic	Shallow	Medium	Deep	Enhanced	+/-	Throws	DME	Total	Rank
2003	Min	17	139.0	25	0	1.000	-	-	7	5	.714	0	21	-1	0	+1	-2	-1	-1	-1	-	-2	-
2004	Min	8	49.0	13	0	1.000	1	1	4	2	.500	0	10	0	0	0	0	-1	-1	0	0	-1	-
2005	Min	20	159.0	35	0	1.000	3	1	7	3	.429	0	35	+3	+1	0	+4	+6	3	0	0	3	-
2006	Min	142	1227.1	260	5	.981	16	18	113	45	.398	7	245	-13	+4	+2	-33	-28	-16	4	2	-10	34
2007	Min	140	1224.1	279	4	.986	24	15	129	50	.388	12	256	-12	+1	-4	-18	-22	-13	10	3	0	19
2008	Min	58	501.2	130	1	.992	18	14	51	21	.412	5	123	-4	+2	-3	-7	-8	-5	3	0	-2	21
2009	Min	117	991.2	206	2	.990	13	12	95	39	.411	2	199	-7	0	-2	-13	-15	-9	0	1	-8	31
2010	Min	66	539.1	124	2	.984	10	8	41	18	.439	4	117	-10	+3	-4	-23	-24	-14	2	2	-10	31
2011	Min	77	639.1	152	4	.974	15	8	63	32	.508	3	142	-8	-1	-3	-14	-19	-11	0	1	-10	34
		645	5470.2	1224	18	.985	100	77	510	215	.422	33	1148	-52	+10	-13	-106	-112	-67	18	9	-40	33

Alejandro De Aza

		BASIC							THROWING					PLUS/MINUS					RUNS SAVED				
								Opps to	Extra				Outs								GFP/		
Year	Team	G	Inn	TC	E	Pct	GFP	DM	Advance	Bases	Pct	Kills	Made	Basic	Shallow	Medium	Deep	Enhanced	+/-	Throws	DME	Total	Rank
2010	CWS	5	19.0	6	0	1.000	0	1				0	6	0	0	-1	0	0	0	0	0	0	-
2011	CWS	31	202.1	48	0	1.000	7	5	15	8	.533	1	46	+3	+2	+2	+1	+5	3	0	0	3	-
		36	221.1	54	0	1.000	7	6	15	8	.533	1	52	+3	+2	+1	+1	+5	3	0	0	3	-

David DeJesus

		BASIC							THROWING					PLUS/MINUS					RUNS SAVED				
								Opps to	Extra				Outs								GFP/		
Year	Team	G	Inn	TC	E	Pct	GFP	DM	Advance	Bases	Pct	Kills	Made	Basic	Shallow	Medium	Deep	Enhanced	+/-	Throws	DME	Total	Rank
2003	KC	1	1.0	0	0	-	-	-				0										0	-
2004	KC	6	32.0	6	0	1.000	0	1	3	2	.667	0	6	0		0	-3	-2	-1	0	0	-1	-
2008	KC	23	123.0	23	0	1.000	1	2	13	7	.538	0	23	0	0	-1	+2	+1	1	0	0	1	-
2009	KC	2	10.0	6	0	1.000	0	0	3	2	.667	0	6	0	0	+1	0	+1	1	0	0	1	-
2010	KC	70	597.1	137	0	1.000	12	6	52	31	.596	2	133	-1	0	+1	-3	-3	-2	-2	2	-2	22
2011	Oak	116	992.2	241	4	.983	29	11	102	55	.539	6	231	+6	-3	+9	+7	+13	7	-3	1	5	5
		218	1756.0	413	4	.990	42	20	173	97	.561	8	399	+5	-3	+10	+3	+10	6	-5	3	4	-

Chris Denorfia

		BASIC							THROWING					PLUS/MINUS					RUNS SAVED				
								Opps to	Extra				Outs								GFP/		
Year	Team	G	Inn	TC	E	Pct	GFP	DM	Advance	Bases	Pct	Kills	Made	Basic	Shallow	Medium	Deep	Enhanced	+/-	Throws	DME	Total	Rank
2005	Cin	2	16.1	9	0	1.000	1	1	2	1	.500	0	9	+1	+1	0	0	+1	1	0	0	1	-
2006	Cin	15	118.1	36	0	1.000	1	2	11	2	.182	2	34	+3	+1	+3	0	+5	3	2	0	5	-
2008	Oak	2	10.0	2	0	1.000	0	0	2	1	.500	0	2	-1		0	-1	-1	-1	0	0	-1	-
2009	Oak	1	2.0	0	0	-	0	0	0	0	-	0	0	0				0	0	0	0	0	-
2010	SD	18	116.0	24	0	1.000	2	2	6	2	.333	1	23	+2	+1	+2	0	+3	2	1	0	3	-
2011	SD	62	445.0	109	2	.982	10	9	46	23	.500	4	101	+3	+2	+5	-5	+3	2	0	1	3	9
		100	707.2	180	2	.989	14	14	67	29	.433	7	169	+8	+5	+10	-6	+11	7	3	1	11	-

Matt Diaz

		BASIC							THROWING					PLUS/MINUS					RUNS SAVED				
								Opps to	Extra				Outs								GFP/		
Year	Team	G	Inn	TC	E	Pct	GFP	DM	Advance	Bases	Pct	Kills	Made	Basic	Shallow	Medium	Deep	Enhanced	+/-	Throws	DME	Total	Rank
2004	TB	1	9.0	3	0	1.000	0	0	2	2	1.000	0	3	-2	0		-3	-3	-2	-1	0	-3	-
2005	KC	2	11.0	4	0	1.000	0	0	0	0	-	0	4	0		0	0	0	0	0	0	0	-
2006	Atl	6	13.0	3	0	1.000	0	0	1	1	1.000	0	3	0		0	+1	+1	1	0	0	1	-
2007	Atl	5	15.2	3	0	1.000	1	0	1	1	1.000	0	3	+1	0	0	0	+1	1	0	0	1	-
2009	Atl	66	540.2	93	2	.978	8	13	63	28	.444	0	89	-2	-2	0	-5	-7	-4	-1	-1	-6	27
2011	2 tms	54	335.2	65	1	.985	5	9	31	14	.452	2	61	-1	+1	+2	-6	-4	-2	0	0	-2	-
		134	925.0	171	3	.982	14	22	98	46	.469	2	163	-4	-1	+2	-13	-12	-6	-2	-1	-9	-

379

Right Fielders

J.D. Drew

	BASIC							THROWING				PLUS/MINUS						RUNS SAVED				
Year	Team	G	Inn	TC	E	Pct	GFP	DM	Opps to Advance	Extra Bases	Pct	Kills	Outs Made	Basic	Shallow	Medium	Deep	Enhanced	+/-	Throws	GFP/DME	Total	Rank
2003	StL	53	391.0	107	1	.991	-	-	35	22	.629	3	90	+1	-1	+5	-2	+2	1	-1	-	0	-
2004	Atl	138	1193.0	291	3	.990	22	19	123	61	.496	5	272	+10	+8	+10	+11	+24	14	-1	0	13	3
2005	LAD	44	382.0	88	2	.977	6	3	53	24	.453	2	83	-1	-7	+2	+5	+3	2	1	1	4	-
2006	LAD	135	1118.0	292	5	.983	9	21	104	48	.462	2	284	+6	-4	+1	+15	+12	7	-2	-1	4	12
2007	Bos	133	1062.0	220	5	.977	7	15	84	43	.512	2	212	0	-5	+5	+5	+5	3	-2	-3	-2	21
2008	Bos	106	886.0	194	4	.979	13	13	87	52	.598	4	184	-5	0	-7	0	-7	-4	-3	-1	-8	30
2009	Bos	131	1083.1	249	2	.992	10	18	112	60	.536	3	243	+12	+2	+4	+14	+20	12	-5	0	7	5
2010	Bos	133	1102.2	236	1	.996	11	22	95	43	.453	1	234	+9	-2	-1	+24	+21	12	-2	-2	8	5
2011	Bos	76	587.1	149	0	1.000	4	9	52	28	.538	1	146	+1	-5	+4	+3	+3	2	-4	0	-2	17
		949	7805.1	1826	23	.987	82	120	745	381	.511	23	1748	+33	-14	+23	+75	+83	49	-19	-6	24	7

Lucas Duda

	BASIC							THROWING				PLUS/MINUS						RUNS SAVED				
Year	Team	G	Inn	TC	E	Pct	GFP	DM	Opps to Advance	Extra Bases	Pct	Kills	Outs Made	Basic	Shallow	Medium	Deep	Enhanced	+/-	Throws	GFP/DME	Total	Rank
2011	NYM	42	335.1	74	1	.986	2	15	29	16	.552	1	72	-8	-3	+1	-13	-15	-9	0	-3	-12	-

Andre Ethier

	BASIC							THROWING				PLUS/MINUS						RUNS SAVED				
Year	Team	G	Inn	TC	E	Pct	GFP	DM	Opps to Advance	Extra Bases	Pct	Kills	Outs Made	Basic	Shallow	Medium	Deep	Enhanced	+/-	Throws	GFP/DME	Total	Rank
2007	LAD	102	779.2	188	4	.979	20	8	90	55	.611	6	177	+7	-1	+5	+12	+16	9	-4	3	8	6
2008	LAD	109	881.0	179	0	1.000	11	14	90	46	.511	3	171	-13	-9	-4	-5	-19	-11	-2	0	-13	34
2009	LAD	158	1365.1	292	7	.976	21	21	111	58	.523	5	279	-6	-2	-5	+5	-3	-2	-5	-1	-8	30
2010	LAD	132	1151.1	230	1	.996	22	13	112	59	.527	2	223	-11	-5	-6	-5	-16	-9	-5	0	-14	34
2011	LAD	126	1091.1	251	0	1.000	20	14	93	53	.570	6	243	-1	-9	+5	+13	+9	5	-2	1	4	7
		627	5268.2	1140	12	.989	94	70	496	271	.546	22	1093	-24	-26	-5	+20	-13	-8	-18	3	-23	29

Ben Francisco

	BASIC							THROWING				PLUS/MINUS						RUNS SAVED				
Year	Team	G	Inn	TC	E	Pct	GFP	DM	Opps to Advance	Extra Bases	Pct	Kills	Outs Made	Basic	Shallow	Medium	Deep	Enhanced	+/-	Throws	GFP/DME	Total	Rank
2007	Cle	5	28.0	6	0	1.000	0	0	3	2	.667	0	6	0	0	0	0	+1	1	0	0	1	-
2008	Cle	32	230.0	53	2	.962	6	2	26	9	.346	4	46	-2	0	+1	-4	-3	-2	3	0	1	-
2009	2 tms	18	122.0	27	0	1.000	3	4	19	11	.579	1	26	-1	0	+1	-1	-2	-2	0	0	-2	-
2010	Phi	20	113.2	28	0	1.000	1	2	12	8	.667	0	28	-1	-1	0	-1	-2	-1	-1	0	-2	-
2011	Phi	55	445.0	91	2	.978	5	11	43	22	.512	2	86	-5	-2	-1	-6	-9	-6	1	-2	-7	29
		130	938.2	205	4	.980	15	19	103	52	.505	7	192	-9	-3	+1	-12	-15	-10	3	-2	-9	-

Jeff Francoeur

	BASIC							THROWING				PLUS/MINUS						RUNS SAVED				
Year	Team	G	Inn	TC	E	Pct	GFP	DM	Opps to Advance	Extra Bases	Pct	Kills	Outs Made	Basic	Shallow	Medium	Deep	Enhanced	+/-	Throws	GFP/DME	Total	Rank
2005	Atl	67	589.0	149	5	.966	15	9	65	28	.431	10	131	+6	+1	+2	+10	+11	6	8	4	18	1
2006	Atl	162	1421.2	338	9	.973	33	26	169	77	.456	9	317	+3	+5	+4	-5	+3	2	3	0	5	8
2007	Atl	162	1440.2	351	5	.986	34	17	129	53	.411	11	328	+7	+5	+7	-2	+10	6	10	4	20	1
2008	Atl	152	1328.2	300	4	.987	16	18	115	50	.435	6	284	-3	-3	+4	-13	-12	-7	2	1	-4	23
2009	2 tms	154	1338.1	306	1	.997	23	31	120	52	.433	8	296	+2	0	+6	-2	+5	3	4	4	11	3
2010	2 tms	131	1070.0	254	3	.988	22	17	100	30	.300	7	240	+5	-2	-6	+22	+13	8	8	1	17	2
2011	KC	153	1352.0	348	5	.986	28	29	144	68	.472	11	328	-7	+1	-15	+2	-12	-7	5	3	1	13
		981	8540.1	2046	32	.984	171	147	842	358	.425	62	1924	+13	+7	+2	+12	+18	11	40	17	68	3

Kosuke Fukudome

	BASIC							THROWING				PLUS/MINUS						RUNS SAVED				
Year	Team	G	Inn	TC	E	Pct	GFP	DM	Opps to Advance	Extra Bases	Pct	Kills	Outs Made	Basic	Shallow	Medium	Deep	Enhanced	+/-	Throws	GFP/DME	Total	Rank
2008	ChC	137	1103.2	256	5	.980	25	12	104	49	.471	4	246	+2	+8	+2	-8	+1	1	-1	2	2	15
2009	ChC	44	263.1	80	0	1.000	9	1	9	4	.444	1	79	+4	0	+2	+5	+7	4	0	1	5	-
2010	ChC	110	816.2	195	1	.995	15	19	73	37	.507	3	190	+3	+5	0	-2	+2	1	-1	-1	-1	19
2011	2 tms	131	1061.0	274	3	.989	20	23	120	52	.433	5	265	0	+6	-7	-3	-4	-3	3	-2	-2	19
		422	3244.2	805	9	.989	69	55	306	142	.464	13	780	+9	+19	-3	-8	+6	3	1	0	4	17

Carlos Gonzalez

	BASIC							THROWING				PLUS/MINUS						RUNS SAVED				
Year	Team	G	Inn	TC	E	Pct	GFP	DM	Opps to Advance	Extra Bases	Pct	Kills	Outs Made	Basic	Shallow	Medium	Deep	Enhanced	+/-	Throws	GFP/DME	Total	Rank
2008	Oak	36	160.2	43	0	1.000	5	1	7	1	.143	0	43	+3	+2	+1	+3	+6	3	1	0	4	-
2009	Col	8	28.2	4	0	1.000	1	2	3	2	.667	1	3	-1		-1	-1	-2	-1	1	0	0	-
2010	Col	40	299.2	58	0	1.000	5	6	24	12	.500	2	56	0	+1	-4	+3	-1	0	0	0	0	-
2011	Col	34	295.1	67	0	1.000	9	7	32	17	.531	2	63	+3	+2	+1	+5	+7	4	0	0	4	-
		118	784.1	172	0	1.000	20	16	66	32	.485	5	165	+5	+5	-3	+10	+10	6	2	0	8	-

Right Fielders

Corey Hart

Year	Team	G	Inn	TC	E	Pct	GFP	DM	Opps to Advance	Extra Bases	Pct	Kills	Outs Made	Basic	Shallow	Medium	Deep	Enhanced	+/-	Throws	GFP/DME	Total	Rank
2005	Mil	3	27.0	10	1	.900	1	1	4	2	.500	1	8	0	0	-1	+2	0	0	0	0	0	-
2006	Mil	37	266.0	65	0	1.000	2	8	30	21	.700	0	63	+1	0	+3	-1	+2	1	-3	0	-2	-
2007	Mil	113	864.1	257	1	.996	19	10	105	52	.495	0	253	+6	-1	+1	+10	+10	6	-4	5	7	8
2008	Mil	156	1376.2	315	5	.984	22	27	122	64	.525	5	304	0	+7	-3	-3	0	0	-3	0	-3	22
2009	Mil	112	930.1	195	5	.974	12	12	61	30	.492	2	189	-3	-3	+1	+3	+1	1	-2	-1	-2	21
2010	Mil	141	1199.0	281	2	.993	24	25	111	53	.477	4	272	+5	-3	+4	+7	+8	5	-1	-1	3	12
2011	Mil	126	1087.2	256	2	.992	20	22	82	43	.524	2	252	+5	-2	+8	+3	+8	5	-4	-2	-1	15
		688	5751.0	1379	16	.988	100	105	515	265	.515	14	1341	+14	-2	+13	+21	+29	18	-17	1	2	18

Jason Heyward

Year	Team	G	Inn	TC	E	Pct	GFP	DM	Opps to Advance	Extra Bases	Pct	Kills	Outs Made	Basic	Shallow	Medium	Deep	Enhanced	+/-	Throws	GFP/DME	Total	Rank
2010	Atl	140	1196.1	246	6	.976	17	14	104	56	.538	4	236	+17	+3	-6	+36	+33	19	-5	1	15	3
2011	Atl	122	990.1	228	6	.974	12	14	86	47	.547	2	218	+14	+1	+3	+29	+32	19	-2	-2	15	1
		262	2186.2	474	12	.975	29	28	190	103	.542	6	454	+31	+4	-3	+65	+65	38	-7	-1	30	4

Torii Hunter

Year	Team	G	Inn	TC	E	Pct	GFP	DM	Opps to Advance	Extra Bases	Pct	Kills	Outs Made	Basic	Shallow	Medium	Deep	Enhanced	+/-	Throws	GFP/DME	Total	Rank
2010	LAA	46	410.0	110	2	.982	8	10	30	16	.533	2	106	-4	-4	+2	-4	-5	-3	0	2	-1	20
2011	LAA	136	1179.1	278	3	.989	36	23	125	68	.544	14	259	-4	-12	+1	+11	+1	1	5	3	9	2
		182	1589.1	388	5	.987	44	33	155	84	.542	16	365	-8	-16	+3	+7	-4	-2	5	5	8	

Conor Jackson

Year	Team	G	Inn	TC	E	Pct	GFP	DM	Opps to Advance	Extra Bases	Pct	Kills	Outs Made	Basic	Shallow	Medium	Deep	Enhanced	+/-	Throws	GFP/DME	Total	Rank
2011	2 tms	31	232.2	55	1	.982	13	5	17	7	.412	1	52	+4	+1	+1	+3	+6	4	1	1	6	-

Jon Jay

Year	Team	G	Inn	TC	E	Pct	GFP	DM	Opps to Advance	Extra Bases	Pct	Kills	Outs Made	Basic	Shallow	Medium	Deep	Enhanced	+/-	Throws	GFP/DME	Total	Rank
2010	StL	61	381.2	74	1	.986	7	6	44	23	.523	2	70	+1	+1	+1	-2	0	0	-2	0	-2	-
2011	StL	56	303.2	85	0	1.000	10	7	31	19	.613	1	84	+8	+4	+5	+5	+13	8	-2	1	7	-
		117	685.1	159	1	.994	17	13	75	42	.560	3	154	+9	+5	+6	+3	+13	8	-4	1	5	

Reed Johnson

Year	Team	G	Inn	TC	E	Pct	GFP	DM	Opps to Advance	Extra Bases	Pct	Kills	Outs Made	Basic	Shallow	Medium	Deep	Enhanced	+/-	Throws	GFP/DME	Total	Rank
2003	Tor	71	532.1	95	3	.968	-	-	56	29	.518	4	86	-2	+2	-1	-7	-5	-3	0	-	-3	25
2004	Tor	53	382.2	92	1	.989	3	4	54	25	.463	1	84	0	-1	+3	-5	-1	-1	-1	0	-2	-
2005	Tor	35	247.0	53	1	.981	5	2	17	8	.471	1	51	-2	0	-1	-3	-4	-2	0	0	-2	-
2006	Tor	30	242.1	67	0	1.000	5	3	15	6	.400	2	64	+4	+1	+2	+4	+7	4	1	1	6	-
2007	Tor	8	71.2	14	0	1.000	1	4	16	8	.500	0	13	+1	0	0	+2	+2	1	0	-1	0	-
2008	ChC	6	23.1	4	0	1.000	2	0	4	2	.500	0	4	+1	0		+3	+2	1	0	0	1	-
2009	ChC	7	37.0	4	0	1.000	1	1	5	2	.400	0	4	-1	0	0	-1	-1	-1	0	1	0	-
2010	LAD	22	141.0	32	0	1.000	3	4	6	1	.167	0	28	-4	-1	-1	-8	-10	-6	0	-1	-6	-
2011	ChC	44	266.0	66	1	.985	3	4	26	13	.500	1	63	+3	+2	0	+2	+4	2	-1	-1	0	-
		276	1943.1	423	6	.986	23	22	199	94	.472	9	397	0	+3	+2	-13	-6	-5	-1	0	-6	

Garrett Jones

Year	Team	G	Inn	TC	E	Pct	GFP	DM	Opps to Advance	Extra Bases	Pct	Kills	Outs Made	Basic	Shallow	Medium	Deep	Enhanced	+/-	Throws	GFP/DME	Total	Rank
2007	Min	1	8.0	3	0	1.000	0	0	1	0	.000	0	3	+1	0	+1	+1	+2	1	0	0	1	-
2009	Pit	39	343.1	80	0	1.000	5	8	36	13	.361	0	76	+7	+5	+2	+3	+9	5	0	0	5	-
2010	Pit	48	397.2	105	3	.971	11	8	36	14	.389	2	98	+4	+2	+3	0	+5	3	3	0	6	-
2011	Pit	90	659.0	158	1	.994	11	12	70	32	.457	2	154	-6	-2	-1	-2	-5	-3	-1	0	-4	24
		178	1408.0	346	4	.988	27	28	143	59	.413	4	331	+6	+5	+5	+2	+11	6	2	0	8	

Matt Joyce

Year	Team	G	Inn	TC	E	Pct	GFP	DM	Opps to Advance	Extra Bases	Pct	Kills	Outs Made	Basic	Shallow	Medium	Deep	Enhanced	+/-	Throws	GFP/DME	Total	Rank
2008	Det	25	161.0	43	1	.977	3	2	21	10	.476	0	42	+2	0	+3	0	+3	2	-1	-1	0	-
2009	TB	5	36.0	6	0	1.000	1	0	2	1	.500	0	6	-1	0	0	-1	-2	-1	0	0	-1	-
2010	TB	52	397.0	106	3	.972	12	4	38	14	.368	0	100	+3	0	+6	-3	+3	2	2	2	6	-
2011	TB	126	1006.1	222	3	.986	22	18	89	43	.483	5	211	+1	+4	-2	-11	-9	-5	0	3	-2	20
		208	1600.1	377	7	.981	37	25	150	68	.453	9	359	+5	+4	+7	-15	-5	-2	1	4	3	

Right Fielders

Mark Kotsay

Year	Team	G	Inn	TC	E	Pct	GFP	DM	Opps to Advance	Extra Bases	Pct	Kills	Outs Made	Basic	Shallow	Medium	Deep	Enhanced	+/-	Throws	GFP/DME	Total	Rank
2008	Bos	19	151.2	32	0	1.000		3	8	5	.625	0	32	0	0	-2	0	-2	-1	-1	-1	-3	-
2009	2 tms	12	62.2	15	0	1.000	2	2	7	5	.714	1	14	+1	0	-1	+2	+1	1	0	0	1	-
2010	CWS	8	48.0	11	0	1.000	3	3	12	9	.750	1	9	-3	-1	-1	-1	-3	-2	0	2	0	-
2011	Mil	30	223.1	49	1	.980	3	0	20	7	.350	0	48	+2	-1	+2	+6	+7	4	-1	0	3	-
		69	485.2	107	1	.991	8	8	47	26	.553	2	103	0	-2	-2	+7	+3	2	-2	1	1	-

Jason Kubel

Year	Team	G	Inn	TC	E	Pct	GFP	DM	Opps to Advance	Extra Bases	Pct	Kills	Outs Made	Basic	Shallow	Medium	Deep	Enhanced	+/-	Throws	GFP/DME	Total	Rank
2004	Min	8	44.0	11	0	1.000	0	0	2	1	.500	0	7	0	0	0	-2	0	0	0	0	0	-
2006	Min	7	40.0	7	0	1.000	0	1	5	2	.400	0	7	0	0	0	0	0	0	0	0	0	-
2008	Min	32	238.2	76	1	.987	2	8	25	15	.600	0	74	-1	-2	+3	-5	-5	-3	-3	0	-6	-
2009	Min	30	219.1	52	0	1.000	1	3	18	7	.389	0	52	+1	+3	-2	+1	+2	1	0	0	1	-
2010	Min	83	670.0	152	4	.974	20	11	63	38	.603	5	142	-6	+1	-2	-13	-15	-8	-1	0	-9	28
2011	Min	50	413.2	105	1	.990	11	7	46	21	.457	0	95	-8	-3	+1	-13	-15	-9	5	1	-3	23
		210	1625.2	403	6	.985	34	30	159	84	.528	12	377	-14	-1	0	-32	-33	-19	1	1	-17	-

Brent Lillibridge

Year	Team	G	Inn	TC	E	Pct	GFP	DM	Opps to Advance	Extra Bases	Pct	Kills	Outs Made	Basic	Shallow	Medium	Deep	Enhanced	+/-	Throws	GFP/DME	Total	Rank
2010	CWS	1	1.0	1	0	1.000	0	0				0	1	0	0	0	0	0	0	0	0	0	-
2011	CWS	43	203.0	45	0	1.000	6	0	21	13	.619	0	45	+3	+2	-2	+7	+7	4	-2	1	3	-
		44	204.0	46	0	1.000	6	0	21	13	.619	0	46	+3	+2	-2	+7	+7	4	-2	1	3	-

Nick Markakis

Year	Team	G	Inn	TC	E	Pct	GFP	DM	Opps to Advance	Extra Bases	Pct	Kills	Outs Made	Basic	Shallow	Medium	Deep	Enhanced	+/-	Throws	GFP/DME	Total	Rank
2006	Bal	126	913.1	248	1	.996	17	16	102	50	.490	5	240	+1	-3	+5	+2	+3	2	0	3	5	8
2007	Bal	161	1399.2	318	2	.994	38	16	157	75	.478	10	303	-6	-1	+2	-6	-5	-3	2	5	4	12
2008	Bal	156	1367.0	347	3	.991	41	12	153	67	.438	14	329	+7	+10	+4	-4	+11	6	10	6	22	2
2009	Bal	161	1402.0	317	6	.981	36	25	136	66	.485	10	303	-6	-2	-2	-8	-12	-7	2	2	-3	25
2010	Bal	159	1402.1	342	3	.991	34	22	151	66	.437	9	332	-12	-3	-3	-13	-18	-11	0	0	-11	33
2011	Bal	157	1389.2	325	0	1.000	38	18	137	68	.496	9	312	-6	-4	-5	-1	-10	-6	2	6	2	11
		920	7874.0	1897	15	.992	204	109	836	392	.469	53	1819	-22	-3	+1	-30	-31	-19	16	22	19	9

Darnell McDonald

Year	Team	G	Inn	TC	E	Pct	GFP	DM	Opps to Advance	Extra Bases	Pct	Kills	Outs Made	Basic	Shallow	Medium	Deep	Enhanced	+/-	Throws	GFP/DME	Total	Rank
2004	Bal	8	48.1	14	0	1.000	1	2	7	2	.286	0	14	+3	+1	0	+4	+5	3	1	0	4	-
2007	Min	3	25.0	3	0	1.000	0	1	3	1	.333	0	2	0	0	0	0	0	0	0	0	0	-
2009	Cin	10	66.2	25	0	1.000	2	1	11	7	.636	0	24	+1	0	0	+1	+1	1	-1	0	0	-
2010	Bos	34	201.0	46	1	.978	3	4	24	16	.667	0	44	-3	-3	0	+3	-1	-1	-2	-2	-5	-
2011	Bos	37	207.1	41	1	.976	2	4	28	17	.607	0	39	+2	0	+1	+3	+4	2	-2	0	0	-
		92	548.1	129	2	.984	8	12	73	43	.589	0	123	+3	-2	+1	+11	+9	5	-4	-2	-1	-

Mitch Moreland

Year	Team	G	Inn	TC	E	Pct	GFP	DM	Opps to Advance	Extra Bases	Pct	Kills	Outs Made	Basic	Shallow	Medium	Deep	Enhanced	+/-	Throws	GFP/DME	Total	Rank
2010	Tex	7	45.0	11	1	.909	1	1	5	2	.400	0	10	+1	0	+1	+1	+2	1	0	0	1	-
2011	Tex	34	244.1	56	1	.982	2	4	21	11	.524	0	55	-3	0	+1	-5	-4	-2	0	0	-2	-
		41	289.1	67	2	.970	3	5	26	13	.500	0	65	-2	0	+2	-4	-2	-1	0	0	-1	-

David Murphy

Year	Team	G	Inn	TC	E	Pct	GFP	DM	Opps to Advance	Extra Bases	Pct	Kills	Outs Made	Basic	Shallow	Medium	Deep	Enhanced	+/-	Throws	GFP/DME	Total	Rank
2006	Bos	2	9.1	2	0	1.000	0	0	0	0	-	0	2	0	0	0	0	0	0	0	0	0	-
2007	2 tms	15	80.0	18	0	1.000	2	0	9	4	.444	2	14	0	-1	-1	+1	0	0	1	0	1	-
2008	Tex	56	407.1	109	6	.981	6	5	47	20	.426	1	107	+7	+3	+4	+4	+11	6	-2	0	4	-
2009	Tex	10	74.0	23	1	.957	0	2	7	3	.429	0	20	-1	+1	0	-3	-2	-1	1	0	0	-
2010	Tex	51	381.1	83	0	1.000	9	5	33	21	.636	1	80	+1	+3	-5	+2	0	0	-2	1	-1	-
2011	Tex	32	247.1	48	0	1.000	3	3	20	8	.400	1	47	+3	0	0	+5	+5	3	0	0	3	-
		166	1199.1	283	2	.993	20	15	116	56	.483	7	270	+10	+6	-2	+9	+14	8	-2	1	7	-

Right Fielders

Magglio Ordonez

Year	Team	G	Inn	TC	E	Pct	GFP	DM	Opps to Advance	Extra Bases	Pct	Kills	Outs Made	Basic	Shallow	Medium	Deep	Enhanced	+/-	Throws	GFP/DME	Total	Rank
2003	CWS	154	1324.2	325	2	.994	-	-	129	59	.457	7	311	0	-7	+4	+14	+11	6	2	-	8	7
2004	CWS	43	364.0	96	1	.990	8	5	38	22	.579	0	94	-6	-7	+1	+8	-3	-2	-2	0	-4	-
2005	Det	81	672.1	145	1	.993	7	7	86	47	.547	2	139	+2	-3	-1	-2	+4	2	0	0	2	14
2006	Det	148	1268.0	274	7	.974	12	26	113	45	.398	6	258	-11	-3	-3	-12	-16	-9	5	-3	-7	30
2007	Det	143	1221.0	266	1	.996	16	22	105	44	.419	3	261	+3	+5	+3	-5	+3	2	0	-1	1	16
2008	Det	135	1144.0	233	5	.979	10	18	143	72	.503	3	220	-5	-9	-3	+7	-5	-3	-2	-1	-6	27
2009	Det	104	796.1	157	2	.987	9	9	85	42	.494	2	149	-8	-3	-4	-11	-18	-10	-1	-1	-10	32
2010	Det	71	608.2	145	3	.979	5	10	75	34	.453	3	135	-6	-1	+3	-16	-14	-8	-1	-1	-10	30
2011	Det	69	471.2	92	0	1.000	8	13	54	28	.519	5	87	-10	-6	+1	-12	-16	-10	1	0	-9	33
		948	7870.2	1733	22	.987	75	110	828	393	.475	31	1654	-41	-34	+1	-29	-54	-32	2	-5	-35	32

Xavier Paul

Year	Team	G	Inn	TC	E	Pct	GFP	DM	Opps to Advance	Extra Bases	Pct	Kills	Outs Made	Basic	Shallow	Medium	Deep	Enhanced	+/-	Throws	GFP/DME	Total	Rank
2009	LAD	3	12.0	1	0	1.000	1	0	0	0	-	0	1	0	0			0	0	0	0	0	-
2010	LAD	15	101.0	21	1	.952	3	3	4	0	.000	0	20	0	-1	0	+2	+1	1	1	-1	1	-
2011	2 tms	72	274.1	61	1	.984	5	7	32	14	.438	0	60	-1	+1	-3	+1	0	-1	0	-1	-2	-
		90	387.1	83	2	.976	9	10	36	14	.389	0	81	-1	0	-3	+3	0	0	1	-2	-1	

Hunter Pence

Year	Team	G	Inn	TC	E	Pct	GFP	DM	Opps to Advance	Extra Bases	Pct	Kills	Outs Made	Basic	Shallow	Medium	Deep	Enhanced	+/-	Throws	GFP/DME	Total	Rank
2007	Hou	14	115.2	38	2	.947	1	0	11	6	.545	0	36	+1	0	0	+1	+1	1	-1	0	0	-
2008	Hou	156	1366.1	357	1	.997	27	27	116	46	.397	11	341	+5	+7	-2	-7	-2	-1	8	2	9	8
2009	Hou	157	1375.2	337	5	.985	29	29	132	53	.402	9	317	+13	+10	+3	+2	+15	9	6	2	17	1
2010	Hou	155	1370.1	355	6	.983	22	30	141	64	.454	5	341	+11	+3	+8	-4	+7	4	-1	-1	2	16
2011	2 tms	153	1342.2	301	6	.980	28	33	137	59	.431	7	285	0	+8	-5	-9	-7	-4	5	0	1	12
		635	5570.2	1388	20	.986	107	119	537	228	.425	32	1320	+30	+28	+4	-17	+14	9	17	3	29	5

Carlos Quentin

Year	Team	G	Inn	TC	E	Pct	GFP	DM	Opps to Advance	Extra Bases	Pct	Kills	Outs Made	Basic	Shallow	Medium	Deep	Enhanced	+/-	Throws	GFP/DME	Total	Rank
2006	Ari	44	389.0	101	2	.980	12	6	47	23	.489	2	96	-2	+2	-5	+1	-3	-2	0	2	0	16
2007	Ari	75	577.0	141	1	.993	10	7	55	23	.418	1	138	+1	-1	+1	+3	+3	2	-1	1	2	15
2010	CWS	104	897.0	195	8	.959	15	16	91	58	.637	2	183	-16	-2	-12	-11	-25	-15	-7	-2	-24	35
2011	CWS	102	854.2	180	1	.994	13	11	77	45	.584	0	177	+9	+8	+6	-1	+13	7	-6	-1	0	14
		325	2717.2	617	12	.981	50	40	270	149	.552	5	594	-8	+7	-10	-8	-12	-8	-14	0	-22	28

Josh Reddick

Year	Team	G	Inn	TC	E	Pct	GFP	DM	Opps to Advance	Extra Bases	Pct	Kills	Outs Made	Basic	Shallow	Medium	Deep	Enhanced	+/-	Throws	GFP/DME	Total	Rank
2009	Bos	10	35.0	10	1	.900	1	1	4	2	.500	0	9	0	+1	0	-1	-1	-1	0	0	-1	-
2010	Bos	15	66.2	13	0	1.000	2	3	7	5	.714	1	12	+1	+1	+1	0	+2	1	0	0	1	-
2011	Bos	56	432.2	111	4	.964	5	9	35	22	.629	3	103	+8	+2	+3	+10	+15	9	-1	-1	7	4
		81	534.1	134	5	.963	8	13	46	29	.630	4	124	+9	+4	+4	+9	+16	9	-1	-1	7	

Cody Ross

Year	Team	G	Inn	TC	E	Pct	GFP	DM	Opps to Advance	Extra Bases	Pct	Kills	Outs Made	Basic	Shallow	Medium	Deep	Enhanced	+/-	Throws	GFP/DME	Total	Rank
2003	Det	6	49.0	17	2	.882	-	-	7	3	.429		15	-1	0	0	-1	-1	-1	0	-	-1	-
2005	LAD	9	52.1	15	1	.933	1	1	7	5	.714	1	12	0	+1	0	0	+1	1	0	0	1	-
2006	2 tms	34	234.2	52	1	.981	4	8	24	10	.417	2	49	-3	-6	0	+2	-4	-2	1	0	-1	-
2007	Fla	19	106.1	33	1	.970	4	0	14	5	.357	2	30	0	0	0	0	0	0	2	1	3	-
2008	Fla	35	153.2	38	1	.974	4	3	10	3	.300	2	37	+3	+1	+1	+3	+6	3	0	-1	2	-
2009	Fla	57	450.0	107	1	.991	6	9	49	26	.531	2	104	+4	+1	+1	+4	+5	3	0	0	3	18
2010	2 tms	54	432.2	114	2	.982	6	5	29	13	.448	2	110	+6	+3	+1	+6	+10	6	0	0	6	9
2011	SF	35	268.0	49	0	1.000	4	9	17	12	.706	2	47	-2	+3	-2	-6	-5	-3	-1	0	-4	-
		249	1746.2	425	9	.979	29	35	157	77	.490	11	404	+7	+3	+1	+8	+12	7	2	0	9	

Nate Schierholtz

Year	Team	G	Inn	TC	E	Pct	GFP	DM	Opps to Advance	Extra Bases	Pct	Kills	Outs Made	Basic	Shallow	Medium	Deep	Enhanced	+/-	Throws	GFP/DME	Total	Rank
2007	SF	30	229.1	49	1	.980	4	5	20	12	.600	0	48	+4	+1	0	+7	+8	5	-2	-1	2	-
2008	SF	19	161.2	41	0	1.000	7	3	17	12	.706	0	40	+4	+2	+2	+5	+9	5	-2	0	3	-
2009	SF	86	597.2	147	2	.986	17	17	55	26	.473	7	136	+6	+4	-2	+5	+7	4	2	0	6	7
2010	SF	109	542.1	126	1	.992	14	20	46	20	.435	6	118	+3	+1	-1	+2	+2	1	4	0	5	10
2011	SF	96	703.2	152	2	.987	13	13	64	30	.469	4	142	-9	-2	-6	-7	-16	-9	1	0	-8	31
		340	2234.2	515	6	.988	55	58	202	100	.495	17	484	+8	+6	-7	+12	+10	6	3	-1	8	16

Right Fielders

Seth Smith

Year	Team	G	Inn	TC	E	Pct	GFP	DM	Opps to Advance	Extra Bases	Pct	Kills	Outs Made	Basic	Shallow	Medium	Deep	Enhanced	+/-	Throws	GFP/ DME	Total	Rank
2007	Col	1	2.0	0	0	-	0	0				0	0	0					0	0			0	-
2008	Col	14	86.0	19	0	1.000	3	2	14	8	.571	0	18	-1	0	0	-1	-1	-1	-1	-1	-3	-
2010	Col	33	223.2	50	1	.980	4	6	27	15	.556	0	182	+2	+2	-1	0	+1	1	-2	-2	-3	-
2011	Col	107	867.1	188	5	.973	13	21	80	49	.613	0	248	0	-5	0	+8	+3	2	-5	-3	-6	27
		155	1179.0	257	6	.977	20	29	121	72	.595	0		+1	-3	-1	+7	+3	2	-8	-6	-12	

Ryan Spilborghs

Year	Team	G	Inn	TC	E	Pct	GFP	DM	Opps to Advance	Extra Bases	Pct	Kills	Outs Made	Basic	Shallow	Medium	Deep	Enhanced	+/-	Throws	GFP/ DME	Total	Rank
2005	Col	1	8.0	7	0	1.000	0	0	1	1	1.000	1	6	0	0	0	0	+1	1	0		1	-
2006	Col	15	99.1	20	1	.950	3	3	13	7	.538	1	18	-1	0	0	-1	-1	-1	1	-1	-1	-
2007	Col	20	124.1	25	0	1.000	2	4	10	5	.500	0	25	-1	0	-1	+1	-1	-1	-1	1	-1	-
2008	Col	22	146.0	39	2	.949	3	2	17	7	.412	1	37	-2	0	-1	-3	-5	-3	-1	-1	-5	-
2009	Col	37	192.1	39	1	.974	6	8	24	10	.417	1	37	+1	+1	0	0	+1	1	0	-1	0	-
2010	Col	62	401.2	85	4	.953	5	7	36	26	.722	0	81	-4	-1	-2	-2	-4	-2	-4	-2	-8	-
2011	Col	29	209.1	37	0	1.000	4	4	21	14	.667	1	35	-1	-1	-1	+2	0	0	-1	-1	-2	-
		186	1181.0	252	8	.968	23	28	122	70	.574	4	239	-8	-1	-5	-3	-9	-5	-6	-5	-16	-

Mike Stanton

Year	Team	G	Inn	TC	E	Pct	GFP	DM	Opps to Advance	Extra Bases	Pct	Kills	Outs Made	Basic	Shallow	Medium	Deep	Enhanced	+/-	Throws	GFP/ DME	Total	Rank
2010	Fla	98	854.2	233	4	.983	25	16	102	48	.471	8	219	+6	-2	+3	+16	+17	10	2	1	13	4
2011	Fla	142	1219.0	296	6	.980	25	43	120	51	.425	5	280	+8	+5	-4	+7	+9	5	2	-4	3	8
		240	2073.2	529	10	.981	50	59	222	99	.446	13	499	+14	+3	-1	+23	+26	15	4	-3	16	12

Ichiro Suzuki

Year	Team	G	Inn	TC	E	Pct	GFP	DM	Opps to Advance	Extra Bases	Pct	Kills	Outs Made	Basic	Shallow	Medium	Deep	Enhanced	+/-	Throws	GFP/ DME	Total	Rank
2003	Sea	159	1367.0	351	2	.994	-	-	140	53	.379	8	333	+7	+2	+4	+10	+15	9	6	-	15	2
2004	Sea	158	1405.1	387	3	.992	25	15	146	55	.377	7	367	+22	+14	+1	+4	+32	19	6	5	30	1
2005	Sea	158	1388.1	392	2	.995	34	11	168	88	.524	6	383	+7	+5	+8	0	+10	6	-5	6	7	9
2006	Sea	121	1061.2	260	2	.992	13	9	119	55	.462	4	250	+7	+1	+1	+13	+14	8	1	2	11	2
2008	Sea	91	788.1	186	4	.978	24	14	93	39	.419	6	176	+7	+5	+6	+2	+13	8	3	1	12	5
2009	Sea	145	1291.0	326	4	.988	31	14	124	58	.468	4	317	+6	+4	+8	-4	+8	5	-5	3	3	15
2010	Sea	160	1412.0	365	4	.989	28	22	144	74	.514	4	353	+3	+1	+10	-8	+3	2	-5	2	-1	18
2011	Sea	151	1333.0	274	4	.985	23	10	127	71	.559	5	263	-4	-2	+7	-9	-4	-2	-3	2	-3	21
		1143	10046.2	2541	25	.990	178	95	1061	493	.465	42	2442	+55	+30	+45	+8	+91	55	-2	21	74	1

Nick Swisher

Year	Team	G	Inn	TC	E	Pct	GFP	DM	Opps to Advance	Extra Bases	Pct	Kills	Outs Made	Basic	Shallow	Medium	Deep	Enhanced	+/-	Throws	GFP/ DME	Total	Rank
2004	Oak	4	28.0	7	2	.714	0	1	5	2	.400	0	5	0	0	0	0	-1	-1	0	-1	-2	-
2005	Oak	121	1027.1	204	2	.990	23	13	83	41	.494	4	197	+7	+4	-4	+8	+4	2	-1	2	3	13
2006	Oak	1	3.0	1	0	1.000	0	0	0	0		0	1	0	0			0	0	0	0	0	-
2007	Oak	57	413.2	109	0	1.000	5	6	36	19	.528	2	109	+6	+5	+2	-2	+5	3	0	0	3	13
2008	CWS	18	118.0	26	1	.962	4	1	12	7	.583	0	25	+1	+1	-1	+1	+1	1	-2	0	-1	-
2009	NYY	130	1052.2	246	5	.980	17	25	91	39	.429	2	239	+1	+2	+3	-8	-3	-2	-2	-3	-7	28
2010	NYY	134	1102.0	279	6	.986	25	25	105	53	.505	4	265	-4	+5	-5	-5	-6	-3	2	0	-1	20
2011	NYY	141	1190.1	283	1	.996	28	22	131	53	.405	3	273	-4	+4	-3	-15	-13	-8	3	1	-4	26
		606	4935.0	1155	15	.987	102	93	463	214	.462	17	1114	+7	+21	-8	-21	-13	-8	0	-1	-9	25

Eric Thames

Year	Team	G	Inn	TC	E	Pct	GFP	DM	Opps to Advance	Extra Bases	Pct	Kills	Outs Made	Basic	Shallow	Medium	Deep	Enhanced	+/-	Throws	GFP/ DME	Total	Rank
2011	Tor	27	223.0	57	1	.982	4	8	25	10	.400	1	55	0	+3	+2	-8	-3	-2	1	-2	-3	-

Justin Upton

Year	Team	G	Inn	TC	E	Pct	GFP	DM	Opps to Advance	Extra Bases	Pct	Kills	Outs Made	Basic	Shallow	Medium	Deep	Enhanced	+/-	Throws	GFP/ DME	Total	Rank
2007	Ari	42	315.1	71	5	.930	5	4	29	16	.552	1	65	+2	0	0	+3	+3	2	-1	0	1	-
2008	Ari	101	860.1	192	11	.943	11	27	82	38	.463	6	175	0	-2	+1	+4	+3	2	1	-3	0	19
2009	Ari	136	1180.0	310	12	.961	13	32	120	52	.433	2	294	+4	-4	-2	+23	+17	10	-1	-5	4	11
2010	Ari	128	1117.0	270	4	.985	16	16	118	58	.492	0	265	+6	-2	+6	+12	+16	9	-5	-2	2	15
2011	Ari	159	1366.2	357	13	.964	23	36	128	62	.484	3	340	+9	-6	+1	+34	+29	17	-5	-4	8	3
		566	4839.1	1200	45	.963	68	115	477	226	.474	12	1139	+21	-14	+6	+76	+68	40	-11	-14	15	13

Right Fielders

Will Venable

	BASIC							THROWING				PLUS/MINUS						RUNS SAVED				
Year Team	G	Inn	TC	E	Pct	GFP	DM	Opps to Advance	Extra Bases	Pct	Kills	Outs Made	Basic	Shallow	Medium	Deep	Enhanced	+/-	Throws	GFP/DME	Total	Rank
2009 SD	68	493.2	126	1	.992	10	7	56	21	.375	2	123	+4	+2	0	+4	+7	4	0	-1	3	16
2010 SD	89	600.1	148	3	.980	7	16	54	24	.444	1	144	+9	+1	+12	-1	+12	7	0	0	7	8
2011 SD	91	662.2	151	2	.987	10	9	44	21	.477	2	147	+8	+5	+1	+4	+10	6	0	-1	5	6
	248	1756.2	425	6	.986	27	32	154	66	.429	5	414	+21	+8	+13	+7	+29	17	0	-2	15	-

Casper Wells

	BASIC							THROWING				PLUS/MINUS						RUNS SAVED				
Year Team	G	Inn	TC	E	Pct	GFP	DM	Opps to Advance	Extra Bases	Pct	Kills	Outs Made	Basic	Shallow	Medium	Deep	Enhanced	+/-	Throws	GFP/DME	Total	Rank
2010 Det	29	151.1	26	0	1.000	4	2	13	10	.769	2	24	0	0	+3	-2	+2	1	1	0	2	-
2011 2 tms	58	274.1	64	1	.984	4	3	21	9	.429	2	61	+1	0	+2	0	+1	0	1	0	1	-
	87	425.2	90	1	.989	8	5	34	19	.559	4	85	+1	0	+5	-2	+3	1	2	0	3	-

Jayson Werth

	BASIC							THROWING				PLUS/MINUS						RUNS SAVED				
Year Team	G	Inn	TC	E	Pct	GFP	DM	Opps to Advance	Extra Bases	Pct	Kills	Outs Made	Basic	Shallow	Medium	Deep	Enhanced	+/-	Throws	GFP/DME	Total	Rank
2003 Tor	19	99.0	22	0	1.000	-	-	14	7	.500	1	16	-1	-1	0	0	-1	-1	1	-	0	-
2004 LA	14	74.0	19	0	1.000	2	1	2	2	1.000	0	19	+1	-1	0	+1	+1	1	-1	0	0	-
2005 LAD	43	291.0	74	0	1.000	3	3	24	11	.458	3	71	+3	+3	-1	-2	+2	1	2	0	3	-
2007 Phi	58	446.0	118	2	.983	17	8	47	13	.277	3	109	+3	+1	+2	+4	+7	4	5	2	11	4
2008 Phi	88	661.1	150	0	1.000	12	10	50	20	.400	6	143	+2	+3	+1	-4	0	0	4	2	6	10
2009 Phi	146	1288.2	341	4	.988	16	26	119	49	.412	6	327	+8	+8	+4	-3	+9	5	3	-4	4	12
2010 Phi	135	1171.0	261	4	.985	33	24	96	32	.333	5	249	-3	+3	+2	-20	-15	-9	5	2	-2	23
2011 Was	134	1172.2	305	8	.974	31	29	141	62	.440	8	288	-7	0	-2	-8	-11	-6	3	-1	-4	25
	637	5203.2	1290	18	.986	114	101	493	196	.398	32	1222	+6	+16	+6	-32	-8	-5	22	1	18	11

Ben Zobrist

	BASIC							THROWING				PLUS/MINUS						RUNS SAVED				
Year Team	G	Inn	TC	E	Pct	GFP	DM	Opps to Advance	Extra Bases	Pct	Kills	Outs Made	Basic	Shallow	Medium	Deep	Enhanced	+/-	Throws	GFP/DME	Total	Rank
2008 TB	2	7.0	0	0	-	0	0	0	0	-	0	0	0				0	0	0	0	0	-
2009 TB	59	329.1	94	0	1.000	18	5	47	14	.298	5	89	+2	0	+2	+2	+4	2	5	2	9	-
2010 TB	103	749.1	188	0	1.000	21	13	60	24	.400	5	182	+6	+2	+2	+3	+7	4	3	1	8	6
2011 TB	38	289.2	66	0	1.000	9	5	21	8	.381	0	65	+5	0	+4	+4	+8	5	0	1	6	-
	202	1375.1	348	0	1.000	48	23	128	46	.359	10	336	+13	+2	+8	+9	+19	11	8	4	23	-

Pitchers

Alfredo Aceves

Year	Tm	Inn	TC	E	GFP	DM	+/-	SB	CCS	PCS/PPO	CS%	+/-	SB	Bnt	GFP/DME	Tot	Rnk
2008	NYY	30	5	0	1	0	-1	2	2	0	.50	-1	0	1	0	0	-
2009	NYY	84	13	2	0	0	0	10	1	1	.17	0	-1	1	0	0	86
2010	NYY	12	2	0	1	0	+1	3	0	0	.00	1	0	0	0	0	-
2011	Bos	114	11	0	0	1	-1	9	0	0	.00	-1	-1	0	0	-2	135
		240	31	2	2	1	-1	24	3	1	.14	-1	-2	2	0	-1	-

Mike Adams

Year	Tm	Inn	TC	E	GFP	DM	+/-	SB	CCS	PCS/PPO	CS%	+/-	SB	Bnt	GFP/DME	Tot	Rnk
2004	Mil	53	5	0	0	0	+1	6	0	1	.14	1	0	-1	0	0	-
2005	Mil	13	1	0	0	0	0	1	0	0	.00	0	0	0	0	0	-
2006	Mil	2	0	0	0	0	0	1	0	0	.00	0	0	0	0	0	-
2008	SD	65	14	0	1	1	0	5	1	0	.17	0	0	0	0	0	-
2009	SD	37	6	0	1	1	0	2	1	0	.33	0	0	0	0	0	-
2010	SD	67	10	0	1	0	+1	6	1	0	.14	1	-1	0	0	0	-
2011	2 tms	74	9	0	1	0	-1	9	0	0	.00	-1	-2	0	0	-3	-
		311	45	0	4	2	1	30	3	1	.12	1	-3	-1	0	-3	-

Nathan Adcock

Year	Tm	Inn	TC	E	GFP	DM	+/-	SB	CCS	PCS/PPO	CS%	+/-	SB	Bnt	GFP/DME	Tot	Rnk
2011	KC	60	15	0	1	0	+1	5	1	0	.17	1	0	1	1	3	-

Jeremy Affeldt

Year	Tm	Inn	TC	E	GFP	DM	+/-	SB	CCS	PCS/PPO	CS%	+/-	SB	Bnt	GFP/DME	Tot	Rnk
2003	KC	126	24	1	-	-	-4	14	2	4	.30	-3	0	1	-	-2	147
2004	KC	76	17	2	2	1	+1	2	2	0	.50	1	0	0	0	1	-
2005	KC	50	8	1	2	0	+1	3	0	0	.00	1	0	0	0	1	-
2006	2 tms	97	15	1	1	1	-1	8	0	0	.00	-1	-1	-1	0	-3	159
2007	Col	59	14	0	1	0	+2	7	1	0	.13	2	-1	0	0	1	-
2008	Cin	78	30	1	1	1	+2	7	1	0	.13	2	-1	0	0	1	-
2009	SF	62	17	1	2	1	+4	4	0	1	.20	3	0	0	0	3	-
2010	SF	50	21	3	1	0	-1	2	2	0	.50	-1	0	1	0	0	-
2011	SF	62	18	0	1	2	+2	4	1	0	.20	2	0	0	0	2	-
		660	164	10	11	6	6	51	9	5	.22	6	-3	1	0	4	62

Matt Albers

Year	Tm	Inn	TC	E	GFP	DM	+/-	SB	CCS	PCS/PPO	CS%	+/-	SB	Bnt	GFP/DME	Tot	Rnk
2006	Hou	15	8	0	0	0	0	1	0	0	.00	0	0	0	0	0	-
2007	Hou	111	21	1	0	3	0	11	3	0	.21	0	-1	0	-1	-2	134
2008	Bal	49	11	0	0	1	+1	3	1	0	.25	1	0	0	0	1	-
2009	Bal	67	10	0	0	0	-1	9	3	0	.25	-1	-1	1	0	-1	-
2010	Bal	76	22	1	1	2	+1	8	2	0	.00	1	-1	0	-1	-1	-
2011	Bos	65	10	1	1	1	-1	6	3	1	.40	-1	0	0	0	-1	-
		382	82	3	2	8	0	38	12	1	.25	0	-3	1	-2	-4	-

Henderson Alvarez

Year	Tm	Inn	TC	E	GFP	DM	+/-	SB	CCS	PCS/PPO	CS%	+/-	SB	Bnt	GFP/DME	Tot	Rnk
2011	Tor	64	19	1	2	0	+4	1	2	0	.67	3	1	0	0	4	-

Brett Anderson

Year	Tm	Inn	TC	E	GFP	DM	+/-	SB	CCS	PCS/PPO	CS%	+/-	SB	Bnt	GFP/DME	Tot	Rnk
2009	Oak	175	29	0	0	3	-3	14	0	4	.22	-2	0	0	0	-2	147
2010	Oak	112	36	1	0	1	+1	8	1	4	.38	0	1	1	0	2	51
2011	Oak	83	23	2	1	2	-2	5	2	5	.58	-1	2	0	0	1	88
		371	88	3	5	9	-4	27	3	13	.37	-3	3	1	0	1	-

Jake Arrieta

Year	Tm	Inn	TC	E	GFP	DM	+/-	SB	CCS	PCS/PPO	CS%	+/-	SB	Bnt	GFP/DME	Tot	Rnk
2010	Bal	100	23	2	2	2	+1	11	1	2	.08	1	0	-1	0	0	85
2011	Bal	119	28	3	0	1	+4	11	4	0	.27	3	-1	0	0	2	42
		219	51	5	2	3	5	22	5	2	.19	4	-1	-1	0	2	-

Bronson Arroyo

Year	Tm	Inn	TC	E	GFP	DM	+/-	SB	CCS	PCS/PPO	CS%	+/-	SB	Bnt	GFP/DME	Tot	Rnk
2003	Bos	17	2	0	-	-	0	0	0	0	-	0		-		0	-
2004	Bos	179	42	2	1	0	-3	4	5	0	.56	-2	1	0	0	-1	116
2005	Bos	205	44	2	1	0	-4	4	3	1	.43	-3	1	0	0	-1	134
2006	Cin	241	62	0	4	5	0	5	5	0	.50	0	1	0	0	1	65
2007	Cin	211	39	1	2	4	+1	3	6	2	.67	1	3	-1	0	3	34
2008	Cin	200	50	0	2	2	+2	5	1	2	.29	2	1	2	0	5	9
2009	Cin	220	51	2	3	1	+2	12	5	1	.33	2	0	1	1	4	12
2010	Cin	216	49	0	6	0	+8	6	2	0	.25	6	0	1	1	8	7
2011	Cin	199	56	4	3	0	+3	9	4	0	.31	2	0	2	0	4	18
		1687	395	11	22	15	+9	48	31	6	.41	8	7	6	2	23	12

John Axford

Year	Tm	Inn	TC	E	GFP	DM	+/-	SB	CCS	PCS/PPO	CS%	+/-	SB	Bnt	GFP/DME	Tot	Rnk
2009	Mil	8	1	0	0	0	0	1	0	0	.00	0	0	0	0	0	-
2010	Mil	58	9	0	3	0	-1	2	0	0	.00	0	0	0	0	0	-
2011	Mil	74	10	2	0	0	+1	6	2	0	.25	0	0	0	0	0	-
		139	20	2	3	0	0	9	2	0	.18	0	0	0	0	0	-

Burke Badenhop

Year	Tm	Inn	TC	E	GFP	DM	+/-	SB	CCS	PCS/PPO	CS%	+/-	SB	Bnt	GFP/DME	Tot	Rnk
2008	Fla	47	12	0	0	0	+3	4	3	0	.43	2	0	0	0	2	-
2009	Fla	72	15	0	1	1	0	4	0	0	.00	0	0	1	0	1	-
2010	Fla	68	23	1	0	2	+1	1	2	0	.67	1	1	0	-1	1	-
2011	Fla	64	13	0	1	0	-2	2	1	1	.33	-1	1	0	1	1	-
		250	63	1	2	3	2	11	6	1	.35	2	2	1	0	5	-

Homer Bailey

Year	Tm	Inn	TC	E	GFP	DM	+/-	SB	CCS	PCS/PPO	CS%	+/-	SB	Bnt	GFP/DME	Tot	Rnk
2007	Cin	45	7	1	0	0	-1	9	0	1	.00	-1	-1	0	0	-2	-
2008	Cin	36	6	1	0	1	-1	8	1	0	.11	-1	-1	0	0	-2	-
2009	Cin	113	26	2	1	2	0	10	5	1	.33	0	0	0	1	1	69
2010	Cin	109	22	1	0	2	-2	10	6	1	.38	-2	0	0	0	-2	144
2011	Cin	132	26	1	2	2	-1	9	2	1	.18	-1	0	-1	0	-2	135
		436	87	6	3	7	-5	46	14	4	.23	-5	-2	-1	1	-7	-

Scott Baker

Year	Tm	Inn	TC	E	GFP	DM	+/-	SB	CCS	PCS/PPO	CS%	+/-	SB	Bnt	GFP/DME	Tot	Rnk
2005	Min	54	11	0	1	0	-1	0	3	1	1.00	-1	1	0	0	0	-
2006	Min	83	11	0	0	0	-1	5	3	0	.38	-1	0	0	0	-1	111
2007	Min	144	21	2	1	0	-1	11	4	0	.27	0	-1	2	0	1	73
2008	Min	172	22	1	3	0	-1	8	5	0	.38	-1	0	0	0	-1	118
2009	Min	200	26	0	5	2	+1	10	3	1	.23	1	0	0	1	2	43
2010	Min	170	29	1	0	1	0	3	6	1	.67	0	2	0	0	2	51
2011	Min	135	17	0	1	2	-2	4	5	0	.56	-2	1	-1	0	-2	143
		958	137	4	11	8	-4	41	29	3	.41	-4	3	1	1	1	84

Grant Balfour

Year	Tm	Inn	TC	E	GFP	DM	+/-	SB	CCS	PCS/PPO	CS%	+/-	SB	Bnt	GFP/DME	Tot	Rnk
2003	Min	26	4	0	-	-	+1	2	1	0	.33	1	0	0	0	1	-
2004	Min	39	7	0	0	0	-1	2	2	0	.50	-1	0	0	0	-1	-
2007	2 tms	25	6	0	0	2	0	3	0	2	.25	-2	1	-1	0	-2	-
2008	TB	58	5	0	0	1	0	2	1	0	.33	0	0	0	0	0	-
2009	TB	67	4	0	0	0	-1	6	1	0	.14	-1	0	1	0	0	-
2010	TB	55	4	0	1	0	0	2	2	0	.50	0	0	0	0	0	-
2011	Oak	62	6	0	0	0	-1	1	0	0	.00	0	0	0	0	0	-
		333	36	0	1	4	-4	18	7	2	.31	-3	1	0	0	-2	-

Daniel Bard

Year	Tm	Inn	TC	E	GFP	DM	+/-	SB	CCS	PCS/PPO	CS%	+/-	SB	Bnt	GFP/DME	Tot	Rnk
2009	Bos	49	8	2	0	1	+1	4	0	0	.00	1	-1	-2	0	-2	-
2010	Bos	75	16	2	0	0	-2	8	1	0	.11	-1	-1	0	0	-2	-
2011	Bos	73	17	1	1	1	0	7	1	0	.13	0	-1	-2	0	-3	-
		197	41	5	1	1	-1	19	2	0	.10	0	-3	-4	0	-7	-

Pitchers

Miguel Batista

Year	Tm	Inn	TC	E	GFP	DM	+/-	SB	CCS	PCS/PPO	CS%	+/-	SB	Bnt	GFP/DME	Tot	Rnk
2003	Ari	193	44	3	-	-	0	8	7	1	.50	0	1	-1	-	0	86
2004	Tor	199	49	1	1	2	+2	9	11	0	.55	2	1	-1	0	2	36
2005	Tor	75	9	1	0	0	-4	2	0	0	.00	-3	0	-1	0	-4	-
2006	Ari	206	50	4	1	7	+2	15	5	2	.32	2	0	-3	0	-1	102
2007	Sea	193	43	2	3	5	-1	14	8	1	.39	-1	1	0	-1	-1	113
2008	Sea	115	25	1	3	3	0	19	2	0	.10	0	-3	0	1	-2	135
2009	Sea	71	12	0	0	0	+1	7	2	0	.22	1	0	0	0	1	-
2010	Was	83	14	0	1	2	0	8	3	0	.27	0	0	0	0	0	88
2011	2 tms	60	12	0	1	1	+1	4	0	0	.00	1	0	0	0	1	-
		1195	258	12	10	20	1	86	38	4	.33	2	0	-6	0	-4	108

Heath Bell

Year	Tm	Inn	TC	E	GFP	DM	+/-	SB	CCS	PCS/PPO	CS%	+/-	SB	Bnt	GFP/DME	Tot	Rnk
2004	NYM	24	3	0	0	0	0	2	0	0	.00	0	0		0	0	-
2005	NYM	47	10	0	0	0	0	4	0	0	.00	0	-1	0	0	-1	-
2006	NYM	37	7	0	0	0	0	2	2	0	.50	0	0	0	0	0	-
2007	SD	94	24	0	2	0	+2	8	2	1	.27	2	0	0	0	2	42
2008	SD	78	15	0	1	1	-1	10	2	0	.17	-1	-1	0	0	-2	-
2009	SD	70	16	0	1	0	+1	5	1	1	.17	1	0		0	1	-
2010	SD	70	7	0	1	1	-1	3	3	0	.50	-1	1		0	0	-
2011	SD	63	8	0	0	0	-2	4	0	0	.00	-1	0	1	0	0	-
		482	90	0	5	2	-1	38	10	2	.22	0	-1	1	0	0	88

Brandon Beachy

Year	Tm	Inn	TC	E	GFP	DM	+/-	SB	CCS	PCS/PPO	CS%	+/-	SB	Bnt	GFP/DME	Tot	Rnk
2010	Atl	15	4	0	0	0	0	1	1	0	.50	0	0		0	0	-
2011	Atl	142	23	0	1	0	+2	13	3	2	.24	1	0	0	0	1	65
		156	27	0	1	0		14	4		.26	1	0	0	0	1	-

Joaquin Benoit

Year	Tm	Inn	TC	E	GFP	DM	+/-	SB	CCS	PCS/PPO	CS%	+/-	SB	Bnt	GFP/DME	Tot	Rnk
2003	Tex	105	23	1	-	-	+3	4	5	0	.56	2	1	0	-	3	20
2004	Tex	103	13	1	1	1	-1	4	1	0	.20	-1	0	0	0	-1	109
2005	Tex	87	9	0	0	0	+2	5	2	0	.29	2	0	0	0	2	46
2006	Tex	80	8	0	0	0	0	1	0	0	.00	-1	0	0	0	-1	-
2007	Tex	82	12	0	1	0	0	2	2	0	.50	0	1		0	1	73
2008	Tex	45	7	0	0	0	+1	1	1	0	.50	1	0	-1	0	0	-
2010	TB	60	4	0	1	0	0	2	1	1	.50	0	1		0	1	-
2011	Det	61	5	0	1	0	0	3	2	0	.40	0	0	1	0	1	-
		623	81	2	4	1	4	22	14	1	.41	3	3	0	0	6	53

Pedro Beato

Year	Tm	Inn	TC	E	GFP	DM	+/-	SB	CCS	PCS/PPO	CS%	+/-	SB	Bnt	GFP/DME	Tot	Rnk
2011	NYM	67	17	0	0	2	+2	6	3	0	.33	2	0	0	0	2	-

Brad Bergesen

Year	Tm	Inn	TC	E	GFP	DM	+/-	SB	CCS	PCS/PPO	CS%	+/-	SB	Bnt	GFP/DME	Tot	Rnk
2009	Bal	123	39	0	1	2	+7	1	3	0	.75	5	1	0	0	6	3
2010	Bal	170	33	0	1	0	+5	9	3	0	.25	4	0	0	0	4	16
2011	Bal	101	18	2	1	3	+1	4	4	0	.50	1	1		0	2	47
		394	90	2	3	5	13	14	10	0	.42	10	2	0	0	12	-

Blake Beavan

Year	Tm	Inn	TC	E	GFP	DM	+/-	SB	CCS	PCS/PPO	CS%	+/-	SB	Bnt	GFP/DME	Tot	Rnk
2011	Sea	97	15	0	1	1	0	6	2	1	.33	0	0	0	0	0	100

Rafael Betancourt

Year	Tm	Inn	TC	E	GFP	DM	+/-	SB	CCS	PCS/PPO	CS%	+/-	SB	Bnt	GFP/DME	Tot	Rnk
2003	Cle	38	3	0	-	-	-1	3	0	0	.00	-1	0	0	-	-1	-
2004	Cle	67	5	0	0	1	0	7	2	0	.22	0	-1	0	0	-1	-
2005	Cle	68	6	0	2	0	-1	3	4	0	.57	-1	1		0	0	-
2006	Cle	57	3	0	0	0	-1	8	2	0	.20	-1	-1	0	0	-2	-
2007	Cle	79	6	0	0	0	0	4	4	0	.50	0	0	0	0	0	-
2008	Cle	71	9	1	1	0	-2	10	1	0	.09	-2	-1	1	0	-2	-
2009	2 tms	56	5	0	0	0	0	8	1	0	.11	0	-1		0	-1	-
2010	Col	62	7	0	0	1	0	8	2	0	.20	0	-1	1	0	0	-
2011	Col	62	2	0	0	1	-1	5	0	0	.00	-1	-1	0	0	-2	-
		560	46	1	3	3	-6	56	16	0	.22	-6	-5	2	0	-9	144

Josh Beckett

Year	Tm	Inn	TC	E	GFP	DM	+/-	SB	CCS	PCS/PPO	CS%	+/-	SB	Bnt	GFP/DME	Tot	Rnk
2003	Fla	142	25	1	-	-	-2	5	5	0	.50	-2	1	0	-	-1	127
2004	Fla	157	23	2	2	2	+1	5	5	0	.50	1	1	-1	0	1	58
2005	Fla	179	38	1	1	2	-1	6	6	1	.54	-1	0	0	0	0	99
2006	Bos	205	38	0	1	2	-2	15	1	0	.06	-2	-2	0	0	-4	165
2007	Bos	201	32	2	2	4	-3	14	6	1	.30	-2	0	0	-1	-3	153
2008	Bos	174	35	2	3	0	-1	7	4	1	.42	-1	1	0	0	0	97
2009	Bos	212	27	2	1	5	0	15	3	0	.17	0	-1	0	0	-1	115
2010	Bos	128	30	1	0	3	+3	18	1	0	.05	2	-3	-1	0	-2	130
2011	Bos	193	36	3	3	2	-1	31	4	0	.11	-1	-4	0	0	-5	165
		1590	284	14	13	20	-6	116	35	3	.24	-6	-6	-2	-1	-15	163

Erik Bedard

Year	Tm	Inn	TC	E	GFP	DM	+/-	SB	CCS	PCS/PPO	CS%	+/-	SB	Bnt	GFP/DME	Tot	Rnk
2004	Bal	137	19	0	1	1	-3	10	3	0	.23	-2	-1	0	1	-2	131
2005	Bal	142	29	1	2	2	+4	8	2	2	.33	3	0	-2	0	1	57
2006	Bal	196	34	1	2	3	+3	4	2	0	.33	2	0	0	0	2	38
2007	Bal	182	23	0	1	1	+2	5	2	0	.29	2	0	0	0	2	42
2008	Sea	81	10	0	1	0	+2	5	1	0	.17	2	0	0	1	3	27
2009	Sea	83	10	0	1	0	+1	5	2	1	.38	1	0	0	0	1	60
2011	2 tms	129	15	1	0	2	-1	3	2	2	.50	0	2	-1	0	1	74
		950	140	3	8	9	8	40	14	5	.31	8	1	-3	2	8	40

Chad Billingsley

Year	Tm	Inn	TC	E	GFP	DM	+/-	SB	CCS	PCS/PPO	CS%	+/-	SB	Bnt	GFP/DME	Tot	Rnk
2006	LAD	90	9	0	0	2	-1	5	5	1	.50	-1	1	0	0	0	93
2007	LAD	147	25	0	1	0	0	5	4	2	.55	0	2	0	0	2	57
2008	LAD	201	33	2	4	2	+1	8	4	0	.33	1	0	0	0	1	60
2009	LAD	196	37	4	1	2	-1	7	8	1	.56	-1	2	0	0	1	74
2010	LAD	192	33	1	0	1	0	10	4	1	.33	0	0	-2	0	-2	134
2011	LAD	188	31	2	2	3	+1	9	4	0	.31	1	0	0	0	1	65
		1013	168	9	8	10	0	44	29	5	.43	0	5	-2	0	3	70

Nick Blackburn

Year	Tm	Inn	TC	E	GFP	DM	+/-	SB	CCS	PCS/PPO	CS%	+/-	SB	Bnt	GFP/DME	Tot	Rnk
2007	Min	12	0	0	0	0	0	0	1	0	1.00	-1	0	0		-1	-
2008	Min	193	36	0	3	0	-1	2	2	0	.50	-1	1	1	0	1	77
2009	Min	206	49	1	2	2	-2	12	1	3	.14	-2	0	0	0	-2	147
2010	Min	161	38	2	5	5	+1	4	1	4	.44	1	1	0	0	2	43
2011	Min	148	42	2	4	3	+2	11	9	3	.45	1	2	1	0	4	23
		720	165	5	14	10	-1	30	17	7	.38	-2	4	2	0	4	66

Matt Belisle

Year	Tm	Inn	TC	E	GFP	DM	+/-	SB	CCS	PCS/PPO	CS%	+/-	SB	Bnt	GFP/DME	Tot	Rnk
2003	Cin	9	2	0	-	-	-1	0	0	0		-1	0	0		-1	-
2005	Cin	86	18	2	1	1	-1	7	2	0	.22	-1	0	0	0	-1	120
2006	Cin	40	6	0	0	1	0	1	0	0	.00	0	0	-1	0	-1	-
2007	Cin	178	30	0	3	1	-2	11	6	0	.35	-2	0	0	0	-2	138
2008	Cin	30	8	1	0	0	0	3	1	0	.25	0	0		0	0	-
2009	Col	31	8	0	1	0	0	4	0	0	.00	1	0	0		-1	-
2010	Col	92	16	2	1	0	0	6	1	0	.33	0	0	-1	0	-1	109
2011	Col	72	13	0	1	1	0	0	3	1	1.00	0	1	0	0	1	-
		536	101	5	7	5	-4	28	13	1	.33	-4	0	-2	0	-6	123

Pitchers

Mitchell Boggs

Year	Tm	Inn	TC	E	GFP	DM	+/-	SB	CCS	PCS/PPO	CS%	+/-	SB	Bnt	GFP/DME	Tot	Rnk
2008	StL	34	12	1	0	1	+1	2	0	0	.00	1	0		0	0	-
2009	StL	58	16	0	3	0	+2	3	1	1	.40	2	0	0	0	2	-
2010	StL	67	12	1	0	0	0	2	2	0	.50	0	0	0	0	0	-
2011	StL	61	11	1	2	3	-1	2	2	0	.50	-1	0	0	-1	-2	-
		220	51	3	5	4	2	9	5	1	.40	2	0	0	-1	1	-

Zach Britton

Year	Tm	Inn	TC	E	GFP	DM	+/-	SB	CCS	PCS/PPO	CS%	+/-	SB	Bnt	GFP/DME	Tot	Rnk
2011	Bal	154	32	2	1	2	-1	7	3	0	.30	-1	0	-3	0	-4	160

Clay Buchholz

Year	Tm	Inn	TC	E	GFP	DM	+/-	SB	CCS	PCS/PPO	CS%	+/-	SB	Bnt	GFP/DME	Tot	Rnk
2007	Bos	23	5	1	1	2	-1	0	0	1		-1	1	-1	-1	-2	-
2008	Bos	76	9	0	0	2	-3	3	2	1	.40	-2	1		-1	-2	-
2009	Bos	92	17	1	2	0	-1	6	0	0	.00	-1	-1	0	0	-2	138
2010	Bos	174	47	2	3	4	-1	8	4	3	.43	-1	2	0	-1	0	101
2011	Bos	83	30	1	2	1	+2	6	2	1	.33	2	0	0	0	2	44
		447	108	5	8	9	-4	23	8	6	.32	-3	3	-1	-3	-4	-

Mark Buehrle

Year	Tm	Inn	TC	E	GFP	DM	+/-	SB	CCS	PCS/PPO	CS%	+/-	SB	Bnt	GFP/DME	Tot	Rnk
2003	CWS	230	53	0	-	-	-3	1	2	5	.80	-2	3	1		2	55
2004	CWS	245	72	4	9	3	+7	5	2	10	.62	5	4	0	1	10	3
2005	CWS	237	60	2	8	1	+2	8	1	5	.27	2	2	1	0	5	4
2006	CWS	204	45	1	0	2	+5	4	3	10	.64	4	5	-1	0	8	4
2007	CWS	201	48	1	3	2	+2	2	0	5	.60	2	3	1	0	6	4
2008	CWS	219	52	0	2	3	0	5	2	7	.58	5	4	0	1	5	11
2009	CWS	213	55	1	7	2	+9	4	0	8	.50	7	3	0	0	10	1
2010	CWS	210	50	0	5	2	+8	6	1	11	.50	6	5	1	0	12	2
2011	CWS	205	56	1	1	2	+6	3	3	6	.70	4	4	-1	0	7	5
		1965	491	10	35	17	36	38	14	67	.56	28	33	2	2	65	1

Madison Bumgarner

Year	Tm	Inn	TC	E	GFP	DM	+/-	SB	CCS	PCS/PPO	CS%	+/-	SB	Bnt	GFP/DME	Tot	Rnk
2009	SF	10	3	0	1	0	+1	0	0	0		1	0	0	0	1	-
2010	SF	111	14	1	2	1	0	8	1	1	.20	0	0	0	0	0	88
2011	SF	205	32	3	1	4	-4	12	8	4	.48	-3	2	0	-1	-2	147
		325	49	4	4	5	-3	20	9	5	.39	-2	2	0	-1	-1	-

A.J. Burnett

Year	Tm	Inn	TC	E	GFP	DM	+/-	SB	CCS	PCS/PPO	CS%	+/-	SB	Bnt	GFP/DME	Tot	Rnk
2003	Fla	23	7	0	-	-	0	1	1	0	.50	0	0		-	0	-
2004	Fla	120	28	0	2	4	+3	14	4	2	.26	2	-1	1	0	2	36
2005	Fla	209	31	2	2	4	-3	24	6	1	.20	-2	-2	0	0	-4	164
2006	Tor	136	23	1	3	3	-2	18	4	1	.18	-2	-2	1	0	-3	160
2007	Tor	166	34	2	2	4	-1	31	0	0	.00	-1	-5	0	0	-6	171
2008	Tor	221	54	7	3	2	-2	22	5	5	.29	-2	0	-1	0	-3	151
2009	NYY	207	28	3	1	3	+1	23	10	4	.34	1	1	0	0	2	43
2010	NYY	187	29	4	5	6	-1	37	3	4	.12	-1	-4	-1	-1	-7	174
2011	NYY	190	38	5	0	2	-6	24	5	5	.23	-4	0	0	0	-4	162
		1458	272	24	18	28	-11	194	38	22	.20	-9	-13	0	-1	-23	173

Trevor Cahill

Year	Tm	Inn	TC	E	GFP	DM	+/-	SB	CCS	PCS/PPO	CS%	+/-	SB	Bnt	GFP/DME	Tot	Rnk
2009	Oak	179	36	1	2	0	+3	17	8	2	.37	2	0	1	1	4	12
2010	Oak	197	61	1	8	0	+12	15	2	5	.25	9	1	0	1	11	3
2011	Oak	208	45	1	3	3	+1	28	7	3	.22	1	-2	-2	0	-3	150
		583	142	3	13	3	16	60	17	10	.28	12	-1	-1	2	12	30

Matt Cain

Year	Tm	Inn	TC	E	GFP	DM	+/-	SB	CCS	PCS/PPO	CS%	+/-	SB	Bnt	GFP/DME	Tot	Rnk
2005	SF	46	4	1	0	0		1	1	0	.50	0	0	0	0	0	-
2006	SF	191	35	3	1	3	-2	15	3	0	.17	-2	-1	0	0	-2	142
2007	SF	200	31	0	4	4	-2	8	5	0	.38	-2	1	1	0	0	102
2008	SF	218	38	0	1	4	-2	13	10	0	.43	-2	1	1	0	0	103
2009	SF	218	39	0	2	6	0	11	9	0	.45	0	1	0	-1	0	86
2010	SF	223	35	2	2	0	+2	19	7	3	.34	1	0	1	0	2	43
2011	SF	222	40	3	3	3	+2	18	5	0	.22	2	-1	1	-1	1	62
		1317	222	9	13	20	-2	85	40	3	.34	-3	1	5	-2	1	83

Shawn Camp

Year	Tm	Inn	TC	E	GFP	DM	+/-	SB	CCS	PCS/PPO	CS%	+/-	SB	Bnt	GFP/DME	Tot	Rnk
2004	KC	67	16	0	0	2	+3	3	0	0	.00	2	0	0	0	2	-
2005	KC	49	10	0	1	1	0	3	3	1	.50	0	1	0	0	1	-
2006	TB	75	20	1	0	1	0	6	2	0	.25	0	0	0	0	0	-
2007	TB	40	8	0	0	0	-1	2	0	0	.00	-1	0	1	0	0	-
2008	Tor	39	9	0	1	1	+2	3	0	0	.00	2	0	0	0	2	-
2009	Tor	80	20	2	2	1	+1	0	1	0	1.00	1	1	0	0	2	43
2010	Tor	72	8	1	0	1	-1	7	1	0	.13	0	-1		0	-1	-
2011	Tor	66	24	1	0	0	0	8	1	3	.20	0	0	1	0	1	-
		488	115	4	5	6	4	32	8	4	.22	4	1	2	0	7	44

Matt Capps

Year	Tm	Inn	TC	E	GFP	DM	+/-	SB	CCS	PCS/PPO	CS%	+/-	SB	Bnt	GFP/DME	Tot	Rnk
2005	Pit	4	2	0	0	0	0	2	0	1	.00	0	0	0	0	0	-
2006	Pit	81	16	2	0	2	0	3	3	0	.50	0	0	-1	0	-1	107
2007	Pit	79	9	0	0	2	-3	1	0	0	.00	-2	0	1	0	-1	-
2008	Pit	54	5	0	0	0	-1	4	1	0	.20	-1	0	0	0	-1	-
2009	Pit	54	10	1	0	1	0	6	0	0	.00	0	-1	0	0	-1	-
2010	2 tms	73	11	0	1	0	-1	3	2	0	.40	0	0	0	0	0	-
2011	Min	66	15	0	2	0	+1	2	0	0	.00	1	0	1	0	2	-
		410	68	3	3	5	-4	21	6	1	.22	-2	-1	1	0	-2	-

Chris Capuano

Year	Tm	Inn	TC	E	GFP	DM	+/-	SB	CCS	PCS/PPO	CS%	+/-	SB	Bnt	GFP/DME	Tot	Rnk
2003	Ari	33	10	1	-	-	+2	3	0	2	.00	2	0	0	-	2	-
2004	Mil	88	19	0	1	1	+1	1	0	6	.50	1	3	0	0	4	24
2005	Mil	219	48	4	2	2	-4	2	3	12	.82	-3	6	0	1	4	25
2006	Mil	221	47	2	6	3	+2	1	1	6	.75	2	3	0	1	6	7
2007	Mil	150	38	1	7	2	+2	6	0	2	.00	2	1	2	1	6	4
2010	Mil	66	12	0	0	0	+2	1	0	0	.00	1	0	0	0	1	-
2011	NYM	186	35	0	4	3	0	9	2	3	.36	0	1	0	0	1	74
		963	209	8	20	11	5	23	6	31	.44	5	14	2	3	24	11

Fausto Carmona

Year	Tm	Inn	TC	E	GFP	DM	+/-	SB	CCS	PCS/PPO	CS%	+/-	SB	Bnt	GFP/DME	Tot	Rnk
2006	Cle	75	24	0	0	1	+2	10	1	1	.17	2	-1	0	0	1	-
2007	Cle	215	64	2	4	0	0	13	5	2	.28	0	1	1	0	2	57
2008	Cle	121	32	2	2	3	+2	6	1	0	.14	2	0	0	-1	1	52
2009	Cle	125	29	0	0	3	+1	8	4	0	.33	1	0	0	-1	0	79
2010	Cle	210	63	2	3	5	+8	33	6	0	.15	8	-4	0	-1	1	59
2011	Cle	189	38	0	1	4	+4	15	6	0	.29	3	-1	0	0	2	42
		934	250	6	10	16	17	85	23	3	.22	14	-5	1	-3	7	42

Chris Carpenter

Year	Tm	Inn	TC	E	GFP	DM	+/-	SB	CCS	PCS/PPO	CS%	+/-	SB	Bnt	GFP/DME	Tot	Rnk
2004	StL	182	46	1	1	4	+3	0	3	0	1.00	2	1	1	0	4	18
2005	StL	242	56	1	4	1	+2	1	4	2	.83	2	2	-1	0	3	27
2006	StL	222	36	0	0	3	+3	3	7	0	.70	2	2	0	0	4	18
2007	StL	6	2	0	0	0	0	0	0	0		0	0	0	0	0	-
2008	StL	15	5	0	0	0	0	0	0	0	-	0	0	1	0	1	-
2009	StL	193	40	1	2	5	-6	2	3	1	.67	-5	1	0	0	-4	170
2010	StL	235	65	1	5	1	+3	3	9	0	.75	2	2	0	1	5	14
2011	StL	237	54	3	6	4	-4	5	6	0	.55	-3	2	1	0	0	118
		1331	304	6	18	18	1	14	32	3	.71	0	10	2	1	13	29

Pitchers

Carlos Carrasco

Year	Tm	Inn	TC	E	GFP	DM	+/-	SB	CCS	PCS/PPO	CS%	+/-	SB	Bnt	GFP/DME	Tot	Rnk
2009	Cle	22	9	1	0	2	+1	3	1	3	.50	1	1		-1	1	-
2010	Cle	45	8	0	1	0	+2	5	6	0	.55	1			0	1	-
2011	Cle	125	19	0	1	2	+1	6	1	2	.33	1	1	0	0	2	47
		191	36	1	2	4	4	14	8	5	.46	3	2	0	-1	4	-

Brett Cecil

Year	Tm	Inn	TC	E	GFP	DM	+/-	SB	CCS	PCS/PPO	CS%	+/-	SB	Bnt	GFP/DME	Tot	Rnk
2009	Tor	93	11	1	0	2	+2	4	4	0	.50	2	1	-1	0	2	36
2010	Tor	173	25	1	1	1	0	4	1	1	.33	0	1	1	-1	1	69
2011	Tor	124	14	1	2	1	+2	4	2	0	.33	1	0	0	0	1	65
		389	50	3	3	4	4	12	7	1	.40	3	2	0	-1	4	-

Jhoulys Chacin

Year	Tm	Inn	TC	E	GFP	DM	+/-	SB	CCS	PCS/PPO	CS%	+/-	SB	Bnt	GFP/DME	Tot	Rnk
2009	Col	11	2	0	0	0	0	3	1	0	.25	0	0		0	0	-
2010	Col	137	22	1	0	1	+1	3	0	0	.30	1	0	1	0	2	43
2011	Col	194	69	4	0	2	+9	4	7	1	.64	6	2	-1	0	7	3
		342	93	5	1	2	10	14	11	1	.44	7	2	0	0	9	-

Tyler Chatwood

Year	Tm	Inn	TC	E	GFP	DM	+/-	SB	CCS	PCS/PPO	CS%	+/-	SB	Bnt	GFP/DME	Tot	Rnk
2011	LAA	142	31	0	1	0	+2	12	6	2	.37	2	1	0	0	3	26

Bruce Chen

Year	Tm	Inn	TC	E	GFP	DM	+/-	SB	CCS	PCS/PPO	CS%	+/-	SB	Bnt	GFP/DME	Tot	Rnk
2003	2 tms	24	1	0	-	-	0	2	0	0	.00	0	0	0	-	0	-
2004	Bal	48	11	0	1	0	0	1	0	2	.67	0	1		0	1	-
2005	Bal	197	37	2	4	2	+2	17	4	1	.32	2	0	1	0	3	27
2006	Bal	99	18	0	0	0	0	9	3	3	.40	0	1	0	0	1	65
2007	Tex	10	0	0	0	0	0	0	0	0	-	0	0			0	-
2009	KC	62	13	1	2	1	0	4	0	4	.50	0	1	0	0	1	-
2010	KC	140	29	1	1	1	+3	5	0	8	.58	2	3	1	0	6	10
2011	KC	155	32	0	6	3	+3	12	2	4	.33	2	1	0	0	3	26
		735	141	4	14	7	8	50	9	25	.40	6	7	2	0	15	23

Tyler Clippard

Year	Tm	Inn	TC	E	GFP	DM	+/-	SB	CCS	PCS/PPO	CS%	+/-	SB	Bnt	GFP/DME	Tot	Rnk
2007	NYY	27	4	0	0	0	0	5	0	0	.00	0	-1		0	-1	-
2008	Was	10	0	0	0	0	0	0	0	0	-	0	0			0	-
2009	Was	60	9	0	0	0	0	1	1	0	.50	0	0	1	0	1	-
2010	Was	91	5	0	0	1	-1	5	1	1	.17	-1	0	0	0	-1	119
2011	Was	88	8	0	0	1	0	3	4	1	.63	0	1	0	0	1	74
		277	26	0	0	2	-1	14	6	2	.33	-1	0	1	0	0	-

Phil Coke

Year	Tm	Inn	TC	E	GFP	DM	+/-	SB	CCS	PCS/PPO	CS%	+/-	SB	Bnt	GFP/DME	Tot	Rnk
2008	NYY	15	3	0	2	0	+1	0	0	0	-	1	0		0	1	-
2009	NYY	60	14	2	0	3	+3	2	2	0	.50	2	0	-1	-1	0	-
2010	Det	65	9	1	0	1	-2	1	0	0	.00	-1	0	0	0	-1	-
2011	Det	109	21	2	0	0	-3	10	3	3	.38	-2	1	1	0	0	114
		248	47	5	2	4	-1	13	5	3	.38	0	1	0	-1	0	-

Casey Coleman

Year	Tm	Inn	TC	E	GFP	DM	+/-	SB	CCS	PCS/PPO	CS%	+/-	SB	Bnt	GFP/DME	Tot	Rnk
2010	ChC	57	12	0	0	0	+1	2	2	0	.67	1	0	0	0	2	-
2011	ChC	84	20	0	1	1	+2	8	1	1	.11	1	0	1	0	2	47
		141	32	0	1	2	3	9	3	1	.25	2	1	1	0	4	-

Tim Collins

Year	Tm	Inn	TC	E	GFP	DM	+/-	SB	CCS	PCS/PPO	CS%	+/-	SB	Bnt	GFP/DME	Tot	Rnk
2011	KC	67	10	0	3	2	+1	7	1	0	.13	1	-1	1	-1	0	-

Josh Collmenter

Year	Tm	Inn	TC	E	GFP	DM	+/-	SB	CCS	PCS/PPO	CS%	+/-	SB	Bnt	GFP/DME	Tot	Rnk
2011	Ari	154	24	0	1	1	-1	4	7	0	.64	0	1	0	0	1	74

Bartolo Colon

Year	Tm	Inn	TC	E	GFP	DM	+/-	SB	CCS	PCS/PPO	CS%	+/-	SB	Bnt	GFP/DME	Tot	Rnk
2003	CWS	242	31	3	-	-	-2	1	6	1	.86	-2	2	1	-	0	106
2004	Ana	208	41	3	6	1	-1	3	6	1	.67	-1	2	1	0	2	56
2005	LAA	223	24	0	1	5	-3	2	4	0	.67	-2	1	0	0	-1	127
2006	LAA	56	12	1	0	1	0	1	3	0	.75	0	1	0	0	1	-
2007	LAA	99	12	1	0	2	-4	2	2	0	.50	-3	1	0	0	-2	147
2008	Bos	39	8	2	1	1	-2	0	0	0	-	-2	0	0	0	-2	-
2009	CWS	62	14	1	0	0	0	0	0	1	-	0	0	1	0	1	-
2011	NYY	164	29	1	4	0	0	5	3	1	.38	0	1	0	0	1	74
		1094	171	12	12	10	-12	14	24	4	.63	-10	9	1	0	0	93

Aaron Cook

Year	Tm	Inn	TC	E	GFP	DM	+/-	SB	CCS	PCS/PPO	CS%	+/-	SB	Bnt	GFP/DME	Tot	Rnk
2003	Col	124	38	3	-	-	-1	8	1	1	.11	-1	0	1	-	0	94
2004	Col	97	32	0	1	1	+3	4	1	1	.20	2	0	0	0	2	36
2005	Col	83	21	2	4	0	-3	3	0	0	.00	-2	0		0	-2	141
2006	Col	213	69	2	6	5	+7	4	2	4	.42	2	1	0	0	3	23
2007	Col	166	47	0	3	3	+6	8	2	0	.20	5	0	0	0	5	6
2008	Col	211	60	2	4	4	+4	5	8	4	.62	3	4	0	0	7	4
2009	Col	158	58	4	4	1	+2	4	4	3	.50	2	2	0	0	4	12
2010	Col	128	25	1	2	1	-2	4	0	2	.00	-1	1	0	1	1	78
2011	Col	97	43	1	2	0	+5	4	6	1	.80	4	2	0	0	6	9
		1276	393	15	26	15	16	44	24	14	.36	14	10	1	1	26	7

Francisco Cordero

Year	Tm	Inn	TC	E	GFP	DM	+/-	SB	CCS	PCS/PPO	CS%	+/-	SB	Bnt	GFP/DME	Tot	Rnk
2003	Tex	83	19	1	-	-	+2	5	4	2	.50	2	1	0	-	3	-
2004	Tex	72	14	0	0	0	0	5	1	2	.29	0	0	0	0	0	-
2005	Tex	69	12	0	1	0	0	4	0	0	.00	0	0	0	0	0	-
2006	2 tms	75	11	0	0	1	0	4	2	0	.33	0	0	1	0	1	-
2007	Mil	63	8	0	1	1	-1	3	0	0	.00	-1	0	0	0	-1	-
2008	Cin	70	8	1	1	2	0	7	2	1	.30	0	0	0	0	0	-
2009	Cin	67	13	0	1	0	-1	3	3	1	.57	-1	1	0	0	0	-
2010	Cin	73	12	1	2	2	-1	12	1	0	.08	-1	1	0	0	-3	-
2011	Cin	70	17	0	4	0	0	9	2	0	.18	-1	-1	1	0	-1	-
		641	114	4	10	6	-2	52	15	6	.27	-2	-1	2	0	-1	94

Kevin Correia

Year	Tm	Inn	TC	E	GFP	DM	+/-	SB	CCS	PCS/PPO	CS%	+/-	SB	Bnt	GFP/DME	Tot	Rnk
2003	SF	39	7	0	-	-	0	4	2	0	.33	0	0	0	-	0	-
2004	SF	19	3	0	0	2	-1	3	0	0	.00	-1	0	-1	0	-2	-
2005	SF	58	4	0	0	0	-2	4	2	0	.33	-2	0	-1	0	-3	-
2006	SF	70	6	0	2	0	-1	3	2	1	.50	-1	1	0	0	0	-
2007	SF	102	17	0	1	1	-2	10	3	0	.23	-2	-1		0	-3	153
2008	SF	110	21	1	0	0	-2	4	6	1	.64	-2	2	-1	0	-1	121
2009	SD	198	46	2	3	2	0	7	6	1	.50	0	1	-2	0	-1	115
2010	SD	145	28	2	0	0	+1	11	5	0	.31	0	0	0	0	0	88
2011	Pit	154	33	0	4	2	+2	6	5	1	.50	2	1	-1	0	2	44
		895	165	5	10	7	-5	52	31	4	.40	-6	4	-6	0	-8	136

Pitchers

Jesse Crain

		BASIC						HOLDING				RUNS SAVED					
Year	Tm	Inn	TC	E	GFP	DM	+/-	SB	CCS	PCS/PPO	CS%	+/-	SB	Bnt	GFP/DME	Tot	Rnk
2004	Min	27	6	1	0	0	-1	1	0	0	.00	-1	0	0	0	-1	-
2005	Min	80	29	1	5	1	-1	3	0	0	.00	-1	0	2	1	2	-
2006	Min	77	17	1	1	0	0	4	1	0	.20	0	0	0	0	0	-
2007	Min	16	7	0	1	0	+1	0	1	0	1.00	1	0	0	0	1	-
2008	Min	63	14	3	1	1	+1	6	1	0	.14	1	-1	0	0	0	-
2009	Min	52	14	1	1	1	+1	4	1	1	.20	1	0	0	0	1	-
2010	Min	68	18	1	0	0	0	7	1	1	.13	0	0	1	0	1	-
2011	CWS	65	15	1	5	1	0	13	2	2	.13	0	-1	0	0	-1	-
		447	120	8	14	4	1	38	7	4	.16	1	-2	3	1	3	

Aaron Crow

		BASIC						HOLDING				RUNS SAVED					
Year	Tm	Inn	TC	E	GFP	DM	+/-	SB	CCS	PCS/PPO	CS%	+/-	SB	Bnt	GFP/DME	Tot	Rnk
2011	KC	62	13	1	0	0	-3	6	1	0	.14	-2	0	1	0	-1	-

Johnny Cueto

		BASIC						HOLDING				RUNS SAVED					
Year	Tm	Inn	TC	E	GFP	DM	+/-	SB	CCS	PCS/PPO	CS%	+/-	SB	Bnt	GFP/DME	Tot	Rnk
2008	Cin	174	34	3	1	3	-1	7	6	1	.46	-1	1	0	0	0	97
2009	Cin	171	21	2	2	4	+1	2	3	2	.71	1	2	0	-1	2	43
2010	Cin	186	42	2	2	1	0	3	2	3	.57	0	2	0	0	2	51
2011	Cin	156	46	5	2	1	+1	1	4	2	.80	1	2	0	0	3	33
		687	143	12	7	9	1	13	15	8	.59	1	7	0	-1	7	47

John Danks

		BASIC						HOLDING				RUNS SAVED					
Year	Tm	Inn	TC	E	GFP	DM	+/-	SB	CCS	PCS/PPO	CS%	+/-	SB	Bnt	GFP/DME	Tot	Rnk
2007	CWS	139	23	1	2	0	+2	10	0	2	.09	2	0	0	0	2	42
2008	CWS	195	40	0	2	3	+2	23	2	6	.26	2	0	1	1	4	16
2009	CWS	200	42	2	2	4	+2	18	3	6	.28	2	1	0	-1	2	36
2010	CWS	213	40	0	7	4	+3	6	2	4	.50	2	2	1	-1	4	20
2011	CWS	170	34	0	2	1	-1	15	2	7	.35	-1	2	2	0	3	41
		917	179	3	15	12	8	72	9	25	.29	7	5	4	-1	15	22

Kyle Davies

		BASIC						HOLDING				RUNS SAVED					
Year	Tm	Inn	TC	E	GFP	DM	+/-	SB	CCS	PCS/PPO	CS%	+/-	SB	Bnt	GFP/DME	Tot	Rnk
2005	Atl	88	17	1	1	0	-1	0	2	2	1.00	-1	2	1	0	2	53
2006	Atl	63	8	0	0	0	0	4	1	1	.20	0	0	0	0	0	-
2007	2 tms	136	26	2	3	2	+2	14	3	0	.18	2	-1	-1	0	0	84
2008	KC	113	15	1	1	1	-3	8	1	0	.11	-2	-1	1	0	-2	141
2009	KC	123	22	2	0	2	-1	17	4	1	.19	-1	-1	0	0	-2	138
2010	KC	184	38	2	3	2	-1	17	3	0	.15	-1	-1	0	0	-2	139
2011	KC	61	11	1	1	1	+1	8	2	0	.20	0	-1	-1	0	-2	-
		768	137	9	9	8	-5	68	16	4	.21	-3	-3	0	0	-6	122

Wade Davis

		BASIC						HOLDING				RUNS SAVED					
Year	Tm	Inn	TC	E	GFP	DM	+/-	SB	CCS	PCS/PPO	CS%	+/-	SB	Bnt	GFP/DME	Tot	Rnk
2009	TB	36	5	0	0	0	0	4	1	0	.20	0	0	0	0	0	-
2010	TB	168	37	2	1	0	-3	13	4	2	.28	-3	0	1	0	-2	146
2011	TB	184	29	0	2	0	-1	2	3	2	.67	0	2	1	0	3	40
		388	71	2	3	0	-4	19	8	4	.34	-3	2	2	0	1	-

Rubby de la Rosa

		BASIC						HOLDING				RUNS SAVED					
Year	Tm	Inn	TC	E	GFP	DM	+/-	SB	CCS	PCS/PPO	CS%	+/-	SB	Bnt	GFP/DME	Tot	Rnk
2011	LAD	61	18	2	1	2	-1	9	4	0	.31	-1	-1	0	-1	-3	-

Ryan Dempster

		BASIC						HOLDING				RUNS SAVED					
Year	Tm	Inn	TC	E	GFP	DM	+/-	SB	CCS	PCS/PPO	CS%	+/-	SB	Bnt	GFP/DME	Tot	Rnk
2003	Cin	116	21	3	-	-	-1	1	2	1	.75	-1	1	-1	-	-1	120
2004	ChC	21	6	0	0	0	+1	2	0	0	.00	1	0	0	0	1	-
2005	ChC	92	20	0	1	1	0	6	2	0	.25	0	0	1	0	1	64
2006	ChC	75	12	1	0	2	-1	5	0	0	.00	-1	-1	0	0	-2	-
2007	ChC	67	11	0	0	0	0	9	0	0	.00	0	-1	0	0	-1	-
2008	ChC	207	53	1	5	2	+6	11	4	0	.27	5	0	0	0	5	6
2009	ChC	200	53	3	4	1	+2	16	11	0	.41	2	0	1	0	3	28
2010	ChC	215	47	1	0	3	+2	16	6	0	.27	1	-1	-1	-1	-2	131
2011	ChC	202	52	3	1	4	+1	17	10	0	.37	1	-1	-1	0	0	93
		1194	275	12	11	13	10	83	35	1	.30	8	-2	-1	-1	4	61

Ross Detwiler

		BASIC						HOLDING				RUNS SAVED					
Year	Tm	Inn	TC	E	GFP	DM	+/-	SB	CCS	PCS/PPO	CS%	+/-	SB	Bnt	GFP/DME	Tot	Rnk
2007	Was	1	0	0	0	0	0	0	0	0	-					0	-
2009	Was	76	18	0	1	0	+1	6	0	3	.33	1	1	0	0	2	-
2010	Was	30	8	0	2	0	-1	4	1	1	.33	-1	0	0	0	-1	-
2011	Was	66	9	1	0	1	-1	3	2	0	.40	-1	0	-1	0	-2	-
		172	35	1	3	1	-1	13	3	4	.35	-1	1	-1	0	-1	-

R.A. Dickey

		BASIC						HOLDING				RUNS SAVED					
Year	Tm	Inn	TC	E	GFP	DM	+/-	SB	CCS	PCS/PPO	CS%	+/-	SB	Bnt	GFP/DME	Tot	Rnk
2003	Tex	117	20	0	-	-	+3	7	2	1	.22	2	0	0	-	2	36
2004	Tex	104	31	2	1	1	-1	6	5	4	.45	-1	2	0	0	1	71
2005	Tex	30	10	0	0	0	+3	3	0	0	.00	2	0	0	0	2	-
2006	Tex	3	0	0												0	-
2008	Sea	112	29	0	1	0	+2	6	3	5	.54	2	2	0	0	4	16
2009	Min	64	15	1	0	2	-1	5	1	1	.17	-1	0	0	0	-1	-
2010	NYM	174	61	0	5	1	+8	9	2	1	.25	6	0	1	1	8	7
2011	NYM	209	67	2	3	1	+8	7	2	5	.30	6	2	1	1	10	1
		813	233	5	10	5	22	43	15	17	.33	16	6	2	2	26	6

Kyle Drabek

		BASIC						HOLDING				RUNS SAVED					
Year	Tm	Inn	TC	E	GFP	DM	+/-	SB	CCS	PCS/PPO	CS%	+/-	SB	Bnt	GFP/DME	Tot	Rnk
2010	Tor	17	7	1	0	0	-2	2	1	0	.33	-1	0	0	0	-1	-
2011	Tor	79	23	0	2	1	+2	8	3	4	.27	2	1	1	0	4	18
		95	30	1	2	1	0	10	4	4	.29	1	1	1	0	3	-

Brian Duensing

		BASIC						HOLDING				RUNS SAVED					
Year	Tm	Inn	TC	E	GFP	DM	+/-	SB	CCS	PCS/PPO	CS%	+/-	SB	Bnt	GFP/DME	Tot	Rnk
2009	Min	84	23	0	0	1	+2	1	1	2	.75	2	1	-1	0	2	36
2010	Min	131	30	0	2	1	+4	3	1	1	.25	3	1	1	0	5	13
2011	Min	162	32	4	2	1	-2	6	5	1	.50	-2	1	-1	1	-1	128
		376	85	4	4	3	4	10	7	4	.50	3	3	-1	1	6	-

Danny Duffy

		BASIC						HOLDING				RUNS SAVED					
Year	Tm	Inn	TC	E	GFP	DM	+/-	SB	CCS	PCS/PPO	CS%	+/-	SB	Bnt	GFP/DME	Tot	Rnk
2011	KC	105	17	0	1	1	-2	11	2	7	.45	-1	2	1	0	2	59

Zach Duke

		BASIC						HOLDING				RUNS SAVED					
Year	Tm	Inn	TC	E	GFP	DM	+/-	SB	CCS	PCS/PPO	CS%	+/-	SB	Bnt	GFP/DME	Tot	Rnk
2005	Pit	85	19	0	0	0	+1	1	1	2	.75	1	1	1	0	3	33
2006	Pit	215	61	1	3	2	+7	13	5	7	.48	5	3	1	0	9	3
2007	Pit	107	24	0	1	1	+1	5	3	2	.50	1	1	1	0	3	34
2008	Pit	185	52	2	2	1	+5	6	2	4	.50	4	2	0	0	6	5
2009	Pit	213	53	2	5	2	+3	7	4	4	.53	2	2	0	0	4	12
2010	Pit	159	34	0	1	0	+1	10	1	2	.23	1	0	0	0	1	60
2011	Ari	77	16	0	0	1	-3	0	3	1	1.00	-2	1	0	0	-1	128
		1041	259	5	12	7	15	42	19	22	.49	12	10	3	0	25	9

Pitchers

Mike Dunn

Year	Tm	Inn	TC	E	GFP	DM	+/-	SB	CCS	PCS/PPO	CS%	+/-	SB	Bnt	GFP/DME	Tot	Rnk
2009	NYY	4	0	0	0	0	0	0	0	0	-		0			0	-
2010	Atl	19	1	0	0	0	0	1	0	0	.00	0	0		0	0	-
2011	Fla	63	11	1	0	0	-3	1	0	1	.50	-2	1	-1		-2	-
		86	12	1	0	0	-3	2	0	1	.33	-2	1	-1	0	-2	

Chad Durbin

Year	Tm	Inn	TC	E	GFP	DM	+/-	SB	CCS	PCS/PPO	CS%	+/-	SB	Bnt	GFP/DME	Tot	Rnk
2003	Cle	9	2	1	-	-	0	1	0	0	.00	0	0			0	-
2004	2 tms	61	10	1	0	0	0	6	2	0	.25	0	0	0	0	0	-
2006	Det	6	0	0	0	0	0	0	0	0	-	0				0	-
2007	Det	128	19	0	1	2	+3	5	2	0	.29	2	0	1	0	3	27
2008	Phi	88	18	0	2	0	-1	3	4	1	.57	-1	1	1	0	1	77
2009	Phi	70	10	0	0	0	-1	5	1	0	.17	-1	0	0	0	-1	-
2010	Phi	69	19	0	0	2	+1	3	1	2	.25	1	1	1	0	3	-
2011	Cle	68	10	0	0	4	0	6	3	0	.33	0	0		0	0	-
		497	88	2	3	8	2	29	13	3	.31	1	2	3	0	6	54

Marco Estrada

Year	Tm	Inn	TC	E	GFP	DM	+/-	SB	CCS	PCS/PPO	CS%	+/-	SB	Bnt	GFP/DME	Tot	Rnk
2008	Was	13	3	0	0	1	0	0	1	0	1.00	0	0			0	-
2009	Was	7	0	0	0	0	0	0	0	0	-	0	0			0	-
2010	Mil	11	3	0	0	0	0	3	0	0	.00	0	-1			-1	-
2011	Mil	93	16	0	0	0	-1	8	2	1	.20	-1	0	0	0	-1	123
		124	22	0	0	1	-1	11	3	1	.21	-1	-1	0	0	-2	

Neftali Feliz

Year	Tm	Inn	TC	E	GFP	DM	+/-	SB	CCS	PCS/PPO	CS%	+/-	SB	Bnt	GFP/DME	Tot	Rnk
2009	Tex	31	5	1	0	0	0	1	0	0	.00	0	0			0	-
2010	Tex	69	5	0	0	0	0	0	0	0	-	0	0	0	0	0	-
2011	Tex	62	14	1	0	0	-1	1	3	2	.75	-1	2	0	0	1	-
		162	24	2	0	0		2	3	2	.60	-1	2	0	0		

Doug Fister

Year	Tm	Inn	TC	E	GFP	DM	+/-	SB	CCS	PCS/PPO	CS%	+/-	SB	Bnt	GFP/DME	Tot	Rnk
2009	Sea	61	13	1	2	0	+2	0	1	0	1.00	0			1	3	-
2010	Sea	171	37	1	1	1	-2	2	2	2	.60	-2	2	1	0	1	83
2011	2 tms	216	58	3	9	6	+5	4	2	0	.33	4	1	-1	0	4	15
		448	108	5	12	7	5	6	5	2	.50	4	3	0	1	8	

Gavin Floyd

Year	Tm	Inn	TC	E	GFP	DM	+/-	SB	CCS	PCS/PPO	CS%	+/-	SB	Bnt	GFP/DME	Tot	Rnk
2004	Phi	28	4	0	1	1	0	7	1	0	.13	0	-1	0	0	-1	-
2005	Phi	26	5	0	1	1	-2	2	0	0	.00	-2	0	0	0	-2	-
2006	Phi	54	11	0	1	1	0	11	1	1	.15	0	-1	-1	0	-2	-
2007	CWS	70	12	1	0	0	-1	12	0	0	.00	-1	-2	0	0	-3	-
2008	CWS	206	43	2	4	6	0	37	4	1	.12	0	-5	1	0	-4	160
2009	CWS	193	32	1	2	1	+3	14	4	0	.22	2	-1	0	0	1	57
2010	CWS	187	35	2	2	1	0	7	3	1	.36	0	1	0	0	1	69
2011	CWS	194	35	1	4	0	+2	23	2	1	.08	1	-2	0	0	0	93
		959	177	8	14	12	4	113	15	4	.14	0	-11	0	1	-10	147

Jeff Francis

Year	Tm	Inn	TC	E	GFP	DM	+/-	SB	CCS	PCS/PPO	CS%	+/-	SB	Bnt	GFP/DME	Tot	Rnk
2004	Col	37	8	0	0	0	-1	2	0	0	.00	-1	0	0	0	-1	-
2005	Col	184	25	0	1	1	-1	19	6	5	.37	-1	1	1	0	1	70
2006	Col	199	42	0	1	5	+2	21	3	5	.25	2	0	1	0	3	23
2007	Col	215	45	0	1	1	+5	9	1	4	.31	4	1	0	0	5	9
2008	Col	144	30	1	3	0	+3	9	1	1	.18	2	0	0	0	2	36
2010	Col	104	19	0	0	0	+1	6	1	2	.33	1	0	0	0	1	60
2011	KC	183	35	0	1	1	+5	18	4	1	.22	4	-1	0	0	4	15
		1065	204	1	6	8	14	84	16	18	.28	11	1	3	0	15	21

Jason Frasor

Year	Tm	Inn	TC	E	GFP	DM	+/-	SB	CCS	PCS/PPO	CS%	+/-	SB	Bnt	GFP/DME	Tot	Rnk
2004	Tor	68	16	0	1	1	0	2	1	0	.33	0	0	0	0	0	-
2005	Tor	75	14	1	1	1	+1	5	3	0	.38	1	0	0	0	1	-
2006	Tor	50	13	1	1	0	-1	4	1	0	.20	-1	0	0	0	-1	-
2007	Tor	57	9	0	1	3	+1	5	2	0	.29	1	0	1	-1	1	-
2008	Tor	47	10	0	1	0	+2	5	2	0	.29	2	0		0	2	-
2009	Tor	58	8	0	1	3	0	6	2	0	.25	0	0	0	0	0	-
2010	Tor	64	12	1	0	1	-2	6	1	0	.14	-1	-1	0	0	-2	-
2011	2 tms	60	8	0	0	1	+2	10	2	0	.17	1	-2		0	-1	-
		478	90	3	6	10	3	43	14	0	.25	3	-3	1	-1	0	87

Ernesto Frieri

Year	Tm	Inn	TC	E	GFP	DM	+/-	SB	CCS	PCS/PPO	CS%	+/-	SB	Bnt	GFP/DME	Tot	Rnk
2009	SD	2	0	0	0	0	0	0	0	0	-	0				0	-
2010	SD	32	2	0	0	0	0	2	1	0	.33	0	0		0	0	-
2011	SD	63	5	0	0	0	-1	7	4	1	.42	-1	0	0	0	-1	-
		96	7	0	0	0	-1	9	5	1	.40	-1	0	0	0	-1	

Charlie Furbush

Year	Tm	Inn	TC	E	GFP	DM	+/-	SB	CCS	PCS/PPO	CS%	+/-	SB	Bnt	GFP/DME	Tot	Rnk
2011	2 tms	85	19	0	2	1	+4	11	2	4	.35	3	1	0	0	4	17

Yovani Gallardo

Year	Tm	Inn	TC	E	GFP	DM	+/-	SB	CCS	PCS/PPO	CS%	+/-	SB	Bnt	GFP/DME	Tot	Rnk
2007	Mil	110	26	1	1	0	+2	4	0	2	.20	2	1	0	0	3	27
2008	Mil	24	5	0	0	0	0	0	1	0	1.00	0	0	0	0	0	-
2009	Mil	186	27	0	2	0	-1	19	2	0	.10	-1	-2	1	0	-2	138
2010	Mil	185	37	1	1	0	0	11	5	1	.35	0	0	0	0	0	88
2011	Mil	207	44	2	2	0	+3	14	6	1	.33	3	0	0	0	3	25
		712	139	4	6	0	4	48	14	4	.26	4	-1	1	0	4	63

Freddy Garcia

Year	Tm	Inn	TC	E	GFP	DM	+/-	SB	CCS	PCS/PPO	CS%	+/-	SB	Bnt	GFP/DME	Tot	Rnk
2003	Sea	203	44	1	-	-	-1	6	5	3	.54	-1	2	-1	0	0	94
2004	2 tms	210	49	0	3	2	+5	12	4	2	.29	4	1	0	0	5	10
2005	CWS	228	47	0	1	3	0	19	5	1	.21	0	-1	0	0	-1	112
2006	CWS	216	32	2	0	2	-1	40	2	0	.05	-1	-6	1	0	-6	173
2007	Phi	58	10	0	0	0	0	5	0	1	.00	0	0	-1	0	-1	-
2008	Det	15	1	0	1	0	+1	1	1	0	.50	1	0		0	1	-
2009	CWS	56	10	0	2	1	+2	10	1	0	.09	2	-1		0	1	-
2010	CWS	157	32	2	2	1	-5	20	5	1	.20	-4	-2	0	0	-6	173
2011	NYY	147	31	1	1	1	-1	22	6	1	.24	-1	-2	-1	0	-4	160
		1290	256	6	10	10	3	135	29	9	.20	0	-9	-2	0	-11	152

Jaime Garcia

Year	Tm	Inn	TC	E	GFP	DM	+/-	SB	CCS	PCS/PPO	CS%	+/-	SB	Bnt	GFP/DME	Tot	Rnk
2008	StL	16	3	0	0	0	0	0	0	0	-	0	0		0	0	-
2010	StL	163	28	0	1	2	-1	6	2	2	.33	-1	1	0	0	0	101
2011	StL	195	27	2	2	3	+2	15	0	3	.17	2	0	-1	0	1	62
		374	58	2	3	5	1	21	2	5	.22	1	1	-1	0	1	

Matt Garza

Year	Tm	Inn	TC	E	GFP	DM	+/-	SB	CCS	PCS/PPO	CS%	+/-	SB	Bnt	GFP/DME	Tot	Rnk
2006	Min	50	6	0	0	0	-2	2	0	0	.00	-2	0			-2	-
2007	Min	83	13	2	0	3	-2	1	2	1	.75	-2	1	-2	0	-3	153
2008	TB	185	27	2	0	3	-4	5	1	0	.17	-3	0	-1	0	-4	167
2009	TB	203	22	1	0	4	-2	3	4	0	.57	-2	1	1	0	0	102
2010	TB	205	24	1	2	2	-3	9	3	1	.31	-2	0	0	0	-2	144
2011	ChC	198	32	7	2	3	-3	10	4	1	.33	-2	1	-1	-1	-3	156
		923	124	13	4	15	-16	30	14	3	.36	-13	3	-3	-1	-14	161

Pitchers

Dillon Gee

Year	Tm	Inn	TC	E	GFP	DM	+/-	SB	CCS	PCS/PPO	CS%	+/-	SB	Bnt	GFP/DME	Tot	Rnk
2010	NYM	33	5	0	0	0	+1	0	0	0		1	0	0	0	1	-
2011	NYM	161	30	1	4	3	-1	8	7	0	.47	-1	1	1	0	1	88
		193	35	1	4	3	0	8	7	0	.47	0	1	1	0	2	-

Gio Gonzalez

Year	Tm	Inn	TC	E	GFP	DM	+/-	SB	CCS	PCS/PPO	CS%	+/-	SB	Bnt	GFP/DME	Tot	Rnk
2008	Oak	34	6	0	1	0	0	0	0	2	1.00	2	0	1	0	3	-
2009	Oak	99	16	1	3	2	+1	4	0	2	.33	1	1	-1	-1	0	79
2010	Oak	201	41	1	4	2	0	12	1	2	.20	0	0	1	0	1	69
2011	Oak	202	34	1	5	1	-1	19	2	2	.17	-1	-1	0	0	-2	135
		535	97	3	13	5	0	35	3	8	.24	0	1	1	0	2	75

Tom Gorzelanny

Year	Tm	Inn	TC	E	GFP	DM	+/-	SB	CCS	PCS/PPO	CS%	+/-	SB	Bnt	GFP/DME	Tot	Rnk
2005	Pit	6	3	0	0	0	0	0	0	0		0	0	-1	0	-1	-
2006	Pit	62	24	3	0	0	0	4	0	2	.33	0	0	0	0	0	-
2007	Pit	202	35	1	1	4	-1	17	3	3	.23	-1	0	0	0	-1	113
2008	Pit	105	25	1	2	2	+1	16	2	3	.20	1	-1	0	0	0	88
2009	2 tms	47	10	2	0	4	+1	1	0	0	.00	1	0	0	0	1	-
2010	ChC	136	22	1	1	1	0	18	3	3	.22	0	-1	0	0	-1	109
2011	Was	105	13	2	0	1	-1	8	0	1	.11	-1	0	-1	0	-2	135
		663	132	10	4	12	0	64	7	12	.21	0	-2	-2	0	-4	110

John Grabow

Year	Tm	Inn	TC	E	GFP	DM	+/-	SB	CCS	PCS/PPO	CS%	+/-	SB	Bnt	GFP/DME	Tot	Rnk
2003	Pit	5	0	0	-	-	0	0	0	0	-	0	0		-	0	-
2004	Pit	62	17	0	1	2	+1	3	3	1	.57	1	1	0	0	2	-
2005	Pit	52	9	1	0	1	+2	2	0	1	.33	2	0	0	0	2	-
2006	Pit	70	17	0	0	1	-1	2	1	0	.33	-1	0	0	0	-1	-
2007	Pit	52	6	0	0	0	-1	10	0	0	.00	-1	-2	0	0	-3	-
2008	Pit	76	13	1	1	1	0	3	1	1	.40	0	0	0	0	0	-
2009	2 tms	72	10	1	1	1	-1	5	0	1	.17	-1	0	0	0	-1	-
2010	ChC	26	6	2	1	1	0	6	0	0	.00	0	-1	-1	0	-2	-
2011	ChC	62	8	1	0	0	-3	3	1	2	.50	-2	1	0	0	-1	-
		476	86	6	4	7	-3	34	6	6	.26	-2	-1	-1	0	-4	111

Zack Greinke

Year	Tm	Inn	TC	E	GFP	DM	+/-	SB	CCS	PCS/PPO	CS%	+/-	SB	Bnt	GFP/DME	Tot	Rnk
2004	KC	145	28	0	1	2	+3	5	3	0	.38	2	0	0	0	2	36
2005	KC	183	44	1	3	2	+2	5	3	1	.38	2	1	1	0	4	22
2006	KC	6	1	0	0	0	0	0	0	0		0	0	0	0	0	-
2007	KC	122	18	0	1	1	0	7	3	1	.30	0	0	1	0	1	73
2008	KC	202	36	1	2	1	+4	2	3	3	.67	3	2	-1	0	4	13
2009	KC	229	47	1	7	1	+2	5	8	2	.64	2	3	2	1	8	2
2010	KC	220	49	1	5	0	+4	12	10	3	.48	3	2	3	1	9	6
2011	Mil	172	35	0	4	2	+2	8	5	1	.43	2	1	0	0	4	18
		1279	258	4	23	9	17	44	35	11	.47	14	9	7	2	32	5

Matt Guerrier

Year	Tm	Inn	TC	E	GFP	DM	+/-	SB	CCS	PCS/PPO	CS%	+/-	SB	Bnt	GFP/DME	Tot	Rnk
2004	Min	19	5	0	0	0	0	0	0	0	-	0	0	0	0	0	-
2005	Min	72	24	0	1	0	+2	2	3	1	.60	2	1	0	0	3	-
2006	Min	70	19	1	1	0	0	1	2	1	.75	0	1	0	0	1	-
2007	Min	88	22	0	0	1	+1	6	2	1	.25	1	0	1	0	2	54
2008	Min	76	16	1	1	0	-1	8	1	1	.11	-1	0	-1	0	-2	-
2009	Min	76	20	0	0	1	+4	4	2	0	.33	3	0	0	0	3	-
2010	Min	71	19	0	2	0	-1	1	2	1	.67	-1	1	1	0	1	-
2011	LAD	66	9	0	2	0	-1	7	0	0	.00	-1	0	0	0	-1	-
		538	134	2	7	1		29	12	5	.31	4	2	1	0	7	44

Jeremy Guthrie

Year	Tm	Inn	TC	E	GFP	DM	+/-	SB	CCS	PCS/PPO	CS%	+/-	SB	Bnt	GFP/DME	Tot	Rnk
2004	Cle	12	2	0	0	0	0	1	0	0	.00	0	0		0	0	-
2005	Cle	6	3	0	0	0	-	0	0	0	-	0	-1	0		-1	-
2006	Cle	19	5	0	0	0	+2	2	1	0	.33	2	0	0	0	2	-
2007	Bal	175	38	1	0	3	+1	4	5	1	.56	1	2	0	0	3	34
2008	Bal	191	43	3	2	4	+3	13	4	0	.24	2	1	1	-1	1	52
2009	Bal	200	36	1	3	2	+3	9	2	4	.18	2	1	1	0	4	12
2010	Bal	209	48	4	2	2	+2	5	2	0	.29	1	0	0	0	1	60
2011	Bal	208	49	3	5	2	+4	3	5	1	.67	3	2	1	0	6	10
		1020	224	12	12	14	15	37	19	6	.35	11	4	2	-1	16	17

Roy Halladay

Year	Tm	Inn	TC	E	GFP	DM	+/-	SB	CCS	PCS/PPO	CS%	+/-	SB	Bnt	GFP/DME	Tot	Rnk
2003	Tor	266	74	1			+4	23	4	0	.15	3	-3	0		0	81
2004	Tor	133	31	1	4	3	-3	7	2	0	.22	-2	0	0	1	-1	116
2005	Tor	142	34	1	6	2	0	16	2	0	.11	0	-2	-1	0	-3	152
2006	Tor	220	57	1	3	4	+3	20	5	0	.20	2	-2	0	-1	-1	102
2007	Tor	225	57	2	2	1	-1	20	6	1	.26	-1	-1	1	0	-1	113
2008	Tor	246	60	1	2	1	-1	15	5	0	.25	-1	-1	2	1	1	77
2009	Tor	239	51	1	2	5	-2	18	6	0	.25	-2	-1	0	0	-3	158
2010	Phi	251	57	1	1	2	0	10	5	0	.33	0	0	0	0	0	88
2011	Phi	234	43	1	1	2	-2	18	4	1	.22	-2	-1	0	0	-3	156
		1955	464	10	23	18	-2	147	39	2	.22	-3	-11	2	1	-11	153

Cole Hamels

Year	Tm	Inn	TC	E	GFP	DM	+/-	SB	CCS	PCS/PPO	CS%	+/-	SB	Bnt	GFP/DME	Tot	Rnk
2006	Phi	132	24	0	2	2	+4	9	2	0	.18	3	-1	1	0	3	22
2007	Phi	183	29	1	5	0	-1	14	0	2	.13	-1	-1	0	1	-1	113
2008	Phi	227	47	3	5	2	+3	15	2	2	.12	2	-1	1	0	2	36
2009	Phi	194	34	0	0	3	-2	18	6	5	.38	-2	1	0	-1	-2	147
2010	Phi	209	37	1	3	0	+3	10	5	1	.38	2	1	0	0	3	27
2011	Phi	216	34	1	4	0	+5	23	5	1	.21	4	-2	-1	0	1	61
		1161	205	6	19	9	12	89	18	11	.25	8	-3	1	0	6	50

Jason Hammel

Year	Tm	Inn	TC	E	GFP	DM	+/-	SB	CCS	PCS/PPO	CS%	+/-	SB	Bnt	GFP/DME	Tot	Rnk
2006	TB	44	9	0	0	0	0	2	1	2	.67	0	1		0	1	-
2007	TB	85	13	1	1	1	-1	16	3	0	.16	-1	-2	0	0	-3	149
2008	TB	78	12	0	1	0	0	11	1	0	.08	0	-1	0	0	-1	-
2009	Col	177	31	0	2	1	0	18	2	1	.10	0	-2	0	0	-2	135
2010	Col	178	35	1	3	2	1	18	4	2	.22	-1	-1	0	0	-2	139
2011	Col	170	39	1	1	1	0	16	5	2	.27	0	0	-1	0	-1	121
		732	139	3	8	5	-2	80	17	6	.19	-2	-5	-1	0	-8	134

Brad Hand

Year	Tm	Inn	TC	E	GFP	DM	+/-	SB	CCS	PCS/PPO	CS%	+/-	SB	Bnt	GFP/DME	Tot	Rnk
2011	Fla	60	13	1	0	0	+2	3	1	3	.57	2	1	0	0	3	-

Joel Hanrahan

Year	Tm	Inn	TC	E	GFP	DM	+/-	SB	CCS	PCS/PPO	CS%	+/-	SB	Bnt	GFP/DME	Tot	Rnk
2007	Was	51	5	0	0	0	0	4	2	0	.33	0	0	0	0	0	-
2008	Was	84	11	2	0	0	-1	11	0	0	.00	-1	-2	0	0	-3	149
2009	2 tms	64	11	1	0	1	-1	6	3	0	.33	-1	0	0	0	-1	-
2010	Pit	70	10	0	1	0	-2	7	1	0	.13	-1	-1	0	0	-2	-
2011	Pit	69	13	2	0	2	-2	3	0	0	.00	-2	0	0	0	-2	-
		337	50	5	1	3	-6	31	6	0	.16	-5	-3	0	0	-8	-

Tommy Hanson

Year	Tm	Inn	TC	E	GFP	DM	+/-	SB	CCS	PCS/PPO	CS%	+/-	SB	Bnt	GFP/DME	Tot	Rnk
2009	Atl	128	30	2	0	2	+1	18	7	1	.31	1	-1	0	0	0	79
2010	Atl	203	43	3	0	1	-2	33	3	2	.11	-2	-4	0	0	-6	170
2011	Atl	130	18	2	0	1	-1	30	2	1	.09	0	-4	0	0	-4	159
		460	91	7	0	4	-2	81	12	4	.16	-1	-9	0	0	-10	148

Pitchers

J.A. Happ

		BASIC						HOLDING				RUNS SAVED					
Year	Tm	Inn	TC	E	GFP	DM	+/-	SB	CCS	PCS/PPO	CS%	+/-	SB	Bnt	GFP/DME	Tot	Rnk
2007	Phi	4	0	0	0	0	0	0	0	0	-		0			0	-
2008	Phi	32	5	0	0	0	0	1	0	0	.00	0	0	0	0	0	-
2009	Phi	166	26	0	1	2	-1	4	3	1	.50	-1	1	1	0	1	74
2010	2 tms	87	13	0	2	2	0	1	1	2	.75	0	1	0	0	1	69
2011	Hou	156	17	0	1	0	0	11	2	3	.31	0	1	0	0	1	74
		445	61	0	4	4	-1	17	6	6	.41	-1	3	1	0	3	-

Aaron Harang

		BASIC						HOLDING				RUNS SAVED					
Year	Tm	Inn	TC	E	GFP	DM	+/-	SB	CCS	PCS/PPO	CS%	+/-	SB	Bnt	GFP/DME	Tot	Rnk
2003	2 tms	76	9	0	-	-	+1	8	2	0	.20	1	-1	0	-	0	-
2004	Cin	161	31	0	2	4	0	7	5	0	.42	0	0	1	0	1	66
2005	Cin	212	30	0	1	5	+1	9	9	0	.50	1	1	-1	-1	0	82
2006	Cin	234	46	2	0	0	-4	16	7	1	.33	-3	0	-1	0	-4	169
2007	Cin	232	31	0	1	4	0	13	8	0	.38	0	0	0	0	0	91
2008	Cin	184	28	1	2	2	-4	17	4	0	.19	-3	-2	0	0	-5	173
2009	Cin	162	20	2	2	2	0	13	3	2	.28	0	0	1	0	1	69
2010	Cin	112	20	1	1	2	-2	3	4	1	.57	-2	1	0	0	-1	127
2011	SD	171	29	4	2	3	+1	24	9	2	.29	1	-1	-2	0	-2	132
		1544	244	10	11	22	-7	110	51	6	.33	-5	-2	-2	-1	-10	149

Rich Harden

		BASIC						HOLDING				RUNS SAVED					
Year	Tm	Inn	TC	E	GFP	DM	+/-	SB	CCS	PCS/PPO	CS%	+/-	SB	Bnt	GFP/DME	Tot	Rnk
2003	Oak	75	17	1	-	-	+1	9	2	1	.18	1	-1	0	-	0	-
2004	Oak	190	34	1	1	5	-4	11	5	2	.35	-3	0	0	-1	-3	155
2005	Oak	128	21	1	2	1	0	4	4	0	.50	0	1	-1	0	0	88
2006	Oak	47	13	0	0	1	+1	2	3	0	.60	1	0		0	1	-
2007	Oak	26	3	0	0	0	-1	1	1	0	.50	-1	0		0	-1	-
2008	2 tms	148	15	0	0	2	+1	7	7	0	.50	1	1	0	0	2	41
2009	ChC	141	18	2	0	3	-3	8	4	0	.33	-2	0	-2	0	-4	165
2010	Tex	92	11	1	0	0	-1	1	1	0	.50	-1	1	0	0	0	101
2011	Oak	83	15	2	0	2	-2	4	5	0	.56	-1	1	0	-1	-1	123
		928	147	8	3	14	-8	47	32	3	.41	-5	4	-3	-2	-6	124

Dan Haren

		BASIC						HOLDING				RUNS SAVED					
Year	Tm	Inn	TC	E	GFP	DM	+/-	SB	CCS	PCS/PPO	CS%	+/-	SB	Bnt	GFP/DME	Tot	Rnk
2003	StL	73	8	0	-	-	-1	2	1	0	.33	-1	0	0	-	-1	-
2004	StL	46	10	1	0	0	0	3	0	0	.00	0	0	0	0	0	-
2005	Oak	217	42	2	2	5	-2	19	4	1	.21	-2	-2	0	0	-4	164
2006	Oak	223	44	1	1	1	+3	10	4	1	.29	2	0	0	0	2	38
2007	Oak	223	30	1	1	1	-5	20	6	0	.23	-4	-1	1	0	-4	167
2008	Ari	216	29	0	4	1	-2	9	2	0	.18	-2	0	2	0	0	103
2009	Ari	229	43	0	1	3	+4	18	6	0	.25	3	-1	1	0	3	26
2010	2 tms	235	37	1	2	2	-4	19	8	2	.32	-3	0	1	0	-2	146
2011	LAA	238	48	0	2	1	+5	21	3	3	.19	4	-1	0	0	3	24
		1700	291	6	13	14	-2	121	33	7	.24	-3	-5	5	0	-3	104

Matt Harrison

		BASIC						HOLDING				RUNS SAVED					
Year	Tm	Inn	TC	E	GFP	DM	+/-	SB	CCS	PCS/PPO	CS%	+/-	SB	Bnt	GFP/DME	Tot	Rnk
2008	Tex	84	9	0	0	1	0	3	3	0	.50	0	1		0	1	69
2009	Tex	63	16	0	0	0	+4	3	2	1	.50	3	1	0	0	4	-
2010	Tex	78	11	1	0	0	0	5	1	0	.17	0	0	0	0	0	-
2011	Tex	186	40	4	3	4	-5	3	1	2	.50	-4	1	-1	-1	-5	170
		411	76	5	3	5	-1	14	7	3	.42	-1	3	-1	-1	0	-

Jeremy Hellickson

		BASIC						HOLDING				RUNS SAVED					
Year	Tm	Inn	TC	E	GFP	DM	+/-	SB	CCS	PCS/PPO	CS%	+/-	SB	Bnt	GFP/DME	Tot	Rnk
2010	TB	36	4	0	0	0	-1	2	0	0	.00	0	0		0	0	-
2011	TB	189	31	0	1	2	+1	10	0	3	.09	0	0	0	0	0	100
		225	35	0	1	2	0	12	0	3	.08	0	0	0	0	0	-

Clay Hensley

		BASIC						HOLDING				RUNS SAVED					
Year	Tm	Inn	TC	E	GFP	DM	+/-	SB	CCS	PCS/PPO	CS%	+/-	SB	Bnt	GFP/DME	Tot	Rnk
2005	SD	48	12	1	0	2	-1	1	0	0	.00	-1	0		-1	-2	-
2006	SD	187	44	2	2	4	+1	12	4	1	.25	1	0	-3	0	-2	127
2007	SD	50	17	0	1	0	+1	10	1	0	.09	1	-1	1	0	1	-
2008	SD	39	7	0	1	0	0	4	0	0	.00	0	0	0	0	0	-
2010	Fla	75	14	1	2	2	+2	5	1	0	.17	1	0	0	0	1	-
2011	Fla	68	12	0	0	1	0	4	1	0	.20	0	0	0	0	0	-
		466	106	4	6	9	3	36	7	1	.16	2	-1	-2	-1	-2	97

David Hernandez

		BASIC						HOLDING				RUNS SAVED					
Year	Tm	Inn	TC	E	GFP	DM	+/-	SB	CCS	PCS/PPO	CS%	+/-	SB	Bnt	GFP/DME	Tot	Rnk
2009	Bal	101	14	0	1	1	-1	8	2	0	.20	-1	0	0	0	-1	124
2010	Bal	79	7	0	0	1	0	4	3	0	.43	0	0	-1	0	-1	109
2011	Ari	69	10	1	2	0	0	2	1	0	.33	0	0	-1	0	-1	-
		250	31	1	3	2	-1	14	6	0	.30	-1	0	-2	0	-3	-

Felix Hernandez

		BASIC						HOLDING				RUNS SAVED					
Year	Tm	Inn	TC	E	GFP	DM	+/-	SB	CCS	PCS/PPO	CS%	+/-	SB	Bnt	GFP/DME	Tot	Rnk
2005	Sea	84	27	0	0	0	+2	3	1	2	.40	2	1	0	0	3	27
2006	Sea	191	41	0	0	1	+6	14	4	1	.26	5	0	0	0	5	9
2007	Sea	190	38	1	1	3	-1	10	5	1	.33	-1	1	0	0	0	94
2008	Sea	201	46	1	10	3	+4	19	3	2	.17	3	-1	-1	0	1	51
2009	Sea	239	54	1	4	3	+2	20	7	1	.29	2	-1	0	0	1	57
2010	Sea	250	54	2	2	7	+1	15	5	0	.25	1	0	0	0	1	60
2011	Sea	234	57	2	3	3	-2	31	8	2	.21	-2	-2	-1	0	-5	166
		1388	317	7	20	20	12	112	33	9	.25	10	-2	-2	0	6	49

Livan Hernandez

		BASIC						HOLDING				RUNS SAVED					
Year	Tm	Inn	TC	E	GFP	DM	+/-	SB	CCS	PCS/PPO	CS%	+/-	SB	Bnt	GFP/DME	Tot	Rnk
2003	Mon	233	63	1	-	-	+10	7	4	2	.42	8	1	-1	-	8	1
2004	Mon	255	84	2	5	1	+9	16	9	2	.36	7	1	0	1	9	5
2005	Was	246	62	1	3	6	+4	14	10	2	.44	3	1	-1	-1	2	41
2006	2 tms	216	53	4	1	7	0	14	3	2	.22	0	0	-2	0	-2	129
2007	Ari	204	52	0	3	2	+3	20	5	2	.20	2	-1	2	1	4	15
2008	2 tms	180	40	1	3	3	+2	3	3	2	.63	2	2	0	0	4	16
2009	2 tms	184	47	0	5	2	+3	11	5	3	.35	2	1	1	0	4	12
2010	Was	212	45	0	7	1	-2	4	7	3	.69	-2	3	1	0	2	58
2011	Was	175	45	1	5	3	+3	9	8	1	.50	2	1	0	0	3	26
		1905	491	10	32	25	32	98	54	19	.39	24	9	0	1	34	4

Luke Hochevar

		BASIC						HOLDING				RUNS SAVED					
Year	Tm	Inn	TC	E	GFP	DM	+/-	SB	CCS	PCS/PPO	CS%	+/-	SB	Bnt	GFP/DME	Tot	Rnk
2007	KC	13	5	0	0	0	-1	0	0	0	-	-1	0	0		-1	-
2008	KC	129	18	1	0	2	-2	14	4	0	.22	-2	-1	0	-1	-4	163
2009	KC	143	30	0	1	2	+1	19	2	4	.17	1	-1	1	0	1	60
2010	KC	103	18	1	0	0	-3	16	1	1	.11	-2	-2	0	0	-4	161
2011	KC	198	42	3	1	0	0	20	3	0	.13	0	-2	1	0	-1	121
		585	113	5	1	4	-5	69	10	5	.16	-4	-6	2	-1	-9	140

Derek Holland

		BASIC						HOLDING				RUNS SAVED					
Year	Tm	Inn	TC	E	GFP	DM	+/-	SB	CCS	PCS/PPO	CS%	+/-	SB	Bnt	GFP/DME	Tot	Rnk
2009	Tex	138	23	5	1	1	-3	8	1	3	.27	-2	1	0	1	0	102
2010	Tex	57	13	1	1	1	-2	6	0	3	.14	-1	1	0	0	0	-
2011	Tex	198	41	3	3	2	-8	7	4	5	.56	-6	3	-1	0	-4	163
		393	77	9	5	4	-13	21	5	11	.38	-9	5	-1	1	-4	-

Greg Holland

		BASIC						HOLDING				RUNS SAVED					
Year	Tm	Inn	TC	E	GFP	DM	+/-	SB	CCS	PCS/PPO	CS%	+/-	SB	Bnt	GFP/DME	Tot	Rnk
2010	KC	19	6	0	1	0	0	1	0	0	.00	0	0	0		0	-
2011	KC	60	4	0	0	0	-1	1	0	0	.00	-1	0	0	0	-1	-
		78	10	0	1	0	-1	2	0	0	.00	-1	0	0	0	-1	-

Pitchers

Daniel Hudson

Year	Tm	BASIC Inn	TC	E	GFP	DM	+/-	HOLDING SB	CCS	PCS/PPO	CS%	+/-	SB	Bnt	GFP/DME	RUNS SAVED Tot	Rnk
2009	CWS	19	4	1	0	0	+1	1	0		.00	1	0	-1	0	0	-
2010	2 tms	95	15	0	1	0	0	3	1	0	.25	0	0	0	0	0	88
2011	Ari	222	31	2	1	7	-1	10	10	1	.50	-1	1	-1	0	-1	123
		336	50	3	2	7	0	14	11	0	.44	0	1	-2	0	-1	

Tim Hudson

Year	Tm	BASIC Inn	TC	E	GFP	DM	+/-	HOLDING SB	CCS	PCS/PPO	CS%	+/-	SB	Bnt	GFP/DME	RUNS SAVED Tot	Rnk
2003	Oak	240	74	2	-	-	+3	7	6	2	.46	2	2	0		4	15
2004	Oak	189	49	1	3	4	-3	8	4	1	.33	-2	1	-1	0	-2	131
2005	Atl	192	64	1	4	4	+1	10	6	2	.41	1	1	1	0	3	33
2006	Atl	218	47	0	1	4	-1	23	3	2	.15	-1	-2	0	1	-2	136
2007	Atl	224	70	0	3	3	+5	9	4	2	.31	4	1	1	0	6	3
2008	Atl	142	30	1	0	3	+4	6	4	0	.40	3	0	0	0	3	24
2009	Atl	42	7	0	1	1	-1	1	4	0	.80	-1	1		0	0	-
2010	Atl	229	77	3	5	0	+3	11	11	3	.50	2	2	1	1	6	10
2011	Atl	215	46	2	1	2	-1	16	5	0	.24	-1	-1	0	0	-2	135
		1691	464	10	18	21	10	91	47	12	.35	7	5	2	2	16	18

Phil Hughes

Year	Tm	BASIC Inn	TC	E	GFP	DM	+/-	HOLDING SB	CCS	PCS/PPO	CS%	+/-	SB	Bnt	GFP/DME	RUNS SAVED Tot	Rnk
2007	NYY	73	14	1	0	0	+1	9	3	0	.25	1	-1	0	0	0	-
2008	NYY	34	5	0	1	0	+1	8	0	0	.00	1	-1	0	1	1	-
2009	NYY	86	9	0	0	0	0	5	2	0	.29	0	0	0	0	0	86
2010	NYY	176	20	0	0	0	-1	10	5	0	.33	-1	0	0	0	-1	119
2011	NYY	75	8	0	0	0	-1	7	0	0	.00	-1	-1	1	0	-1	-
		443	56	1	1	0	0	39	10	0	.20	0	-3	1	1	-1	-

Philip Humber

Year	Tm	BASIC Inn	TC	E	GFP	DM	+/-	HOLDING SB	CCS	PCS/PPO	CS%	+/-	SB	Bnt	GFP/DME	RUNS SAVED Tot	Rnk
2006	NYM	2	0	0	0	0	0	1	0	0	.00	0				0	-
2007	NYM	7	0	0	0	0	0	0	0	0	-	0				0	-
2008	Min	12	2	0	0	0	-1	0	0	0	-	-1	0		0	-1	-
2009	Min	9	2	1	0	1	-2	1	0	0	.00	-2	0		0	-2	-
2010	KC	22	1	0	0	0	-1	2	0	0	.00	0	0		0	0	-
2011	CWS	163	28	1	0	3	-5	13	3	0	.19	-3	-1	-1	0	-5	168
		214	33	2	0	4	-9	17	3	0	.15	-6	-1	-1	0	-8	-

Tommy Hunter

Year	Tm	BASIC Inn	TC	E	GFP	DM	+/-	HOLDING SB	CCS	PCS/PPO	CS%	+/-	SB	Bnt	GFP/DME	RUNS SAVED Tot	Rnk
2008	Tex	11	2	1	0	1	-1	1	0	1	.50	-1	0		0	-1	-
2009	Tex	112	18	1	2	0	-2	9	1	1	.25	-2	0	0	1	-1	129
2010	Tex	128	26	1	3	0	-1	5	1	1	.29	-1	0	0	1	0	101
2011	2 tms	85	19	1	1	0	+1	6	3	1	.40	0	1	0	0	1	74
		335	65	4	6	1	-3	21	6	4	.32	-4	1	0	2	-1	-

Edwin Jackson

Year	Tm	BASIC Inn	TC	E	GFP	DM	+/-	HOLDING SB	CCS	PCS/PPO	CS%	+/-	SB	Bnt	GFP/DME	RUNS SAVED Tot	Rnk
2003	LA	22	3	0	-	-	+1	1	0	0	.00	1	0		-	1	-
2004	LA	25	8	0	0	0	+1	2	0	1	.00	1	0		0	1	-
2005	LAD	29	2	0	0	1	0	2	1	0	.33	0	0		0	0	-
2006	TB	36	6	0	0	1	0	3	0	0	.00	0	0	0	0	0	-
2007	TB	161	27	2	0	6	-6	17	4	1	.23	-5	-1	0	-1	-7	172
2008	TB	183	31	1	0	1	-2	12	6	1	.33	-2	1	0	0	-1	121
2009	Det	214	31	4	2	1	-3	23	9	0	.28	-2	-2	0	0	-3	158
2010	2 tms	209	37	5	2	1	-2	19	6	0	.24	-2	-1	-1	0	-4	161
2011	2 tms	200	43	3	1	3	+1	22	1	1	.04	1	-2	-1	0	-2	132
		1079	188	15	5	14	-10	101	27	4	.22	-8	-5	-2	0	-15	164

Chris Jakubauskas

Year	Tm	BASIC Inn	TC	E	GFP	DM	+/-	HOLDING SB	CCS	PCS/PPO	CS%	+/-	SB	Bnt	GFP/DME	RUNS SAVED Tot	Rnk
2009	Sea	93	22	2	0	1	-2	2	1	2	.50	-2	1		0	-1	129
2010	Pit	1	0	0	0	0	0	0	0	0	-	0				0	-
2011	Bal	72	9	0	0	1	-1	2	2	0	.50	-1	0	0	0	-1	-
		166	31	2	0	2	-3	4	3	2	.50	-3	1	0	0	-2	-

Ubaldo Jimenez

Year	Tm	BASIC Inn	TC	E	GFP	DM	+/-	HOLDING SB	CCS	PCS/PPO	CS%	+/-	SB	Bnt	GFP/DME	RUNS SAVED Tot	Rnk
2006	Col	8	2	0	0	0	0	2	1	0	.33	0	0			0	-
2007	Col	82	25	3	1	0	+1	16	0	0	.00	1	-3	0	0	-2	133
2008	Col	199	52	4	2	0	+1	19	2	1	.14	1	-1	-1	0	-1	110
2009	Col	218	61	2	4	3	+1	15	4	2	.29	1	0	2	0	3	31
2010	Col	222	37	1	1	0	+1	12	13	2	.52	1	2	0	0	3	31
2011	2 tms	188	44	2	0	2	+4	24	6	2	.20	3	-2	-1	0	0	92
		916	221	12	8	5	8	88	26	9	.25	7	-4	0	0	3	69

Jim Johnson

Year	Tm	BASIC Inn	TC	E	GFP	DM	+/-	HOLDING SB	CCS	PCS/PPO	CS%	+/-	SB	Bnt	GFP/DME	RUNS SAVED Tot	Rnk
2006	Bal	3	0	0	0	0	0	1	0	0	.00	0				0	-
2007	Bal	2	0	0	0	0	0	0	0	0	-	0				0	-
2008	Bal	69	14	0	0	0	0	3	2	0	.40	0	0		0	0	-
2009	Bal	70	15	1	1	1	+1	4	1	0	.20	1	0	-1	0	0	-
2010	Bal	26	5	0	0	0	-1	0	1	0	1.00	0	0		0	0	-
2011	Bal	91	25	1	3	1	0	4	2	0	.33	0	0	0	0	0	100
		261	59	2	4	2	0	12	6	0	.33	1	0	-1	0	0	-

Josh Johnson

Year	Tm	BASIC Inn	TC	E	GFP	DM	+/-	HOLDING SB	CCS	PCS/PPO	CS%	+/-	SB	Bnt	GFP/DME	RUNS SAVED Tot	Rnk
2005	Fla	12	5	0	0	0	0	5	1	0	.17	0	-1	0	0	-1	-
2006	Fla	157	31	0	0	3	+3	9	6	2	.47	2	1	0	1	4	18
2007	Fla	16	4	1	0	1	-1	1	1	0	.50	-1	0	0	0	-1	-
2008	Fla	87	16	0	0	1	0	5	2	0	.29	0	0	0	0	0	92
2009	Fla	209	50	0	3	1	+1	18	8	0	.31	1	-1	0	1	1	60
2010	Fla	184	39	3	0	1	+1	15	6	2	.35	-1	0	0	0	-1	119
2011	Fla	60	15	0	1	0	+1	5	3	0	.38	0	0	0	0	0	-
		725	160	4	5	6	3	58	27	4	.35	1	-1	1	1	2	74

Jair Jurrjens

Year	Tm	BASIC Inn	TC	E	GFP	DM	+/-	HOLDING SB	CCS	PCS/PPO	CS%	+/-	SB	Bnt	GFP/DME	RUNS SAVED Tot	Rnk
2007	Det	31	4	0	0	0	+1	2	0	0	.00	1	0		0	1	-
2008	Atl	188	45	1	5	1	-1	28	3	0	.10	-1	-4	0	1	-4	161
2009	Atl	215	51	4	4	1	+2	14	7	1	.33	2	0	0	1	3	28
2010	Atl	116	28	1	2	1	+1	6	2	1	.33	1	0	1	0	2	43
2011	Atl	152	38	0	4	1	+2	15	8	1	.38	1	0	1	0	2	47
		702	166	6	15	4	5	65	20	3	.25	4	-4	2	2	4	63

Jeff Karstens

Year	Tm	BASIC Inn	TC	E	GFP	DM	+/-	HOLDING SB	CCS	PCS/PPO	CS%	+/-	SB	Bnt	GFP/DME	RUNS SAVED Tot	Rnk
2006	NYY	43	11	1	0	0	0	2	0	0	.00	0	0		0	0	-
2007	NYY	15	1	0	0	0	0	1	0	0	.00	0	0		0	0	-
2008	Pit	51	11	2	1	0	-1	3	2	1	.50	-1	1	-1	0	-1	-
2009	Pit	108	16	0	1	1	-2	9	2	1	.18	-2	0	-1	0	-3	158
2010	Pit	123	27	0	2	0	+3	8	5	1	.43	2	1	0	0	3	27
2011	Pit	162	36	2	3	1	+1	14	2	0	.13	1	-1	1	0	1	65
		501	102	5	7	2	1	37	11	3	.26	0	1	-1	0	0	88

Kyle Kendrick

Year	Tm	BASIC Inn	TC	E	GFP	DM	+/-	HOLDING SB	CCS	PCS/PPO	CS%	+/-	SB	Bnt	GFP/DME	RUNS SAVED Tot	Rnk
2007	Phi	121	27	0	2	2	+1	8	2	0	.20	1	0	0	0	1	64
2008	Phi	156	43	1	5	1	+7	15	4	1	.25	5	-1	-1	1	4	12
2009	Phi	26	5	1	0	0	0	0	0	0	-	0	0	0	0	0	-
2010	Phi	181	45	3	3	2	+5	4	4	1	.50	4	1	-1	0	4	16
2011	Phi	115	25	1	1	6	0	3	3	0	.50	0	1	-1	0	0	100
		598	145	6	11	11	13	30	13	2	.32	10	1	-3	1	9	35

Ian Kennedy

Year	Tm	BASIC Inn	TC	E	GFP	DM	+/-	HOLDING SB	CCS	PCS/PPO	CS%	+/-	SB	Bnt	GFP/DME	RUNS SAVED Tot	Rnk
2007	NYY	19	2	0	1	0	+1	1	1	0	.50	1	0		0	1	-
2008	NYY	40	7	0	1	0	+1	5	2	1	.29	1	0	0	0	1	-
2009	NYY	1	0	0	0	0	0	0	0	0	-	0			0	0	-
2010	Ari	194	38	1	0	0	+2	12	5	1	.33	2	0	1	0	3	27
2011	Ari	222	36	0	1	2	+1	6	0	1	.00	1	0	1	0	2	47
		475	83	1	3	2	5	24	8	3	.27	5	0	2	0	7	43

394

Pitchers

Clayton Kershaw

Year	Tm	Inn	TC	E	GFP	DM	+/-	SB	CCS	PCS/PPO	CS%	+/-	SB	Bnt	GFP/DME	Tot	Rnk
2008	LAD	108	20	1	5	2	0	5	0	2	.29	0	0	1	0	1	69
2009	LAD	171	27	0	2	3	-2	6	3	7	.54	-2	3	0	0	1	77
2010	LAD	204	36	1	0	2	0	8	1	8	.50	0	3	1	-1	3	35
2011	LAD	233	47	0	5	6	+2	14	2	9	.39	1	3	1	0	5	14
		716	130	2	12	13	0	33	6	26	.44	-1	9	3	-1	10	34

Craig Kimbrel

Year	Tm	Inn	TC	E	GFP	DM	+/-	SB	CCS	PCS/PPO	CS%	+/-	SB	Bnt	GFP/DME	Tot	Rnk
2010	Atl	21	1	1	0	1	-1	3	0	0	.00	0	0		0	0	-
2011	Atl	77	11	0	1	0	0	1	2	1	.75	0	1		0	1	74
		97	12	1	1	1	-1	4	2	1	.43	0	1		0	1	-

Hiroki Kuroda

Year	Tm	Inn	TC	E	GFP	DM	+/-	SB	CCS	PCS/PPO	CS%	+/-	SB	Bnt	GFP/DME	Tot	Rnk
2008	LAD	183	58	2	5	6	+4	7	2	2	.22	3	1	-1	1	4	13
2009	LAD	117	21	1	1	3	-2	10	0	1	.00	-2	-1	0	0	-3	158
2010	LAD	196	36	3	1	5	-1	14	7	1	.33	-1	0	0		-2	139
2011	LAD	202	51	0	5	2	+6	9	4	1	.36	5	1	1	0	7	4
		699	166	6	12	16	7	40	13	5	.26	5	1	0	0	6	52

John Lackey

Year	Tm	Inn	TC	E	GFP	DM	+/-	SB	CCS	PCS/PPO	CS%	+/-	SB	Bnt	GFP/DME	Tot	Rnk
2003	Ana	204	38	3	-	-	0	14	7	1	.36	0	0	-2	-	-2	133
2004	Ana	198	38	0	1	2	-2	15	7	1	.32	-2	0	-1	0	-3	148
2005	LAA	209	33	3	1	1	-3	11	7	2	.42	-2	1	1	0	0	108
2006	LAA	218	35	0	0	3	+5	12	4	0	.25	4	0	1	0	5	10
2007	LAA	224	49	2	0	0	-3	19	5	2	.24	-2	0	0	0	-2	138
2008	LAA	163	24	5	2	2	-4	11	2	1	.21	-3	0	-1	0	-4	167
2009	LAA	176	37	2	5	0	+1	13	3	0	.19	1	-1	0	0	0	79
2010	Bos	215	46	3	0	2	-2	26	8	2	.28	-2	-2	0	0	-4	161
2011	Bos	160	38	3	2	2	-1	33	3	0	.08	-1	-5	0	0	-6	172
		1767	338	21	11	12	-9	154	46	9	.25	-7	-7	-2	0	-16	168

John Lannan

Year	Tm	Inn	TC	E	GFP	DM	+/-	SB	CCS	PCS/PPO	CS%	+/-	SB	Bnt	GFP/DME	Tot	Rnk
2007	Was	35	8	0	1	1	+1	4	1	1	.33	1	0	0	0	1	-
2008	Was	182	43	2	1	4	0	18	2	5	.28	0	0	-1	0	-1	112
2009	Was	206	36	0	1	1	0	10	4	4	.41	0	2	1	0	3	34
2010	Was	143	34	0	3	0	-2	18	2	1	.14	-1	-2	1	1	-1	119
2011	Was	185	43	2	4	2	+2	6	3	1	.40	2	1	1	1	5	13
		751	168	4	9	9	1	56	12	12	.29	2	1	2	2	7	46

Mat Latos

Year	Tm	Inn	TC	E	GFP	DM	+/-	SB	CCS	PCS/PPO	CS%	+/-	SB	Bnt	GFP/DME	Tot	Rnk
2009	SD	51	6	0	0	2	0	4	3	0	.43	0	0	0	-1	-1	-
2010	SD	185	30	1	2	2	-2	7	0	1	.00	-1	0	1	0	0	101
2011	SD	194	39	1	4	2	+2	25	7	1	.24	1	-2	0	0	-1	119
		429	75	2	6	6	0	36	10	2	.23	0	-2	1	-1	-2	-

Brandon League

Year	Tm	Inn	TC	E	GFP	DM	+/-	SB	CCS	PCS/PPO	CS%	+/-	SB	Bnt	GFP/DME	Tot	Rnk
2004	Tor	5	0	0	0	0	0	0	0	0	-	0	0		0		-
2005	Tor	36	8	1	0	0	0	0	0	0	-	0	0		0		-
2006	Tor	43	18	2	0	2	0	1	1	0	.50	0	0	-1		-1	-
2007	Tor	12	5	1	1	1	+1	0	1	0	1.00	1	0		0	1	-
2008	Tor	33	12	0	0	0	0	0	0	0	-	-1	0		0	-1	-
2009	Tor	75	16	2	0	1	-2	9	1	0	.10	-2	-1	-2	0	-5	-
2010	Sea	79	17	0	1	1	-2	5	5	0	.50	-1	1	1	0	1	78
2011	Sea	61	8	3	1	1	-4	5	1	0	.17	-3	0	-1	0	-4	-
		342	84	9	2	6	-8	20	9	0	.31	-6	0	-3	0	-9	-

Mike Leake

Year	Tm	Inn	TC	E	GFP	DM	+/-	SB	CCS	PCS/PPO	CS%	+/-	SB	Bnt	GFP/DME	Tot	Rnk
2010	Cin	138	43	3	2	1	0	5	3	1	.38	0	1	0	1	2	51
2011	Cin	168	40	0	3	3	+3	5	2	2	.29	2	1	1	0	4	18
		306	83	3	5	4	3	10	5	3	.33	2	2	1	1	6	-

Wade LeBlanc

Year	Tm	Inn	TC	E	GFP	DM	+/-	SB	CCS	PCS/PPO	CS%	+/-	SB	Bnt	GFP/DME	Tot	Rnk
2008	SD	21	5	0	0	0	0	1	0	0	.00	0	0	0	0	0	-
2009	SD	46	8	1	0	0	0	1	0	1	.50	0	0	0	0	0	-
2010	SD	146	32	0	1	1	+2	9	2	8	.50	2	3	0	0	5	14
2011	SD	80	19	0	3	3	+1	7	3	3	.46	1	1	1	0	3	33
		293	64	1	1	1	3	18	5	12	.47	3	4	1	0	8	-

Sam LeCure

Year	Tm	Inn	TC	E	GFP	DM	+/-	SB	CCS	PCS/PPO	CS%	+/-	SB	Bnt	GFP/DME	Tot	Rnk
2010	Cin	48	12	0	0	0	0	7	0	1	.13	0	-1	0	0	-1	-
2011	Cin	78	22	0	2	0	+2	4	1	1	.33	1	0	1	0	3	33
		125	34	0	2	0	2	11	1	2	.21	1	-1	1	0	2	-

Cliff Lee

Year	Tm	Inn	TC	E	GFP	DM	+/-	SB	CCS	PCS/PPO	CS%	+/-	SB	Bnt	GFP/DME	Tot	Rnk
2003	Cle	52	7	1	-	-	0	4	2	0	.33	0	0	-1	-	-1	-
2004	Cle	179	12	0	0	2	-2	9	4	1	.36	-2	0	0	0	-2	131
2005	Cle	202	18	3	1	4	-4	7	4	0	.36	-3	0	0	-1	-4	170
2006	Cle	201	23	1	1	0	-2	7	1	2	.30	-2	1	0	0	-1	118
2007	Cle	97	13	1	0	1	-3	4	1	0	.20	-2	0	0	0	-2	138
2008	Cle	223	31	1	4	2	-4	3	0	0	.00	-3	0	0	0	-3	158
2009	2 tms	232	42	2	2	1	-3	7	1	2	.30	-2	1	1	0	0	102
2010	2 tms	212	28	4	2	3	-5	4	3	0	.43	-4	1	0	0	-3	159
2011	Phi	233	34	1	5	2	-1	11	2	2	.27	0	0	0	1	1	74
		1631	208	14	15	15	-24	56	18	7	.31	-18	3	0	0	-15	167

Jon Lester

Year	Tm	Inn	TC	E	GFP	DM	+/-	SB	CCS	PCS/PPO	CS%	+/-	SB	Bnt	GFP/DME	Tot	Rnk
2006	Bos	81	11	0	0	0	-1	9	1	6	.40	-1	2	-1	0	0	93
2007	Bos	63	11	1	2	0	-2	4	1	1	.33	-2	0		0	-2	-
2008	Bos	210	42	2	0	2	-3	8	2	3	.38	-2	1	1	0	0	103
2009	Bos	203	33	2	1	3	+3	19	0	6	.24	2	0	-2	0	0	78
2010	Bos	208	43	3	0	3	+4	22	1	6	.24	3	0	-1	0	2	36
2011	Bos	192	29	1	2	2	-2	14	8	4	.46	-1	2	0	0	1	88
		957	169	9	5	10	-1	76	13	26	.33	-1	5	-3	0	1	82

Colby Lewis

Year	Tm	Inn	TC	E	GFP	DM	+/-	SB	CCS	PCS/PPO	CS%	+/-	SB	Bnt	GFP/DME	Tot	Rnk
2003	Tex	127	21	0	-	-	0	5	6	0	.55	0	1	0	-	1	73
2004	Tex	15	3	0	0	0	0	1	0	0	.00	0	0	0	0	0	-
2006	Det	3	0	0	0	0	0	0	0	0	-		0			0	-
2007	Det	38	4	0	0	0	0	1	0	0	.00	0	0	0	0	0	-
2010	Tex	201	25	5	2	1	-5	13	4	0	.24	-4	-1	0	0	-5	169
2011	Tex	200	20	4	1	1	0	10	7	0	.41	0	1	-1	0	0	100
		584	73	9	3	2	-5	30	17	0	.36	-4	1	-1	0	-4	112

Ted Lilly

Year	Tm	Inn	TC	E	GFP	DM	+/-	SB	CCS	PCS/PPO	CS%	+/-	SB	Bnt	GFP/DME	Tot	Rnk
2003	Oak	178	19	0	-	-	-1	24	0	1	.04	-1	-3	1	-	-3	153
2004	Tor	197	22	2	2	2	-4	7	1	0	.13	-3	0	1	0	-2	144
2005	Tor	126	15	0	1	3	-1	10	0	1	.09	-1	0	0	0	-2	139
2006	Tor	182	32	1	2	6	0	14	1	2	.18	0	-1	-1	0	-2	129
2007	ChC	207	32	4	4	10	+1	14	2	2	.22	1	0	-1	0	0	89
2008	ChC	205	27	0	2	1	-1	12	2	6	.40	-1	2	0	0	1	77
2009	ChC	177	25	5	1	3	+1	12	4	1	.25	1	0	-3	0	-2	134
2010	2 tms	194	33	2	3	0	+4	20	0	1	.05	3	-2	-1	0	0	84
2011	LAD	193	34	2	0	3	+3	35	1	5	.05	2	-5	-1	-1	-5	164
		1658	239	14	15	28	-14	148	11	15	.14	1	-10	-5	-1	-15	162

Pitchers

Tim Lincecum

Year	Tm	Inn	TC	E	GFP	DM	+/-	SB	CCS	PCS/PPO	CS%	+/-	SB	Bnt	GFP/DME	Tot	Rnk
2007	SF	146	24	0	0	2	-2	10	2	0	.17	-2	-1	0	0	-3	153
2008	SF	227	26	0	0	4	-3	20	3	0	.13	-2	-2	0	-1	-5	172
2009	SF	225	40	2	2	4	-4	20	5	0	.20	-3	-2	0	0	-5	171
2010	SF	212	27	2	3	3	-4	27	3	0	.10	-3	-3	0	0	-6	171
2011	SF	217	40	1	3	0	-1	23	12	2	.38	-1	0	1	0	0	110
		1028	157	5	8	13	-14	100	25	2	.21	-11	-8	1	-1	-19	171

Francisco Liriano

Year	Tm	Inn	TC	E	GFP	DM	+/-	SB	CCS	PCS/PPO	CS%	+/-	SB	Bnt	GFP/DME	Tot	Rnk
2005	Min	24	5	0	0	0	0	3	0	1	.25	0	0		0	0	-
2006	Min	121	10	1	0	3	-3	9	0	0	.00	-2	-1	-1	0	-4	165
2008	Min	76	13	0	0	1	-2	6	0	3	.33	-2	-1	0	0	-1	-
2009	Min	137	16	0	3	0	-1	15	3	6	.38	-1	1	0	0	0	96
2010	Min	192	29	1	5	4	-3	12	1	2	.20	-2	0	-1	-1	-4	161
2011	Min	134	22	0	1	1	+1	9	2	3	.36	1	1	0	0	2	47
		683	95	2	9	9	-8	54	6	15	.28	-6	-2	-2	-1	-7	132

Jesse Litsch

Year	Tm	Inn	TC	E	GFP	DM	+/-	SB	CCS	PCS/PPO	CS%	+/-	SB	Bnt	GFP/DME	Tot	Rnk
2007	Tor	111	31	0	5	3	+3	6	3	0	.33	2	0	0	0	2	42
2008	Tor	176	62	3	9	1	+8	3	6	1	.67	6	2	1	0	9	2
2009	Tor	9	2	0	0	0	0	1	1	0	.50	0	0	0	0	0	-
2010	Tor	47	16	0	3	1	0	2	0	0	.00	0	0	0	0	0	-
2011	Tor	75	26	3	4	1	+4	2	1	0	.33	3	0	0	0	3	-
		417	137	6	21	6	15	14	11	1	.44	11	2	1	0	14	-

Kameron Loe

Year	Tm	Inn	TC	E	GFP	DM	+/-	SB	CCS	PCS/PPO	CS%	+/-	SB	Bnt	GFP/DME	Tot	Rnk
2004	Tex	7	2	1	0	0	+1	1	1	0	.50	1	0		0	1	-
2005	Tex	92	30	4	2	1	+1	9	2	0	.18	1	-1	0	0	0	82
2006	Tex	78	16	2	0	2	0	5	0	0	.00	0	-1	0	0	-1	-
2007	Tex	136	40	3	2	3	+4	11	5	1	.31	3	0	0	0	3	26
2008	Tex	31	5	1	0	0		0	0	1	-	0	1	0	0	1	-
2010	Mil	58	17	2	0	0	-1	2	0	0	.00	-1	0	0	0	-1	-
2011	Mil	72	13	1	1	0	-2	2	0	0	.00	-1	0	0	0	-1	-
		474	123	14	5	6	3	30	8	2	.21	3	-1	0	0	2	71

Kyle Lohse

Year	Tm	Inn	TC	E	GFP	DM	+/-	SB	CCS	PCS/PPO	CS%	+/-	SB	Bnt	GFP/DME	Tot	Rnk
2003	Min	201	38	1	-	-	-3	12	3	1	.20	-2	0	-1		-3	155
2004	Min	194	34	0	1	4	-1	16	5	4	.33	-1	1	-1	0	-1	109
2005	Min	179	40	0	3	0	-2	3	3	4	.67	-2	2	0	0	0	108
2006	2 tms	127	36	0	0	0	0	2	2	2	.60	0	1	1	0	2	51
2007	2 tms	193	34	1	3	1	+1	12	8	1	.40	1	1	-1	0	1	64
2008	StL	200	49	0	5	4	-2	9	2	1	.25	-2	0	1	0	-1	121
2009	StL	118	34	1	1	0	+2	4	1	0	.20	2	0	0	0	2	36
2010	StL	92	27	1	0	1	-1	1	2	1	.75	-1	1	1	0	1	78
2011	StL	188	51	0	2	3	0	1	2	0	.67	0	1	0	0	1	74
		1491	343	4	15	13	-6	60	28	14	.38	-5	7	0	0	2	78

Rodrigo Lopez

Year	Tm	Inn	TC	E	GFP	DM	+/-	SB	CCS	PCS/PPO	CS%	+/-	SB	Bnt	GFP/DME	Tot	Rnk
2003	Bal	147	24	2	-	-	-4	21	6	1	.22	-3	-2	0	-	-5	173
2004	Bal	171	36	0	2	4	-3	9	3	3	.31	-2	1	1	0	0	100
2005	Bal	209	52	3	6	5	-3	22	5	1	.21	-2	-2	1	0	-3	153
2006	Bal	189	31	1	0	8	-1	9	9	1	.53	-1	2	0	0	1	72
2007	Col	79	21	0	1	1	+2	8	4	1	.33	2	0	0	0	2	-
2009	Phi	30	3	0	0	0	0	3	1	0	.25	0	0	0	0	0	-
2010	Ari	200	39	4	1	4	-1	22	2	3	.08	-1	-1	0	-1	-3	155
2011	ChC	98	24	0	3	0	0	6	6	2	.54	0	1	0	0	1	74
		1123	230	10	13	22	-10	100	36	12	.29	-7	-1	2	-2	-7	133

Wilton Lopez

Year	Tm	Inn	TC	E	GFP	DM	+/-	SB	CCS	PCS/PPO	CS%	+/-	SB	Bnt	GFP/DME	Tot	Rnk
2009	Hou	19	5	0	0	0	-1	1	0	0	.00	-1	0	0	0	-1	-
2010	Hou	67	22	0	3	2	+2	1	3	0	.75	1	1	0	0	2	-
2011	Hou	71	22	2	1	0	1	1	2	0	.67	0	1	1	0	2	-
		157	49	2	4	2	1	3	5	0	.63	0	2	1	0	3	-

Derek Lowe

Year	Tm	Inn	TC	E	GFP	DM	+/-	SB	CCS	PCS/PPO	CS%	+/-	SB	Bnt	GFP/DME	Tot	Rnk
2003	Bos	203	64	0	-	-	+2	14	2	1	.18	2	-1	1	-	2	36
2004	Bos	183	64	3	2	9	0	34	1	2	.06	0	-4	0	-1	-5	165
2005	LAD	222	70	1	4	5	+3	19	6	0	.24	2	-1	0	0	1	59
2006	LAD	218	70	3	4	6	+1	26	3	1	.13	1	-3	0	0	-2	127
2007	LAD	199	39	0	1	2	+2	14	12	0	.46	2	1	1	0	4	15
2008	LAD	211	56	2	2	2	+1	14	3	0	.18	1	-1	0	0	0	88
2009	Atl	195	43	2	3	6	-7	13	4	2	.24	-5	0	-1	0	-6	174
2010	Atl	194	44	0	0	3	0	10	1	1	.52	0	2	0	0	2	51
2011	Atl	187	44	0	4	2	0	26	3	1	.13	0	-3	0	0	-3	151
		1811	494	11	20	35	2	170	44	8	.22	3	-10	1	-1	-7	127

Cory Luebke

Year	Tm	Inn	TC	E	GFP	DM	+/-	SB	CCS	PCS/PPO	CS%	+/-	SB	Bnt	GFP/DME	Tot	Rnk
2010	SD	18	8	2	0	0	0	0	0	1	1.00	0	1		0	1	-
2011	SD	140	32	0	1	2	+1	11	2	4	.35	1	1	1	0	3	33
		157	40	2	1	2	1	11	2	5	.39	1	2	1	0	4	-

Jordan Lyles

Year	Tm	Inn	TC	E	GFP	DM	+/-	SB	CCS	PCS/PPO	CS%	+/-	SB	Bnt	GFP/DME	Tot	Rnk
2011	Hou	94	24	1	1	2	+1	4	0	1	.00	1	0	0	0	1	65

Ryan Madson

Year	Tm	Inn	TC	E	GFP	DM	+/-	SB	CCS	PCS/PPO	CS%	+/-	SB	Bnt	GFP/DME	Tot	Rnk
2003	Phi	2	0	0	-	-	0	0	0	0					-	0	-
2004	Phi	77	13	0	0	0	-1	6	2	0	.25	-1	0	0	0	-1	-
2005	Phi	87	12	0	0	1	-3	6	2	0	.25	-2	0	0	0	-2	141
2006	Phi	134	29	0	1	0	0	14	6	1	.30	0	0	0	0	0	84
2007	Phi	56	12	0	4	0	+2	1	3	0	.75	2	1	0	0	3	-
2008	Phi	83	16	0	0	0	-1	7	1	0	.13	-1	-1	0	0	-2	139
2009	Phi	77	15	1	0	0	0	5	0	1	.17	-1	0	0	0	-1	-
2010	Phi	53	5	0	1	1	+1	4	0	0	.00	0	0	0	0	0	-
2011	Phi	61	7	1	0	1	0	4	1	0	.20	-1	0	0	0	-1	-
		630	109	2	6	3	-4	47	15	2	.25	-4	0	0	0	-4	112

Paul Maholm

Year	Tm	Inn	TC	E	GFP	DM	+/-	SB	CCS	PCS/PPO	CS%	+/-	SB	Bnt	GFP/DME	Tot	Rnk
2005	Pit	41	7	0	1	1	+2	2	2	0	.50	2	0		0	2	-
2006	Pit	176	53	2	0	2	+1	13	3	9	.46	1	3	2	-1	5	13
2007	Pit	178	37	1	3	2	0	11	5	1	.35	0	0	-1	0	-1	108
2008	Pit	206	39	2	1	3	+3	5	4	3	.58	2	2	1	0	5	9
2009	Pit	195	50	2	5	2	+3	15	3	4	.29	2	1	0	1	4	12
2010	Pit	185	48	3	2	3	0	8	1	2	.20	0	1	0	0	1	69
2011	Pit	162	38	1	2	3	+3	7	1	3	.30	2	1	0	0	3	26
		1143	272	11	14	16	12	61	19	22	.38	9	8	2	0	19	14

Shaun Marcum

Year	Tm	Inn	TC	E	GFP	DM	+/-	SB	CCS	PCS/PPO	CS%	+/-	SB	Bnt	GFP/DME	Tot	Rnk
2005	Tor	8	0	0	0	0	0	0	0	0	-		0			0	-
2006	Tor	78	12	0	0	0	0	2	1	0	.33	0	0	0	0	0	-
2007	Tor	159	46	0	2	1	+3	6	2	1	.25	2	1	1	0	4	15
2008	Tor	151	35	0	0	1	+1	5	2	0	.29	1	0	0	0	1	60
2010	Tor	195	42	0	5	3	+3	7	8	0	.53	2	1	0	0	3	27
2011	Mil	201	40	1	3	0	+1	8	6	1	.43	0	1	0	0	1	74
		792	175	1	10	3	8	28	19	2	.40	5	3	1	0	9	37

Pitchers

Carlos Marmol

Year	Tm	Inn	TC	E	GFP	DM	+/-	SB	CCS	PCS/PPO	CS%	+/-	SB	Bnt	GFP/DME	Tot	Rnk
2006	ChC	77	13	3	0	1	0	11	4	2	.31	0	0	0	0	0	-
2007	ChC	69	11	0	0	2	+1	9	0	1	.00	1	0	0	0	0	-
2008	ChC	87	15	1	2	0	0	3	1	0	.25	0	0	-1	0	-1	112
2009	ChC	74	10	2	2	1	0	2	0	1	.00	0	0	0	0	0	-
2010	ChC	78	5	0	0	0	-2	10	1	0	.09	-2	-1	0	0	-3	-
2011	ChC	74	15	0	1	0	+2	12	1	0	.08	2	-2	0	0	0	-
		459	69	6	5	4	1	47	7	4	.15	1	-4	-1	0	-4	109

Jason Marquis

Year	Tm	Inn	TC	E	GFP	DM	+/-	SB	CCS	PCS/PPO	CS%	+/-	SB	Bnt	GFP/DME	Tot	Rnk
2003	Atl	41	12	1	-	-	+1	1	0	0	.00	1	0	0	-	1	-
2004	StL	201	55	3	5	8	+2	7	4	1	.36	2	1	0	0	3	28
2005	StL	207	43	2	2	1	0	3	6	0	.67	0	1	0	0	1	64
2006	StL	194	44	1	3	5	-2	10	5	0	.33	-2	0	1	0	-1	118
2007	ChC	192	44	2	2	3	+3	20	2	0	.09	2	-1	1	0	1	61
2008	ChC	167	46	1	5	1	+4	11	1	0	.08	3	-1	1	0	3	24
2009	Col	216	56	2	7	4	+6	18	4	0	.18	5	-1	-1	1	4	10
2010	Was	59	11	0	0	0	-2	9	2	0	.18	-2	-1	-1	0	-4	-
2011	2 tms	132	24	1	0	1	-5	6	1	0	.14	-3	0	0	0	-3	158
		1408	335	15	24	23	7	85	25	1	.23	6	-3	1	1	5	56

Sean Marshall

Year	Tm	Inn	TC	E	GFP	DM	+/-	SB	CCS	PCS/PPO	CS%	+/-	SB	Bnt	GFP/DME	Tot	Rnk
2006	ChC	126	25	1	0	0	+2	12	3	2	.29	2	0	0	0	2	38
2007	ChC	103	25	1	0	0	-1	5	1	1	.29	-1	0	0	0	-1	113
2008	ChC	65	12	0	0	2	+1	5	2	0	.29	1	0	-1	0	0	-
2009	ChC	85	23	0	1	2	0	3	1	0	.25	0	0	1	-1	0	86
2010	ChC	75	14	0	0	0	+1	3	0	0	.00	1	0	0	1	-
2011	ChC	76	17	1	1	0	0	9	1	1	.18	0	0	0	0	0	100
		530	116	3	2	4	3	37	8	4	.24	3	0	0	-1	2	71

Cristhian Martinez

Year	Tm	Inn	TC	E	GFP	DM	+/-	SB	CCS	PCS/PPO	CS%	+/-	SB	Bnt	GFP/DME	Tot	Rnk
2009	Fla	26	6	1	1	0	0	0	0	0	-	0	0	-1	0	-1	-
2010	Atl	26	6	0	0	0	-2	1	1	0	.50	-1	0	0	0	-1	-
2011	Atl	78	18	0	0	1	+1	0	0	0	-	1	0	0	0	1	65
		130	30	1	1	1	-1	1	1	0	.50	0	0	-1	0	-1	-

Nick Masset

Year	Tm	Inn	TC	E	GFP	DM	+/-	SB	CCS	PCS/PPO	CS%	+/-	SB	Bnt	GFP/DME	Tot	Rnk
2006	Tex	9	3	0	0	0	0	0	0	0	-	0	0	0	0	-
2007	CWS	39	3	0	1	1	+1	8	1	0	.11	1	-1	0	0	-
2008	2 tms	62	17	3	0	2	-2	2	1	1	.33	-2	0	1	0	-1	-
2009	Cin	76	16	0	0	4	0	2	2	0	.50	0	0	0	-1	-1	-
2010	Cin	77	13	0	0	1	-3	6	2	1	.33	-2	0	1	0	-1	-
2011	Cin	70	21	1	0	1	0	6	1	0	.14	0	0	-1	0	-1	-
		333	73	4	1	9	-4	24	7	2	.25	-3	-1	1	-1	-4	

Justin Masterson

Year	Tm	Inn	TC	E	GFP	DM	+/-	SB	CCS	PCS/PPO	CS%	+/-	SB	Bnt	GFP/DME	Tot	Rnk
2008	Bos	88	14	1	1	0	+2	9	1	0	.10	2	-1	0	0	1	52
2009	2 tms	129	28	2	1	3	-3	15	5	1	.29	-3	-1	0	0	-4	168
2010	Cle	180	61	5	4	3	0	13	6	2	.38	0	1	0	0	1	69
2011	Cle	216	49	2	1	4	-3	14	13	2	.50	-2	2	0	0	0	114
		613	152	10	7	10	-4	51	25	5	.36	-3	1	0	0	-2	102

Brandon McCarthy

Year	Tm	Inn	TC	E	GFP	DM	+/-	SB	CCS	PCS/PPO	CS%	+/-	SB	Bnt	GFP/DME	Tot	Rnk
2005	CWS	67	7	0	0	0	0	2	0	0	.00	0	0	0	0	0	-
2006	CWS	85	15	0	1	2	-1	8	3	0	.27	-1	-1	0	0	-2	136
2007	Tex	102	18	2	0	2	-1	17	5	0	.23	-1	-2	0	0	-3	149
2008	Tex	22	1	0	0	0	0	6	1	0	.14	0	-1	0	0	-1	-
2009	Tex	97	18	1	0	1	0	5	2	0	.29	0	0	0	0	0	86
2011	Oak	171	38	4	0	3	-2	11	3	1	.27	-1	0	-1	0	-2	135
		543	97	7	1	8	-4	49	14	1	.23	-3	-4	-1	0	-8	135

Kyle McClellan

Year	Tm	Inn	TC	E	GFP	DM	+/-	SB	CCS	PCS/PPO	CS%	+/-	SB	Bnt	GFP/DME	Tot	Rnk
2008	StL	76	12	0	1	0	-1	2	1	0	.33	-1	0	0	0	-1	-
2009	StL	67	15	0	0	3	0	0	0	0	-	0	0	0	0	0	-
2010	StL	75	12	0	1	0	0	8	1	1	.20	0	-1	0	0	-1	-
2011	StL	142	35	1	0	1	-2	6	3	3	.33	-2	2	0	0	0	114
		359	74	1	2	4	-3	16	5	4	.27	-3	1	0	0	-2	

Daniel McCutchen

Year	Tm	Inn	TC	E	GFP	DM	+/-	SB	CCS	PCS/PPO	CS%	+/-	SB	Bnt	GFP/DME	Tot	Rnk
2009	Pit	36	7	0	2	1	+1	3	0	1	.00	1	0	0	0	1	-
2010	Pit	68	22	1	2	1	0	8	1	2	.11	0	0	-1	0	-1	-
2011	Pit	85	15	2	1	0	0	9	3	2	.25	0	0	0	0	0	100
		188	44	3	5	2	1	20	4	5	.17	1	0	-1	0	0	-

James McDonald

Year	Tm	Inn	TC	E	GFP	DM	+/-	SB	CCS	PCS/PPO	CS%	+/-	SB	Bnt	GFP/DME	Tot	Rnk
2008	LAD	6	2	0	0	0	0	0	0	0	-	0	0	0	0	0	-
2009	LAD	63	6	0	0	0	-2	4	2	0	.33	-2	0	0	0	-2	-
2010	2 tms	72	15	1	1	0	0	2	2	0	.60	0	1	0	0	1	-
2011	Pit	171	28	1	1	2	-5	17	7	2	.32	-2	0	1	-1	-2	143
		311	51	2	2	2	-5	23	11	4	.36	-4	1	1	-1	-3	

Mark Melancon

Year	Tm	Inn	TC	E	GFP	DM	+/-	SB	CCS	PCS/PPO	CS%	+/-	SB	Bnt	GFP/DME	Tot	Rnk
2009	NYY	16	5	0	1	0	+1	2	0	0	.00	1	0	0	0	1	-
2010	2 tms	21	6	0	0	0	0	0	0	0	-	0	0	0	0	0	-
2011	Hou	74	18	1	0	1	0	6	2	0	.25	0	0	0	0	0	-
		112	29	1	1	1	1	8	2	0	.20	1	0	0	0	1	-

Andrew Miller

Year	Tm	Inn	TC	E	GFP	DM	+/-	SB	CCS	PCS/PPO	CS%	+/-	SB	Bnt	GFP/DME	Tot	Rnk
2006	Det	10	1	0	0	0	0	0	0	0	-	0	0	0	0	0	-
2007	Det	64	12	2	1	2	-2	10	1	0	.09	-2	-1	0	0	-3	-
2008	Fla	107	14	1	2	4	-2	13	2	1	.19	-2	-1	0	0	-3	151
2009	Fla	80	15	1	0	0	0	13	3	0	.19	0	-1	1	0	0	86
2010	Fla	33	5	0	1	1	-1	4	0	0	.00	-1	-1	0	0	-2	-
2011	Bos	65	13	2	0	1	-2	8	1	0	.11	-1	-1	-1	0	-1	-
		359	60	6	4	8	-7	48	7	1	.14	-6	-5	0	0	-11	

Mike Minor

Year	Tm	Inn	TC	E	GFP	DM	+/-	SB	CCS	PCS/PPO	CS%	+/-	SB	Bnt	GFP/DME	Tot	Rnk
2010	Atl	41	4	0	0	0	-1	3	0	2	.40	-1	0	0	0	-1	-
2011	Atl	83	12	0	0	3	-1	2	2	0	.50	-1	1	0	0	0	110
		123	16	0	0	3	-2	5	2	2	.44	-2	1	0	0	-1	

Brandon Morrow

Year	Tm	Inn	TC	E	GFP	DM	+/-	SB	CCS	PCS/PPO	CS%	+/-	SB	Bnt	GFP/DME	Tot	Rnk
2007	Sea	63	3	0	0	1	0	3	2	0	.40	0	0	0	0	0	-
2008	Sea	65	3	0	0	0	0	3	1	0	.25	0	0	0	0	0	-
2009	Sea	70	12	0	1	2	0	5	1	0	.17	0	0	1	0	1	-
2010	Tor	146	16	0	1	1	-1	8	8	1	.53	-1	0	0	1	1	78
2011	Tor	179	24	3	2	3	-6	17	5	0	.23	-5	-1	1	-1	-6	175
		523	58	3	4	7	-7	36	17	1	.33	-6	0	2	0	-4	114

Charlie Morton

Year	Tm	Inn	TC	E	GFP	DM	+/-	SB	CCS	PCS/PPO	CS%	+/-	SB	Bnt	GFP/DME	Tot	Rnk
2008	Atl	75	10	0	0	1	0	7	1	1	.22	0	0	0	0	0	-
2009	Pit	97	18	0	1	2	0	9	3	1	.31	0	0	0	0	0	86
2010	Pit	80	21	3	1	1	0	12	1	1	.14	-1	0	1	0	-2	139
2011	Pit	172	39	1	1	0	-1	16	5	2	.27	-1	0	1	0	0	110
		423	88	4	3	4	-3	44	10	6	.24	-2	-1	1	0	-2	

Pitchers

Guillermo Moscoso

Year	Tm	Inn	TC	E	GFP	DM	+/-	SB	CCS	PCS/PPO	CS%	+/-	SB	Bnt	GFP/DME	Tot	Rnk
2009	Tex	14	1	0	0	0	0	1	0	0	.00	0	0		0	0	-
2010	Tex	1	0	0	0	0	0		0			0			0	0	-
2011	Oak	128	15	2	0	2	0	5	1	1	.29	0	0	-1	-1	-2	134
		142	16	2	0	2	0	6	1	1	.25	0	0	-1	-1	-2	

Dustin Moseley

Year	Tm	Inn	TC	E	GFP	DM	+/-	SB	CCS	PCS/PPO	CS%	+/-	SB	Bnt	GFP/DME	Tot	Rnk
2006	LAA	11	1	0	0	0	0	2	0		.00	0	0		0	0	-
2007	LAA	92	9	1	1	0	-1	6	3	0	.33	-1	0		0	-1	113
2008	LAA	50	11	0	1	0	0	4	1	2	.33	0	1		0	1	-
2009	LAA	15	5	0	1	0	+1	2	1	0	.33	1	0		0	1	-
2010	NYY	65	17	0	1	0	+3	9	2	0	.18	2	-1		0	1	-
2011	SD	120	33	0	4	1	+1	18	4	1	.18	1	-2	0	1	0	93
		353	76	1	8	1	4	41	11	3	.23	3	-2	0	1	2	

Guillermo Mota

Year	Tm	Inn	TC	E	GFP	DM	+/-	SB	CCS	PCS/PPO	CS%	+/-	SB	Bnt	GFP/DME	Tot	Rnk
2003	LA	105	21	1	-	-	+4	8	5	0	.38	3	0	-1	-	2	32
2004	2 tms	97	16	0	0	3	+1	21	2	1	.13	1	-2	0	0	-1	104
2005	Fla	67	7	0	0	0	+1	10	3	0	.23	1	-1		0	0	-
2006	2 tms	56	4	0	0	0	0	9	1	0	.10	0	-1		0	-1	-
2007	NYM	59	16	1	0	1	+4	9	0	0	.00	3	-1	-1	0	1	-
2008	Mil	57	15	0	0	0	+2	4	0	2	.20	2	0		0	2	-
2009	LAD	65	11	0	0	1	+1	6	1	0	.14	1	-1	0	0	0	-
2010	SF	54	8	1	1	1	-1	7	1	0	.13	-1	-1		0	-2	-
2011	SF	80	14	0	2	0	+1	4	2	1	.33	1	1	1	0	3	33
		640	112	3	3	6	13	78	15	4	.18	11	-6	-1	0	4	60

Jason Motte

Year	Tm	Inn	TC	E	GFP	DM	+/-	SB	CCS	PCS/PPO	CS%	+/-	SB	Bnt	GFP/DME	Tot	Rnk
2008	StL	11	2	0	0	0	0	0	0	0	-	0	0		0	0	-
2009	StL	57	10	0	2	0	0	0	0	1	1.00	0	1		1	2	-
2010	StL	52	9	1	1	1	+1	3	0	1	.25	1	0		0	1	-
2011	StL	68	23	0	2	1	+3	6	1	1	.14	2	0	0	1	3	-
		188	44	1	5	2	4	9	1	3	.25	3	1	0	2	6	-

Edward Mujica

Year	Tm	Inn	TC	E	GFP	DM	+/-	SB	CCS	PCS/PPO	CS%	+/-	SB	Bnt	GFP/DME	Tot	Rnk
2006	Cle	18	2	0	0	0	-1	0	0	1	1.00	-1	0		0	-1	-
2007	Cle	13	0	0	0	0	0	1	0	0	.00	0	0			0	-
2008	Cle	39	4	0	2	0	+1	0	1	0	1.00	1	0		0	1	-
2009	SD	94	14	0	2	2	+1	3	3	0	.50	1	1	0	0	2	43
2010	SD	70	10	0	0	1	0	2	0	1	.33	0	0		0	0	-
2011	Fla	76	22	2	4	0	0	7	1	2	.13	0	0	1	0	1	74
		309	52	2	8	3	1	13	5	4	.35	1	1	1	0	3	

Brett Myers

Year	Tm	Inn	TC	E	GFP	DM	+/-	SB	CCS	PCS/PPO	CS%	+/-	SB	Bnt	GFP/DME	Tot	Rnk
2003	Phi	193	42	2	-	-	+4	16	5	0	.24	3	-1	0	-	2	32
2004	Phi	176	38	0	0	5	-1	18	3	0	.14	-1	-2	0	-1	-4	159
2005	Phi	215	50	2	3	4	+4	15	4	2	.21	3	0	0	-1	2	41
2006	Phi	198	38	0	1	3	0	13	3	2	.28	0	0	0	0	0	84
2007	Phi	69	16	0	2	1	0	6	1	0	.14	0	-1	0	0	-1	-
2008	Phi	190	38	0	1	3	+2	17	2	1	.15	2	-2	1	0	1	52
2009	Phi	71	16	0	1	2	0	3	2	2	.50	0	1		0	1	-
2010	Hou	224	57	2	3	2	0	10	6	2	.41	0	1	0	0	1	69
2011	Hou	216	56	4	3	4	-4	15	6	1	.29	-3	0	-2	0	-5	168
		1551	351	10	14	24	5	113	32	10	.25	4	-4	-1	-2	-3	103

Chris Narveson

Year	Tm	Inn	TC	E	GFP	DM	+/-	SB	CCS	PCS/PPO	CS%	+/-	SB	Bnt	GFP/DME	Tot	Rnk
2006	StL	9	1	0	0	0	0	1	1	0	.50	0	0		0	0	-
2009	Mil	47	9	0	1	0	+2	5	1	0	.17	2	0		0	2	-
2010	Mil	168	34	2	6	3	+2	10	5	3	.44	1	1	-2	0	0	85
2011	Mil	162	33	1	3	3	+2	12	2	6	.40	2	2	0	0	4	18
		385	77	3	10	6	6	28	9	9	.39	5	3	-2	0	6	-

Juan Nicasio

Year	Tm	Inn	TC	E	GFP	DM	+/-	SB	CCS	PCS/PPO	CS%	+/-	SB	Bnt	GFP/DME	Tot	Rnk
2011	Col	72	21	1	1	3	+1	7	0	1	.13	1	-1	0	0	0	-

Jeff Niemann

Year	Tm	Inn	TC	E	GFP	DM	+/-	SB	CCS	PCS/PPO	CS%	+/-	SB	Bnt	GFP/DME	Tot	Rnk
2008	TB	16	1	0	0	1	0	2	1	0	.33	0	0		0	0	-
2009	TB	181	21	0	0	1	-3	24	6	1	.20	-2	-2	0	0	-4	165
2010	TB	174	23	1	0	0	-4	21	0	2	.09	-3	-2	0	0	-5	168
2011	TB	135	31	0	2	1	0	16	4	1	.24	0	-1	1	0	0	100
		506	76	1	2	3	-7	63	11	4	.18	-5	-5	1	0	-9	141

Jonathon Niese

Year	Tm	Inn	TC	E	GFP	DM	+/-	SB	CCS	PCS/PPO	CS%	+/-	SB	Bnt	GFP/DME	Tot	Rnk
2008	NYM	14	4	0	1	0	0	0	0	0	-	0	0	0	0	0	-
2009	NYM	26	4	0	1	1	-1	1	1	1	.67	0	0	0	0	0	-
2010	NYM	174	34	1	0	4	+2	0	3	1	1.00	2	2	-1	-1	2	39
2011	NYM	157	40	0	2	1	+3	7	1	0	.13	2	0	1	0	3	26
		370	82	1	4	6	4	8	5	2	.47	3	3	0	-1	5	-

Ricky Nolasco

Year	Tm	Inn	TC	E	GFP	DM	+/-	SB	CCS	PCS/PPO	CS%	+/-	SB	Bnt	GFP/DME	Tot	Rnk
2006	Fla	140	25	4	0	4	-1	6	6	0	.50	-1	1	-1	0	-1	111
2007	Fla	21	2	0	0	0	-2	1	2	0	.33	-2	0	-1	0	-3	-
2008	Fla	212	29	0	1	6	-2	7	5	0	.42	-2	1	1	-1	-1	121
2009	Fla	185	31	0	1	2	-1	13	3	1	.24	-1	-1	0	0	-2	138
2010	Fla	158	30	3	3	2	-1	5	4	2	.55	-1	1	-2	0	-2	139
2011	Fla	206	34	1	0	3	0	12	2	0	.14	0	-1	-2	0	-3	151
		922	151	8	5	17	-7	45	21	3	.35	-7	1	-5	-1	-12	156

Bud Norris

Year	Tm	Inn	TC	E	GFP	DM	+/-	SB	CCS	PCS/PPO	CS%	+/-	SB	Bnt	GFP/DME	Tot	Rnk
2009	Hou	56	4	0	0	0	-1	1	0	1	.00	-1	1		0	0	-
2010	Hou	154	36	3	5	1	+2	12	5	1	.29	2	0	1	1	4	20
2011	Hou	186	54	3	4	4	+2	16	6	3	.27	1	0	0	0	1	65
		395	94	6	9	5	3	29	11	5	.28	2	1	1	1	5	-

Ivan Nova

Year	Tm	Inn	TC	E	GFP	DM	+/-	SB	CCS	PCS/PPO	CS%	+/-	SB	Bnt	GFP/DME	Tot	Rnk
2010	NYY	42	11	1	0	0	-1	3	0	0	.00	-1	0	0	0	-1	-
2011	NYY	165	37	0	1	3	+2	10	8	0	.44	2	1	0	-1	2	44
		207	48	1	1	3	1	13	8	0	.38	1	1	0	-1	1	-

Eric O'Flaherty

Year	Tm	Inn	TC	E	GFP	DM	+/-	SB	CCS	PCS/PPO	CS%	+/-	SB	Bnt	GFP/DME	Tot	Rnk
2006	Sea	11	2	0	0	0	0	0	0	0		0	0		0	0	-
2007	Sea	52	10	0	1	3	0	2	1	1	.50	0	1		0	1	-
2008	Sea	7	4	0	0	0	0	3	0	1	.25	0	0		0	0	-
2009	Atl	56	5	0	0	5	-2	4	2	1	.43	-2	0	0	-2	-4	-
2010	Atl	44	6	0	0	2	+1	3	0	0	.00	1	0	0	0	1	-
2011	Atl	74	16	0	0	2	+1	5	1	1	.29	1	0	0	-1	0	-
		244	43	0	1	13	0	17	4	4	.32	0	1	0	-3	-2	-

Pitchers

Alexi Ogando

		BASIC						HOLDING				RUNS SAVED					
Year	Tm	Inn	TC	E	GFP	DM	+/-	SB	CCS	PCS/PPO	CS%	+/-	SB	Bnt	GFP/DME	Tot	Rnk
2010	Tex	42	7	1	1	1	-1	6	1	0	.14	0	-1	-1	0	-2	-
2011	Tex	169	20	0	1	0	-2	2	3	0	.60	-2	1	1	0	0	114
		210	27	1	2	1	-3	8	4	0	.33	-2	0	0	0	-2	

Logan Ondrusek

		BASIC						HOLDING				RUNS SAVED					
Year	Tm	Inn	TC	E	GFP	DM	+/-	SB	CCS	PCS/PPO	CS%	+/-	SB	Bnt	GFP/DME	Tot	Rnk
2010	Cin	59	20	1	1	2	0	0	2	0	1.00	0	1	0	0	1	-
2011	Cin	61	19	1	2	1	0	4	1	0	.20	0	0	0	0	0	-
		120	39	2	3	3	0	4	3	0	.43	0	1	0	0	1	

Roy Oswalt

		BASIC						HOLDING				RUNS SAVED					
Year	Tm	Inn	TC	E	GFP	DM	+/-	SB	CCS	PCS/PPO	CS%	+/-	SB	Bnt	GFP/DME	Tot	Rnk
2003	Hou	127	23	0	-	-	-4	1	4	1	.83	-3	1	0	-	-2	147
2004	Hou	237	49	3	0	3	+2	6	4	1	.45	2	1	1	0	4	18
2005	Hou	242	50	0	2	5	-1	3	4	1	.57	-1	1	1	0	1	70
2006	Hou	221	44	1	1	1	-1	5	5	1	.55	-1	1	1	0	1	72
2007	Hou	212	56	0	3	3	+1	5	1	0	.17	1	0	1	0	2	54
2008	Hou	209	54	0	2	1	+3	1	1	0	.50	2	1	0	1	4	16
2009	Hou	181	40	0	0	2	+1	2	1	0	.33	1	1	1	0	3	31
2010	2 tms	212	46	2	3	1	+4	15	5	1	.29	3	-1	1	0	3	26
2011	Phi	139	24	1	2	0	-1	11	0	0	.00	0	-1	1	0	0	100
		1779	386	7	13	16	4	49	25	5	.37	4	4	7	1	16	19

Juan Oviedo

		BASIC						HOLDING				RUNS SAVED					
Year	Tm	Inn	TC	E	GFP	DM	+/-	SB	CCS	PCS/PPO	CS%	+/-	SB	Bnt	GFP/DME	Tot	Rnk
2005	KC	54	11	0	0	1	-2	2	2	1	.60	-2	1	0	0	-1	-
2006	KC	13	3	0	0	0	+1	0	0	0	-	1	0	0	0	1	-
2007	KC	44	2	0	0	1	-1	5	0	0	.00	-1	-1	0	0	-2	-
2008	KC	48	6	1	0	0	0	1	0	1	.50	0	0	-1	0	-1	-
2009	Fla	69	9	1	1	0	-2	8	1	0	.11	-2	-1	0	0	-3	-
2010	Fla	65	14	0	0	0	-3	2	3	1	.67	-2	1	0	0	-1	-
2011	Fla	64	11	0	1	0	+1	6	1	0	.14	1	0	0	0	-1	-
		357	56	2	2	2	-6	24	7	3	.29	-5	0	-1	0	-6	

Micah Owings

		BASIC						HOLDING				RUNS SAVED					
Year	Tm	Inn	TC	E	GFP	DM	+/-	SB	CCS	PCS/PPO	CS%	+/-	SB	Bnt	GFP/DME	Tot	Rnk
2007	Ari	153	28	2	3	3	-1	4	3	0	.43	-1	1	1	0	1	78
2008	Ari	105	26	1	2	0	+3	3	2	0	.40	2	0	1	0	3	27
2009	Cin	120	30	2	0	1	0	7	2	0	.22	-1	0	-1	0	-1	115
2010	Cin	33	7	0	2	0	0	2	1	0	.33	0	0	0	1	1	-
2011	Ari	63	12	1	0	1	+1	2	2	1	.50	1	1	-1	0	1	-
		473	103	6	7	5	3	18	10	1	.36	2	2	0	1	5	57

Jonathan Papelbon

		BASIC						HOLDING				RUNS SAVED					
Year	Tm	Inn	TC	E	GFP	DM	+/-	SB	CCS	PCS/PPO	CS%	+/-	SB	Bnt	GFP/DME	Tot	Rnk
2005	Bos	34	5	0	0	0	0	1	4	0	.80	0	1		0	1	-
2006	Bos	68	8	1	0	0	-1	4	1	0	.20	-1	0		0	-1	-
2007	Bos	58	4	0	0	0	-1	4	0	0	.00	-1	0		0	-1	-
2008	Bos	69	13	3	0	2	-5	2	0	1	.00	-4	0	0	0	-4	-
2009	Bos	68	6	1	0	0	0	10	1	0	.09	0	-1		0	-1	-
2010	Bos	67	10	1	1	0	-2	11	0	0	.00	-1	-2	0	0	-3	-
2011	Bos	64	6	1	0	0	-1	6	0	0	.00	-1	-1	0	0	-2	-
		429	52	7	1	2	-10	38	6	1	.14	-8	-3	0	0	-11	

David Pauley

		BASIC						HOLDING				RUNS SAVED					
Year	Tm	Inn	TC	E	GFP	DM	+/-	SB	CCS	PCS/PPO	CS%	+/-	SB	Bnt	GFP/DME	Tot	Rnk
2006	Bos	16	4	0	0	3	0	0	0	0	-	0	0		0	0	-
2008	Bos	12	1	0	0	1	-1	2	0	0	.00	-1	0		0	-1	-
2010	Sea	91	14	0	0	2	-1	8	0	0	.00	-1	-1	-1	0	-3	155
2011	2 tms	74	14	0	0	1	0	5	3	0	.38	0	0	0	0	0	-
		193	33	0	0	7	-2	15	3	0	.17	-2	-1	-1	0	-4	

Felipe Paulino

		BASIC						HOLDING				RUNS SAVED					
Year	Tm	Inn	TC	E	GFP	DM	+/-	SB	CCS	PCS/PPO	CS%	+/-	SB	Bnt	GFP/DME	Tot	Rnk
2007	Hou	19	5	0	0	0	0	0	0	0	-	0	0	0	0	0	-
2009	Hou	98	16	0	0	0	-3	2	1	3	.50	-2	2	0	0	0	102
2010	Hou	92	18	2	0	0	-4	7	4	0	.36	-3	0	1	0	-2	146
2011	2 tms	139	30	3	3	4	-1	11	2	2	.21	-1	0	0	-1	-2	135
		347	69	5	3	4	-8	20	7	5	.31	-6	2	1	-1	-4	

Carl Pavano

		BASIC						HOLDING				RUNS SAVED					
Year	Tm	Inn	TC	E	GFP	DM	+/-	SB	CCS	PCS/PPO	CS%	+/-	SB	Bnt	GFP/DME	Tot	Rnk
2003	Fla	201	40	0	-	-	+2	17	3	0	.15	2	-2	-1	-	-1	112
2004	Fla	222	40	0	1	4	-1	16	5	0	.24	-1	-1	0	0	-2	125
2005	NYY	100	13	0	1	0	-2	11	4	0	.27	-2	-1	0	0	-3	153
2007	NYY	11	3	0	0	0	0	3	0	0	.00	0	-1		-	-1	-
2008	NYY	34	7	0	0	1	-1	5	1	0	.17	-1	-1	0	0	-2	-
2009	2 tms	199	33	0	1	0	+1	33	6	0	.15	1	-4	0	0	-3	156
2010	Min	221	45	0	1	2	0	31	6	2	.21	0	-3	0	0	-3	152
2011	Min	222	57	2	5	4	+3	24	5	2	.19	2	-1	0	0	1	62
		1211	238	2	9	11	2	140	30	4	.19	1	-14	-1	0	-14	159

Jake Peavy

		BASIC						HOLDING				RUNS SAVED					
Year	Tm	Inn	TC	E	GFP	DM	+/-	SB	CCS	PCS/PPO	CS%	+/-	SB	Bnt	GFP/DME	Tot	Rnk
2003	SD	195	40	3	-	-	-1	7	1	0	.13	-1	-1	1	-	-1	120
2004	SD	166	35	1	6	3	+1	16	1	0	.06	1	-2	1	1	1	58
2005	SD	203	35	1	1	1	+2	19	5	1	.21	2	-2	0	0	0	77
2006	SD	202	44	2	2	3	+1	25	6	0	.19	1	-3	0	1	-1	104
2007	SD	223	48	0	3	5	+5	21	2	1	.09	4	-2	0	0	2	41
2008	SD	174	40	2	6	0	0	18	8	1	.33	0	-1	1	1	1	69
2009	2 tms	102	19	1	4	1	+1	9	2	0	.18	1	-1	0	1	1	60
2010	CWS	107	24	0	2	2	0	12	1	3	.20	0	0	0	0	0	88
2011	CWS	112	16	1	2	1	-4	10	5	0	.33	-3	0	1	0	-2	147
		1483	301	11	26	16	5	137	31	6	.20	5	-12	4	4	1	79

Mike Pelfrey

		BASIC						HOLDING				RUNS SAVED					
Year	Tm	Inn	TC	E	GFP	DM	+/-	SB	CCS	PCS/PPO	CS%	+/-	SB	Bnt	GFP/DME	Tot	Rnk
2006	NYM	21	4	0	0	1	0	2	1	0	.33	0	0	0	0	0	-
2007	NYM	73	8	0	0	2	-2	8	0	1	.00	-2	-1	-1	-1	-5	-
2008	NYM	201	47	0	0	2	-1	5	6	4	.55	-1	3	1	0	3	33
2009	NYM	184	39	2	2	3	-3	16	4	2	.27	-2	0	-1	1	-2	147
2010	NYM	204	48	2	0	5	-1	12	5	2	.29	-1	1	-1	0	-1	119
2011	NYM	194	41	2	2	3	-2	29	2	1	.06	-1	-4	-1	0	-6	172
		876	187	6	4	16	-9	72	18	10	.22	-7	-1	-3	0	-11	154

Brad Penny

		BASIC						HOLDING				RUNS SAVED					
Year	Tm	Inn	TC	E	GFP	DM	+/-	SB	CCS	PCS/PPO	CS%	+/-	SB	Bnt	GFP/DME	Tot	Rnk
2003	Fla	196	32	1	-	-	-2	11	3	0	.21	-2	-1	0	-	-3	155
2004	2 tms	143	31	1	4	1	-2	14	4	0	.22	-2	-1	0	1	-2	131
2005	LAD	175	36	0	1	2	-2	17	4	1	.23	-2	-1	2	0	-1	127
2006	LAD	189	30	1	1	1	-2	20	7	2	.29	-2	-1	0	0	-3	160
2007	LAD	208	36	0	4	2	-2	14	5	0	.26	-2	0	1	0	-1	124
2008	LAD	95	24	1	1	1	-3	8	3	0	.27	-2	0	0	0	-2	141
2009	2 tms	173	29	1	1	3	-5	28	2	1	.10	-4	-4		-1	-9	175
2010	StL	56	11	0	1	1	-1	1	1	0	.50	-1	0	1	0	0	-
2011	Det	182	35	1	1	0	-2	16	4	2	.27	-2	0	0	0	-2	143
		1417	264	6	14	11	-21	129	33	6	.23	-19	-8	4	0	-23	174

Joel Peralta

		BASIC						HOLDING				RUNS SAVED					
Year	Tm	Inn	TC	E	GFP	DM	+/-	SB	CCS	PCS/PPO	CS%	+/-	SB	Bnt	GFP/DME	Tot	Rnk
2005	LAA	35	7	0	0	0	0	1	1	2	.67	0	1	0	0	1	-
2006	KC	74	10	0	0	0	-3	4	1	0	.20	-2	0	0	0	-2	-
2007	KC	88	11	0	0	0	-1	8	0	1	.00	-1	-1	0	0	-2	136
2008	KC	53	5	0	0	2	-2	3	1	0	.25	-2	0	0	0	-2	-
2009	Col	25	6	1	1	0	0	2	0	1	.00	0	0	1	0	1	-
2010	Was	49	5	0	1	0	-1	3	0	1	.00	0	0	0	0	0	-
2011	TB	68	9	0	0	0	0	5	2	1	.29	0	0	0	0	0	-
		390	53	1	2	4	-7	26	5	6	.19	-5	0	1	0	-4	

Pitchers

Luis Perez

Year	Tm	Inn	TC	E	GFP	DM	+/-	SB	CCS	PCS/PPO	CS%	+/-	SB	Bnt	GFP/DME	Tot	Rnk
2011	Tor	65	10	2	1	2	-3	2	3	0	.60	-2	1	0	0	-1	-

Rafael Perez

Year	Tm	Inn	TC	E	GFP	DM	+/-	SB	CCS	PCS/PPO	CS%	+/-	SB	Bnt	GFP/DME	Tot	Rnk
2006	Cle	12	3	1	0	1	0	3	0	0	.00	0	0	0	0	0	-
2007	Cle	61	11	2	1	1	-1	2	1	0	.33	-1	0	0	0	-1	-
2008	Cle	76	19	1	1	6	0	2	3	0	.60	0	1	-1	0	0	-
2009	Cle	48	11	1	0	0	+1	4	2	0	.33	1	0	0	0	1	-
2010	Cle	61	14	1	3	3	0	5	1	0	.17	0	0	-2	-1	-3	-
2011	Cle	63	24	3	0	1	+1	2	4	0	.67	1	1	1	0	3	-
		321	82	9	5	12	1	18	11	0	.38	1	2	-2	-1	0	-

Glen Perkins

Year	Tm	Inn	TC	E	GFP	DM	+/-	SB	CCS	PCS/PPO	CS%	+/-	SB	Bnt	GFP/DME	Tot	Rnk
2006	Min	6	1	0	0	0	0	0	0	0	-	0		0	0	0	-
2007	Min	29	3	0	0	1	0	1	1	0	.50	0		0	0	0	-
2008	Min	151	28	1	3	2	+3	3	1	3	.57	2	2	0	0	4	16
2009	Min	96	12	1	1	2	-3	7	0	0	.00	-2	-1	0	0	-3	158
2010	Min	22	10	0	1	0	+1	2	0	1	.33	1	0	0	0	1	-
2011	Min	62	11	1	2	1	-1	3	1	1	.40	-1	0	1	0	0	-
		365	65	3	7	6	0	16	3	5	.33	0	1	1	0	2	-

Vinnie Pestano

Year	Tm	Inn	TC	E	GFP	DM	+/-	SB	CCS	PCS/PPO	CS%	+/-	SB	Bnt	GFP/DME	Tot	Rnk
2010	Cle	5	1	0	0	0	0	1	0	0	.00	0	0	0		0	-
2011	Cle	62	5	0	0	0	+1	1	0	0	.00	1	0	0		1	-
		67	6	0	0	0	1	2	0	0	.00	1	0	0		1	-

Michael Pineda

Year	Tm	Inn	TC	E	GFP	DM	+/-	SB	CCS	PCS/PPO	CS%	+/-	SB	Bnt	GFP/DME	Tot	Rnk
2011	Sea	171	26	1	1	3	-3	10	10	0	.50	-2	1	0	0	-1	128

Joel Pineiro

Year	Tm	Inn	TC	E	GFP	DM	+/-	SB	CCS	PCS/PPO	CS%	+/-	SB	Bnt	GFP/DME	Tot	Rnk
2003	Sea	212	45	1	-	-	+4	11	2	0	.15	3	-1	1	0	3	19
2004	Sea	141	24	1	0	2	0	11	3	0	.21	0	-1	0	0	-1	106
2005	Sea	189	42	1	1	1	0	7	2	0	.22	0	0	1	0	1	64
2006	Sea	166	36	0	1	1	+1	8	3	0	.27	1	0	-1	0	0	81
2007	2 tms	98	28	2	3	1	+6	4	2	0	.33	5	0	0	0	5	6
2008	StL	149	44	1	4	2	+1	5	3	2	.44	1	1	-1	0	1	60
2009	StL	214	59	1	5	0	+4	1	4	0	.80	3	1	0	0	4	11
2010	LAA	152	38	1	3	2	+3	3	1	0	.25	2	0	0	0	2	39
2011	LAA	146	22	1	0	1	-1	5	2	1	.38	-1	1	0	0	0	110
		1465	338	9	17	10	18	55	22	3	.30	14	1	0	0	15	20

Rick Porcello

Year	Tm	Inn	TC	E	GFP	DM	+/-	SB	CCS	PCS/PPO	CS%	+/-	SB	Bnt	GFP/DME	Tot	Rnk
2009	Det	171	38	2	1	7	-2	8	2	1	.20	-2	0	0	-1	-3	158
2010	Det	163	25	1	3	2	-5	10	5	0	.33	-4	0	0	0	-4	166
2011	Det	182	38	2	2	2	-1	16	4	0	.20	-1	-1	1	0	-1	123
		515	101	5	6	11	-8	34	11	1	.24	-7	-1	1	0	-8	138

David Price

Year	Tm	Inn	TC	E	GFP	DM	+/-	SB	CCS	PCS/PPO	CS%	+/-	SB	Bnt	GFP/DME	Tot	Rnk
2008	TB	14	1	0	0	0	0	0	0	0	-	0	0	0	0	0	-
2009	TB	128	23	1	2	3	0	8	3	3	.43	0	1	0	0	1	69
2010	TB	209	30	0	2	0	-1	13	4	3	.35	-1	1	1	1	2	57
2011	TB	224	40	4	5	2	-1	20	4	1	.20	-1	-1	1	0	-1	123
		575	94	5	9	5	-2	41	11	7	.31	-2	1	2	1	2	77

Chad Qualls

Year	Tm	Inn	TC	E	GFP	DM	+/-	SB	CCS	PCS/PPO	CS%	+/-	SB	Bnt	GFP/DME	Tot	Rnk
2004	Hou	33	4	0	0	1	-1	1	1	0	.50	-1	0		0	-1	-
2005	Hou	80	19	0	1	2	0	4	2	1	.33	0	0	-1	0	-1	-
2006	Hou	89	19	0	2	0	-2	3	3	1	.57	-2	1	-1	0	-2	142
2007	Hou	83	19	0	1	0	-4	7	4	1	.42	-3	1	0	0	-2	147
2008	Ari	74	13	2	2	0	-1	3	0	0	.00	-1	0	-1	1	-1	-
2009	Ari	52	11	0	0	1	0	3	0	0	.00	0	0	0	0	0	-
2010	2 tms	59	12	2	2	2	-4	5	1	0	.17	-3	-1	-1	0	-5	-
2011	SD	74	18	0	1	1	0	10	4	1	.29	0	0	0	0	0	-
		543	115	4	9	7	-12	36	15	4	.32	-10	1	-4	1	-12	157

Ramon Ramirez

Year	Tm	Inn	TC	E	GFP	DM	+/-	SB	CCS	PCS/PPO	CS%	+/-	SB	Bnt	GFP/DME	Tot	Rnk
2006	Col	68	10	1	0	0	-1	2	0	0	.00	-1	0		0	-1	-
2007	Col	17	3	0	0	0	-1	3	0	0	.00	-1	0	0	0	-1	-
2008	KC	72	11	1	0	0	0	3	0	1	.25	0	0	0	0	0	-
2009	Bos	70	12	1	0	0	0	6	0	0	.00	0	-1	0	0	-1	-
2010	2 tms	69	13	2	0	0	0	5	1	0	.17	0	0	0	0	0	-
2011	SF	69	12	2	0	0	-2	13	2	0	.13	-2	-2	0	0	-4	-
		364	61	7	0	1	-4	32	3	1	.11	-4	-3	0	0	-7	-

Chris Resop

Year	Tm	Inn	TC	E	GFP	DM	+/-	SB	CCS	PCS/PPO	CS%	+/-	SB	Bnt	GFP/DME	Tot	Rnk
2005	Fla	17	2	0	0	0	-1	1	1	0	.50	-1	0		0	-1	-
2006	Fla	21	1	0	0	0	0	3	1	0	.25	0	0	0	0	0	-
2007	LAA	4	0	0	0	0	0	0	0	0	-	0	0	0		0	-
2008	Atl	18	3	0	0	0	-2	1	0	0	.00	-2	0	0	0	-2	-
2010	2 tms	21	4	0	0	0	0	2	0	0	.00	0	0	0	0	0	-
2011	Pit	70	6	1	1	1	-2	9	3	0	.25	-2	-1	0	1	-2	-
		151	16	1	1	1	-5	16	5	0	.24	-5	-1	0	1	-5	-

Jo-Jo Reyes

Year	Tm	Inn	TC	E	GFP	DM	+/-	SB	CCS	PCS/PPO	CS%	+/-	SB	Bnt	GFP/DME	Tot	Rnk
2007	Atl	51	8	0	0	1	+1	2	0	1	.33	1	0	0	0	1	-
2008	Atl	113	16	0	0	0	0	9	3	1	.31	0	0	0	0	0	92
2009	Atl	27	4	1	0	0	-1	1	0	0	.00	-1	0	0	0	-1	-
2010	Atl	3	0	0	0	0	0	0	0	0	-	0	0	0	0	0	-
2011	2 tms	141	21	0	2	2	+2	14	1	1	.13	1	-1	1	0	1	65
		334	49	1	2	4	2	26	4	3	.21	1	-1	1	0	1	-

Clayton Richard

Year	Tm	Inn	TC	E	GFP	DM	+/-	SB	CCS	PCS/PPO	CS%	+/-	SB	Bnt	GFP/DME	Tot	Rnk
2008	CWS	48	13	3	0	1	0	6	0	0	.00	0	-1	0	0	-1	-
2009	2 tms	153	38	3	0	2	-5	13	2	9	.43	-4	3	-2	-1	-4	169
2010	SD	202	43	4	3	4	+1	8	2	6	.47	1	3	-1	0	3	31
2011	SD	100	29	3	0	1	+1	5	2	5	.50	0	2	0	0	2	55
		502	123	13	3	8	-3	32	6	20	.41	-3	7	-3	-1	0	91

Mariano Rivera

Year	Tm	Inn	TC	E	GFP	DM	+/-	SB	CCS	PCS/PPO	CS%	+/-	SB	Bnt	GFP/DME	Tot	Rnk
2003	NYY	70	21	2	-	-	0	3	2	0	.40	0	0	-1	-	-1	-
2004	NYY	79	41	1	2	0	+4	5	1	0	.17	3	0	1	0	4	-
2005	NYY	78	29	0	3	0	+3	6	3	0	.33	2	0	1	0	2	-
2006	NYY	75	25	0	1	1	+3	3	3	0	.50	2	0	1	0	3	-
2007	NYY	71	16	0	1	0	0	2	1	0	.33	0	0	0	0	0	-
2008	NYY	71	14	0	1	0	-1	6	1	0	.14	-1	-1	0	0	-2	-
2009	NYY	66	18	0	1	1	+4	4	1	0	.33	3	0	0	0	3	-
2010	NYY	60	18	0	2	0	+4	8	0	1	.00	1	0	1	0	2	-
2011	NYY	61	13	0	3	0	+2	5	1	0	.17	1	0	1	0	2	-
		632	195	3	14	2	19	40	13	1	.25	13	-2	2	0	13	25

Pitchers

David Robertson

Year	Tm	Inn	TC	E	GFP	DM	+/-	SB	CCS	PCS/PPO	CS%	+/-	SB	Bnt	GFP/DME	Tot	Rnk
2008	NYY	30	4	0	0	0	-2	4	3	0	.43	-2	0		0	-2	-
2009	NYY	44	3	0	0	0	-3	2	1	1	.50	-2	0		0	-2	-
2010	NYY	61	5	0	0	2	-1	6	1	0	.14	-1	0		0	-1	-
2011	NYY	67	7	1	0	1	-1	16	2	0	.11	-1	-2	0	0	-3	-
		202	19	1	0	3	-7	28	7	1	.22	-6	-2	0	0	-8	-

Aneury Rodriguez

Year	Tm	Inn	TC	E	GFP	DM	+/-	SB	CCS	PCS/PPO	CS%	+/-	SB	Bnt	GFP/DME	Tot	Rnk
2011	Hou	85	15	2	0	0	-1	13	1	0	.07	-1	-2	0	0	-3	154

Francisco Rodriguez

Year	Tm	Inn	TC	E	GFP	DM	+/-	SB	CCS	PCS/PPO	CS%	+/-	SB	Bnt	GFP/DME	Tot	Rnk
2003	Ana	86	15	0	-	-	0	6	3	1	.40	0	0	0	-	0	86
2004	Ana	84	14	0	2	1	0	4	2	0	.33	0	0	1	0	1	66
2005	LAA	67	12	1	0	0	-1	2	0	0	.00	-1	0	0	0	-1	-
2006	LAA	73	10	0	0	1	+1	2	1	1	.33	1	1	0	0	2	-
2007	LAA	67	6	0	0	0	-1	12	1	0	.08	-1	-2		0	-3	-
2008	LAA	68	12	2	1	1	0	8	0	0	.00	0	-1	-1	0	-2	-
2009	NYM	68	8	0	0	0	-1	7	2	0	.22	-1	-1	0	0	-2	-
2010	NYM	57	9	0	0	0	-2	4	1	1	.20	-2	0		0	-2	-
2011	2 tms	72	12	0	1	1	-3	11	1	0	.08	-2	-1	0	0	-3	-
		643	98	3	4	4	-7	56	11	3	.18	-6	-4	0	0	-10	150

Henry Rodriguez

Year	Tm	Inn	TC	E	GFP	DM	+/-	SB	CCS	PCS/PPO	CS%	+/-	SB	Bnt	GFP/DME	Tot	Rnk
2009	Oak	4	1	0	0	1	0	1	0	0	.00	0	0		0	0	-
2010	Oak	28	3	0	0	0	0	8	0	0	.00	0	-1		0	-1	-
2011	Was	66	9	0	2	1	-1	13	0	0	.00	-1	-2	1	0	-2	-
		97	13	0	2	2	-1	22	0	0	.00	-1	-3	1	0	-3	-

Wandy Rodriguez

Year	Tm	Inn	TC	E	GFP	DM	+/-	SB	CCS	PCS/PPO	CS%	+/-	SB	Bnt	GFP/DME	Tot	Rnk
2005	Hou	129	31	2	2	2	+3	5	4	2	.55	2	1	0	0	3	27
2006	Hou	136	22	1	2	0	0	6	3	4	.50	-1	2	-1	1	1	72
2007	Hou	183	37	1	2	0	+2	13	3	6	.41	2	2	-1	0	3	27
2008	Hou	137	23	0	1	0	0	4	2	1	.43	0	1	0	0	1	69
2009	Hou	206	32	0	3	2	+1	3	1	5	.57	1	1	0	0	2	43
2010	Hou	195	41	1	6	3	+4	13	9	2	.46	3	1	0	0	4	18
2011	Hou	191	37	0	3	1	+1	20	3	0	.13	1	-2	1	0	0	93
		1176	223	5	19	8	10	64	26	16	.40	8	6	-1	1	14	24

Esmil Rogers

Year	Tm	Inn	TC	E	GFP	DM	+/-	SB	CCS	PCS/PPO	CS%	+/-	SB	Bnt	GFP/DME	Tot	Rnk
2009	Col	4	0	0	0	0	0	0	0	0	-		0		0	0	-
2010	Col	72	17	2	4	0	-1	6	3	1	.40	-1	0	0	0	1	-
2011	Col	83	21	0	1	2	-1	2	3	0	.60	-1	1	1	0	1	88
		159	38	2	5	2	-2	8	6	1	.47	-2	1	1	0	1	-

Ricky Romero

Year	Tm	Inn	TC	E	GFP	DM	+/-	SB	CCS	PCS/PPO	CS%	+/-	SB	Bnt	GFP/DME	Tot	Rnk
2009	Tor	178	42	2	3	4	-1	9	5	4	.44	-1	2	1	0	2	54
2010	Tor	210	57	3	4	3	+8	4	3	3	.56	6	2	2	0	10	4
2011	Tor	225	53	1	3	2	+5	18	1	6	.28	3	1	1	0	5	12
		613	152	6	10	9	12	31	9	13	.38	8	5	4	0	17	15

James Russell

Year	Tm	Inn	TC	E	GFP	DM	+/-	SB	CCS	PCS/PPO	CS%	+/-	SB	Bnt	GFP/DME	Tot	Rnk
2010	ChC	49	8	0	0	3	-1	3	0	1	.25	-1	0	0	0	-1	-
2011	ChC	68	12	1	1	2	-1	5	1	2	.38	-1	1	0	0	0	-
		116	20	1	1	5	-2	8	1	3	.33	-2	1	0	0	-1	-

Marc Rzepczynski

Year	Tm	Inn	TC	E	GFP	DM	+/-	SB	CCS	PCS/PPO	CS%	+/-	SB	Bnt	GFP/DME	Tot	Rnk
2009	Tor	61	12	0	1	2	+1	7	1	2	.30	1	0	0	0	1	-
2010	Tor	64	5	0	0	2	-1	5	3	0	.38	-1	0		0	-1	-
2011	2 tms	62	19	2	1	2	+2	2	0	2	.50	1	0	-2	0	-1	-
		187	36	2	2	6	2	14	4	4	.36	1	0	-2	0	-1	-

CC Sabathia

Year	Tm	Inn	TC	E	GFP	DM	+/-	SB	CCS	PCS/PPO	CS%	+/-	SB	Bnt	GFP/DME	Tot	Rnk
2003	Cle	198	28	2	-	-	0	5	7	2	.64	0	2	0	-	2	46
2004	Cle	188	18	0	1	2	-1	17	5	1	.26	-1	-1	0	-1	-2	125
2005	Cle	197	21	2	2	2	-5	11	5	2	.39	-4	1	0	0	-3	162
2006	Cle	193	25	3	1	2	-2	14	5	0	.26	-2	-1	1	0	-2	142
2007	Cle	241	26	1	4	8	+1	10	9	1	.50	1	2	0	-2	1	64
2008	2 tms	253	34	1	5	4	-2	12	1	2	.20	-2	0	0	-1	-3	151
2009	NYY	230	31	0	4	7	0	13	4	3	.35	0	1	0	-2	-1	115
2010	NYY	238	35	1	2	4	0	15	1	2	.17	0	-1	0	-1	-2	134
2011	NYY	237	27	3	0	4	-8	11	5	1	.35	-6	1	0	0	-5	171
		1974	245	13	19	33	-17	108	42	14	.34	-14	4	1	-6	-15	166

Fernando Salas

Year	Tm	Inn	TC	E	GFP	DM	+/-	SB	CCS	PCS/PPO	CS%	+/-	SB	Bnt	GFP/DME	Tot	Rnk
2010	StL	31	8	0	0	0	+1	2	0	0	.00	0	0	0	0	0	-
2011	StL	75	13	0	0	0	0	2	0	0	.00	0	0	0	0	0	-
		105	21	0	0	0	1	4	0	0	.00	0	0	0	0	0	-

Chris Sale

Year	Tm	Inn	TC	E	GFP	DM	+/-	SB	CCS	PCS/PPO	CS%	+/-	SB	Bnt	GFP/DME	Tot	Rnk
2010	CWS	23	1	0	0	0	-1	0	0	0	-	-1	0	0	0	-1	-
2011	CWS	71	20	0	0	3	0	3	1	3	.57	0	1	1	0	2	-
		94	21	0	0	3	-1	3	1	3	.57	-1	1	1	0	1	-

Jeff Samardzija

Year	Tm	Inn	TC	E	GFP	DM	+/-	SB	CCS	PCS/PPO	CS%	+/-	SB	Bnt	GFP/DME	Tot	Rnk
2008	ChC	28	7	0	1	1	0	5	0	1	.17	0	0	0	0	0	-
2009	ChC	35	9	1	0	0	0	3	1	0	.25	0	0	-1	0	-1	-
2010	ChC	19	3	0	0	0	0	4	1	0	.20	0	0	0	0	0	-
2011	ChC	88	15	1	1	1	-1	16	2	0	.11	-1	-2	0	0	-3	154
		169	34	2	2	2	-1	28	4	1	.15	-1	-2	-1	0	-4	-

Brian Sanches

Year	Tm	Inn	TC	E	GFP	DM	+/-	SB	CCS	PCS/PPO	CS%	+/-	SB	Bnt	GFP/DME	Tot	Rnk
2006	Phi	21	1	0	0	0	0	0	1	0	1.00		0		0	0	-
2007	Phi	15	1	0	0	0	0	1	2	0	.67		0		0	0	-
2008	Was	11	1	0	0	0	0	1	0	0	.00	0	0		0	0	-
2009	Fla	56	9	1	0	0	+1	6	3	0	.33	1	0	-1	0	0	-
2010	Fla	64	11	0	0	1	+1	5	1	0	.17	1	0	0	0	1	-
2011	Fla	62	6	0	0	0	0	12	2	0	.14	0	-2		0	-2	-
		228	29	1	0	1	2	25	9	0	.26	2	-2	-1	0	-1	-

Anibal Sanchez

Year	Tm	Inn	TC	E	GFP	DM	+/-	SB	CCS	PCS/PPO	CS%	+/-	SB	Bnt	GFP/DME	Tot	Rnk
2006	Fla	114	29	1	0	5	+2	6	1	0	.14	2	0	0	-1	1	58
2007	Fla	30	12	2	0	1	0	1	0	0	.00	0	0	0	0	0	-
2008	Fla	52	11	4	1	0	-1	7	0	1	.00	-1	-1	-1	0	-3	-
2009	Fla	86	18	2	0	1	+1	11	1	0	.08	1	-1	-1	0	-1	110
2010	Fla	195	44	5	1	2	-6	11	3	0	.21	-4	0	2	0	-2	150
2011	Fla	196	45	1	4	1	+1	15	2	2	.12	1	0	1	1	3	33
		673	159	15	6	10	-3	51	7	3	.12	-1	-2	1	0	-2	100

Pitchers

Jonathan Sanchez

Year Tm	Inn	TC	E	GFP	DM	+/-	SB	CCS	PCS/PPO	CS%	+/-	SB	Bnt	GFP/DME	Tot	Rnk
2006 SF	40	2	0	0	1	0	9	0	1	.00	0	-1	0		-1	-
2007 SF	52	6	0	0	1	-2	1	3	1	.80	-2	1	1	0	0	-
2008 SF	158	17	0	1	1	0	19	2	1	.14	0	-2	0	0	-2	135
2009 SF	163	18	0	0	1	+1	24	3	2	.17	1	-2	0	0	-1	110
2010 SF	193	28	1	1	1	-2	17	5	5	.35	-2	1	0	0	-1	127
2011 SF	101	21	2	1	1	+1	12	2	3	.29	1	0	-1	0	0	93
	708	92	3	3	6	-2	82	15	12	.24	-2	-3	0	0	-5	118

Ervin Santana

Year Tm	Inn	TC	E	GFP	DM	+/-	SB	CCS	PCS/PPO	CS%	+/-	SB	Bnt	GFP/DME	Tot	Rnk
2005 LAA	134	20	0	0	0	0	8	4	1	.38	0	0	0	0	0	88
2006 LAA	204	27	2	0	2	-2	5	8	1	.64	-2	2	0	0	0	99
2007 LAA	150	19	0	0	1	-1	11	3	0	.21	-1	0	0	0	-1	113
2008 LAA	219	32	0	2	3	-5	16	4	0	.20	-4	-1	1	0	-4	170
2009 LAA	140	16	1	1	3	-2	15	5	0	.25	-2	-1	0	0	-3	158
2010 LAA	223	32	0	3	2	-5	36	8	1	.18	-3	-4	1	0	-6	171
2011 LAA	229	36	5	3	0	-2	28	5	0	.15	-2	-3	-2	1	-6	174
	1297	182	8	9	10	-17	119	37	3	.25	-14	-7	0	1	-20	172

Sergio Santos

Year Tm	Inn	TC	E	GFP	DM	+/-	SB	CCS	PCS/PPO	CS%	+/-	SB	Bnt	GFP/DME	Tot	Rnk
2010 CWS	52	8	0	1	1	-3	4	0	1	.20	-2	0	1	0	-1	-
2011 CWS	63	9	0	1	0	+1	5	0	0	.00	1	-1	0	1	1	-
	115	17	0	2	1	-2	9	0	1	.10	-1	-1	1	1	0	-

Joe Saunders

Year Tm	Inn	TC	E	GFP	DM	+/-	SB	CCS	PCS/PPO	CS%	+/-	SB	Bnt	GFP/DME	Tot	Rnk
2005 LAA	9	0	0	0	0	0	1	0	0	.00	0	0	0		0	-
2006 LAA	71	11	0	0	3	-2	1	2	1	.75	-2	1	1	0	0	-
2007 LAA	107	17	0	0	2	-1	7	2	2	.36	-1	1		0	0	94
2008 LAA	198	41	0	3	6	+2	18	4	3	.28	2	0	0	-1	1	52
2009 LAA	186	32	1	3	3	+1	4	3	4	.28	1	0	0	0	1	60
2010 2 tms	203	53	1	4	0	0	9	3	3	.53	0	3	1	0	4	25
2011 Ari	212	49	0	3	2	+4	9	8	4	.57	3	3	1	0	7	6
	986	203	2	13	16	4	63	22	22	.41	3	8	3	-1	13	28

Max Scherzer

Year Tm	Inn	TC	E	GFP	DM	+/-	SB	CCS	PCS/PPO	CS%	+/-	SB	Bnt	GFP/DME	Tot	Rnk
2008 Ari	56	10	1	2	0	0	0	1	0	1.00	0	0	0	0	0	-
2009 Ari	170	35	2	2	2	-2	10	5	1	.38	-2	1	-1	0	-2	147
2010 Det	196	30	2	2	3	-2	17	12	1	.43	-1	0	0	0	-1	119
2011 Det	195	23	0	2	1	-6	12	6	3	.43	-5	2	1	0	-2	149
	617	98	5	8	6	-10	39	24	5	.43	-8	3	0	0	-5	119

James Shields

Year Tm	Inn	TC	E	GFP	DM	+/-	SB	CCS	PCS/PPO	CS%	+/-	SB	Bnt	GFP/DME	Tot	Rnk
2006 TB	125	29	0	0	0	0	7	2	4	.36	0	1	1	0	2	51
2007 TB	215	55	1	4	2	+2	9	6	0	.40	2	1	0	0	3	27
2008 TB	215	39	1	2	0	-1	7	6	1	.46	-1	1	0	0	1	77
2009 TB	220	43	2	4	4	-1	5	2	1	.29	-1	1	0	0	0	96
2010 TB	203	39	4	2	4	-5	10	3	2	.23	-4	1	-1	0	-4	166
2011 TB	249	54	3	2	4	+1	6	4	13	.45	0	6	1	0	7	8
	1227	259	11	14	14	-4	44	23	21	.37	-4	11	2	0	9	39

Alfredo Simon

Year Tm	Inn	TC	E	GFP	DM	+/-	SB	CCS	PCS/PPO	CS%	+/-	SB	Bnt	GFP/DME	Tot	Rnk
2008 Bal	13	7	0	0	0	-1	1	0	0	.00	-1	0		0	-1	-
2009 Bal	6	2	0	1	0	+1	1	1	0	.50	1	0		0	1	-
2010 Bal	49	9	0	0	0	-2	5	2	0	.29	-2	0	0	0	-2	-
2011 Bal	116	24	1	3	0	+1	10	8	0	.44	1	0	0	1	2	47
	184	42	1	4	0	-1	17	11	0	.39	-1	0	0	1	0	-

Tony Sipp

Year Tm	Inn	TC	E	GFP	DM	+/-	SB	CCS	PCS/PPO	CS%	+/-	SB	Bnt	GFP/DME	Tot	Rnk
2009 Cle	40	6	0	1	0	0	3	0	0	.00	0	0	1	0	1	-
2010 Cle	63	11	0	0	1	+1	8	0	6	.43	1	1	0	0	2	-
2011 Cle	62	15	1	0	1	+1	13	0	2	.13	1	-1	1	0	1	-
	165	32	1	1	2	2	24	0	8	.25	2	0	2	0	4	-

Joe Smith

Year Tm	Inn	TC	E	GFP	DM	+/-	SB	CCS	PCS/PPO	CS%	+/-	SB	Bnt	GFP/DME	Tot	Rnk
2007 NYM	44	11	0	1	2	0	5	1	0	.17	0	0		0	0	-
2008 NYM	63	21	0	3	0	+4	6	2	0	.25	3	0	1	0	4	-
2009 Cle	34	12	0	2	0	+3	1	0	0	.00	2	0		0	2	-
2010 Cle	40	9	0	2	1	+2	6	0	1	.14	1	0		0	1	-
2011 Cle	67	26	1	2	0	+7	4	2	3	.43	5	1	0	0	6	-
	248	79	1	10	3	16	22	5	4	.24	11	1	1	0	13	-

Joakim Soria

Year Tm	Inn	TC	E	GFP	DM	+/-	SB	CCS	PCS/PPO	CS%	+/-	SB	Bnt	GFP/DME	Tot	Rnk
2007 KC	69	14	1	2	0	+2	0	0	1		2	1	0	0	3	-
2008 KC	67	12	0	2	0	0	2	2		.33	0	1		1	2	-
2009 KC	53	8	1	0	0	0	0	1	0	1.00	0	0	0	0	0	-
2010 KC	66	19	0	0	1	+1	1	1	0	.50	1	0	0	0	1	-
2011 KC	60	12	0	0	2	+1	0	1	0	1.00	1	1	0	0	2	-
	315	65	2	3	3	4	3	3	3	.57	4	3	0	1	8	-

Tim Stauffer

Year Tm	Inn	TC	E	GFP	DM	+/-	SB	CCS	PCS/PPO	CS%	+/-	SB	Bnt	GFP/DME	Tot	Rnk
2005 SD	81	16	0	1	0	0	1	2	0	.67	0	0		0	0	88
2006 SD	6	0	0	0	0	0	0	1	0	1.00	0	0		0	0	-
2007 SD	8	0	0	0	0	0	0	0	0		0	0		0	0	-
2009 SD	73	13	0	1	0	0	1	2	0	.67	0	1	1	0	2	-
2010 SD	83	12	0	1	1	+1	1	2	0	.67	1	1	0	0	2	43
2011 SD	186	65	1	4	0	+4	5	7	1	.62	3	2	1	0	7	6
	436	106	1	7	1	5	8	14	1	.65	4	4	2	1	11	-

Zach Stewart

Year Tm	Inn	TC	E	GFP	DM	+/-	SB	CCS	PCS/PPO	CS%	+/-	SB	Bnt	GFP/DME	Tot	Rnk
2011 2 tms	67	16	2	2	2	0	6	2	0	.25	0	-1	0	0	-1	-

Drew Storen

Year Tm	Inn	TC	E	GFP	DM	+/-	SB	CCS	PCS/PPO	CS%	+/-	SB	Bnt	GFP/DME	Tot	Rnk
2010 Was	55	8	0	0	0	0	2	1	0	.33	0	0	0	0	0	-
2011 Was	75	16	0	1	0	0	3	0	0	.00	0	0	1	0	1	-
	130	24	0	1	0	0	5	1	0	.17	0	0	1	0	1	-

Michael Stutes

Year Tm	Inn	TC	E	GFP	DM	+/-	SB	CCS	PCS/PPO	CS%	+/-	SB	Bnt	GFP/DME	Tot	Rnk
2011 Phi	62	11	3	1	0	-1	7	3	1	.30	0	0	0	0	0	-

Anthony Swarzak

Year Tm	Inn	TC	E	GFP	DM	+/-	SB	CCS	PCS/PPO	CS%	+/-	SB	Bnt	GFP/DME	Tot	Rnk
2009 Min	59	7	0	1	0	0	1	2	0	.67	0	1		0	1	-
2011 Min	102	10	0	0	2	0	3	3	0	.50	0	1	0	0	1	74
	161	17	0	1	2	0	4	5	0	.56	0	2	0	0	2	-

Pitchers

Hisanori Takahashi

Year	Tm	Inn	TC	E	GFP	DM	+/-	SB	CCS	PCS/PPO	CS%	+/-	SB	Bnt	GFP/DME	Tot	Rnk
2010	NYM	122	21	1	0	0	+2	3	4	1	.57	1	1	0		2	43
2011	LAA	68	15	1	0	0	+2	7	1	1	.22	2	0	0	0	2	-
		190	36	2	0	0	+4	10	5	1	.38	3	1	0	0	4	-

Mitch Talbot

Year	Tm	Inn	TC	E	GFP	DM	+/-	SB	CCS	PCS/PPO	CS%	+/-	SB	Bnt	GFP/DME	Tot	Rnk
2008	TB	10	2	0	0	0	0	2	0	0	.00	0	0			0	-
2010	Cle	159	31	1	2	0	+1	4	11	1	.73	1	3	-1	0	3	31
2011	Cle	64	12	0	0	3	-3	7	3	1	.36	-2	0	0	0	-2	-
		232	45	1	2	3	-2	13	14	2	.54	-1	3	-1	0	0	-

Chris Tillman

Year	Tm	Inn	TC	E	GFP	DM	+/-	SB	CCS	PCS/PPO	CS%	+/-	SB	Bnt	GFP/DME	Tot	Rnk
2009	Bal	65	6	0	2	0	0	1	5	0	.83	0	1		0	1	-
2010	Bal	54	14	1	0	0	0	3	1	0	.25	0	0		0	0	-
2011	Bal	62	8	0	1	2	-4	5	3	0	.38	-3	0	0	0	-3	-
		180	28	1	3	2	-4	9	9	0	.50	-3	1	0	0	-2	-

Josh Tomlin

Year	Tm	Inn	TC	E	GFP	DM	+/-	SB	CCS	PCS/PPO	CS%	+/-	SB	Bnt	GFP/DME	Tot	Rnk
2010	Cle	73	13	0	1	1	+2	2	3	0	.60	1	1	0	0	2	-
2011	Cle	165	43	2	1	1	+1	0	0	1	-	1	1	-1	0	1	65
		238	56	2	2	2	3	2	3	1	.60	2	2	-1	0	3	-

Koji Uehara

Year	Tm	Inn	TC	E	GFP	DM	+/-	SB	CCS	PCS/PPO	CS%	+/-	SB	Bnt	GFP/DME	Tot	Rnk
2009	Bal	67	5	0	2	0	0	4	0	1	.00	0	0	0	0	0	-
2010	Bal	44	5	0	0	1	0	1	0	0	.00	0	0	1	0	0	-
2011	2 tms	65	6	0	0	0	0	0	0	1	-	0	0	0	0	0	-
		175	16	0	2	1	0	5	0	2	.00	0	0	1	0	1	-

Jose Valverde

Year	Tm	Inn	TC	E	GFP	DM	+/-	SB	CCS	PCS/PPO	CS%	+/-	SB	Bnt	GFP/DME	Tot	Rnk
2003	Ari	50	4	0	-	-	0	6	0	0	.00	0	-1		-	-1	-
2004	Ari	30	8	2	0	1	-1	1	0	0	.00	-1	0	0	0	-1	-
2005	Ari	66	10	0	0	0	+1	1	0	1	.50	1	0		0	1	-
2006	Ari	49	2	0	0	0	-1	1	0	0	.00	-1	0	0	0	-1	-
2007	Ari	64	7	0	0	0	0	4	1	1	.33	0	0	0	0	0	-
2008	Hou	72	10	1	0	0	-1	8	0	0	.00	-1	-1		0	-2	-
2009	Hou	54	3	0	0	1	-3	5	3	0	.38	-2	0	0	0	-2	-
2010	Det	63	8	0	1	1	-1	3	1	0	.25	-1	0		0	-1	-
2011	Det	72	7	1	0	0	-1	9	3	0	.25	-1	-1	-1	0	-3	-
		521	59	5	1	3	-7	38	8	2	.21	-6	-3	-1	0	-10	150

Jason Vargas

Year	Tm	Inn	TC	E	GFP	DM	+/-	SB	CCS	PCS/PPO	CS%	+/-	SB	Bnt	GFP/DME	Tot	Rnk
2005	Fla	74	15	0	0	0	+2	11	0	1	.00	2	-1	0	0	1	-
2006	Fla	43	8	0	1	2	+2	6	0	0	.00	2	-1	0	-1	0	-
2007	NYM	10	0	0	0	1	-1	2	0	0	.00	-1	0		0	-1	-
2009	Sea	92	16	0	2	1	+2	2	5	2	.75	2	2	0	0	4	12
2010	Sea	193	26	0	7	3	+1	9	1	1	.10	1	0	0	0	1	60
2011	Sea	201	29	1	1	3	+2	18	3	2	.22	1	-1	0	0	0	93
		612	94	1	11	10	8	48	9	6	.20	7	-1	0	-1	5	55

Javier Vazquez

Year	Tm	Inn	TC	E	GFP	DM	+/-	SB	CCS	PCS/PPO	CS%	+/-	SB	Bnt	GFP/DME	Tot	Rnk
2003	Mon	231	45	2	-	-	0	3	1	1	.40	0	1		-	2	46
2004	NYY	198	48	2	4	3	+3	2	4	3	.71	2	2	1	0	5	12
2005	Ari	216	45	3	2	2	-2	6	1	1	.25	-2	0	1	0	-1	127
2006	CWS	203	36	0	0	0	0	10	2	2	.29	0	0	2	0	2	51
2007	CWS	217	40	2	3	1	+2	6	4	0	.40	2	1	0	0	3	27
2008	CWS	208	46	0	2	1	+5	9	2	1	.25	4	0	-1	0	3	23
2009	Atl	219	40	0	4	2	+2	7	5	0	.42	2	1	0	0	4	12
2010	NYY	157	37	0	3	2	+7	4	4	0	.50	5	1	1	0	7	9
2011	Fla	193	28	1	1	0	+1	8	0	0	.00	1	-1	0	0	0	93
		1841	365	10	19	11	18	55	23	8	.35	14	5	6	0	25	8

Jonny Venters

Year	Tm	Inn	TC	E	GFP	DM	+/-	SB	CCS	PCS/PPO	CS%	+/-	SB	Bnt	GFP/DME	Tot	Rnk
2010	Atl	83	19	2	1	0	+3	3	2	0	.40	2	0		0	2	39
2011	Atl	88	27	2	2	4	+3	2	2	0	.50	2	0	1	0	3	26
		171	46	4	3	4	6	5	4	0	.44	4	0	1	0	5	-

Jose Veras

Year	Tm	Inn	TC	E	GFP	DM	+/-	SB	CCS	PCS/PPO	CS%	+/-	SB	Bnt	GFP/DME	Tot	Rnk
2006	NYY	11	1	0	0	0	0	2	1	0	.33	0	0		0	0	-
2007	NYY	9	0	0	0	0	0	2	0	0	.00	0	0			0	-
2008	NYY	58	9	0	0	0	+1	5	3	0	.38	1	0	1	0	2	-
2009	Fla	50	10	1	0	0	0	4	1	0	.20	0	0	1	0	1	-
2010	Fla	48	10	1	1	0	0	4	1	0	.20	0	0	0	0	0	-
2011	Pit	71	8	0	0	0	-1	5	1	0	.17	0	0	0	0	0	-
		247	38	2	1	0	0	22	7	0	.24	1	0	2	0	3	-

Justin Verlander

Year	Tm	Inn	TC	E	GFP	DM	+/-	SB	CCS	PCS/PPO	CS%	+/-	SB	Bnt	GFP/DME	Tot	Rnk
2005	Det	11	5	1	0	0	0	1	0	0	.00	0	0		0	0	-
2006	Det	186	39	3	1	2	+1	1	4	8	.83	1	5	0	0	6	8
2007	Det	202	24	0	1	2	-2	4	1	2	.20	-2	1	0	0	-1	124
2008	Det	201	33	2	2	1	+4	8	8	2	.53	3	2	0	0	5	7
2009	Det	240	36	2	2	1	-3	9	15	3	.64	-2	4	1	0	3	35
2010	Det	224	51	2	5	1	+4	24	7	3	.23	3	-1	0	0	2	36
2011	Det	251	50	5	2	0	+5	10	4	2	.33	4	1	-1	1	5	11
		1315	237	15	13	7	9	57	39	20	.43	7	12	0	1	20	13

Carlos Villanueva

Year	Tm	Inn	TC	E	GFP	DM	+/-	SB	CCS	PCS/PPO	CS%	+/-	SB	Bnt	GFP/DME	Tot	Rnk
2006	Mil	54	11	0	0	0	+3	2	0	0	.00	2	0		0	2	-
2007	Mil	114	11	0	0	1	-2	6	2	1	.33	-2	0	1	0	-1	124
2008	Mil	108	22	1	0	2	+1	5	2	0	.29	1	0	0	0	1	60
2009	Mil	96	20	0	1	2	+1	5	1	0	.17	1	0	1	0	2	43
2010	Mil	53	6	0	0	0	0	8	1	0	.11	0	-1	0	0	-1	-
2011	Tor	107	17	1	0	1	+3	13	1	0	.07	2	-2	-2	0	-2	131
		532	87	2	1	6	6	39	7	1	.17	4	-3	0	0	1	80

Ryan Vogelsong

Year	Tm	Inn	TC	E	GFP	DM	+/-	SB	CCS	PCS/PPO	CS%	+/-	SB	Bnt	GFP/DME	Tot	Rnk
2003	Pit	22	7	1	-	-	-1	1	0	0	.00	-1	0	0	-	-1	-
2004	Pit	133	22	0	0	1	-2	5	1	0	.17	-2	0	0	0	-2	131
2005	Pit	81	13	0	0	0	-1	3	1	0	.25	-1	0	0	0	-1	120
2006	Pit	38	14	0	0	0	+3	6	1	0	.14	2	-1	1	0	2	-
2011	SF	180	32	0	0	2	+1	12	3	1	.20	0	0	0	0	0	100
		454	88	1	0	3	0	27	6	1	.18	-2	-1	1	0	-2	-

Pitchers

Edinson Volquez

Year	Tm	Inn	TC	E	GFP	DM	+/-	SB	CCS	PCS/PPO	CS%	+/-	SB	Bnt	GFP/DME	Tot	Rnk
2005	Tex	13	1	0	0	0	-1	1	0	0	.00	-1	0	0		-1	-
2006	Tex	33	6	0	0	0	0	4	1	0	.20	0	0	0		0	-
2007	Tex	34	2	0	0	0	-2	2	0	0	.00	-2	0	0		-2	-
2008	Cin	196	35	1	1	3	+1	21	12	0	.36	1	-1	0	-1	-1	110
2009	Cin	50	13	2	0	1	+2	2	0	0	.00	2	0	0		1	-
2010	Cin	63	12	0	1	1	+1	4	1	0	.20	1	0	0		2	-
2011	Cin	109	16	2	0	1	-3	16	4	0	.20	-2	-2	-1	0	-5	166
		497	85	5	2	6	-2	50	18	0	.26	-1	-3	-1	-1	-6	121

Chris Volstad

Year	Tm	Inn	TC	E	GFP	DM	+/-	SB	CCS	PCS/PPO	CS%	+/-	SB	Bnt	GFP/DME	Tot	Rnk
2008	Fla	84	13	0	1	1	-2	12	2	0	.14	-2	-1	-1	0	-4	163
2009	Fla	159	38	1	0	4	+1	21	9	1	.32	1	-1	0	0	0	79
2010	Fla	175	32	0	2	1	-1	29	4	1	.12	0	-3	0	0	-3	152
2011	Fla	166	35	1	3	2	-3	10	4	1	.29	-2	0	0	0	-2	143
		584	118	2	6	8	-5	72	19	3	.22	-3	-5	-1	0	-9	139

Tim Wakefield

Year	Tm	Inn	TC	E	GFP	DM	+/-	SB	CCS	PCS/PPO	CS%	+/-	SB	Bnt	GFP/DME	Tot	Rnk
2003	Bos	202	37	1	-	-	+2	23	8	0	.26	2	-2	0	-	0	82
2004	Bos	188	42	4	3	0	-2	33	7	3	.20	-2	-3	0	0	-5	167
2005	Bos	225	52	2	1	1	+1	18	6	1	.28	1	-1	0	0	0	82
2006	Bos	140	25	0	3	1	+2	24	4	2	.14	2	-2	0	0	0	77
2007	Bos	189	36	0	3	3	+1	41	8	0	.16	1	-6	0	0	-5	169
2008	Bos	181	23	1	0	1	+2	27	10	1	.27	2	-2	0	0	0	85
2009	Bos	130	21	0	0	2	0	23	3	0	.12	0	-3	0	0	-3	157
2010	Bos	140	26	2	1	1	-1	24	3	3	.17	-1	-2	-1	1	-3	155
2011	Bos	155	26	0	0	1	+2	12	7	3	.43	2	1	0	0	3	26
		1550	288	10	11	10	7	225	56	13	.22	7	-20	-1	1	-13	158

Jordan Walden

Year	Tm	Inn	TC	E	GFP	DM	+/-	SB	CCS	PCS/PPO	CS%	+/-	SB	Bnt	GFP/DME	Tot	Rnk
2010	LAA	15	6	0	0	0	0	2	0	0	.00	0	0	0		0	-
2011	LAA	60	10	1	0	0	-1	13	1	1	.13	-1	-2	0	0	-3	-
		75	16	1	0	0	-1	15	1	1	.12	-1	-2	0	0	-3	-

Chien-Ming Wang

Year	Tm	Inn	TC	E	GFP	DM	+/-	SB	CCS	PCS/PPO	CS%	+/-	SB	Bnt	GFP/DME	Tot	Rnk
2005	NYY	116	43	1	3	2	+5	9	4	0	.31	4	0	1	0	5	8
2006	NYY	218	58	1	2	6	+1	9	10	1	.55	1	2	0	0	3	30
2007	NYY	199	45	0	1	2	+7	14	7	0	.33	5	0	0	0	5	6
2008	NYY	95	20	0	2	0	0	8	3	0	.27	0	0	-1	0	-1	112
2009	NYY	42	10	0	0	1	-2	10	2	1	.23	-2	-1	0	0	-3	-
2011	Was	62	10	1	0	0	-1	4	3	0	.43	0	0	0	0	0	-
		733	186	3	8	11	10	54	29	2	.36	8	1	0	0	9	36

Jered Weaver

Year	Tm	Inn	TC	E	GFP	DM	+/-	SB	CCS	PCS/PPO	CS%	+/-	SB	Bnt	GFP/DME	Tot	Rnk
2006	LAA	123	17	2	0	2	0	11	3	0	.21	0	-1	0	0	-1	107
2007	LAA	161	29	2	4	1	-3	19	2	1	.10	-2	-2	0	0	-4	164
2008	LAA	177	23	2	2	3	-2	20	5	2	.20	-2	-1	0	0	-3	151
2009	LAA	211	30	1	3	1	+1	19	5	3	.24	1	0	0	0	1	60
2010	LAA	224	28	0	2	0	0	27	3	3	.13	0	-2	0	0	-2	134
2011	LAA	236	34	2	0	2	-1	10	6	6	.41	-1	3	0	0	2	59
		1131	161	9	11	9	-5	106	24	15	.20	-4	-3	0	0	-7	130

Randy Wells

Year	Tm	Inn	TC	E	GFP	DM	+/-	SB	CCS	PCS/PPO	CS%	+/-	SB	Bnt	GFP/DME	Tot	Rnk
2008	2 tms	5	0	0	0	0	0	0	0	0		0		0		0	-
2009	ChC	165	34	1	0	3	-5	14	4	0	.22	-4	-1	-1	0	-6	173
2010	ChC	194	48	5	1	2	0	14	3	2	.22	0	0	0	-1	-1	109
2011	ChC	135	19	2	2	0	-2	12	5	0	.29	-1	0	0	0	-2	135
		500	101	8	3	5	-7	40	12	2	.25	-5	-1	-2	-1	-9	141

Jake Westbrook

Year	Tm	Inn	TC	E	GFP	DM	+/-	SB	CCS	PCS/PPO	CS%	+/-	SB	Bnt	GFP/DME	Tot	Rnk
2003	Cle	133	30	1	-	-	+3	11	4	1	.27	2	0	0	-	2	36
2004	Cle	216	76	3	4	4	+11	8	6	1	.43	8	1	1	0	10	2
2005	Cle	211	82	2	6	4	+5	13	2	2	.24	4	0	1	0	5	8
2006	Cle	211	74	1	4	4	+3	16	1	3	.16	2	0	1	0	3	23
2007	Cle	152	48	0	2	2	+2	14	7	2	.33	2	1	1	0	4	15
2008	Cle	35	12	1	1	1	+3	0	1	1	1.00	2	1	0	0	3	-
2010	2 tms	203	65	2	6	3	+14	15	8	0	.35	11	0	1	0	12	1
2011	StL	183	74	2	1	1	+7	13	3	4	.24	6	1	1	0	8	2
		1343	461	12	24	19	48	90	32	14	.30	37	4	5	1	47	2

Dontrelle Willis

Year	Tm	Inn	TC	E	GFP	DM	+/-	SB	CCS	PCS/PPO	CS%	+/-	SB	Bnt	GFP/DME	Tot	Rnk
2003	Fla	161	23	4	-	-	0	3	3	3	.50	0	2	0	-	2	46
2004	Fla	197	51	2	6	3	+2	12	4	5	.37	2	1	0	2	5	12
2005	Fla	236	48	3	5	3	+7	1	4	1	.83	5	2	1	1	9	2
2006	Fla	223	60	5	8	5	+4	6	4	2	.45	3	2	0	0	5	11
2007	Fla	205	48	5	9	2	+3	6	1	1	.14	2	1	0	1	4	15
2008	Det	24	2	0	1	0	0	0	0	0		0	0	0	0	0	-
2009	Det	34	11	0	1	3	+1	4	0	0	.00	1	0	0	0	0	-
2010	2 tms	66	10	0	0	3	0	9	2	1	.25	-1	0	0	-1	-2	-
2011	Cin	76	17	0	1	0	0	0	0	3	1.00	0	2	0	0	2	55
		1221	270	19	31	21	17	41	19	16	.41	12	9	1	3	25	9

C.J. Wilson

Year	Tm	Inn	TC	E	GFP	DM	+/-	SB	CCS	PCS/PPO	CS%	+/-	SB	Bnt	GFP/DME	Tot	Rnk
2005	Tex	48	12	0	0	0	0	1	0	0	.00	0	0	0	0	0	-
2006	Tex	44	7	0	1	0	1	5	2	1	.38	0	0	0	0	0	-
2007	Tex	68	17	1	0	1	-1	1	0	0	.00	-1	0	0	0	-1	-
2008	Tex	46	13	1	2	2	+1	1	1	0	.50	1	0	0	0	1	-
2009	Tex	74	18	2	3	2	+1	4	2	0	.33	1	0	-1	0	0	-
2010	Tex	204	35	2	3	3	0	21	7	1	.28	0	-1	-1	0	-2	134
2011	Tex	223	30	1	1	3	0	24	7	0	.23	0	-2	0	-1	-3	151
		708	132	7	10	12	1	58	19	2	.27	1	-3	-2	-1	-5	116

Randy Wolf

Year	Tm	Inn	TC	E	GFP	DM	+/-	SB	CCS	PCS/PPO	CS%	+/-	SB	Bnt	GFP/DME	Tot	Rnk
2003	Phi	201	40	3	-	-	+1	8	2	0	.20	1	0	-1	-	0	84
2004	Phi	136	24	2	0	1	+1	6	0	0	.00	1	-1	0	0	0	82
2005	Phi	80	11	0	1	0	0	1	1	0	.50	0	0	0	0	0	-
2006	Phi	57	12	0	0	0	+2	3	2	0	.40	2	0	0	0	2	-
2007	LAD	103	17	0	1	2	+1	4	3	0	.43	1	1	1	0	3	34
2008	2 tms	190	35	2	1	2	-2	8	4	2	.38	-2	1	0	0	-1	121
2009	LAD	214	42	1	1	6	+4	7	3	2	.42	3	1	1	0	5	6
2010	Mil	216	53	0	4	4	+6	11	1	1	.15	4	0	1	0	5	12
2011	Mil	212	44	4	5	4	+2	18	0	1	.05	1	-2	0	0	-1	119
		1409	278	12	13	16	15	66	15	7	.24	11	0	2	0	13	26

Blake Wood

Year	Tm	Inn	TC	E	GFP	DM	+/-	SB	CCS	PCS/PPO	CS%	+/-	SB	Bnt	GFP/DME	Tot	Rnk
2010	KC	50	11	0	0	1	+1	10	2	1	.23	1	-1		0	0	-
2011	KC	70	16	0	0	0	-2	6	1	2	.33	-1	0	-1	0	-2	-
		119	27	0	0	1	-1	16	3	3	.27	0	-1	-1	0	-2	-

Travis Wood

Year	Tm	Inn	TC	E	GFP	DM	+/-	SB	CCS	PCS/PPO	CS%	+/-	SB	Bnt	GFP/DME	Tot	Rnk
2010	Cin	103	13	3	2	0	+2	0	0	0		1	0	0	0	1	60
2011	Cin	106	19	0	1	0	+1	5	2	3	.50	1	1	1	0	3	33
		208	32	3	3	0	3	5	2	3	.50	2	1	1	0	4	-

Vance Worley

Year	Tm	Inn	TC	E	GFP	DM	+/-	SB	CCS	PCS/PPO	CS%	+/-	SB	Bnt	GFP/DME	Tot	Rnk
2010	Phi	13	4	0	0	0	+1	0	1	0	1.00	1	0	0	0	1	-
2011	Phi	132	24	0	3	1	+2	2	0	0	.00	1	0	0	1	2	47
		144	28	0	3	1	3	2	1	0	.33	2	0	0	1	3	-

Pitchers

Jamey Wright

		BASIC						HOLDING					RUNS SAVED				
Year	Tm	Inn	TC	E	GFP	DM	+/-	SB	CCS	PCS/PPO	CS%	+/-	SB	Bnt	GFP/DME	Tot	Rnk
2003	KC	25	4	0	-	-	0	5	0	1	.00	0	0	0	-	0	-
2004	Col	79	25	0	0	1	+2	13	2	4	.13	2	0	1	0	3	-
2005	Col	171	37	2	1	3	-2	25	7	6	.22	-2	0	-2	0	-4	164
2006	SF	156	40	2	0	3	-7	13	3	7	.38	-5	2	0	0	-3	164
2007	Tex	77	20	1	3	0	+1	4	4	1	.50	1	1	0	0	2	-
2008	Tex	84	35	2	5	2	+1	9	1	2	.10	1	0	-1	0	0	88
2009	KC	79	19	2	0	0	+1	7	3	2	.30	1	1	0	0	2	43
2010	2 tms	58	21	0	0	1	+3	13	0	1	.00	3	-2	-1	0	0	-
2011	Sea	68	18	1	0	0	-2	8	2	2	.27	-2	0	0	0	-2	-
		798	219	10	9	10	-3	97	22	26	.22	-1	2	-3	0	-2	100

Carlos Zambrano

		BASIC						HOLDING					RUNS SAVED				
Year	Tm	Inn	TC	E	GFP	DM	+/-	SB	CCS	PCS/PPO	CS%	+/-	SB	Bnt	GFP/DME	Tot	Rnk
2003	ChC	214	68	4	-	-	0	3	5	1	.63	0	2	0	-	2	46
2004	ChC	210	49	2	5	4	0	7	3	1	.36	0	0	2	0	2	54
2005	ChC	223	57	2	2	5	+1	1	9	3	.90	1	4	0	0	5	14
2006	ChC	214	49	4	4	5	-2	2	3	1	.60	-2	1	1	0	0	99
2007	ChC	216	49	1	5	4	-1	4	3	1	.43	-1	1	0	0	0	94
2008	ChC	189	45	3	2	1	-1	10	9	3	.47	-1	2	0	0	1	77
2009	ChC	169	45	3	3	4	+1	5	8	2	.62	1	3	1	0	5	9
2010	ChC	130	32	3	3	2	0	9	3	1	.25	0	0	0	0	0	88
2011	ChC	146	21	1	2	2	0	4	0	2	.00	0	1	1	0	2	55
		1710	415	23	26	27	-2	45	43	15	.49	-2	14	5	0	17	16

Jordan Zimmermann

		BASIC						HOLDING					RUNS SAVED				
Year	Tm	Inn	TC	E	GFP	DM	+/-	SB	CCS	PCS/PPO	CS%	+/-	SB	Bnt	GFP/DME	Tot	Rnk
2009	Was	91	24	1	3	1	+3	8	4	2	.38	2	1	0	0	3	28
2010	Was	31	5	2	0	0	+1	3	1	0	.25	1	0		0	1	-
2011	Was	161	36	0	1	4	-1	3	6	3	.67	0	3	0	-1	2	55
		283	65	3	4	5	3	14	11	5	.46	3	4	0	-1	6	-

One-Year Register

When we released *The Fielding Bible Volume II*, we added pitcher and catcher registers. While we considered adding Designated Hitter registers this time around, we thought blank registers would look a little odd. Instead, we beefed up the existing registers by adding more data and doing a little reorganization. We added so much valuable data into these registers, we almost had to use fold-out pages for the register. Can you imagine the third base register as a centerfold?

To make it a little easier on the eyes, rather than list every player at each position in this volume, we split the position tables in two: regulars and everyone else. It's much easier to compare players in this format. In the regulars table, you'll find the players who played full-time or near full-time (i.e. the 35 players with the most innings). These players are also the guys that we rank by their total Runs Saved.

The updated design contains three key sections: basic data, position-specific evaluations, and each player's Runs Saved numbers broken down by component. The basic section is the same for every position. We have games played, innings, total chances (abbreviated as TC), errors, and fielding percentage. Since Good Fielding Plays (GFP) and Defensive Misplays (DM) have become critical pieces to our evaluations, we also add these totals to the basic section.

The final group of columns in the one year register for all positions are the Runs Saved columns. These are the most important columns in the entire table. If you want to know who was good, who was bad, and who was worse than Jeter, look here. Every applicable Runs Saved component for each position is displayed, followed by a player's Total Runs Saved and his ranking. Non-regulars aren't ranked. Each component of Runs

Saved has its own chapter in this book which provides a complete explanation of the data. They are:

- Plus/Minus Runs Saved, which measures the fielder's range: his ability to convert batted balls into outs.
- Bunt Runs Saved, which evaluates a corner infielder or catcher's skill in converting bunts to outs.
- Double Play Runs Saved, which judges an infielder's ability to start and turn double plays.
- Throwing Arm Runs Saved, which assesses the run prevention ability of an outfielder's throwing arm.
- Adjusted Earned Runs Saved, which measures a catcher's pitcher handling ability behind the plate.
- Pitcher Stolen Base Runs Saved, which evaluates the ability of a pitcher to control the running game.
- Catcher Stolen Base Runs Saved, which evaluates the ability of a catcher to control the running game.
- Good Play/Misplay Runs Saved, which measures a fielder's good plays and misplays.

Catchers

For each position, we display specific evaluations that are key to fielding that position. For catchers, these sections are on bunts, pitcher handling, and stolen bases. The latter two sections also appeared in Volume II but the bunt evaluations are brand new for catchers. The three bunt categories we're displaying are opportunities (Opp), Sac Hits, and Bunt Hits. For the purposes of the register, a Sac Hit is any bunt in a sacrifice situation where the batter is credited with a sacrifice. All other bunt hits are listed under the "Bunt Hits" column. For more on our bunt evaluations, check out our bunt section on page 299.

Under Pitcher Handling, we're displaying wins and losses, winning percentage, earned runs allowed, the player's Catcher ERA, and pitch blocks. When we were working with our Good Fielding Play/Defensive Misplay data, we found that pitch blocking ability is a major piece of our catcher evaluations.

We also evaluate a catcher's ability to control the running game. Under the stolen bases section, we display stolen bases against (SB), catcher caught stealing (CCS), pitcher caught stealing (PCS), catcher pickoffs (CPO), caught stealing percentage (CS%), and stolen bases saved. Houston's Humberto Quintero picked off four runners in 2011 to lead all regular catchers. Fielding Bible Award winner Matt Wieters led all catchers with seven stolen bases saved.

Corner Infielders

Since Volume II, we've published data on first basemen and third basemen fielding bunts. We're still displaying that data here in the one-year register, but in this book we're adding double play evaluations for those fielders. We've listed opportunities (Opp), number of double plays (GDP), and a percentage of successful double plays (Pct). Angels first baseman Mark Trumbo led all regulars with a .778 double play percentage. This is the percentage of successful double plays he started out of 18 opportunites. He'll have to translate his defensive skills to a new position in 2012 with Albert Pujols now wearing a halo on his hat.

The Plus/Minus section for corner infielders provides familiar data. Outs made, a fielder's Plus/Minus on balls to his right, straight on, and balls to his left are the first four columns in the Plus/Minus section. The data labeled "to his right", "straight on", and "to his left" is particularly interesting, as it really showcases a fielder's strengths and weaknesses. 2010 National League MVP Joey Votto was +12 on balls to his right but -4 on balls to his left. Across the diamond, Evan Longoria was +15 on balls to his right, but -5 on balls straight on. The next two columns are a player's ratings on groundballs and balls in the air. Pablo "Kung Fu Panda" Sandoval was best on grounders at +20. Sandoval was a whopping 45 plays better on groundballs than Aramis Ramirez, who was -25. We round out the plus/minus section with a player's Total and Enhanced Plus/Minus numbers. Enhanced Plus/Minus is an estimate of the number of bases involved with plays that are made or missed.

Middle Infielders

The middle infielders also utilize the revamped double plays section. We don't calculate an Enhanced Plus/Minus for middle infielders, but the rest of the Plus/Minus section is identical to corner infielders. What immediately jumps off the page is Hanley Ramirez's -21 on balls hit to his right. It looks like Ramirez will be moving to third base to accommodate Miami's signing of Jose Reyes (-19 to his right). Ramirez and Reyes have nearly identical left/straight on/right splits so it will be interesting to check in on the Marlins' shortstop and third base defense during the next few years. On the other side of the base is Pirates second baseman Neil Walker. Walker is an average second baseman at balls hit straight on but is extremely good (+20) on balls to his right and extremely bad on balls to his left (-18).

Outfielders

The position-specific section for outfielders is an evaluation of their throwing arms. We display opportunities to advance, extra bases taken, advancement percentage (Pct), and base runner Kills. Remember that a base runner Kill is unassisted. Torii Hunter led all outfield regulars with 14 Kills while Shane Victorino and Carl Crawford each played over 1,000 innings without recording a Kill.

An outfielder's Plus/Minus section shows his outs made, Basic Plus/Minus, Enhanced Plus/Minus, and Shallow, Medium, and Deep splits. Michael Bourn is the Neil Walker of the outfield...at least in 2011. Bourn was weak on shallow (-15) and medium (-3) balls, but was excellent on balls hit deep (+22). Austin Jackson, winner of his first Fielding Bible Award in 2011, was also better as the ball was hit deeper (+27), but didn't have the trouble Bourn had on shallow and medium balls (+1 shallow, +12 medium).

Pitchers

Pitchers, like catchers, are evaluated on their ability

to control the running game. We have stolen base attempts and caught stealing data in the pitcher register along with runners putout by throws by the pitcher: pitcher pickoffs and pitcher caught stealing. While we also evaluate pitchers on bunts now, we just couldn't fit that data into the chart. We could have, if you wanted to read the book with a magnifying glass, but who carries one of those around anyway? His Bunt Runs Saved number is there, just not the more granular data. We rank 175 pitchers and lucky #175 in 2011 was Brandon Morrow of the Blue Jays. Yes, he struck out over 200 hitters this season, but he was a sub-par fielder. He cost his team an estimated six runs because of defense.

Catchers - Regulars

BASIC									BUNTS			PITCHER HANDLING						STOLEN BASES						RUNS SAVED					
Name	Team	G	Inn	TC	E	Pct	GFP	DM	Opp	Sac Hits	Bunt Hits	W	L	Pct	ER	CERA	Pitch Block	SB	CCS	PCS	CPO	CS%	SB Saved	Adj ER	SB	Bunt	GFP/ DME	Total	Rnk
Matt Wieters	Bal	132	1150.0	930	5	.995	12	35	14	9	1	57	72	.442	583	4.56	435	58	32	2	0	.36	7	9	5	1	2	17	1
Jeff Mathis	LAA	91	698.0	568	3	.995	13	28	12	5	2	45	34	.570	252	3.25	405	48	12	6	1	.20	0	3	1	-1	5	8	2
Chris Iannetta	Col	105	943.2	817	2	.998	10	41	9	6	0	51	54	.486	442	4.22	417	70	26	4	1	.27	4	4	3	1	0	8	2
Russell Martin	NYY	125	1044.1	972	10	.990	18	51	7	3	2	67	51	.568	429	3.70	618	95	35	5	0	.27	3	0	2	-1	6	7	4
H. Quintero	Hou	77	642.0	589	5	.992	7	13	10	3	2	25	48	.342	329	4.61	293	48	11	3	4	.19	-1	1	1	0	4	6	5
Miguel Montero	Ari	134	1169.1	997	11	.989	21	35	25	9	3	82	49	.626	468	3.60	356	48	28	4	2	.37	3	3	3	0	-1	5	6
Nick Hundley	SD	76	654.1	567	6	.989	10	22	9	4	2	30	43	.411	257	3.53	258	57	24	8	1	.30	3	-1	2	0	4	5	6
Brayan Pena	KC	69	537.0	444	2	.995	14	22	7	2	2	22	35	.386	268	4.49	215	48	16	11	0	.25	2	-1	2	-1	3	3	8
Kelly Shoppach	TB	86	625.2	525	3	.994	5	19	4	2	1	39	32	.549	262	3.77	266	26	15	3	1	.37	6	-2	5	-1	1	3	8
Rod Barajas	LAD	88	733.1	701	2	.997	9	25	12	10	1	44	41	.518	291	3.57	371	60	14	6	0	.19	-1	-1	-1	-1	5	2	10
Lou Marson	Cle	78	667.0	524	5	.990	9	22	9	2	1	36	38	.486	319	4.30	185	48	24	6	0	.33	5	0	3	1	-2	2	10
Carlos Ruiz	Phi	128	1051.0	1022	4	.996	15	16	19	10	1	70	43	.619	357	3.06	351	77	18	5	1	.19	-3	-4	-2	1	5	0	12
Ryan Hanigan	Cin	89	687.1	574	4	.993	8	23	4	3	0	38	35	.521	303	3.97	209	34	13	5	0	.28	-1	4	-1	0	-3	0	12
Drew Butera	Min	93	670.2	461	5	.989	8	26	8	3	0	27	48	.360	369	4.95	272	48	20	2	2	.29	3	-6	3	2	0	-1	14
Jason Varitek	Bos	68	574.2	551	4	.993	2	24	3	0	1	42	22	.656	228	3.57	283	73	10	2	0	.12	-7	2	-5	0	2	-1	14
Geovany Soto	ChC	122	1041.2	994	13	.987	13	36	20	13	0	49	70	.412	499	4.31	371	85	30	6	0	.26	2	-2	1	1	-1	-1	14
Kurt Suzuki	Oak	129	1132.1	976	7	.993	20	48	8	3	2	55	72	.433	476	3.78	471	98	23	15	1	.19	0	-4	1	0	2	-1	14
Matt Treanor	2 tms	72	565.2	447	4	.991	9	36	5	2	2	30	34	.469	284	4.52	220	42	11	3	0	.21	0	2	0	-2	-2	-2	18
Alex Avila	Det	133	1157.0	1018	5	.995	20	59	11	6	2	78	52	.600	499	3.88	462	85	26	14	0	.23	-2	3	-2	0	-3	-2	18
Eli Whiteside	SF	81	583.2	541	5	.991	9	23	4	1	0	33	31	.516	214	3.30	203	53	13	5	0	.20	-2	-2	-1	1	0	-2	18
John Jaso	TB	82	603.1	509	4	.992	6	30	5	3	2	39	28	.582	226	3.37	240	50	8	2	0	.14	-4	2	-3	-1	-1	-3	21
J. Saltalamacchia	Bos	101	856.0	740	6	.992	9	50	10	3	2	47	49	.490	439	4.62	274	83	28	9	0	.25	6	-2	4	-1	-5	-4	22
Brian McCann	Atl	126	1083.0	1061	5	.995	8	48	23	11	3	60	58	.508	434	3.61	463	104	22	7	0	.17	-4	-2	-3	2	-1	-4	22
Josh Thole	NYM	102	793.1	703	2	.997	9	31	16	13	0	45	46	.495	373	4.23	284	65	14	3	0	.18	-6	-1	-4	0	1	-4	22
Carlos Santana	Cle	95	786.1	630	7	.989	7	36	5	2	0	44	44	.500	366	4.19	239	56	15	3	1	.21	-2	0	-1	0	-3	-4	22
Yadier Molina	StL	138	1150.0	929	5	.995	11	48	20	13	1	72	60	.545	499	3.91	657	46	15	4	2	.25	-1	-6	0	-1	3	-4	22
R.Hernandez	Cin	82	658.0	549	1	.998	4	29	11	4	1	34	42	.447	310	4.24	249	39	18	5	0	.32	0	-3	0	2	-3	-4	22
J.P. Arencibia	Tor	122	1059.2	900	6	.993	11	69	11	3	2	55	63	.466	507	4.31	517	87	18	10	1	.17	-9	1	-5	1	-2	-5	28
Wilson Ramos	Was	108	951.2	744	5	.993	6	42	14	8	1	54	52	.509	394	3.73	386	48	19	4	0	.28	2	-2	1	-1	-3	-5	28
Jonathan Lucroy	Mil	132	1043.2	1046	7	.993	10	65	7	2	1	68	46	.596	421	3.63	647	77	21	9	0	.21	-5	0	-4	0	-1	-5	28
John Buck	Fla	135	1144.0	1055	5	.995	5	37	12	7	3	60	69	.465	496	3.90	357	83	15	2	1	.15	-5	0	-3	0	-2	-5	28
Ronny Paulino	NYM	68	511.0	412	7	.983	3	26	9	4	0	22	34	.393	254	4.47	147	47	10	2	0	.18	-4	-1	-3	2	-4	-6	32
A.J. Pierzynski	CWS	120	1008.0	886	4	.995	7	48	12	6	4	54	58	.482	453	4.04	405	94	14	10	0	.13	-4	-2	-3	-1	-3	-9	33
Miguel Olivo	Sea	127	1064.1	917	11	.988	14	74	15	4	2	54	66	.450	446	3.77	427	79	25	6	1	.24	-4	0	-3	0	-6	-9	33
Yorvit Torrealba	Tex	98	823.2	732	9	.988	8	28	13	6	2	49	46	.516	394	4.31	251	56	21	6	0	.27	-1	-5	-1	-4	-2	-12	35
2011 MLB Totals						.992	523	1842		265	54					3.94						.23							

First Basemen - Regulars

BASIC									BUNTS			GDP			PLUS/MINUS								RUNS SAVED					
Name	Team	G	Inn	TC	E	Pct	GFP	DM	Opp	Sac Hits	Bunt Hits	Opp	GDP	Pct	Outs Made	To His Right	Straight On	To His Left	GB	Air	Total	Enhanced	+/-	Bunt	GDP	GFP/ DME	Total	Rk
Adrian Gonzalez	Bos	156	1352.2	1351	4	.997	56	16	14	8	1	18	8	.444	287	+2	-2	+9	+6	+1	+7	+9	7	3	0	2	12	1
James Loney	LAD	150	1203.2	1208	5	.996	71	21	14	5	5	16	9	.563	242	+2	+5	+1	+8	+2	+10	+10	7	0	1	3	11	2
Albert Pujols	StL	146	1260.1	1430	11	.992	67	18	16	8	4	21	11	.524	271	0	+5	+2	+7	+3	+10	+9	7	0	1	2	10	3
Mark Trumbo	LAA	149	1257.1	1384	10	.993	48	19	9	6	2	18	14	.778	281	+6	+4	0	+10	0	+10	+10	7	0	2	0	9	4
Daniel Murphy	NYM	52	419.0	459	4	.991	31	9	13	8	0	10	6	.600	74	+4	+2	0	+6	+2	+8	+8	6	1	0	1	8	5
Todd Helton	Col	119	987.2	1092	3	.997	35	11	13	11	2	18	12	.667	222	-4	+4	+7	+8	-1	+7	+6	5	-1	1	2	7	6
Carlos Lee	Hou	79	624.1	658	5	.992	33	15	7	5	0	13	8	.615	130	+4	+2	+1	+6	-1	+5	+6	5	1	1	0	7	6
Gaby Sanchez	Fla	153	1354.0	1368	5	.996	50	24	19	13	2	17	5	.294	263	+2	+5	-2	+5	+2	+7	+6	5	0	0	0	5	8
Brett Wallace	Hou	96	768.2	742	6	.992	34	12	13	5	2	7	0	.000	140	+2	+4	-4	+2	+2	+4	+5	4	0	-1	2	5	9
Joey Votto	Cin	160	1427.2	1520	6	.996	61	28	22	14	3	21	5	.238	292	+12	+3	-4	+14	0	+14	+11	8	-1	-1	-2	4	10
Daric Barton	Oak	65	568.1	643	8	.988	40	11	8	5	0	6	3	.500	141	-2	+4	+3	+2	0	+2	+5	4	0	0	0	4	11
Mark Teixeira	NYY	147	1274.0	1306	4	.997	79	25	12	6	3	15	4	.267	251	+9	-2	-1	+9	-1	+8	+5	4	0	-1	0	3	12
Casey Kotchman	TB	146	1222.1	1201	2	.998	53	18	6	1	4	13	7	.538	215	0	-2	+5	+1	-1	0	+2	1	-1	0	3	3	13
Aubrey Huff	SF	120	1032.2	1067	5	.995	43	18	23	17	1	4	1	.250	187	-3	+3	+4	+1	-1	0	+3	2	-1	0	1	2	14
Jesus Guzman	SD	53	434.0	419	4	.990	15	11	7	4	1	5	2	.400	73	+1	+3	-1	+3	-2	+1	+1	1	0	0	-1	0	15
Xavier Nady	Ari	52	391.1	407	3	.993	21	4	4	2	0	2	0	.000	61	-2	-3	+2	-2	-1	-3	-3	-3	1	0	2	0	16
Brandon Allen	2 tms	51	440.1	439	4	.991	19	13	5	4	1	5	3	.600	100	-1	+2	-1	0	0	0	0	0	0	0	-1	-1	17
Carlos Pena	ChC	153	1258.1	1212	8	.993	77	27	32	22	4	15	5	.333	200	+6	-4	-3	0	0	0	-1	-1	0	0	0	-1	18
Justin Smoak	Sea	108	926.2	950	7	.993	36	11	5	1	2	13	5	.385	165	+1	+1	0	-1	-3	-4	-2	-1	-1	0	1	-1	18
Carlos Santana	Cle	66	565.0	669	4	.994	37	13	5	1	2	11	5	.455	125	-3	0	+2	-2	-1	-3	-2	-2	1	0	-1	-2	20
Mitch Moreland	Tex	99	799.0	789	4	.995	30	12	6	2	0	5	2	.400	129	0	-6	+2	-4	0	-4	-4	-3	1	0	0	-2	21
Freddie Freeman	Atl	156	1370.1	1415	6	.996	70	24	15	10	3	8	1	.125	234	-2	-4	+1	-6	+1	-5	-5	-3	0	0	1	-2	21
Justin Morneau	Min	56	479.1	485	1	.998	21	9	2	2	0	7	4	.571	83	-3	-1	+1	-3	+1	-2	-2	-2	0	0	-1	-3	23
Derrek Lee	2 tms	113	984.0	1021	8	.992	45	20	12	6	1	14	4	.286	170	+2	-2	-1	-1	-3	-4	-4	-3	1	0	-1	-3	24
Miguel Cabrera	Det	152	1322.0	1379	13	.991	52	15	11	5	4	23	13	.565	226	-7	0	+1	-7	-2	-9	-7	-5	-1	1	2	-3	25
Juan Miranda	Ari	46	401.0	395	4	.990	7	6	6	3	0	4	3	.750	65	-1	-1	0	-2	0	-2	-2	-1	-2	0	-1	-4	26
Adam Lind	Tor	109	965.1	1020	4	.996	48	18	4	2	1	13	4	.308	166	-2	-2	+1	-4	0	-4	-3	-2	0	-1	-1	-4	27
Paul Konerko	CWS	111	963.1	1048	5	.995	32	15	8	3	3	16	12	.750	170	-4	+1	-3	-7	+1	-6	-5	-4	-1	1	0	-4	28
Lyle Overbay	2 tms	109	917.0	994	8	.992	34	13	11	7	0	18	9	.500	153	-7	0	-1	-9	+2	-7	-7	-5	1	0	0	-4	29
Conor Jackson	2 tms	53	392.0	372	1	.997	14	6	1	0	0	3	1	.333	74	-3	-1	-3	-5	-1	-6	-7	-5	0	0	0	-5	30
Michael Morse	Was	85	723.1	793	6	.992	35	10	12	9	2	11	5	.455	135	-1	-4	-5	-8	+1	-7	-9	-7	-1	0	1	-7	31
Eric Hosmer	KC	127	1135.2	1182	8	.993	69	26	13	6	3	17	3	.176	205	-4	-2	-3	-7	0	-7	-9	-7	-1	-1	0	-9	32
Prince Fielder	Mil	159	1394.2	1431	15	.990	48	27	12	7	1	17	7	.412	253	-3	-5	-2	-9	0	-9	-9	-7	0	0	-2	-9	32
Matt LaPorta	Cle	97	802.2	855	7	.992	32	16	8	3	4	11	6	.545	170	-5	-2	-5	-12	+2	-10	-10	-7	-3	0	-1	-11	34
Ryan Howard	Phi	149	1309.0	1361	9	.993	58	24	28	19	3	12	7	.583	234	-8	-10	+2	-16	-2	-18	-17	-12	1	0	-2	-13	35
2011 MLB Totals						.994	1996	778		300	83			.426														

Second Basemen - Regulars

Name	Team	G	Inn	TC	E	Pct	GFP	DM	Opps	GDP	Pct	Outs Made	To His Right	Straight On	To His Left	GB	Air	Total	+/-	GDP	GFP/DME	Total	Rank
				BASIC						GDP			PLUS/MINUS							RUNS SAVED			
Ben Zobrist	TB	131	1058.1	535	6	.989	39	22	98	65	.663	330	+15	0	+5	+19	+10	+29	22	1	0	23	1
Dustin Pedroia	Bos	159	1392.1	722	7	.990	66	15	131	82	.626	456	+7	+7	+9	+23	-4	+19	15	-1	4	18	2
Ian Kinsler	Tex	144	1269.0	677	11	.984	54	27	142	102	.718	442	+9	+3	+2	+13	+7	+20	15	3	0	18	2
Mark Ellis	2 tms	123	1054.2	636	3	.995	46	13	129	84	.651	390	+6	+5	-1	+11	+5	+16	12	1	4	17	4
Howie Kendrick	LAA	108	937.2	483	4	.992	35	16	89	59	.663	318	+5	+7	+9	+21	-7	+14	10	0	0	10	5
Dustin Ackley	Sea	86	741.0	375	6	.984	25	12	70	48	.686	251	0	+2	+12	+13	-2	+11	9	1	0	10	6
Chase Utley	Phi	100	887.2	488	5	.990	28	18	86	50	.581	315	+5	+5	0	+10	0	+10	8	-1	0	7	7
Brandon Phillips	Cin	148	1324.0	721	6	.992	57	28	153	94	.614	428	+6	+2	+4	+11	-2	+9	7	-1	0	6	8
Danny Espinosa	Was	158	1393.0	784	14	.982	65	33	136	89	.654	488	+5	+2	+1	+8	-1	+7	5	0	0	5	9
Robert Andino	Bal	94	724.1	402	4	.990	28	16	90	58	.644	242	-4	+4	+3	+3	+2	+5	4	1	0	5	10
Omar Infante	Fla	146	1283.1	734	8	.989	54	28	111	72	.649	514	+1	+4	0	+6	0	+6	4	0	0	4	11
Ramon Santiago	Det	75	434.2	237	1	.996	12	6	46	26	.565	143	-1	+3	0	+2	+3	+5	4	0	0	4	11
Gordon Beckham	CWS	149	1307.2	723	8	.989	64	26	130	80	.615	463	-8	+3	+12	+6	0	+6	4	0	-1	3	13
Jose Altuve	Hou	55	460.2	217	2	.991	22	5	37	26	.703	145	-1	0	+2	+1	0	+1	1	1	1	3	14
Aaron Hill	2 tms	137	1198.1	635	7	.989	40	21	130	80	.615	392	+2	-2	+5	+5	-2	+3	3	0	-1	2	15
Darwin Barney	ChC	135	1110.1	619	12	.981	47	30	100	56	.560	373	-3	+1	+3	+1	+3	+4	3	-2	0	1	16
Robinson Cano	NYY	157	1340.0	777	10	.987	68	40	139	96	.691	461	+11	-5	-5	+1	-1	0	-1	0	2	1	17
Ruben Tejada	NYM	55	457.1	245	4	.984	29	9	47	33	.702	150	-5	+1	0	-3	+2	-1	-1	0	2	1	18
Alexi Casilla	Min	56	470.2	265	6	.977	25	8	53	36	.679	186	-2	+2	-1	-1	0	-1	-1	0	2	1	18
Kelly Johnson	2 tms	141	1224.0	627	10	.984	33	18	118	82	.695	358	-2	-1	-1	-4	+1	-3	-3	2	2	1	20
Jonathan Herrera	Col	62	499.0	247	2	.992	19	9	39	28	.718	173	+1	-3	0	-2	+2	0	0	0	0	0	21
Chris Getz	KC	110	894.1	494	6	.988	23	19	108	65	.602	297	-3	-1	+5	+2	-3	-1	-1	0	-1	-2	22
Aaron Miles	LAD	72	519.0	260	2	.992	15	15	41	24	.585	161	-4	+2	-1	-3	0	-3	-2	0	0	-2	23
Skip Schumaker	StL	95	739.0	397	7	.982	29	15	71	43	.606	273	-3	0	-5	-8	+6	-2	-2	-1	0	-3	24
Neil Walker	Pit	159	1382.1	781	6	.992	58	31	172	106	.616	448	+20	0	-18	+3	-10	-7	-5	-1	3	-3	25
Orlando Cabrera	2 tms	85	709.1	400	6	.985	21	22	67	42	.627	264	+4	+1	-3	+3	-5	-2	-2	0	-2	-4	26
Rickie Weeks	Mil	115	974.0	481	15	.969	31	25	93	63	.677	286	+4	-8	+7	+3	-7	-4	-3	1	-3	-5	27
Maicer Izturis	LAA	49	422.2	249	4	.984	19	8	49	35	.714	158	-3	-2	-7	-11	+1	-10	-8	1	2	-5	28
Jemile Weeks	Oak	96	849.1	422	13	.969	28	20	70	45	.643	286	-3	-2	+1	-5	-4	-9	-6	0	0	-6	29
Freddy Sanchez	SF	58	514.1	244	3	.988	15	13	39	30	.769	143	-3	-1	-8	-12	+3	-9	-7	1	0	-6	30
Orlando Hudson	SD	114	959.2	550	4	.993	30	23	111	65	.586	323	-7	+2	-2	-7	0	-7	-5	-3	0	-8	31
Jamey Carroll	LAD	81	549.1	256	5	.980	16	13	46	33	.717	161	-9	-5	+2	-12	-4	-16	-12	1	1	-10	32
Jeff Keppinger	2 tms	93	791.0	390	5	.987	18	15	60	31	.517	252	-7	-2	-5	-14	+4	-10	-7	-2	-2	-11	33
Justin Turner	NYM	78	642.1	358	4	.978	26	15	66	35	.530	219	-6	-2	-3	-10	0	-10	-8	-3	-2	-13	34
Dan Uggla	Atl	159	1431.2	749	15	.980	45	38	140	82	.586	448	-2	+4	-10	-8	-5	-13	-10	-1	-2	-13	35
2011 MLB Totals						.984	1700	962	4395	2808	.639												

Third Basemen - Regulars

Name	Team	G	Inn	TC	E	Pct	GFP	DM	Opp	Sac Hits	Bunt Hits	Opp	GDP	Pct	Outs Made	To His Right	Straight On	To His Left	GB	Air	Total	Enhanced	+/-	Bunt	GDP	GFP/DME	Total	Rk
				BASIC						BUNTS			GDP			PLUS/MINUS							RUNS SAVED				
Evan Longoria	TB	130	1124.2	367	14	.962	49	16	17	6	2	42	28	.667	296	+15	-5	+3	+8	+5	+13	+19	14	4	1	3	22	1
Pablo Sandoval	SF	106	904.2	295	10	.966	42	17	8	5	0	24	11	.458	246	+12	+8	+1	+20	-1	+19	+20	15	1	0	1	15	2
Adrian Beltre	Tex	112	980.1	312	11	.965	35	21	9	4	2	30	19	.633	260	+6	+6	+7	+19	-1	+18	+18	14	0	0	-1	13	3
Alex Rodriguez	NYY	89	762.0	225	6	.973	26	11	13	3	5	18	10	.556	190	+6	+11	-1	+15	-3	+12	+14	11	1	0	1	13	4
Scott Rolen	Cin	63	547.1	161	4	.975	15	10	4	1	1	12	8	.667	133	-4	+11	+3	+10	-1	+9	+9	7	0	1	2	10	5
Placido Polanco	Phi	118	1044.2	345	8	.977	33	17	18	11	5	32	13	.406	295	+14	+4	-3	+14	-1	+13	+13	10	0	-1	0	9	6
Jack Hannahan	Cle	104	819.0	296	5	.983	30	14	9	2	5	29	13	.448	247	+7	+6	-4	+10	-1	+9	+9	7	0	-1	0	6	7
Juan Uribe	LAD	59	462.2	136	3	.978	23	6	8	6	1	8	2	.250	111	+4	+3	-1	+5	+1	+6	+7	5	1	0	-1	5	8
Alberto Callaspo	LAA	129	1139.1	365	15	.959	37	21	21	10	9	33	22	.667	303	+5	+7	-5	+7	-3	+4	+4	4	0	1	-1	4	9
Miguel Cairo	Cin	58	432.1	143	4	.972	7	12	2	2	0	15	9	.600	121	-2	0	+5	+3	+1	+4	+4	3	0	0	0	3	10
Lonnie Chisenhall	Cle	58	461.0	168	10	.940	12	10	7	3	1	14	6	.429	141	-4	+4	+2	+1	0	+1	+2	2	1	0	0	3	11
Casey McGehee	Mil	147	1233.1	347	20	.942	32	20	9	5	2	22	15	.682	289	-2	0	+2	+2	0	+2	-1	0	0	1	2	3	12
Mike Moustakas	KC	89	778.0	240	11	.954	19	15	10	2	7	16	10	.625	198	0	+6	-2	+4	+1	+5	+5	4	-2	0	0	2	13
Brent Morel	CWS	125	1058.0	297	14	.953	44	14	16	7	7	24	9	.375	247	-4	+1	+4	+2	+1	+3	+2	1	0	-1	2	2	14
Chase Headley	SD	107	895.1	272	11	.960	33	14	9	7	2	15	10	.667	213	-7	+2	+4	0	+2	+2	0	0	-1	0	2	1	15
Kevin Youkilis	Bos	112	948.2	273	9	.967	29	15	14	5	5	15	7	.467	224	+8	-7	+1	0	0	0	+2	2	0	-1	-1	0	16
Chone Figgins	Sea	80	679.2	185	11	.941	22	21	9	5	2	10	7	.700	148	-4	+1	+2	-5	0	-5	-2	-1	1	0	-1	-1	17
Ty Wigginton	Col	68	520.1	133	4	.970	15	11	8	1	5	18	11	.611	109	-2	0	-2	-4	+1	-3	-3	-2	0	0	1	-1	18
David Freese	StL	88	674.0	204	12	.941	24	14	8	5	3	24	19	.792	170	-3	+1	-1	-1	-1	-2	-3	-2	0	1	0	-1	18
Brandon Inge	Det	99	730.2	248	9	.964	16	15	11	2	7	17	11	.647	209	-3	+4	+2	+3	-1	+2	+1	1	-2	0	-1	-2	20
Chipper Jones	Atl	116	1006.1	248	6	.976	21	18	9	5	2	20	11	.550	211	-5	-2	+3	-2	-1	-3	-5	-3	0	0	0	-3	21
Aaron Miles	LAD	61	459.2	111	8	.928	13	11	9	5	3	9	5	.563	87	-5	0	-1	-5	-1	-6	-7	-5	1	0	-1	-5	22
Ryan Zimmerman	Was	97	866.2	278	12	.957	29	12	21	12	5	19	11	.579	214	-5	-4	-2	-12	0	-12	-10	-8	1	0	2	-5	23
David Wright	NYM	101	893.2	267	19	.929	31	13	13	5	4	15	6	.400	202	-5	-3	+8	0	-4	-4	-4	-3	-1	-1	-1	-6	24
Daniel Descalso	StL	117	666.0	182	6	.967	22	13	6	3	2	19	13	.684	145	+2	-6	+1	-3	-4	-7	-7	-5	-1	0	0	-6	25
Wilson Betemit	2 tms	87	696.0	208	11	.947	13	15	17	6	6	20	9	.450	170	+1	-5	-5	-10	+2	-8	-8	-6	0	1	0	-7	26
Ryan Roberts	Ari	107	902.1	281	10	.964	30	20	12	5	5	19	12	.632	242	+3	-11	-3	-9	+4	-5	-7	-6	-1	0	0	-7	26
Kevin Kouzmanoff	2 tms	71	576.1	181	13	.928	33	21	11	4	4	15	9	.600	141	0	-1	-7	-9	-1	-10	-10	-7	0	0	0	-7	28
Greg Dobbs	Fla	100	755.0	192	11	.943	15	17	11	7	10	12	7	.583	154	-1	-2	-6	-9	-1	-10	-9	-7	-2	0	0	-9	29
Pedro Alvarez	Pit	66	549.0	214	14	.935	24	17	11	4	5	22	10	.455	167	-3	-3	-4	-8	0	-8	-10	-8	-1	-1	-1	-11	30
Scott Sizemore	Oak	91	782.0	196	13	.934	24	22	13	5	8	13	8	.615	157	-7	-4	-2	-11	+1	-10	-11	-9	-1	0	-1	-11	31
Chris Johnson	Hou	101	841.1	237	15	.937	18	13	9	6	2	23	14	.609	184	-4	-5	-8	-15	-2	-17	-18	-14	1	0	1	-12	32
Danny Valencia	Min	147	1280.2	351	18	.949	28	26	20	8	10	34	20	.588	300	-2	-5	-7	-14	0	-14	-15	-11	-1	0	1	-11	33
Aramis Ramirez	ChC	145	1241.0	298	14	.953	38	34	21	11	5	24	12	.500	249	-8	-13	-5	-25	+2	-23	-24	-18	2	-1	-1	-18	34
Mark Reynolds	Bal	114	984.1	253	26	.897	29	31	12	5	7	25	16	.640	198	-8	-13	-2	-21	-1	-22	-23	-18	-3	1	-2	-22	35
2011 MLB Totals						.954	1373	864		287	222			.569														

Shortstops - Regulars

Name	Team	G	Inn	TC	E	Pct	GFP	DM	Opps	GDP	Pct	Outs Made	To His Right	Straight On	To His Left	GB	Air	Total	+/-	GDP	GFP/DME	Total	Rank
				BASIC						GDP				PLUS/MINUS						RUNS SAVED			
Brendan Ryan	Sea	123	1060.2	572	15	.974	59	26	122	81	.664	386	+18	+5	-2	+21	0	+21	16	1	1	18	1
Clint Barmes	Hou	122	1058.1	539	12	.978	44	19	98	65	.663	369	0	+12	+5	+18	+1	+19	14	-1	1	14	2
Troy Tulowitzki	Col	140	1208.1	684	6	.991	67	23	146	104	.712	434	+12	+1	-2	+11	-3	+8	6	2	3	11	3
Alcides Escobar	KC	158	1387.1	745	15	.980	77	32	169	97	.574	492	+19	+5	-5	+19	-4	+15	11	-3	2	10	4
Alex Gonzalez	Atl	149	1316.0	633	12	.981	62	25	116	76	.655	465	+3	+3	+3	+10	+2	+12	9	-1	1	9	5
J.J. Hardy	Bal	129	1133.0	620	6	.990	46	17	123	73	.593	429	+9	+8	-10	+6	+4	+10	8	-1	1	8	6
Yunel Escobar	Tor	132	1121.0	539	14	.974	35	25	121	77	.636	363	+8	0	+2	+12	-2	+10	8	0	-1	7	7
Reid Brignac	TB	91	680.2	328	7	.979	32	14	62	41	.661	239	+12	-9	+3	+6	+3	+9	7	0	0	7	8
Elvis Andrus	Tex	147	1261.1	677	25	.963	54	15	148	109	.736	434	+13	+1	-10	+4	+3	+7	5	3	-1	7	9
Alexei Ramirez	CWS	155	1382.0	690	16	.977	64	30	136	95	.699	481	+16	-3	-4	+2	+4	+5	4	3	0	7	10
Paul Janish	Cin	103	743.1	392	10	.974	36	12	84	46	.548	270	+1	+9	+4	+15	-4	+11	8	-2	0	6	11
Ronny Cedeno	Pit	125	1050.1	601	13	.978	39	26	114	65	.570	432	0	0	+12	+12	0	+12	9	-2	-2	5	12
Brandon Crawford	SF	65	507.1	248	7	.972	24	12	43	29	.674	184	-3	+3	+4	+5	0	+5	3	0	0	3	13
Asdrubal Cabrera	Cle	151	1326.2	617	15	.976	62	25	117	73	.624	416	-1	-5	+7	+2	+1	+3	2	-1	2	3	14
Stephen Drew	Ari	84	731.1	345	7	.980	38	11	71	46	.648	245	+1	0	-3	-1	+2	+1	0	1	2	3	15
Jhonny Peralta	Det	145	1245.0	608	7	.988	26	26	125	81	.648	409	-6	+8	+8	+10	-4	+6	4	0	-2	2	16
Edgar Renteria	Cin	86	628.0	316	13	.959	19	13	64	37	.578	231	-7	0	+13	+6	-2	+4	3	-1	-1	1	17
Marco Scutaro	Bos	109	928.2	428	12	.972	28	23	94	59	.628	299	+6	-1	-2	+3	-1	+2	2	0	-1	1	18
Willie Bloomquist	Ari	59	501.0	235	5	.979	21	6	54	32	.593	169	-2	+2	-1	-1	+1	0	0	0	1	1	19
Erick Aybar	LAA	142	1262.0	658	13	.980	56	30	154	107	.695	437	-4	-1	-2	-7	+1	-6	-4	2	1	-1	20
Ian Desmond	Was	152	1317.2	686	23	.966	48	35	140	84	.600	474	-13	+3	-1	-10	+7	-3	-2	-1	0	-3	21
Dee Gordon	LAD	54	446.1	218	10	.954	28	13	37	21	.568	149	-7	0	+2	-5	+3	-2	-2	-1	0	-3	21
Rafael Furcal	2 tms	85	726.2	394	14	.964	40	18	92	62	.674	261	-3	-6	+6	-2	-2	-4	-4	0	-1	-5	23
Jamey Carroll	LAD	66	504.2	214	4	.981	10	7	40	26	.650	149	-3	0	-1	-4	-3	-7	-5	0	0	-5	24
Emilio Bonifacio	Fla	67	543.2	261	9	.966	19	12	51	31	.608	177	-10	-5	+3	-12	+5	-7	-5	0	0	-5	24
Yuniesky Betancourt	Mil	149	1278.2	606	21	.965	47	19	124	83	.669	426	+18	-14	-14	-10	-1	-11	-9	2	0	-7	26
Jimmy Rollins	Phi	138	1207.0	581	7	.988	38	16	122	88	.721	426	-15	+9	-6	-13	+1	-12	-9	2	0	-7	26
Ryan Theriot	StL	91	755.0	388	17	.956	22	20	84	54	.643	262	+3	-7	-5	-9	-1	-10	-8	0	0	-8	28
Jason Bartlett	SD	138	1211.0	612	18	.971	39	26	131	83	.634	417	+3	-2	-10	-10	-1	-11	-8	0	-1	-9	29
Cliff Pennington	Oak	147	1272.1	612	22	.964	50	26	138	97	.703	394	+5	-11	-7	-13	-1	-14	-10	1	0	-9	30
Starlin Castro	ChC	158	1398.2	742	29	.961	69	56	139	78	.561	505	-7	-6	-1	-13	+5	-8	-6	-2	-2	-10	31
Tsuyoshi Nishioka	Min	60	508.1	278	10	.964	22	21	64	34	.531	180	-3	-3	-1	-7	-2	-9	-7	-2	-3	-12	32
Hanley Ramirez	Fla	86	754.2	329	14	.957	35	19	73	42	.575	211	-21	+2	+7	-12	-4	-16	-12	-1	0	-13	33
Jose Reyes	NYM	124	1087.0	554	18	.968	45	21	131	84	.641	365	-19	+4	+4	-11	-7	-18	-14	0	1	-13	34
Derek Jeter	NYY	122	1047.1	432	12	.972	31	19	103	63	.612	291	-15	+3	-5	-17	0	-17	-13	-1	-1	-15	35
2011 MLB Totals						.972	1819	948	4545	2893	.637												

Left Fielders - Regulars

Name	Team	G	Inn	TC	E	Pct	GFP	DM	Opps to Advance	Extra Bases	Pct	Kills	Outs Made	Basic	Shallow	Medium	Deep	Enhanced	+/-	Throws	GFP/DME	Total	Rank
				BASIC						THROWING					PLUS/MINUS						RUNS SAVED		
Brett Gardner	NYY	149	1158.2	305	4	.987	33	19	89	27	.303	5	294	+26	+19	+11	+7	+36	20	3	0	23	1
Alex Gordon	KC	148	1309.0	335	3	.991	31	23	126	34	.270	12	313	+5	+4	+7	-1	+10	5	13	2	20	2
Tony Gwynn	LAD	110	624.1	132	1	.992	17	9	58	25	.431	3	124	+5	-7	+5	+20	+18	10	0	2	12	3
Gerardo Parra	Ari	125	1018.0	281	2	.993	31	25	106	35	.330	10	267	+11	+1	+6	+10	+17	9	2	0	11	4
Sam Fuld	TB	75	604.2	170	3	.982	30	16	48	14	.292	4	162	+4	+5	+5	-7	+4	2	4	3	9	5
Michael Brantley	Cle	66	558.1	125	2	.984	10	8	52	14	.269	4	118	+8	+2	+8	0	+10	6	2	0	8	6
Martin Prado	Atl	100	854.0	180	3	.983	15	10	74	26	.351	6	171	+1	-3	+5	+5	+6	4	2	1	7	7
Carlos Lee	Hou	80	645.1	131	2	.985	20	9	74	24	.324	6	118	+2	+4	0	-1	+3	2	3	2	7	8
Laynce Nix	Was	73	504.1	110	2	.982	8	8	47	12	.255	4	102	-1	-2	-2	+8	+4	2	4	0	6	9
Brennan Boesch	Det	57	424.0	108	2	.981	11	9	58	23	.397	4	102	+1	0	-5	+7	+3	1	2	2	5	10
Josh Hamilton	Tex	85	709.0	161	4	.975	19	8	65	22	.338	2	153	+5	+4	+1	+1	+7	4	0	0	4	11
Ryan Braun	Mil	147	1250.0	268	1	.996	19	20	106	48	.453	5	259	+7	+2	+4	+7	+14	8	-6	1	3	12
Jose Tabata	Pit	76	626.0	145	1	.993	8	11	69	25	.362	4	140	+6	0	+4	+7	+12	7	-3	-1	3	13
Desmond Jennings	TB	53	467.0	104	1	.990	13	8	31	12	.387	2	100	+6	+5	0	+2	+7	4	0	-1	3	14
Juan Rivera	2 tms	56	414.2	80	0	1.000	4	7	33	10	.303	2	77	-2	0	-4	+4	0	0	3	0	3	15
Alex Presley	Pit	48	406.0	74	1	.986	7	8	64	21	.328	0	71	+2	-2	0	+9	+6	3	0	-1	2	16
Carlos Gonzalez	Col	61	518.0	99	1	.990	17	8	48	12	.250	4	93	-2	0	-5	+3	-2	-1	2	1	2	17
J.D. Martinez	Hou	51	436.1	98	1	.990	13	7	45	14	.311	4	92	-2	+3	-1	-7	-4	-2	2	2	2	18
David Murphy	Tex	78	556.1	129	4	.969	8	4	61	31	.508	0	123	+2	-3	+3	+11	+10	6	-4	-1	1	19
Jonny Gomes	2 tms	73	550.1	117	2	.983	7	8	63	16	.254	3	114	-1	-6	+1	+6	+1	1	1	-2	0	20
Josh Willingham	Oak	96	829.1	164	2	.988	14	9	80	25	.313	3	159	-6	-1	-1	-4	-6	-3	0	3	0	21
Michael Morse	Was	55	421.0	94	1	.989	7	7	37	12	.324	2	89	-4	0	-1	-5	-5	-3	1	2	0	21
Matt Holliday	StL	115	990.2	203	3	.985	10	13	97	42	.433	4	197	-4	-11	-2	+13	+1	0	-2	1	-1	23
Carl Crawford	Bos	127	1098.1	239	3	.987	17	19	112	35	.313	0	235	-1	+3	+14	-21	-4	-2	0	0	-2	24
Nolan Reimold	Bal	73	593.2	155	3	.981	10	14	70	27	.386	3	147	0	+3	-6	-1	-5	-3	-1	2	-2	25
Delmon Young	2 tms	115	994.1	228	7	.969	12	13	101	39	.386	4	214	-2	-6	0	+7	+1	1	-3	-1	-3	26
Jason Bay	NYM	122	1053.1	226	2	.991	26	14	102	36	.353	3	220	-4	-2	+4	-11	-9	-5	0	2	-3	27
Ryan Ludwick	2 tms	117	1005.0	200	1	.995	22	17	85	36	.424	3	190	0	+4	-9	+1	-4	-3	-3	1	-5	28
Cody Ross	SF	83	530.0	114	1	.991	8	10	54	18	.333	4	109	-4	+5	-8	-10	-13	-7	2	0	-5	29
Vernon Wells	LAA	111	930.2	248	3	.988	14	17	86	32	.372	2	241	-5	-4	-12	+11	-5	-3	-2	-3	-8	30
Eric Thames	Tor	52	456.1	93	1	.989	10	13	37	19	.514	1	91	-2	0	+1	-10	-9	-5	-2	-2	-9	31
Alfonso Soriano	ChC	128	1007.0	202	7	.965	6	22	93	32	.344	5	187	-2	+3	-1	-13	-11	-6	1	-4	-9	32
Juan Pierre	CWS	155	1365.0	290	7	.976	23	22	113	44	.389	2	278	-7	-1	+9	-19	-11	-6	-4	-1	-11	33
Raul Ibanez	Phi	134	1196.2	214	1	.995	17	22	107	41	.383	3	208	-18	-5	-10	-17	-32	-18	-3	-2	-23	34
Logan Morrison	Fla	119	1021.1	218	5	.977	17	42	95	30	.316	4	207	-21	-9	-10	-22	-40	-23	1	-4	-26	35
2011 MLB Totals						.984	862	797	4230	1523	.360	182											

Center Fielders - Regulars

Name	Team	G	Inn	TC	E	Pct	GFP	DM	Opps to Advance	Extra Bases	Pct	Kills	Outs Made	Basic	Shallow	Medium	Deep	Enhanced	+/-	Throws	GFP/ DME	Total	Rank
Austin Jackson	Det	152	1264.0	390	3	.992	20	14	104	56	.538	5	379	+20	+1	+12	+27	+40	23	2	4	29	1
Chris Young	Ari	155	1373.1	401	3	.993	23	15	123	69	.561	1	393	+19	+2	+10	+27	+39	22	-3	1	20	2
Cameron Maybin	SD	136	1173.0	349	5	.986	27	21	108	62	.574	2	342	+18	+15	+3	+14	+32	18	-2	-1	15	3
Carlos Gomez	Mil	87	569.0	188	0	1.000	22	16	49	19	.388	3	184	+13	+9	+3	+4	+17	9	3	3	15	4
Peter Bourjos	LAA	147	1269.1	361	4	.989	29	19	98	45	.459	4	351	+3	+4	+4	+2	+10	6	3	3	12	5
Franklin Gutierrez	Sea	92	763.0	244	0	1.000	20	6	69	44	.638	5	237	0	-9	+9	+8	+9	5	1	4	10	6
Denard Span	Min	67	585.1	208	1	.995	12	9	51	32	.627	0	206	+15	+8	+5	+11	+24	13	-3	-1	9	7
Rick Ankiel	Was	105	785.1	243	1	.996	19	14	72	30	.417	7	234	0	+5	0	-7	-2	-1	8	1	8	8
Jacoby Ellsbury	Bos	154	1358.1	394	0	1.000	19	25	125	78	.624	3	388	+12	+3	+3	+11	+17	9	-2	0	7	9
Andrew McCutchen	Pit	155	1353.2	430	7	.984	28	22	132	73	.553	3	414	+3	-5	-5	+20	+14	8	-3	0	5	10
Jon Jay	StL	75	570.0	174	3	.983	19	8	41	25	.610	2	167	+8	+7	+2	-1	+8	4	0	0	4	11
Nyjer Morgan	Mil	95	724.2	222	2	.991	15	14	82	46	.561	0	216	+4	-2	-1	+15	+13	7	-2	-2	3	12
Shane Victorino	Phi	130	1150.2	296	0	1.000	10	15	71	32	.451	0	296	+8	+13	+8	-17	+5	3	-1	0	2	13
Ezequiel Carrera	Cle	55	426.0	117	3	.974	8	14	45	26	.578	1	112	-1	-1	0	+7	+6	3	0	-2	1	14
Coco Crisp	Oak	133	1134.1	324	1	.997	26	16	96	62	.646	1	321	-4	-4	-2	+10	+4	2	-3	2	1	15
Endy Chavez	Tex	66	514.1	130	1	.992	11	3	33	17	.515	1	126	0	-2	+4	+1	+2	1	-1	0	0	16
Marlon Byrd	ChC	118	998.0	284	3	.989	18	12	93	56	.602	4	273	-4	-7	+4	-4	-8	-4	2	2	0	17
Ben Revere	Min	89	776.1	252	6	.976	14	16	89	56	.629	3	244	+3	0	-6	+13	+7	4	-3	-2	-1	18
Dexter Fowler	Col	122	1072.2	323	8	.975	13	22	83	55	.663	3	309	0	-12	-4	+23	+6	3	-2	-4	-3	19
Michael Bourn	2 tms	156	1359.0	376	3	.992	16	23	131	75	.573	2	367	-4	-15	-3	+22	+5	2	-3	-2	-3	20
Andres Torres	SF	106	776.0	205	3	.985	11	9	54	35	.648	2	196	0	+7	-3	-8	-4	-2	0	-1	-3	21
Colby Rasmus	2 tms	127	1092.2	312	6	.981	12	20	85	52	.612	1	302	-1	+3	+3	-8	-2	-1	-2	-1	-4	22
Drew Stubbs	Cin	157	1329.0	377	3	.992	15	26	124	66	.532	8	365	-9	-12	+8	-10	-14	-8	5	-1	-4	23
Adam Jones	Bal	148	1281.0	403	8	.980	24	27	141	78	.553	13	380	-7	+4	-6	-19	-21	-12	8	0	-4	24
Matt Kemp	LAD	159	1380.0	361	5	.986	28	23	109	59	.541	8	346	-14	-9	+2	-13	-20	-11	4	2	-5	25
Grady Sizemore	Cle	56	479.1	126	2	.984	8	7	54	27	.500	4	123	-4	+1	-5	-5	-9	-5	-1	0	-6	26
Melky Cabrera	KC	144	1265.2	332	3	.991	26	27	139	90	.647	8	316	-10	-4	0	-9	-13	-7	-1	2	-6	27
Curtis Granderson	NYY	155	1348.0	368	3	.992	30	19	122	60	.492	5	355	-5	+9	-18	-10	-19	-11	2	3	-6	28
Nate McLouth	Atl	55	498.0	131	2	.985	13	13	37	21	.568	2	129	-2	-1	-2	-3	-6	-3	-2	-2	-7	29
Jordan Schafer	2 tms	79	672.0	194	2	.990	9	13	68	40	.588	1	191	-2	-1	-2	-3	-6	-4	-1	-2	-7	30
B.J. Upton	TB	151	1326.1	391	3	.992	26	24	114	63	.553	5	381	-4	+6	-11	-7	-12	-7	1	-1	-7	31
Angel Pagan	NYM	121	1045.0	317	10	.968	17	26	128	74	.578	1	302	-10	-2	-12	+4	-9	-5	-1	-2	-8	32
Alex Rios	CWS	143	1230.0	357	3	.992	17	27	144	79	.549	2	349	-6	-3	-5	-3	-11	-6	-1	-1	-9	33
Rajai Davis	Tor	79	652.0	178	2	.989	11	9	53	33	.623	0	174	-7	-9	+4	-6	-11	-6	-4	1	-9	33
Chris Coghlan	Fla	65	568.1	160	0	1.000	9	11	44	30	.682	2	157	-10	0	-2	-20	-22	-12	-1	0	-13	35
2011 MLB Totals						.989	811	795	4022	2268	.564	139											

Right Fielders - Regulars

Name	Team	G	Inn	TC	E	Pct	GFP	DM	Opps to Advance	Extra Bases	Pct	Kills	Outs Made	Basic	Shallow	Medium	Deep	Enhanced	+/-	Throws	GFP/ DME	Total	Rank
Jason Heyward	Atl	122	990.1	228	6	.974	12	14	86	47	.547	2	218	+14	+1	+3	+29	+32	19	-2	-2	15	1
Torii Hunter	LAA	136	1179.1	278	3	.989	36	23	125	68	.544	14	259	-4	-12	+1	+11	+1	1	5	3	9	2
Justin Upton	Ari	159	1366.2	357	13	.964	23	36	128	62	.484	2	340	+9	-6	+1	+34	+29	17	-5	-4	8	3
Josh Reddick	Bos	56	432.2	111	4	.964	5	9	35	22	.629	3	103	+8	+2	+3	+10	+15	9	-1	-1	7	4
David DeJesus	Oak	116	992.2	241	4	.983	29	11	102	55	.539	6	231	+6	-3	+9	+7	+13	7	-3	1	5	5
Will Venable	SD	91	662.2	151	2	.987	10	9	44	21	.477	2	147	+8	+5	+1	+4	+10	6	0	-1	5	6
Andre Ethier	LAD	126	1091.1	251	0	1.000	20	14	93	53	.570	6	243	-1	-9	+5	+13	+9	5	-2	1	4	7
Mike Stanton	Fla	142	1219.0	296	6	.980	25	43	120	51	.425	5	280	+8	+5	-4	+7	+9	5	2	-4	3	8
Shin-Soo Choo	Cle	85	735.1	185	4	.978	15	20	78	39	.500	6	172	0	+1	+1	+1	+3	2	2	-1	3	9
Chris Denorfia	SD	62	445.0	109	2	.982	10	9	46	23	.500	1	101	+3	+2	+5	-5	+3	2	0	1	3	10
Nick Markakis	Bal	157	1389.2	325	0	1.000	38	18	137	68	.496	9	312	-6	-4	-5	-1	-10	-6	2	6	2	11
Hunter Pence	2 tms	153	1342.2	301	6	.980	28	33	137	59	.431	7	285	0	+8	-5	-9	-7	-4	5	0	1	12
Jeff Francoeur	KC	153	1352.0	348	5	.986	28	29	144	68	.472	11	328	-7	+1	-15	+2	-12	-7	5	3	1	13
Carlos Quentin	CWS	102	854.2	180	1	.994	13	11	77	45	.584	0	177	+9	+8	+6	-1	+13	7	-6	-1	0	14
Corey Hart	Mil	126	1087.2	256	2	.992	20	22	82	43	.524	2	252	+5	-2	+8	+3	+8	5	-4	-2	-1	15
Brennan Boesch	Det	51	366.2	92	1	.989	8	4	32	19	.594	1	88	-1	+2	0	-2	0	0	-1	0	-1	16
J.D. Drew	Bos	76	587.1	149	0	1.000	4	9	52	28	.538	1	146	+1	-5	+4	+3	+3	2	-4	0	-2	17
Jay Bruce	Cin	155	1371.0	320	4	.988	16	22	128	62	.484	5	306	+4	+6	+1	-7	+1	0	-2	0	-2	18
Kosuke Fukudome	2 tms	131	1061.0	274	3	.989	20	23	120	52	.433	5	265	0	+6	-7	-3	-4	-3	3	-2	-2	19
Matt Joyce	TB	126	1006.1	222	3	.986	22	18	89	43	.483	5	211	+1	+4	-2	-11	-9	-5	0	-3	-2	20
Carlos Beltran	2 tms	134	1153.2	241	1	.996	22	26	114	56	.491	4	230	-3	-1	-8	+6	-3	-2	0	-1	-3	21
Ichiro Suzuki	Sea	151	1333.0	274	4	.985	23	10	127	71	.559	5	263	-4	-2	+7	-9	-4	-2	-3	2	-3	21
Jason Kubel	Min	50	413.2	105	1	.990	11	7	46	21	.457	7	95	-8	-3	+1	-13	-15	-9	5	1	-3	23
Garrett Jones	Pit	90	659.0	158	1	.994	11	12	70	32	.457	2	154	-6	-2	-1	-2	-5	-3	-1	0	-4	24
Jayson Werth	Was	134	1172.2	305	8	.974	31	29	141	62	.440	8	288	-7	0	-2	-8	-11	-6	3	-1	-4	25
Nick Swisher	NYY	141	1190.1	283	1	.996	28	22	131	53	.405	3	273	-4	+4	-3	-15	-13	-8	3	1	-4	26
Seth Smith	Col	107	867.1	188	5	.973	13	21	80	49	.613	3	182	0	-5	0	+8	+3	2	-5	-3	-6	27
Nelson Cruz	Tex	109	863.2	225	5	.978	16	14	71	37	.521	3	216	-1	+3	-3	-5	-5	-3	-3	0	-6	28
Ben Francisco	Phi	55	445.0	91	2	.978	5	11	43	22	.512	2	86	-5	-2	-1	-6	-9	-6	1	-2	-7	29
Jose Bautista	Tor	116	1014.0	252	6	.976	21	26	97	49	.505	10	233	-8	0	-3	-20	-23	-13	3	3	-7	30
Nate Schierholtz	SF	96	703.2	152	2	.987	13	13	64	30	.469	4	142	-9	-2	-6	-7	-16	-9	1	0	-8	31
Domonic Brown	Phi	52	451.0	82	4	.951	3	8	33	17	.515	0	78	-5	-4	-2	-3	-8	-5	-2	-2	-9	32
Magglio Ordonez	Det	69	471.2	92	0	1.000	8	13	54	28	.519	5	87	-10	-6	+1	+12	-16	-10	1	0	-9	33
Michael Cuddyer	Min	77	639.1	152	4	.974	15	8	63	32	.508	3	142	-8	-1	-3	-14	-19	-11	0	1	-10	34
Lance Berkman	StL	110	865.1	180	4	.978	12	20	80	41	.513	1	173	-10	-2	-8	-14	-24	-14	-2	-2	-18	35
2011 MLB Totals						.985	844	846	4180	2065	.494	209											

All Other Catchers

		BASIC							BUNTS			PITCHER HANDLING						STOLEN BASES						RUNS SAVED					
Name	Team	G	Inn	TC	E	Pct	GFP	DM	Opp	Sac Hits	Bunt Hits	W	L	Pct	ER	CERA	Pitch Block	SB	CCS	PCS	CPO	CS%	SB Saved	Adj ER	SB	Bunt	GFP/ DME	Total	Rnk
Eliezer Alfonzo	Col	19	159.1	145	5	.966	2	8	2	1	0	8	10	.444	87	4.91	56	10	5	0	0	.33	2	0	1	1	0	2	-
John Baker	Fla	1	3.0	2	0	1.000	0	0				0	0	-	1	3.00	-	0	0	0	0	-	0	0	0			0	-
Josh Bard	Sea	25	201.0	170	2	.988	2	6				8	15	.348	88	3.94	78	15	7	2	0	.32	0	0	0		0	0	-
Henry Blanco	Ari	37	274.0	192	1	.995	0	10	2	1	0	12	19	.387	141	4.63	113	13	8	3	0	.38	2	-1	2	0	-1	0	-
J.C. Boscan	Atl	3	18.0	19	0	1.000	0	1				1	1	.500	8	4.00	7	2	1	0	0	.33	1	0	0		0	0	-
Dusty Brown	Pit	10	78.0	52	0	1.000	1	5	1	1	0	2	6	.250	36	4.15	32	6	1	0	0	.14	0	0	0	0	0	0	-
Robinson Cancel	Hou	2	16.0	14	0	1.000	0	0				1	1	.500	9	5.06	12	2	0	0	0	.00	0	0	0		0	0	-
Welington Castillo	ChC	4	31.2	20	2	.900	0	2				0	4	.000	21	5.97	21	1	2	0	0	.67	1	0	0		0	0	-
Ramon Castro	CWS	21	174.1	122	1	.992	1	4				9	11	.450	83	4.28	29	16	2	2	1	.11	-1	0	0		-1	-1	-
Francisco Cervelli	NYY	41	316.1	302	6	.980	5	13				25	10	.714	123	3.50	155	24	4	0	0	.14	-5	1	-3		1	-1	-
R. Chirinos	TB	19	132.0	123	0	1.000	1	3				8	7	.533	65	4.43	64	21	2	0	0	.09	-1	0	-1		2	1	-
Steve Clevenger	ChC	2	12.0	13	0	1.000	0	0				0	1	.000	6	4.50	3	1	0	0	0	.00	0	0	0		0	0	-
Hank Conger	LAA	56	450.0	355	6	.983	7	20	5	3	0	24	24	.500	192	3.84	233	53	10	2	1	.16	-5	-1	-3	0	3	-1	-
Carlos Corporan	Hou	50	411.1	407	6	.985	5	20	4	4	0	14	32	.304	183	4.00	245	43	9	0	0	.17	-2	1	-1	-1	3	2	-
Tony Cruz	StL	20	99.0	96	0	1.000	1	8	3	3	0	5	3	.625	33	3.00	52	2	2	0	0	.50	0	0	0	-1	-1	-2	-
Ryan Doumit	Pit	60	461.1	353	6	.983	5	21	3	2	0	21	32	.396	245	4.78	183	41	11	2	0	.21	-1	-3	-1	-1	-1	-6	-
A.J. Ellis	LAD	29	221.2	178	0	1.000	0	10	1	0	0	14	11	.560	89	3.61	75	11	2	2	0	.15	-1	0	-1	0	-2	-3	-
Tim Federowicz	LAD	7	40.0	44	1	.977	0	1	1	1	0	2	2	.500	14	3.15	31	3	2	0	0	.40	1	0	1	0	1	2	-
Jesus Flores	Was	22	193.0	151	1	.993	1	9	1	0	0	10	11	.476	72	3.36	89	16	4	0	0	.20	0	0	0	0	0	0	-
Tyler Flowers	CWS	31	256.2	260	2	.992	1	10				16	12	.571	113	3.96	120	25	6	2	0	.19	1	1	1		1	3	-
Jake Fox	Bal	10	57.0	39	0	1.000	1	4				2	4	.333	49	7.74	22	5	0	0	0	.00	-2	0	-1		0	-1	-
Eric Fryer	Pit	8	61.2	48	1	.979	2	3	1	1	0	2	5	.286	21	3.06	16	7	3	0	1	.30	2	0	2	0	0	2	-
Chris Gimenez	Sea	20	152.0	120	0	1.000	4	7				4	13	.235	83	4.91	53	14	6	0	0	.30	2	-1	1		1	1	-
Hector Gimenez	LAD	1	9.0	8	0	1.000	0	1				0	1	.000	10	10.00	9	1	0	0	0	.00	0	0	0		0	0	-
Brett Hayes	Fla	50	312.2	274	0	1.000	5	13	5	3	0	12	21	.364	144	4.14	97	20	5	2	1	.20	-1	0	0	0	-1	-1	-
Koyie Hill	ChC	45	349.0	340	6	.982	4	17	2	1	0	22	16	.579	166	4.28	154	25	7	1	0	.22	-1	1	-1	0	0	0	-
Steve Holm	Min	6	43.0	34	0	1.000	2	2				1	4	.200	26	5.44	12	5	0	0	0	.00	-1	0	-1		0	-1	-
Jason Jaramillo	Pit	14	73.2	67	0	1.000	1	6				4	3	.571	31	3.79	31	5	1	0	1	.17	0	0	0		-1	-1	-
Rob Johnson	SD	63	475.0	429	2	.995	8	21	14	5	1	22	32	.407	173	3.28	196	49	11	4	3	.18	-4	1	-2	2	2	3	-
Don Kelly	Det	1	6.0	3	0	1.000	0	0				0	0	-	4	6.00	-	0	0	0	0	-	0	0	0		0	0	-
George Kottaras	Mil	36	253.0	179	0	1.000	1	5	1	1	0	20	11	.645	102	3.63	101	18	3	0	0	.14	-2	0	-2	0	1	-1	-
Erik Kratz	Phi	1	10.0	10	0	1.000	1	0	1	0	0	0	1	.000	4	3.60	2	1	0	0	0	.00	0	0	0	0	0	0	-
Gerald Laird	StL	31	213.0	197	3	.985	1	10	7	4	0	13	9	.591	83	3.51	102	16	3	1	0	.16	-1	0	-1	-1	0	-2	-
Ryan Lavarnway	Bos	8	26.2	25	0	1.000	1	0				1	1	.500	13	4.39	10	0	1	0	0	1.00	1	0	1		1	2	-
Jose Lobaton	TB	14	88.0	94	1	.989	0	2				5	4	.556	24	2.45	46	7	2	1	0	.22	0	0	0		1	1	-
Donny Lucy	CWS	3	21.0	24	0	1.000	3	1				0	2	.000	16	6.86	16	0	0	1	0	-	0	0	0		1	1	-
Martin Maldonado	Mil	3	3.0	4	0	1.000	0	0				0	0	-	0	0.00	1	0	0	0	0	-	0	0	0		0	0	-
Luis Martinez	SD	19	148.1	129	0	1.000	1	3	2	1	1	10	6	.625	55	3.34	60	14	3	2	0	.18	-2	0	-2	-1	0	-3	-
Victor Martinez	Det	26	219.0	160	2	.988	3	11				13	13	.500	128	5.26	94	29	7	1	0	.19	-1	-1	-1		0	-2	-
Joe Mauer	Min	52	408.2	313	4	.987	2	19	5	2	0	21	26	.447	201	4.43	146	28	10	2	0	.26	-1	1	0	1	-2	0	-
Michael McKenry	Pit	58	485.0	388	5	.987	6	20	2	1	0	26	28	.481	201	3.73	199	39	10	3	0	.20	0	0	0	0	1	1	-
Devin Mesoraco	Cin	16	122.1	112	3	.973	4	7				7	6	.538	65	4.78	32	8	2	1	0	.20	-1	0	-1		-1	-2	-
Gustavo Molina	NYY	3	19.0	10	0	1.000	0	0				1	1	.500	5	2.37	8	1	1	0	0	.50	0	0	0		0	0	-
Jose Molina	Tor	48	399.0	367	1	.997	5	21				26	18	.591	194	4.38	108	24	12	0	2	.33	0	1	1		-4	-2	-
Jesus Montero	NYY	3	22.0	13	0	1.000	1	2				1	2	.333	19	7.77	13	4	1	0	0	.20	0	0	0		0	0	-
Adam Moore	Sea	2	15.2	12	0	1.000	0	0				1	1	.500	6	3.45	4	2	0	0	0	.00	-1	0	0		0	0	-
Jose Morales	Col	17	151.2	130	5	.962	1	6	5	0	1	10	7	.588	63	3.74	76	9	4	2	0	.31	1	0	1	-1	0	0	-
Mike Napoli	Tex	61	506.1	458	2	.996	5	17	3	1	1	42	15	.737	178	3.16	153	21	10	2	1	.32	1	2	1	0	-2	1	-
Dioner Navarro	LAD	54	428.0	455	7	.985	14	20	4	2	0	22	24	.478	163	3.43	165	41	10	4	5	.20	-3	1	0	0	0	1	-
Mike Nickeas	NYM	20	143.2	124	0	1.000	2	6	1	1	0	10	5	.667	47	2.94	51	9	2	2	0	.18	0	1	0	0	0	1	-
Wil Nieves	Mil	17	129.0	118	1	.992	3	5	4	3	0	7	9	.438	55	3.84	77	7	2	1	0	.22	0	0	0	0	1	1	-
Jordan Pacheco	Col	2	10.0	9	0	1.000	0	1				1	0	1.000	5	4.50	3	2	0	0	0	.00	0	0	0		0	0	-
Matt Pagnozzi	2 tms	9	74.0	51	0	1.000	1	3	3	2	0	0	9	.000	65	7.91	37	11	2	3	0	.15	-1	0	-1	0	0	-1	-
Salvador Perez	KC	39	338.2	314	3	.990	10	21	4	2	0	19	20	.487	159	4.23	187	26	5	2	3	.16	0	-1	1	0	1	1	-
Kyle Phillips	SD	24	171.2	155	3	.981	3	5	1	1	0	9	10	.474	67	3.51	74	21	7	1	1	.25	0	0	0	0	1	1	-
Manny Pina	KC	4	36.0	34	0	1.000	0	5				2	2	.500	11	2.75	12	1	1	0	0	.50	1	0	1		-1	0	-
Jorge Posada	NYY	1	6.0	9	0	1.000	0	1				0	0	-	5	7.50	4	0	1	0	0	1.00	1	0	1		0	1	-
Buster Posey	SF	41	361.0	359	2	.994	1	13	1	1	0	23	18	.561	134	3.34	133	27	11	4	0	.29	3	0	2	0	1	3	-
Landon Powell	Oak	33	273.1	254	2	.992	3	10	1	1	0	18	12	.600	82	2.70	76	16	6	3	0	.27	2	2	1	0	-1	2	-
Anthony Recker	Oak	5	42.0	46	1	.978	1	3				1	4	.200	39	8.36	27	5	0	0	0	.00	1	0	0		1	1	-
Mike Rivera	Mil	1	13.0	15	0	1.000	0	0				1	0	1.000	5	3.46	3	0	1	0	0	1.00	1	0	0		0	0	-
Rene Rivera	Min	44	299.1	250	3	.988	4	9	4	2	0	14	21	.400	130	3.91	126	15	6	4	0	.29	0	2	0	1	0	3	-
Ivan Rodriguez	Was	37	304.2	266	3	.989	5	13	5	4	1	16	18	.471	111	3.28	106	12	12	1	0	.50	4	1	3	-1	-1	2	-
Austin Romine	NYY	8	50.2	50	1	.980	1	2				3	1	.750	24	4.26	19	4	1	1	0	.20	0	0	0		0	0	-
Wilin Rosario	Col	14	123.0	104	1	.990	1	14				3	11	.214	66	4.83	68	3	5	0	0	.63	2	0	1		-2	-1	-
David Ross	Atl	49	378.2	372	3	.992	5	15	7	7	0	28	14	.667	131	3.11	133	22	10	1	1	.31	3	1	3	0	-1	3	-
Hector Sanchez	SF	11	63.0	54	0	1.000	0	3	1	1	0	3	3	.500	37	5.29	43	10	2	2	0	.17	-1	0	-1	0	0	-1	-
Omir Santos	Det	10	58.0	51	0	1.000	1	3				4	2	.667	16	2.48	14	5	1	0	0	.17	0	0	0		0	0	-
Dane Sardinha	Phi	15	107.0	92	0	1.000	1	7				4	8	.333	36	3.03	23	8	3	0	0	.27	0	0	0		-1	-1	-
Brian Schneider	Phi	40	309.0	287	1	.997	0	8	4	4	0	28	8	.778	99	2.88	97	20	3	0	0	.13	-4	1	-3	0	-1	-3	-
Chris Snyder	Pit	33	265.2	218	0	1.000	0	10	4	2	0	16	14	.533	100	3.39	97	17	5	1	0	.23	-1	1	-1	0	-1	-1	-
Chris Stewart	SF	63	460.1	485	7	.986	9	21	6	5	0	27	24	.529	138	2.70	205	34	19	3	2	.36	7	3	6	1	2	12	-
Craig Tatum	Bal	30	239.2	226	3	.987	6	6	4	1	0	10	17	.370	159	5.97	121	20	8	0	0	.29	1	-1	1	0	3	3	-
Taylor Teagarden	Tex	14	85.1	68	0	1.000	0	3				3	5	.375	30	3.16	32	6	5	2	0	.45	2	0	2		0	2	-
Wyatt Toregas	Pit	2	10.0	6	0	1.000	0	1				1	0	1.000	4	3.60	3	2	1	0	0	.33	0	0	0		0	0	-
J.R. Towles	Hou	51	365.2	312	6	.981	4	6	5	4	0	16	25	.390	198	4.87	165	38	6	2	0	.14	-3	-1	-2	1	3	1	-
Bobby Wilson	LAA	47	317.0	266	1	.996	4	14	3	1	0	17	18	.486	137	3.89	195	25	8	2	1	.24	0	-1	1	1	2	3	-
2011 MLB Totals						.992	523	1842		265	54					3.94						.23							

All Other First Basemen

BASIC									BUNTS			GDP			PLUS/MINUS								RUNS SAVED					
Name	Team	G	Inn	TC	E	Pct	GFP	DM	Opp	Sac Hits	Bunt Hits	Opp	GDP	Pct	Outs Made	To His Right	Straight On	To His Left	GB	Air	Total	Enhanced	+/-	Bunt	GDP	GFP/ DME	Total	Rk
Dustin Ackley	Sea	1	6.2	8	0	1.000	1	0				0	0	-	0	0	0	0	0	0	0	0	0		0	0	0	-
Erick Almonte	Mil	2	2.0	3	0	1.000	0	0				0	0	-	2	0	0	0	0	0	0	0	0		0	0	0	-
Yonder Alonso	Cin	3	13.0	11	0	1.000	0	1	1	1	0	1	0	.000	2	0	0	0	0	0	0	0	0	0	0	0	0	-
Lars Anderson	Bos	6	15.0	16	1	.938	2	0				0	0	-	5	0	0	0	0	0	0	0	0		0	0	0	-
Jeff Baker	ChC	19	126.0	121	0	1.000	2	2	1	1	0	0	0	-	19	0	+1	+1	+1	0	+1	+1	1	0	0	0	1	-
Brandon Belt	SF	31	203.0	214	1	.995	9	3	1	0	0	1	1	1.000	32	0	+1	+1	+1	0	+1	+1	1	0	0	1	2	-
Lance Berkman	StL	21	145.0	170	2	.988	8	3	4	2	1	4	2	.500	25	+1	-2	-1	-2	0	-2	-2	-1	0	0	0	-1	-
Wilson Betemit	KC	3	27.0	25	0	1.000	0	0				2	0	.000	6	0	-1	0	-1	0	-1	-1	-1		0	0	-1	-
Brian Bixler	Was	2	3.0	3	0	1.000	0	0				0	0	-	0	0	0	0	0	0	0	0	0		0	0	0	-
Casey Blake	LAD	8	50.0	49	1	.980	2	1	2	1	0	0	0	-	8	0	0	0	0	-1	-1	-1	-1	0	0	0	-1	-
Kyle Blanks	SD	13	83.0	73	0	1.000	3	0	1	1	0	1	0	.000	10	+1	0	0	+1	0	+1	+1	1	0	0	0	1	-
John Bowker	2 tms	2	6.0	5	0	1.000	0	1				0	0	-	2	0	0	0	0	0	0	0	0		0	0	0	-
Russell Branyan	2 tms	25	159.0	161	1	.994	8	1				4	0	.000	29	+1	-1	+1	+1	+2	+3	+3	2		0	0	2	-
Manny Burriss	SF	2	8.0	10	0	1.000	0	0				0	0	-	1	0	0	0	0	0	0	0	0		0	0	0	-
Billy Butler	KC	11	94.2	94	0	1.000	1	1	1	0	0	2	0	.000	12	-1	-1	-1	-3	+1	-2	-2	-2	0	0	0	-2	-
Miguel Cairo	Cin	5	9.0	11	0	1.000	0	0				0	0	-	2	0	0	0	0	0	0	0	0		0	0	0	-
Jorge Cantu	SD	26	190.2	208	2	.990	5	0	3	3	0	1	0	.000	32	0	0	+1	+1	0	+1	+1	1	0	0	0	1	-
Mike Carp	Sea	34	263.2	269	2	.993	13	7	3	1	0	3	1	.333	47	+2	-3	0	-1	-1	-2	-2	-1	0	0	0	-1	-
Chris Carter	Oak	11	71.1	69	1	.986	1	3				1	1	1.000	15	0	0	0	0	0	0	0	0		0	0	0	-
Eric Chavez	NYY	3	16.0	13	0	1.000	0	2				0	0	-	2	0	0	0	0	0	0	0	0		0	0	0	-
R. Chirinos	TB	1	3.0	3	0	1.000	0	0				0	0	-	2	0	0	0	0	0	0	0	0		0	0	0	-
Tyler Colvin	ChC	4	22.1	23	0	1.000	1	0				1	1	1.000	4	0	0	-1	0	0	0	0	0		0	0	0	-
Brooks Conrad	Atl	1	1.2	3	0	1.000	0	0				0	0	-	0	0	0	0	0	0	0	0	0		0	0	0	-
David Cooper	Tor	15	105.0	110	4	.964	5	3	1	1	0	2	0	.000	20	0	-1	+1	0	0	0	0	0	0	0	-1	-1	-
Alex Cora	Was	9	16.0	16	2	.875	2	0				0	0	-	3	0	-1	-1	-1	0	-1	-1	-1		0	0	-1	-
Allen Craig	StL	2	4.0	6	0	1.000	0	0				0	0	-	0	0	0	0	0	0	0	0	0		0	0	0	-
Tony Cruz	StL	2	10.0	8	0	1.000	0	0				0	0	-	0	0	0	0	0	0	0	0	0		0	0	0	-
Michael Cuddyer	Min	46	352.2	380	2	.995	11	2	3	2	1	3	0	.000	72	0	+2	-1	+1	-1	0	+1	0	0	0	1	1	-
Johnny Damon	TB	1	1.0	2	0	1.000	0	0				0	0	-	0							0			0	0	0	-
Chris Davis	2 tms	31	221.2	240	0	1.000	7	5	2	0	0	2	1	.500	36	0	-2	-2	-3	0	-3	-4	-3	1	0	0	-2	-
Ike Davis	NYM	36	317.0	322	1	.997	8	12	4	4	0	5	0	.000	74	+2	+1	0	+1	+1	+2	+3	2	0	0	-1	1	-
Mark DeRosa	SF	10	36.0	36	0	1.000	3	0				0	0	-	5	0	0	0	0	0	0	0	0		0	0	0	-
Greg Dobbs	Fla	4	28.0	24	0	1.000	2	0	1	1	0	0	0	-	6	0	0	+1	+1	0	+1	+1	1	0	0	0	1	-
Matt Downs	Hou	13	42.0	41	0	1.000	3	1	1	1	0	1	0	.000	8	+1	0	0	+2	0	+2	+2	1	0	0	0	1	-
Lucas Duda	NYM	43	323.1	367	2	.995	15	8	6	3	1	4	2	.500	69	-1	+1	-1	-1	0	-1	-1	0	1	0	-1	0	-
Shelley Duncan	Cle	7	52.2	51	1	.980	3	1				0	0	-	11	-1	+1	+1	0	0	0	+2	1		0	0	1	-
Adam Dunn	CWS	35	284.2	287	4	.986	9	7	2	1	1	3	3	1.000	39	-1	0	-1	-3	0	-3	-3	-2	-1	0	-1	-4	-
Mark Ellis	Oak	2	14.2	18	0	1.000	2	0				0	0	-	5	+1	0	0	+1	0	+1	+1	1		0	0	1	-
E. Encarnacion	Tor	25	190.0	205	4	.980	8	4	2	1	0	0	0	-	24	0	-1	0	-2	-1	-3	-2	-1	-1	0	-1	-3	-
Nick Evans	NYM	45	337.2	398	3	.992	24	2	12	9	0	5	0	.000	71	+1	+5	0	+7	+2	+9	+8	7	1	-1	2	9	-
Tyler Flowers	CWS	3	21.0	21	0	1.000	0	0				1	1	1.000	5	0	0	0	+1	0	+1	+1	1		0	0	1	-
Jake Fox	Bal	6	34.1	26	0	1.000	2	0				0	0	-	4	0	0	0	0	0	0	0	0		0	0	0	-
Todd Frazier	Cin	1	9.0	11	0	1.000	0	0				0	0	-	1	0	0	0	0	-1	-1	-1	-1		0	0	-1	-
David Freese	StL	5	14.0	8	0	1.000	1	0				0	0	-	2	0	0	0	0	0	0	0	0		0	0	0	-
Mat Gamel	Mil	2	15.0	19	0	1.000	0	0				0	0	-	2	+1	0	0	+1	0	+1	+1	1		0	0	1	-
Jason Giambi	Col	23	170.0	214	1	.995	8	5	2	2	0	2	0	.000	36	0	0	+1	+1	0	+1	+1	1	0	0	-1	0	-
Chris Gimenez	Sea	2	16.0	16	0	1.000	2	0				0	0	-	1	0	0	-1	-1	0	-1	-1	-1		0	0	-1	-
Ross Gload	Phi	10	64.0	74	1	.986	4	1	1	1	0	0	0	-	7	0	-1	-2	-1	0	-1	-2	-1	0	0	0	-1	-
Paul Goldschmidt	Ari	43	368.0	373	0	1.000	29	7	2	0	2	6	2	.333	60	-2	-1	-1	-4	-2	-6	-6	-5	-1	0	3	-3	-
Alberto Gonzalez	SD	4	17.0	18	0	1.000	1	0				0	0	-	2	0	-1	0	-1	0	-1	-1	0		0	0	0	-
Alex Gordon	KC	7	23.0	28	1	.964	1	0	1	1	0	0	0	-	4	0	0	-2	-1	0	-1	-2	-1	0	0	0	-1	-
Carlos Guillen	Det	1	2.0	2	0	1.000	0	0				0	0	-	1	0	0	0	0	0	0	0	0		0	0	0	-
Mark Hamilton	StL	8	25.2	24	0	1.000	1	0				0	0	-	6	0	0	0	0	0	0	0	0		0	0	0	-
Jack Hannahan	Cle	8	33.0	32	0	1.000	3	1				1	1	1.000	9	0	0	+1	0	0	0	+1	1		0	0	1	-
Brad Hawpe	SD	44	383.0	404	4	.990	18	6	8	5	1	8	3	.375	72	+1	0	-2	0	0	0	-1	-1	0	0	0	-1	-
Brett Hayes	Fla	1	3.0	3	0	1.000	0	0				0	0	-	0	0	0	0	0	0	0	0	0		0	0	0	-
Wes Helms	Fla	5	13.2	7	0	1.000	0	2	1	0	1	0	0	-	1	-1	0	+1	0	0	0	0	0	0	0	-1	-1	-
Diory Hernandez	Atl	1	2.0	1	0	1.000	0	0				0	0	-	0							0			0	0	0	-
R. Hernandez	Cin	1	9.0	8	0	1.000	1	0				0	0	-	0	0	0	0	0	0	0	0	0		0	0	0	-
Eric Hinske	Atl	13	83.1	89	0	1.000	3	2	1	1	0	0	0	-	20	+1	+1	+1	+2	-1	+1	+1	1	0	0	0	1	-
Luke Hughes	Min	36	274.0	292	1	.997	17	8				3	1	.333	51	-1	+2	+1	+1	0	+1	+1	1		0	-1	0	-
Chris Iannetta	Col	2	2.0	4	0	1.000	0	0				0	0	-	0	0	0	0	0	0	0	0	0		0	0	0	-
Dan Johnson	TB	21	151.1	165	1	.994	12	4	1	0	0	1	0	.000	37	+2	0	-1	+1	0	+1	+1	1	0	0	0	1	-
Elliot Johnson	TB	2	2.1	1	0	1.000	0	0				0	0	-	0	0	0	0	0	0	0	0	0		0	0	0	-
Garrett Jones	Pit	34	260.1	277	3	.989	11	11	2	0	2	1	0	.000	39	0	-1	0	-1	+1	0	0	0	-1	0	-2	-3	-
Kila Ka'aihue	KC	19	171.0	198	2	.990	4	5				4	2	.500	35	-1	+2	+1	+2	0	+2	+2	1		0	-3	-2	-
Don Kelly	Det	15	56.0	55	0	1.000	0	2				2	1	.500	18	+1	0	-1	+1	0	+1	0	0		0	0	0	-
Howie Kendrick	LAA	17	113.2	130	1	.992	11	3	1	0	0	4	3	.750	22	0	0	+2	+2	-2	0	0	0	0	0	1	1	-
Adam Kennedy	Sea	36	218.0	243	2	.992	15	6	3	2	0	3	0	.000	49	+4	-1	-1	+2	0	+2	+2	2	0	0	1	3	-
Mark Kotsay	Mil	11	24.0	28	0	1.000	1	1				1	0	.000	3	0	+1	0	+1	0	+1	+1	0		0	0	0	-
Bryan LaHair	ChC	4	19.2	15	0	1.000	0	0				0	0	-	1	0	0	0	0	0	0	0	0		0	0	0	-
Brandon Laird	NYY	3	20.1	22	1	.955	2	0				2	1	.500	4	+1	+1	-1	0	0	0	0	0		0	0	0	-
Gerald Laird	StL	1	1.0	1	0	1.000	0	0				0	0	-	0							0			0	0	0	-
Adam LaRoche	Was	43	375.0	412	0	1.000	17	5	4	4	0	9	3	.333	90	+2	+1	+3	+6	+1	+7	+7	5	0	0	0	5	-
Andy LaRoche	Oak	1	8.0	15	0	1.000	1	0				0	0	-	1	0	0	0	0	0	0	0	0		0	0	0	-
DJ LeMahieu	ChC	1	8.0	8	0	1.000	1	0				0	0	-	1	0	+1	0	+1	-1	0	0	0		0	0	0	-
Brent Lillibridge	CWS	22	127.0	127	2	.984	4	1				3	1	.333	28	0	+2	-1	+2	0	+2	+2	1		0	0	1	-
Felipe Lopez	TB	6	40.0	43	1	.977	2	1				0	0	-	9	0	+1	0	+1	-1	0	0	0		0	-1	-1	-
Jose Lopez	Fla	8	53.0	45	0	1.000	5	2	1	1	0	1	0	.000	10	0	0	-1	0	0	0	-1	-1	0	0	0	-1	-
Jed Lowrie	Bos	4	12.0	12	0	1.000	0	0				0	0	-	1	0	0	-1	-1	0	-1	-1	-1		0	0	-1	-
Nick Markakis	Bal	3	18.0	16	0	1.000	1	1				1	0	.000	5	+1	0	0	+1	0	+1	+1	1		0	0	1	-
Chris Marrero	Was	31	264.1	270	2	.993	10	4	7	5	1	1	1	1.000	46	-1	0	+1	-1	+1	0	0	0	0	0	-1	-1	-
Victor Martinez	Det	6	52.0	48	0	1.000	1	0				0	0	-	13	+1	0	-1	+1	0	+1	+1	1		0	0	1	-
Joe Mather	Atl	1	9.0	11	0	1.000	0	0				0	0	-	1	0	-1	0	-1	0	-1	-1	-1		0	0	-1	-
Joe Mauer	Min	18	141.0	170	1	.994	10	6	2	0	1	3	0	.000	35	+1	+2	+2	+4	0	+4	+5	3	0	0	-2	1	-

		BASIC							BUNTS			GDP			PLUS/MINUS								RUNS SAVED					
Name	Team	G	Inn	TC	E	Pct	GFP	DM	Opp	Sac Hits	Bunt Hits	Opp	GDP	Pct	Outs Made	To His Right	Straight On	To His Left	GB	Air	Total	Enhanced	+/-	Bunt	GDP	GFP/DME	Total	Rk
John Mayberry	Phi	18	100.0	96	1	.990	3	3	2	1	0	2	1	.500	15	0	0	0	0	-1	-1	-1	-1	0	0	0	-1	-
Casey McGehee	Mil	5	5.0	6	0	1.000	0	0				0	0	-	1	0	0	0	0	0	0	0	0	0	0	0	0	-
Dallas McPherson	CWS	6	8.0	7	0	1.000	1	0				0	0	-	3	0	0	0	0	0	0	0	0	0	0	0	0	-
Russ Mitchell	LAD	6	35.0	32	1	.969	2	1				0	0	-	7	0	0	0	0	0	0	0	0	0	0	-1	-1	-
Yadier Molina	StL	2	2.0	4	1	.750	0	0				0	0	-	0	-1	0	0	-1	0	-1	-1	0	0	0	0	0	-
Melvin Mora	Ari	1	1.0	3	0	1.000	1	0				0	0	-	1	0	0	0	0	0	0	0	0	0	0	0	0	-
Logan Morrison	Fla	1	8.0	6	0	1.000	0	0				0	0	-	0	0	0	0	0	0	0	0	0	0	0	0	0	-
Mike Napoli	Tex	35	246.1	243	1	.996	9	7				2	1	.500	38	+2	0	-2	+1	-1	0	-1	0	0	-1	-1	-1	-
Efren Navarro	LAA	8	29.0	41	0	1.000	0	0				0	0	-	5	0	0	0	0	0	0	0	0	0	0	0	0	-
Laynce Nix	Was	9	47.1	48	0	1.000	0	0	1	0	1	0	0	-	11	+1	+1	-1	+1	0	+1	0	0	0	0	0	0	-
David Ortiz	Bos	2	13.0	18	0	1.000	0	0				0	0	-	1	0	0	0	0	0	0	0	0	0	0	0	0	-
Jordan Pacheco	Col	13	97.0	109	1	.991	3	3				1	1	1.000	18	-1	+2	-4	-4	-1	-5	-4	-3	0	0	0	-3	-
Chris Parmelee	Min	20	173.2	178	2	.989	8	1	3	0	2	4	1	.250	47	0	+2	+2	+3	+1	+4	+4	3	-1	0	0	2	-
Val Pascucci	NYM	1	7.0	5	1	.800	1	0				0	0	-	1	0	-1	0	-1	0	-1	-1	-1	0	0	0	-1	-
Steve Pearce	Pit	16	83.0	91	1	.989	5	0	2	2	0	3	1	.333	14	-1	+1	0	0	0	0	0	0	0	0	1	1	-
Jhonny Peralta	Det	1	2.0	1	0	1.000	0	0				0	0	-	1	0	0	0	0	0	0	0	0	0	0	0	0	-
Brett Pill	SF	14	110.2	115	0	1.000	7	1	3	2	0	2	2	1.000	24	+1	+1	+2	+3	0	+3	+3	2	1	1	1	4	-
Trevor Plouffe	Min	1	1.0	0	0	-	0	0				0	0	-	0							0		0	0	0	0	-
Jorge Posada	NYY	14	104.0	81	1	.988	3	3				0	0	-	14	0	-1	0	0	-1	-1	-1	0	0	0	0	0	-
Buster Posey	SF	2	18.0	18	0	1.000	0	1				1	1	1.000	3	0	0	0	+1	0	+1	+1	0	0	0	0	0	-
Landon Powell	Oak	1	8.0	10	0	1.000	0	0				0	0	-	2	0	0	0	+1	0	+1	+1	0	0	0	0	0	-
Martin Prado	Atl	2	13.1	13	0	1.000	2	0				0	0	-	2	0	0	0	0	0	0	0	0	0	0	0	0	-
Ryan Raburn	Det	2	6.0	6	0	1.000	0	0				0	0	-	1	0	0	0	0	0	0	0	0	0	0	0	0	-
Mark Reynolds	Bal	44	375.2	392	5	.987	31	8	2	1	0	3	1	.333	69	-2	0	-1	-4	0	-4	-3	-2	0	1	0	-1	-
Juan Rivera	2 tms	38	303.2	305	3	.990	11	2	2	0	1	3	1	.333	54	0	-1	+1	0	0	0	0	0	0	0	0	0	-
Anthony Rizzo	SD	45	341.2	344	2	.994	13	6	5	4	0	5	1	.200	62	+1	-1	+2	+3	-1	+2	+2	2	0	0	0	2	-
Ivan Rodriguez	Was	1	1.0	1	0	1.000	0	0				0	0	-	0							0		0	0	0	0	-
Luis Rodriguez	Sea	1	2.0	3	0	1.000	0	0				0	0	-	0							0		0	0	0	0	-
Sean Rodriguez	TB	5	29.0	25	0	1.000	1	0	2	0	0	0	0	-	7	+1	0	-1	0	0	0	0	0	0	0	0	0	-
Adam Rosales	Oak	5	38.0	38	0	1.000	0	1				2	0	.000	6	-1	0	0	-1	+1	0	0	0	0	0	0	0	-
Pablo Sandoval	SF	6	51.2	60	0	1.000	2	2				0	0	-	11	+1	0	0	+1	0	+1	+1	1	0	0	-1	0	-
Jerry Sands	LAD	6	26.0	28	0	1.000	1	0	1	1	0	0	0	-	4	0	0	0	0	0	0	0	0	0	0	0	0	-
Josh Satin	NYM	8	44.0	53	0	1.000	4	0	2	0	2	0	0	-	13	+1	0	+1	+1	0	+1	+2	1	0	0	0	1	-
Luke Scott	Bal	12	95.0	90	0	1.000	2	1				2	2	1.000	17	0	0	-2	0	0	0	-1	-1	0	0	0	-1	-
Brandon Snyder	Bal	5	40.0	45	1	.978	2	0	1	1	0	0	0	-	6	0	0	-1	-1	0	-1	-1	-1	0	0	0	-1	-
Matt Stairs	Was	4	19.1	12	0	1.000	0	1				1	0	.000	2	0	-1	0	-1	0	-1	-1	-1	0	0	0	-1	-
Chris Stewart	SF	3	8.0	5	0	1.000	0	0				0	0	-	1	0	0	0	0	0	0	0	0	0	0	0	0	-
Drew Sutton	Bos	5	12.0	14	0	1.000	0	0				1	0	.000	3	0	0	0	0	0	0	0	0	0	0	0	0	-
Nick Swisher	NYY	11	44.0	31	0	1.000	5	0				0	0	-	4	0	0	-3	-1	0	-1	-3	-2	0	0	0	-2	-
Craig Tatum	Bal	1	2.0	1	0	1.000	0	1				0	0	-	0	0	0	0	0	0	0	0	0	0	0	0	0	-
Mark Teahen	2 tms	18	44.0	49	0	1.000	2	1	1	0	0	0	0	-	8	-1	-1	0	-2	0	-2	-2	-1	0	0	0	-1	-
Dayan Viciedo	CWS	4	21.0	19	0	1.000	0	2				0	0	-	4	0	0	0	0	0	0	0	0	0	0	-1	-1	-
Omar Vizquel	CWS	1	3.0	2	0	1.000	0	0				0	0	-	2	0	0	0	0	0	0	0	0	0	0	0	0	-
Matt Wieters	Bal	1	8.0	4	0	1.000	0	0				0	0	-	0	0	0	0	0	0	0	0	0	0	0	0	0	-
Ty Wigginton	Col	36	191.0	193	0	1.000	5	5	1	0	0	4	1	.250	37	-1	-3	0	-4	0	-4	-5	-3	0	0	0	-3	-
Bobby Wilson	LAA	6	11.0	7	0	1.000	0	0				0	0	-	1	0	0	0	0	0	0	0	0	0	0	0	0	-
Josh Wilson	Mil	1	1.0	0	0	-	0	0				0	0	-	0							0		0	0	0	0	-
Brandon Wood	2 tms	10	41.0	45	0	1.000	2	0				0	0	-	10	0	0	0	0	0	0	0	0	0	0	0	0	-
Kevin Youkilis	Bos	6	44.2	42	0	1.000	2	0	2	2	0	0	0	-	9	0	+1	0	+1	0	+1	+1	1	0	0	0	1	-
Michael Young	Tex	36	302.0	283	3	.989	8	8	2	1	1	4	3	.750	33	-1	-1	-3	-4	+1	-3	-4	-3	0	0	-2	-5	-
2011 MLB Totals						.994	1996	778		300	83			.426														

All Other Second Basemen

Name	Team	BASIC							GDP			PLUS/MINUS							RUNS SAVED				
		G	Inn	TC	E	Pct	GFP	DM	Opps	GDP	Pct	Outs Made	To His Right	Straight On	To His Left	GB	Air	Total	+/-	GDP	GFP/DME	Total	Rank
Ryan Adams	Bal	26	213.0	111	2	.982	10	7	22	14	.636	63	-3	-2	0	-5	+1	-4	-3	0	0	-3	-
Alexi Amarista	LAA	14	93.2	56	2	.964	7	2	11	8	.727	31	-1	0	0	-2	+2	0	0	0	0	0	-
Alfredo Amezaga	2 tms	16	127.0	74	1	.986	10	6	9	7	.778	44	-1	-2	+2	-1	-1	-2	-2	0	0	-2	-
Mike Aviles	2 tms	27	191.2	113	3	.973	8	11	26	14	.538	70	-2	0	+2	0	+2	+2	2	-1	-2	-1	-
Jeff Baker	ChC	18	119.2	64	1	.984	2	2	14	8	.571	38	+2	+1	-1	+2	-2	0	1	-1	0	0	-
Wilson Betemit	KC	1	5.0	4	0	1.000	0	0	2	1	.500	1	0	0	-1	-1	0	-1	-1	0	0	-1	-
Andres Blanco	Tex	5	19.0	15	0	1.000	0	0	1	1	1.000	9	+1	0	0	+1	0	+1	1	0	0	1	-
Willie Bloomquist	Ari	1	8.0	1	0	1.000	0	1	0	0	-	0	-1	0	0	-1	-1	-2	-1	0	0	-1	-
Emilio Bonifacio	Fla	5	28.0	12	0	1.000	1	1	2	1	.500	8	-1	0	0	-1	+1	0	0	0	0	0	-
Jason Bourgeois	Hou	2	7.0	3	0	1.000	1	0	1	1	1.000	2	-1	0	0	-1	0	-1	0	0	0	0	-
Manny Burriss	SF	39	230.0	142	3	.979	15	4	33	23	.697	75	0	-4	+2	-2	+1	-1	-1	1	0	0	-
Miguel Cairo	Cin	13	80.0	40	0	1.000	1	3	9	6	.667	31	+1	+2	+2	+5	-1	+4	3	0	0	3	-
Jorge Cantu	SD	1	1.0	0	0	-	0	0	0	0	-	0						0		0		0	-
Juan Castro	LAD	4	23.0	14	0	1.000	2	0	1	1	1.000	11	-1	-1	0	-2	0	-2	-1	0	0	-1	-
Ronny Cedeno	Pit	1	9.0	3	0	1.000	0	0	1	0	.000	3	0	0	0	0	0	0	0	0	0	0	-
Francisco Cervelli	NYY	1	2.0	1	0	1.000	0	0	1	0	.000	1	0	0	0	0	0	0	0	0	0	0	-
Brooks Conrad	Atl	10	45.1	21	0	1.000	3	0	4	4	1.000	11	0	0	0	-1	0	-1	-1	0	0	-1	-
Alex Cora	Was	5	24.2	10	1	.900	0	1	1	0	.000	3	0	0	-1	-1	+1	0	0	0	-1	-1	-
Craig Counsell	Mil	25	107.2	55	0	1.000	5	1	11	9	.818	36	+1	0	+2	+3	+1	+4	3	1	0	4	-
Allen Craig	StL	8	41.0	17	0	1.000	1	2	3	1	.333	12	-1	0	0	-1	0	-1	0	0	0	0	-
Tony Cruz	StL	1	1.0	0	0	-	0	0	0	0	-	0						0		0		0	-
Michael Cuddyer	Min	17	140.0	88	1	.989	5	8	17	7	.412	65	+1	+1	-7	-5	-1	-6	-5	-2	0	-7	-
Chase d'Arnaud	Pit	1	3.0	2	0	1.000	0	0	0	0	-	1	0	0	0	0	0	0	0	0	0	0	-
Blake Davis	Bal	18	140.0	62	2	.968	5	3	9	7	.778	39	+2	0	+1	+3	0	+3	2	0	0	2	-
Ivan De Jesus	LAD	11	62.2	34	1	.971	3	0	6	3	.500	26	-1	-1	-2	-4	+2	-2	-2	-1	0	-3	-
Mark DeRosa	SF	2	2.1	2	0	1.000	0	0	0	0	-	1	0	0	+1	+1	0	+1	1	0	0	1	-
Daniel Descalso	StL	18	82.2	58	0	1.000	4	2	9	6	.667	36	0	-3	+2	0	-1	-1	-1	0	0	-1	-
Blake DeWitt	ChC	19	126.2	80	2	.975	7	3	16	8	.500	39	+1	-1	-1	-1	+1	0	0	-1	0	-1	-
Brian Dinkelman	Min	11	89.0	56	0	1.000	2	3	14	9	.643	32	0	0	-3	-3	-2	-5	-3	0	0	-3	-
Jason Donald	Cle	19	169.2	87	1	.989	5	7	18	10	.556	59	+1	+1	-1	+1	+1	+2	1	0	-1	0	-
Matt Downs	Hou	27	162.0	86	3	.965	6	6	13	8	.615	51	-2	-2	-2	-6	-1	-7	-6	0	0	-6	-
Brad Emaus	NYM	11	83.1	53	0	1.000	2	6	11	5	.455	38	-1	+1	0	-1	-1	-2	-1	-1	-1	-3	-
Eduardo Escobar	CWS	2	3.0	3	0	1.000	2	0	1	1	1.000	1	0	0	0	0	0	0	0	0	0	0	-
Adam Everett	Cle	8	44.1	28	3	.893	0	1	5	3	.600	17	-1	-3	+2	-1	0	-1	-1	0	0	-1	-
Mike Fontenot	SF	23	155.2	82	3	.963	4	4	11	6	.545	54	-1	-1	-2	-4	0	-4	-3	0	-1	-4	-
Logan Forsythe	SD	23	147.1	84	4	.952	13	2	17	12	.706	36	-2	0	+1	-2	+3	+1	1	0	1	2	-
Todd Frazier	Cin	2	8.0	3	0	1.000	0	0	1	1	1.000	2	0	0	0	0	0	0	0	0	0	0	-
Esteban German	Tex	2	10.0	3	0	1.000	0	0	1	1	1.000	3	0	0	0	0	0	0	0	0	0	0	-
Johnny Giavotella	KC	46	385.1	177	5	.972	23	12	27	16	.593	119	0	-3	+2	-1	-1	-2	-1	-1	1	-1	-
Alberto Gonzalez	SD	41	243.1	116	2	.983	11	3	17	13	.765	65	-1	-4	+4	0	0	0	0	1	0	1	-
Taylor Green	Mil	7	26.0	15	0	1.000	0	0	1	0	.000	11	0	0	+1	+1	0	+1	1	0	0	1	-
Tyler Greene	StL	25	136.1	60	3	.950	4	5	11	6	.545	40	-2	-3	+2	-3	-1	-4	-3	0	0	-3	-
Carlos Guillen	Det	25	215.2	119	2	.983	3	6	22	18	.818	71	-1	-1	-2	-4	0	-4	-2	1	0	-1	-
Jerry Hairston	2 tms	30	199.2	102	3	.971	10	2	12	10	.833	63	+1	0	+1	+2	-1	+1	1	1	1	3	-
Scott Hairston	NYM	1	0.2	0	0	-	0	0	0	0	-	0						0		0		0	-
Bill Hall	2 tms	51	387.2	197	6	.970	15	14	42	18	.429	101	-4	0	-6	-11	+4	-7	-5	-3	0	-8	-
Willie Harris	NYM	10	66.1	32	0	1.000	0	1	4	2	.500	20	-1	+1	-2	-2	-1	-3	-2	0	0	-2	-
Josh Harrison	Pit	6	41.0	26	2	.923	3	0	3	3	1.000	16	+1	0	-1	0	0	0	1	0	-1	0	-
Wes Helms	Fla	2	7.0	2	0	1.000	0	0	1	0	.000	1	0	0	0	0	0	0	0	0	0	0	-
Chin-lung Hu	NYM	10	29.2	17	1	.941	0	0	2	1	.500	11	-1	0	0	-1	0	-1	-1	0	0	-1	-
Luke Hughes	Min	37	301.1	189	2	.989	11	2	36	25	.694	111	-2	+2	+1	+1	+2	+3	3	1	1	5	-
Joe Inglett	Hou	3	16.0	15	0	1.000	3	3	6	3	.500	8	0	-1	-1	-2	0	-2	-1	0	1	0	-
Cesar Izturis	Bal	3	22.1	11	1	.909	0	2	2	0	.000	8	0	+1	-1	0	0	0	0	0	-1	-1	-
Paul Janish	Cin	5	44.0	22	1	.955	5	0	6	5	.833	11	+1	-1	-1	-1	-1	-2	-1	0	1	0	-
Elliot Johnson	TB	9	38.0	18	1	.944	1	2	1	0	.000	15	0	-1	+1	0	0	0	0	0	0	0	-
Adam Kennedy	Sea	34	293.2	148	1	.993	10	6	25	20	.800	100	-4	0	+1	-3	0	-3	-2	1	-1	-2	-
Jason Kipnis	Cle	36	305.0	164	6	.963	11	10	29	13	.448	112	-1	+1	-1	-1	-1	-2	-1	-1	0	-2	-
Pete Kozma	StL	10	28.2	19	0	1.000	4	1	3	3	1.000	11	+1	0	-1	+1	0	+1	1	0	0	1	-
Andy LaRoche	Oak	8	48.0	16	0	1.000	1	2	5	2	.400	11	+1	0	-1	0	0	0	0	0	0	0	-
DJ LeMahieu	ChC	15	77.2	38	0	1.000	3	1	8	5	.625	23	+1	+1	-1	+1	-2	-1	-1	0	1	0	-
Brent Lillibridge	CWS	6	19.0	9	0	1.000	0	1	2	2	1.000	6	-1	0	-2	-3	0	-3	-2	0	0	-2	-
Steve Lombardozzi	Was	3	20.0	11	0	1.000	0	0	0	0	-	8	0	0	+1	0	0	0	0	0	0	0	-
Felipe Lopez	Mil	11	82.0	43	1	.977	2	1	9	4	.444	28	0	0	+1	0	+1	+1	1	0	0	1	-
Jose Lopez	2 tms	20	129.0	63	0	1.000	4	1	18	11	.611	38	+1	+1	0	+1	0	+1	1	0	0	1	-
Jed Lowrie	Bos	1	3.0	2	0	1.000	0	0	0	0	-	2	0	0	0	0	0	0	0	0	0	0	-
Julio Lugo	Atl	2	2.2	0	0	-	0	0	0	0	-	0	0	0	0	0	0	0	0	0	0	0	-
Russell Martin	NYY	1	2.0	1	0	1.000	0	0	0	0	-	0	0	0	0	0	0	0	0	0	0	0	-
Michael Martinez	Phi	19	83.0	48	1	.979	3	2	9	8	.889	34	+2	0	+1	+3	+1	+4	3	0	0	3	-
Mike McCoy	Tor	10	84.0	49	1	.980	5	3	8	3	.375	37	0	0	+1	+1	+2	+3	2	-1	0	1	-
John McDonald	Tor	21	148.2	82	1	.988	7	6	15	12	.800	57	+2	-2	+3	+3	+1	+4	3	0	-1	2	-
Jose Morales	Col	2	3.0	2	0	1.000	0	0	0	0	-	2	0	0	0	+1	0	+1	1	0	0	1	-
Daniel Murphy	NYM	24	168.1	93	2	.978	6	5	8	4	.500	67	0	0	0	0	-2	-2	-2	0	0	-2	-
Donnie Murphy	Fla	1	1.0	0	0	-	0	0	0	0	-	0						0		0		0	-
Chris Nelson	Col	29	208.2	97	3	.969	6	6	24	16	.667	59	-2	-4	-2	-7	-1	-8	-6	0	0	-6	-
Tsuyoshi Nishioka	Min	6	49.2	26	2	.923	2	2	10	8	.800	8	-2	0	-2	-3	0	-3	-3	0	0	-3	-
Jayson Nix	Tor	4	15.1	10	0	1.000	0	0	2	1	.500	9	0	0	0	0	0	0	0	0	0	0	-
Eduardo Nunez	NYY	16	82.0	40	0	1.000	2	2	8	4	.500	31	+1	+1	-2	0	+1	+1	0	0	0	0	-
Pete Orr	Phi	29	188.2	114	2	.982	11	3	21	14	.667	67	+1	0	-1	0	+1	+1	0	0	0	0	-
Jordan Pacheco	Col	2	16.0	4	0	1.000	0	1	0	0	-	3	0	0	-1	-1	0	-1	-1	0	0	-1	-
Andy Parrino	SD	3	25.0	15	0	1.000	1	0	2	2	1.000	10	-1	0	+1	0	+1	+1	1	0	0	1	-
Eric Patterson	SD	10	73.0	41	2	.951	1	3	11	7	.636	16	0	0	-1	-1	0	-1	0	0	-1	-1	-
Ramiro Pena	NYY	7	31.1	16	0	1.000	1	0	5	2	.400	9	0	0	-1	-2	0	-2	-1	0	0	-1	-
Cord Phelps	Cle	20	153.0	75	5	.933	3	4	19	8	.421	45	-2	-2	0	-4	0	-4	-3	-1	-2	-6	-
Trevor Plouffe	Min	17	127.0	69	1	.986	3	8	20	9	.450	39	-6	0	0	-6	-2	-8	-6	-1	-1	-8	-
Placido Polanco	Phi	1	1.0	1	0	1.000	0	0	0	0	-	0						0		0		0	-

417

		BASIC							GDP			PLUS/MINUS							RUNS SAVED				
Name	Team	G	Inn	TC	E	Pct	GFP	DM	Opps	GDP	Pct	Outs Made	To His Right	Straight On	To His Left	GB	Air	Total	+/-	GDP	GFP/ DME	Total	Rank
Jorge Posada	NYY	1	1.0	1	0	1.000	0	0	0	0	-	1	0	0	0	0	0	0	0	0	0	0	-
Nick Punto	StL	45	243.0	151	2	.987	9	6	34	24	.706	95	0	0	+3	+2	+1	+3	2	0	1	3	-
Omar Quintanilla	Tex	5	23.0	11	0	1.000	0	1	3	2	.667	7	0	0	0	0	-1	-1	0	0	0	0	-
Ryan Raburn	Det	56	401.0	201	10	.950	13	10	34	20	.588	123	0	-1	-5	-6	-3	-9	-7	0	-1	-8	-
Edgar Renteria	Cin	4	7.0	6	0	1.000	0	0	0	0	-	6	0	0	0	+1	0	+1	0	0	0	0	-
Will Rhymes	Det	24	187.1	91	2	.978	8	5	14	12	.857	61	-4	-2	0	-6	+1	-5	-4	1	0	-3	-
Brian Roberts	Bal	39	347.0	191	3	.984	17	5	37	23	.622	125	0	-2	+1	-1	+1	0	0	0	1	1	-
Ryan Roberts	Ari	28	212.2	125	4	.968	6	2	27	17	.630	72	+1	0	0	+1	-1	0	0	0	0	0	-
Josh Rodriguez	Pit	1	5.0	4	0	1.000	0	0	0	0	-	3	0	0	0	0	0	0	0	0	0	0	-
Luis Rodriguez	Sea	7	32.0	21	1	.952	2	0	5	2	.400	10	0	-2	0	-2	0	-2	-2	0	0	-2	-
Sean Rodriguez	TB	48	352.2	180	2	.989	25	9	30	23	.767	113	+2	-2	+1	+1	+1	+2	2	1	0	3	-
Adam Rosales	Oak	3	19.0	7	0	1.000	0	0	2	1	.500	5	+1	0	0	+1	0	+1	1	0	0	1	-
Angel Sanchez	Hou	19	134.1	79	0	1.000	6	1	21	18	.857	42	+3	+2	+2	+6	+1	+7	5	1	1	7	-
Marco Scutaro	Bos	2	18.0	10	1	.900	0	0	1	0	.000	6	0	+1	0	+1	0	+1	0	0	0	0	-
Kyle Seager	Sea	3	24.0	9	0	1.000	0	0	0	0	-	8	0	0	-1	-1	0	-1	0	0	0	0	-
Justin Sellers	LAD	12	90.2	49	0	1.000	8	2	7	3	.429	30	0	0	0	+1	+3	+4	3	0	0	3	-
Scott Sizemore	2 tms	18	151.1	84	3	.964	8	3	13	11	.846	61	+3	-1	0	+2	-1	+1	1	1	0	2	-
Eric Sogard	Oak	3	27.0	15	1	.933	4	1	2	2	1.000	10	0	+1	0	+1	0	+1	1	0	0	1	-
Nate Spears	Bos	1	1.0	0	0	-	0	0	0	0	-	0						0		0		0	-
Drew Sutton	Bos	7	18.0	9	1	.889	0	1	2	0	.000	4	0	-2	-1	-3	0	-3	-2	0	0	-2	-
Miguel Tejada	SF	4	33.0	18	0	1.000	2	2	2	2	1.000	12	0	0	-1	-1	0	-1	-1	0	0	-1	-
Ryan Theriot	StL	35	190.1	113	1	.991	2	4	27	24	.889	65	+1	0	+2	+4	-2	+2	2	1	-1	2	-
Joe Thurston	Fla	1	9.0	7	0	1.000	0	0	1	1	1.000	5	0	0	0	0	0	0	0	0	0	0	-
Matt Tolbert	Min	36	244.0	142	3	.979	14	3	24	20	.833	78	-2	0	+2	+1	+3	+4	3	1	1	5	-
Juan Uribe	LAD	18	137.0	68	6	.912	6	2	17	12	.706	40	+1	0	-1	0	0	0	0	0	0	0	-
Chris Valaika	Cin	1	4.2	4	0	1.000	0	0	0	0	-	3	-1	0	0	-1	0	-1	0	0	0	0	-
Luis Valbuena	Cle	11	81.0	43	0	1.000	3	1	11	7	.636	22	-1	+1	0	0	0	0	0	0	0	0	-
Wilson Valdez	Phi	45	316.2	175	2	.989	12	9	33	19	.576	106	+1	+3	-7	-3	-3	-6	-5	0	-1	-6	-
Gil Velazquez	LAA	2	11.0	7	0	1.000	0	0	1	1	1.000	5	0	0	0	+1	0	+1	1	0	0	1	-
Eugenio Velez	LAD	11	50.1	23	0	1.000	0	1	5	2	.400	17	0	0	0	0	0	0	0	0	0	0	-
Omar Vizquel	CWS	16	130.1	61	1	.984	5	3	12	7	.583	42	-3	-1	+2	-1	0	-1	-1	0	-1	-2	-
Jack Wilson	Sea	45	342.1	192	0	1.000	5	5	37	25	.676	114	+2	+2	+2	+5	+3	+8	7	0	0	7	-
Josh Wilson	Mil	10	64.0	33	0	1.000	2	4	6	5	.833	22	+1	0	+1	+1	0	+1	1	0	0	1	-
Brandon Wood	Pit	3	9.0	3	0	1.000	0	0	1	0	.000	1	0	0	0	0	0	0	0	0	0	0	-
Chris Woodward	Tor	2	11.0	5	0	1.000	0	0	1	1	1.000	5	0	0	0	0	0	0	0	0	0	0	-
Danny Worth	Det	15	53.0	20	0	1.000	0	0	4	2	.500	13	0	0	0	0	0	0	0	0	0	0	-
Eric Young	Col	7	43.0	22	1	.955	2	1	5	5	1.000	10	-1	0	0	-1	0	-1	0	0	0	0	-
Michael Young	Tex	14	120.1	57	0	1.000	0	3	17	9	.529	26	-1	-1	-1	-4	0	-4	-3	0	0	-3	-
2011 MLB Totals						.984	1700	962	4395	2808	.639												

All Other Third Basemen

BASIC									BUNTS			GDP			PLUS/MINUS								RUNS SAVED					
										Sac	Bunt				Outs	To His	Straight	To His								GFP/		
Name	Team	G	Inn	TC	E	Pct	GFP	DM	Opp	Hits	Hits	Opp	GDP	Pct	Made	Right	On	Left	GB	Air	Total	Enhanced	+/-	Bunt	GDP	DME	Total	Rk
Yonder Alonso	Cin	1	9.0	0	0	-	0	0				0	0	-	0	0	0	0	0	0	0	0	0		0		0	-
Alfredo Amezaga	Col	2	4.1	0	0	-	0	0				0	0	-	0	0	0	0	0	0	0	0	0		0		0	-
Robert Andino	Bal	22	172.0	58	1	.983	8	3	2	0	2	4	3	.750	49	0	+3	-2	+2	0	+2	+2	1	0	0	0	1	-
Alex Avila	Det	1	8.0	2	1	.500	0	0	1	0	1	0	0	-	1	-1	0	0	0	0	0	0	0	-1	0	0	-1	-
Mike Aviles	2 tms	46	347.2	106	8	.925	11	8	9	4	4	12	4	.333	87	-2	0	0	-2	+1	-1	-1	-1	0	0	0	-1	-
Jeff Baker	ChC	11	54.0	10	0	1.000	0	1	2	0	1	0	0	-	7	-1	0	-3	-3	0	-3	-3	-3	0	0	0	-3	-
Jose Bautista	Tor	25	205.0	81	2	.975	7	4	1	0	1	5	1	.200	74	+3	+2	+2	+6	+2	+8	+8	6	-1	0	0	5	-
Josh Bell	Bal	21	134.0	43	3	.930	9	8	2	1	0	3	1	.333	34	-1	0	+1	-1	+1	0	+1	0	-1	0	-1	-2	-
Brian Bixler	Was	14	48.1	14	1	.929	1	0	1	0	0	0	0	-	10	+1	-1	0	0	0	0	0	0	0	0	0	0	-
Casey Blake	LAD	45	383.2	112	6	.946	7	0	2	1	1	8	4	.500	85	+2	+3	-2	+3	0	+3	+4	3	0	0	1	4	-
Andres Blanco	Tex	6	18.0	5	1	.800	0	0				0	0	-	4	0	0	0	0	-1	-1	-1	-1		0	0	-1	-
Geoff Blum	Ari	14	103.0	29	0	1.000	2	3	4	2	2	3	2	.667	26	0	0	0	+1	0	+1	+1	0	0	0	0	0	-
Emilio Bonifacio	Fla	36	245.2	67	3	.955	5	5	7	5	1	9	8	.889	51	-3	+4	+1	+1	+1	+2	+3	2	0	0	-2	0	-
Russell Branyan	LAA	2	3.0	1	0	1.000	0	0				1	0	.000	1	0	0	0	0	0	0	0	0		0	0	0	-
Manny Burriss	SF	2	17.0	7	1	.857	0	0				0	0	-	6	0	-1	0	-1	0	-1	-1	0		0	0	0	-
Sean Burroughs	Ari	20	132.0	38	1	.974	3	1	1	0	1	6	5	.833	35	-3	0	+2	+1	0	+1	-1	0	0	0	0	0	-
Orlando Cabrera	2 tms	5	29.0	4	0	1.000	0	2				0	0	-	3	-2	0	0	-2	0	-2	-3	-2		0	0	-2	-
Jorge Cantu	SD	10	84.0	20	1	.950	2	3	3	1	1	2	1	.500	16	+1	+1	-1	+1	0	+1	+1	1	0	0	0	1	-
Matt Carpenter	StL	5	39.0	13	0	1.000	2	3	2	1	1	0	0	-	12	-1	0	0	-1	0	-1	-1	-1	0	0	0	-1	-
Juan Castro	LAD	1	7.0	3	0	1.000	0	0	2	1	1	0	0	-	2	0	0	0	0	0	0	0	0	-1	0	0	-1	-
Francisco Cervelli	NYY	2	2.0	0	0	-	0	0				0	0	-	0							0			0		0	-
Eric Chavez	NYY	42	305.2	86	0	1.000	12	3	8	3	2	7	6	.857	73	+3	0	-2	0	+1	+1	+2	2	0	1	0	3	-
Pedro Ciriaco	Pit	2	6.0	3	0	1.000	0	0				1	1	1.000	3	0	+1	0	+1	0	+1	+1	1		0	0	1	-
Brooks Conrad	Atl	8	56.0	20	1	.950	1	0	1	0	0	1	0	.000	14	+1	+1	0	+1	0	+1	+1	1	0	0	0	1	-
Alex Cora	Was	31	167.2	46	1	.978	6	2	1	0	0	5	5	1.000	41	+1	-2	+2	+1	0	+1	+1	1	0	1	0	2	-
Craig Counsell	Mil	14	86.0	25	1	.960	3	1	2	0	1	0	0	-	20	+1	+1	+1	+2	0	+2	+2	2	0	0	0	2	-
Allen Craig	StL	2	11.0	2	0	1.000	0	1				0	0	-	2	0	0	-1	-1	0	-1	-1	-1		0	0	-1	-
Tony Cruz	StL	3	11.0	2	0	1.000	0	0				0	0	-	2	0	0	0	+1	0	+1	+1	0		0	0	0	-
Chase d'Arnaud	Pit	12	95.0	42	3	.929	5	0	2	2	0	4	4	1.000	35	+1	+3	-1	+2	0	+2	+3	2	0	0	0	2	-
James Darnell	SD	12	88.1	22	2	.909	0	3	1	0	1	4	1	.250	16	-1	-3	+1	-3	0	-3	-3	-2	0	0	0	-2	-
Blake Davis	Bal	1	8.0	3	2	.333	0	2				1	1	1.000	1	-2	-1	0	-3	-1	-4	-4	-3		0	0	-3	-
Chris Davis	2 tms	26	222.1	57	8	.860	2	1	2	0	2	5	4	.800	44	-4	+1	-2	-5	0	-5	-6	-3	-1	0	1	-3	-
Mark DeRosa	SF	16	121.0	34	2	.941	4	3	2	1	0	3	2	.667	26	-2	0	0	-1	+1	0	-1	-1	0	0	0	-1	-
Blake DeWitt	ChC	14	79.0	33	5	.848	2	4	1	1	0	3	2	.667	23	-3	0	+1	-2	0	-2	-2	-2	0	0	-1	-3	-
Matt Dominguez	Fla	16	122.0	29	2	.931	2	6				2	1	.500	25	0	-1	-1	-1	-2	-3	-4	-3		0	0	-3	-
Jason Donald	Cle	4	30.2	8	0	1.000	0	0				1	0	.000	8	+1	0	0	+1	-1	0	0	0		0	0	0	-
Matt Downs	Hou	19	126.0	25	2	.920	3	4	1	0	1	3	3	1.000	19	0	0	-1	-2	-1	-3	-3	-2	0	0	0	-2	-
E. Encarnacion	Tor	36	273.2	74	8	.892	4	5				4	1	.250	57	-2	-4	+1	-6	-1	-7	-5	-4		0	0	-4	-
Nick Evans	NYM	2	3.0	1	0	1.000	0	0	1	1	0	0	0	-	0	0	0	0	0	0	0	0	0	0	0	0	0	-
Adam Everett	Cle	16	114.2	31	1	.968	5	1				6	4	.667	28	+1	0	-1	+1	0	+1	+1	1		0	0	1	-
Mike Fontenot	SF	8	30.0	6	0	1.000	2	0	1	1	0	1	1	1.000	5	0	0	0	0	0	0	0	0	0	0	0	0	-
Logan Forsythe	SD	26	184.0	67	1	.985	10	2	4	1	0	5	4	.800	56	+2	+2	0	+5	+1	+6	+5	4	1	0	0	5	-
Juan Francisco	Cin	24	186.2	52	2	.962	3	6	2	1	1	2	1	.500	43	0	+3	-1	+1	0	+1	+2	1	0	0	-2	-1	-
Todd Frazier	Cin	27	207.2	64	2	.969	7	3	3	1	1	4	1	.250	49	0	+1	+2	+3	-1	+2	+2	1	0	0	0	1	-
Mat Gamel	Mil	3	19.0	6	1	.833	0	0				0	0	-	4	0	0	0	0	0	0	0	0		0	0	0	-
Esteban German	Tex	4	13.0	3	0	1.000	0	1				0	0	-	3	+1	0	-1	0	0	0	0	0		0	0	0	-
Conor Gillaspie	SF	4	22.0	3	0	1.000	1	0				0	0	-	2	0	0	0	0	-1	-1	-1	-1		0	0	-1	-
Alberto Gonzalez	SD	21	129.1	33	1	.970	5	1	2	0	1	4	2	.500	30	+2	+1	0	+3	0	+3	+3	2	0	0	0	2	-
Taylor Green	Mil	5	31.0	9	0	1.000	0	2				2	2	1.000	9	-1	+1	0	0	-1	-1	-2	-1		0	0	-1	-
Jerry Hairston	2 tms	49	370.0	102	6	.941	8	8	5	3	2	7	3	.429	80	0	-4	+1	-3	0	-3	-3	-2	-1	0	1	-2	-
Willie Harris	NYM	7	48.0	16	1	.938	3	2	2	1	1	5	0	.000	13	-2	-1	0	-3	0	-3	-4	-3	0	-1	0	-4	-
Josh Harrison	Pit	50	363.1	137	6	.956	15	7	5	3	0	9	6	.667	114	+7	+1	+1	+9	+1	+10	+10	8	1	0	0	9	-
Wes Helms	Fla	33	179.0	48	3	.938	6	0	2	1	0	1	0	.000	37	+1	-2	-1	-3	0	-3	-3	-2	0	0	1	-1	-
Diory Hernandez	Atl	6	37.0	7	2	.714	0	2	1	0	1	0	0	-	5	-1	+1	-1	-1	0	-1	-1	-1	0	0	0	-1	-
Jonathan Herrera	Col	9	28.2	5	0	1.000	1	0				0	0	-	5	0	0	0	+1	-1	0	0	0		0	0	0	-
Brandon Hicks	Atl	6	16.1	3	1	.667	0	0				0	0	-	2	0	0	0	0	0	0	0	0		0	0	0	-
Luke Hughes	Min	13	104.0	39	2	.949	3	6	1	0	1	4	2	.500	35	0	0	+1	0	+1	+1	+3	2	0	0	0	2	-
Chris Iannetta	Col	1	1.0	0	0	-	0	0				0	0	-	0	0	0	0	0	0	0	0	0		0		0	-
Joe Inglett	Hou	2	4.0	1	0	1.000	0	1				0	0	-	1	-1	0	0	-1	0	-1	-1	-1		0	0	-1	-
Cesar Izturis	Bal	1	1.0	0	0	-	0	0				0	0	-	0	0	0	0	0	0	0	0	0		0		0	-
Maicer Izturis	LAA	37	301.2	84	3	.964	10	3	4	2	1	2	1	.500	68	-1	+3	+1	+3	0	+3	+3	2	0	0	0	2	-
Conor Jackson	2 tms	7	29.2	10	0	1.000	4	0	1	1	0	2	0	.000	9	0	0	0	+1	0	+1	+1	1	0	0	0	1	-
Paul Janish	Cin	8	51.2	9	1	.889	1	0				0	0	-	8	0	-1	0	-1	0	-1	-1	-1		0	0	-1	-
Dan Johnson	TB	3	3.0	2	0	1.000	0	0				0	0	-	2	0	0	0	0	0	0	0	0		0	0	0	-
Don Kelly	Det	45	325.0	103	4	.961	8	5	4	0	2	12	5	.417	82	0	-1	+5	+2	+1	+3	+5	4	0	0	0	4	-
Adam Kennedy	Sea	27	210.2	57	2	.965	5	6	2	0	0	3	2	.667	46	0	-1	-1	-1	-1	-2	-3	-2	1	0	0	-1	-
Pete Kozma	StL	1	1.0	0	0	-	0	0				0	0	-	0							0			0		0	-
Brandon Laird	NYY	9	40.0	10	0	1.000	0	0				2	1	.500	9	+1	0	0	+1	-1	0	0	0		0	0	0	-
Andy LaRoche	Oak	27	159.0	42	4	.905	5	0	3	3	0	5	3	.600	32	0	-3	-2	-5	0	-5	-4	-3	1	0	0	-2	-
Brett Lawrie	Tor	43	380.1	164	6	.963	19	12	4	2	1	12	5	.417	138	+3	+7	+9	+18	+1	+19	+20	15	0	-1	0	14	-
DJ LeMahieu	ChC	11	60.0	22	4	.818	2	1				3	3	1.000	17	-1	+1	0	0	0	0	0	0		0	0	0	-
Alex Liddi	Sea	14	110.0	35	1	.971	9	1				3	2	.667	30	+2	+1	-2	+1	0	+1	+1	1		0	0	1	-
S. Lombardozzi	Was	3	27.2	12	1	.917	1	0	1	1	0	0	0	-	10	-1	+1	0	+1	0	+1	+1	1	0	0	0	1	-
Felipe Lopez	2 tms	24	157.0	43	2	.953	4	3	3	0	1	1	1	1.000	36	0	-2	0	-1	0	-1	-1	-1	0	0	1	0	-
Jose Lopez	2 tms	39	288.1	78	5	.936	4	2	2	2	0	7	3	.429	67	0	0	-1	-1	0	-1	-1	0	0	-1	0	-1	-
Jed Lowrie	Bos	33	268.1	97	5	.948	5	4	5	2	2	8	5	.625	77	+5	-1	0	+3	-1	+2	+2	2	0	0	0	2	-
Julio Lugo	Atl	8	53.0	17	0	1.000	0	0	1	1	0	2	0	.000	15	0	+1	+1	+3	+1	+4	+4	3	0	0	0	3	-
Russell Martin	NYY	3	4.0	2	1	.500	0	0				0	0	-	1	0	0	0	-1	0	-1	0	0		0	0	0	-
Michael Martinez	Phi	26	218.2	63	2	.968	10	5				1	1	1.000	56	0	-3	-1	-4	+1	-3	-3	-3		0	0	-3	-
Osvaldo Martinez	Fla	1	1.0	0	0	-	0	0				0	0	-	0							0			0		0	-
Joe Mather	Atl	1	2.0	1	0	1.000	0	0				0	0	-	1	0	0	0	0	0	0	0	0		0	0	0	-
Mike McCoy	Tor	16	64.2	16	0	1.000	3	1	2	1	0	0	0	-	12	-1	0	+1	0	+1	+1	+1	0	0	0	1	1	-
John McDonald	Tor	26	162.1	58	1	.983	9	5	1	1	0	8	6	.750	51	+2	-3	+1	0	0	0	0	1	0	0	-1	0	-
Michael McKenry	Pit	1	1.0	0	0	-	0	0				0	0	-	0							0			0		0	-
Dallas McPherson	CWS	5	28.1	11	0	1.000	1	0				1	0	.000	9	0	0	0	0	0	0	0	0		0	0	0	-

		BASIC							BUNTS			GDP			PLUS/MINUS								RUNS SAVED					
Name	Team	G	Inn	TC	E	Pct	GFP	DM	Opp	Sac Hits	Bunt Hits	Opp	GDP	Pct	Outs Made	To His Right	Straight On	To His Left	GB	Air	Total	Enhanced	+/-	Bunt	GDP	GFP/ DME	Total	Rk
Russ Mitchell	LAD	11	82.2	30	0	1.000	2	1	2	2	0	0	0	-	23	0	-1	+1	0	0	0	0	0	0	0	0	0	-
Melvin Mora	Ari	31	270.1	86	3	.965	6	6	3	2	1	5	1	.200	73	+1	-1	-1	-1	0	-1	-2	-1	0	-1	-1	-3	-
Daniel Murphy	NYM	28	220.2	60	4	.933	7	1	4	2	1	4	4	1.000	48	-2	+1	+3	+1	0	+1	+2	2	0	0	0	2	-
Donnie Murphy	Fla	15	79.2	27	1	.963	1	1	3	2	1	1	0	.000	20	+1	0	0	0	0	0	0	0	-1	0	0	-1	-
Yamaico Navarro	2 tms	16	100.0	28	2	.929	1	2	4	1	1	2	1	.500	19	0	-3	0	-3	0	-3	-3	-1	0	0	0	-1	-
Chris Nelson	Col	24	130.2	48	4	.917	12	1	1	0	0	4	1	.250	40	-1	+1	+2	+3	0	+3	+2	1	0	0	1	2	-
Jayson Nix	Tor	41	334.2	118	3	.975	12	7	2	0	0	10	6	.600	99	+2	+2	+7	+11	+2	+13	+13	9	0	0	0	9	-
Eduardo Nunez	NYY	40	285.1	74	6	.919	6	5	2	1	0	7	5	.714	59	0	-3	0	-5	0	-5	-3	-2	0	0	0	-2	-
Pete Orr	Phi	3	18.0	7	0	1.000	2	0	1	0	0	0	0	-	6	+1	+1	0	+2	0	+2	+2	1	0	0	0	1	-
Jordan Pacheco	Col	7	57.0	21	2	.905	3	2				0	0	-	15	0	0	0	0	0	0	0	0	0	0	0	0	-
Jimmy Paredes	Hou	46	390.2	107	5	.953	15	17	9	6	3	4	3	.750	79	-3	-1	+3	-1	-1	-2	-2	-2	-1	0	2	-1	-
Andy Parrino	SD	11	68.1	22	0	1.000	1	0				4	2	.500	20	+2	+3	+1	+5	0	+5	+5	4		0	0	4	-
Steve Pearce	Pit	10	57.1	19	2	.895	3	1	3	0	1	1	1	1.000	12	0	-1	0	-1	0	-1	-1	-1	0	0	0	-1	-
Ramiro Pena	NYY	13	59.1	25	3	.880	1	1	2	1	0	2	2	1.000	17	-2	-1	-1	-5	0	-5	-4	-3	0	0	0	-3	-
Martin Prado	Atl	41	297.0	101	5	.950	9	5	8	4	2	10	6	.600	85	-1	+6	+2	+7	-2	+5	+5	4	1	0	1	6	-
Albert Pujols	StL	7	33.2	17	3	.824	2	1	1	1	0	3	2	.667	11	-2	+1	0	-1	0	-1	-1	-1	0	0	0	-1	-
Nick Punto	StL	7	26.1	13	1	.923	0	0	1	1	0	0	0	-	9	0	0	0	+1	0	+1	+1	0	0	0	0	0	-
Omar Quintanilla	Tex	3	13.0	4	0	1.000	0	0				0	0	-	4	0	0	0	0	0	0	0	0		0	0	0	-
Ryan Raburn	Det	4	30.0	11	1	.909	0	0	1	1	0	1	1	1.000	7	-3	0	-1	-3	0	-3	-3	-2	0	0	0	-2	-
Cody Ransom	Ari	6	35.2	21	2	.905	3	0	1	1	0	2	0	.000	13	-1	-1	+1	-1	0	-1	-1	-1	0	0	0	-1	-
Luis Rodriguez	Sea	11	88.0	17	0	1.000	1	2	1	0	1	2	2	1.000	14	+2	-3	0	-2	0	-2	-2	-1	0	0	0	-1	-
Sean Rodriguez	TB	30	172.1	60	0	1.000	10	5	2	1	1	8	5	.625	52	+2	0	+1	+3	+1	+4	+4	3	0	0	0	3	-
Andrew Romine	LAA	3	18.0	3	0	1.000	1	1				1	1	1.000	3	0	0	0	0	0	0	0	0	0	0	0	0	-
Adam Rosales	Oak	6	43.1	12	2	.833	1	2	1	0	1	1	1	1.000	9	-1	+1	-1	-2	0	-2	-2	-1	0	0	0	-1	-
Carlos Ruiz	Phi	1	1.0	0	0	-	0	0				0	0	-	0							0			0		0	-
Angel Sanchez	Hou	10	73.0	20	0	1.000	1	2				4	2	.500	18	-1	0	-1	-2	0	-2	-2	-1		0	0	-1	-
Ramon Santiago	Det	5	12.0	3	0	1.000	0	0				0	0	-	3	0	0	+1	+1	0	+1	+1	1		0	0	1	-
Josh Satin	NYM	1	5.0	0	0	-	0	0				0	0	-	0							0			0		0	-
Kyle Seager	Sea	42	335.2	120	4	.967	10	6	5	2	2	8	2	.250	104	+2	-3	+2	0	+2	+2	+3	2	0	0	0	2	-
Justin Sellers	LAD	5	36.1	15	0	1.000	1	0	2	1	0	1	0	.000	13	+1	0	0	+2	0	+2	+2	1	0	0	0	1	-
Eric Sogard	Oak	10	70.0	18	0	1.000	3	2				2	0	.000	18	+1	+1	+1	+3	+1	+4	+4	3		0	0	3	-
Ian Stewart	Col	42	284.0	85	6	.929	8	3	2	1	0	5	2	.400	65	-2	+1	+1	+1	+1	+2	+1	1	1	0	1	3	-
Drew Sutton	Bos	8	46.0	15	0	1.000	1	0	1	0	1	1	1	1.000	15	0	+1	+1	+3	0	+3	+2	2	0	0	0	2	-
Mark Teahen	2 tms	32	219.2	68	0	1.000	11	3	9	1	4	5	2	.400	57	+1	+2	0	+3	+1	+4	+4	3	0	0	0	3	-
Miguel Tejada	SF	44	372.1	130	2	.985	18	6	11	7	1	15	9	.600	105	+2	+1	+3	+6	+1	+7	+7	5	1	0	1	7	-
Jim Thome	Cle	1	0.0	0	0	-	0	0				0	0	-	0							0			0		0	-
Matt Tolbert	Min	6	37.0	5	0	1.000	0	2	1	0	1	1	1	1.000	5	0	0	0	0	0	0	0	0	-1	0	-1	-2	-
Justin Turner	NYM	36	277.2	79	4	.949	8	8	5	2	2	5	3	.600	61	-2	+3	-3	-1	+1	0	-1	-1	0	0	0	-1	-
Chris Valaika	Cin	4	33.0	17	0	1.000	2	1	1	0	1	4	2	.500	16	+1	0	-1	+1	0	+1	+1	1	0	0	0	1	-
Wilson Valdez	Phi	24	194.2	49	3	.939	1	3	5	4	1	5	4	.800	34	-1	-5	0	-5	0	-5	-5	-4	0	0	0	-4	-
Gil Velazquez	LAA	2	3.0	2	0	1.000	0	0				0	0	-	2	0	0	0	0	0	0	0	0	0	0	0	0	-
Omar Vizquel	CWS	29	182.0	44	0	1.000	2	4	4	1	2	5	2	.400	37	+3	-1	-1	0	0	0	+1	1	0	0	0	1	-
Jack Wilson	2 tms	4	21.0	7	0	1.000	2	0	1	0	1	1	1	1.000	5	0	0	0	+1	-1	0	0	0	0	0	0	0	-
Josh Wilson	Mil	13	33.1	8	1	.875	1	1	1	1	0	1	1	1.000	6	0	-1	0	-1	-1	-2	-2	-1	0	0	0	-1	-
Brandon Wood	Pit	61	377.2	113	3	.973	10	14	8	3	5	12	6	.500	97	0	+1	-1	0	-2	-2	-2	-2	-2	-1	-1	-6	-
Chris Woodward	Tor	2	10.0	2	0	1.000	0	0				0	0	-	1	0	0	0	0	0	0	0	0	0	0	0	0	-
Danny Worth	Det	13	56.1	18	1	.944	2	0				4	3	.750	15	0	-1	0	-1	0	-1	-1	-1	0	0	0	-1	-
Michael Young	Tex	40	342.0	101	5	.950	12	5	7	0	4	11	7	.636	81	-3	+1	-1	-2	-1	-3	-5	-4	0	0	1	-3	-
2011 MLB Totals						.954	1373	864	287		222			.569														

All Other Shortstops

Name	Team	G	Inn	TC	E	Pct	GFP	DM	Opps	GDP	Pct	Outs Made	To His Right	Straight On	To His Left	GB	Air	Total	+/-	GDP	GFP/ DME	Total	Rank
			BASIC						GDP				PLUS/MINUS						RUNS SAVED				
Alexi Amarista	LAA	1	3.0	0	0	-	0	0	0	0	-	0								0		0	-
Alfredo Amezaga	Col	2	15.1	7	1	.857	0	0	0	0	-	6	-1	0	0	-1	0	-1	-1	0	0	-1	-
Robert Andino	Bal	30	223.1	133	5	.962	16	6	25	17	.680	104	+4	+2	-4	+2	+2	+4	3	0	0	3	-
Mike Aviles	2 tms	14	91.0	39	1	.974	2	1	6	3	.500	29	+1	-1	+1	+1	0	+1	0	0	0	0	-
Darwin Barney	ChC	5	35.2	15	0	1.000	1	0	4	2	.500	14	+2	0	-1	+1	0	+1	1	0	0	1	-
Brian Bixler	Was	2	7.0	5	0	1.000	1	0	0	0	-	4	0	0	0	0	0	0	0	0	0	0	-
Andres Blanco	Tex	23	147.0	71	3	.958	8	3	13	12	.923	54	+1	-2	-1	-2	+1	-1	0	1	1	2	-
Manny Burriss	SF	9	48.0	18	1	.944	5	2	3	2	.667	12	0	0	+1	0	0	0	0	0	0	0	-
Everth Cabrera	SD	2	17.0	9	0	1.000	1	2	6	0	.000	5	0	-1	-1	-2	0	-2	-1	-1	0	-2	-
Orlando Cabrera	2 tms	39	309.1	155	5	.968	18	12	37	22	.595	110	-2	+1	+4	+3	0	+3	2	0	1	3	-
Alexi Casilla	Min	36	306.2	162	5	.969	8	8	31	22	.710	112	+6	-4	-4	-2	-2	-4	-3	0	0	-3	-
Pedro Ciriaco	Pit	7	34.1	29	1	.966	4	2	3	2	.667	24	+1	0	0	0	-1	-1	-1	0	0	-1	-
Alex Cora	Was	16	114.2	69	0	1.000	8	4	14	10	.714	47	+1	0	0	+1	+1	+2	2	0	-1	1	-
Craig Counsell	Mil	23	120.0	50	1	.980	6	3	12	7	.583	28	+1	-2	0	0	0	0	-1	0	1	0	-
Zack Cozart	Cin	11	77.1	63	0	1.000	5	1	11	7	.636	40	+2	+2	+1	+5	0	+5	4	0	0	4	-
Chase d'Arnaud	Pit	29	206.2	94	6	.936	13	6	22	12	.545	68	-1	-3	-2	-6	+1	-5	-4	-1	0	-5	-
Blake Davis	Bal	2	4.0	4	0	1.000	0	0	3	2	.667	3	-1	0	+1	0	+1	+1	0	0	0	0	-
Daniel Descalso	StL	13	97.0	54	2	.963	6	4	13	7	.538	35	-2	+3	0	+1	+1	+2	1	-1	0	0	-
Jason Donald	Cle	16	103.2	50	3	.940	2	2	14	6	.429	33	+3	-3	-1	-2	+2	0	0	0	0	0	-
Matt Downs	Hou	2	10.0	5	1	.800	0	0	1	0	.000	3	0	0	0	0	0	0	0	0	0	0	-
Eduardo Escobar	CWS	3	6.0	4	0	1.000	0	0	0	0	-	3	0	0	0	+1	0	+1	0	0	0	0	-
Adam Everett	Cle	4	7.0	4	0	1.000	0	0	0	0	-	1	0	0	0	0	0	0	0	0	0	0	-
Tommy Field	Col	15	113.0	66	1	.985	8	4	12	9	.750	51	-3	0	+4	+1	+3	+4	3	0	0	3	-
Pedro Florimon	Bal	4	18.2	10	1	.900	0	1	1	1	1.000	9	-1	-1	0	-1	0	-1	-1	0	0	-1	-
Mike Fontenot	SF	37	284.0	126	4	.968	10	7	22	16	.727	87	-6	+3	+2	0	+2	+2	1	1	-1	1	-
Logan Forsythe	SD	1	2.1	0	0	-	0	0	0	0	-	0	0	0	0	0	0	0	0	0		0	-
Todd Frazier	Cin	2	3.0	3	0	1.000	2	0	1	0	.000	1	0	0	0	0	0	0	0	0	0	0	-
Chris Getz	KC	4	26.0	17	1	.941	1	0	2	1	.500	11	-1	0	+2	+2	0	+2	1	0	0	1	-
Hector Gomez	Col	2	11.0	6	1	.833	1	0	0	0	-	5	-1	0	0	-1	0	-1	-1	0	1	0	-
Alberto Gonzalez	SD	30	199.0	105	1	.990	11	4	21	9	.429	71	0	-1	+1	+1	0	+1	0	-1	1	0	-
Tyler Greene	StL	20	111.1	57	2	.965	4	4	10	7	.700	41	0	+1	0	+1	-2	-1	-1	0	0	-1	-
Jerry Hairston	2 tms	2	9.0	4	0	1.000	0	0	1	1	1.000	2	+1	0	0	+1	0	+1	1	0	0	1	-
Diory Hernandez	Atl	3	13.0	5	0	1.000	0	0	2	1	.500	4	0	0	+1	0	0	0	0	0	0	0	-
Jonathan Herrera	Col	21	78.0	35	1	.971	4	1	6	5	.833	25	+3	0	0	+3	0	+3	3	0	0	3	-
Brandon Hicks	Atl	3	21.0	11	1	.909	1	2	5	3	.600	7	0	-1	0	0	0	0	0	0	0	0	-
Chin-lung Hu	NYM	1	1.0	0	0	1.000	0	0	1	0	.000	0						0		0	0	0	-
Jose Iglesias	Bos	8	18.2	5	0	1.000	0	0	0	0	-	5	0	0	0	-1	0	-1	0	0	0	0	-
Cesar Izturis	Bal	12	67.2	49	0	1.000	4	2	20	15	.750	33	+2	+1	+2	+5	0	+5	4	0	-1	3	-
Maicer Izturis	LAA	16	132.0	69	1	.986	6	2	11	8	.727	49	0	0	+3	+3	-2	+1	1	0	-1	0	-
Elliot Johnson	TB	52	337.2	149	1	.993	14	5	24	17	.708	110	+5	-2	+4	+7	+2	+9	7	1	0	8	-
Pete Kozma	StL	3	15.0	3	0	1.000	0	0	1	0	.000	2	0	0	0	0	0	0	0	0	0	0	-
Andy LaRoche	Oak	9	44.2	29	1	.966	1	2	7	2	.286	25	+5	0	-2	+3	0	+3	2	0	-1	1	-
Steve Lombardozzi	Was	1	9.0	2	0	1.000	0	0	0	0	-	1	0	-1	0	-1	0	-1	-1	0	0	-1	-
Jed Lowrie	Bos	49	398.0	181	10	.945	14	6	34	21	.618	123	+6	0	-6	-1	-3	-4	-3	0	0	-3	-
Julio Lugo	Atl	5	38.1	12	0	1.000	0	0	2	1	.500	7	-1	0	-1	-1	0	-1	-1	0	0	-1	-
Michael Martinez	Phi	13	82.0	40	2	.950	3	1	10	7	.700	26	+1	-1	+3	+4	-1	+3	2	0	0	2	-
Osvaldo Martinez	Fla	6	21.0	4	1	.750	1	0	0	0	-	3	-1	0	0	-1	0	-1	-1	0	0	-1	-
Mike McCoy	Tor	26	211.0	118	4	.966	7	4	21	12	.571	79	-2	+2	+5	+5	-1	+4	3	0	0	3	-
John McDonald	2 tms	38	264.2	150	2	.987	16	7	31	19	.613	107	+5	+1	+3	+10	0	+10	8	0	2	10	-
Aaron Miles	LAD	1	3.1	0	0	-	0	0	0	0	-	0						0		0		0	-
Donnie Murphy	Fla	18	140.1	74	1	.986	5	1	17	9	.529	46	-1	+2	0	+1	-1	0	0	0	0	0	-
Yamaico Navarro	2 tms	4	27.0	6	0	1.000	0	2	2	1	.500	4	0	0	0	0	0	0	0	0	-1	-1	-
Chris Nelson	Col	2	22.0	7	1	.857	1	0	1	0	.000	6	+1	0	+1	+1	0	+1	1	0	0	1	-
Eduardo Nunez	NYY	50	386.1	161	14	.913	7	11	30	14	.467	109	-2	-5	-2	-9	0	-9	-7	-1	-1	-9	-
Andy Parrino	SD	4	20.0	11	0	1.000	4	1	2	2	1.000	8	0	0	+1	+1	0	+1	1	0	0	1	-

Name	Team	G	Inn	TC	E	Pct	GFP	DM	Opps	GDP	Pct	Outs Made	To His Right	Straight On	To His Left	GB	Air	Total	+/-	GDP	GFP/ DME	Total	Rank
Ramiro Pena	NYY	4	24.2	15	2	.867	0	0	3	2	.667	8	-1	-2	0	-3	0	-3	-2	0	0	-2	-
Trevor Plouffe	Min	45	396.2	195	11	.944	9	10	51	31	.608	125	-5	0	-11	-15	-2	-17	-13	0	-1	-14	-
Nick Punto	StL	8	61.1	23	0	1.000	2	0	4	2	.500	16	-1	+1	-1	0	0	0	0	0	0	0	-
Omar Quintanilla	Tex	3	25.0	19	0	1.000	1	0	2	2	1.000	12	0	0	-1	0	-1	-1	-1	0	0	-1	-
Cody Ransom	Ari	8	46.0	24	1	.958	3	2	3	2	.667	17	-1	0	+1	0	0	0	0	0	0	0	-
Ryan Roberts	Ari	1	3.0	0	0	-	0	0	0	0	-	0	0	0	0	0	0	0	0	0		0	-
Josh Rodriguez	Pit	4	24.0	11	0	1.000	0	1	2	2	1.000	6	0	-1	0	-1	+1	0	0	0	0	0	-
Luis Rodriguez	Sea	23	185.2	95	3	.968	15	4	20	16	.800	58	-4	+2	0	-1	+1	0	0	0	1	1	-
Sean Rodriguez	TB	60	430.2	169	9	.947	16	6	36	22	.611	116	0	-2	+1	-1	+1	0	0	0	0	0	-
Andrew Romine	LAA	7	30.0	20	1	.950	2	0	3	3	1.000	15	0	-1	-1	-1	0	-1	-1	0	0	-1	-
Adam Rosales	Oak	7	51.2	23	2	.913	3	0	5	3	.600	11	+1	-1	-1	-1	-1	-2	-1	0	0	-1	-
Angel Sanchez	Hou	46	366.2	194	7	.964	9	10	40	22	.550	130	-9	+2	0	-7	0	-7	-6	-1	0	-7	-
Ramon Santiago	Det	27	195.0	117	2	.983	6	6	22	14	.636	80	0	+1	+4	+5	-1	+4	3	0	0	3	-
Kyle Seager	Sea	10	74.0	36	2	.944	5	5	6	6	1.000	22	-3	0	-1	-3	0	-3	-3	0	0	-3	-
Justin Sellers	LAD	19	151.2	74	1	.986	9	3	20	15	.750	50	+3	0	+1	+2	+2	+4	3	0	0	3	-
Eric Sogard	Oak	14	79.0	38	1	.974	3	2	5	2	.400	25	+1	0	-2	0	+1	+1	0	0	0	0	-
Drew Sutton	Bos	4	32.0	13	1	.923	0	1	3	2	.667	8	0	-1	-1	-2	+1	-1	-1	0	0	-1	-
Miguel Tejada	SF	42	334.1	162	8	.951	14	9	18	13	.722	111	-3	0	-3	-6	0	-6	-4	0	-1	-5	-
Ruben Tejada	NYM	41	353.0	181	8	.956	30	10	43	19	.442	126	-7	+1	+8	+1	+2	+3	2	-3	0	-1	-
Matt Tolbert	Min	31	210.0	110	3	.973	3	2	24	18	.750	72	-4	+1	-1	-4	+1	-3	-2	1	0	-1	-
Justin Turner	NYM	1	5.0	5	1	.800	0	0	1	0	.000	3	0	0	0	0	0	0	0	0	-1	-1	-
Juan Uribe	LAD	4	21.2	8	0	1.000	0	0	2	2	1.000	2	0	0	0	0	0	0	0	0	0	0	-
Chris Valaika	Cin	2	16.0	3	0	1.000	1	0	2	1	.500	2	0	0	+1	+1	0	+1	1	0	0	1	-
Luis Valbuena	Cle	1	1.0	0	0	-	0	0	0	0	-	0						0		0		0	-
Wilson Valdez	Phi	25	188.0	91	4	.956	6	4	23	17	.739	61	0	0	+2	+2	-1	+1	1	0	-1	0	-
Omar Vizquel	CWS	9	72.0	26	0	1.000	3	2	5	3	.600	19	0	0	-2	-2	0	-2	-1	0	0	-1	-
Jack Wilson	2 tms	26	204.0	116	2	.983	8	4	22	14	.636	72	+1	-2	-1	-2	+1	-1	0	0	-1	-1	-
Josh Wilson	2 tms	11	58.0	33	1	.970	4	2	8	4	.500	16	0	-1	0	-1	0	-1	0	0	0	0	-
Brandon Wood	2 tms	24	172.0	90	2	.978	6	2	26	18	.692	58	-5	-1	+2	-4	0	-4	-3	1	0	-2	-
Chris Woodward	Tor	1	1.0	0	0	-	0	0	0	0	-	0						0		0		0	-
David Wright	NYM	1	2.0	1	0	1.000	0	0	0	0	-	0	0	0	0	0	0	0	0	0	0	0	-
Michael Young	Tex	1	8.0	3	0	1.000	0	0	1	1	1.000	1	0	0	0	0	-1	-1	-1	0	0	-1	-
2011 MLB Totals						.972	1819	948	4545	2893	.637												

		BASIC							THROWING				PLUS/MINUS						RUNS SAVED				
Name	Team	G	Inn	TC	E	Pct	GFP	DM	Opps to Advance	Extra Bases	Pct	Kills	Outs Made	Basic	Shallow	Medium	Deep	Enhanced	+/-	Throws	GFP/DME	Total	Rank
Bobby Abreu	LAA	18	143.1	22	0	1.000	2	4	12	2	.167	2	20	-5	-3	-2	-2	-8	-4	3	0	-1	-
Yonder Alonso	Cin	16	112.2	24	1	.958	1	6	19	9	.474	0	22	-4	-4	+1	-3	-6	-3	-1	-2	-6	-
Alexi Amarista	LAA	8	43.1	10	0	1.000	1	1	5	2	.400	0	9	0	0	0	+1	+1	1	0	0	1	-
Alfredo Amezaga	Fla	4	11.0	1	0	1.000	0	0				0	1	0	0	0	0	0	0	0	0	0	-
Robert Andino	Bal	3	11.0	2	0	1.000	0	0				0	2	0	0	0	0	0	0	0	0	0	-
Matt Angle	Bal	14	65.0	24	2	.917	0	4	5	3	.600	0	22	0	+1	0	-1	0	0	-1	-1	-2	-
Mike Aviles	Bos	1	9.0	4	0	1.000	0	3	1	0	.000	0	4	0	0	0	-2	-1	-1	0	-1	-2	-
Jeff Baker	ChC	1	6.0	2	0	1.000	1	1	2	0	.000	0	2	-1	0	0	-2	-2	-1	0	-1	-2	-
Mike Baxter	NYM	3	5.0	2	0	1.000	0	0				0	2	+1	0	0	+1	+1	1	0	0	-1	-
Josh Bell	Bal	1	1.0	0	0	-	0	0														0	-
Brandon Belt	SF	31	231.0	50	3	.940	2	2	22	8	.364	1	46	+3	+3	+2	-4	+1	1	0	0	1	-
Joe Benson	Min	11	88.0	20	1	.950	1	2	11	2	.182	0	19	0	+1	-2	0	-1	0	0	0	0	-
Lance Berkman	StL	16	131.0	22	0	1.000	1	3	13	3	.231	0	21	+2	0	0	+4	+4	2	0	0	2	-
Roger Bernadina	Was	36	175.0	45	0	1.000	7	2	13	6	.462	0	43	+2	0	-3	+6	+3	2	-1	0	1	-
Brian Bixler	Was	27	79.1	22	0	1.000	2	0	1	1	1.000	0	22	+3	+1	0	+4	+5	3	0	0	3	-
Charlie Blackmon	Col	25	198.1	41	0	1.000	2	4	23	9	.391	0	39	-1	-2	-2	+4	0	0	0	-1	-1	-
Casey Blake	LAD	2	3.1	0	0	-	0	0														0	-
Kyle Blanks	SD	37	300.0	66	1	.985	5	4	37	10	.270	3	63	+2	+3	-3	+6	+6	3	2	2	7	-
Willie Bloomquist	Ari	25	197.1	41	0	1.000	6	1	17	7	.412	0	41	0	-1	-2	+5	+2	1	-1	1	1	-
Brandon Boggs	Mil	2	3.0	0	0	-	0	0					0	0	0	0	0	0	0			0	-
Brian Bogusevic	Hou	13	47.0	12	0	1.000	2	0	2	1	.500	0	12	+1	0	+1	+2	+2	1	0	0	1	-
Emilio Bonifacio	Fla	32	247.1	57	1	.982	3	6	19	5	.263	1	54	-1	-1	0	-4	-5	-3	2	0	-1	-
Jason Bourgeois	Hou	34	124.2	29	1	.966	2	6	24	6	.250	0	28	0	0	+3	-2	+1	0	1	-1	0	-
Milton Bradley	Sea	26	213.0	55	2	.964	6	6	25	10	.400	0	53	-3	+1	+1	-8	-7	-4	-1	-1	-6	-
Travis Buck	Cle	25	192.0	43	0	1.000	2	1	18	3	.167	0	43	+2	0	+2	+4	+6	4	0	0	4	-
Pat Burrell	SF	54	349.2	59	4	.932	3	3	22	9	.409	1	53	+1	+1	-2	+2	+2	1	0	-1	0	-
Manny Burriss	SF	2	2.0	2	0	1.000	0	0	1	0	.000	0	2	0	0	0	0	0	0	0	0	0	-
Melky Cabrera	KC	12	63.0	15	0	1.000	0	0	10	1	.100	0	15	0	-1	+2	0	0	0	0	0	0	-
Mike Cameron	Bos	4	9.0	2	0	1.000	1	0	1	1	1.000	0	2	0	+1	0	0	+1	0	1	0	1	-
Tony Campana	ChC	35		17	1	.941	3	0	6	2	.333	1	15	+1	+2	0	0	+2	1	1	0	2	-
Mike Carp	Sea	27	216.2	55	4	.927	9	5	22	9	.409	0	49	0	-1	-4	-5	-10	-5	-1	-1	-7	-
Ezequiel Carrera	Cle	9	60.0	13	1	.923	1	0	9	4	.444	0	12	0	0	-1	0	-1	0	0	0	0	-
Adron Chambers	StL	6	7.0	1	0	1.000	0	1				0	1	0	0	0	0	0	0	0	0	0	-
Endy Chavez	Tex	12	32.0	3	0	1.000	0	0	3	2	.667	0	3	-1	-1	0	0	-1	-1	0	0	-1	-
Lonnie Chisenhall	Cle	1	0.0	0	0	-	0	0														0	-
Justin Christian	SF	6	29.0	9	0	1.000	2	3	4	1	.250	0	9	+1	+1	0	-1	+1	1	0	1	2	-
Pedro Ciriaco	Pit	2	5.1	1	0	1.000	0	0	1	0	.000	0	1	0	0	0	0	0	0	0	0	0	-
Tyler Colvin	ChC	10	43.1	10	0	1.000	0	0	3	3	1.000	0	10	+1	0	0	+3	+3	2	-1	0	1	-
Jose Constanza	Atl	17	113.2	32	1	.969	5	2	9	7	.778	0	31	+4	0	+1	+4	+6	3	-1	-1	1	-
Craig Counsell	Mil	1	2.0	0	0	-	0	0														0	-
Scott Cousins	Fla	4	20.2	3	0	1.000	2	2	3	2	.667	1	2	+1	+1	0	0	+1	0	1	0	1	-
Collin Cowgill	Ari	18	138.0	44	0	1.000	2	2	18	8	.444	0	43	+6	+3	+2	+5	+10	6	-1	-1	4	-
Allen Craig	StL	26	190.2	40	0	1.000	2	6	20	7	.350	0	39	+2	+5	+2	-4	+2	1	0	-1	0	-
Trevor Crowe	Cle	10	51.0	7	0	1.000	2	3	5	1	.200	0	7	0	0	0	0	0	0	0	-1	-1	-
Nelson Cruz	Tex	18	135.0	31	1	.968	1	1	8	3	.375	1	29	0	+1	0	-1	0	0	1	0	1	-
Aaron Cunningham	SD	13	61.2	7	0	1.000	2	0	4	2	.500	0	7	+1	+1	-1	+1	+1	1	0	0	1	-
Johnny Damon	TB	16	84.0	19	0	1.000	2	3	5	2	.400	0	19	-3	0	-1	-5	-5	-3	0	0	-3	-
James Darnell	SD	3	15.1	3	0	1.000	0	0				0	3	0	0	-1	+1	-1	0	0	0	0	-
Rajai Davis	Tor	4	36.0	5	0	1.000	0	0	1	0	.000	0	5	0	-1	0	0	0	0	0	0	0	-
Alejandro De Aza	CWS	4	21.0	9	0	1.000	0	0	2	0	.000	0	9	0	-1	0	+1	0	0	0	0	0	-
Chris Denorfia	SD	34	128.2	30	1	.967	4	2	16	4	.250	1	29	0	+1	+2	-3	+1	0	0	0	0	-
Blake DeWitt	ChC	23	155.0	34	1	.971	3	7	15	4	.267	1	33	-1	-3	+1	+1	-1	-1	1	0	0	-
Matt Diaz	2 tms	18	104.2	18	1	.944	1	0	10	3	.300	0	17	-1	-3	+1	+1	-1	-1	1	0	0	-
Chris Dickerson	NYY	14	43.1	9	0	1.000	0	1	5	2	.400	0	9	0	0	0	-2	-1	-1	0	0	-1	-
Brian Dinkelman	Min	5	40.2	13	0	1.000	2	0	7	5	.714	0	13	0	0	0	-1	-1	-1	0	0	-1	-
Andy Dirks	Det	38	236.2	67	1	.985	4	6	24	12	.500	1	66	+5	-1	-4	+17	+12	7	0	0	7	-
Greg Dobbs	Fla	3	27.0	9	0	1.000	0	0	5	2	.400	0	9	0	0	0	0	0	0	0	0	0	-
Lucas Duda	NYM	4	29.0	3	0	1.000	0	1	1	1	1.000	0	3	0	0	0	0	0	0	0	0	0	-
Shelley Duncan	Cle	37	253.1	61	1	.984	4	7	29	7	.241	1	58	-8	-4	-4	-6	-14	-8	2	0	-6	-
Nick Evans	NYM	1	1.0	0	0	-	0	0					0	0	0	0	0	0	0			0	-
Chone Figgins	Sea	2	8.0	2	0	1.000	0	0	2	1	.500	0	2	0	0	0	-1	-1	0	0	0	0	-
Jake Fox	Bal	5	35.0	5	0	1.000	1	3	3	0	.000	0	5	-1	0	-2	+2	-1	-1	0	0	0	-
Ben Francisco	Phi	14	109.0	19	1	.947	2	3	7	2	.286	1	17	-3	-1	-1	-2	-4	-2	1	0	-2	-
Todd Frazier	Cin	4	18.0	4	0	1.000	1	0	2	0	.000	1	3	+1	0	+2	+1	+2	1	1	0	2	-
Mat Gamel	Mil	2	3.1	1	0	1.000	0	0				0	1	0	0	0	0	0	0	0	0	0	-
Cole Garner	Col	2	10.0	3	0	1.000	0	0				0	3	0	0	0	0	0	0	0	0	0	-
Joey Gathright	Bos	4	5.0	2	0	1.000	0	0	1	0	.000	0	2	+1	+1	0	0	+1	1	0	0	1	-
Craig Gentry	Tex	2	9.0	1	0	1.000	0	0				0	1	0	0	0	0	0	0	0	0	0	-
Jay Gibbons	LAD	10	71.0	12	0	1.000	1	1	9	1	.111	0	12	-2	-1	0	-1	-2	-1	0	0	-1	-
Cole Gillespie	Ari	2	10.0	3	0	1.000	0	0	2	1	.500	0	3	0	0	0	0	0	0	0	0	0	-
Chris Gimenez	Sea	3	9.2	0	0	-	0	0	2	1	.500	0	0	0	0	0	0	0	0	0	0	0	-
Greg Golson	NYY	4	8.1	1	0	1.000	0	0				0	1	-1	0	-2	0	-2	-1	0	0	-1	-
Tyler Greene	StL	2	3.0	0	0	-	0	0				0	0	0	0	0	0	0	0	0	0	0	-
Brandon Guyer	TB	3	20.0	7	0	1.000	1	0	1	0	.000	0	7	0	+1	+1	-1	0	0	0	0	0	-
Jesus Guzman	SD	6	47.0	13	0	1.000	1	2	2	1	.500	0	13	+1	+1	-2	+2	+1	1	0	-1	0	-
Jerry Hairston	2 tms	23	129.0	37	2	.946	3	2	12	5	.417	0	35	+2	+3	+1	0	+4	2	0	-1	1	-
Scott Hairston	NYM	10	48.1	11	1	.909	0	0	8	3	.375	0	10	-2	-2	0	0	-2	-1	0	0	-1	-
Bill Hall	SF	1	4.0	2	0	1.000	0	0	1	1	1.000	0	2	0	0	0	+1	+1	0	0	0	0	-
Greg Halman	Sea	29	162.1	39	0	1.000	2	3	14	7	.500	0	39	-1	-2	+1	+1	0	0	-1	0	-1	-
Mark Hamilton	StL	2	2.0	0	0	-	0	0				0	0	0	0	0	0	0	0	0	0	0	-
Robby Hammock	Ari	1	3.0	0	0	-	0	0					0	0	0	0	0	0	0			0	-
Willie Harris	NYM	33	241.1	48	0	1.000	1	8	31	12	.387	0	48	-4	-4	-1	0	-5	-3	-1	-1	-5	-
Brett Hayes	Fla	1	1.0	0	0	-	0	0				0										0	-
Jerad Head	Cle	9	62.0	16	1	.938	0	0	9	2	.222	0	15	+1	+2	0	0	+1	1	0	0	1	-
Chris Heisey	Cin	88	393.0	88	2	.977	3	9	29	15	.517	1	85	+3	+4	+4	-6	+1	1	-2	-1	-2	-

423

		BASIC							THROWING				PLUS/MINUS						RUNS SAVED				
									Opps to	Extra			Outs								GFP/		
Name	Team	G	Inn	TC	E	Pct	GFP	DM	Advance	Bases	Pct	Kills	Made	Basic	Shallow	Medium	Deep	Enhanced	+/-	Throws	DME	Total	Rank
Jeremy Hermida	Cin	3	25.0	5	0	1.000	0	0				0	5	0	0	-1	0	-1	-1	0	0	-1	-
Eric Hinske	Atl	32	211.0	42	0	1.000	3	2	17	5	.294	0	41	0	-2	-1	+4	+1	0	0	1	1	-
Jamie Hoffmann	LAD	1	8.0	3	0	1.000	0	0	1	0	.000	0	3	0	0	0	-1	-1	-1	0	0	-1	-
Kyle Hudson	Bal	8	60.2	13	1	.923	0	0	10	3	.300	0	12	0	0	0	0	0	0	0	0	0	-
Aubrey Huff	SF	9	37.2	10	0	1.000	1	2	4	2	.500	0	10	0	0	+1	0	+1	1	0	-1	0	-
Conor Jackson	2 tms	23	162.0	33	0	1.000	6	3	18	11	.611	1	31	0	+1	+1	-2	-1	0	-1	0	-1	-
Jon Jay	StL	19	115.1	22	0	1.000	1	4	15	6	.400	0	22	-1	0	+1	-3	-2	-1	-1	0	-2	-
Elliot Johnson	TB	1	0.1	0	0	-	0	0														0	-
Reed Johnson	ChC	27	76.0	13	1	.923	2	0	8	4	.500	0	12	+1	+1	0	-1	0	0	-1	0	-1	-
Andruw Jones	NYY	39	247.0	60	1	.983	3	1	16	4	.250	0	59	+1	+1	-3	+3	+1	1	-1	0	0	-
Matt Joyce	TB	15	86.2	20	0	1.000	1	3	9	5	.556	0	20	+1	0	+1	-1	+1	0	-1	-1	-2	-
Austin Kearns	Cle	36	264.1	70	0	1.000	6	6	27	8	.296	0	70	-3	+4	0	-12	-8	-4	1	-1	-4	-
Don Kelly	Det	17	57.0	16	0	1.000	1	1	5	1	.200	0	16	-1	+1	-1	-2	-2	-1	0	0	-1	-
Howie Kendrick	LAA	23	175.0	34	0	1.000	2	9	12	5	.417	0	33	-3	0	-5	0	-5	-3	-1	-1	-5	-
Mark Kotsay	Mil	19	131.1	26	4	.846	3	0	15	6	.400	2	20	0	-1	+2	0	0	0	0	0	0	-
Jason Kubel	Min	9	70.0	15	0	1.000	0	2	7	3	.429	0	15	+1	+1	+1	0	+1	1	-1	0	0	-
Bryan LaHair	ChC	5	41.0	4	0	1.000	0	0	4	1	.250	0	4	-1	-1	0	0	-1	-1	0	0	-1	-
Ryan Langerhans	Sea	5	34.2	8	0	1.000	0	0	3	0	.000	0	8	0	0	0	0	+1	0	0	0	0	-
Fred Lewis	Cin	45	315.2	79	0	1.000	8	3	38	17	.447	2	76	+7	+1	+4	+9	+14	8	-2	1	7	-
Brent Lillibridge	CWS	9	60.0	16	0	1.000	4	2	3	1	.333	0	16	+2	+1	0	+3	+4	2	0	2	4	-
Adam Loewen	Tor	1	7.0	1	1	.000	0	1				0	0	-1	-2	0	-1	-2	-1	0	0	-1	-
Mitch Maier	KC	11	79.1	26	0	1.000	0	2	8	2	.250	0	25	-1	0	-1	0	0	0	0	0	0	-
Fernando Martinez	NYM	1	1.0	1	1	.000	0	0	1	1	1.000	0	0	0	0	0	0	0	0	0	0	0	-
Michael Martinez	Phi	2	10.0	3	0	1.000	1	1	3	1	.333	0	2	-2	-1	0	-2	-3	-2	0	0	-2	-
Joe Mather	Atl	4	12.1	2	0	1.000	0	0					2	0	0	0	0	0	0	0	0	0	-
Hideki Matsui	Oak	27	232.1	57	1	.982	8	2	22	4	.182	2	53	-5	-4	+2	-4	-6	-3	2	2	1	-
John Mayberry	Phi	21	161.1	31	0	1.000	1	1	15	5	.333	1	30	+2	+1	+2	0	+3	1	0	0	1	-
Darnell McDonald	Bos	23	126.0	31	2	.935	3	3	13	3	.231	1	28	0	+1	+1	-3	-1	0	1	0	1	-
Nate McLouth	Atl	26	202.0	38	0	1.000	6	0	14	7	.500	0	38	+3	+2	-1	+2	+4	2	-1	0	1	-
Jason Michaels	Hou	26	158.0	37	0	1.000	1	4	18	6	.333	0	37	+1	-4	+1	+4	+1	0	-1	0	-1	-
Lastings Milledge	CWS	2	11.0	7	0	1.000	0	1	5	4	.800	0	7	-1	0	-2	0	-2	-1	-1	0	-2	-
Lou Montanez	ChC	10	31.1	5	0	1.000	0	0	2	0	.000	0	5	-1	0	-1	0	-1	-1	0	0	-1	-
Jeremy Moore	LAA	2	13.0	4	0	1.000	1	0	1	0	.000	1	3	0	0	+1	-1	0	0	1	0	1	-
Nyjer Morgan	Mil	17	35.0	5	0	1.000	1	1	7	4	.571	0	5	0	0	-1	+2	+1	1	0	0	1	-
Daniel Murphy	NYM	1	2.0	1	0	1.000	0	0				0	1	0	0	0	0	0	0	0	0	0	-
Xavier Nady	Ari	10	52.0	11	0	1.000	2	1	3	1	.333	1	10	+1	+1	+1	-1	+1	0	1	0	1	-
Yamaico Navarro	Bos	3	21.0	6	0	1.000	0	1	4	0	.000	0	6	+1	0	+1	0	+1	0	1	0	1	-
Jayson Nix	Tor	1	4.0	0	0	-	0	0					0	0	0	0	0	0	0			0	-
Eduardo Nunez	NYY	1	1.0	0	0	-	0	0	1	1	1.000		0	0	0	0	0	0	0	0	0	0	-
Trent Oeltjen	LAD	13	65.2	16	1	.938	0	2	8	2	.250	0	15	-2	-1	-2	0	-3	-2	1	-1	-2	-
Andy Parrino	SD	1	1.0	0	0	-	0	0														0	-
Corey Patterson	2 tms	56	396.2	96	0	1.000	10	7	37	12	.324	2	93	-2	-2	0	-5	-6	-4	0	0	-4	-
Eric Patterson	SD	4	18.0	7	0	1.000	0	0	1	0	.000	0	7	+1	+1	0	0	+2	1	0	0	1	-
Xavier Paul	2 tms	27	164.1	35	0	1.000	4	6	18	10	.556	4	31	-1	-2	-1	+3	0	1	1	0	2	-
Carlos Peguero	Sea	40	325.2	83	1	.988	9	7	25	11	.440	2	79	0	-3	+2	+3	+3	1	0	2	3	-
Wily Mo Pena	Ari	1	1.0	0	0	-	0	0	1	0	.000	0	0	0	0	0	0	0	0	0	0	0	-
Bryan Petersen	Fla	22	109.1	20	0	1.000	1	1	12	4	.333	1	18	0	+1	-2	0	-1	-1	0	0	-1	-
Felix Pie	Bal	67	349.2	90	0	1.000	7	14	52	21	.404	1	89	-10	-8	-9	+1	-16	-9	-2	0	-11	-
Trevor Plouffe	Min	3	19.0	4	0	1.000	0	1	1	0	.000	0	4	0	0	-2	0	-1	-1	0	0	-1	-
Jason Pridie	NYM	13	67.0	10	0	1.000	0	2	2	0	.000	0	10	0	0	-1	+1	0	0	0	0	0	-
Ryan Raburn	Det	52	335.2	95	3	.968	11	9	30	12	.400	2	89	+3	+4	0	+1	+5	3	0	1	4	-
Wilkin Ramirez	Atl	5	37.0	4	0	1.000	0	0				0	4	0	0	0	0	0	0	0	0	0	-
Josh Reddick	Bos	21	148.0	38	1	.974	7	2	12	3	.250	1	36	+3	+3	0	+1	+4	2	1	1	4	-
Jason Repko	Min	24	128.0	24	0	1.000	2	2	12	2	.167	0	23	0	0	+1	-1	0	0	1	0	1	-
Ben Revere	Min	13	112.1	34	1	.971	4	1	10	5	.500	0	33	-3	0	+2	-6	-5	-3	-1	0	-4	-
Ryan Roberts	Ari	3	17.0	4	0	1.000	0	0	2	0	.000	0	4	+1	0	0	+2	+2	1	0	0	1	-
Shane Robinson	StL	1	1.0	0	0	-	0	1	1	0	.000	0	0	0	0	0	0	-1	-1	0	0	-1	-
Trayvon Robinson	Sea	30	230.0	60	3	.950	10	7	31	16	.516	2	55	-1	-1	+1	-1	-1	0	-1	2	1	-
Sean Rodriguez	TB	2	3.0	1	0	1.000	0	0				0	1	0	0	0	0	0	0	0	0	0	-
Adam Rosales	Oak	2	7.0	4	0	1.000	0	0				0	4	0	0	0	0	0	0	0	0	0	-
Vinny Rottino	Fla	1	8.0	1	0	1.000	0	1	4	3	.750	0	0	0	0	0	0	0	0	0	0	0	-
Aaron Rowand	SF	46	219.2	34	1	.971	7	5	19	6	.316	0	32	-1	0	0	-1	-2	-1	0	1	0	-
Justin Ruggiano	TB	27	183.1	49	0	1.000	7	5	15	4	.267	0	49	+5	+1	0	+6	+8	4	0	2	6	-
Jerry Sands	LAD	41	288.0	65	0	1.000	5	9	29	12	.414	3	61	-3	-2	-3	-1	-7	-4	1	1	-2	-

Name	Team	G	Inn	TC	E	Pct	GFP	DM	Opps to Advance	Extra Bases	Pct	Kills	Outs Made	Basic	Shallow	Medium	Deep	Enhanced	+/-	Throws	GFP/DME	Total	Rank
Dave Sappelt	Cin	31	194.2	46	0	1.000	7	4	22	8	.364	1	44	+3	0	+4	-2	+3	2	0	0	2	-
Michael Saunders	Sea	12	67.0	21	0	1.000	2	0	2	0	.000	0	21	+2	+2	+1	-1	+2	1	0	0	1	-
Nate Schierholtz	SF	8	61.0	17	1	.941	1	1	8	3	.375	1	15	+2	+1	0	0	+2	1	1	0	2	-
Skip Schumaker	StL	6	16.0	1	0	1.000	0	0				0	1	0	0	0	0	0	0	0	0	0	-
Luke Scott	Bal	45	330.2	83	1	.988	5	4	36	14	.389	0	82	+1	-4	0	+7	+3	2	-2	3	3	-
J.B. Shuck	Hou	6	23.2	4	0	1.000	0	1	1	0	.000	0	4	-1	0	0	0	0	0	0	0	0	-
Seth Smith	Col	25	186.2	38	0	1.000	5	5	19	10	.526	2	34	-1	-1	-1	+1	-1	-1	-1	0	-2	-
Travis Snider	Tor	44	367.0	83	3	.964	8	5	43	11	.256	2	77	-1	0	+2	-1	0	0	3	0	3	-
Brad Snyder	ChC	1	6.0	0	0	-	0	0					0	0	0	0	0	0	0			0	-
Nate Spears	Bos	1	5.0	1	0	1.000	0	0				0	1	0	0	0	0	0	0	0	0	0	-
Ryan Spilborghs	Col	29	126.1	15	0	1.000	2	0	16	6	.375	1	13	0	-1	0	+2	+1	1	0	0	1	-
Drew Sutton	Bos	3	16.0	7	1	.857	1	0	1	1	1.000	0	6	-1	+1	-2	-1	-2	-1	0	0	-1	-
Ryan Sweeney	Oak	41	219.0	42	0	1.000	3	1	6	3	.500	1	41	+7	+3	+4	+3	+9	5	0	0	5	-
Michael Taylor	Oak	3	18.0	3	0	1.000	0	2	4	2	.500	0	3	0	0	-1	0	0	0	-1	-1	-2	-
Mark Teahen	2 tms	6	17.0	4	1	.750	0	0	3	2	.667	0	3	-1	-2	0	+1	-1	-1	0	0	-1	-
Blake Tekotte	SD	3	11.0	2	0	1.000	0	1	1	0	.000	0	2	-1	0	0	-2	-2	-1	0	0	-1	-
Marcus Thames	LAD	17	99.0	27	1	.963	1	1	10	3	.300	0	26	-1	-1	0	0	-1	-1	-1	0	-2	-
Andres Torres	SF	1	4.0	0	0	-	0	0					0	0	0	0	0	0	0			0	-
Rene Tosoni	Min	38	321.0	92	3	.967	9	4	49	19	.388	3	85	-2	+1	-2	-7	-7	-4	0	0	-4	-
Mike Trout	LAA	10	75.0	21	0	1.000	1	0	6	2	.333	0	21	0	0	+1	-1	0	0	0	0	0	-
Mark Trumbo	LAA	1	2.0	0	0	-	0	0					0	0	0	0	0	0	0			0	-
Luis Valbuena	Cle	2	12.1	2	0	1.000	0	1	6	3	.500	0	2	-2	-1	0	-2	-2	-1	0	0	-1	-
Eugenio Velez	LAD	4	15.0	5	1	.800	0	0	1	0	.000	0	4	+1	0	+1	+2	+2	1	0	0	1	-
Will Venable	SD	7	38.0	7	0	1.000	0	0	1	1	1.000	0	7	-1	0	0	0	-1	0	0	0	0	-
Casper Wells	2 tms	21	159.0	51	1	.980	7	2	13	5	.385	3	47	+3	0	+2	+3	+5	3	2	2	7	-
Ty Wigginton	Col	21	139.0	18	2	.889	1	0	17	5	.294	0	16	-2	-2	0	+1	-1	-1	-1	0	-2	-
Reggie Willits	LAA	19	82.2	23	0	1.000	0	0	7	4	.571	0	23	0	0	-1	+1	0	0	-1	0	-1	-
Josh Wilson	Mil	3	16.0	2	0	1.000	0	0					2	0	0	0	+1	+1	0	0	0	0	-
Mike Wilson	Sea	5	42.0	9	0	1.000	2	0	6	2	.333	1	8	0	0	0	-1	-1	-1	0	0	-1	-
DeWayne Wise	2 tms	13	21.0	3	0	1.000	1	0	2	2	1.000	0	3	0	+1	0	-2	-1	-1	0	0	-1	-
Eric Young	Col	35	269.1	51	1	.980	4	5	34	15	.441	0	50	-1	0	+1	-2	-1	0	-3	-1	-4	-
Matt Young	Atl	9	35.1	8	0	1.000	3	1	6	2	.333	0	8	0	+1	-1	0	0	0	0	0	0	-
2011 MLB Totals						.984	862	797	4230	1523	.360	182											

All Other Center Fielders

Name	Team	G	Inn	TC	E	Pct	GFP	DM	Opps to Advance	Extra Bases	Pct	Kills	Outs Made	Basic	Shallow	Medium	Deep	Enhanced	+/-	Throws	GFP/ DME	Total	Rank
Matt Angle	Bal	16	124.2	37	0	1.000	3	4	11	8	.727	0	37	-3	0	-1	-7	-8	-5	-1	-1	-7	-
Joe Benson	Min	2	17.0	5	0	1.000	0	1	2	1	.500	0	5	-1	-2	0	0	-2	-1	0	0	-1	-
Roger Bernadina	Was	56	420.2	107	0	1.000	10	11	42	22	.524	3	103	-8	-4	+1	-9	-12	-7	2	3	-2	-
Brian Bixler	Was	4	31.0	7	0	1.000	0	0	7	3	.429	0	7	-1	0	-1	-2	-2	-1	0	0	-1	-
Charlie Blackmon	Col	2	16.0	4	0	1.000	1	1	1	1	1.000	0	4	-1	-1	-3	+2	-1	-1	0	0	-1	-
Brandon Boggs	Mil	1	9.0	1	0	1.000	0	0	1	0	.000	0	1	0	0	0	0	0	0	0	0	0	-
Emilio Bonifacio	Fla	16	89.0	25	0	1.000	0	6	12	8	.667	0	25	-2	-3	+3	-3	-3	-2	-1	-2	-5	-
Julio Borbon	Tex	32	243.1	72	1	.986	6	9	24	9	.375	1	70	-3	+1	-3	-5	-7	-4	1	0	-3	-
Jason Bourgeois	Hou	34	244.0	63	0	1.000	0	3	21	14	.667	0	63	+2	+2	-1	0	+1	0	-2	0	-2	-
Michael Brantley	Cle	52	412.2	119	1	.992	3	7	40	23	.575	0	118	+2	+2	+2	-4	-1	0	-1	-1	-2	-
Travis Buck	Cle	7	8.0	5	0	1.000	0	0				0	5	+1	0	+1	+1	+2	1	0	0	1	-
Lorenzo Cain	KC	2	17.0	2	0	1.000	0	0				0	2	0	0	-1	0	-1	0	0	0	0	-
Mike Cameron	2 tms	42	350.0	97	0	1.000	8	13	34	24	.706	2	94	+5	+6	+3	-4	+5	3	-1	-1	1	-
Tony Campana	ChC	29	208.2	54	0	1.000	5	8	18	10	.556	0	54	+3	+2	-2	+2	+2	1	0	-1	0	-
Brett Carroll	Mil	1	8.0	3	0	1.000	1	0	1	1	1.000	0	3	0	0	0	-1	-1	0	0	0	0	-
Adron Chambers	StL	5	8.1	6	1	.833	0	0				0	5	-1	0	-1	0	-1	-1	0	0	-1	-
Justin Christian	SF	10	76.0	18	0	1.000	3	0	10	5	.500	1	17	+2	0	+2	+1	+4	2	0	0	2	-
Tyler Colvin	ChC	8	67.0	19	0	1.000	0	0	7	3	.429	0	19	-1	0	+1	-1	-1	0	0	0	0	-
Jose Constanza	Atl	4	28.0	6	0	1.000	1	1	2	2	1.000	0	6	-1	0	-2	+1	-1	-1	0	0	-1	-
Scott Cousins	Fla	5	25.0	9	0	1.000	1	1				1	8	0	0	0	+1	+1	0	1	0	1	-
Collin Cowgill	Ari	10	60.0	16	0	1.000	2	0	3	1	.333	1	15	0	-1	+1	+2	+2	1	1	1	3	-
Allen Craig	StL	5	29.0	11	0	1.000	3	1	5	4	.800	0	9	+1	+2	0	-1	+1	1	0	0	1	-
Trevor Crowe	Cle	7	29.0	8	0	1.000	1	1	2	1	.500	0	8	+1	0	+1	0	+2	1	0	0	1	-
Alejandro De Aza	CWS	19	153.1	50	1	.980	1	2	16	8	.500	0	49	+2	-2	+4	+1	+4	2	0	0	2	-
David DeJesus	Oak	8	62.2	9	0	1.000	1	3	4	1	.250	0	9	-4	-4	+1	-4	-7	-4	0	0	-4	-
Chris Denorfia	SD	15	86.2	32	0	1.000	2	4	4	1	.250	0	32	+1	0	0	+1	+1	0	0	1	1	-
Andy Dirks	Det	16	115.0	32	1	.969	2	0	17	13	.765	1	30	-4	-2	-5	0	-7	-4	0	0	-4	-
Luis Durango	Hou	2	17.0	3	0	1.000	0	0	2	1	.500	0	3	0	0	0	0	0	0	0	0	0	-
Jarrod Dyson	KC	17	98.2	31	0	1.000	1	3	8	4	.500	0	31	+4	0	+5	+2	+8	4	0	0	4	-
Darren Ford	SF	15	43.2	11	0	1.000	2	1	1	0	.000	0	11	+2	0	+3	+1	+4	2	0	0	2	-
Kosuke Fukudome	2 tms	13	104.1	31	1	.968	4	1	15	6	.400	1	29	-4	-4	-1	0	-5	-3	2	0	-1	-
Sam Fuld	TB	7	37.2	14	0	1.000	1	1	2	1	.500	0	14	+1	0	0	0	+1	0	0	0	0	-
Brett Gardner	NYY	18	92.1	29	1	.966	3	1	3	1	.333	0	28	+1	+1	0	-1	+1	1	0	-1	0	-
Craig Gentry	Tex	55	313.2	104	1	.990	6	2	33	18	.545	0	103	+9	+3	+4	+9	+16	9	-1	0	8	-
Greg Golson	NYY	3	18.0	5	0	1.000	0	0	2	0	.000	0	5	-1	-1	-1	0	-2	-1	0	0	-1	-
Carlos Gonzalez	Col	30	248.1	66	0	1.000	8	7	32	16	.500	3	63	0	0	+2	-2	-1	0	2	0	2	-
Tony Gwynn	LAD	12	46.0	17	0	1.000	2	1	3	1	.333	1	16	+2	+1	+2	+1	+3	2	1	0	3	-
Jerry Hairston	2 tms	20	123.1	36	0	1.000	4	4	23	9	.391	2	34	-1	+3	0	-7	-3	-2	3	1	2	-
Scott Hairston	NYM	10	59.1	19	0	1.000	0	1	6	2	.333	0	17	-1	-1	-1	+2	0	0	1	0	1	-
Greg Halman	Sea	9	61.0	20	0	1.000	1	2	5	3	.600	0	20	-1	0	-1	-3	-4	-2	0	0	-2	-
Josh Hamilton	Tex	35	259.0	73	1	.986	6	4	19	9	.474	0	71	0	+2	+3	-9	-3	-2	0	0	-2	-
Willie Harris	NYM	7	31.0	9	0	1.000	0	1	2	1	.500	0	9	0	+1	0	-3	-1	-1	0	0	-1	-
Chris Heisey	Cin	18	118.2	32	1	.969	3	1	8	5	.625	0	31	-1	0	0	-1	-2	-1	-1	2	0	-
Kyle Hudson	Bal	2	8.0	1	0	1.000	0	0	1	0	.000	0	1	0	0	0	0	0	0	0	0	0	-
Cedric Hunter	SD	2	3.2	0	0	-	0	0				0	0	0	0	-1	0	-1	0	0	0	0	-
Torii Hunter	LAA	1	8.2	4	0	1.000	1	1				0	4	-1	0	-1	0	0	0	0	0	0	-
Desmond Jennings	TB	8	64.0	18	0	1.000	1	0	6	1	.167	0	18	0	+1	+1	-4	-2	-1	0	0	-1	-
Elliot Johnson	TB	1	1.0	0	0	-	0	0														0	-
Reed Johnson	ChC	24	153.2	45	1	.978	5	6	14	9	.643	1	41	-2	0	-1	-2	-4	-2	0	1	-1	-
Don Kelly	Det	4	25.0	9	0	1.000	0	2	2	1	.500	0	9	-2	-3	-2	+1	-4	-2	0	0	-2	-
Mark Kotsay	Mil	10	58.0	11	0	1.000	0	0	6	4	.667	0	11	-2	-3	0	+1	-2	-1	-1	0	-2	-
Ryan Langerhans	Sea	12	97.0	23	0	1.000	1	2	14	8	.571	0	23	-5	-2	-2	-7	-11	-6	0	0	-6	-
Brent Lillibridge	CWS	11	76.2	26	0	1.000	2	2	5	3	.600	0	26	+1	-1	0	+4	+3	2	0	-1	1	-
Adam Loewen	Tor	3	24.0	8	1	.875	0	0	3	1	.333	0	7	0	0	0	0	0	0	0	0	0	-
Mitch Maier	KC	9	70.0	24	0	1.000	2	1	8	5	.625	0	24	+1	-1	+2	+1	+3	2	0	0	2	-
Leonys Martin	Tex	8	19.0	7	0	1.000	1	0	1	1	1.000	0	7	-1	0	0	-1	-1	-1	0	0	-1	-
Michael Martinez	Phi	12	79.2	22	1	.955	1	2	8	5	.625	0	21	0	+1	-1	+1	0	0	0	0	0	-
Darin Mastroianni	Tor	1	9.0	2	0	1.000	0	2	2	0	.000	0	2	-1	0	-1	0	-1	-1	0	0	-1	-
Joe Mather	Atl	3	20.0	11	0	1.000	1	0				0	11	+1	+1	+1	0	+1	1	0	0	1	-
John Mayberry	Phi	32	246.2	64	2	.969	2	7	18	9	.500	0	62	-3	-2	-2	+2	-2	-1	-1	-2	-4	-
Mike McCoy	Tor	16	116.1	38	0	1.000	2	6	15	7	.467	0	36	-1	0	0	-2	-2	-1	0	-1	-2	-
Darnell McDonald	Bos	13	60.0	23	0	1.000	1	0	4	2	.500	0	23	+3	+4	0	-1	+3	1	0	0	1	-
Jai Miller	Oak	3	5.0	0	0	-	0	0				0	0	0	0	0	0	0	0			0	-
Lou Montanez	ChC	1	1.0	0	0	-	0	0														0	-
David Murphy	Tex	13	92.0	23	0	1.000	2	1	13	6	.462	2	21	-1	+1	0	-4	-3	-2	1	1	0	-
Laynce Nix	Was	4	8.1	0	0	-	0	0				0	0	0	0	-1	0	-1	0	0	0	0	-
Trent Oeltjen	LAD	1	4.0	1	0	1.000	0	0				0	1	0	0	0	0	0	0	0	0	0	-
Gerardo Parra	Ari	2	10.0	3	1	.667	0	0	1	1	1.000	0	2	-2	0	0	-3	-2	-1	0	0	-1	-
Corey Patterson	2 tms	40	287.2	74	0	1.000	5	7	25	16	.640	0	74	+2	+3	+5	-5	+2	1	0	-1	0	-
Eric Patterson	SD	7	47.0	12	0	1.000	1	2	8	4	.500	0	12	0	+1	-1	-2	-2	-1	0	0	-1	-
Xavier Paul	Pit	9	46.1	12	0	1.000	1	1	3	2	.667	1	11	-2	-1	0	-1	-2	-1	1	0	0	-

426

		BASIC							THROWING				PLUS/MINUS						RUNS SAVED				
Name	Team	G	Inn	TC	E	Pct	GFP	DM	Opps to Advance	Extra Bases	Pct	Kills	Outs Made	Basic	Shallow	Medium	Deep	Enhanced	+/-	Throws	GFP/DME	Total	Rank
Bryan Petersen	Fla	42	316.2	76	2	.974	6	6	27	17	.630	3	71	-1	0	-2	-1	-3	-2	2	0	0	-
Felix Pie	Bal	6	33.0	6	0	1.000	0	1	1	0	.000	0	6	0	0	-1	0	-1	-1	0	0	-1	-
Alex Presley	Pit	5	32.1	6	0	1.000	0	1	1	0	.000	0	6	-1	0	-2	-1	-3	-2	0	0	-2	-
Jason Pridie	NYM	43	312.2	88	2	.977	2	7	38	23	.605	1	85	+4	+1	+3	+5	+9	5	-1	-2	2	-
Ryan Raburn	Det	2	3.0	2	0	1.000	0	0				0	2	0	0	0	0	0	0	0	0	0	-
Josh Reddick	Bos	3	21.0	6	0	1.000	0	2	2	0	.000	0	6	0	0	+1	-2	-1	-1	0	0	-1	-
Jason Repko	Min	5	43.0	13	1	.923	2	4	12	6	.500	1	11	-3	-1	-2	-3	-6	-3	0	0	-3	-
Shane Robinson	StL	5	14.2	1	0	1.000	0	0				0	1	0	0	0	0	0	0	0	0	0	-
Trayvon Robinson	Sea	16	109.2	29	3	.897	1	3	12	10	.833	0	25	-3	0	-3	-3	-6	-4	-1	-1	-6	-
Cody Ross	SF	22	158.2	29	0	1.000	2	3	11	8	.727	1	27	-1	+1	-3	-2	-4	-2	0	0	-2	-
Aaron Rowand	SF	60	413.2	125	0	1.000	7	4	41	22	.537	1	123	+3	+5	-8	+5	+2	1	0	1	2	-
Justin Ruggiano	TB	4	20.0	7	0	1.000	2	0	3	2	.667	1	6	0	0	0	+1	+1	0	1	0	1	-
Jerry Sands	LAD	1	2.0	0	0	-	0	0				0	0	0	0	0	0	0	0	0	0	0	-
Dave Sappelt	Cin	4	20.0	7	0	1.000	1	1	2	1	.500	0	7	0	0	+2	-1	+1	0	0	0	0	-
Michael Saunders	Sea	46	376.1	119	0	1.000	7	5	37	22	.595	0	118	+1	0	+3	0	+3	2	-1	2	3	-
Logan Schafer	Mil	1	2.0	0	0	-	0	0				0							0	0	0	0	-
Skip Schumaker	StL	5	13.0	2	0	1.000	0	0	1	0	.000	0	2	0	0	0	0	0	0	0	0	0	-
J.B. Shuck	Hou	9	58.2	25	1	.960	2	0	5	3	.600	1	24	0	0	0	0	0	0	0	0	0	-
Travis Snider	Tor	6	36.0	12	0	1.000	2	2	8	5	.625	1	11	0	0	0	+1	+1	0	0	0	0	-
Ryan Spilborghs	Col	13	71.2	30	0	1.000	1	3	6	5	.833	0	30	-1	-1	+1	-1	-2	-1	-1	0	-2	-
Mike Stanton	Fla	1	1.0	2	0	1.000	0	0				0	2	0	0	0	+1	+1	0	0	0	0	-
Ryan Sweeney	Oak	34	245.2	75	0	1.000	5	2	25	14	.560	0	75	-4	-2	0	-5	-7	-4	-1	0	-5	-
Jose Tabata	Pit	2	17.0	3	1	.667	0	0	3	1	.333	0	2	0	0	0	-1	-1	0	0	0	0	-
Blake Tekotte	SD	7	46.0	6	0	1.000	0	2	5	3	.600	0	6	-2	-1	0	-3	-3	-2	-1	0	-3	-
Mike Trout	LAA	13	107.2	38	1	.974	2	1	9	5	.556	1	37	+1	+1	+1	+1	+3	2	0	0	2	-
Will Venable	SD	14	93.0	23	0	1.000	1	4	7	3	.429	0	22	0	-2	-1	+3	+1	0	0	1	1	-
Casper Wells	2 tms	9	59.0	22	0	1.000	1	0	4	1	.250	0	20	0	-1	0	+2	+1	0	0	0	0	-
Vernon Wells	LAA	12	79.1	24	0	1.000	1	1	12	6	.500	0	24	-2	-3	0	0	-3	-2	0	0	-2	-
Jayson Werth	Was	19	151.2	56	0	1.000	4	1	14	7	.500	0	55	+1	+3	+2	-2	+3	1	0	0	1	-
DeWayne Wise	2 tms	37	195.2	70	2	.971	11	5	13	8	.615	1	67	+2	+2	0	0	+1	1	0	0	1	-
Eric Young	Col	5	39.0	12	1	.917	1	3	4	3	.750	0	11	0	0	-2	+1	-1	-1	0	-1	-2	-
Matt Young	Atl	3	18.0	3	0	1.000	0	0	3	3	1.000	0	3	0	0	0	0	0	0	-1	0	-1	-
2011 MLB Totals						.989	811	795	4022	2268	.564	139											

All Other Right Fielders

		BASIC							THROWING				PLUS/MINUS						RUNS SAVED				
Name	Team	G	Inn	TC	E	Pct	GFP	DM	Opps to Advance	Extra Bases	Pct	Kills	Outs Made	Basic	Shallow	Medium	Deep	Enhanced	+/-	Throws	GFP/DME	Total	Rank
Bobby Abreu	LAA	10	81.1	10	1	.900	0	0	6	2	.333	0	9	-3	-2	-2	+1	-3	-2	0	0	-2	-
Erick Almonte	Mil	7	45.0	2	0	1.000	0	1	3	1	.333	0	2	-2	-2	0	-3	-5	-3	0	0	-3	-
Alfredo Amezaga	Col	2	2.2	0	0	-	0	0					0	0	0	0	0	0	0			0	-
Matt Angle	Bal	2	9.0	3	0	1.000	1	0				0	3	+1	0	+1	0	+1	1	0	0	1	-
Rick Ankiel	Was	9	59.2	12	0	1.000	1	0	10	4	.400	0	11	0	-1	+1	+1	0	0	1	0	1	-
Mike Aviles	Bos	4	10.0	1	0	1.000	0	0	1	0	.000	0	1	-1	0	0	0	-1	0	0	0	0	-
Jeff Baker	ChC	10	46.0	9	0	1.000	0	1	3	0	.000	0	9	0	0	0	0	0	0	0	0	0	-
Mike Baxter	NYM	10	68.0	11	0	1.000	6	4	7	2	.286	1	10	+2	+2	+1	-2	+1	1	1	0	2	-
Josh Bell	Bal	1	2.0	0	0	-	0	0														0	-
Brandon Belt	SF	1	10.2	5	0	1.000	1	0	1	1	1.000	1	4	0	0	0	-1	-1	-1	1	0	0	-
Joe Benson	Min	7	59.2	21	1	.952	0	4	10	5	.500	0	20	-2	-2	0	-3	-4	-2	-1	-1	-4	-
Roger Bernadina	Was	10	63.2	14	1	.929	1	1	4	2	.500	0	13	+2	+1	+1	0	+2	1	0	0	1	-
Brian Bixler	Was	6	14.0	3	0	1.000	1	1	3	1	.333	1	2	0	0	0	0	0	0	1	0	1	-
Andres Blanco	Tex	1	5.0	1	0	1.000	0	0				1	0	-1	-1	0	0	-1	0	1	0	1	-
Brandon Boggs	Mil	2	10.0	1	0	1.000	0	0				0	1	0	0	0	0	0	0	0	0	0	-
Brian Bogusevic	Hou	40	277.0	79	2	.975	13	3	31	18	.581	6	67	+1	-1	0	+3	+3	2	4	4	10	-
Emilio Bonifacio	Fla	15	106.0	28	0	1.000	3	1	6	5	.833	2	26	+2	+1	-1	+2	+3	2	1	1	4	-
Jason Bourgeois	Hou	13	95.1	26	0	1.000	2	2	7	0	.000	1	25	+3	+2	+1	0	+3	2	1	0	3	-
John Bowker	2 tms	2	8.0	4	0	1.000	0	0	1	1	1.000	0	4	0	0	0	+1	+1	0	0	0	0	-
Andrew Brown	StL	7	40.0	10	0	1.000	0	0	6	1	.167	0	10	0	-1	0	0	0	0	0	0	0	-
Travis Buck	Cle	14	100.2	33	1	.970	0	2	9	6	.667	0	32	+1	0	+1	+2	+3	2	-1	0	1	-
Melky Cabrera	KC	2	11.0	0	0	-	0	0	1	0	.000	0	0	0	0	0	0	0	0	0	0	0	-
Lorenzo Cain	KC	4	34.2	5	0	1.000	0	1	4	1	.250	0	5	0	0	+1	0	+1	1	0	0	1	-
Mike Cameron	Bos	25	194.0	46	1	.978	2	8	19	9	.474	0	45	-1	-1	-2	+3	0	0	-1	-1	-2	-
Tony Campana	ChC	5	26.2	16	0	1.000	1	0				0	16	+4	+2	+2	+2	+6	4	0	0	4	-
Mike Carp	Sea	1	3.0	0	0	-	0	0														0	-
Ezequiel Carrera	Cle	6	20.0	4	0	1.000	0	0	1	0	.000	0	4	0	0	0	0	0	0	0	0	0	-
Adron Chambers	StL	1	2.0	1	0	1.000	0	0				0	1	+1	+1	0	0	+1	0	0	0	0	-
Endy Chavez	Tex	6	41.0	4	0	1.000	0	1	4	1	.250	0	4	0	0	0	-1	-1	0	0	0	0	-
Justin Christian	SF	3	8.0	1	0	1.000	0	0	1	1	1.000	0	1	-1	-1	0	0	-1	0	0	0	0	-
Tyler Colvin	ChC	44	314.2	79	1	.987	6	5	35	12	.343	2	76	0	-1	0	+3	+2	1	2	1	4	-
Jose Constanza	Atl	16	114.1	30	0	1.000	1	0	15	10	.667	0	30	+1	+1	-1	+2	+2	1	-1	0	0	-
Scott Cousins	Fla	12	36.2	11	0	1.000	1	2	4	2	.500	1	10	+2	+1	0	+2	+3	2	0	0	2	-
Allen Craig	StL	18	106.0	26	0	1.000	2	0	8	3	.375	0	26	+1	+1	0	0	+2	1	0	1	2	-
Tony Cruz	StL	2	6.0	1	0	1.000	1	0	1	1	1.000	0	1	0	0	0	0	0	0	0	0	0	-
Aaron Cunningham	SD	18	105.2	29	0	1.000	0	2	11	5	.455	0	29	+2	-1	+2	+2	+4	2	0	0	2	-
Rajai Davis	Tor	8	62.0	18	0	1.000	0	1	7	4	.571	0	18	0	0	+1	0	+1	1	0	0	1	-
Alejandro De Aza	CWS	31	202.1	48	0	1.000	7	5	15	8	.533	1	46	+3	+2	+2	+1	+5	3	0	0	3	-
Matt Diaz	2 tms	54	335.2	65	1	.985	5	9	31	14	.452	2	61	-1	+1	+2	-6	-4	-2	0	0	-2	-
Chris Dickerson	NYY	42	119.1	27	2	.926	1	0	13	7	.538	0	25	+2	+2	+1	+2	+4	2	0	0	2	-
Brian Dinkelman	Min	5	22.0	7	0	1.000	1	0	3	3	1.000	0	7	0	0	0	0	0	0	0	0	0	-
Andy Dirks	Det	22	140.1	34	0	1.000	0	2	8	4	.500	1	33	+3	+3	0	+1	+3	2	0	-1	1	-
Greg Dobbs	Fla	4	27.0	3	0	1.000	1	0	2	1	.500	0	3	-1	0	-1	-1	-2	-1	0	0	-1	-
Matt Downs	Hou	3	25.0	4	0	1.000	0	0	2	0	.000	0	4	0	0	+1	0	+1	0	0	0	0	-
Lucas Duda	NYM	42	335.1	74	1	.986	2	15	29	16	.552	0	72	-8	-3	+1	-13	-15	-9	0	-3	-12	-

427

		BASIC							THROWING				PLUS/MINUS						RUNS SAVED				
Name	Team	G	Inn	TC	E	Pct	GFP	DM	Opps to Advance	Extra Bases	Pct	Kills	Outs Made	Basic	Shallow	Medium	Deep	Enhanced	+/-	Throws	GFP/DME	Total	Rank
Shelley Duncan	Cle	2	16.0	1	0	1.000	0	0	5	3	.600	0	1	0	0	0	0	0	0	0	0	0	-
Adam Dunn	CWS	2	14.0	1	0	1.000	0	0				0	1	+1	0	0	+1	+1	1	0	0	1	-
Nick Evans	NYM	8	45.0	9	0	1.000	1	0	2	0	.000	0	9	-2	-1	-1	0	-2	-1	0	0	-1	-
Tommy Field	Col	1	3.0	1	0	1.000	0	0				0	1	0	0	0	0	0	0	0	0	0	-
Sam Fuld	TB	9	40.0	14	0	1.000	1	0	5	0	.000	0	14	0	+1	-2	+1	0	0	1	0	1	-
Cole Garner	Col	1	6.1	3	0	1.000	0	0				0	3	0	0	0	+1	+1	0	0	0	0	-
Craig Gentry	Tex	7	40.0	6	1	.833	0	0	4	2	.500	0	5	0	0	0	0	+1	0	0	0	0	-
Jay Gibbons	LAD	4	29.0	5	0	1.000	1	1	1	0	.000	1	4	-2	-1	0	-1	-2	-1	1	0	0	-
Cole Gillespie	Ari	2	3.2	0	0	-	0	0					0	0	0	0	0	0	0			0	-
Ross Gload	Phi	3	21.0	5	0	1.000	2	0				1	4	0	0	0	0	0	0	1	0	1	-
Greg Golson	NYY	3	8.0	1	0	1.000	0	0					1	0	0	0	0	0	0	0	0	0	-
Jonny Gomes	Was	11	49.1	13	0	1.000	0	1	3	1	.333	0	13	-1	0	-1	0	-1	-1	0	0	-1	-
Adrian Gonzalez	Bos	2	13.0	0	0	-	0	0				0	0	0	0	0	0	0	0	0	0	0	-
Carlos Gonzalez	Col	34	295.1	67	0	1.000	9	7	32	17	.531	2	63	+3	+2	+1	+5	+7	4	0	0	4	-
Tyler Greene	StL	8	14.0	6	0	1.000	0	0					6	0	0	0	0	0	0	0	0	0	-
Brandon Guyer	TB	11	74.0	13	0	1.000	2	0	5	1	.200	0	13	+2	+1	+1	0	+2	1	0	0	1	-
Jesus Guzman	SD	1	4.0	0	0	-	0	0					0	0	0	0	0	0	0			0	-
Tony Gwynn	LAD	2	6.2	0	0	-	0	0				0	0	0	0	0	0	0	0	0	0	0	-
Scott Hairston	NYM	15	85.1	18	1	.944	0	4	11	7	.636	0	17	0	0	-1	+2	0	0	0	-1	-1	-
Greg Halman	Sea	2	12.0	0	0	-	0	0					0	0	0	0	0	0	0			0	-
Willie Harris	NYM	6	22.1	6	0	1.000	0	0	7	2	.286	0	6	-3	-2	-1	-1	-4	-2	0	0	-2	-
Brad Hawpe	SD	7	61.0	11	0	1.000	0	2	3	2	.667	0	11	0	-1	0	+1	+1	0	0	0	0	-
Brett Hayes	Fla	1	1.0	0	0	-	0	0					0	0	0	0	0	0	0			0	-
Chris Heisey	Cin	10	70.1	19	0	1.000	2	0	6	2	.333	1	19	+3	+2	+2	0	+4	2	1	0	3	-
Jeremy Hermida	2 tms	14	104.1	25	0	1.000	2	1	5	1	.200	1	24	+2	+1	0	+2	+3	2	1	0	3	-
Eric Hinske	Atl	16	110.0	25	0	1.000	4	1	13	8	.615	0	24	-1	-2	+1	+1	0	0	-1	0	-1	-
Aubrey Huff	SF	13	86.0	13	0	1.000	2	5	11	8	.727	0	12	-7	-2	-4	-5	-11	-7	-1	0	-8	-
Conor Jackson	2 tms	31	232.2	55	1	.982	13	5	17	7	.412	1	52	+4	+1	+1	+3	+6	4	1	1	6	-
Jon Jay	StL	56	303.2	85	0	1.000	10	7	31	19	.613	1	84	+8	+4	+5	+5	+13	8	-2	1	7	-
Desmond Jennings	TB	1	1.0	0	0	-	0	0														0	-
Reed Johnson	ChC	44	266.0	66	1	.985	3	4	26	13	.500	1	63	+3	+2	0	+2	+4	2	-1	-1	0	-
Andruw Jones	NYY	19	123.2	30	1	.967	3	0	10	9	.900	1	29	0	+2	0	-2	0	0	0	0	0	-
Austin Kearns	Cle	19	150.1	37	1	.973	2	2	13	7	.538	1	35	+1	+2	0	-3	-1	0	1	0	1	-
Don Kelly	Det	39	154.2	36	1	.972	5	0	10	4	.400	1	34	0	0	0	0	0	0	1	1	2	-
Mark Kotsay	Mil	30	223.1	49	1	.980	3	0	20	7	.350	0	48	+2	-1	+2	+6	+7	4	-1	0	3	-
Bryan LaHair	ChC	9	66.0	20	1	.950	1	1	5	3	.600	0	19	0	+1	+1	-1	+1	0	0	0	0	-
Ryan Langerhans	Sea	1	8.0	2	0	1.000	0	0	1	1	1.000	0	2	0	0	0	0	0	0	0	0	0	-
Fred Lewis	Cin	4	21.1	6	1	.833	0	0	2	1	.500	0	5	-1	0	-1	0	-1	0	0	0	0	-
Brent Lillibridge	CWS	43	203.0	45	0	1.000	6	0	21	13	.619	0	45	+3	+2	-2	+7	+7	4	-2	1	3	-
Adam Loewen	Tor	4	28.0	13	1	.923	0	0				0	12	0	0	+1	0	+1	0	0	0	0	-
Ryan Ludwick	2 tms	14	106.0	29	1	.966	3	3	17	8	.471	0	27	-1	-1	0	-2	-4	-2	-1	0	-3	-
Mitch Maier	KC	10	53.2	16	0	1.000	3	3	7	2	.286	1	15	+2	0	0	+3	+3	2	1	0	3	-
Fernando Martinez	NYM	3	17.0	4	0	1.000	0	0	4	1	.250	0	4	0	0	0	0	0	0	0	0	0	-
J.D. Martinez	Hou	1	9.0	1	0	1.000	0	0				0	1	0	0	0	0	0	0	0	0	0	-
Joe Mather	Atl	21	122.0	20	1	.950	0	4	13	5	.385	0	19	-1	-1	-1	0	-2	-1	0	0	-1	-
Joe Mauer	Min	1	9.0	3	0	1.000	0	0				0	3	0	0	0	0	0	0	0	0	0	-
John Mayberry	Phi	10	66.1	13	0	1.000	2	2	8	3	.375	1	12	0	0	+1	-1	0	0	1	0	1	-
Mike McCoy	Tor	5	15.0	4	0	1.000	1	0	2	0	.000	0	4	0	0	0	-1	-1	0	0	0	0	-
Darnell McDonald	Bos	37	207.1	41	1	.976	2	4	28	17	.607	0	39	+2	0	+1	+3	+4	2	-2	0	0	-
Nate McLouth	Atl	3	18.0	2	0	1.000	0	1	4	3	.750	0	2	-1	0	0	-1	-1	-1	0	0	-1	-
Jason Michaels	Hou	16	95.0	23	0	1.000	5	1	11	6	.545	0	23	+5	+2	+4	+3	+8	5	-1	0	4	-
Jai Miller	Oak	2	17.0	2	0	1.000	0	0				0	2	0	0	0	0	0	0	0	0	0	-
Russ Mitchell	LAD	1	1.0	0	0	-	0	0														0	-
Lou Montanez	ChC	14	85.0	21	0	1.000	1	2	12	4	.333	0	20	0	0	+1	-1	-1	0	0	0	0	-
Jeremy Moore	LAA	3	5.0	1	0	1.000	0	0				0	1	0	0	0	0	0	0	0	0	0	-
Mitch Moreland	Tex	34	244.1	56	1	.982	2	4	21	11	.524	0	55	-3	0	+1	-5	-4	-2	0	0	-2	-
Nyjer Morgan	Mil	20	74.2	24	0	1.000	3	0	3	2	.667	1	23	+2	+1	0	+3	+4	2	1	0	3	-
Brandon Moss	Phi	1	4.0	2	0	1.000	0	0	1	1	1.000	0	2	+1	+1	+1	0	+2	1	0	0	1	-
David Murphy	Tex	32	247.1	48	0	1.000	3	3	20	8	.400	1	47	+3	0	0	+5	+5	3	0	0	3	-
Laynce Nix	Was	12	90.0	21	0	1.000	1	4	9	5	.556	1	20	0	+1	0	-2	-1	-1	0	0	-1	-
Eduardo Nunez	NYY	3	17.0	4	0	1.000	0	0	2	2	1.000	0	4	0	0	0	0	0	0	-1	0	-1	-
Trent Oeltjen	LAD	11	49.1	9	0	1.000	0	1	4	2	.500	0	9	-2	-2	-1	0	-2	-1	0	0	-1	-
Gerardo Parra	Ari	14	73.0	19	0	1.000	3	1	4	1	.250	0	19	+4	0	+3	+3	+6	4	0	0	4	-
Andy Parrino	SD	4	12.2	5	0	1.000	0	1	1	0	.000	0	5	-1	-3	0	+2	-2	-1	0	0	-1	-
Corey Patterson	2 tms	25	82.2	24	1	.958	0	1	9	3	.333	0	22	+1	+2	-1	+1	+3	1	0	0	1	-
Eric Patterson	SD	6	45.0	15	0	1.000	2	1	3	2	.667	0	15	-1	0	-1	+1	0	0	0	0	0	-
Xavier Paul	2 tms	72	274.1	61	1	.984	5	7	32	14	.438	0	60	0	+1	-3	+1	-1	-1	0	-1	-2	-
Steve Pearce	Pit	5	32.1	5	1	.800	1	0	6	5	.833	0	4	0	0	0	0	0	0	-1	0	-1	-
Carlos Peguero	Sea	3	11.0	3	0	1.000	0	0				0	3	0	0	0	0	0	0	0	0	0	-
Bryan Petersen	Fla	10	60.0	17	0	1.000	0	1	4	3	.750	0	16	0	0	+1	-2	-1	-1	0	0	-1	-
Felix Pie	Bal	3	19.0	5	0	1.000	0	0	1	0	.000	0	5	0	0	0	0	0	0	0	0	0	-
Trevor Plouffe	Min	11	72.0	16	0	1.000	2	1	12	5	.417	1	15	0	+1	0	-2	-1	-1	1	1	1	-
Jason Pridie	NYM	21	84.2	26	0	1.000	4	2	10	5	.500	1	25	+1	+1	+1	-1	0	0	1	0	1	-
Ryan Raburn	Det	20	81.1	19	3	.842	0	0	10	7	.700	1	15	-2	-1	0	-3	-3	-2	0	-1	-3	-
Wilkin Ramirez	Atl	2	17.0	4	1	.750	0	1				0	3	0	0	0	0	0	0	0	0	0	-
Nolan Reimold	Bal	8	27.0	3	0	1.000	0	2	4	3	.750	0	3	-1	0	+1	-2	-1	-1	-1	0	-2	-
Jason Repko	Min	27	157.2	44	0	1.000	6	2	18	8	.444	0	44	+3	+1	0	+5	+6	3	0	1	4	-
Ben Revere	Min	5	37.0	9	0	1.000	0	0	2	1	.500	0	9	+2	+1	0	+2	+3	2	0	0	2	-
Juan Rivera	2 tms	17	130.1	30	0	1.000	2	2	6	4	.667	0	30	0	-2	0	+3	+2	1	-1	-1	-1	-

		BASIC							THROWING				PLUS/MINUS						RUNS SAVED				
Name	Team	G	Inn	TC	E	Pct	GFP	DM	Opps to Advance	Extra Bases	Pct	Kills	Outs Made	Basic	Shallow	Medium	Deep	Enhanced	+/-	Throws	GFP/DME	Total	Rank
Shane Robinson	StL	3	3.0	1	0	1.000	0	0				0	1	0	0	0	0	0	0	0	0	0	-
Cody Ross	SF	35	268.0	49	0	1.000	4	9	17	12	.706	2	47	-2	+3	-2	-6	-5	-3	-1	0	-4	-
Vinny Rottino	Fla	2	10.0	1	0	1.000	0	0	1	0	.000	0	1	0	0	0	0	0	0	0	0	0	-
Aaron Rowand	SF	3	16.2	2	0	1.000	0	0				0	2	0	0	0	0	0	0	0	0	0	-
Justin Ruggiano	TB	6	38.0	9	0	1.000	0	2	1	0	.000	0	9	0	0	0	-1	-1	-1	0	0	-1	-
Jerry Sands	LAD	22	153.1	30	0	1.000	2	1	8	2	.250	1	28	0	-2	0	0	-1	-1	1	1	1	-
Logan Schafer	Mil	1	1.0	0	0	-	0	0														0	-
Skip Schumaker	StL	31	79.0	21	1	.952	2	2	7	2	.286	1	19	+1	+1	0	0	+2	1	1	0	2	-
J.B. Shuck	Hou	16	73.1	17	0	1.000	2	2	9	6	.667	0	17	0	0	-1	0	0	0	-1	0	-1	-
Travis Snider	Tor	3	24.0	3	0	1.000	0	1				0	3	0	0	0	0	0	0	0	0	0	-
Ryan Spilborghs	Col	29	209.1	37	0	1.000	4	4	21	14	.667	1	35	-1	-1	-1	+2	0	0	-1	-1	-2	-
Ryan Sweeney	Oak	23	153.1	36	0	1.000	6	4	17	7	.412	1	34	-5	-4	-2	-4	-10	-6	1	1	-4	-
Jose Tabata	Pit	15	106.0	15	0	1.000	0	4	16	8	.500	0	15	-2	0	+1	-6	-5	-3	-1	0	-4	-
Michael Taylor	Oak	8	65.0	22	2	.909	2	3	4	3	.750	0	20	-1	0	-1	+1	0	0	0	0	0	-
Mark Teahen	2 tms	9	38.0	3	0	1.000	1	1	5	3	.600	0	3	0	0	-1	0	0	0	0	0	0	-
Blake Tekotte	SD	1	9.0	2	0	1.000	0	0				0	2	0	0	0	0	0	0	0	0	0	-
Eric Thames	Tor	27	223.0	57	1	.982	4	8	25	10	.400	1	55	0	+3	+2	-8	-3	-2	1	-2	-3	-
Andres Torres	SF	4	11.2	8	0	1.000	0	0	3	2	.667	0	8	+2	0	0	+3	+4	2	-1	0	1	-
Rene Tosoni	Min	4	11.1	2	0	1.000	0	0	3	1	.333	0	2	0	0	0	0	0	0	0	0	0	-
Mike Trout	LAA	13	109.0	23	1	.957	3	3	14	6	.429	0	22	+1	-1	+2	+2	+3	2	-1	-1	0	-
Mark Trumbo	LAA	10	21.0	3	0	1.000	0	0	2	1	.500	0	3	-1	0	-2	+1	-1	-1	0	0	-1	-
Dayan Viciedo	CWS	21	163.0	28	0	1.000	2	3	23	6	.261	1	26	-1	+1	-2	0	-1	-1	2	0	1	-
Casper Wells	2 tms	58	274.1	64	1	.984	4	3	21	9	.429	2	61	+1	0	+2	0	+1	0	1	0	1	-
Vernon Wells	LAA	10	66.1	16	0	1.000	1	1	6	4	.667	0	16	-1	0	-4	+3	-2	-1	0	0	-1	-
Ty Wigginton	Col	6	46.2	9	0	1.000	1	3	1	0	.000	1	9	0	0	0	-1	0	0	1	0	1	-
Reggie Willits	LAA	1	3.0	0	0	-	0	0											0			0	-
Mike Wilson	Sea	2	17.0	2	0	1.000	0	0				0	2	0	0	0	0	0	0	0	0	0	-
DeWayne Wise	Tor	2	8.0	1	0	1.000	0	0	1	0	.000	0	1	0	0	0	0	0	0	0	0	0	-
Wesley Wright	Hou	1	0.1	0	0	-	0	0														0	-
Eric Young	Col	3	17.0	7	1	.857	0	0	5	2	.400	2	5	0	0	0	-1	-1	0	2	0	2	-
Matt Young	Atl	7	49.0	7	0	1.000	0	0	1	1	1.000	0	7	+1	0	0	+2	+2	1	0	0	1	-
Ben Zobrist	TB	38	289.2	66	0	1.000	9	5	21	8	.381	0	65	+5	0	+4	+4	+8	5	0	1	6	-
2011 MLB Totals						.985	844	846	4180	2065	.494	209											

429

Pitchers

BASIC								HOLDING				RUNS SAVED					
Player	Tm	Inn	TC	E	GFP	DM	+/-	SB	CCS	PCS/PPO	CS%	+/-	SB	Bnt	GFP/DME	Tot	Rk
F Abad	Hou	20	5	2	0	0	0	1	0	0	.00	0	0	-1	0	-1	-
J Abreu	Hou	7	1	0	0	0	0	0	0	0	-	0	0		0	0	-
J Accardo	Bal	38	6	0	0	0	+1	5	0	0	.00	0	-1	0	0	-1	-
A Aceves	Bos	114	11	0	0	1	-1	9	0	0	.00	-1	-1	0	0	-2	135
M Acosta	NYM	47	6	0	1	1	-1	5	3	0	.38	-1	0	0	0	-1	-
M Adams	2 tms	74	9	0	1	0	-1	9	0	0	.00	-1	-2	0	0	-3	-
N Adcock	KC	60	15	0	1	0	+1	5	1	0	.17	1	0	1	1	3	-
J Affeldt	SF	62	18	0	1	2	+2	4	1	0	.20	2	0	0	0	2	-
M Albers	Bos	65	10	1	1	1	-1	6	3	1	.40	-1	0	0	0	-1	-
Alburquerque	Det	43	6	0	0	0	0	5	1	0	.17	0	0	0	0	0	-
H Alvarez	Tor	64	19	1	2	0	+4	1	2	0	.67	3	1	0	0	4	-
B Anderson	Oak	83	23	2	1	2	-2	5	2	5	.58	-1	2	0	0	1	88
J Arredondo	Cin	53	11	0	0	0	-2	2	4	0	.67	-1	1	0	0	0	-
J Arrieta	Bal	119	28	3	0	1	+4	11	4	0	.27	3	-1	0	0	2	42
B Arroyo	Cin	199	56	4	3	3	+3	9	4	0	.31	2	0	2	0	4	18
J Ascanio	Pit	6	0	0	0	0	-1	0	0	0	-	-1	0			-1	-
J Asencio	Atl	10	5	0	0	0	+1	0	0	0	-	1	0		0	1	-
S Atchison	Bos	30	6	1	0	1	+1	1	3	0	.75	1	1		-1	1	-
M Atkins	Bal	11	1	0	0	0	0	0	0	0	-	0	0		0	0	-
B Augenstein	StL	6	1	0	0	0	0	0	1	0	1.00	0	0	0	0	0	-
D Axelrod	CWS	19	7	0	0	0	0	1	0	0	.00	0	0	0	0	0	-
J Axford	Mil	74	10	2	0	0	+1	6	2	0	.25	0	0	0	0	0	-
L Ayala	NYY	56	13	0	1	1	+1	4	0	0	.00	1	0	0	0	1	-
B Badenhop	Fla	64	13	0	1	0	-2	2	1	1	.33	-1	1	0	1	1	-
D Baez	Phi	36	7	0	1	0	0	7	0	0	.00	0	-1		0	-1	-
A Bailey	Oak	42	5	0	1	1	-1	5	0	0	.00	-1	-1	0	0	-2	-
H Bailey	Cin	132	26	1	2	2	-1	9	2	1	.18	-1	0	-1	0	-2	135
S Baker	Min	135	17	0	1	2	-2	4	5	0	.56	-2	1	-1	0	-2	143
C Balester	Was	36	3	1	0	1	-1	5	1	0	.17	-1	-1	0	0	-2	-
G Balfour	Oak	62	6	0	0	0	-1	1	0	0	.00	0	0		0	0	-
D Bard	Bos	73	17	1	1	0	0	7	1	0	.13	0	-1	-2	0	-3	-
A Bass	SD	48	18	0	1	0	+2	5	1	0	.17	2	0	0	1	3	-
A Bastardo	Phi	58	4	1	0	1	+1	2	0	0	.00	1	0	-1	0	0	-
M Batista	2 tms	60	12	0	1	1	+1	4	0	0	.00	1	0	0	0	1	-
B Beachy	Atl	142	23	0	1	0	+2	13	3	2	.24	1	0	0	0	1	65
P Beato	NYM	67	17	0	0	2	+2	6	3	0	.33	2	0	0	0	2	-
B Beavan	Sea	97	15	0	1	1	0	6	2	1	.33	0	0	0	0	0	100
C Beck	Tor	2	0	0	0	0	0	0	0	0	-		0			0	-
J Beckett	Bos	193	36	3	3	2	-1	31	4	0	.11	-1	-4	0	0	-5	165
E Bedard	2 tms	129	15	1	0	2	-1	3	2	2	.50	0	2	-1	0	1	74
J Beimel	Pit	25	1	0	0	1	0	1	0	0	.00	0	0	-1	0	-1	-
M Belisle	Col	72	13	0	1	1	0	0	3	1	1.00	0	1	0	0	1	-
H Bell	SD	63	8	0	0	0	-2	4	0	0	.00	-1	0	1	0	0	-
T Bell	LAA	34	5	0	0	0	-2	0	3	0	1.00	-2	1		0	-1	-
D Below	Det	29	2	0	0	0	-1	2	0	1	.33	-1	0		0	-1	-
J Benoit	Det	61	5	0	1	0	0	3	2	0	.40	0	0	1	0	1	-
J Berg	ChC	12	2	0	0	0	0	0	1	0	1.00	0	0		0	0	-
B Bergesen	Bal	101	18	2	1	3	+1	4	4	0	.50	1	1		0	2	47
J Berken	Bal	47	8	0	0	0	0	1	0	0	.00	0	0		0	0	-
D Betances	NYY	3	0	0	0	0	0	1	0	0	.00		0		0	0	-
R Betancourt	Col	62	2	0	0	1	-1	5	0	0	.00	-1	-1	0	0	-2	-
B Billings	2 tms	7	2	0	0	1	0	0	0	0	-	0	0		0	0	-
C Billingsley	LAD	188	31	2	2	3	+1	9	4	0	.31	1	0	0	0	1	65
N Blackburn	Min	148	42	2	4	3	+2	11	9	3	.45	1	2	1	0	4	23
J Blanton	Phi	41	9	0	1	1	-1	4	0	0	.00	0	-1	0	0	-1	-
J Blevins	Oak	28	3	0	0	0	0	1	0	0	.00	0	0	0	0	0	-
M Boggs	StL	61	11	1	2	3	-1	2	2	0	.50	-1	0	0	-1	-2	-
M Bowden	Bos	20	3	0	0	0	0	2	1	0	.33	0	0		0	0	-
B Boyer	NYM	7	1	0	0	1	0	1	0	0	.00	0	0	0	0	0	-
B Brach	SD	7	0	0	0	0	0	0	0	0	-	0	0			0	-
A Brackman	NYY	2	0	0	0	0	0	0	0	0	-	0	0			0	-
Z Braddock	Mil	17	0	0	0	0	0	2	0	0	.00	0	0			0	-
D Braden	Oak	18	1	0	0	0	-1	0	3	0	1.00	-1	1		0	0	-
B Bray	Cin	48	5	1	1	0	-1	4	2	0	.33	-1	0	1	0	0	-
Y Brazoban	Ari	6	0	0	0	0	0	0	0	0	-		0			0	-
C Breslow	Oak	59	10	1	1	1	-2	3	2	5	.70	-1	2	0	0	1	-
Z Britton	Bal	154	32	2	1	2	-1	7	3	0	.30	-1	0	-3	0	-4	160
B Broderick	Was	12	4	0	0	0	+1	1	1	0	.50	0	0	0	0	0	-
R Brothers	Col	41	3	2	0	0	0	6	1	0	.14	0	-1		0	-1	-
J Broxton	LAD	13	4	0	0	0	+1	0	0	0	-	1	0		0	1	-
B Bruney	CWS	20	4	0	0	0	-1	4	1	0	.20	-1	0	0	0	-1	-
C Buchholz	Bos	83	30	1	2	1	+2	6	2	1	.33	2	0	0	0	2	44
T Buchholz	NYM	26	4	0	0	0	0	4	1	0	.20	0	0	0	0	0	-
M Buehrle	CWS	205	56	1	1	2	+6	3	3	6	.70	4	4	-1	0	7	5
J Buente	2 tms	5	2	0	0	0	+1	0	1	0	1.00	0	0		0	0	-
J Bulger	LAA	9	4	1	0	0	0	3	0	0	.00	0	-1		0	-1	-
M Bumgarner	SF	205	32	3	1	4	-4	12	8	4	.48	-3	2	0	-1	-2	147
A Burnett	NYY	190	38	5	0	2	-6	24	5	5	.23	-4	0	0	0	-4	162
A Burnett	Min	51	10	1	1	0	+2	7	1	0	.13	1	-1	0	0	0	-
S Burnett	Was	57	23	0	3	0	+3	2	0	0	.00	2	0	0	0	2	-
B Burres	Pit	14	2	0	0	0	0	1	0	0	.00	0	0	0	0	0	-
J Burton	Cin	5	0	0	0	0	0	2	0	0	.00	0	0			0	-
D Bush	Tex	37	10	0	3	1	+1	8	1	0	.11	1	-1	0	0	0	-
T Byrdak	NYM	38	5	0	0	3	0	1	0	1	.50	0	0	0	-1	-1	-
T Cahill	Oak	208	45	1	3	3	+1	28	7	3	.22	1	-2	-2	0	-3	150
M Cain	SF	222	40	3	3	3	+2	18	5	0	.22	2	-1	1	-1	1	62
S Camp	Tor	66	24	1	0	0	0	8	1	3	.20	0	0	1	0	1	-
M Capps	Min	66	15	0	2	0	+1	2	0	0	.00	1	0	1	0	2	-
C Capuano	NYM	186	35	0	4	3	0	9	2	3	.36	0	1	0	0	1	74
A Carignan	Oak	6	1	0	0	0	0	1	0	0	.00	0	0		0	0	-
B Carlyle	NYY	8	1	0	0	0	0	0	1	0	1.00		0		0	0	-
F Carmona	Cle	189	38	0	1	4	+4	15	6	0	.29	3	-1	0	0	2	42
C Carpenter	StL	237	54	3	6	4	-4	5	6	0	.55	-3	2	1	0	0	118
C Carpenter	ChC	10	3	1	0	0	0	1	1	0	.50	0	0		0	0	-
D Carpenter	Hou	28	8	0	0	0	+1	1	0	0	.00	1	0	1	0	2	-
D Carpenter	2 tms	15	1	0	0	0	-1	2	1	0	.33	-1	0		0	-1	-
C Carrasco	Cle	125	19	0	1	2	+1	6	1	2	.33	1	1	0	0	2	47
D Carrasco	NYM	49	9	1	0	0	0	6	2	0	.25	0	0		0	0	-
J Carreno	Tor	16	2	0	0	0	+1	0	1	0	1.00	1	0		0	1	-
A Cashner	ChC	11	1	0	0	0	0	0	0	0	-	0	0		0	0	-
S Casilla	SF	52	6	0	1	0	-1	3	0	0	.00	-1	0	0	0	-1	-
B Cassevah	LAA	40	6	0	0	0	0	5	1	0	.17	0	0	0	0	0	-
A Castillo	Ari	12	4	0	0	0	+1	1	0	0	.00	0	0		0	0	-
B Cecil	Tor	124	14	1	2	1	+2	4	2	0	.33	1	0	0	0	1	65
J Ceda	Fla	20	2	0	0	1	0	1	0	0	.00	0	0		0	0	-
X Cedeno	Hou	2	0	0	0	0	0	0	0	0	-	0	0			0	-
J Chacin	Col	194	69	4	0	2	+9	4	7	1	.64	6	2	-1	0	7	3
J Chamberlain	NYY	29	7	0	1	0	0	2	1	0	.33	0	0		0	0	-
A Chapman	Cin	50	15	4	1	1	-1	2	0	4	.67	-1	2	1	0	2	-
T Chatwood	LAA	142	31	0	1	0	+2	12	6	2	.37	2	1	0	0	3	26
J Chavez	KC	8	0	0	0	0	0	1	0	0	.00	0	0			0	-
B Chen	KC	155	32	0	6	3	+3	12	2	4	.33	2	1	0	0	3	26
R Choate	Fla	25	12	1	1	0	0	2	0	0	.00	0	0	0	0	0	-
S Cishek	Fla	55	13	4	0	1	0	5	0	0	.00	0	-1	-2	0	-3	-
M Cleto	StL	4	0	0	0	0	0	0	0	0	-	0	0			0	-
T Clippard	Was	88	8	0	0	1	0	3	4	1	.63	0	1	0	0	1	74
A Cobb	TB	53	12	1	0	5	-1	11	0	0	.00	0	-2	0	0	-2	-
T Coffey	Was	60	8	1	0	1	-2	2	1	0	.33	-1	0	0	0	-1	-
P Coke	Det	109	21	2	0	0	-3	10	3	3	.38	-2	1	1	0	0	114
C Coleman	ChC	84	20	0	1	1	+2	8	1	1	.11	1	0	1	0	2	47
L Coleman	KC	60	7	1	0	0	-2	2	4	0	.67	-1	1	1	0	1	-
T Collins	KC	67	10	0	3	2	+1	7	1	0	.13	1	-1	1	-1	0	-
J Collmenter	Ari	154	24	0	1	1	-1	4	7	0	.64	0	1	0	0	1	74
B Colon	NYY	164	29	1	4	0	0	5	3	1	.38	0	1		0	1	74
J Contreras	Phi	14	0	0	0	0	0	2	1	0	.33	0	0			0	-
A Cook	Col	97	43	3	2	0	+5	1	4	1	.80	4	2	0	0	6	9
R Cook	Ari	8	3	0	0	0	0	3	0	1	.00	0	0		0	0	-
F Cordero	Cin	70	17	1	4	0	-1	9	2	0	.18	-1	-1	1	0	-1	-
L Cormier	LAD	14	7	1	0	0	+1	0	0	0	-	1	0		0	1	-
K Correia	Pit	154	33	0	4	2	+2	6	5	1	.50	2	1	-1	0	2	44
D Cortes	Sea	11	4	0	1	0	0	2	1	0	.33	0	0		0	0	-
J Crain	CWS	65	15	1	5	1	0	13	2	2	.13	0	-1	0	0	-1	-
B Cramer	Oak	8	0	0	0	0	-1	0	0	0	-	0	0			0	-
M Crotta	Pit	11	1	0	0	0	0	2	1	0	.33	0	0		0	0	-
A Crow	KC	62	13	1	0	0	-3	6	1	0	.14	-2	0	1	0	-1	-
J Cruz	TB	49	7	0	1	1	-1	8	3	0	.27	-1	-1	0	0	-2	-
M Cuddyer	Min	1	0	0	0	0	0	0	0	0	-					0	-
J Cueto	Cin	156	46	5	2	1	+1	1	4	2	.80	1	2	0	0	3	33
M Daley	Col	6	1	0	0	0	-1	0	0	0	-	0	0	0	0	0	-
J Danks	CWS	170	34	0	2	1	-1	15	2	7	.35	-1	2	2	0	3	41
K Davies	KC	61	11	1	1	1	-1	8	2	0	.20	0	-1	-1	0	-2	-
D Davis	ChC	46	8	1	1	1	0	3	0	1	.00	0	0	-1	0	-1	-
W Davis	TB	184	29	0	2	0	-1	2	3	2	.67	0	2	1	0	3	40
J De Fratus	Phi	4	1	0	0	0	0	0	0	0	-		0	0	0	0	-
F de la Cruz	Mil	13	0	0	0	0	0	1	0	0	.00	0	0			0	-
D de la Rosa	TB	7	0	0	0	0	0	0	1	0	1.00	0	0			0	-
J de la Rosa	Col	59	12	0	0	0	0	10	2	0	.17	0	-1	0	0	-1	-
R de la Rosa	LAD	61	18	2	1	2	-1	9	4	0	.31	-1	-1	0	-1	-3	-
De Los Santos	Oak	33	5	0	1	0	0	6	1	0	.14	0	-1	0	0	-1	-
S Deduno	SD	3	2	0	0	0	0	2	0	0	.00	0	0		0	0	-
E Del Rosario	Hou	53	13	0	0	1	-2	10	1	0	.09	-2	-1	0	0	-3	-
S Delabar	Sea	7	0	0	0	0	-1	0	2	0	1.00	0	0			0	-
R Delaney	TB	5	1	0	0	0	0	1	0	0	.00	0	0		0	0	-
R Delgado	Atl	35	10	0	1	0	0	2	1	0	.33	0	0	0	0	0	-
S Demel	Ari	26	3	0	0	0	-4	1	1	0	.50	-3	0		0	-3	-
R Dempster	ChC	202	52	3	1	4	+1	17	10	0	.37	1	0	-1	0	0	93
R Detwiler	Was	66	9	1	0	1	-1	3	2	0	.40	-1	0	-1	0	-2	-
J Devine	Oak	23	0	0	0	0	-1	5	0	0	.00	0	-1			-1	-
S Diamond	Min	39	4	0	0	0	+1	2	0	0	.00	0	0	0	0	0	-
R Dickey	NYM	209	67	2	3	1	+8	7	2	5	.30	6	2	1	1	10	1
B Dickson	StL	8	0	0	0	0	0	0	0	0	-	0	0			0	-
M DiFelice	Mil	3	1	0	0	0	0	1	0	0	.00	0	0		0	0	-
T Dillard	Mil	29	10	0	0	0	+2	2	2	0	.50	1	0	0	0	1	-
R Dolis	ChC	1	1	0	0	0	0	0	0	0	-		0		0	0	-
O Dotel	2 tms	54	6	1	0	1	0	1	0	1	.50	0	1	-1	0	0	-
F Doubront	Bos	10	2	0	0	0	0	2	1	2	.60	0	1		0	1	-
S Downs	LAA	54	19	0	1	1	+3	0	0	0	-	2	0	0	0	2	-
K Drabek	Tor	79	23	0	2	1	+2	8	3	4	.27	2	1	1	0	4	18
B Duensing	Min	162	32	4	2	1	-2	6	5	1	.50	-2	1	-1	1	-1	128
D Duffy	KC	105	17	0	1	1	-2	11	2	7	.45	-1	2	1	0	2	59
Z Duke	Ari	77	16	0	0	1	-3	0	3	1	1.00	-2	1	0	0	-1	128
P Dumatrait	Min	41	9	0	0	4	+1	5	1	0	.17	1	0	-1	0	0	-
M Dunn	Fla	63	11	1	0	0	-3	1	0	1	.50	-2	1	-1	0	-2	-
C Durbin	Cle	68	10	0	0	4	0	6	3	0	.33	0	0		0	0	-
S Edlefsen	SF	11	4	0	0	0	0	0	0	0	-	0	0		0	0	-
M Ekstrom	TB	1	0	0	0	0	0	0	0	0	-		0			0	-
S Elbert	LAD	33	2	0	0	0	-2	1	1	0	.50	-1	0		0	-1	-
J Ely	LAD	13	2	1	0	0	0	2	1	0	.33	0	0		0	0	-
B Enright	Ari	38	7	0	1	0	+1	1	0	0	.00	1	0		0	1	-
N Eovaldi	LAD	35	8	0	0	0	+2	2	0	2	.33	2	1		0	3	-
C Eppley	Tex	9	5	0	0	0	0	1	1	0	.50	0	0	0	0	0	-
E Escalona	Col	26	6	0	1	0	+1	2	1	0	.33	1	0	0	0	1	-
S Escalona	Hou	28	9	1	0	0	-1	5	1	0	.17	0	-1	0	0	-1	-
M Estrada	Mil	93	16	0	0	0	-1	8	2	1	.20	-1	0	0	0	-1	123

BASIC								HOLDING				RUNS SAVED					
Player	Tm	Inn	TC	E	GFP	DM	+/-	SB	CCS	PCS/PPO	CS%	+/-	SB	Bnt	GFP/DME	Tot	Rk
D Eveland	LAD	30	8	0	0	0	0	2	1	1	.50	0	0	0	0	0	-
W Eyre	Bal	18	4	0	0	1	0	1	1	0	.50	0	0	0	0	0	-
K Farnsworth	TB	58	15	1	0	0	0	2	1	0	.33	0	0		0	0	-
D Farquhar	Tor	2	0	0	0	0	0	0	0	0	-		0			0	-
S Feldman	Tex	32	10	0	0	0	+2	3	4	0	.57	2	0		0	2	-
N Feliz	Tex	62	14	1	0	0	-1	1	3	2	.75	-1	2	0	0	1	-
M Fiers	Mil	2	2	0	0	0	0	1	0	1	.50	0	0		0	0	-
N Figueroa	Hou	29	7	3	0	0	-1	6	0	0	.00	-1	-1	0	0	-2	-
C Fisher	Cin	24	6	1	0	0	+1	2	1	0	.33	1	0	0	0	1	-
D Fister	2 tms	216	58	3	9	6	+5	4	2	0	.33	4	1	-1	0	4	15
G Floyd	CWS	194	35	1	4	0	+2	23	2	1	.08	1	-2	0	1	0	93
J Francis	KC	183	35	0	1	1	+5	18	4	1	.22	4	-1	1	0	4	15
F Francisco	Tor	51	5	1	0	0	0	13	1	0	.07	0	-2	0	0	-2	-
R Franklin	StL	28	11	0	0	0	0	0	0	0	-	0	0	0	0	0	-
J Frasor	2 tms	60	8	0	0	1	+2	10	2	0	.17	1	-2		0	-1	-
E Frieri	SD	63	5	0	0	0	-1	7	4	1	.42	-1	0	0	0	-1	-
B Fuentes	Oak	58	11	1	0	2	+3	6	0	1	.14	2	0	0	-1	1	-
J Fulchino	2 tms	35	6	0	0	1	0	9	0	0	.00	0	-1	0	0	-1	-
C Furbush	2 tms	85	19	0	2	1	+4	11	2	4	.35	3	1	0	0	4	17
A Galarraga	Ari	43	7	0	0	0	0	1	0	0	.00	0	0	0	0	0	-
Y Gallardo	Mil	207	44	2	2	0	+3	14	6	1	.33	3	0	0	0	3	25
F Garcia	NYY	147	31	1	1	1	-1	22	6	1	.24	-1	-2	-1	0	-4	160
J Garcia	StL	195	27	2	2	3	+2	15	0	3	.17	2	0	-1	0	1	62
J Garland	LAD	54	16	0	0	0	+4	2	1	0	.33	3	0	0	0	3	-
S Garrison	NYY	1	0	0	0	0	0	0	0	0	-					0	-
M Garza	ChC	198	32	7	2	3	-3	10	4	1	.33	-2	1	-1	-1	-3	156
J Gaub	ChC	3	1	0	0	0	0	0	0	0	-	0	0		0	0	-
C Gaudin	Was	8	0	0	0	0	0	1	1	0	.50	0	0			0	-
C Gearrin	Atl	18	1	0	0	0	0	3	0	0	.00	0	0		0	0	-
D Gee	NYM	161	30	1	4	3	-1	8	7	0	.47	-1	1	1	0	1	88
J Germano	Cle	13	5	0	1	0	+2	0	0	0	-	1	0	0	0	1	-
G Godfrey	Oak	25	7	0	0	1	-1	0	0	0	-	-1	0	0	0	-1	-
B Gomes	TB	37	6	0	0	0	0	3	1	0	.25	0	0	0	0	0	-
J Gomez	Cle	58	17	1	3	1	+3	6	3	1	.40	2	0		0	2	-
E Gonzalez	Col	2	1	0	0	0	0	0	0	0	-	0	0		0	0	-
E Gonzalez	Det	9	2	0	0	0	-1	0	1	0	1.00	-1	0		0	-1	-
G Gonzalez	Oak	202	34	1	5	1	-1	19	2	2	.17	-1	-1	0	0	-2	135
M Gonzalez	2 tms	53	7	0	1	2	-1	4	0	0	.00	-1	-1	1	0	-1	-
B Gordon	NYY	10	1	0	0	0	-1	0	2	0	1.00	0	0	0	0	0	-
T Gorzelanny	Was	105	13	2	0	1	-1	8	0	1	.11	-1	0	-1	0	-2	135
J Grabow	ChC	62	8	1	0	0	-3	3	1	2	.50	-2	1	0	0	-1	-
J Gray	2 tms	48	14	3	2	1	0	3	3	0	.50	1	0		-1	0	-
S Green	Mil	12	1	0	0	0	0	3	0	0	.00	0	0		0	0	-
L Gregerson	SD	56	24	2	1	1	+2	5	0	0	.00	2	-1	0	0	1	-
K Gregg	Bal	60	11	0	0	0	0	6	2	0	.25	0	0		0	0	-
Z Greinke	Mil	172	35	0	4	2	+2	8	5	1	.43	2	1	1	0	4	18
J Grilli	Pit	33	10	0	0	0	+2	0	0	1	-	2	1		0	3	-
J Guerra	LAD	47	12	1	2	0	-3	0	0	1	1.00	-2	1	0	0	-1	-
M Guerrier	LAD	66	9	0	2	0	-1	7	0	0	.00	0	-1	0	0	-1	-
J Guthrie	Bal	208	49	3	5	2	+4	3	5	1	.67	3	2	1	0	6	10
J Gutierrez	Ari	18	3	2	0	0	-3	2	0	0	.00	-2	0		0	-2	-
E Hacker	Min	5	1	0	0	0	0	0	0	0	-	0	0		0	0	-
N Hagadone	Cle	11	1	0	0	0	-1	0	0	1	1.00	-1	0		0	-1	-
R Halladay	Phi	234	43	1	1	2	-2	18	4	1	.22	-2	-1	0	0	-3	156
M Hamburger	Tex	8	0	0	0	0	0	1	0	0	.00	0	0			0	-
C Hamels	Phi	216	34	1	4	2	+5	23	5	1	.21	4	-2	-1	0	1	61
J Hammel	Col	170	39	1	1	1	0	16	5	2	.27	0	0	-1	0	-1	121
E Hamren	SD	12	4	1	0	0	0	0	1	0	1.00	0	0	0	0	0	-
B Hand	Fla	60	13	1	0	0	+2	3	1	3	.57	2	1	0	0	3	-
J Hanrahan	Pit	69	13	2	0	2	-2	3	0	0	.00	-2	0	0	0	-2	-
T Hanson	Atl	130	18	2	0	1	-1	30	2	1	.09	0	-4	0	0	-4	159
J Happ	Hou	156	17	0	1	0	0	11	2	3	.31	0	1	0	0	1	74
A Harang	SD	171	29	4	2	3	+1	24	9	2	.29	1	-1	-2	0	-2	132
R Harden	Oak	83	15	2	0	2	-2	4	5	0	.56	-1	1	0	-1	-1	123
D Haren	LAA	238	48	0	2	1	+5	21	2	3	.19	4	-1	0	0	3	24
L Harrell	2 tms	18	7	1	0	0	0	0	0	0	-	0	0	0	0	0	-
M Harrison	Tex	186	40	4	3	4	-5	3	1	2	.50	-4	1	-1	-1	-5	170
C Hatcher	Fla	10	0	0	0	0	-1	0	0	0	-	-1	0			-1	-
L Hawkins	Mil	48	12	1	1	1	-1	2	1	0	.33	-1	0	-1	0	-2	-
B Hawksworth	LAD	53	9	0	1	1	+1	5	1	0	.17	1	0	0	0	1	-
A Heilman	Ari	35	8	1	0	1	-1	1	0	0	.00	-1	0	0	0	-1	-
J Hellickson	TB	189	31	0	1	2	+1	10	0	3	.09	0	0	0	0	0	100
M Hendrickson	Bal	11	6	0	0	0	0	1	0	0	.00	0	0	0	0	0	-
L Hendriks	Min	23	6	0	0	0	+2	0	0	0	-	1	0		0	1	-
C Hensley	Fla	68	12	0	0	1	0	4	1	0	.20	0	0	0	0	0	-
D Hernandez	Ari	69	10	1	2	0	0	2	1	0	.33	0	0	-1	0	-1	-
F Hernandez	Sea	234	57	2	3	3	-2	31	8	2	.21	-2	-2	-1	0	-5	166
L Hernandez	Was	175	45	1	5	3	+3	9	8	1	.50	2	1	0	0	3	26
D Herndon	Phi	57	14	0	0	1	+1	3	2	0	.40	1	0	1	0	2	-
D Herrera	2 tms	10	1	0	0	0	-1	0	0	0	-	-1	0		0	-1	-
K Herrera	KC	2	2	0	0	0	0	0	0	0	-	0	0	0	0	0	-
F Herrmann	Cle	56	3	0	0	0	-2	7	0	0	.00	-2	-1	0	0	-3	-
R Hill	Bos	8	1	0	0	0	0	1	0	0	.00	0	0		0	0	-
L Hochevar	KC	198	42	3	0	0	0	20	3	0	.13	0	-2	1	0	-1	121
J Hoey	Min	25	4	0	1	0	-1	3	1	0	.25	-1	0		0	-1	-
D Holland	Tex	198	41	3	3	2	-8	7	4	5	.56	-6	3	-1	0	-4	163
G Holland	KC	60	4	0	0	0	-1	1	0	0	.00	-1	0	0	0	-1	-
J Horst	Cin	15	2	0	0	1	0	0	0	0	-	0	0		0	0	-
T Hottovy	Bos	4	0	0	0	0	0	1	0	0	.00	0	0			0	-
J Howell	TB	31	5	0	0	0	+1	5	0	1	.17	1	0		0	1	-
D Hudson	Ari	222	31	2	1	7	-1	10	10	0	.50	-1	1	-1	0	-1	123
T Hudson	Atl	215	46	2	1	2	-1	16	5	0	.24	-1	-1	0	0	-2	135
D Huff	Cle	51	4	0	0	1	+1	4	0	0	.00	1	0		0	1	-

BASIC								HOLDING				RUNS SAVED					
Player	Tm	Inn	TC	E	GFP	DM	+/-	SB	CCS	PCS/PPO	CS%	+/-	SB	Bnt	GFP/DME	Tot	Rk
D Hughes	Min	13	2	0	1	0	-1	0	1	1	1.00	0	1		0	1	-
J Hughes	Pit	11	4	0	0	0	+1	2	0	0	.00	1	0	0	0	1	-
P Hughes	NYY	75	8	0	0	0	-1	7	0	0	.00	-1	-1	1	0	-1	-
P Humber	CWS	163	28	1	0	3	-5	13	3	0	.19	-3	-1	-1	0	-5	168
T Hunter	2 tms	85	19	1	1	0	+1	6	3	1	.40	0	1	0	0	1	74
R Igarashi	NYM	39	10	0	0	2	+1	3	1	0	.25	1	0	0	0	1	-
J Isringhausen	NYM	47	7	0	0	0	-1	10	1	2	.17	-1	-1	0	0	-2	-
E Jackson	2 tms	200	43	3	1	3	+1	22	1	1	.04	1	-2	-1	0	-2	132
Jakubauskas	Bal	72	9	0	0	1	-1	2	2	0	.50	-1	0	0	0	-1	-
C James	Min	10	2	0	0	0	+1	0	0	0	-	0	0		0	0	-
K Jansen	LAD	54	5	0	0	0	+1	7	0	0	.00	1	-1	1	0	1	-
C Janssen	Tor	56	17	2	1	2	+2	2	3	0	.60	2	1	0	0	3	-
J Jeffress	KC	15	5	1	1	0	0	0	1	1	1.00	0	1	0	0	1	-
B Jenks	Bos	16	4	0	1	0	0	2	0	0	.00	0	0	0	0	0	-
K Jepsen	LAA	13	3	0	0	0	-1	1	0	0	.00	-1	0		0	-1	-
C Jimenez	Sea	7	1	0	0	0	0	0	0	0	-	0	0		0	0	-
U Jimenez	2 tms	188	44	2	0	2	+4	24	6	2	.20	3	-2	-1	0	0	92
W Joaquin	SF	6	0	0	0	0	0	0	1	0	1.00	0	0			0	-
A Johnson	Col	4	2	0	0	0	0	0	0	0	-	0	0		0	0	-
J Johnson	Bal	91	25	1	3	1	0	4	2	0	.33	0	0	0	0	0	100
J Johnson	Fla	60	15	0	1	0	+1	5	3	0	.38	0	0	0	0	0	-
J Judy	Cle	14	1	0	0	0	0	2	0	0	.00	0	0	0	0	0	-
J Jurrjens	Atl	152	38	0	4	1	+2	15	8	1	.38	1	0	1	0	2	47
J Karstens	Pit	162	36	2	3	1	+1	14	2	0	.13	1	-1	1	0	1	65
S Kazmir	LAA	2	1	0	0	0	+1	2	0	0	.00	1	0		0	1	-
S Kelley	Sea	13	1	1	0	0	-1	0	0	0	-	-1	0		0	-1	-
D Kelly	Det	0	0	0	0	0	0	0	0	0	-					0	-
K Kendrick	Phi	115	25	1	1	6	0	3	3	0	.50	0	1	-1	0	0	100
I Kennedy	Ari	222	36	0	1	2	+1	6	0	1	.00	1	0	1	0	2	47
C Kershaw	LAD	233	47	0	5	6	+2	14	2	9	.39	1	3	1	0	5	14
C Kimball	Was	14	2	0	0	0	-1	0	1	0	1.00	0	0		0	0	-
C Kimbrel	Atl	77	11	0	1	0	0	1	2	1	.75	0	1		0	1	74
J Kinney	CWS	18	4	0	0	0	+1	0	0	0	-	1	0		0	1	-
B Kintzler	Mil	15	3	0	0	0	0	0	0	0	-	0	0		0	0	-
M Kirkman	Tex	27	6	0	1	0	+2	1	0	0	.00	2	0	0	0	2	-
C Kluber	Cle	4	0	0	0	0	0	0	0	0	-		0			0	-
M Kohn	LAA	12	3	1	0	1	-1	2	0	0	.00	0	0		0	0	-
G Kontos	NYY	6	0	0	0	0	0	1	1	0	.50	0	0			0	-
Z Kroenke	Ari	4	1	0	0	0	0	0	0	0	-	0	0		0	0	-
H Kuo	LAD	27	2	1	0	1	0	4	1	0	.20	0	0	-1	0	-1	-
H Kuroda	LAD	202	51	0	5	2	+6	9	4	1	.36	5	1	1	0	7	4
J Lackey	Bos	160	38	3	2	2	-1	33	3	0	.08	-1	-5	0	0	-6	172
A Laffey	2 tms	53	18	0	2	0	+2	2	0	0	.00	0	0	0	1	1	-
J Lannan	Was	185	43	2	4	2	+2	6	3	1	.40	2	1	1	1	5	13
M Latos	SD	194	39	1	4	2	+2	25	7	1	.24	1	-2	0	0	-1	119
B League	Sea	61	8	3	0	1	-4	5	1	0	.17	-3	0	-1	0	-4	-
M Leake	Cin	168	40	0	3	3	+3	5	2	2	.29	2	1	1	0	4	18
W LeBlanc	SD	80	19	0	0	0	+1	7	3	3	.46	1	1	1	0	3	33
S LeCure	Cin	78	22	0	2	0	+2	4	1	1	.33	1	0	1	1	3	33
W Ledezma	Tor	6	0	0	0	0	-1	0	0	0	-	-1	0			-1	-
C Lee	Phi	233	34	1	5	2	-1	11	2	2	.27	0	0	0	1	1	74
C Leroux	Pit	25	4	0	0	0	-1	2	1	0	.33	-1	0	0	0	-1	-
J Lester	Bos	192	29	1	2	2	-2	14	8	4	.46	-1	2	0	0	1	88
C Lewis	Tex	200	20	4	1	1	0	10	7	0	.41	0	1	-1	0	0	100
R Lewis	Tor	5	1	0	0	0	0	0	0	0	-	0	0		0	0	-
B Lidge	Phi	19	3	0	0	0	-1	6	1	0	.14	-1	-1	0	0	-2	-
T Lilly	LAD	193	34	2	0	3	+3	35	1	1	.05	2	-5	-1	-1	-5	164
T Lincecum	SF	217	40	1	3	0	-1	23	12	2	.38	-1	0	1	0	0	110
B Lincoln	Pit	48	16	0	1	0	0	4	2	0	.33	0	0	0	0	0	-
J Lindblom	LAD	30	5	0	0	0	-1	1	5	0	.83	0	1	1	0	2	-
S Lindsay	CWS	6	2	0	0	0	0	1	0	0	.00	0	0		0	0	-
M Lindstrom	Col	54	16	1	2	0	+1	10	2	1	.17	1	-1	0	0	0	-
S Linebrink	Atl	54	10	2	0	2	-2	6	3	0	.33	-1	0	-1	0	-2	-
F Liriano	Min	134	22	0	1	1	+1	9	2	3	.36	1	1	0	0	2	47
J Litsch	Tor	75	26	3	4	1	+4	2	1	0	.33	3	0	0	0	3	-
J Locke	Pit	17	5	0	0	0	+1	3	0	1	.25	1	0	0	0	1	-
K Loe	Mil	72	13	1	1	0	-2	2	0	0	.00	-1	0	0	0	-1	-
B Logan	NYY	42	12	1	1	0	0	3	0	2	.40	0	1	0	0	1	-
K Lohse	StL	188	51	0	2	3	0	1	2	0	.67	0	1	0	0	1	74
J Lopez	SF	53	21	1	2	1	+3	3	1	1	.40	2	0	0	0	2	-
R Lopez	ChC	98	24	0	3	0	0	6	6	2	.54	0	1	0	0	1	74
W Lopez	Hou	71	22	2	1	0	0	1	2	0	.67	0	1	1	0	2	-
D Lowe	Atl	187	44	0	4	2	0	26	3	1	.13	0	-3	0	0	-3	151
M Lowe	Tex	45	6	0	0	0	-1	1	3	0	.75	-1	1		0	0	-
C Luebke	SD	140	32	0	1	2	+1	11	2	4	.35	1	1	1	0	3	33
J Lueke	Sea	33	3	0	1	0	-1	1	0	0	.00	-1	0	1	0	0	-
J Lyles	Hou	94	24	1	1	2	+1	4	0	1	.00	1	0	0	0	1	65
L Lynn	StL	35	4	0	0	1	-2	2	1	0	.33	-2	0		0	-2	-
B Lyon	Hou	13	7	0	0	0	0	2	0	0	.00	0	0	1	0	1	-
M MacDougal	LAD	57	13	3	0	0	-4	5	2	0	.29	-3	0	0	0	-3	-
R Madson	Phi	61	7	1	0	1	-1	4	1	0	.20	-1	0	0	0	-1	-
T Magnuson	Oak	15	5	0	0	0	+1	1	0	0	.00	1	0		0	1	-
P Maholm	Pit	162	38	1	2	3	+3	7	1	3	.30	2	1	0	0	3	26
M Maier	KC	1	1	0	0	0	0	0	0	0	-				0	0	-
S Maine	ChC	7	0	0	0	0	0	0	0	0	-	0	0			0	-
M Maloney	Cin	19	7	0	1	0	+2	0	0	0	-	1	0		0	1	-
J Manship	Min	3	1	0	0	0	0	1	0	0	.00	0	0		0	0	-
S Marcum	Mil	201	40	1	3	0	+1	8	6	1	.43	0	1	0	0	1	74
C Marmol	ChC	74	15	0	1	0	+2	12	1	0	.08	2	-2	0	0	0	-
J Marquez	NYY	4	1	1	0	0	-1	0	0	0	-	0	0		0	0	-
J Marquis	2 tms	132	24	1	0	1	-5	6	1	0	.14	-3	0	0	0	-3	158
S Marshall	ChC	76	17	1	1	0	0	9	1	1	.18	0	0	0	0	0	100
L Marte	Det	4	0	0	0	0	0	0	0	0	-	0	0			0	-

BASIC								HOLDING				RUNS SAVED					
Player	Tm	Inn	TC	E	GFP	DM	+/-	SB	CCS	PCS/PPO	CS%	+/-	SB	Bnt	GFP/DME	Tot	Rk
C Martinez	Atl	78	18	0	0	1	+1	0	0	0	-	1	0	0	0	1	65
N Masset	Cin	70	21	1	0	1	0	6	1	0	.14	0	0	-1	0	-1	-
J Masterson	Cle	216	49	2	1	4	-3	14	13	2	.50	-2	2	0	0	0	114
M Mateo	ChC	23	1	0	0	0	-1	2	2	0	.50	-1	0	0	0	-1	-
S Mathieson	Phi	5	1	0	0	0	0	0	0	0	-	0	0	0	0	0	-
D Matsuzaka	Bos	37	2	0	0	0	-1	6	0	0	.00	-1	-1		0	-2	-
R Mattheus	Was	32	2	0	0	1	-1	3	1	0	.25	-1	0	0	0	-1	-
B Matusz	Bal	50	3	0	0	0	-1	8	2	0	.20	-1	-1	0	0	-2	-
Y Maya	Was	33	7	0	0	0	-1	1	2	0	.67	-1	0	0	0	-1	-
V Mazzaro	KC	28	4	0	0	1	-1	4	1	1	.20	-1	0	-1	0	-2	-
Z McAllister	Cle	18	2	1	0	0	-3	1	1	1	.50	-2	1		0	-1	-
B McCarthy	Oak	171	38	4	0	3	-2	11	3	1	.27	-1	0	-1	0	-2	135
K McClellan	StL	142	35	1	0	1	-2	6	3	3	.33	-2	2	0	0	0	114
M McClendon	Mil	14	4	0	0	0	+1	0	0	0	-	1	0		0	1	-
M McCoy	Tor	1	0	0	0	0	0	0	0	0	-					0	-
D McCutchen	Pit	85	15	2	1	0	0	9	3	2	.25	0	0	0	0	0	100
D McDonald	Bos	1	1	0	0	0	0	0	0	0	-	0	0		0	0	-
J McDonald	Pit	171	28	1	1	2	-3	17	7	2	.32	-2	0	1	-1	-2	143
J McGee	TB	28	3	0	0	0	0	4	0	0	.00	0	-1	0	0	-1	-
D McGowan	Tor	21	2	0	0	1	0	4	0	0	.00	0	-1		0	-1	-
K Medlen	Atl	2	2	0	1	0	+1	0	0	0	-	1	0		0	1	-
E Meek	Pit	21	9	0	0	0	+2	0	0	0	-	2	0	0	0	2	-
M Melancon	Hou	74	18	1	0	1	0	6	2	0	.25	0	0	0	0	0	-
L Mendoza	KC	15	5	0	0	0	0	0	2	0	1.00	0	0	0	0	0	-
K Mickolio	Ari	7	1	0	0	0	+1	1	0	0	.00	1	0		0	1	-
J Mijares	Min	49	7	1	0	0	-1	2	1	2	.60	-1	1	0	0	0	-
W Miley	Ari	40	6	1	0	1	-1	3	1	1	.40	-1	0	-1	0	-2	-
A Miller	Bos	65	13	2	0	1	-2	8	1	0	.11	-1	-1	-1	0	-3	-
J Miller	Col	7	0	0	0	0	0	0	0	0	-	0	0			0	-
T Miller	3 tms	21	8	0	0	0	0	1	1	0	.50	-1	0	1	0	0	-
B Mills	Tor	18	3	0	0	0	0	0	0	0	-	0	0	0	0	0	-
K Millwood	Col	54	12	1	2	0	-1	1	3	0	.75	-1	1	-1	0	-1	-
T Milone	Was	26	5	0	0	0	+1	1	0	1	.50	1	0	0	0	1	-
M Minor	Atl	83	12	0	0	3	-1	2	2	0	.50	-1	1	0	0	0	110
P Misch	NYM	7	3	0	0	0	0	0	0	0	-	0	0		0	0	-
S Mitre	2 tms	38	10	1	0	0	-1	8	1	0	.11	-1	-1		0	-2	-
M Moore	TB	9	2	0	0	0	0	0	0	0	-	0	0		0	0	-
F Morales	2 tms	46	9	0	1	0	0	6	0	4	.00	0	1	0	0	1	-
B Morrow	Tor	179	24	3	2	3	-6	17	5	0	.23	-5	-1	1	-1	-6	175
C Mortensen	Col	58	13	1	0	0	+1	4	1	2	.43	1	1	0	0	2	-
C Morton	Pit	172	39	1	1	0	-1	16	5	2	.27	-1	0	1	0	0	110
G Moscoso	Oak	128	15	2	0	2	0	5	1	1	.29	0	0	-1	-1	-2	134
D Moseley	SD	120	33	0	4	1	+1	18	4	1	.18	1	-2	0	1	0	93
D Moskos	Pit	24	6	2	1	1	0	3	0	0	.00	0	0	-1	0	-1	-
G Mota	SF	80	14	0	2	0	+1	4	2	1	.33	1	1	1	0	3	33
J Motte	StL	68	23	0	2	1	+3	6	1	1	.14	2	0	0	1	3	-
P Moylan	Atl	8	2	0	0	1	0	0	0	0	-	0	0		0	0	-
E Mujica	Fla	76	22	2	4	0	0	7	1	2	.13	0	0	1	0	1	74
B Myers	Hou	216	56	4	3	4	-4	15	6	1	.29	-3	0	-2	0	-5	168
C Narveson	Mil	162	33	1	3	3	+2	12	2	6	.40	2	2	0	0	4	18
J Nathan	Min	45	9	0	0	1	+1	8	0	0	.00	1	-1	0	0	0	-
P Neshek	SD	25	2	0	0	0	+1	3	0	0	.00	1	0		0	1	-
J Nicasio	Col	72	21	1	1	3	+1	7	0	1	.13	1	-1	0	0	0	-
J Niemann	TB	135	31	0	2	1	0	16	4	1	.24	0	-1	1	0	0	100
J Niese	NYM	157	40	0	2	1	+3	7	1	0	.13	2	0	1	0	3	26
H Noesi	NYY	56	8	0	0	0	+1	6	3	0	.33	1	0	-1	0	0	-
R Nolasco	Fla	206	34	1	0	3	0	12	2	0	.14	0	-1	-2	0	-3	151
J Norberto	Oak	7	1	1	0	0	-1	0	0	0	-	-1	0		0	-1	-
B Norris	Hou	186	54	3	4	4	+2	16	6	3	.27	1	0	0	0	1	65
I Nova	NYY	165	37	0	1	3	+2	10	8	0	.44	2	1	0	-1	2	44
M O'Connor	NYM	7	0	0	0	0	0	1	0	0	.00	0	0			0	-
D O'Day	Tex	17	5	1	1	0	0	4	0	0	.00	0	-1		0	-1	-
E O'Flaherty	Atl	74	16	0	0	2	+1	5	1	1	.29	1	0	0	-1	0	-
A Ogando	Tex	169	20	0	1	0	-2	2	3	0	.60	-2	1	1	0	0	114
R Ohlendorf	Pit	39	5	0	0	0	-1	7	1	1	.22	-1	0	0	0	-1	-
W Ohman	CWS	53	7	0	0	1	-2	2	0	1	.33	-2	0	0	0	-2	-
H Okajima	Bos	8	5	0	0	0	0	2	0	0	.00	0	0	1	0	1	-
A Oliver	Det	10	1	0	0	1	+1	4	1	0	.20	1	-1		0	0	-
D Oliver	Tex	51	9	2	0	0	-2	4	0	2	.33	-2	0	-1	0	-3	-
L Oliveros	2 tms	21	3	0	0	0	+1	0	0	0	-	0	0		0	0	-
G Olson	Pit	4	1	1	0	0	0	0	0	0	-		0	-1	0	-1	-
L Ondrusek	Cin	61	19	1	2	1	0	4	1	0	.20	0	0	0	0	0	-
R Ortiz	ChC	33	8	0	0	1	+2	1	0	0	.00	1	0	0	0	1	-
S O'Sullivan	KC	58	12	1	0	0	+1	1	4	0	.80	1	1	-1	0	1	-
R Oswalt	Phi	139	24	1	2	0	-1	11	0	0	.00	0	-1	1	0	0	100
J Outman	Oak	58	14	1	1	0	0	3	0	2	.40	0	1	0	0	1	-
J Oviedo	Fla	64	11	0	1	0	+1	6	1	0	.14	1	0	0	0	1	-
M Owings	Ari	63	12	1	0	1	+1	2	2	1	.50	1	1	-1	0	1	-
V Padilla	LAD	9	1	0	1	0	0	0	0	0	-	0	0	0	0	0	-
M Palmer	LAA	16	5	0	1	0	0	0	1	0	1.00	0	0	0	0	0	-
J Papelbon	Bos	64	6	1	0	0	-1	6	0	0	.00	-1	-1	0	0	-2	-
J Parker	Ari	6	1	0	0	0	0	0	0	0	-		0	0	0	0	-
B Parnell	NYM	59	13	1	2	2	-1	9	0	0	.00	-1	-1	0	-1	-3	-
J Paterson	Ari	34	14	1	1	0	0	2	0	0	.00	0	0	1	0	1	-
T Patton	Bal	30	4	0	0	0	-3	1	0	0	.00	-2	0	0	0	-2	-
D Pauley	2 tms	74	14	0	0	1	0	5	3	0	.38	0	0	0	0	0	-
F Paulino	2 tms	139	30	3	3	4	-1	11	2	2	.21	-1	0	0	-1	-2	135
C Pavano	Min	222	57	2	5	4	+3	24	5	2	.17	2	-1	0	0	1	62
B Peacock	Was	12	1	0	0	0	-1	0	0	0	-	0	0		0	0	-
J Peavy	CWS	112	16	1	2	1	-4	10	5	0	.33	-3	0	1	0	-2	147
M Pelfrey	NYM	194	41	1	2	3	-2	29	2	1	.06	-1	-4	-1	0	-6	172
T Pena	CWS	20	2	0	0	0	0	2	0	0	.00	0	0	0	0	0	-
L Pendleton	2 tms	19	1	0	0	0	0	0	0	0	-	0	0		0	0	-

BASIC								HOLDING				RUNS SAVED					
Player	Tm	Inn	TC	E	GFP	DM	+/-	SB	CCS	PCS/PPO	CS%	+/-	SB	Bnt	GFP/DME	Tot	Rk
B Penny	Det	182	35	1	1	0	-2	16	4	2	.27	-2	0	0	0	-2	143
J Peralta	TB	68	9	0	0	0	0	5	2	1	.29	0	0	0	0	0	-
C Perez	Cle	60	14	1	1	1	-1	8	0	0	.00	-1	-1	0	0	-2	-
J Perez	Phi	5	0	0	0	0	0	0	0	0	-		0			0	-
L Perez	Tor	65	10	2	1	2	-3	2	3	0	.60	-2	1	0	0	-1	-
R Perez	Cle	63	24	3	0	1	+1	2	4	0	.67	1	1	1	0	3	-
G Perkins	Min	62	11	1	2	1	-1	3	1	1	.40	-1	0	1	0	0	-
R Perry	Det	37	5	0	0	0	0	2	1	0	.33	0	0	0	0	0	-
V Pestano	Cle	62	5	0	0	0	+1	1	0	0	.00	1	0		0	1	-
B Petersen	Fla	1	0	0	0	0	0	0	0	0	-		0			0	-
Z Phillips	Bal	8	1	0	0	0	0	0	0	0	-	0	0		0	0	-
M Pineda	Sea	171	26	1	1	3	-3	10	10	0	.50	-2	1	0	0	-1	128
J Pineiro	LAA	146	22	1	0	1	-1	5	2	1	.38	-1	1	0	0	0	110
D Pomeranz	Col	18	1	0	0	0	0	1	1	0	.50	0	0		0	0	-
R Porcello	Det	182	38	2	2	2	-1	16	4	0	.20	-1	-1	1	0	-1	123
D Price	TB	224	40	4	5	2	-1	20	4	1	.20	-1	-1	1	0	-1	123
S Proctor	2 tms	40	5	0	0	0	0	2	0	0	.00	0	0	0	0	0	-
D Purcey	3 tms	34	6	0	1	0	+1	3	0	1	.25	0	0		0	0	-
Z Putnam	Cle	7	0	0	0	0	0	0	0	0	-	0	0			0	-
J Putz	Ari	58	13	0	1	0	-1	7	1	0	.13	-1	-1	1	0	-1	-
C Qualls	SD	74	18	0	1	1	0	10	4	1	.29	0	0	0	0	0	-
H Ramirez	LAA	9	4	0	1	0	0	1	0	1	.00	0	0		0	0	-
R Ramirez	SF	69	12	2	0	0	-2	13	2	0	.13	-2	-2	0	0	-4	-
C Ramos	TB	44	12	0	0	0	+2	4	0	0	.00	1	0		0	1	-
C Rapada	Bal	16	3	0	1	0	0	0	0	1	1.00	0	0		0	0	-
J Rauch	Tor	52	9	0	0	1	0	1	1	0	.50	0	0	0	0	0	-
C Ray	Sea	33	6	0	2	1	-1	6	1	0	.14	-1	-1		0	-2	-
A Reed	CWS	7	0	0	0	0	0	0	0	0	-	0	0			0	-
C Reineke	Cin	7	0	0	0	0	0	1	1	0	.50	0	0			0	-
C Resop	Pit	70	6	1	1	1	-2	9	3	0	.25	-2	-1	0	1	-2	-
D Reyes	Bos	2	1	0	0	0	0	0	0	1	1.00	0	0		0	0	-
J Reyes	2 tms	141	21	0	2	1	+2	14	1	1	.13	1	-1	1	0	1	65
G Reynolds	Col	32	8	0	0	0	+2	1	0	0	.00	1	0		0	1	-
M Reynolds	Col	51	7	0	0	1	0	5	1	2	.38	0	0	0	0	0	-
A Rhodes	2 tms	33	4	0	1	0	0	1	1	0	.50	-1	0		0	-1	-
C Richard	SD	100	29	3	0	1	+1	5	2	5	.50	0	2	0	0	2	55
G Richards	LAA	14	5	0	0	0	0	1	1	1	.50	0	1		0	1	-
S Richmond	Tor	0	0	0	0	0	0	0	0	0	-					0	-
M Rivera	NYY	61	13	0	3	0	+2	5	1	0	.17	1	0	1	0	2	-
D Robertson	NYY	67	7	1	0	1	-1	16	2	0	.11	-1	-2	0	0	-3	-
F Rodney	LAA	32	6	1	0	3	-2	5	0	0	.00	-2	-1		-1	-4	-
A Rodriguez	Hou	85	15	2	0	0	-1	13	1	0	.07	-1	-2	0	0	-3	154
F Rodriguez	Hou	52	9	0	2	0	0	7	0	1	.13	0	-1	0	0	-1	-
F Rodriguez	2 tms	72	12	0	1	1	-3	11	1	0	.08	-2	-1	0	0	-3	-
F Rodriguez	LAA	14	2	0	0	1	+1	1	0	0	.00	0	0		0	0	-
H Rodriguez	Was	66	9	0	2	1	-1	13	0	0	.00	-1	-2	1	0	-2	-
W Rodriguez	Hou	191	37	0	3	1	+1	20	3	0	.13	1	-2	1	0	0	93
J Roenicke	Col	17	1	0	0	0	0	1	0	0	.00	0	0		0	0	-
E Rogers	Col	83	21	0	1	2	-1	2	3	0	.60	-1	1	1	0	1	88
J Romero	2 tms	25	7	0	0	1	0	1	0	2	.50	0	1		0	1	-
R Romero	Tor	225	53	1	3	2	+5	18	1	6	.28	3	1	1	0	5	12
S Romo	SF	48	3	0	0	1	0	3	1	0	.25	0	0	0	0	0	-
S Rosario	Fla	4	1	0	0	0	0	0	0	0	-	0	0		0	0	-
T Ross	Oak	36	7	1	2	0	0	1	0	0	.00	0	0	0	1	1	-
C Ruffin	2 tms	18	1	0	0	0	0	3	0	0	.00	0	0	0	0	0	-
D Runzler	SF	27	7	1	1	0	0	6	1	2	.33	0	0	0	0	0	-
J Rupe	Bal	14	1	0	0	0	-1	0	0	0	-	-1	0		0	-1	-
A Russell	TB	33	5	0	0	1	-1	5	1	0	.17	-1	-1	0	0	-2	-
J Russell	ChC	68	12	1	1	2	-1	5	1	2	.38	-1	1	0	0	0	-
Rzepczynski	2 tms	62	19	2	1	2	+2	2	0	2	.50	1	0	-2	0	-1	-
C Sabathia	NYY	237	27	3	0	4	-8	11	5	1	.35	-6	1	0	0	-5	171
T Saito	Mil	27	2	0	0	0	-2	1	0	0	.00	-1	0	0	0	-1	-
F Salas	StL	75	13	0	0	0	0	2	0	0	.00	0	0	0	0	0	-
C Sale	CWS	71	20	0	0	3	0	3	1	3	.57	0	1	1	0	2	-
J Samardzija	ChC	88	15	1	1	1	-1	16	2	0	.11	-1	-2	0	0	-3	154
A Sanabia	Fla	11	1	0	0	0	0	1	0	0	.00	0	0		0	0	-
B Sanches	Fla	62	6	0	0	0	0	12	2	0	.14	0	-2		0	-2	-
A Sanchez	Fla	196	45	1	4	1	+1	15	2	2	.12	1	0	1	1	3	33
E Sanchez	StL	30	3	0	0	0	0	1	0	0	.00	0	0		0	0	-
J Sanchez	SF	101	21	2	1	1	+1	12	2	3	.29	1	0	-1	0	0	93
A Sanit	NYY	7	2	0	0	0	0	0	0	0	-	0	0		0	0	-
E Santana	LAA	229	36	5	3	0	-2	28	5	0	.15	-2	-3	-2	1	-6	174
H Santiago	CWS	5	1	0	0	0	0	0	0	0	-	0	0		0	0	-
S Santos	CWS	63	9	0	1	0	+1	5	0	0	.00	1	-1	0	1	1	-
J Saunders	Ari	212	49	0	3	2	+4	9	8	4	.57	3	3	1	0	7	6
J Savery	Phi	3	1	0	0	0	0	0	0	0	-		0	0	0	0	-
M Scherzer	Det	195	23	0	2	1	-6	12	6	3	.43	-5	2	1	0	-2	149
D Schlereth	Det	49	10	1	1	0	0	5	2	1	.38	0	0	0	0	0	-
S Schumaker	StL	1	0	0	0	0	0	0	0	0	-		0			0	-
M Schwimer	Phi	14	1	0	1	1	0	0	1	0	1.00	0	0	0	0	0	-
C Schwinden	NYM	21	4	1	0	1	-1	2	0	0	.00	-1	0	1	0	0	-
E Scribner	SD	14	3	0	0	0	0	1	0	0	.00	0	0		0	0	-
A Severino	Was	5	0	0	0	0	-1	1	0	0	.00	-1	0			-1	-
B Shaw	Ari	28	13	1	0	1	0	1	1	1	.67	0	1	0	0	1	-
G Sherrill	Atl	36	8	0	0	1	-3	0	1	1	1.00	-2	1	0	0	-1	-
J Shields	TB	249	54	3	2	4	+1	6	4	13	.45	0	6	1	0	7	8
A Simon	Bal	116	24	1	3	0	+1	10	8	0	.44	1	0	0	1	2	47
T Sipp	Cle	62	15	1	0	1	+1	13	0	2	.13	1	-1	1	0	1	-
A Slama	Min	2	1	1	0	0	0	1	0	0	.00		0		0	0	-
D Slaten	Was	16	5	0	0	1	0	0	0	0	-	0	0		0	0	-
K Slowey	Min	59	9	0	1	0	-2	4	1	0	.20	-1	0	0	0	-1	-
J Smith	Cle	67	26	1	2	0	+7	4	2	3	.43	5	1	0	0	6	-
J Smith	Cin	20	0	0	0	0	-1	0	1	0	1.00	-1	0			-1	-

BASIC / HOLDING / RUNS SAVED

Player	Tm	Inn	TC	E	GFP	DM	+/-	SB	CCS	PCS/PPO	CS%	+/-	SB	Bnt	GFP/DME	Tot	Rk
A Sonnanstine	TB	36	9	0	0	0	0	1	2	0	.67	0	0	0	0	0	-
J Soria	KC	60	12	0	0	2	+1	0	1	0	1.00	1	1	0	0	2	-
R Soriano	NYY	39	3	0	0	1	-2	6	2	0	.25	-2	0	0	0	-2	-
H Sosa	Hou	53	13	0	0	1	+1	3	2	1	.50	1	1	0	0	2	-
J Spence	SD	30	4	0	0	1	0	1	1	0	.50	0	0	0	0	0	-
C Stammen	Was	10	3	0	0	0	+1	1	0	0	.00	1	0	0	0	1	-
T Stauffer	SD	186	65	1	4	0	+4	5	7	1	.62	3	2	1	1	7	6
M Stetter	Mil	7	0	0	0	0	0	1	0	0	.00	0	0			0	-
J Stevens	ChC	7	2	0	0	0	0	0	2	0	1.00	0	0			0	-
Z Stewart	2 tms	67	16	2	2	2	0	6	2	0	.25	0	-1	0	0	-1	-
J Stinson	NYM	13	0	0	0	1	0	1	0	0	.00	0	0	0	0	0	-
D Storen	Was	75	16	0	1	0	0	3	0	0	.00	0	0	1	0	1	-
S Strasburg	Was	24	3	0	0	0	0	1	0	0	.00	0	0	0	0	0	-
H Street	Col	58	16	1	2	0	+3	2	1	0	.33	2	0	0	0	2	-
P Strop	2 tms	22	3	0	0	0	0	3	0	0	.00	0	0	-1	0	-1	-
E Stults	Col	12	1	0	0	0	0	0	0	0	-	0	0			0	-
M Stutes	Phi	62	16	1	3	0	-1	7	3	1	.30	0	0	0	0	0	-
E Surkamp	SF	27	9	2	0	0	-1	6	3	1	.40	0	0	0	0	0	-
A Swarzak	Min	102	10	0	0	2	0	3	3	0	.50	0	1	0	0	1	74
H Takahashi	LAA	68	15	1	0	0	+2	7	1	1	.22	2	0	0	0	2	-
M Talbot	Cle	64	12	0	0	3	-3	7	3	1	.36	-2	0	0	0	-2	-
B Tallet	2 tms	13	6	0	1	0	+1	1	0	0	.00	1	0	0	0	1	-
Y Tateyama	Tex	44	7	0	0	0	0	3	2	0	.40	0	0	0	0	0	-
J Tazawa	Bos	3	0	0	0	0	0	0	0	0	-					0	-
E Teaford	KC	44	5	0	0	0	+1	3	1	0	.25	1	0		0	1	-
J Teheran	Atl	20	6	0	0	0	0	3	0	0	.00	0	0			0	-
R Tejeda	KC	7	0	0	0	0	0	0	0	0	-	0	0	-1	0	-1	-
K Texeira	KC	6	1	0	0	1	0	0	0	0	-	0	0			0	-
J Thatcher	SD	10	1	0	0	0	-1	1	0	1	.50	-1	0		0	-1	-
D Thayer	NYM	10	4	0	0	0	0	1	0	0	.00	0	0			0	-
B Thomas	Det	11	1	0	0	1	-2	0	0	0	-	-1	0		0	-1	-
A Thompson	Pit	8	2	0	0	0	0	3	0	0	.00	0	0	0	0	0	-
D Thompson	Cin	3	2	0	0	0	0	0	0	0	-	0	0			0	-
R Thompson	LAA	54	7	0	0	0	-1	6	0	2	.14	-1	0	0	0	-1	-
M Thornton	CWS	60	12	0	0	0	-2	13	1	1	.13	-1	-2	0	0	-3	-
C Tillman	Bal	62	8	0	1	2	-4	5	3	0	.38	-3	0	0	0	-3	-
M Tobin	Tex	5	0	0	0	0	0	0	0	0	-	0	0			0	-
B Tomko	Tex	18	1	0	0	0	0	1	0	0	.00	0	0	0	0	0	-
J Tomlin	Cle	165	43	2	1	1	+1	0	0	1	-	1	1	-1	0	1	65
A Torres	TB	8	0	0	0	0	-1	1	1	0	.50	-1	0			-1	-
R Troncoso	LAD	23	2	0	1	0	-1	2	0	0	.00	-1	0		0	-1	-
R Tucker	Tex	5	0	0	0	0	0	1	0	0	.00	0	0	0	0	0	-
J Turner	Det	13	1	0	0	2	0	7	0	0	.00	0	-1		0	-1	-
K Uehara	2 tms	65	6	0	0	0	0	0	0	1	-	0	0	0	0	0	-
R Valdes	2 tms	12	3	0	1	0	0	0	1	0	1.00	0	0	0	0	0	-
J Valdez	Hou	14	4	0	0	0	+1	1	0	0	.00	1	0	0	0	1	-
M Valdez	Tex	4	0	0	0	0	-1	1	0	0	.00	-1	0			-1	-
W Valdez	Phi	1	0	0	0	0	0	0	0	0	-	0	0			0	-
J Valverde	Det	72	7	1	0	0	-1	9	3	0	.25	-1	-1	-1	0	-3	-
R VandenHurk	Bal	9	0	0	0	0	0	1	1	0	.50	0	0			0	-
J Vargas	Sea	201	29	1	1	3	+2	18	3	2	.22	1	-1	0	0	0	93
A Varvaro	Atl	24	4	0	0	0	0	2	0	1	.33	0	0	0	0	0	-
A Vasquez	Sea	29	5	2	0	0	+1	1	0	1	.50	1	0	-2	0	-1	-
E Vasquez	Ari	30	8	1	1	1	+2	1	0	0	.00	1	0	0	0	1	-
J Vazquez	Fla	193	28	1	1	0	+1	8	0	0	.00	1	-1	0	0	0	93
J Venters	Atl	88	27	2	2	4	+3	2	2	0	.50	2	0	1	0	3	26
J Veras	Pit	71	8	0	0	0	-1	5	1	0	.17	0	0	0	0	0	-
J Verlander	Det	251	50	5	2	0	+5	10	4	2	.33	4	1	-1	1	5	11
C Villanueva	Tor	107	17	1	0	1	+3	13	1	0	.07	2	-2	-2	0	-2	131
E Villanueva	Fla	3	0	0	0	0	0	0	0	0	-	0	0			0	-
B Villarreal	Det	16	8	2	1	0	+2	4	0	2	.00	1	0		0	1	-
P Viola	Bal	4	0	0	0	0	0	0	0	0	-	0	0			0	-
A Vizcaino	Atl	17	2	0	0	0	-1	0	0	0	-	0	0	0	0	0	-
R Vogelsong	SF	180	32	0	0	2	+1	12	3	1	.20	0	0	0	0	0	100
E Volquez	Cin	109	16	2	0	1	-3	16	4	0	.20	-2	-2	-1	0	-5	166
C Volstad	Fla	166	35	1	3	2	-3	10	4	1	.29	-2	0	0	0	-2	143
C Wade	NYY	40	4	0	0	1	-1	2	2	0	.50	-1	0	0	0	-1	-
N Wagner	Oak	5	0	0	0	0	0	0	0	0	-	0	0			0	-
T Wakefield	Bos	155	26	0	0	1	+2	12	7	3	.43	2	1	0	0	3	26
J Walden	LAA	60	10	1	0	0	-1	13	1	1	.13	-1	-2	0	0	-3	-
K Waldrop	Min	11	2	0	0	0	-1	1	0	0	.00	-1	0	0	0	-1	-
P Walters	2 tms	5	2	0	0	0	0	0	0	0	-	0	0			0	-
C Wang	Was	62	10	1	0	0	-1	4	3	0	.43	0	0	0	0	0	-
T Watson	Pit	41	11	0	0	1	+1	8	0	1	.11	1	-1	1	0	1	-
J Weaver	LAA	236	34	2	0	2	-1	10	6	6	.41	-1	3	0	0	2	59
R Webb	Fla	51	9	1	0	2	+1	9	1	0	.10	1	-1	0	0	0	-
K Weiland	Bos	25	2	0	0	1	-1	0	1	0	1.00	-1	0		0	-1	-
R Weinhardt	Det	2	0	0	0	0	0	0	0	0	-	0	0			0	-
R Wells	ChC	135	19	2	2	0	-2	12	5	0	.29	-1	0	-1	0	-2	135
J Westbrook	StL	183	74	2	1	1	+7	13	3	4	.24	6	1	1	0	8	2
D Wheeler	Bos	49	3	0	0	0	-2	1	2	0	.67	-1	0		0	-1	-
K Whelan	NYY	2	1	0	0	0	0	0	0	0	-	0	0			0	-
A White	2 tms	51	7	2	0	2	-3	3	4	0	.57	-2	0	0	0	-2	-
T Wilhelmsen	Sea	33	8	1	0	0	+1	3	0	1	.25	1	0	0	0	1	-
A Wilk	Det	13	1	0	0	0	-1	0	0	0	-	0	0	0	0	0	-
J Williams	LAA	44	8	2	0	1	-3	3	1	1	.40	-2	0	0	0	-2	-
R Williams	Bos	8	0	0	0	0	0	1	0	0	.00	0	0			0	-
D Willis	Cin	76	17	0	1	2	0	1	0	3	1.00	0	2	0	0	2	55
B Wilson	SF	55	6	0	0	1	-3	1	1	0	.50	-2	0	0	0	-2	-
C Wilson	Tex	223	30	1	1	3	0	24	7	0	.23	0	-2	0	-1	-3	151
R Wolf	Mil	212	44	4	5	4	+2	18	0	1	.05	1	-2	0	0	-1	119
B Wood	KC	70	16	0	0	0	-2	6	1	2	.33	-1	0	-1	0	-2	-
K Wood	ChC	51	8	1	1	1	-2	3	1	1	.25	-1	0	-1	0	-2	-
T Wood	Pit	8	2	0	0	0	0	1	0	0	.00	0	0	0	0	0	-
T Wood	Cin	106	19	0	1	0	+1	5	2	3	.50	1	1	1	0	3	33
V Worley	Phi	132	24	0	3	1	+2	2	0	0	.00	1	0	0	1	2	47
M Worrell	Bal	2	0	0	0	0	0	1	0	0	.00	0	0			0	-
J Wright	Sea	68	18	1	0	0	-2	8	2	2	.27	-2	0	0	0	-2	-
W Wright	Hou	12	2	0	0	0	0	2	0	0	.00	0	0	0	0	0	-
M Wuertz	Oak	34	3	0	0	0	-1	10	1	0	.09	0	-2	0	0	-2	-
C Young	NYM	24	2	0	0	0	-1	4	0	1	.20	0	0	0	0	0	-
M Zagurski	Phi	3	0	0	0	0	-1	0	0	0	-	-1	0			-1	-
C Zambrano	ChC	146	21	1	2	2	0	4	0	2	.00	0	1	1	0	2	55
B Ziegler	2 tms	58	23	3	1	1	0	6	3	0	.33	0	0	-1	0	-1	-
J Zimmermann	Was	161	36	0	1	4	-1	3	6	3	.67	0	3	0	-1	2	55
B Zito	SF	54	12	1	1	0	0	4	2	2	.50	0	1	0	0	1	-
2011 MLB Totals					491	486		987	414		.28						

METHODOLOGIES

Baseball Info Solutions' Data Collection

Bill James, John Dewan and Steve Moyer have been collecting baseball data together for many years. At STATS, Inc., they sent scorers to each major league stadium to sit in the press box and record information about each play. Scorers recorded trajectory information for each ball in play as well as the "zone" to which the ball was hit.

When forming Baseball Info Solutions (BIS) in 2002, they decided to start recording a litany of information from video. In addition to pitch type, velocity and location data, they began recording each batted ball location as a pixel on a computer screen, rather than as a zone. Using recorded video gave their video scouts the ability to rewind as many times as necessary to record accurate information.

In the BIS database, we record the pixel coordinate of each recorded batted ball location. We also translate these (x,y) coordinates into a "Vector" and "Distance," which are more intuitive for certain types of analysis. The Vector and Distance coordinates reflect a polar coordinate system. Vector refers to the degree-wide angle of the recorded location, with 135 representing the first base line, 180 as straight-away center field, and 225 as the third base line. Distance refers to the distance from home plate, rounded to the nearest foot.

In the early years of BIS, each batted ball was classified by velocity (soft, medium, hard) and type (groundball, line drive, flyball or bunt). Combining this information with hit locations, John Dewan and cohorts developed the original Plus/Minus System for evaluating defenders.

In 2006, the company added a more detailed description of the trajectory of each batted ball for clients. We added a new trajectory, "fliner", to describe the balls higher than a typical line drive but lower than an average flyball. BIS decided to split line drives and flyballs into four distinct categories: line drives, fliner-liner, fliner-fly and flyballs. In the Plus/Minus system, the two categories of fliners were grouped together.

Around that time, Bill James developed a new system for tracking previously-unrecorded details about defensive play. We now know this information as Good Fielding Plays and Defensive Misplays. BIS has been able to record this information back to 2004, marking every ball scooped out of the dirt and every missed cutoff man, among other things.

The following year, Baseball Info Solutions began tracking balls hit off outfield walls. No longer would left fielders be penalized for flyballs that hit 20 feet up the Green Monster.

In 2010, BIS began tracking the location of the catcher's target before every pitch. We're only beginning to discover the insights this data has to offer.

After completing *The Fielding Bible—Volume II*, BIS decided to record even more information about every ball in play. Now, BIS video scouts put a stop watch to every batted ball, giving us a more objective description of the ball's speed and trajectory. Groundballs are timed from contact with the bat until they are touched by a fielder or cross into the outfield grass, whichever comes first. Flyballs and line drives are timed until they are caught or land untouched.

While expanding the variety of data collected in an effort to satisfy the desire for more data, the company has also increased its expectations of data quality. In addition to automated quality control checks and auditing reports, BIS video scouts now complete a minimum of three passes through each major league game.

Criticisms of BIS Hit Location Data

Michael Humphreys, author of the book *Wizardry: Baseball's All-Time Greatest Fielders Revealed*, wrote an article for *The Hardball Times Baseball Annual 2012* in which he spelled out the basics of his system for evaluating every fielder in baseball. His Defensive Regression Analysis (DRA) system utilizes only publicly available data, with the intention of allowing motivated readers to do the math for themselves. He also elects to ignore any form of hit location data because he doesn't trust its accuracy.

He elaborates later on in the article, citing claims that any manually collected hit location data has biases that render the data, and all analysis based on the data, inaccurate. In Humphreys' own words:

"It appears that stringers coding location data, regardless of who they work for, may be 'anchoring' their estimates by reference to the position of the fielder.

One possible indirect result of this anchoring effect is that if a fielder catches the ball, the coders may tend to locate the ball close to the fielder's position, while if the fielder does not catch the ball, the coder will tend to code the ball as having been farther away.

If you think about it a little bit, that would mean that a rangy fielder's great plays would tend to be coded as close to his position, and a non-rangy fielder's hits allowed would tend to be coded as having been difficult to reach. Any such 'range bias,' as [Baseball Prospectus analyst] Colin Wyers has called it, would systematically pull defensive runs estimates toward the mean."

To clarify, neither Humphreys nor anyone else would claim that BIS or any other company is marking bad locations intentionally. They claim the alleged bias is subconscious, and that the video scouts wouldn't even realize they're doing it. If a scorer wasn't being careful enough, they might see a flyball to the left fielder handled routinely and mark it a few feet closer to the regular left field position.

For each play, a few feet may not seem like much. However, a few feet on tens of thousands of flyballs can add up pretty quickly.

Without having actual BIS hit location data, these claims are based on snapshots seen from various clients. Shane Jensen, a professor at Wharton and the University of Pennsylvania, purchased 2002-05 play-by-play data with hit locations from BIS to develop his own fielding analysis, named Spatial Aggregate Fielding Evaluation (SAFE).

In a 2009 paper, Jensen laid out the details of SAFE, including an overview of Baseball Info Solutions data. He included a couple of graphs to illustrate the plotted hit locations (see below for one of his graphs). The graph below is a contour plot, with the circles surrounding each of the outfield positions representing the higher number of hit locations plotted in those regions.

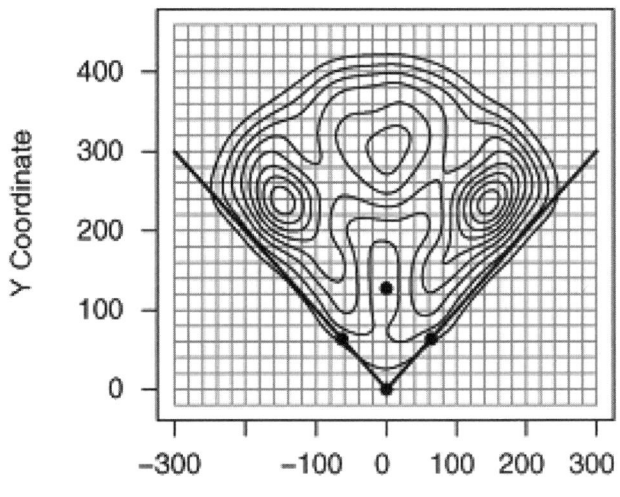

Flyballs

The graph (using 2002-05 BIS data) indicates that, for whatever reason, more hit locations were plotted directly at each outfield position than were plotted in the gaps.

Investigation

Using the BIS database, we prepared graphs of outfield flyballs by vector, looking at the distribution year by year. In the following graphs, Vector 225 represents the left field foul line, Vector 180 is straight-away center field, and Vector 135 is the right field line. We have combined groups of 10 vectors together to smooth out much of the noise.

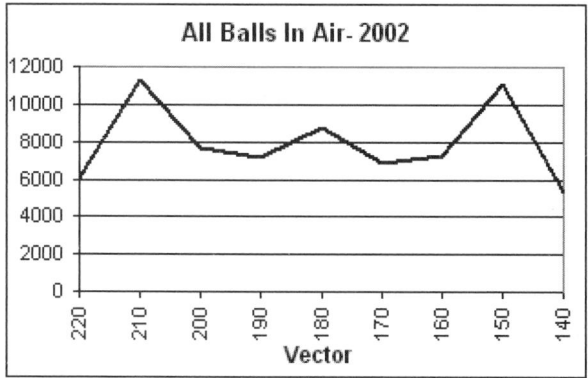

In this graph from 2002, we see clear peaks in line with each outfield position. The first peak, around vector 210, is roughly the angle the left fielder typically occupies before each pitch. The graph indicates that we marked nearly 12,000 flyballs around vector 210, compared to under 8,000 about ten degrees into the gap in left-center.

The center fielder lines up near straight-away center, of course, and we see a smaller peak of nearly 9,000 flyballs there. And in right field, the graph shows another large peak of 11,000 flyballs at vector 150, compared to the 7,500 and 5,000 on either side.

Fast-forward to 2006, where the same chart features far smaller peaks and valleys.

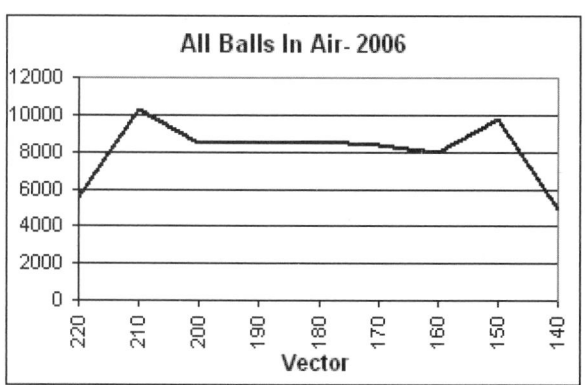

Now let's look at the most-recent season of data:

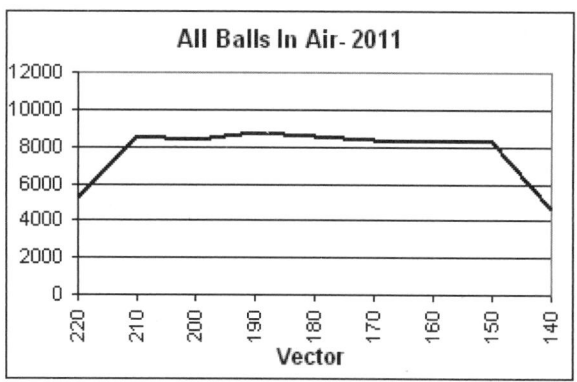

By 2011, the peaks and valleys had smoothed out entirely. Every group of vectors (except down the foul lines) contains between 8,000 and 9,000 flyballs.

We also looked at groundball distributions season by season and saw a similar effect. As with flyballs, the peaks and valleys smoothed out in the most recent seasons of data.

"No Video" Plays

One important observation relates to the nature of the BIS data collection process. When BIS started collecting data in 2002, video feeds were not the quality, high-definition feeds we're accustomed to today. Certain teams, most notably the Montreal Expos, did not televise their full schedule of games, leaving us to rely on their opponents' television broadcasts. If neither team televised the game, our scorers would resort to radio broadcasts to log the play-by-play.

We were up-front with our clients, explaining the limitations of our data in those early years. From our clients' perspective, any hit location was better than no hit location; therefore, we plotted the hit locations based on the descriptions available to us, even if that was just a radio broadcast. If there was a flyout to the left fielder, we'd mark it somewhere near where the left fielder usually stands. Knowing a ball was hit to left field is better than not knowing anything at all about its location.

There are also games where television feeds exist, but for whatever reason they miss a few pitches. They occasionally have technical problems, or they come back from a commercial break late. If we have an alternate video feed of the game, we can switch for any plays we missed. However, especially for the earlier years, an alternate feed was not always available.

This issues have been less and less prevalent in recent years. In 2002, we marked about 8 percent of batted balls as "No Video" plays. That figure had dropped to 2 percent by 2006, under 1 percent by 2008, and essentially 0 percent in 2011. The Expos moved to Washington, solidified their financial standing, and secured a long-term television contract. Other teams also expanded their television coverage to include more games, especially on the road. In recent seasons, almost all games have more than one video broadcast available.

In those early seasons, we did make a note when video footage of a play was unavailable. For the most precise analyses, it might be useful to remove these plays from consideration. For example, our Plus/Minus System specifically excludes "No Video" plays before 2006. We're evaluating a slightly smaller sample of plays, but we're removing that potential bias from our numbers.

Additional Quality Control

BIS has gone to great lengths to improve data quality. Over the years we've:

- Improved the accuracy of our park diagrams several times, including larger fields, seating diagrams, and customized infields as reference points when plotting hit locations
- Added an independent second record of the hit location for comparison
- Added a third pass of hit location auditing to sort out discrepancies between the first two
- Lowered the threshold of the hit location differences, adding more plays to the auditing process
- Switched to newer, better scoring software customized to our needs
- Increased our overall understanding of hit location data quality
- Increased the video scout's overall awareness of data quality issues
- Improved communication and consistency among all scorers

Considering all of these improvements and more over the past decade, it's no surprise that our data quality has improved to its current level.

Conclusions

The concerns raised by Michael Humphreys and others may have some validity, especially when using data from earlier years with estimated hit locations. However, as technology and video feeds have improved, so has our data quality.

By no means do we believe that our most-recent data is perfect. It's possible, even likely, that there are other forms of bias or error that we haven't even considered yet. Fortunately, we've also begun to collect more objective data, such as the batted ball timer, to reduce the room for error. Stronger data collection will ultimately produce better analysis and improve our understanding and appreciation for Major League Baseball.

Methodology:
The Run Matrix

Through three volumes of *The Fielding Bible*, we've developed metrics which significantly improve our understanding of defense in baseball. In order to make these metrics more meaningful, we have converted our eight separate evaluation systems into a common currency: runs.

Baseball is all about runs. Runs determine the score and consequently the winner of each game. Runs are all over the statistics. How many runs did he drive in? What's his earned run average? Now, we can add, "How many runs did he save (or cost) his team defensively?" In order to convert each rating system into runs, we made use of a tool developed in the 1970's called the 24 States Run Matrix.

24 States Analysis (or The Run Matrix)

Take your pick. What do you want to call it? Somteimes it's called "24 States Analysis." I'm a big fan of *The Matrix* movie series so I'll go with "The Run Matrix." It sounds like a complicated concept, but in reality it's not that difficult. The basic premise is simple: at any point in an inning (defined by the current baserunners and number of outs), how many runs can we expect the offense to score, on average, before the third out is made?

Well, we can figure that out, can't we? There are eight combinations of men on base: none out, man on first, man on second, man on third, men on first and second, men on first and third, men on second and third, and bases loaded. There can be either zero, one, or two

outs at any point in the inning, so three options there. Eight base-situations times three out-situations gives you 24 states. For each of these situations, we can count how many runs scored through the end of that half inning. The end result is a chart that tells you, at any point in time, how many runs we can expect the offense to score by the end of the inning. Here's the Run Matrix for 2011:

The Run Matrix (2011)

Runners	0 Outs	1 Out	2 Outs
None	0.477	0.258	0.099
First only	0.839	0.500	0.220
Second only	1.061	0.647	0.317
Third only	1.453	0.944	0.312
First & Second	1.402	0.867	0.421
First & Third	1.750	1.146	0.476
Second & Third	1.932	1.334	0.543
Bases Loaded	2.142	1.475	0.763

The number in the chart corresponding to nobody on and no outs is 0.477. That simply means that anytime this situation occurred in an inning during 2011, an average of 0.477 runs were scored from that point until the end of the inning. Sometimes the offense scored one run, sometimes two, sometimes ten, and often zero. But on average, 0.477.

Or, take the bases loaded with one out, when the run expectancy is 1.475. Considering every one of these situations in 2011, we find that 1.475 runs scored on average after a team had the bases loaded and one out.

The key way that we use this chart is to look at it before and after a play. Let's say there's a man on first with one out. The expected runs at that point are 0.500.

The next play is a groundball to the shortstop. He boots it for an error and we now have men on first and second with one out. The expected runs went from 0.500 to 0.867. That's an increase of 0.367 runs; thus, the error cost the defensive team an expected 0.367 runs. We don't have to follow it through and count the rest of the inning. We know what the value of the ending state is and can use it.

Let's go back to that first situation: a runner on first base with one out. What if, rather than making an error, the shortstop got the forceout at second base? The starting run expectancy is still 0.500, but with two outs and a runner on first (the batter, after reaching on the fielder's choice) the run expectancy drops to 0.220, a difference of -0.280 runs. According to Newton's Third Law, for every force there is an equal and opposite reaction. Similarly, that fielder's choice groundball affected the offense -0.280 expected runs while helping the defense +0.280 runs.

What if the defense turned a double play? This result (three outs) ends the half inning and the offense's chance to score. While the offense was expected to score an average of 0.500 runs before the end of the inning, they scored none. The run value of the play, the change in run expectancy, is -0.500. The difference between turning a double play (+0.500 from the defense's perspective) and booting the ball (-0.367) is huge: 0.867, almost a full run! If a particular shortstop turns 20 errors or base hits into outs over the course of the season, you can see how the runs will start to add up.

It's important to note that every error isn't going to be worth exactly +0.367 runs, and every double play isn't worth -0.500 runs. With the bases loaded and nobody out, an error will be more costly (and a double play will be more valuable) than with the bases empty. If we wanted to find the run value of the average error made, we could compare the run expectancy states from before and after every error made last season. The average change in run expectancy is the approximate run value of an error.

We can apply similar logic to estimate the run impact of any baseball event, including doubles, double plays, fly outs, sacrifice bunts, baserunner kills, and stolen bases. We use these average run values in our various Defensive Runs Saved components to determine the appropriate run effect on each aspect of defensive play.

Methodology: Plus/Minus

The Plus/Minus System is the primary component of Defensive Runs Saved, responsible for rating each fielder's success at turning batted balls into outs. The basic premise of the system is to approximate the proportion of the league's fielders who would have successfully made any given play, then to appropriately reward or penalize each fielder for his efforts.

The system indirectly measures several skills which are crucial to a fielder's ability to record outs. Each outfielder's positioning, reactions, reads, routes, range/speed and hands, are important elements to catching flyballs. Infielders need those same skills plus a quick and smooth glove-to-hand transfer as well as a strong and accurate throw to successfully turn groundballs into groundouts. The combination of these individual skills determines whether a particular fielder can make the plays to help his team.

A play is considered "made" by the fielder if he gets a putout or assist on the batted ball. This includes catching the ball on the fly, throwing out the batter at first or retiring a runner via force out (among other things). A play is considered "not made" when the fielder doesn't get a putout or assist on the play AND no other fielder had the first putout, assist or error. For example, if the third baseman fields a groundball towards the third base/shortstop hole, we don't count this play for or against the shortstop. We assume that he didn't have an opportunity to make the play and award no credit or penalty.

Let's say we're watching a Dodgers game, and Matt Kemp is patrolling center field. We might estimate that a particular play is made by the league's center fielders 42 percent of the time (we'll come back to the details of that

calculation later). If Kemp makes this play, it's a nice play. A sizable 58 percent of center fielders did NOT make the play. We reward him for this; specifically, we reward him 0.58 Basic Plus/Minus points (or "plays"). If Kemp does not make the play, we penalize him according to the proportion of fielders who did make the play, 0.42. In this case, Kemp would get -0.42 Basic Plus/Minus points on the play.

Because giving up doubles and triples is obviously more costly than allowing singles, we also calculate Enhanced Plus/Minus to estimate how many bases a fielder saved or cost his team on these plays. When this particular play was not made, the batter got an average of 1.50 bases on the play. Since the center fielders who made this play were rewarded with 0.58 Basic Plus/Minus points (plays), and each play saved 1.50 bases, we can say that a center fielder saved 0.58 * 1.50 = 0.87 bases (Enhanced Plus/Minus points) by making the catch.

If center fielder Kemp did not make the play, he is penalized by 0.42 plays times the number of bases he allowed the batter to reach. If he doesn't make the catch but plays it well and holds the batter to a single, he's penalized -0.42 * 1 = -0.42 Enhanced Plus/Minus bases. If he lollygags and allows the batter a double, he is penalized -0.42 * 2 = -0.84 Enhanced Plus/Minus points. If he completely overruns the ball and turns it into a triple, he'll be docked 1.26 Enhanced Plus/Minus bases.

Lastly, we estimate how many runs a player saved or cost his team. Using the 24 Run Expectancy states (see Run Matrix Methodology on page 439), we calculated, for each position, the average number of runs that each Enhanced Plus/Minus point is worth. We can then multiply the Enhanced Plus/Minus credit or penalty by the runs factor for the position, and we call this the player's Plus/Minus Runs Saved on the play.

Plus/Minus Runs Saved Factors

Position	Factor
Pitcher	0.75
First Base	0.73
Second Base	0.76
Third Base	0.76
Shortstop	0.76
Left Field	0.56
Center Field	0.56
Right Field	0.58
Note that the Runs Saved Factors reflect the run value per base (Enhanced Plus/Minus point), not the per play (Basic Plus/Minus point).	

In our hypothetical example, Matt Kemp was credited with .87 bases for a successful catch according to Enhanced Plus/Minus. He is awarded 0.87 * 0.56 = 0.49 Plus/Minus Runs Saved. However, if he didn't make the catch, and the batter got a double out of it, Kemp receives a penalty of -0.84 * 0.56 = -0.47 runs (a single would dock him -0.42 * 0.56 = -0.24 runs, while a triple would dock him -1.26 * 0.56 = -0.71 Plus/Minus Runs Saved).

We then add up the credits and penalties from every play over the course of the entire season to arrive at a rating for any particular fielder. We use different units to cite a fielder's Plus/Minus rating, including plays, bases and runs. The average fielder will have a rating of 0 plays, 0 bases and 0 runs.

We might quote a player's Basic Plus/Minus score as +20, meaning the fielder made about 20 more plays than we'd expect from the average fielder at his position. Another fielder might cost his team 24 bases, translating to a -24 Enhanced Plus/Minus score. Depending on the plays and the position, the first fielder might finish the season with 15 Plus/Minus Runs Saved, meaning we estimate that his team allowed 15 fewer runs than they would have with a league-average fielder at the position thanks to this fielder's range and ability to convert batted balls into outs. On the other hand, -15 Plus/Minus Runs Saved means the fielder cost the team 15 runs due to his inability to record outs.

Approximating the difficulty of an individual play is part science and part art. To do so, we take into account a number of factors, including the location, trajectory and velocity of the given batted ball. We also account for a few specific factors that affect each position differently.

Infield Groundball Plus/Minus

We rate pitchers, first basemen, second basemen, third basemen and shortstops on their ability to field groundballs.

The original Plus/Minus System, introduced in *The Fielding Bible* (2006), used two primary components, "vector" and "velocity," to approximate the difficulty of each play. "Vector" is the term for a one degree-wide angle at which the groundball was hit. "Velocity" refers to the recorded speed of the groundball, either soft, medium, or hard. (For more information on vector, velocity, and BIS data collection, see page 435.)

In 2011, there were 408 medium groundballs marked at Vector 206, 19 degrees off of the third base line (roughly 45 feet) and towards the shortstop side of the hole. We'll say that these 408 groundballs comprise one "bucket" of very similar grounders which we'll consider together. Out of those 408 plays, the shortstop made 192 of them, roughly 47 percent. We'd expect to see good shortstops make this play more often than not, but a poor shortstop will rarely convert the out.

First basemen have a unique challenge in that they typically stand right next to first base when holding a runner close. This greatly restricts his range on groundballs, through little fault of his own. Therefore, when there is a runner on first base with second base open, we make the assumption that the first baseman was likely holding the runner at the base. Accordingly, for first basemen we consider these plays separately from all other groundballs by grouping them in separate buckets.

As one of baseball's oldest strategies, hit-and-run plays usually affect middle infielders. We consider any play where the runner on first is breaking towards second a hit-and-run play. It may have been intended as a straight steal, but if the batter hits the ball, it becomes a hit-and-run in practice, at least from the standpoint of the defense. The Plus/Minus System also considers these plays separately from other groundballs.

Lastly, while corner infielders can make plays down the lines to save potential doubles and triples, pitchers and middle infielders are going for balls that almost always turn into simple singles. For shortstops, second basemen and pitchers, we assume that every groundball saved or cost the team one base. Therefore, we don't calculate a separate Enhanced Plus/Minus score; instead, we multiply their Basic Plus/Minus score (rather than his

Enhanced Plus/Minus score) by his position's Runs Saved factor to derive his Plus/Minus Runs Saved.

Enhancements for Volume III

For infielders, the Plus/Minus System remained unchanged through *The Fielding Bible—Volume II.* However, for this book, we have reevaluated the system and implemented a few changes and enhancements to the system, reflected in the 2010-11 numbers.

When Baseball Info Solutions began collecting batted ball timer data for groundballs, we wanted to incorporate this more objective information to get a more accurate measure of how hard each batted ball was hit. BIS Video Scouts record the time from when the ball makes contact with the bat until either the point a fielder first touches the ball or when it passes by the infield/outfield dirt/grass cutoff (whichever comes first). The Plus/Minus System then divides the distance the ball travelled to that point (in feet) by the time (in seconds) and converts to miles per hour (mph).

It's certainly true that groundballs lose some of their speed while bouncing through the infield, and their average speed will decline as they progress. However, the difference in the average speed of a single groundball when fielded at different distances is relatively small when compared to the overall variance among groundball speeds.

We take each groundball's average speed and group it into one of six timer groups (see chart).

Timer Groups for Groundballs

Timer Group	Min (mph)	Max (mph)
1	0	25
2	25	45
3	45	55
4	55	65
5	65	75
6	75	-

As you might expect, the slowest and fastest groundballs give fielders the most trouble. Infielders have the easiest time with groundballs which travel between 25 and 45 miles per hour. Infielders can range far to both sides, and they usually have enough time left that a good throw will retire the batter or runner. The harder a ball is hit, however, the more a fielder's range is limited. Unless it's hit right at him, he won't have the time to get to the ball before it passes through the infield.

With the batted ball timer data, we moved to a rolling two-year base to increase the sample size of plays considered in each bucket. Increasing the size of the buckets is a tradeoff between accuracy and precision; we want to increase the sample size to decrease the random noise within each bucket, but at the same time we want to keep the buckets small so that the included plays are as similar as possible, and we're getting precise estimates of a play's difficulty. We feel more confident with the accuracy and precision of the new base.

As a result of the multi-year base, the average fielder isn't guaranteed to sit exactly at zero when initially calculated; therefore, we re-center the league so that a rating of zero represents the average fielder at the position for each season.

We also compared out rates on groundballs from right-handed batters to those from left-handed batters. We found that the out rates shifted over a few vectors for opposite-handed hitters, due to fielders' leaning and/or positioning themselves differently. As a result of that analysis, we elected to treat groundballs from right-handed and left-handed hitters separately by forming distinct buckets.

Lastly, in reviewing the hit-and-run groundballs, we decided to group each set of three vectors together to increase the sample size when evaluating the difficulty of these plays, giving us more accurate assessments of each play.

Infield Flyball Plus/Minus

We also rate first basemen, second basemen, third basemen and shortstops on their ability to field flyballs and line drives.

As of *The Fielding Bible—Volume II,* the Plus/Minus System considered infield flyballs based on type (liner, fliner, fly), velocity (soft, medium, hard), and location (grouped into roughly 3 feet by 3 feet zones).

For 2010 and 2011 plus/minus numbers, we made two changes. First, we replaced the recorded type and velocity information with hang-time data, and divided the plays into six hang-time groups. We also reviewed the system and found that zones of roughly 8 feet by 8 feet gives us more plays in each bucket and therefore a better approximation of the difficulty of each play.

Outfield Plus/Minus

We measure each outfielder's success at catching flyballs and line drives. The system introduced in *The Fielding Bible* utilized three pieces of information to assess each play's difficulty: type (flyball or line drive), velocity (soft, medium, hard) and location.

In 2006, Baseball Info Solutions began tracking a category of plays between line drives and flyballs, termed "fliners," to further separate the easy outs (high flyballs) from sure hits (hard liners).

In 2007, BIS began tracking balls hit unreachably high off outfield walls, and the Plus/Minus System correspondingly added the "Manny Adjustment." Outfielders have no chance on balls high off the Green Monster, for example, where no fielder could reach without a cape and the ability to leap tall buildings in a single bound. Our system appropriately removes these plays from consideration.

In 2009 we incorporated the new hang-time data for outfield flyballs, replacing type and velocity information. Each flyball or line drive is split into one of six Timer Groups based on its hang-time. Obviously, the longer a ball hangs in the air, the more likely it will be caught for an out.

Timer Groups for Flyballs (Center Fielders)

Timer Group	Min (sec)	Max (sec)
1	0.0	2.7
2	2.7	3.0
3	3.0	3.5
4	3.5	4.2
5	4.2	5.0
6	5.0	-

While we formerly considered each flyball within a region of about 5 feet by 5 feet (5 feet deep by one vector wide), for 2010 and 2011 we switched to roughly 10 by 10 regions (10 feet by two vectors). We also moved to a rolling two-year base. As mentioned previously, we believe this increases the accuracy of our estimates without compromising the precision of smaller buckets.

As a result of the unadjusted multi-year base, the average fielder isn't guaranteed to sit exactly at zero when initially calculated; therefore, we re-center the league so that a rating of zero represents the average fielder at the position for each season.

Methodology:
Outfield Arm Runs Saved

Under the old system of evaluating outfield throwing arms, we examined three types of plays: first to third on a single, second to home on a single, and first to home on a double. We counted the results of these plays. We break these results into three categories:

1) Moved: Anytime a runner takes an extra base on a hit (i.e. two bases on a single, three bases on a double), we say that the runner has "Moved."

2) Did Not Move: If the runner goes station-to-station on the hit, we call that "Did Not Move."

3) Thrown Out: If the runner gets thrown out trying to take the extra base, that's "Thrown Out."

We look at the frequencies of these events, and then we add a fourth category, Miscellaneous Kills. A Miscellaneous Kill is anytime a runner is thrown out on the basepaths by an outfielder (without a relay) that doesn't involve base hit. For example, a runner who is thrown out trying to score on a flyout would be a Miscellaneous Kill. The four categories put together comprise an outfielder's Throwing Arm Runs Saved.

This time around, we dug a little deeper. While we still examine the same three key types of plays: first to third on a single, second to home on a single, or first to home on a double, we felt that, for example, all first to third advancements are not created equal. Let's look at two plays to understand why all first to third plays are not the same. The first play is a bloop single to shallow right field near the foul line with two outs and a runner on first. The old system treats this the same as our second play, a medium-distance line drive single toward the right-center

field gap with no one out and a runner on first.

2011 First to Third Plays

Play	Moved	Did Not Move	Thrown Out
Bloop Single	90%	10%	0%
Line Drive	38%	62%	0%

Our old system grouped these two plays together for our evaluations. The information in the chart above shows that these two plays are very different. On the bloop single, the runner advances 90 percent of the time. This makes sense because there were two outs, so the runner should be more aggressive, and the ball landed in a spot a bit far from the right fielder. There's little the right fielder can do to prevent the advancement. The line drive was hit to medium right-center, much closer to the right fielder, and there were no outs, so it made sense for the runner to be more cautious. In this situation, runners only advanced 38 percent of the time.

These two plays highlight our additional classifications for each ball in play. First, we separate flyballs from grounders and use a slightly different technique for each. If the ball in play was a flyball, we then determine if there are two outs. With two outs, we would expect a runner to be more aggressive, and he is.

2011 First to Third Plays:
Line Drive to Medium Right-Center

Play	Moved	Did Not Move	Thrown Out
Two Outs	62%	38%	0%
Less Than Two Outs	38%	62%	0%

Using our medium-distance line drive to right-center, we find that the Moved percentage and the Did Not Move percentage flip. That's the reason we isolate two-out plays.

Next, we establish the location of the ball in play. On flyballs, each outfield position is split into nine zones that resemble a tic-tac-toe board. Three are shallow, three are medium, and three are deep.

If we group all flyballs based on outs and location, we have 18 categorizations, or buckets, for flyballs for each situation (first to third, second to home, first to home) and each outfield position. We use a rolling one year of data to get our league average Moved percentage, Did Not Move percentage and Thrown Out percentage for each bucket in each situation for each position. When tabulating Thrown Out numbers, we only give the outfielder half credit for relay outs, i.e. runners that were Thrown Out with the help of a relay man.

The next step is calculating a player's opportunities. To get his opportunities, we add the number of times baserunners Moved against him to the number of times they Did Not Move to the number of times a runner was Thrown Out. Relay outs are counted as half an opportunity. His opportunities are multiplied by the league average percentages in each bucket to get his expected Moved, Did Not Move and Thrown Out numbers. The difference between the expected numbers and the player's actual numbers are multiplied by the run value of each play. Add that up and we have his Throwing Arm Runs Saved for flyballs, but that's only half the equation.

The other half of the equation is groundballs, where we get to showcase our batted ball timer data. We don't separate two-out balls in play from non-two-out balls in play for groundballs, nor do we use distance for ground balls. Rather than use distance, which the fielder has some control over, we split the field into slices of pie that start from home plate. Each position gets six slices of pie (mmm...yummy!) for first to third and second to home situations. Let's compare two grounders of the same velocity hit to right field, one toward the middle of right field and the other down the line, to show why location is still important for grounders.

2011 Grounders to Right Field 55 to 65 MPH

Play	Moved	Did Not Move	Thrown Out
Mid-Right	62%	38%	0%
Down the Line	100%	0%	0%

Just as we saw with flyballs, the location matters. Everyone advanced from first to third on grounders hit down the line, while not as many advanced on balls hit to the middle of right field.

In first to third and second to home situations, we also group the balls in play by velocity. There are four velocity groups: 0 to 45 MPH, 45 to 55 MPH, 55 to 65 MPH and 65+ MPH. Let's look at that same grounder to mid-right but with two different MPH groupings.

2011 Grounders to Mid-Right Field

Play	Moved	Did Not Move	Thrown Out
45 to 55 MPH	71%	25%	4%
65+ MPH	55%	44%	1%

This makes sense. A hard-hit ball is likely to get picked up quicker by a fielder than a soft-hit ball. That reduces the chances of a baserunner advancing from first to third on a single. Using both velocity and vector creates 24 buckets for each outfield position on both first to third and second to home situations, respectively.

First to home situations on grounders are the odd-ball, the cousin Oliver from the Brady Bunch. They just don't belong. We classified only four grounders as first to home plays for center fielders for 2011. We obviously can't split those four balls into 24 buckets. The dearth of grounders that produce first to home situations led us to significantly alter the methodology for these situations. First, the velocity doesn't matter here, so we threw it out. Then we had to address the location buckets. For center field, we merged all 24 buckets to create one super bucket. We don't care about the location because there are so few plays. For corner outfielders, instead of six buckets, we have three asymmetrical buckets. Think about it for a second. Where would a groundball need to be hit in order for the runner to try to take two extra bases? The answer is down the line. Anything could happen on a grounder down the line. A fielder would have to run a significant distance to get to the ball and/or it could rattle around in the corner to give the runner extra time to advance. For each corner outfield position, we put a bucket on each side of the foul line and a catch-all bucket for everything else toward the middle of the field.

To get the groundball share of an outfielder's Throwing Arm Runs Saved, we perform a calculation similar to that for flyballs. First, we use balls from a rolling one year of data to get our league average Moved percentage, Did Not Move percentage and Thrown Out percentage for each bucket in each situation for each position. The league numbers are then multiplied by a player's opportunities (Moved + Did Not Move + Thrown Out) in each bucket to get his expected Moved,

Did Not Move and Thrown Out. We still only give outfielders half credit for relay outs, and we only count those plays as half of an opportunity. The difference between the expected and the individual player's actual numbers are multiplied by the run value of each play. Add that up to get the grounders portion of his throwing Runs Saved.

So that's both halves of our Throwing Arm Runs Saved, but there's actually a third half. Yes, a third half. We have to reward outfielders for the runners they throw out, unassisted, that is not a first to third, second to home, or first to home situation. These plays we group into a category called Miscellaneous kills. Under our original Throwing Arm Runs Saved methodology, we rewarded an outfielder with .75 Runs Saved for each Miscellaneous Kill. We're still going to do that this time, but we're going to compare a player's Miscellaneous Kills to his expected number. We first calculate the league average Miscellaneous Kills per touch which is the sum of Miscellaneous Kills over the total number of touches. We take the league number and multiply that by a player's touches. That gives us an expected number for the fielder. The difference between the player's actual total and the expected total is multiplied by our run value (.75) to get a player's Miscellaneous Kills runs saved.

A player's total Throwing Arm Runs Saved is then the sum of our three halves: flyballs Runs Saved + groundballs Runs Saved + Miscellaneous Kills Runs Saved.

Methodology:
Double Play Runs Saved

Our original GDP system measured double play conversion rates, compared each player to the average, and converted to Runs Saved. This system worked well considering its simplicity, highlighting double play savants like Mark Grudzielanek and pointing out the weak links like Jeff Kent. But we wanted to do better.

Utilizing our batted ball timer data, we developed a new system for evaluating double play groundballs. We implemented this new double plays system for seasons in which BIS batted ball timer data is available (2009 to the present); for previous seasons, we continue to use the original GDP Runs Saved system introduced in *The Fielding Bible—Volume II*.

Original System (used for 2008 and prior)

Using the definitions from the original *Fielding Bible*:

GDPs: How many times the player was involved in a groundball double play, either starting the double play or as the "pivot" man.

GDP Opps: How many times the player was involved in a fielding play on a groundball in a double play situation (man on first with less than two outs). This includes DPs, force outs, errors, etc.

Pivots: How many times the player made the double play pivot (for second basemen: 6-4-3, 5-4-3, 1-4-3, etc.).

Pivot Opps: How many times the player accepted a force out at second in a situation that could have been a double play (for second basemen: 6-4, 5-4, 1-4, etc.).

Pivots and Pivot Opps are included in GDPs and GDP Opps, but are also listed separately because of the different set of skills required. We include a pivot rating for shortstops as well (yeah, I know, a shortstop doesn't usually pivot physically like a second basemen does, but you get the idea).

Now we need to determine the run value of the successful and unsuccessful double play. It turns out the changes in base-out run expectancies are very close for both positions:

Average Run Expectancy Change on Double Play Attempts

	Shortstop	Second Baseman
DP	0.80	0.81
Missed DP	0.23	0.23
DP %	59%	51%

By Run Expectancy Change (RE), we mean, for example, that on a completed double play involving the shortstop, the number of expected runs that the offense will score in the inning has dropped by 0.80 runs. If the fielder doesn't get the double play and only gets a force out, the run expectancy only drops by 0.23 runs. (For more details on run expectancy and the 24 States Run Matrix, see page 439.)

Note that shortstops converted a higher percentage of DP Opps into double plays. The offense's run expectancy based on all GDP Opps (whether completed or not) drops by an average of 0.80 * 0.59 + 0.23 * (1 - 0.59) = .57 runs on a GDP Opp fielded by an average shortstop, but only .51 runs when fielded by an average second baseman. Since we are putting Runs Saved on an above-average scale, the run value awarded to each play will subtract out the average run expectancy change on GDP Opps. For shortstops, a completed DP is worth 0.80 - 0.57 = 0.23 runs, and a Missed DP is 0.23 - 0.57 = -0.34 runs.

However, we're not quite through. A typical double play involves more than one fielder to complete. A 6-4-3 double play requires both the shortstop and the second baseman. In fact, by awarding the full run value we are double-counting all such double plays. How much credit should we give to each? Let's split it 50/50 and call it even:

Run Values Applied on Double Play Attempts

	Shortstop	Second Baseman
DP	0.12	0.15
Missed DP	-0.17	-0.15

These are the values we apply to each player's DPs and Missed DPs to find out how many runs each middle infielder helped or hurt his team on double play opportunities.

New Timer System (used from 2009 to the present)

We recently redesigned our system to measure the approximate difficulty level of each double play opportunity. First, we redefined double play opportunities slightly so we can better measure a fielder's performance on traditional chances. Then we consider both the angle (Batted Ball Vector) and speed (the time it took to reach the original fielder) to form the basis of the play's difficulty. Each set of six degrees (vectors) and three-tenths of a second are grouped together to form buckets of similar plays.

The accounting works very similar to the Plus/Minus System. For example, 87 percent of the double play opportunities that reached the shortstop at vector 192 in 1.8 seconds (right at the normal shortstop in double play depth) were converted successfully. On these double plays, we award 1 - 0.87 = 0.13 points, split between the original fielder and the pivot man. If only the force out was recorded, we debit the fielders -0.87 points, again split between the two.

By comparison, a 2.1-second groundball about 20 feet further to the shortstop's right (vector 204) is converted for a double play just 17 percent of the time. The double play and pivot man split 1 - 0.17 = 0.83 points for a successful double play. If only the force out was recorded, we dock the fielders -0.17 points, or -0.085 each.

From there, we multiply by the average run value difference between failed and successful double plays. Across all positions, we found that the average difference between successful and failed double plays was .58 runs.

In the new system, we also measure the run impact of corner infielders' double play opportunities. While corner infielders rarely function as the middle man on a double play, they still have an opportunity to get the ball to second base quickly and cleanly and should be rewarded or penalized appropriately. As you might expect, the range between the best and worst corner infielders on double play attempts is small.

Lastly, we apply a minor adjustment to ensure that the average player at each position centers at exactly zero Double Plays Runs Saved. This new Timer Double Plays system is in place from 2009 to the present.

Methodology: Bunts Runs Saved

We are introducing several enhancements to the Bunt Runs Saved calculation that was presented in Volume II.

The previous methodology was based on a bunt rating system which Bill James developed for *The Fielding Bible*. In Bill's system, bunt events were separated into five categories: Sacrifice, Base Hit, Pure Out (no base advancement), Error, and Double Play. A point value was assigned to each outcome, and the average of the point values gives the Bunt Score, with the average around .500. To give you an idea of how to interpret the Bunt Score, each was awarded a letter grade from A+ to F.

In Volume II we made a couple of improvements to Bill's system, converting each of these five bunt outcomes into runs saved. For example, a sacrifice bunt to the third baseman converted into an out at first base (allowing the runners to advance) actually lowered the batting team's expected number of runs scored by 0.17 runs (compared to the average bunt to third). We give the third baseman a +0.17 for his effort.

We felt like we could still do better, though, so for Volume III we have made some changes to our methodology in which we more specifically define bunt type events, and thereby create a clearer picture of how good players are at fielding bunts. We are also now calculating Bunt Runs Saved for catchers and pitchers in addition to first basemen and third basemen. All seasons (back to 2003) have been restated according to the new system.

In the new methodology, each bunt event is first classified as a sacrifice bunt attempt or a non-sacrifice bunt attempt based on the game situation. We consider a bunt a sacrifice attempt if there is at least one runner on base with less than two outs. It is obviously possible for a player to decide on his own to try to bunt for a hit in what would otherwise be considered a sacrifice situation, but without the ability to know exactly what the batter intended, these classifications provide a pretty sturdy basis from which to work.

Each bunt is then further classified according to three other parameters:

- the direction the ball is hit
- the defensive position of the player who fields the ball
- whether the batter was a pitcher or not

The direction of the bunt is measured as a vector coming off of home plate, with the vectors grouped into six equally sized zones that span between the first base line and the third base line. This basically creates six equally sized pie slices of the infield between the first base line and the third base line, where the center of the pie is at home plate.

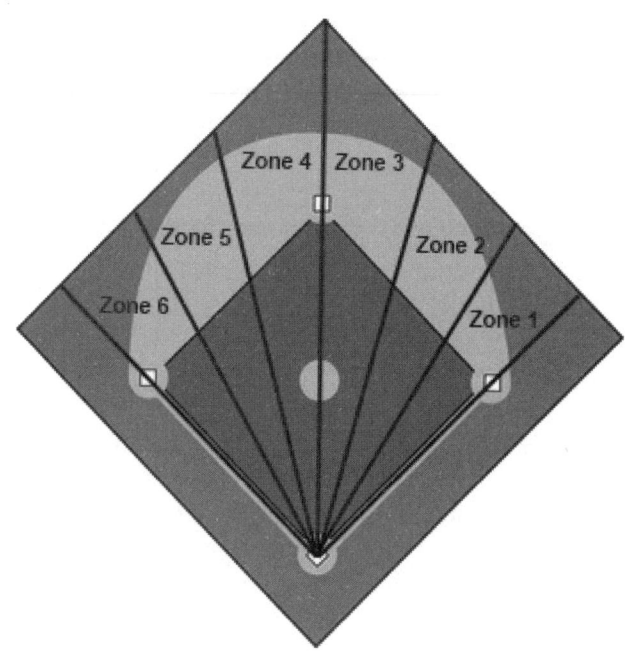

The defensive position of the player who fields the ball is self-explanatory. Third base, first base, catcher, or pitcher.

We found that when pitchers bunt for a sacrifice, the defense had a much easier time converting the out than on non-pitcher bunts. Presumably, pitchers are easier to retire because they jog to first to conserve their stamina for the mound, or they simply don't bunt as well as position players. For this reason, we evaluate pitcher bunts separately.

We group bunts into different sets, or "buckets," based on these distinct qualities: sacrifice/non-sacrifice, direction, fielder position, and pitcher/non-pitcher batting. Within each bucket, the bunt attempts are then categorized as one of the following bunt outcomes.

Sacrifice Bunt Attempts:

- *Sac Out* - The player that fields the ball is credited with a putout or an assist, no baserunners are out on the play, and at least one baserunner advances. Using the 24 States Run Matrix (see page 439), these plays are worth -0.18 runs on average.
- *Out No Advance* - The player that fields the ball is credited with a putout or an assist, no baserunners are out on the play, and no baserunners advance. This includes situations where the fielder catches the bunt in the air or otherwise retires the batter without allowing baserunner advancement. These plays are worth -0.43 runs on average.

- *Fielder's Choice* - The player that fields the ball is credited with a putout or an assist, the batter safely reaches base, and a baserunner is out on the play. On average, these plays were worth -0.45 runs.
- *Bunt DP* - A bunt play on which the batter is out and at least one baserunner is out OR the batter reaches safely and two baserunners are out. These plays cost the offense an average of -0.85 runs.
- *All Safe* - The player that fields the ball does not record a putout or an assist. This includes base hits (batter beats out the throw), fielder's choices where all the runners are safe, plays on which the fielder makes a fielding error, and plays on which the fielder makes a throwing error. These plays help the offense increase their run expectation an average of 0.63 runs.

Non-Sacrifice Bunt Attempts:

- *Pure Out* - The player that fields the ball is credited with a putout or an assist in a non-sacrifice situation. The offense's run expectancy decreases an average of -0.21 runs on these plays.
- *All Safe* - The player that fields the ball does not record a putout or an assist. This includes bunt hits, fielder's choices with two outs where all the runners are safe, plays on which the fielder makes a fielding error, and plays on which the fielder makes a throwing error. These plays are worth an average of 0.32 runs.

Note: if the fielder makes a play but no out is recorded due to another fielder's error, we give the original fielder credit for making the play successfully.

Using our play-by-play data going back to 2003, we determined the likelihood of each bunt outcome occurring within each bucket.

For example, for the bucket represented by:
- A sacrifice bunt attempt
- Hit to Zone 1 (near the first base line)
- Fielded by the first baseman
- With a non-pitcher batting

The results look like this:
- 74 percent of the time the fielder records a Sac Out
- 12 percent of the time everyone is safe (All Safe)

- 7 percent of the time the fielder records an Out No Advance
- 6 percent of the time the fielder records a Fielder's Choice
- 1 percent of the time the fielder records a Double Play

Within each bucket, a player is debited or credited based on the actual plays he makes compared to what was expected based on the percentages. The aggregate of those debits and credits are then converted to runs based on the run values (as determined by changes in run expectancy) associated with each bunt event type.

If we multiply each bunt outcome's frequency by the corresponding run value, we find the average run value for this particular bunt (-0.12). Let's say our first baseman completed the sacrifice out on this play. Because a sacrifice out is worth -0.18 runs for the offense, we can attribute the small decrease in run expectancy [-0.18 - (-0.12) = -0.06 runs for the offense, or +0.06 runs for the defense] to the first baseman for getting the out.

Instead of recording the sacrifice out, what if the first baseman had gotten the lead runner for a fielder's choice? We can subtract the run expectation for the play (-0.12) from the run value of a fielder's choice (-0.45) to find that the play cost the offense -0.45 - (-0.12) = -0.33 runs. In other words, the first baseman saved a third of a run by nabbing the lead runner.

The same is done for each play that a fielder faces over the course of the season. Each bunt classification bucket has its own set of percentages and expected run value; the difference between the bunt outcomes and expectations yields a fielder's total Bunt Runs Saved.

Throwing errors, while captured in the two All Safe categories and the Out No Advance category, require a secondary run value adjustment due to additional baserunner advancement. This adjustment is handled similarly to the other bunt type events. For each bucket, there is an associated likelihood of a throwing error

occurring. A fielder's actual number of throwing errors is compared to his expected number of throwing errors, for which he receives a debit or a credit, and that difference is then converted to runs based on the run value of the throwing error. The run value of the throwing error has been calculated with the run value of the All Safe or Out No Advance removed so that there is no double counting.

So let's go back to the example that we were using earlier—a sacrifice bunt attempt, bunted by a non-pitcher, bunted to zone 1, and fielded by the first baseman. Let's say that this time the first baseman tries to throw out the lead runner going to second base, but throws the ball away. This would be categorized as an All Safe because all baserunners will have advanced safely. We subtract the expected run value from the play (-0.12) from the run value of an All Safe outcome (0.63) to find that the play helped the offense an expected 0.75 runs, so we penalize the first baseman three-quarters of a run.

Now, if this had been a case where the runner simply beat the throw to the bag, we would be done. However, the first baseman also made a throwing error, which likely means that runners were able to advance further. In this situation there is a 1 percent likelihood of a throwing error occurring. Therefore, the first baseman has made 1 – 0.01 = 0.99 more throwing errors than expected. The ADDITIONAL change in run expectancy of making the throwing error (on top of the run value of the All Safe) is 0.35 runs for the offense. This means that the first baseman has cost his team an additional 0.99 x 0.35 = 0.3465 runs. So with the All Safe plus the throwing error, the first baseman cost his team a total of 0.75 + 0.35 = 1.10 runs on this play.

Because we are using a multi-year base for evaluating bunts, there is no guarantee that any individual season will center with the average fielder at each position at zero Runs Saved when initially calculated. Therefore, we make an additional adjustment to force the league average to zero for each season.

Methodology:
Good Play/Misplay Runs Saved

The release of *The Fielding Bible—Volume II* featured Defensive Runs Saved (DRS), the "next generation" of defensive evaluations. DRS took the Plus/Minus System, which must seem like an antique by now, and other elements of fielding—an outfielder's throwing arm, a pitcher's ability to control the running game, etc.— and translated these metrics into runs. Another cornerstone of that book was the introduction of Bill James' Defensive Misplays and Good Fielding Plays system. Good Fielding Plays (GFP) and Defensive Misplays (DM) were defined by James as "a very specific observation of a very narrowly defined event, created in such a way as to keep the scorer's use of judgment to an absolute minimum." Examples of these specific observations would be a catcher blocking the ball in the dirt, an outfielder robbing a home run, or a player losing the ball in the lights and allowing a catchable ball to drop in for a hit. We treat errors the same as we treat Misplays. Rather than classify an error vaguely as an error, we get a little more specific. An error could be a "groundball through infielder" or "bad throw," among other types.

We dipped our toe in the water of converting Good Fielding Plays and Defensive Misplays and Errors to Runs Saved with home run robberies back in Volume II, but in the three years since the publication of Volume II, we have converted our other GFP and DM data to the familiar Runs Saved scale, adding another layer to our defensive evaluations. Let's take a look behind the curtain and see how it's done.

We have over 80 total GFP/DM types. Some of these types are not converted to Runs Saved. This was done purposefully because including them would result in a play getting unreasonably double-counted. For instance, we have a Misplay type "Groundball Through Infielder." Let's say a batter hits a ball down the first base line. Let's call the first baseman Bill Buckner. If the ball, which should be fielded easily, gets through Buckner (which, let's face it, isn't likely), he gets penalized via the Plus/Minus System for not cleanly fielding the ball and recording the out. We felt that penalizing Buckner a second time for his Misplay would be egregious. He simply did not field the ball. There was no boneheaded play (like kicking the ball) that resulted in Buckner not fielding the ball or no unusual event that prevented him from making the play.

The flip side of the Buckner play is the Good Fielding Play "robs home run." Robbing a home run requires an extraordinary effort that goes above and beyond what is necessary to record a standard flyball out. In the 2002 All-Star Game, Torii Hunter leaped and caught a sure home run off the bat of Barry Bonds. Hunter's elbow was at the top of the Milwaukee center field wall, so his glove was more than a foot above that. That was no ordinary out. Had Hunter's catch been made in the regular season, he would have been rewarded for making the play in the Plus/Minus System, but it would look like an ordinary fly out. He gets additional credit for robbing a home run through Good Play/Misplay Runs Saved.

"Robs home run" was its own Runs Saved category in Volume II, and we rewarded each robbery with 1.6 Runs Saved. Here in Volume III, we rolled home run robberies back into Good Play/Misplay Runs Saved where they belong and updated the methodology a bit to center the data. Many of the Good Play/Misplay types we converted to DRS use a similar methodology.

Each GFP/DM type that we convert to DRS is centered at zero, meaning if you add up the home run robbery Runs Saved over every player at a particular position for a particular season, you get zero. Home run robberies center on opportunities, usually a player's fielding touches or innings, depending on the Good Play or Misplay. We compare a player's actual home run robberies to an expected number based on his touches or innings. The difference, multiplied by the run value of the play, is his Runs Saved for that category.

If we are trying to calculate the home run robbery portion of Torii Hunter's Good Play/Misplay Runs Saved for 2011, we take the following steps:

- Find the league average home run robbery per opportunity for right fielders in 2011. All we do here is add up the number of home run robberies across the league for right fielders in 2011 and divide by the total number of touches by those same players. This is our league average home run robbery rate.
- We multiply the league average home run robbery rate by Hunter's touches to get his expected number of home run robberies for 2011. Because of the infrequency of home run robberies, this number is .14.
- Then, we use the expected number of home run robberies and compare that to Hunter's actual home run robberies. Hunter, in his old age, didn't rob any home runs this year.
- We find that his actual robberies minus expected robberies is -.14.
- Multiply -.14 by the run value of robbing a home run (still 1.6 runs) and we get -.22, which is Hunter's home run robbery Runs Saved.

Hunter has somewhere in the neighborhood of three Runs Saved from other categories since his GFP/DME Runs Saved for 2011 is three.

We repeat this process for the other Good Play, Misplay and error types, except the three involved in first basemen scoops and the three involved with catchers preventing wild pitches and passed balls, which are handled a bit differently. Let's go over our methodology to estimate runs saved for making difficult catches on throws. Most of these kind of catches are scoops on throws in the dirt made by first basemen, so we often refer to this in shorthand as Scoops.

A scoop is really two different plays—a bad throw and a nice play that saves a throwing error. We developed our methodology for the scoops portion of Good Play/Misplay Runs Saved with this in mind.

The first half of a scoop play is the throw. In the Plus/Minus System, an infielder gets rewarded for plays that he makes—even if that made play was a result of his own bad throw that was scooped by a first baseman. If a first baseman is saving his team runs picking throws out of the dirt, the corresponding fielder that was making poor throws deserves to be penalized. Since the thrower gets credit for making the play in the Plus/Minus System, we dock a portion of his plus/minus credit, relative to the scoop percentage on the play, as part of his Good Play/ Misplay Runs Saved. Since we penalize bad throws, we also need to credit the thrower on failed scoops. We do this in the same way, based on the plus/minus on the play, relative to the league average scoop percentage.

The second half of the play is the scoop itself. If a first baseman (or usually the first baseman, any fielder can have to manage a bad throw) picks a low throw out of the dirt or lunges to save a wild throw from giving runners a shot at extra bases, we give him credit with a Good Fielding Play for handling a difficult throw or catching a wild throw. However, if the ball is within the fielder's reach and he doesn't come up with it, he receives a Defensive Misplay for failing to catch the throw. To measure the receiving fielder's credit, we calculate the percentage of each of these three plays where he handled a difficult throw, caught a wild throw, or failed to catch the throw. Our denominator would be the sum of all three of these type of plays. We compare a player to the league average to get his scoop runs saved.

Once we have a player's Runs Saved number for each Good Play/Misplay type, we add that all up to get his GFP/DME Runs Saved.

Methodology:
Catcher Stolen Base Runs Saved

In the discussion of a pitcher's control over the running game on page 457, we illustrate how pitchers vary wildly in their ability to prevent stolen bases. Consequently, when evaluating a catcher's effect on baserunners we need to adjust for the pitcher's impact on each potential stolen base.

To do so, we revisit the pitcher's entire history of allowing stolen bases. We credit the catcher for every stolen base better (or worse) than the pitcher's career rate.

We'll walk through the example of 2011 Fielding Bible Award winner Matt Wieters. The young Oriole caught 1,150 innings behind the plate, nabbing 32 of 90 potential basestealers. (We ignore "Pitcher Caught Stealing," when the runner is thrown out without a pitch to the plate, since the catcher had no part in the play.) The league threw out 23 percent of basestealers in 2011, so Wieters' 36 percent certainly stands out. Further, when you compare each pitcher's career caught-stealing rate with their rate when Wieters caught them in 2011, you see that Wieters threw out a higher percentage more often than not.

Player	With Wieters, 2011			With All Catchers, Career
	SB	CCS	CS Pct	CS Pct
Alfredo Simon	8	5	38%	39%
Jake Arrieta	7	4	36%	19%
Zach Britton	6	3	33%	30%
Kevin Gtregg	6	2	25%	19%
Jeremy Guthrie	2	5	71%	34%
Tommy Hunter	3	3	50%	22%
Chris Tillman	3	3	50%	50%
Jim Johnson	3	2	40%	33%
Jeremy Accardo	5	0	0%	16%
Mike Gonzalez	4	0	0%	8%
Brad Bergesen	2	1	33%	43%
Chris Jakubauskas	1	2	67%	43%
Brian Matusz	2	1	33%	11%
Willie Eyre	1	1	50%	56%
Pedro Strop	2	0	0%	0%
Jason Berken	1	0	0%	0%
Jo-Jo Reyes	1	0	0%	13%
Mark Worrell	1	0	0%	0%

Let's walk through the Wieters-Guthrie case. Over his career, Guthrie has allowed 37 stolen bases in 56 attempts, a 66 percent stolen base success rate. With Wieters in 2011, however, Guthrie allowed just 2 steals in 7 attempts. Based on his career rate, we would have expected 7 * 0.66 = 4.6 successful steals; instead, Wieters allowed just 2. The difference, 2.6, is the number of stolen bases Wieters saved with Guthrie on the mound.

Repeating this calculation for every pitcher Wieters

caught in 2011, we find that Wieters saved about 6.8 stolen bases for Orioles pitchers.

Utilizing the 24 States Run Matrix (see page 439), we found the run value of a stolen base to be about 0.22 runs and catcher caught stealing plays (excluding pitcher caught stealing) to be worth about -0.48 runs. Because each stolen base saved is the difference between a successful stolen base and a catcher caught stealing, we attribute the 0.70 run difference to the catcher. In Wieters' case, we multiply the 6.8 stolen bases saved by 0.70 to get approximately 5 runs saved on stolen base attempts.

Since offensive levels rise and fall from year to year, the 24 states run values for stolen bases and caught stealing may change depending on which time frame you're focusing on. When we recalculate the run values for stolen bases and caught stealing, we find the difference has dropped to 0.62 based on more recent seasons. While the values in this book use 0.70 per stolen base saved, we will be moving to 0.62 runs per stolen base saved for future seasons.

Additionally, many catchers fire directly to a base after a pitch in an effort to catch runners napping. Each pickoff is worth approximately .46 runs. While Wieters did not pick off any runners in 2011, Dioner Navarro led the league with five catcher pickoffs. Yadier Molina is the king of catcher pickoffs, with 13 over the past three seasons. Defensive-specialist Humberto Quintero trails Molina with 11 in half as many innings behind the plate.

Methodology:
Pitcher Stolen Base Runs Saved

The toughest pitcher to run against over the past six years was Kenny Rogers. Though he retired after 2008, opposing baserunners only attempted 10 stolen bases with Rogers on the mound over 2006-08 and were successful only twice, for a 80 percent caught stealing rate. On the other hand, we have Chris Young, who has not been able to stop the run. Over six years he has allowed 126 stolen bases in 133 attempts, a 5 percent caught stealing rate. Rogers' rate is an incredible 75 percentage points higher than Young's, while the gap between the best and worst catchers (Yadier Molina and Josh Bard, at 37 percent and 13 percent, respectively) is just 24 percentage points.

The mission is to convert pitcher stolen base data into runs saved. To do this, we need to break it into two components, caught stealing rate and stolen base frequency.

The first component of Pitcher Stolen Base Runs Saved is calculated based on how often runners were caught by way of a catcher caught stealing, pitcher caught stealing, or pitcher pickoff. The second component is based on how often runners attempt to steal on the pitcher.

Using the 24 States Run Matrix (see page 439), we found the average run value of a stolen base was 0.19 runs (obviously a positive event for the offense), while the average run value of a pickoff or caught stealing was -0.43 runs.

Based on the relative variance in their caught stealing rates, we then assigned 65 percent of the responsibility for stolen bases and catcher caught stealing to the pitcher and 35 percent to the catcher. Pitcher caught stealing and pickoff plays were credited entirely to the pitcher. Stolen bases are counted as $-0.19 \times 0.65 = -0.1235$ runs per occurrence (restated as a negative because we're evaluating Runs Saved from the perspective of the pitcher). Catcher caught stealing are $0.43 \times 0.65 = 0.2795$ runs per occurrence. Pitcher caught stealing and pickoffs are 0.43 runs per occurrence.

For example, Mark Buehrle allowed three steals in six attempts as well as four pitcher caught stealings and two pickoffs. This amounts to $(3 * -0.19 * 0.65) + (3 * 0.43 * 0.65) + (4 * 0.43) + (2 * 0.43) = 3.05$ runs saved on these twelve plays.

On the other hand, Tommy Hanson allowed 30 steals in 32 attempts, with one pitcher caught stealing. He receives $(30 * -0.19 * 0.65) + (2 * 0.43 * 0.65) + (1 * 0.43) + (0 * 0.43) = -2.72$ runs saved on these 33 plays.

Additionally, we examine how often opposing baserunners attempted stolen bases in the first place. For example, Kenny Rogers limited opposing baserunners to a 20 percent success rate, but only 10 runners were foolish enough to even try to run against him in three seasons. What about those other would-be basestealers who were afraid to try in the first place? Rogers and similar pitchers should be credited for that, too.

We counted the number of stolen base opportunities (defined as any situation with a runner on first and second base open) against each pitcher. We then compared the number of stolen base attempts to the average number of stolen base attempts in the same number of opportunities. For every stolen base attempt allowed less than average, we credit him with the average run value of a stolen base attempt (as calculated from the 24 States Run Matrix).

For example, runners had 222 opportunities to steal bases against Mark Buehrle in 2011. An average pitcher in Buehrle's shoes would have allowed 21.6 stolen base attempts, but the lefty allowed just 6. He allowed 21.6 - 6 = 15.6 attempts fewer than expected, the most in Major League Baseball. Including both successful steals and failed attempts, the average stolen base was worth about 0.047 runs last year. We award Buehrle 15.6 * 0.047 = 0.73 additional runs of credit, bringing his total to 3.78 Runs Saved.

If a pitcher allowed more stolen base attempts than league average, they lose the other 35 percent of the runs we were attributing to the catcher for attempts above league average. For example, Tommy Hanson allowed 32 stolen base attempts in 111 stolen base opportunities last year. Given that many opportunities, we would have expected 10.8 attempts, 21.2 fewer than he actually allowed (the biggest difference in baseball last year). We've already penalized Hanson for 65 percent of all 32 stolen base attempts; we additionally penalize him 21.2 / 32 * (30 * -0.19 * 0.35) = -1.32 for the additional stolen bases and 21.2 / 32 * (2 * 0.43 * 0.35) * -1 = -0.20 to remove credit for the additional caught stealing. This additional -1.52 penalty, on top of the -2.72 runs saved from the first part, means that Hanson cost himself about 4.2 runs on stolen base attempts in 2011.

Lastly, we apply a small adjustment so the league average pitcher centers at exactly zero Stolen Base Runs Saved.

Methodology:
Adjusted Earned Runs Saved

The evaluation of catcher defense, specifically the handling of the pitching staff, has been the subject of much debate over the years. Craig Wright introduced Catcher ERA in his book *Diamond Appraised*, comparing catchers on the same team to gauge pitchers' effectiveness when throwing to different pitch callers. Many analysts, including Keith Woolner formerly of Baseball Prospectus and now with the Cleveland Indians, have questioned the validity of Catcher ERA and similar statistics.

In *The Fielding Bible—Volume II*, we introduced a method called Adjusted Earned Runs Saved. Our goal is to assess each catcher's ability to handle the pitching staff, saving runs with intelligent pitch calling, framing pitches, and anything else he can do to help each pitcher be more effective. The idea is similar to Catcher ERA, with some very important adjustments.

First, we park-adjust each pitcher's seasonal ERA. For example, let's take a look at Tim Hudson of the Atlanta Braves. The former Auburn Tiger allowed 77 earned runs and a 3.22 ERA; however, Hudson pitched primarily in pitcher-friendly Turner Field last year. We park adjust his total by dividing his earned runs allowed in each ballpark by its park factor, then adding them up to get 82.4 adjusted earned runs and a 3.45 Adjusted ERA.

We then look specifically at each pitcher's performance with each catcher. We perform the same park adjustment calculation to find how many adjusted earned runs the pitcher allowed with each catcher. Brian McCann caught Hudson for 118 innings last year and allowed 49 earned runs. Those 49 earned runs turn into 53.3 adjusted earned runs after applying the park factors.

Next, we take the pitcher's full season Adjusted Earned Run Average, multiply by the number of innings thrown to that particular catcher, and divide by nine to get the expected number of (adjusted) earned runs allowed by that pitcher/catcher duo. We then subtract the actual number of adjusted earned runs for that tandem to find the number of adjusted earned runs saved for that catcher. Back to our Hudson/McCann example, Hudson's full season Adjusted ERA was 3.45, multiply by 118 and divide by nine to get...45.2. They actually allowed 53.3 adjusted earned runs, a difference of -8.1 adjusted earned runs.

We do the same calculation for every pitcher-catcher combination in baseball, then add up the adjusted earned runs saved for each catcher. For Brian McCann, this amounts to -6.5 adjusted earned runs saved.

There's one final adjustment. The scale of adjusted earned runs can vary quite a bit, especially in smaller sample sizes. There is a lot of random noise in a single season of pitcher ERA, let alone the variation between catchers. If a pitcher has a bad day and gives up six runs in six innings for one particular backup catcher, that might be three runs more than expected. However, those extra three runs could be attributed to any number of things that have nothing to do with the catcher. The wind might be blowing out that day, the pitcher could be going through a dead-arm period and not have his best stuff, or he might have forgotten to eat his Wheaties for breakfast. Because of all the variables outside of the catcher's control, we apply a credibility factor. We take the catcher's adjusted earned runs saved, multiply by the number of innings he caught that year, then divide by three times the number of innings caught in a full season behind the plate. For 2011, this number was 1,451. For McCann, we multiply -6.5 * 1,083 / (1,451 * 3) = -1.6, which rounds to -2 Adjusted Earned Runs Saved.

Methodology:
Centering Runs Saved

You have in your hands a book full of numbers, specifically numbers related to defensive analysis of baseball. Each number means something, and it's our job as the authors to convey that meaning to you. You might want the 30-second explanation, or you might want to know every detail; we are trying to provide both as best we can.

Regardless of your thirst for details, you need some sort of context or baseline to know what the numbers mean. If I told you a player hit 20 home runs, is that good or bad? What if I told you he hit 20 homers in just 300 at-bats? What if it took five seasons and 3,000 at bats to reach 20 homers? What if he hit his 20 bombs in the majors as a shortstop? What if he did that in the low levels of the minors, in an extreme hitters' park, as a first baseman? We need some sort of baseline to help us account for the context of the 20 home runs.

Sometimes we use counting statistics, such as home runs or strikeouts, where a player starts at zero and goes up. We still need to know the context to put the number into perspective. We also use rate statistics, such as batting average or ERA, where we divide a numerator (hits or earned runs) by a denominator (at bats or innings) as another way of providing context. Growing up, we've come to learn that a major league player with a .300 batting average or 40 homers in a season is good, while a .230 average or a 6.00 ERA is bad.

The original *Fielding Bible* featured rating systems to measure an outfielder's range (Plus/Minus and Enhanced Plus/Minus) and his throwing arm (Extra Base Percentage) but on entirely different scales. If we wanted to compare right fielders J.D. Drew and Alex Rios, we could say with some confidence that Drew had superior range but Rios had the better arm. Which was more important? Did Drew's superior range outweigh Rios' stronger throws? We could only speculate.

Three years ago in *The Fielding Bible—Volume II*, we converted Plus/Minus, Outfield Arms, and six other components of defense into the same currency: runs. With everything on one scale, we learned that Rios' arm was so good that it more than made up for Drew's negligible Plus/Minus advantage. Since we knew the run impact of a player's or team's defensive effort, we could also start comparing fielders to pitchers and hitters.

Since Volume II, we realized that the baseline of our Defensive Runs Saved metric wasn't as precisely defined as it could have been. In general, good defenders were above zero and bad fielders were below zero; however, some components of Runs Saved (most notably Outfield Arms) tended to be skewed one way or the other.

Additionally, the demand for up-to-date and accurate defensive numbers grew. The Plus/Minus System combines similar plays into "buckets" for the purpose of estimating each play's difficulty. While the Plus/Minus System had traditionally used only plays from the current season as a basis, the sample sizes of the buckets early in the season were smaller than we liked. We elected to move to a rolling one-year basis for the system during the season to give more meaning to the numbers in April and May. One consequence of the rolling basis was a potential league-wide skew in the numbers. While we liked the additional accuracy the new basis brought, we were slightly uncomfortable when the average shortstop was +5 plays. After all, the Plus/

Minus system was designed with 0 as the league average.

The skew intensified when we added Good Play/Misplay Runs Saved to our Team Fielding Bible product. Because Good Fielding Plays and Defensive Misplays don't occur in equal proportion for every position, we witnessed an additional skew to the numbers.

Lastly, as the sabermetric community advanced in recent years, there has been great progress in establishing context to new statistics. Many new defensive statistics had rigid baselines, most often with the league average fielder at each position equal to zero.

For all of these reasons, we made the decision to center each of the eight components of Defensive Runs Saved at zero when we update the numbers nightly. Depending on the component, we use slightly different techniques to ensure that the average fielder at each position is centered at zero. More details of these calculations are included in the methodology section of this book beginning on page 434.

Some readers may observe that the league totals for each position in this book are very close to zero but might not add exactly to zero. First, while we have re-run the categories with the largest skews, for a variety of reasons we have not recalculated every component of Runs Saved. For instance, we have re-run the 2003-2008 Outfield Arms, Pitcher Stolen Bases, Bunts, and Good Play/Misplay Runs Saved numbers, but we have not re-run the GDP, Catcher Stolen Bases, Catcher Adjusted Earned Runs, or Plus/Minus components for those seasons. Secondly, there is some rounding error. We feel comfortable citing a player's Runs Saved score to the nearest integer; however, we believe that citing Runs Saved to one or more decimal places implies a level of precision that just isn't there. As much as we've learned about defense in the past nine years, we still have miles to go.

Acknowledgements

We'd probably still be working on this book if it weren't for Rob Burckhard. As with the *Bill James Handbook*, Rob has the thankless task of assembling the book piece by piece and personally changing every minor revision or edit that strikes our fancy. On top of that, he still managed to make significant analytical contributions to several components of Defensive Runs Saved and wrote several sections of this book. We cannot thank him enough.

Steve Moyer and the entire Baseball Info Solutions team (BaseballInfoSolutions.com) has been nothing but supportive. Mike Piekarski, Dan Casey, Todd Radcliffe, Jon Vrecsics and Jim Swavely head the data collection operation. They were called on to review thousands of plays during their offseason to make sure we got the data right. They've also been invaluable stat-checkers and proofreaders, especially for the Defensive Scouting Reports. Jeff Spoljaric, Patrick Coyle and Andrew Gibson comprise the IT Department, constantly improving our internal database. Andrew was especially helpful with writing, proofreading and stat-checking. Jim Capuano is the Director of Business Development.

Michael Schatz and Joe Rosales interned for Rob and Ben in the Research & Development department over the past year. Joe in particular had the unenviable task of working with us through a *Handbook* and most of a *Fielding Bible*. We're happy to report that both Michael and Joe are now contributing to major league teams and doing well in the baseball world.

Maxwell Cook, Tani Cohen, Will Cohen, Jason Eisele, Mike Fecteau, Adam Hayes, Andy Johnson, Brady Johnston, Christian Karayannides, Ian Kenyon and Craig Vanderkam contributed defensive scouting reports to the book. These guys watched more baseball games last year than just about anyone in professional baseball.

Bill James, as always, inspires much of our analysis. Almost anything he writes is a must-read. He contributed two pieces and countless ideas to this book.

Chris Dial and Mitchel Lichtman, both known for their own contributions to the field of defensive analytics, have also graciously contributed new articles. With their additions, we believe this book is the best collection of cutting-edge fielding research to date.

Greg Pierce and the rest of the gang at ACTA Sports (ACTASports.com) do a fantastic job getting this book from us to the printers and back again. The rest of the gang includes Amanda Modelski, Donna Ryding, Mary Eggert, Richard Struben and Brendan Gaughan. Charles Fiore and David Barlow spent countless hours proofreading this book.

Our innumerable friends in the industry provide feedback and keep us in business. Our partners at ESPN, Fangraphs, Baseball-Reference and The Hardball Times (especially Dave Studenmund) are fantastic advocates of our defensive metrics and the baseball analytics industry as a whole.

Lastly, a special thanks to Sue Dewan, Amy Pucklavage, Kelsey Sidlo and all of the friends and family we've neglected in recent weeks and months. This book is dedicated to you.

Baseball Info Solutions

Baseball Info Solutions has been supplying top notch, timely, and in-depth baseball data and analytics to its customers for the last ten years. BIS collects a statistical snapshot of every important moment of every Major League Baseball game with the most advanced technology, resulting in a database that includes traditional data, pitch-by-pitch data, and defensive positioning data. The company also has the highest quality pitch charting data available anywhere, including pitch type, location, and velocity.

BIS provides comprehensive services to about half of the 30 Major League Baseball teams, as well as many sports agents, media, fantasy services, game companies and private individuals.

John Dewan, the principal owner of BIS, has been on the cutting edge of baseball analysis for over 25 years. His experience goes all the way back to his days as Executive Director of Project Scoresheet, the Bill James-led effort that pioneered the new wave of baseball statistics that are now common terminology.

President Steve Moyer brings 20 years of baseball industry experience to BIS. His hands-on, can-do business demeanor helps set BIS apart from its competition.

The rest of the BIS team includes former professional and collegiate baseball players as well as research, programming and database management experts. Over the last five seasons, BIS has more than tripled its full-time staff.

BIS continues to grow within the industry while emphasizing personal attention to its customers.

To contact BIS:

Baseball Info Solutions
41 S. 2nd Street
Coplay, PA 18037
610-261-2370
www.baseballinfosolutions.com